HANDBOOK
OF
SOCIALIZATION
THEORY
AND
RESEARCH

Contributors

Joan Aldous, *University of Minnesota*
Alan Ross Anderson, *University of Pittsburgh*
Justin Aronfreed, *University of Pennsylvania*
Alfred L. Baldwin, *New York University*
Albert Bandura, *Stanford University*
Jerome S. Bruner, *Harvard University*
Ernest Q. Campbell, *Vanderbilt University*
Leonard S. Cottrell, Jr., *University of North Carolina*
Anne Foner, *Rutgers—The State University*
John H. Gagnon, *State University of New York, Stony Brook*
Jacob L. Gewirtz, *National Institute of Mental Health*
David A. Goslin, *Russell Sage Foundation*
Patricia Marks Greenfield, *Harvard University*
Susan Harter, *Yale University*
Beth Hess, *Rutgers—The State University*
Reuben Hill, *University of Minnesota*
Alex Inkeles, *Harvard University*
James J. Jenkins, *University of Minnesota*
Jerome Kagan, *Harvard University*
Lawrence Kohlberg, *Harvard University*
Robert A. LeVine, *University of Chicago*
Boyd R. McCandless, *Emory University*
Daniel R. Miller, *University of Michigan*
Omar Khayyam Moore, *University of Pittsburgh*
Wilbert E. Moore, *Russell Sage Foundation*
Paul H. Mussen, *University of California, Berkeley*
Francis H. Palmer, *City University of New York*
Harriet L. Rheingold, *University of North Carolina*
Stephen A. Richardson, *Association for the Aid of Crippled Children*
Matilda White Riley, *Rutgers—The State University*
Robert A. Scott, *Princeton University*
William Simon, *Institute for Juvenile Research*
Marcia L. Toby, *Rutgers—The State University*
Eugene A. Weinstein, *State University of New York, Stony Brook*
Stanton Wheeler, *Yale University*
Herman A. Witkin, *State University of New York, Downstate Medical Center*
Donald R. Young, *The Rockefeller University*
Edward F. Zigler, *Yale University*

HANDBOOK OF SOCIALIZATION THEORY AND RESEARCH

Edited by
David A. Goslin
Russell Sage Foundation

RAND McNALLY AND COMPANY · CHICAGO

Rand McNally Sociology Series
Edgar F. Borgatta, Advisory Editor

Handbook of Personality Theory and Research
   Edgar F. Borgatta and William W. Lambert, Eds.
Handbook of Marriage and the Family
   Harold T. Christensen, Ed.
Handbook of Modern Sociology
   Robert E. L. Faris, Ed.
Handbook of Socialization Theory and Research
   David A. Goslin, Ed.
Handbook of Organizations
   James G. March, Ed.

Preface

The *Handbook of Socialization Theory and Research* was conceived, early in 1964, as "a collection of short, tightly-written, essentially theoretical essays on various topics related to the general area of socialization." The major aim of the book was, "to bring together in a form that would challenge the imagination of both graduate students and experienced researchers, relevant concepts and data concerning the acquisition of social skills from a variety of theoretical positions and contextual viewpoints." Unlike most "handbooks" it was not intended primarily to be an exhaustive review of the literature, but rather to provide a fresh outlook on how existing ideas might contribute to our understanding of the socialization process and identify crucial issues for further research.

How close we have come to achieving those goals is a matter for the reader to judge for himself. It is clear that, at least in one respect, we have deviated significantly from the original conception; namely in the length of many articles. I do not, incidentally, regard this as a fault, but rather as a tribute to the interest and devotion of the authors. Moreover, while a claim of exhaustiveness is not warranted, many of the contributions provide extensive reviews of existing literature. Taken as a whole, it is my undoubtedly biased view that no more extensive or stimulating set of essays on socialization currently exists.

The credit, if credit is to be given, for this accomplishment belongs in largest measure to the authors. It is their book, not mine, although I assume full responsibility for whatever shortcomings in overall conceptual organization, balance, or style may be discerned. The edited collection of original papers has become an increasingly familiar phenomenon in social science publishing. While I believe such books can and do serve a useful function (otherwise I would not have undertaken this project), my sympathies lie entirely with those overworked individuals who, in a moment of weakness, agree to write a "handbook" chapter, and then must put up with an editor's badgering until their contribution is completed. The patience, fortitude, and good humor of the authors of this volume were unshakable; more important, their contributions are uniformly the product of considerable creative energy and impeccable scholarship. To each I would like to express my gratitude.

Apart from the authors, many individuals have contributed in important ways to this book. My colleague, David C. Glass, took a major part of the responsibility for developing and initiating this project as coeditor. Professional obligations ultimately forced him to resign this role, but his continued unstinting assistance and wise counsel are reflected throughout the volume. In large measure, this book is also the result of the enthusiasm and persuasive powers of Edgar F. Borgatta, who conceived the idea and, along with John Applegath, succeeded in convincing us of the need.

A large part of the success of any handbook may be attributed to the logic (if any) underlying the Table of Contents and the selection of authors. I am indebted to M. Brewster Smith, John A. Clausen, Harold W. Stevenson, Orville G. Brim, Jr. and William Sewell for their encouragement and informed judgments regarding this *Handbook's* organization and implementation. Without their assistance this would be a far less useful book.

The production of a book this size is a monumental task. In the present instance it was accomplished with exceptional care and highest quality in record time. Major credit for this achievement belongs to Marianne Clark, Managing Editor of the College Department at Rand McNally, and Stella Jenks, whose editorial skills and devotion to the project kept the production wheels turning on schedule.

Finally, I should like to express my gratitude to my secretaries, Elisabeth Groenendijk and Alice P. Roberts, without whose calm competence, moral support, and organizational expertise this book would not have been possible.

David A. Goslin
Russell Sage Foundation

May 28, 1968

Acknowledgements

I wish to express my thanks to the following authors and publishers who have given permission to quote from their works:

To Dr. Mary D. Ainsworth and the Merrill-Palmer Institute for the quotations in Chapter 2 from the *Merrill-Palmer Quarterly;*

To Appleton-Century-Crofts for the quotation in Chapter 20 from *The Campus* by Robert Cooley Angell;

For permission to quote in Chapter 9 from R. F. Hefferline, "Learning Theory and Clinical Psychology—An Eventual Symbiosis?" in *Experimental Foundations of Clinical Psychology,* edited by A. J. Bachrach, Basic Books, Inc., Publishers, New York, 1962;

To Donald M. Baer and the Society for the Experimental Analysis of Behavior, Inc., for permission to reproduce Figure 3.1 from the *Journal of the Experimental Analysis of Behavior,* 1967, 10, p. 413. Copyright 1967, by the Society for the Experimental Analysis of Behavior, Inc.;

To the American Psychological Association for permission to reproduce Figure 3.2 by Albert Bandura from the *Journal of Personality and Social Psychology,* 1965, 1, p. 592;

To Holt, Rinehart and Winston, Inc., for quotations in Chapters 7 and 15 from *Social Learning and Personality Development* by Albert Bandura and Richard H. Walters;

To Schenkman Publishing Company for quotations in Chapter 8 from D. T. Campbell, "Variation and Selective-Retention in Sociocultural Evolution," in *Social Change in Developing Areas: A Re-Interpretation of Evolutionary Theory* by H. R. Barringer, G. I. Blanksten and R. W. Mack;

To the Russell Sage Foundation for quotations in Chapter 8 from *Education for Child Rearing* by O. G. Brim, Jr.;

To *Psychology Today Magazine* for quotations in Chapter 2 from N. Chomsky, "Language and the Mind," in the February 1968 issue, copyright Communications/Research/Machines/Inc.;

To The Free Press and to Methuen & Company, Ltd., London, for quotations in Chapter 28 from A. M. Clarke and J. Tizard in *Mental Deficiency: The Changing Outlook* by A. M. Clarke and A. D. B. Clarke, copyright 1958 by The Free Press, a division of The Macmillan Company;

To the *American Journal of Orthopsychiatry* for quotations in Chapter 26 from M. J. Cole and L. H. Taboroff, Vol. 25, No. 3, July, 1955, pp. 627-639. Copyright 1955 by the American Orthopsychiatric Association, Inc., and reproduced by permission;

To The Free Press for quotations in Chapter 20 from J. S. Coleman, *The Adolescent Society,* copyright 1961 by The Free Press, a division of The Macmillan Company;

To the American Association on Mental Deficiency for the quotations in Chapter 28 from L. A. Dexter which appeared in the *American Journal of Mental Deficiency,* 1958, Vol. 62;

To John Wiley & Sons, Inc., for the quotation from *The Adolescent Experience* by E. Douvan and J. Adelson, in Chapter 20;

To International Universities Press, Inc., for quotations in Chapter 26 from Dorothy Burlingham in Vol. 16, 1961, and Anne-Marie Sandlar in Vol. 18, 1963, of *Psychoanalytic Study of the Child,* edited by Ruth S. Eissler et al.;

To McGraw-Hill Book Company for quotations in Chapter 28 from S. L. Garfield and B. A. Maher which appeared in the *Handbook of Mental Deficiency,* edited by N. R. Ellis;

To Dr. Erik H. Erikson and International Universities Press, Inc., for the portion of Figure 19.1 which appeared in the *Journal of the American Psychoanalytic Association,* 1956, 4, p. 75;

To John Wiley & Sons, Inc., for the quotation in Chapter 2 from J. Bowlby's comment which appeared in *Determinants of Infant Behaviour,* edited by B. M. Foss;

To Rand McNally & Company for the quotation in Chapter 20 from W. W. Charters, Jr., in *Handbook of Research on Teaching,* edited by N. L. Gage;

To John Wiley & Sons, Inc., for the quotation in Chapter 25 from R. Giallombardo's *A Study of a Women's Prison;*

To Prentice-Hall for quotations in Chapter 27 from Erving Goffman, *Stigma: Notes on the Management of Spoiled Identity,* copyright 1963, Prentice-Hall, Inc., Englewood Cliffs, New Jersey;

To the Russell Sage Foundation for quotations in Chapter 15 from Jerome Kagan which appeared in *Review of Child Development Research,* Vol. 1, edited by M. L. Hoffman and L. W. Hoffman;

To John Wiley & Sons, Inc., for the quotation in Chapter 16 from *Birth to Maturity,* by J. Kagan and H. A. Moss;

To Holt, Rinehart and Winston, Inc., for the quotation from *Social Psychology* by Alfred R. Lindesmith and Anselm L. Strauss in Chapter 17;

To Dr. Berthold Lowenfeld and The Council for Exceptional Children for quotations in Chapter 26 from *Exceptional Children,* 1949, 16;

To the Stanford University Press for use of the quotations in Chapter 2 and Chapter 15 of Lawrence Kohlberg and W. Mischel from *The Development of Sex Differences,* edited by Eleanor E. Maccoby;

To Methuen & Company, Ltd., London, for the quotation in Chapter 6 from *An Introduction to Social Psychology* by W. McDougall;

To Dr. William Meyer of the Institute of Child Behavior, University of Iowa, Iowa City, for the use of his picture in Chapter 28;

To The Ronald Press Company for quotations in Chapter 15 from *Learning Theory and Personality Dynamics—Selected Papers* by O. Hobart Mowrer, copyright 1950 by The Ronald Press Company, New York;

To Clark University Press for quotations from John Dewey in Chapter 6 from *Psychologies of 1930,* edited by C. Murchison;

To The Free Press for the quotation in Chapter 20 from *The Social System* by Talcott Parsons, copyright 1951 by The Free Press, a division of The Macmillan Company;

To the Houghton Mifflin Company and *Daedalus* for the quotation in Chapter 29 by O. Handlin from *The Negro American,* by T. Parsons and K. B. Clark;

To Sidgwick & Jackson, Ltd., London, for the quotation in Chapter 28 from *The Biology of Mental Defect* by L. S. Penrose;

To Alfred A. Knopf for the quotation from G. E. McClearn in Chapter 28 from *Psychology in the Making,* edited by L. Postman;

To the Houghton Mifflin Company for use of Lawrence Kohlberg's Tables 6.2, 6.4, and 6.7 which appeared in *Religion and Public Education* by T. Sizer;

To the Oxford University Press, London, for the quotations in Chapter 27 from *Community Services for the Mentally Handicapped* by J. Tizard;

To Appleton-Century-Crofts for the quotations in Chapter 28 from A. L. Benton and R. F. Heber which appeared in *The Exceptional Child* by P. E. Trapp and P. Himelstein;

To the American Academy of Arts and Sciences for the quotation in Chapter 29 from Paul Weiss which appeared in *Daedalus,* Journal of The American Academy of Arts and Sciences, Boston, Mass., Winter, 1960, "The Visual Arts Today";

To Prentice-Hall for the quotation in Chapter 29 from Robin M. Williams, Jr., *Strangers Next Door: Ethnic Relations in American Communities,* copyright 1964, by Prentice-Hall, Inc., Englewood Cliffs, New Jersey;

And to the Hafner Publishing Company for quotations in Chapter 26 from Berthold Lowenfeld which appeared in *Blindness, Modern Approaches to the Unseen Environment* by Paul A. Zahl.

Table of Contents

HANDBOOK
OF
SOCIALIZATION
THEORY
AND
RESEARCH

INTRODUCTION

DAVID A. GOSLIN

Russell Sage Foundation

A wide range of viewpoints, intellectual styles, and subject areas are represented in this book. The aspects of socialization are approached from divergent theoretical perspectives as well as at significantly different levels of analysis; sociological and anthropological frames of reference are imposed along with more traditional developmental psychological points of view. Several chapters focus on narrowly defined aspects of socialization, while others treat the topic from a broader theoretical perspective. Some of the contributions provide extremely detailed analyses of basic processes and theories; others take more general views.

This diversity is the result of a deliberately open charge to authors: within the confines of a general topic, to deal with those issues each author felt held the greatest promise for advancing our knowledge about socialization, either in terms of present research findings and theories or with respect to directions in which future work might proceed. The result is an extraordinary collection of essays, albeit one which reviewers may find to be uneven and in places frustrating, since far more questions are raised than answered.

In a very real sense this volume accurately reflects the current state of theory and research in the field of socialization as a whole. A major problem has been the difficulty in integrating sociological, anthropological and psychological conceptions of the social-learning process. Historically, the systematic study of socialization has its roots in all three fields[1]; psychology focusing on the development of individual characteristics relevant to social behavior as well as on the basic processes through which these behavioral tendencies are learned, sociology concentrating on characteristics of specific groups or institutions in which socialization occurs and on the common social skills acquired by individuals in varying contexts, and anthropology viewing socialization from the standpoint of the broader culture which helps to determine the overall boundaries of socialization experiences. Obviously these differences in approach encompass many theoretical issues, among them (1) the relative influence of early as opposed to later experiences on behavior; (2) the relative emphasis to be placed on individual drives, motives, and needs as energizers of behavior as opposed to the influence of the social apparatus (group, institution, culture as a whole); (3) the relative emphasis to be placed on process as opposed to content as a basis for predicting

---

[1]For an excellent history of the development of the concept of socialization, see Clausen, 1968.

and understanding social behavior; (4) the extent to which one focuses on unique aspects of socialization experiences as opposed to their common properties; and (5) whether one's primary concern is with the causes of deviations from behavioral norms, with measurement of the extent of deviation, or with forces that tend to produce conformity to normative expectations.

The Nature of Socialization

Despite these differences, however, the basis for our interest in socialization remains clear. In the most general sense we are concerned with discovering how individuals learn to participate effectively in social interaction, why some individuals have difficulties and what makes some groups function better than others. Basic courses in sociology, anthropology and psychology introduce students to the simple notion that societies and groups would not be possible without an extraordinary degree of conformity by group members to commonly held expectations regarding what constitute appropriate behaviors, attitudes, and values in a wide range of situations. At the same time conformity to social norms and value standards is regarded as a variable, and individual differences in social behavior are not only acknowledged but regarded as a major problem requiring explanation.

Historically, many specific definitions of socialization have been offered and the reader will encounter several in the following chapters. As a starting point, however, we take socialization to refer to "the process by which individuals acquire the knowledge, skills, and dispositions that enable them to participate as more or less effective members of groups and the society" (Brim, 1966). We are interested in social learning, not only during childhood, but throughout the life cycle and within each of the various group and organizational contexts that provide settings for social behavior. It is obvious that the great bulk of human behavior does not occur in social isolation. Even acts performed while an individual is alone (for example, reading, taking a shower, shaving and the like) are to a large degree influenced by significant others in the individual's life space. Socialization is, therefore, an extremely broad topic; some might say too broad. It could be argued, for example, that a distinction between learning and social learning is unnecessary; that it obscures one's view of essential features of all learning by shifting the focus from process to content. Yet if one is interested in understanding and, ultimately, predicting the behavior of individuals in social groups, or of social groups as such, content is of more than casual interest. *What* people learn and *why* they learn it is as important as *how* they learn it. Furthermore, it is worth entertaining the notion that even basic processes by which human beings learn may be modified by characteristics of their social context.

Although current usage of the term *socialization* and a conception of social learning as a specific field of enquiry are the product of developments in psychology and sociology occurring primarily during the last three decades, an interest in child-rearing and social development is as old as man. Scientific investigation of these processes and the development of more precise theories to explain research findings is a more recent phenomenon. The elaboration of, and experimentation on, alternative conceptions of learning; the growth of psychoanalysis and its translation into specific theories of personality development; and the development of techniques for systematically studying social interaction both in and outside of the laboratory all contributed to the evolution of socialization into a distinguishable field of study. This book provides one of the first assessments of the present state of knowledge and theory in this field along with speculations on what may turn out to be the most profitable lines of research to pursue in the future.

Major Issues and a Central Theme

The great diversity of theoretical approaches to socialization represented in this volume already has been noted. While making an overall synthesis difficult, this diversity provides a set of issues organized around a central theme that serves as the basis for this introduction. In simplest terms, this theme is the longstanding difference between the disciplines of psychology and sociology in their respective approaches to social phenomena. What is especially interesting is the emergence of a few concrete issues that serve to illuminate the sources of these differences in approach and, more important, the beginnings of an apparent convergence among theorists representing each group in their conceptualizations of socialization processes.

Both these tendencies toward convergence and remaining areas of disagreement are reflected in two major categories of problems that are dealt with either implicitly or explicitly by nearly all of our authors. One set of problems is generated by different views of characteristics of the learner in the socialization process. Many psychologically oriented theorists have tended to conceptualize the activities of the learner in essentially irrational or behaviorist terms; the individual is perceived as responding in more or less automatic and stable ways, as a consequence of prior experiences, to configurations of stimuli coming both from the external environment and from within the learner himself. Theoretical explorations of the dynamics of behavior changes vary considerably from writer to writer, but in most cases the focus is on the individual as responding to, rather than initiating, social interaction and concomitant learning experiences. Sociologists, on the other hand, often tend to hold a more rational, externally oriented conception of the individual learner. The learner is more often viewed as consciously making choices, seeking out new roles, and deciding as well as being unconsciously induced to acquire new skills or alter existing behaviors.

The chapters that follow make it clear that this issue arises in large part from the propensity of theorists to concentrate on different aspects of the socialization process rather than from fundamentally different conceptions of human nature. The age-old controversy over free will versus determinism rears its head hardly at all in this volume, at least in any recognizable form. In fact both points of view may be considered to be equally deterministic. What is apparent, however, is that a focus on the content or context of socialization experiences leads one to a far more rationalistic conception of process. The sociologically oriented theorists, while acknowledging the importance of prior experience, established response patterns, and the like, frequently take as a starting point an individual who is viewed as being capable of making rational decisions, weighing the consequences of his acts, and optimizing his chances for achieving consciously determined personal goals. On the other hand, those theorists who concern themselves primarily with attempting to answer the hard questions about how special characteristics of an individual's external social environment and the quality of his experiences with this environment are translated into more or less unique configurations of responses to new and different situations find themselves conceptualizing the actor's social behavior as essentially unconscious.

Despite these differences, tendencies toward theoretical convergence may be noted. For example, as James J. Jenkins points out in Chapter 13 on language learning, the psychological view has moved from simple to complex association learning and, finally, to the apprehension of systems and structures, i.e., rule-governed behavior. The latter, of course, involves a lot of association, but is not wholly explicable in such terms. A seeking, creating, system-building mind must be postulated. Similar views of the cognitive capacities of the learner are implied in the contributions by Justin Aronfreed (Chapter 4), Alfred Baldwin (Chapter 5), Lawrence Kohlberg (Chapter 6), Omar K. Moore and Alan Ross Anderson (Chapter 10), and Patricia Marks Greenfield and Jerome S. Bruner (Chapter 12), along with several others. Finally, in Chapter 8, Robert A. LeVine calls attention to the existence of culturally defined boundaries between those aspects of behavior that are assumed to be more or less "automatic" or "nativistic" (in the sense of the old issue of nativism versus empiricism), and those that are presumed to be the result of conscious planning on the part of individuals.

A number of subsidiary issues arise, of course, as a result of the previous difference in approach. Among others, these include recognition of the distinction between how, on the one hand, individuals *acquire* the skills, knowledge and dispositions necessary for effective social participation and, on the other hand, how they are induced to *perform* socially prescribed acts based on what they have learned. This problem underscores the tendency of theorists to focus primarily on either the means by which the external system exerts control over individual behavior or on the process of internalization, through which societal prescriptions and proscriptions become more or less autonomous energizers of behavior. Although these issues are real ones, what is especially interesting about many of the following chapters is the extent to which theorists approaching this problem from initially divergent perspectives or who concentrate on different aspects of socialization have attempted to take into account opposing viewpoints.

A second major category of issues is generated by a conceptualization of socialization as a two-way process, a process in which both socializer (whether individual or group) and socializee may be changed in significant ways. This concept leads to an explication of the contractual characteristics of social interaction and an examination of such issues as the opportunities open to participants for negotiation over their respective social roles. In addition, the consequences of socialization for groups, organizations and the society as a whole become an important topic for consideration. Finally, the problem of goodness of fit between the individual and his social environment may be raised, leading to an analysis of the relation between individual characteristics and attributes of groups into which they are being socialized.

The following two sections deal, first, with the issues arising from a conceptualization of socialization as a two-way process and, second, with the problem of alternative views of the learner and the learning process. A point made earlier will be apparent immediately in the discussion that follows; namely, the rational bias of a sociological theorist. At the same time, although no claim of completeness can be made, an attempt will be made to point out the areas of agreement and disagreement among the various approaches.

SOCIALIZATION AS A TWO-WAY PROCESS

As we have noted, traditional experimental studies of the learning process typically have focused primarily on changes in the behavior of the learner. Whether a rat, pigeon, or human being, the learner is viewed as developing patterns of responses to stimuli coming from the environment. Depending on one's theoretical persuasion, establishment of a connection between stimulus and response may be attributed simply to temporal contiguity between a stimulus and some act (response) on the part of the learner, to the occurrence of a reward (variously defined, but usually conceived either as a pleasurable sensation or cessation of an unpleasant sensation) immediately following a stimulus and behavioral response on the part of the learner, or some combination of the two. An enormous body of experimental data gathered over the course of the last half century indicates that, despite the existence of many important unanswered questions concerning the precise nature of learning experiences, human beings, as well as other organisms, can and do acquire behavioral dispositions in accordance with the general principles noted above. Further, as will be seen in succeeding chapters by Francis H. Palmer (Chapter 1), Jacob L. Gewirtz (Chapter 2), Albert Bandura (Chapter 3), Aronfreed (Chapter 4), and Daniel R. Miller (Chapter 7), these basic principles are as relevant to the acquisition of social skills as they are to the learning of nonsense syllables or responses to essentially impersonal stimuli.

An important, albeit obvious, fact about social learning, is that it takes place in a social environment. More significant is the fact that the learner is an integral part of that environment. Just as the learner is responding to stimuli from others around him, his responses constitute significant stimuli for those responsible for socializing him. To a variable but nonetheless considerable extent, therefore, the individual helps to shape his own social environment and in an important respect becomes socializer as well as socializee. Harriet L. Rheingold (Chapter 18) makes this point eloquently in describing the socializing effect of the infant on its family. Miller (Chapter 7) notes that ". . . both partners in a relationship have to be socialized. Not only must the three-year-old learn to control his aggression more than he did in the previous age grade; his mother must also learn to act differently than she did when he was more passive ..." (p. 497). LeVine (Chapter 8) hypothesizes that an important factor in the desire on the part of parents in modern societies to teach children verbal skills at an early age is so that they (parents) can obtain feedback from their children regarding the adequacy of their socializing acts and make appropriate modifications thereof. Even more dramatic instances of the influence of the learner on his social environment are noted by Robert A. Scott (Chapter 26), Stephen A. Richardson (Chapter 27), Edward F. Zigler and Susan Harter (Chapter 28), and Donald R. Young (Chapter 29) in their discussions of the socialization of the blind, physically disabled, the mentally retarded, and minority groups, respectively.

One way of approaching this problem is through a conceptualization of socialization in role-developmental terms. A social role has been defined as the behavior expected of an individual occupying a given social position (Gross, Mason & McEachern, 1958, p. 60). In accordance with this definition, practically all social acts may be thought of as constituting role behavior in the sense that the individual actor is presumed to be responding to perceived legitimate expectations regarding his performance from significant others in his social environment. From this standpoint, socialization refers to the process whereby individuals learn to play various social roles necessary for effective participation in the society; that is, how they acquire the knowledge, skills and dispositions that enable them to perform in accordance with the expectations of others as they move from position to position in the social order over time, from infant to child to adult, from student to worker, from son or daughter to husband or wife, to father or mother, and as they occupy several positions simultaneously; for example, adult, worker, son, husband, father, citizen.

It may be postulated that in every interactional system each of the participants influences the behavior of each other participant in significant ways. Thus we may not realistically talk about role-learning without also considering role-teaching. This is not a new idea, yet, as we have suggested, traditional approaches have tended to focus on modifications in the behavior of only one member of the interactional system, while ignoring the fact that such modifications are nearly always the result of a process of negotiation in which all participants alter their behavior to some degree. George Herbert Mead (1934), among others, including Leonard S. Cottrell, Jr., in Chapter 9 of this volume, have conceptualized the intra- and inter-personal dynamics of this process. Parsons and Shils (1951), Merton (1957) and others (Gross et al., 1958; Biddle & Thomas, 1966) have added the notion that every social position normatively has attached to it both a role (behavior legitimately expected of the occupant) and a status (behavior the occupant legitimately is entitled to demand of specified others). More recently Thibaut and Kelley (1959), Goffman (1959), and Eugene A. Weinstein (Chapter 17) have focused on the problem of how an individual goes about getting others to accept his definition of the situation in general and his perception of his role in particular. Finally, it should be noted that most modern social learning theorists, for example, Bandura (Chapter 3) postulate a reciprocal influence process. Thus we see further evidence for assuming a degree of convergence among psychologically and sociologically oriented students of socialization processes.

Role Negotiation

A conception of socialization as a two-way process leads us to a consideration of some of the factors affecting the extent to which the behavior of individuals in social groups, including the individual being socialized, may be subject to bargaining or negotiation among the participants. Occupancy of a social position involves both responding to the expectations of significant others in the interactional system *and* exercising one's rights to expect certain behaviors from other participants. Thus, the stability of any interactional system depends upon the agreement of the participants to a "contract" specifying what each may demand of the other. This contract may take one of several different forms. One major dimension along which interactional contracts vary is the degree to which the behaviors specified by the contract are institutionalized by the society or group in advance of the participants' entry into the situation. Under conditions of high institutionalization, there is relatively little opportunity for any of the participants to deviate from established expectations concerning their behavior (given their position in the system), or to make demands on the other participants different from those they are legitimately permitted to make under the terms of the agreement. Thus, both rights and duties are to some degree spelled out in advance. Adequate performance by the participants of their respective roles may depend upon internal or external sanctions, or both, but socialization for such roles is concerned mainly with learning of existing role prescriptions rather than the negotiation of a new contract. The reciprocal roles of teacher and student, factory worker and foreman, store clerk and shopper, and (sometimes to a lesser extent) boss and secretary, are examples of such relationships. It should be emphasized, however, that even the most highly institutionalized positions, for example, that of a Cardinal in the Roman Catholic Church, permit some negotiation on the part of the individual occupant with respect to how he will play his role vis-a-vis various positions in his role set.

On the other hand, individuals typically participate in many interactional systems that are composed of positions initially containing only very general institutionalized prescriptions concerning the behavior of the occupant. Friendships, husband-wife relationships, many of our casual social interactions and often even relationships between children and their parents fall into this category. Societal norms, even though highly institutionalized, as in the case of marriage, may be, nevertheless, relatively unspecific regarding one's behavior in a variety of frequently encountered situations. Personality variables may be adduced to explain much of behavior occurring under such conditions. However, to the extent that roles are not clearly specified by the group or society in advance of an individual's participation in the interactional system, some mutually satisfactory pattern of role accommodation often must be achieved through a process of negotiation between the individual and other participants before successful interaction can take place. In a sense, reciprocal roles must be created and tacitly accepted by the participants. Under these conditions individuals must possess skills appropriate to establishing and maintaining a situational identity (role) and to recognizing the identities (roles) that other participants are attempting to create. Socialization in this instance means something quite different from learning how little boys or corporation presidents are supposed to behave.

Several points may be made regarding role negotiation:

(1) It should be emphasized that some negotiation is possible and/or necessary in the establishment of every interactional relationship, no matter how highly institutionalized the role may be.

(2) In stressing the concept of negotiability, we should not lose sight of the fact that in probably even a majority of the instances in which negotiation takes place, one or all of the parties may be unaware that it is going on. Rheingold's example in Chapter 18 of the socializing influence of the infant on the mother provides a clear case in which negotiation (in the unconscious sense) of the role relationship may be assumed to be taking place. At the other extreme we find examples of situations in which one or more members of the system explicitly and consciously attempt to structure the relationship in such a way as to attain their own ends with respect to the role they wish to play and the roles they wish other participants to play.

(3) Correlative to the previous two points is the notion that an important aspect of any role relationship is whether any or all of the participants perceive the possibility of negotiation (whether or not this is a realistic perception) and, if so, which aspects of their role and the role of the other are viewed as being subject to negotiation. Obviously, this perception need not be shared by all of the members of the interactional system; when it is not, it may be hypothesized that those who accurately assess the negotiability of role expectations have a significant advantage over the other participants. Most children quickly learn that they possess significant negotiating power in their relationships with their parents, teachers and peers. It may be hypothesized that the acquisition of this awareness is facilitated by nonauthoritarian child-rearing practices which encourage children to express their own feelings and in which explicit recognition is given to the rights of the child.[2] Palmer (Chapter 1), Baldwin (Chapter 5), Kohlberg (Chapter 6), Greenfield and Bruner (Chapter 12), Herman A. Witkin (Chapter 14), and Boyd R. McCandless (Chapter 19), all deal with various aspects of this process, as do many of the other authors, indirectly. Some treat the problem from the standpoint of the development of cognitive skills, others from the point of view of emotional stability and independence training. It is clear, however,

---

[2]It should be noted, however, that under certain conditions, highly institutionalized or rigid socialization settings may foster, out of necessity, the development of extremely sophisticated tactics of negotiation. A minimal degree of freedom in the exercise of one's role and the absence of extreme punishments must be postulated however, especially in childhood socialization.

that a variety of experiences may serve in an important way as an introduction to the tactics of role negotiation. Not only does the child become aware that negotiation is frequently possible, but he begins to acquire specific techniques for conducting himself in role-bargaining situations. The advantages and disadvantages of such learning are apparent. Children who have great freedom to bargain and do so with frequent success are likely to experience considerable frustration when they encounter situations in which negotiation is not possible. They may lack the ability to distinguish between situations in which negotiation is possible and those in which it is not (and they cannot tolerate the latter). On the other hand, children who have too little opportunity to experiment with the techniques of role negotiation are likely to be at a considerable disadvantage when they enter situations in which bargaining is necessary, not only because they lack the techniques, but also because they may be unable to recognize negotiable contracts when they see them. The preceding argument leads us to the second major point concerning an individual's capacity for role negotiation; namely the extent to which individuals possess the necessary techniques. Goffman (1959), Cottrell (Chapter 9), Weinstein (Chapter 17), and others have examined in detail many of the tactics by which individuals attempt to shape their own roles and those of others.

(4) An important and related aspect of interactional systems is the distribution of power in the relationship. Presumably the teacher has greater influence over his student's role than vice versa, and the neighborhood bully more to say about his victims' behavior than the weaker child does about how the bully will act. Analysis of this aspect of role relationships is not easy, however. Possession of a great deal of legitimate power (President of the United States, General of the Army, etc.) may carry with it so many obligations that one has relatively little freedom regarding one's own role. Thus individuals in designated subordinate roles frequently may be in a better bargaining position regarding their own role than are their supporters. This leads us to reemphasize the important point that when and if negotiation occurs, it occurs within the structural constraints imposed by the formal role.

Reuben Hill and Joan Aldous (Chapter 22) provide a relatively detailed discussion of mutual socialization where power relations are symmetrical and degree of commitment is considered as a variable (for example, going steady versus engagement and marriage). Equal distribution of power in the system tends to produce much improvising of appropriate roles and frequent attempts to shape others' roles.

Control of needed resources is often a critical factor in role negotiations giving the member who possesses such resources considerable bargaining power, regardless of the formal or informal distribution of authority or power. An excellent summary of current research and theoretical developments relating to the strategies of interpersonal bargaining may be found in Jones and Gerard (1967). Missing from this discussion, however, is a concern with the process by which interactional contracts that specify reciprocal roles evolve in interactional systems and are maintained over time.

(5) Finally, it should be noted that the internalization of values and standards of conduct may restrict, to a significant degree, one's absolute freedom to negotiate one's role. This would appear to be especially true in those instances where establishment of the relationship depends less on adherence to institutionalized role prescriptions and more on the exercise of personal power. To be an effective Machiavellian requires, therefore, that the individual possess an extensive repertoire of techniques of role negotiation without the restricting influence of a well-established, internalized, set of values regarding one's conduct vis-a-vis others (except, of course, the overriding value of self-enhancement). Moreover, individuals often find themselves committed to playing some roles in specific ways as a consequence of having played them that way for a period of time, in the process relinquishing what may have been an initial option to engage in negotiation. The husband, for example, who has washed dishes for five years cannot arbitrarily decide to discontinue doing so without arousing multiple repercussions, even though most husbands do not wash dishes.

Socialization for Socialization

The preceding notions suggest that an important part of the socialization process is the acquisition of certain skills, attitudes, and the like, which facilitate subsequent socialization. At the most elementary level, for example, verbal skills are a prerequisite for learning most roles. In general, as individuals get older, they are expected to possess a larger and larger repertoire of skills which facilitate the acquisition and performance of new roles. Role development is thus cumulative ; new roles building upon, modifying, and elaborating previous roles, each of which has resulted in the individual acquiring certain skills, dispositions and values that contribute to his ability to learn a new role.

Previously acquired skills may be divided roughly into those that facilitate learning and those that are prerequisite to ultimate successful performance. Into the first category fall such things as verbal skills, one's ability to perceive oneself as others perceive one, and one's ability to differentiate between real and ideal role expectations. The latter category includes a great variety of specific skills necessary to the performance of a given role; for example, typing or baseball-throwing ability. This distinction is, of course, far from perfect since many skills are relevant both to role acquisition and performance. Highly developed verbal skills are necessary, for example, both for learning how to play the role of salesman and for adequate performance in the role itself. On the other hand, typing skill is a less important prerequisite for learning what is expected of a secretary than it is for performance in the secretarial role. With respect to institutionalized roles, at least, the distinction may be operationally clarified in part by asking what skills an individual must possess in order to be permitted even to enter training for the role. Confusion frequently results, however, from the fact that entry into a position often requires that individuals possess both skills necessary to learn new behaviors expected of occupants of that position and, at least, some of the skills that ultimately will be required in the actual performance of the role. Thus the woman who applies for a job as a secretary must already have certain skills appropriate to the role of secretary, as generally defined, but must also be able to learn what is expected of her in the particular position for which she is applying. In other words, partial role-learning is often necessary before an individual can acquire all of the skills, dispositions, and the like, involved in fully adequate performance. In this sense, possession of certain role specific skills may be a prerequisite for the acquisition of new skills.

Considering just those skills and abilities necessary for role-learning (as opposed to role-performance or initial entry to the role), it is apparent that individuals differ widely with respect to the qualities they bring to situations in which role-learning and/or role-negotiation is necessary. First, some individuals possess greater verbal and cognitive symbolic skills than others. Obvious differences exist as a function of age, prior training, and experience. Since a great part of role-learning (not to mention role-negotiation) is mediated by symbolic processes of one sort or another, we may expect to find considerable differences between individuals in their ability to learn many roles according to their facility with language and the degree of their conceptual development generally (Kohlberg, Chapter 6; Greenfield and Bruner, Chapter 12; Jenkins, Chapter 13). Second, the acquisition of most roles requires that the learner have the ability to understand how others perceive him and his behavior (Cottrell, Chapter 9; Moore and Anderson, Chapter 10). Unless one possesses such understanding, it is difficult for one to evaluate the implications of situational cues pertaining to the adequacy of one's performance. The child may realize that he is being punished, but may not fully realize why unless he understands how his acts were interpreted by his mother. Furthermore, knowing how others will interpret one's behavior before one acts is of fundamental importance in choosing from among alternative behaviors, even if the individual knows what behavior is expected. Finally, significant differences often exist between what is actually expected of an individual in a given situation and the ideal role (Weinstein, Chapter 17). Students quickly learn, for example, that they need not live up to the ideal conception of the student role all of the time in order to get through school or, frequently, even to get good grades. The recognition of disparities between actual expectations and ideal roles frequently makes possible the resolution of role conflict and is nearly always a necessary skill when one is attempting to learn a new role. Usually one is unable to live up to ideal role expectations at first in any case. Realizing how closely one's behavior is expected to approximate the ideal is consequently of critical importance.

One implication to be drawn from the foregoing analysis, however tentative it may be, is that a crucial variable in determining the outcome of socialization experiences is the degree of "fit" between the individual and his immediate socializing environment. As individuals develop and move from one stage or setting to another, the amount of behavioral baggage they carry with them continually increases. In general, we characterize individuals as having a personality structure that predisposes them to behave in certain ways under varying circumstances. As we have suggested, however, much of this baggage is a prerequisite for subsequent learning, for example, symbolic and cognitive skills, a concept of self, information and specific motor skills, a repertoire of interpersonal tactics, and so on. Where critical elements are missing from the individual's store of response capabilities, serious discontinuities and disruptions of the socialization process may result when the individual attempts to learn new roles.

Furthermore, existing well-established response patterns may turn out to be dysfunctional as the individual shifts from one context to another, and very difficult to alter without placing severe strain on the individual as well as others around him. Adult socialization requires that individuals not merely continue to learn new roles. They must also learn to reconcile many conflicting demands imposed by the multiple roles confronted in middle life. Moreover, they must learn over the life course to relinquish a succession of roles (as student, parent, worker, spouse) by a process that is in many respects the reverse of the better understood process of learning to play new roles (Matilda White Riley, Anne Foner, Beth Hess and Marcia L. Toby, Chapter 23; Paul H. Mussen, Chapter 15; and William Simon and John H. Gagnon, Chapter 16).

Thus, we may talk about the consequences of socialization, or lack thereof, not only for the individual, but also for society as a whole and for specific groups and institutions in society. Several of the chapters in this volume, mainly those focusing on the stages and contexts of socialization and the problem of transition from one stage or context to another, deal directly with this problem (for example, Miller, Chapter 7; LeVine, Chapter 8; Ernest Q. Campbell, Chapter 20; Wilbert E. Moore, Chapter 21; Hill and Aldous, Chapter 22; Riley, Foner, Hess and Toby, Chapter 23; Jerome Kagan, Chapter 24; and Stanton Wheeler, Chapter 25).

CONCEPTIONS OF THE LEARNER
AND THE LEARNING PROCESS

Socialization clearly involves both conscious and unconscious learning on the part of the individual being socialized. The previous discussion of role-negotiation has tended to overemphasize the conscious, rational, and essentially purposive aspects of socialization. Much of the time, however, the individual may be viewed as a more or less passive agent in the process of role-learning and perform-ance; one who responds in various ways to situational demands, automatically tends to model his behavior after that of significant reference figures in the environment, and, in turn, makes little conscious effort to shape emerging role relationships in accordance with already established personal goals, values and conceptions of the role itself. Even in those situations where individuals appear to be making rational and conscious decisions about what roles they wish to play, what reference figures to emulate, and what expectations to incorporate into their behavioral repertoire, an essentially mechanistic conception of the process by which responses are linked to patterns of stimuli may, as we have suggested, go a long way toward enabling us to predict, or at least understand, in retrospect, social behavior. At the same time, if the degree of awareness of the individual of what is going on around him is taken as a significant intervening variable in the process, our attention is drawn to several additional factors that increase our understanding of socialization processes.

For example, as we have suggested, one important consequence of awareness on the part of the learner is enhanced attentiveness to situational cues pertinent to understanding what new behaviors are expected of him and the adequacy of his performance (Bandura, Chapter 3; Baldwin, Chapter 5). Correlative to this is the probability that the learner will display increased motivation to perform in accordance with role demands (assuming that he had some choice about entering the position in the first place). In particular, the learner is likely to pay special attention to cues indicating that external sanctions are impending unless behavior is altered. In addition, awareness often leads the learner to attempt to elicit responses from others aimed at confirming or denying the appropriateness of his behavior (for example, "I hope this was what you wanted," or "Is my dress all right?"), or to obtain specific instructions concerning his behavior in advance (for example, "What should I wear?" or "How long do you want the paper to be?").

It is interesting to note that explicit selection of role models is often encouraged by one's social group or by the society itself. Children are frequently asked to say who they most want to be like when they grow up, adolescents compare choices of figures to be emulated. Institutionalized role models such as the hero in the Western movie abound in the society. Parents often direct the attention of children to the behavior of siblings, suggesting, for example, that the younger child make use of his older brother as either a negative or positive reference figure.

The Problem of Social Control

Regardless of whether one conceptualizes socialization in more or less rationalistic terms, one must come to grips with the problem of social control. By what process or processes are individuals induced to behave in accordance with normative expectations of groups and the society? It is clear that both role-learning and adequate performance depend in part on the effectiveness of sanctions, both internal and external to the individual. The view one takes of the learner, however, leads to somewhat different interpretations of the function of sanctions in the socialization process. From a sociological point of view, for example, the occurrence of rewards or punishment may be thought of in terms of providing the learner with cues enabling him consciously to evaluate the adequacy of his performance and modify his behavior where necessary. Further, expectations on the part of individuals that they will be rewarded or punished for specified acts are conceived as important energizers or inhibitors of behavior. A more mechanistic or unconscious conception of the individual learner, however, results in concentration on how punishing and/or rewarding experiences facilitate the establishment of links between external (or internal) stimuli and behavioral responses (Gewirtz, Chapter 2). In addition, more emphasis is likely to be placed on internal as opposed to external sanctions and on the process by which external rewards and punishments become, over time, internalized.

A focus on characteristics of situations in which socialization occurs helps to make clear this distinction as well as provide a partial basis for integrating the two points of view. At the outset, situations may be characterized simply according to the extent to which role-learning and subsequent performance depend upon internal as opposed to external sanctions; that is, rewards and punishments imposed on the individual by others. Where the likelihood of externally imposed rewards or punishment for inappropriate role performance is low, learning may be hypothesized to depend more on identificatory processes (Bandura, Chapter 3; Miller, Chapter 7) and subsequent performance to depend on internalized dispositions. In those situations characterized by a high degree of external social control, both learning and at least the initial motivation to perform are likely to be a function of the type and effectiveness of sanctions present.

It is very clear that great variation exists between situations with respect to this variable. The insurance of adequate role performance in childhood, for example, probably depends more heavily on the availability and employment of external sanctions than does performance in most adult roles. As individuals get older an increasing proportion of their behavior may be assumed to become independent of external control; i.e., to become based on internalized dispositions (Aronfreed, Chapter 4; Miller, Chapter 7; Kagan, Chapter 24). At the same time it is apparent that external rewards and punishments play an important part in the internalization process itself.

External Sanctions

The majority of the contributions to this volume deal explicitly in part with the role of external sanctions in socialization. Regardless of whether the learner is assumed to be responding more or less automatically to environmental stimuli or consciously selecting among perceived alternative behaviors; or whether rewards and punishments are viewed primarily as energizers of behavior, as cues enabling individuals to distinguish between adequate and inadequate role performance, or as providing the mechanism by which responses are linked to stimuli; they are conceived as playing an integral part in social learning. Taken as a group the following chapters point to a number of important dimensions on which sanctions or the context in which they occur may vary, each having implications for the learning process. These include the strength of sanctions, whether they are positive or negative, when they occur in relation to the learner's acts, their frequency and consistency, and the form they take (for example, verbal versus physical; vicarious or direct). It is apparent that sanctions encountered by individuals in the performance or acquisition of a role may vary considerably in intensity and consistency of intensity. The experimental literature on punishment and reward indicates clearly the complexity of the relationship between strength of sanction and rate of learning, retention, discrimination, internalization, and motivation to respond to similar stimulus configurations. Extremely strong negative sanctions, for example, as in the avoidance learning paradigm, have been shown to result in the acquisition of response dispositions that are highly resistant to extinction, and are accompanied by high motivation to perform.

On the other hand, there is evidence that the ability to make subtle discriminations among stimuli is inhibited by very strong punishment, as is the ability of the learner to modify responses acquired under such conditions, even when it is appropriate for him to do so. These findings dramatize a potential inherent conflict between the factors that facilitate learning (especially subsequent learning) and those that affect motivation to perform. One explanation for this is that strong sanctions produce in the learner strong emotional responses (for example, anxiety) in addition to whatever connection may be established between stimulus and specific overt behaviors. The arousal of powerful emotions by a stimulus often results in high motivation to perform, but it may also serve to complicate subsequent discrimination on the part of the learner by, in effect, adding a new and dominating element (emotion) to the stimulus field. Thus, the child often learns something the adult did not intend rather than something he did. Psychoanalytic theory, as Miller (Chapter 7) points out, is especially sensitive to fortuitous associations created by timing and common contexts rather than the adults' intentions. Mild sanctions, on the other hand, permit full concentration on "relevant" stimuli, but may not result in high motivation to perform.

The preceding point suggests the importance of distinguishing situations according to whether they contain predominantly positive or negative sanctions. Again the distinction between acquisition and performance is an important cross-cutting variable. Given comparable levels of intensity (a difficult matter to establish independent of measures of the organism's responses), it may be hypothesized that positive and negative sanctions function with equal effectiveness as cues enabling the learner to discriminate appropriate from inappropriate responses. If one takes a drive reduction view of motivation, however, performance tendencies will depend more upon the current drive state of the organism in the case of positive sanctions than in the case of negative sanctions since we may postulate the existence of a more or less constant drive to avoid extreme pain or punishment.

A number of experiments have focused on the relationship between the timing of sanctions relative to the learner's acts and the effectiveness of the sanctions. In general, the findings indicate that closer temporal contiguity between act and reward or punishment results in more rapid acquisition of desired responses by the learner. In part this may be explained in discrimination terms; immediate sanctions make discrimination easier.

A fourth set of situational variables relating to external sanctions are the regularity and consistency with which such sanctions occur in response to individual acts. Are particular behaviors always followed by rewards or punishment from the environment; if not, do sanctions occur randomly or in accordance with some regular pattern; and, when sanctions follow behavior, how consistent are they with regard to intensity, type, timing, and the like? It may be hypothesized that the more frequent and consistent sanctions are, the easier it will be for the learner to discriminate appropriate from inappropriate acts. On the other hand, the literature on partial reinforcement indicates that, at least for some kinds of learning, stronger (in the sense of more persistent) response tendencies are acquired when sanctions are consistent in nature, but random in probability of occurrence.

In regard to each of the previous four points, it should be noted that conclusions drawn from experimental studies of learning may only be marginally relevant for analyzing certain development processes, particularly results pertaining to performance factors such as motivation, retention, and persistence of response. Under conditions in which the learner is strongly motivated in advance to learn a role (or to create a role relationship in conjunction with one or more other individuals), external sanctions will perform a primarily discriminating as opposed to motivating function (unless they are so intense as to affect the individual's prior commitment to the situation, either positively or negatively).

Finally, external sanctions vary significantly in form and immediacy of their impact on individuals. A simple distinction may be made between sanctions that are mediated by symbolic processes and those that involve a direct physical impact on the individual. Similarly, sanctions may be categorized according to whether they are experienced directly by the individual or vicariously through observation of what happens to others.

The preceding discussion has stressed the psychological characteristics of external sanctions; that is, their impact on the behavior of individuals. From a more sociological perspective, however, sanctions and sanctioning power also must be considered in terms of their availability to socializing agents in specific institutional settings and as resources subject to exchange among members of groups. As such, as I have noted, sanctions are an integral part of the process of role-negotiation and the distribution and redistribution of sanctioning power is a major factor in determining the outcome of this process. Moreover, when viewed in essentially economic terms, sanctioning power turns out to be a valuable commodity that may be competed for both within and between groups, thereby accounting for a great deal of intra- and inter-group behavior.

The Process of Internalization

It has been suggested that as an individual gets older an increasing proportion of his behavior may become independent of external control and be based instead on internalized dispositions. Internalization processes are discussed at length by a number of authors in this volume, especially Aronfreed (Chapter 4). Psychoanalytic interpretations are analyzed by Miller in Chapter 7. In general, several conclusions may be cited that lend support to the previous notions concerning reward and punishment. First, data from animal studies indicate that punishment (avoidance learning) serves as a more powerful influence on internalization than do positive rewards. Second, partial reinforcement may be assumed to play an important role in internalization, especially if one takes the view that symbolic processes function as vital mediators in internalization (Aronfreed, Chapter 4). Third, the contributions to this volume make it clear that internalization is not synonymous with freedom from stimulus control of the external environment; i.e., without stimulus cues from the environment we cannot expect individuals to display internalized behaviors. Fourth, much behavior that appears to be internally motivated may in fact be regulated by the actor's perception of surveillance by real or imagined agents of social control who are not physically present, for example, God. Fifth, with respect to the role of punishment in internalization, many studies indicate that immediacy of punishment produces greater internalization. This finding is consistent with Aronfreed's view of internalization as being primarily mediated by "cognitive representations which serve as a common intrinsic stimulus bridge across the entire sequence of proprioceptive and external cues that unfold as an act is initiated and completed" (Chapter 4, p. 275). Thus, the intensity and availability of discriminatory cues are critical to the internalization process. Finally, an interesting and somewhat different perspective on internalization is provided by W. E. Moore (Chapter 21) who suggests, in the context of an analysis of occupational socialization, that strong internal commitment to professional norms is a likely consequence of extremely arduous socialization experiences occurring under certain specified conditions.[3]

Whatever theoretical perspective one favors regarding characteristics of the learner, the convergence of opinions presented in the following chapters on the importance of symbolic or cognitive processes as mediators between the individual and his social environment is striking. It should be noted that this is due in part to a bias in the sample of theoreticians represented. Nevertheless, it represents an important development in socialization theory; one which portends the possibility of productive collaboration between those sociologists and social psychologists who take a symbolic interactionist position (for example, Cottrell, Chapter 9; and Moore and Anderson, Chapter 10) and more traditionally oriented psychological social-learning theorists. Both of the former take a naturalistic view of social learning, postulating the emergence of the social self (in G. H. Mead's, 1934, terms) as a consequence of interaction between the individual and significant others in his social environment (assuming the existence of certain critical features of the interactional system). While they tend to concentrate more on the conditions that lead to development than on the internal mechanisms that mediate social learning, their assumptions about the symbolic and cognitive capacities of human beings are very similar to those held by theorists such as Palmer (Chapter 1), Bandura (Chapter 3), Aronfreed (Chapter 4), Baldwin (Chapter 5), and Kohlberg (Chapter 6). An extensive reminder of the fact that alternative theories exist is provided by Gewirtz (Chapter 2), who examines the considerable contributions of S-R reinforcement theory in some detail.

---

[3]This is a position similar to dissonance theory explanations of changes in attitudes and behavior following severe initiations (see, for example, Aronson & Mills, 1959).

Characteristics of Socialization Settings

A major conclusion to be drawn from the preceding discussion is the importance of paying attention to characteristics of settings in which socialization takes place, especially those features of the social environment that facilitate or inhibit the learner's assessment of his own behavior and provide him with more or less explicit information concerning what is expected of him (Alex Inkeles, Chapter 11). From a sociological, and therefore admittedly rationalistic, perspective, it is apparent that interactional systems vary significantly with respect to the likelihood of the participants receiving information concerning the adequacy of their role performance. As we have suggested, external sanctions are an important part of the process whereby individuals are able to evaluate the appropriateness of their behavior. We may, however, distinguish situations along four additional dimensions relevant to the availability of information to the person socialized. These include: the extent to which the situation contains institutionalized mechanisms for teaching new members how to play their role; the frequency of informal cues (other than external sanctions) that help the learner to evaluate his own performance and that of others in the system; the rate of interaction in the system; and contextual characteristics of the system itself.[4]

Very often when an individual takes on a new position (and with it a new role) the group or even the society at large makes explicit provisions for helping the individual to learn his role by providing formal instruction in the skills, values, and normative expectations that are necessary for adequate performance. Executive or sales training programs operated by large corporations and orientation programs for college freshmen are good examples of such institutionalized attempts to provide the socializee with information about what will be expected of him in his new position (W. E. Moore, Chapter 21). On a somewhat less formal, but nevertheless still institutionalized level, is the "instruction" likely to be received by the prospective bride and bridegroom concerning the behavior that will be expected of them in their roles as husband and wife (Hill and Aldous, Chapter 22). In this case, family, friends, and occasionally "experts" such as the family doctor; priest, minister, or rabbi; or a marriage counselor take responsibility for providing information. It may be hypothesized that formal instruction (in the training-program sense) is more likely and possible for roles or aspects of roles that are relatively nonnegotiable and dependent upon external sanctions as opposed to internal control mechanisms. On the other hand, informal instruction is likely to stress the negotiable aspects of the role and may actually be directed to both (or all) participants in the system simultaneously, as in the case of the minister counseling the bride and bridegroom as a couple. Similarly, the new prison inmate is likely to receive formal instruction from the warden and the guards with respect to the nonnegotiable elements of his role, and informal instruction from his fellow inmates regarding the negotiable aspects of his role (Wheeler, Chapter 25).

---

[4]In considering each of these dimensions, it is important to keep in mind the fact that stage of socialization is a significant cross-cutting variable.

In learning a new role individuals pay attention to formal and informal instructions or advice and also to sanctions that facilitate discrimination between adequate and inadequate performance. Such discriminations are aided, however, by a multiplicity of informal cues given by other participants in the interactional system. Cues may, for example, serve to warn the learner that sanctions are impending unless he alters his behavior or may identify a particular act within a set of behaviors as the reason why sanctions were exercised. Informal cues are particularly important in situations where reciprocal roles must be negotiated since they provide participants with information about whether the course of action being followed in the negotiation is having the desired result on the other participant(s). Further, informal cues are a vital part of the process of role-taking, observational learning and, ultimately, internalization, since they make it possible for the learner to interpret the behavior of others (particularly alter's responses to ego) in terms of the learner's own feelings and emotions.

It is obvious that effective socialization is impossible under conditions where the individual is isolated from the system into which he is being socialized. Accordingly, it may be postulated that ease of role-learning and/or role development will be directly related to the rate of interaction among the participants in the system. Interaction serves several important functions with respect to role development. First, the exercise of external sanctions is difficult under conditions of low interaction except in highly formalized settings such as the military where infrequent contact between authority figures and other members of the system may actually facilitate sanctioning behavior. Second, infrequent interaction makes it difficult for participants in the system to find out by experimentation whether acquired behaviors are appropriate or not, and whether their interpretation of how their role should be played coincides with the interpretation of others. Third, motivation for adequate performance is difficult to sustain under conditions of low interaction, unless high internalization is postulated. Finally, role negotiation is virtually impossible unless the rate of interaction is high.

Some qualification must be made, however. Homans (1950) and others have pointed out that, other factors being equal, degree of interaction is directly related to the affective (emotional) content of the relationship. It may be assumed, therefore, that frequent interaction tends to lead to more affective involvement of the participants in the relationship—either positive or negative. In situations where the institutionalized roles attached to positions in the system are supposed to be nonemotional in character (secondary), high rates of interaction may fundamentally alter the character of the roles themselves and, as a result, be potentially disrupting to the system. For example, negotiation may become both possible and necessary. If negotiation then fails, the system as a whole may suffer. In addition, the more interaction, the more complex becomes the interchange of informal cues which requires that the participants in the system have the capacity to deal with increasingly subtle indicators of role expectations. If this capacity is not equally distributed among the participants in the system, the possibility emerges of explicit exploitation of the relationship by those who are able to interpret behavioral cues accurately and who possess the interpersonal techniques necessary for sophisticated role negotiations. Finally, as interaction continues at a high rate over time, the relationship acquires a history. This history may have important constraining effects on the behavior of the participants, particularly when changes in the external situation necessitate alterations in the roles of one or more participants or even renegotiation of the relationship itself.

Socialization settings may be distinguished further according to a number of structural characteristics that affect, in important ways, the availability of information to individuals within the system. In his discussion of formally organized socialization settings, Wheeler (1966) has called attention to a number of these variables, including, among others, whether the socializee is alone in learning his role or in the company of other new members of the system, whether the role he is learning is a new role or whether others have been socialized into it before him, and the extent to which responsibility for socialization of new members is formally allocated to specific members of the system. In addition, situations vary significantly in regard to the extent to which they provide the socializee with role models whose behavior may be emulated by the learner.

Implicit in a great many of the points made above is the notion that an important variable affecting the success of socialization experiences throughout the life cycle, but especially during childhood, is the extent to which individuals have an opportunity to experiment (consciously or unconsciously) with alternative behavioral responses to environmental stimuli without suffering dire consequences if they choose inappropriately in the beginning. From one perspective, therefore, optimally effective socializing environments may be thought of as protected settings designed to provide maximum feedback to the individual regarding the consequences of his acts (Moore and Anderson, Chapter 10).

CONCLUSION

The preceding discussion brings into clear focus, I think, some of the issues raised by sociological as opposed to psychological perspectives on socialization. During the course of development human beings acquire more or less stable sets of responses to a variety of environmental stimuli. Although there is disagreement among theorists concerning the principal mechanisms by which the link between a stimulus and a response is established, evidence indicates that learning may take place in several different ways. Moreover, it is apparent that both naturalistic, essentially unconscious, learning takes place, as well as learning in which the socializee takes an active part in attempting to consciously modify his own behavior and the behavior of others around him. Finally, social learning takes place in an interactional and cultural context that often is characterized by institutionalized mechanisms designed to facilitate acquisition by the learner of specific skills, dispositions, and values. Once certain response capabilities have been established, maintenance and regulation of appropriate behavior patterns may occur either through continued exercise of externally imposed rewards and punishments, or as a result of processes internal to the individual that may be considered to be a product of the original learning experiences. Thus the individual may be viewed not only as responsive to external stimuli, but also as producing stimuli, to which he himself, along with others, responds.

These and other issues are dealt with in considerably greater detail in the chapters that follow. The relatively simplistic perspectives provided above should not be permitted to lull the reader into imagining that social learning processes are not exceedingly complex or that major disagreements among theorists as to the nature of these processes still do not exist. As a focus of scientific inquiry, socialization is still in its infancy. As with any infant (as this volume makes abundantly clear) the factors that may be expected to influence its continued growth and development are numerous and not always in accord with one another. Out of this process, however, will someday emerge a mature discipline. It is my hope that this volume will have contributed in some measure to speeding up the maturational process, if not to the ultimate shape of the discipline itself.

REFERENCES

ARONSON, E., & MILLS, J. The effect of severity of initiation on liking for a group. *Journal of Abnormal and Social Psychology,* 1959, 59, 177-181.

BIDDLE, B. J., & THOMAS, E. J. (Eds.) *Role theory: Concepts and research.* New York: Wiley, 1966.

BRIM, O. G., JR. Socialization through the life cycle. In O. G. Brim, Jr., & S. Wheeler, *Socialization after childhood.* New York: Wiley, 1966.

CLAUSEN, J. A. A historical and comparative view of socialization theory and research. In J. A. Clausen (Ed.), *Socialization and society.* Boston: Little, Brown & Co., 1968.

GOFFMAN, E. *The presentation of self in everyday life.* New York: Doubleday, 1959.

GROSS, N. C., MASON, W. S., & McEACHERN, A. W. *Explorations in role analysis: Studies of the school superintendency role.* New York: Wiley, 1958.

HOMANS, G. C. *The human group.* New York: Harcourt, Brace, 1950.

JONES, E. E., & GERARD, H. B. *Foundations of social psychology.* New York: Wiley, 1967.

MEAD, G. H. *Mind, self and society: From the standpoint of a social behaviorist.* Chicago: Univer. of Chicago Press, 1934.

MERTON, R. K. *Social theory and social structure: Toward the codification of theory and research.* Glencoe, Ill.: Free Press of Glencoe, 1957.

PARSONS, T., & SHILS, E. A. (Eds.) *Toward a general theory of action.* Cambridge, Mass.: Harvard Univer. Press, 1951.

THIBAUT, J. W., & KELLEY, H. H. *The social psychology of groups.* New York: Wiley, 1959.

WHEELER, S. The structure of formally organized socialization settings. In O. G. Brim, Jr., & S. Wheeler, *Socialization after childhood.* New York: Wiley, 1966.

PART I
THEORETICAL APPROACHES
TO THE
SOCIALIZATION PROCESS

CHAPTER **1**

Inferences To The Socialization
Of The Child From Animal Studies:
A View From The Bridge

Francis H. Palmer

City University of New York

From the time that John B. Watson fled the for him tumultuous academic life at Johns Hopkins University to the relatively quiet and protected life of Madison Avenue to the April day in 1957 when Harry Harlow (1958) first reported publicly on "The Nature of Love," a curious void existed between the results of animal studies and the deliberations of those concerned with the intellective growth of children. Those who followed in Watson's path denied the need to extend their results to human behavior, and those concerned with children were only vaguely aware of what animal investigators were doing. But Harlow's graphic documentation of the behavior of infant monkeys reared with man-made surrogate mothers made it virtually impossible for his audience to leave without speculating about the implication of those data to the intellective and emotional development of the child.

Exposed to the sound of a noisy tin toy, monkeys reared with wire mother surrogates exhibited maladaptive behavior as severe as those associated with studies of experimental neurosis, and the antecedents of that behavior did not involve conditioning techniques and physical trauma. Other monkeys, provided contact comforts by a foam rubber and terry cloth mother, were momentarily frightened by the same toy and then explored the stimulus as good monkeys do. Subsequent research by Harlow and his colleagues lead him to modify some of his conclusions and reinstate the mother in the nature of love. But perhaps more important, those first reports created an atmosphere within which one could publicly speculate on the relevance of animal studies to human behavior.

The unpublished data referred to in this chapter is from a larger longitudinal study not yet completed. That study is supported by grant HD-02253, National Institute of Health. Partial support for the first year was from the Center for Urban Education, New York City. The research was done in the Harlem Research Center of the Institute for Child Development and Experimental Education of The City University of New York.

Generalization from animal studies was raised on the hierarchy of allowable inference.

While behavioral scientists were beginning to speak their private thoughts aloud, the awkward American concern for relating politics with humanity was seeking something new to assuage our guilt and to provide a rallying cry for votes to support the Great Society. The rallying point became poverty and its truly iniquitous effects, and what aspect of poverty is better suited to attract the American voter than the disadvantaged child? From Harvard was heard a voice even more eloquent than Watson's, under proper conditions and instructions the child could be taught any task at any age. Regardless of the dearth of data to solidly support that hypothesis, society was handed a touchstone where political action and the frustrated drives of scientists, educators and legislators could be joined at last.

The preschool child is IN, and while the reasons may be more outside social science than in it, social scientists are benefiting by an increase in research funds and access to children for study. We can anticipate an enormous increase in the number of children who will be involved in some form of preschool training. The number of preschools as they exist today will increase. For good or bad, programs designed to deal with younger and younger children will be developed. Curricula and materials related to intellective growth will be made available to mothers for more systematic training in the home. As the number of preschool programs increase, the impact of those programs as a socialization agent will increase. Indeed, if the relationship between very early experience and subsequent behavior is as strong as this chapter suggests, preschool programs may change the socialization process of our children as few things have done in this century.

The increased number of preschool programs will also increase the number of two- and three-year-old children who are accessible for research. Data will be forthcoming which will more clearly delineate the age at which socioeconomic variables begin to accelerate or decelerate intellective and social growth, and specific stimuli within the socioeconomic environment which stimulate or retard growth will be identified.

If the mushrooming preschool movements are to have the above effects, the assumptions behind that movement deserve examination. What are these assumptions? Deutsch (1965) has recently suggested that there are at least four which underlie the development of the modern preschool: (a) Earlier intervention is superior to later intervention. (b) Any intervention is better than none. (c) A rich program for a limited period of time will ignite growth until then dormant. And, (d) diverse compensatory stimulation is required when the child's environmental background is limited.

Whether or not these assumptions are related to the expansion of the preschool movement may be debated, but there is no doubt that they are hypotheses widely held by many persons actively engaged with preschool children. As such they should be examined from several points of view, to include the extent to which they are substantiated by research on the growth of young animals.

There is a long history of animal research with implications for intellective growth of the child, and in the last decade such research has been pursued with increased vigor and imagination. Because it appears to be particularly relevant to the above assumptions, this chapter will examine so much of the animal data as is related to the effects of early deprivation, and the concept of critical periods of development.

The deprivation literature is particularly provocative because the effects of deprivation have been shown to be relatively consistent across species. Different studies vary with respect to the stage of development of the organism when deprivation is introduced, the length and intensity of deprivation, and the categories of behavior affected. A typical design provides for a control and experimental group, where the animals in the latter are prevented from gratifying needs associated with primary or secondary drives or from stimulation normally found in the organism's environment, or both, and where the dependent variable is related to cognitive, perceptual, emotional or social behavior. There is, as we shall see, an orderliness to the results of these studies, and there is strong implication that, as the phylogenetic scale is ascended, the relationship between early stimulation and subsequent social and emotional behavior increases. It is this relationship which makes the data so pertinent for socialization theory. If stimulation or lack of it plays a major role in emotional and social as well as intellective development, it is an intermediary which prepares the host for the shaping influences of socialization forces.

In examining the data on animal deprivation it is useful to use the distinction between drive and stimulus deprivation. Bronfenbrenner (1968) has shown that the distinction is important in the formation of hypotheses about the unique but interacting roles of the two, and his recent summary of these data has expedited the writing of this chapter considerably. His definitions of drive and stimulus deprivation are below:

Drive deprivation: "At an early period in its life the organism is prevented from normal gratification of hunger, sucking, etc., or secondary drives acquired through learning."

Stimulus deprivation: "During infancy the organism is prevented from experiencing stimuli normally encountered in the course of early life."

Since it is not the purpose of this chapter to review the literature, but to examine the results of animal studies for implications about the development of the preschool child, illustrative studies of drive and stimulus deprivation are summarized below for the reader who is unacquainted with the deprivation literature. Those interested in a wider selection are referred to Bronfenbrenner (1968).

Drive deprivation.   Elliot and King (1960) investigated the effects of early food deprivation on subsequent behavior toward food and other dependent variables. They divided 14 dogs into two groups equated in breed, litter, and sex. Each group of seven was raised in a room equipped with wire stalls which provided for individual eating. The deprived group was fed twice

each day for periods of five minutes, within the individual stalls. The nondeprived group was allowed two ten-minute feedings each day within the stalls,
but in addition was fed *ad libitum* when not in the stalls. The treatment was
continued from four to seven weeks of age, after which both groups were fed
ad libitum for six weeks under conditions where surplus food was continuously
left in the room. The effects were measured in terms of subsequent reactions
to familiar and unfamiliar human beings, food consumption after 23 hours
of deprivation, motivation to reach unattainable food, and learning an avoidance response to food. It was found that the deprived dogs responded with
more frequent approaches and fewer avoidances to both familiar and unfamiliar persons, and that they ate faster and were more active in trying
to obtain food. While many of these effects tended to dissipate rapidly and
the results of the study are meaningful only when put into the perspective of
others, the procedure is illustrative of the traditional approach to studies of
drive deprivation.

Stimulus deprivation.   Riesen (1947) investigated the effects of extreme
visual deprivation on the development of two infant chimpanzees. The animals
were raised in total darkness until the age of 16 months except for a 45-second
period each day for care of the animals. At 16 months they were exposed
to light periodically during testing, and at 21 months the female was placed
in an illuminated environment permanently, but the male was provided light
only during meals and tests. At 16 months the animals had developed postural
and locomotor skills roughly comparable to chimpanzees reared under conditions of normal illumination, and the pursuit of moving light with eyes and
head were normal; however, the ability to fixate on light and to make visually
mediated responses was impaired. Their learning of an avoidance response to
electric shock and the acquisition of visually mediated responses was extremely
slow. The male was consistently slower in learning such responses than the
female.

Interaction of drive and stimulus deprivation.   Harlow and Zimmerman (1958) investigated the effects of tactile stimulation to include contact
comfort on the behavior of infant monkeys. Since they did not control for the
stimulus deprivation the monkeys were subjected to as a function of being separated from the mother, the study is an example of deprivation of the opportunity to acquire the dependency drive as well as deprivation of kinaesthetic
and tactile stimulation normally provided by the mother.

Infant monkeys were separated from their natural mothers six to twelve
hours after birth and were placed in separate cages with surrogate mothers.
One surrogate was a wire mesh cylinder, the other a wooden cylinder covered
with terry cloth. Each surrogate had a different "face" attached but all were
equipped with nipples in the "chest." The surrogates were placed in a cubicle
adjoining the living cage for each individual animal at a 45-degree angle to
facilitate normal monkey clinging. Some surrogate mothers of both types pro-

vided milk through the nipples and some did not. After 165 to 190 days, the infants were separated from their mother surrogates to measure the effects of separation. Other measures were taken while the animals were living with their surrogate mothers.

Measures were taken of the time spent on the surrogate mother, reaction to fear-producing stimuli both in the living cage and in an open field situation, and the number of times the infant opened a door to look at various objects to include the surrogate. They found that infants reared on the terry cloth surrogates spent more time on that object whether or not the surrogate lactated, and that infants opened the door to look at the terry cloth mother much more frequently. The incidence of clinging to the terry cloth surrogate as compared to the wire mesh surrogate was interpreted by the investigators as the development of a dependency drive. When exposed to a novel stimulus, those reared with the terry cloth mothers clung to the mother and then left her to investigate the stimulus; those reared on the wire mesh mother did not go to the surrogate, did not exhibit normal curiosity toward the stimulus, and evidenced extremely deviant behavior to fear-producing stimuli. This was the first of a series of studies by Harlow and his colleagues which have contributed immensely to our understanding of the role of contact comfort variables in animal development.

Because the concept of critical periods in the development of the child has been particularly attractive to practitioners and investigators alike, the literature on that subject will be discussed and its usefulness examined. It states that specific stimulation must occur within a limited period of time if responses associated with the stimulation are to become part of the child's repertoire of behavior, and if the stimulation occurs before or after that time, its effects will be limited if they exist at all. Clearly, the all or none implications of the critical periods hypothesis has relevance for preschool development. Some of the assumptions underlying the development of modern preschool programs imply that there are data which show that intellective growth can be triggered or ignited by a rich experience during a limited period of the child's early life. If our knowledge of infrahuman organisms does not support that assumption, that fact should be communicated to practitioners for whom the term "critical period" has strong attraction.

DRIVE DEPRIVATION

Studies of drive deprivation have for the most part considered the effects upon the organism of preventing it from normal gratification of hunger (e.g., Hunt, 1941), sucking (e.g., Ross, 1951), and tactile stimulation and body contact as well as dependency on the mother (e.g., Harlow & Zimmerman, 1958). Change in behavior resulting from manipulation of drive has been studied with respect to learning capacity, general activity, aggressiveness, hoarding, and emotionality (in rats); and the organisms relationship to humans and other animals of its species, degree of nonnutritive sucking, manipulatory behavior,

TABLE 1.1

TYPICAL DRIVES, BEHAVIORAL MEASURES AND ORGANISMS
USED IN DRIVE DEPRIVATION STUDIES*

Measure	Drive				
	Food and/or Water Deprivation	Maternal Deprivation	Social Deprivation	Sucking	Thermal & Tactual Stimulation
Activity Level/Exploratory Behavior	Mice—53	Dogs—29	Dogs—91		Dogs—91 Rats—18,23,24
Consummatory Behavior	Dogs—28				Rats—55,56
Dependency Behavior (Maternal)				Dogs—51	Monkeys—41,42,43
Emotional Behavior		Rats—22,71	Dogs—68,93	Cats—90 Rats—1	Dogs—67,68 Monkeys—41,42,43,89 Rats—20,24,86
Gastric Ulcers				Rats—2	
Hoarding Behavior	Rats—48,49,63, 65,95				
Learning Ability/Problem Solving Ability	Mice—53 Rats—3,4,13,21			Cats—90	Dogs—14,92 Rats—7,8,16,19,57
Maternal Behavior		Rats—10			
Oral Activity		Cats—82		Cats—81 Dogs—59,83,88 Monkeys—6	
Pecking Behavior	Chicks—60				
Sexual Behavior		Monkeys—40	Rats—5		
Social Behavior	Dogs—28	Cats—82 Monkeys—40	Mice—35	Cats—90	Dogs—69
Survival Rate/Body Weight					Rats—58

*The numbers in the body of the table refer to studies in the list of references.

aggressiveness, emotionality, and learning ability (in cats, dogs, and monkeys).
Table 1.1 shows the range of measures used to study the various drives, and
representative organisms on which such studies have been conducted.

What have these studies found about drive deprivation in infrahuman
organisms? From a recent review by Bronfenbrenner (1968), the following
summary statements can be made:

Early drive deprivation leads to increased drive level both in general and
particularly with respect to the specific need previously deprived. Drive
strength is a function of the development of the organism, the degree of deprivation, and the strength of the drive at the time of initial deprivation. Increased drive resulting from early deprivation can have a facilitating or inhibiting effect on a given behavior pattern depending on how well-organized
the pattern was before deprivation. Thus, a behavior pattern organized before
deprivation can be facilitated through increased drive, and a pattern poorly
organized or not yet organized before deprivation will be organized later with
greater difficulty. High drive and an unorganized behavior pattern before deprivation will lead to frustration manifested by anxiety, inhibition of exploratory and manipulatory behavior, fear, aggressiveness, etc., when faced with
learning the behavior in the future.

As a consequence of reinforcement of body contact and associated primary drives, the organism develops a successively stronger secondary drive for
contact with the mother (frequently referred to as the dependency drive).
Secondary drives have the properties of primary drive where the effects of
deprivation are concerned. Separation from the mother thus has the effect of
drive deprivation. Within undetermined limits the more reinforcement the dependency drive has had through contact with the mother, the stronger the
drive and the more pronounced the effects of separation. Where behavior patterns are fixed before separation from the mother and the dependency drive is
high, subsequent development of the pattern may be expected to be facilitated.
Where they are not fixed before separation, and the dependency drive is high,
we may expect drive frustration manifested in the aberrant behaviors listed
above. Where the dependency drive is low because of lack of reinforcement
through mother-child contact, the effects of separation from the mother will
be less of a facilitator for already fixed patterns and less of an inhibitor for
those not yet established or poorly established.

If we assume that strength of dependency drive in the infant is a function
of the intensity and frequency of tactile, kinaesthetic, visual and auditory stimulation provided largely by the mother, presumably the number and nature of
mother-child interactions will be related to the amount of drive strength.

When a child is separated from his mother in order to attend a preschool,
it is usually the first such separation for a protracted time or in a systematic
sense. The separation deprives the child of the relationship he has had with
his mother until then. We may also expect that, upon separation, new conditions arise which alter that relationship further. Consequently, we can hypoth-

esize that the change in the child's behavior upon being frustrated by separation is a function of antecedent and new conditions which surround separation. Antecedent conditions which affect the type of behavior the child will exhibit upon separation include the intensity of the dependency drive and the extent to which habit patterns which are relevant to the demands on the child at separation are fixed. New conditions include modifiers of the environment at the time of separation, such as (a) the extent to which the mother-child relationship changes as the result of part-time separation, (b) remedial action taken by the mother to meet problems associated with the separation, and (c) the extent to which the preschool situation provides an environment related to the child's existing behavior patterns. The effects of separation will be two: an increased drive state, the intensity of which is a function of previous mother-child interaction, and a response to frustration upon separation, which is a function of antecedent and existing conditions.

From the animal literature we would expect the intensity of drive upon separation to be positively related to the degree of frustration, and the degree of frustration to manifest itself in behavior such as aggression, regression, withdrawal, and emotional reactions to include persistent crying and thumb and object sucking. Presumably where the mother-child relationship is altered least and where the mother's and teacher's remedial actions are well executed, the nonfacilitative components of separation frustration will be minimized. This does not mean that drive level per se will be reduced, but that the nonproductive responses will be reduced.

Furthermore we can hypothesize that in the case of the child with high dependency drive, initial reaction to frustration will be with the nonproductive responses listed above, regardless of the extent to which behavior patterns relevant to the new situation have been fixed. However, the duration of such responses will be determined partly by pre-established patterns. Where antecedent and concurrent modifiers of the environment are equal, the child with established and relevant patterns of behavior will more quickly be guided to productive responses within the preschool situation, and the high drive level will generalize to school-related activities. Where the drive level is high and relevant behavior patterns have not been established, nonproductive responses associated with separation from the mother will continue. In extreme cases of high drive and poorly established patterns of behavior, we would predict increasingly maladaptive responses toward a preschool situation and lasting negative associations to environments similar to it.

Low dependency drive will result in low frustration upon initial separation and in fewer and less intense elicitations of interfering of nonproductive responses. The child will be more adaptable to the preschool situation and because of the absence of such responses may at first progress better than the high drive child regardless of pre-established patterns of behavior. In the uncommon instance of low drive and well-established patterns of behavior we would predict slow but steady progress in preschool situations, at least until other secondary drives associated with that environment could be developed with greater intensity. Low dependency drive and poorly established patterns of behavior will result in fewer interfering responses initially, but progress in a preschool situation will be slow and the child will be vulnerable to other problems associated with being unable to meet that new situation's criteria. It is in this latter group that the truly disadvantaged may be found. They are underdeveloped with respect to prerequisite behaviors and low in drive. The problem for formal schooling at any level is compounded.

Finally, we would hypothesize that learning and emotional problems associated with schooling have as their origin the lack of relevant and fixed patterns of behavior when separation from the mother occurs, and that such problems will be most intense for children on the extremes of the strength of dependency drive continuum.

Interaction between level of dependency drive and level of organization of relevant behavior patterns should provide a basis for predicting when a child should begin a preschool and what the preschool should provide the child.

The child with high dependency and low organization of relevant behavior would appear to be a poor candidate. Intervention should first occur at home, by stressing to the mother that she must accompany her interactions with instruction in responses relevant to behavior patterns the child will need in the preschool environment. What some of these behaviors are and how mothers might obtain information designed to guide appropriate instruction will be dealt with later.

Children with high dependency drive and well-established patterns of behavior, or with low drive whether relevant behaviors are established or not, would benefit from preschool experience which begins as early as is practical. The former are equipped with respect to drive and behavior and are prepared for more complex socialization to include interaction with peers; low drive children are unlikely to be exposed to more intense mother-child interaction in the home and preschool situations may provide possibilities for developing other secondary drives which can subsequently be related to school-related behavior.

This framework provides a reasonable explanation for the occasional child from the large illiterate slum family who does do well in school situations. Despite his background of low socioeconomic status, patterns of behavior have been organized which are transferable to the school situation, and the mother-child relationship has been intense. It could also account for the child from the middle-class home who in his earliest school experience is retarded, but who has no somatic defect. The mother-child relationship has not been adequate for the development of an unspecified level of dependency drive, behavior patterns which are school-relevant have not been developed, or both. The two are not unlikely correlates. Where the mother has not developed an adequate interaction with the child, presumably there is less opportunity to help the child develop patterns of behavior.

In this manner we can conclude that in most cases earlier intervention is superior to later intervention. However, where the child has a high dependency drive and poorly organized school-relevant behaviors, intervention should not occur in the form of preschool. Intervention should be in the form of manipulating the mother to develop those behaviors, and preschool should be delayed, with the mother's cooperation. The argument for earlier and earlier intervention by the preschool is best when the dependency drive is low, to allow for the development of other secondary drives relevant to subsequent schooling.

Our inferences from the drive deprivation literature with animals have been made to apply to the child in a single instance, the secondary drive associated with dependency upon the mother. That secondary drive implicitly depends on primary drives related to kinaesthetic and tactile stimulation. That emphasis does not preclude the probability that other primary drives may influence the child and his socialization. However, specific hypotheses are more difficult to come by for deprivation of hunger and thirst due to the difficulty of identifying children who have been exposed to such deprivation and of measuring the amount. Mother-child interaction is measurable in terms of duration, rate and intensity of stimulation associated with such variables as visual, auditory, kinaesthetic and tactile contact.

The interaction between level of dependency drive and level of previously established behavior patterns relevant to the preschool situation allows for specific working hypotheses.

Hypothesis 1. High dependency drive is a function of the frequency and intensity of previous auditory, visual, kinaesthetic and tactile contact with the mother.

Hypothesis 2. The child with high dependency drive upon initial separation from the mother will manifest withdrawal, hyperexcitability, and anxiety responses, the duration of which will be a function of the extent to which patterns of behavior appropriate for the situation surrounding separation have been previously fixed.

Hypothesis 3. The child with low dependency drive will not elicit the maladaptive responses of the high dependent child upon initial separation of the mother regardless of the level to which behavior patterns appropriate to the situation have been fixed.

Hypothesis 4. The child with high dependency drive and a low level of fixed patterns of behavior appropriate for preschool situations will persist in maladaptive responses to school situations and is a candidate for subsequent behavioral problems.

Hypothesis 5. The child with low dependency drive and low fixed patterns of behavior appropriate for preschool situations will become a low achiever in subsequent schooling at the preschool and primary level.

Hypothesis 6. The direction of behavior associated with frustration from initial separation will be modified by:

a) The extent to which the mother-child relationship is altered by the conditions surrounding separation.

b) Remedial action taken by the mother or new caretaker to meet problems associated with separation.

c) The extent to which the new situation provides mother surrogate relationships, or

d) The extent to which the new situation identifies already existing behavior patterns and is reinforcing for their continued use and development.

STIMULUS DEPRIVATION

In our considerations of the effects of drive deprivation on the preschool child we have emphasized the interaction of one drive, dependency, and the extent to which the child has developed relevant patterns of behavior for the new environment he meets upon separation from the mother. Clearly the question is what behavior patterns should be established before separation which are relevant to the preschool situation, and how are they established. The animal literature on stimulus deprivation has implications for that question. Table 1.2 shows typical stimulus modalities and behavioral measures used in studies of stimulus deprivation, and lists representative organisms on which such studies have been conducted.

The results of stimulus deprivation studies from Bronfenbrenner (1968) may be summarized as follows:

The infant organism has a drive for perceptual motor stimulation which increases with exposure to stimuli. Except for the possibility of deleterious effects of overstimulation about which we know little, the more stimulation he gets, the more he seeks. However, organisms which have been deprived of stimuli when very young are subsequently more active and excitable when exposed to new stimuli. This apparent contradiction between an increase in drive for stimulation with exposure to stimuli and activity and excitability in the deprived animal has been shown to be due to the fact that the normal animal is more quickly satiated with a new stimulus. Where the deprived organism is undifferentiated in his responses to a new stimulus and continues to be excited by it, the normal animal more quickly adapts and ceases to be excited by it.

The debilitating effects of sensory deprivation increase as the organism shifts from passive to active participation with its environment, then decrease with respect to a specific modality as the behavior patterns associated with it become more organized. While there are no data to bear directly on the subject, we might expect that altricial species, dependent on the mother for initial sustenance, would be less vulnerable to deprivation during early life than precocial species, who are self-sustaining from birth. In any event, once behavior patterns are developed through interaction with the environment, deprivation of stimuli related to those behaviors has less effect.

To the extent that deprivation occurs early in life and continues, cognitive

TABLE 1.2

TYPICAL STIMULUS MODALITIES, BEHAVIORAL MEASURES AND ORGANISMS
USED IN STIMULUS DEPRIVATION STUDIES*

Measure	Stimulus Modality			
	Motor	Motor and Sensory	Tactual	Visual
Activity Level/Exploratory Behavior	Rats—74	Dogs—91 Rats—61		
Emotional Behavior	Rats—32	Dogs—66,67,93		Rats—32
Learning Ability/Problem Solving Ability	Rats—32,33	Dogs—14 Rats—9,15,30,31,46, 50,61		Rats—32
Psychological Measures				Chimps—76
Sensori-motor Coordination		Cats—47	Chimps—69	Chicks—71 Rats—53
Social Behavior				Dogs—68
Visual Discrimination		Cats—47,78		Cats—78,79 Chimps—12 Monkeys—36 Rats—34,37,38,44,45, 64,94

*The numbers in the body of the table refer to studies in the list of references.

and emotional defects are more severe, and the success of remedial treatment diminishes. Thus it is the duration of deprivation interacting with the stage of development of the organism which is significant. The longer the deprivation during the period of life when the organism normally more and more actively engages the environment, the more serious the effects, and stimulus exposure to those previously deprived is more remedially effective where the deprivation period has been shorter.

Cognitive impairment is manifested in attention span, ability to differentiate between stimuli and responses, learning ability, and problem solving. Emotional disturbances occur as reduced capacity for differentiation, anxiety, withdrawal and/or hyperexcitability, and an impaired capacity for engaging in normal social and sexual interaction with other animals. Thus stimulus deprivation results in not only cognitive deficit but in emotional effects reminiscent of the responses found from frustration from separation from the mother, and in long term effects in the sexual and social domains.

The similarity of some of the effects of stimulus deprivation and of separation from the mother raises the question of interaction between the two variables. Many studies have withdrawn the mother as a condition of stimulus deprivation thereby confounding the two. It has been clearly shown, however, that control groups provided with stimulus variability in the absence of the mother develop cognitive and emotional behavior superior to animals deprived of relevant stimuli and the mother. While withdrawal of the mother unquestionably reduces the stimulus variability available to the young organism, environments have frequently been contrived whereby stimulation of a specific modality is adequate for normal or near normal development. Thus there is no question but that the presence of the mother and other animals provides an enriched stimulus situation for the infant organism. But neither is there question but that stimulus deprivation per se results in behavioral deficit.

Comparing results across species indicates that certain effects are more or less significant as the phylogenetic scale is ascended. In higher species the mother and other animals play a greater role in providing stimulus variation, the vulnerability to stimulus deprivation is greater, and the organism more readily responds to remedial treatment. Thus, the effects of stimulus deprivation are more severe for monkeys than for rats, but the monkey can repair the deficit more effectively when exposed to stimuli formerly deprived.

The Development of Relevant Behavior Patterns

Earlier it was suggested that the child's ability to cope with a new environment which included separation from the mother depended on at least two variables: the intensity of mother-child interaction prior to separation, and the previous development of behavior patterns relevant to the new environment. There are four summary statements from the animal literature which appear highly relevant to that development:

(a) the infant organism has a drive for stimulation which increases with exposure to stimuli;

(b) the effects of stimulus deprivation increase as the organism becomes less passive and more actively interacts with his environment;

(c) the effects of deprivation increase with its duration, and with the development of the organism, until relevant patterns of behavior are established; and

(d) as the phylogenetic scale is ascended, stimulus deprivation has more severe effects, but the success of remedial treatment increases.

From the above, certain working hypotheses can be developed about the growth of the child which appear to be directly relevant to the establishment of behaviors referred to previously as prerequisites for subsequent development. Such hypotheses must, of course, be made with certain caveats. Until data is available about the relationship between deprivation of specific sensory modalities in the human infant and subsequent deficit, generalizing from infrahuman species to human is tenuous. Even if the generalizations prove to be correct, the specific stimulus modalities critical for infrahuman growth may be different for the human in kind or degree. Also, increased ability to respond to remedial treatment as we ascend the phylogenetic scale may imply that higher organisms are more capable of mobilizing intact behavior for the repair of deficit resulting from deprivation of a specific modality, in which case the human may be less vulnerable to deprivation of a specific modality providing that stimulation of other modalities has been adequate. Also, there are undoubtedly stimulus dimensions critical for human development which have not been studied with animals, such as those associated with the development of language.

Nor is there a body of knowledge about the effects of overstimulation on the young organism. Studies exist which show deterioration of receptors and even of central nervous system mechanisms as a result of intense physical stimulation, but none have demonstrated their deficit results from a high frequency of moderate stimulation. It seems unlikely that too much pattern vision, for example, might have a harmful effect on the young organism provided that the intensity of stimulation was moderate, but we don't know. More important are questions about what constitutes an adequate amount of stimulation, and what are the periods in development when stimulation is most critical.

A. The Child Needs Increasingly Complex Levels of Stimulation

If we accept the animal literature and infer to the development of the child, we can develop:

Hypothesis 7. The human infant has a drive for stimulation which increases with exposure to stimuli.

This statement introduces the problem of what stimulation and in what sequence. Since there are few examples of research on stimulus components which have specific effects in the subsequent development of the infant or child, our best estimates for the infant are those which have been shown to be essential for the normal development of animals. Simple and varied stimulation of the auditory, visual, kinaesthetic and tactile modalities, within moderate intensities, would presumably satisfy the infant's initial need.

The one study known to the author which has examined longitudinally the effects of such variables is by Rubenstein (1966), who demonstrated that the frequency and variety of auditory and tactile contacts between mother and child at three months is positively related to responsiveness to novel stimuli at six months. Hopefully, Rubenstein's work will provoke more interest in such difficult research and information will become available as to what specific early stimulation is related to what specific responses later.

If the above hypothesis is valid, however, its most important message is not simply that the infant needs stimulation, but that the more he gets, the more he needs, and stimuli must be increasingly complex for continued development. This suggests that an environment adequate for one level of development is inadequate for another, and has implications for individual differences within and across cultures as well as for profound questions about the optimum human potential.

What stimulation is optimally effective for the child and the sequencing of increasingly complex levels of stimulation is, of course, an open question. However, the animal literature would suggest that the kinaesthetic, tactile, auditory and visual senses must be stimulated and our present knowledge of the general levels of learning through which the average child proceeds may be used as first approximations of sequencing. Concepts associated with his immediate environment regardless of his culture would seem to be fundamental to subsequent learning. Discrimination between *big* and *little* is learned before *far* and *near* in this culture, and while the hierarchy of such concepts may vary somewhat by culture it is difficult to imagine a child in any culture not having to learn *big, little, far,* and *near* before he can cope with more complex learning peculiar to a given culture. Presumably the earlier a child can distinguish between two objects of different sizes the sooner he will be ready to learn a more complex concept such as *same* and *different*. Thus we have a first approximation for sequencing what the child should learn, and from the information related to the four sense modalities above we can infer the objects and materials through which he can learn.

From this discussion deprivation may be interpreted somewhat differently from the usual emphasis in the animal literature. In that literature visual deprivation is usually defined as complete or partial withdrawal of stimulation at some point in the animal's development. We submit that the absence of stimulation is detrimental to human development, but that much more frequently deficit occurs when the child is unable to fulfill the need for increasingly complex stimulation:

Hypothesis 8. Where deficit from lack of stimulation occurs, it more frequently results from the lack of increasingly complex stimulation related to subsequent demands by his environment than from the withdrawal of stimulation per se.

B. At What Age Is Increasingly Complex Stimulation Important?

As we dealt with the what and in what sequence of stimulation, we should also consider *when* the child should be exposed to increasingly complex stimuli.

Hypothesis 9. The child requires, and can develop responses to, increasingly complex stimuli from birth.

Traditionally the neonate has been viewed as a passive organism and the early infant only a little less so. That view holds that so long as the organism has food, oxygen and warmth there is little that can damage it irreparably or expedite its development. It is cousin to the notion that there are few experiences worth giving the infant systematically, because when he has further matured, he can benefit from the same experiences more efficiently.

If we accept the animal data, this position is valid only to the extent that the neonate is passive. If at a given age he demonstrates that he can interact with his environment systematically, he gives evidence that he is ready to develop responses to increasingly complex stimulation. Thus, the age at which the human can interact with his environment is of considerable importance.

There is a growing body of evidence that the neonate is not passive at all. While a neonate he can be conditioned, a response can be extinguished, he can discriminate between different auditory or visual stimuli and respond differentially (Papousek, 1967). The development of his visual perception has been shown to be dependent on visual stimulation and his interaction with it (Salapatek & Kessen, 1966). It is safe to predict that further research will confirm our conclusion that from birth the human is capable of responding to stimulation and of developing increasingly complex responses to increasingly complex stimulation. These conclusions do not preclude the possibility that the same stimulation later may be adequate for so-called normal development, but they raise profound questions about optimal sequencing, rate of intellective, social and emotional growth, individual differences, and the ultimate capacity of the individual.

C. The Earlier and More Prolonged the Deprivation, the Greater the Deficit in the Child

Until patterns of behavior relevant to a new situation are established in the child, the effects of deprivation increase with its duration. Once established we might expect the new situation to provide the increasingly complex stimuli which will continue the development of more and more complex responses. In this context, however, the definition of deprivation at a given stage of growth may take on new dimensions. It is unlikely that deprivation for the neonate and for the older infant constitute the same levels of stimulation. An environment completely adequate for the former may not offer the variety of stimulation sufficient to satisfy the needs of the latter. While this concept may be continued *ad absurdum* throughout the life span, and be related to the case of the productive individual who suddenly ceases to grow and contribute, it is perhaps most meaningful at an early age when the varieties of stimulation possible are relatively limited. Deprivation for the preschool child may occur if the environment is limited to stimulation for which the child has already developed responses. The longer he is in an environment which is not increasingly complex, the more severe the deficit, and presumably the less effective remedial treatment will be. Hence, an unchallenging preschool can be a form of deprivation, and the intellectively advanced child could be deprived of his needs by a school adequate for stimulating others, and the length of that deprivation could have the effects of stimulus deprivation more commonly conceived.

Dennis (1938, 1960) in his studies of foundling homes in the Middle East has data which supports the animal results indicating that the effects of deprivation increase with duration. He has shown that some institutions from which children are adopted provide little or no stimulation for the child. The age of adoption, or the amount of time the child has spent in the institution, is significantly related to IQ scores at a specified amount of time after adoption. He concludes that the mean developmental quotient for children in such institutions is established by the duration of their stay. While there they develop on the average at one-half of the normal rate, or an IQ of 50. Furthermore, with adoption they develop at a normal rate, a mean of one year mental age per year of chronological age. Thus a child who spent the first two years in the institution (MA = 1.0), adopted on his second birthday, would have by age 10 an IQ of 90 on the average. One who spent the first four years of life in the institution (MA = 2.0), adopted on his fourth birthday, would have by age 10 an IQ of 80 on the average. While his reported samples are small thus far, his data fit this model.

Hypothesis 10. The longer the child is without increasingly complex stimulation, the more severe the deficit in intellective and emotional behavior.

D. The Prognosis for Remedial Treatment

The animal data show that the effects of stimulus deprivation increase as the phylogenetic scale is ascended and that the effectiveness of remedial treatment also increases. Thus, provided that both the stimulus modality and the level of complexity where deprivation occurred can be identified, we might expect to implement successful remedial treatment for the child. However, the detection of deficit and the identification of modality and level of complexity is a problem of some magnitude.

Deficit may exist early in life but not be suspected until later when the environment demands more complex responses which the child cannot develop. Its early detection is made more difficult by the inverse relationship which exists between age of the child and the reliability of his responses to a given stimulus, a fact which also deters the design of adequate measures of early deficit. For these reasons deficit in the very young is frequently suspected rather than established. Where deficit is suspected, however, previous stimulus deprivation or the lack of increasingly complex stimulation must be considered as a possible antecedent.

Ideally, if stimulus deprivation has occurred, a specification of the modalities deprived and the age and level of growth when it occurred should be obtained. However, remedial treatment is not entirely dependent on an accurate history of the deprivation, since we can assume that the child's present level of response is indicative of the modality and level of complexity when deprivation occurred and development was arrested. However, since the duration and intensity of deprivation is related to emotionality upon presentation of a novel stimulus, stimulation without regard to those factors could conceivably do more harm than good. For the practitioners this implies that continued hyperexcitability to novel stimuli is a warning that treatment should proceed slowly, with considerable caution, and with extended efforts to obtain further information about the nature of the suspected deprivation.

Hypothesis 11. Success of remedial treatment will be a function of:
(a) duration and intensity of deprivation;
(b) level of development at the time of deprivation; and
(c) the extent to which treatment begins in the modality and at the level of complexity where deprivation occurred.

In the above contexts we can reexamine the assumptions underlying the modern preschool movement with respect to the development of behavior patterns:

(a) "Early intervention is superior to later intervention." With respect to the establishment of behavior patterns this assumption appears to be fully supported by the animal literature. Since the duration of deprivation is related to the severity of deficit, we may assume that the earlier the deficit is detected and acted upon the better. However, intervention should consist of stimulation specific to the modalities concerned and the level of development when deprivation occurred.

(b) "Any intervention is better than none." Since the deprived organism is hyperexcitable to novel stimuli in the modality previously deprived, and presumably is less able to develop adequate responses to the novel stimulus, intervention could be detrimental to the child if not carefully programmed to the length and intensity of deprivation and the level of development of the child. If the assumption is interpreted that any stimulation for the deprived child is better than none regardless of age and level of development, the assumption must be rejected.

(c) "A rich program for a limited period of time will ignite growth until then dormant." This assumption appears to be vulnerable on at least two points: that a rich program will necessarily provide stimulation for the specific modality and level of development required for the individual child, and that a limited period of stimulation is sufficient to repair the effects of deprivation. Even if the program concerned was appropriate to relevant modalities and levels of complexity, there is serious question as to whether brief exposure to stimulation would substantially benefit the child with significant deficit. Furthermore, the phrase "ignite growth until then dormant" appears to be in direct contradiction of the data which imply that continued growth requires increasingly complex stimulation from the present level of development.

(d) "Diverse compensatory stimulation is required when the child's environment has been limited." In practice this assumption would appear useful in that diverse compensatory stimulation may at random benefit the child in the modality and at the level of the complexity of previous deprivation. In fact, stimulation more specific to the deficit and accompanied by information about the duration and intensity of deprivation is required for efficient remedial treatment of a specific child.

Of the four, the first is most valid. The other three, if seen in the perspective of what modern programs usually are, could be detrimental to a specific child although they may well be beneficial to most. They are useful to the extent that the nature of deprivation is established and the treatment is appropriate for the individual child's previous deprivation by modality and level of development.

CRITICAL PERIODS OF DEVELOPMENT

Attractive to investigators in child development as well as practitioners in the preschool has been the hypothesis that some responses may be acquired most effectively during a specified period of development regardless of previous experience, and that if the response is not acquired during that period it will be acquired later with great difficulty or not at all. This hypothesis, derived from the animal research on imprinting originally conducted by Lorenz (1937), deserves examination because of its obvious relevance to the assumption that "a rich program for a limited period of time will ignite growth until then dormant."

Lorenz found that there was a specified time in the young gosling's life when exposure to a moving object, be it goose or human caretaker, resulted in a following-response which remained remarkably stable throughout the remainder of the animal's existence. If the gosling was not exposed to this type of stimulus during the specified period, the animal never developed the following-response. The all or none nature of this response has been demonstrated in several species, although it has been shown that the specific time when imprinting occurs is subject to minor modifications under experimentally contrived environmental conditions.

The term "critical period" of development was first used by Scott and Marston (1950) in describing the results of a deprivation study with puppies. He used the term in the embryological sense wherein organs and tissues develop in an invariable sequence or not at all. The rigorous application of the term has been violated by many investigators to refer to any period of development when an organism is most receptive to stimuli related to the acquisition of a given response. The distinction between these interpretations and their relative contribution to the literature on development has been discussed by Denenberg (1964), who describes the interpretation used by Scott as ". . . certain limited time periods in development during which a particular class of stimuli will have particularly profound effects, and that the same stimulation before or after this interval will have little, if any, effect on the organism." The less precise use of the term states "the same physical stimulation at different ages has different effects upon the *S;* this states, simply, that *S*'s age is an important parameter and can scarcely be questioned."

It is the first of these interpretations, in the context of Lorenz and Scott, which could generate particularly unique hypotheses about early development if the animal data were entirely convincing and relevant observations on humans were consistent with these data. Unfortunately, Denenberg (1964) after reviewing the literature has concluded that the data supporting the critical periods hypothesis in the context of Scott and Lorenz is inconclusive, even for the animals, and suggests that these data are better interpreted as a complex function of the amount of stimulation to which the organism has been exposed rather than as a critical period of development. Thus it may be, as Riesen has suggested (1961) that the term *critical stimulation* is more validly inferred from the data, and that it is the exposure of the organism to specific stimulus complexities as it matures which is most intimately associated with the acquisition of responses regardless of the stage of development.

If one accepts Denenberg and Riesen it is difficult to justify the classical critical periods hypothesis as a valid explanation of response acquisition in the child, or to support the assumption "that a rich program for a limited period of time will ignite growth until then dormant." However, in generating hypotheses about response acquisition in the child it is not necessary to limit oneself to the two possibilities which result from this dichotomy, that is, to assume that time and the stage of development is all important *or* that the amount of stimulation and its order of presentation are the sole variables responsible for response acquisition. The misuse of the term "critical periods" when referring to data which show that the organism is more responsive to given stimuli at one time than another does not derogate the validity of such findings. Such data are more significant than stating "simply, that *S*'s age is an important parameter" of growth. The subtle interaction between the stage of development of the organism and the stimulation to which it is exposed may indeed have greater import than that suggested by Riesen. The discussion below will illustrate a stage of development in the human where response to stimulation cannot be explained by previous exposure to stimulation alone.

A MODEL FOR PRESCHOOL TRAINING

Presumably there is a point in the development of every child when he would benefit most from attending a preschool providing that the preschool programmed for him increasingly complex learning situations. It has been suggested above that the time for a specific child will be a function of the intensity of drive related to his dependency on his mother, and the extent to which relevant behavior patterns for the new situation have been established. To that we can add that while critical periods in the classical sense may not be relevant to such timing, there are probably periods of development in every child's life when specific stimulation would have more pronounced and durable effects than others. Apart from individual differences among children, at what age should preschool training outside the home begin for the average child, and what should occur in the home before he begins preschool?

Almost all children begin to speak between eighteen months and three years of age, but speech alone does not appear a sufficient criterion for entrance in preschools. Presumably the child who speaks at an early age is provided with an additional dimension of behavior with which he can explore increasingly complex stimuli, although there are no definitive studies to show that early speech is related to subsequent superior intellective skills. Furthermore, while there is a relationship between concept development and language facility at age two, many children score high on tests of the former before they speak at all. The correlation among 120 Negro males tested for concept formation and language facility within one month of their second birthday has been shown to be .55 (Palmer, 1968). Thus the ability to respond to directions about operations related to his environment ("put the *big* horse on the table") clearly precedes verbal output for many children, as does the child's ability to differentiate between *big* and *little*. Surely the mastery of such basic concepts is as important to the child faced with the demands of the preschool as is his ability to speak. Indeed, he may obtain more from a preschool if his knowledge of such concepts is high and his verbal facility low, than vice versa. Therefore, it is suggested that knowledge of operations symbolized by prepositions and adjectives (*up, full, low, over, on top of*, etc.), hereafter referred to in this chapter as "prepads," are the prerequisites to profitable participation in the preschool. For children, it is suggested that these represent the fixed patterns of behavior to which we have referred above. Fortunately for questions related to preschool intervention for the disadvantaged, there are no differences by social class in the Negro sample cited above with respect to language facility *or* concept development at age two.

These data provide a model from which hypotheses follow with respect to those factors that specifically account for the increasing differences in intellective function by class and with age. For example, the poorly educated mother is equally capable of providing increasingly complex stimulation for her child until he begins to acquire speech, after which she is at a disadvantage which increases with the level of development of the child. Or, the middle-class mother has the resources for providing a wider range of stimulus variability and complexity *after* the child's development has reached a stage where he is more mobile. Until the child is mobile, her superior resources do not contribute significantly to the level of stimulus complexity which the child needs.

It has repeatedly been shown that social class differences already exist at age five in almost every domain of intellective behavior. While it has not been shown that within-class differences increase from age two to five, this is a reasonable assumption. Inadequate mothers of two- and three-year-old children are certainly not limited to low socioeconomic groups, and presumably the middle-class child with an inadequate mother is as deprived of increasingly complex stimulation as his lower-class peer.

This emphasis on the relative criticality during the period the child is acquiring speech and increasing his adventuresomeness does not, of course, detract from the importance of stimulation at even earlier ages. Since there are large individual differences at age two, unrelated to social class, with respect to verbal facility and the understanding of relational concepts, presumably part of those differences may be attributable to stimulation before the age of two.

Home Training

It is before the child begins to actively engage the environment outside the home that the mother has the greatest control in shaping individual differences. Once peer pressures and other socializing agents become part of the child's environment, she is no longer the relatively autonomous designer of his world. A model for preschool training must consider the stimulus requirements of the child from birth, and the suggestions from the animal literature for that period of growth seem to be clear. The neonate and infant must be provided with increasingly varied sources of auditory, visual, kinaesthetic and tactile stimuli with particular reference to direct contact between the child and the mother or caretaker. Aids to the caretaker or mother in the form of objects and toys for providing such stimulation are currently as scarce as is literature related to the need. Existing toys seem to be designed more as pacifiers than as stimulators. However, as literature related to the need for infant stimulation becomes better known, presumably the more creative toy manufacturers will begin to market items which will allow for greater variability for feeling, seeing, hearing and manipulating.

As the child approaches age two a strong dependency on the mother *and* fixed patterns of behavior relevant to subsequent environments he must face without her become increasingly important. With respect to the former, presumably the early need for physical contact between mother and child becomes less important and other intense affective relationships become more important. We have little evidence about the nature of these needs, but Kagan (1967) has suggested that the character of the conversation from mother to child becomes increasingly important. For her to verbalize to the child without providing a condition which includes some other affective bond has a different effect than if the interaction involves both. Thus the quantity of verbalization has less to do with the development of the relationship (and language?) than what he calls *distinctive verbalization,* verbalization accompanied by affect involving such behaviors as direct visual contact, holding, patting, etc. Observations of children in a day-care center being "taught" as a group, and under conditions where a given child is in a one-to-one relationship with an adult, bear this out. More is transpiring in the one-to-one relationship, providing that the interaction has affective involvement for both, than the mere presentation of words or materials which the child is to learn. We suggest that it is such intense affective interactions which increase the dependency drive, and that where that interaction is accompanied with the teaching of the concepts described above, the desired combination of high drive and established behavior patterns occurs.

But if she is to provide, under these conditions, increasingly complex stimuli associated with the prepads mentioned above, is there evidence for a sequence for their relative difficulty? For the 120 two-year-old Negro males the percentage responding correctly to instructions to "give me," "point to," "show me," etc., (whichever the child had demonstrated was in his repertoire prior to testing) on items related to 43 prepads is shown in Table 1.3.

These prepads, which range in difficulty, would appear to provide a first approximation to the sequencing of home training. If *open* or *closed* is learned earlier by more children than *same* and *different,* one may reasonably assume that the latter are more difficult for the average child and training in that concept should be delayed until *open, closed,* and others more frequently in the young child's repertoire have been learned.

With lists of prepads of increasing difficulty for the average child, the mother can readily determine at what level her child is, and interact with the child using objects and contrivances designed to give him experience with increasingly difficult concepts. She should also be instructed that the understanding of a prepad may be situation-bound. That is, when presented with a big and little ball he can give, upon request, the big ball, but he cannot respond correctly when asked to give her the bigger of two cups. Before she convinces herself that he can distinguish between *big* and *little* she should repeat her question with a variety of objects.

As the child masters increasingly difficult prepads we can hypothesize that he is readying himself for even more difficult concepts such as those related to mass, length, and number. Again, as a first approximation to this sequencing, we infer that the concept of conservation of mass must be antedated by such relatively difficult prepads as *same* and *different.*

It is fundamental to this model of preschool training that the learning of increasingly difficult prepads constitutes a large part of what we have previously referred to as behavioral patterns that are prerequisites for success in the next environment the child will encounter. Within the cognitive domain, the extent to which the child can benefit from more formal schooling is highly dependent on his understanding of these concepts.

TABLE 1.3

PERCENTAGE OF SUBJECTS AGE TWO
WHO UNDERSTAND CONCEPT (N=120)

Concept	Per Cent Responding Correctly	Concept	Per Cent Responding Correctly
1. On top of	86.7	22. Little	30.5
2. Into	81.5	23. One	30.5
3. Open	67.5	24. Many	29.0
4. Out of	67.0	25. Dry	28.5
5. Closed	62.0	26. Hard	28.0
6. Wet	55.0	27. High	27.5
7. Down	48.5	28. Black	26.5
8. Through	48.0	29. White	26.5
9. Circle	48.0	30. Fat	26.5
10. Soft	44.0	31. Heavy	26.5
11. Full	41.0	32. Light	26.5
12. Dirty	40.0	33. Short	25.5
13. Big	38.5	34. Long	24.0
14. Up	38.0	35. Skinny	23.5
15. Loud	37.0	36. Littlest	23.0
16. Clean	34.0	37. Soft	23.0
17. Fast	34.0	38. Under	22.5
18. Square	33.5	39. Rough	20.5
19. Low	33.0	40. Smooth	19.0
20. Over	32.5	41. Biggest	19.0
21. Empty	32.0	42. Slow	16.5
		43. Around	8.5

Furthermore, the implications for maternal behavior are probably more reasonable and understandable to the mother than more elegant models. Given lists of increasingly difficult prepads and suggestions about those objects, indigenous to the home, which she can use as teaching materials, she has a meaningful framework for home instruction which applies to several years of the child's growth. Furthermore, this framework provides a structure for introducing new objects and labeling. As the child acquires new words to represent his environment, they are acquired in what may be a more meaningful context.

The Preschool

Presently the concept of the preschool is an extension of public schooling in that one or more instructors deal with children in groups of various sizes. Assuming that most children have spent most of their prior time in the home, interacting primarily with parents and siblings, the transition to a school-type situation seems to place more demands on the child at the time of separation from his family than is necessary. Probably for the first time he is exposed to a number of his peers. His total time away from home is suddenly increased by many hours each week. And he must learn how to interact with adults until then unfamiliar to him and follow their instructions. There are probably few times in life when the individual experiences greater environmental change, and for many children the change may not facilitate learning or may disrupt it. Some interim step between home instruction and preschool would appear desirable.

At age two most children can understand simple instructions related to play whether they can speak intelligently or not. They are also capable, contrary to popular belief, of relating to a strange adult in play situations for periods up to one hour. Furthermore, after adaptation periods in the presence of the mother, most are able to interact productively with a strange adult in the absence of the mother.

The author has had 120 Negro children who began, at exactly age two, attending a preschool situation for one hour periods twice weekly for eight months (Palmer, 1968). Half the children were seen individually by an instructor who was well informed about his level of attainment on the aforementioned prepads, and who decided before each session what prepads would be taught and with what toys. The other half of the group were also seen individually, but systematic teaching of prepad relationships was not emphasized. Rather, with the same toys and materials present, the instructor was told only to answer questions the child had and to play with him in a manner similar to the normal nursery school. Seventy additional children of the same age were tested at the end of the eight-month program, none of whom had been in the program during the year.

On nonverbal measures of performance after the eight months training (two hours per week) the group who had been systematically taught prepad concepts were superior to the "discovery" group. No differences between these groups existed on verbal measures. Both groups who had participated in the eight-month program were highly superior to the control group of seventy on all measures used, verbal and nonverbal. Furthermore, the lower-class children in the experimental group were equal to or superior to middle-class children in the discovery group on nonverbal measures, and lower-class children who participated in either eight-month treatment were superior to middle-class control children.

Thus with two hours per week, the two-year-old child benefits greatly from individual instruction. We hypothesize that the intensity of interaction between adult and child, without exposing him simultaneously to the more drastic change of the usual preschool situation, not only taught him many of the fundamentals of learning he will need for other new environmental demands, but also taught him to follow adult instructions and persevere in learning tasks. We predict that these children will be better prepared for the demands of the more traditional nursery or preschool situation as a result of their experience.

Since both training and discovery groups outperformed their controls on all measures of performance at the end of the eight months' period, the training of prepads does not account for the superiority of the discovery group over the controls. While the study was not designed to answer specifically the question of the effects of one-to-one training, it is our opinion that the intensity of the relationship between child and adult, developed over sequential forty-five minute periods of interaction, was an extremely important part of both groups' achievement. Nothing was *taught* in the discovery group, but progress slightly less than that through teaching was achieved. We believe that the affect associated with an adult and a two-year-old child in a one-to-one relationship served to effectively redirect the already existing drive among high dependent children toward performance in their new environment, and that many low dependent children acquired a drive compatible with the demands of the preschool situation.

Consequently we conclude that the one-to-one relationship when accompanied by distinctive verbalization and undisturbed affective involvement is a significant contribution to the child's ability to make the transformation from the home to the preschool situation. This can be implemented by the one hour twice weekly situation used in the study above, or possibly by imbedding the one hour twice weekly one-to-one relationship within the regular preschool program.

However, not all children at age two are ready for this exposure, as all at age four are not ready for traditional preschool exposure.

The animal data suggest, and our observations confirm, that when a child can benefit from individual instruction in the traditional preschool is a function of the intensity of the mother-child relationship and the extent to which relevant behavior patterns have been fixed. We hypothesize that children with high dependency needs for the mother and well-developed patterns of behavior have initial problems on separation but quickly adapt to the demands of the individual instruction. Where the mother-child interaction is intense, but the child is inadequately prepared with respect to such simple concepts as *up, down,* etc., we hypothesize that individual or preschool instruction outside the home should be delayed. Where the dependency drive is low but patterns of behavior are well established, a not-frequent combination, individual or preschool instruction outside the home should begin as early as possible. Where dependency drive is low and behavior patterns relevant to the new environment have not been learned, the truly disadvantaged child is found, be he in lower- or middle-class homes, and intervention by out-of-the-home programs is urgent.

With proliferation of preschool programs and the tendency to have younger and younger children involved, we are faced with a new socialization agent which because of the very early age it reaches the child may be of considerable moment to coming generations. Presently some preschool programs may be as limiting for the child's development as the institutions found in Dennis' (1960) work. At best, preschool programs consuming many hours per week fall short of developing activities which are known to contribute to intellective, affective, and social development. Little is known about what variables combine to let us decide when a given child should make the break from home training to the preschool, or what programs are best suited to a given child. As there has been an increased willingness to examine the animal literature for hypotheses about how the child's intellect and affect develops, at the same time there has occurred an increased tendency for well-trained investigators to feel respectable working with children in the home and the school. This first approximation of a model for preschool training has provided hypotheses some of which are currently being tested.

REFERENCES

1. ADER, R. The effects of early experience on subsequent emotionality and resistance to stress. *Psychological Monographs*, 1959, 73, No. 2 (Whole No. 472).

2. ADER, R. Social factors affecting emotionality and resistance to disease in the animals: III. Early weaning and susceptibility to gastric ulcers in the rat: A control for nutritional factors. *Journal of Comparative and Physiological Psychology*, 1962, 55, 600–602.

3. ANDERSON, J. E., & SMITH, A. H. The effect of quantitative and qualitative stunting upon maze learning in the white rat. *Journal of Comparative Psychology*, 1926, 6, 337–359.

4. ANDERSON, J. E., & SMITH, A. H. The relation of performance to age and nutritive condition in the white rat. *Journal of Comparative Psychology*, 1932, 13, 409–446.

5. BEACH, F. A. Comparison of copulatory behavior of male rats raised in isolation, cohabitation and segregation. *Journal of Genetic Psychology*, 1942, 60, 121–136.

6. BENJAMIN, L. S. The effect of bottle and cup feeding on the nonnutritive sucking of the infant Rhesus monkey. *Journal of Comparative and Physiological Psychology*, 1961, 54, 230–237.

7. BERNSTEIN, L. A note on Christie's "Experimental naivete and experiential naivete." *Psychological Bulletin*, 1952, 49, 38–40.

8. BERNSTEIN, L. The effects of variations in handling upon learning and retention. *Journal of Comparative and Physiological Psychology*, 1957, 50, 162–167.

9. BINGHAM, W. E., & GRIFFITHS, W. J., JR. The effect of different environments during infancy on adult behavior in the rat. *Journal of Comparative and Physiological Psychology*, 1952, 45, 307–312.

10. BIRCH, H. G. Sources of order in the maternal behavior of animals. *American Journal of Orthopsychiatry*, 1956, 26, 279–284.

11. BRONFENBRENNER, U. Early deprivation in mammal and man. In G. Newton (Ed.), *Early experience and behavior*. Springfield, Ill.: Charles C Thomas, 1968, in press.

12. CHOW, K. L., & NISSEN, H. W. Intervocular transfer of learning in visually naive and experienced infant chimpanzees. *Journal of Comparative and Physiological Psychology*, 1955, 48, 224–237.

13. CHRISTIE, R. The effects of some early experiences in the latent learning of adult rats. *Journal of Experimental Psychology*, 1952, 43, 281–288.

14. CLARKE, R. S., HERON, W., FEATHERSTONHAUGH, M. L., FORGAYS, D. G., & HEBB, D. O. Individual differences in dogs: Preliminary reports on the effects of early experience. *Canadian Journal of Psychology*, 1951, 5, 150–156.

15. COOPER, R. M., & ZUBEK, J. P. Effects of enriched and restricted early environments on the learning ability of bright and dull rats. *Canadian Journal of Psychology*, 1958, 12, 159–164.

16. DENENBERG, V. H. An attempt to isolate critical periods of development in the rat. *Journal of Comparative and Physiological Psychology*, 1962, 55, 813–815.

17. DENENBERG, V. H. Critical periods, stimulus input and emotional reactivity: A theory of infantile stimulation. *Psychological Review*, 1964, 71, 335–351.

18. DENENBERG, V. H., & MORTON, J. R. C. Effects of environmental complexity and social groupings upon modification of emotional behavior. *Journal of Comparative and Physiological Psychology*, 1962, 55, 242–246. (a)

19. DENENBERG, V. H., & MORTON, J. R. C. Effects of preweaning and postweaning manipulations upon problem-solving behavior. *Journal of Comparative and Physiological Psychology*, 1962, 55, 1096–1098. (b)

20. DENENBERG, V. H., MORTON, J. R. C., KLINE, N. J., & GROTA, L. J. Effects of duration of infantile stimulation upon emotionality. *Canadian Journal of Psychology*, 1962, 16, 72–76.

21. DENENBERG, V. H., & NAYLOR, J. C. The effects of early food deprivation upon adult learning. *Psychological Record*, 1957, 7, 75–77.

22. DENENBERG, V. H., OTTINGER, D. R., & STEPHENS, M. W. Effects of maternal factors upon growth and behavior of the rat. *Child Development*, 1962, 33, 65–71.

23. DENENBERG, V. H., & SMITH, S. A. Effects of infantile stimulation and age upon behavior. *Journal of Comparative and Physiological Psychology*, 1963, 56, 307–312.

24. DENENBERG, V. H., & WHIMBEY, A. E. Infantile stimulation and animal husbandry: A methodological study. *Journal of Comparative and Physiological Psychology*, 1963, 56, 877–878.

25. DENNIS, W. Infant development under conditions of restricted practice and of minimum social stimulation. *Journal of Genetic Psychology*, 1938, 53, 149–158.

26. DENNIS, W. Causes of retardation among institutional children: Iran. *Journal of Genetic Psychology*, 1960, 96, 47–59.

27. DEUTSCH, M. Social intervention and malleability of the child. *Fourth Annual School of Education Lecture*. Ithaca, N.Y.: Cornell Univer., 1965.

28. ELLIOT, O., & KING, J. A. Effect of early food deprivation upon later consummatory behavior in puppies. *Psychological Report*, 1960, 6, 391–400.

29. ELLIOT, O., & SCOTT, J. P. The development of emotional distress reactions to separation in puppies. *Journal of Genetic Psychology*, 1961, 99, 3–22.

30. FORGAYS, D. G., & FORGAYS, J. W. The nature of the effect of free environmental experience in the rat. *Journal of Comparative and Physiological Psychology*, 1952, 45, 322–328.

31. FORGAYS, D. G., & REED, J. M. Crucial periods for per-environmental experience in the rat. *Journal of Comparative and Physiological Psychology*, 1962, 55, 816–818.

32. FORGUS, R. H. The effect of early perceptual learning on the behavioral organization of adult rats. *Journal of Comparative and Physiological Psychology*, 1954, 47, 331–336.

33. FORGUS, R. H. Influence of early experience on maze learning with and without visual cues. *Canadian Journal of Psychology*, 1955, 9, 207–214.

34. FORGUS, R. H. Advantage of early over late perceptural experience in improving form discrimination. *Canadian Journal of Psychology*, 1956, 10, 147–155.

35. FREDERICKSON, E. Competition: The effects of infantile experience upon adult behavior. *Journal of Abnormal and Social Psychology*, 1951, 46, 406–409.

36. GANZ, L., & RIESEN, A. H. Stimulus generalization to hue in the dark-reared macaque. *Journal of Comparative and Physiological Psychology*, 1962, 55, 92–99.

37. GAURON, E. F., & BECKER, W. C. The effects of early sensory deprivation on adult rat behavior under competition stress: An attempt at replication of a study of Alexander Wolf. *Journal of Comparative and Physiological Psychology*, 1959, 52, 689–693.

38. GIBSON, E. J., & WALK, R. D. The effect of prolonged exposure to visually presented patterns on learning. *Journal of Comparative and Physiological Psychology,* 1956, 49, 239–242.

39. HARLOW, H. F. The nature of love. *American Psychology,* 1958, 13, 673–685.

40. HARLOW, H. F. Development of the second and third affectional systems in macaque monkeys. In T. T. Tourlentes, S. L. Pollack, & H. D. Himwich (Eds.), *Research approaches to psychiatric problems.* New York: Grune, 1962. Pp. 209–229.

41. HARLOW, H. F., HARLOW, M. K., & HANSEN, E. W. The maternal affectional system of Rhesus monkeys. In H. L. Rheingold (Ed.), *Maternal behavior in mammals.* New York: Wiley, 1963. Pp. 254–281.

42. HARLOW, H. F., & ZIMMERMAN, R. R. The development of affectional responses in infant monkeys. *Proceedings of the American Philosophical Society,* 1958, 102, 501–509.

43. HARLOW, H. F., & ZIMMERMAN, R. R. Affectional responses in the infant monkey. *Science,* 1959, 130, 421–432.

44. HEBB, D. O. The innate organization of visual activity: I. Perception of figures by rats reared in darkness. *Journal of Genetic Psychology,* 1937, 51, 101–126. (a)

45. HEBB, D. O. The innate organization of visual activity: II. Transfer of response in the discrimination of brightness and size by rats reared in total darkness. *Journal of Comparative Psychology,* 1937, 24, 277–299. (b)

46. HEBB, D. O. The effects of early experience on problem-solving at maturity. *American Psychology,* 1947, 2, 306–307.

47. HELD, R., & HEIN, A. Movement produced stimulation in the development of visually guided behavior. *Journal of Comparative and Physiological Psychology,* 1963, 56, 872–876.

48. HUNT, J. McV. The effects of infant feeding–frustration upon hoarding in the albino rat. *Journal of Abnormal and Social Psychology,* 1941, 36, 338–360.

49. HUNT, J. McV., SCHLOSBERG, H., SOLOMON, R. L., & STELLAR, E. Studies of the effects of infantile experience on adult behavior in rats. *Journal of Comparative and Physiological Psychology,* 1947, 40, 291–304.

50. HYMOVITCH, B. The effects of experimental variations on problem-solving in the rat. *Journal of Comparative and Physiological Psychology,* 1952, 45, 313–321.

51. IGEL, G. J., & CALVIN, A. D. The development of affectional responses in infant dogs. *Journal of Comparative and Physiological Psychology,* 1960, 53, 302–305.

52. KAGAN, J. On cultural deprivation. Paper read at Russell Sage & Rockefeller Conference, April, 1967.

53. KOCH, A. M., & WARDEN, C. J. The influence of quantitative stunting on learning ability in mice. *Journal of Genetic Psychology,* 1936, 48, 215–217.

54. LASHLEY, K. S., & RUSSELL, J. T. The mechanism of vision: XI. A preliminary test of innate organization. *Journal of Genetic Psychology,* 1934, 45, 136–144.

55. LEVINE, S. Infantile experience and consummatory behavior in adulthood. *Journal of Comparative and Physiological Psychology,* 1957, 50, 609–612.

56. LEVINE, S. Noxious stimulation in infant and adult rats and consummatory behavior. *Journal of Comparative and Physiological Psychology,* 1958, 51, 230–233.

57. LEVINE, S., CHAVALIER, J. A., & KORCHIN, S. J. The effects of early shock and handling on later avoidance learning. *Journal of Personality,* 1956, 24, 475–493.

58. LEVINE, S., & OTIS, L. S. The effects of handling before and after weaning on the resistance of albino rats to later deprivation. *Canadian Journal of Psychology,* 1958, 12, 103–108.

59. LEVY, D. M. Experiments on the sucking reflex and social behavior in dogs. *American Journal of Orthopsychiatry*, 1934, 4, 203–224.

60. LEVY, D. M. On instinct satiation: An experiment of the pecking behavior of chickens. *Journal of Genetic Psychology*, 1938, 18, 327–348.

61. LORENZ, K. The companion in the bird's world. *Aak*, 1937, 54, 245–273.

62. LUCHINS, A. S., & FORGUS, R. H. The effect of differential post-weaning environments on the rigidity of an animal's behavior. *Journal of Genetic Psychology*, 1955, 86, 51–58.

63. MANDLER, J. M. Effects of early food deprivation on adult behavior in the rat. *Journal of Comparative and Physiological Psychology*, 1958, 51, 513–517.

64. MASSERMAN, J. H. *Behavior and neurosis: An experimental psychoanalytic approach to psychobiologic principles.* Chicago, Ill.: University of Chicago Press, 1943.

65. McKELVEY, R. K., & MARX, N. H. Effects of infantile food and water deprivation on adult hoarding in the rat. *Journal of Comparative and Physiological Psychology*, 1951, 44, 423–430.

66. MEIER, G. W., & McGEE, R. K. A re-evaluation of the effect of early perceptual experience on discrimination performance during adulthood. *Journal of Comparative and Physiological Psychology*, 1959, 52, 390–395.

67. MELZACK, R. A. The genesis of emotional behavior: An experimental study of the dog. *Journal of Comparative and Physiological Psychology*, 1954, 47, 166–168.

68. MELZACK, R. A., & SCOTT, T. H. The effects of early experience on the response to pain. *Journal of Comparative and Physiological Psychology*, 1957, 50, 155–161.

69. MELZACK, R. A., & THOMPSON, W. R. Effects of early experience on social behavior. *Canadian Journal of Psychology*, 1956, 10, 82–90.

70. NISSEN, H. W., CHOW, K. L., & SEMMES, J. Effects of restricted opportunity for tactual, kinesthetic, and manipulative experience on the behavior of a chimpanzee. *American Journal of Psychology*, 1951, 64, 485–507.

71. OTTINGER, D. R., DENENBERG, V. H., & STEPHENS, M. W. Maternal emotionality, multiple mothering, and emotionality in maturity. *Journal of Comparative and Physiological Psychology*, 1963, 56, 313–317.

72. PADELLA, S. G. Further studies on delayed pecking in chicks. *Journal of Comparative Psychology*, 1935, 20, 413–443.

73. PALMER, F. H. Intellective growth in the two-year-old. In preparation, 1968.

74. PAPOUSEK, H. Experimental studies of appetitional behavior in human newborns and infants. In H. W. Stevenson, E. H. Hess, & Harriet L. Rheingold (Eds.), *Early behavior: Comparative and developmental approach.* New York: Wiley, 1967. Pp. 249–278.

75. PATRICK, J. R., & LAUGHLIN, R. N. Is the wall-seeking tendency in the white rat an instinct? *Journal of Genetic Psychology*, 1934, 44, 378–389.

76. RIESEN, A. H. The development of visual perception in man and chimpanzee. *Science*, 1947, 106, 107–108.

77. RIESEN, A. H. Post-partum development of behavior. *Chicago Medical School Quarterly*, 1951, 13, 17–24.

78. RIESEN, A. H. Critical stimulation and optimum period. Paper read at American Psychology Association, New York, September, 1961.

79. RIESEN, A. H., & AARONS, F. Visual movement and intensity discrimination in cats after early deprivation of pattern vision. *Journal of Comparative and Physiological Psychology*, 1959, 52, 142–149.

80. RIESEN, A. H., KURKE, M. I., & MELLINGER, J. C. Interocular transfer of habits learned monocularly in visually naive and experienced cats. *Journal of Comparative and Physiological Psychology,* 1953, 46, 166–172.

81. ROSENBLATT, J. S., & SCHNEIRLA, T. C. The behavior of the cat. In E. S. E. Hafez (Ed.), *The behavior of domestic animals.* London: Bailliere, Tindall, and Cox, 1962. Pp. 453–488.

82. ROSENBLATT, J., TURKEWITZ, G., & SCHNEIRLA, T. C. Early socialization in the domestic cat as based on feeding and other relationships between female and young. In B. Foss (Ed.), *Determinants of infant behavior.* London: Methuen, 1963. Pp. 51–74.

83. ROSS, S. Sucking frustration in neonate puppies. *Journal of Abnormal and Social Psychology,* 1951, 46, 142–149.

84. RUBENSTEIN, JUDITH. Maternal attentiveness and subsequent exploratory behavior in the infant. Unpublished doctoral dissertation, Boston University, 1966.

85. SALAPATEK, P., & KESSEN, W. Visual scanning of triangles by the human newborn. *Journal of Experimental Child Psychology,* 1966, 3, 151–167.

86. SCOTT, J. H. Some effects at maturity of gentling, ignoring or shocking rats during infancy. *Journal of Abnormal and Social Psychology,* 1955, 51, 412–414.

87. SCOTT, J. P., & MARSTON, M. V. Critical periods affecting the development of normal and maladjustive social behavior in puppies. *Journal of Genetic Psychology,* 1950, 77, 25–60.

88. SCOTT, J. P., ROSS, S., & FISHER, A. E. The effects of early enforced weaning on sucking behavior of puppies. *Journal of Genetic Psychology,* 1959, 95, 261–281.

89. SEAY, B., HANSEN, E., & HARLOW, H. F. Mother-infant separation in monkeys. *Journal of Child Psychology and Psychiatry,* 1962, 3, 123–132.

90. SEITZ, P. F. D. Infantile experience and adult behavior in animal subjects: II. Age of separation from the mother and adult behavior in the cat. *Psychosomatic Medicine,* 1959, 21, 353–378.

91. THOMPSON, W. R., & HERON, W. The effect of early restriction on activity in dogs. *Journal of Comparative and Physiological Psychology,* 1954, 47, 77–82. (a)

92. THOMPSON, W. R., & HERON, W. The effects of restricting early experience on the problem-solving capacity of dogs. *Canadian Journal of Psychology,* 1954, 8, 17–31. (b)

93. THOMPSON, W. R., MELZACK, R., & SCOTT, T. H. "Whirling behavior" in dogs as related to early experience. *Science,* 1956, 123, 939.

94. WOLF, A. The dynamics of the selective inhibition of specific functions in neurosis: A preliminary report. *Psychosomatic Medicine,* 1943, 5, 27–38.

95. WOLFE, J. B. An exploratory study of food-storing in rats. *Journal of Comparative Psychology,* 1939, 28, 97–108.

CHAPTER **2**

Mechanisms Of Social Learning: Some Roles Of Stimulation And Behavior In Early Human Development

Jacob L. Gewirtz

National Institute of Mental Health

.

PREFACE

In this chapter, current social concepts which have largely derived from informal cognitive, quasi-cognitive, motivational, socialization, and clinical theories, as well as from more formal social-learning approaches, will be examined, and an attempt will be made to cast the phenomena with which they deal into a consistent, operational, and parsimonious framework. To this end, simple and well-defined conditioning concepts will be used, in a way that readily meets the canons of objectivity and parsimony, to order behaviors ranging from the simple responses of infants to the complex responses of adults in complicated settings. The issues dealt with in this chapter are thus generic for all theories of social development, regardless of their orientations, their heuristic flavor, or their degree of formality.

We will begin our attempt by detailing some of the basic building-block concepts of a conditioning analysis, demonstrating their plausibility with examples from both research and life settings. For those readers who remain with us through this didactic introduction, our operational-learning approach will then be applied to a wide variety of substantive and practical issues, and analyses will be made of some focal behavior systems in life settings in a context where extant theories in the area have been characteristically informal or unsystematic and often posed in obscure cognitive or motivational terms. For these purposes, this chapter has been divided into the following main sections: an introduction to the

Constructive critical comments on segments of the first draft of this paper were made by D. M. Baer and A. J. Caron. I am also indebted to Karen Stingle for her assistance in the earliest phase of the writing of this paper, to Solomon Schimmel for his help in the final phase, and to Laura Rosenthal and Danielle Spiegler who provided dedicated and discriminating assistance at all phases of its preparation. The opinions expressed herein are those of the author, and do not necessarily represent the position of NIMH.

milieu of social-learning theory; the definition of the social environment; key constructs of social-learning analyses and their operating modes; additional implications of the approach for life settings; the effects on behavior of gross shifts in the maintaining environment, and of privation and deprivation; an evaluation of abstractions often employed in social-learning analyses; two key social-learning processes—imitation-identification and dependence-attachment; and an evaluation of the role of motivational conceptions in social-learning analyses.

INTRODUCTION

The Milieu of Social-Learning Theory

Stimulus-response (S-R) approaches to the social learning and socialization of the child commonly attempt to order, in terms of basic S-R concepts and principles, many of the same phenomena and issues that have been highlighted by clinical-developmental theories, which have characteristically used less formal or explicit approaches to theory development and less systematic research procedures. Indeed, the early S-R social-learning approaches were inspired particularly by Freudian psychoanalytic theory with its implicit emphasis on learning conceptions and its explicit emphasis on the importance of early experience in determining later behavior systems, as well as by its treatment of specific issues, like anxiety, in the clinical literature.

Several general S-R approaches have set the tone for consideration of social learning in the past quarter century. In the 1940's and early 1950's, approaches in the Hullian tradition perhaps did most to attempt to bridge the gap between the laboratory and the life setting (cf., e.g., Hull, 1943). The outstanding contributions in that tradition were those of Dollard, Doob, Miller, Mowrer and Sears (1939), Miller and Dollard (1941), McClelland (1942, 1951), Mowrer and Kluckhohn (1944), Sears (1943, 1944, 1951), Miller (1944, 1948a, 1948b, 1951, 1959, 1963), Dollard and Miller (1950), Mowrer (1950, 1960a, 1960b), and Whiting and Child (1953). From the late 1940's to the present, Skinner (1948, 1953) began attempts to extend his general conceptions and mode of approach to the social case, and was rapidly joined by researchers and theorists influenced by him (e.g., Bijou, 1955; Bijou & Baer, 1961, 1965; Ferster, 1961, 1963). Their work has contributed much to the contemporary flavor of the field of social behavior and learning. And, in the 1950's, Rotter (1954) and his followers began to publish their applications of learning principles to social behavior, although to date their approach has not had its full impact on the field.

The present analysis will concentrate mainly on issues and potential solutions stemming from the learning traditions of Hull and Skinner. A number of writers have approached social learning and development from views not very different from those taken in this chapter, and some of these are noted throughout this chapter for both background and detail. A recent summary and appraisal of S-R strategies and tactics and social-learning theories of child development, written at an introductory level, can be found in A. L. Baldwin (1967); while a well-balanced systematic consideration of the scope of personality study (which overlaps social learning), the role of theory in it, and its relation to learning approaches can be found in Farber (1964).

In the last decade and a half, important technological advances have been made in the practical application to life problems of the concepts of acquired stimulus control over behavior, and the stimulus conditions (for the most part social) which maintain that behavior. Stemming mainly from the utility of Skinner's (1938, 1953, 1954) operational concepts, these advances were made in the applied areas of behavior modification and education. The impact of this technology has also served to confirm and broaden our understanding of generic stimulus-control issues in social-learning contexts (e.g., Ferster, 1961, 1968; Ullmann & Krasner, 1965; Baer, Peterson & Sherman, 1967; Lovaas, 1967; Etzel & Gewirtz, 1967). There have also been a number of specific attempts to devise, improve or update particularly the "motivational" constructs of social-learning approaches (McClelland, 1951; Skinner, 1953; J. S. Brown, 1953; McClelland, Atkinson, Clark & Lowell, 1953; Rotter, Seeman & Liverant, 1962; Miller, 1959, 1963; Hill, 1960; Bandura, 1962; Bandura & Walters, 1963; and Gewirtz, 1961b, 1967a, 1967b, 1968a, 1968b). Attention has also been given to the conditions which can function as *social reinforcers* (e.g., Bijou & Sturges, 1959; Gewirtz, 1956b, 1961a, 1961b; Bijou & Baer, 1963; Stevenson, 1965; Zigler, 1963b), and to *setting* (context) conditions which qualify the functioning of stimuli in their several roles, in particular stimuli from social sources (e.g., Gewirtz & Baer, 1958a, 1958b; Walters & Ray, 1960; Stevenson & Odom, 1961, 1962; Landau & Gewirtz, 1967; Gewirtz, 1967a, 1967b, 1969).

In the past decade there have also been conceptual and empirical advances in the substantive area of *early* social development and learning (e.g., Brackbill, 1958; Rheingold, Gewirtz & Ross, 1959; Gewirtz, 1961b, 1965, 1968b; Weisberg, 1963; Bijou & Baer, 1965; Walters & Parke, 1965; Etzel & Gewirtz, 1967), as well as in social-learning analyses and applications performed under a number of key, partially overlapping social-learning rubrics, including among others: *achievement* (e.g., McClelland et al., 1953); *aggression* (e.g., Sears, Whiting, Nowlis & Sears, 1953; Bandura & Walters, 1963; Walters & Parke, 1967); *attachment* (e.g., Gewirtz, 1961b; Walters & Parke, 1965); *conflict* and *displacement* (Miller, 1944, 1948b; Dollard & Miller, 1950); *conscience* and *morality* (e.g., Sears, 1957; Sears, Maccoby & Levin, 1957; Burton, Maccoby & Allinsmith, 1961; Aronfreed, 1963; Aronfreed & Reber, 1963); *delay of reward* (self-imposed) (Mischel, 1966b); *dependence* (e.g., Sears et al., 1953; Beller, 1955, 1959; Gewirtz, 1956b, 1961b; Sears et al., 1957; Bandura & Walters, 1963; Walters & Parke, 1964); *fear* and *anxiety* (e.g., Miller, 1948a, 1951, 1959; Farber, 1954; Bandura & Walters, 1963); *imitation* and *identification* (e.g., Miller & Dollard, 1941; Mowrer, 1950, 1960b; Seward, 1954; Sears, 1957; Whiting, 1960; Bandura, 1962, 1969; Bandura & Walters, 1963; Sears, Rau & Alpert, 1965; Gewirtz & Stingle, 1968); and *sex role* and *sex typing* (e.g., Sears et al., 1957; Maccoby, 1959; Burton & Whiting, 1961; Sears et al., 1965; Mischel, 1966a; Bandura, 1969). Finally, a variety of analyses and reports published by theorists operating within traditions which have not emphasized learning conceptions (for instance, "cognitive-developmental" or psychoanalytic) may bear directly on social-learning issues or conceptions (e.g., A. L. Baldwin, 1955; Bronfenbrenner, 1960; Kohlberg, 1966, 1969; Lewin, 1946, 1951; Piaget, 1950, 1952; White, 1959).

Scope of this Chapter

In analyses of social learning, nonbehavioral theorists have used complex and often seemingly inefficient (unparsimonious) constructs to order the overlapping areas of cognitive and personality development, parent-child relationships, social learning, and socialization. A considerable gap has existed between the variables used in their empirical studies and the sequential details of stimulus-response interchanges required for learning analyses. In this chapter we attempt to bridge much of this gap. Rather than emphasize global concepts like environments or traits, which summarize stimuli or responses through lengthy time spans, our approach calls for a finer analysis of stimuli, responses, their interchange at a particular moment, and the sequences of such interactions across successive moments.

Empirical work to date shows that it is both reasonable and profitable to conceive of social behavior as following the general laws of behavior, but with the relevant stimuli mediated by the behavior of persons rather than by other environmental sources. On this basis, our study of human social behavior proceeds in the same way as learning-based studies of other behavior classes: by analysis of the variables in the environment, both in the present and of the past, that *control* behavior. Such concepts can provide a flexible model for ordering the complex developmental patterns characterizing the child's socialization, by detailing the changing conditions of environmental stimulation in family, school, and peer group settings accompanying this development. The changing capacities of the child through developmental processes such as those indexed in naturalistic approaches by the terms "organismic maturation," "stages," "critical periods," and the like (e.g., Piaget, 1951), might qualify this approach but would not change its essential features.

In this chapter, we emphasize mainly conditioning concepts for positive stimulus control, as they apply to social behavior systems. While fear- and conflict-based concepts are considered as a proper part of this, a detailed examination of those concepts and of the techniques of aversive control on which they are based is put off for another occasion. As it is unlikely that any significant features of social development and socialization are based exclusively on such mechanisms, this tack simplifies the analysis, and seems to result in little loss of explanatory power or scope. Indeed, it permits a more detailed consideration of the topics covered and a more complete treatment of some key methodological and theoretical issues. Finally, given that a minimal number of modifications of the basic concepts are introduced, this tack makes possible a relatively unencumbered evaluation of the plausibility or adequacy of the use of basic operational concepts to understand how variations in environmental conditions (i.e., differential experience with stimuli) can affect social-behavior outcomes in early human development.

DEFINITION OF THE SOCIAL ENVIRONMENT

The terms "environment" and "stimulation" occur often in everyday discourse. These terms also occur frequently in analyses of child development, where, similarly, they have been employed more intuitively than precisely. Characterized as "wholesome" or "rich," these terms are frequently invoked as causes of certain patterns of development, and occasionally as labels for experimental or remedial treatments. However, there are neither universal definitions nor consensually defined operational indices of environment and stimulation, or of their derivatives "love" or "warmth," and as a corollary, such dimensions as "environmental wealth," that extend from poor or deficient to rich or abundant, can have no *a priori* meaning. Without behavioral criteria, these concepts are essentially useless both for understanding human social development and behavior technology, and may be best suited to literary ventures.

To be useful in an analysis of the impact of experience on the child's behavior, the concept of environment must have a basis in functional criteria, specifically the control of or impact on behavior by stimuli. Emphasis must be placed simultaneously on the environment and the behavior of the organism, for there can be no fruitful independent definition either of stimuli or of behavior. Environment, under our functional definition, is restricted to those stimuli impinging upon the organism that affect his behavior in some way. Under this conception, a large number of physical events that have no detectable effect on the organism's behavior would not be considered part of his environment; and, similarly, movements by the organism are not considered responses until they are observable and are shown to be under the control of stimuli.

The *social environment* consists of those functional stimuli which are provided by people; and *social behaviors* are those under the actual or potential control of social stimuli, in either their acquisition or maintenance, or both. It is arbitrary whether learning that occurs in a social context, but that is, or subsequently comes, under the control of nonsocial stimuli, is labeled social. Except that stimuli occurring in natural settings are likely to be more variable than stimuli in contrived laboratory experiments, and that the term social stimuli usually denotes those occurring in natural settings, there is nothing intrinsically special about stimuli provided by people or about social settings as contexts for learning. Thus, the term "social learning" simply defines a category of learning that involves stimuli provided by people but that follows the same principles as nonsocial learning.

We do not mean to imply, however, that because it has no special inherent qualities, social learning is not an important topic for study. Because of the nature of civilization, social learning, which is involved in man's dealings with other human beings, is perhaps the most indispensable class of human learning and accounts for many of the distinctive behavioral qualities of human beings. So much cueing and reinforcement in complex human-learning situations is of a social nature, e.g., discriminative settings for parental, teacher, or peer approval, that if social stimuli have not acquired strong discriminative and reinforcing value for the child, his learning may not reach appropriate levels. Those who have a major deficiency in social learning are thus unable to fend for themselves in society; and they are, in some instances, called "autistic." For these reasons, the study of the social environment and of social stimuli and responses is most important. And this study must be carried out in the same way as the study of nonsocial learning: with a careful analysis of stimulus-response processes. For social learning is, after all, learning.

KEY CONSTRUCTS OF
A SOCIAL-LEARNING THEORY
AND THEIR OPERATING MODES

Before looking at socialization processes per se, it is essential to define the key constructs of an operational learning approach and to illustrate their basic operating modes. This will enable us to delineate our problems more clearly. These constructs are the same as those that have been used in analyses of other classes of behaviors. As typically used, learning concepts order environmental operations that effect systematic and reversible changes in definable, observable behaviors. The operational concepts employed in this chapter do not differ markedly from the empirical concepts of alternative S-R associative approaches to learning. The number of constructs and operations and the labels assigned to them in a learning analysis are arbitrary. Further, the area is open to the addition of new concepts and to the differentiation and refinement of already existing concepts. In this analysis, we will stress the paradigm of operant (instrumental) conditioning as being most relevant to social-behavior functions (including "perception"), although assuming that respondent (classical) conditioning may operate concurrently and be responsible for many types of social learning.[1] The list that follows is not intended to be exhaustive, but only to give an idea of typical learning procedures and to suggest how these terms and procedures may be applied to situations in the life setting.[2]

Responses

In instrumental learning, the concept of the response (operant) is one of the two basic concepts. A response is any movement of the organism that is under the

---

[1]Although we will treat operant and respondent conditioning as independent paradigms to simplify the didactic presentation of this chapter, we recognize that they may approach and even overlap each other at several key points.

[2]The technical conditioning terms and symbols used are derived mainly from Skinner (1938, 1953) and Keller and Schoenfeld (1950). Our usage parallels that of Bijou and Baer (1961, 1965), among others.

control of environmental stimuli. Thus, although a movement of the organism is not necessarily a response, it has the potential to become one. A major assumption in our approach is that at no level of analysis is there validity in specifying responses without close attention to the controlling aspects (stimuli) in the environment that affect those responses. Emphasis must be on the stimulus-response unit; a response can only be defined in terms of the preceding and following stimuli that control it, and a stimulus can be defined only in terms of the responses it controls.

Because the meaning of a response is given by its functional relation to the stimuli that control it (and vice versa), in a given context even an otherwise trivial response like a bar press, button push, ear-lobe pull, or eye blink can gain a functional status comparable to that of freely occurring clearly social behaviors in human interaction in representative life settings. For example, these responses may acquire a functional equivalence to an attention-getting dependence behavior or an imitative-identificatory behavior.

In the natural course of events in ordinary social environments, many responses of the developing child come to acquire considerable strength and social meaning, and some of these will routinely change in topography with the increasing capacities of the child. These responses include orienting, regarding, tracking, reaching for, holding, clinging, vocalizing, smiling, laughing, and the like. Furthermore, as we shall note repeatedly in later sections, there have been successful attempts in the laboratory to condition various socially meaningful responses in the very young human infant with diverse, mainly social, reinforcing stimuli (summarized in Horowitz, 1968; Lipsitt, 1963, 1967). These include eye contact, smiles, and decreases in crying by two months (Etzel & Gewirtz, 1967), and smiles (Brackbill, 1958) and vocalizations (Rheingold et al., 1959; Weisberg, 1963) around three to four months. (Further, there has been speculation that differences [Gewirtz, 1965] detected in smiles to a human face at four weeks of life between groups of infants from kibbutz and institution settings may be due to differences in conditioning opportunities before that time.) These social responses are in addition to a variety of responses that do not ordinarily become social in life settings but which also have been instrumentally conditioned in the laboratory in the first months of life. The latter include: head turning, conditioned as early as the first month (Papousek, 1967) for milk-formula reinforcement and at four months (Siqueland, 1964), and at two and three months for social and nonsocial visual-display reinforcement (Koch, 1965, 1968; R. F. Caron, 1967); nonnutritive sucking as well as nutritive sucking for milk-formula reinforcement (Kaye, 1967); and manipulative responses maintained by visual displays (e.g., Rheingold, Stanley & Cooley, 1962; Lipsitt, Pederson & DeLucia, 1966). Respondent conditioning of various autonomic responses has been demonstrated in the first weeks and months of life (as described in Brackbill, Fitzgerald & Lintz, 1967; Lipsitt, 1963, 1967; Horowitz, 1968; Papousek, 1965, 1967), but will not be emphasized in our treatment in this chapter for reasons that will be detailed later.

Stimuli

Stimuli are environmental events that affect the responses of the organism. They can play a number of roles defined by their temporal relation to the response (contingency): they may function to evoke, cue, or reinforce behavior. Before the immediate or long-term response outcome of a stimulus can be predicted, the role of the stimulus in the particular situation must be specified. It is axiomatic that no *acquisition* can occur in the absence of stimuli, and the limiting case for predicting acquisition, therefore, occurs when there are no stimuli available. Further, when reinforcing stimuli are available, their effects on behavior are qualified by such factors as the temporal gradients of delay between response and stimulus, schedules of reinforcement, and the program or temporal sequence of application, as well as by whether or not there are background events present that mask (or change) either the stimuli presented or competing responses to those stimuli. Thus, when environmental events do not occur in such a way as to affect behavior, they are not *functional* insofar as they do not constitute stimuli for the organism (Gewirtz, 1968a, 1968b).

Discriminative stimuli.   A stimulus that systematically precedes a reinforced response can thus signal that the response, if emitted, is likely to be reinforced, and is termed a *discriminative stimulus* or *cue* (S^D). It controls the probability that the response will occur in the manner required by the reinforcement schedule. For example, a child may become conditioned to respond (e.g., by reaching out and smiling) to the appearance of his mother's face if these responses, when she appears, are systematically followed by functional reinforcers. In this case, the appearance of the mother's face would be said to function as the discriminative stimulus for the child's reaching out and smiling. The absence of this stimulus, or the presentation of other stimuli in whose presence responses are systematically not followed by reinforcement, is conventionally indicated by the label S^Δ ("S delta"). If stimuli are to merit these labels, the probability of the child's emitting the response must increase in the presence of the S^D and decrease in the presence of the S^Δ, as a result of such systematic differential association with reinforcement.

Reinforcing stimuli.   Reinforcement represents one basic way that systematic changes in behavior can be affected by differential experience with recurring stimuli. When the critical stimulus apparently responsible for the strengthening or maintenance of some index of a response is identified in an operational learning approach, it is ordinarily termed a "reinforcing stimulus." There are at least two major paradigms for the operation of such stimuli. In the most frequently used paradigm, that of operant (instrumental) conditioning, a reinforcing stimulus is an event which systematically makes more or less probable (i.e., "strengthens" or "weakens") an identified response when made repeatedly contingent upon it. This usage has come to give the term reinforcement much of its contemporary tone. Under the respondent-conditioning (Pavlovian, classical) paradigm, each presentation of a previously neutral (to be conditioned) stimulus is followed by an unconditioned stimulus that elicits an unconditioned response. This procedure is termed reinforcement when the result is a systematic increase in the probability that the originally neutral stimulus will elicit a response similar to or a derivative of the unconditioned response. Some experimental characteristics are unique to each paradigm; others operate in both. While the respondent-conditioning reinforcing operation is of a different order than the operant, both have been termed "reinforcing."

Thus, under an operational approach, any recurring event is labeled "reinforcing" if it makes systematically more (or less) probable a response which it regularly precedes (in the respondent paradigm) or follows (in the operant paradigm). The class of reinforcing operations is open, and the distinction between the labels "reinforcement" and "conditioning" is, for most purposes, one of semantics. Thus, under each conditioning paradigm any of a large number of stimulus-response contingency operations may in principle be classified as reinforcing when response strength is systematically affected by the provision of a stimulus. Also, there exist a large number of conditions (stimulus deprivations, response sets, and the like) which can qualify the effectiveness of reinforcing events. The remainder of this section is devoted to a detailed treatment of reinforcing stimuli as they function under the operant-conditioning paradigm.

Under the operant-conditioning paradigm, any stimulus is termed a *reinforcer* (S^R) when its presentation or removal contingent upon (i.e., immediately following) a response systematically affects certain attributes of that response (e.g., its probability, rate, amplitude, latency, resistance to extinction). A contingent stimulus whose systematic presentation leads to an increase in the strength of a response and whose removal leads to a decrease in its strength is termed a *positive reinforcer* (in the past often termed a "reward"[3]). And when the removal of a stimulus contingent upon a response leads to an increase in response strength and its presentation leads to a decrease in response strength, the stimulus is termed a *negative reinforcer*. Thus, the presentation of a positive reinforcer and the removal of a negative reinforcer by definition have a similar effect which may be termed *reinforcement*. For example, the removal of negative reinforcers, such as when the parent stops an older child from hitting his younger sibling, can be potent reinforcement for the child's seeking help from the parent (behaviors typically labeled "dependent," the acquisition of which is considered later.) The contingent presentation of a negative reinforcer and the contingent withdrawal of a positive reinforcer that has been previously available, similarly lead to a decrease in response strength and may be termed "punishment."

---

[3]The terms "reward" and "punishment," although flavored with hedonic tone, have often been employed by psychologists. As used in this chapter, these terms can provide historical context for some issues. However, my preference is to use in their stead the more neutral terms reinforcement, positive and negative reinforcers, contingent aversive stimuli, and the like.

It remains an empirical question which of the myriad potential stimuli in the human infant's milieu emerge at each growth point to function as unconditioned ("primary")[4] positive reinforcers for his behaviors to effect learning. Even so, it appears thus far that a very large variety of events can function as positive reinforcers in early human life, in addition to those which are thought to meet such organismic needs as food, water, and the removal of aversive cutaneous conditions including pain, cold, and wetness. However, with the exception of "food" (i.e., a milk formula) which has been studied extensively in the past decade (e.g., Papousek, 1965, 1967; Siqueland, 1964; Siqueland & Lipsitt, 1966; Kaye, 1967), even those positive reinforcing stimulus classes that have been emphasized most in social-learning approaches are only relatively well understood.

Thus, potential reinforcing stimuli that remain to be studied include the sensory stimuli provided through diverse tactile, olfactory, taste, auditory, and visual receptors. In certain contexts, some of these may be even more effective than food and water. Such events could also acquire discriminative (cue) value for behavior. It is likely that the potential stimulus events involving the different receptor systems will vary in terms of the absolute numbers of each which will occur in the infant's environment. Further, due simply to the mechanics of the receptors, different proportions of these potential stimulus events will actually come to function as stimuli for the infant. Thus, assuming that the events provided are above threshold level, the position of the head in relation to the visual event source and whether or not the eyelids are closed are examples of mechanical "gates" in the visual receptor system; whether or not there is an obstruction between the ears and a sound source is an example for the auditory system; and whether or not clothing can interfere with skin-contact events is a limiting factor for the reception of tactile events. Further, competitive or masking events for potential stimuli may be more frequent in the visual than in the auditory realms, and more frequent in the latter area than in the tactile sector. In this sense, when tactile events occur, they may provide more potent stimuli than auditory ones, and auditory events may provide more potent stimuli than visual ones.

It is recalled that in his early writings, Freud (1938b) speculated that contact stimuli to "erotogenic zones" of the body provided through rocking, stroking, kissing, and the like were very likely to be potent. In the conditioning language of this chapter, such events would be likely to function as reinforcing (as well as discriminative) stimuli. Further, there is evidence that visual stimuli can also function as potent reinforcers, at least for three-month-old children, as demonstrated by studies on the reinforcing efficacy of changing visual displays (Rheingold et al., 1962; R. F. Caron, 1967). Finally, there is suggestive evidence that even simple vocal and/or tactile replies can reinforce such infant responses as vocalizations, smiles, and eye contact (Rheingold et al., 1959; Etzel & Gewirtz,

---

[4]When a functional reinforcing stimulus terminating a chain has an unknown history, it is sometimes termed "primary" or "unconditioned" (e.g., appetitive stimuli, strong noxious stimuli).

1967). It is also likely that what some would term the "intrinsically interesting" (or "self-reinforcing") gross motor behaviors of the infant, such as his staring at gross movements of his hands or fingers, can be maintained by such specifiable extrinsic consequences (i.e., reinforcing stimuli) as breaking beams of light and making and changing patterns of visual stimuli.

Further, it has been shown that the opportunity for a response can function as a positive reinforcer for some other unrelated response that occurs at a lower rate, when the more frequent response is made contingent upon the occurrence of the less frequent one (Premack, 1959, 1962). Conversely, making a lower-rate response contingent upon a higher-rate response is equivalent to punishment of the latter (Weisman & Premack, 1966). This relationship, originally isolated in rats, provides a basis for the evocation and reinforcement of diverse child behaviors in social settings, with minimal concern for the stimuli which might be maintaining those behaviors. This principle is often implicitly used by socializing agents to bring infrequent behaviors into a child's repertory. Thus, in life settings a child who understands verbal instructions is often told that he will be permitted to engage in what is, for him, a frequent behavior *only* *after* he exhibits (a given rate of) an infrequent behavior or a specified novel response (one which he might not exhibit in the ordinary course of events). For instance, going out to play may serve to reinforce doing homework, reading, practicing a musical instrument, or repairing the deck. In a preliminary application in a nursery-school setting, Homme, de Boca, Devine, Steinhorst and Richert (1963) increased the rate of originally low-probability behaviors, such as sitting quietly in a chair and looking at the blackboard, by making contingent upon them such high-probability responses as running around the room, screaming, pushing chairs, or working jigsaw puzzles.

The association of a stimulus with a reinforcer can take various forms. By temporal association with an already functional reinforcer, a previously neutral stimulus can acquire functional reinforcing value, in which case it is termed a *conditioned (acquired, secondary) reinforcer* (S^r). Presenting a functional (e.g., terminal) reinforcer on an intermittent schedule with respect to a conditioned reinforcer will make that reinforcer more durable in maintaining responses (cf., e.g., J. Zimmerman, 1963). Thus, schedules can be devised to minimize, but never to preclude, the requirement for a conditioned reinforcer to be systematically associated with a functional reinforcer; at least occasional pairing will always be necessary. The conditioned reinforcer may thus function as a probabilistic "promise" that the functional reinforcer with which it is associated will follow. (This parallels the definition of a discriminative stimulus which, as we have seen, may be conceived as a cue that promises a certain probability of reinforcement *if* the correct response is emitted.)

A corollary of the concept of conditioned reinforcement (and the S-R chaining conception that is examined later) is that, relative to its efficacy in reinforcing a novel response (or a remote response in an S-R chain), a conditioned reinforcing stimulus will be more effective in maintaining the response that immediately preceded it in the original conditioning situation (in the chain in which it acquired its reinforcing value), and it will do so as long as the contingency between it and the functional (terminal) reinforcing stimulus is maintained (assuming the latter retains its value for a child). The reinforcing efficacy of conditioned reinforcers (and chain stimuli generally) has been fleeting in many conditioning-test settings because researchers, often overlooking these properties, have at the same time both employed an entirely new response (with a very different topography) and removed the contingency between the conditioned reinforcer being tested and relevant functional reinforcers. Under such conditions, the conditioned reinforcer must, of necessity, rapidly decrease in effectiveness at the same time and through the same process by which it is evaluated.[5] (This issue will be elaborated further in our consideration of the concept of *functional autonomy of motives.*)

Analogous to the conditioned positive reinforcer, a *conditioned aversive stimulus* (or conditioned negative reinforcer) is a stimulus that systematically precedes the occurrence of an aversive stimulus and thus acquires many of the properties of that aversive stimulus. It can decrease responses when presented contingent upon them and increase responses when removed contingent upon them. It similarly requires at least occasional pairing with the functional noxious reinforcer to maintain its potency.

It is likely that under typical life conditions, a stimulus will be paired with more than one functional reinforcing stimulus. Such conditioned reinforcing stimuli, which could thus be effective under a wide range of setting conditions (for instance, different kinds and degrees of deprivation), have been termed *generalized reinforcers* (Skinner, 1953). It has been proposed that relative to a conditioned reinforcer associated with only one functional reinforcer, a generalized reinforcer is more effective in maintaining responses that precede it, its reinforcing efficacy is less likely to be qualified by the momentary conditions of the organism (e.g., deprivations), and it will be more resistant to loss of reinforcing value when no longer paired with a particular functional reinforcer.[6]

Many of the stimulus events which are reinforcing for behavior are supplied by people and thus may be termed *social reinforcers.* They represent stimulus complexes or elements, which for the most part are assumed to have acquired their generalized positive or negative reinforcing value for the young child by

---

[5] In addition to tests of conditioned reinforcer efficacy under extinction conditions and in contexts where the contingencies between such a stimulus and the functional reinforcer are maintained as in life settings (e.g., chained schedules), a third procedure is also available for examining the reinforcing efficacy of a conditioned reinforcer: the concurrent scheduling of primary and conditioned reinforcement. J. Zimmerman (1963) has found that a response can be indefinitely maintained by a conditioned reinforcer when a second response is concurrently maintained by the primary reinforcer with which the conditioned reinforcer is repeatedly associated. Like the chained schedule of reinforcement, and perhaps even more so, the concurrent schedule is typical of real life situations and thus a more rational mode of examining conditioned reinforcement than extinction procedures.

[6] Some researchers (e.g., Wike & McNamara, 1955, and Myers & Trapold, 1966) have found that the reinforcing value of generalized reinforcers (based on two primary reinforcers) has not been greater than that of reinforcers associated with only one functional reinforcer. Even so, this hypothesis has been supported by several studies (e.g., Wike & Barrientos, 1958; and Kanfer, 1960) and is still open to further experimental investigation.

being consistently discriminative for (or associated with) not one but a variety of functioning reinforcers, including such vital stimuli as food, water, and the removal of painful stimuli,[7] as well as other tactile, visual, and auditory events. (Social reinforcers, however, need not be generalized, as it is possible that, under certain conditions, they would be associated with only one functional reinforcing stimulus.) The human infant, helpless in early life, receives many of the stimuli which are reinforcing for his behaviors through caretaking. Moreover, concurrently in the interaction context, an infant will be responded to by adults, even when he does not exhibit an apparent "need," as when he has emitted a response which delights the adult, or at times simply because the caretaker thinks him "charming." These conditions are assumed to lead to the acquisition of strong reinforcing value by social stimuli provided by a caretaker or parent, for instance, her near presence, attention, approval, and component responses like her smile. Similarly, aversive social stimulus complexes, such as verbal disapproval, and component responses like frowns, acquire generalized aversive properties by being paired with various functional noxious reinforcers for the individual.

Whichever stimuli caretakers consistently provide preceding or concomitant with functional reinforcement to a young child are those which should subsequently function as social reinforcers for him. Hence, particular social stimuli will be differentially reinforcing for different children. Thus, attention or approval may become a positive reinforcer for one child, a negative rein-

---

[7] It is possible that even the conditions of the appearance of food or moderate degrees of environmental change per se may be effective as reinforcing stimuli not on an unconditioned basis but rather as conditioned reinforcers. Moreover, their reinforcing value should be extinguishable if the sequence in which they constitute an important occasion for reinforcement could be broken at some point. Thus, although the reinforcing effectiveness of food appears to be under the control of periodic, homeostatic conditions, the stimuli provided by its appearance, smell, taste, and the sounds accompanying its presentation, may each have acquired reinforcer value for behavior solely on the basis of its position in the usually invariant sequence of events which leads ultimately to some terminal "unconditioned" reinforcing event. This possibility is generally compatible with the informal observations made by researchers that rhesus monkeys only slowly learn to eat food. Perhaps the stimuli provided by food come to function as conditioned discriminative and reinforcing stimuli for the successive responses in S-R eating chains.

Similarly, *environmental change* in moderate degrees may be conditioned as a reinforcing stimulus class. As the child grows, an increasing number of his responses will be reinforced by a growing number of both apparently unconditioned and conditioned reinforcing stimuli provided by the increasingly direct effects of his ever-increasing success in operating on the environment. As a function of its contiguous occurrence with a large variety of potent reinforcing stimuli (perhaps even before most conditioned reinforcing stimuli have developed as such for a child), moderate environmental change per se may become a potent conditioned (generalized) reinforcing stimulus capable of maintaining the behaviors of the child under a wide range of conditions (Gewirtz, 1961b; Bijou & Baer, 1965). Thus, also, other stimuli which have generally been thought to operate on unconditioned bases, such as those provided the child through contact-holding, as when he is picked up to distract or otherwise quiet him at times when he is in apparent pain, or for feeding and other caretaking, may have acquired some portion of their reinforcing power through their association for the child with the potent reinforcing stimuli provided by the disappearance (through distraction) of the pain, by "interesting" environmental changes, or by feeding and other caretaking.

forcer for a second (as when it has consistently been made discriminative for aversive stimuli), and nonfunctional for a third. Apart from standing for particular stimulus complexes, terms like attention and approval often serve as helpful abstractions that loosely organize the great variety of component stimuli which the caretaking environment can provide incidental to reinforcement. These stimuli include those provided by diverse combinations of speaking, hugging, kissing, humming, singing, squeezing, smiling, nonsense vocalizing, and grimacing. When such abstractions are reduced, as they must be, to their component stimulus elements, it may be found that for some children, verbal approval may operate as a potent reinforcer for behavior whereas nods or smiles, also intended by an adult to indicate approval, may not be effective (Gewirtz, 1961b; Bijou & Baer, 1963). Even within such classes of social stimuli, the responsiveness of children will vary depending upon their differential experiences with specific stimuli. Thus, for a particular child one variant of an approval word may be a more effective reinforcer than another variant (e.g., *good* as opposed to *correct*), or than the mere absence of verbal disapproval. It is also likely that the reinforcing efficacy of social stimuli will vary according to the similarity of a given setting to the one in which the stimuli initially acquired their reinforcing value. Further, as will be seen in a later section on setting conditions, the source of social reinforcers may also determine or qualify their functional value for the recipient, depending on his experiential history with that source person. When provided by different people, what appears to be otherwise the same social stimulus could have quite different effects on the behavior of a young child. Thus, stimulus complexes which are intended to constitute "love" by the dispensing agency would not operate as reinforcing stimuli for a child if they had not been conditioned as such for him with respect to that particular reinforcing agent. Moreover, as will be seen subsequently, this child will also differ from others as to what constitutes a "sufficient" supply of the stimulus, the rate at which he has been conditioned to receive it, and the like (Gewirtz, 1961b).

S-R Chains

Responses and stimuli usually occur in S-R chains of varying lengths terminating with a functional reinforcer (S^R). The smallest functional chain consists of at least S^D–R–S^R. In longer operant chains, a response which occurs in the presence of a discriminative stimulus is followed by the discriminative stimulus for the next response. Since each discriminative stimulus can act as a conditioned reinforcer for the response it follows, stimuli that originally may have been neutral may acquire reinforcing value as they acquire cue value.[8] As long as their rela-

---

[8]There has been some controversy concerning the conditions for establishing a stimulus as a conditioned reinforcer (i.e., whether a stimulus need be discriminative in order to acquire conditioned reinforcing value). Keller and Schoenfeld (1950) cite the studies of Schoenfeld, Antonitis and Bersh (1950) and Dinsmoor (1950) as evidence that discriminative stimuli and conditioned reinforcers are co-existent: a stimulus can function as a conditioned reinforcer only if it has also been established as a discriminative stimulus for some response. However, Kelleher and Gollub (1962) and Kelleher (1966) have cited

tionship to the functional reinforcer is maintained at least occasionally, these conditioned reinforcers can maintain behaviors preceding them in chains, and hence can support new learning (i.e., reinforce new responses when made contingent upon them).[9] Thus, each originally neutral stimulus in an S-R chain preceding the terminal reinforcer typically acquires two functions: it serves both as a discriminative stimulus for the response that follows it and as a reinforcer for the response that precedes it in the chain.

Traditionally, social learning analyses have emphasized the reinforcing role of chain stimuli. A stimulus that is found in many varied S-R chains will be discriminative for more than one functional reinforcing stimulus (as is the case with a large number of social stimuli such as attention or approval), and thus it may function as a *generalized reinforcer*. Since it can condition and maintain diverse approach responses under a wide range of conditions, the reinforcing value of a chain stimulus when it occurs relatively late in diverse chains is also emphasized in the present analysis. However, response strength in a chain may testify not only to the value of the conditioned reinforcer following it but also to the value of the preceding stimulus that functions as a cue for the next chain stimulus and for the terminal chain stimulus. Thus, when it characteristically occurs at points near the beginning of numerous chains of diverse composition, we will emphasize the discriminative value of a chain stimulus. In such instances, it can set the occasion for the occurrence of numerous response-reinforcement sequences, and thus, for our heuristic purpose, may be termed a *generalized discriminative stimulus*. Such generalized discriminative stimuli may perhaps have two additional roles: they may effect increases in any of the instrumental responses that have occurred in that context (conditioned facilitation), and they may become discriminative for conditioned approach responses specific to the person dispensing the stimuli. These two stimulus functions are corollaries of the chaining conception, but to date have seldom received conceptual or empirical emphasis.

Aversive chain stimuli can acquire generalized discriminative and reinforcing properties which are reciprocally analogous to the properties just noted for

---

studies (e.g., Ferster & Skinner, 1957; and Stein, 1958) in which stimuli were found to function as conditioned reinforcers without necessarily also functioning as discriminative stimuli. Moreover, it was found that discriminative stimuli occurring early in long operant chains did not necessarily function as conditioned reinforcers. Although the evidence on this issue is not yet conclusive, stimuli in S-R chains appear generally to function both as conditioned reinforcers for responses preceding them and as discriminative stimuli for responses following them.

[9]In passing, we note that several writers have remarked that the conditions determining the operation of conditioned reinforcement (particularly in the absence of the terminal "primary" reinforcer of the S-R chain) are operationally identical with frustration conditions, i.e., interference in an S-R chain of directed activity, even though conditioned reinforcement has equilibrium and approach connotations and frustration has disequilibrium and aversive connotations (e.g., Bower, 1963; Lott, 1967). As the issue is moot, and the possible operation of frustration is confounded with conditioned reinforcement on the level of analysis at which we are operating and does not affect our case, it may reasonably be ignored in our exposition here. When frustration is considered in a later section, note will be taken of Amsel's (1962) thesis that after reward conditions have become routine, non-reward can produce a frustration drive state affecting the incidence of responses generally.

conditioned positive discriminative and reinforcing stimuli. In addition to the effects of the contingent provision or removal of such (generalized) conditioned aversive stimuli, and their discriminative value for a variety of responses, they can have at least two other independent effects, depending on their relations to behaviors: they can decrease various ongoing responses in the context even without their contingent presentation (conditioned suppression), and they can become discriminative for behaviors avoiding the conditioned (or unconditioned) aversive stimuli (and decreasing or eliminating concurrent emotional respondents).

Whole chains or large segments of chains may come under the control of several different generalized discriminative and reinforcing stimuli, and may occur so regularly that they appear to be unlearned. When generalized discriminative and reinforcing stimuli are social, they come to control much of the interchange between people. The conditioned discriminative and reinforcing stimulus concept as used here can be employed to order the phenomena ordinarily classified under "acquired drive," and on that basis alone is a key concept for an operational analysis of social learning.[10]

It follows from our joint emphasis on the importance of co-defining stimuli and responses that our approach requires detailed attention to the sequential ordering of stimuli and responses in the study of interactions between two or more people, and that this approach has greater explanatory power than a "one-sided" approach that attends only to one person's responses (sometimes through lengthy time spans) and therefore misses important functional relationships operating between the interactors. Only by attending to the sequence of stimuli and responses is it possible to specify the conditions under which a response will occur, and then to modify the response by changing those conditions; thus the S-R chain is the most appropriate (and hence potentially useful) unit of analysis in social learning.

Stimulus Generalization and Discrimination

Stimulus generalization. The phenomenon whereby a response conditioned in the presence of one particular stimulus (which thus comes to be discriminative for it) is also emitted in the presence of stimuli which were not

---

[10]The occurrence of various originally unconditioned autonomic responses (i.e., "emotional" respondents such as increased heart rate, respiration, perspiration, or excretory acts) in the presence of such conditioned aversive stimuli, together with some of the just-noted properties of conditioned aversive stimuli, have sometimes been taken to reflect the presence of conditioned "fear" (where there is an identifiable aversive stimulus) or "anxiety" (where there is not, or where the effects of the stimulus are highly generalized). Moreover, they have served for some as indices of a "drive state," whose removal-reduction has been equated to reinforcement (Dollard & Miller, 1950; Miller, 1951). A critique of the adequacy of the discriminative and reinforcement facets of the conditioned reinforcer concept is considered in a later section on the role of motivation in social-learning approaches, where the postulation of "drive" is often gratuitous. The concept of "functional autonomy of motives" provides the focus for this evaluation, in which the bases for the introduction of terms like "drive" and "motive" are also considered.

earlier associated with the response, in proportion to their similarity to that training stimulus, is termed stimulus generalization. It is assumed that the response will be emitted (i.e., be generalized) to such new stimuli because of their "similarity" to the training stimulus, that is, because these stimuli may contain, along with irrelevant components, varying proportions of the relevant aspects of the training stimulus which acquired control over the response in the original acquisition context. Thus, also, it may be assumed that new stimuli, because they may be in new contexts or vary along irrelevant dimensions, will often appear to be different from the original training stimulus, although they are actually functionally identical to it.[11] Thus, stimulus generalization is likely to occur to the degree that the organism has *not* been consistently nonreinforced for responding to stimuli varying along salient similarity dimensions from the training stimulus. For instance, when a child conditioned to respond to the appearance of his mother's face by reaching out and smiling is presented with another face, the probability of his reaching out and smiling should at first be a function of the similarity of that face to his mother's; and subsequently a function of whether or not his smiles to that new face are reinforced. If the conditioned response either to the training stimulus or to its variants is not reinforced, extinction of the response will result. Generalization along a stimulus dimension which is defined not in terms of physical similarity but rather in terms of a learned functional similarity by the child (e.g., different words while varying along possible dimensions all belong to the same class) has sometimes been termed *mediated generalization.*

Stimulus discrimination.   In contrast to generalization, the occurrence of a response to a training stimulus or in one stimulus situation, with a corresponding absence of that response to stimuli varying from the training stimulus, or in other stimulus situations, as a result of differential reinforcement, is termed stimulus discrimination. When the child is reinforced for responding to, or in the presence of, a particular stimulus (S^D) (or specifiable aspect of stimulation) but is not reinforced for responses in the absence of the original stimulus or in the presence of stimuli that vary in salient features from the original cue stimulus (S^Δ), or when he is reinforced for not responding to those different stimuli, his response comes under the control of the presence or absence of the stimulus. Responses under such stimulus control are said to be discriminated operants.

Extending our earlier example, if the child's reaching out and smiling to the mother's face is frequently followed by functional reinforcers such as may be provided by hugs, caresses, food, etc., and these stimuli are not provided (or are provided to a lesser degree) when he reaches out and smiles to others, the probability that the child will respond to others will decrease and a discrimination

---

[11]Such cases in which generalization maintains to the new stimuli which appear to be different from the training stimulus seldom appear in the basic stimulus generalization literature, but may ordinarily be found in other literatures, such as that on concept acquisition. They may, however, be basic for the use of "generalization" and "transfer" conceptions to explain the acquisition of complex behavior systems, such as language.

may be said to have been established. Hypothetically, if reinforcing stimuli were provided to a child nondifferentially by each of a large number of care-takers, the occasion for discrimination learning would be less likely to occur, and the child should be equally responsive to all caretakers (and perhaps to strangers as well). A child reared under such conditions, which would be more likely to occur in institutions than in family settings, would also not be given the optimal circumstances for acquiring differential "attachments" to people (which process will be discussed in a later section).

Thus, generalization and discrimination represent *reciprocal* definitions of the same phenomenon and provide convenient foci for the consideration of variations of the basic acquisition process of stimulus control of responses. Indeed, there can be postulated a dimension of treatment conditions involving varying degrees of differential reinforcement for the response to a stimulus, ranging from those which yield pure stimulus generalization (i.e., no discrimi-nation) at the start of a test series to conditions which yield pure stimulus dis-crimination (i.e., no generalization). Gradients of response across stimulus di-mensions are expected to fall more steeply from a maximum at the training stimulus as training (and test) conditions approach those for discrimination (Gewirtz, Jones & Waerneryd, 1956). In this context, it can be seen how the types of experiences a child has with the stimuli in his environment can affect his subsequent learning and the degree to which his responses will come under stimulus control. As much of social learning involves the acquisition by stimuli of discriminative control over the responses of the developing child, the dis-crimination-learning process outlined is particularly important in early life. Moreover, it provides a useful model for studying the development of early di-mensional learning by the young child.

Dimensional learning. It is readily assumed that the discrimination-learning trials in which responses are followed by reinforcement constitute dimensional-learning trials. However, it is our contention that dimensional learning is also dependent upon the discrimination-learning trials in which responses are *not* followed by reinforcement. The assumption is that, in discrim-ination learning, the child learns to discriminate not only the occasions for reinforcement (S^D) but, at the same time, the occasions for nonreinforcement (S^Δ). On this basis, it is thought that a child comes to discriminate between stimuli varying along salient dimensions (e.g., height, area, brightness), and that his responding to sets of stimuli in terms of such dimensions constitutes dimensional learning. Moreover, it is assumed that the efficiency with which the child comes to discriminate these salient differences is a direct function of the positive S^D and negative S^Δ instances he has experienced, in terms of their number and range, the proportion of each set, and like factors.

It is therefore important that a child be provided with a wide range of diverse environmental events, through which he can acquire many varied dimen-sional discriminations. To facilitate such dimensional learning, environments might be designed to provide stimulus instances that fall much closer to each other along salient (simple and compound) stimulus dimensions (i.e., instances of negative discriminative stimuli that are increasingly similar to the positive discriminative stimulus), thereby requiring ever finer discriminations by the child. Insofar as the child is able to discriminate more and more subtle differences among stimuli varying along growing numbers of dimensions, the child's behavior systems come increasingly under more subtle and varied discriminative stimulus control.

Complex discriminations. Complex discriminations can be established that govern a subject's responses to a wide range of discriminative stimuli varying in content. Some have termed this learning "concept formation," and a useful label for many purposes appears to be *"conditional discrimination"* (Lashley, 1938; Cumming & Berryman, 1965). In simple discrimination acquisitions (involving simultaneous or successive contrasts), the correct response is made entirely on the basis of the presence or absence of a single discriminative stimulus (attribute) that sets the occasion for reinforcement of the response. In a conditional-discrimination situation, however, the correct response is made on the basis of attributes of two or more stimuli, for instance, the standard (i.e., the conditional stimulus) and comparison stimuli in the matching-to-sample conditioning case. In the general case, these would be termed the *conditional* stimulus and *discriminative* stimuli, and the relationship between the two stimulus sets need not be one of matching. Thus, the discriminative stimulus is not homogeneous as in simple discrimination learning where it is but a standard cue in whose presence the response may be reinforced and in whose absence it will not be; rather it varies across discrimination trials relative to the conditional stimulus which thus comes to function as a set or selector for discriminations. The conditional discrimination is therefore a setting concept that can provide the presumed basis for many complex behavior systems: the conditional stimulus(i) sets the occasion for the stimulus dimension(s) or the value(s) along the dimensions that control the response, i.e., it defines the discriminative stimuli for reinforcement. The analysis of imitation-identification made later describing two key complex social-learning processes is based on a matching-to-sample conditional-discrimination paradigm. Further, as is also noted later on, language acquisition may abound with conditional discriminations, which (through generalization-induction) function as grammatical rules; for instance, verbs are inflected one way in a present context and another way in a past context.

Acquisition and its Facilitation

Shaping. One process that can facilitate response acquisition is shaping or response differentiation. This procedure, which involves the differential reinforcement of successively closer approximations to the desired response (Skinner, 1953), is a means by which desired behavior outcomes previously unobserved in a child's repertoire can be fostered. Initially, appropriate evoking stimuli may be necessary to facilitate the occurrence of primitive behavior elements that can then be modified through shaping. In the child's socialization, his behaviors are continually being shaped as his changing capacities permit. However, it is often difficult, and for many purposes irrelevant, to specify which is the cause and which the effect, as shaping procedures may be responsible to a large degree for many of these changes in "capacities."

Fading.   A process that is complementary to shaping, but involves a progressive change in the stimuli controlling the response rather than in the response itself, is stimulus fading. This fading process could involve changing from continuous to intermittent reinforcement, from a high potency reinforcer in acquisition to a lower-potency reinforcer in maintenance, or from one discriminative stimulus to another. For example, in discriminative-stimulus fading, an initially neutral stimulus can come to function as a discriminative stimulus for behavior when it is presented simultaneously with a functioning discriminative stimulus which is gradually withdrawn. By this method, the subject can learn difficult discriminations without acquiring the tendency to respond occasionally to the negative discriminative stimulus (i.e., to make errors), as is the case when the discrimination is learned by trial and error methods (Terrace, 1963a, 1963b). Fading methods can be especially useful for bringing behaviors under the control of verbal commands or requests. For example, Baer, Peterson and Sherman (1965, 1967) reported that an experimenter-model taught children to imitate his behavior by saying "Do this," emitting the desired response, and physically assisting the child to make the same response. On each trial, they lessened (i.e., faded) the amount of assistance provided until the child came to respond to the cues in the verbal command and the model's response alone.

A combination of both shaping and fading methods can be an effective procedure to facilitate the child's verbal learning, which is one of the most important components of socialization. A cogent example of the use of these techniques is the Lovaas, Berberich, Perloff and Schaeffer (1966) method for teaching initially nonverbal schizophrenic children to speak. In the initial stages of learning, the experimenters used shaping methods to make the sounds emitted by the child become more and more like those modeled by the experimenter. Once the child had learned to imitate the experimenter's vocalizations, the next step was to teach him to answer questions. Here fading procedures were used: the experimenter asked questions and prompted the child by telling him the answers. The experimenter then gradually faded out the prompt cue by saying the answer more and more softly, until the child learned to answer the question without prompting. Similarly, after speech was established in autistic echolalic children by shaping and imitation training, that speech behavior was transferred from imitative to appropriate stimulus control by fading in new stimuli and fading out the verbal prompts (Risley & Wolf, 1967).

Schedules of reinforcement.   The contingency patterns in which reinforcing stimuli are provided play significant roles in the acquisition and maintenance of behavior (Ferster & Skinner, 1957). Reinforcement schedules illustrate one form of control that stimuli can acquire over behavior, in that they determine the rate at which behavior is emitted. This reinforcement-pattern control, however, is secondary to the control over behavior exercised directly by reinforcing stimuli. The simplest reinforcement schedule is that of *continuous reinforcement* (CRF), in which a given response is reinforced each time it occurs. It was the schedule typically employed in the early studies, which attended to simple relationships between the response and reinforcement. Acquisition and extinction under CRF can provide baselevels in terms of which a consideration of intermittent reinforcement schedules can proceed. Under CRF, a response will be acquired most rapidly and will extinguish most quickly if reinforcement is withheld. Intermittent reinforcement schedules vary along two basic dimensions: ratio or interval, and fixed or variable. In ratio schedules, the reinforcer is presented according to the number of times the response is emitted, whereas in interval schedules the reinforcer is presented according to the amount of elapsed time since the previous reinforcement of the response. Furthermore, reinforcement according to either of these two types of schedules may be presented on a fixed or variable basis.[12] In general, ratio schedules result in high response rates with "bursts" of responding, and interval schedules produce low, steady response rates. A variety of other reinforcement schedules have been and can be devised, including differential reinforcement of low response rates (DRL) or simultaneous or successive combinations of any of these schedules.

Because under intermittent reinforcement a response becomes more resistant to extinction, these schedules may be thought of as a means of "fortifying" the organism against changes in response rate when contingent stimulation is removed or changed in provision rate. Most reinforcement in the child's development can be assumed to be on some sort of intermittent schedule, since the caretaker is often occupied with other children or with some task and is not able to reinforce (continuously) every one of the child's behaviors; or occasionally the caretaker may deliberately withhold reinforcement from the child to avoid "spoiling" him.

Correlated or conjugate reinforcement. Some ordered attribute of performance (e.g., response latency, duration, amplitude, rate) may directly determine the magnitude of a reinforcer or the speed with which it is dispensed following a response. The more closely a performance approaches the defined criterion, the greater the amount of reinforcement or the faster it is provided.

---

[12]In a *fixed ratio* (FR) schedule, every Nth response is reinforced, as compared to a *variable ratio* (VR) schedule, where on the average every Nth response is reinforced, but the actual number of response occurrences between reinforcement occasions varies randomly about the average characterizing ratio. *Fixed interval* (FI) and *variable interval* (VI) schedules are analogous to ratio schedules, except that in interval schedules the first response occurring after a fixed or variable time interval is reinforced; in VI schedules the time between reinforced responses varies randomly around some average interval. Under an FI schedule, "scalloping" tends to occur, with the response rate decreasing immediately following a reinforcement, and increasing as the time approaches for the next reinforcement occasion.

This mode of reinforcement provision has been termed "*correlated*" by Logan (1960), "*conjugate*" by Lindsley (e.g., 1963), and "*titration*" by Weiss and Laties (1963). For instance, panel-pressing was conditioned in 12-month-old children when the intensity of the reinforcing event, a light to permit the viewing of a moving object in a box, was increased in proportion to response rate (Lipsitt et al., 1966).

Correlated or conjugate reinforcement studies differ from instrumental conditioning studies employing the standard modes of reinforcement (previously discussed) in several ways. In the latter studies, ineffective low or possibly noxious high values of a potential positive reinforcing stimulus are ordinarily discarded from experimental procedures, after either an examination of the lore or prior pilot research (although these informal checks are usually only implied in the experimental report), and a single value of the reinforcer is then made contingent upon a single, defined value of the response. However, when correlated or conjugate reinforcement is used, both those values of the intended reinforcing event that may, and those that may not, function as reinforcers (under a standard setting condition) are provided within the same procedure. And *any* response, whether it be close to or (within a defined wide range) remote from the criterion level chosen for maximal reinforcement, is followed by some value of the intended reinforcing event. In such studies, therefore, it is the span of values of the intended reinforcing stimulus, known from previous lore or prior pilot research to function as strong positive reinforcers of behavior, that is coordinated with the response range around the criterion value (that value selected to receive maximal reinforcement). This is done either explicitly, as in Logan's (1960) work, where a defined intermediate response value provides the criterion that is to be maximally reinforced, or implicitly, as in the work of Lindsley (1963) or of Lipsitt et al. (1966), where some unspecified but high value of the response unit receives maximal reinforcement.

"Intrinsic" or "self" reinforcement.   It is axiomatic that behavior acquisition and maintenance require the presence of stimuli. However, there are sometimes situations in which a systematic change in some aspect of behavior is identified but the extrinsic reinforcing stimuli (i.e., stimuli provided by environmental agents) strengthening or maintaining it are not. Such behaviors have sometimes been labeled gratuitously as "self-reinforcing" or "intrinsically reinforcing," this usage implying that the responses at issue occur "for their own sake" (e.g., Harlow, 1950; Aronfreed, 1967, 1969; Kohlberg, 1963). In a not dissimilar vein, others have written that such responses are "intrinsically motivated," based on a "motive" to exhibit the behavior, e.g., the motive of exploration, of curiosity, or the "manipulation drive" of Harlow, Harlow and Meyer (1950), and that organisms have a "need" for the sensory stimulation which ensues as a consequence. Kohlberg (1966) has conceived that "effectance" or "competence-mastery" motives or a motive for "interesting" events underlies "intrinsically reinforced" behaviors, a conception like White's (1959) "competency striving." However, the analysis in this chapter assumes that many behaviors that

appear to be acquired on these bases may, in fact, be conceived as functionally attributable to the operation of extrinsic reinforcement provided by opportunities to manipulate or to attain specific consequences that may be assumed to involve mastery or interesting events. Thus, by using such labels for responses as "intrinsically reinforcing" or "self-reinforcing" and "intrinsically motivated" or "self-motivated," researchers may ignore some relevant observable determinants of a response's strength which may be of a different order from the ones usually involved in conventional reinforcement analyses. Further, under a competence-effectance approach as presently conceived by its various proponents, there is no provision for specifying, in advance of its occurrence, those conditions that will maintain a response. Such a conception seems to be more a device for discussing behavior that has occurred outside of the range of behaviors maintained by organismically relevant reinforcing consequences than a means for advancing detailed, directional hypotheses. Thus, also, Aronfreed (1968, 1969) has postulated that "pleasurable affective change" induced by the positive conse-quences of instrumental learning may become directly attached (conditioned) to the intrinsic correlates of a response so that the response's reinforcing affective consequences come to be elicited by the intrinsic perceptual cues or cognitive representations which are associated with performance of the act. For Aronfreed, the affective values of these intrinsic correlates provide the basis for the inherent reinforcing properties for the overt response in a process which he labels "internalization," in that he assumes "the behavior becomes independent to some extent of its external consequences" (although how behavior can become independent "to some extent" is unclear to me). Exactly what the scientific status is of these affective properties (e.g., in terms of independent indices), and how these properties which make acts intrinsically reinforcing can be removed so that the response, once established, can become extinguished, is not made clear in Aronfreed's thesis. Yet some responses do extinguish. (These issues are fur-ther discussed in later sections.)

Another proposed explanation for the continued occurrence of responses after the removal of extrinsic reinforcement is the notion advanced by some conditioning theorists that a behavior can be maintained by its response-produced cues which, having systematically preceded extrinsic reinforcers, acquire reinforc-ing properties (cf., e.g., Staats & Staats, 1963). This conception is perhaps more parsimonious than Aronfreed's, insofar as it does not contain his unobserved, hedonistically flavored processes. Even so, in assuming that a stimulus attribute of the response acquires conditioned-reinforcer value, thereby maintaining the response in the absence of extrinsic reinforcement, the conception has a limitation very similar to that of Aronfreed's: it confounds the conditioned reinforcer with the response whose occurrence it explains, thus precluding the conditioned reinforcer's having the independent status required for differential prediction. At the same time, this conditioned-reinforcer conception does not provide an appreciably better explanation for a functional analysis of behavior maintenance, in the apparent absence of extrinsic reinforcement, than does the simple concep-tion of intermittent reinforcement schedules. In fact, emphasizing such a concept in intermittent, extrinsic-reinforcement contexts can detract from the parsimony of a functional analysis. What such conditioning approaches must assume but do not emphasize is that the conditioned reinforcer will inevitably lose its reinforcing value if it is not, at least occasionally, paired with strong, active functioning reinforcers. It follows, since any conditioned reinforcer alone can maintain a response only for a limited number of trials, that the key to the explanation of behavior maintenance in the absence of identified reinforcers must be the (at least) occasional occurrence of extrinsic reinforcement.

In the present analysis, therefore, it is argued that use of the concepts intrinsic reinforcement or motivation, mastery-interest motives, or the conditioned reinforcement of response-produced cues is unnecessary, as the classes of outcomes for which they so imprecisely account appear to be readily explainable in an operational-learning analysis with the conceptions of functional response classes acquired and maintained under intermittent, extrinsic reinforcement. Moreover, the intrinsic-motivation or intrinsic-reinforcement concepts do nothing to expedite the tactical problem that provides the rationale for their being advanced or determining the environmental conditions (i.e., extrinsic reinforcers) that differentially affect acquisition and maintenance of the child's responses. To determine precisely the dimensions of those reinforcing consequences, and, where necessary, the relevant setting conditions that qualify them and the antecedent determinants of their efficacy, systematic empirical study is necessary. Our approach is further illustrated in a later section on the acquisition and maintenance of generalized imitation, where it is shown that imitative responses that have been assumed by some to involve intrinsic reinforcement and/or intrinsic motivation can be accounted for by intermittent, extrinsic reinforcement of members of the imitative response class. Nevertheless, these nonstandard conditioning examples can illustrate ways in which the reinforcement concept has been used and for our present didactic purposes can identify some interesting substantive issues that these uses index. The parsimony of intrinsic motivation concepts like effectance and of other drive concepts as used in analyses of human development and socialization is considered in detail near the end of this chapter.

Elimination of Behavior

Reinforcing incompatible responses. In the preceding sections, procedures for the acquisition of instrumental behavior, in which the incidence of a particular response is systematically increased through its reinforcement, were enumerated. It follows that reinforcement can be employed alone, or in combination with extinction or punishment (as will be detailed in the next two sections) to lower the incidence of, or to eliminate, an undesired response (whether or not the contingencies maintaining it have been identified) if the response selected for reinforcement is alternative to, or incompatible with, the undesired one. In cases where the contingencies maintaining the undesirable response are known but where it is not practical or (for some reason) desirable to withhold the reinforcer, the reinforcement of alternative responses is a viable alternative to extinction. It would, of course, be necessary to make contingent on the alternative response a positive reinforcer that is significantly more potent than the one maintaining the undesired response.

Extinction.   A basic procedure by which responses are eliminated is extinction, which involves the decrease in the rate of a conditioned response to its earlier baselevel when the contingent reinforcing stimulus previously maintaining it is withheld. Unlike *forgetting* in which the response does not generally occur, extinction is an active process in which the response occurs but is not reinforced. The extinction pattern of a response is determined by the schedule of reinforcement on which it was earlier maintained. Relative to continuous reinforcement (if the number of reinforcements has been constant under conditioning), extinction is prolonged after intermittent reinforcement, the type of schedule most often found in life settings.[13] Moreover, as will be seen in the next section, a response previously strengthened by the removal of a strong negative reinforcer will often be more resistant to extinction than one strengthened by the presentation of a strong positive reinforcer (the number of reinforcement trials having been constant).

Extinction of a response may be facilitated by reinforcing responses that are incompatible with the undesirable response. Socializing agents often find it difficult to remove contingencies maintaining undesired behaviors, perhaps because it is so hard for the well-intentioned adult not to respond to a child who may be "suffering" or in "need," as when he is crying, or "charming" when he exhibits other undesired behaviors. However, they can find extinction of an undesired response mixed with the reinforcement of incompatible positive responses much easier to implement unambivalently (Gewirtz, 1968b). Thus, after caretaker attention was identified as the reinforcing stimulus for such objectionable behaviors as high-rate operant crying, the attention was withheld, and the extinction process was facilitated by evoking and reinforcing eye contact and smiling responses to the experimenter's face at the same time that the attention contingency maintaining the infant crying was removed (Etzel & Gewirtz, 1967).

Punishment.   A controversial means through which socializing agents may attempt to eliminate undesired behaviors is punishment. Punishment has been defined as either the contingent presentation of a noxious stimulus or the withdrawal of a positive reinforcer (e.g., Skinner, 1953). However, in this section the term will be employed to refer mainly to the contingent presentation of an aversive stimulus. Unlike extinction, in which the identity of the stimulus maintaining the response must be known so that it can be removed, for punishment

---

[13]Extinction following continuous reinforcement is relatively rapid with bursts of relatively few responses. Following ratio schedules, it is also fairly rapid but many responses are emitted at a high rate. Following interval schedules, it is prolonged with responses emitted at a low sustained rate.

knowledge of the contingency maintaining the response is not critical, since a noxious stimulus, whether or not earlier related to the response, is made contingent upon the response. Even so, such knowledge could be useful to socializing agents in that it would permit an estimate of how potent an aversive stimulus must be, relative to the reinforcing stimulus maintaining the undesired response, in order for it to eliminate that response when presented contingent upon it. Furthermore, in view of the reservations that will be made in this section about the effects of punishment on behavior, withdrawing the previous, continuously available maintaining stimulus may be a more effective procedure than punishment.

The use of punishment can be illustrated with the social-response class termed aggression,[14] which is often punished by socializing agents. An aversive stimulus, if strong enough, presented contingent upon a response class like aggression may suppress it. Also, pre-aversive stimuli, which may include response-produced cues from aggression and verbalizations about aggression in addition to events in the presence of which aggression has been punished, can become discriminative for avoidance, escape, and/or conditioned emotional responses (which some would term "fear" or even "anxiety") that are incompatible with emitting aggression. As conditioned aversive stimuli, they may also function to suppress the response class upon which they are contingently presented.

The use of aversive stimuli as in punishment is not infrequently employed by socializing agents as a means of eliminating (undesirable) behavior more rapidly than via extinction.[15] Punishment may also be employed by caretakers because often they understand better how to implement punishment than extinction, or because they hold the theory that a child is or may become evil if his transgressions are not dealt with immediately and sternly. However, the usually immediate suppressive effect of the contingent presentation of aversive stimuli may be only short-term. Indeed, after punishment, the response may recur in varying degrees ranging from no recovery to complete recovery of the original response strength (Solomon, 1964).

---

[14]Behaviors are ordinarily termed aggressive if they are maintained (by stimuli provided) by the hurt or damage caused to another (others). These "hurting" consequences may be physical or social in character. It is commonly thought that the aggressive response may be acquired on the basis that initially undirected physical acts prove to be instrumentally effective in removing noxious stimuli, including those stimuli that block ongoing behaviors or prevent S-R chains from going through all their cycles (i.e., frustration), and that the annoyance or pain cues from caretakers which follow the instrumental responses in the chain and are discriminative for the terminal reinforcement acquire conditioned reinforcer value for aggressive behaviors. Sometimes an infant's thrashing about and emitting high-amplitude verbal responses can be effective not only in removing a noxious stimulus, but can also result in other positive reinforcing stimuli, like "soothing" skin contact and similar unconditioned and conditioned stimuli received from the caretaking environment. The reinforcement contingencies listed here can establish the aggressive response class as a strong one for an individual.

[15]A study evaluating the relative effectiveness of procedures designed to eliminate behavior was performed by Holz and Azrin (1963). Stimulus change, extinction, satiation, physical restraint, and punishment were evaluated on the criteria of the immediacy, duration, extent, and irreversibility of response reduction. It was found that extinction was the only procedure which did not produce an immediate reduction of behavior.

Any outcome within this range can be produced by merely varying the intensity of the noxious stimulus (Azrin & Holz, 1961). However, the efficacy of punishment in eliminating behavior may also be determined by other important factors: the duration and frequency of the noxious stimulus, the delay in its presentation, whether its intensity is sudden or gradual, the strength of the response, the way in which it was initially acquired (usually difficult to specify in the case of long-standing responses), on what schedule it is being maintained, and whether or not an alternative response is reinforced during the response suppression period. In fact, in most experiments where punishment has been found to have only a temporary suppressive effect, the subject did not have (was not offered) an alternative for obtaining the positive reinforcer that was maintaining the punished response (Solomon, 1964). Although response suppression appears initially to generalize to other settings, ordinarily it is subsequently restricted to the setting in which the response has been punished. A reasonable assumption is that a response suppressed by punishment will be less likely to occur in settings varying from the punishment setting when an incompatible or alternative response has been positively reinforced in the punishment setting by the same reinforcer as maintained the punished response, or sometimes even by a different one. Another variable which may determine the effectiveness of aversive stimuli in controlling child behavior is the relationship between the agent of punishment and its recipient. The ways in which contextual factors like these can operate as setting conditions to determine or qualify the efficacy of stimuli for child behavior are considered in detail elsewhere (Gewirtz, 1967a), and are surveyed in a subsequent section.

In settings where escape or avoidance is possible, the punishment process may lead to behaviors which remove the organism from the controlling aversive stimuli and decrease or eliminate concurrent emotional respondents. Stimuli associated with the dispensers of punishment (i.e., socializing agents), as systematically part of the punishment setting, become discriminative for these escape and avoidance behaviors. Since a punished child may subsequently withdraw from interaction with socializing agents, the use of punishment can have socially disruptive side effects. A case known to me which involves the punishment of thumb-sucking behavior in a six-year-old child can serve to illustrate these points. The child's parent attempted to eliminate this undesired behavior by making contingent upon it verbal disapproval (in the form of shaming) and/or the physical removal of the child's thumb from his mouth. Subsequently, whenever that parent approached the child or entered his vicinity, the child would remove his thumb from his mouth or hide himself from the parent. Thus, the aversive stimuli employed by the parent seem to have controlled the child's thumb-sucking only in the parent's presence and even then only when the child did not attempt to hide his thumb-sucking from his parent. While the child did not cease his thumb-sucking completely, thumb-sucking and hiding behavior came under the control of the sight of his parent.

We have already noted that the use of aversive stimuli (and stimuli which systematically precede them) in the control of behavior, particularly when avoidance or escape behaviors from the aversive stimuli are not possible in the setting, often evokes undesirable emotional and aggressive behaviors which may be incompatible with desired behaviors and thus disruptive for new learning involving these or other behaviors in the setting. The aggressive-behavior outcomes may include instrumental aggression directed against the punishment source as well as nondirected aggression against persons and objects present in the setting.

Concerning these emotional-behavior outcomes, it is important to note that Azrin and Holz (1966) have concluded from a summary of experimentation with animals and gross observations with humans that relatively few emotional-behavior outcomes of punishment persist as chronic maladjustive patterns. Even so, if the effects of punishment can be long lasting as many others have assumed, then the use of punishment may merely result in the exchange of one undesired behavior for another, that is, emotional, aggressive and/or escape-avoidance behaviors for the response that punishment was being made contingent upon to eliminate, precluding the acquisition of desired behaviors. While punishment is often employed by socializing agents in the belief that it will benefit the child, the advantage which may result from the cessation of the undesirable behavior may only be momentary and may be beneficial or reinforcing only for the punishing agent, while the effects for the child may be mainly detrimental and possibly long lasting. It is clear, however, that if punishment is used, it is likely to be maximally effective with minimal side effects when it is presented *immediately* contingent upon the objectionable response, and an alternative, preferably incompatible, response is positively reinforced.

In extreme cases, where undesired behaviors are so probable in the child's repertory that alternative reinforceable behaviors are not likely to occur until the objectionable behaviors are suppressed, the use of punishment (rather than positive reinforcement of alternative responses) would be unquestionably indicated. Thus, also, punishment may be necessary in order to suppress a response of the child that places him in great immediate personal danger. However, it will certainly be more effective in eliminating responses (even severe problem behaviors) and probably less likely to bring on emotional and aggressive behaviors as by-products when supplemented by the positive reinforcement of alternative, and preferably incompatible, responses. For example, the behaviors of "autistic" children have been effectively modified by presenting strong electric shock contingent upon obsessively repeated self-injurious behaviors and by removing the shock contingent upon the appearance of socially valued approach responses that are incompatible with the former behaviors (Lovaas, 1967).

A readily applied alternative to contingent noxious stimulation for eliminating a behavior is the *contingent withdrawal of a previous continuously available positive reinforcing stimulus*. Unlike extinction, which is the complete removal of the positive reinforcer which had previously maintained the conditioned response, this procedure involves the contingent removal of a reinforcing stimulus which is present in the setting prior to each emission of the response, regardless of whether or not the stimulus was involved in the acquisition of the response. An example is provided by a study in which the rate of thumb-sucking was systematically reduced by turning off (i.e., removing from the screen) an animated-cartoon reinforcer whenever the child inserted his thumb into his mouth (Baer, 1962). As in the case of the contingent removal of an aversive stimulus (Lovaas, 1967), this disciplinary technique can be extremely effective in modifying behavior and less difficult for the socializing agent to administer when its termination is made contingent upon desirable behavior. Thus, Baer (1962) found that contingent reinstatement of the reinforcing event was highly effective in modifying behavior in directions desired by the experimenter. Another variation on the withdrawal of positive reinforcement is the use of "time out" sessions, occasions on which the response is never reinforced. This procedure has also been found to be especially effective in eliminating a response when there is an alternative response available that is maintained by the same reinforcer as maintained the response being eliminated (Holz, Azrin & Ayllon, 1963).

Thus, the main effect of the contingent removal of positive reinforcement on the response being modified appears generally similar to the main effect of contingent aversive stimulation, and it is suspected that many or all of the emotional responses which frequently accompany negative stimulation may be absent following the withdrawal of positive reinforcement that previously was continuously available. However, comparison of all of the effects of these two procedures remains an empirical question for each experimental case (just as it does when the operations of presenting two aversive stimuli are compared). A recent survey of the effects on child social behavior of punishment and related disciplinary techniques can be found in Walters and Parke (1967).

On the Relative Potency of Positive and Negative Reinforcing Stimuli

There has been frequent speculation about the relative potency of positive and negative reinforcing stimulus classes in terms of their effect on behavior. Thus, Miller (1944, 1948b, 1964) has directed attention to the fact that when the locomotor avoidance response to a training stimulus followed by an aversive reinforcer is stronger than or equal to the approach response to it followed by a positive reinforcer, steeper ("generalization") gradients across spatial stimulus dimensions occur for the former avoidance response than for the latter approach response. Further, a locomotor approach response may require many more training trials, with positive reinforcing stimuli, to attain the same strength that a locomotor avoidance response may reach with only one or two noxious contingency trials. However, the traditional paradigms for studying the effects on behavior of negative reinforcing stimuli have often been different and more varied than those used to study the effects of positive reinforcing stimuli, and thus some of the distinctions between the two types of reinforcing stimuli may be due mainly to differences in the operations used to study them. Thus, the identity of reinforcers is often confounded with their effects: escape and avoidance behaviors which are typically maintained by aversive stimuli are emphasized relatively more than are approach behaviors maintained by positive reinforcers, particularly in natural settings.

Speculation as to whether noxious stimuli which function as negative reinforcers are generally more or less potent than stimuli which ordinarily function as positive reinforcers may be of limited theoretical consequence. Although aversive stimuli within the range of intensity values and setting conditions ordinarily studied generally do have a more potent (in the sense of rapid) effect on behavior than do positive reinforcing stimuli, in principle one could devise parallel paradigms for the study of positive and negative reinforcers such that they would be considered equivalent in potency, or even reversed. In such instances, the removal of the former could have the same impact on behavior as the presentation of the latter, and vice versa, particularly when setting-context conditions are also manipulated (as considered in the next section). Moreover, in such cases these operations may not only lead to equivalent outcomes in the behavior monitored, but they may also have equivalent concurrent responses associated with them. Frequently, however, it would be of limited utility to compare the general effects of positive and negative reinforcing stimuli, or to wonder if, in general, the withdrawal of positive reinforcement and the presentation of negative reinforcement have different emotional behavioral concomitants.

There is still a further sense in which the comparison of positive and negative stimuli is indeterminate if approached as a general case. Stimuli ordinarily conceived to function as positive or as negative reinforcers may do so only within a limited range of intensity values or setting conditions. For instance, stimulus events which normally function as aversive stimuli at high intensities can function as positive reinforcers at low intensities (e.g., a tingling shock). Further, there are stimuli that may function as positive reinforcers under one value of a setting condition and as nonreinforcers or as negative reinforcers under another value. Thus, food stimuli function as positive reinforcers primarily after they have been unavailable to the organism for a sufficient period, but as negative reinforcers when the food-satiated organism cannot avoid receiving them. Thus, almost any event can come to function as a strong reinforcing stimulus, a relatively weak one, as no stimulus at all, or even as a stimulus with reinforcing properties opposite to those ordinarily expected, depending upon its intensity-value or setting-condition context, such as an individual's condition of deprivation or satiation. The effects of setting conditions on stimulus efficacy and how they are qualified by an individual's long-term maintenance pattern for a stimulus are discussed in detail in the next section.

Contextual Determinants of Momentary Stimulus Efficacy

The effectiveness of stimuli for controlling behavior on a particular occasion, by evoking, cueing, or reinforcing it, is typically dependent upon the contextual aspects of stimulus provision and may be enhanced or decreased by manipulating these contextual-setting conditions. Some of the most familiar of them involve the deprivation and satiation of appetitive stimuli (i.e., food and water). An often neglected context has to do with the circumstance (ground) present when stimuli (figures) are provided, as in perceptual research where the ground is often varied systematically to increase or decrease the salience of the stimulus figure. However, in learning experiments, which usually involve the attempt to vary performance to some set of focal stimuli, background stimuli are sometimes held constant and often overlooked. Although discriminative and reinforcing stimuli are usually described in sufficient detail in studies of child learning, the setting conditions that qualify the efficacy of those stimuli are rarely made explicit. All too frequently these conditions (e.g., time of deprivation for the stimulus class being tested, the subject's adaptation or maintenance level for that class, or the specific or general status of the person dispensing a discriminative or reinforcing stimulus) are only implied in descriptions of experimental conditioning procedures with humans.

The conditions which heighten or lower the salience of stimuli for behavior may operate: (1) at one time point concurrent with the functional focal stimulus (e.g., as the ground for the stimulus figure, or as masking effects) ; (2) immediately before the point of stimulus functioning (e.g., as a cue to the region in which the focal stimulus will appear) ; and (3) across time points before focal stimulus functioning (e.g., as deprivation or satiation contexts for a stimulus, or as fatigue effects). Further, we have noted in an earlier section on generalization and discrimination that the stimuli controlling higher-order discriminated operants (conditional discriminations) may also function essentially as setting conditions to qualify stimulus efficacy for behavior.

To illustrate how contextual factors may, in time, come to operate prior to the testing of stimulus functioning, the next two sections will emphasize deprivation-satiation functions governing the efficacy of given stimuli and the maintenance levels for given stimuli which, through some as yet poorly understood form of learning, can apparently also qualify their efficacy. We may thus concentrate here on some other conditions which operate concurrently with or immediately preceding the presentation of a stimulus to qualify its reinforcing efficacy. There is evidence that various stimulus attributes of the person dispensing a stimulus, including his sex, social-, or role-status, may come to qualify the reinforcing efficacy of that stimulus for behavior. In a number of studies, reinforcing stimuli dispensed by men have been found more effective in altering the behavior of girls than of boys, and the opposite effect has been found when women dispensed the reinforcers (e.g., Gewirtz, 1954 ; Gewirtz & Baer, 1958a, 1958b ; Patterson, Littman & Hinsey, 1964). Some research and speculations about the role in the modification of child behavior of such characteristics of socializing agents are reported by Patterson (1967).

Furthermore, such setting conditions which operate concurrently with focal stimulus functioning can stem from an individual's history of reinforcement (e.g., the role the reinforcing source has played there), and thus, like the stimulus maintenance conditions which will be discussed subsequently, must have their bases in learning factors.[16] An agent may routinely have been the source only of positive reinforcement, only of aversive stimulation, or of both stimulus types; or the types of interaction a child experiences with an adult experimenter during a single prior treatment session may have been positive, negative, or neutral. These prior conditions can qualify the efficacy for the child's behavior of both positive and negative reinforcing stimuli. For instance, positive and negative reinforcers were each found to be more effective for child subjects after sessions of positive interaction than after sessions of neutral or impersonal contact with an experimenter (see McCoy & Zigler, 1965, for positive, and Parke & Walters, 1967, for negative reinforcers). However, positive reinforcing stimuli were less effective for child performance after a positive- than after a negative-interaction experience with an adult (Berkowitz, Butterfield & Zigler, 1965). Furthermore, the absence of any reaction from an adult experimenter could come to function as a positive reinforcer for children who in an earlier session had received negative verbal reinforcement or as a negative reinforcer for children who had earlier received positive reinforcement (Crandall, Good & Crandall, 1964).

A stimulus can also come to function as a positive or negative reinforcer if it has been selectively associated with positive or negative reinforcement. Further, in a context in which an organism must respond and can choose between responses that have been followed by two different but nevertheless strong noxious stimuli, the weaker noxious stimulus can function as a positive reinforcer for the response upon which it is contingent. Thus, such setting conditions as an individual's previous experience with focal and/or ground stimuli or the matrix of his alternatives may qualify the efficacy of stimuli in controlling behavior, even to the point where a stimulus can come to function with reinforcing properties opposite to those ordinarily expected.

Although it has been generally assumed that stimuli of inherently high salience are not readily susceptible to modification, even the efficacy of these stimuli can be qualified, as shown by Bevan and Adamson (1960) who modified the reinforcing efficacy of cutaneous electric shock for human adults by earlier giving them different intensity distributions and average levels of shock. However, the concurrent or preceding setting conditions must themselves be quite strong to effect a change in the efficacy of such potent stimuli. Perhaps more important for social learning, an otherwise trivial stimulus may be made to function as a potent discriminative or reinforcing stimulus for behavior, if the contextual aspects of the environment are considered and properly manipulated. Indeed,

---

[16]There are diverse headings, including some more conventional learning categories, under which we might have listed the learning-*qua*-experience factors implied in the conception of maintenance-level or maintenance-pattern reference standards and of stimulus sources as qualifiers of stimulus efficacy. However, for convenience in this didactic presentation, we have arbitrarily chosen to emphasize how the outcomes of such experience factors can come to qualify stimulus functioning in ways that have no direct relevance to their experimental roles in a given investigation. Hence we have opted here to deal with these issues under the heading of setting conditions, and to leave their implications for the forms of learning that must be involved to a subsequent conceptualization.

these conditions must be considered if the potentially discriminative or reinforcing stimuli are to function effectively and uniformly, particularly in social contexts (Gewirtz, 1967a).

If successive presentations of a stimulus were to lead consistently to the same response, it would be unnecessary to consider the contextual aspects of the environment in which the stimulus was presented. Because this homogeneity in response attributes is rare, it is important to consider the conditions under which a stimulus is provided and the response which results. Many of these conditions have been labeled, or attributed by some to, "drive," but because of the often ambiguous (excess) meanings of that term, we have termed them "setting" conditions as some others have also done (e.g., Kantor, 1959; Bijou & Baer, 1963). Once the relevant setting conditions have been identified, and the functional relationships specified between them as background stimuli, the focal stimulus, and the response, the use of the term "drive" or of similar terms would be superfluous for many purposes.

Deprivation and satiation. Short-term deprivation and satiation relationships are illustrative of how setting conditions can operate across time points to qualify the effectiveness for behavior of stimuli presented on any particular occasion, e.g., as reinforcers. Deprivation of a stimulus refers to its removal, or to a decrease in the rate of its provision, leading to an increase in its effectiveness; and satiation for a stimulus refers to its repeated presentation, or an increase in the rate of its provision, leading to a decrease in its effectiveness. So defined, deprivation and satiation are reciprocal operations. Recovery from satiation, which involves an increase in stimulus efficacy brought about by a period (following satiation) during which the stimulus is not provided, is thereby the conceptual equivalent of deprivation. The reinforcing efficacy of a stimulus will thus be a direct function of the degree of the organism's deprivation for it at that particular moment, usually indicated by the length of time that the reinforcing stimulus has been withheld. Although it is conventional to consider stimuli such as food (or social stimuli such as approval or attention) as positive reinforcers, most such stimuli function in this role only within a narrow range of conditions, in particular when the organism for whom they can function as stimuli has recovered from being satiated for them (i.e., after having been appropriately deprived of them). Indeed, if an infant is well satiated for any one of a large number of stimuli which normally (i.e., in a wide range of settings) function as positive reinforcers (whether or not they occur as consequences of his behavior), he may find the stimulus aversive, whether it be food, light, sound, or a cutaneous stimulus (Gewirtz, 1961b, 1967a). Conversely, for an infant limited from receiving what is for him an important positive reinforcing stimulus, a normally aversive contingent stimulus may function as a positive reinforcer. For instance, "negative attention" from parents (via scolding) may positively reinforce a behavior of a child, especially if he is otherwise ignored by them.

Traditionally, deprivation-satiation functions were thought by many to hold uniquely for appetitive stimuli, with effects typically identified in the reinforcing efficacy of these stimuli. Recently, however, deprivation and satiation relationships have been found to function for nonappetitive stimuli, such as visual and auditory events (Glanzer, 1953, 1958; Butler, 1957; Jones, 1964; Odom, 1964), word meanings (Lambert & Jakobovits, 1960; Jakobovits & Lambert, 1962), and a person's passive presence (Bacon & Stanley, 1963). Similar functions, involving the evocative or discriminative effectiveness of stimuli, have also been identified under the headings of *curiosity-exploration* and stimulus *novelty* (e.g., Montgomery, 1953; Berlyne, 1955, 1957) and response *habituation* or *adaptation* (Berlyne, 1955; Hinde, 1960; Welker, 1956). Moreover, similar short-term functional relations have also been identified for social stimuli (Gewirtz, 1967a, 1969; Landau & Gewirtz, 1967). Thus, the reinforcing efficacy of the stimulus word *good* (from a woman experimenter) in conditioning was an inverse function of the number of times it was presented to boy subjects during a treatment session immediately preceding the conditioning test (i.e., the degree of their satiation for the stimulus), and a direct function of the recovery interval between satiation treatment and conditioning test. While satiation and recovery for a social stimulus produced opposite, additive effects like those which characterize satiation and recovery (i.e., deprivation) functions for appetitive stimuli, it would be superfluous to apply in addition the term "drive," as has traditionally been done. Having identified a dimension of setting conditions, the description of the functional relation is sufficient for most requirements. The series of experiments just described on nonappetitive stimuli represents only a beginning in the identification of potentially many types of deprivation-satiation functions.[17]

The role of maintenance levels for stimulation. An individual's prior experiences with stimuli may also provide contextual determinants of stimulus efficacy at any given moment, with long-term performance implications. In particular, the summary abstraction (e.g., a central tendency) of some characteristic level of an individual's long-term maintenance pattern for a stimulus, for instance, the number, variety, range, or rate of stimuli experienced, may function as a reference standard to determine the efficacy of an implemented level of the stimulus for his behavior, even to the point where it can exercise close control over behaviors related to basic organismic requirements. This conception has been advanced by a number of theorists in diverse areas of psychology and stimulated much research (e.g., Baron, 1966; Bevan & Adamson,

---

[17]In connection with the deprivation-satiation conception, there remain empirical questions about: (a) the identities of the stimuli whose efficacy can be affected by deprivation-satiation manipulations; (b) the form of the functional relationship between each set of deprivation-satiation manipulations and the efficacy of each stimulus affected; (c) the identities of other setting operations that can produce comparable effects; (d) whether such operations affect different stimulus functions in the same or in different ways; and (e) the way in which the long-term pattern of maintenance conditions for a stimulus can provide referents that determine the impact of deprivation-satiation operations on the efficacy of that stimulus for an organism. When compared to the mass of functional relationships explored for performance and learning, it becomes evident that remarkably little attention has been devoted by behavioral approaches to the conditions (apart from those directly involved in learning) that determine the momentary efficacy of stimuli for behavior. But if a further understanding of the determinants of behavior (including social behavior) is to be acquired, it is these very setting conditions which theorists cannot afford to overlook.

1960, 1963; Gewirtz, 1967a; Glanzer, 1958; Helson, 1964; McClelland et al., 1953; Premack & Collier, 1962). A survey of various incongruity hypotheses and some problems in their use can be found in Harvey (1963).

An example of a stimulation-level summarizing concept is Helson's (1964) "adaptation level." Helson demonstrated how, for diverse stimulus-response systems, the weighted average of salient stimulus attributes the organism has experienced (and hence, as some would say, he comes to "expect"), may acquire the capacity (through some as yet inadequately identified learning process) to function as a reference standard or context to qualify the functioning of a subsequently presented stimulus of that class in determining behavior. For example, the organism may more readily respond to the average level of a distribution of an experienced stimulus than to an extreme, infrequently experienced value of that stimulus; or he may respond in a manner that will maintain or restore the level of stimulation when it deviates from the adaptation or maintenance pattern or level.

On the basis of this maintenance-level conception, one could predict an organism's approach to diverse stimuli, including a stimulus such as food, in the sense that its "hunger" at any given time would depend on temporal conditioning factors, based perhaps on some average time span between earlier feedings and the average number or amount of food stimuli received per feeding. If as we have been proposing, the momentary efficacy of diverse classes of stimuli may be qualified by an individual's long term maintenance level for them, then the deprivation-satiation functions of food and diverse other stimuli, and, indeed, their operational definitions, would also depend upon such reference levels. That is, 18 hours of food deprivation may be said to operate as a relative *deprivation* condition for organisms regularly fed more frequently (e.g., every 12 hours) and as a relative *satiation* condition for organisms regularly fed less frequently (e.g., every 24 hours). This outcome may constitute a paradox under the more conventional conceptions for the functioning of stimuli, for drive and setting conditions, and the like.

Overlooking what may be the irrelevant fact that stimuli like food are required for organismic survival, it is quite possible that operations for stimulus classes other than food may be similarly qualified by the distributional characteristics of the subject's experience with a particular stimulus commodity or with the range and other distributional characteristics of those classes of stimuli (Gewirtz, 1967a). For example, Gewirtz et al. (1956) found that subjects' generalization-discrimination response gradients for visual-angle stimuli within a particular range were displaced in the direction of the range of stimuli they had earlier experienced. (These findings are also consistent with what would be expected on the central-tendency basis of the concept of adaptation level.) Moreover, learned maintenance levels or standards may provide the context for an organism's responding to novel stimuli. One notion has been that elements sufficiently incongruent with stimuli presented in the past might evoke fear and avoidance behaviors, whereas more congruent but still novel elements might evoke curiosity and investigatory behaviors (cf., Hebb, 1946, 1949). For instance, Hebb (1966) reported that chimpanzees typically displayed strong fear responses when presented with extraordinary (i.e., in terms of previous main-tenance contexts) stimuli (e.g., the severed head of a chimpanzee or a model of one).

Thus, apparently through some as yet inadequately identified process of learning, the organism becomes conditioned to the maintenance pattern of the classes, rates, frequencies, ranges, and types of stimuli received, which can them-selves function to control behavior. (This learning should occur readily when the rate of stimulation is regular rather than intermittent.) The control acquired over behavior by these maintenance levels as setting conditions might for the moment be included under the flexible rubric of learning we have been using. One of our early empirical tasks will be to investigate systematically how reference standards for aspects of stimulation are acquired. Although many approaches contain terms, such as novelty, whose meanings depend on the learning of back-ground contexts and levels of stimulation, there is, as yet, no approach which can adequately account for them. If we are to gain a full understanding of human development, however, these contextual factors must be considered and adequately incorporated into any learning approach to the outcomes of early experience.

Ecological determinants of social behavior and learning. Social behavior and learning are affected by the physical and social ecology of a setting and can be facilitated or limited by the manipulation of ecological factors. As used here, the term ecology stands for the gross conditions of an environment which determine which events and behaviors can occur in a setting, and specifically whether or not a child can receive a stimulus or emit a response. Such facilitators and constraints are therefore as much setting conditions as are, for instance, deprivation-satiation operations for food stimuli. The amount of floor space available, the positions of walls and of furniture, all represent *physical* conditions that can grossly determine behavior systems. Similarly, the rules and regulations in a setting (explicit and implicit) represent *social* facilitators or constraints on behavior systems. Thus, ecological conditions can insulate a child against, or cause him to be exposed to, adults, other children, or their specific activities, and in that way can determine whether or not he can emit particular responses or "seek" particular ends.

The physical and social ecology of a setting can therefore impose effective constraints on behavior systems. In group settings, social rules and physical limitations can be employed to decrease the likelihood that individual children would interfere with group activities or with the activities of a particular child. In effect, such procedures prevent an undesired behavior from occurring simply by removing the individual from the situation in which the response may occur. However, that behavior will not be suppressed when the "motivation" set and opportunity for responding are again present. Social or physical confinement will be most effective in suppressing undesired behaviors only when combined with other procedures, particularly the strengthening of alternative, incompatible behaviors. (This issue was discussed earlier in the section on punishment.)

The ecology of a setting can also be employed to facilitate social learning.

Thus, in a group setting, the probability of various positive interactions among the children and of particular activities (as role or thematic play) can be increased by manipulating the number of children in a limited area. It is also possible to manipulate the kind of props and their ratio to space in order to foster constructive use of them or particular patterns of interactions. Further, the social ecology of a child's setting can be an important factor in his socialization. For instance, the availability of active adults and/or older children in a child's environment provides a range of behaviors for the child to use as models for his own behavior (as will be explored in a later section on generalized imitation and identification). Thus, in groups containing children of heterogeneous ages, caretaker-models are more apt to exhibit nurturant responses to young children which the older children may copy. Moreover, socialization-by-imitation (modeling) is simpler for the young child when there are a large number of older individuals in his environment who exhibit a variety of behaviors that he can copy, and for which he can often be reinforced, particularly when these models are of the same sex as the child.

Whether a child is part of a family unit or in a group-care setting, if the socialization process occurs in the *absence* of older models who could both provide examples for, and directly reinforce, a child's behaviors, it is more difficult for him to acquire the increasingly mature behaviors expected of him. In that nonmodeling context, the socialization process would have to depend almost entirely on direct instrumental training. Considering the number of response systems to be modified, this process would be time and energy consuming, for the socializing agent would have to monitor continuously the child's behaviors and be prepared to respond to them, and decide, on the basis of those behaviors assumed appropriate for the child's age level (or for the next higher age level), taking into account his existing behavior repertory and level of social (and physical) development, which of his behaviors to reinforce differentially.

Thus, the occurrence of various undesirable behavior systems may be inhibited and the occurrence of various desirable behaviors may be facilitated and subsequently reinforced by conditions brought about by systematic manipulations of the available space, the type and number of materials positioned in that space, and the type and number of peers and adults in that space (e.g., their status for the child, as described earlier). Although principles underlying such ecological manipulations are not as yet well understood, an illustration of their utility can be found in Shure (1963).

ADDITIONAL IMPLICATIONS
OF THE APPROACH FOR LIFE SETTINGS

Emotional Behaviors and
Conditioning in Social Contexts

Over and above their particular discriminative or reinforcing effects upon instrumental responses, conditioned and unconditioned positive and aversive stimuli may have many wide-ranging effects on a number of important response repertories. While in molar-behavior analyses, the effects of presentations of positive (approach) or negative (aversive) social stimuli are indexed by changes in ongoing behavior systems, emotional behaviors (including autonomic respondents) are frequent by-products of their provision, particularly of aversive events. Moreover, even though there is no evidence that emotional behaviors or their autonomic correlates are critical determinants of instrumental responses (i.e., are more than concurrent with them) and it is likely that extreme and wide-ranging changes in many instrumental response systems often occur without such concurrent autonomic response changes, emotional-behavior sets are often considered to be causes of diverse instrumental responses.[18] Thus, it is often said that one does something for the "joy" it will bring him, or doesn't do it because he is "afraid." Further, caretakers are often even more concerned with emotional responses (particularly those assumed to be associated with "distress") than with more routine operants. Hence, apart from being concurrent with operants, emotional behaviors (or their expressive correlates) may be reinforced (as operants) by consequences like the receipt of "affection" or "sympathy" from others.

It is well known that it is often impossible to separate such emotional-respondent sets from one another without taking into account the controlling stimuli, the particular settings in which the behaviors are observed, or sometimes also their expressive-behavior correlates (e.g., facial or bodily appearance), even though the latter are known to vary widely with culture-group norms (sometimes more than with the stimulus context of the presumed emotional "state" being described). Indeed, in the context of knowledge of an individual's experiential history, such expressive responses may differentially index sets of emotional behaviors.[19] However, it is recognized only occasionally that the terms used to

---

[18]Emotional behavior, which appears to be largely respondent, has often been neglected in behavioral analyses. This is perhaps a result of the conceptual distinction between respondent and operant behavior and the greater attention typically given to the latter. However, the original distinction between the two paradigms, based on the conception that operants are skeletal responses while respondents are muscular or glandular responses under the control of the autonomic nervous system with only a few instances of overlap (e.g., Skinner, 1938) is, as has been pointed out increasingly in recent years (e.g., Hefferline, 1962), an oversimplification. Conditioned emotional behavior may accompany and even be involved in the maintenance of many behavior systems, and further, there is increasing evidence that some emotional responses can be instrumentally conditioned. However, even given these considerations, the fact that emotional responses often appear to follow straightforwardly the classical conditioning paradigm supports the possible utility for behavioral analyses of maintaining a heuristic emphasis on a distinct paradigm of classical conditioning. Thus, while our didactic analysis of social learning in this chapter emphasizes the operant-conditioning paradigm, at the very least it should be noted that the respondent-conditioning paradigm may operate concurrently with many instrumental behavior systems.

[19]Indeed, expressive behaviors like smiles and laughs seem to be readily conditionable early in human development, both on respondent and operant bases (discussed in Gewirtz, 1965). Thus, if the appearance of a (parent's) face (conditioned stimulus) is followed systematically by acts like lifting or tickling (unconditioned stimuli) which produce smiles and laughter in the child, or if his smiles to that face (discriminative stimulus) are followed by reinforcing stimuli, subsequent presentations of the face can come to evoke those "joyful" expressive behaviors from the child (Leuba, 1941; Etzel & Gewirtz, 1967). When such behaviors are concurrent with the receipt of positive reinforcement, they are likely to be reinforcing to, and reinforced by, the socializing agent dispensing the reinforcing stimuli.

describe emotional states are but labels for different families of functional stimulus-response relations. Thus, our everyday language is replete with overlapping terms for various sets of such emotional behaviors emitted in specific stimulus contexts, viz., anger, rage, frustration, fear, fright, anxiety, terror, guilt, shame, sorrow, sadness, depression, joy, happiness. And subjects' verbal behaviors concurrent with these emotional response sets may vary with the conditions under which they occur (i.e., that produce them). Thus, emotional behaviors and changes in directed behaviors following separation from a loved one (e.g., through his death) may be termed *sorrow* or *melancholia*,[20] while a similar behavior set following presentation of an identified aversive stimulus may be termed *fear* and one to generalized (i.e., many) stimuli where the controlling aversive stimulus is not apparent, may be termed *anxiety;* and responses occurring after a strong ongoing behavior chain is blocked may be termed *frustration*.

Thus, we have noted that, as respondents, emotional behaviors may be concurrent with various expressive behaviors and with the receipt of positive or negative reinforcers contingent upon instrumental responses. It is also thought that, as instrumental responses, they can come under the control of discriminative and reinforcing stimuli. Moreover, emotional responses may have an effect upon behaviors that do not appear to be related to the instrumental response that has been (positively or negatively) reinforced, i.e., the occurrence of emotional responses may increase the incidence of those behaviors that are compatible with them and decrease the incidence of those that are not.

Frustration.   Operationally, conditions which interfere (block, interrupt) with a stimulus-response chain have been termed frustrating. Emotional behaviors are frequent concomitants or results of such interference (as will also be noted in a subsequent section on deprivation-separation as shifts in the maintaining environment). J. S. Brown and Farber (1951), who did much to introduce a conception of frustration within a larger theoretical framework (that of Hull-Spence), assumed that its operations added to general drive level to have a simultaneous impact on many responses and that it provided internal stimuli with which responses could become associated. Amsel (1962) has mostly explored nonreward (after reward) as frustration operations with drive results (see also the section on setting conditions). Insofar as incompatible responses to a stimulus in a conflict setting may involve the blocking of one response by the other, a frustration operation would be involved, and concurrent emotional responses and

---

[20]As will be seen in a later section on effects of shifts in the maintaining environment (and in Gewirtz, 1961b), effects termed sadness, melancholia, depression, and the like, may not represent emotional-behavior outcomes so much as they reflect simply the absence of a child's behaviors due to the removal of the stimuli controlling them, particularly the relevant discriminative stimuli which set the occasions for behaviors to occur but also the reinforcing stimuli which maintain them. When only the behaviors under the control of the earlier environment and not a wide range of behaviors are weakened, it is likely that these grief patterns reflect more the simple withdrawal of the relevant discriminative stimuli for a large proportion of the child's behavior systems than emotional "states" involving emotional behaviors incompatible with responding in the new setting.

other consequences might result. Thus, conflict phenomena could be subsumed under frustration for many theoretical purposes, particularly under a notion of frustration operations contributing to a theoretical concept of general drive level. However, as that issue is tangential to the purposes of the didactic analysis of this chapter, the issues involved and the approaches which emphasize it are only being mentioned here.

In an early social-learning analysis, Dollard et al. (1939), in their book *Frustration and Aggression,* postulated that frustration was an antecedent to aggression, whether or not that response was overtly exhibited. This postulate, however, was not derived from the social-learning theory within which these authors were working (and which several of them subsequently codified), but apparently stemmed from a conception of Freud. Even while their analysis was criticized at a number of points, it was a useful catalyst for diverse social-learning analyses.

Conflict. Consistent findings from various studies on deviant behavior indicate that many social behavior classes, generally considered undesirable, are maintained by reinforcing schedules provided by the social environment (Patterson, 1967; Gewirtz & Etzel, 1967). Indeed, it can often be observed that behavior classes like aggression are positively reinforced by socializing agents as well as punished by them. Moreover, at the same time that a child's deviant behavior may be punished by a teacher or parent, it may be reinforced by a peer or younger sibling. Consequently, in natural settings the discriminative stimuli controlling such response classes may come to be cues for incompatible approach and avoidance responses by the child, in which case a conflict situation is said to exist. It has been noted earlier that conflict often results in emotional responses (taken by some to index "fear" or "anxiety"), vacillation, and similar responses. (It has also been noted that after aversive stimulation contingent upon the response, events in the presence of which the response has been punished and cues from the occurrence of the response [and from verbal responses about it] can come to function as conditioned aversive stimuli to suppress the response.) The resolution of the conflict which can result from such mixed reinforcement patterns can take different forms, depending on the pattern of response strengths of the incompatible behaviors.

Extending some of Freud's (1920) and Lewin's (1938, 1946, 1951) conflict notions, Miller (1944) explored the effects of conflict involving several patterns of incompatible approach and avoidance responses along a spatial-distance dimension originating with the conditioned stimulus, under various combinations of positive and negative reinforcement. For example, positive and negative reinforcement for responses to a single stimulus will lead to approach-avoidance conflict. And when two stimuli associated with different combinations of positive and negative reinforcement are simultaneously presented, the results may be approach-approach, avoidance-avoidance, and double-approach-avoidance conflict. These patterns of conflict and their features of equilibrium (or disequilibrium) have proved to be heuristically useful in approaching a variety of social-behavior systems (e.g., Dollard & Miller, 1950).

Apart from implications of his useful conflict paradigm for the behavior outcomes of a frustration "drive," Miller (1948b) has applied it to the question of how objects of aggressive behavior are determined. Miller assumed a steeper slope and narrower generalization range of the avoidance (inhibition, based on punishment) than of the approach (excitation, based on reward) generalization gradient, and used the algebraic sums of response strengths at different points along that stimulus-dissimilarity dimension, points that differed increasingly from the parent socializers and corresponded to possible objects of aggression, to predict the identities of the objects to which aggression would be *displaced*. Thus, if parents sometimes strongly reinforce a child's aggressive responses and sometimes strongly punish that response class, assuming the resultant avoidance gradient is higher than the approach gradient at their point of origin, the response may occur (i.e., generalize) to objects increasingly dissimilar to the parents along some dimension of similarity from them. Thus, an aggressive response might be displaced to another child or to an inanimate doll like the parent in appearance (Miller, 1948b; Sears, 1951; Sears et al., 1953). Further, the response itself may be displaced by being transformed topographically into one less overt, e.g., a verbal epithet instead of direct physical hurting.

The Place of Verbal Responses in Social Learning[21]

The classes of responses with which we deal in this chapter include both motor and vocal (including verbal-language) responses. Although verbal responses need not be singled out for special emphasis in a general analysis of social learning like ours, such responses are involved in an important way in the human socialization process, and first-language acquisition is a significant correlate and outcome of that socialization. Indeed, some may view language as the central outcome of socialization. Further, language learning and usage is a key behavior characteristic often used to distinguish humans from other species, as not even the most advanced of the subhuman-primate species which have peripheral speech apparatuses similar to that of man speak or use language as we know it.

Yet, there appears to be nothing inherently special about verbal responses which could serve to differentiate the process of their acquisition from that of motor and other responses in humans. Indeed, motor gestures frequently play known language roles (and, in fact, provide the only basis for the language of deaf mutes), and motor responses are very often concurrent with or correlates of verbal responses. And although the concept of grammar is usually reserved for verbal-language processes, grammatical systems could be proposed for motor and other responses as well, though this may never have been done, apart from

---

[21]I am indebted to the Drs. Donald Boomer, Albert J. Caron, and Murray Glanzer for instructive discussions on language learning and for a critical reading of an earlier draft of this section. Dr. Caron was particularly helpful on the role of "induction."

the routine gathering of such phenomena into sets of functional relationships (Lashley, 1951).

Verbal behavior and language.   Much work on language structure has been done in the academic discipline of linguistics. Hence, attention has been given through the years to many of the complex facets of languages, and some of the dimensions and features of the structure of language and its complexities are known to everyone, if only at an intuitive level. While a good deal of psychological research has been done on verbal behavior and its acquisition, and on language insofar as it is made up of verbal responses, very little systematic empirical work and theoretical analysis has been done thus far on the specifics of this system (e.g., on sequential and temporal patterns of responses [including verbal ones], on criteria of meaning of responses as symbols, and the like). In this context, relative to the various other important behavior systems, which are in principle at least equally as complex, the complexities of language structure and acquisition have become, as it were, "prematurely" visible. This condition is asynchronous, for the identified complexities of language are not readily explained by the extant simple principles which have otherwise been serving us well, and those principles thus tend to appear simplistic and less than adequate. Functional relationships based on these principles, however, have been identified in various other psychological areas which in principle involve systems at least as complex as verbal behavior systems termed languages, and in which the issues have been far less visible than those of verbal-language structure and acquisition. While there are as yet only primitive "grammars" identified for such systems (as, for example, involving visual-pattern discriminations or size constancy processes, where context "inflects" the nature of the figure seen [see the earlier section on setting conditions and Gewirtz, 1967a], or as involving generalized imitation or attachments), and although, at the moment, the principles we can bring to the organization of these systems appear commonplace, we expect nevertheless that a finite number of such simple principles will one day provide very adequate accountings of the complex aspects involved in each case. It is therefore likely that the turmoil of the "premature" exposure of the complexities of language would have a wholesome, catalytic effect, especially if, in identifying the great gap our principles must bridge, the scope of the problem obscures neither the fact that much systematic empirical work must yet be done nor the utility in other problem areas of the principles employed.

Language acquisition—innate or learned?   There is considerable controversy about whether or not a straight experiential analysis of verbal-behavior acquisition, with extrinsic reinforcement and inductive principles playing a central role, is sufficient, or even able, to account for language learning and performance, which is perhaps the most complex behavior system characterizing the human. Indeed, it is thought in some quarters that the organization of verbal responses in language may depend upon an innate, nativistic, and maturational structure (Chomsky, 1959, 1965, 1968; Fodor, 1967; Lenneberg, 1967).[22] Those theorists who have taken such a nativistic position on language acquisition have, on several grounds, questioned the utility of simple conditioning assumptions and models to order the generative grammars that an acquisition model for language behavior must explain. Thus, Chomsky (1965) has assumed that language acquisition is based on the child's innate knowledge of a theoretical model—a generative grammar—of his language, "many of the concepts and principles of which are only remotely related to experience by long and intricate chains of unconscious quasi-inferential steps." He has further contended that the limited sample of utterances to which the child is exposed, as compared to the complexity of the grammar acquired, and its independence of intelligence[23] and motivation leave little doubt that language structure cannot be acquired by a child without the operation of innate schemata. Thus, the general language structure is thought by Chomsky to reflect not so much experience as one's innate ideas and principles. He concludes that the "child cannot know at birth which language he is going to learn. But he must 'know' that its grammar must be of a predetermined form . . ." (1968, p. 66). Chomsky therefore further contends that what "evidence is now available supports the view that all human languages share deep-seated properties of organization and structure. These properties—these linguistic universals—can be plausibly assumed to be an innate mental endowment rather than the result of learning" (1968, p. 68).

Thus, these nativist critics have faulted the inductive principles of generalization and transfer in conditioning approaches as being unable to account for a speaker's ability to produce and instantly understand sentences dissimilar to those previously heard, and hence for not bridging the wide gap between associative principles and the apparent complexities of human language development, and as falling far short in handling the nuances implied in concepts of language structure.[24] However, in the context where there is a large gap between conditioning principles and the complexities of language behavior, and in the absence of any given definitive evidence for the claimed innate homogeneity of languages which could be evaluated, a researcher working in an empiricist tradition would approach this issue wondering whether, if homogeneity in any aspect were ever identified across languages, it might be due not to an "innate mental endowment"

---

[22]A succinct summary of several of the issues separating the innate versus the experiential theoretical approaches to first-language acquisition can be found in a recent book review by R. Brown (1968).

[23]Those who take the nativist approach to language have assumed a discontinuity between the intellective mechanisms of problem solving and those of language. A functional analysis like ours, on the other hand, approaches language behavior and its complexities no differently from problem solving and intellective behavior systems generally. In principle, we would expect under our posture to find performances in the higher segment of the quality range of problem solutions for individuals within some subhuman species that are superior to lower-range performance of some humans.

[24]Several features of this argument are not dissimilar from those which some theorists of complex human personality have earlier skeptically advanced regarding the utility of conditioning principles in accounting for complex personality functions (e.g., Allport, 1937).

so much as to the homogeneous experiences involved in the pan-human conditions of socialization (also possibly responsible for the degree to which infant dependence patterns seem homogeneous in diverse human groups).

We have seen that the claim of some nativists is that the structure and processes comprising the child's native endowment provides the basis for his acquiring the ability to speak his community's language. However, underlying such approaches there is a marked paucity of theory that specifies how and at what levels the innate substrate of language ability interacts with experience as learning. Further, no genetic process has been detailed that is capable of transmitting the types of endowed information that nativistic theories have postulated to underlie language acquisition. Hence, the approach of many who favor innate factors as the basis for first-language acquisition may come down to little more than the claim that language acquisition is the outcome of a brain, a voice box, a mouth, and two ears being innately present (and functional) in the child. If in fact this is the case, the utility of such an approach to language acquisition may be diluted. It is well realized that the empirical approach of this chapter is far from a complete solution to the problem. Even so, our contention is that, however incomplete an empirically based approach to first-language acquisition may be at present, it offers a reasonable posture that is potentially more profitable than a rational approach based on intuitive evidence.

Learning, verbal behavior, and language.[25] Shaping and fading procedures (which were discussed earlier), and direct imitative training and generalized imitation (which are discussed in a later section), can all play fundamental roles in the learning of language responses. However, it is the more advanced conditioning concepts in the area of stimulus control, in which "generalization-transfer" is viewed as the direct product of complex discriminated-operant or conditional-discrimination mechanisms (which were earlier described in the section on complex discriminations) (Lashley, 1938; Cumming & Berryman, 1965; Goldiamond, 1966; Terrace, 1966), that appear to provide a more promising basis for understanding the acquisition of distinctive cue and class values in language and of their operating roles. The potential role of complex discriminated operants and their *direct* "induction" to stimuli which, because they may be in new contexts or vary along irrelevant dimensions, only *appear* to be different from the control stimuli in the acquisition context, has been appreciated too little by both partisans and critics of learning approaches as providing a potentially important basis for an improved conditioning account of language acquisition and performance.

Language is characterized by grammatical rules which may stem from, or

---

[25]Examples of diverse conditioning approaches to language acquisition, more or less compatible with the one presented in this chapter, have been advanced by Skinner (1957), Braine (1963), Osgood (1963), Staats and Staats (1963), Jenkins and Palermo (1964), and Crothers and Suppes (1967), among others. It came to my attention after this section was completed that Crothers and Suppes (1967) have presented a critique, more formal than that made here, of the assumptions underlying some nativistic approaches to language acquisition.

be equivalent to, generalized conditional discriminations. Thus, the tense of a verb depends on the specific context in which it occurs, and is affected one way in the present context and another way in the past. In terms of conditional discriminations, "generalization" would derive from communalities in conditional stimuli, in comparison stimuli which contain the discriminative stimulus (e.g., verb inflections), in the relationships among them, or in the broader contexts in which both comparison and conditional stimulus classes appear. While experimental work has thus far rarely approached the level of complexity implied in such contexts-within-contexts discriminations, the concept of conditional discrimination and its derivatives provides a plausible basis for the acquisition of grammars, a basis continuous with the conditioning analysis of this chapter.

However, even this emphasis on the direct induction of straightforward stimulus-control concepts as a plausible empirical basis for accounting for language learning may constitute for critics a limitation of the conditioning model, insofar as it must carry so much explanatory weight and its implications are not yet entirely understood. On this last point, however, we note that there exist few scientific concepts that are in final form (including the nativistic concepts favored by some critics). And there has been an increasing awareness in recent years of the potential power of the conception of direct induction of stimulus-control functions on which conditioning analyses rely. Moreover, this conception of direct induction has recently successfully served the generalization function: a simple model like that for generalized-imitation learning, presented later in this chapter and in Gewirtz and Stingle (1968), can effectively illustrate how a simple variant of a basic instrumental-training conception (and the conditional-discrimination concept) can plausibly bridge the broad gap between simple conditioning settings and what many had considered to be a rather complex personality process, namely generalized imitation and identification (which processes would seem also to be involved in first-language learning).

In this context, and especially because conditioning assumptions seem to have relatively more constructive implications for ways of facilitating language development than do the alternative conceptual approaches, we feel it appropriate to illustrate in our analysis the continuity between verbal and all other functional response classes. It is our contention that both nonverbal and verbal responses can be conceived as following the same laws of learning, and it is therefore reasonable to include both in any detailed analysis of the mechanisms of social learning. The approach outlined here is particularly appropriate for the inclusion of the learning of verbal responses, for it is oriented to the interaction process between child and socializing agent, which means between "talker" and "listener" with these roles cycling between the two (whether motor or verbal responses or both are involved in an interchange). As such, the present approach can conceive of the verbal responses of one person as constituting both discriminative and reinforcing stimuli for the verbal responses of the other person. (Some of the responses involved may be imitative, a general process which will be considered in a subsequent section on imitation and identification.) Once verbal responses are acquired, they will be maintained by responses made to them in conversational interchanges, according to the same principles as account for the maintenance of other responses.

The Child Conditions and Is Conditioned

The child as conditioner of his environment. It is axiomatic that the caretaker-child interaction setting provides many occasions for mutual stimulation and reinforcement. It follows as a corollary of the conception of interchange that *both* interactors can change, and that the stimuli they provide can acquire control over behaviors of the other, i.e., condition them. Thus, the socializing environment is also socialized! This conception of the behaviors of socializing agents adapting to the behaviors of the child has received little emphasis to date in analyses of caretaker-child interaction, where the orientation has usually been on how the caretaking environment affects child behaviors.[26] Yet, just as the caretaker can condition the child's behaviors by providing consequences that are valued by the child, so also can the child's behaviors mediate reinforcing stimuli that can condition behaviors of the caretaker. The child's smiling, vocalizing, reaching toward, eating "well," or ceasing to cry can heavily reinforce many of the adult's behaviors (Gewirtz, 1968b).

On this basis, "baby talk" or outlandish grimaces can enter the caretaker's behavior repertory, as a function of differential reinforcement provided by the infant. And a caretaker may become "attached" to her charge on the same conditioned-reinforcement basis that is thought to underlie the child's "attachment" to his caretaker: stimuli provided by the young child become conditioned reinforcers for the caretaker's behaviors because they are associated with diverse potent reinforcers (for her behavior).

Some of the conditioning of the behavior of the caretaking environment has unconstructive implications for socialization, as can be illustrated by the environment's response to high-rate instrumental crying of infants. Such crying has strong aversive qualities for most adults, and they will often stop some activity (in an institution, for instance, the care of another infant) to attend to the crier in the attempt to stop his crying. When a caretaker succeeds in stopping (the aversive stimuli provided by) his crying, she is heavily reinforced, and the likelihood increases of her picking up or attending to that child when he again cries. However, picking up the crying infant also constitutes a potent reinforcer for his crying. Thus, even though there is momentary relief for a caretaker each time

---

[26]For exceptions, see papers by Gewirtz, by Rheingold, and by Bell. Gewirtz (1961b) emphasized the ways the infant normally acquires considerable control over, and modifies, the environmental conditions impinging upon him, and how caretaker-parents become socially dependent upon and attached to their charges. Rheingold (1966) has similarly emphasized how the infant modifies the behavior of other persons in his environment. Bell (1968) reinterpreted the direction of effects in diverse researches on socialization outcomes, questioning whether child-behavior "outcome" variables thought to be determined by caretaking behaviors as "antecedents" might not often be equally well conceived as determinants of those caretaker behaviors.

the infant ceases to cry when he is attended to, the long-range effect is to increase the incidence of the very behaviors of the infant that are aversive for the caretaker. Gewirtz and Etzel (1967) have presented a detailed analysis of the mutual conditioning process inherent in such cases.

The environment as conditioner of the child. As is noted at several points in this chapter, there are unfortunate consequences that can result when a caretaker responds indiscriminately to a child in an attempt to show her "love" and "affection." Some of these detrimental effects, for both the caretaker and the child, can often be eliminated by modification of the caretaker's pattern of responsiveness to the child. If discriminative and reinforcing stimuli (the care-taker's "love" and "attention") are provided to the child under optimal condi-tions, in terms of an operational-conditioning model such as has been outlined, desirable results for both the child and the caretaker can be achieved simul-taneously.

One desirable result is the child's acquisition of a variety of socially valued behavior patterns, including those which will not only insure that he will benefit maximally from his experiences, but will also allow him to learn to manipulate his environment to bring on such experience, independent of his caretaking setting. For example, when the child's high-rate instrumental crying is reacted to by extinction procedures rather than by caretaker "attention," his more socially desired behaviors, such as smiles or vocal responses, can be reinforced and thereby acquired as functional responses.

The second desirable result of the provision of optimal learning conditions is the satisfaction experienced by parent-caretakers when they feel that they are taking an active role in evoking and reinforcing the child's socially desirable behaviors. It is our experience that most caretakers are well-intentioned (i.e., "warm and loving") persons, but that they are often ambivalent to a child when they must respond to him on his terms, particularly given the vehemence of the injunctions and prescriptions in our society regarding the proper adult orienta-tion to their charges. What such caretakers require is the means by which to translate their "love" for the child into effective reinforcement conditions, to be provided contingent upon those behaviors deemed desirable and important for him to acquire. By employing simple operational-conditioning procedures, the caretaker may thus experience considerable satisfaction from knowing *how* and *when* to provide her "attentive concern, care, and love" for the child. We have already seen that if this reasoning is not applied, and the caretaker only responds to the child on his terms, she may find herself in the paradoxical (and unsatisfy-ing) position of reinforcing the very behaviors of the child she wishes to eliminate, that is, his immature or antisocial behaviors, such as his disruptive instrumental crying. Taking a focused, disciplined role by reinforcing particular socially desirable behavior patterns and not reinforcing antisocial or immature responses may require a greater sensitivity on the part of the caretaker than does undis-ciplined responding to the child, but it should also prove to be more satisfying and to involve less ambivalence than should attempts to follow such vague maxims as "be good to the child" or "give infants as much tender loving care as they need."

Some Limitations of Conditioning Concepts for Social Learning

The learning relationships and theories, which are the basis of the conditioning approach to the impact of environment on early human adaptive and social behavior, are derived both from work with lower organisms and from simplified situations with humans in each of which a few apparently salient aspects of naturally occurring phenomena are systematically manipulated. In this approach, attempts are made simply to identify both the stimulus events in the environment and the key behaviors which they appear to control. There is, however, a fundamental limitation in this approach which often goes unrecognized when basic learning paradigms are applied uncritically to early human development and learning.

Typically, in investigations modeled on basic stimulus-response acquisition and performance paradigms with either lower organisms or humans in highly abstracted settings, some salient conditions are systematically manipulated in an *extreme* way, keeping minimal the number of cues or competing responses in a task setting, and employing operations to make the stimuli involved maximally salient for the organism (e.g., by manipulating background contrast factors). For example, if food is to be employed as a discriminative or reinforcing stimulus in a discrimination task with pigeons, the subjects are frequently reduced to about 80 per cent of their normal body weight and are, in addition, deprived of food for 24 or 36 hours. Further, the food stimulus is then dispensed in relatively small amounts, so as to preclude the subject's satiating markedly for it during the experimental session and to insure its homogeneous effectiveness throughout the session. Thus, in this example, the salience of the food stimulus for the organism is maximized by the implementation of conditions which fall toward the extreme of a postulated dimension of operations for food salience.

In experiments with young humans, however, it is rarely possible to implement such extreme conditions, and more than minimal operations along this dimension are seldom attempted. The impact of discriminative and reinforcing stimuli on their behaviors must be studied within the intensity ranges permitted by everyday conditions in those environments. Thus, experiments and systematic observational studies with humans often cannot be carried out as efficiently as can studies with lower organisms in highly contrived situations.

Only a surface aspect of the limitation inherent in the approach questioned here, however, is indicated by this last point. The basic reason for the limited scope of most of the work accomplished with lower organisms is, paradoxically, the success with which these contrived and extreme experimental conditions have been implemented. In the conditioning literature and in the deprivation-satiation motivation literature as well, remarkably little attention has been devoted to the functioning for behavior of stimuli through the lower and intermediate segments of their intensity ranges. The young, rapidly developing human, however, is normally subjected only to stimuli of lower and intermediate intensity values (e.g., he is not deprived of food for more than a very few hours) in situations with several competing stimuli and with only minimal contrast (setting) conditions that can operate to heighten stimulus discriminability. Hence, the generalizations that can be drawn from experimental work can only apply minimally to the developing infant. Thus, an understanding of the operation of stimuli in this *lower* portion of the stimulus-attribute ranges is precisely what is required for a more complete understanding of the impact of the environment on the behaviors of the young organism, and paradoxically, it is about this lower portion that we know very little. Although, in attempts to understand the impact on behavior of these less extreme conditions, the tendency has been to use concepts like "attention" and "vigilance," these concepts contain considerable excess meaning and have proved gross and unwieldy. They can aid little in providing an understanding of the human adult behavior for which they were devised, and much less in the understanding of the stimulus-response relationships that are focal in early life.

It is for these reasons that we have, earlier in this chapter, emphasized the variety of setting conditions that could qualify the impact of stimuli on behaviors (even in the lower portion of the intensity range of their functioning), including the apparently learned long-term background contexts for some classes of setting conditions. If we are to understand the functioning of stimuli in the lower segments of their intensity ranges and hence through the gamut of conditions in life settings, a deliberate attempt must be made in the study of early human development and learning to identify setting operations which qualify the functioning of stimuli for behaviors of the young organism.

SOCIAL LEARNING
AND THE CONCEPT OF DEVELOPMENT

It was noted earlier that the changing behavior capacities of the child through developmental processes indexed by terms like "organismic maturation," "stages," and "critical periods" might qualify the behavior-development approach of this chapter but would not change its essential features. Similar assumptions are made in this chapter about various other factors which also, in principle, must be accounted for in analyses of the impact of experience on the behavioral development of young humans, and which also would qualify the present approach. These include apparently unlearned S-R associations, species-specific behaviors, individual differences in initial characteristics, and like factors. In recent years, behavioral scientists have found it of very limited utility (if not indeterminate) to attempt to separate behavior functioning from environmental context, as was the emphasis in, for instance, the nature versus nurture controversies of a few decades back. Thus, it has come to be realized that concepts like "ability," "capacity," and "level of functioning" have limited meaning independent of behavior as it occurs and comes to be controlled within an environmental context. The relevant issue for all approaches to child development is therefore the modifiability of behavioral development. As A. L. Baldwin (1955) has observed, once it has been established in a given situation that both the factors ordinarily termed "heredity" and those termed "environment" play some role in determining a behavior system, the question of their relative effects may become insignificant for many purposes. We would add that this would be so at least relative to such questions as which stimuli control the behavior system at issue.

The Status of Developmental Laws in a Functional Learning Analysis

Our line of reasoning turns on the notion that there may be no fundamental difference between the laws characterizing behavior changes in early life and those characterizing behavior changes during other, later, time spans. All involve the determination of sequential, functional relations between stimulus input and behavior output in the individual's experience.[27] The term "development" in a molar psychological analysis is an abstraction for systematic changes in specific S-R patterns. Throughout the entire life history of an organism,

---

[27]There are several reasons why it is difficult to have a reasonable operational concept of development which can apply to the entire human life span, or even only to early life. The specification of those behavior systems whose sequential changes are taken to reflect development is arbitrary. Also arbitrary are the directional criteria usually employed for development, such as increasing behavioral *adaptiveness* and *complexity*. This is because relevant indices of these criteria will vary with (a) different environmental contexts, and (b) the portion of the life span being considered (i.e., behavior changes in early life may be scored in a different, even opposite way from behavior changes in later life). Further, measures of these criteria may not intercorrelate. Moreover, implicit in the concept of development as it has often been used is the assumption that behavior changes are *irreversible,* a notion which is incompatible with much recent thought in substantive areas that attempt to explain behavior change (e.g., in learning and perception).

Numerous exceptions can be found to the common assumption that advances in developmental level with age are reflected in the direction of increased *complexity* of behavior systems. Holding stimulus level constant, some inefficient responses that are complex, in the sense of being undifferentiated, unfocused, or of containing many components, may give way with experience to focused, simple and efficient responses. Thus, the direction of a systematic developmental change may be from the "complex" to the "simple," and thus may run counter to what is often considered a developmental advance. Similarly, holding the response level constant, a child's increased experience (learning) with a gross stimulus complex often results in his selecting out the salient stimulus elements. Hence, while his response steadily increases in efficiency by becoming controlled by fewer, simpler, and relevant stimulus elements, he attends decreasingly to irrelevant elements of the stimulus complex. Thus, here too what is often termed development may reflect changes in the direction of simplifying (rather than making more complex) aspects of a behavior system, in this case the controlling stimuli for responses.

Having questioned the directional criteria for defining development operationally, adaptiveness and changes toward complexity, and the assumption of irreversibility, it appears that developmental processes are not distinct from the processes underlying

training conditions can be implemented to produce behavior outcomes either quickly or slowly, relative to some "norm." As we shall demonstrate, providing the young organism with experience that is focused with reference to a particular outcome can facilitate the acquisition of behavior systems that, in the natural course of events within the range of settings ordinarily observed, characterize much older organisms. We also note the opposite possibility (which one would usually seek to avoid) of providing an older organism with patterns of experiences to retard or reverse (extinguish) the acquisition of behavior systems so that his behaviors would be like those ordinarily characterizing much younger organisms.

Some theorists seem to have stressed explicitly or implicitly the study of sequential and often rapid behavior changes comprising *early* development mainly because of the assumed unique dependence of those changes upon (or at least, their correlation with) gross changes in body structure (e.g., Munn, 1965), while failing to note that gross biological changes also occur during other segments of the life span, some of which undoubtedly correlate with behavior changes as rapid as those typically noted in early life. Hence, while there is a valid place for diverse research strategies and tactics directed to the biological substrate of molar receptor and effector functions, and to coordinating such variables with molar behavior, it must be noted that because changes in biological substrates and in behavior systems occur both in early and in later segments of the life span, the laws characterizing early development should in no way be different either in general flavor or in detail from the laws governing other psychological areas in which change in behavior provides the dependent variable.

Research issues in early development are distinguished from those in other areas of psychology, however, in that an organism in the first phase of his life has had relatively *little* cumulative commerce with his environment, and thus the context for the impact of experience on his behavior will be different from that of organisms in later phases of life who have had more cumulative experience. (However, it should be noted that there may be life sectors in which an older organism may have had little experience relative to a particular behavior outcome and, consequently, the impact of some new experiences upon that older organism may be functionally similar to the impact of new experience on

---

sequential behavior change studied under the aegis of process areas like those labeled perception, learning, cognition, and personality. The single, unique aspect of developmental psychology thus appears to be only that a variety of researchers, for diverse value reasons, have oriented their attention to identifying primarily those behavior changes that vary with gross chronological age units, and have labeled their interest developmental. The validity of this age orientation is questioned in the next section, where it is argued that process functions underlying behavior systems, and not age-related functions, should be the focus of study now, even for those researchers who are interested eventually in reducing these age-related behavior changes to process laws in which age is not a varible. For even though age-related functions can be reduced to process functions, they may still be biased to an unknown degree by factors that also happen to correlate with age but are irrelevant to the behavior systems in question.

the very young organism.) In view of this limited-experience context for the impact of experience on behavior, certain special issues that do not greatly characterize such other psychological areas as learning or motivation may characterize more the study of early development. These issues include maturation-learning and those involved in the requirement of stimulus input for certain structural systems to become and remain functional.

When a systematic short-term change in behavior cannot be attributed routinely to what is consensually termed a learning operation (i.e., the implementation of some recurring environmental stimulus contingent upon a response) or to some short-term performance operation (e.g., the implementation of changes in some setting or ecological condition), that behavior change has often been classified residually as due to "maturation." While the term maturation has been used in diverse ways, it is conventionally thought to apply in at least two behavior-change contexts: (a) when a topographically complete behavior suddenly appears in (enters) the child's repertory, either with or without an identified stimulus basis; or (b) when a primitive approximation of a behavior suddenly appears in a child's repertory, with or without an identified stimulus, that, with monitored practice or simply with the passage of time, approaches the behavior's final topographic form. An important implication of the maturation conception is that, within the normal range of conditions, the behavior change is essentially irreversible, in contrast to the corollary of reversibility inherent in the learning conception (i.e., that a behavior will revert to its original level when the conditions maintaining it are removed).

Thus, behaviors which appear to enter the growing child's repertory suddenly are often attributed to maturation, the innately determined unfolding with age of a gradual plan of development independent of experience. However, the sudden appearance of a new behavior may often be due to a rapidly implemented learning procedure unnoticed by observers, to other effects of experience not usually conceptualized as learning, or to other factors underlying the behavior such as changes in stimulus threshold ("capacity") that may also be conceived to be possible experiential-learning phenomena. The inability of a molar analysis, which emphasizes the impact of environmental stimuli on behavior, to specify plausibly the determinants of new behaviors in terms of experience and learning effects may imply only that the currently available concepts and observational and research techniques require improvement. It follows that the premature labeling of effects which are unexplainable under a given posture as due either to maturation or to learning may be unwarranted as it explains little and may obscure much.[28] In such cases, the introduction of

---

[28]Under a given conceptual posture, many questions may be phrased in an all-or-none manner (e.g., as behavior determinants being *all* maturation or *all* learning) to emphasize their conceptual salience, even though the researchers operating under that posture realize that it may be difficult to arrive at empirical answers that do not lie somewhere between the extreme alternatives they have posed, if only because all relevant factors are rarely taken into account in the early approaches to an issue. Thus, what may be considered unexplained variance ("error" factors) under one all-or-none posture (e.g., all learning) may be considered evidence by researchers under another all-or-none posture (e.g., all organismic maturation), and vice versa. While it is generally recognized, if only implicitly,

the maturation concept to account for behavior variations not readily explained, especially when it is *un*accompanied by a systematic focus on the environmental events that may affect the behavior, may prematurely preclude the search for an explanatory principle based upon specification of antecedent-consequent relationships, and may be tantamount to the notion that age is the independent variable in developmental psychology.

Limitations of the Age Variable in Developmental Analyses

Chronological age has functioned for many as the central variable in the study of developmental functions because of its supposed convenience, as an ordered variable, in indexing successive changes both in physical structure and in behavioral systems of the organism. Spiker (1966) and Zigler (1963a) have viewed age as an index of the medium of time in which various processes can occur. On the other hand, Berlyne (1966) has maintained that chronological age almost automatically describes the developmental condition of the subject, and as such, is a necessary part (or qualifier) of any behavioral law. He feels that it is "... often impossible to predict what kinds of responses will be evoked by particular stimuli unless we also know the subject's age" (p. 72). However, age is actually a residual independent variable (of last resort, as it were), for it provides a relatively pure index only of the passage of time in the physical world. As it, by its nature, but imperfectly indexes changes in biological structure, in sequences and combinations of experience and in the resulting behavior systems, age does not provide the required indices of *processes* occurring in time and hence can only be an incidental variable for the sequential phenomena comprising development. A child will have cumulative, differential commerce with stimuli, representing a sequence of learning procedures (although not necessarily provided optimally for the organism). In this sequence, forms of learning may occur in which stimuli acquire control (direct and conditional) over instrumental responses, and may vary in terms of the order, salience or other criteria for the efficacy with which they have been presented to the organism. And while, on the average, these sequential processes may occur at different age points in a specifiable environmental group, there is no necessary correlation between their occurrence and age-*qua*-time. Under this conception, then, the "correct" time for implementing an environmental procedure to facilitate development is a *point in a sequence of experiences* and only incidentally a point in physical time. A corollary of this conception is that, insofar as the sequential order of a response system provides no clear evidence for a time-linked course, age would be of limited utility for process-linked issues.

---

that, in the extreme form in which they have been posed, such questions (as maturation vs. learning, heredity vs. environment) may be basically indeterminate, the increased salience of the question affected by an extreme posture can give direction to research and can aid in the eduction of diverse functional relationships under the aegis of the issue. And it is these relationships which inevitably facilitate refining the issue further, despite the fact that the issue initially may be couched in all-or-none terms.

I have noted elsewhere (Gewirtz, 1961b) that learning procedures to which the child is exposed in life settings are seldom optimally efficient in facilitating his acquisition of key behavior systems. This point becomes even more salient when one considers that optimizing development requires the efficient, rapid presentation to the child of a correct sequence of learning experiences. For instances, A. J. Caron (1968) has shown that seven-year-old performance on a conceptual-transfer task could be brought about in three-year-old pre-linguistic children by subjecting them to relatively rapid dimension-highlighting training, which stood, as it were, for the four years of relevant experience that seven-year-olds ordinarily receive between the ages of three and seven. That Caron was able to achieve this level of performance within such a relatively short time span dramatically demonstrates that those four years of experience in the life setting are ordinarily provided inefficiently, insofar as they involve inadequate and poorly sequenced learning procedures unfocused with respect to this type of task. In the context of results like Caron's, those (e.g., Zigler, 1963a) who have attempted to differentiate learning from development on the basis of the length of time (prescribed number of trials versus several years) required for a response change may in effect be equating development with the relatively inefficient learning in life settings that is often measured in large time units. The routine attention to age-linked performance changes would have missed entirely functional relations like the one Caron identified in this performance sector.[29]

An emphasis on the charting of assumed age-linked *performance changes* in standard stimulus settings, therefore, tends to preclude both an emphasis upon the *process* of development and an awareness of the relative *rapidity* with which a given process may effect a behavior outcome. An alternative approach is to focus upon the determination of *what combination and sequence of experiences can be provided by the environment* (in terms of stimuli and their contingencies with behaviors) in order for the organism to attain some given performance level[30] (which level may be age-associated, i.e., one that is ordinarily characteristic of individuals older than a given child). Given our cur-

---

[29]After this section was completed, my attention was drawn to the fact that an argument much like the one presented in this paragraph and the next was made by Baer (1966) in an articulate, unpublished talk. Baer presented an example similar to ours of how early discrimination learning was facilitated, thus providing a dramatic illustration of how, when an experimenter perseveres, responses some would think impossible to facilitate could be brought into the child's repertory.

[30]Because the term *stage* often appears to have been used to represent a plateau within ordered sequences of behaviors that, by implication, characterizes an individual's performance for a lengthy time period and is ordinarily associated with an age range, the terms *point* or *level* are preferred for our use here. When stage is employed, as it were, as a still-photograph of a level in a continuous process of development, it would be synonymous with our usage of the terms level or point in an ordered sequence, and we would thus have no quarrel with that use of the term. However, some have employed the term stage to emphasize more the fixity, length of span, and/or association with given age levels of a behavior system. Thus, a convenient term which for some theorists seems to have heuristically evolved to indicate momentary points in sequential changes in development, for others appears to imply heuristically a long-term "stopping" of development in a process during which relevant sequential changes are implicitly assumed not to be taking place.

rent understanding of behavior technology, we have seen that when there is such a systematic joint focus on behavior and the differential environmental conditions provided to facilitate its occurrence, procedures may conceivably be implemented that would take rather few trials during sessions lasting only minutes or hours to produce any of a number of specified effects that, in the natural course of events, would occur only after many months or even years. Furthermore, there are also sequential behavior changes that may occur very rapidly in the life of the organism (e.g., within days, hours or even minutes) in natural as well as experimental settings which will rarely correlate with the larger age units typically used in developmental analyses, such as years, months or even weeks. These sequential behavior changes may be basically no different from those which, because they correlate with age, are routinely labeled developmental. When considered with the already noted possibility of facilitating or retarding the time course of diverse behavior sequences, the fact that sequential behavior change can occur in very brief periods of time also argues against the use of chronological age as a standard independent variable in the study of development, or, indeed, even as an important variable.

Hence, it is precisely because we are in general accord with such theorists as Spiker (1966) who view chronological age as merely a measure of the time during which diverse processes can occur and as a variable that will not be required in advanced theories of development, that we question the utility of an age-variable focus even now. In fact, we suspect that its current use may obscure rather than facilitate uncovering the process variables determining the ordered changes in behavior that are consensually termed developmental. We must therefore question Spiker's unqualified notion (and the similar implication from Zigler's [1963a] distinction between development and learning) that the concept of development be restricted to behavior changes that normally accompany increases in chronological age. It is possible that Spiker means his position to serve only as an initial definitional tactic of directing research towards the assembling of sequential behavior patterns by the identification and study of age-correlated behavior changes, which for him would comprise the "developmental" laws ultimately to be reduced into the advanced process-oriented theories of development that dispense with age as a variable. Even so, there are at least two grounds on which the utility of such an initial tactic could be questioned. First, unqualified by sampling considerations, such an approach to development can imply a homogeneity of experiential differences correlated with age, as well as resulting homogeneity of behavior outcomes among subsamples of subjects readily identified in terms of independent criteria. Therefore, such an unqualified age-related approach would be impeached by the identification of any behavior system for which there are found subgroup differences in age course, of which many examples can be found in the literature (e.g., Anastasi, 1958; Gewirtz, 1965; H. B. Gewirtz & J. L. Gewirtz, 1968a). Further, those behavior changes that do correlate with age and are consequently selected to characterize development initially, may be biased to an unknown extent by those conditions that, while they also happen to correlate with age, are irrelevant to the processes underlying the behavior changes in question. Second, there is the possibility of arranging conditions (as Spiker has also suggested) that would greatly accelerate or that would retard development of a behavior system, once its determinants have been identified.[31]

Thus, in the conceptual context of this chapter, developmental level is used to stand not simply for the passage of time since the beginning of extra-uterine existence (as indexed by age) but rather for an ordered point in the sequence of receptor and effector response occurrences cumulatively affected by stimuli. The fundamental question for many theoretical purposes then is to ask what sequences and combinations of systematically manipulated experiences can enhance (or compensate for) the routine experiences that children ordinarily receive in selected life settings to facilitate the acquisition of specific key behavior systems. This procedure is more in keeping with modal scientific approaches, for time is considered to be nothing more than an index of the occasions and the limits for the process of environmental impact on behavior, and never itself to be the major variable. Further, this concentration on process contributes more to a general understanding of behavior functioning and can yield clear principles that are immediately useful in providing engineering bases for bringing out the "full potential" of children as well as for "up-grading" the behavior systems of children from all types of life settings (including disadvantaged ones).

Important systematic changes in the S-R systems of children can be indexed in a number of ways. (Many of these changes would be conventionally termed "advances in developmental level.") Focusing upon the responses of the child, there can be increases in the number of sequences, in their length, in the smoothness or skill of their execution, or in the number of simultaneous responses occurring, and in the inhibition of certain responses and the occurrence of others in the presence of discriminative stimuli. However, in analyzing the sequential changes in the child's behavior, it would be an incomplete approach to focus on the response side of the S-R sequential unit to the neglect of the

---

[31]Our reservation about an age-defined concept of development has been seen to stem from the assumption that it is not age per se but rather the processes which normally occur with age in natural environments, but which can be expedited or delayed at various ages by environmental conditions, that are the immediate, relevant variables in the study of developmental psychology. Further, we have noted that age-related behavior changes may be biased in unknown ways by conditions which, while they happen also to correlate with age, are irrelevant to a behavior change being studied. Nevertheless, we recognize the possible use of age as a preliminary vehicle for identifying sequences of behavior or systematic behavior changes ordinarily taken to characterize development, in a context where the qualifications of such an approach are explicitly taken into account by the researcher and where the limited aim of such initial screening is merely to expedite immediate process-oriented studies of the pattern of environmental variables which account for the ordered behavior changes identified. This use of age as an initial screening variable is not unlike the use of classifications in process-oriented approaches to comparative and differential psychology, for the purpose of initially identifying culture or species differences in behavior (even though such classifications, unlike age, are usually not initially ordered along dimensions). The main research task for process-oriented approaches in both instances is to identify the determinants of differential behavior outcomes, i.e., to specify the process underlying those outcomes.

stimulus side, as has often been the case. Behavior changes can often be accounted for by increased "responsivity" to stimuli, increasingly fine discriminations between stimuli (Bijou & Baer, 1963), and by the increasing complexity of the stimulus patterns (e.g., number, type, range, and spatial and temporal relationship of the stimuli) that acquire control over various behaviors. For example, upon hearing any auditory stimulus, an infant may initially orient its head in the direction in which its mother is usually found, but will eventually perform this response only to particular tones, appearing at certain intervals of the day and in conjunction with a variety of other stimuli. Thus, the discriminative stimulus for head turning, insofar as it comes to involve a conditional discrimination, changes while the single head-turning response it controls remains unchanged. By directing attention to changes in the stimulus side of the S-R unit, it may often be found that systematic increases in the complexity of an older child's behavior, relative to that of a younger child's, are primarily due to systematic increases in the complexity of the stimuli provided by the controlling environment (in part, perhaps, because parents or teachers assume that only the older child is capable of responding to complex stimuli, although for many behavior systems this may not necessarily be so). Thus, the characteristics (some would term "developmental level") of a child's response systems could be determined by the range of functional stimuli to which he has been exposed (cf., e.g., Vince, 1961). That is, the development of the child's behaviors may often be limited by the nature of the stimuli provided by the controlling environment rather than by the child's "potential." Often, actually, a child might have exhibited the more complex and effective behaviors at an earlier chronological age if the more complex stimuli had been provided systematically then. An analysis of changes in the behavior *of the controlling environment* in such instances may explain more about the child's development than would an analysis focused only on the child's behaviors.

Such behavioral changes can be facilitated by continuous differential reinforcement of successive approximations of the child's responses to a desired level of complexity (or simplicity). Also, at any given level of complexity his responses can be differentially reinforced so that they come increasingly under the control of differentiated discriminative and reinforcing stimuli. Those unconditioned and conditioned stimuli which are discriminative and reinforcing for a child at any developmental-sequence point, in terms of their types, numbers, range, and spatial and temporal patterning, will then function to shape his responses in the direction of more efficiently attaining positive reinforcing stimulus consequences (both nonsocial and social), which subsequently will maintain those behaviors. At first, the child's performances will have only limited effects on the environment, but through approximations of increasingly differentiated and efficient responses, they become increasingly efficient in bringing on reinforcing consequences (Gewirtz, 1961b, 1968b). In this context, it is worth noting that Zigler's (1963a) view that a unique interest of developmental psychology (as distinguished from the interests of behavior theory), demanding approaches, methodologies and theories having particular character-istics, is the study of "changes in the form or organization of responses over time as contrasted with the changes in the strength or accuracy of the response" (p. 345), may have lost sight of the long-standing concern of conditioning researchers, particularly those working on operant behavior, with changes in the topography of responses prior to and during shaping procedures.

In connection with changes in behavior capacities, however, it is axiomatic that the individual cannot perform tasks which require responses he is physi-cally incapable of making. In a similar vein, unconditioned and conditioned stimuli must surely exhibit the beginnings of their effectiveness at different cumulative-experience points in the course of a child's development. Until a child's receptor and effector skills are sufficiently advanced on whatever basis, the number and types of stimuli from all sources to which he can respond and which can reinforce his responses are limited (Gewirtz, 1961b). That is, learn-ing cannot occur until physical growth ("maturation") has reached the ap-propriate point (Hebb, 1966). (And, in keeping with what was earlier noted, even such conditions at best can be indexed only imperfectly by the chrono-logical age of the child.) Further, as the child grows, some reinforcing stimuli may drop out functionally, to be superseded by others, or their relative im-portance for him may change. Thus, food may decrease in reinforcing effec-tiveness relative to (a small degree of) *environmental change* per se. Thus, also, it is likely that the essential nature of the event pattern which constitutes the reinforcing property of certain stimuli for the infant changes as he moves from one capacity "level" to a higher one. To illustrate, those stimulus changes which could be effected by rather gross movements of an infant's hands or fingers (e.g., interfering with light sources), originally produced by the most complex behaviors of which he was capable, might become increasingly less effective as reinforcing stimuli in the context of his increasingly complex response repertory. Thus, also, the conditioned social reinforcing stimulus of attention may be superseded in importance by that of approval (to be at-tained from the caretaker-parent by successively more complex performances) in restricted settings in which the caretaker's approval response mediates the receipt by the young child of most of the reinforcing stimuli which are impor-tant for him. A developmental analysis, such as the one proposed here, would examine the origins and changes in reinforcing stimuli as functions of the roles they play in behavior chains important for the child in the context of changes in the child's receptor and effector capacity due to sequences of experience.

Early Experience

There are several reasons why early (or, more generally, earlier) experience may significantly influence the development of behavior systems later in life. As has been noted, some structural systems which underlie behavior systems appear to require stimulus input in order that they become (or remain) functional. For example, a physically developed eye may not be functional until it has been exposed to the light (Hinde, 1966). Second, many behavior systems of the organism depend directly upon the previous acquisition of component response systems. Thus, all forms of ambulatory behavior require the earlier acquisition of the ability to stand and maintain balance. Third, and perhaps most salient for our purposes in this chapter, certain later behavior systems would appear to be more effectively established when supported by behavior systems that are usually learned early in life (such as eye contact, visual following, smiling, and vocalizing), and that can subsequently become the elements of diverse response complexes and S-R chains, including those directed at people.

These later behavior systems are often maintained by the same stimuli as maintained the earlier acquired responses, and on this basis, behavior systems acquired early in life may become pervasive, and may often appear permanent and irreversible. Nevertheless, it should be noted that these systems would extinguish if the conditions maintaining them were removed (Gewirtz, 1961b). Thus, the strength of these behavior systems is often due *not* to their "irreversibility," but rather to the *locking in* of the behavior of the environment with the child's behavior, so that, from the earliest acquisitions onward, the maintaining contingencies might not even appear to be operating to the untrained observer. Further, in this locking-in process, the appearance of irreversibility of some behavior systems may result from the transfer of stimulus control from the initial sets of maintaining stimuli to different sets, which, to the untrained observer, similarly might not appear to be operating (Etzel & Gewirtz, 1967). While strict elimination of reinforcement for such pervasive response classes is often unlikely to be implemented in life settings, it is possible in principle.

The effects of experience in early life are likely to be qualified by a variety of limiting conditions, and hence no general principle about early experience appears warranted. First, the assumption that later experience builds upon the results of earlier experience does not apply uniquely to the young child, but may hold for any time span in the life of an organism. It is also possible that the effects of only some early experiences are particularly important for development, in the sense that they directly or indirectly become the bases for later behavior systems considered important, or are required for some structural systems to become functional. On the other hand, the long-range effects of many other experiences of the young organism may be much less important. Thus, an older organism learning a new skill, involving long and complex S-R chains that must be mastered sequentially, may find that the experiences involved in learning the earlier part of a chain are more critical for learning later parts than are diverse experiences it may have had early in life in contexts dissimilar from that in which the new learning is taking place. Further, while certain kinds of stimulation may be required early in life to make some structural systems functional, stimulation may also be required throughout life in order to maintain the functioning of these and other systems.

The emphasis of the approach of this chapter upon experience is not meant to negate the effects of "heredity" upon the development of behavior

systems. It is obvious that certain learnings are guided (i.e., facilitated or inhibited) by structural and constitutional factors. Thus, some behaviors which
appear to be unlearned, perhaps because of the suddenness of their appearance,
may be partially explained by the hereditarily determined growth of the receptor and/or effector systems which make possible the very rapid learning of
the behavior.

However, as noted above, it is our assumption that many of the behavior
systems that may appear unlearned are dependent upon experience and hence
learning to a much larger degree than is usually acknowledged. Thus, as Hebb
(1966) notes, while a baby does not have to learn a temper tantrum (in the
sense of practicing it or witnessing it in others) in order to perform it definitively on the first try, the baby must previously have learned to value something that is now beyond his reach or being withheld from him. Further, the
behavior is modifiable insofar as the child's value matrix of relevant objects
may be changed, and positive or aversive consequences may be made contingent
upon the tantrum behavior (Etzel & Gewirtz, 1967).

Homogeneities in the early experience of children may also be responsible
to a large degree for the common features of certain human behaviors which
have caused some to consider them unlearned, "species-specific" behaviors.
Perhaps because of the emphasis which many such theorists have placed on
"instinctive" or "innate" behaviors, there has often been the failure to recognize the dependence of such behaviors on the experiences with stimuli that are
normally inevitable for all members of a species, and on the common learning
which can result from such opportunities (Gewirtz, 1956b). Thus, as we note
at a number of places in this chapter, the extreme helplessness of the human
infant in early life and the care he requires simply to remain alive constitute
a pan-human circumstance which could lead to some relatively homogeneous
outcome patterns in human behavior. These learned response patterns, then,
would only appear unlearned and species-specific.

Critical and sensitive periods.   The concept of *critical* period has often
been applied to time spans, particularly in the early life of an organism,
during which the organism's capacity for the acquisition of certain behavior
systems may be assumed to be permanently lost if relevant experience does
not occur then.[32] A related concept is that of *sensitive* period which has been
applied to time spans during which it has been assumed that relatively large
or rapid behavioral effects can be produced by lower magnitudes of environmental stimulation than would be required to produce such effects at other,
presumably nonsensitive, time periods.

These concepts of critical and sensitive periods have often referred to a
particular span (or spans) of time in the life of the organism bounded by

---

[32]At an orthogonal level of conceptual analysis, which is fundamentally irrelevant for
a functional analysis of behavior growth, that time span may follow the assumed or known
development of the underlying structures involved, whether that development be at birth
or at some later growth point (e.g., Hebb, 1966).

numerical chronological-age points. Although use of these concepts may be coupled with mention of the significance of the sequential experiences that enable an organism to acquire specific behaviors during a presumed critical or sensitive period, often it is the time spans bounded by specific age points that have received focal emphasis and have been termed sensitive or critical. The usage of such age-linked time spans appears to connote a high degree of precision, yet the age limits involved are often qualified by such terms as "around," "about," "roughly," or "approximately."

Particularly as applied to the human, the age-linked conceptions of critical and sensitive periods are often tied only to those naturally occurring environmental conditions that are considered by observers, and thus may reflect with fidelity little more than the failure of those observers to find exceptions in this sampling context. That is, the labeling of a period as *critical* may stem solely from such negative evidence as not noting the appearance of the behavior system in question outside of the age limits within which it has appeared in the samples that happened to be studied. The label *sensitive* often appears to have been assigned to a norm-derived age span based almost entirely on the central tendency and dispersion or range of ages for the appearance of the behavior under scrutiny, and therefore, so used, this term too would be qualified by any limitations in subject or environment sampling conditions upon which observations were based.

Nevertheless, these age spans have often served as guideposts in practical application. For instance, the casually documented notions that infants cannot acquire attachments to an adult after "about" nine months of life if they have not acquired one before or that they may not be able to transfer their attachment if they have acquired one, and/or that they display an "eight-months' anxiety" involving a fear of strangers (e.g., Spitz, 1950), have sometimes guided foster- and adoptive-home placement procedures. In such cases, the more relevant and useful age-independent behavioral indices of the infant's capacity to adapt successfully to a new caretaker environment have appeared to be more or less neglected. At the infrahuman level, Scott's (1968) prescription for a dog (regardless of species) to establish satisfactory social relationships both with dogs and people is simply that he be taken from the litter and adopted into human society when between six and eight weeks of age.

As has been argued in the preceding sections with reference to development, any age-defined concept must be limited in utility to the extent that it ignores the relevant behavioral and environmental events occurring in time. A number of ethologists and psychologists now emphasize (to greater or lesser extents) the inadequacy of age-defined or even maturation-defined critical or sensitive period concepts, and maintain, as we do here, that the focus of research must be on process, and that a detailed analysis of organism-environment interaction is required (Caldwell, 1962; Hinde, 1966; Moltz, 1960). Once the *processes* whereby cumulative experience affect behavior systems are examined, we find that the notions of critical and sensitive periods lose the connotations of precision which their age-linked time limits suggest to many.

Thus, with reference to the postulated critical period for imprinting in duck-lings, it has been demonstrated that the time during which it is possible to initiate the following-pattern indicating imprinting to a stimulus object can be extended considerably by reducing an animal's visual experience prior to its initial introduction to the imprinting situation (Moltz & Stettner, 1961). Similarly, the critical period for imprinting in chicks can be extended by rearing them in isolation (Sluckin, 1962).

In this context, a process-oriented theorist may still wish to retain a con-cept like critical period, or more accurately a concept of critical experience, notwithstanding its lack of functional precision, for the purpose of labeling and making salient certain features of development. Thus, he may use that con-cept to label a sequence of S-R experiences without which the capacity for a potential or actual behavior system could appear to be lost, i.e., due to the lack of experiences assumed necessary to insure that the behavior system can be acquired or become functional. The developmental points bounding the interval would be defined in terms of the relevant behavior systems in the organism's repertory. The loss of capacity to acquire the behavior system in question may be attributed to any of a number of factors, such as the acquisi-tion of incompatible behavior systems or simply to the failure of the appropriate conditions for learning to present themselves at any time in the natural environ-ment. Another possible basis for considering a span as critical could be that a behavior system acquired during the span may appear irreversible, due to its being maintained by environmental contingencies that have become routine and, for this or other reasons, are not readily apparent to an observer. An additional basis for process theorists to use sensitive or critical period terms may be to label some span between developmental-sequence points during which the acquisition of certain behavior systems could begin to occur, or could occur most rapidly, as a result of the child's receptor and/or effector systems having reached appropriate levels, as manifested in his being more receptive-responsive to particular stimulus conditions. These levels would reflect experience up to that point.

From a process-oriented point of view, even more important than demon-strating the ability to extend the length of an assumed critical period (as in some of the studies cited) is the general implication from such demonstra-tions that specification of the conditions that prevent the acquisition of a behavior system at any point or that give it the appearance of irreversi-bility may make it possible for the learning to be facilitated, or for the apparently irreversible behavior outcome to be reversed, through the use of appropriate techniques. This implication would further impeach the utility of a critical period concept. Thus, behaviors which have not been acquired during an assumed critical or sensitive period and therefore have appeared to some to be forever beyond the potentiality of the organism to acquire, could possibly be learned at later points in the life span by the deliberate manipulation of variables involved in the processes underlying their acquisition. For instance, if it could be shown that the acquisition of incompatible responses was the factor preventing or impeding the acquisition of a particular behavior system, then techniques could in principle be devised to eliminate (for long or short periods) these incompatible responses from the organism's repertory. This tactic could facilitate learning of the desired behavior system (cf., e.g., Lovaas et al., 1966; Baer et al., 1967; Risley & Wolf, 1967). An example from the imprinting literature is relevant. It is assumed that chicks or ducklings fail to engage in object-following after some point because, having learned the details of the environment in which they are reared, they may then recognize objects as strange, which evokes distress responses and fleeing, the latter response being incompatible with following. On this basis, Hinde (1966) has suggested that enforced proximity to a strange object could result in habituation of the fowls' attempts to flee with a consequent increase in the tendency to follow.

The sensitive period concept of a unique time span of heightened or maximum susceptibility to particular environmental influences is similarly of questionable utility. The organism is changing continuously due to experience and to organismic factors, and its capacity to learn will therefore vary throughout its life span. Further, even within a narrow segment of the life span, the probability of learning at any given moment may vary greatly as a function of diverse setting conditions (Gewirtz, 1967a). Moreover, it has been noted that sensitive periods are usually not sharply defined and that the factors which define sensitive periods for learning are as diverse as the types of behavior involved (Hinde, 1966). Finally, the position taken in this chapter with reference to the use of the age variable and to the critical period applies to the sensitive period as well. That is, it is the process(es) which underlie any particular heightened sensitivity of the organism at one point relative to another that must be determined. And once determined, a process may be made to occur more efficiently, so that the receptivity and responsivity of the organism may be heightened and the relevant acquisition processes may thereby be facilitated.

EFFECTS ON BEHAVIOR OF GROSS SHIFTS
IN THE MAINTAINING ENVIRONMENT

It is axiomatic that a child will bring to a new environmental setting into which he is placed behavior systems that have been maintained by (and possibly acquired on the basis of) the stimuli in the setting from which he has come. It follows that the child's initial behavior in response to stimuli in the new setting will be a function of the similarity of those stimuli to the stimuli that controlled his behavior in the earlier context. If the new stimuli are markedly dissimilar from the discriminative stimuli in his former setting, the child may infrequently respond there. When the child does respond, his behaviors will provide the basis for new adaptive learning in connection with the stimuli available in the new setting.

There are a number of possible outcomes of such environmental shifts. A sudden extreme shift from a setting in which the child's behavior systems have been under close stimulus control to a setting in which they are not may lead to a considerable weakening or even a cessation of many of his behaviors. That is, because the former controlling stimuli are no longer available or are not provided in functional relations with the child's responses, behaviors exhibited by the child and the discriminations made by him in the new setting may be less complex, even primitive, relative to his behaviors under stimulus control in the previous setting. Behaviors in the new setting are also determined by the rate at which the child's responses to novel stimulus conditions will habituate, which may be a slow process with disruptive effects if the child is very young and the new environment contains abundant startle and noxious stimuli.

New Environments

The nature of the child's adjustment to the new social environment depends on whether or not the significant figures there (e.g., caretakers) recognize the relevant discriminative and reinforcing stimuli for his behaviors and provide them appropriately; whether or not the child, through learning occasions that are provided in the new caretaking setting, acquires responses appropriate to that setting; and whether or not stimuli in that setting (e.g., social stimuli from a new caretaker) acquire discriminative and reinforcing value for the child's behaviors. If caretakers in the new setting are inflexible and fail to shape the child's simple behaviors into behaviors appropriate to the new setting, the child may not acquire an acceptable substitute behavior repertory. These conditions may result in a vicious cycle: a caretaker responds to the child in terms of expectations based on the behaviors of other children of that age group whose maintaining environment has not been shifted, and if these responses of the caretaker are not appropriate to that child's present level of learning and thus do not function as discriminative or reinforcing stimuli for new learning by the child, the child will drop even farther behind in his behavioral development. These conditions may thus eventuate in the child's being labeled "unteachable." Another possible outcome is that nonreinforcement of formerly reinforced responses may lead to emotional responses or other maladaptive behaviors, which if reinforced by the caretaker's attention may become more and more likely in the new setting. Because these responses may be incompatible with new adaptive learning, another vicious cycle then occurs, which will probably also eventuate in a labeling of the child as "unteachable," but this time due to "emotional disturbance." A survey of adaptations to new environments and conditions for the establishment of substitute behavior repertories and attachments to new object persons is to be found in Gewirtz (1961b).

Another unfortunate, but not infrequent, problem-behavior outcome in children can stem from the arbitrary conclusions drawn by caretakers about charges recently placed in their care (or by parents about their offspring). On the basis of what they take to be the children's behavior limitations or from information supplied by some diagnostic procedure, these caretakers may conclude that the children are afflicted with some organismic anomaly (brain impairment or injury) or simply (and residually) that they are retarded (Gewirtz, 1968a). However, the children's "backward" behavior patterns may actually be the result of adverse reinforcement histories due to a paucity of functional stimuli during their lives up to that point (in a later section, such patterns will be termed *privation*) ; or the behavior patterns may result merely from the consistent absence of coordination between some stimulus classes provided (which might otherwise have been ample in number and type) and some child response classes (Gewirtz, 1961b).

This process wherein caretakers or parents define their charges as "backward" may be self-fulfilling, as the caretakers may then continue, or begin, to offer a restricted stimulus diet to their charges on the assumption that "backward" children cannot benefit from the stimulation it is possible to provide, or will even be harmed by it. An alternative possibility in this context has been noted by Bijou (1963). Under the rationale that such an arbitrarily defined "deficient" child "needs" more than the usual amount of attention because he is "handicapped," the parent-caretakers may differentially reinforce the child's dependent behaviors, both instrumental and social-emotional, and, at the same time under their humane rationale, may systematically extinguish or mildly punish independent activities of the child. This pattern would preclude the child's acquiring effective, resourceful, and mature behavior patterns and insure that he will remain helpless and infantile. Clearly this type of caretaking process soon justifies itself in terms of its outcomes: children who might otherwise have functioned rather well come to require the stifling "help" that has been imposed on them by their well-intentioned caretakers (Gewirtz & Etzel, 1967). Thus, because of the attitudes of their parents and caretakers more than because of their presumed or actual afflictions, these children frequently acquire stilted behavior patterns, having been made passive in child-rearing settings in which as active, responsive children they could otherwise have developed fully.

Indeed, whether or not a child's affliction is a real one (e.g., he is actually brain injured or limited in his motor coordination), the engineering problem remains the same: to optimize the environmental conditions so as to bring the child's performance up to their highest (asymptotic) levels. In fact, given the inefficiency of conditioning procedures in natural settings (which point is discussed in a later section), it is conceivable that when acquisition and setting conditions are optimized, the performances of so-called "afflicted" children may often be brought to functional levels higher than those characterizing the behaviors of so-called "normals" (e.g., for certain motor or verbal behaviors, etc.).

Concurrent Multiple Environments

A special case of changes of stimulus control conditions involves independent but sometimes overlapping environmental settings that differ in their discriminative and reinforcing stimulus control of the child's behavior (as in "multiple mothering"). Each caretaker essentially provides a different caretaking setting for the child, defined by the discriminative and reinforcing stimuli provided and the responses considered appropriate by each caretaker. The child then has the problem of discriminating between caretakers and caretaker roles in the different environments. Difficulties may arise when a certain response to a stimulus is considered appropriate by one caretaker but inappropriate by another. For the child in an institution, or for one who is in a nursery school during the day or is raised jointly by several persons in a household (parent, relative, maid), these issues may be important.

I have suggested elsewhere (Gewirtz, 1968b) that infants in the care of busy or ambivalent caretakers, as in some institutions or family settings, might be subjected to a conditioning program so as to strengthen those responses in their repertoires (e.g., eye contact, reaching toward, smiles, selected vocal responses) that are likely to function as potent reinforcers for the behaviors of caretakers. In this way, infants would be in a position to "compete" more effectively for the caretaker's limited attention, and a fertile interaction basis could be established to facilitate the mutual acquisitions of constructive attachment patterns by child and caretaker.

Privation and Deprivation as
Environment-Deficiency and Shift Conditions

The environment-deficiency conceptions "privation" and "deprivation" have occupied a central role in formulations which have attempted to relate deficiency conditions of stimulation in early childhood, as antecedents, to aberrations in later behavior patterns of children as consequences (e.g., Bakwin, 1942, 1949; Bowlby, 1940, 1951, 1953b; Goldfarb, 1945a, 1945b, 1955; Levy, 1937; Spitz, 1946a, 1946b, 1949, 1954; Yarrow, 1961).

Following our earlier operational analysis (Gewirtz, 1961a, 1961b), we will reserve the term stimulus *privation* for a paucity of all, or particular, classes of stimuli through long time spans, usually early in life at the very time stimuli could support the early foundation learning that is being laid down. In some instances, abundant stimuli may be available but are nonfunctional because of an absence of appropriate setting or context conditions or because of an inept mode of provision (e.g., noncontingent on behavior). For example, if social stimuli are not made discriminative for behavior, they will not acquire cue or reinforcer value, and privation of social stimuli will be said to have occurred. The child developing under these conditions may become generally responsive to nonsocial stimuli but unresponsive to social discriminative and reinforcing stimuli. Children displaying these characteristics are usually termed "autistic" (Kanner, 1949; Ferster, 1961). As we have used the term, privation does not index conditions involving a gross shift in the maintaining environment. Nevertheless, it is surveyed here to provide a context for the concept of deprivation which can involve such a shift.

We will use the term stimulus *deprivation* to encompass both long-term and short-term effects of gross shifts or changes in the maintaining environment brought about by the removal of stimuli that have become functionally significant for key behavioral systems of the child. This involves either lowering the level of stimulation from the child's accustomed level, making key stimuli from stimulus-response chains unavailable, blocking responses, changing the quality of stimulation by changing its source, or removing the setting conditions that enhance the efficacy of key stimuli. An example is a child's separation from a person to whom he is strongly attached or that person's sudden and continuing rejection of the child. As a result of such situations, the child may at first exhibit behavior patterns not unlike those usually found in the initial stages of experimental extinction, i.e., an initial increase in frequency of the response compared to the rate exhibited under reinforcement conditions, as well as irrelevant emotional responses, which may further disrupt the response pattern and preclude the learning of new adaptive behaviors.[33]

The deficiency conception. Attempts to explain the assumed consequences of privation and especially of deprivation conditions have generally been centered around a deficiency conception, which focuses attempts to order long-term phenomena according to a short-term homeostatic drive model. This latter model, however, is ordinarily used to order an organism's recurring and reversible requirements for food and water, but has been extended by adherents of a deficiency conception to include "hungers" or "needs" for such things as affection or love, and stimulation. Generally, this model seems to involve the assumption that if young children receive an inadequate supply of "essential" stimuli from their caretaking environments, they will develop atypical patterns of responsiveness to nonsocial stimuli, of dependence and attachment behaviors, or of adaptive behavior generally. The "deficient" stimulus supply may have been received from early life onward or it may have been implemented abruptly and continued for a period following an earlier adequate supply. These behavior-outcome patterns would include developmental arrest, depression, and apathy in younger children; and in others, no requirements, or apparently insatiable (and sometimes indiscriminate) ones, for the formerly deficient commodities (e.g., attention, affection) and a limited capacity for social relationships (attachments). For instance, Levy (1937) has written of behaviors characterized by a lack of "emotional response" and a "shallowness of affect."

One implicit motivational analogue of the deficiency model often used to explain the above outcomes is that of *hunger*. For example, Levy (1937) coined the phrase "primary affect hunger," and Spitz (1949) has written of "emotion-

---

[33]The conception of stimulus deprivation emphasized briefly in this section involves the unavailability in a setting of mostly conditioned stimuli which have maintained selected behavior systems there. As such, this usage differs systematically from one in which behavior aberrations result from shifts to such unusual environments as those that become unstructured or involve usually short-term stimulus impoverishment (sometimes termed "sensory deprivation"), as described, for instance, by Bevan (1967). A consideration of the results of the very extreme curtailment or rearrangement of stimulation often involved in such (often contrived) settings is beyond the scope of this chapter.

ally starved" children. This usage can be illustrated by Levy's (1937) classic statement:

> . . . affect hunger is . . . an emotional hunger for maternal love and those other feelings of protection and care implied in the mother-child relationship . . . a state of privation due primarily to a lack of maternal affection with a resulting need, as for food in a state of starvation (pp. 643-644).

This presumably analogous homeostatic hunger-drive model has usually been applied in other contexts to order the periodic and readily reversible requirements of organisms for such indispensable stimuli as food and water. An analysis of the hunger model, however, indicates that it cannot possibly order the reported conditions and results of regular, long-term deprivation: it operates only through hours, or at most a very few days; and it implies complete satiability after periodic deprivation, with no residual effects that could cumulate in time and manifest themselves in systematic changes in behaviors for the events of which the organism was earlier deprived. In fact, a close analysis of long-term food starvation effects indicates that a short-term homeostatic model is totally inadequate to handle even food deprivation if effected for protracted periods (Keys, Brozek, Henschel, Michelsen & Taylor, 1950). The deficiency model attempts to order through months and (more typically) years, not periodic and reversible but cumulating effects of recurring conditions of deprivation in the early life of the child, which result in systematic changes in some of his behaviors with reference to the stimulus commodities deprived. This model thus emphasizes a "need for stimuli" which through time can build up in strength if unrequited, i.e., if less than some (unspecified) adequate level is supplied to the child over relatively many occasions through the longer term, on either a regular or irregular basis. As earlier noted, the "need" which builds up in this way may lead later to the child's exhibiting apparently insatiable requirements for (and even the hoarding of) the stimulus commodities earlier provided in deficient supply, but sometimes it may lead to apathy or other aberrant behavior outcomes. In addition to the inherent difficulties of attempting to order long-term phenomena according to a short-term model, there is the further limitation that the drive concept inherent in these models carries irrelevant (excess) and even misleading meaning which derives from the usage of the short-term homeostatic drive model in contexts which are quite different in their essential properties from those in which the term "childhood deprivation" has been applied.

Application of the deficiency conception. Despite these arguments against the use of the deficiency model for ordering long-term phenomena, the model is still often used implicitly or explicitly by theorists, therapists, and caretakers alike. Under the deficiency model, the solution for dealing with inadequate conditions would be to provide a large number of stimuli without regard to their relationships with the behaviors emitted by the child. If this prescription were followed to the letter, the infrequent contingencies between responses and stimuli would minimally affect response acquisition, but could change the long-term maintenance level for stimulation in proportion to the rate of stimulus provision. A less likely outcome could be "superstitious" behavior: responses that happen to occur just before stimulus provision could increase in probability, and because of their increased frequency would be likely to be inadvertently reinforced again.

In actuality, however, it is unlikely that a caretaker or therapist will ignore the child's behaviors when she provides stimuli. Rather, the caretaker is likely to provide the stimuli, if only inadvertently, in some functional relation to particular response classes of the child, and the response classes that are reinforced may vary from one caretaker to another. Thus, without a predetermined specification of the desired responses, there are a number of possible behavioral outcomes. If the stimuli intended to constitute "sufficient" attention and love are provided contingent upon the child's disruptive or attention-seeking behaviors, those responses will be strengthened, and the result may be an unfavorable response pattern that precludes the learning of more appropriate adaptive behaviors. If, on the other hand, the caretaker provides those stimuli contingent upon more socially valued responses, such as responses typical of the child's age group or responses oriented more toward autonomy and achievement, these responses will be strengthened and the outcome will be more favorable.

Ironically, both of these behavior shifts can be used by advocates of the deficiency model to index the inadequacy of the previous setting. A high or increased incidence of attention-seeking behaviors or disruptive emotional responses could be assumed to indicate that the child has a "hunger" for those stimuli believed to have been inadequately provided previously, and to require even more stimulation to satiate or reverse. The opposite outcome, the relative increase in appropriate behaviors, may lead to the assumption that the new, more adequate environment has satisfied (satiated) the child's hunger for the stimuli, for he no longer appears to "need" as much attention and love and therefore appears more "secure," a result which is also interpreted as validation for the principles of the deficiency model.

The routine use of a deficiency model, whether for appetitive or non-appetitive (including social) conditions, is disadvantageous in that it discourages close attention to environmental stimuli and behaviors at the level of detail required by a differentiated learning analysis. By focusing on what appear to be minimal conditions for behavioral development, this model considers neither its range nor its potential upper limit. It also plays down the concepts required for ordering systematic and cumulative changes in behavior effected by recurring conditions (contingencies) of the environment, i.e., learning concepts. The deficiency model uses the network of empirical relationships implied in the reversible homeostatic-motivational conception, and, as such, is only aimed at, and capable of, summarizing recurring regularities in selected organismic behaviors involving no residual effects. Further, it tends to emphasize few behavior indices, which are assumed to return periodically to some routine level. This emphasis on few indices may reflect an implicit concern at a reduced analytic level with a physiological process that is a key to organismic survival. Hence, the conception is misleading for ordering either chronic starvation effects or cumulative long-term functional relationships between the availability of stimuli and effects on relevant behaviors.

In contrast, a learning analysis would first specify the conditions of stimulus control over responses existing prior to the removal of stimulus classes in deprivation, as well as the changed contingencies between the child's behaviors and the stimuli provided in the new setting. Thus, the outcomes of environmental shifts earlier considered would be regarded in a learning analysis as reflecting an adjustment of the rate of the child's behaviors to the changed conditions of stimulus provision in the new setting, which includes new learning by the child resulting from changed response-reinforcement contingencies in the new setting. The basic assumption of a learning analysis overlooked by proponents of a deficiency conception is that, in order to understand the development of human social motivation under both normal and deficiency conditions of stimulation, it is not sufficient to focus simply on which or how many stimuli are provided to the child. Rather, one must take account of the circumstances under which given stimuli are made available, and in particular, whether these stimuli are functional and enter into effective learning contingencies with the child's behaviors.

ABSTRACTIONS OFTEN EMPLOYED
IN SOCIAL-LEARNING ANALYSES

One-sided and Two-sided Summary or Index Variables

Nearly all extant theories of parent-child interaction and socialization are process-oriented. They therefore imply a focus on the sequential details of the interchange between the child and his caretaking environment, wherein stimuli provided by the appearance or behavior of the caretaker evoke or are consequences of the child's behaviors. Each S-R interchange unit involved is conceived to represent a point in a sequence and to contribute to the next point, within and across interchange episodes. Thus emphasis is on the *process* of interaction, and on the systematic changes in the child's behaviors (i.e., his learning) resulting from the provision of stimuli articulated at successive points with them. As has been noted earlier in the section on the infant conditioning the behavior of the environment, there is also a parallel learning process involved: the behaviors of the parent can systematically change too (see also Sears, 1951; Gewirtz, 1961b). However, as has been noted earlier, caretaker-socializer learning is hardly emphasized at all in approaches to parent-child interaction.

Yet when many process-oriented theories of parent-child relationships and the researches carried out under their auspices are examined, it is noted that neither their theoretical constructs nor the empirical constructs which are related to the theoretical terms via (usually implied but occasionally explicit) coordinating definitions are at a level of analysis that is optimally efficient for the level required by the emphasis on process pervading the theories. Rather than the direct indices of process required under these theories, the empirical constructs instead only summarize through time spans (often lengthy ones) either the environmental events presumed to constitute the stimuli that are functional for the child's behaviors (e.g., "nurturance"), *or* those child behaviors (e.g., "dependence"), but not the interchange S-R units that are required to index successive points in the process of change. Indeed, even approaches to the process and outcomes of parent-child interaction that lean heavily or exclusively upon social-learning assumptions (e.g., Sears et al., 1957) have sometimes employed mainly "one-sided" (although defined) summary variables in research. Such constructs are relatively insensitive to the sequential details of interaction conditions that make possible studying the direct impact of the stimuli provided upon the child's responses, and are for most purposes, therefore, less than optimal indices of the learning-change considerations that pervade a process theory like learning.[34]

Furthermore, generalized-response trait variables for each side of the interaction process at best emphasize only the "average" response tendencies of the environment or of the child across situations and thus reflect minimally the successive details of the highly differentiated discriminative control that social stimulus settings can acquire over child behavior. Although approaches using such variables may find some differential relations both among the summary behavior indices used and between them and environmental variables, uniformly high relations or even homogeneous ones are seldom found, and, indeed, in most cases, should not be expected. This is because there is always the possibility that one response measure can enter into a higher association with independent variables than another, or simply enter into a different functional-relation form with them. This condition is attenuated when theoretical concepts are imprecisely defined and used, overlap each other in meaning and overlap differentially on particular questions, as well as when measures are differentially reliable. Further, such concepts are often imprecise, and what appear upon closer analysis to be fundamentally different phenomena are often grouped under one such concept (e.g., achievement, attachment, aggression, dependence, dominance, imitation, identification). Hence, at the very least, the discrepancy between the level of abstraction of the one-sided global summary variables and the level implied in learning concepts must inevitably limit progress in both theory and empirical research. The use of such summary variables within otherwise relatively articulate process theories (like learning) tends to limit the possibilities for the modification and improvement of such theories, particularly in terms of their internal consistency and the coordination of empirical indices with the concepts of those theories. Further, reconciliation of such a theory with the empirical relationships found between stimulus and response variables is unduly complicated by the use of summary terms, and discrepancies in the levels of analysis can result in inefficient utilization of research resources. Of course, the utility of these con-

---

[34]As will be seen later in the present section, this apparently inconsistent usage might be explained by occasional research purposes for which the use of summarizing and one-sided trait variables can be efficient and fruitful, even under an approach whose ultimate aim is to attend to successive details of the mother-infant interaction process.

cepts for research can be improved by delimiting the functional relationships which they summarize. In the present chapter, however, we concentrate instead on reducing such concepts to functional relationships.

Examples of one-sided variables frequently used to summarize aspects of the *environment* that can have impact on particular behavior systems often have as their assumed indices such demographic classifications as geographic area, culture group, institutional membership, social class, father's presence or absence, child's age, sex category, and sibling-status pattern, as well as mother's age, whether primiparous or multiparous, and whether or not she is employed outside the home, has household help, or there are several generations residing in the household. Caretaker-role variables, which include nurturance, warmth, love, and acceptance (often qualified by consistency, frustration, or conflict), are another type of variable used to summarize relevant environmental details. One-sided variables summarizing the child's *responses* are most usually typified by "trait" concepts, which index response classes likely to be emitted by him in diverse stimulus settings. Some examples of trait-like concepts summarizing child behaviors are dependence, dominance, and hostility (sometimes also qualified by anxiety, consistency, frustration, or conflict). Under a learning approach, such one-sided variables have limited utility except for preliminary purposes like summarizing and data-grouping operations or subject selection, as they only grossly index attributes of the stimuli that have been functional for a child; and, while in principle these gross terms are reducible to patterns of stimulation and their interchange with child behaviors (J. L. Gewirtz & H. B. Gewirtz, 1965; H. B. Gewirtz & J. L. Gewirtz, 1968a, 1968b), their use can preclude or delay specification of those required details. These global terms are thus not sufficiently differentiated to be more than minimally useful under a learning model. A statement of the amount of stimulation a child receives or has received cumulatively must therefore be supplemented by a functional analysis of the behavior relevance of the provision of those stimuli. Such an analysis would attend to such aspects as the discriminability and the pattern of provision of stimuli, the sequences of stimuli and responses which constitute S-R chains, the delay interval between behavior and reinforcement, the acquisition of discriminative and reinforcing value by previously neutral cues, the setting conditions affecting the efficacy of the stimuli, and like factors.

The utility of one-sided variables is further reduced by the fact that measures of them are usually derived from such sources as parent interviews or questionnaires, which are sometimes administered years after the occurrence of the parent-child interchanges being assessed, or from specific or global rating scales or projective tests. Even if these methods were to give reliable measures of verbal performance, it is often questionable (and rarely determined) whether they actually reflect the behaviors they are intended to assess. Furthermore, the parental values, attitudes, or child-rearing traits (or personality organization or conflicts) that such assessment devices describe may correlate only slightly (if at all) with the actual stimuli impinging on the child that are relevant to a behavior system under study. Similar to the measurement of stimulus summary variables, the presence of a trait is often inferred from retrospective parental reports of the frequency of these response classes. Often no attempt is made to assess the events leading to and following members of such response classes or to take account of the stimulus conditions which differentially control the response class.

Thus, the limited value of a caretaker-role variable such as "love" or "warmth" is illustrated by the fact that the amount of love or warmth evidenced in the parent's attitude toward his child as expressed in interview or question-naire data, global or specific rating scales, or projective tests may bear little direct relationship to the functional stimuli actually received by the child. To the young child with little or no appreciation of subtle verbal distinctions, stimulus qualities like love can only be perceived in the form of functional physical stimuli, e.g., as visual and sound patterns, skin contact, etc. The infant or young child does not discriminate "attitudes" or "feelings"; however, he may discriminate ani-mated from expressionless faces, soothing from harsh sounds, gentle from hard squeezes, gradual from sudden movements, or one complex of these events from another. If the events implied by a gross variable are not discriminated by the child (or his caretaker) and do not affect in any way his (their) behaviors which are of theoretical interest, then they are irrelevant to a social-learning analysis of the child's behavior systems (and of the caretaker's). As the child's symbolic processes develop, he may at a later age come to discriminate increasingly subtle indications of approval and love. Even so, these stimuli, e.g., verbal ones, will have no relevance for his behavior if their value has not been conditioned by the functional provision of discriminable stimulation at an earlier age (Gewirtz, 1961b, 1968b, 1968c).

Further, the use of such one-sided variable labels can sometimes have unfortunate consequences when applied uncritically in the life setting. The labeling of a child's response class as a "trait" is sometimes accompanied by a belief that the trait is possibly innate, and will persist throughout life in some form or another. (The assumption of "motives" for the child's behaviors is fundamentally identical to this usage of traits.) Such beliefs will often result in self-fulfilling prophecies: a teacher who has been warned by another teacher that a particular child is hostile would tend to expect hostile behavior from that child and might, therefore, interpret his behaviors as reflecting the hostility which she expects of him. If, as is often the case, her negative attention functions as a positive reinforcer for the child, she will inadvertently increase the rate of his emission of hostile behaviors. Similarly, if she has been led to believe that a randomly chosen child is intelligent or creative, she will very likely prime and reinforce those of his behaviors that appeal to her notion of intelligence and creativity (Rosenthal, 1966).

The limitations of one-sided trait variables become clearly evident when one reviews the studies concerned with the relative importance in accounting for behavior in a given setting of the trait variable and the stimuli present in the period preceding an action. The latter were often found to be critical determi-nants of a child's behavior, and may be better predictors of consequent behaviors than more long-term trait variables. Thus Rotter (1960) surveyed studies in which situational variables predicted an individual's behaviors as well as or better than test performance or other summarizing behavior indices; Raush (1965) found that when a child's immediately preceding interaction was considered together with setting variables, the combination constituted a more effective predictor of whether another child's behavior would be friendly or hostile than did individual differences among the children; Barker and Wright (1955) showed how specific settings can instigate interaction and how variations in structure of the environment can account for differences in interaction behavior; and Gellert (1962) found that the frequency of a child's dominant behaviors depended upon the behaviors of the person with whom he was in interaction—that is, his dominant behaviors increased in incidence when he was paired with the less assertive of two peers. Thus, both the setting conditions and the behavior of the first interactor (e.g., the parent) can differentially control the type of response emitted by the second interactor (e.g., the child). As will be seen subsequently, some behaviors of the parent might therefore result in copying behaviors by the child, whereas others might lead to complementary or antagonistic responses. Differential functional relationships such as these are obscured by long-term one-sided trait variables that measure only across settings and only the behaviors of one of two or more interactors.

Some uses of abstract summary variables.   In general, inexplicit abstract concepts tend to be inefficient, and the phenomena they summarize can be dealt with best if they are reduced to, and thereby replaced by, more explicit variables (see the next section for such an approach to identification). Nonetheless, there may be research strategies for which the use of reasonably well-defined one-sided summary variables might be plausible, and even fruitful, at least at first. For example, even under an approach that attends directly to the successive details of the mother-child interaction process, the use of a gross trait variable for behavior might occasionally be a necessary research compromise, if only to facilitate data processing, including grouping and reduction, or to select subjects that would vary along some dimension of responses to and for stimuli. Further, demographic environmental variables may be gross indicators of the environmental constraints that limit parent-child interplay. For example, the sex of the adult determines to some degree his behavior toward the child, and the sex of the child determines some of the stimuli he receives as well as the behavior he emits. Similarly, the birth order of a child may influence the child's environment in that the experience of the mother in child-rearing and the amount of attention and time she could devote to the child would be affected (J. L. Gewirtz & H. B. Gewirtz, 1965). Moreover, by grouping subjects (parents and/or children) in terms of levels of index variables such as social-class strata or sibling-status groups, one could be reasonably assured of sampling widely disparate points along postulated dimensions of stimulation mediated by parents to their children. Such indices, therefore, might be useful in (or a by-product of) the first stages of an empirical analysis under a theoretical model that relates environment and behaviors at an abstract level. For example, if one is interested in defining levels of a social-class variable, or in correlating social-class levels with parent-child behaviors, or parental attitudes or child-rearing practices with child behavior, a variable yielding a more heterogeneous distribution of scores may be more appropriate than even those that directly index stimulus-response interchange in the parent-child interaction process.

In those instances where it may be plausible to use summary variables, however, two-sided variables, which simultaneously emphasize both the environment and behavior, would have greater utility in principle than one-sided variables. Examples of such two-sided concepts that require further development are A. L. Baldwin's (1955) concept of "dispositional trait" and R. R. Sears' (1963) conception of "action system," which involve the organization of child or adult behaviors in terms of their relation to classes of stimulus events. Such two-sided summary variables may avoid some of the disadvantages of one-sided summary variables, such as the de-emphasis of the stimulus settings that exert differential control over behavior systems and the obscuring of the analysis of contexts in the controlling environment. Nevertheless, any gross variable may constitute a multiple predictor at a particular level of analysis, a predictor for which the various components may not even have been identified, much less precisely defined, and for which the loadings of the various factors are unknown and possibly indeterminate at that level of analysis. More precisely defined, limited variables, therefore, would still be more advantageous and beneficial for most purposes of both research and theory than even the best of two-sided summary variables.

Some Brief Comments on Theory

In approaches to child social development, there has been insufficient recognition of the distinction between what Reichenbach (1938, 1951) has termed the contexts of "discovery" and "justification" in the development of scientific theories. In using the verification criterion of empirical meaning, psychology has the same task as the other sciences: its concepts, however derived, must be reducible to observable conditions—stimuli and responses, and antecedents and consequents.

In this context, there are at least two functions of theory in psychology, the economic and the integrative (e.g., Farber, 1964). Under the *economic* function, a theorist may develop and use concepts to reconcile assumed relationships among operations in order to facilitate identification of the functional relations between determinants and effects that characterize a process. This function appears to be the one emphasized by Tolman (1938) and Spence (1948) in their use of "intervening-variable" terms as calculational devices, and it has been suggested that Skinner's (1953) occasional use of derived terms like "drive" to classify various antecedents under the same heading in terms of their homogeneous effects on behavior rate may similarly be economic (Miller, 1959; Farber, 1964). (However, as Estes [1955] has noted, one difficulty with the calculational-device type of construct is its flexibility, for once advanced it could encompass or explain each new empirical turn with the help of *ad hoc* assumptions.) The *integrative* or unifying function of theories is to organize empirical relations within and among domains. Where the coordinating statements between empirical and theoretical concepts are sufficiently detailed, deductions for further empirical relations can be extensive and novel implications many. And it is always possible that one such theory may become integrated into another, even one that has quite different theoretical constructs and labels, and which organizes sets of empirical relations that were not thought related earlier (Spence, 1948, 1956, 1957).

When examining how these two functions of theory, the economic and the integrative, have been involved in psychological theorizing, and specifically in the area of the impact of environment on child behavioral development, it is noted that apart from the use of operationally tied-down concepts from the field of conditioning and of derived terms closely related to them, it is doubtful that child-development theories have often benefited from either the economic or the integrative utility function. Further, while a basis for choosing between two theoretical approaches or concepts would be their heuristic utility, such as the degree to which they generate new research, organize many and diverse phenomena, and yield general principles (Maltzman, 1966), such criteria have almost never been applied to theories in the domain of environment-child interaction. For the most part, researchers appear to emphasize or adhere to theories with which they are comfortable, on personal-value rather than on utilitarian grounds. Thus, many seem to favor concepts because of their mentalistic-reflective-cognitive flavor or their uniquely human flavor.

The development and use of theories by psychological researchers has long been valued, and, during the past four decades, there has been an increasingly self-conscious approach to theory in psychology. Our thinking has been that a theory generates research questions and then requires that the empirical answers be referred back to it and be taken into account to modify the theory as necessary. A good theory might be said to fit the Piaget assimilation-accommodation model: derived from existing observational facts, it assimilates new empirical data as they are, but also accommodates to them when required to do so. And, given its utilitarian purpose, a theory must be discarded when it fails to accommodate to new empirical data. It is often said that only a theory, however inadequate or preliminary, can point to the relationships among events that are important and provide guidelines for identifying and controlling irrelevant factors. It is also recognized that it would be nearly impossible to gather data independent of a theory (or theories), however informal or preliminary, or however difficult it may be for the investigator to articulate it. Thus, we have been schooled in ways to develop and evaluate theories and in how to judge the logical and psychological adequacy of the concepts and assumptions of a theory.

In their zeal to emphasize the utility of theory, however, many psychological theorists have ignored or played down other criteria for the efficiency of research, particularly prescriptions for the relationships between theoretical assumptions and research operations. To the degree that such criteria are met, it becomes possible to make selective modification of the theory for purposes of consistency, of increasing precision of the concepts, or of fairly readily developing a more parsimonious statement within the framework of the theory. Hence, there is an emphasis on the adequacy or degree of coordination between the theory's terms and the empirical variables.

It is with these criteria in mind that the argument is made here for a more self-conscious emphasis on the articulation between empirical and theoretical concepts as the means of strengthening research approaches to parent-child interaction conditions and outcomes. For, there have been theories of socialization in child development that seem to emphasize neither operational definitions underlying their empirical terms, explicit definitions of their theoretical terms, nor coordinating definitions between theoretical and empirical terms that specify unambiguously the circumstances under which theoretical terms are to be used (i.e., their referents). We have in mind, for instance, diverse approaches to development which emphasize mainly cognitive and motivational concepts, like some that are soon to be noted in this analysis. As Farber (1964), using Reichenbach's distinction, has observed, theories that appear comprehensive through the use of terms with no specific referents may have suggestive value for the scientist operating privately in the context of discovery, but the ambiguity of these terms precludes rigorous test of their purported relations for the purpose of the scientist's justifying his theory to others.

Labels Are Not Explanations

One difficulty which is encountered when inexplicit, abstract concepts are employed is that there is often an obscuring of their ties to antecedent and consequent factors, with one result being that a label for the behavior process at issue may come to serve as the "explanation" of that process, e.g., the concept of "schema." Such concepts may also be used in theories containing a number of terms with no specific referents that, therefore, only appear to be comprehensive. While these ambiguous terms may facilitate the researcher's hunches about potentially interesting relationships as he operates within the pre-scientific context of discovery, it remains necessary for him to verify empirically the functional relations involved and to show through a sequence of discrete steps how his theoretical terms relate to his empirical ones. Otherwise, his continuing to use ambiguous terms would be a form of self-indulgence, for by remaining, as it were, within or on the fringes of the context of discovery, the researcher could not readily justify his theory to the scientific community (except perhaps to those who may believe they share his immediate experience and pre-scientific concept language). In addition, this researcher would benefit neither from the economic nor the organizing power of a theory, nor from its ability to generate new kinds of research. I shall consider this issue of explanatory terms in two parts, first for cognitive approaches and then, more briefly, for motivational approaches.

On some cognitive labels. The confusion of labels with explanation is especially evident in many cognitive approaches, for instance, in Aronfreed's (1967, 1969), Kohlberg's (1966), and Whiting's (1960; Burton & Whiting,

1961) approaches to identification, which are considered in detail in the next section. Thus, in attempting to explain the acquisition of identification behaviors by children, Aronfreed has assumed that children fairly rapidly form a "cognitive template" or "representational cognition" of the model's behavior, which serves for storage and retrieval of performance. However, he has proposed no clear basis for the acquisition of a "cognitive template," except to imply that it depends (in an unspecified way) on the capacity to exert verbal control over behavior and that it may be acquired through a form of observational learning; nor did he tie this term to imitative-identificatory behaviors. He has provided no coordinating definitions between his theoretical terms and operations indexing environmental and behavioral phenomena. This "cognitive template" concept, therefore, seems to offer an explanation for the acquisition of identification behaviors only insofar as we are told that the acquisition of one is the basis for the acquisition of the other. In a more general vein than Aronfreed's, Kohlberg (1966) has written of his theory being ". . . cognitive in that it stresses the active nature of the child's thought as he organizes his role perceptions and role learnings around his basic conceptions of his body and his world" (p. 83), and he stresses observational learning involving intrinsic rather than extrinsic reinforcement of one's own responses as ". . . cognitive in the sense that it is selective and internally organized by relational schemata rather than directly reflecting associations or events in the outer world" (p. 83).

In cognitive-developmental approaches, therefore, it appears that intrapsychic cognitive-act euphemisms phrased in common-sense or immediate-experience language are often employed to characterize heuristically the bases for a subject's behavior in a given context. However, in such instances, it is often difficult for a reader to determine where the line is drawn that separates such heuristic variables from the required empirical variables, between observation and inference, between interpretations and concepts, and between the private, pre-scientific context of discovery and the public, scientific context of verification. In the process, it is far from obvious whether the locus of such heuristic terms is meant to be the head of the subject or (the theory) of the scientist, or the immediate experience of the subject or of the scientist as if he were the subject. Thus, the distinction between the statement of a problem and its explanation can be obscured, and empirical questions can lose their importance or appear to be solved simply by the application of cognitive labels to them.

The notion advanced here and illustrated throughout this chapter is that well-defined and extensively used conditioning concepts can order social-behavior phenomena as well as or better than can more abstract, less explicit, cognitive terms (or motivational terms, as will be noted in the next section). This very brief consideration of the form of the concepts employed in some cognitive approaches can close with our taking note of what Maltzman (1966) has observed in another evaluative context. The heuristic value of the cognitive approach to development is not necessarily greater than that of alternative theoretical approaches nor does it contain a greater number of testable concepts or more assertions that have been proven true by test, nor have there been under the aegis of theories using cognitive-flavored concepts any discoveries, empirical relations, or new environmental or response variables which logically could not be treated within some behavioristic approach, for instance, like the one outlined in this chapter.

On some motivation labels. A similar difficulty is often encountered in approaches where motivational (drive) terms are employed to account for a behavior process. As motivation is considered in greater detail in a subsequent section on its role in social learning, our discussion at this point will serve merely to highlight some limitations of motive labels in explanations of behavior, to parallel our consideration of the limitations of cognitive labels.

In principle, there is no argument being advanced against the use of cognitive or motivational terms per se, for they are only words and words can be employed constructively or obscurely, explicitly or loosely. What is being criticized here, however, is the imprecise, gratuitous, and uncritical manner in which cognitive and motivational terms are often employed in analyses of social development and learning, and the often inadvertent consequences of these usages. One inevitable result is an obscuring of the relevant functional relationships. Another is a decrease in the researcher's attention to the fine grain of the organism's behavior, to the details of the environment operating on the behavior, and to the contingencies between environmental stimuli and behavior. Expressed in such terms as secondary, acquired, or learned drives, motivational concepts have often been advanced to order behavior systems that appear only to be the outcomes of learning conditions occurring through long time spans. As is seen in a later section, these terms have often been employed in analyses of pervasive behavior systems, such as imitation-identification (e.g., Miller & Dollard, 1941; Bronfenbrenner, 1960; Sears, 1957; Hindley, 1957; Kohlberg, 1963) and dependence-attachment (Sears et al., 1953; Sears, 1963; McClelland, 1951; Whiting & Child, 1953). Further, various conceptions of innate drives "for" stimuli or for the attainment of certain goals have entered extensively into theoretical analyses of early social development (cf., e.g., Berlyne, 1950; Harlow, 1950, 1953; Hendrick, 1942; Hunt, 1963; Kohlberg, 1966; Montgomery, 1951; Ribble, 1943, 1944, 1965; White, 1959, 1963).

This preoccupation of psychologists to explain myriad behavior phenomena through the use of such diverse notions, which involve gross abstractions that only summarize the effectiveness for the child's behaviors of various social stimuli (e.g., those from his parent) and refer so imperfectly to one side of an interchange between a child and his environment, has resulted in a lack of parsimony and in confusion, and has severely limited the conveyance of meaningful information regarding the development of adaptive and social behavior systems. This inconsistent, inexact, and thus inefficient use of motivational terms has led not only to definitional ambiguity and an explanatory impotence, but also to a loss of precision in the specification of the functional relationships sought, the reasons for seeking them, and the theoretical language used to order these phenomena. As we have already seen and will further see in the subsequent sections of this chapter, the behavior systems to which motivational (and cognitive) concepts have been applied can be both completely and parsimoniously accounted for in terms of the simple learning mechanism of acquired stimulus control over behavior. Thus, the addition of such concepts to these cases is, at best, gratuitous.

TWO KEY SOCIAL-LEARNING PROCESSES

This section will be devoted to a detailed examination of abstractions for a pair of two-phased acquisition processes and behavior systems which are focal in social learning: the first is imitation (including vicarious reinforcement and observational learning) and identification (including sex-typing); and the second is dependence and attachment. A consideration of these focal processes can illuminate the roles of the acquisition and maintenance of behavior, and can at the same time illustrate the stimulus and response content of socialization.

1. Imitation-Identification

There are conventionally thought to be at least two types of processes by which children acquire social-behavior patterns, and the values and attitudes these patterns reflect. Up to this point in our survey, we have emphasized only the first of these processes wherein social learning is based on *direct* instrumental training (tuition). In this direct training, reinforcing agencies tend to have particular socialization goals in view and are relatively more explicit about the responses the child must acquire, which they attempt to shape via differential reinforcement. This direct-training process may be more or less efficient. (A by-product of this process is emphasized in the section that follows, which deals with the acquisition and maintenance of behavior systems ordinarily termed dependence and attachment.) There is, however, a second type of socialization learning which is thought by some to proceed *without* direct tuition, at least without the type of explicit training that involves both differential reinforcement of child responses and relatively clear goals of socializing agents (e.g., Bandura, 1963), and to comprise the greater portion of socialization learning. This learning occurs through the process ordinarily termed *imitation,* in which the child *matches* his responses to the cues provided by the responses of another person (a "model").

Some Background on Imitation[35]

Miller and Dollard (1941) did much to bring imitation into a behavior-theory framework by suggesting that it is based on both the individual's capacity

---

[35]There is a relatively large literature on imitation and identification, a portion of which is summarized in a paper by Gewirtz and Stingle (1968), with extensive summaries and treatments to be found in chapters by Aronfreed, Bandura, and Kohlberg in this *Handbook.* Approaches to imitation have been presented by Humphrey (1921), Holt (1931), Miller

to learn to imitate and environmental conditions that have positively reinforced him for such learning. Copying, which by their definition involves the copier's knowing when his response is the same as the model's, is learned in a trial-and-error fashion when an external "critic" (reinforcing agent) positively reinforces randomly occurring similarity and punishes dissimilarity, or when copying is followed by the same reinforcer that followed the model's response. Eventually, as the copier's discrimination improves, he emits anticipatory discrimination responses that produce anxiety if his copying response is different from the model's response or reduce anxiety if his copying response is the same. Thus, the copier in time becomes his own critic.

Also, in a learning-theory framework, Mowrer's (1950, 1960b) theory of imitative learning postulates that imitation (particularly of vocal behaviors) of a model occurs because cues from that model's behaviors have acquired reinforcing value through their pairing with primary reinforcers, and through generalization their imitation acquires secondary reinforcement value for the copier and is thereby maintained. Thus, imitation is learned through a process of self-contained trial-and-error learning, without direct (extrinsic) reinforcement for imitation.[36] In a preliminary analysis, Skinner (1953) briefly sketched how the cues from models' responses can become discriminative for the extrinsic reinforcement of matching responses but he did not develop the case for a functional matching-response class maintained by intermittent reinforcement.

The mechanism for the acquisition of imitative (-identificatory) behaviors stressed by Bandura (1962, 1965b, 1969) is that of *observational learning*, in which matching behaviors are acquired by an observer through simple exposure to a model's response, independent of the observer's overt response or of its reinforcement. Specifically, Bandura assumes that stimuli from the model's behavior elicit perceptual responses in the observer that become associated on the basis of the temporal contiguity of the stimuli provided by the environment (e.g., the model's behavior). After repeated contiguous stimulation, these perceptual responses come to form verbal or imaginal representations of the stimuli involved. These representational systems mediate response retrieval and reproduction in that they provide cues which elicit or are discriminative for overt responses corresponding to those of the model. Thus, according to Bandura, it is primarily on the basis of stimulus contiguity and symbolic mediation that imitative behaviors

---

and Dollard (1941), Piaget (1951), Maccoby (1959), and Baer et al. (1967). Approaches to identification have been presented by Sears (1957), Sears et al. (1965), Kagan (1958), Bronfenbrenner (1960), Whiting (1960), and Kohlberg (1963, 1966). Attempts to relate the concepts of imitation and identification have been made by Mowrer (1950, 1960b), Lazowick (1955), Sanford (1955), Hill (1960), Gewirtz (1961b), and Bandura (1962, 1969). A review of determinants of imitative-identificatory behaviors is presented by Bandura in Chapter 3.

[36]Mowrer (1960b) also lists but does not develop a form of "empathetic," observational learning in which the witness of the reinforced response of a model becomes inclined to reproduce the model's response. Our later evaluation of the concept of observational learning will apply as well to Mowrer's "empathetic" learning.

are acquired.[37] The rate and level of observational learning are conceived to be determined by a variety of what Bandura terms perceptual, motoric, cognitive, and incentive variables. Included under such categories are setting conditions (e.g., the saliency and complexity of modeling cues), the availability of necessary component responses in the observer's behavior repertory, and overt and covert rehearsal of the matching response. However, Bandura assumes that performance of imitative responses, once they are learned, is primarily governed by extrinsic, self-administered, or vicariously experienced reinforcing events. Bandura's conceptualization of observational learning is considered further in a subsequent section.

Varying cognitive approaches to imitation (and identification) have also been put forth by Piaget (1951), and more recently in different ways by Kohlberg (1966) and Aronfreed (1967, 1968, 1969). Kohlberg rejects an S-R instrumental-learning conception apparently on the basis of a narrow conception in which reinforcement is equated with organismic drive reduction. And although Aronfreed does not deny the role of instrumental learning for certain behaviors, he does qualify the learning mechanism with unindexed "representational" processes (as was earlier noted). Both theorists, however, minimize the importance of extrinsic reinforcement of the child's responses for imitative learning. Instead, they stress *observational learning* (as does Bandura), and *intrinsic reinforcement* of responses. As has been noted in passing in earlier sections and as is further detailed subsequently, Kohlberg assumes intrinsic reinforcement to result somehow from "motives" for "competence-mastery" and "interesting"

---

[37]As is argued later in this section, when an organism acquires a functional response class, in a sense a discrimination of similarity is made between his present response and his past responses that have been reinforced in the discriminative context (e.g., as in bar-pressing or in imitative matching responses). Thus, there is a sense in which all organisms must somehow bridge the gap between relevant experience and later response performance that depends on the earlier experience. What is not obvious, however, is the means by which this is accomplished; and theoretical approaches may differ in whether they attempt to bridge this gap only with their theory or also with operations that index successive aspects of the postulated process. They may also differ as to the utility of postulating such gap-bridging processes, particularly when indexing operations are not involved for assumed events thought to occur at different points in a long chain. For most heuristic purposes it has typically been assumed by conceptualizers of human and subhuman learning to be unnecessary to posit a special discriminative process over and above that implied in the functional response class as defined by the subject's overt responding. For, unless an independent operation is specified and ultimately employed to index a postulated representational or cognitive process, the parsimony and utility of positing the occurrence of such an implicit process to bridge the time gap between experience and subsequent performance is questionable, both for infrahuman and human subjects.

Bandura has assumed that his implicit cue-producing response mediators can be independently manipulated, and that they are conditionable and extinguishable according to the same laws as those governing explicit forms of behavior. Thus, he has shown that various setting conditions, such as attentional-highlighting or dimensional-appreciation procedures, or even an observer's verbalizing or attempting to visually code the details of the behaviors of a model while he is viewing them, can be implemented during prior training (observation) to facilitate subsequent test performance (e.g., Bandura, Grusec & Menlove as cited in Bandura, 1965b). (The functional relations into which these setting operations enter with imitative behaviors constitute a contribution to the body of available data about consequences, while Aronfreed assumes that it derives from the child's observation of the model's behavior and the "affective" value that becomes attached (conditioned) to the model and his behavior as well as to the child's "cognitive representation" or "template" of the model's behavior. This last-mentioned implicit response representational concept appears to be not dissimilar to the concepts of Bandura surveyed earlier.

Explanations of imitative response acquisition in terms of observational learning may have stemmed from the difficulty some have experienced, under instrumental-training conceptions, in specifying some salient features of the imitative process. Such explanations may be due, at least in part, to the problem of identifying a matching response class whose content changes from trial to trial, but also in part to the difficulty of identifying the reinforcing stimuli for that response class when it has been specified. Explanations of the imitative process in terms of S-R contiguity learning (Holt, 1931; Humphrey, 1921; Maccoby, 1959; Piaget, 1951) may also have stemmed in part from the difficulty in specifying extrinsic reinforcing conditions for imitation. Possibly for these reasons also, covert rehearsal of the model's behavior has sometimes been suggested as essential in the learning of imitative behavior (Sears et al., 1957; Maccoby, 1959; Burton & Whiting, 1961).

An experiment by Baer et al. (1965, 1967) provides a dramatic demonstration of imitation learning with implications for practical application, as well as a useful point of departure for the conceptualization of imitation we shall propose. By physically assisting the child to make the desired imitative responses

---

the imitative process, and thus have a utility independent of Bandura's theory.) However, as the only indices of implicit response processes are the very imitative-behavior outcomes the implicit responses are postulated to explain (or the differential operations that established them), it is difficult for us to see how the manipulation of such setting conditions (in what is termed an observational-learning setting) can be conceived as the independent manipulation of implicit responses. Nor do such operations necessarily provide support for the notion that imaginal or representational processes mediate the recall of copying responses. Indeed, explaining the effects on behavior of such training conditions in terms of implicit representational or cognitive responses that remain unindexed, however intuitively plausible such processes might seem to the researcher operating within his prescientific context of discovery (e.g., as if he were the subject, human or not), is gratuitous and can often be detrimental to the search for the relevant functional relationships at issue. These comments apply as well to Aronfreed's (1968, 1969) similar assumptions about cognitive representations and unindexed affective mechanisms, that have been discussed in the previous section of this chapter on abstractions (and particularly labels as explanations) and are again considered in the sections that follow.

Our purpose here, however, is to detail for the seemingly complex behavior systems of imitation and identification an instrumental-learning model that is parsimonious, operational, and reasonably complete, and that readily lends itself to empirical test. Hence, it is appropriate for us to attend primarily to relevant learning issues, and to leave to a subsequent analysis the more definitive comparison of simple conditioning theories like the one we detail with approaches that posit representational or cognitive processes. Such a confrontation would necessarily involve questions about the efficiency and parsimony of such implicit concepts relative to that of conditioning concepts like ours that are closely tied to stimuli, responses, and their sequential relationships. As was noted in the earlier section on abstractions in which such a comparison was begun, this issue has implications far beyond those of a simple analysis of imitation-identification.

initially and reinforcing each such response immediately, Baer et al. taught imitative responses to retarded children whose behavior repertoires had been observed closely for a period and did not appear to include imitation. After training on a number of such responses, each subject could then imitate new modeled responses, and eventually response chains, without assistance. Further, the rate of a generalized imitative response that was never directly reinforced, but had been maintained when interspersed with reinforced imitative responses, declined when reinforcement was withdrawn from the imitative behaviors that were previously reinforced. Lovaas et al. (1966) have successfully used a similar paradigm for conditioning imitation of verbal responses in initially nonverbal schizophrenic children.

An Updated Social-Learning Approach

Our consideration of this topic can be introduced by a legendary story concerning the Rabbi of Kotzk. A townsman had requested that the Rabbi pray to insure that his sons would study the Torah diligently. In reply to this man's request, the Rabbi said: "If your sons will see that you are a diligent student, they will imitate you. But if you neglect your own studies, and merely wish your sons to study, the result will be that they will do likewise when they grow up; they will neglect the Torah themselves and desire that their sons do the studying." By implication, the Rabbi's assumption was that the father-model's exemplary behaviors, which could be imitated by his sons without extrinsic reinforcement, would provide a better basis for their acquiring studious behavior patterns than would direct training via reinforcement of the desired behaviors, implemented by the parent or by others. Without going into the merits of this assumption here, this charming story can set the stage for a consideration of the important twofold socialization topic of imitation and identification.

It is thought by many that, while a significant portion of children's socialization experiences occurs through direct training, by far the largest portion, and the most pervasive, significant, and long lasting of such patterns, is acquired through the active process of children's imitation of parent-models' behaviors. These often rapidly acquired imitative-behavior patterns (frequently also termed identification) are assumed to be matched to behaviors which socializing agents do not ordinarily attempt to teach directly, and indeed may not know how to train or even wish to train at all. These patterns may therefore be the opposites of those emphasized in direct training via differential reinforcement, and it is thought can often partially or completely nullify that direct tuition. Thus, the example of the nonstudious pattern set by the townsman of Kotzk might in certain contexts nullify much or all of his sons' studious behavior pattern that is maintained by direct reinforcement. It remains an empirical question whether or not a response in a given context can be acquired more efficiently or rapidly via direct instrumental training or via imitative learning (as conventionally conceived or in the matched instrumental-training sense as we conceive it in the sections that follow). In fact, instances of direct tuition to the child at the same time may represent occasions for imitative learning, with the effects due to either process. For instance, physical punishment of a child for hitting others, which is intended as training that he should refrain from such acts in the future, may also provide the child with an example from a parent-model of how to hurt others, which behavior the child might subsequently exhibit when the appropriate social occasion arises (Bandura, 1962, 1969).[38]

My thesis in this chapter, however, is the *opposite* of the widely held current position that imitative responses and generalized imitation are acquired *without* direct instrumental training (e.g., Aronfreed, 1967; Bandura, 1963; Sears, 1957; and others). Using a basic operant-learning conception for the shaping and acquisition of functional response classes, my assumption is, rather, that imitative responses are simply instrumental responses that are matched to the cues provided by the responses of models, that the functional response class they constitute for the child (which we term *generalized imitation*) is acquired through extrinsic reinforcement from socializing agents, and that this functional response class is maintained by intermittent extrinsic reinforcement. It is my thesis then that matching or imitation learning is only a special case of instrumental learning, and that it is illusory to hold that the second type of socialization learning, generalized imitation and identification, takes place without the direct instrumental training from socializing agents that defines the first type (direct tuition). (The issue involved, of course, represents an empirical question which, in principle, can be tested through systematic observation in life settings.)

It is further assumed in this chapter that if socializers tend to focus less on particular socialization goals and to be less explicit about the responses the child must acquire through the imitative type of socialization learning, it is but an *artifactual* outcome of the very different and more general orientation in the imitative case as compared to the focus in instrumental training on single clearly defined responses and discriminable reinforcing stimuli in a well-defined discriminative context—i.e., with clearly specified outcomes. Indeed, the orientation in imitation learning is more toward a response class containing a potentially unlimited number of responses, varied in content and often matched to response-provided cues from many models (but which may be focused on one model), and often occurring in situations where the model is absent or where there is no extrinsic reinforcement for imitation. Because of the very large number of potential responses at issue, very few of the outcomes involved are specified in detail.

I shall now move on to a conceptual analysis of the process of generalized imitation and the conditions for its acquisition and maintenance, as well as of identification for which generalized imitation is the assumed basis. At the same time, I shall examine the process of observational learning and, relying heavily on

---

[38]It is assumed that the child will more readily match those of the model's responses that are of classes relatively high in the child's response hierarchy or that will occur in situations in which there are no strong incompatible-response tendencies.

assumptions and considerations emphasized by Gewirtz and Stingle (1968), shall attempt to account for this process by showing that it may be identical to the learning of generalized imitation.

Generalized Imitation

It has been noted that after the response of another (a "model") has been witnessed by a child, he will often exhibit a response resembling that of the model. Such a response (class) is termed *imitative* when it is emitted to match the cues provided by the model's response and not because of common stimulus antecedents or environmental constraints. Imitative responses, therefore, are not classifiable by content or by similarity alone. The term *generalized imitation* can be applied when many different responses of a model are copied in diverse situations, often in the absence of extrinsic reinforcement. My approach to generalized imitation assumes that a very simple learning model can encompass the complex behavior outcomes ordered under that concept and also many grouped under the heading of observational learning. A paradigm as elementary as the one that is presented here, in which imitation represents one variety of stimulus control over instrumental responses and is acquired on the basis of direct extrinsic reinforcement of imitative behaviors, has not been fully developed before now as the basis for the acquisition and maintenance of either imitative behaviors or observational learning (much less as the basis for identification).

The first imitative responses must occur by chance, through direct physical assistance, or through direct training (with shaping or fading procedures applied by a reinforcing agent to occurring responses). When such responses occur, they are strengthened and maintained by direct extrinsic reinforcement from environmental agents. After several imitative responses become established in this manner, a class of diverse but *functionally equivalent* behaviors is acquired and is maintained by extrinsic reinforcement on an intermittent schedule. Differences in response content of the imitative behaviors are thought to play a minimal role as long as the responses are members of the imitative response class as defined functionally *by reinforcing agents*. This process is thought to be the same as the way in which, for example, variations in the content of successively emitted plural nouns or first-person pronouns or even in the seemingly homogeneous free-operant bar-pressing output are irrelevant as long as most of the response variants are members of the response class reinforced.

Much past work on imitation (and even more on identification) has emphasized imitative responses as such, with only an implicit consideration of the relevant environmental stimuli that give that response class its functional meaning. The important difference between those approaches and the one presented here is that, in addition to an emphasis on the environmental stimuli (from the model's responses and discriminative settings) that cue the occurrence of imitative responses, we emphasize also those stimuli that maintain (reinforce) them as essential in the process. Thus, the term imitation implies for us just one type of stimulus control over responses. As with any functional response class under some kind of stimulus control, the response class has no special intrinsic value independent of the stimulus conditions controlling it. In a given context, an otherwise trivial response class like bar-pressing can gain a functional status comparable to that of imitative responses in life settings.

An even better analogy to the functional class of generalized imitation is provided by the *matching-to-sample* conditional-discrimination learning paradigm. When a conditional (standard, "sample") stimulus and an array of discriminative comparison stimuli are varied from trial to trial, the subject's task is to respond to the comparison stimulus (i.e., the discriminative stimulus) that is the same as (or similar to) the previously presented conditional stimulus. Through extrinsic reinforcement of the class of matching responses (i.e., those made to each matching comparison stimulus), the subject acquires the relevant matching-response class that then governs his responses to a wide range of stimuli differing in content. Some may term this a "concept" of identity or similarity, while, if a label must be used to provide historical context, we would favor "conditional discrimination" (Lashley, 1938; Cumming & Berryman, 1965).[39]

On each trial, the subject's response to the comparison-discriminative stimulus from the finite number in the array that matches the conditional stimulus (the sample) is analogous to his selecting from his own repertory the response that matches the model's response in its stimulus context, i.e., the imitative response. Since reinforced matching responses in the functional imitative class are diverse, discrimination between matched behaviors which are reinforced and those which are not is unlikely to occur, and some copying responses that are never directly reinforced will persist, therefore, unless they are specifically punished or are incompatible with stronger responses in the child's repertory.

In principle, conditions could prevail such that imitative responses that are never reinforced could be discriminated from those responses that are reinforced, and thus they would not become part of the functional response class defined by extrinsic reinforcement from the environment. However, with the content of reinforced imitative responses differing from one occasion to the next and the functional response class being maintained on a schedule of intermittent extrinsic reinforcement, it is unlikely that efficient conditions for discrimination would frequently prevail. Then, insofar as there are recurring instances of reinforcement for imitative responses and ineffective conditions for subclass discrimination, even those imitative responses that are *never* themselves directly

---

[39]This is because unlike simple simultaneous or successive discrimination learning, in which the correct response is made on the basis of the presence or absence of a single discriminative stimulus that sets the occasion for the reinforcement of the response, in the (complex discriminated operant) matching-to-sample situation the correct response must be made in terms of the properties of two or more stimuli (the conditional or standard stimulus and the discriminative comparison stimuli). The significance of the discriminative stimulus varies with successive discrimination trials, changing relative to the conditional stimulus which preceded it, with the conditional stimulus thus coming to function more as a differential cue or selector of discriminations (or as a differential setting condition for them) than as a simple cue for individual responses.

reinforced may become part of the functional response class. On this basis, new matching responses will continue to enter the functional imitation class in the child's repertory.[40]

Some Issues Resolved by
Our Generalized-Imitation Mechanism

Intrinsic versus extrinsic reinforcement.   Our analysis with regard to the stimuli and responses in the imitative behavior chain was in part stimulated by earlier analyses by Baer and his associates (Baer & Sherman, 1964 ; Baer et al., 1965). However, our analysis differs from theirs (and from the approach of Staats & Staats, 1963, that is similar to it) [41] mainly in respect to which component details are emphasized, and in the fact that their heuristic account appears to emphasize an intrinsic-reinforcement mechanism and ours does not. In their analysis, conditioned-reinforcer value is assumed to become associated with the imitator's (unassessed) discrimination of similarity between his response and one previously emitted by the model, while the unit of our emphasis is the entire S-R chain, of which all elements are maintained by terminal extrinsic reinforcement.[42] (These elements could include the discrimination response and its assumed reinforcing value emphasized by Baer and his associates.) Our simpler assumption that a lack of discrimination between reinforced and nonreinforced members of the imitative response class serves the heuristic purpose equally well is similar to the usual conceptual accounts of behavior, and does not necessitate the introduction of an additional construct. The functional value of each element in the imitative S-R chain is due entirely to its association with the terminal reinforcer. Thus, a key feature of our analysis is that the environmental agency (and not the imitator himself) determines the occasion for reinforcement.

---

[40]In this context, it should be noted that the acquisition of the functional generalized-imitation response class, derived from the communality in responses as defined by extrinsic reinforcing agents, could have aspects in common with what, in the conceptual context of language acquisition and use, involves the organization of responses according to transformational grammars.

[41]It was brought to my attention, after this chapter (and Gewirtz & Stingle, 1968) were prepared, that in a brief analysis of the formation of verbal discriminations via matching, Staats and Staats (1963) have proposed that an organism could learn to match a stimulus produced by his own response to a stimulus produced by someone else and that the stimulus provided by the *match* could acquire conditioned-reinforcer value as a result of its being discriminative for extrinsic reinforcement. Thus, correct response matching itself produces secondary reinforcement. Although this point is not made explicitly by the Staatses in their approach to matching as a basis for verbal discriminations, or by Baer et al. (1967) in their conception, such a similarity stimulus would have to be followed often enough by active reinforcers for its conditioned reinforcer value to maintain. The reservations we will advance about the latter approach in the present didactic analysis would seem to apply as well to that of the Staatses.

[42]We have termed extrinsic any reinforcing stimuli provided by the environment. Even if a terminal reinforcing stimulus has acquired its reinforcer value through conditioning, it differs from the conditioned-reinforcement value that is assumed to be associated with the stimulus of similarity in the Baer et al. (1965) analysis, in that it can be observed in the chain, measured along some dimension, and controlled by a reinforcing agent.

In discussions in the literature of other functional classes, such as relatively simple bar-pressing on an intermittent reinforcement schedule by nonverbal organisms, there is usually no special heuristic emphasis on the subject's discrimination that he has performed a response like those that have led to reinforcement in that setting in the past. Although such a discrimination may be involved, and its assumed conditioned-reinforcer value has occasionally been used to account for continued responding between reinforcements in intermittent schedules (e.g., Denny, 1946; Kimble, 1961), operations are rarely if ever introduced for its study. In the same vein, the singled-out unindexed conditioned reinforcer based on a judgment of similarity does not seem critical for the Baer et al. (1965, 1967) analysis of what they consider to be a relatively complex case of imitative learning, and certainly not for an overall heuristic analysis. Indeed, as used by these authors, the intrinsic conditioned-reinforcer concept may carry surplus "cognitive" meaning. Even if the ultimate behavioral analysis of these implications proves more complex, for the moment at least Baer and his colleagues have made no case for treating the imitator's discriminative judgment any differently than analyses of the acquisition of other functional response classes would treat an organism's discrimination of the similarity between an emitted response and responses previously reinforced in that setting.[43]

It is similarly difficult to see the value of some other intrinsic-reinforcement concepts that have been postulated to account for imitation in the apparent absence of extrinsic reinforcement. These concepts include Aronfreed's (1967, 1968, 1969) "affective value," Kohlberg's (1966) "motives" for "mastery" and "interesting" consequences, and the conditioned-reinforcement concept as used by Mowrer (1950, 1960b). As they have no independent operational status in the imitation context, these concepts as presently formulated can only be inferred from the very imitative behaviors they have been devised to explain. Therefore, in no way do such concepts advance the analyses or facilitate the research purposes of those theorists, for each of them still has the tactical problem of determining the environmental conditions that differentially affect acquisition and maintenance of the child's imitative responding.

In contrast, our functional analysis has assumed that many behaviors that appear to be acquired on the basis of observational learning in the presence of "intrinsic" reinforcement may in fact be functionally attributable to the operation

---

[43]Their stress on the conditioned reinforcer apparently had two purposes: to explain the emergence of new, topographically different imitative behaviors prior to any reinforcement of them; and to account for the continued strength of those behaviors thereafter despite consistent nonreinforcement of them. D. M. Baer (personal communication) has indicated that the emphasis on the role of the assumed conditioned reinforcer in the Baer et al. (1965) analysis represents a preliminary attempt to conceptualize the mode of acquisition of functional response classes, and is thus concerned with the general issue involving the formation of all such classes and not just with imitation. In this connection also, the argument that systematic improvement in the topography of an imitative response without extrinsic reinforcement operating (as reported, e.g., by Lovaas et al., 1966) requires a conditioned-reinforcer concept like that of Baer and his associates is not tenable, without ruling out many conditions confounded with practice that could be the basis for this improvement.

of extrinsic reinforcers. It assumes also that mastery sequences and interesting consequences can (be isolated to) function as extrinsic reinforcers for child behavior. Hence, it represents one solution to the deficiencies noted in the above intrinsic-reinforcement approaches. The simpler model proposed in this section appears to be the most parsimonious of the extant models to account for the original acquisition and the subsequent maintenance of the imitative response class. It is based on relatively few, well-defined concepts that are the same as those used in analyses of less complex animal behavior, and it does not single out for special emphasis concepts that in principle should be observable, without making independent provision in the experimental context to index such concepts operationally.

Observational learning.   Through the years, there has been considerable controversy among learning approaches, in the realms of both theory and research, as to whether or not (observational) learning can occur in the absence of responses by the viewing organism (and of reinforcement) (Kimble, 1961). Comparative-psychological research has also not been definitive as to whether or not (observational) learning can occur in some subhuman species independent of prior matching-response occurrence and reinforcement. In this context, Bandura (1962, 1965b, 1969) has catalogued evidence that children exhibit matching responses (even after delays) following observation of models' responses (whether reinforced or not), when there has been no apparent opportunity for the occurrence (practice) of the observing child's matching responses and therefore no extrinsic reinforcing stimuli provided contingent on those responses. On the basis of this evidence and the S-S learning assumptions he favors, Bandura has therefore opted to emphasize "no-trial" observational learning as the mechanism for the acquisition of imitative responses by children. In this context, he has faulted instrumental-conditioning theories for requiring that matching responses be performed and reinforced before they can be acquired. It has been noted that Aronfreed (1967, 1968, 1969) and Kohlberg (1966) similarly emphasize, although perhaps on different grounds, observational learning as the basis for the acquisition of imitation.

Even so, Bandura (1965a) has noted that extrinsic reinforcement of matching responses is inevitable during human social development, where models typically exhibit responses from cultural repertoires proved effective in the stimulus settings. As he himself has observed, observational-learning effects apparently demonstrated in experimental work with children may thus simply reflect prior instrumental learning, for which the requisite control conditions cannot be implemented practically. (In fact, Bandura believes that definitive tests of this theoretical issue may require the use of infrahuman Ss whose reinforcement histories can be readily controlled.)

Given the current theoretical indeterminacy of the issue of learning without response occurrence in instrumental life settings, and the fact that assumed observational-learning effects that are clearly free of prior positive (or even negative) extrinsic reinforcement for responses matched to those of models are improbable in early-childhood contexts, we have chosen to emphasize how what Bandura and others have termed observational-learning outcomes can be plausibly explained by the routine intermittent extrinsic reinforcement of overt matching responses that provides the basis for generalized imitation. Our heuristic concern is thus to illustrate, in a manner continuous with analyses in the literature of other functional response classes in simple organisms and settings, how basic instrumental-conditioning procedures thought to be commonly involved in adult-child interaction can credibly account for the acquisition and maintenance of responses matched to (cues provided by) models' responses. That is, we attempt to show how one must *learn* to learn through exposure to models' responses.

It is our conception that intermittent extrinsic reinforcement for imitation of the varied responses of a range of models can account for the child's frequent (generalized) imitation of both the reinforced and nonreinforced responses of a model. The appearance that the child has not exhibited the response, and that he has not received extrinsic reinforcement when he did imitate, can be explained by the facts that: (a) there can be lengthy delays between the model's response and the child's imitation of it; (b) the functional, matching-response class will vary in content; and (c) the reinforcement is intermittent. Both observational learning and our concept of generalized imitation involve the subject's matching his response to the response of a model in a given discriminative context, and, in our view, therefore, may be functionally equivalent through the range of settings in which the two terms are used. As the generalized-imitation concept can account, in terms of a few key assumptions, for most or all of the phenomena grouped under the observational learning of young humans, and because extrinsically reinforced imitative performance is likely to characterize a child's experience in life settings prior to his exposure to a model in observational-learning research designs where this factor has been typically uncontrolled, the generalized-imitation concept would seem to be a parsimonious one for approaching the general problem of explaining behavioral matching. This concept can provide a useful context for much of the research that remains to be done, and, at the very least, a context for the controls that remain to be implemented in research on the question of observational learning in young humans.

Vicarious reinforcement is a special case of observational learning, in which positive *reinforcement* administered *to a model* contingent upon a particular behavior is said to increase the likelihood that an observing child will copy that behavior (cf., e.g., Hill, 1960; Bandura, 1962; Bandura, Ross & Ross, 1963). In our view a parsimonious (and plausible) explanation of this phenomenon is that the responses by the child which are similar to those for which a model is reinforced are frequently likely to be extrinsically reinforced in the same settings, whether emitted independently or matched to a model's responses; whereas the child's responses like those for which a model is not reinforced or for which he is punished are *not* likely to be reinforced. Often unknown to the viewer, therefore, the model's reinforced response is already in the child's repertoire due to its having been extrinsically reinforced earlier. This is possible particularly if the response is a likely one in the given context, and if extrinsic reinforcement is also likely there. Furthermore, after the child has been reinforced for imitation of several of a model's reinforced responses in a given context, reinforcement provided contingent upon a particular behavior of a model should come to function as a generalized cue for a high probability of extrinsic reinforcement to the child when he imitates that behavior. (Walters, Parke & Cane [1965] have similarly regarded reinforcement to the model in an experimental context as a cue indicating the "permissibility"of reproducing that behavior.) This conception would be one way to account for Bandura's (1965a) finding that, after observing a film in which various hostile-hurting behaviors of the model were reinforced, children emitted a greater variety of such imitative responses than did those children who saw the model's aggressive responses punished. Indeed, Bandura (1965b, 1969) and Aronfreed (1969) have noted this and several other ways in which reinforcing stimuli contingent upon the model's behavior could provide discriminative stimuli that facilitate or inhibit imitative behaviors, particularly in ambiguous settings.

In terms of this analysis, it would be expected that if the child has not already learned this discrimination pattern, its acquisition will depend only on his subsequent exposure to the proper discriminative occasions. Furthermore, if discriminative conditions were reversed, that is, if the observer were reinforced relatively less often for imitating behaviors for which the model is reinforced and more often for alternative behaviors, reinforcement to the model could come to serve as a discriminative stimulus for alternative behaviors, and vicarious reinforcement could thus be ineffective or its effects reversed in relation to the observer's behavior. For example, Miller and Dollard (1941) demonstrated that children could learn nonimitation of a choice response for which a peer model was reinforced, and that this learning could generalize to other situations.

Life Conditions for Learning Generalized Imitation

Conditions in life settings make our analysis particularly appropriate in accounting for the rapid acquisition of topographically accurate imitative behavior sequences that typically occurs. Theorists like Mowrer (1960b) and Bandura (1962) have argued that a trial-and-error process would be too slow to account for this rapid acquisition. However, that point does not seem cogent when one considers the abundance of extrinsic reinforcement occasions and efficient shaping processes during all stages of the child's development, particularly for response classes like imitation. Because these reinforcers come from a variety of sources, on an intermittent schedule overall, and for diverse imitative behaviors, generalized imitation will be acquired relatively early in the child's socialization, maintained at high strength, and be relatively resistant to change. This is in keeping with the observation that gross imitative behaviors appear to occur early in life (Walters & Parke, 1965). Although, as a learned social behavior, imitation should be reversible, its extinction would rarely occur, since strict elimination of reinforcement for such pervasive response classes is unlikely to be implemented in complex life settings.

Parents often deliberately set out to teach the child to imitate, using direct tuition, shaping, and fading of the sort employed by Baer et al. (1965, 1967) or Lovaas et al. (1966). The child's imitation can be highly reinforcing *to* parents or models (i.e., when contingent on their behaviors). Sometimes a parent may himself imitate the child, either as a spontaneous response or as a step in the process of teaching him to imitate. Among other effects, this may facilitate the child's discrimination of the degree of similarity between his and the model's responses, and can constitute steps in a shaping procedure wherein the child's response is matched to the model's with increasing closeness through successive approximations. This procedure very likely plays an important role in the child's language learning.

Indeed, it is thought that generalized imitation constitutes a most important basis for the initial occurrence and acquisition of many language responses by the child, and for the subsequent expansion of his language repertory, and may play an even more important role in this acquisition than does simple direct instrumental training without matching. Once such verbal responses are acquired, they will be maintained by responses made to them in conversational inter-changes, according to the same principles that account for the maintenance of any other responses.

Behaviors of the child that are in the direction of increasing competence and are thus reinforced by socializing agents are almost invariably behaviors the child has observed older models perform (e.g., walking, talking, writing), and his performance of those behaviors is frequently reinforced in the presence of models who are exhibiting them. In a sense, these behaviors are also imitative. Thus, reinforcement for progress toward increasing competence can at the same time be reinforcement for generalized imitation. As the child is subjected increasingly to the socialization process with age, the behaviors for which he is reinforced will change with his growing capacities. The agents reinforcing him will also vary and increase in number, each reinforcing on a different schedule and for different behaviors. In the face of this continual change, one thing remains constant for the child: the imitative response class continues to be reinforced at a high rate throughout his development.

Like other social behaviors, the appropriateness of imitative responses varies from one situation to another. Thus, the imitative behavioral unit usually includes a *discriminative occasion* indicating that an imitative response is likely to be reinforced. Reinforceable occasions may be preceded by an explicit verbal cue, like "Susy, do this" of Baer et al. (1965, 1967), or by a less explicit cue indicating that imitation is appropriate. The imitator learns to discriminate those cue stimuli from cues indicating that noncopying, complementary interactive responses—for instance, dependence—are appropriate. For example, based on differential reinforcement of the child's behaviors in the past, the model's *being oriented toward* the child (physically or otherwise), or his *not being occupied* in some ongoing activity, may acquire discriminative stimulus value for the child's emitting *complementary* interaction responses and for suppressing copying responses, which would be clearly inappropriate. Imitative behaviors are more likely to be reinforced when the model is busily engaged in a *solitary* activity and can more readily reinforce the child's parallel behaviors (like imitation) than his approach or interactive behaviors (like dependence), since the model can then continue his activity without long interruption. If the child is frequently reinforced for making disruptive (dependency) initiations in this situation, he may not learn to discriminate that such behaviors are inappropriate and may interrupt the model at will, thus in extreme cases becoming what could be termed "spoiled." It is possible that such children do not learn to imitate to as great an extent as children whose models discourage interruptions of the model's task. It is also likely that at the same time they do not acquire autonomous task-oriented behavior patterns independent of frequent reinforcement from their socializing agents.

There remains a considerable need for a detailed analysis of the discriminative cues that indicate to the child, in specific and more general cases, when it is appropriate to imitate (i.e., when imitation is likely to be reinforced) and which model it is most appropriate to imitate when alternative models are available. An analysis from our intentionally simple approach would attend only in passing to developmental changes in imitative behaviors and learning that occur in typical life settings. Our conception of generalized-imitation learning is not incompatible with cognitive-developmental analyses based on observation of life settings, like Piaget's (1951) conception of "stages" of imitation (with developmental increases in its generality and autonomy) and other naturalistic approaches that stress changes in the child's capacities during the early years as well as developmental differences in the organization of imitative behaviors. However, we assume that the basic mode of acquisition and maintenance of imitation is not altered by such developmental changes.

Focused versus nonfocused generalized imitation. The generalized-imitation paradigm as we have used it until now has been relatively *non*focused with regard to the model imitated, summarizing imitation of diverse responses of many models. Yet an important case where such imitation appears to be *focused* on one particular model more than on others often occurs. This model is usually a parent, and the focused imitation involved is thought to provide an important basis for identification, as will be detailed in a coming section of this chapter. Such a selective imitation pattern can result from a combination of relatively frequent or even exclusive contact with (and chances to observe) one model and frequent reinforcement by the model or by others for imitating a variety of the behaviors of that model. That model's behaviors will therefore acquire discriminative value for the child, indicating that his imitation of them has an even higher probability of being reinforced than does imitation in general.

Much of the child's early socialization takes place in the family setting, where he interacts with parents and siblings. Although a differential distribution of the child's interaction with the members of his family is bound to result, it should be less important for his generalized-imitation learning than should differential reinforcement for imitation of those members. Children of both sexes typically interact more with their mothers than with their fathers, but the boy comes to imitate his father and the girl her mother because of differential reinforcement for copying each of them. As noted earlier, the child will be reinforced for imitating different models in diverse contexts. In the family setting, however, on the basis of being differentially reinforced for imitation, he will discriminate which single model it is usually most appropriate to imitate; and because of frequent chances to observe that model, the child will imitate an extensive range of his behaviors. More will be said on this issue in a subsequent section on sex-typing.

This distinction between focused and nonfocused generalized imitation is analogous to the one between focused attachment (to a particular object-person) and nonfocused social dependence (on a class of persons) made earlier (Gewirtz, 1961b), and is elaborated in the subsequent section on dependence-attachment.

Generalized Imitation Extended

We have shown thus far that generalized-imitation learning based on extrinsic reinforcement (a) can account plausibly for the acquisition and maintenance of imitative responses in the apparent absence of extrinsic reinforcement (a condition that has been termed "intrinsic" reinforcement by a number of writers), (b) can be facilitated by the heavy extrinsic reinforcement of developmental behavioral advances by the child in the presence of models performing those responses, (c) can be focused on a single model under the proper circumstances, and (d) can come under the discriminative control of gross behavioral settings in which the model is engaged. The generalized-imitation concept can account for related behavioral phenomena which will be relevant to our analysis of identification. These include imitation of the model's behavior in his absence, imitation of a large portion of a model's behavior role in play settings, and wide-ranging similarities in abstract values or attitudes.

Imitation in the model's absence. Delayed imitation, which includes imitation of the model's behavior in his absence, can be regarded as a simple variant of the generalized-imitation paradigm. Also pertinent to observational learning, this point becomes clearer when one considers that all imitative behaviors occur *after* the model's performance, providing the relevant cues, has terminated and often while the child is not looking at the model, and in that sense they are *always* performed in the absence of the model. The delay between the model's performance and the imitative behavior may be further lengthened through shaping techniques, implemented either deliberately or in an unplanned way by reinforcing agents. Immediate direct reinforcement for delayed imitation in the model's absence may frequently be provided by agents other than the model, and sometimes in the form of statements like "you are acting just like your father" or "like a big boy." In addition, the agent may indicate explicitly that what is being reinforced is not only performance of the response, but its performance in the model's absence.

Imitation of the model in play.   Imitation of large segments of a model's behavior role in play situations where the model is not present may also be facilitated by ecological factors. Props given to the child can be appropriate to the model's role, as in the case of toy kitchen utensils being made available to a young girl. Reinforcement can be provided through the reciprocal role play of other children, or through occasional direct reinforcement by the model or other adult witnesses. These toys may serve a dual purpose, in that they can also provide a sanctioned discriminable context for the child's imitation of a model's behaviors in his absence when these behaviors might be hazardous or inappropriate in their usual context.

Generalized imitation of values.   The generalized-imitation concept can also be extended readily to account for wide-ranging similarities in abstract values (attitudes, life styles, or motives). For example, often a child will act as the model might in a situation even if he has not actually witnessed the model in that situation, or he will strive for the same goals as the model. (We shall see in the next section that these behaviors are often termed identification.)

An example of a model's value is "tidy housekeeping." A mother's behavior may exemplify that value, and her daughter either may be directly reinforced for nonimitative tidying responses or may exhibit these responses through simple generalized imitation (with or without extrinsic reinforcement). An important assumption for extending our analysis is that a daughter generally reinforced for acting like her mother may come to discriminate the common elements of responses exhibited by the model in a class of related stimulus contexts (such as housekeeping), which she might also inductively characterize with a statement like, "Mom keeps a tidy house." The child's value is based on her discrimination of such a functional class of the model's responses (some would term it a "concept"), which would then apply to situations in which the child, as generalized-imitator, may not actually have seen the model perform. The daughter may also exhibit verbal responses that reflect the value, for instance, "It's good to keep the house tidy," which have been acquired together with tidy housekeeping responses via generalized-imitation learning. Although some of the daughter's responses may be quite different in topography from those of her mother (because of changed climatic conditions, technological and socio-economic levels, etc.), they will produce the same outcome: a tidy house. Once the value has been acquired in this manner, the mother and other environmental agents are likely to reinforce the resulting responses, and the value will be maintained. As is true of all learned behaviors, however, the performance of a value will depend on the continuation of the same reinforcement matrix for the class of responses implying that value, and thus it is potentially subject to change.

Thus far, the analysis has stressed primarily those situations in which cues from the model and extrinsic reinforcement to the child provide the context for the child's imitative behaviors. The above examples show the potential utility of the generalized-imitation paradigm in situations where some of the relevant discriminative and reinforcing stimuli for imitation are absent.

Identification

The concept of *identification* has been used, particularly in psychoanalytic approaches, to indicate the child's acquisition of the values, ideals, roles, and conscience of an important other person (the model), particularly those of his parents and especially the same-sex parent. The term has been used variously to refer to the process by which these characteristics are acquired, to the person's desire to possess the characteristics of the model and his belief that he does, and to the resulting similarity of behavior patterns. Several of these usages are often found in the same analysis. The identification term has also been used as if it were a unitary concept that involves a single, incompletely specified complex paradigm with demographically defined independent variables (e.g., gender of subject in an intact nuclear family) and no consensually valid dependent variable. In this analysis, the generalized-imitation paradigm, as detailed in the preceding section, becomes a parsimonious basis for the phenomena usually grouped under the identification concept.

The earliest approaches to the phenomena of identification occurred within the frame of psychoanalytic theory, and much of identification theory still relies on these early attempts. While Freud dealt with identification in a scattered way through half a century of his writing, and there were apparent variations in his approach, he seems to have employed the term in at least two ways: as a *process* and as the behavior-similarity *outcome* of that process. Thus, Freud (1933) regarded identification as the process by which "one ego becomes like another one, which results in the first ego behaving . . . in certain respects in the same way as the second; it imitates it, and as it were takes it into itself" (p. 90). And, in one of his writings, Freud's (1920) index of the outcome of identification was imitation of the model's behaviors. When assumed to result from complete instrumental dependence upon and an emotional tie to the model (typically the parent), identification has been termed "anaclitic" in Freud's approach and by Sears (1957; Sears et al., 1965) and "developmental" by Mowrer (1950); while "aggressive" or "defensive" identification (A. Freud, 1937; Mowrer, 1950) is assumed to result from fear of punishment from the model, with the child avoiding punishment by becoming like the model. The child's super-ego, the locus of self-observation, conscience, and ideals, is assumed to be based largely on this type of identification and to be built upon the model of the parents' super-ego rather than on their actual behavior.

Although many would agree that the child can learn to imitate a range of behaviors on the basis of simple instrumental (trial-and-error) learning (as involved in generalized imitation), imitation has typically been treated in the literature as somehow distinct from identification. Thus, despite an early instance where Freud (1920) used imitation to index identification, the typical psycho-analytic view appears to be that the relatively precise matching to the model's overt behavior in imitation is a transient, symptomatic, surface process, whereas the wider ranging, less precise behavioral matching in identification results from a more fundamental and dynamic underlying process.

Kohlberg (1963) has proposed that identification differs from imitation in three ways: (1) identification is a "motivated disposition" because of the intrinsic reinforcing properties of perceived similarity to the model; (2) similarity between the behaviors of the subject and the model often occurs in the absence of the model; and (3) many aspects of the model's behavior are reproduced. These factors appear to have been the bases for many theorists' considering identification as a "higher-order" process than generalized imitation.[44]

Within the learning-theory tradition, Miller and Dollard (1941) in a brief comment suggested that imitation mechanisms are also involved in identification, while Seward (1954) suggested that identification is a high-level abstraction from numerous imitative habits. Bandura (1962) and Bandura and Walters (1963) have noted that observational learning is often termed imitation in behavior-theory approaches to personality development and identification in more traditional personality theories, with no substantial differences between the two usages. In our similar view, often the only reason that generalized-imitation learning is assumed inadequate to account for identification phenomena is that factors like a motivation to be like, an emotional attachment to, or envy of, the model that are assumed relevant for identification are just not considered at all relevant to generalized imitation and are often thought to be outside the sphere of simple learning.

Generalized imitation as the basis for identification.   Such distinctions may have made the analysis of identification needlessly complex. They also point up the necessity for a more systematic approach to identification phenomena and their underlying mechanism(s). It was shown earlier that: (a) the seemingly intrinsic reinforcing property of certain behavior classes, including imitation, depends entirely upon occasional extrinsic reinforcement of members of that class; and that (b) the performance of diverse imitative behaviors in the absence of the model is also accountable by straightforward application of the generalized-imitation paradigm, as is (c) the tendency to focus generalized imitation on one model and to imitate not only a range of his overt behaviors, but also behaviors implied in such general dispositions as are often termed motives, values, or attitudes. In this way, it has been automatically proposed under the functional approach of this chapter that most, if not all, of the phenomena usually grouped under the rubric of identification may reasonably be assumed to be the direct consequences of generalized-imitation training, and thus can be reduced to that more parsimonious instrumental-training conception.

---

[44]More recently, Kohlberg (1966) has proposed that attachment follows (generalized) imitation, and that the combination of these two factors leads to identification, but it is not clear what the roles of the above three criteria are in his recent approach.

It appears that another distinction implicit in most definitions of imitation and identification is that while both terms refer to behaviors matched to those of a model, the latter behaviors are maintained exclusively by social stimuli while the former may be maintained by both social and nonsocial ones. Thus, all identificatory acts may be imitative but not all imitative acts are identificatory. Because the specification of which stimulus contexts and reinforcers are social is often arbitrary, we contend that in a similar manner the distinction between identification and imitation is to a large degree an arbitrary semantic one with no fundamental differences in the way in which they are learned. Under a learning analysis, the major reason we would prefer to use a single term like social imitation rather than both imitation and identification is that the use of both terms implies that such differences exist and are meaningful, an implication that can only cloud the issue. The use of more learning-oriented terms precludes such interpretations and facilitates the fitting of existing and future data on identification processes into a framework that allows us to tie in other important aspects of the learning process more easily.

Thus, it often appears that the only real distinction between identification and generalized imitation may be in the less precise, more complex, and more inclusive way that the identification process is typically defined: the major response class subsumed under the identification concept is that of generalized imitation, controlled by the discriminative stimuli provided by the model's behaviors. (For some, this apparent identity would eliminate the need for a separate concept of identification.) Further, a large number of loosely related and often overlapping terms at varying levels of conceptual analysis, like introjection, incorporation, internalization, modeling, rote copying, and sex-typing, all of which lead to similarities between the model's and the identifier's behavior patterns, are included under identification. This situation has further complicated the concept of identification and appears to have implied, as an artifact, a larger number of seemingly distinct processes than is warranted. The level from which such concepts typically are approached makes it difficult to make clear-cut differentiations between identification and overlapping concepts like introjection or sex-typing. Reduction of these terms to the same level of analysis in basic paradigms open to a learning analysis is necessary and may show that apparent differences among them can be attributed to the methods of measurement, the segments of the stream of behavior emphasized, the particular stimuli evoking the responses, and the functional reinforcers available, factors that do not ordinarily justify separate paradigms. Such a reduction can be implemented by regarding identification concepts as based on the simpler generalized-imitation paradigm, with behavioral similarity as the outcome. For example, *introjection* is often defined as the act of incorporating a value system in its entirety, with identification as its result (Fuchs, 1937). Thus, while introjection appears to refer to the acquisition process and identification to its result, those terms may only reflect emphasis on different stages in the behavior process by which generalized imitation is learned and maintained, with introjection pointing to a somewhat earlier phase of the learning than does identification. The use of two different terms therefore seems to emphasize arbitrarily what may for most purposes be a trivial distinction.

Similarly, *sex-typing* usually denotes identification by the child with models of his own sex, and has itself been broken down further into sex-role identification, sex-role preference, and sex-role adoption (Lynn, 1959). Thus, the term sex-typing refers to the shaping of the child's behaviors to match behaviors specifically appropriate to his gender. These behaviors are usually assumed to be acquired through observation of a model or a class of models. So defined, they can be regarded as the result of generalized imitation, with the gender of the model serving as a discriminative stimulus for a higher frequency of extrinsic (immediate or delayed) reinforcement for imitation. Kohlberg (1966) has reported that a shift from generalized imitation of the mother to imitation of the father typically occurs in boys between ages four and seven, which he interpreted as reflecting changes in boys' conceptualization of age and sex roles. The approach being advanced in this chapter is open to such possibilities, but we would conceive them as resulting from a systematic shift in the discriminative conditions under which imitative behaviors are reinforced. Mischel (1966a) has reviewed a number of other results of sex-typing studies done to date and interpreted them from a learning approach very much like ours.

At this point in its evolution, the research area of identification can benefit from a deliberate approach, both theoretical and operational. In the context of a profusion of overlapping concepts and the need to reduce the frequently used demographic independent variables to component functional stimuli, the salient issues for our analysis must be operational, such as whether or not discriminative stimuli for imitation are present and whether or not functional extrinsic reinforcers follow imitative responses. In addition to reducing demographic variables to a more useful level of analysis, such factors can provide the basis for distinguishing among possibly diverse paradigms. By attending to the actual stimuli, responses, and the sequential details of their interaction, this level of analysis makes possible a flexible, individual-oriented approach to identification phenomena. Although in representative life settings some general outcomes do occur, e.g., children typically do imitate behaviors appropriate to their sex category, this approach provides greater precision and flexibility in detailing the history of the individual child in question in terms of what similarity behaviors have been acquired and how they are evoked and maintained. But equally important, it can also highlight the conditions responsible for a failure to acquire particular identification behaviors and the conditions that may facilitate, extinguish, or otherwise modify such behaviors. Reversibility or change in identification-behavior patterns is almost never assumed or tested, yet is a perfectly reasonable corollary of the conception of learning, in representative life settings as in the laboratory. A functional analysis such as we propose would also make it possible to determine which antecedent process determines a particular behavior-similarity outcome and whether or not there are different combinations of antecedents that could lead to an identical outcome. The continuous differentiation process involved would lead routinely to new concept groupings and labels, with previously unidentified but relevant phenomena brought under the identification concept and ordered by novel or derived paradigms.

Empirical research studies of identification have quite reasonably employed behavioral similarity[45] between the child and his parents as a measure of identification (though often, when verbal reports have provided these indices, the variables generated were at too removed a level to allow precise leverage on the process). At the level of analysis emphasized here, direct measures of similarity between the child's and the adult's responses (including those summarized as traits) in structured stimulus settings would be useful operational indices of identification, with variations in discriminative and reinforcement parameters as independent variables. It will be necessary to show in such settings that the behaviors of the child that are termed identification are acquired under the control of the discriminative cues provided by the model's behaviors rather than being determined by environmental constraints or independent but parallel acquisition processes, and that they are, in the absence of the model, under the control of the same discriminative stimuli as were the model's behaviors.

The present approach, then, regards the development of identification behaviors as due to extrinsic reinforcement of the child's imitation of his parent's (or model's) behaviors. The degree to which a child is identified with a particular model is thus grossly determined by the value to the child of the reinforcers contingent upon his imitation of that person's behavior. His identification will also be a function of the amount of exposure to other potential models and reinforcement for imitating them, the frequency of reinforcement for original, nonimitative behaviors, and the value of the reinforcers provided for each of these behavior classes. In this way, as is seen in a later section on whether or not dependence-attachment and imitation-identification are sequentially related, attachment may enter peripherally, in that it grossly abstracts the discriminative and reinforcing value of stimuli dispensed by a particular person. Identification with the model at the level of abstract values may require finer discriminations by the child but, as has already been shown, should follow the same principles as generalized imitation.

The advantages of this functional approach are evident when one looks at such work as that by Lovaas (1967) with schizophrenic children. Besides teaching the children to imitate vocalizations and to converse, as was described earlier, Lovaas reinforced nonverbal imitation in order to teach behaviors in the areas of personal hygiene, games, drawing, and affectionate behavior, with the intention of eventually shifting the control of these behaviors (by fading procedures) away from the model to control by more appropriate or general stimuli. Noting that the behaviors learned by these children were neither as representative nor did they occur in as wide a range of settings as those covered by such terms as identification, Lovaas nevertheless implied that bringing about this more extensive imitation is not incompatible with the procedures he has been using and may primarily involve increasing the reinforcing value of stimuli from the model and

---

[45]For instance, in responses to projective tests or paper and pencil questionnaires.

others. Thus, besides permitting a more precise evaluation of the factors involved in the child's failure to identify, this approach suggests specific areas of attack to remedy the deficiencies.

Let me at this point summarize the argument developed thus far in this chapter. After basic instrumental-conditioning and S-R chaining concepts were employed to order many of the assumed complexities of generalized imitation, it was proposed that the phenomena usually grouped under the rubric of identification can also be reduced, under a discriminated-operant learning model, to this more parsimonious conception of generalized imitation and its direct extensions. We have not advocated this approach for the sake of reduction per se, but rather to bring these phenomena to a level at which they will be dealt with more productively. Since identification phenomena involve systematic changes in behavior effected by recurring environmental conditions, a learning analysis is appropriate, and its use makes immediately available a wealth of knowledge about the functioning of stimuli and responses. Under a systematic learning approach to identification phenomena, the relevant behaviors are potentially subject to acquisition, discrimination, facilitation, extinction, and other modifications, according to well-established laws of behavior. The study of such modifications would be in contrast to the typical approach to identification, in which the effects are for the most part assumed to be long-term, and reversibility or change in the process is never tested and almost never even assumed.

The role of motivation in identification.   Hindley (1957) has assumed that an acquired drive underlies imitation when, following acquisition based on extrinsic reinforcement, it continues to occur in the absence of extrinsic reinforcement. Bronfenbrenner (1960) has argued that the identification concept cannot be reduced to a notion like "acquired similarity" because in the process one would risk losing sight of Freud's view of identification as what Bronfenbrenner termed a "sweeping and powerful phenomenon" involving the tendency of the child to take on a *total* pattern of the parental model's behavior with an emotional intensity that implies a powerful "motive in the child to become like the parent" (p. 27). Within a learning framework, Sears (1957) has written similarly of a *motive* to become like the model as the basis for the child's adopting total patterns of the parent model's behavior without apparent specific training (although he later questioned the utility of the motive construct [Sears et al., 1965]). As the mother's nurturant responses become secondary (conditioned) reinforcers for the child, he is conceived by Sears to acquire a secondary dependency drive and can partially gratify this drive by performing similar responses himself (an assumption not unlike Mowrer's [1950]).

Apart from these remarks, neither Bronfenbrenner nor Sears has detailed the implications of the use of a motivational concept for identification. They may intend it only to reflect the pervasiveness of the imitative behaviors across many behavior contents and settings or, with Hindley (1957) and Kohlberg (1963), to reflect the apparent intrinsically reinforcing properties of such behaviors, or with Kohlberg to reflect its involving a particular model. However, we have seen that the generalized-imitation response class discussed in this chapter is also pervasive, can occur without apparent extrinsic reinforcement, and can be focused on one model. Moreover, Kohlberg (1966) has recently written of the acquisition and performance of imitation and identification as being motivated by a "drive" for "competence-mastery" and "interesting" events. This conception in no way advances his analysis either, for there still remains the tactical problem of determining the conditions that differentially affect the child's imitative responding. Finally, because of their excess meaning, there is no advantage to introducing motivational terms in analyses such as these, when these terms can be readily replaced by concepts more coordinated to operations—like intermittently reinforced generalized imitation indexed by behavioral similarity.

The role of reinforcement in identification.   One issue on which the approach to identification in this chapter differs from many others is in the importance we assign to extrinsic reinforcement of imitative behaviors in the acquisition of identification. Our approach also differs from some others in that they implicitly or explicitly employ cognitive-flavored abstractions or intrapsychic euphemisms as mechanisms to account for identification phenomena, while we rely entirely on sets of responses maintained by extrinsic reinforcement. Thus, Kagan (1958) has assumed that the child identifies with an adult whom he sees being rewarded because he *believes* that by possessing the model's characteristics and thus becoming similar to the model he, too, will command the attractive goal states that the model controls. In a similar vein, regarding the caretaker as the mediator of valued resources, Whiting (1960) and Burton and Whiting (1961) have assumed that the child's identification with the caretaker (as in learning his role) is motivated by *envy* of him because he can withhold the resources from the child or receive and consume them himself (implying control). In both analyses, extrinsic reinforcement of the child's imitative behaviors is only implied and is not considered essential for identification.

A basic assumption in our approach is that the child comes to copy diverse responses performed by his parent-models because he is consistently reinforced directly for diverse representatives of that class of behaviors, perhaps even more consistently than for behaviors that he initiates on his own. The class of copying responses is highly likely to culminate in extrinsic reinforcers in a variety of settings and from many sources, both social and nonsocial. The assumption here is that many imitative behaviors may occur without extrinsic reinforcement, but only *after* the response class has initially been established in the child's behavioral repertoire by direct reinforcement and only if it is still being directly reinforced at least occasionally. Then will the child appear to fit Kagan's or Whiting's specifications. Regardless of how often the model is rewarded in the presence of the child, we do not conceive of the child's imitating him (identifying) unless the child himself is at least occasionally rewarded for it. Likewise, the withholding of reinforcement from the child can be effective only if in other situations or for other behaviors such reinforcement is not withheld. In the terms of our analysis, the model would make the withheld resources available to the child contingent upon various classes of behavior, one of which is likely to be imitation. What seems appreciated too little by many theorists is the ability of intermittent, even infrequent, extrinsic reinforcement to maintain an extensive class of behaviors, many of which are *never* reinforced, as has been well established by the research of Baer et al. (1965, 1967) and Lovaas et al. (1966) and the context of behavioral technology from which these studies spring. At the same time, such research clearly demonstrates the necessity of at least occasional reinforcement in the acquisition and maintenance of a behavior class.

Fear and identification.   For heuristic simplicity, this analysis has avoided the use of "fear" concepts (e.g., of rejection or of punishment, or "anxiety") often used in identification theories. An example is the assumed fear basis of defensive identification (A. Freud, 1937; Mowrer, 1950). The paradigms for those defensive concepts are compatible with the ones advanced for the acquisition and maintenance of generalized imitation, except that they may imply different classes of reinforcers, such as the removal or avoidance of a noxious stimulus. Self-critical responses and others labeled "guilt" or "resistance to temptation" reflecting "internalized controls" or "conscience" can undoubtedly be reinforced by such consequences, but they can also be acquired through the direct positive reinforcement processes we have emphasized.

2. Dependence-Attachment

In this section, we examine some theoretical and research issues that have characterized the behavior systems grouped under the rubrics of dependence and attachment. We have already seen that the problem for the molar behaviorist is to articulate the manner in which differential stimulation facilitates and comes to control the behaviors of the organism. Under this logic, and with the results of the research to date kept in the forefront, the attempt is made to reduce to simple terms the complexities of the behaviors which characterize dependence and attachment, and to posit basic acquisition processes to relate those behaviors to the multiplicity of environmental conditions to which children are typically subject. As did our earlier examination of imitation-identification, the analysis proceeds in simple conditioning terms, using the concepts of responses, discriminative and reinforcing stimuli, and the conception of sequential contingencies or chaining.

An analysis of the behavior organizations termed dependence and attachment is considered fundamental for an understanding of the key controlling attributes of human social life, at all developmental points. In our previous survey of instrumental learning in social contexts and its application to generalized imitation, emphasis was placed mainly on the principles of behavior acquisition and maintenance, and hardly at all on content. However, the analysis of dependence and attachment upon which we are now embarking emphasizes the identities (content) of classes of stimuli and responses in addition to assumptions about behavior acquisition and maintenance, and promises another basis for bridging the present gaps between basic learning and performance concepts and principles that have been identified, and the actual conditions of earliest parent-child interaction. Our purpose, then, continues to be the eduction of some specific laws of learning to the special case of the developing human, but in this case, in addition, it involves an increased emphasis on stimulus and response content.

Meaning and Usage of Dependence and Attachment

To date, few articulate theories have been advanced on the nature or dimensionality of socioemotional *dependence* (dependency) and *attachment* (relationship, bond, tie) or on their antecedents. It seems reasonable to approach questions about the mechanisms underlying the development of dependence and attachment in terms of assumptions about the nature of social learning and to order the conditions characterizing the acquisition of and changes in relationships between the initially helpless child and the persons in his environment in terms of conditioning concepts. This is done with a view toward charting the acquisition of various forms of dependence and attachment, in the context of transformations in response systems and changes in the identity of other persons involved as occur during the course of an individual's development.

In such an analysis, dependence and attachment are best conceptualized as abstractions for classes of functional relationships involving the positive stimulus control over a wide variety of an individual's responses by stimuli provided either by a class of persons (dependence) or by a particular person (attachment). Thus, in dependence, an individual's behavior systems are controlled by discriminative and reinforcing stimuli which may be dispensed by any member of a *class* of persons who share certain stimulus characteristics (e.g., as those involved in sex, race, age, or caretaking role). In contrast, in attachment, the efficacy of discriminative and reinforcing stimuli in controlling an individual's behavior systems depends upon the unique physical and/or behavioral characteristics of a *particular* "object" person dispensing those stimuli (e.g., his facial stimuli, tactile characteristics). In principle, a child could be said to form attachments to more than one person, in the sense that certain of his behavior systems could be controlled by the (discriminative and reinforcing) stimuli provided by the unique characteristics of a particular person, while other of his behavior systems could be determined by different stimuli provided by the unique characteristics of another person. This type of differential control by a very few individuals is not to be confused with the pattern of stimulus control over child behaviors that we have termed dependence, which involves the homogeneous power over a set of child behaviors that is exhibited by the common stimuli that may be provided by any one member of a large class of persons. This distinction between nonfocused social dependence and focused attachment points up the differences between the two sets of phenomena, but it also emphasizes the similarities and overlap as well as the probable communalities of antecedents. That is, attachment can be conceived as a form of (social) dependence of the behavior systems of one person upon the unique physical and behavioral stimuli provided by a particular other person (or a very few individuals), for instance, a child and his parent or caretaker.

Instrumental dependence involves the acquisition by the child of help-seeking responses, based on his requiring physical help in a variety of contexts. While this concept provides, in one way or another, an important basis for nearly all approaches that are to be listed here, writers and researchers in this area have emphasized in addition *either* nonfocused social dependence (e.g., Sears, 1951, 1963; Sears et al., 1953; Whiting & Child, 1953; Heathers, 1955a, 1955b; Beller, 1955, 1957, 1959; Gewirtz, 1956a, 1956b; Sears et al., 1957; Kagan & Moss, 1962; Bandura & Walters, 1963; Sears et al., 1965) *or* focused attachment (e.g., Bowlby, 1958; Ainsworth, 1963, 1964; Schaffer & Emerson, 1964), but not both social dependence and attachment. (An exception can be found in Gewirtz, 1961b, who distinguished among all three concepts.) These two terms have therefore been subject to variable and inexplicit usage, and have often been employed idiosyncratically in research, so that they are sometimes used to order the same phenomena with the distinction between social dependence and attachment ignored.

A number of writers, in different ways, have also made the distinction that we emphasize in this analysis between "instrumental" or "task-oriented" dependence and "social," "emotional," "affectional," or "person-oriented" dependence (cf., e.g., Heathers, 1955a; Gewirtz, 1956b, 1961b; Kagan & Moss, 1962; Bandura & Walters, 1963). In the present discussion, the term social dependence is used synonymously with the term dependence, as that term has been commonly used, and instrumental and social dependence are defined orthogonally. The essence of instrumental dependence is that some response of another person is required in order for the individual (e.g., child) to attain some stimulus (like food or the removal of a noxious stimulus) that is reinforcing independent of the characteristics of either the helping response (e.g., attention) or the appearance of the helping agent (e.g., mother). This distinction therefore depends upon the identification of the reinforcing stimulus. That is, if a young child requests help from a parent in obtaining an object from a high shelf only because it is physically impossible for him to reach, this would be an instance of instrumental dependence. If, however, that same child asks for help in obtaining an object which he has at other times gotten himself (or if he is seen placing an object on a shelf only to ask for it when his parent appears), this would be classified as an instance of social dependence. The identification of the reinforcing stimulus, which is necessary in principle if the dependent act is to be properly classified as instrumental or social, is therefore sometimes difficult to make in life settings. In this context, it is not surprising that different theorists may occasionally have made little attempt to distinguish between these two types of dependence (cf., e.g., Beller, 1955; Stendler, 1954). In those cases where writers have made such a distinction, it has most often been thought that the form of social interaction involved in instrumental dependence may constitute the main basis for the acquisition of noninstrumental, social dependence on people in general, as well as of attachments to particular persons.

Perhaps as a result of the abstract and vague way in which the concept of dependence has often been used and of the inadequacies of the indices employed to identify it, there has often been difficulty in defining the limits of its dimensional features. Thus, regardless of whether or not a distinction has been made between instrumental and social dependence, there has often been the tendency to view "independence" (self-reliance, autonomous achievements, assertiveness) as the opposite of dependence, and several authors have written of or implied bipolar (and confounded) dimensions for instrumental independence-dependence and socioemotional independence-dependence, extending to "overdependence" (e.g., Levy, 1943; Stendler, 1954). When the term independence refers to the quality and types of behaviors employed by the child for (i.e., that are maintained by) various reinforcers, social and nonsocial, in a particular context, it would seem less confusing for most purposes to adopt the convention of transforming the implied bipolar dimension(s) into unipolar one(s), and to classify behaviors as instrumental or social dependence. Under such a unipolar conception, the assumed dimensions would extend from low to high instrumental dependence and from low to high social dependence, with individuals having a relatively high incidence of self-reliant, self-assertive, autonomous behaviors assumed to fall at points in the lower portions of those scales. Under this convention, autonomous, achievement-oriented behaviors apparently maintained by (performed for) others' approval would be characterized as involving relatively low instrumental dependence but relatively high social dependence; and similar behaviors that appear oriented to mastery of tasks and self-assertion and not to the receipt of someone's approval would be conceived to reflect, in addition to low instrumental dependence, low social dependence (or "emotional independence" as Heathers [1955a] has termed it).

Analyses and research dealing with dependence-attachment phenomena have often involved variables (like deprivation) too extreme or too vaguely understood to be well implemented experimentally with humans. The terms dependence and attachment are themselves gross abstractions or summary variables which are perhaps only properly used as open-ended headings to group various classes of behavior or to label an area of scientific interest. Nevertheless, the tendency has been to use these terms as though they represented a unitary process, a conception which, through the inclusion of loosely defined motivation (drive) terms and of terms like affection and reassurance, has often amplified the imprecision of research on human development. (As we shall detail in a later section, the drive concept itself has usually contained surplus meaning in that the operations implied in its use are generally inexplicit, numerous, often incompatible, and may not represent clear alternatives to one another.) As a consequence of the use of inexact terminology and the inclusion of imprecise motivational terms, there has often been a failure in developmental and parent-child relationship research to distinguish observation from inference, definition from explanation.

The acquisition of dependence and attachment. Through roughly the first half of this century, the theory most generally held in connection with the acquisition of social motivation, dependence, and attachment (particularly of the child's bond to his mother), was that of "acquired" or "secondary drive." The central features of this theory were the concepts of discriminative and conditioned (generalized) reinforcing stimuli (e.g., provided by incidental care-taker appearance characteristics) which acquired and maintained their reinforcing value by being discriminative for a limited set of apparently unconditioned reinforcing stimuli conventionally thought to be satisfiers of physiological needs (in particular food, water, and the removal of noxious stimuli). In general, the responses that were cued and maintained by the conditioned stimuli and that comprised the dependence-attachment behaviors received little emphasis, and by implication could be of almost any class. This appealingly simple secondary-drive approach was at the core both of Freud's (e.g., 1938a, 1938b; Fenichel, 1945; A. Freud, 1954) theory of cathexis and object formation and of standard conditioning approaches to acquired motivation (e.g., Miller & Dollard, 1941; Mowrer & Kluckhohn, 1944; Dollard & Miller, 1950; Sears, 1951, 1963).

In addition to what may be the gratuitous use of the term "drive" in this formulation (since the behaviors which are assumed to be determined by an infant's motivation could be accounted for completely in terms of conditioned discriminative and/or reinforcing stimulus control), in the past two decades the adequacy of the "secondary drive" theory has come to be questioned on two main grounds: the first question, influenced by ethological research on unconditioned and sometimes species-specific behavior patterns (and by conditioning studies of response topography), concerned the nature and organization of the responses involved in dependence attachment; and the second question, influenced by conditioning and performance research in a number of topical areas showing that diverse stimuli functioned as reinforcers, as well as by the posture of the operational approach to conditioning, was whether there was not a greater diversity of functional reinforcers operating for the behaviors of the developing infant than those that seemed organismically relevant.

Because of the findings of such research, an operational approach like the one in this chapter emphasizes the assumption that many and diverse classes of events can come to function as discriminative and reinforcing stimuli for numerous child behaviors, in addition to the limited number of stimulus events provided through caretaking that are thought to relate directly to organismic survival. Thus, it is our assumption that diverse near (i.e., proximal) events as well as events provided at a distance (i.e., distal), may function initially as unconditioned stimuli, or may come to acquire conditioned value, as evoking, discriminative, or reinforcing stimuli for the acquisition and maintenance of an increasing variety of infant behaviors. These behaviors include approaches, visual orienting, regard, and tracking, as well as smiles and vocalizations. In addition to the proximal stimuli such as are provided through the infant's being touched, held, caressed, and raised in the air, or through warmth and similar conditions, the distal stimuli may include visual events like those provided by the sight of people, and such aspects of their appearance as hair color, facial features, size, and their characteristic behaviors like gait, approach, and successive movements in space; auditory stimuli like sounds made by approaches and other movements, and by speech; and olfactory stimuli.[46]

It is our thesis that the behavior classes termed dependence and attachment are initially acquired and subsequently maintained on these pervasive bases. It is assumed also that the behaviors of the object person or persons who function in a caretaking-socializing role at the same time will come under the control of appearance and behavior stimuli provided by the child. These processes will account for progressively longer S-R interaction chains between the infant's responses and the stimuli provided by his caretaking environment. Some of the stimuli and responses will be parts of one or of very few chains, while others will occur in many different chains and, hence, will acquire generalized value (which process was earlier described in the section on key social-learning constructs and their operating modes).

We have noted that the concepts dependence and attachment represent gross, preliminary, and often vague abstractions for a set of functional relationships which characterize the control[47] over a wide variety of the behaviors of the child exercised by the discriminative and reinforcing stimuli provided by the appearance and behaviors of a class of persons (dependence) or a particular other person (attachment). The acquisition process for dependence and attachment, therefore, summarizes the details of two intimately correlated processes which begin when the infant is helpless and relatively immobile: the conditioning of various behavior systems, including remaining near, touching, smiling, vocalizing, approaching, eye and facial orienting, and visual regarding and tracking with respect to a class of persons or a person (like the caretaker-mother) according to the principles outlined; and the conditioning of the physical and behavioral appearance characteristics of those persons as discriminative and reinforcing stimuli (many of which are generalized), that maintain the child's behaviors and can account for the acquisition and maintenance of many new behaviors as well. Thus, at the very same time that the conditioning of appearance aspects of the mother-caretaker as generalized reinforcing stimuli is

---

[46]Although there have been writers (e.g., Bowlby, 1953a, 1958) who have proposed that some stimuli in the preceding list have unconditioned ("releasing") value for infant approach behaviors, this general assumption (which is testable in principle), need not concern us in the present social-learning analysis.

[47]Though we shall emphasize positive control in this analysis, situations characterized by negative control are also relevant (and, indeed, may play key roles, as in attachment associated with defensive identification), though we imagine most often they comprise a lesser portion of the functional relationships that characterize the behavior systems of dependence or attachment.

taking place, the child is heavily reinforced by diverse stimuli for approaching, following, orienting toward her, clinging, and generally for proximity responses which preclude the caretaker's getting out of sight or earshot, the complexity of his responses increasing with his developing capacities.

It follows as a corollary from this conception that (1) the greater the number of behavior systems of the child under the stimulus control of persons or of a particular person, (2) the greater the number of behaviors under their stimulus control *relative* to behaviors under the stimulus control of others, (3) the greater the degree of control over each behavior system, and (4) the greater the number of stimulus settings in which the control operates, the *"stronger"* the dependence or attachment may be said to be. This notion would apply where an overall summary statement is required by a researcher. Further, for the purposes of a particular analysis, one might define subvarieties of dependence or attachment to cover particular patterns of behavior or of stimulus control conditions. For the didactic purposes of the present illustrative social-learning analysis, however, such distinctions are premature.

Some *"pre-learning"* approaches to attachment.

The preceding line of reasoning may be usefully illustrated in some detail by an examination of the attachment conceptions of Bowlby and Ainsworth. In their present state, both may be termed "pre-learning" approaches because, although they are entirely compatible with learning considerations in that reciprocal interaction is emphasized very generally in both positions, they stop short of specifying the role of learning in attachment formation. Both approaches also differ from the one proposed in this chapter in that they reflect quite different theoretical orientations and less of a concern with method. Further, their definition of attachment may overlap that of social dependence in terms of our distinction.

Recent thought on the process of infant attachment to significant figures has been influenced greatly by Bowlby's approach. In place of the traditional secondary-drive learning conception,[48] Bowlby (1958, 1960a, 1960b) has proposed that, like that of many lower species, the initial attachment or bond exhibited by the human infant to his mother involves a number of primary, un-

---

[48]Bowlby's (1958) critique of the early "secondary drive" conditioning approach to attachment (and its psychoanalytic counterpart which he has faulted for its emphasis on orality and its view that the child's relation to his mother is initially one of "cupboard love"), which was already being challenged and superseded by the open-ended, operational approach to instrumental learning before Bowlby's 1958 paper was written, was in great part based on his notion that the class of reinforcers that could operate in the acquisition of attachment under a secondary drive or conditioning approach was limited to include only those provided through caretaking, namely food, water, and the removal of noxious stimuli. He pointed out that other unlearned behavior systems (and by implication reinforcing stimuli), which had little if anything to do with the appetitive stimuli that the early secondary-drive conditioning theories emphasized, as well as stimuli for mothers' behaviors, appeared to play critical roles in the formation of human attachments. However, Bowlby's implicit equation of the functioning of a limited set of organismic reinforcing stimuli with a conditioning approach (the secondary-drive theory) was unfortunate in a context where an operational-learning approach to attachment acquisition (like that emphasized in this chapter) remains completely *open* with respect to the identities of the

learned component "species-specific behavior patterns" (that he also labels "instinctual response systems") in the infant's repertory, that are readily evoked by available stimuli. These are originally independent of each other, mature and develop at different times and rates during the child's first year, and together have high survival value. Of the five instinctual-response systems Bowlby identified, those in which the infant is the active partner, which insure close proximity and caretaking, and which require only a limited reciprocal response from the mother are *sucking, clinging,* and visual, auditory, and locomotor *following* (i.e., not letting her out of sight or earshot). These instinctual-response systems lead the infant "to attach himself with vigour at first to any mother-figure and later to a particular mother-figure and to remain so attached for a long time" (Bowlby, 1960a, p. 314). In the normal course of development, these response systems become integrated, focused on a single mother-figure between about three and six months of age through (an unspecified form of) learning, and form the basis for the strong attachment of the infant to his mother, which Bowlby assumes does not begin to wane until around the infant's third birthday. Bowlby (1958) identified the remaining two instinctual-response systems, in which the infant's responses provide releasing stimuli to activate or evoke the unlearned instinctual behavior patterns of the mother and to bind her reciprocally to the child, as *crying* and *smiling.* (These two systems were not emphasized in some of Bowlby's later analyses [1960a, 1960b, 1961].) [49]

The instinctive response systems in Bowlby's approach may be intended to

---

stimuli and the behaviors involved in the acquisition and maintenance of attachment at different points in early human development, and emphasizes (as he does implicitly) the reciprocal interaction between infant and mother-figure.

It has been brought to my attention that Bowlby appears to make precisely the same error in a recent manuscript of a book on attachment and loss that has been circulated privately prior to its impending publication. Bowlby still appears to be unaware of operational, open-ended instrumental conditioning approaches. This is remarkable considering that he commented appreciatively in print (Bowlby, 1961) on precisely such an approach to attachment which I made (Gewirtz, 1961b). Ainsworth (1964) takes a similar posture to that of Bowlby regarding the secondary-drive theory of attachment, and appears to be similarly unaware of open-ended conditioning theories like the one mentioned. This is a pity, for, as we shall see, neither Bowlby's nor Ainsworth's related approaches are incompatible with learning assumptions. Indeed, the weakness of their analyses in great part stems from a limited appreciation of the ways in which experiential learning can affect their behavior indices.

[49]It is my understanding that, in an as yet unpublished manuscript, Bowlby goes farther than he has in earlier papers in specifying organizational and sequential details of child and parent behaviors that are relevant to their attachment for different ages of the child. He apparently includes additional responses as contributing to attachment (which he now views as one context for interaction) and organizes them into classes based on which responses will be "evoked" by what he conceives to be low and high overall intensities of attachment. It also appears that he postulates that, while the same five behavior patterns listed above remain important, during the first year of life they become incorporated into more sophisticated goal-directed systems that are organized and activated to maintain a child in proximity to his mother; and to take some account of situational determinants (e.g., mother's whereabouts) for the various behaviors which he feels mediate attachment and for various other responses (e.g., exploration) which are incompatible with attachment behaviors. Thus, some of the criticisms in this chapter, based on Bowlby's published works, might be qualified when his forthcoming theoretical statement is published.

represent more possible contexts for mother-infant interaction from which the attachment develops than specific behavior indices of attachment. Even so, by implication, the composite strengths of sucking, clinging, and following, as well as crying and smiling, the primary "instinctual response systems mediating attachment to a mother-figure" (Bowlby, 1960a, p. 315), would reflect the child's attachment to her. From soon after birth onward, conditions of isolation tend first to activate crying and later clinging and following; and "until he [the infant] is in close proximity to his familiar mother-figure these instinctual response systems do not cease motivating him" (1960b, p. 93). Bowlby maintains that until the infant attains proximity to his mother, his subjective experience is that of "primary anxiety"; when he is close to her, it is that of "comfort." Thus, Bowlby has also assumed that, once these instinctual response systems are activated, any interference (e.g., through separation from the mother) with their termination must lead to distress and anxiety, as will frustration of other "primary instincts." Hence, the distress and protest responses to separation from the mother reflect "primary anxiety," and are related to the fear responses exhibited by many species to aversive (often including novel) stimuli, in that both are reduced not simply by avoidance behaviors but by escape to a place of safety, like that provided by the mother. (When separation continues, the result includes despair, and later, emotional detachment.)[50] Thus, after an attachment is acquired, Bowlby assumes that the distress brought about by either separation from the mother or the presence of aversive stimuli may be reduced by the same condition: physical proximity to the mother. Hence, the same behavior systems which Bowlby holds are involved in, and, we presume, index, attachment may, in the context of threatened or of actual separation from the mother, also index distress and may be viewed as disorganization behaviors.[51]

Ainsworth (1963, 1964), whose approach derives from Bowlby's, identified thirteen behavior patterns that she took to mediate the attachment of the infant to his mother. Of these thirteen indices, eleven reflected positive stimulus control. Each of these responses normally enters children's repertoires at different time points during the first half-year of life, and the indices may thus involve several

---

[50]Bowlby has conceived of *protests* as involving especially the issue of separation anxiety, *despair* that of grief and mourning, and *detachment* that of defense (Bowlby, 1960b). Schaffer's (Schaffer & Emerson, 1964) results for protest responses suggest to Bowlby that the child's separation anxiety on losing his mother is not exhibited by him before about 28 weeks. These findings are considered later in this section. The earlier section which questions the utility of age variables in the study of development is pertinent here also.

[51]Harlow's approach to the reciprocal attachment pattern of the rhesus macaque infant and mother, which details the developmental course of these systems, appears to be conceptually rather similar to Bowlby's. Thus, Harlow (1959, 1961, 1963; Harlow & Harlow, 1965, 1966) has described the affectional system of the infant macaque for his mother as proceeding through a series of overlapping developmental stages (that reciprocally complement the maternal stages). These developmental stages he has termed: reflex, comfort and attachment, security, and separation or independence. (We will consider primarily the first two stages here, as they relate to Bowlby's assumptions. The reciprocal maternal stages are: attachment and protection; transition or ambivalence; and separation or rejection.) During the first 10-20 days of life, the neonate's survival is insured by his "reflex" behaviors, which include those that facilitate his proper orientation to the mother's body, nourishment (via sucking), and physical support (via hand and foot grasping, clasping, etc.). The basic social

developmental levels. The eleven positive stimulus-control indices Ainsworth used were differential smiling, differential vocalization, visual-motor orientation, following, "scrambling" over mother, burying face in mother's lap, exploration from mother as a secure base, clinging, lifting arms in greeting, clapping hands in greeting, and approaching through locomotion. Her two negative indices were differential crying (crying when held or comforted by another person relative to crying shown to mother), and crying when mother departs. Ainsworth assumed that during the first year of life infants pass through four partially overlapping social-behavior phases, which are indexed by different patterns of the thirteen indices: undiscriminating responsiveness to people; differential responsiveness to the mother; sharply defined attachment to the mother, with striking waning of undiscriminating friendliness; and attachment to one or more familiar figures other than the mother.

Bowlby bypassed the issue of the interrelationships among attachment indices (which, at most, he only implied) ; and while Ainsworth informally grouped subsets of indices, like Bowlby she detailed neither the acquisition process for attachment nor the relationship between social dependence and attachment. For reasons that are not specified but which Ainsworth indicates stem from her conception that attachment involves affection and discrimination as to object person, and that its formation depends upon active interchange with the object whose response is reciprocally affected, she implicitly treats the term attachment as a gross rubric for the study of various interaction-response patterns between mother and child. Hence, while Ainsworth has written of attachment as if it were an entity reflecting a single underlying dimension, with all thirteen attachment-behavior patterns somehow becoming organized together in relation to the mother as object (through an unspecified process), she has also written that attachment soon afterwards becomes directed to other "favorite figures" (which, unspecified as to form, may border on what we have termed social dependence and hence may obscure the distinction between nonfocused and focused dependence), and that not all thirteen behavior patterns need be included in, or essential for, a particular attachment. On this last point, Ainsworth reported that "the attachments of some infants seemed chiefly mediated by crying when mother leaves, by following, and later by clinging. The attach-

---

relationship between infant and mother develops after the second week of life, during the comfort and attachment stage. The infant's responses are now mostly under voluntary control, and he maintains close physical contact with the mother through nursing and particularly through clinging. (This latter response is also the most prevalent behavior of the infant during the security stage, as evidenced by the observation that mere contact with the mother-figure is apparently sufficient to alleviate the infant's fear [of strange objects or surroundings].) Further, the infant follows (by both visual and locomotor means) the mother and imitates her behaviors, a facet of his development which Harlow considers an important factor for macaque socialization.

Harlow considers these basic mechanisms that bind the macaque infant to his mother as homologous to those Bowlby (1958) has described for the human infant: primary object sucking, clinging, and following. Further, it would seem that Harlow (like Bowlby) considers the differential behaviors of the infant for his mother, and particularly those falling under the headings listed, as the indices of the attachment (and as the behaviors which result from separation from the object of attachment).

ment of others seemed more conspicuously mediated by greeting, smiling, vocalization, and visual-motor orientation" (1964, p. 57). While in this report she did not attempt to classify these or other outcome patterns as distinct varieties of attachment, in an earlier study. Ainsworth (1963) classified infants with outcome patterns like the above as "insecure attached" and "secure attached," and termed a third pattern "non-attached." Thus, it is not actually clear whether Ainsworth preferred to assume that diverse subpatterns nevertheless reflect a unidimensional conception of attachment, or whether she preferred to classify them as distinct varieties of attachment.

It has been seen that both Bowlby and Ainsworth in their complementary approaches to the emergence of attachment state that the various component behaviors of the infant they have emphasized become organized and focused on the mother figure through learning (i.e., experience with the environment). However, as we have noted, neither theorist details the conditions for the acquisition of attachment in even a preliminary fashion to show the form of the learning through which those component responses become integrated and focused, nor do they detail whether those responses undergo topographic changes during development. It has been shown that responses like those Ainsworth used and Bowlby implied as indices, particularly eye contact, smiling, vocalizing and crying, can be instrumentally conditioned (or extinguished) in the early weeks of life (e.g., Brackbill [1958] for smiling; Rheingold et al. [1959] and Weisberg [1963] for vocalizing; Etzel & Gewirtz [1967] for eye contact, smiling, and crying), and that the age of their onset and selective discriminative control may vary in diverse environmental settings (Gewirtz [1965] for smiling). However, Ainsworth did not attempt to detail the impact of learning on her response indices except to argue (gratuitously) that the behavioral components of attachment patterns initially "are clearly unlearned"; and like Bowlby, she conceives of these responses as becoming "tied into attachment patterns . . . only when they become differentially directed towards different figures . . ." (Ainsworth, 1964, p. 57), but does not detail how this organization comes about. This may be tantamount to saying that a child will be conceived to have an attachment whenever any of the thirteen response indices are directed differentially toward persons.

Further, we have noted that although Bowlby's five instinctual response systems (and Ainsworth's parallel behavior patterns highlight some key settings for intensive mother-infant interaction in which there are potentially many recurring conditioning opportunities that a sequential-learning approach to attachment must ultimately detail, Bowlby makes no attempt to detail the learning processes involved. Yet there is an extensive research literature which suggests the countless ways in which learning (in the sense of systematic increases of behaviors in particular discriminative contexts) can readily be affected by recurring stimulus conditions. Thus, various S-R sequences are surely involved in the complex clinging context, with sequentially occurring responses in the presence of sequentially provided stimulus events; and the component responses of these chains would be in the position to be potently reinforced, for instance, by stimuli provided via contingent physical contact from the mother. At the same time, those appearance characteristics of the mother that are discriminative for such reinforcement could become conditioned reinforcing stimuli; thus constituting an aspect of attachment learning. The interaction settings of Bowlby and Ainsworth and the latter's phases and selected indices all reflect the stimulus control (mostly positive) over the behaviors of the child that is exercised by the appearance and behaviors of the object mother (and a very few others) that I have argued is the essence of an attachment and can be analyzed in the simple learning terms outlined.

Despite the fertile context for rapid conditioning that the reciprocal social interaction setting comprises, the assumption that the infant's crying and smiling behaviors innately release species-specific attention and care patterns in the mother was strongly reaffirmed by Bowlby (1961) in his rejoinder to my attempt to fault that position (Gewirtz, 1961b). Bowlby argued that ". . . the suddenness with which maternal feelings often make their appearance and the overwhelming compulsion they bring to attend to and care for the baby seem to require some other explanation [than learning]. Since species-specific behaviour patterns are so clearly at work in other mammalian species, why need we baulk at postulating their presence in man?" (pp. 301-302).[52]

In this rejoinder, Bowlby ignored the difficulties which I had pointed out (Gewirtz, 1961b, pp. 233-234) in postulating innate releasers of species-specific caretaking behaviors. These were: first, Bowlby's assumption would be difficult to validate, for it requires that we exercise a sufficient degree of control (which is not easily done) over the histories of human adults to rule out the possibility that the control exercised over caretaking behaviors by the stimuli provided by infant smiling and crying is not acquired through learning. On the basis of abundant evidence that, relative to lower animals, a rather large proportion of human adult behavior systems would seem to be determined by experiential

---

[52]Scott's (1967) view of social attachment is not unlike Bowlby's and Harlow's. Like Bowlby, Scott contends that such responses as crying and smiling are elicited by innate releasers (e.g., the presentation of a face) and are neither products of learning nor contributors to an attachment formation in accordance with operational-learning conceptions. (Scott feels he does differ from Bowlby, however, in that the five child responses the latter emphasized do not themselves mediate the attachment bond, but rather, they represent positive behavioral mechanisms which lead to close contact with the mother and thus make possible the formation of the bond, the basic requirement being merely prolonged contact between child and mother.) Further, Scott appears to share Bowlby's narrow view that the class of reinforcers that can operate under a conditioning approach is limited to food, water, and the removal of noxious stimuli. Thus, as evidence of the inability of an operational learning approach to explain attachment formation, he cites studies like Harlow's (1958) which have been interpreted by Harlow to indicate that feeding by the mother is an unnecessary prerequisite for the formation of an attachment-bond between child and mother. And Scott therefore concludes that the process of social attachment is "something which takes place entirely within the animal, not being under the control of external stimulation" (1967, p. 503). While the findings cited by Scott are not disputed, they do not provide sufficient evidence to invalidate an approach like ours, for what Scott and others holding a similar view have neglected to consider is the wide variety of other reinforcers dispensed by the mother that could function in the formation of the attachment in accordance with the operational-learning principles described in this chapter.

learning, it is at least equally plausible to assume that the possibly homogeneous aversion (negative reinforcing properties) of infant crying or the uniform delight (positive reinforcing properties) of infant smiling for parent-caretakers of both sexes, could be products of learning that may reflect the nearly universal value orientations placed on these infant behaviors. There are several possible reasons for the reinforcing effectiveness of infant smiling and crying for caretaker behaviors. First, the human infant is, generally speaking, an enigma to his caretakers. His smiling and crying (which are similar to the responses of adults in certain contexts) can serve to communicate to them important information about his overall well-being, which is of great concern to them. Thus, caretakers will consider a child's crying as a response to (the presence of) aversive stimuli which they must remove. Crying can also be aversive to the caretaker because of its implication of inadequate caretaking behavior on her part. On the other hand, an infant's smiles to his caretaker could provide positive reinforcers for her behaviors (as she may associate the smiles with the valued conditions of being liked, appreciated, recognized, or preferred to strangers). Smiling may also serve as a discriminative cue for the adults that other (interesting and charming) reinforcing stimuli may be forthcoming, such as vocalizing or reaching for them (as objects). Thus, caretaker behaviors which are followed by the cessation of crying or by the initiation of smiling can be strengthened, whereas those which are followed by the cessation of smiling and the initiation of crying can be weakened.

We reiterate then, that while unlearned and species-specific behavior systems of the human infant or of his mother might well be involved in their early interaction, as Bowlby and Ainsworth have proposed, it is a fundamental assumption of a conditioning approach like ours that these systems would more likely establish the context and limits for the reciprocal social dependence or attachment learning of the infant and of his mother, but do not in a direct manner themselves represent dependence or attachment. As the assumptions of Bowlby and Ainsworth can readily be translated into the standard social-learning principles discussed in this chapter, it is assumed that the organization and focusing that, for them, is the key to attachment formation would take place according to such conditioning principles, and that the interaction arenas they emphasized provide key opportunities for that acquisition.

In the conditioning approach advocated, the issues remain open concerning the specific organization of behavior systems under the headings of dependence and attachment. Hence, the following issues remain to be resolved: which stimuli for the infant's behaviors are initially unconditioned (releasers); which unconditioned infant responses are most likely to occur to the stimuli that are initially present in the child's vicinity; whether any of these responses are species-specific; which developmental changes occur in receptor systems (i.e., discriminative capacities) and effector systems (i.e., responses); which reinforcing stimuli are likely to condition cue aspects of the mother-figure as conditioned reinforcing stimuli; and which of the attachment behaviors (e.g., orientation, approach, and following responses) come to be maintained by those conditioned-reinforcing stimuli. It is kept in mind that some of these questions are also applicable to the reciprocal attachment formation of the mother-caretaker and others to their charges. Further, our conditioning approach does emphasize (and is open to) the potential reinforcing efficacy of stimuli provided through the response of following (e.g., those termed environmental changes) and through skin and other contacts (e.g., via clinging) (Harlow, 1960, 1961, 1963; Harlow & Zimmermann, 1959). Hence, on these issues, Bowlby's ethologically influenced theory would complement a learning approach like the one proposed, and would seem completely compatible with it, given the current level of specificity of his theory and the openness of the learning approach.[53]

The choice of relevant attachment-dependence indices. Given the present limited degree of specificity of theoretical contexts in which such concepts as dependence and attachment have evolved, and the consequent absence of close coordination between the theoretical terms and the empirical operations, we have seen that there are often what appear to be fundamentally different phenomena that could be grouped under each concept. Yet the two concepts are often defined identically. However, if they are defined at the same level of abstraction, attachment and dependence behavior indices need not correlate with each other, or within themselves, in any simple manner, or even at all. In the context where the relevant theories have not progressed sufficiently to detail the behavior chains characterizing the sequential contingencies in interactions, many and diverse behaviors might be reasonable indices of either attachment or dependence, or simultaneously of both.

The typical behavioral indices of dependence are naturally occurring approach responses which are maintained by positive stimuli provided via the

[53]The preceding points, together with a number of others that have been involved in considerations of the acquisition of dependence and particularly of attachment, have been detailed in an earlier extensive analysis in social-learning terms of the acquisition and maintenance processes at issue, as well as of the modes of operation of possible unconditioned stimuli in early human life (Gewirtz, 1961b). In addition, that analysis considered such related issues as: the implications for dependence and attachment of ethological research on releasing stimuli, species-specific behaviors, and species differences; the apparently unconditioned and conditioned reinforcing stimuli that may operate in the early months for the human infant; the similarities between imprinting and attachment learning (which analysis was misinterpreted by Salzen [1967], who cited my position as emphasizing the critical importance [rather than merely the likely operation] of contact for attachment learning in humans and in animals); forms of substitute attachments and how they are acquired; the role of a limited environment ("privation") or a gross shift in the maintaining conditions of the environment ("deprivation," as through separation) upon outcomes in dependence and attachment behaviors; the role of particular infant response systems (e.g., clinging, orienting toward, smiling, vocalizing) in possible human imprinting, and in the acquisition of dependence and attachment; a critique of Bowlby's (1958) ethological approach to infant attachment, which included suggestions about various points in Bowlby's conception of the formation of an attachment at which instrumental-learning considerations could enter; and lastly, possible bases were considered for the acquisition of a dependence and/or an attachment by parent-caretakers *to* their infant charges. Some of these issues are also considered in two of my recent papers (Gewirtz, 1968a, 1968b).

behavior of other persons, and hence index positive stimulus control. Included are responses such as bodily contact, nearness, appeals for reassurance, and seeking attention or approval (including the approach index of deviation [from standard] or annoyance behaviors for attention) (e.g., Beller, 1948, 1955, 1959; Gewirtz, 1948, 1954, 1956a; Sears et al., 1953; Sears, 1963) that may be stratified, for instance, by object class (whether made to adults or children) or by degree of mother's availability (Sears et al., 1965). On the other hand, the behavioral indices of attachment may include similar direct indices of the positive stimulus control acquired by the object person over a child's behaviors, but they also typically include, and may be almost entirely restricted to, emotional behavior (symptom) indices which reflect behavior disorganization effected by disruptions in the opportunities for the child to exhibit those responses (reflecting positive stimulus control) he ordinarily would show in the presence of the stimuli provided, either because the stimuli are simply no longer forthcoming in that context, e.g., through removal (separation) from the child's proximity of the "object" person who has typically provided those stimuli, or because the child is blocked from receiving the stimulus or from making a response to stimuli from the object person. These disruptive emotional responses may include protests, crying, anxiety, and tantrums, as well as misery, apathy and emotional detachment as the separation continues (cf., e.g., Bowlby, 1958, 1960a, 1960b; Ainsworth, 1964; Schaffer & Emerson, 1964; Cairns, 1966). (Some of the determinants and effects of behavioral disorganization were detailed in an earlier section on the effects of shifts in the maintaining environment.) Cues provided by the mother's departure (which Bowlby [1960b] regards as evoking a form of "primary anxiety") or by the presence of stimuli that are for any reason aversive to the infant may also evoke responses which, while in other circumstances may function simply as approach behaviors maintained by positive stimuli, in these stimulus contexts may be viewed by some as "security-getting" behaviors. These may include approaching, remaining near, and physical contact (including clinging) responses, which are often strong and can seriously disrupt ongoing S-R sequences.

It is clear that both diverse approach responses (including approaches for security) and diverse disorganization responses could provide plausible indices of dependence and of attachment, that a given orientation could emphasize indices from both classes, and that depending on their particular purposes, it could be an efficient tactic for theoretical orientations to emphasize some particular index or different sets and proportions of indices from each of the two classes. Thus, we have seen that Ainsworth (1964) used eleven approach and two disorganization indices for her purposes. In my earlier analysis (Gewirtz, 1961b), I opted implicitly for a strategic emphasis on diverse, simple approach response indices rather than either approach indices based on security behaviors or disorganization indices. My underlying assumption was that, relative to disorganization indices, approach indices more directly, and hence more efficiently, reflect the positive stimulus control process at issue. Even so, it could be an efficient tactic to emphasize security behaviors or disorganization indices in a research approach whose purpose is not to deal directly with issues of positive stimulus control over relevant behaviors as such, but rather to understand the disorganization brought on by interference with attachment behaviors, or disorganization generally.

There are serious problems concerning the choice of behavioral indices and the generality of inferences to be drawn from them. For one, explicit recognition is almost never given to there being, under the standard conceptions of dependence or attachment, many and diverse potential indices of those concepts, a factor that should qualify inferences from any set of indices that are not representative under the theory of a researcher. Further, a number of tactical assumptions are often at issue in the use of indices in research done under abstractions like dependence and attachment. An implicit and unwarranted assumption that is often made is that the various indices of each of these two concepts are alternative measures of the same unitary process, that, therefore, they should intercorrelate highly (in principle, unity), and that the values of a single intercorrelation matrix should characterize all subjects in all situations. However, by the very fact that such numbers of variegated indices are used for each concept, many of which appear to have been selected somewhat arbitrarily for use by earlier investigators (e.g., Beller, 1948; Gewirtz, 1948), there is bound to be some overlap among these indices and they should intercorrelate on this artifactual basis alone. Another implicit and often unwarranted assumption is that there is independence between the occurrence of a behavior (index) and the settings sampled. Where that assumption is not tenable, the intercorrelation matrix would be biased by the sample of behavior settings that happen to be selected. If, in fact, in a given situation or across settings the indices represent either mutually exclusive or alternative responses (i.e., either one particular response, or any of a set of alternative responses, is appropriate in the setting), the correlations among responses for any group of subjects could be either positive, negative, or zero order, depending upon the imperatives and constraints in the situations represented and the relative response strengths based on the reinforcement histories of the subjects involved. Closely related to these points is the often neglected consideration that independently defined subcategories may overlap in physical stimulus qualities. Thus, it is difficult to conceive of a case where a child is held or caressed by an adult when he is not simultaneously touched or provided with positive attention, if not also with approval or affection. Similarly, a child who ordinarily or frequently would exhibit a behavior that is maintained by positive attention might, in a situation in which those around him are quite busy, exhibit negative deviations for attention. What often seems to be missing from analyses using such indices, however, is an awareness of these factors, a deficiency which often makes the research on dependence and attachment artifactually complex as well as arbitrary.

Thus, an expectation of finding that one set of correlation-matrix values will characterize the response interrelationships for some set of randomly selected subjects in a group may be an oversimplification. By the very nature of the life setting with which we are dealing, it seems reasonable to suppose that the individual histories of children would differ in regard to each of the responses comprising the subcategories of such summary variables as dependence or attachment. On this basis, different subgroups may be expected in any sample of children studied, each with its unique characteristic intercorrelation matrix for behavior indices to reflect the different conditioning histories that could be involved. Thus, while in a sample or across samples of children we may find, on the average, a particular pattern of interrelationships among these subcategories (which finding, to be sure, would be of limited utility), we would expect there to be large individual differences among children on the interrelationship of these variables in a particular stimulus context. Consequently, generalizations about the relationship among the indices or between them and environmental settings would be limited due to these factors that would determine (bias) the intercorrelation matrix.

A number of studies in the past 15 years have all approached dependence in a fairly homogeneous manner, some of them using the same five behavior categories for dependency or slight variations on them (Beller, 1948; Gewirtz, 1948; Sears et al., 1953; Sears et al., 1957; Sears, 1963). Under an open-ended definition of dependence similar to Murray's *n succorance* (1938), these categories included behavior for physical contact, nearness, positive attention, negative (deviation for) attention, and reassurance, and the sum of all was taken to constitute a total dependency score. While the emphasis in these studies was generally directed to examining relationships between the total dependency score and various demographic and historical variables, attention was often given to the organization of dependence, i.e., the relationships among the five (or more) subcategories, the implicit thesis apparently being that the dependence subcategories should intercorrelate highly, at one time, across several time points, and across situations[54] (excepting as some might be less reliable than others or that the sampling conditions might have been more conducive to the occurrence of some subcategories than of others). Such subcategory intercorrelations or those between gross summary indices like total dependence and, e.g., some identification score, however, may prove to be of little theoretical consequence when abstractions like dependence and identification are reduced to their component functional relationships involving acquired stimulus control over responses. Only at this level of a functional analysis can one avoid what are difficulties at the more abstract levels, for instance, the fact that individual children display different or opposite patterns of behaviors or that some emit behaviors which are accounted for by the indices used, and others do not.

Further, while there might be something like a standard S-R interaction

---

[54]More recently, Sears (1963) has interpreted his analyses of the dependency subcategories to indicate that it is not warranted to conceive of the organization of dependency subcategories as reflecting the existence of a common trait (in Allport's [1937] sense), but rather that it would be more fruitful to consider each of the five subcategories separately with respect to its origins. Nevertheless, for his sample Sears, too, intercorrelated the five subcategories and correlated each of them with assorted demographic and historical measures.

chain that characterizes sequential attachment behaviors for an identified sample of children homogeneous in history or within a particular setting, it is plausible that the behaviors of individual children would be organized according to quite different patterns of interaction chains, and further that some responses used as indices may have a certain relation to other responses in the chain, for instance, one response may be a precondition for another response. Thus, in the standard (and perhaps artificial) setting in which assessments are made, Child A might be (misleadingly) scored higher on nearness behaviors and lower on negative attention-seeking (crying) behaviors than Child B, simply because the first response of Child A to stimuli early in an attention-seeking chain pattern might be moving near while that of Child B might be crying. Further, at later phases in the learning, there may be "short-circuiting" of the chain as it becomes more efficient, with fewer behavior steps leading to, for instance, approval or attention, than had been involved at an earlier point. There are also dynamic implications from the standpoint that if a response to a stimulus close to the end point of the chain cannot occur (due, for example, to the imposition of some barrier), it is possible that the child would employ with greater frequency a response to the stimulus which occurs earlier in the organization of the sequence. Thus, if only selected responses are observed while the entire S-R chain and its history are overlooked, an incomplete, even misleading, impression of the child's behavior pattern may be obtained.

A conception of a common S-R chain can illustrate some of the reasons why we would not expect the subcategories of dependence or attachment to relate to each other in a homogeneous way, or necessarily even at all, especially for children selected for study without regard to their S-R chain histories. Furthermore, the particular situational conditions in which behaviors occur may dramatically affect the operation of a chain. That is, in some environmental settings (such as those involved when a child is ill) one set of segments or patterns of chain responses would be likely to occur, while in another environmental setting a quite different organization of the subcategories might occur. Further, the momentary setting conditions involved (such as when a child is hungry) would differentially affect the efficacy of stimuli and hence the behaviors for which they are discriminative or reinforcing. Thus, an understanding of the stimulus conditions comprising the situation, and of the setting conditions operating, is critical for the comprehension and prediction of the pattern in which the dependence or attachment responses are organized.

There is a further issue with regard to the behaviors which generally serve as indices of dependence or attachment. There have been many laboratory studies of the reinforcing efficacy of social stimuli as reflected in changes in the attributes of responses upon which those stimuli were made contingent. While such reinforcing stimuli (e.g., the word *good*) and the responses they control are not ordinarily considered to be related to dependence behaviors usually studied in life situations, these stimuli are often similar to, or identical with, those maintaining behaviors classified under dependence. Hence, it should be instructive to examine the functional relationships into which these social stimuli enter.

At the very least, they may illustrate the utility of using a single response (index) in research.

As has been shown, there are in use many and variegated indices of dependence. Some detrimental consequences of using uncritically a large number of such indices have already been noted. One point should perhaps be reemphasized, however: the use of several presumed indices of a process is not in itself detrimental, *if* the possible consequences of this practice and the complexities involved are taken into consideration. A related point that is only too seldom considered in the dependence-attachment research area is the possibility of using a single behavior index (e.g., all attempts to get some response from another person) and a single measure of that behavior (e.g., its rate or latency on each trial). This tactic (which is a convenient one), based on the finding that various alternative measures of response strength relate only imperfectly to each other,[55] has often been fruitfully used in conditioning studies, e.g., of bar-pressing. Thus, a single response class may be sufficient for a researcher's purposes if found (1) to be reliable, (2) to be either representative of the range of the stimulus control process or reflective of response(s) that are representative, and (3) to enter into some reasonable relationships with independent variables under the researcher's expectations.

In contrast to the half-dozen or so behaviors typically used to index dependence, the number of attachment indices (with the exception of the thirteen used by Ainsworth [1964]) may be small (even one, as might be the case when a protest or fear index upon separation is employed). The practice of employing few indices is not, in principle, unreasonable, for, as has already been noted, there are research contexts in which a single representative response index may make possible considerable research progress, such as the finding of significant relationships with independent variables that are important under a given theoretical approach. Thus, much has been made of the differential reinforcing efficacy of the word *good* for a choice response following differential deprivation and satiation pretreatments to which subjects were exposed (Gewirtz, 1967a, 1969; Landau & Gewirtz, 1967). There are, however, still several reservations which should be noted regarding the use of a small number of attachment indices. The first consideration already noted stems from the fact that attachment indices have been mostly disorganization responses, and because they are indirect may be less sensitive to a stimulus-control conception, and in that sense less efficient than are direct stimulus-control response indices. Since disorganization indices may not operate in the lower portion of a hypothetical disorganization dimension (e.g., due to there being an operative threshold), it might require a large degree of disorganization to provide a nonzero score on that index. A potential limitation like this one would be less likely to operate were direct indices of positive stimulus control used.

---

[55]It is recalled that Osgood (1953) reports that the correlations among indices like resistance to extinction, latency, and amplitude are heterogeneous; and that Hull (1943) emphasized primarily resistance to extinction as his index of response strength.

A second consideration when a single response is used to index attachment in life settings is that the response could actually be under some special form of social-stimulus control independent of that implied in attachment. Thus, the utility of single indices is limited by the difficulty of insuring that they are not simply reflections of idiosyncratic conditions in children's unique conditioning histories, for, in the case where they are, these single indices may be unrepresentative of the broader set of positive stimulus-control functions that is implied by the term attachment under most theoretical orientations. For instance, we have already noted that Etzel and Gewirtz (1967) have shown that crying can be very easily maintained (i.e., reinforced) by caretaker attention (i.e., her hovering around the child, talking, picking him up) even in the early weeks of life (which is also well before the time many would conceive that an "attachment" could have been acquired). Thus, if a single index is used as in the Schaffer and Emerson research (1964), such as one that summarizes (interview) reports of the occurrence, intensity, and direction of protests after seven different separations of children from the parent, the single crying-fussing response index of attachment under this practice may in reality reflect merely the fact that the children had been heavily reinforced for displaying such behaviors in similar (or certain other) situations (for instance, whenever their mother was about to leave their vicinity.).[56] In this case, therefore, protests in separation situations, which might otherwise index the children's strong tie to their mother, would only reflect the limited fact that their mother reinforced protest behaviors and that such behaviors were merely a part of the child's conditioned response repertory. Indeed, differences in such specific training conditions, particularly in the discriminability of the unique cues provided by the object mother, might account, in part at least, for the pronounced individual differences in the age of onset of specific attachment found by Schaffer and Emerson. Further, a single index might be extremely unrepresentative, as children might show rather little attachment by other indices that reflect either positive or negative stimulus control. We have already seen that different subject histories in regard to the responses comprising subcategories of such global variables as dependence and attachment confound the difficulties of interpreting the results of studies which rely on a method such as that of intercorrelating indices for an unselected sample. A functional behavior-oriented analysis of the stimulus conditions that have acquired control of relevant responses of the individual could help to eliminate such confounding factors (whether single or multiple indices are used).

The basic point to be made is that the use of such abstractions as dependence and attachment can obscure the fundamental characteristics of the processes

[56]This possibility is not listed for the purpose of impeaching the Schaffer and Emerson findings on the relationships between age and protest scores (and age and scores from systematic observations of the infant's response to various degrees of approach by the interviewer), for by employing their response index in various situations they may have had the equivalent of several indices. However, in studies conducted in life settings, the validity of research findings may be qualified by the use of a single index of attachment when account is not taken of the issues raised here.

loosely grouped under these rubrics. Thus, the emphasis of theorists using such gross abstractions has been primarily on summarizing behavior, and almost not at all on the stimuli which control and maintain such behavior. And even when stimulus conditions have been considered under summary abstractions, the moment-to-moment differences in behavior caused by the moment-to-moment changes in the controlling stimuli have not been considered. Neither has there been an adequate tie-up between presumed dependence or attachment behaviors as outcomes and various extreme conditions as antecedents. Research approaches in the past have tended to rely on the method of studying generalized patterns of stimulation provided by the environment, such as nurturance, consistency, and frustration, and of relating them to comparable traits in the behavior of children, such as dependency, insecurity, and attention-seeking. These gross abstractions have by their nature limited the analyses of both the stimulus conditions and the behavior of the child. This is because they have tended to index only some average characteristics of the behaviors through extended time spans and have precluded the necessary articulation between the stimuli provided by the environment and the relevant behaviors of the child. That is, by dealing with the environmental stimuli and the child's behaviors under such generalizations, researchers have tended to neglect the sequential relationships of the discrete stimuli and the discrete responses. Such a method cannot help but miss the subtleties that various of the extant theoretical approaches would consider relevant and important.

Progress in the direction of understanding dependence and attachment would seem to require that more careful attention be given, for instance, under the social-learning theoretical formulation we have outlined in this chapter, to specifying more clearly the indices for these abstractions and examining more closely the empirical relationships involved. For example, as has been noted it is necessary to discover which unique (physical appearance and behavioral) aspects of the object person could serve (1) to reinforce and subsequently to maintain a variety of the child's approach and other behavior sequences, and (2) to provide, in the context of the child's behaviors, discriminative stimuli in the appropriate sequential order for the many interaction behavior chains which would be involved. It would be important to know also under which conditions the removal of particular stimuli provided by the object(s) might lead to crying, "sadness," disorganization and the like. This required analysis would encompass the identities, frequencies, varieties, and ranges of stimuli provided, and, for an analysis of the learning process, their sequential and timing relationships with such behaviors as smiles, which could constitute opportunities for those behaviors to become conditioned according to the classical or operant paradigms. The moment-to-moment impact on, and control of, behaviors, both by preceding and consequent stimuli—the meshing and interweaving of sequential environmental events (provided by the behaviors of the parent) with sequential behaviors of the child, in effect, the very essence of the interaction process—has often been directly ignored in analyses which employ gross variables, and is in fact at issue whenever summary concepts are employed.

Are Dependence-Attachment and
Imitation-Identification Sequentially Related?

It has been common for theorists of social learning to assume a relationship between the two focal social-behavior systems we have considered in detail, dependence-attachment and imitation-identification. The factors assumed to contribute or relate to a child's identification with his parent-model, i.e., his pervasive imitation of the model's behaviors, include nurturance or love from, or social-emotional dependence on, the parent, and a personal attachment, strong tie, emotional intensity, or warm relationship between the child and the parent (e.g., Freud, 1933; Miller & Dollard, 1941; Mowrer, 1950, 1960b; Whiting & Child, 1953; Sears, 1957; Sears et al., 1957; Kagan, 1958; Bronfenbrenner, 1960; Sears et al., 1965). An alternative possibility suggested by Walters and Parke (1965) and Kohlberg (1966) is that imitative behaviors may precede the learning of specific attachments and that, by increasing the child's responsiveness to others, may thus directly or indirectly contribute to attachment learning. In our view, these issues may be artifacts of the gross level of conceptual analysis from which imitative-identificatory and dependence-attachment phenomena have been typically approached.

In life settings, social dependence-attachment behaviors and imitative-identificatory behaviors may be acquired concurrently or sequentially from identical or similar stimulus conditions, as both behavior classes are emitted in the presence of many of the same discriminative stimuli and are maintained by many of the same reinforcers provided by the parents. As changes in the social stimuli (and their efficacy) provided by the parents may be reflected in both imitative-identificatory and dependence-attachment behaviors, the acquisition of these two processes is not likely to be independent. Even so, one behavior class is not necessary for the acquisition of the other; they involve separate response systems that in theory can be represented by distinct paradigms, interdependent only in their use of some of the same stimulus elements for their acquisition and maintenance. Indeed, although the imitative response class is ordinarily defined more in terms of response similarity than in terms of the social stimuli that cue or maintain the matched responses, imitation is like other response classes that are under the type of social stimulus control implied and summarized by the concepts of dependence and attachment. In this special sense, imitation-identification behaviors that are evoked and maintained by social stimuli may be considered a subset of dependence-attachment behaviors, insofar as the former behaviors are a means by which the child can attain social stimuli from a parent (model).[57]

---

[57]There is no reason to expect, however, that the person to whom the child is most strongly attached—i.e., from whom discriminative and reinforcing stimuli (e.g., approval) should be most effective for his behaviors—will necessarily be the model for the child's behaviors. However, through differential reinforcement that person may determine who the model will be, as in the case of the mother who reinforces her young son for acting as his father does.

Thus, from our functional approach, the existence of a dependence or attachment to the parent-model, the quality of the relationship with him, or the degree to which nurturance and affection were earlier received are gross abstractions which summarize and index social-stimulus efficacy from a person (e.g., the parent) or a class of persons in functioning as discriminative stimuli and generalized reinforcers for the child's responses, *including* his imitative-identificatory ones. But such broad concepts are inevitably nonspecific about the details of these contingencies. It follows that, because a large class of imitative behaviors are maintained by social discriminative and reinforcing stimuli, the correlation between the strengths of imitative and attachment behaviors may be high, but this should not be taken to indicate that attachment is a precondition for generalized imitation, or vice versa. The search for such correlations, e.g., by Sears et al. (1957) and Payne and Mussen (1956), among others, may therefore provide information that is of limited theoretical relevance when both abstractions are reduced to functional relationships involving acquired stimulus control over responses, as in the functional analysis of this chapter.

THE ROLE OF MOTIVATION
IN SOCIAL LEARNING

The phenomena usually grouped under *motivation* (the terms "drive," "need," and "motive" are assumed to be synonymous for our purposes) are important or relevant for nearly all theoretical approaches. In recent years, however, there has been an increasing realization that even our best conceptualizations of those phenomena have been far from adequate. Motivational terms have been used to serve diverse functions, and there has often been confusion as to which function a particular motivational term has been advanced to serve at a particular time. For example, drive concepts have sometimes reflected a focus on an energizing function for behavior, at other times, a focus on a reinforcing function or simply on the persistence of behavior. Further, drive concepts have sometimes been used to stand for assumed physiological states and sometimes simply to order or label specific antecedent operations assumed related to those states (e.g., deprivation-satiation for food or water). At the same time, drive terms have served as intervening variables or abstractions that focus in a loose way on organizations of specific behaviors or changes in their characteristics. These varied usages of motivational terms have led to a lack of parsimony and confusion. In this context, Cofer (1959) has wondered whether a distinct concept of motivation might not disappear as functionally unnecessary; and Skinner (1938, 1953) has routinely found the need for a special concept of motivation essentially unnecessary.

There is no argument in this chapter against the study of the events usually grouped under the heading of motivation, for they include most of the phenomena which our approach to social learning and those of others ordinarily attempt to order. Nor is there an argument against the use of motivation labels, for a label is only a word, and words and the syntactical relations in which they occur can be employed tightly or loosely, constructively or obscurely. However, after taking note in this section of various ways in which drive terms have been used in early adaptive- and social-learning analyses and the often inadvertent consequences of these usages, it is our thesis that diverse concepts commonly grouped under the heading of conditioning can provide a more adequate heuristic account of most social-behavior phenomena, including a substantial portion of those ordinarily grouped under the heading of drive, than can less explicit motivation terms. The advantages of such an approach have been illustrated in an earlier section, in which relatively well-defined and extensively used conventional learning concepts were generally found better suited to the heuristic explanation of long-term privation and deprivation outcomes than was the short-term, deficiency-homeo-static, motivation model.

The consequences of various uses of drive conceptions are considered in this section under two main headings: unlearned motives in early social development, in particular so-called "natural motivation," and learned drives. And for the most part without employing drive terms, alternative and seemingly more parsi-monious ways are presented that heuristically account for long-term and some short-term phenomena that such motivational terms are often posited to order. In the main, concepts that reflect acquired stimulus control of social behavior will be emphasized.

Some Unlearned Drives in Early Social Development

Various conceptions of innate "drives" for stimuli or for the attainment of certain goals have entered extensively in theoretical analyses of early social devel-opment. Several theorists have attempted to explain the functioning of selected stimulus events for infant behavior by postulating instinctive "needs," such as an "innate need of the child for a loving relationship" (Ribble, 1943, 1944, 1965), an "attachment need" as the motivational force behind the tendency to seek proximity with members of one's species (Schaffer & Emerson, 1964), or a need to value things that are consistent with or like the self (Kohlberg, 1966). As we noted earlier, drive terms have also been used in connection with behavior patterns labeled "curiosity" (Berlyne, 1950) and "exploration" (Montgomery, 1951) as conceived in the drive-reduction tradition, and those labeled "intrinsic motivation" (Harlow, 1950, 1953; White, 1959) and "manipulation" (Harlow et al., 1950) as conceived in the need-for-stimulation context. Various over-lapping conceptions which attempt to subsume other nonphysiological drives, and which in many cases have been employed as explanations for such social phenomena as imitation or attachment, have included White's (1959) "compe-tence" or "effectance" motivation (also Kohlberg, 1966) and Hunt's (1963) "information-processing" motivation. These terms have been introduced to account for empirical evidence accumulating during the past two decades which stands in contrast to the widely held homeostatic view, represented particularly by the approaches of Freud and Hull, that the organism whose biological needs (in the traditional meaning of that term) are satisfied and who is not threatened (by noxious events) is passive and essentially unresponsive.

In the psychoanalytic tradition, there have been parallel attempts to introduce an energy basis for ego psychology. Thus, sources of ego energy have been postulated ranging from Freud's tentative notions of desexualized libido, as broadened and systematized by Hartmann, Kris, and Lowenstein (1964) since 1939 to include the reversible neutralization of both sexual and aggressive drives, through Hendrick's (1942) postulation of an independent ego instinct of "mastery," and White's (1959, 1963) broadening of it to a position holding that the ego has energies of its own whose expenditure brings natural satisfaction (e.g., in dealing with reality).

The preoccupation of psychologists with homeostatic drives, drive reduction, energy, manipulatory-exploratory drives, mastery motives, and the like to explain the occurrence in early life of behaviors oriented to or maintained by stimuli has resulted in a lack of parsimony and in confusion. In all of these instances, the *only* index of the postulated drive is the occurrence of the behaviors that the drive itself has been posited to explain. Moreover, the gratuitous use of explanatory drive notions, which refer so imperfectly to only one side of the interchange between a child and his environment, has severely limited the conveyance of meaningful information regarding the early development of social phenomena.

Since "natural motivation" conceptions appear to have been postulated by theorists only to stand broadly for the occurrence of nonorganically driven behavior (Kohlberg, 1966), a parsimonious alternative would be to rid ourselves of the extraneous gear of "drives," "needs," "motives," "energies," and "urges" and to make the straightforward assumption that it is a fundamental property of a species like man, at all ages, to be potentially responsive to and in active commerce with the myriad stimuli in the environment, even when organismic requirements (for food, water, sleep, and the removal of noxious stimulation) are satisfied. This conception that responsiveness and action are simply part of the definition of the living organism is not a new one and has been advanced in very different ways, implicitly or explicitly, by theorists and researchers from diverse conceptual traditions (e.g., J. M. Baldwin, 1906; Piaget, 1952; Skinner, 1938; Woodworth, 1958; White, 1959), by researchers on animal and child play (e.g., Beach, 1945; Welker, 1961), and by collectors of normative data on infant responses to diverse stimuli (e.g., Gesell & Thompson, 1934).

It thus seems reasonable to propose that the organism's responses can be evoked and maintained by a great variety of environmental stimuli (both conditioned and unconditioned) that have no apparent survival value, at least in terms of traditional conceptions of organic drives. Once this *property of the species* is specified and listed in its proper place, the behavioral researcher, now unencumbered by imprecise drive notions, can instead concentrate on the strategic and tactical problems of determining the conditions under which a child is differentially responsive to particular environmental stimuli functioning in their evocative, discriminative, or reinforcing roles. In the last analysis it remains necessary to specify the conditions under which events are differentially "interesting" or worthy of "mastery."

A similar line of reasoning is applicable to the psychoanalytic notion of *neutralization of energy,* which postulates that libidinal or aggressive energies can be turned from their original aims and can become useful to achieve the aims of the ego. For the researcher, once the energy is transformed the original aims are of no consequence, and he is still left with the problem of empirically identifying the new aims for which the energy is utilized. Thus, the energy conception is not only superfluous in this case, but may actually interfere with the careful specification of observable events.

An unfortunate consequence of the use of drive terms in this context of "innate drives for stimuli" is that these conceptions tend to obfuscate the reasonable assumption, which is perfectly compatible with operational analyses of learning, that various unconventional consequences (very different from food, water, and the removal of noxious stimulation) may account for the acquisition and maintenance of behaviors, i.e., function as reinforcing stimuli. The proposal made when this topic was first touched upon in our discussion of intrinsic reinforcement in the section on key constructs and their operating modes was that the outcomes for which such underlying "effectance" drive notions have been postulated can be conceived as functionally attributable to the operation of extrinsic reinforcement provided by opportunities to manipulate or to attain specific consequences. Thus, when "interesting" or "mastery" consequences are identified, they can simply be conceived as discriminative and reinforcing events. So defined, the competence-mastery drive approach of White, Kohlberg, Hunt, and others would be entirely compatible with operational analyses of the determinants of behavior and learning (like Skinner's [e.g., 1953] or our own similar approach to the issues in this chapter).

Further, the behavior ordered by such notions as competence or mastery motives may be conceived, under the operational-learning model being emphasized in this chapter, as resulting from certain pan-human conditions of learning, for it is certainly likely that in almost any caretaking situation various active behaviors in relation to the environment are heavily reinforced. On this basis, therefore, a competence or mastery motive would simply be a learned response tendency.

In this context, it is remarkable that explorations of short-term conditions (which have been termed "setting" or "drive" conditions) that determine the momentary impact of both conditioned and unconditioned stimuli on behavior have been so few in number and so narrow in range. This is noteworthy considering that (a) the functional relations involving those short-term conditions, especially deprivation and satiation effects, are perhaps the only set of relations many theorists would agree to classify as drive functions, and (b) the determinants of the "interesting" or "novelty" qualities of a stimulus could function as short-term setting conditions to affect its reinforcing efficacy (Gewirtz, 1967a). However, it may be that so little attention has been devoted to setting conditions in social-learning analyses because the casual use of the drive term has resulted in a loss of precision and a confusion in objectives, and has obscured the important relationships involved. Alternatively, given that the drive term has been applied so readily to setting conditions for appetitive stimuli, this lack of attention may reflect the narrow belief on the part of many researchers that setting conditions are relevant only for stimuli pertinent to organismic needs.

An approach oriented to stimulus control would attend to the stimuli impinging on the child in early infancy, their temporal relationships with the child's behaviors, and the contextual conditions that account for variations in their discriminability and efficacy. It would concentrate on cataloguing the behavior of infants in terms of the number and variety of stimuli that potentially may evoke and reinforce behaviors in early life, rather than on singling out and perhaps reifying a few vaguely defined stimuli from the very large number that might be operating. Thus, a functional learning analysis such as we propose would have directional implications, which are lacking under drive models of social behavior, to indicate which behaviors will be affected and in what manner.

Learned Drives

Motivational concepts, also, have often been advanced to order behavior systems that are thought to be the outcomes of learning occurring through long time spans. These concepts have been expressed in such terms as *secondary, acquired,* or *learned* drives, which many have held affect human behavior even more than do recurrent organismic drives. These drive notions have been used in diverse ways and to explain myriad behavior phenomena in human development, contributing to definitional confusion and ambiguity as well as to an overlapping of concepts, surplus and inexact meanings, and an explanatory impotence. In particular, the inefficient use of motivational terms to explain the operation of simple conditioned reinforcers has led to a loss of precision in the specification of the functional relationships sought, the reasons for seeking them, and the theoretical language used to order these phenomena. The addition of the concept of learned drive to an analysis, while intended to serve a theoretical purpose, is often little more than gratuitous. Clearly, the functional relationships involved do not generally warrant the additional implications that stem from bestowing drive terms to the functioning of stimuli in the control of behavior.

In Hull's tradition, Dollard et al. (1939), Dollard and Miller (1950), Miller (1951), Miller and Dollard (1941), and Mowrer (1950) have written of "learned drive" and "conditioned fear," and Sears has advanced models for social learning parent-infant interaction employing concepts like nurturance "drive" (e.g., 1951). The points to be made here can be illustrated with the work of Miller and of Sears, whose drive conceptions appear to derive in part from Hull's notion of the "fractional anticipatory goal response" (r_g-s_g) mechanism by which the internal stimuli (s_g) assume drive value and can become associated with a variety of responses. Miller assumed that "learnable" drives are the product of responses that produce strong stimulation, and that conditioned reinforcement is the result of responses that reduce strong stimulation. Sears has conceived that the fractional anticipatory goal response-produced stimuli become integrated into the total stimulus constellation that instigates future behavior sequences. Although only the results of conventional learning operations appear to be at issue in nearly all such analyses, with the behaviors involved completely explicable in terms of acquired stimulus control and with no unique effects on performance involved, the concept of drive has been retained. This usage of the drive concept may represent an attempt to be consistent within a particular theoretical approach (in the case of the theorists just cited, Hull's) or with labeling conventions that have long been established and maintained in given conceptual areas despite their ambiguities. As a consequence, some attention has been diverted from the stimulus control operations occurring and is instead concentrated on inferences regarding internal processes and the relative strength of various drive tendencies.

Motivation is treated not too differently by Rotter (1954; Crowne & Marlow, 1964) as an abstraction in his social-learning theory. Although Rotter has not employed drive terminology in his experimental analyses, he has introduced drive concepts into his theoretical work such as the highly connotative term "need," which he often uses to replace his habit terminology. He has defined a "need" or "motive" as a functionally related set of behaviors directed toward the attainment of a goal, which is conceived to be a set of operationally conceptualized, related reinforcers. (The determination of major goals or needs, assumed to be acquired through the law of effect and through association with physiological "primary" drives, is an empirical problem.) The means by which these needs eventually function autonomously to direct behavior remain unspecified, and Rotter's use of the term "need" may therefore be gratuitous, as it functions only to label behaviors under the control of a family of reinforcers.

Some learning theorists have attempted to explain certain persistent habit systems by postulating an avoidance-conditioning paradigm based on noxious stimulation that results in a motive to respond because of "fear" or "anxiety" (McClelland, 1942; Miller, 1951, 1959). Others have proposed that such an anxiety conception may be a basis for social-approach behavior systems, like those termed "affiliative" (e.g., Schachter, 1959), or that anxiety is the drive that energizes behaviors for money, prestige, achievement, or affection (J. Brown, 1953). These theorists apparently found the simpler conception of aversive stimulus control an insufficient basis for explaining such behavior systems. Their conceptions, however, tend to group behaviors with indeterminate terminology, thereby leaving the actual details of the relationship between various behaviors and environmental events unclarified.

The aversive paradigm, and not that involving positive reinforcement, has been emphasized for acquired drives in part because experimental attempts aimed at definitively establishing an "externalization of drive" (Anderson, 1941) based on positive appetitive reinforcement were either not sufficiently controlled (e.g., Calvin, Bicknell & Sperling, 1953) or have failed (e.g., Myers & Miller, 1954), whereas a "drive" based on aversive stimulation is easily established (Miller, 1948a, 1951). The justifications that have been given for the use of a drive label are that avoidance conditioning shows little extinction over many unpunished trials and that new responses can come under the control of the stimuli whose presentation cued the original avoidance response and whose removal reinforced it. However, both characteristics may simply reflect the organism's failure to discriminate between extinction and maintenance conditions (thus delaying the extinction which must eventually occur if there are no further aversive contingencies), and the natures and relative potencies of the negative and positive reinforcers typically used in such experiments. The use of drive terms here, therefore, may be gratuitous, as the reinforcement of behavior by the removal of a noxious stimulus is solely a question of stimulus (reinforcer) control.[58] Further, although some persistent habits may fit an avoidance-learning paradigm, there is no evidence that all of them do or that a positive-reinforcement paradigm does not simultaneously affect those habit systems. An attempt to place all learned approach behaviors under this rubric would ignore a variety of other equally likely possibilities, many of which may be both more parsimonious and more inclusive of phenomena.

Many secondary drives proposed in the learning tradition appear to be little more than terminological transformations of what were at one time considered unlearned "instincts" or "purposive actions" (e.g., James, 1890; McDougall, 1950). As a consequence of Bernard's (1924) survey of these instinct systems which indicated that they invariably involved learning, many behavior systems classified as instinctive appear to have been simply transformed conceptually into learned-motive systems (e.g., Shaffer, 1936). Further, other learned motives, of which Murray's (1938) "psychogenic needs" seem representative, have been added to the large inventory. These needs include, among others, aggression, dominance, affiliation, succorance, and nurturance (the last three of which we have considered earlier together with behavior systems termed attachment or dependence). In such instances as these, therefore, the postulation of learned drives may have been more a relabeling of terms than a conceptual or theoretical advance.

We have seen in an earlier section that motivational terms have traditionally also been applied to *pervasive* behavioral systems such as imitation-identification, particularly when a behavior, acquired on the basis of extrinsic reinforcement, systematically continues to occur in the apparent *absence of that reinforcement.* Thus, Hindley (1957) applied the acquired-drive term to imitation occurring in situations without apparent reward, a usage bearing some resemblance to Allport's functional autonomy conception (to be examined in the next section), and Kohlberg (1963) has similarly proposed that one way in which identification differs from imitation is that the former is a "motivated disposition" because perceived similarity to the model has "intrinsic" reinforcing properties.[59] In the analysis of generalized imitation and identification presented at earlier points in

---

[58]It was not until much later that Miller (1963) formally considered the possibility that such drive terms and the theoretical framework from which they were derived may have been entirely unnecessary for the functional relationships at issue. At that time he formulated a new system built around a "go mechanism," which does not seem to differ substantially from an operational conception of reinforcer functioning.

[59]Kohlberg (1966) has subsequently proposed that the motivation for imitation is the same sort as that involved in curiosity, exploratory and mastery behaviors. This motive conception has been critically examined in several earlier sections of this chapter.

this chapter, however, it was proposed that the response class comprising generalized imitation (and identification) is acquired through extrinsic reinforcement of its members by reinforcing agents, and that it is maintained by intermittent extrinsic reinforcement. This very simple learning mechanism for acquired stimulus control over generalized imitation can account for its pervasiveness and strength, its focus on one model, and its occurrence in situations where the model is absent or where there is no extrinsic reinforcement for imitative responses, the very details of a response system that have prompted theorists like Bronfenbrenner (1960), Hindley (1957), Kohlberg (1963) and others to apply to it the term "acquired drive" or "motivated disposition." The application of drive conceptions to imitative-identificatory learning is therefore also unnecessary.

In a similar vein, Sears (1963) has referred to dependency as an acquired drive, and McClelland (1951) has postulated various learned needs, such as approval and succorance, which underlie such behavioral systems as dependence-attachment. We have seen in an earlier section that in each of these cases the use of drive conceptions may be gratuitous, as the approaches involve the use of gross abstractions which only summarize the effectiveness for the child's behaviors of various social stimuli, e.g., those from his parent or another adult. The phenomena involved could be better accounted for on the basis of the discriminative and reinforcing roles of stimuli, as the only factors at issue are those of acquired stimulus control over behavior, i.e., learning.

Some have felt that the use of a drive term is justified by the pervasiveness, strength, and persistence of learned behavior systems, even though such researchers treat their data as they would simple outcomes of learning. Ironically, a basic inconsistency in all these systems is probably the term "learned drive" itself, for in a sense it represents a contradiction in terms in a learning approach: the typical and least disputed usage of the term "drive" is in reference to shorter-term or momentary performance effects, while "learning" typically refers to longer-term systematic acquisition effects. This distinction between learning and performance has arisen and evolved in learning analyses and should nowhere be as valid as in learning approaches where, as my illustrations have shown, it is often obscured. In this context, there seem to be only two meanings of the term "learned drive" that are at all consistent with the consensus of the way setting or drive conditions that affect response performance have been employed. The first, referred to by Brown (1961) writing in Hull's tradition as "learned sources of drive," is that manipulation of a conditioned stimulus or response will affect other responses in the same way as will standard motivational operations like food deprivation, either by increasing "nonspecific drive" and affecting all responses, by producing distinctive cues, or both. How the determinants of the learning of a response operate as motivational variables when the response interacts with other responses is the question at issue in this usage. The second use of the term "learned drive" consistent with consensual usage is the labeling of a setting operation for a conditioned stimulus (e.g., deprivation or satiation) that heightens or lowers the efficacy of that stimulus (Gewirtz, 1967b). Both of these uses, however, require a precise specification of the stimulus operations and the responses they affect, an approach which has not been routine in drive analyses.

The functional autonomy of motives.   The persistence of various learned behavior systems in life situations that is said to reflect the complex "motive" structure characterizing the human adult has given rise to the notion of *functional autonomy of motives* (Allport, 1937). Allport conceived that these learned behavior systems come to be functionally independent of the maintaining-reinforcing conditions (and biological, tension-based needs) from which they were originally derived in early childhood, and become transformed in adulthood into varied, self-sustaining motive systems which are different in character and purpose. This process of "transformation of motives" Allport termed "functional autonomy." Observations of this phenomenon have been reported by Allport even under seemingly unfavorable conditions, such as when behaviors under those systems are punished or when they require much time or effort and lead to no identifiable extrinsic reward. This loosely formulated principle evoked considerable interest when it was first advanced, and it continues to play a role, if only to index the weakness of alternative learning conceptions. Even so, the functional-autonomy conception has been criticized on a number of grounds (e.g., Bertocci, 1940; McClelland, 1942; Rethlingshafer, 1943). And there have been ambivalent emphases on functional autonomy as a model for the acquisition of motives, probably due in part to the difficulty of subjecting the conception to experimental test. The functional-autonomy conception will be dealt with in detail in this section for two complementary reasons: to illustrate how basic learning principles can be used to account for important, contemporaneous human behavior systems and, at the same time, how the gap can be bridged between basic learning conceptions and complex personality functions.

Allport's anecdotal illustrations for functional autonomy reflect rather complex phenomena and settings where relationships between outcomes and their presumed antecedents are postulated many years after the original learning was assumed to have taken place. Because the level of the human behavior systems to which the term "motives" has been applied is remote from the level of the acquisition of stimulus control over responses of lower organisms typical of experimental analyses of conditioned reinforcement, some seem to have overlooked the fact that the phenomena at both levels have much in common. Reinforcement occasions, which can be so readily controlled in the laboratory, may and do often occur in life settings, but their control is harder to manipulate and their identity thus harder to establish there. Another difficulty lies in the fact that the reinforcement in the life setting is often intermittent, thereby making the discrimination between maintenance and extinction conditions difficult for both the subject and the observer. It is quite possible, therefore, that what appears to be functional autonomy is simply the result of an observer's failure to identify the reinforcers that are, in reality, maintaining a behavior system. Indeed, examples have been presented throughout this chapter of cases in which the maintaining conditions for a behavior system have not been obvious. In most of these cases, observers, using various nonoperational theoretical frameworks, have routinely failed to identify the reinforcers operating.

A notion like functional autonomy for complex personality functions, even in the apparent absence of extinction, is thus premature[60] to a thoroughgoing analysis of the factors that may be responsible for the maintenance of a behavior in question. As has been suggested by McClelland (1942) and by Dollard and Miller (1950), we need first ask such questions as whether or not the original controlling stimuli were correctly identified and are now really absent, and then we must determine the effect of changes in contextual conditions on the retardation of the extinction process, for extinction may be occurring but so slowly as to go unnoticed. In addition, we must consider the possibility that in cases where the original reinforcing stimuli have been removed, the control of the behavior may have been transferred to a different set of maintaining stimuli, the process being unnoticed by the observer.

Rather than concentrate on the more constructive theoretical issue of whether or not reinforcement conditions for a behavior were maintained, some learning theorists have tended to concentrate on the lesser of the issues involved, the failure to find behavioral evidence of the extinction of "motives" in the complex contexts discussed by Allport (e.g., Dollard & Miller, 1950). Under laboratory conditions, responses followed by conditioned reinforcing stimuli that were previously on a continuous reinforcement schedule but are no longer functionally paired with effective, terminal reinforcers (as in S-R chains) undergo a rapid decrease in their rate of emission, signifying the loss of power by the conditioned reinforcing stimuli.[61] Although it is unreasonable to assume that this rapid loss in reinforcing value by the conditioned stimulus on a continuous reinforcement schedule provides a proper baseline for the functioning of conditioned reinforcers on intermittent reinforcement schedules in life settings, many motivational theorists have made this unreasonable assumption.

Because conditioned reinforcement is the key concept by which conditioning approaches account for much of human behavior, Hall (1961) has called for the demonstration of the efficacy of conditioned reinforcers over long time spans without their even occasional association with primary reinforcers. Some learning theorists, therefore, have felt it necessary to attempt to show that conditioned

---

[60]This argument parallels the one earlier advanced when we considered the utility of conditioning principles for understanding another complex behavior system, first-language acquisition and performance.

[61]If in this issue the focus is on the removal of the terminal, functional reinforcer in the chain that has followed the conditioned reinforcer and the preceding response it maintains, then the relevant behavior paradigm for the decrease in the rate of the response monitored would seem to be that of *extinction:* all responses in the chain undergo extinction. However, when the emphasis is on the fact that, with successive contingent presentations of a reinforcing stimulus, whether it be of unknown history, apparently unconditioned, or conditioned, a new response (e.g., one that was *not* part of the original S-R chain in which a conditioned reinforcer may have acquired its value) systematically decreases in its rate of emission, the paradigm that fits this phenomenon most closely is that of *habituation.* Even so, this loss of reinforcing value for behavior by the contingent conditioned stimulus has sometimes been indiscriminately termed "extinction."

reinforcement value, when acquired and maintained on an intermittent schedule with respect to primary reinforcement (conditions thought to be characteristic of those available in life settings), can be made more resistant to extinction than ever before shown. By implication, these results would provide the required demonstration of how, in the life setting, conditioned reinforcers can maintain responses almost indefinitely. For instance, Mowrer (1960b) and others have emphasized the finding of D. W. Zimmerman (1957) that by creating S-R chains in which each stimulus element is on an intermittent schedule with respect to the next, behaviors can be maintained for a relatively long period in the absence of functional, terminal ("primary") reinforcement. A succession of such intermittent schedules appears not unlike that of the life setting in which functional reinforcers follow the conditioned reinforcers dispensed by a caretaker only intermittently, and these conditioned reinforcers in turn follow the child's behaviors only intermittently.

Such results as these have clearly extended our knowledge. However, even with potent conditioned reinforcers operating in the life setting, their loss of reinforcing power for responses must eventually, and rapidly, occur if the original maintaining conditions are removed and there has been no substitution for them. Thus, demonstrating a heightened resistance to loss of reinforcing power by conditioned reinforcers in the life setting does not take incisive hold of the main issue implied in Allport's (1937) postulate that the relationship between acquisition conditions and behavior outcomes is historical rather than functional, with the behavior systems involved assumed to be autonomous of the acquisition conditions. Nor does this demonstration take into account the questioning within conditioning approaches of the adequacy of the conditioned-reinforcement concept. In a context where it is not recognized that the conditioned reinforcer must rapidly lose its efficacy in the absence of at least occasional pairing with a functional reinforcer, the utility of the conditioned-reinforcer concept as well as the general utility of conditioning approaches to complex human behavior for which this concept is the cornerstone is impeached.

Both these issues are resolved in our treatment. It is our contention that effective pairings between conditioned and functional reinforcers continue to occur in life settings, as do the conditioned-reinforcement contingencies maintaining key behavior systems, so that the conditioned reinforcers retain their value and the behavior systems they maintain do not extinguish. Further, many conditioned stimuli become generalized as they function in many S-R chains. This basic condition is apart from the fact already noted that reinforcement in life settings is often intermittent, thereby making the discrimination between maintenance and extinction conditions difficult for both the subject and the observer. It is quite possible, therefore, that the de-emphasis of these basic points and the misplaced emphasis on the failure to observe extinction have been detrimental to social-learning analyses, in that they have made it easier for many to cling unnecessarily to a functional autonomy notion and to miss the stimulus-response contingencies that are likely to be operating in the acquisition and maintenance of social behavior.

Some Additional Consequences of the Use of Drive Notions

Sampling some of the diverse ways in which the term "drive" has been used in analyses of human adaptive and social learning, we have seen how behaviors exhibited in connection with certain stimuli have by fiat been taken to reflect "unlearned drives" for those stimuli, how similarly, learned response systems have often been gratuitously characterized as "drive" systems, and how "drives" have often been nothing more than labels for behaviors they purported to explain. We have also noted that the inconsistent and inexact use of motivational terms has led to a loss of precision in the specification of the functional relationships sought, the reasons for seeking them, and the theoretical language used to order these phenomena; and that the relationships sought under this usage may not even be the most pertinent.

Casual usage of drive terms can be even further illustrated by the practice in the literature of presenting a lawful relation between several measures, and assuming that one of these measures reflects a construct, like that of a "learned social need" for approval (Crowne & Strickland, 1961; Crowne & Marlowe, 1964) or "need achievement" (McClelland, 1951; McClelland et al., 1953; Atkinson, 1965). Thus, a social-desirability questionnaire to assess "approval need" or TAT performance to assess "achievement need" has been used to predict the reinforcing efficacy of approval stimuli or performance under an achievement set. Such research merely provides a straightforward "response-response" relationship between data for two or more seemingly alternative empirical operations for the importance of a set of stimuli constituting approval or achievement, as some of the theorists involved occasionally have noted (e.g., Crowne & Marlowe, 1964). However, even when this is realized, the researchers may still fail to give sufficient attention to the possibility that both response variables may be joint outcomes of the same antecedents, which issue they generally do not attempt to study. There is, therefore, a tendency to disregard and even to question the utility of close analyses of stimulus control and reinforcer efficacy and to concentrate instead on the less interesting problem of relating responses as a means of validating a system's constructs; and a commonplace relationship may be reified by its presumed support of a drive conception. Thus, the postulation of a learned social need, which researchers such as Crowne and Marlowe consider to give theoretical consistency to results, may sometimes obscure the relevance of a search for what would be more interesting causal relationships. And although the empirical relationships found may have their valid place, the level of theory involved may not be very productive and the results disappointing, even in the context of the expressed purpose of investigators like those just listed. Finally, if findings such as these are used as a basis for construct validation for a learned motive, a more complete theoretical network must be devised to account for antecedents, changes in the relationship, or negative findings. Even in that case, however, the term "motive" is most often gratuitous, especially in the unqualified way it is frequently introduced.

It is paradoxical that even some researchers who ordinarily use a learning approach have often seemed to ignore standard learning concepts of acquired stimulus control as they proceed to postulate drives in their analyses of social learning. This has been true not only in their research, but also in their attempts to deal with such special engineering problems as maternal-environmental-cultural deprivation, separation from the mother, shifts in the maintaining environment, differences between institutional and family environments, and the like. As we have emphasized, when a researcher postulates a drive in the organism or when he places an emphasis upon cognitive processes (perhaps together with competence or novelty motivation) as determinants of behavior, the result seems almost inevitably to be a decrease in his attention to the search for the functional relationships involving contingencies between environmental stimuli and the behavior system under scrutiny. The resulting de-emphasis of the conditions governing the acquisition and maintenance of behavior makes it easy for difficult-to-test assumptions like the functional autonomy of motives to be retained. Under these casual approaches to social learning, it is difficult to design new and improved environments or to effect child therapy, and it is not hard to be pessimistic about the possibility of systematically changing a child's behavior. Only under an approach that strictly separates learning from performance-drive functions can we clearly distinguish how a behavior comes under the control of the environment through long time spans (acquisition), how that control can be reversed when the maintaining conditions no longer exist (extinction or counter-conditioning), and how a variety of short-term contextual-setting conditions can determine momentary stimulus efficacy for performance. In summary, then, a functional-learning analysis obviates any supposed necessity for postulating either externally or internally aroused drives to explain an organism's response to external stimuli. In most instances, we need only know that the organism is alive, and, therefore, has the potential for behavior. Our focus then becomes stimuli, responses, and the conditions of their interchange.

SUMMARY

An approach has been outlined in this chapter for conceptualizing the roles of environmental stimulation and social experience as they affect child behavior and social learning in early development. It has been our assumption that to be meaningful in such an approach, the concept "environment" must be defined in terms of stimuli which affect behavior, and, at the same level of analysis, behavior must be defined in terms of its functional relationships to controlling stimuli. Global concepts like environment or trait, which only summarize through lengthy time spans the occurrence of either stimuli or responses but not both facets of the S-R interchange, are typically removed from the level of analysis required by the process theories which have spawned their use in research. Rather than emphasize such summarizing concepts, our approach to human social learning has proceeded as a detailed functional analysis of stimuli and responses, their interchange at a particular moment (i.e., the stimulus-response unit), and the sequences of interaction across successive moments (i.e., the stimulus-response chain). The conditioning concepts we have employed thus order environmental operations that effect systematic and reversible changes in observable behaviors. And the approach we have detailed remains open to the addition of new concepts as required, and to the differentiation and refinement of the concepts in current use.

While assuming that the respondent-conditioning paradigm may operate concurrently, we have emphasized the operant-conditioning paradigm as being most relevant to social behavior functioning, stressing its key constructs and their operating modes. We have considered the various functions of stimuli in controlling behavior, i.e., evocative, (generalized) discriminative, and (generalized) reinforcing stimuli, and how these stimulus roles are acquired. Contextual factors (also termed "setting" conditions) which can affect the momentary efficacy of stimuli were also detailed. As a by-product, various conditioning procedures were outlined for fostering socially valued behavior systems and for eliminating undesirable ones. These procedures provide conceptual leverage on training techniques for bringing out the full potential of children in both privileged and underprivileged settings, one of the most important problems of our age. Further, conditioning concepts were used in attempting to posit a plausible account of the child's acquisition of verbal-language (in a milieu where the nativistic approach of Chomsky and his associates has done much to set the recent tone) and emotional behaviors. It was seen, too, how at the same time that the child is being conditioned by his environment, he comes to control that environment by effectively dispensing reinforcers valued by parents and caretakers.

The place of developmental changes in an approach to the adaptive and social learning in early life was also considered. Development was conceived to represent points in a sequence of experiences (i.e., receptor and effector response occurrences cumulatively affected by stimuli) and only incidentally as points in physical time. It was thus proposed that diverse concepts commonly grouped under the heading of learning can provide a parsimonious, yet flexible, model for ordering the complex developmental patterns characterizing the child's socialization. By detailing the changing conditions of environmental stimulation accompanying development, this approach appears to index focal aspects of those changes in the child's behavior systems ordinarily termed development more effectively than does an index like age.

Behavior changes due to *deprivation* (involving gross and often dramatic shifts in the maintaining environment, as in separation) and to *privation* conditions of stimulation (involving an inadequate supply of functional stimuli for the child during the early years) were also considered. In this context, it was suggested that "backward" behavior patterns by a child may result from severe limitations in the number and variety of functional stimuli made available to him, as well as by reinforcement of his instrumental dependence.

As it has been our contention that an operational-learning approach is potentially more fruitful for understanding and enhancing the process of environment-child interchange than are approaches using abstract, "one-sided" summary concepts, only basic instrumental-conditioning and S-R chaining concepts have been employed to order many of the assumed complexities of the two-phased acquisition processes of imitation and identification (including sex-typing) as well as of dependence and attachment. Under a conditional-discrimination learning paradigm, imitative responses were conceived to be simply instrumental responses varied in content and matched to the cues provided by the responses of models, constituting a functional response class for the child which contains a potentially unlimited number of responses (which we have termed *generalized imitation*) that is acquired through extrinsic reinforcement by socializing agents of some members of that response class and is subsequently maintained by intermittent extrinsic reinforcement. This conception can account for the pervasiveness of imitation, its focus on one model, its occurrence when the model is absent or when there is no extrinsic reinforcement for it, and its resulting in behaviors that can be quite different topographically from the model's. A functional learning approach, therefore, can account for the very phenomena which have prompted others to postulate seemingly unparsimonious and nonempirical principles such as the operation of intrinsic reinforcement or cognitive processes as well as of observational learning and vicarious reinforcement. Further, without the use of conventional motivational constructs, the generalized-imitation paradigm can parsimoniously account for the phenomena usually grouped under the process of identification, by which the child is said to acquire the motives, ideas, and values of another (or others).

Dependence and attachment have also been evaluated critically and models advanced for their acquisition and maintenance. These phenomena were thought best conceptualized as classes of functional relationships involving the (mostly) positive stimulus control over a wide variety of an individual's responses by stimuli provided either by a class of persons (dependence) or by a particular person (attachment). When the phenomena classified under these two terms are not conceptualized in a functional way, the distinction between the terms and their fundamental characteristics may be obscured. As gross abstractions, dependence and attachment can be indexed by various combinations of approach (positive stimulus control) and disorganization (following separation) behaviors, and considerations have been detailed for the selection of indices under different research strategies and tactics. Under a functional approach, rather than being either a precondition for, or an outcome of, imitation-identification, dependence-attachment was conceived to be relevant to imitation-identification only insofar as it can index the discriminative and reinforcing value for the child of stimuli dispensed by the model or others.

In the realm of motivation, the concepts of innate drives for stimuli (i.e., "natural motivation") and learned drives and their utility in analyses of generalized imitation and identification as well as of emotional dependence and attachment have been examined. Our approach was critical of the innate drives, including competence or effectance motives, that have been postulated as underlying various components of infant responsiveness and of learned drives, and has led to the conclusion that these uses of the drive conception in analyses of socialization are gratuitous and actually detrimental in that simple, routine learning concepts can order efficiently most of the phenomena that those drive concepts have been advanced to explain.

It has thus been argued that diverse social behaviors of the child which have been "explained" by cognitive, intrinsic-reinforcement, motivational, and observational-learning concepts may in fact be efficiently accounted for by conditioning concepts in common use. These social-behavior phenomena are functionally attributable to the operation of explicit, extrinsic stimulus control, and can be more adequately characterized by parsimonious statements of the functional relationships involved. A functional learning approach such as we propose, which requires emphasis upon the sequential details of environment-organism interaction, i.e., stimuli, responses, and their interchanges, focuses upon the environmental conditions by which child behaviors can be acquired, maintained, extinguished, or otherwise modified, and thus upon the conditions by which the behavioral development and social learning of the young child may be enhanced.

REFERENCES

AINSWORTH, M. D. The development of infant-mother interaction among the Ganda. In B. M. Foss (Ed.), *Determinants of infant behaviour II*. London: Methuen (New York: Wiley), 1963. Pp. 67-112.

AINSWORTH, M. D. Patterns of attachment behavior shown by the infant in interaction with his mother. *Merrill-Palmer Quarterly*, 1964, 10, 51-58.

ALLPORT, G. W. *Personality: A psychological interpretation*. New York: Holt, 1937.

AMSEL, A. Frustrative nonreward in partial reinforcement and discrimination learning: Some recent history and a theoretical extension. *Psychological Review*, 1962, 69, 306-328.

ANASTASI, A. *Differential psychology*. (3rd Ed.) New York: Macmillan, 1958.

ANDERSON, E. E. The externalization of drive: I. Theoretical considerations. *Psychological Review*, 1941, 48, 204-224.

ARONFREED, J. The effects of experimental socialization paradigms upon two moral responses to transgression. *Journal of Abnormal and Social Psychology*, 1963, 66, 437-448.

ARONFREED, J. Imitation and identification: An analysis of some affective and cognitive mechanisms. Paper presented at the biennial meeting of the Society for Research in Child Development, New York, March, 1967.

ARONFREED, J. *Conduct and conscience: The socialization of internalized control over behavior*. New York: Academic Press, 1968.

ARONFREED, J. The concept of internalization. In D. A. Goslin (Ed.), *Handbook of socialization theory and research*. Chicago: Rand McNally, 1969. Chapter 4.

ARONFREED, J., & REBER, A. The internalization of social control through punishment. Unpublished manuscript, University of Pennsylvania, 1963.

ATKINSON, J. W. Some general implications of conceptual developments in the study of achievement-oriented behavior. In M. R. Jones (Ed.), *Human motivation*. Lincoln, Neb.: Univer. of Nebraska Press, 1965. Pp. 3-31.

AZRIN, N. H., & HOLZ, W. C. Punishment during fixed interval reinforcement. *Journal of the Experimental Analysis of Behavior*, 1961, 4, 343-347.

AZRIN, N. H., & HOLZ, W. C. Punishment. In W. K. Honig (Ed.), *Operant behavior: Areas of research and application.* New York: Appleton-Century-Crofts, 1966. Pp. 380-447.

BACON, W. E., & STANLEY, W. C. Effect of deprivation level in puppies on performance maintained by a passive person reinforcer. *Journal of Comparative and Physiological Psychology,* 1963, 56, 783-785.

BAER, D. M. Laboratory control of thumbsucking by withdrawal and re-presentation of reinforcement. *Journal of the Experimental Analysis of Behavior,* 1962, 5, 525-528.

BAER, D. M. An age-irrelevant concept of development. Paper presented to the annual meeting of the American Psychological Association, 1966.

BAER, D. M., PETERSON, R. F., & SHERMAN, J. A. Building an imitative repertoire by programming similarity between child and model as discriminative for reinforcement. Paper presented at the biennial meeting of the Society for Research in Child Development, Minneapolis, March, 1965.

BAER, D. M., PETERSON, R. F., & SHERMAN, J. A. The development of generalized imitation by reinforcing behavioral similarity to a model. *Journal of the Experimental Analysis of Behavior,* 1967, 10, 405-416.

BAER, D. M., & SHERMAN, J. A. Reinforcement control of generalized imitation in young children. *Journal of Experimental Child Psychology,* 1964, 1, 37-49.

BAKWIN, H. Loneliness in infants. *American Journal of Diseases of Children,* 1942, 63, 30-40.

BAKWIN, H. Emotional deprivation in infants. *Journal of Pediatrics,* 1949, 35, 512-521.

BALDWIN, A. L. *Behavior and development in childhood.* New York: Dryden, 1955.

BALDWIN, A. L. *Theories of child development.* New York: Wiley, 1967.

BALDWIN, J. M. *Mental development in the child and the race: Methods and processes.* New York: Macmillan, 1906.

BANDURA, A. Social learning through imitation. In M. R. Jones (Ed.), *Nebraska symposium on motivation: 1962.* Lincoln: Univer. of Nebraska Press, 1962. Pp. 211-269.

BANDURA, A. The role of imitation in personality development. *Journal of Nursery Education,* 1963, 18.

BANDURA, A. Influence of models' reinforcement contingencies on the acquisition of imitative responses. *Journal of Personality and Social Psychology,* 1965, 1, 589-595. (a)

BANDURA, A. Vicarious processes: A case of no-trial learning. In L. Berkowitz (Ed.), *Advances in experimental social psychology.* Vol. 2. New York: Academic Press, 1965. Pp. 1-55. (b)

BANDURA, A. Social-learning theory of identificatory processes. In D. A. Goslin (Ed.), *Handbook of socialization theory and research.* Chicago: Rand McNally, 1969. Chapter 3.

BANDURA, A., ROSS, D., & ROSS, S. A. Vicarious reinforcement and imitative learning. *Journal of Abnormal and Social Psychology,* 1963, 67, 601-607.

BANDURA, A., & WALTERS, R. H. *Social learning and personality development.* New York: Holt, Rinehart & Winston, 1963.

BARKER, R. G., & WRIGHT, H. F. *Midwest and its children.* New York: Harper & Row, 1955.

BARON, R. M. Social reinforcement effects as a function of social reinforcement history. *Psychological Review,* 1966, 73, 527-539.

BEACH, F. A. Current concepts of play in animals. *American Naturalist,* 1945, 79, 523-541.

BELL, R. Q. A reinterpretation of the direction of effects in studies of socialization. *Psychological Review,* 1968, 75, 81-95.

BELLER, E. K. Dependency and independence in young children. Unpublished doctoral thesis, State Univer. of Iowa, 1948.

BELLER, E. K. Dependency and independence in young children. *Journal of Genetic Psychology,* 1955, 87, 25-35.

BELLER, E. K. Dependency and autonomous achievement striving related to orality and anality in early childhood. *Child Development,* 1957, 28, 287-315.

BELLER, E. K. Exploratory studies of dependency. *Transactions of the New York Academy of Sciences,* 1959, 21, 414-426.

BERKOWITZ, H., BUTTERFIELD, E. C., & ZIGLER, E. The effectiveness of social reinforcers on persistence and learning tasks following positive and negative social interactions. *Journal of Personality and Social Psychology,* 1965, 2, 706-714.

BERLYNE, D. E. Novelty and curiosity as determinants of exploratory behavior. *British Journal of Psychology,* 1950, 41, 68-80.

BERLYNE, D. E. The arousal and satiation of perceptual curiosity in the rat. *Journal of Comparative and Physiological Psychology,* 1955, 48, 238-246.

BERLYNE, D. E. Attention to change, conditioned inhibition $(_sI_R)$ and stimulus satiation. *British Journal of Psychology,* 1957, 48, 138-140.

BERLYNE, D. E. The delimitation of cognitive development. In H. W. Stevenson (Ed.), Concept of development: A report of a conference commemorating the fortieth anniversary of the Institute of Child Development, University of Minnesota. *Monographs of the Society for Research in Child Development,* 1966, 31, No. 5 (Whole No. 107), 71-81.

BERNARD, L. L. *Instinct: A study in social psychology.* New York: Holt, 1924.

BERTOCCI, P. A. A critique of G. W. Allport's theory of motivation. *Psychological Review,* 1940, 47, 501-532.

BEVAN, W. Behavior in unusual environments. In H. Helson & W. Bevan (Eds.), *Contemporary approaches to psychology.* Princeton, N. J.: Van Nostrand, 1967. Pp. 385-418.

BEVAN, W., & ADAMSON, R. Reinforcers and reinforcement: Their relation to maze performance. *Journal of Experimental Psychology,* 1960, 59, 226-232.

BEVAN, W., & ADAMSON, R. Internal referents and the concept of reinforcement. In N. F. Washburne (Ed.), *Decisions, values, and groups.* Vol. 2. New York: Pergamon Press, 1963. Pp. 453-472.

BIJOU, S. W. A systematic approach to an experimental analysis of young children. *Child Development,* 1955, 26, 161-168.

BIJOU, S. W. Theory and research in mental (developmental) retardation. *Psychological Record,* 1963, 13, 95-110.

BIJOU, S. W., & BAER, D. M. *Child development, Vol. I: A systematic and empirical theory.* New York: Appleton-Century-Crofts, 1961.

BIJOU, S. W., & BAER, D. M. Some methodological contributions from a functional analysis of child development. In L. P. Lipsitt & C. C. Spiker (Eds.), *Advances in child development and behavior.* Vol. 1. New York: Academic Press, 1963. Pp. 197-231.

BIJOU, S. W., & BAER, D. M. *Child development, Vol. II: Universal stage of infancy.* New York: Appleton-Century-Crofts, 1965.

BIJOU, S. W., & STURGES, P. T. Positive reinforcers for experimental studies with children—consumables and manipulatables. *Child Development,* 1959, 30, 151-170.

BOWER, G. H. Secondary reinforcement and frustration. *Psychological Reports,* 1963, 12, 359-362.

BOWLBY, J. The influence of early environment in the development of neurosis and neurotic character. *International Journal of Psychoanalysis,* 1940, 21 (2), 154-178.

BOWLBY, J. Maternal care and mental health. *Bulletin of the World Health Organization,* 1951, 3, 355-534.

BOWLBY, J. Critical phases in the development of social responses in man and other animals. *New Biology,* 14. London: Penguin Books, 1953. Pp. 25-32. (a)

BOWLBY, J. Some pathological processes set in train by early mother-child separation. *Journal of Mental Science,* 1953, 99, 265-272. (b)

BOWLBY, J. The nature of the child's tie to his mother. *International Journal of Psychoanalysis,* 1958, 39, 1-34.

BOWLBY, J. Ethology and the development of object relations. *International Journal of Psychoanalysis,* 1960, 41, 313-317. (a)

BOWLBY, J. Separation anxiety. *International Journal of Psychoanalysis,* 1960, 41, 89-113. (b)

BOWLBY, J. Comment on paper by Dr. Gewirtz. In B. M. Foss (Ed.), *Determinants of infant behaviour.* London: Methuen (New York: Wiley), 1961. Pp. 301-303.

BRACKBILL, Y. Extinction of the smiling response in infants as a function of reinforcement schedule. *Child Development,* 1958, 29, 115-124.

BRACKBILL, Y., FITZGERALD, H. E., & LINTZ, L. M. A developmental study of classical conditioning. *Monographs of the Society for Research in Child Development,* 1967, 32, No. 8.

BRAINE, M. D. S. On learning the grammatical order of words. *Psychological Review,* 1963, 70, 323-348.

BRONFENBRENNER, U. Freudian theories of identification and their derivatives. *Child Development,* 1960, 31, 15-40.

BROWN, J. S. Problems presented by the concept of acquired drives. In *Current theory and research in motivation, a symposium.* Lincoln, Neb.: Univer. of Nebraska Press, 1953. Pp. 1-23.

BROWN, J. S. *The motivation of behavior.* New York: McGraw-Hill, 1961.

BROWN, J. S., & FARBER, I. E. Emotions conceptualized as intervening variables—with suggestions toward a theory of frustration. *Psychological Bulletin,* 1951, 48, 465-480.

BROWN, R. In the beginning was the grammar. (Review of F. Smith & G. A. Miller [Eds.], *The genesis of language: A psycholinguistic approach.* Cambridge, Mass.: MIT Press, 1966.) *Contemporary Psychology,* 1968, 13, 49-51.

BURTON, R. V., MACCOBY, E. E., & ALLINSMITH, W. Antecedents of resistance to temptation in four-year-old children. *Child Development,* 1961, 32, 689-710.

BURTON, R. V., & WHITING, J. W. M. The absent father and cross-sex identity. *Merrill-Palmer Quarterly,* 1961, 7, 85-95.

BUTLER, R. A. The effect of deprivation of visual incentives on visual exploration in monkeys. *Journal of Comparative and Physiological Psychology,* 1957, 50, 177-179.

CAIRNS, R. B. Attachment behavior of mammals. *Psychological Review,* 1966, 73, 409-426.

CALDWELL, B. M. The usefulness of the critical period hypothesis in the study of filiative behavior. *Merrill-Palmer Quarterly,* 1962, 8, 229-242.

CALVIN, J. S., BICKNELL, E. A., & SPERLING, D. S. Establishment of a conditioned drive based on the hunger drive. *Journal of Comparative and Physiological Psychology,* 1953, 46, 173-175.

CARON, A. J. Conceptual transfer in preverbal children as a consequence of dimensional training. *Journal of Experimental Child Psychology,* 1968.

CARON, R. F. Visual reinforcement of head-turning in young infants. *Journal of Experimental Child Psychology,* 1967, 5, 489-511.

CHOMSKY, N. Review of B. F. Skinner's *Verbal Behavior. Language,* 1959, 35, 26-58.

CHOMSKY, N. *Aspects of the theory of syntax.* Cambridge, Mass.: MIT Press, 1965.

CHOMSKY, N. Language and the mind. *Psychology Today,* 1968, 1 (9), 48-51, 66-68.

COFER, C. N. Motivation. *Annual Review of Psychology,* Vol. 10. Stanford, Calif.: Stanford Univer. Press, 1959. Pp. 173-202.

CRANDALL, V. C., GOOD, S., & CRANDALL, V. J. The reinforcement effects of adult reactions and nonreactions on children's achievement expectations: A replication study. *Child Development,* 1964, 35, 485-497.

CROTHERS, E., & SUPPES, P. *Experiments in second-language learning.* New York: Academic Press, 1967.

CROWNE, D. P., & MARLOWE, D. *The motive for approval: Studies in evaluative dependence.* New York: Wiley, 1964.

CROWNE, D. P., & STRICKLAND, B. R. The conditioning of verbal behavior as a function of the need for social approval. *Journal of Abnormal and Social Psychology,* 1961, 63, 395-401.

CUMMING, W. W., & BERRYMAN, R. The complex discriminated operant: Studies of matching-to-sample and related problems. In D. Mostofsky (Ed.), *Stimulus generalization.* Stanford, Calif.: Stanford Univer. Press, 1965. Pp. 284-330.

DENNY, M. R. The role of secondary reinforcement in a partial reinforcement learning situation. *Journal of Experimental Psychology,* 1946, 36, 373-389.

DINSMOOR, J. A. A quantitative comparison of the discriminative and reinforcing functions of a stimulus. *Journal of Experimental Psychology,* 1950, 40, 458-472.

DOLLARD, J., DOOB, L. W., MILLER, N. E., MOWRER, O. H., & SEARS, R. R. *Frustration and aggression.* New Haven: Yale Univer. Press, 1939.

DOLLARD, J., & MILLER, N. E. *Personality and psychotherapy.* New York: McGraw-Hill, 1950.

ESTES, W. K. Statistical theory of spontaneous recovery and regression. *Psychological Review,* 1955, 62, 145-154.

ETZEL, B. C., & GEWIRTZ, J. L. Experimental modification of caretaker-maintained high-rate operant crying in a 6- and a 20-week-old infant *(Infans tyrannotearus):* Extinction of crying with reinforcement of eye contact and smiling. *Journal of Experimental Child Psychology,* 1967, 5, 303-317.

FARBER, I. E. Anxiety as a drive state. In *Current theory and research in motivation, a symposium.* Lincoln, Neb.: Univer. of Nebraska Press, 1954. Pp. 1-55.

FARBER, I. E. A framework for the study of personality as a behavioral science. In P. Worchel & D. Byrne (Eds.), *Personality change.* New York: Wiley, 1964. Pp. 3-37.

FENICHEL, O. *The psychoanalytic theory of neurosis.* New York: Norton, 1945.

FERSTER, C. B. Positive reinforcement and behavioral deficits of autistic children. *Child Development,* 1961, 32, 437-456.

FERSTER, C. B. Part three: Essentials of a science of behavior. In J. I. Nurnberger, C. B. Ferster & J. P. Brady (Eds.), *An introduction to the science of human behavior.* New York: Appleton-Century-Crofts, 1963. Pp. 199-345.

FERSTER, C. B. An operant reinforcement analysis of infantile autism. In S. Lesse (Ed.), *An evaluation of the results of the psychotherapies.* Springfield, Ill.: Thomas, 1968. Chapter 12.

FERSTER, C. B., & SKINNER, B. F. *Schedules of reinforcement.* New York: Appleton-Century-Crofts, 1957.

FODOR, J. A. Why we are nativists. Paper presented at the annual meeting of the American Psychological Association, Washington, D. C., 1967.

FREUD, A. *The ego and the mechanisms of defense.* London: Hogarth, 1937.

FREUD, A. Psychoanalysis and education. *Psychoanalytic Study of the Child,* 1954, 9, 9-15.

FREUD, S. *A general introduction to psychoanalysis.* Garden City: Garden City Publishing Co., 1920.

FREUD, S. *New introductory lectures on psychoanalysis.* London: Hogarth, 1933.

FREUD, S. *An outline of psychoanalysis.* London: Hogarth, 1938. (a)

FREUD, S. Three contributions to the theory of sex. (1905) In A. A. Brill (Translator), *The basic writings of Sigmund Freud.* New York: Modern Library, 1938. Pp. 553-629. (b)

FUCHS, S. H. On introjection. *International Journal of Psychoanalysis,* 1937, 18, 269-293.

GELLERT, E. The effect of changes in group composition on the dominant behaviour of young children. *British Journal of Social and Clinical Psychology,* 1962, 1, 168-181.

GESELL, A., & THOMPSON, H. *Infant behavior: Its genesis and growth.* New York: McGraw-Hill, 1934.

GEWIRTZ, H. B., & GEWIRTZ, J. L. Caretaking settings, background events, and behavior differences in four Israeli child-rearing environments: Some preliminary trends. In B. M. Foss (Ed.), *Determinants of infant behaviour IV.* London: Methuen, 1968. Pp. 229-252. (a)

GEWIRTZ, H. B., & GEWIRTZ, J. L. Visiting and caretaking patterns for *kibbutz* infants: Age and sex trends. *American Journal of Orthopsychiatry,* 1968, 38, 427-443. (b)

GEWIRTZ, J. L. Succorance in young children. Unpublished doctoral thesis, State Univer. of Iowa, 1948.

GEWIRTZ, J. L. Three determinants of attention-seeking in young children. *Monographs of the Society for Research in Child Development,* 1954, 14, 5-48.

GEWIRTZ, J. L. A factor analysis of some attention-seeking behaviors of young children. *Child Development,* 1956, 27, 17-37. (a)

GEWIRTZ, J. L. A program of research on the dimensions and antecedents of emotional dependence. *Child Development,* 1956, 27, 205-221. (b)

GEWIRTZ, J. L. A learning analysis of the effects of affective privation in childhood. *Acta Psychologica,* 1961, 19, 404-405. (a)

GEWIRTZ, J. L. A learning analysis of the effects of normal stimulation, privation and deprivation on the acquisition of social motivation and attachment. In B. M. Foss (Ed.), *Determinants of infant behaviour.* London: Methuen (New York: Wiley), 1961. Pp. 213-299. (b)

GEWIRTZ, J. L. The course of infant smiling in four child-rearing environments in Israel. In B. M. Foss (Ed.), *Determinants of infant behaviour III.* London: Methuen (New York: Wiley), 1965. Pp. 205-260.

GEWIRTZ, J. L. Deprivation and satiation of social stimuli as determinants of their reinforcing efficacy. In J. P. Hill (Ed.), *Minnesota symposia on child psychology.* Vol. 1. Minneapolis: Univer. of Minnesota Press, 1967. Pp. 3-56. (a)

GEWIRTZ, J. L. Detrimental usage of drive in social-learning theory. Paper presented at the annual meeting of the American Psychological Association, Washington, D. C., September, 1967. (b)

GEWIRTZ, J. L. The role of stimulation in models for child development. In L. L. Dittmann (Ed.), *Early child care: The new perspectives.* New York: Atherton, 1968. Chapter 7. Pp. 139-168. (a)

GEWIRTZ, J. L. On designing the functional environment of the child to facilitate behavioral development. In L. L. Dittmann (Ed.), *Early child care: The new perspectives.* New York: Atherton, 1968. Chapter 8. Pp. 169-213. (b)

GEWIRTZ, J. L. On the choice of relevant variables and levels of conceptual analysis in environment-infant interaction research. Paper presented at the Merrill-Palmer Institute Conference on Research and Teaching of Infant Development, 1968. (c)

GEWIRTZ, J. L. Potency of a social reinforcer as a function of satiation and recovery. *Developmental Psychology,* 1969, 1 (1).

GEWIRTZ, J. L., & BAER, D. M. Deprivation and satiation of social reinforcers as drive conditions. *Journal of Abnormal and Social Psychology,* 1958, 57, 165-172. (a)

GEWIRTZ, J. L., & BAER, D. M. The effect of brief social deprivation on behaviors for a social reinforcer. *Journal of Abnormal and Social Psychology,* 1958, 56, 49-56. (b)

GEWIRTZ, J. L., & ETZEL, B. C. Contingent caretaking as a solution for some child-rearing paradoxes. Paper read at the biennial meeting of the Society for Research in Child Development, New York City, March, 1967.

GEWIRTZ, J. L., & GEWIRTZ, H. B. Stimulus conditions, infant behaviors, and social learning in four Israeli child-rearing environments: A preliminary report illustrating differences in environment and behavior between the "only" and the "youngest" child. In B. M. Foss (Ed.), *Determinants of infant behaviour III.* London: Methuen (New York: Wiley), 1965. Pp. 161-184.

GEWIRTZ, J. L., JONES, L. V., & WAERNERYD, K. E. Stimulus units and range of experienced stimuli as determinants of generalization-discrimination gradients. *Journal of Experimental Psychology,* 1956, 51, 51-57.

GEWIRTZ, J. L., & STINGLE, K. G. The learning of generalized imitation as the basis for identification. *Psychological Review,* 1968, 75.

GLANZER, M. Stimulus satiation: An explanation of spontaneous alternation and related phenomena. *Psychological Review,* 1953, 60, 257-268.

GLANZER, M. Curiosity, exploratory drive, and stimulus satiation. *Psychological Bulletin,* 1958, 55, 302-315.

GOLDFARB, W. Effects of psychological deprivation in infancy and subsequent stimulation. *American Journal of Psychiatry,* 1945, 102, 18-33. (a)

GOLDFARB, W. Psychological privation in infancy and subsequent adjustment. *American Journal of Orthopsychiatry,* 1945, 15, 247-255. (b)

GOLDFARB, W. Emotional and intellectual consequences of psychologic deprivation in infancy: A re-evaluation. In P. H. Hoch & J. Zubin (Eds.), *Psychopathology of children.* New York: Grune & Stratton, 1955. Pp. 105-119.

GOLDIAMOND, I. Perception, language and conceptualization rules. In B. Kleinmuntz (Ed.), *Problem solving: Research method and theory.* New York: Wiley, 1966.

HALL, J. F. *Psychology of motivation.* Philadelphia, Pa.: Lippincott, 1961.

HARLOW, H. F. Learning and satiation of response in intrinsically motivated complex puzzle performance by monkeys. *Journal of Comparative and Physiological Psychology,* 1950, 43, 289-294.

HARLOW, H. F. Motivation as a factor in the acquisition of new responses. In *Current theory and research in motivation, I.* Lincoln, Neb.: Univer. of Nebraska Press, 1953. Pp. 24-49.

HARLOW, H. F. The nature of love. *American Psychologist,* 1958, 13, 673-685.

HARLOW, H. F. Love in infant monkeys. *Scientific American,* 1959, 200, 68-74.

HARLOW, H. F. Primary affectional patterns in primates. *American Journal of Orthopsychiatry,* 1960, 30, 676-684.

HARLOW, H. F. The development of affectional patterns in infant monkeys. In B. M. Foss (Ed.), *Determinants of infant behaviour.* London: Methuen (New York: Wiley), 1961. Pp. 75-97.

HARLOW, H. F. The maternal affectional system. In B. M. Foss (Ed.), *Determinants of infant behaviour II.* London: Methuen (New York: Wiley), 1963. Pp. 3-33.

HARLOW, H. F., & HARLOW, M. K. The affectional systems. In A. M. Schrier, H. F. Harlow & F. Stollnitz (Eds.), *Behavior of nonhuman primates.* Vol. 2. New York: Academic Press, 1965. Pp. 287-334.

HARLOW, H. F., & HARLOW, M. K. Learning to love. *American Scientist,* 1966, 54, 244-272.

HARLOW, H. F., HARLOW, M. K., & MEYER, D. R. Learning motivated by the manipulation drive. *Journal of Experimental Psychology,* 1950, 40, 228-234.

HARLOW, H. F., & ZIMMERMANN, R. R. Affectional responses in the infant monkey. *Science,* 1959, 130, 421-432.

HARTMANN, H., KRIS, E., & LOWENSTEIN, R. M. Papers on psychoanalytic psychology. *Psychological issues, Monograph 14.* Vol. 4, No. 2. New York: International Universities Press, 1964.

HARVEY, O. J. Concluding comments on the current status of the incongruity hypothesis. In O. J. Harvey (Ed.), *Motivation and social interaction.* New York: Ronald Press, 1963. Pp. 289-300.

HEATHERS, G. Acquiring dependence and independence: A theoretical orientation. *Journal of Genetic Psychology,* 1955, 87, 277-291. (a)

HEATHERS, G. Emotional dependence and independence in nursery school play. *Journal of Genetic Psychology,* 1955, 87, 37-57. (b)

HEBB, D. O. On the nature of fear. *Psychological Review,* 1946, 53, 259-276.

HEBB, D. O. *The organization of behavior.* New York: Wiley, 1949.

HEBB, D. O. *A textbook of psychology.* Philadelphia: W. B. Saunders, 1966.

HEFFERLINE, R. F. Learning theory and clinical psychology—an eventual symbiosis? In A. J. Bachrach (Ed.), *Experimental foundations of clinical psychology.* New York: Basic Books, 1962. Pp. 97-137.

HELSON, H. *Adaptation-level theory.* New York: Harper, 1964.

HENDRICK, I. Instinct and ego during infancy. *Psychoanalytic Quarterly,* 1942, 11, 33-58.

HILL, W. F. Learning theory and the acquisition of values. *Psychological Review,* 1960, 67, 317-331.

HINDE, R. A. Factors governing the changes in strength of a partially inborn response, as shown by the mobbing behaviour of the Chaffinch *(Fringilla Coelebs)*: III. The interaction of short-term and long-term incremental and decremental effects. *Proceedings of the Royal Society,* Series B, 1960, 153, 398-420.

HINDE, R. A. *Animal behaviour: A synthesis of ethology and comparative psychology.* New York: McGraw-Hill, 1966.

HINDLEY, C. B. Contributions of associative learning theories to an understanding of child development. *British Journal of Medical Psychology,* 1957, 30, 241-249.

HOLT, E. B. *Animal drive and the learning process.* Vol. 1. New York: Holt, 1931.

HOLZ, W. C., & AZRIN, N. H. A comparison of several procedures for eliminating behavior. *Journal of the Experimental Analysis of Behavior,* 1963, 6, 399-406.

HOLZ, W. C., AZRIN, N. H., & AYLLON, T. Elimination of behavior of mental patients by response-produced extinction. *Journal of the Experimental Analysis of Behavior,* 1963, 6, 407-412.

HOMME, L. E., DE BOCA, P. C., DEVINE, J. V., STEINHORST, R., & RICHERT, E. J. Use of the Premack principle in controlling the behavior of nursery school children. *Journal of the Experimental Analysis of Behavior,* 1963, 6, 544.

HOROWITZ, F. D. Infant learning and development: Retrospect and prospect. *Merrill-Palmer Quarterly,* 1968, 14, 101-120.

HULL, C. L. *Principles of behavior.* New York: Appleton-Century, 1943.

HUMPHREY, G. Imitation and the conditioned reflex. *Pedagogical Seminary,* 1921, 28, 1-21.

HUNT, J. McV. Piaget's observations as a source of hypotheses concerning motivation. *Merrill-Palmer Quarterly,* 1963, 9, 263-275.

JAKOBOVITS, L. A., & LAMBERT, W. E. Semantic satiation in an addition task. *Canadian Journal of Psychology*, 1962, 16, 112-119.

JAMES, W. *Principles of psychology.* New York: Holt, 1890.

JENKINS, J. J., & PALERMO, D. S. Mediation processes and the acquisition of linguistic structure. In U. Bellugi & R. W. Brown (Eds.), The acquisition of language. *Monographs of the Society for Research in Child Development,* 1964, 29, No. 1. Pp. 79-92.

JONES, A. Drive and incentive variables associated with the statistical properties of sequences of stimuli. *Journal of Experimental Psychology,* 1964, 67, 423-431.

KAGAN, J. The concept of identification. *Psychological Review,* 1958, 65, 296-305.

KAGAN, J., & MOSS, H. A. *Birth to maturity: A study in psychological development.* New York: Wiley, 1962.

KANFER, F. H. Incentive value of generalized reinforcers. *Psychological Reports,* 1960, 7, 531-538.

KANNER, L. Problems of nosology and psychodynamics of early infantile autism. *American Journal of Orthopsychiatry,* 1949, 19, 416-426.

KANTOR, J. R. *Interbehavioral psychology.* Bloomington, Ind.: Principia Press, 1959.

KAYE, H. Infant sucking behavior and its modification. In L. P. Lipsitt & C. C. Spiker (Eds.), *Advances in child development and behavior.* Vol. 3. New York: Academic Press, 1967. Pp. 1-52.

KELLEHER, R. T. Chaining and conditioned reinforcement. In W. K. Honig (Ed.), *Operant behavior: Areas of research and application.* New York: Appleton-Century-Crofts, 1966. Pp. 160-212.

KELLEHER, R. T., & GOLLUB, L. R. A review of positive conditioned reinforcement. *Journal of the Experimental Analysis of Behavior,* 1962, 5, 543-597.

KELLER, F. S., & SCHOENFELD, W. N. *Principles of psychology.* New York: Appleton-Century-Crofts, 1950.

KEYS, A., BROZEK, J., HENSCHEL, A., MICHELSEN, O., & TAYLOR, H. L. *The biology of human starvation.* 2 Vols. Minneapolis: Univer. of Minnesota Press, 1950.

KIMBLE, G. A. *Hilgard and Marquis' conditioning and learning.* New York: Appleton-Century-Crofts, 1961.

KOCH, J. The development of conditioned orienting reaction to humans in 2-3 month infants. *Activitas Nervosa Superior,* 1965, 7, 141-142.

KOCH, J. Conditioned orienting reactions to persons and things in 2-5 month old infants. *Human Development,* 1968, 11, 81-91.

KOHLBERG, L. Moral development and identification. In H. W. Stevenson (Ed.), *Child psychology: The sixty-second yearbook of the National Society for the Study of Education.* Chicago: Univer. of Chicago Press, 1963. Pp. 277-332.

KOHLBERG, L. A cognitive-developmental analysis of children's sex-role concepts and attitudes. In E. E. Maccoby (Ed.), *The development of sex differences.* Stanford, Calif.: Stanford Univer. Press, 1966. Pp. 82-173.

KOHLBERG, L. Stage and sequence: The cognitive-developmental approach to socialization. In D. A. Goslin (Ed.), *Handbook of socialization theory and research.* Chicago: Rand McNally, 1969. Chapter 6.

LAMBERT, W. E., & JAKOBOVITS, L. A. Verbal satiation and changes in the intensity of meaning. *Journal of Experimental Psychology,* 1960, 60, 376-383.

LANDAU, R., & GEWIRTZ, J. L. Differential satiation for a social reinforcing stimulus as a determinant of its efficacy in conditioning. *Journal of Experimental Child Psychology,* 1967, 5, 391-405.

LASHLEY, K. S. Conditional reactions in the rat. *Journal of Psychology,* 1938, 6, 311-324.

LASHLEY, K. S. The problem of serial order in behavior. In L. A. Jeffress (Ed.), *Cerebral mechanisms in behavior: The Hixon symposium.* New York: Wiley, 1951. Pp. 112-136.

LAZOWICK, L. M. On the nature of identification. *Journal of Abnormal and Social Psychology,* 1955, 51, 175-183.

LENNEBERG, E. H. *Biological foundations of language.* New York: Wiley, 1967.

LEUBA, C. Tickling and laughter: Two genetic studies. *Journal of Genetic Psychology,* 1941, 58, 201-209.

LEVY, D. M. Primary affect hunger. *American Journal of Psychiatry,* 1937, 94, 643-652.

LEVY, D. M. *Maternal overprotection.* New York: Columbia Univer. Press, 1943.

LEWIN, K. The conceptual representation and measurement of forces. *Contributions to Psychological Theory,* 1938, 1 (4).

LEWIN, K. Behavior and development as a function of the total situation. In L. Carmichael (Ed.), *Manual of child psychology.* New York: Wiley, 1946. Pp. 791-844.

LEWIN, K. *Field theory in social science.* New York: Harper, 1951.

LINDSLEY, O. R. Experimental analysis of social reinforcement: Terms and methods. *American Journal of Orthopsychiatry,* 1963, 33, 624-633.

LIPSITT, L. P. Learning in the first year of life. In L. P. Lipsitt & C. C. Spiker (Eds.), *Advances in child development and behavior.* Vol. 1. New York: Academic Press, 1963. Pp. 147-194.

LIPSITT, L. P. Learning in the human infant. In H. W. Stevenson, E. H. Hess & H. L. Rheingold (Eds.), *Early behavior.* New York: Wiley, 1967. Pp. 225-247.

LIPSITT, L. P., PEDERSON, L. J., & DeLUCIA, C. A. Conjugate reinforcement of operant conditioning in infants. *Psychonomic Science,* 1966, 4, 67-68.

LOGAN, F. A. *Incentive.* New Haven: Yale Univer. Press, 1960.

LOTT, D. F. Secondary reinforcement and frustration: A conceptual paradox. *Psychological Bulletin,* 1967, 67, 197-198.

LOVAAS, O. I. Behavior therapy approach to treatment of childhood schizophrenia. In J. P. Hill (Ed.), *Minnesota symposia on child psychology.* Vol. 1. Minneapolis: Univer. of Minnesota Press, 1967.

LOVAAS, O. I., BERBERICH, J. P., PERLOFF, B. F., & SCHAEFFER, B. Acquisition of imitative speech by schizophrenic children. *Science,* 1966, 151, 705-707.

LYNN, D. B. A note on sex differences in the development of masculine and feminine identification. *Psychological Review,* 1959, 66, 126-135.

MACCOBY, E. E. Role-taking in childhood and its consequences for social learning. *Child Development,* 1959, 30, 239-252.

MALTZMAN, I. Awareness: Cognitive psychology vs. behaviorism. *Journal of Experimental Research in Personality,* 1966, 1, 161-165.

McCLELLAND, D. C. Functional autonomy of motives as an extinction phenomenon. *Psychological Review,* 1942, 49, 272-283.

McCLELLAND, D. C. *Personality.* New York: Sloane, 1951.

McCLELLAND, D. C., ATKINSON, J. W., CLARK, R. A., & LOWELL, E. L. *The achievement motive.* New York: Appleton, 1953. Pp. 6-96.

McCOY, N., & ZIGLER, E. Social reinforcer effectiveness as a function of the relationship between child and adult. *Journal of Personality and Social Psychology,* 1965, 1, 604-612.

McDOUGALL, W. *An introduction to social psychology.* (30th ed.) London: Methuen, 1950. (Originally published in 1908.)

MILLER, N. E. Experimental studies of conflict. In J. McV. Hunt (Ed.), *Personality and the behavior disorders.* Vol. 1. New York: Ronald, 1944. Pp. 431-465.

MILLER, N. E. Studies of fear as an acquirable drive: I. Fear as motivation and fear-reduction as reinforcement in the learning of new responses. *Journal of Experimental Psychology,* 1948, 38, 89-101. (a)

MILLER, N. E. Theory and experiment relating psychoanalytic displacement to stimulus-response generalization. *Journal of Abnormal and Social Psychology,* 1948, 43, 155-178. (b)

MILLER, N. E. Learnable drives and rewards. In S. S. Stevens (Ed.), *Handbook of experimental psychology.* New York: Wiley, 1951. Pp. 435-472.

MILLER, N. E. Liberalization of basic S-R concepts: Extension to conflict behavior, motivation and social learning. In S. Koch (Ed.), *Psychology: A study of a science.* Vol. 2. New York: McGraw-Hill, 1959. Pp. 196-292.

MILLER, N. E. Some reflections on the law of effect to produce a new alternative to drive reduction. In M. R. Jones (Ed.), *Nebraska symposium on motivation:1963.* Lincoln, Neb.: Univer. of Nebraska Press, 1963. Pp. 65-113.

MILLER, N. E. Some implications of modern behavior therapy for personality change and psychotherapy. In P. Worchel & D. Byrne (Eds.), *Personality change.* New York: Wiley, 1964. Pp. 149-175.

MILLER, N. E., & DOLLARD, J. *Social learning and imitation.* New Haven: Yale Univer. Press, 1941.

MISCHEL, W. A. A social-learning view of sex differences in behavior. In E. E. Maccoby (Ed.), *The development of sex differences.* Stanford, Calif.: Stanford Univer. Press, 1966. Pp. 56-81. (a)

MISCHEL, W. A. Theory and research on the antecedents of self-imposed delay of reward. In B. A. Maher (Ed.), *Progress in experimental personality research.* Vol. 3. New York: Academic Press, 1966. Pp. 85-132. (b)

MOLTZ, H. Imprinting: Empirical basis and theoretical significance. *Psychological Bulletin,* 1960, 57, 291-314.

MOLTZ, H., & STETTNER, L. J. The influence of patterned-light deprivation on the critical period for imprinting. *Journal of Comparative and Physiological Psychology,* 1961, 54, 279-283.

MONTGOMERY, K. C. The relation between exploratory behavior and spontaneous alternation in the white rat. *Journal of Comparative and Physiological Psychology,* 1951, 44, 582-589.

MONTGOMERY, K. C. Exploratory behavior as a function of "similarity" of stimulus situations. *Journal of Comparative and Physiological Psychology,* 1953, 46, 129-133

MOWRER, O. H. *Learning theory and personality dynamics.* New York: Ronald Press, 1950.

MOWRER, O. H. *Learning theory and behavior.* New York: Wiley, 1960. (a)

MOWRER, O. H. *Learning theory and the symbolic process.* New York: Wiley, 1960. (b)

MOWRER, O. H., & KLUCKHOHN, C. Dynamic theory of personality. In J. McV. Hunt (Ed.), *Personality and the behavior disorders.* Vol. 1. New York: Ronald, 1944. Pp. 69-135.

MUNN, N. L. *The evolution and growth of human behavior* (2nd Ed.). Boston: Houghton Mifflin, 1965.

MURRAY, H. A. *Explorations in personality.* New York: Oxford Univer. Press, 1938.

MYERS, A. K., & MILLER, N. E. Failure to find a learned drive based on hunger; evidence for learning motivated by "exploration." *Journal of Comparative and Physiological Psychology,* 1954, 47, 428-436.

MYERS, W. A., & TRAPOLD, M. A. Two failures to demonstrate superiority of a generalized secondary reinforcer. *Psychonomic Science,* 1966, 5, 321-322.

ODOM, R. D. Effects of auditory and visual stimulus deprivation and satiation on children's performance in an operant task. *Journal of Experimental Child Psychology,* 1964, 1, 16-25.

OSGOOD, C. E. *Method and theory in experimental psychology.* New York: Oxford Univer. Press, 1953.

OSGOOD, C. E. On understanding and creating sentences. *American Psychologist,* 1963, 18, 735-751.

PAPOUSEK, H. The development of higher nervous activity in children in the first half-year of life. In P. H. Mussen (Ed.), European research in cognitive development. *Monographs of the Society for Research in Child Development,* 1965, 30, No. 2 (Whole No. 100), 102-111.

PAPOUSEK, H. Experimental studies of appetitional behavior in human newborns and infants. In H. W. Stevenson, E. H. Hess & H. L. Rheingold (Eds.), *Early behavior.* New York: Wiley, 1967. Pp. 249-277.

PARKE, R. D., & WALTERS, R. H. Some factors influencing the efficacy of punishment training for inducing response inhibition. *Monographs of the Society for Research in Child Development,* 1967, 32, (Whole No. 109).

PATTERSON, G. R. Social learning: An additional base for developing behavior modification technologies. In C. Frank (Ed.), *Assessment and status of the behavior therapies and associated developments.* New York: McGraw-Hill, 1967.

PATTERSON, G. R., LITTMAN, R., & HINSEY, W. C. Parental effectiveness as reinforcers in the laboratory and its relation to child rearing practices and child adjustment in the classroom. *Journal of Personality,* 1964, 32, 180-199.

PAYNE, D. E., & MUSSEN, P. H. Parent-child relations and father identification among adolescent boys. *Journal of Abnormal and Social Psychology,* 1956, 52, 358-362.

PIAGET, J. *Psychology of intelligence.* New York: Harcourt, Brace, 1950.

PIAGET, J. *Play, dreams and imitation in childhood.* New York: Norton, 1951.

PIAGET, J. *The origins of intelligence in children.* New York: International Universities Press, 1952.

PREMACK, D. Toward empirical behavior laws: I. Positive reinforcement. *Psychological Review,* 1959, 66, 219-233.

PREMACK, D. Reversibility of the reinforcement relation. *Science,* 1962, 136, 255-257.

PREMACK, D., & COLLIER, G. Analysis of nonreinforcement variables affecting response probability. *Psychological Monographs,* 1962, 76, No. 5 (Whole No. 524).

RAUSH, H. L. Interaction sequences. *Journal of Personality and Social Psychology,* 1965, 2, 487-499.

REICHENBACH, H. *Experience and prediction.* Chicago: Univer. of Chicago Press, 1938.

REICHENBACH, H. *The rise of scientific philosophy.* Berkeley, Calif.: Univer. of California Press, 1951.

RETHLINGSHAFER, D. Experimental evidence for functional autonomy of motives. *Psychological Review,* 1943, 50, 397-407.

RHEINGOLD, H. L. The development of social behavior in the human infant. In H. W. Stevenson (Ed.), Concept of development: A report of a conference commemorating the fortieth anniversary of the Institute of Child Development, University of Minnesota. *Monographs of the Society for Research in Child Development,* 1966, 31, No. 5 (Whole No. 107), 2-17.

RHEINGOLD, H. L., GEWIRTZ, J. L., & ROSS, H. W. Social conditioning of vocalizations in the infant. *Journal of Comparative and Physiological Psychology,* 1959, 52, 68-73.

RHEINGOLD, H. L., STANLEY, W. C., & COOLEY, J. A. Method for studying exploratory behavior in infants. *Science,* 1962, 136, 1054-1055.

RIBBLE, M. A. *The rights of infants*. New York: Columbia Univer. Press, 1943.

RIBBLE, M. A. Infantile experience in relation to personality development. In J. McV. Hunt (Ed.), *Personality and the behavior disorders*. New York: Ronald, 1944. Pp. 621-651.

RIBBLE, M. A. *The rights of infants: Early psychological needs and their satisfaction*. New York: Columbia Univer. Press, 1965.

RISLEY, T., & WOLF, M. Establishing functional speech in echolalic children. *Behavior Research and Therapy*, 1967, 5, 73-88.

ROSENTHAL, R. *Experimenter effects in behavioral research*. New York: Appleton-Century-Crofts, 1966.

ROTTER, J. B. *Social learning and clinical psychology*. New York: Prentice-Hall, 1954.

ROTTER, J. B. Some implications of a social learning theory for the prediction of goal directed behavior from testing procedures. *Psychological Review*, 1960, 67, 301-316.

ROTTER, J., SEEMAN, M., & LIVERANT, S. Internal versus external control of reinforcements: A major variable in behavior theory. In N. F. Washburne (Ed.), *Decisions, values, and groups*. New York: Pergamon Press, 1962. Pp. 473-516.

SALZEN, E. A. Imprinting in birds and primates. *Behaviour*, 1967, 28 (3-4), 232-254.

SANFORD, N. The dynamics of identification. *Psychological Review*, 1955, 62, 106-118.

SCHACHTER, S. *The psychology of affiliation*. Stanford, Calif.: Stanford Univer. Press, 1959.

SCHAFFER, H. R., & EMERSON, P. E. The development of social attachments in infancy. *Monographs of the Society for Research in Child Development*, 1964, 29, 1-77.

SCHOENFELD, W. N., ANTONITIS, J. J., & BERSH, P. J. A preliminary study of training conditions necessary for secondary reinforcement. *Journal of Experimental Psychology*, 1950, 40, 40-45.

SCOTT, J. P. The process of primary socialization in canine and human infants. In *Exceptional infant: The normal infant*. Vol. 1. Seattle, Wash.: Special Child Publications, 1967.

SCOTT, J. P. *Early experience and the organization of behavior*. Belmont, Calif.: Brooks/Cole (Wadsworth), 1968.

SEARS, R. R. *Survey of objective studies of psychoanalytic concepts*. New York: Social Science Research Council, 1943. Bulletin No. 51.

SEARS, R. R. Experimental analysis of psychoanalytic phenomena. In J. McV. Hunt (Ed.), *Personality and the behavior disorders*. Vol. 1. New York: Ronald, 1944. Pp. 306-332.

SEARS, R. R. A theoretical framework for personality and social behavior. *American Psychologist*, 1951, 6, 476-483.

SEARS, R. R. Identification as a form of behavioral development. In D. B. Harris (Ed.), *The concept of development*. Minneapolis: Univer. of Minnesota Press, 1957. Pp. 149-161.

SEARS, R. R. Dependency motivation. In M. R. Jones (Ed.), *Nebraska symposium on motivation: 1963*. Lincoln, Neb.: Univer. of Nebraska Press, 1963. Pp. 25-65.

SEARS, R. R., MACCOBY, E. E., & LEVIN, H. *Patterns of child rearing*. Evanston, Ill.: Row, Peterson, 1957.

SEARS, R. R., RAU, L., & ALPERT, R. *Identification and child rearing*. Stanford, Calif.: Stanford Univer. Press, 1965.

SEARS, R. R., WHITING, J. W. M., NOWLIS, V., & SEARS, P. S. Some child-rearing antecedents of aggression and dependency in young children. *Genetic Psychology Monographs*, 1953, 47, 135-234.

SEWARD, J. P. Learning theory and identification: II. Role of punishment. *Journal of Genetic Psychology*, 1954, 84, 201-210.

SHAFFER, L. F. *The psychology of adjustment.* New York: Houghton Mifflin, 1936.

SHURE, M. B. Psychological ecology of a nursery school. *Child Development,* 1963, 34, 979-993.

SIQUELAND, E. R. Operant conditioning of head turning in four-month infants. *Psychonomic Science,* 1964, 1, 223-224.

SIQUELAND, E. R., & LIPSITT, L. P. Conditioned head-turning in human newborns. *Journal of Experimental Child Psychology,* 1966, 3, 356-376.

SKINNER, B. F. *The behavior of organisms.* New York: Appleton-Century, 1938.

SKINNER, B. F. *Walden two.* New York: Macmillan, 1948.

SKINNER, B. F. *Science and human behavior.* New York: Macmillan, 1953.

SKINNER, B. F. The science of learning and the art of teaching. *Harvard Educational Review,* 1954, 24, 86-97.

SKINNER, B. F. *Verbal behavior.* New York: Appleton-Century-Crofts, 1957.

SLUCKIN, W. Perceptual and associative learning. *Symposia of the Zoological Society of London,* 1962, 8, 193-198.

SOLOMON, R. L. Punishment. *American Psychologist,* 1964, 19, 239-253.

SPENCE, K. W. The methods and postulates of "behaviorism." *Psychological Review,* 1948, 55, 67-78.

SPENCE, K. W. *Behavior theory and conditioning.* New Haven: Yale Univer. Press, 1956.

SPENCE, K. W. The empirical basis and theoretical structure of psychology. *Philosophy of Science,* 1957, 24, 97-108.

SPIKER, C. The concept of development: Relevant and irrelevant issues. In H. W. Stevenson (Ed.), Concept of development: A report of a conference commemorating the fortieth anniversary of the Institute of Child Development, University of Minnesota. *Monographs of the Society for Research in Child Development,* 1966, 31, No. 5 (Whole No. 107), 40-54.

SPITZ, R. A. Anaclitic depression. In R. S. Eissler, A. Freud, H. Hartmann & M. Kris (Eds.), *The psychoanalytic study of the child.* Vol. 2. New York: International Universities Press, 1946. Pp. 313-342. (a)

SPITZ, R. A. Hospitalism: A follow-up report. In R. S. Eissler, A. Freud, H. Hartmann & M. Kris (Eds.), *The psychoanalytic study of the child.* Vol. 2. New York: International Universities Press, 1946. Pp. 113-117. (b)

SPITZ, R. A. The role of ecological factors in emotional development in infancy. *Child Development,* 1949, 20, 145-156.

SPITZ, R. A. Anxiety in infancy: A study of its manifestations in the first year of life. *International Journal of Psychonanalysis,* 1950, 31, 138-143.

SPITZ, R. A. Unhappy and fatal outcomes of emotional deprivation and stress in infancy. In I. Galdston (Ed.), *Beyond the germ theory.* New York: Health Education Council, 1954. Pp. 120-131.

STAATS, A. W., & STAATS, C. K. *Complex human behavior.* New York: Holt, Rinehart & Winston, 1963.

STEIN, L. Secondary reinforcement established with subcortical reinforcement. *Science,* 1958, 127, 466-467.

STENDLER, C. B. Possible causes of overdependency in young children. *Child Development,* 1954, 25, 125-146.

STEVENSON, H. W. Social reinforcement of children's behavior. In L. P. Lipsitt & C. C. Spiker (Eds.), *Advances in child development and behavior.* Vol. 2. New York: Academic Press, 1965. Pp. 97-126.

STEVENSON, H. W., & ODOM, R. D. Effects of pretraining on the reinforcing value of visual stimuli. *Child Development,* 1961, 32, 739-744.

STEVENSON, H. W., & ODOM, R. D. The effectiveness of social reinforcement following two conditions of social deprivation. *Journal of Abnormal and Social Psychology,* 1962, 65, 429-431.

TERRACE, H. S. Discrimination learning with and without "errors." *Journal of the Experimental Analysis of Behavior,* 1963, 6, 1-27. (a)

TERRACE, H. S. Errorless transfer of a discrimination across two continua. *Journal of the Experimental Analysis of Behavior,* 1963, 6, 223-232. (b)

TERRACE, H. S. Stimulus control. In W. K. Honig (Ed.), *Operant behavior: Areas of research and application.* New York: Appleton-Centruy-Crofts, 1966. Pp. 271-345.

TOLMAN, E. C. The determiners of behavior at a choice point. *Psychological Review,* 1938, 45, 1-41.

ULLMANN, L. P., & KRASNER, L. (Eds.) *Case studies in behavior modification.* New York: Holt, Rinehart & Winston, 1965.

VINCE, M. A. Developmental changes in learning capacity. In W. H. Thorpe & O. L. Zangwill (Eds.), *Current problems in animal behaviour.* Cambridge: Cambridge Univer. Press, 1961. Pp. 225-247.

WALTERS, R. H., & PARKE, R. D. Social motivation, dependency, and susceptibility to social influence. In L. Berkowitz (Ed.), *Advances in experimental social psychology.* Vol. 1. New York: Academic Press, 1964. Pp. 231-276.

WALTERS, R. H., & PARKE, R. D. The role of the distance receptors in the development of social responsiveness. In L. P. Lipsitt & C. C. Spiker (Eds.), *Advances in child development and behavior.* Vol. 2. New York: Academic Press, 1965. Pp. 59-96.

WALTERS, R. H., & PARKE, R. D. The influence of punishment and related disciplinary techniques on the social behavior of children: Theory and empirical findings. In B. A. Maher (Ed.), *Progress in experimental personality research.* Vol. 4. New York: Academic Press, 1967. Pp. 179-228.

WALTERS, R. H., PARKE, R. D., & CANE, V. A. Timing of punishment and the observation of consequences to others as determinants of response inhibition. *Journal of Experimental Child Psychology,* 1965, 2, 10-30.

WALTERS, R. H., & RAY, E. Anxiety, social isolation, and reinforcer effectiveness. *Journal of Personality,* 1960, 28, 358-367.

WEISBERG, P. Social and non-social conditioning of infant vocalizations. *Child Development,* 1963, 34, 377-388.

WEISMAN, R., & PREMACK, D. Punishment and reinforcement produced by reversal of the probability relation between two responses. *Program of the Seventh Annual Scientific Meeting of the Psychonomic Society,* 1966, 20-21. (Abstract)

WEISS, B., & LATIES, V. G. Characteristics of aversive thresholds measured by a titration schedule. *Journal of the Experimental Analysis of Behavior,* 1963, 6, 563-572.

WELKER, W. I. Variability of play and exploratory behavior in chimpanzees. *Journal of Comparative and Physiological Psychology,* 1956, 49, 181-185.

WELKER, W. I. An analysis of exploratory and play behavior in animals. In D. W. Fiske & S. R. Maddi (Eds.), *Functions of varied experience.* Homewood, Ill.: Dorsey, 1961. Pp. 175-226.

WHITE, R. W. Motivation reconsidered: The concept of competence. *Psychological Review,* 1959, 66, 297-333.

WHITE, R. W. Ego and reality in psychoanalytic theory. *Psychological issues, Monograph 11.* Vol. 3, No. 3. New York: International Universities Press, 1963. Pp. 1-210.

WHITING, J. W. M. Resource mediation and learning by identification. In I. Iscoe & H. W. Stevenson (Eds.), *Personality development in children.* Austin: Univer. of Texas Press, 1960. Pp. 112-126.

WHITING, J. W. M., & CHILD, I. L. *Child training and personality.* New Haven: Yale Univer. Press, 1953.

WIKE, E. L., & BARRIENTOS, G. Secondary reinforcement and multiple drive reduction. *Journal of Comparative and Physiological Psychology,* 1958, 51, 640-643.

WIKE, E. L., & McNAMARA, H. J. A quest for the generalized conditioned reinforcer. *Psychological Reports,* 1955, 1, 83-91.

WOODWORTH, R. S. *Dynamics of behavior.* New York: Holt, 1958.

YARROW, L. J. Maternal deprivation: Toward an empirical and conceptual re-evaluation. *Psychological Bulletin,* 1961, 58, 459-490.

ZIGLER, E. Metatheoretical issues in developmental psychology. In M. H. Marx (Ed.), *Theories in contemporary psychology.* New York: Macmillan, 1963. Pp. 341-369. (a)

ZIGLER, E. Social reinforcement, environmental conditions, and the child. *American Journal of Orthopsychiatry,* 1963, 33, 614-623. (b)

ZIMMERMAN, D. W. Durable secondary reinforcement: Method and theory. *Psychological Review,* 1957, 64, 373-383.

ZIMMERMAN, J. Technique for sustaining behavior with conditioned reinforcement. *Science,* 1963, 142, 682-684.

CHAPTER **3**

Social-Learning Theory
Of Identificatory Processes

Albert Bandura

Stanford University

Among the various processes involved in socialization, identificatory learning is generally assigned a prominent role regardless of whether explanatory theories favor psychological or sociological variables. There are several reasons for this emphasis. It is evident from informal observation that the complex repertoires of behavior displayed by members of society are to a large extent acquired with little or no direct tuition through observation of response patterns exemplified by various socialization agents. This is particularly true of behavior for which there is no reliable eliciting stimulus apart from the cues furnished by the responses of others.

The provision of social models is also an indispensible means of transmitting and modifying behavior in situations where errors are likely to produce costly or fatal consequences. Indeed, if social learning proceeded exclusively on the basis of rewarding and punishing consequences, most people would never survive the socialization process. Even in cases where nonsocial stimuli can be relied upon to elicit some approximation of the desired behavior, and errors do not result in perilous outcomes, people are customarily spared exceedingly tedious and often haphazard trial-and-error experimentation by emulating the behavior of socially competent models. In fact, it would be difficult to imagine a socialization process in which the language, mores, vocational and avocational patterns, the familial customs of a culture, and its educational, social, and political practices were shaped in each new member by selective reinforcement without the response guidance of models who exhibit the accumulated cultural repertoires in their own behavior. To the extent that people successfully match the behavior of appropriate societal models, the social-learning process can be greatly accelerated and the development of response patterns by differential reinforcement can be short-circuited.

Much of the research reported in this chapter was supported by Research Grant M-5162 from the National Institutes of Health, United States Public Health Service.

DEFINITION AND MEASUREMENT OF IDENTIFICATION

Although wide differences of opinion exist among personality theorists in what they consider to be the most suitable reference events for identification, it is generally agreed that identification refers to a process in which a person patterns his thoughts, feelings, or actions after another person who serves as a model. The present chapter deals mainly with the conceptual scheme, strategies of research, and major findings based on a social-learning theory of identification. However, some consideration will be given to other theoretical approaches, particularly in instances where several alternative explanations of specific modeling phenomena are indicated.

Measures of Identification
Based on Actual or Assumed Similarity

In empirical investigations of modeling processes, the degree of similarity between a subject's self-description on some type of personality questionnaire and his description of his parents on the same or a similar test is occasionally employed as an index of parental identification (Heilbrun, 1965; Sopchak, 1952). A more commonly used variant of this procedure operationally defines identification in terms of the degree of correspondence in self-description scores on an inventory completed independently by the subject and the person who presumably is taken as the model (Cass, 1952; Gray & Klaus, 1956; Helper, 1955; Lazowick, 1955; Payne & Mussen, 1956). In other instances identification scores are obtained by comparing ratings of the participants' personality characteristics by one or more observers who are well-acquainted with the persons under study (Hetherington, 1965).

The interpretation of these types of difference scores and the various possible combinations of actual and assumed resemblances as valid measures of identification has been seriously questioned on numerous grounds by Bronfenbrenner (1958) and Cronbach (1955). First, self-descriptions and ratings by observers are susceptible to response biases which may artificially inflate or diminish identification scores. The issue of rater contamination is particularly serious in cases where the same person evaluates both himself and the model. Second, questionnaire techniques measure similarity only in self-descriptive responses which, in many cases, may have little relationship to respondents' actual social behavior. Accuracy of self-definition is affected not only by response sets and item ambiguity, but also by adequacy of self-observation. Third, the use of global indices, in which responses to a heterogeneous set of test items are combined into a single identification score, assumes a high degree of generality between modeling outcomes presumably mediated by a unitary identification process. Contrary to the unitary theory, evidence to be cited later in this chapter clearly indicates that persons are quite discriminative in the types of behaviors they select to reproduce. Consequently, intercorrelations among different classes of matching responses tend to be relatively low. Fourth, measures derived from difference scores involving self-ratings are affected by statistical artifacts such as the lack of independence of errors of measurement, regression effects, and treatment of data measured in ordinal scales as though the points had equivalent meaning and represented equal intervals to different raters.

Even if ingenious procedures could be devised to overcome the numerous psychometric problems, measures of real or assumed similarity as indices of identification would still have serious limitations. All parent-child resemblances in attitudes or behavior do not necessarily represent outcomes of a modeling process. Many behavioral similarities undoubtedly result from direct tuition, selective exposure to environmental settings and activities, and the influence of common reinforcement contingencies in specific cultural subgroups.

Sex-role behavior, for example, which is generally attributed to identificatory processes, provides an excellent example of active parental training in sex-appropriate interests and modes of behavior before young children have much opportunity to observe and to discriminate accurately the sexual appropriateness of response patterns displayed by adult males and females. Sex-role differentiation usually commences immediately after birth when the baby is named and both the infant and the nursery are given the blue or pink treatment depending upon the sex of the child. Thereafter, indoctrination into masculinity and femininity is diligently promulgated by adorning children with distinctive clothes and hair styles, selecting sex-appropriate play materials and recreational activities, promoting associations with same-sex playmates, and through nonpermissive parental reactions to deviant sex-role behavior. In view of the extensive discrimination training, peer modeling, and frequent maternal demonstrations of masculine activities at times when the father is absent, it seems highly improbable that a three-year-old child looks and behaves like a boy primarily as a result of identifying with a 35-year-old man whom he can observe for relatively brief periods mainly during leisure-time activities if the commuting schedule happens to be favorable.

In most instances behavioral similarities are attributable in large part to modeling processes. The problem of identifying the sources of emulated behavior, however, is complicated by the fact that children are repeatedly exposed to multiple models including teachers, other adults in the immediate neighborhood, peer companions, and a host of prestigeful models presented mainly through television and films. It is therefore extremely doubtful that children rely exclusively on parents as models for the diverse response patterns that are characteristically displayed at different periods of development. Moreover, the findings of Lazowick (1955) and Helper (1955) that people show no greater similarity to their actual parents than to randomly matched parental figures suggest that measures of identification based on personality questionnaires primarily assess general culturally conditioned patterns of behavior basic to all members of the same sex, or to raters' sex-linked stereotypes.

Identification Measured in Terms of
Adult-Role Behavior, Sex-Typing and
Behavioral Manifestations of Self-Control

A second major approach to the study of modeling processes focuses attention on hypothesized products of identification rather than on actual behavioral similarities between parent and child. According to this theoretical formulation, which is most clearly explicated by Sears and his associates (Sears, Rau & Alpert, 1965), a single mediating process of identification governs the development of diverse types of responses including sex-role behavior, prosocial aggression, adult-like attitudes and conduct, resistance to deviation, and guilt reactions following transgression. Research guided by this point of view attempts to link child-rearing antecedents supposedly determining the hypothetical process of identification to their presumed behavioral manifestations. Various measures of identificatory behavior are typically employed in these studies including use of male or female dolls as agents of doll-play actions (Levin & R. R. Sears, 1956; P. S. Sears, 1953), choices between responses portrayed by doll models in doll-play situations (Hartup, 1964), projective tests of sex-role preference (Mussen & Distler, 1959), and responses to vocational interest tests (Mussen, 1961). Identification is also frequently inferred from the presence of adult-like attitudes and behavior, sex-typed characteristics, and indices of self-control based on behavioral observations, projective tests, parental interviews, and semi-structured parent-child interactions (Sears et al., 1965).

Both the conceptual structure and the dependent variables of psychodynamically-based approaches to identification are beleaguered by serious problems, not the least of which is evidence that the myriad behaviors presumably generated by the single mediating process are not positively intercorrelated to any appreciable degree (Bandura & Walters, 1963; Sears et al., 1965). A single unitary mediator cannot possibly account for the remarkable variety of heterogeneous responses and changes in their occurrence under different stimulus conditions, toward different persons, and at different times. It would seem that a considerably more complex theory of modeling is required.

As in the case of similarity measures, the major methodological difficulties with most of the popular indices of identification arise from failure to establish the source of children's responses, or to demonstrate that they are in fact products of a modeling process. There is substantial evidence from laboratory studies (Aronfreed, 1967; Bandura & Walters, 1963), for example, that reinforcement variables can be influential in establishing resistance to deviation and self-punitive responses following transgression. Moreover, the reinforcement contingencies required for the acquisition of these two modes of response differ markedly. Therefore it is not surprising that no consistent relationships between resistance to temptation and guilt have emerged from numerous studies in which both variables have been measured, and that the child-rearing antecedents of these indices of moral development are somewhat different (Hoffman, 1963).

The evidential value of linkages between child-rearing practices and behavioral qualities attributed to identification for a theory of modeling is difficult to evaluate when the most critical set of variables—namely, the actual content of the attitudes, values, and social behavior displayed by parental models—is not directly and intensively assessed, as is often the case. Thus, a boy who deviates readily and experiences little or no guilt over violation of prohibitions would be considered deficient in identificatory behavior even if this resulted from emulating antisocial attitudes of a deviant parental model. Similarly, the presence of feminine interests, mannerisms, and personality characteristics in a boy who identified strongly with an effeminate father would receive low scores on paternal identification. It is apparent from these examples that identificatory behavior has no intrinsic defining properties and consequently, it cannot be identified or validly measured independently of the behavior of the persons who have been emulated. The specific origin of social behavior is further obscured by the fact that after particular responses have been acquired observationally, they may later be evoked by a variety of models and appropriate situational cues. When there exists considerable homogeneity in the behavior displayed by societal models, there is no reliable means of determining whether a given pattern of behavior was originally adapted from parents, peers, teachers, other adults or even from influential televised characters.

Definition and Measurement of
Identificatory Processes in Social-Learning Theory

In social-learning theory an identificatory event is defined as the occurrence of similarity between the behavior of a model and another person under conditions where the model's behavior has served as the determinative cue for the matching responses.[1] Although the matching process frequently involves reproduction of specific patterns of behavior, in many instances a common attribute abstracted from diverse responses is modeled. It should be noted that both the characteristics of the behavior and its antecedents are the principal defining properties of identification. The reason for considering the stimulus source of behavior is that two or more persons may exhibit identical responses to the same environmental cues without the occurrence of any identification (e.g., when several motorists stop their automobiles the moment a red signal light flashes).

Pseudo-identification is also involved in cases where differential situational cues independently elicit similar patterns of behavior in different participants.

---

[1] The term "behavior" is employed in the broad sense to include motoric, cognitive, and physiological classes of response.

This point is dramatically illustrated in a story, definitely apocryphal, about a big-game hunter who, after many days of fruitless search for wild animals, finally came face to face with a ferocious lion. As he prepared to shoot the onrushing beast, the gun jammed. Helpless and terrified, the hunter promptly closed his eyes and began to pray rapidly. Moments passed and, much to his surprise, nothing happened. Puzzled by this unexpected turn of events, the hunter cocked his head, and slowly opened his eyes to find the lion also bowed in prayer. The jubilant hunter loudly exclaimed, "Thank God, you are responding to my prayers!" The lion promptly replied, "Not at all, I'm saying grace."

In dealing with naturally occurring events it is exceedingly difficult to establish precisely the stimulus sources of a person's social behavior. Consequently, laboratory studies in which models exhibit novel responses that do not exist in observers' behavioral repertoires can provide the most definitive information about the conditions regulating identificatory learning. Moreover, to the extent that investigators can successfully generate and modify identificatory behavior by systematic manipulation of variables considered germane to the phenomenon by their theory, one can place considerable confidence in the validity of the guiding theoretical principles.

Regardless of how identification may be defined, the actual behavioral phenomenon encompassed by the construct (i.e., the occurrence of matching behavior as a function of exposure to modeling cues) is no more complicated nor elusive than most other psychological events. Even a cursory review of the relevant literature discloses, however, that the phenomenon has become hopelessly entangled in semantics as a result of efforts to differentiate various forms of matching behavior. For example, on the basis of numerous arbitrary criteria, one finds distinctions among "identification," "imitation," "introjection," "incorporation," "internalization," "copying," and "role-taking," to mention only a few of the more popular varieties.

Identification has been most frequently differentiated from imitation in terms of outcome variables on the assumed basis that imitation involves the reproduction of discrete responses whereas identification involves the adoption of either diverse patterns of behavior (Kohlberg, 1963; Parsons, 1955; Stoke, 1950), symbolic representations of the model (Emmerich, 1959), or similar meaning systems (Lazowick, 1955). Sometimes the distinction is made in terms of differential antecedent or maintaining variables as illustrated in Parsons' (1951) view that a "generalized cathectic attachment" is a necessary precondition for identification but is unessential or absent in the case of imitation; Kohlberg (1963), on the other hand, reserves the term identification for matching behavior that is presumed to be maintained by the intrinsic reinforcement of perceived similarity and the construct imitation for instrumental responses supported by extrinsic rewards. Others define imitation as matching behavior occurring in the presence of the model, while endowing identification with the performance of the model's behavior in the latter's absence (Kohlberg, 1963; Mowrer, 1950). Not only is there little consensus with respect to differentiating criteria, but some theorists assume that imitation produces identification, whereas others contend, with equally strong conviction, that identification gives rise to imitation.

Unless it can be shown that vicarious learning of different classes of matching behavior is governed by separate independent variables, distinctions proposed in terms of forms of emulated responses are not only gratuitous, but breed unnecessary confusion. Limited progress would be made in elucidating behavioral change processes if, for example, fundamentally different learning mechanisms were invoked, without adequate empirical basis, to account for the acquisition of one social response and ten interrelated social responses that are designated as various aspects of a given role. Results of numerous studies to be reviewed later demonstrate that the acquisition of isolated matching responses and entire behavioral repertoires is determined by the same antecedent conditions. Further, retention and delayed reproduction of even discrete matching responses require representational mediation of modeling stimuli. There is also little reason to suppose, either on empirical or theoretical grounds, that different principles and processes are involved in the acquisition of matching responses that are subsequently performed in the presence or in the absence of the model. Indeed, if the diverse criteria enumerated above were seriously applied, either singly or in various combinations, in categorizing modeling outcomes, most instances of matching behavior that have been labelled imitation would qualify as identification, and much of the naturalistic data cited as evidence of identificatory learning would be reclassified as imitation.

Although it is possible to draw distinctions among descriptive terms based on antecedent, mediating, or behavioral variables, one might question whether it is advantageous to do so, since there is every indication that essentially the same learning process is involved regardless of the content and generality of what is learned, the models from whom the response patterns are acquired, and the stimulus conditions under which emulative behavior is subsequently performed. Therefore, in the interests of clarity and parsimony the terms "identification," "imitation," and "observational learning" will be employed interchangeably to refer to behavioral modifications resulting from exposure to modeling stimuli.

LEARNING MECHANISM
UNDERLYING MODELING PROCESSES

In evaluating theories of identification or modeling phenomena, it is essential to distinguish between *acquisition* and spontaneous *performance* of matching behavior because these events are determined by different sets of variables. Traditional theories of identification devote a great deal of attention to familial conditions that may be conducive to modeling performance, but these formulations rarely specify the basic learning mechanisms by which persons acquire response patterns through exposure to the behavior of models. An adequate theoretical account of identification must designate the variables regulating observational response acquisition, the factors influencing long-term retention of previously learned matching responses, and the conditions affecting degree of behavioral reproduction of modeling stimuli.

A number of theorists, in their efforts to explain imitation, have offered detailed analyses of modeling phenomena in terms of instinctual propensities (Morgan, 1896; Tarde, 1903; McDougall, 1908), associative and classical conditioning mechanisms (Allport, 1924; Holt, 1931; Humphrey, 1921; Mowrer, 1960; Piaget, 1951), or reinforcement theories of instrumental conditioning (Miller & Dollard, 1941; Skinner, 1953; Baer & Sherman, 1964). As discussed at length elsewhere (Bandura, 1965a), the latter theoretical formulations account satisfactorily for the control of previously learned matching responses. However, they fail to explain how new response patterns are acquired observationally, particularly under conditions where an observer does not overtly perform the model's responses during the acquisition phase, reinforcers are not administered either to the model or to the observer, and the first appearance of the acquired response may be delayed for days, weeks, or even months. Since observers can acquire only perceptual and other symbolic responses resembling the sequences of modeling stimuli while they are occurring, internal representational processes which mediate subsequent behavioral reproduction obviously play a prominent role in observational learning.

Mechanisms of Observational Learning

Recent theoretical analyses of observational learning (Bandura, 1962, 1965a; Sheffield, 1961)—which is the basic learning process underlying identification, however defined—assign a prominent role to representational mediators that are assumed to be acquired on the basis of a contiguity learning process. According to my formulation observational learning involves two representational systems—an *imaginal* and a *verbal* one. After modeling stimuli have been coded into images or words for memory representation they function as mediators for response retrieval and reproduction.

Imagery formation is assumed to occur through a process of sensory conditioning. That is, during the period of exposure, modeling stimuli elicit in observers perceptual responses that become sequentially associated and centrally integrated on the basis of temporal contiguity of stimulation. If perceptual sequences are repeatedly elicited, a constituent stimulus acquires the capacity to evoke images of the associated stimulus events even though they are no longer physically present (Conant, 1964; Ellson, 1941; Leuba, 1940). These findings indicate that, in the course of observation, transitory perceptual phenomena produce relatively enduring, retrievable images of modeled sequences of behavior. Later, reinstatement of imaginal mediators serves as a guide for reproduction of matching responses.

The second representational system, which probably accounts for the notable speed of observational learning and long-term retention of modeled contents by humans, involves verbal coding of observed events. Most of the cognitive processes that regulate behavior are primarily verbal rather than visual. To take a simple example, the route traversed by a model can be acquired, retained, and later reproduced more accurately by verbal coding of the visual information into a sequence of right-left turns (e.g., RRLRLL) than by reliance upon visual imagery of the itinerary. After modeled sequences of responses have been transformed into readily utilizable verbal symbols, performances of matching behavior on later occasions can be effectively controlled by covert verbal self-directions.

The influential role of symbolic representation in observational learning is disclosed in a study (Bandura, Grusec & Menlove, 1966) in which children were exposed to complex sequences of modeled behavior on film during which they either watched attentively, verbalized the novel responses as they were performed by the model, or counted rapidly while watching the film to prevent implicit coding of modeling cues. A subsequent test of observational learning disclosed that children who generated verbal equivalents of modeled stimuli reproduced significantly more matching responses than those in the viewing alone condition who, in turn, showed a higher level of acquisition than children who engaged in competing symbolization.

Further supporting evidence for the influence of symbolic coding operations in the acquisition and retention of modeled responses is furnished by Gerst (1968). Subjects observed a filmed model perform motoric responses varying in the ease with which they can be verbally coded and they were instructed to transform the items into either vivid images, concrete verbal descriptions of the response elements, or convenient summary labels that incorporate the essential ingredients of the responses. Compared to the performance of controls who had no opportunity to generate symbolic mediators, all three coding operations enhanced observational learning. Concise labeling and imaginal codes were equally effective in aiding immediate reproduction of modeled responses and both systems proved superior in this respect to the concrete verbal form. However, a subsequent test for retention of modeled responses showed concise labeling to be the best coding system for memory representation. Subjects in the latter condition retained most of what they learned, whereas those who relied upon imagery and concrete verbalization displayed a substantial loss of matching responses.

Results of a program of research utilizing a nonresponse acquisition procedure (Bandura, 1965a) indicate that the organization of behavior elements into novel patterns resembling modeled stimulus compounds can occur at a central level without motoric responding. The present theory assumes, however, that *stimulus contiguity is a necessary, but not a sufficient, condition for acquisition and performance of modeled patterns of behavior.* Modeling phenomena, in fact, involve complex interactions of numerous subprocesses each with its own set of controlling variables. A comprehensive theory of identification must therefore encompass the various subsystems governing the broader phenomena. The subprocesses that markedly influence the degree and content of observational learning are discussed next.

Attentional processes. At the sensory registration level, it is exceedingly unlikely that a person could reproduce modeling stimuli if he did not attend to, recognize, and differentiate the distinctive features of the model's responses. Considerable research is needed to evaluate the effects on observational learning of visual exposure variables including the frequency, duration, rate, saliency, multiplicity, and complexity of modeling cues.

In the case of highly intricate response systems such as linguistic behavior, children encounter considerable difficulty in acquiring linguistic structures because the identifying characteristics of different grammatical constructions cannot be readily distinguished within extremely diverse and complex utterances. Given high occurrence of observing responses and the presence of adequate discriminative cues, relatively complicated response patterns can be acquired observationally (Bandura & Harris, 1966; Sheffield & Maccoby, 1961).

Simply exposing persons to distinctive sequences of modeling stimuli is no guarantee that they will attend closely to the cues, that they will necessarily select from the total stimulus complex only the most relevant stimuli, or that they will even perceive accurately the cues to which their attention has been directed. Motivational conditions, prior training in discriminative observation, and the presence of incentive-oriented sets may strongly determine those features of the social environment which will be of greatest interest and to which the person will pay closest attention. In addition, observer characteristics and other social factors that affect association preferences will determine to a large degree the types of models who are selected for observation and consequently, the modes of behavior that will be most thoroughly learned.

Retention processes. Another basic component function involved in observational learning, but one that has been virtually ignored in theories of identification, concerns the long-term retention of coded modeling events. This is a particularly interesting problem in cases where children, for example, acquire patterns of behavior observationally and retain them over extended periods even though the response tendencies have rarely, if ever, been activated into overt performance until the persons reach the age or social status that makes the activity appropriate and permissible.

Among the numerous variables governing retention processes, rehearsal operations effectively stabilize and strengthen acquired responses. The level of observational learning can be considerably enhanced through overt practice or rehearsal of modeled response sequences (Margolius & Sheffield, 1961). Of greater import is evidence that covert rehearsal, which can be readily engaged in when overt participation is either impeded or impracticable, may likewise enhance retention of acquired matching responses (Michael & N. Maccoby, 1961).

The influential function of covert role-practice of modeled behaviors has received greatest emphasis in E. E. Maccoby's (1959) account of the identification process. According to this view, controlling, nurturant, and caretaking activities require explicit reciprocal behaviors on the part of parents and children. Consequently, in the course of frequent mutually dependent interactions, both participants learn, anticipate, and covertly rehearse each other's customary responses. In addition to the frequency and intimacy of social interactions, the degree of power exercised by the model over desired resources is considered to be an important determinant of the frequency of fantasy role-playing. In this theory, vicarious role-rehearsal primarily serves a defensive function; that is, in an effort to guide his behavior toward models who possess controlling power, a person will imagine different courses of action for receiving help or avoiding censure, and he will try to anticipate as accurately as possible the model's probable responses to these approaches. On the other hand, there would be little incentive to prepare oneself for, or to practice covertly, the behavior of models who command no rewarding or punishing power.

Anticipatory implicit rehearsal of modeled responses may be supported by role reciprocity and threat from resource controllers, but it should be noted that persons will also be inclined to practice modeled responses that are effective in producing rewarding outcomes. Moreover, according to social-learning theory, the behavior of powerful models will be attended to, rehearsed, and reproduced even though observers have had no direct interaction with them (Bandura, Ross & Ross, 1963b), because their behavior is likely to have high utilitarian value. This is particularly true in the case of models who possess expert power in particular specialties. It would be unnecessary, for example, for a novice to establish a complementary role relationship with a qualified automobile mechanic in order to master his skills through observation during apprentice training. Rehearsal processes are undoubtedly governed by different types of incentive conditions, some of which may be entirely independent of the model whose behavior is being emulated.

Symbolic coding operations, to which reference was made earlier, may be even more efficacious than rehearsal processes in facilitating long-term retention of modeled events. During exposure to stimulus sequences observers are inclined to recode, classify and reorganize elements into familiar and more easily remembered schemes. These coding devices may take various forms such as representing stimulus events in vivid imagery, translating action sequences into abbreviated verbal systems, or grouping constituent patterns into larger integrated units.

Motoric reproduction processes.   The third major component of modeling phenomena involves the utilization of symbolic representations of modeled patterns in the form of imaginal and verbal contents to guide overt performances. It is assumed that reinstatement of representational schemes provides a basis for self-instruction on how component responses must be combined and sequenced to produce new patterns of behavior. The process of representational guidance is essentially the same as response learning under conditions where a person behaviorally follows an externally depicted pattern or is directed through a series of instructions to enact novel response sequences. The only difference is that, in the latter cases, performance is directed by external cues whereas, in delayed modeling behavioral reproduction is monitored by symbolic counterparts of absent stimuli.

The rate and level of observational learning will be partly governed, at the motoric level, by the availability of necessary component responses. Responses of high-order complexity are produced by combinations of previously learned components which may, in themselves, represent relatively intricate compounds. Modeling outcomes are most readily achieved when they primarily involve the synthesis of previously acquired behavioral elements into new patterns exhibited by models. On the other hand, observers who lack some of the necessary components will, in all probability, display only partial reproduction of a model's behavior. In such cases the constituent elements are first established through modeling and then in a stepwise fashion increasingly complex compounds are acquired imitatively.

The above modeling procedure is frequently employed in the treatment of gross behavioral deficits, such as autism, childhood schizophrenia, and severe social or mental retardation. A model may repeatedly exhibit desired patterns of behavior, but these displays often have relatively little impact on the children (Baer, Peterson & Sherman, 1967; Lovaas, Berberich, Perloff & Schaeffer, 1966). This lack of responsivity often results from such great inattention to social stimuli that the children fail to observe adequately the modeled events. Even on occasions when the children attend closely to modeling cues, given an impoverished behavioral repertoire their reproductions of the therapist's behavior are deficient because many of the required components for the modeled responses are lacking. In addition to the use of graduated modeling, powerful incentives are employed to enhance attentiveness and to activate into performance the responses that have been acquired as a function of exposure to the modeling cues.

In many instances modeled responses have been acquired and retained in representational forms but they cannot be enacted behaviorally because of physical limitations. Few basketball enthusiasts could ever successfully match the remarkable performance of a Wilt Chamberlain regardless of their vigilance and dutiful rehearsal.

Accurate behavioral enactment of modeling cues is also difficult to achieve under conditions where the model's performance is governed by subtle adjustments of internal responses that are unobservable and not easily communicable. An aspiring operatic singer may benefit considerably from observing an accomplished voice instructor; nevertheless, skilled vocal reproduction is hampered by the fact that the model's laryngeal and respiratory muscular responses are neither readily observable nor easily described verbally. The problem of behavioral reproduction is further complicated in the case of highly coordinated motor performances (e.g., golf) in which a person cannot observe many of the responses he is making and must therefore primarily rely upon proprioceptive feedback cues.

Incentive or motivational processes. A person may acquire, retain, and possess the capabilities for skillful execution of identificatory behavior, but the learning is rarely activated into overt performance due to negative sanctions or inadequate positive reinforcement. When favorable incentives are introduced, observational learning promptly emerges in action (Bandura, 1965b). As noted earlier, incentive conditions can, of course, affect learning and retention as well as performance. Since most theories of identification are built around performance-related variables, the factors presumed to control identificatory performances will be discussed at length in succeeding sections.

It is evident from the foregoing discussion that observers do not function as passive video-tape recorders which register indiscriminately and store symbolic representations of all modeling stimuli encountered in everyday life. Identificatory learning constitutes a multiprocess phenomenon that is determined by factors regulating sensory registration of modeling stimuli, their transformation to representational forms, subsequent stabilization and retrieval of modeling contents, response capabilities, and motivational processes.

VARIABLES GOVERNING PERFORMANCE OF IDENTIFICATORY RESPONSES

A thorough review of the literature on theories of identification discloses a remarkably narrow range of conditions that supposedly regulate spontaneous performance of modeling behavior. According to psychoanalytic theory, which has provided the most widely accepted explanation of modeling phenomena, there exist two sets of familial conditions, both frustrative or aversive, that induce a child to identify with his parents (Bronfenbrenner, 1960; Freud, 1923, 1925). These hypothesized processes, labeled *anaclitic* and *defensive* identification, are discussed, along with pertinent experimental findings, in the sections that follow.

Nurturance Withdrawal

Anaclitic identification (Freud, 1925) is believed to occur during the first few years of life when a nurturant adult, usually the mother, to whom the child has developed a nonsexual attachment withdraws affectional gratifications. The resulting threat of loss of love then motivates the child to "introject" the parent's behavior and attributes. This general formulation has been reinterpreted and elaborated in terms of learning theory by Mowrer (1950, 1958) and Sears (1957) to furnish more empirically verifiable implications.

According to Mowrer's reformulation (1950), when a parent mediates the child's primary gratifications her behavior gradually takes on secondary reward value as a function of repeated contiguous association with rewarding experiences. On the basis of stimulus generalization, responses that resemble those of the parent generate positively reinforcing effects in proportion to their similarity when performed by the child. Consequently, the child can produce self-rewarding experiences when the parent is absent or withdraws her attentions simply by reproducing as closely as possible the parent's positively valenced behavior.

Sears (1957; Sears et al., 1965) likewise considers a nurturant interaction between a caretaking adult and a child as a necessary precondition for identification. Through this basic relationship the child learns to want and to value the maternal behaviors that have accompanied rewarding caretaking activities and, by the end of the first year of life, the child acquires a dependency motive. However, for reasons of social necessity and the need to develop the child's independence, the mother begins reducing or withholding affectionate interaction and nurturance. The consequent dependency frustration leads the child to adopt the method of role practice as a means of reinstating the maternal nurturant responses. The child thus secures self-rewards by imitating or role-playing maternal behaviors that possess conditioned reward value. In the earlier formulation (Sears, 1957) it was further hypothesized that, as a function of repeated association of imitation with direct or self-produced rewards, identification becomes an acquired drive for which the satisfying goal response is behaving like another person. More recently, however, Sears (Sears et al., 1965) has conceptualized identification as a generalized habit of role practice rather than as a secondary drive.

There is evidence from naturalistic studies of child-rearing antecedents of identification that, compared to boys whose fathers were relatively nonnurturant, boys of warm affectionate fathers display a higher degree of male-role preference (Mussen & Distler, 1959), stronger masculine vocational interests (Mussen, 1961), and greater father-son similarity in response to items on a personality inventory (Payne & Mussen, 1956); more often assume the father role in doll-play activities (P. S. Sears, 1953); and more frequently perceive themselves as thinking and acting like their fathers (Bandura & Walters, 1959).

In naturalistic relationships nurturance may exert its effects upon modeling through means other than the endowment of self-reinforcing properties to modeled behavior. Warm affectionate parents are more likely than cold aloof ones to engage in frequent and extensive interactions with their children thus providing them with more opportunities to observe and to learn parental patterns. Moreover, influence processes are typically bidirectional, in which case children who express parental values and emulate their behavior might be expected to increase the level of both parental affection and interpersonal contact. Several modeling studies have been conducted in which the rewarding quality of the model is manipulated experimentally, the amount of exposure to the modeling cues is controlled, and the influence of reciprocal reinforcement is eliminated (Bandura & Huston, 1961; Henker, 1964; Mischel & Grusec, 1966). In accord with correlational findings, these experiments have generally shown that an adult who is warm and nurturant elicits considerably more imitative behavior from children than a model who lacks rewarding qualities. Similar results are also obtained when parents, preselected on the basis of high or low nurturance, serve as models for their children on imitation performance tasks (Hetherington & Frankie, 1967; Mussen & Parker, 1965).

Although the available data generally support the hypothesized relationship between nurturance and identification, finer analyses of matching performances indicate that the theory of anaclitic identification may require substantial qualification. First, modeling outcomes are considerably less generalized or pervasive than the theory assumes. Mischel and Grusec (1966), for example, found that a prior nurturant interaction with the model enhanced children's spontaneous reproduction of the model's socially neutral behaviors, but it did not increase their willingness to perform matching responses that possessed aversive qualities. Some further evidence of the differential effects of nurturance on reproduction of different classes of modeling behavior is provided in a study by Bandura and Huston (1961). Whereas the model's rewarding quality facilitated imitation of verbal and stylistic responses, children readily adopted aggressive responses regardless of the degree of the model's nurturance. The foregoing results, and data that will be cited later, demonstrate that the rewarding property of a model is often a facilitative but not a necessary condition for imitation, and that children typically display imitative response specificity rather than a generalized disposition to emulate the behavior of others.

The problem is further complicated by the fact that a high degree of nurturance may, in fact, *diminish* identification, depending upon the pattern of behavior that is being transmitted. This is clearly illustrated in an experiment (Bandura, Grusec & Menlove, 1967b) designed to identify conditions under which children willingly adopt high standards of achievement that result in negative self-evaluations and self-denial of available rewarding resources.

Most learning interpretations of the socialization process emphasize the role of extrinsic reinforcement in the modification and maintenance of social behavior. A highly important, but largely ignored, reinforcement phenomenon is evident when a person adopts a standard of what constitutes a worthy performance and rewards himself when he attains his self-imposed standard, but engages in self-critical or self-punitive behavior when his performances fall short of self-prescribed norms.

It has been shown in a series of studies that self-monitoring reinforcement systems can be readily transmitted to children through exposure to the self-reinforcement patterns displayed by adults and peers (Bandura & Kupers, 1964). However, children are inclined to reject superior models who set themselves relatively high standards (Bandura & Whalen, 1966). In order to determine whether the rejection process could be counteracted, we introduced, in a subsequent experiment, social variables that would be expected to enhance modeling. One group of children experienced a highly rewarding interaction with an adult model who subsequently exhibited high criteria for self-reward and was praised for adhering to high standards. With other groups of children the model assumed a nonnurturant attitude or received no social recognition for high standard-setting behavior. In addition, half the children in each condition also observed a peer who displayed a low standard of behavior in order to determine the effects of exposure to conflicting modeling cues.

This experiment disclosed, among other things, that children who had experienced a highly nurturant and rewarding interaction with the adult model were more inclined to accept the low standards set by the peer than if the adult were less beneficent. In this case, high nurturance was conducive to ready self-gratification rather than to modeling the stringent achievement demands self-imposed by the rewarding adult.

Finally, it should be noted that the experimentation establishing a covariation between nurturance and identification is based almost entirely upon modeling studies utilizing two-person groups. There is some evidence (Bandura et al., 1963b) that developmental principles based upon a two-person paradigm may be subject to stringent limitations, since the introduction of additional social variables can produce significant changes in the functional relationships between the rewarding properties of a model and children's matching behavior.

In the experiment referred to above, which employed triads, one adult served as a controller of highly rewarding resources, and another adult and a child were placed in a competitive situation so that rewards given to one person precluded their availability for the other. Children who were treated generously by the controller subsequently exhibited more total imitation (i.e., the number of characteristics of both adult models that were reproduced) than children who lost out in the competition and were ignored. However, the effect of combining direct gratification of the child with resource ownership by the female model was primarily to increase imitation of the neglected male, rather than to enhance imitation of the model who generously provided the child with food, attractive toys, and a great deal of positive attention. In fact, boys who were the recipients of the generous treatment from the female model tended to favor slightly the ignored male as their object of imitation. Post-experimental interviews revealed that the rewarded boys felt sympathetic toward the neglected male and were mildly critical of the controller for not being more charitable with her bountiful resources. However, children exhibited a marked preference in imitating the behavior of the rewarding model under conditions where they received the same nurturant treatment but the other adult was excluded by choice rather than through competitiveness. Thus, the same absolute level of the model's rewarding quality exerted a differential effect upon children's degree and pattern of imitation, depending upon whether they were provided gratifications within a competitive or a nonrivalrous interpersonal setting. These findings indicate that modeling may be affected to a greater extent by interpersonal contrast of rewarding treatment in interaction with other social variables than by the absolute magnitude of reward.

It would appear from the over-all evidence based on research conducted within a social-learning framework that the developmental or anaclitic theory of identification, which assumes that nurturance promotes modeling, may be valid only under certain limiting conditions. The findings of other studies also raise questions concerning the interpretation of the process of defensive identification, or identification with the aggressor, which is frequently invoked to account for modeling outcomes.

Fear of the Aggressor

The theory of defensive or aggressive identification (Freud, 1923) presumably applies only to boys. This form of identification is viewed as the outcome of the resolution of the Oedipus complex, in which the boy reduces anxiety deriving from anticipated punishment by castration for his incestuous wishes toward his mother, and rivalrous feelings toward his father, by emulating the characteristics of the threatening father. Although this theory suggests an incentive, other than feared loss of love, for identification, it provides no satisfactory explanation as to why modeling the behavior of a threatening competitor should reduce anxiety. Indeed, it is highly probable that the reproduction of aversive modeled behavior would generate negative effects and, except for adoption of paternal prohibitions, behaving like a menacing antagonist would accent the rivalry and thus augment rather than attenuate anticipatory fear of punishment.

Whiting (1959, 1960) has recently proposed an extension of Freud's defensive identification hypothesis in which envy and vicarious gratification rather than anxiety reduction are presumed to be the major motivational and reinforcing mechanisms for identificatory behavior. In his status-envy theory, Whiting depicts identification as an outcome of a rivalrous interaction between the child and the parent who occupies an envied status. While Freud presents the child as competing with the father primarily for the mother's sexual and affectional attention, Whiting regards any forms of reward, maternal or social, as valued resources around which rivalry may develop. This theory further assumes that the more strongly a child envies the status of another person in respect to the consumption of desired resources of which he feels himself to be deprived, the more he will enact the role of that person in fantasy. Hence, when a child competes unsuccessfully with an adult for affection, attention, food, and care, he will envy the adult consumer and consequently identify with him.

In contrast to the status-envy interpretation of modeling, a social power theory of identification (Maccoby, 1959; Mussen & Distler, 1959; Parsons, 1955) would predict that the controller, rather than the consumer, of rewarding resources would be selected as the primary model for emulation.

In order to test predictions derived from these opposing theories of identification, an experiment was conducted (Bandura et al., 1963b) with the use of three-person groups representing prototypes of the nuclear family. In one condition of the experiment an adult assumed the role of controller of highly rewarding resources including attractive play materials, appetizing foods, and high status objects. Another adult was the recipient of these resources, while the child, a participant observer in the triad, was seated at a distant table and totally ignored. In a second experimental condition one adult controlled the resources; the child, however, was the recipient of the positive attention and rewarding resources, while the other adult, who was assigned the subordinate role, was neglected.

An adult male and an adult female served as models in each of the triads. For half the boys and girls in each condition the male model controlled and dispensed the rewarding resources, simulating the husband-dominant family; for the remaining children, the female model mediated the positive resources as in the wife-dominant home. Following the experimental social interactions, the two adult models performed several tasks in the presence of the child, during which they exhibited divergent motoric and verbal patterns of behavior, and differential preferences for colors, pictorial items, and apparel. The child then performed the same tasks in the absence of the two adults, and measures were obtained of the degree to which he patterned his behavior after that of either model.

The results of this experiment reveal that children tend to identify with the source of rewarding power rather than with the envied competitor for rewards. Moreover, power inversions on the part of the male and female models produced cross-sex imitation, particularly in girls. These findings suggest that the distribution of rewarding power within the family may be a major determinant of the development of both sex-appropriate behavior and deviant sex-role tendencies.

Whiting's reformulation of the defensive identification process stresses the envy aspects of the psychoanalytic interpretation. However, the original theory (Freud, 1923) and supporting anecdotal evidence presented by Anna Freud (1946) and Bettelheim (1943) emphasize the anxiety-provoking and aggressively threatening qualities of the model. It is evident from the illustrative case data provided by Anna Freud and Bettelheim that the conditions under which identification with the aggressor is presumed to occur differ from those originally proposed by Freud. Moreover, most of the examples of aggressive behavior can be adequately accounted for without invoking a mediating identificatory process.

In a number of Anna Freud's cases, for example, the person who sup-posedly serves as the model in fact displays no aggression and the therapist simply assumes that the aggressive child is expecting physical attack. While the child's anticipatory aggression could be interpreted as a defensive maneuver, it could hardly represent identification with the aggressor any more than swatting a mosquito represents insect identification on the part of a threatened adult. In others of Freud's illustrations a child who was accidentally hurt by a games-master in an outdoor game at school wears military apparel the following day, and a boy who had undergone dental treatment subsequently displays aggressively demanding and destructive behavior during a therapeutic session. It is, of course, entirely possible that the boys' behavior and the previous experience of being hurt are totally unrelated and, even if a contingency were involved, it is unclear from the illustration why the boys failed to reenact the behavior of the dentist or the games-master. The clearest example that Freud gives of actual imitative behavior involves the case of a boy who mimicked his teacher's angry grimaces while the latter was punishing or reproving him. Freud's interpretation that the boy "through his grimaces was assimulating himself to or identifying himself with the dreaded external object" (p. 118) is complicated by the fact that the boy's imitative grimaces provoked bursts of laughter from his classmates, thus providing strong social reinforcement for the matching facial expressions. It is therefore doubtful, even in the latter case, that the imitative behavior was maintained by anxiety-reducing mechanisms.

It is likewise apparent in Bettelheim's (1943) account of prisoners' behavior in a Nazi concentration camp, which is also frequently cited as evidence for the occurrence of identification with the aggressor, that most of the behavioral outcomes described may not, in fact, have involved identificatory processes. For example, Bettelheim reports that many of the older prisoners were verbally and physically aggressive toward newcomers and potential troublemakers, sometimes behaving more aggressively than their guards when placed in charge of others; they enforced nonsensical rules that the Gestapo had at one time or another imposed on the group; some of the older captives even modified their uniforms to resemble those of the guards and resented sympathetic foreign correspondents who criticized the Germans.

It is true that the old prisoners often imposed on their fellow captives aversive controls similar to those that they themselves had endured, but it is by no means clear whether their behavior represented identification with the aggressor, in the sense that the concept is employed in psychoanalytic theory. The Gestapo consistently imposed group-oriented punishments in which the transgressions of any individual resulted in brutal torture of the entire group. When two prisoners attempted to escape, for example, all the prisoners were punished by being forced to stand at attention in a snow storm without overcoats for hours, during which many died from exposure, and several hundred later had to undergo amputations of their badly frozen extremities. Since the group consequences were generally extremely aversive and the demands of the guards highly capricious, it is not surprising that, in order to escape brutal and degrading treatment, experienced prisoners often enforced demands that were unpredictably imposed by the Gestapo officers. The prisoners' punitive rule enforcement may thus represent straightforward avoidance behavior designed to suppress transgressions that would endanger the whole group, rather than emulative behavior. Indeed, the explicit purpose of the hostage and group-punishment system was to make every prisoner feel responsible for the acts committed by other group members.

Similarly, antagonism toward foreign correspondents and former fellow-prisoners who had publicly reported cruelties perpetrated in the concentration camps, also interpreted by Bettelheim as an example of identification with the aggressor's ideology, may have been due simply to the fact that newspaper accounts written by these persons brought severe punishment on the prisoners.

Bettelheim does provide evidence that, in some cases, prisoners went to great lengths to emulate the guards. Some of the old captives, for example, collected pieces of Gestapo uniforms and sewed their own uniforms so as to resemble those of the guards. However, such imitative behavior was punished by the guards and therefore could hardly have served as anxiety-reducing or defensive functions. Indeed, since this particular modeling behavior persisted in spite of the explicit negative sanctions, it seems to furnish disconfirmatory evidence for the defensive identification hypothesis and perhaps to suggest that the prisoners were, in accordance with social-power theory, emulating the Gestapo elite who possessed potent rewarding and coercive power. Based on experimental evidence provided by Epstein (1966), that persons who display high authoritarianism are prone to imitate punitive behavior of aggressive models, one might expect that prisoners who had developed authoritarian attitudes before their imprisonment (some were formerly prominent politicians) would be predisposed to admire and imitate these attributes in the guards. Striving to emulate the elite who possess control over desired resources is a characteristic also of upwardly mobile persons who, like the prisoners in question, tend to persist in their imitative behavior in spite of rebuffs that they incur from their peers and admired models.

The case material discussed above, and empirical investigations of aggressive identification (Sarnoff, 1951), illustrate the vague and loose criteria that are typically employed in designating aggressive response patterns as outcomes of a defensive identificatory process. Even in cases where aggression is clearly imitative, findings of controlled experiments present some basis for questioning whether the matching behavior is maintained by anxiety-reducing mechanisms.

There is considerable evidence that both children and adults readily imitate aggressive models presented on film who obviously constitute no threat whatever (Bandura, Ross & Ross, 1963a; Hartmann, 1965; Hicks, 1965; Walters & Thomas, 1963). Moreover, studies in which the model's aggressive behavior incurs either rewarding or punishing consequences (Bandura, 1965b; Bandura, Ross & Ross, 1963c) demonstrate that the success of the model's behavior is a crucial factor in determining the degree to which an aggressive pattern of behavior will be spontaneously reproduced by observers. On the basis of the response-consequences interpretation of modeling effects, it would be predicted that if the behavior of an aggressive model is highly effective in gaining control over rewarding resources, observers will identify with the aggressor, even though they may dislike the model's attributes (Bandura et al., 1963c). If, on the other hand, the aggressor's behavior fails to gain power and control over persons and their resources, or in fact produces punishing outcomes, identification with the aggressor will not occur.

In most naturalistic situations the possible influence of the threat value of modeled aggression and its effectiveness in producing rewarding outcomes are confounded. That is, an aggressor may not only be fear-provoking, but he provides repeated demonstrations that by dominance through physical and verbal force he can gain possession of material resources, he can change rules to fit his own needs and wishes, he may gain control over and extract subservience from others, and he can level barriers which impose blocks or delays in gratification. Evidence that the behavior of domineering models is extensively emulated (Bandura et al., 1963c; Hetherington & Frankie, 1967; Hoffman, 1960) does not necessarily establish anxiety reduction as the underlying mechanism governing the identificatory performances. An alternative explanation can be offered in terms of the utilitarian value of power-assertiveness. Although it has been shown that fear of a punitive model is not a necessary condition for identification with aggressors, the question of whether fear is a facilitative, impeding, or irrelevant factor in the identification process can be best answered through laboratory studies in which threat and rewarding and punishing consequences to the model are independently manipulated.

According to the theories of identification reviewed in the preceding sections, in order to get a boy to emulate a baseball player such as Mickey Mantle, it would be necessary for the youngster to develop an intense attachment to the brawny model, who would then withhold affectional responsiveness, thereby motivating the child to incorporate the modeled stylistic behavior. Or the athletic youngster would have to develop strong incestuous desires toward Mrs. Mantle, hostile rivalrous feelings toward the baseball slugger, and, as a way of reducing anxieties generated by his libidinal feelings and the anticipated threat of castration, the boy would begin to swat home runs and otherwise behave like his threatening competitor.

It is evident from informal observation that youngsters emulate athletic models extensively without any direct personal contact or Oedipal entanglements with them. One would predict from the social-learning theory of vicarious reinforcement (Bandura, 1965a) that boys will strive to duplicate the roles and stylistic performances of baseball players who maintain an impressive batting average and are therefore the recipients of public adulation. If, on the other hand, the players' athletic achievements and social applause should wane, they would quickly be abandoned as models for emulation.

A social-learning theory of observational learning is not confined to imitation of models to whom the observer has a cathectic attachment, but is designed to encompass a diversity of modeling outcomes based upon direct and vicarious experiences with actual and symbolic models. In this formulation the incentive conditions impinging upon the model and imitative response feedback variables, as well as the model's competence, rewarding quality, and social power, are regarded as important determinants of overt expression of identificatory responses. These incentive variables, and other parameters governing the performance of modeling behavior, are considered next.

Reinforcement Control of Identificatory Behavior

The extent of utilization of identificatory response patterns is greatly influenced by the reinforcing consequences and the social sanctions associated with imitative behavior. Thus, for example, in a series of studies by Kanareff and Lanzetta (1958, 1960; Lanzetta & Kanareff, 1959), in which the functional value of imitative responses was systematically varied, the level of matching behavior was found to increase with increasing probability of positive reinforcement. Conversely, when matching responses are consistently nonrewarded (Baer & Sherman, 1964; Miller & Dollard, 1941) or negatively sanctioned (De Rath, 1964; Kanareff & Lanzetta, 1958), imitative behavior is extinguished or inhibited.

Positive reinforcement of specific identificatory responses may not only increase the spontaneous performance of rewarded matching behavior, but it can, under certain conditions, also establish a generalized imitative response tendency. The phenomenon of generalized imitation has been interpreted by Baer and his associates (Baer & Sherman, 1964) in terms of self-reinforcing mechanisms. It is assumed that if accurate reproduction of modeling stimuli is consistently rewarded, behavioral similarity per se acquires secondary reinforcing properties. Thereafter a person will tend to display a high incidence of precisely imitative behaviors which, due to their acquired reward value, will be strengthened and sustained in the absence of extrinsic reinforcement.

In one study (Baer & Sherman, 1964) designed to demonstrate reinforcement control of generalized imitation, three imitative responses (head nodding, mouthing, and novel verbalizations) were established in young children by social reinforcement from a puppet who had explicitly instructed the subjects to match his modeling behavior. For a subgroup of children who showed an increase in imitative responding the puppet displayed nonreinforced bar-pressing interspersed among the other three rewarded matching responses. Under these circumstances, some of the children imitated bar-pressing in varying amounts even though this particular response was never positively reinforced. In order to further demonstrate the dependence of generalized imitation on direct reinforcement of other matching responses, social approval for imitative head nodding, mouthing and novel verbalizations was discontinued with two children. This extinction procedure resulted in decreased imitative bar-pressing in one of the two children; when reinforcement of the other three modeling responses was reinstated, imitative bar-pressing also reappeared.

The frequent references to the above study as providing dramatic evidence of reinforcement control of generalized imitation overlook the fact that, even under the strong situational demands, the imitative behavior of one-third of the children was unaffected by the reinforcement operations, and of the remaining children whose data are presented, half of them showed increments in reinforced imitative behavior, but they failed to perform the nonreinforced modeled response to any significant degree. Since reinforcement exerted no clearly predictable effects on the occurrence of generalized imitation it must have been largely determined by other unmeasured and uncontrolled variables.

Using similar reinforcement procedures with social models and more powerful incentives, Baer, Peterson and Sherman (1967) were able to establish generalized imitativeness in three severely retarded children who initially displayed a very low level of matching behavior. After an extensive period of imitation-contingent reinforcement had markedly increased modeling behavior in these children, some matching responses could be effectively maintained without reinforcement by randomly interspersing them among positively reinforced imitations. However, both types of matching responses rapidly declined when social approval and food were given to the children on a temporal basis rather than contingent upon imitative behavior (Figure 3.1). It was further shown that both types of matching responses could be quickly restored to their previously high level by reintroduction of response-contingent reinforcement.

In testing the efficacy of modeling procedures for establishing language in mute schizophrenic children, Lovaas and his coworkers (Lovaas et al., 1966) likewise demonstrated that the children could acquire and maintain Norwegian words imitatively without any reinforcement as long as they were rewarded for English words when correctly reproduced.

A generalized disposition to model the behavior of others can be developed by having different persons reinforce diverse types of responses in a variety of situations. However, the hypothesis that behavioral similarity becomes inherently endowed with reinforcing properties through rewarding practices requires more direct verification. If this were in fact the governing mechanism, matching responses should not undergo such abrupt and marked extinction (Figure 3.1) the moment that reinforcement for the larger subclass of imitative

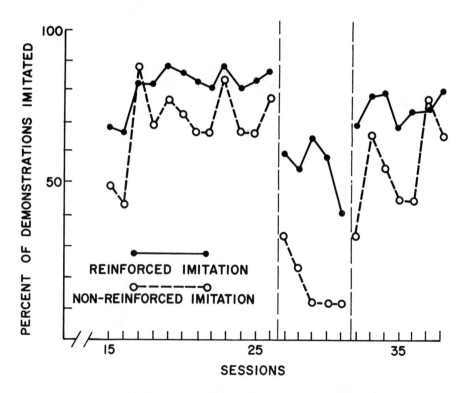

FIGURE 3.1. Per cent of reinforced and nonreinforced modeled responses reproduced by one child during periods when rewards were made contingent upon either the occurrence of matching responses or after a certain period of time had elapsed. Adapted from Baer, Peterson and Sherman, 1967.

responses is withdrawn, since one would not expect similarity cues to lose their reinforcing properties that suddenly. Rather, the intrinsic rewards arising from precise response duplication should sustain imitative behavior for some time in the absence of externally administered reinforcers.

An alternative explanation for the occurrence of generalized imitation can be offered in terms of discrimination rather than secondary reinforcement processes. When a few nonrewarded modeled responses are randomly embedded in a large number that are consistently reinforced, the two sets of modeling responses cannot be easily distinguished and are therefore likely to be performed with similar frequency. If, on the other hand, the discriminative complexity of the modeling task were reduced by having the model portray a series of reinforced responses, followed by the set of readily discriminable responses that are never rewarded, the observer would eventually recognize that the latter responses never produce positive consequences and he would, in all likelihood, discontinue reproducing them. A discrimination hypothesis thus leads to a prediction which is opposite to that derived from the principle of secondary reinforcement. According to the acquired reward interpretation, the longer imitative responses are positively reinforced, the more strongly behavioral similarity is endowed with reinforcing properties, and consequently, the greater is the resistance to extinction of nonrewarded matching responses. In contrast, discrimination theory would predict that the longer the differential reinforcement practices are continued, the more likely the observer is to distinguish between rewarded and nonreinforced imitative behaviors resulting in rapid extinction of nonreinforced imitative responsivity.

The occurrence of generalized modeling is also probably determined in part by the invariant conditions under which laboratory tests are conducted. Reinforced and nonrewarded responses are typically exhibited by the same model, in the same social setting, during the same period of time, and after subjects have been strongly urged to behave imitatively. On the other hand, under naturally occurring conditions which are highly variable and more easily distinguishable, there appears to be considerable specificity to modeling behavior. If close matching does in fact become self-reinforcing, then its occurrence should not be as restricted in generality. The issue would appear to be one of performance rather than learning, since persons do know how to match. Performance is primarily a function of anticipated outcomes which, in turn, is partly determined by the degree of similarity between new situations and situations in the past in which the particular response has been reinforced.

Although the influential role of reinforcement in maintaining the modifying identificatory behavior has been amply demonstrated, the major determinants of generalized modeling have not been adequately established.

Influence of Vicarious Reinforcement on Modeling

In social-learning theory special consideration is given to the role of vicarious reinforcement, as evidenced by changes in the behavior of observers as a function of witnessing reinforcing stimuli administered to performers. There is considerable experimental evidence (Bandura, 1965a) that observation of rewarding or punishing consequences to a model can substantially affect the extent to which observers willingly engage in identificatory behavior. Indeed, comparative investigations of the relative efficacy of vicarious and direct reinforcement reveal that the behavioral changes displayed by observers are generally of the same magnitude as those achieved by reinforced performers (Kanfer & Marston, 1963) or, under certain conditions, may even exceed them (Berger, 1961). Moreover, vicarious reinforcement effects are governed by such variables as the percentage (Kanfer, 1965; Marston & Kanfer, 1963), intermittency (Rosenbaum & Bruning, 1966), and magnitude (Bruning, 1965) of reward in essentially the same manner as when they are applied directly to a performing subject.

The effect of observing response consequences to a model on the acquisition and spontaneous performance of matching responses is illustrated by a study (Bandura, 1965b) in which children observed a film-mediated model who exhibited a number of novel physical and verbal aggressive responses. In one condition the model was severely punished following the display of aggressive behavior; in a second treatment the model was generously praised and rewarded; the third condition depicted no response consequences to the model. A post-exposure test for spontaneous imitation revealed that the reinforcement contingencies applied to the model's aggression produced differential degrees of matching behavior. Children who had observed the model rewarded, or having suffered no adverse consequences, for his behavior displayed a significantly greater variety of imitative responses than children who saw the model punished. Moreover, boys emulated substantially more of the model's behavioral repertoire than girls; these differences were particularly marked when modeled aggression resulted in punishing consequences (Figure 3.2).

Some additional findings of this study again highlight the necessity for distinguishing between identificatory learning and spontaneous performance of matching behavior. Following the performance test, children in all three groups were offered highly attractive incentives contingent upon their reproducing the model's responses, in order to counteract the inhibiting effects of vicarious punishment and thus to actualize the modes of behavior that the children had acquired observationally. As shown in Figure 3.2, the introduction of positive incentives completely eliminated the previously observed performance differences, revealing an equivalent amount of identificatory learning among children in the model-rewarded, model-punished, and the no-consequences conditions. Similarly, the initially large sex difference in imitative aggression also was virtually eliminated.

Discrepancies between extent of response acquisition and perfor~
level are most likely to obtain under conditions where behavior is
sanctioned. Thus, the children who displayed significant increme~
when the behavior was positively reinforced were boys wh
aggressive model punished, and girls for whom, in

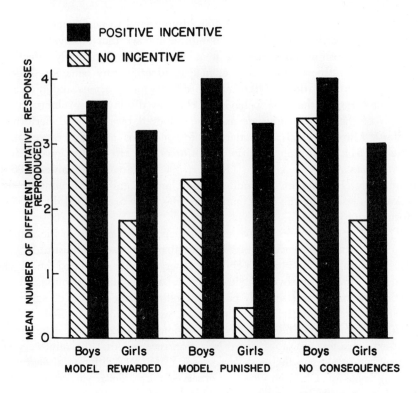

FIGURE 3.2.   Mean number of different matching responses reproduced by children as a function of response consequences to the model and positive incentives. Bandura, 1965b.

aggressive behavior is typically labelled sex-inappropriate or is negatively sanctioned.

Most differences existing in the behavior of boys and girls are often explained in terms of differential masculine and feminine identification. It would appear from evidence that positive incentives essentially eliminate sex disparity in performed aggression, that most sex differences may primarily reflect differences in willingness to exhibit observationally-learned behavior because of the nature of prevailing social sanctions, rather than deficits in identificatory sex-role learning.

Under most conditions people readily adopt appropriate modeled responses. However, in some problem-solving and achievement-like situations they display strong counter-imitation tendencies for fear that matching behavior will be considered cheating, copying, or subservience and, therefore, socially disapproved (Lanzetta & Kanareff, 1959; Luchins & Luchins, 1961; Schein, 1954). The inhibiting effect of anticipated negative sanctions for imitation can be overcome in observers through positive reinforcement of the model's responses (Clark, 1965). Further evidence that imitative behavior can be enhanced or inhibited by observation of reinforcing consequences to a model's responses is provided by Walters and his associates (Walters & Parke,

1964; Walters, Parke & Cane, 1965). In the latter studies children who witnessed a peer model transgress with rewarding or no adverse consequences deviated more readily and more often than those who saw the same model punished for engaging in the socially disapproved behavior.

In cases where a model displays reprehensible behavior, it is interesting to note that the nonoccurrence of anticipated punishing consequences may influence the observer's responses to the same degree as witnessed rewarding outcomes. These findings suggest that nonreaction to formerly prohibited activities may take on, through contrast, positive qualities. Similar contrast-of-reinforcement effects have been demonstrated in studies of direct reinforcement (Buchwald, 1959a, 1959b; Crandall, 1963; Crandall, Good & Crandall, 1964) in which nonreward following punishment had functioned analogously to a positive incentive, whereas the occurrence of nonreward subsequent to a series of rewards had operated as a negative reinforcer. In fact, even a weak positive incentive, when contrasted with more rewarding prior events, may acquire punishing properties (Buchwald, 1960). The reinforcing effects of witnessed outcomes on matching behavior may therefore be determined to a large extent by the context in which the events occur and the customary sanctions associated with particular modeled response patterns.

Because previous studies have utilized deviant modes of behavior, which may be readily disinhibited through omission of negative consequences, the results provide no clear evidence for the occurrence of positive vicarious reinforcement. However, findings of a recent experiment (Bandura, Grusec & Menlove, 1967b) involving modeled behavior that is usually positively sanctioned reveal that social rewards dispensed to a model can have a strong impact on observers' identificatory behavior. Children who had observed an adult model adopt high achievement standards for self-reward, and receive social recognition for adhering to such exacting norms, subsequently imposed on themselves higher achievement demands than children who had witnessed the model portray the same stringent pattern of self-reward with no socially rewarding consequences. The enhancement of modeling through vicarious social reinforcement is particularly striking in this case, considering that the self-imposition of exceedingly high standards occurred in the absence of any social agents, and the emulative behavior resulted in increased negative self-evaluation and considerable self-denial of freely available rewards.

The discussion so far has been primarily concerned with the extent to which other persons are affected by rewards or punishments administered to the performing model by external social agents. Results of investigations concerned with the social transmission of self-reinforcing behavior (Bandura & Kupers, 1964; Bandura & Whalen, 1966) disclose that discriminative patterns of inhibition of self-rewarding responses can be acquired through observation of achievement-contingent rewards and punishments self-administered by the model. These findings suggest that observers' self-controlling responses can be modified and reinforced by models' self-evaluative and self-punitive reactions to deviation.

Although the influence of vicarious reinforcement on identificatory behavior is well-established, the behavioral changes displayed by observers may be interpreted in several ways (Bandura, 1965a). Response consequences experienced by another person undoubtedly convey information to the observer about the probable reinforcement contingencies associated with analogous performances in similar situations. Reinforcing stimuli presented to the model may therefore serve to facilitate or inhibit emulative behavior through their discriminative or informative function. Knowledge gained from witnessing the outcomes experienced by models would be particularly influential in regulating behavior under conditions where considerable ambiguity exists about what constitutes permissible or punishable actions, and where the observer believes that the model's contingencies apply to himself as well. It is highly unlikely, for example, that witnessing social approval for physical aggression exhibited by a person occupying a unique role, such as a policeman, would evoke imitative aggressiveness in observant citizens to any great extent. If the predictability of social-learning theory is to be further increased, experiments are needed that test the magnitude of vicarious reinforcement effects as a function of comparability of social sanctions customarily applied to models and observers.

A model's responses are often differentially reinforced depending upon the persons toward whom the behavior is directed or the social settings in which it is expressed. When differential consequences are correlated with different stimulus conditions, observation of the pattern of reinforcement associated with the model's responses helps the observer to identify the social or environmental stimuli controlling the model's behavior. These may be difficult to distinguish without the observed informative feedback. Hence, through repeated exposure to the outcomes of others, an observer not only acquires knowledge of predictable reinforcement contingencies, but may also discern the cues for the model's correct responses. The resultant discrimination learning can later facilitate the performance of appropriate matching responses in the presence of the cues to which the model previously had been responding with favorable consequences (Church, 1957; McDavid, 1962).

Observation of reinforcing outcomes and the model's concomitant reactions may also have important activating or motivational effects on an observer. The mere sight of highly valenced reinforcers can produce anticipatory arousal which, in turn, will affect the level of imitative performance. Similarly, variations in the magnitude of observed reinforcers, although providing equivalent information about the permissibility of matching responses, have different motivational effects on observers (Bruning, 1965). As in the case of direct reinforcement, incentive-produced motivation in observers is most likely to affect the speed, intensity, and persistence with which matching responses are executed.

The affective expressions of models undergoing rewarding or punishing experiences generally elicit corresponding emotional responses in viewers (Dysinger & Ruckmick, 1933). These vicariously aroused emotional responses can readily become conditioned, through repeated contiguous association either to the modeled responses themselves, or to environmental stimuli (Bandura & Rosenthal, 1966; Berger, 1962) that are regularly correlated with the model's affective reactions. Similarly, the nonoccurrence of anticipated aversive consequences to a model can extinguish in observers previously established emotional responses that are vicariously aroused by threatening modeled displays (Bandura, Grusec & Menlove, 1967a; Bandura & Menlove, 1968; Bandura, Blanchard & Ritter, 1967). It is therefore possible that the facilitative or suppressive effects of observing the affective consequences accruing to the model may be partly mediated by the vicarious arousal or extinction of emotional responses.

Finally, reinforcements administered to another person may have important social evaluative consequences. Punishment is apt to devalue the model and his behavior, whereas models who are recipients of praise and admiration tend to be attributed high prestige, status, and competence (Hastorf, 1965). Model status changes, in turn, can significantly affect observers' subsequent performance of matching responses. A particular vicarious reinforcement event, depending on its nature and context, may thus produce behavioral changes in observers through any one or more of the five processes outlined.

Further research is needed to separate the relative contribution of cognitive, emotional, and other factors governing vicarious reinforcement effects. The available evidence nevertheless presents some basis for assuming that the principle of vicarious reinforcement, together with the stabilizing effect of covert rehearsal, can explain the persistence of identificatory behavior in observers without overt responding or the support of direct reinforcement. Indeed, children frequently acquire and retain on a long-term basis adult-rewarded but child-prohibited behavior patterns that are not reproduced until the child has reached the age or social status that makes the activity appropriate or acceptable.

Influence of Model Status Cues
Signifying Differential Reinforcing Outcomes

Overt performance of identificatory behavior is influenced not only by immediate response consequences to the model, but also by distinctive status-conferring symbols and model attributes; these are usually dealt with by social psychology in terms of such variables as prestige, power, competence, socioeconomic status, and expertise (Asch, 1948; Campbell, 1961).

The strong control exercised by discriminative characteristics of a model on imitative behavior is well-documented in social-psychological research. For example, models who have demonstrated high competence (Gelfand, 1962; Mausner, 1954a, 1954b; Mausner & Bloch, 1957; Rosenbaum & Tucker, 1962), who are purported experts (Mausner, 1953) or celebrities (Hovland, Janis & Kelley, 1953), and who possess symbols of socioeconomic success (Lefkowitz, Blake & Mouton, 1955) are imitated to a considerably greater degree by both children and adults than models who lack these qualities. Other discriminative properties of the model, such as age (Bandura & Kupers, 1964; Hicks, 1965; Jakubczak & Walters, 1959), sex (Bandura et al., 1963a; Rosenblith, 1959, 1961), social power (Bandura et al., 1963b; Mischel & Grusec, 1966), and ethnic status (Epstein, 1966), which are generally associated with predictable reinforcing outcomes, likewise influence the degree to which social attitudes and behavior will be reproduced by others.

In learning analyses of modeling phenomena as a function of status variables (Miller & Dollard, 1941), stimulus generalization and differential reinforcement are utilized as the main explanatory principles. According to this interpretation, social models differ in the extent to which their behavior is likely to be successful in producing favorable outcomes. Hence, persons are most frequently rewarded for matching the behavior of models who are intelligent, who possess certain social and technical competencies, and who, by virtue of their adroitness, occupy high positions in various status hierarchies. On the other hand, the behaviors of models who are ineffectual, uninformed, and who have attained low vocational, intellectual, and social status, are apt to have considerably less utilitarian value. As a result of repeated differential reinforcement for matching models who possess diverse attributes, the identifying characteristics gradually come to serve as discriminative stimuli that signify the probable consequences associated with behavior modeled by different social agents. Moreover, through the process of stimulus generalization, the effect of a model's prestige carries over from one area of behavior to another (an effect that is exploited in advertising), and imitative responses tend to generalize to unfamiliar persons to the extent that they share similar characteristics with past reward-producing models.

The foregoing theoretical assumptions have been verified by a series of studies (Miller & Dollard, 1941) in which the history of differential reinforcement for matching the behavior of models possessing diverse characteristics was experimentally manipulated. However, questions of the generality of the theory in its present form arise from the fact that only a relatively narrow range of social conditions has been investigated, the models characteristically display socially neutral behaviors, and negative sanctions are not imposed for emulation of high-status persons. As Miller and Dollard (1941) point out in another context, subordinate individuals are more inclined to imitate the social patterns and linguistic styles of models who occupy adjacent, rather than the most prestigeful, positions in a status hierarchy, because of social barriers against marked upward mobility, and lack of the resources necessary for long periods to acquire proficiency in the elaborate customs and mannerisms of highly discrepant social groups. Under the latter conditions one would expect to find a nonmonotonic relationship between prestige level of the model and amount of matching behavior.

Also, some recent evidence (Epstein, 1966) suggests that characteristics of the recipients of the model's actions may be highly influential in defining probable response consequences and thus attenuating the effects of prestige generalization. Epstein found that white college students displayed more imitative punitiveness toward a Negro after they had observed an aggressive Negro model than when the punitive behavior was initially exhibited by a Caucasian. Since it seems reasonable to assume that people would have been rewarded most often for imitating ethnically similar models, the latter findings are not explainable in terms of generalization from prior differential reinforcement associated with model attributes alone. It is highly probable that an attack on a minority-group member by one of his own group implies greater culpability of the victim, and thus signifies to the observer more justification and permissibility for aggression than a similar assault by a representative of a majority outgroup whose actions would more likely be viewed as prejudicial and censurable. Without independent ratings of the target of aggression, and diversity in the ethnic status of observers and victims, it is not possible to determine the validity of this interpretation. The available data, however, indicate the need for systematic variation of the attributes of both the models and the targets of their behavior in order to determine the manner in which more complex relational cues and other aspects of the social situation govern generalization of imitation to unfamiliar models.

The preceding discussion has been primarily concerned with the influence of status variables on modeling of socially neutral or prosocial response patterns. There is some evidence (Lefkowitz et al., 1955) that prohibited or socially disapproved behavior can likewise be increased by exposure to high-status deviant models. Traffic signal violations by a high-status person attired in a freshly pressed suit, shined shoes, white shirt and tie produced a higher pedestrian violation rate than the same transgression performed by the same model when dressed in soiled patched trousers, scuffed shoes, and a blue denim shirt. The differential reduction in restraints is probably attributable to the fact that violations by persons who occupy a high position in a prestige hierarchy are likely to be punished less frequently and less severely, due to earned gratitude or their power to counter-aggress, than prohibited acts performed by low-status transgressors. The differential leniency is apt to be extended temporarily to the imitator as well, provided that he displays the matching behavior at the same time the protective model is disregarding the prohibition.

If, in fact, model status facilitates imitative transgression through assumed protection from punishment, the findings of a study by Wiggins, Dill and Schwartz (1965) suggest that the latter variables are not related in a simple linear fashion. Compared to individuals of intermediate status, high-status persons tend to receive less punishment for minor deviations, but are treated more severely when their transgressions produce serious consequences for group members. These findings are somewhat analogous to naturalistic situations in which severe and well-publicized punishments are administered for major transgressions by models who occupy prestigeful positions in society in an effort to deter similar behavior in observers.

The prestige qualities of a model may not only increase the probability of matching behavior, but also produce stable value changes through the process of higher-order vicarious conditioning (Bandura, 1965a, 1968b). If a model who elicits positive affective responses in viewers expresses strong preference for certain stimulus objects and makes pleasant evaluative statements about them, the positive reinforcing value of the objects is likely to be increased. Conversely, negative valences may become strongly conditioned to objects that are habitually associated with unpleasant evaluations portrayed by highly esteemed models.

The process of value modification through prestigeful modeling is strikingly illustrated in an ingenious experiment by Duncker (1938). In an initial test of food preferences nursery school children chose powdered chocolate with a pleasant lemon flavor over a very sweet sugar with a disagreeable medicinal taste. Later, a story was read to the children in which a stalwart astute hero abhorred a sour-tasting foodstuff similar to the children's preferred food and enthusiastically relished a sweet-tasting substance. The reactions of the admired hero reversed the children's initial food preference, as measured immediately after the story session and in six successive tests in which the children chose between powdered chocolate and sugar. Moreover, brief recall of the story reinstated the experimentally induced value change that had declined gradually over time. Although there is reason to believe, from findings cited earlier, that the prestigeful properties of the model were a significant determinant of changes in preferences, in the absence of data based on a low-status model its contribution in the present study cannot be evaluated.

More recently, Bandura, Blanchard and Ritter (1967) found that negative attitudes of long duration were drastically altered by having phobic adults observe modeled positive responses toward the repugnant attitude object without any adverse consequences accruing to the performing model. And Carlin (1965) demonstrated that young children showed a greater preference for deferred gratification after having observed an adult model display positive affective reactions while waiting for delayed rewards than when the model expressed negative emotional reactions during the imposed delay period and devalued the goal object. Results of these studies are sufficiently promising to warrant further investigation of the modification of evaluative meanings of objects and activities through their contiguous association with affective modeling cues.

Modeling as a Function of Observer-Model Similarity

The research reviewed in the preceding section examined generalization of matching responses to unfamiliar persons on the basis of their similarity to past reward-producing models. Under certain conditions, modeling can also be significantly influenced by real or assumed similarity between the observer and the model.

Stotland and his coworkers (Burnstein, Stotland & Zander, 1961; Stotland & Hillmer, 1962; Stotland & Patchen, 1961; Stotland, Zander & Natsoulas, 1961) have conducted a series of experiments on the process of identification, in each of which some subjects are initially led to believe that they are similar in one or more attributes to a model, while other subjects are given information suggesting that they are dissimilar to the model in social background, preferences, or personality characteristics. The subjects are later informed of the model's preferential choices on a new task, and the number of matching responses induced in high and low similarity groups are compared. The results generally show that persons told they have some qualities in common with a model are more inclined to imitate additional new responses portrayed by the model than subjects who initially share no common characteristics. Moreover, within the range of conditions tested, generalized matching behavior has been found to occur without any prior acquaintance or direct social interaction with the model, and even when the relationship between the classes of modeled responses is entirely arbitrary, the possession of the initial similar attributes is a matter of chance, and the new modeled responses have no inherent rewarding properties.

According to Stotland's theoretical interpretation of identification, generalization of similarity results from a cognitive process that is characterized as follows: Individuals have a strong need to achieve cognitive consistency in their self-concepts. Therefore, when a person conceives of himself as having some characteristics in common with a model, he will introject other attributes of the model into his self-concept in order to maintain cognitive or perceptual consistency.

Although the studies by Stotland furnish some suggestive evidence for generalization of similarities, this cognitive theory of identification receives weak empirical support even in the limited conditions under which it has been tested. Several of the studies include significant attributes, but in most cases the symbolically modeled responses are of a relatively inconsequential nature (e.g., preference for musical selections, nonsense syllables or diving styles) and, following a widely accepted tradition in social psychology, the dependent measures generally involve simple self-ratings that are highly subject to response biases, rather than changes in actual social behavior. Moreover, the elusiveness of the phenomenon itself is revealed in studies (Burnstein et al., 1961; Stotland & Hillmer, 1962) that include a control condition in which no attempt is made to induce interpersonal resemblance. Whereas in many comparisons subjects in high and low similarity conditions display differential self-ratings, the two groups usually do not differ significantly from the controls. Considering that both the similarity induction and the identification model are typically presented in verbal form by the same researcher in the same situation, the relatively weak response-generalization effects may be a function of an experimentally induced set for agreement, rather than internal pressures for cognitive consistency.

It should also be noted, in this connection, that the experiments simply demonstrate generalization of imitation across different classes of modeled responses. Interpretations of these data in terms of cognitively induced motivations, perceptual processes, introjective mechanisms, and self-concept reorganization appear superfluous because, except for self-evaluative ratings which yield equivocal results, the hypothesized mediating processes are never assessed. An alternative interpretation is that similarity facilitates modeling primarily through interpersonal attraction rather than as a consequence of striving for cognitive consistency. Byrne (1968) has shown in a series of experiments that perceived similarity between a given individual and a stranger increases attraction toward the stranger. Conversely, dissimilarity manipulations that portray the divergent model as favoring contrary interests may reduce matching behavior by arousing antipathy toward the model. Data from a condition in which the model is clearly dissimilar but possesses attributes that the subject admires and aspires to have would be particularly relevant to these alternative formulations. The cognitive consistency and the attraction hypotheses lead to opposite predictions regarding imitation of admired dissimilar models.

Even if empirical findings had strongly substantiated the cognitive-consistency interpretation of modeling, a more inclusive theory of identification would still be needed to account adequately for both the generalization of similarity across a wide range of socially significant responses and the absence of generalized matching when high initial similarity exists between observers and a model. In Stotland's theory it is assumed that new modeled responses will not be acquired through identification if they are contradictory to, or incompatible with, already existing attributes in the observer. Since this condition may obtain only rarely in socially significant areas of behavior, this theoretical formulation places severe limitations on the behavioral changes that can be achieved through the influence of models. The theory also implies that individuals would be continually reorganizing their self-concepts and changing their behavior on the basis of casual contacts with unfamiliar models who happen to share some common characteristics. Finally, there are numerous studies (Bandura & Kupers, 1964; Hicks, 1965; Jakubczak & Walters, 1959) in which children are more imitative of adults than peers—who obviously display a considerably greater number of common attributes—and adults may be more inclined to match some behaviors of ethnically dissimilar models than those of similar ethnic and socioeconomic status (Epstein, 1966). These types of findings are not explicable in terms of a cognitive theory which assumes prompt generalization of similarities.

The diverse results discussed above can be encompassed within the framework of social-learning theory in terms of stimulus generalization from prior experiences involving *analogous* reinforcement contingencies. One would expect people who possess similar characteristics to share many experiences and outcomes in common. Results of experiments with infrahuman subjects reveal that the experience of repeated common consequences is an important determinant of matching responsivity. Church (1959), for example, found that animals subjected to paired aversive consequences subsequently displayed more emotional responsivity to the pain cues emitted by another animal than a group of subjects that had received the same amount of aversive stimulation, but unassociated with the pain responses of another member of their species. Moreover, Murphy, Miller and Mirsky (1955) employing a cooperative avoidance conditioning procedure, demonstrated that emotional responses in monkeys could be vicariously elicited not only by the sight of affective cues from their experimental counterpart, but also through stimulus generalization to another monkey who was never involved in the original aversive contingencies. Findings of these laboratory studies indicate that repeated association of similarity cues with analogous reinforcing outcomes would establish likeness as a discriminative stimulus for generalized identificatory behavior.

On the other hand, if people who share common characteristics rarely experience concordant outcomes, but emulation of dissimilar models produces favorable consequences, one would predict high imitation of new attributes portrayed by a divergent model. These are precisely the conditions under which children in Miller and Dollard's (1941) experiments learned to match the behavior of an adult rather than a peer model, and subsequently generalized this differential identificatory preference to other unfamiliar adults. This process would, of course, eventually result in high observer-model resemblance.

In either case, whether initial similarity or dissimilarity facilitates generalized matching behavior may primarily depend on the extent to which these cues have been associated in the past with paired consequences or paired opposing outcomes for models and observers. The relative influence of similarity and analogous outcomes on identification could be best evaluated by an experiment in which similar people experience opposite consequences prior to the test for imitation, whereas dissimilar people encounter identical outcomes. It would be predicted from social-learning theory that discrepant outcomes would override previously established discriminative functions of modeling stimuli. The highest level of identification would be expected to occur under conditions of high subject-model similarity and common consequences.

Role of Social-System Variables and Other Extra-Familial Influences in Identification

Traditional psychological theories of socialization would lead one to believe that social behavior can be acquired vicariously only through identification with real-life models; that interpersonal relationship factors are necessary preconditions for identificatory learning; that parents serve as decisive role models and, at least during the early developmental period, siblings, peers, and nonfamilial adults are minor sources of social behavior; that the behavioral transmission process is unidirectional (i.e., children adapt behavior exhibited by parents, but not vice versa) ; and that social organizational systems do not exist as sources of values and conduct. Research based on social-learning theory and analyses of behavior as a function of social-structure variables indicates that a broad range of modeling influences, both actual and symbolized, must be incorporated in a comprehensive theory of behavioral transmission.

The peer group is perhaps one of the most neglected sources of social learning in psychological accounts of the identification process. In training their children parents frequently demonstrate specific skills and desired child-appropriate behaviors, and they may also furnish play materials suitable for enacting adult roles. However, because of the wide age disparity most of the social-response patterns spontaneously portrayed by parental and other adult figures can serve, at the most, as general guides for young children in their daily social interactions. Children must, consequently, rely to some extent on older siblings and peers as models for specific modes of behavior that parents do not ordinarily provide. Indeed, in some cultures (Bronfenbrenner, 1962) peers supersede parental figures as the principal models and agents of socialization.

The identification process becomes more complicated under conditions in which children are exposed to both parental and peer models who display conflicting standards in the same areas of behavior. Thus, in the experiment mentioned earlier (Bandura, Grusec & Menlove, 1967b), children who simultaneously observed an adult set himself high standards of achievement and a peer adopt low norms subsequently imposed less stringent standards on themselves than children who were exposed only to the behavior of the adult model. The influence of the peer's self-indulgent pattern could be effectively counteracted, however, by social reinforcement of the model's high standard-setting behavior.

The deleterious effect of conflicting identifications arising from incompatible value systems of parents and peer reference figures has received considerable attention in theories of adolescent socialization. It should therefore be emphasized in passing that selection of peer models is greatly influenced by the values prevailing in the home. Children tend to choose friends who share similar values and who are therefore more likely to reinforce familial standards of conduct than to serve as sources of conflict (Bandura, 1964; Bandura & Walters, 1959; Elkin & Westley, 1955).

As children grow older, they must draw even more heavily upon peers and other extra-familial models for several reasons. In the first place, under conditions of rapid social and technological change, many parental interests, attitudes, and role behaviors that were serviceable at an earlier period may have little functional value for members of the younger generation. New complex patterns of behavior must therefore be learned from other social agents whenever major disruptive changes introduce wide disparities among age groups. One suspects that fox-trotting parents will not necessarily prove to be the most idolized or effective models for Watusi-swinging adolescents. Indeed, in many instances, adolescents function as models for their parents, especially in a culture like ours which sets a high value on the activities and symbols of youth.

Social mobility also places severe limitations on the extent of familial transmission of behavior patterns. This is most clearly evident in studies (Ellis & Lane, 1963; Krauss, 1964) investigating the sources of high educational aspirations among lower-class children. In these families the parents themselves cannot provide satisfactory models for class-typed habits of speech, customs, social skills, and attitudes that are required for successful upward mobility. The parents usually initiate the mobility process by encouraging and supporting high educational aspirations; admired teachers further reinforce, by approval and example, college ambitions in lower-class youths; and selective association with college-oriented middle-class peers provides the social-learning conditions for the gradual development of attitudes, belief systems, and complex behavioral repertoires necessary for achieving the desired status.

During later periods of development people must continue to draw extensively upon a variety of nonfamilial models in preparing themselves for new vocational, professional, and social roles that cannot be transmitted within the family no matter how versatile its members may be. Identification should therefore be viewed as a continuous process involving multiple modeling, rather than a phenomenon that primarily occurs in relationship to parents during early childhood, producing enduring and pervasive changes in personality characteristics.

Another neglected influential source of social learning is the abundant and diverse symbolic modeling provided in television and other audio-visual displays. Since response patterns can be acquired on a purely observational basis, it is not surprising to find in comparative studies that models provided by filmed displays can be as influential as their real-life counterparts in shaping children's behavior (Bandura et al., 1963a). In fact, many of the experiments reviewed earlier, demonstrating extensive modeling effects in both children and adults, utilized pictorially presented models.

In view of the efficacy of symbolic modeling and the large amount of time that most young people spend watching televised productions (Schramm, Lyle & Parker, 1961), mass media may play a more important part in shaping behavior and in modifying social norms than has generally been assumed. To the extent that conduct norms modeled by parental transmitters are contradicted by those exemplified by prestigeful televised transmitters, the socialization influence of the family is attenuated for better or for worse, depending on the types of behavior that are repeatedly portrayed. It is highly probable that with further advances in communication technology, parents, teachers, and other socialization agents may become relatively less influential role models as increasing use is made of symbolic models. Some changes in this direction have already occurred in educational practice.

Much social learning is fostered through exposure to *behavioral modeling cues* in actual or pictorial forms. However, after adequate language development is achieved, persons rely extensively upon *verbal modeling cues* for guiding their behavior. Thus, for example, one can usually assemble relatively complicated mechanical equipment, acquire rudimentary social and vocational skills, and learn appropriate ways of behaving in almost any situation simply by matching the responses described in instructional manuals. If the relevant cues are specified clearly and in sufficient detail, verbally symbolized models may have effects that are quite similar to those induced by analogous behavioral displays. Bandura and Mischel (1965) found that children's willingness to defer gratification could be modified to an essentially comparable degree by having them either observe an adult model exhibit delay behavior that was counter to the children's orientation, or read a verbal account of his delay pattern. The use of verbal forms of modeling makes it possible to transmit an almost infinite variety of values and response patterns that would be exceedingly difficult and time-consuming to portray behaviorally.

Normative systems that describe in detail appropriate conduct in given situations and the consequences for deviation also represent a prevalent means of influencing and regulating the social behavior of both parents and children. The interpretation of normative injunctions as a special case of symbolic modeling provides a link between conceptualizations of behavioral control favored by sociologists and those that predominate among psychologists.

FAMILIAL AND SOCIAL-SYSTEMS TRANSMISSION OF BEHAVIORAL PATTERNS

In a provocative paper Reiss (1966) contrasts theories of behavioral transmission based upon the family unit with those emphasizing institutionally organized systems, and he enumerates several reasons why the former model cannot adequately explain socialization outcomes.

As noted earlier, most personality theories maintain that values, attitudes, and patterns of behavior are primarily transmitted through the parent-child relationship. Assuming a 20-year difference between generations, a relatively long period intervenes between parental input of social values and the time when the supposedly internalized contents can be passed on to succeeding descendants. Under these conditions the rate of social change would be exceedingly slow whereas, in fact, extensive society-wide shifts in normative behavior often occur within a single generation. Reiss therefore argues that the parent-child relationship cannot be the major agency of cultural transmission. Rather, standards of conduct are disseminated by institutionally organized systems (e.g., religious, political, legal, and educational agencies) and regulated by collectively enforced sanctions. Innovation, according to Reiss's view, originates at the social organization level, whereas changes emerging within the family are of minor social consequence. Thus, for example, discriminative practices in schools, public accommodations, and voting rights are more effectively eliminated by invoking Supreme Court decisions than by waiting for bigoted parents to inculcate in their children tolerant attitudes which might result in more compassionate behavior towards Negroes when the offspring become members of school boards or motel operators twenty years later.

In general agreement with Reiss's main thesis, the theory of behavioral transmission outlined in the present chapter and elsewhere (Bandura, 1968a) assumes that social behavior is, in large part, developed through exposure to modeling cues and regulated by reinforcement contingencies, many of which are prescribed by one's organizational affiliations. Because social agencies are given a great deal of power to administer potent rewarding and punishing consequences to their members, collectively enforced sanctions can produce rapid and widespread changes in behavior. However, a systems theory alone is insufficient to explain the varied socialization outcomes that typically exist even in relatively homogeneous sub-cultures. These differences occur because organizational prescriptions for conduct must be implemented by parents and other societal agents. Parents who, for whatever reason, do not subscribe to organizationally sanctioned codes of behavior, and who themselves display deviant characteristics, generally produce children who are also socially deviant. In addition, the child-rearing practices employed by socially conforming parents can affect indirectly the success of group control. Parental methods of training may fail to endow social and symbolic cues with the reinforcing functions required for effective socialization, and establish in children strong defiant, avoidant, or overinhibited response tendencies that serve as barriers to societal influences (Bandura & Walters, 1959; McCord, McCord & Zola, 1959). Finally, in cases where strong sanctions are not employed by governing agencies to enforce advocated changes, parents generally resist adoption of new customs, technologies, and values for some time.

In discussing the limitations of personality theories of socialization, Reiss states that, in such approaches, social changes can arise only through failures in transmission between generations. This criticism may apply to radical theories that assume that parental characteristics are introjected by children *in toto* and later passed on in unmodified forms to their progeny. In fact, social learning is a continuous process in which established patterns of behavior are often extinguished or extensively elaborated, and new modes of response are adopted. The behavioral contents transmitted by parents to children therefore include not only some aspects of their social heritage, but also response tendencies acquired from numerous sources during later periods of development. Hence, considerable modifications in characteristic patterns of behavior can emerge across generations on the basis of a familial transmission process.

The limitations regarding intergenerational changes that Reiss attributes to personality theories of socialization also imply certain assumptions about modeling phenomena (i.e., homogeneity of modeling cues, extremely narrow selection of models, unmodifiability of matching responses, etc.) that are not confirmed by recent findings from research in social-learning theory. According to the observational-learning interpretation of modeling, children have repeated opportunities to observe and to learn the behavior and values not only of parents, but also of siblings, peers, and other significant persons. Consequently, when a child is exposed to a variety of models, he may select one or more of them as the principal sources of social behavior, but he rarely reproduces all elements of a single model's repertoire or confines his imitation to that person. In the experiment (Bandura et al., 1963b) that utilized three-person groups, for example, although children adopted many characteristics of the model who possessed rewarding power, they also reproduced some of the attributes exhibited by the model who occupied a subordinate role. The children therefore displayed a relatively novel pattern of behavior representing amalgams of elements from both models. Moreover, the specific admixture of behavioral elements varied from child to child. Thus, within the same family even same-sex siblings may exhibit quite different personality characteristics resulting from having selected for imitation different elements of parental and sibling behavior. It may seem paradoxical, but under conditions of high diversity of modeling patterns, much innovation of social behavior can occur entirely through identification. On the other hand, in homogeneous cultures in which models display essentially similar patterns of behavior, and deviants are ostracized, placed in confinement, or otherwise punished, one would expect little change across successive generations. Although questions can be raised about the validity of some of the criticisms levied by Reiss against the family transmission model, nevertheless his major contention that perpetuation and change of behavioral norms are primarily controlled by social-system conditions, and not by parental agents, appears to be well-grounded.

GENERALITY OF MODELING INFLUENCES

It is widely assumed, on the basis of evidence that people often produce new responses which they have never formed or seen before, that innovative behavior cannot be accounted for on the basis of learning theory principles. This limitation may apply to theoretical formulations that depict the learning process exclusively in terms of selective reinforcement of spontaneously emitted variations in behavior. However, theories employing modeling principles have often been similarly criticized on the mistaken assumption that exposure to the behavior of others can produce, at the most, mimicry of specific modeled responses.

In most experimental investigations of identificatory processes a single model exhibits a limited set of responses, and observers are subsequently tested for the amount of precise response duplication under similar or identical stimulus conditions. These restricted experimental paradigms can yield only specific imitative outcomes that do not extend beyond the particular responses demonstrated. On the other hand, studies employing more complex procedures indicate that innovative behavior, generalized behavioral orientations, and principles for generating novel combinations of responses can be transmitted to observers through exposure to modeling cues. As has been shown earlier, under conditions in which children are provided opportunities to observe the behavior of heterogeneous models (Bandura et al., 1963b), observers typically display novel patterns of behavior representing diverse combinations of elements from the different models. Illustrations of the efficacy of modeling procedures for developing generalized conceptual and behavioral propensities are provided in studies designed to modify moral judgmental orientations (Bandura & McDonald, 1963) and delay-of-gratification patterns of behavior (Bandura & Mischel, 1965). In these experiments the models and observers respond to entirely different sets of stimuli in the social-influence setting, and tests for generalized identificatory effects are conducted by different experimenters in different settings with the models absent, and with different stimulus items. The results disclose that observers respond to new stimulus situations in a manner consistent with the models' dispositions even though the subjects had never witnessed the model's behavior in response to the same stimuli.

In the higher-order form of modeling described above the observer acquires a common verbally labelled attribute or a rule exemplified in a variety of modeling responses that may differ in many other aspects. Subsequent responses generated by the subject that embody the observationally derived rule are likely to resemble the behavior that the model would be inclined to exhibit under similar circumstances. The abstraction of rules from modeling cues is achieved through vicarious discrimination learning (Bandura & Harris, 1966) in which the responses of models that contain the relevant attribute are reinforced, whereas those that lack the critical feature are consistently nonrewarded.

Although modeling variables play an important role in the development of most social behaviors, their position with respect to language learning is almost unique. Since children cannot acquire words and syntactical structures without exposure to verbalizing models, it is obvious that some amount of modeling is indispensable for language acquisition. However, because of the highly generative character of linguistic behavior, it is usually assumed that imitation cannot possibly play much of a part in language development and production. The main argument, which is based on the mimicry view of modeling, is as follows: Children can construct an almost infinite variety of sentences that they have never heard. Consequently, instead of imitating and memorizing specific utterances that they may have heard at one time or another, children learn sets of rules, on the basis of which they can generate an unlimited variety of grammatical sentences.

It is obvious that rules about grammatical relations between words cannot be learned unless they are exemplified in the verbal behavior of models. An important question therefore concerns the conditions that facilitate abstraction of rules from verbal modeling cues. The principle underlying a model's varied responses can be most readily discerned if its identifying characteristics are repeated in responses involving a variety of different stimuli. If, for example, one were to place a series of objects on tables, chairs, boxes, and other places, and simultaneously verbalize the common prepositional relationship between the objects, a child would eventually discern the grammatical principle. He could then easily generate a novel grammatical sentence if a toy hippopotamus were placed on a piano and the child were asked to describe the enacted stimulus event.

Unlike social responses which are often readily acquired, language learning is considerably more difficult because sentences represent complex stimulus patterns in which the identifying features of syntactic structures cannot be easily discriminated. The influential role of both modeling and discrimination processes in language development is shown by findings of an experiment (Bandura & Harris, 1966) designed to alter the syntactic style of young children who had no formal grammatical knowledge of the linguistic features that were manipulated. The grammatical constructions chosen to be modified were the prepositional phrase, which has a high base rate of occurrence, and the passive voice, which is grammatically more complex and rarely displayed by young children.

As might be expected, social reinforcement, even when combined with a strong attentional set to identify the characteristics of "correct" sentences, was ineffective in increasing the use of passives in sentences generated by the children in response to a set of simple nouns. The majority of subjects did not produce a single passive sentence, and consequently, no responses occurred that could be reinforced. Nor were the children able to discern, within the relatively brief exposure period, the critical syntactic category simply from observing a model construct a series of passive sentences. In contrast, children generated significantly more passives when verbal modeling cues were combined with procedures designed to increase syntactic discriminability. The most powerful treatment condition was one in which the attentional set was induced, modeled passive constructions were interspersed with some sentences in the active voice so as to enhance differentiation of relevant grammatical properties, and both the model and the children were rewarded for passive constructions. In the case of a syntactic category as common as prepositional phrases, reinforcement together with an active attentional set were effective in altering children's usage of prepositions, but modeling cues were not a significant contributory factor.

Children who show gross behavioral deficits, and whose discriminative and attentive capacities are limited, may benefit little from repeated exposure to verbal modeling cues alone, even though they may be easily discriminable. In such cases, highly explicit and concrete modeling procedures must be utilized, as is well-exemplified in the therapeutic program devised by Lovaas (1966) to establish grammatical speech in schizophrenic children.

The program consists essentially of rewarding the child's discriminative responsivity to verbally or behaviorally modeled events. Whenever the child fails to respond or responds incorrectly he is aided by verbal and physical prompts which are gradually faded out on succeeding trials. Prepositional training will serve to illustrate the three basic discriminations that are developed. Initially the adult gives a verbal instruction involving a preposition (e.g., "Put the block inside the box") and the child is promptly rewarded for performing the motor response appropriate to the verbal stimulus. If the child fails to execute the response correctly, the therapist moves the child's hand with the block to the box while repeating the corresponding verbal response. In the second discrimination, objects are arranged in a particular way and the child verbally describes the relationships between the objects, using the proper preposition. In the third step, the child gives grammatical verbal responses to sentences spoken by the adult. Children are later taught to generalize the linguistic rule by modeling a variety of objects in a variety of prepositional relationships. Essentially the same modeling procedures have been successfully employed by Lovaas to establish other types of syntactic patterns in mute schizophrenic children.

CONCLUDING COMMENTS

The theory of identification outlined in the present chapter assigns a prominent role to observational learning, which is assumed to mediate identificatory outcomes. According to this theoretical formulation, matching behavior is acquired on the basis of contiguity of modeling stimulus sequences and symbolic verbal coding of observational inputs. These representational symbolic events, in conjunction with appropriate environmental cues, later guide overt enactment of appropriate matching responses. Performance of observationally learned identificatory responses, on the other hand, is primarily governed by reinforcing events that may be externally applied, self-administered, or vicariously experienced. Moreover, emphasis is given to the differential consequences of emulating the behavior of models possessing distinctive characteristics. These come to function as discriminative stimuli for regulating generalization of identificatory responses toward unfamiliar models, in different social situations, and across different classes of behavior displayed by the same model.

The conceptualization of modeling processes in terms of social-learning principles differs in several important respects from most personality theories of identification. Traditional approaches generally depict identification as a pervasive and more or less unitary modeling outcome that is firmly established early in a child's life, and which results from nurturant and threatening interactions with parental figures. In contrast, social-learning theory not only posits a different type of learning process, and a different set of controlling variables for identification, but also assumes a considerably more complex model of behavioral transmission. Identification, according to this view, is a continuous process in which new responses are acquired and existing repertoires of behavior are modified to some extent as a function of both direct and vicarious experiences with a wide variety of actual or symbolic models, whose attitudes, values, and social responses are exemplified behaviorally, or in verbally coded forms. Although a family can provide general prescriptions for conduct, parental models cannot possibly serve as primary sources of the elaborate skills and modes of behavior required at different stages of social development. Complex cultural patterns of behavior are, in large part, transmitted and regulated at a social-systems level.

The conceptual scheme presented here appears to be sufficiently inclusive to encompass a large set of variables that have been shown to influence identificatory phenomena. Moreover, if the worth of a psychological theory is judged by the efficacy of the behavioral modification procedures that it produces, as theory ultimately should be, then preliminary results from clinical applications of modeling techniques based on social-learning principles indicate this approach holds considerable promise.

REFERENCES

ALLPORT, F. H. *Social psychology.* Cambridge, Mass.: Riverside Press, 1924.

ARONFREED, J. Conduct and conscience. A natural history of internalization. Unpublished manuscript, Univer. of Pennsylvania, 1967.

ASCH, S. E. The doctrine of suggestion, prestige, and imitation in social psychology. *Psychological Review,* 1948, *55,* 250–277.

BAER, D. M., PETERSON, R. F., & SHERMAN, J. A. The development of imitation by reinforcing similarity to a model. *Journal of the Experimental Analysis of Behavior,* 1967, *10,* 405–416.

BAER, D. M., & SHERMAN, J. A. Reinforcement control of generalized imitation in young children. *Journal of Experimental Child Psychology,* 1964, *1,* 37–49.

BANDURA, A. Social learning through imitation. In M. R. Jones (Ed.), *Nebraska symposium on motivation: 1962.* Lincoln: Univer. Nebraska Press, 1962. Pp. 211–269.

BANDURA, A. The stormy decade: Fact or fiction? *Psychology in the Schools,* 1964, *1,* 224–231.

BANDURA, A. Vicarious processes: A case of no-trial learning. In L. Berkowitz (Ed.), *Advances in experimental social psychology,* Vol. II. New York: Academic Press, 1965. Pp. 1–55. (a)

BANDURA, A. Influence of models' reinforcement contingencies on the acquisition of imitative responses. *Journal of Personality and Social Psychology,* 1965, *1,* 589–595. (b)

BANDURA, A. *Principles of behavioral modification.* New York: Holt, Rinehart & Winston, 1968 (in press). (a)

BANDURA, A. Modelling approaches to the modification of phobic disorders. In *Ciba Foundation Symposium. The role of learning in psychotherapy.* London: Churchill, 1968 (in press). (b)

BANDURA, A., BLANCHARD, E. B., & RITTER, BRUNHILDE J. Relative efficacy of modeling and desensitization therapeutic approaches for inducing behavioral, attitudinal and affective changes. Unpublished manuscript, Stanford Univer., 1967.

BANDURA, A., GRUSEC, JOAN E., & MENLOVE, FRANCES L. Observational learning as a function of symbolization and incentive set. *Child Development,* 1966, *37,* 499–506.

BANDURA, A., GRUSEC, JOAN E., & MENLOVE, FRANCES L. Vicarious extinction of avoidance behavior. *Journal of Personality and Social Psychology,* 1967, *5,* 16–23. (a)

BANDURA, A., GRUSEC, JOAN E., & MENLOVE, FRANCES L. Some social determinants of self-monitoring reinforcement systems. *Journal of Personality and Social Psychology,* 1967, *5,* 449–455. (b)

BANDURA, A., & HARRIS, MARY B. Modification of syntactic style. *Journal of Experimental Child Psychology,* 1966, *4,* 341–352.

BANDURA, A., & HUSTON, ALETHA C. Identification as a process of incidental learning. *Journal of Abnormal and Social Psychology,* 1961, *63,* 311–318.

BANDURA, A., & KUPERS, CAROL J. Transmission of patterns of self-reinforcement through modeling. *Journal of Abnormal and Social Psychology,* 1964, *69,* 1–9.

BANDURA, A., & McDONALD, F. J. The influence of social reinforcement and the behavior of models in shaping children's moral judgments. *Journal of Abnormal and Social Psychology,* 1963, *67,* 274–281.

BANDURA, A., & MENLOVE, FRANCES L. Factors determining vicarious extinction of avoidance behavior through symbolic modeling. *Journal of Personality and Social Psychology*, 1968, *8*, 99–108.

BANDURA, A., & MISCHEL, W. Modification of self-imposed delay of reward through exposure to live and symbolic models. *Journal of Personality and Social Psychology*, 1965, *2*, 698–705.

BANDURA, A., & ROSENTHAL, T. L. Vicarious classical conditioning as a function of arousal level. *Journal of Personality and Social Psychology*, 1966, *3*, 54–62.

BANDURA, A., ROSS, DOROTHEA, & ROSS, SHEILA A. Imitation of film-mediated aggressive models. *Journal of Abnormal and Social Psychology*, 1963, *66*, 3–11. (a)

BANDURA, A., ROSS, DOROTHEA, & ROSS, SHEILA A. A comparative test of the status envy, social power, and secondary reinforcement theories of identificatory learning. *Journal of Abnormal and Social Psychology*, 1963, *67*, 527–534. (b)

BANDURA, A., ROSS, DOROTHEA, & ROSS, SHEILA A. Vicarious reinforcement and imitative learning. *Journal of Abnormal and Social Psychology*, 1963, *67*, 601–607. (c)

BANDURA, A., & WALTERS, R. H. *Adolescent aggression*. New York: Ronald, 1959.

BANDURA, A., & WALTERS, R. H. *Social learning and personality development*. New York: Holt, Rinehart & Winston, 1963.

BANDURA, A., & WHALEN, CAROL K. The influence of antecedent reinforcement and divergent modeling cues on patterns of self-reward. *Journal of Personality and Social Psychology*, 1966, *3*, 373–382.

BERGER, S. M. Incidental learning through vicarious reinforcement. *Psychological Reports*, 1961, *9*, 477–491.

BERGER, S. M. Conditioning through vicarious instigation. *Psychological Review*, 1962, *69*, 450–466.

BETTELHEIM, B. Individual and mass behavior in extreme situations. *Journal of Abnormal and Social Psychology*, 1943, *38*, 417–452.

BRONFENBRENNER, U. The study of identification through interpersonal perception. In R. Tagiuri & L. Petrullo (Eds.), *Person perception and interpersonal behavior*. Stanford: Stanford Univer. Press, 1958. Pp. 110–130.

BRONFENBRENNER, U. Freudian theories of identification and their derivatives. *Child Development*, 1960, *31*, 15–40.

BRONFENBRENNER, U. Soviet methods of character education: Some implications for research. *American Psychologist*, 1962, *17*, 550–564.

BRUNING, J. L. Direct and vicarious effects of a shift in magnitude of reward on performance. *Journal of Personality and Social Psychology*, 1965, *2*, 278–282.

BUCHWALD, A. M. Extinction after acquisition under different verbal reinforcement combinations. *Journal of Experimental Psychology*, 1959, *57*, 43–48. (a)

BUCHWALD, A. M. Experimental alterations in the effectiveness of verbal reinforcement combinations. *Journal of Experimental Psychology*, 1959, *57*, 351–361. (b)

BUCHWALD, A. M. Supplementary report: Alteration of the reinforcement value of a positive reinforcer. *Journal of Experimental Psychology*, 1960, *60*, 416–418.

BURNSTEIN, E., STOTLAND, E., & ZANDER, A. Similarity to a model and self-evaluation. *Journal of Abnormal and Social Psychology*, 1961, *62*, 257–264.

BYRNE, D. E. Attitudes and attraction. In L. Berkowitz (Ed.), *Advances in experimental social psychology*. Vol. IV. New York: Academic Press, 1968 (in press).

CAMPBELL, D. T. Conformity in psychology's theories of acquired behavioral dispositions. In I. A. Berg & B. M. Bass (Eds.), *Conformity and deviation*. New York: Harper, 1961. Pp. 101–142.

CARLIN, M. T. The effects of modeled behavior during imposed delay on the observer's subsequent willingness to delay rewards. Unpublished doctoral dissertation, Stanford Univer., 1965.

CASS, LORETTA K. An investigation of parent-child relationships in terms of awareness, identification, projection, and control. *American Journal of Orthopsychiatry,* 1952, *22,* 305–313.

CHURCH, R. M. Transmission of learned behavior between rats. *Journal of Abnormal and Social Psychology,* 1957, *54,* 163–165.

CHURCH, R. M. Emotional reactions of rats to the pain of others. *Journal of Comparative and Physiological Psychology,* 1959, *52,* 132–134.

CLARK, BARBARA S. The acquisition and extinction of peer imitation in children. *Psychonomic Science,* 1965, *2,* 147–148.

CONANT, M. B. Conditioned visual hallucinations. Unpublished manuscript, Stanford Univer., 1964.

CRANDALL, VIRGINIA C. The reinforcement effects of adult reactions and non-reactions on children's achievement expectations. *Child Development,* 1963, *34,* 335–354.

CRANDALL, VIRGINIA C., GOOD, SUZANNE, & CRANDALL, V. J. The reinforcement effects of adult reactions and non-reactions on children's achievement expectations: A replication study. *Child Development,* 1964, *35,* 485–497.

CRONBACH, L. J. Processes affecting scores on "understanding of others" and "assumed similarity." *Psychological Bulletin,* 1955, *52,* 177–194.

DE RATH, G. W. The effects of verbal instructions on imitative aggression. *Dissertation Abstracts,* 1964, *25,* 624–625.

DUNCKER, K. Experimental modification of children's food preferences through social suggestion. *Journal of Abnormal and Social Psychology,* 1938, *33,* 489–507.

DYSINGER, W. S., & RUCKMICK, C. A. *The emotional responses of children to the motion-picture situation.* New York: Macmillan, 1933.

ELKIN, F., & WESTLEY, W. A. The myth of adolescent culture. *American Sociological Review,* 1955, *20,* 680–684.

ELLIS, R. A., & LANE, W. C. Structural supports for upward mobility. *American Sociological Review,* 1963, *28,* 743–756.

ELLSON, D. G. Hallucinations produced by sensory conditioning. *Journal of Experimental Psychology,* 1941, *28,* 1–20.

EMMERICH, W. Parental identification in young children. *Genetic Psychology Monographs,* 1959, *60,* 257–308.

EPSTEIN, R. Aggression toward outgroups as a function of authoritarianism and imitation of aggressive models. *Journal of Personality and Social Psychology,* 1966, *3,* 574–579.

FREUD, ANNA. *The ego and the mechanisms of defense.* New York: International Univer. Press, 1946.

FREUD, S. *The ego and id.* London: Hogarth, 1923.

FREUD, S. Mourning and melancholia. In *Collected papers,* Vol. IV. London: Hogarth, 1925. Pp. 152–170.

GELFAND, DONNA M. The influence of self-esteem on rate of verbal conditioning and social matching behavior. *Journal of Abnormal and Social Psychology,* 1962, *65,* 259–265.

GERST, M. S. Symbolic coding operations in observational learning. Unpublished doctoral dissertation, Stanford Univer., 1968.

GRAY, SUSAN W., & KLAUS, R. The assessment of parental identification. *Genetic Psychology Monographs,* 1956, *54,* 87–114.

HARTMANN, D. The influence of symbolically modeled instrumental aggression and pain cues on the disinhibition of aggressive behavior. Unpublished doctoral dissertation, Stanford Univer., 1965.

HARTUP, W. W. Patterns of imitative behavior in young children. *Child Development,* 1964, *35,* 183–191.

HASTORF, A. H. The "reinforcement" of individual actions in a group situation. In L. Krasner & L. P. Ullmann (Eds.), *Research in behavior modification.* New York: Holt, Rinehart & Winston, 1965. Pp. 268–284.

HEILBRUN, A. B., JR. The measurement of identification. *Child Development,* 1965, *36,* 111–127.

HELPER, M. M. Learning theory and the self-concept. *Journal of Abnormal and Social Psychology,* 1955, *51,* 184–194.

HENKER, BARBARA A. The effect of adult model relationships on children's play and task imitation. *Dissertation Abstracts,* 1964, *24,* 4797.

HETHERINGTON, E. MAVIS. A developmental study of the effects of sex of the dominant parent on sex-role performance, identification, and imitation in children. *Journal of Personality and Social Psychology,* 1965, *2,* 188–194.

HETHERINGTON, E. MAVIS, & FRANKIE, G. Effects of parental dominance, warmth, and conflict on imitation in children. *Journal of Personality and Social Psychology,* 1967, *6,* 119–125.

HICKS, D. J. Imitation and retention of film-mediated aggressive peer and adult models. *Journal of Personality and Social Psychology,* 1965, *2,* 97–100.

HOFFMAN, M. L. Power assertion by the parent and its impact on the child. *Child Development,* 1960, *31,* 129–143.

HOFFMAN, M. L. Childrearing practices and moral development: Generalizations from empirical research. *Child Development,* 1963, *34,* 295–318.

HOLT, E. B. *Animal drive and the learning process.* Vol. 1. New York: Holt, 1931.

HOVLAND, C. I., JANIS, I. L., & KELLEY, H. H. *Communication and persuasion.* New Haven: Yale Univer. Press, 1953.

HUMPHREY, G. Imitation and the conditioned reflex. *Pedagogical Seminary,* 1921, *28,* 1–21.

JAKUBCZAK, L. F., & WALTERS, R. H. Suggestibility as dependency behavior. *Journal of Abnormal and Social Psychology,* 1959, *59,* 102–107.

KANAREFF, VERA T., & LANZETTA, J. T. The acquisition of imitative and opposition responses under two conditions of instruction-induced set. *Journal of Experimental Psychology,* 1958, *56,* 516–528.

KANAREFF, VERA T., & LANZETTA, J. T. Effects of task definition and probability of reinforcement upon the acquisition and extinction of imitative responses. *Journal of Experimental Psychology,* 1960, *60,* 340–348.

KANFER, F. H. Vicarious human reinforcement: A glimpse into the black box. In L. Krasner & L. P. Ullmann (Eds.), *Research in behavior modification.* New York: Holt, Rinehart & Winston, 1965. Pp. 244–267.

KANFER, F. H., & MARSTON, A. R. Human reinforcement: Vicarious and direct. *Journal of Experimental Psychology,* 1963, *65,* 292–296.

KOHLBERG, L. Moral development and identification. In H. W. Stevenson (Ed.), *Child psychology: The sixty-second yearbook of the National Society for the Study of Education.* Part I. Chicago: The National Society for the Study of Education, 1963. Pp. 277–332.

KRAUSS, I. Sources of educational aspirations among working-class youth. *American Sociological Review,* 1964, *29,* 867–879.

LANZETTA, J. T., & KANAREFF, VERA T. The effects of a monetary reward on the acquisition of an imitative response. *Journal of Abnormal and Social Psychology,* 1959, *59,* 120–127.

Lazowick, L. On the nature of identification. *Journal of Abnormal and Social Psychology,* 1955, *51,* 175–183.

Lefkowitz, M. M., Blake, R. R., & Mouton, Jane S. Status factors in pedestrian violation of traffic signals. *Journal of Abnormal and Social Psychology,* 1955, *51,* 704–706.

Leuba, C. Images as conditioned sensations. *Journal of Experimental Psychology,* 1940, *26,* 345–351.

Levin, H., & Sears, R. R. Identification with parents as a determinant of doll play aggression. *Child Development,* 1956, *27,* 135–153.

Lovaas, O. I. A program for the establishment of speech in psychotic children. In J. K. Wing (Ed.), *Childhood autism.* Oxford: Pergamon Press, 1966. Pp. 115–144.

Lovaas, O. I., Berberich, J. P., Perloff, B. F., & Schaeffer, B. Acquisition of imitative speech by schizophrenic children. *Science,* 1966, *151,* 705–707.

Luchins, A. S., & Luchins, Edith H. Imitation by rote and by understanding. *Journal of Social Psychology,* 1961, *54,* 175–197.

Maccoby, Eleanor E. Role-taking in childhood and its consequences for social learning. *Child Development,* 1959, *30,* 239–252.

Margolius, G. J., & Sheffield, F. D. Optimum methods of combining practice and filmed demonstration in teaching complex response sequences: Serial learning of a mechanical-assembly task. In A. A. Lumsdaine (Ed.), *Student response in programmed instruction: A symposium.* Washington, D. C.: National Academy of Science–National Research Council, 1961. Pp. 33–53.

Marston, A. R., & Kanfer, F. H. Group size and number of vicarious reinforcement in verbal learning. *Journal of Experimental Psychology,* 1963, *65,* 593–596.

Mausner, B. Studies in social interaction: III. Effect of variation in one partner's prestige on the interaction of observer pairs. *Journal of Applied Psychology,* 1953, *37,* 391–393.

Mausner, B. The effect of prior reinforcement on the interaction of observer pairs. *Journal of Abnormal and Social Psychology,* 1954, *49,* 65–68. (a)

Mausner, B. The effect of one partner's success in a relevant task on the interaction of observer pairs. *Journal of Abnormal and Social Psychology,* 1954, *49,* 557–560. (b)

Mausner, B., & Bloch, B. L. A study of the additivity of variables affecting social interaction. *Journal of Abnormal and Social Psychology,* 1957, *54,* 250–256.

McCord, W., McCord, Joan, & Zola, I. K. *Origins of crime: A new evaluation of the Cambridge-Somerville Youth Study.* New York: Columbia Univer. Press, 1959.

McDavid, J. W. Effects of ambiguity of environmental cues upon learning to imitate. *Journal of Abnormal and Social Psychology,* 1962, *65,* 381–386.

McDougall, W. *An introduction to social psychology.* London: Methuen, 1908.

Michael, D. N., & Maccoby, N. Factors influencing the effects of student participation on verbal learning from films: Motivating versus practice effects, "feedback," and overt versus covert responding. In A. A. Lumsdaine (Ed.), *Student response in programmed instruction: A symposium.* Washington, D. C.: National Academy of Science–National Research Council, 1961. Pp. 271–293.

Miller, N. E., & Dollard, J. *Social learning and imitation.* New Haven: Yale Univer. Press, 1941.

Mischel, W., & Grusec, Joan. Determinants of the rehearsal and transmission of neutral and aversive behaviors. *Journal of Personality and Social Psychology,* 1966, *2,* 197–205.

Morgan, C. L. *Habit and instinct.* London: E. Arnold, 1896.

Mowrer, O. H. *Learning theory and personality dynamics.* New York: Ronald, 1950.

Mowrer, O. H. Hearing and speaking: An analysis of language learning. *Journal of Speech Disorders*, 1958, *23*, 143–152.

Mowrer, O. H. *Learning theory and the symbolic processes.* New York: Wiley, 1960.

Murphy, J. V., Miller, R. E., & Mirsky, I. A. Interanimal conditioning in the monkey. *Journal of Comparative and Physiological Psychology*, 1955, *48*, 211–214.

Mussen, P. H. Some antecedents and consequents of masculine sex-typing in adolescent boys. *Psychological Monographs*, 1961, *75*, No. 2, (Whole No. 506).

Mussen, P. H., & Distler, L. Masculinity, identification, and father-son relationships. *Journal of Abnormal and Social Psychology*, 1959, *59*, 350–356.

Mussen, P. H., & Parker, Ann L. Mother-nurturance and girls' incidental imitative learning. *Journal of Personality and Social Psychology*, 1965, *2*, 94–97.

Parsons, T. *The social system.* New York: Free Press, 1951.

Parsons, T. Family structure and the socialization of the child. In T. Parsons & R. F. Bales, *Family, socialization, and interaction process.* Glencoe, Ill.: Free Press, 1955. Pp. 35–131.

Payne, D. E., & Mussen, P. H. Parent-child relations and father identification among adolescent boys. *Journal of Abnormal and Social Psychology*, 1956, *52*, 358–362.

Piaget, J. *Play, dreams, and imitation in childhood.* New York: Norton, 1951.

Reiss, A. J., Jr. Social organization and socialization: Variations on a theme about generations. Unpublished manuscript, Univer. of Michigan, 1966.

Rosenbaum, M. E., & Bruning, J. L. Direct and vicarious effects of variations in percentage of reinforcement on performance. *Child Development*, 1966, *37*, 959–966.

Rosenbaum, M. E., & Tucker, I. F. The competence of the model and the learning of imitation and nonimitation. *Journal of Experimental Psychology*, 1962, *63*, 183–190.

Rosenblith, Judy F. Learning by imitation in kindergarten children. *Child Development*, 1959, *30*, 69–80.

Rosenblith, Judy F. Imitative color choices in kindergarten children. *Child Development*, 1961, *32*, 211–223.

Sarnoff, I. Identification with the aggressor: Some personality correlates of anti-Semitism among Jews. *Journal of Personality*, 1951, *20*, 199–218.

Schein, E. H. The effect of reward on adult imitative behavior. *Journal of Abnormal and Social Psychology*, 1954, *49*, 389–395.

Schramm, W., Lyle, J., & Parker, E. F. *Television in the lives of our children.* Stanford: Stanford Univer. Press, 1961.

Sears, Pauline S. Child-rearing factors relating to playing sex-typed roles. *American Psychologist*, 1953, *8*, 431 (abstract).

Sears, R. R. Identification as a form of behavioral development. In D. B. Harris (Ed.), *The concept of development.* Minneapolis: Univer. Minnesota Press, 1957. Pp. 149–161.

Sears, R. R., Rau, Lucy, & Alpert, R. *Identification and child rearing.* Stanford: Stanford Univer. Press, 1965.

Sheffield, F. D. Theoretical considerations in the learning of complex sequential tasks from demonstration and practice. In A. A. Lumsdaine (Ed.) *Student response in programmed instruction: A symposium.* Washington, D. C.: National Academy of Sciences–National Research Council, 1961. Pp. 13–22.

Sheffield, F. D., & Maccoby, N. Summary and interpretation of research on organizational principles in constructing filmed demonstrations. In A. A. Lumsdaine (Ed.), *Student response in programmed instruction: A symposium.* Washington, D. C.: National Academy of Sciences–National Research Council, 1961. Pp. 117–131.

SKINNER, B. F. *Science and human behavior.* New York: Macmillan, 1953.

SOPCHAK, A. L. Parental "identification" and "tendencies toward disorder" as measured by the MMPI. *Journal of Abnormal and Social Psychology,* 1952, *47,* 159–165.

STOKE, S. An inquiry into the concept of identification. *Journal of Genetic Psychology,* 1950, *76,* 163–189.

STOTLAND, E., & HILLMER, M. L., JR. Identification, authoritarian defensiveness, and self-esteem. *Journal of Abnormal and Social Psychology,* 1962, *64,* 334–342.

STOTLAND, E., & PATCHEN, M. Identification and changes in prejudice and in authoritarianism. *Journal of Abnormal and Social Psychology,* 1961, *62,* 265–274.

STOTLAND, E., ZANDER, A., & NATSOULAS, T. The generalization of interpersonal similarity. *Journal of Abnormal and Social Psychology,* 1961, *62,* 250–256.

TARDE, G. *The laws of imitation.* New York: Holt, 1903.

WALTERS, R. H., & PARKE, R. D. Influence of response consequences to a social model on resistance to deviation. *Journal of Experimental Child Psychology,* 1964, *1,* 269–280.

WALTERS, R. H., PARKE, R. D., & CANE, VALERIE A. Timing of punishment and the observation of consequences to others as determinants of response inhibition. *Journal of Experimental Child Psychology,* 1965, *2,* 10–30.

WALTERS, R. H., & THOMAS, E. L. Enhancement of punitiveness by visual and audio-visual displays. *Canadian Journal of Psychology,* 1963, *17,* 244–255.

WHITING, J. W. M. Sorcery, sin, and the superego. In M. R. Jones (Ed.), *Nebraska symposium on motivation.* Lincoln: Univer. Nebraska Press, 1959. Pp. 174–195.

WHITING, J. W. M. Resource mediation and learning by identification. In I. Iscoe & H. W. Stevenson (Eds.), *Personality development in children.* Austin: Univer. Texas Press, 1960. Pp. 112–126.

WIGGINS, J. A., DILL, F., & SCHWARTZ, R. D. On "status-liability." *Sociometry,* 1965, *28,* 197–209.

CHAPTER 4

The Concept Of Internalization

Justin Aronfreed

University of Pennsylvania

Even the casual observer of socialization can see that the external contingencies in the child's immediate social environment exercise a profound control over the modification and maintenance of its behavior. The more remarkable consequence of socialization is that it gives the child's acquired behavioral dispositions a stability that shows an increasing independence of external control. The young child's social behavior is initially highly dependent on its experience of external events which are transmitted through the presence and activity of its socializing agents. But its behavior gradually comes to be governed, to a very considerable extent, by internal monitors. These internal monitors appear to carry many of the functions of the external controls which were originally required to establish the behavior. The mechanisms through which the internal monitors become established provide much more than an account of how the child's behavior is maintained once it has been acquired. These mechanisms are fundamental to a general understanding of the very nature of the phenomena of learning in the origins of social behavior.

Terms such as "internalization" or "interiorization" sometimes have been used to refer to a process whereby behavior that was once public and overt becomes represented with an internal cognitive model (Piaget, 1951; Vygotsky, 1962). This usage actually pertains to a powerful and special case of a much broader array of affective and cognitive mechanisms which can translate the child's social learning into its capacity for internalized control over its behavior. These mechanisms carry the motivational and informational functions of many of the externally structured determinants of the child's earlier experience. They are superimposed upon, and sometimes displace, the functional properties of concrete external events. And they take a variety of forms, many of which are relatively simple transformations of the affective and cognitive input that

Some recent experiments which have been conducted by the author and his associates are reported in this chapter. The experiments were supported in part by Research Grant MH-06671 from the National Institutes of Health, United States Public Health Service.

the child has received from its social environment. Cognitive models for the storage of complex patterns of behavior, which may sometimes replace behavior at the level of covert representation, are a particularly interesting type of transformation of social experience. But great repertoires of behavior which remain overt and active come under internalized control through the simpler transformations of conditioning and direct training, as well as through various kinds of cognitive transmission of social information which are less imposing than a representational model.

After a general introduction to the phenomena which require a concept of internalization, we will examine two major channels of socialization which produce and maintain the child's internalized controls over its social behavior. The first channel of socialization is the shaping of behavior through positive or aversive outcomes which are contingent on the child's overt acts. The second channel of socialization is observational learning, which does not require outcomes of the child's overtly emitted behavior. The types of observational learning which have been studied most extensively are the imitation of social models and the behavioral effects of observing the consequences of the behavior of others. Following an extended theoretical and experimental analysis of some of the phenomena of these two basic channels of socialization, we will look at certain rough confirmations of their broader outlines in the findings of studies which have attempted to assess the naturalistic antecedents of children's internalized behavioral dispositions.

A number of different kinds of evidence will be used here to demonstrate the utility of a concept of internalization. However, there are two bodies of empirical work which bear most directly on the problem of how socialization produces internalized control of behavior. The first kind can be found in many recent investigations which have used experimental paradigms of socialization. The results of such investigations often make it possible to draw inferences about the conditions of learning which facilitate internalized control over behavior. A few of the experiments examine the parameters of the learning process closely enough to test explicit conceptions of mechanisms of internalization. This kind of evidence is taken primarily, though not exclusively, from experiments which focus on the behavior of children. The second major body of evidence appears in naturalistic surveys of the relationships between the child-rearing practices of parents and the behavior of their children. Such surveys usually employ the parents' verbal report of their own behavior, but often use more direct observational techniques to assess the child's dispositions.

BEHAVIORAL AND COGNITIVE ASPECTS
OF INTERNALIZATION

The concept of internalization is often used to refer to the child's adoption of social norms or roles as its own, and to the resulting control of its behavior by the most complex mediational functions of cognitive and verbal processes (see, for example, Newcomb, 1950, or Parsons & Bales, et al., 1955). The empirical findings which bear most directly on this conception come from assessments of those products of internalization which appear in the child's verbal expressions of conscience and, even more specifically, in its moral judgment (Kohlberg, 1969; Piaget, 1948). Although such a conception emphasizes that evaluative cognition is sometimes a powerful determinant of social behavior, it does not begin to contain the broader conceptual resources which we need in order to understand the total spectrum of ways in which social experience produces internalized control over the child's conduct. The place of values in the control of behavior can be more accurately estimated if we first take into account that human beings are highly conditionable, and that large areas of social behavior can be subjected to internalized control with little or no engagement of evaluative decision-making processes.

Common observation compels us to see that standards for the evaluation of conduct are not a prerequisite to internalized control of behavior. The young preverbal child is capable of some acquired control over its behavior in the absence of social surveillance—for example, if it has had earlier experience with any form of punishment for touching dangerous objects or running into the street. Very young children will frequently show distress when they have committed an act for which they have been punished previously, or will show pleasure in reaction to an act for which they have been previously rewarded, even when it seems highly unlikely that socializing agents would originally have communicated a cognitive standard for evaluating the act in question.

These observations are confirmed by the findings of a number of experiments in which older children have been used as subjects. It has been shown, for example, that behavioral suppression can be brought under effective internalized control in training paradigms where children are punished for their choices of attractive toys without being given any explanation or further criterion for punishment (Aronfreed, 1966). Another experiment, which was designed to examine the origin of self-criticism, has demonstrated the conditions under which a child will reproduce a verbal component of social punishment, and apply the component to its own punished behavior, when the child has had no previous experience of either the verbal label or the behavior in an evaluative context (Aronfreed, 1964). The findings of other experiments indicate that children are more likely to suppress behavior that is under some social constraint if they first have observed the punitive consequences of another person's performance of the same behavior (Bandura, 1965a; Walters & Parke, 1964). These experiments also include less effective attempts to demonstrate facilitation of children's behavior by observation of the rewarding consequences of another person's corresponding behavior. In this type of experiment, no direct attempt is made to change the child's evaluative standards in the direction of the reported behavioral effects. Bandura, Ross and Ross (1963c) reported, in fact, that some children who had expressed disapproval of the aggressive behavior which they observed nevertheless behaved in a similar fashion if they had seen the behavior produce socially rewarding consequences for the other person.

Internalized control of behavior is also evident in the persistence of certain forms of learned behavior in animals. The persistence is especially impressive in the case of avoidance behavior, which can sometimes be sustained during the prolonged absence of the original conditions of aversive learning under which it was acquired. Avoidance behavior may be very stable even though shock is no longer the consequence of failure to make the avoidance response (Sidman, 1955; Solomon & Wynne, 1954). It may be highly resistant to change even after shock has become the consequence of its performance rather than of its nonperformance (Brown, Martin & Morrow, 1964; Gwinn, 1949; Solomon, Kamin & Wynne, 1953). In contrast, behavioral changes which are acquired through positive reinforcement do not seem to have the persistence that is sometimes seen in the results of aversive learning (Myers, 1958; Wike, 1966). Behavior that has been shaped by positive reinforcement may show some stability when the reinforcement is withdrawn (Wolfe, 1936; Zimmerman, 1957). But the stability appears to be quite limited in duration. The contrast with aversive learning may be an instructive source of inference about the relative strength and durability of those components of human social learning which are derived, respectively, from positive and aversive experience. Such an extrapolation should be made cautiously, however, since the long-term effects of human socialization may not be entirely predictable from the effects of the nonsocial medium that is generally used to study learning in animals. For example, Lovaas, Freitag, Kinder, Rubenstein, Schaeffer and Simmons (1966) recently have used hungry autistic children to demonstrate that the positive value of social stimuli can be first established through their association with food and then used to independently maintain repetitive behavior over an impressive duration of time.

It is commonly thought that people have a much greater capacity than animals for internalized control over their behavior, and that they are able to maintain the control for long periods of time. It may be that people can more easily maintain the value of their conduct through intrinsically reinforcing consequences which have the advantage of being carried in the cognitive representations for which humans are so uniquely equipped. But human behavior may be less free than it appears to be of the external reinforcement that is usually required to sustain learned behavior in animals. Human social behavior may often have the benefit of schedules of infrequent reinforcement for cumulative or serial performances, of the kind which can also be used to make the learned behavior of animals somewhat more tenacious (Ferster & Skinner, 1957). Many forms of conduct may have their value continually reinstated by external social reinforcements which are not easily observable. A person's behavior may be externally controlled not only by explicit reward or punishment, but also by various subtle indicators of social approval or disapproval which are conveyed in the behavior of others. Moreover, the internalized control which people exercise over their conduct is probably seldom placed in direct competition with behavioral dispositions whose motivation is strong enough to jeopardize the control. The suppressive effects of electric shock on an animal's behavior may extinguish fairly quickly, for example, when the behavior leads to reduction of a strong hunger drive and the suppression is no longer instrumental to shock-avoidance (Estes, 1944; Miller, 1959). In human society, behavioral suppression is only infrequently put to such a severe test. But under conditions of unusual stress, people do sometimes relinquish patterns of behavior which appeared to have been firmly internalized (Bettelheim, 1943; Milgram, 1963; Schein, 1957).

A number of recent experiments with children have demonstrated a variety of conditions of learning which can be used to induce some degree of internalized control over behavior (Aronfreed, 1964; Aronfreed & Paskal, 1966; Aronfreed & Reber, 1965; Bandura, 1965a; Bandura & Kupers, 1964; Parke & Walters, 1967; Walters & Parke, 1964; Walters, Parke & Cane, 1965). These experiments generally do not attempt to assess persistence of internalized behavioral control over any substantial period of time. But their tests for internalization bear some relationship to the criterion of resistance to extinction, which is commonly used to test the persistence of learned behavior over time. The experiments examine the behavioral effects of socialization in test situations which appear to be entirely private, or in which it is at least clear that the subject's actions will not produce social reward or punishment. The results of such experiments also illustrate quite clearly the situational specificity of the effects of learning, and thus emphasize that internalization is not synonymous with freedom from the stimulus control of the external environment. Even the most highly internalized forms of social behavior must remain dependent on external situational cues.

When the concept of internalization is used in reference to the absence of observable external conditions for the maintenance of an act, it is anchored only to the absence of *consequences* of the act which are socially transmitted and have some affective value for the actor. External cues continue to determine internalized conduct not only through their control over the individual's selection of appropriate behavior, but also through their specification of whether a particular form of behavior will maintain its intrinsic value. For example, it is quite common to find that a young child will effectively suppress an act that has been punished, even in the subsequent absence of external surveillance, but that it may then show no evidence of suppression when environmental cues are slightly different from those under which it was originally punished. Such discriminations are, of course, a pervasive feature of socialization. They serve to facilitate the accuracy with which the child's acquisition of internalized controls reflects social reality, since there are very few acts to which socializing agents will always respond in the same way regardless of the situational context in which they occur.

A criterion of internalization which is tied only to social surveillance, or to the immediate outcomes of an act for the actor, focuses on the direct control of behavior by external events such as reward or punishment. Such a criterion does not permit the full range of distinctions which it is possible to make if we take into account the various cognitive schemata with which people may represent and evaluate their conduct. These schemata vary in the concreteness of abstraction of their reference to the external outcomes of an act, and also in the directness with which they translate outcomes into their value for the individual. When we allow for the cognitive structures which may be superimposed upon concrete external stimulus events, we can distinguish a number of different kinds of evaluative control over conduct, which may be thought of as lying along a continuum of *internal versus external orientation*. For example, even in situations which are objectively private and without risk of surveillance, a child's conduct may be governed by its anticipation of later positive or aversive outcomes for itself, or by its cognitive representation of how other people may have reacted to its behavior in the past. Whiting (1959) provides excellent examples of societies in which adults characteristically behave in accordance with their perception of surveillance by both real and imaginary agents of social control who are not physically present. Such cognitive interventions may be regarded as being highly externally oriented.

In contrast, a number of other cognitive criteria for the evaluation of conduct, which are much less externally oriented, may control a person's behavior without any concrete reference to its rewarding or punitive consequences. These criteria are especially visible in verbal expressions of conscience, when either children or adults are asked to give rationales for the evaluation of different forms of conduct in hypothetical situations (see particularly the detailed analysis of these expressions by Kohlberg, 1963). People may evaluate their actions with respect to the standards or practices of those whom they hold in esteem or authority. They may evaluate the consequences of their actions in accordance with their standards for the maintenance of satisfactory affiliative or contractual relationships within a social system. Or they may apply broader principles which are oriented toward the intrinsic goodness or rightness of their actions with respect to the welfare of others.

Many forms of social behavior which remain highly dependent on external reinforcing consequences for their maintenance are also under the cognitive control of evaluative structures. Rotter (1966) has shown that the effects of external reinforcement on behavior in various tasks are systematically influenced by the individual's expectations about how closely the reinforcement will be determined by his own performance. Rotter's findings are but one instance of the broader observation that the value of social reward or punishment is not entirely a function of the concrete stimulus properties of the external outcomes of an act. Their value may be mediated in part by the cognitive processes which they engage. Reward and punishment may serve as cues, for example, to elicit an individual's evaluation of the consequences of his actions for others, or to evoke other cognitive dimensions of value which will control subsequent behavior. Similar distinctions may be made when a person's conduct has no direct external consequences for himself, but is dependent rather on its actual or anticipated consequences for others. The conduct may be reinforced by the person's empathic or vicarious response to observable external cues which indicate its immediate effect on others (for example, cues which indicate pleasure or relief of distress). The reinforcement value of the conduct may also be more indirectly mediated by cognitive processes which represent and evaluate its effects on others, quite independently of whether the effects are directly observable.

Although it is generally assumed that values are the most significant source of control over social conduct (Thibaut & Kelley, 1959), the available evidence usually points to great discrepancies between the verbal expression of evaluative standards and actual behavior in a real social context. Hartshorne and May (1928) found only a small degree of correlation between the child's knowledge of common social standards and its internalized control over behavior in situations which were designed to test honesty. Other investigators (Brogden, 1940; Terman et al., 1925) also have observed that the child's verbalized knowledge of social standards is often discrepant with its actual resistance to the opportunity to cheat when it is ostensibly not under surveillance. There appears to be no greater predictive power in children's descriptions of the application of their evaluative cognition to specific situations. Children in Western society are frequently reported to show an increasingly internalized orientation of conscience, as they advance in age, when they are asked to evaluate the determinants and consequences of conduct (Boehm, 1962; Kohlberg, 1963; Lerner, 1937; MacRae, 1954; Piaget, 1948). But there do not appear to be corresponding age-related increments in the effectiveness with which children control their own behavior in resistance-to-temptation situations (Hartshorne & May, 1928; Sears, Rau & Alpert, 1965, Ch. 6). Likewise, altruistic and sympathetic behavior do not seem to show consistent changes of frequency or extent in children who are beyond the age of five or six years (Handlon & Gross, 1959; Murphy, 1937; Turner, 1948; Ugurel-Semin, 1952; Wright, 1942).

In one study in which conduct and conscience were assessed for the same children, Grinder (1964) found that an increasingly internalized orientation of conscience with advancing age was not paralleled by an increase of internalized behavioral conformity to the rules of an achievement game. Medinnus (1966) also has reported an absence of relationship between behavioral and cognitive indices of internalization for the same children. There are other studies, however, which map the conscience of children in greater detail, and which suggest that social behavior is not insensitive to cognitive control through evaluative standards. Kohlberg (1964, 1969) has reported an inverse relation between cheating and the degree of internalized orientation that characterizes the child's moral decisions in hypothetical conflict situations. Hoffman (1963, 1968) has found that children differ in their internalized dispositions to react to their own transgressions, in ways which are related to the classification of their dominant conscience orientations as being externalized, conventional, or humanistic. The inconsistencies between these findings and those which are cited above may be partially attributable to complex motivational linkages between values and behavior, which are differentially activated by variations in the cognitive and affective impact of specific social stimulus situations. An understanding of how these linkages operate may require close theoretical and experimental analyses of their mediational properties, rather than attempts to simply correlate behavioral and cognitive indices of internalization.

INTERNALIZED CONTROL OF BEHAVIOR THROUGH DIRECT TRAINING

A very great part of socialization takes place through the reinforcing and suppressive effects of positive or aversive outcomes of the child's overt behavior (Skinner, 1953; Solomon, 1964). Although such outcomes may be socially transmitted in a variety of ways, many of which do not require the child to perceive the act-outcome contingency as an intentional attempt to influence its behavior, reward and punishment are often the most convenient generic terms to use in reference to large classes of reinforcing or suppressive consequences of an act. It should be noted, however, that termination of positive or aversive events also may have corresponding suppressive or reinforcing effects on the child's behavior.

The theoretical base that is required for a concept of internalization is the assumption that the effects of external events on the child's behavioral dispositions over time are a function of their induction of changes in the child's affectivity. Internalization takes place to the extent that changes of affective state become transferred from the mediation of external events to the mediation of monitors which are more intrinsically associated with the child's own behavior. This transfer of control over affectivity is in itself essentially a conditioning process. The internal monitors to which affective control becomes attached may be proprioceptive (response-produced) cues which are immediately inherent in the performance of an overt act. But internal monitors also take a much more powerful form in the informational properties of cognitive processes which give the child the capacity to represent and evaluate both its behavior and the external stimulus environment in which its behavior occurs. Internalization through direct training is initially dependent on the child's experience of the outcomes of its own overt behavior. When socialization utilizes a verbal and cognitive medium, the duration of time over which the outcomes of an act may be effective becomes greatly expanded. Verbal mediation also makes it possible for large repertoires of the child's social behavior to be controlled by the affective value that can become attached to the intentional or anticipatory representations which precede overt acts.

There is a remarkable scarcity of work on children's acquisition of internalized control over their behavior through the direct training that can be imposed by social reward or other kinds of positive external reinforcement.

Despite the great number of recent experimental studies of the effects of positive social reinforcement on children's learning and performance (see the review by Stevenson, 1965), there are very few studies which bear directly on internalization. In contrast, there have been many empirical studies which give detailed attention to the internalized aversive control that can be produced either by the disciplinary habits of parents or by punishment in experimental paradigms (Aronfreed, 1968; Walters & Parke, 1967). It is possible that the emphasis on the child's experience of punishment reflects with some accuracy the respective contributions which positive and aversive affective control make to those patterns of social behavior which remain most autonomous over substantial periods of time. But the emphasis may be disproportionate, since common observation makes it apparent that positive reinforcement is a very extensive source of at least the immediate external control which socializing agents can exercise over the child's behavior.

A number of experiments have shown that adult subjects can assume accurate and effective control over the reinforcing outcomes of their own performance in a task, after they first have been exposed to externally controlled positive reinforcement of their learning of the task (Kanfer, Bradley & Marston, 1962; Kanfer & Marston, 1963b; Marston & Kanfer, 1963). Although these experiments are interesting demonstrations of the capacity of human subjects to allocate their own external reinforcements, their relevance to the internalization process is difficult to interpret. The self-reinforcement paradigm is essentially one in which the subject assumes complete control over the occurrence of a concrete external event. The external event retains the same significance, as an indicator of correct performance, that was originally given to it by social instruction. And there is no evidence that value becomes independently attached to any intrinsic correlates of performance in the task. The situation that is used to test the effectiveness of the subject's own control over the reinforcement of his performance appears to elicit his already established disposition to provide himself with reinforcing external information about his behavior. It does not appear to establish the internalized value of the behavior itself.

There are similar problems in the interpretation of the results of experiments with children, in which the child's direct experience of success or failure at a task, or its exposure to externally imposed criteria of good performance, is shown to influence the frequency, magnitude, or timing of the external rewards which it subsequently controls or administers to itself (Bandura & Whalen, 1966; Mischel & Liebert, 1966; Mischel & Staub, 1965). The behavioral choices which are observed during the test situations of these experiments may well have some intrinsic value that is independent of external consequences. Following certain of the training conditions, for example, the children maintain high performance criteria for self-reward, or choose delayed rewards, even though their behavior is apparently no longer under external constraint. However, the experimental designs make it difficult to ascertain whether the training conditions actually induce, or only elicit, the children's internalized behavioral control. Two of the experiments which are cited above employed a broader design that also examined the effects of the child's observation of another person's self-rewarding behavior. The overall patterns of results suggested that the children might have been making decisions primarily about how to best utilize available external rewards. The children seemed to be choosing from among their already well-internalized evaluative structures on the basis of information that was provided both in their own past performance and in the observed behavior of others.

Cooperation (and competition) is another type of social behavior that has been shown to be malleable to positive social reinforcement, but without much evidence that the behavior can be brought under internalized control. Many experiments have demonstrated that socially controlled rewards will establish and maintain cooperative or sharing behavior between children (Azrin & Lindsley, 1956; Fischer, 1963; Weingold & Webster, 1964), between human adults (Kelley, Thibaut, Radloff & Mundy, 1962; Sidowski, Wyckoff & Tabory, 1956), and between other primates (Boren, 1966; Mason, 1959; Nissen & Crawford, 1936). A few of these studies indicate that the induced cooperative behavior may have some temporary stability when external reinforcement is withdrawn (during extinction). But none of the studies provide evidence that the behavior acquires intrinsic correlates of affective value which become independent of the definition of the situation as one in which external reward is potentially available for the subject—in contrast to the kind of internalized value that appears to govern behavior when it is sustained, for example, by the individual's empathic or vicarious response to its consequences for others (see the later discussion of altruistic and sympathetic behavior).

A phenomenon that may actually reveal somewhat more evidence of internalization than does cooperative behavior is the social attachment across species that has been demonstrated in experiments on the effects of early rearing conditions upon the behavior of various mammals (Cairns & Johnson, 1965; Denenberg, Hudgens & Zarrow, 1964; Kuo, 1960). Once positive attachments have been formed between members of different species, they appear to show a considerable independence of the concrete behavior of the object of attachment, and they also tend to supplant agonistic or flight reactions which would otherwise occur under natural conditions. That social attachment may impose some internalized affective value on the external behavioral properties of the object of attachment is also suggested by the resistance of attachment within mammalian species to conditions which are ordinarily expected to produce extinction or suppression (Cairns, 1966; Harlow & Harlow, 1965). It should be noted, however, that social attachments seem to be formed through conditioning to specific forms of experience at critical junctures in development, rather than through the kind of direct training that requires outcomes which are contingent on the young organism's behavior.

Internalization of social control is often demonstrated in the extensive body of observations which uses the suppression of socially prohibited behavior, in the absence of external surveillance, as an index of conformity for either children or adults (Burton, Maccoby & Allinsmith, 1961; Grinder, 1962; Kimbrell & Blake, 1958; Lefkowitz, Blake & Mouton, 1955; Sears et al., 1965, Ch. 6; Walters, Leat & Mezei, 1963). These situational observations cannot be used, however, to provide any direct information about the learning processes which underlie internalization. The same limitation appears to apply to studies in which behavioral or cognitive conformity is experimentally induced by direct exposure of the subject to varying degrees of social pressure (Allen & Crutchfield, 1963; Asch, 1956; Endler, 1966; Jacobs & Campbell, 1961; Milgram, 1964). It is very difficult to estimate the extent to which the subject's own choices in such experiments are attributable to his direct positive or aversive experience of other people's behavior or judgments, or alternatively to his use of the observed behavior or judgment of others as an informational model for his own conformity. An interesting feature of the results of some of these experiments is the apparent persistence of the induced conformity for a period of time after the original exposure to social influence. But the observations of persistence generally are made under conditions in which the subject might well perceive that there is external surveillance or knowledge of his behavior. Other studies which have introduced controlled variations in privacy have shown that social conformity is greater when the subject's choices are exposed to the observation or knowledge of others (Argyle, 1957; Gerard, 1964; Kelman, 1958). Stone (1967) recently has shown that the influence of the judgments of others on an individual's autokinetic perceptual norms can be easily and quickly overcome by subsequent exposure of the individual's judgments to verbal conditioning.

One segment of a recent series of experiments in progress (Aronfreed, 1968) illustrates a method for the direct study of the internalization process in the context of behavior-contingent learning under social reward. Eight- to ten-year-old boys and girls are placed in an experimental paradigm of socialization, in which they must choose repeatedly between a highly attractive small toy and a relatively unattractive toy over the course of ten training trials. The pairs of toys vary over trials. The adult socializing agent, either a male or a female, rewards the child with verbal approval (*Good!*) and candy whenever it chooses the unattractive toy, but gives no reaction when the child chooses the attractive toy. After two or three training trials, the children are generally consistent in picking up the unattractive toys. In an immediately subsequent test situation, the agent leaves the room on a pretext. The child is left alone with another pair of toys, under conditions of complete privacy which are carefully designed to convey that there is no prospect of reward or even of external knowledge of the child's behavior. Children who have been rewarded immediately upon reaching for unattractive toys during training pick up the unattractive test object more quickly than do children who have been rewarded only after they have already picked up the unattractive toys during training. Such a simple delay-of-reinforcement effect, when it extends to conditions in which opportunity for social reward is withdrawn, supports the inference that positive affective value has become directly attached to the intrinsic correlates of the rewarded act. The magnitude of the positive affect that would become conditioned to the intentional or motoric precursors of a previously rewarded act would be expected to be a function of how early the reward originally occurred in the course of the onset and performance of the act.

The learning processes which produce internalization through direct training have been more extensively explored for aversive control of behavior. Aronfreed and Reber (1965) have shown that the punishment training of children induces an internalized behavioral suppression that is very sensitive to the original timing of punishment with respect to the initiation and completion of the punished behavior. The nature of the effect, and its implications for the mechanisms of internalization, can best be illustrated by a much more extensive set of experiments (Aronfreed, 1966), in which essentially the same method was used. Eight- to ten-year-old children were exposed to one of four punishment training paradigms, in which they chose between an attractive toy and an unattractive toy on each of ten training trials. The pairs of toys varied over trials. The adult agent of socialization instructed the child to pick up and describe the toy in each pair that it wished to tell about. But the child was given no further explanation or criterion of punishment. Whenever the child chose an attractive toy, the agent responded with verbal disapproval (No!) and deprivation of candy. In contrast, the child was permitted to pick up and describe the unattractive toys freely. The four experimental paradigms were designed so as to produce four successive values for the timing of punishment: when the child had reached for the toy, when the child had completed the act of lifting the toy, six seconds after the child had lifted the toy, and after the child had described the toy (roughly 10–12 seconds after the toy had been lifted). Although almost all of the children quickly conformed to a pattern of consistent unattractive choices during training, the strength of their behavioral suppression during an immediately subsequent test of internalization was directly proportionate to the immediacy of the punishment that they had experienced previously. During the test situation, which gave the children what appeared to be complete freedom from surveillance or risk of punishment, covert monitors recorded the occurrence and latency of the transgression of picking up or handling an extremely attractive toy object (which was again paired with an unattractive object). The strength of the internalized suppression during the test was reliably sensitive to differences between each two adjacent values on the parameter of timing of punishment. This effect was obtained for both boys and girls, and was replicated with both male and female socializing agents.

The diminishing strength of internalized behavioral suppression with increasing delay of punishment during training has also been observed in other experiments with children, which have been conducted by Walters and his colleagues (Parke & Walters, 1967; Walters & Demkow, 1963; Walters et al., 1965). The experimental effect provides strong support for a conception that has been set forth elsewhere in more detail (Aronfreed, 1968): that internalized behavioral suppression is motivated as a function of the intensity of an aversive affective state that becomes conditioned by punishment to the intrinsic proprioceptive or cognitive correlates of an incipient or ongoing punished act. It is convenient to use anxiety as a generalized motivational term for this affective state, although the qualitative experience of the state may actually assume a number of different forms. The effect also provides some support for the view that anxiety-reduction (and consequent reinforcement value) becomes attached to the intrinsic correlates of nonpunished behavioral alternatives to a punished act. This conceptual formulation is consistent with findings from experimental studies of the more general effects of delayed punishment and reinforcement on aversive learning in children (Penney, 1967; Walters, 1964). It is also consistent with the findings of experiments on punishment learning in the animal laboratory (Church, 1963; Kamin, 1959; Solomon & Brush, 1956; Mowrer, 1960a, Ch. 2; Mowrer, 1960b, pp. 399–404).

Further confirmation of the role of anxiety-reduction in the reinforcement of internalized behavioral suppression is provided by the results of another paradigm which employed the same punishment training method as was used in the experimental series described above (Aronfreed, 1966). In the additional paradigm, the timing of punishment was identical to the delayed value that had been used in the third of the original four paradigms. But safety signals for choices of unattractive toys were transmitted to the child, through the agent's behavior, at an earlier point than that at which they had originally occurred. Children who were trained under the early safety signal showed more prolonged internalized suppression of the act of picking up the attractive test object than did the children for whom both punishment and safety signal had been equally delayed in the original baseline paradigm. This finding clearly suggests that the external social cues which follow nonpunished behavior acquire anxiety-reducing reinforcement value during punishment training, and that the conditioning of this value to the intrinsic correlates of nonpunished behavior is a function of the immediacy with which the cues originally occur as outcomes of the behavior.

The fact that internalization is so sharply affected by the timing of outcomes of the child's behavior indicates that it can be partially understood in terms of mechanisms of conditioning and behavior-contingent learning. At the same time, there are many reasons to think that the internalized consequences of variations in even the simplest kinds of direct training cannot be fully understood without taking into account the representational function of the child's cognitive capacities. The medium of verbal communication that is used so pervasively by socializing agents greatly dilutes the importance of the intrinsic monitors which are available in the proprioceptive topography of the child's overt behavior. Internalized affective control of behavior can be much more effectively carried by cognitive representations which serve as a common intrinsic stimulus bridge across the entire sequence of proprioceptive and external cues that unfolds as an act is initiated and completed. Verbal mediation also makes it possible for intentions or other precursors of the child's behavior to be represented, in direct conjunction with socially rewarding or punitive outcomes of the behavior, at points in time which are well beyond the completion of an act. The affective value that is acquired by such representations can then intercede on subsequent occasions to control the occurrence of the same behavior even before it is performed.

The profound impact of cognitive structure on internalized control of behavior is demonstrated in a number of extensions of the punishment training paradigms which have been already described (Aronfreed, 1966). In the extension series, equal numbers of boys and girls were again used, and the experimental socializing agent was a male. The procedure was identical to that used in the original timing-of-punishment paradigms, with punishment being given for choice of an attractive toy. But various cognitive structures were now injected into paradigms which had a common baseline of delayed punishment (six seconds after the child lifted an attractive toy). During the instructions, and contiguous with each administration of punishment during training, the agent briefly verbalized references to a cognitive structure that focused on a continuum of ease versus difficulty. It was made clear to the child that punishment was associated with its choice of toys which were difficult to tell about and therefore appropriate only for older children. During the test for internalization that immediately followed training, children who were exposed to this cognitive structure showed consistently stronger suppression of the punished transgression of picking up (or even handling) the attractive toy than did children who were trained under the corresponding original paradigm in which the same timing of punishment was used without cognitive structure. Another group of children was then trained in a paradigm in which the agent's verbal communication of the same cognitive structure occurred 10–12 seconds after each punishment (in the intertrial interval that followed a punished choice), rather than in direct conjunction with the punishment. This paradigm produced reliably more internalized suppression than did the baseline timing paradigm which included no cognitive structure, but reliably less internalized suppression than the paradigm in which the agent's cognitive structuring was given in direct association with punishment. The entire pattern of findings clearly supports the inference that cognitive structure facilitates internalized suppression by serving as an intrinsic mediator of anxiety which can intercede before the commission of a punished act, even though the original socialization process may generally transmit cognitive structure after the punished act has been committed.

Some striking findings emerged from additional paradigms in which the cognitive structure of ease versus difficulty was further elaborated to focus on the children's intentions. In all but one of these additional paradigms, punishment was administered six seconds after the child had lifted an attractive toy, in the verbal context of the toy being too difficult for the child to describe. Some of the paradigms used a verbal medium which also conveyed to the child, during instructions and in conjunction with each punishment, that it was being punished for *wanting* to *pick up* the toys which were difficult to describe. In other paradigms, the child was told that it was being punished for *wanting* to *tell* about the difficult choices. Children who were exposed to a verbal medium that focused on their intentions did show markedly stronger suppression, during the test for internalization, than did the children who had been exposed to a cognitive structure that focused only on ease versus difficulty without any reference to their intentions. The distinct effect of associating punishment with the children's intentions was obtained, however, only when a paradigm had been designed in such a way as to permit the relevant intention, but not the intended behavioral component, to have already occurred at the moment of punishment. Children who were trained under these conditions actually showed a frequency of complete internalized suppression of transgression that was equivalent to the frequency for children who were punished upon reaching for an attractive toy, but who were given no verbal medium of punishment (the immediate punishment paradigm of the original timing series). But the paradigms in which punishment followed the behavioral component that was linked by cognitive structuring to the children's intentions were no more effective in producing internalized test suppression than were the paradigms in which children were given only the cognitive structure of ease versus difficulty. Apparently, the verbal representation of a child's intention facilitates internalized behavioral suppression only when the actual occurrence of punishment is closely attached in time to the occurrence of the intention. A focus on intentions appears to contribute nothing to internalization, beyond the generalized mediational properties of any cognitive structure, when punishment does not separate intentions from the performance of the intended behavior. The strength of the internalized suppression that can be produced by attaching punishment directly to intentions is quite remarkable, particularly in view of the significant place that is commonly given to intentions in accounts of the child's acquisition of moral judgment (Kohlberg, 1964; Piaget, 1948).

Although punishment learning can sometimes produce effective internalized suppression in the absence of a verbal medium of socialization, its usual suppressive effects may be disrupted in unexpected ways if successful learning requires information for which the child does not have an adequate cognitive representation. Some of the effects which may occur under these conditions are suggested in an unpublished study by Aronfreed and Leff (1963), in which six- and seven-year-old boys were exposed to different values of intensity of punishment and complexity of discrimination. Procedures were similar in many respects to those which have been already described. The toys between which the children were required to choose were comparable in attractiveness, however, and differed consistently in other cues which the children could use to distinguish between punished and nonpunished choices. All of the children were punished at the point where they had just touched a forbidden toy. Two groups of children were exposed to a simple discrimination between red and yellow toys, and two groups were exposed to a complex and difficult discrimination between toys which represented passive containers and toys which represented objects with active internal mechanisms. No cognitive structure was provided for the discriminant properties of the toys or for the contingency between choice and punishment. The punishment of the male socializing agent was compounded of verbal disapproval, deprivation of candy, and activation of a buzzer that could be varied in loudness in order to control the intensity of the punishment.

During the common test for internalization that followed the various training paradigms described above, the children were confronted with a highly attractive toy in a pair that was similar to either of the two types of pairs which had been used in training. Children who had been trained under a simple discrimination were much more likely to show complete suppression of handling of the attractive toy if they had been exposed to intense punishment than if they had been exposed to mild punshiment. But children who were trained under a complex discrimination were more likely to transgress if they had been intensely punished than if they had been mildly punished. The reversal between the two effects, both of which were highly reliable, is quite remarkable. It suggests the possibility that children who experience intense punishment, under conditions where it is difficult for them to discriminate punished and nonpunished acts, may be equally likely to commit either class of act on subsequent occasions—perhaps because both punitive and nonpunitive consequences have become effective markers for the reduction of anticipatory anxiety, and have thus attached some intrinsic anxiety-reducing value to a number of behavioral dispositions which include the transgression itself. It is interesting to note that the effects of the complex discrimination are not unlike those which have been observed in the behavior of animals who are exposed to punishment or frustration under the conditions of a difficult or insoluble task (Amsel & Ward, 1965; Farber, 1948; Maier, 1949). The findings of the series of experiments which have been conducted by Parke and Walters (1967) also suggest that the effectiveness of internalized suppression is directly related to intensity of punishment when children are given clearly discriminable alternatives, but that the intensity effect is obscured when punishment is arbitrarily assigned to the child's acts in such a way as to deprive it of discriminant cues.

Direct external reinforcement and punishment also play an important role in the child's learning of reactions to its already committed transgressions. These reactions are acquired during the course of socialization, and are often internalized, because they can exercise some control over the punitive consequences of transgression, even though the transgression has been already committed because its suppression has been ineffective or only poorly established. Just as in the case of behavioral suppression, internalized reactions to transgression are initially motivated by an aversive affective state that becomes attached to transgression as a result of punishment. However, reactions to transgression take a number of distinct forms—for example, self-criticism, confession, reparation, and reactions which are oriented toward an external punitive resolution of transgression. The relative probabilities of these specific reactions will tend to be dependent, to some extent, on the cognitive housing of the aversive affect that is aroused by a transgression. This housing may determine whether the affect is experienced as fear, shame, or guilt. Nevertheless, the concept of anxiety may be used to designate the generalized motivational role of the aversive affective state.

Various social stimulus events which are transmitted in the behavior of socializing agents come to mark the resolution of committed transgressions, from the child's point of view, and thus acquire anxiety-reducing reinforcement value as outcomes which can be produced by the child's own reactions to transgression. The anxiety-reducing value of these external events can then become directly attached, through the mechanisms of internalization, to the intrinsic correlates of the child's reactions (Aronfreed, 1961). This general pattern of contingencies is actually often effected through imitation and other forms of observational learning which are essential, for example, to the learning of self-criticism. But it is more appropriate to introduce reactions to transgression in an outline of internalization through direct training, because they appear to be so extensively shaped by learning that is dependent on the outcomes of the child's overt behavior. For example, confession and attempts to either avoid or elicit punishment are very common reactions to transgression, which frequently become internalized to the extent that they become independent of external knowledge of the transgression or objective risk of punishment. Reports of observations which have included these reactions as indices of internalization in children (for example, Aronfreed, 1961, or Sears, Maccoby & Levin, 1957, Ch. 10) suggest the possibility that they acquire intrinsic anxiety-reducing value because they originally either avoid or produce punitive consequences. Both of these outcomes have the common reinforcing effect of reducing the anticipatory anxiety which the child already has acquired as a response to its previously punished actions. A much more detailed analysis of the learning of internalized reactions to transgression, and of the cognitive controls which may be exercised by fear, shame, and guilt, can be found in a forthcoming monograph (Aronfreed, 1968).

The effect of direct reinforcement on the learning of reparative behavior has been studied in two closely related experiments (Aronfreed, 1963), in which ten-year-old boys and girls were repeatedly punished for their aggressive actions during a training task. For some groups, the experimental socializing agent decided how many candies were to be taken from the child, in apparent proportion to a concrete visible index of how much aggression had occurred, and then removed the candy. Other groups made their own evaluations of their aggressive behavior and removed the number of candies that they judged appropriate. The punishment sequence on each trial, which included the experimental agent's verbal observations on the child's aggressive behavior, was always terminated by the deprivation of candy. And in the case of the children who administered their own deprivation, the removal of the candy was followed by verbal approval. Immediately following the training trials, there was a test trial on which each child apparently broke a doll that had been an object of protection during training. While surveying the damage, the agent casually verbalized a series of standardized open-ended queries about how best to proceed at that point. Children who had been given control over their own punishment much more frequently proposed ways of repairing the doll, or volunteered other reparative suggestions, than did children whose punishment had been externally controlled. The children's generalized reparative dispositions during the test were sharply influenced, then, by direct external reinforcement specifically for self-administered punishment during training. This finding also suggests the importance of verbal or cognitive mediation between original conditions of socialization and later stimulus situations which elicit the child's reactions to committed social transgressions.

INTERNALIZED CONTROL OF BEHAVIOR THROUGH OBSERVATIONAL LEARNING

Children acquire many of their stable patterns of social behavior on the basis of their observation of the behavior of others. The foundations of this kind of learning appear to lie in the conditions of observation, rather than in the modification of the child's overtly emitted behavior by positive or aversive external outcomes. Observational learning takes a number of forms, all of which appear to require the child's cognitive capacities for processing and storing information from its social environment. A great deal of attention has been given recently to children's imitative reproduction of certain of the specific behavioral characteristics of a social model. Although imitation of a model is only one of the ways in which observation of others can produce behavioral change in the child, it is a convenient initial reference point for a brief summary of the implications of observational learning for a concept of internalization. A more extended discussion of these implications can be found elsewhere (Aronfreed, 1968).

It is very common to see children reproduce a detailed sequence of the relatively idiosyncratic behavior of a model, after having observed the behavior on only a few occasions, under conditions where it is obvious that the reproduction could not previously have been subjected to external social reinforcement. The child's imitation may not require even the cues which would be provided by the presence of the model, and it may be privately repeated many times without reinforcing social consequences. The imitation of children is also highly selective. They do not imitate all of the behavior of the potential models whom they observe. Moreover, imitation is often very persistent. Children will sometimes show precise imitation of a social model repeatedly, over long periods of time, when it does not appear that the fidelity of their behavior is instrumental in producing reinforcing external consequences. All of these characteristics of imitative behavior indicate that imitation may have intrinsically reinforcing properties which derive from the affective value that has become attached to the child's representation of the model during the period of observation. The role of intrinsic affective value in imitative learning is difficult to evaluate empirically, however, in part because we know very little about the nature and magnitude of the value which a great variety of social stimuli may impart to the behavior of a model. Nevertheless, experimental studies can sometimes be designed so as to uncover the acquired intrinsic value of imitative behavior.

The behavior of the child's parents, and of its other potential models, occurs in a pervasive context of socially transmitted stimuli which have a strong affective impact on the child. This conjunction will often result in the direct attachment (conditioning) of intrinsic affective value to the child's cognitive representation of the behavior, and also to the reproducible components of the behavior itself. The behavior thus acquires a value that is no longer dependent on its place in an external social medium which induces changes of affectivity in the child. The child may then reproduce the behavior of the model, under the control of appropriate external cues, if the acquired intrinsic value of the behavior corresponds to a reinforcing change of affective state. The stimulus events which originally induce changes of affectivity in the child, in contiguity with the observed behavior of a model, may be directly carried in the potentially replicable components of the model's behavior—as, for example, in certain expressive features of a mother's affectionate behavior. They may also be transmitted through other aspects of the model's behavior which are closely interwoven in time with the behavioral components that the child will imitate. Social stimuli may elicit affective responses in the child, and may attach corresponding value to the behavior of a model, even when they are not directly experienced by the child—for example, when the child can respond empathically or vicariously to the actions of other people or to the consequences of those actions. But regardless of how the affective value of the model's behavior is established, the child's imitation will tend to have intrinsically reinforcing consequences immediately upon its first performance, since it produces behavioral stimuli and cognitive representations which have already acquired value during the child's observation of the model. Some indirect support for the kind of mechanism of affective conditioning that is outlined here may be found in studies of animal learning in which relatively neutral stimulus events are shown to acquire positive or aversive properties, through their association with other events of established value, in the absence of the overt acts which are subsequently used to control the occurrence of the stimuli and to demonstrate their value (Jenkins, 1950; Rescorla & LoLordo, 1965; Solomon & Turner, 1962; Stein, 1958).

Although the contingencies which relate the observed behavior of a model to changes of affective state in the child may account for the acquired intrinsic value of imitation, they do not explain the child's capacity to store and reproduce an overt performance of the behavior. Under certain conditions, the concrete stimulus properties of a model's behavior may be very close to corresponding properties of behavior which the child would be strongly disposed to emit quite independently of the provision of a model, so that the child's behavior simply gains an increment of intrinsic reinforcement from the acquired value of the model's behavior. Mowrer (1950, Ch. 24; 1960b, Ch. 3) suggested that the vocalization of infants could become intrinsically reinforcing through essentially such a simple form of imitation. But children characteristically reproduce

the most varied and complex sequences of the observed motoric and verbal behavior patterns of their models. They appear to have the capacity to program
a rather high-fidelity replication of the exact topography of a model's behavior.
Their imitation often emerges with remarkable suddenness and accuracy, after
only very limited exposure to a model, and it is sometimes an innovative departure from any behavior that is likely to occur spontaneously. It therefore
seems necessary to assume that children can form fairly rapidly a *cognitive
template* of the behavior of a model. Under such an assumption, the affective
value of the stimulus context in which the model's behavior has been observed
would become attached to the template. And the intrinsically reinforcing consequences of the imitation would be a function of the match between the template and the flow of imitative behavior.

Because imitation often seems to produce remarkably rapid and accurate
modifications of the child's behavior, without the opportunity for externally
reinforced practice, some theorists have suggested that the child engages in
covert rehearsal of the model's actions (Logan, Olmstead, Rosner, Schwartz &
Stevens, 1955, pp. 149–151; Maccoby, 1959; Sears et al., 1957, Ch. 10). A
representational or symbolic rehearsal process would undoubtedly be useful in
accounting for the child's ability to assemble and structure the behavioral elements in an imitative program (see, for example, the experiment that is reported
by Bandura, Grusec & Menlove, 1966). But covert rehearsal would not appear
to explain the topographical precision which children are capable of showing
in their imitative performance of novel and complex patterns of behavior, unless the rehearsal also included private or miniaturized practice that engaged
overt motor components of behavior. It seems very likely, in fact, that a detailed analysis of a child's initial reproductions of a model's behavior would
reveal only a low fidelity of imitation of those behavioral components which
are entirely foreign to its repertoire. However, under the assumption that imitative performance is affectively controlled, the imitation would tend to
increase in fidelity with repeated practice. One would expect the intrinsic reinforcement value of the imitation to be proportionate, along a gradient of generalization, to the accuracy with which it represented those original properties
of the model's behavior to which affective value had become attached.

The fact that imitative learning so often occurs under conditions where
external reinforcing events cannot be identified has suggested to other theorists
that it can be understood in terms of contiguity mechanisms (Holt, 1931, pp.
112–119; Humphrey, 1921; Maccoby, 1959; Piaget, 1951, Part I; Sheffield,
1961). It is possible that young children do acquire a disposition to respond to
the stimulus of another person's act, under certain conditions, with a corresponding act of their own (see, for example, Holt, and Piaget). But such a
disposition would hardly account for the child's imitation of programmatic
sequences of observed behavior, or for the occurrence of any kind of imitation
when the model is no longer present. If a contiguity mechanism were interpreted in the conventional sense of a close temporal association between stim-

ulus and overt response, then it would not appear to be the effective mechanism in the control of imitative behavior, since imitative learning can occur when the child observes without performing during its exposure to the model. If a contiguity concept is applied to an association between external stimuli and the child's perceptual or cognitive "responses" in observing the model (for example, Bandura, 1962), then there is still the question of how such an association would control the child's subsequent overt behavior. It is obvious that imitation requires the child to observe and attend to a model's behavior, and that perceptual contiguities would establish the power of external cues to elicit the child's cognitive representation of the behavior on subsequent occasions. However, perceptual contiguity in itself does not provide an account of how imitative performance is governed by the child's cognitive representation of the model. Nor does it make any provision for affective control of the child's behavior.

A number of theorists have proposed that the child's early experience of nurturance and affection establishes the positive affective value of the stimulus attributes of its social models, and thus fosters the child's disposition to reproduce the attributes in its own behavior (Mowrer, 1950, Ch. 21; Mowrer, 1960b, Ch. 3; Sears et al., 1957, Ch. 10; Sears et al., 1965; Whiting & Child, 1953, Ch. 11). There are some experimental findings which do indicate that children are more inclined to reproduce the actions of a nurturant model than those of a nonnurturant model (Bandura & Huston, 1961; Bandura, Ross & Ross, 1963b; Mussen & Parker, 1965). However, the nurturance of a model has not been found to facilitate children's imitative behavior in other studies (Aronfreed, 1964; Rosenhan & White, 1967; Stein & Wright, 1964). Some of the evidence from these latter studies suggests that a child's imitative dispositions may be more sensitive to continuity or change in the level of nurturance to which it has become adapted than they are to the sheer amount of nurturance that it receives.

For reasons which will be pointed out later, the nurturance of a model would be expected to be an important determinant of the potential affective value of imitation. But it would not be a fundamental or a unique determinant. Experimental paradigms of socialization have been used recently to demonstrate how children learn to reproduce the verbal criticism of a model, or the sympathetic actions of a model, under conditions which establish a close contiguity between the model's behavior and termination of the child's experience of either anticipatory anxiety or distressful noxious stimulation (Aronfreed, 1964; Aronfreed & Paskal, 1966). The effects which are obtained in these experiments are not contingent on first establishing the nurturant attributes of a model. Two other recent studies (Grusec, 1966; Mischel & Grusec, 1966) do suggest that nurturance may facilitate the child's disposition to reproduce the verbal components of a model's punitive behavior. But it seems more plausible to suppose that the generally nurturant behavior of a model would enhance the effectiveness of withdrawal of affection as a component of punishment, and thus intensify the anxiety that motivates the child's imitation, than it does to assume that nurturance attaches positive value even to the model's punitive behavior.

The nurturance of socializing agents may also establish the positive affective value of a great variety of other social stimuli which can be transmitted in their behavior, such as expressive gestures or verbal indicators of approval, because of the original relationship between such stimuli and the child's early experience of care and affection. These stimuli may then impart their own acquired positive value to the observed behavior of a potential model. In many instances, a child's imitative disposition may be controlled by its empathic or vicarious response to social cues which convey the affectivity inherent in the behavior of others or in the consequences of their behavior. The range of social stimuli which may have such a function can be greatly expanded when we consider that many stimuli which we do not ordinarily think of as pleasurable may nevertheless have positive affective value for the child. It is possible, for example, that recent demonstrations of the influence of an aggressive model on children's behavior (Bandura & Walters, 1963a) are effective in part because of the children's pleasurable reaction to the interesting forms of aggression which are emitted by the model.

The problem of determining the reinforcement value of the truly imitative act can be seen somewhat more clearly in the context of the kind of learning paradigm in which the behavior of one organism becomes attached, through repeated performance and external reinforcement, to the cues which are transmitted in the corresponding behavior of another organism. This phenomenon has been demonstrated many times in both animals and children (Bayroff & Lard, 1944; Church, 1957; Miller & Dollard, 1941; Stein & Wright, 1964). Baer and Sherman (1964) recently have reported a particularly impressive demonstration of the effectiveness with which direct social reinforcement can be used to induce children to match their overt actions to those which are displayed by another person. There is a limitation, however, on the behavioral correspondence that can be attained through gradual shaping of behavior which is based on the discrimination of social cues and direct reinforcement. The correspondence generally appears to be restricted to the relatively gross matching of simple behavioral choices. It does not seem to extend to the child's capacity to reproduce the more precise structural sequence and topography of the observed behavior of others. And even when social reinforcement does appear to contribute to a more precise match between the child's behavior and the behavior of a model, there is still the problem of accounting for the child's use of its observation to meet the criterion of behavioral precision that will be reinforced.

The cues which are transmitted in the behavior of others pervade all forms of social modification of the child's behavior. Such cues may elicit corresponding behavior from the child without necessarily requiring that the child use the other person's behavior as a *model*. Their mode of transmission will very often not be essential to their function, which may be to convey information about the social environment and the consequences of the child's behavioral choices. The observed behavior of others is an extensive source of informational cues and motivational stimuli, and will often serve to elicit behavioral dispositions which the child has already acquired as a result of its past history of conditioning and behavior-contingent reinforcement. A child's behavior will therefore frequently correspond to the observed behavior of another person, at the gross level of common choice among alternative acts, without showing anything like the exact matching that would correspond to imitative modeling. Such a simple behavioral correspondence might just as well have been mediated by non-social cues or by direct verbal instruction to the child about the outcomes of its actions (see, for example, Skinner, 1953, pp. 119–122). In the case of true imitation, however, the behavior of another person functions as a *representation* of the behavior to be performed by the child. There are cues intrinsic to the structure of the behavior itself which quite literally serve as a model for the changes which may occur in the child's behavioral repertoire.

The problem of imitative learning, then, is one of accounting for both the child's motivation and its capacity to reproduce the topography and structure of a model's behavior with great fidelity, under conditions where the precision of the imitation may often be well beyond that required to elicit reinforcing consequences from the social environment. Behavioral dispositions which are established by direct social reinforcement ordinarily have a considerable latitude in the precise forms which they take. Whatever intrinsic value they may acquire will be essentially the same among a number of closely related and finely differentiated acts, because socializing agents have not made their reinforcement selectively contingent on the exact topography of the acts. In contrast, imitation on the basis of observational learning tends to reproduce the behavioral properties of a model more exactly, because its intrinsic reinforcement value is more narrowly bound to those properties. The intrinsic value of forms of behavior which are only grossly equivalent will be differentially determined by their fidelity to the precise features of the model's behavior which were most closely associated with reinforcing changes of affective state for the child.

Of course, imitative dispositions which are acquired initially through observational learning will often be subjected to the subsequent external reinforcing or suppressive consequences of their overt expression. Many of a child's imitative acts may have reinforcing outcomes which are inherent in the social or nonsocial effects that they necessarily produce in the external environment. For example, the child's imitation of an aggressive model may produce effects on an object of aggression which already have acquired reinforcing affective value for the child as a result of its past experience with the consequences of aggression. Reward and other forms of direct social reinforcement may also selectively control the occurrence of behavior that the child has originally learned on an imitative basis. Bandura (1965a) has demonstrated that external incentives can be used to induce further behavioral evidence of what children have retained from their observation of another person's aggressive actions, after they have first been given an opportunity to reproduce the actions spontaneously. Grusec (1966) has recently shown that termination of punishment can be used to enhance the probability of children's verbalized self-critical reactions to their transgressions, after the reactions have first been acquired on the basis of observation of a model. These effects of direct social reinforcement emphasize that the child's imitative performance is jointly controlled by its intrinsic value and by the external reinforcement structure of specific situations.

This outline of imitative learning is useful in making certain distinctions among a number of recent experiments which demonstrate that the behavior of children can be influenced by their observation of the behavior of others. These demonstrations, which are briefly summarized below, are effective in producing various kinds of control over the child's behavior. Generally speaking, the tests for the behavioral effects of observation are carried out in situations where the child's behavioral choices are not explicitly supported by direct social rewards or punishments. In some cases, the test situations are apparently private, from the child's point of view. Nevertheless, it is often difficult to judge the extent to which the behavioral correspondence between child and model is attributable to the intrinsic representational value of an imitative act. Even the simplest discrete choices among alternative acts can be shown to have acquired some internalized reinforcement value, through the child's observation of a model, when experimental contingencies have been carefully designed to permit the necessary inferences to be drawn about the locus of affective control over the child's behavior. In the absence of such contingencies, it is usually easier to discern that internalized value has become directly attached to the child's reproduction of the model's behavior if the behavior has some differentiable elements of structure or sequence. For the child may then reproduce these elements with a fidelity that is obviously not instrumental in producing external effects. Some of the recent experiments on observational social learning do provide the child with the opportunity to reproduce structural or sequential components of the model's behavior. But even when such an opportunity is provided, the reported descriptions leave much uncertainty, in some cases, about the innovative features of the child's behavior and about its topographical fidelity to the model. The problem of interpretation is not one of whether the children would have shown the same behavior spontaneously, without the eliciting cues which were provided by observation of another person's behavior (clearly, they would not). It is rather one of whether the child has acquired new behavioral dispositions, and of whether these dispositions have acquired some intrinsic value which is a function of their representation of an external model.

There are some experiments on observational learning in children which do appear to demonstrate imitation through the representational use of a model, since the children reproduce with some precision the stylistic and relatively idiosyncratic features of the behavior which they have observed. Bandura and Huston (1961) found that children for whom a positive affective relationship had been established to a nurturant model were more likely to imitate the model's stylistic task-irrelevant behavior than were children whose model had assumed a nonnurturant role. In a similar experiment, Mussen and Parker (1965) observed that the disposition of girls to adopt the task-irrelevant expressive behavior of their mothers was directly related to the level of nurturance which characterized the mother's relationship to the child. However, Stein and Wright (1964) did not find that the nurturance of a model facilitated children's dispositions to reproduce expressive motoric patterns which were incidental to the model's performance in a task. Two other experiments suggest specific behavioral effects of observing another person's control over pleasurable experience or rewards. Bandura et al. (1963b) reported that children were more disposed to repeat some of the unusual behavior patterns of adult agents who had controlled and dispensed nurturant resources (to either the child or another adult) than they were to repeat the behavior of other adults who had subordinate or consumer roles. Bandura and Kupers (1964) found that children who were given control over dispensation of rewards for their performance tended to adopt some of the same self-approving and self-critical verbal statements, along with relevant performance criteria, which had been displayed previously in the self-rewarding behavior of adult or peer models. It is interesting to note that some of the behavioral effects which were observed in these last two experiments may have been produced through empathic or vicarious experience, since the experiments included conditions in which the children observed rewarding or nurturant events which were experienced by another person rather than directly by themselves. Finally, an experiment by Grusec and Mischel (1966) provides some particularly suggestive evidence of the role of intrinsic affective value in the child's formation and retrieval of its cognitive representation of a model's expressive behavior. This experiment showed that children were better able to recall the actions of a rewarding model than those of a nonrewarding model, even though strong external incentives were offered for reproduction of the actions of either model.

It is somewhat more difficult to ascertain the evidence for representational imitation in the findings of another group of experiments, which have demonstrated the effects of the observation of aggression on children's expression of their own aggressive dispositions (Bandura, 1965a; Bandura, Ross & Ross, 1961; Bandura, Ross & Ross, 1963a; Bandura et al., 1963c; Hicks, 1965). These experiments reveal some striking similarities between observed and performed aggression, which could be taken as evidence that imitation of a model's expressive mode of aggression had acquired some intrinsic functional value for the children. However, the evidence is uncertain, because the eliciting cues which were provided in the observed behavior of the other person, and the presence of a highly attractive target for aggression (for example, a large inflated doll that was specifically designed to invite physical aggression), might have predetermined the children's disposition to perform aggressive acts which were like those they had observed. It is possible that many of these aggressive acts may have been already prepotent in the children's repertoires, and may have been also selectively invited by situational supports, so that their performance did not really require the children to learn very much through the representational use of a model.

There have also been a great number of experiments in which it seems quite clear that the child's observation of the behavior of others, and in some cases its observation of the consequences of their behavior, functions primarily to elicit or suppress its choices among simple acts or judgments which are already available to it (Bandura & McDonald, 1963; Bandura & Mischel, 1965; Rosenhan & White, 1967; Sgan, 1967; Walters et al., 1963; Walters & Parke, 1964). A variety of similar experiments with adults also have demonstrated the matching of simple behavioral choices on the basis of observation (Marston, 1965; O'Connell, 1965; Walters, Bowen & Parke, 1964). Some of the experiments with children focus on forms of behavior which are commonly taken to be indices of internalized control over conduct—for example, the suppression of socially prohibited acts (Walters et al., 1963; Walters & Parke, 1964), charitable actions toward others (Rosenhan & White, 1967), and judgments of transgressions in terms of their intentions or their consequences (Bandura & McDonald, 1963). The findings of most of these experiments may be taken as evidence of observational control that is based on the child's capacity for cognitive representation of act-outcome contingencies. But none of the experiments is designed to provide evidence that the observed behavior serves as a representational model for the child's learning of new behavioral dispositions. The observed behavior appears rather to be the source of cues which indicate the appropriateness and potential consequences of the subject's choices among different objects, verbalized judgments, or distributions of rewarding resources. Other experiments of the same general type (Bandura & Whalen, 1966; Mischel & Liebert, 1966) indicate that the criteria which children use in rewarding themselves are as sensitive to the information that has been provided by externally imposed outcomes of their own past performance as they are to the information that has been provided by the previously observed self-rewarding behavior of others.

An experimental study of the origin of self-criticism (Aronfreed, 1964) provides an example of one kind of design that can be used to establish the internalized value of the child's imitation of even a simple discrete element of a model's behavior, when the contingencies for learning are arranged to permit inferences about affective control of the imitation. This experiment is also an instructive demonstration of imitative aversive learning. A variety of experimental paradigms of socialization were used to investigate the conditions under which nine- and ten-year-old girls would acquire the disposition to use the label "blue," in reference to their own punished actions, after the label had been used repeatedly as a verbal component of the punishment of a female socializing agent. Each child was engaged in a guessing game in which she indicated her choices, on each of ten training trials, by pushing down some of the four levers on a choice box. In the punishment paradigms, the child was punished by sharp verbal disapproval and deprivation of candy, ostensibly for the manner in which she pushed the levers, on five of the ten trials. Since the occurrence of a transgression was artificially controlled, and the child had no behavioral cues which identified it, a buzzer was used as an external signal of transgression. Both the signal and the punishment were initiated immediately upon the child's completion of the movement of a lever, and both the signal and the punishment terminated together. In one paradigm, the agent used the label "blue," in reference to the child's punished act, just at the termination of buzzer and punishment, where the label was expected to acquire anxiety-reducing value for the child, since it had the position of a signal that marked the end of an interval of anticipatory anxiety. In a second paradigm, the label was used at the very onset of the buzzer and punishment, in a position where it was expected that anticipatory anxiety would not yet have attained any substantial intensity. In a control paradigm in which no punishment was used, the buzzer signaled only the agent's use of the label "blue," and the label occurred at termination of the buzzer.

Immediately following these training paradigms, the children were placed in a common test situation, during which they were given the opportunity to overtly verbalize the label "blue," in reference to their continuing performance in operating the levers, when the buzzer sounded but the socializing agent had temporarily suspended her punitive role. Children who had been exposed to the label at termination of transgression signal and punishment used the label with a much higher frequency than did children who had been exposed to the label at onset of signal and punishment. Among children who had been exposed to the control paradigm, the use of the label was very infrequent. When additional groups of children were trained under the label-at-termination paradigm, the children almost invariably acquired the disposition to use the word "blue" to refer to their own transgressions. These children continued to verbalize the self-critical label, whenever their behavior produced the buzzer that signaled transgression, throughout various extinction procedures in which external punishment was eliminated or was given an entirely different temporal relationship to the occurrence of the label.

Comparison of the effects of the various paradigms which are described above clearly indicates that self-criticism is a form of behavior that may be initially acquired entirely on the basis of its internalized reinforcement value. It appears that children may sometimes imitate in order to produce representations of social stimuli which have acquired intrinsic value through their previous external occurrence in conjunction with the termination of anxiety. This imitative disposition can be extended to certain components of social punishment. The underlying mechanism that would be required for the establishment of such a disposition receives some indirect confirmation from the findings of experiments on aversive learning in animals (Beck, 1961; Brown, 1965; Campbell, Smith & Misanin, 1966; Dinsmoor & Clayton, 1966). These experiments also suggest that various external stimulus events, including the occurrence of punishment itself, may acquire potential reinforcement value through their association with the reduction of anticipatory anxiety. It is important to emphasize, however, that the interval between the onset of anxiety and the occurrence of a cue component of punishment is the critical temporal factor in determining whether the component will acquire value for the reduction of anticipatory anxiety. If the interval is sufficiently long, and punishment is not too intense or prolonged, then verbal components which occur even at the onset of punishment may acquire such value and be reproduced by the child under subsequent conditions of anxiety following a transgression. It is just this point that appears, in fact, to have been recently demonstrated in an experiment which is reported by Grusec (1966), although the findings are mistakenly interpreted as evidence that the learning of self-criticism is not controlled by anxiety-reduction (on the grounds that children reproduced a model's verbal criticism even when it did not coincide with termination of punishment). The same experiment also shows that the frequency of overtly verbalized self-criticism can be increased by the reinforcement of punishment-termination, once the child has acquired the response through imitation of a model. Hill (1960) has argued that children originally acquire self-criticism through direct training because it is effective in producing reinstatement of parental affection. But the experiments which are cited above, as well as others (Bandura & Kupers, 1964; Mischel & Grusec, 1966), clearly demonstrate that direct training could hardly be the primary channel for the learning of self-criticism. Since the self-critical response is generally not overtly expressed by the child, under the conditions of naturalistic socialization, it cannot easily be subjected to reinforcing external outcomes. And even when it does sometimes appear overtly in the behavior of the very young child, its initial emergence often has the speed and vigor of a response that is already well established.

The overall pattern of findings from the experiment which varied the temporal position of the label "blue" (Aronfreed, 1964) demonstrated that the learning of self-criticism rests on aversive control of the child's imitative behavior, and not on generalization of the positive control which can be exercised by nurturant or affectionate models. This inference appears to be confirmed by the findings in yet another paradigm of the original experiment, in which the agent (and potential model) generally displayed much affection and approval toward the child, but withdrew her nurturance when she administered punishment. The nurturance of the agent did not facilitate the children's disposition to reproduce her use of the critical label "blue," which was placed at onset of transgression signal and punishment during training. The frequency with which the label was used during the test trials which followed the nurturance paradigm was comparable to the low frequency of its use among children who had been trained with the label in the same temporal position, but who had experienced no nurturance from the agent. This finding does not lead to the conclusion that the nurturance of parents has no effect on the child's reproduction of their critical or punitive behavior. It does indicate, however, that the child will imitate the punitive behavior of a model only to the extent that contingencies of aversive learning permit the behavior to acquire some intrinsic representational value, and that nurturance can influence this kind of imitation only to the extent that it affects the aversive learning process. The experiments which are reported by Grusec (1966), and by Mischel and Grusec (1966), suggest that the nurturance of a model can facilitate the child's imitation of verbal criticism, when the criticism is given a temporal position at which it can coincide with attenuation of the child's anxiety. This facilitation would be expected, as will be pointed out later, on the basis of the effect that nurturance might have on the salience of punishment or on its effectiveness in producing anxiety.

The experiment which induced children to apply the label "blue" to their own actions produced one other finding which also indicated that imitation of a model's verbal evaluative behavior must be under the control of the specific affective context in which the behavior occurs. In all of the paradigms which have been described, the agent used the label "red" in reference to the child's behavior in operating the levers on all trials on which the behavior was not labeled as "blue." The "red" label was simply associated with absence of punishment in the two basic punishment paradigms, but it was associated with verbal praise and physical affection in the punishment paradigm for which the agent had assumed a generally nurturant role. Only a few of the children from any of these paradigms used the label "red" to refer to their own behavior, when they were given the opportunity to do so during test trials. This finding indicates that the children who did reproduce the label "blue," following the appropriate contingencies of training, had not acquired a generalized disposition to imitate the verbalization of the experimental agent. Apparently, their self-criticism had acquired an intrinsic reinforcement value that was governed by the affective conditions under which external criticism had occurred originally. It may be somewhat surprising that the label "red" was not reproduced by children who had been exposed to it in the nurturant context of verbal approval and physical affection. However, they had no external signal that was associated with reward for their "red" behavior (in contrast to the buzzer that signaled "blue" behavior on both training and test trials). And the positive affective properties of an evaluative label that was associated with reward may have been difficult to establish for the child in a learning situation that was so largely defined by punishment and anxiety. The same finding would support the inference that the evaluative properties of any verbal (or non-verbal) behavior are not fully defined by its cognitive context. The affective conditions under which evaluative behavior is acquired must also be taken into account. It seems certain that children in all of the paradigms had a clear cognition of the distinction between the "blue" and "red" labels. But the affective correlates which would motivate and reinforce their overt verbal application of the labels to their own behavior were present in different degrees for the two labels.

The findings of another experiment (Aronfreed, Cutick & Fagen, 1963), which was carried out with nine- to ten-year-old boys and male socializing agents, again demonstrate some of the conditions of socialization which maximize the disposition of children to apply verbal criticism to their own previously punished behavior. The children were individually engaged in a task in which they had to knock down some toy soldiers in order to protect a nurse. On each of ten training trials, the child was punished by deprivation of candy, apparently in proportion to how many soldiers had been knocked down. In two of the training paradigms, the agent made frequent verbal references to the child's performance, along the dimensions of "careful-careless" and "gentle-rough," during instructions and just at the termination of each punishment. In two other paradigms, the agent did not use this cognitive structuring. Within each of these two pairs of paradigms, two levels of variation were introduced in the agent's nurturance toward the child. When the agent assumed a nurturant role, he was solicitous toward the child, occasionally replenished the child's supply of candy, and commented on his overt attempts to make the child's task easier by placement of the soldiers. The agent's nonnurturant role included none of these features. Following all of the four training paradigms, there was a common test trial on which the doll that represented the nurse appeared to break as a result of the vigor of the child's task-oriented aggressive behavior. Children who had been punished under the verbalized cognitive structure of "careful-careless" and "gentle-rough" significantly more often held their own behavior responsible for the breaking of the nurse-doll than did children who had been punished without cognitive structure (even though they rarely used the specific critical labels which had been employed by the agent). But there were no significant differences in the use of self-criticism which were attributable to variations of nurturance. Although this experiment was not designed to uncover mechanisms of internalization, it does provide some confirmation of the findings of the later experiment which induced children to use the label "blue" (Aronfreed, 1964).

Empathic and Vicarious Experience

Although the terms empathic and vicarious are often used synonymously, they can be usefully distinguished. Empathy may be used to refer to the child's affective experience when it is elicited by cues of a corresponding affective state in the expressive behavior of another person. The term vicarious is more appropriate when the child's affective experience is elicited by its observation of the stimulus events which impinge upon another person. The two forms of experience would, of course, often be interwoven. These criteria for both empathic and vicarious experience emphasize the affective response of the observer. They require only a similarity between the observer's affective state and the affective experience which the observer perceives (or cognizes) another person to be having. They do not require that the observer have an identity of cognitive viewpoint with the other person, or even that the observer perceive himself to be in the other person's role (cf. Mowrer, 1960b, p. 115). There are many reasons why the exact quality of affective states may not be transmitted with high fidelity from the actual experience of one person to the empathic or vicarious experience of another. However, constraints on cognitive matching do not limit empathic and vicarious experience only to a gross correspondence between two people in the general direction of their affective states. Since the specific quality of an affective state is determined by its cognitive housing (Schachter, 1964), empathic or vicarious experience will require some similarity between the cognitive substance of the observer's affect and the cognitive elements which are perceived to be present in another person's experience.

Very early in the course of their development, children begin to show evidence of pleasurable or aversive affective responses both to the expressive cues which indicate the corresponding affective experience of others and to the stimulus events to which others are exposed. The establishment of empathic and vicarious dispositions may be thought of as a kind of internalization process, since it enables the child's behavior to become somewhat independent of the control of its direct experience of social reward and punishment. Allport (1924, p. 235) and Humphrey (1922) many years ago suggested that the basic mechanism for the attachment of a child's affective responses to the perceived experience of another person was essentially a social conditioning process that rested on a close and repeated association between cues which conveyed the experience of others and stimulus events which had direct affective consequences for the child. Socialization provides many contingencies which would support such an association—for example, in the simultaneous experience of certain pleasurable or aversive stimulus events by both the child and another person, or in the probability of coincidence between the affective states of socializing agents and their disposition to behave in ways which directly induce corresponding states in the child. The cues which indicate the affective experience of the other person may be initially subordinated, in the child's perception, to the total complex of stimuli which it directly experiences as the source of affective arousal. But as the cues become increasingly discriminable to the child, they can acquire their own capacity to elicit the child's affective experience, under conditions where they are no longer perceived by the child as having direct consequences for itself.

It is often difficult to identify truly empathic or vicarious control of behavior. A child's affective response to another person's expressive cues, or to the events which impinge upon that person, may be partially attributable to the child's direct experience of the positive or aversive properties of the observed stimuli. Such a phenomenon would be quite common. It could occur because of some generalization from the child's own direct past experience with similar stimulus events, or because the observed events are perceived as signals which portend events of corresponding affective value to be directly experienced by the child. The concepts of "empathic" and "vicarious" can be applied accurately only to those components of the child's affective states which are elicited by its perception of the affective experience of others—that is, to those components which are independent of the social stimuli which it perceives as having a direct impact upon itself. The application of this criterion clearly would be highly dependent on the child's cognition of concrete stimulus events. For example, the criteria of empathic experience are not fully met in recent studies in which animals have been shown to produce various response indices of aversion to the distress cues which are emitted by other animals (Church, 1959; Miller, 1961; Miller, Banks & Ogawa, 1963). These studies assess the effects of a prior association between the observed distress cues and the direct experience of pain by the observing animal, in situations where the cues might well continue to function as signals which convey directly aversive consequences for the observer.

The most direct demonstrations of empathic and vicarious experience have used peripheral autonomic indices of affective arousal, when the affective state is presumed to be anxiety or distress, in response to cues of pain from another person or to indicators of the painful stimuli to which others are exposed (Bandura & Rosenthal, 1966; Berger, 1962; Haner & Whitney, 1960; Lazarus, Speisman, Mordkoff & Davison, 1962). Another approach has been to examine the generalized arousal effect of another person's pain cues on the observer's responses in a simple reaction time task (DiLollo & Berger, 1965). These demonstrations have not been addressed to the question of how empathic and vicarious experience contribute to internalized control of social behavior by reducing the requirements for maintenance of the behavior by direct reward and punishment. But a great number of other studies have attempted to use the effects of social stimuli on the overt behavior of an observer to draw inferences about empathic or vicarious control of the behavior (Bandura, 1965a; Bandura, Grusec & Menlove, 1967; Bandura et al., 1963c; Jones, 1924; Kobasigawa, 1965; Walters et al., 1963; Walters & Parke, 1964; Walters et al., 1965). All of these experiments have been conducted with children, and many of them are clearly relevant to the child's internalized control over its socially constrained behavioral dispositions. The general strategy of the experiments assumes that the child's empathic or vicarious affective experience of the positive or aversive outcomes of another person's behavior has been demonstrated when the child's observation of the outcomes has no immediate consequences for itself, but does result in subsequent facilitation or suppression of its own corresponding behavior.

Some recent summaries of the experimental literature (Bandura, 1965b; Kanfer, 1965) appear to assume a form of rapid observational learning, based on the empathic or vicarious experience of reward and punishment, to account for virtually any evidence that an individual's behavior has been influenced by observation of the outcomes of another person's actions. The criteria for empathic and vicarious experience which have been suggested here, however, would not permit their presence to be inferred from such evidence. The experimental design of a few of the studies which are cited above would not support inferences beyond those which are warranted by a demonstration that the activity of one organism is enhanced by the mere presence or activity of another (Zajonc, 1965). Some of the studies do clearly demonstrate the behavioral effects of observing the consequences of another person's actions. However, the sheer information that is conveyed by the observed reward or punishment of another person's behavior would be sufficient to elicit or suppress a child's already established behavioral dispositions, without requiring the occurrence either of learning or of empathic or vicarious experience. Demonstrations of the influence of social observation on the child's behavior almost always reveal the child's capacity for cognitive representation of information from its environment. But such demonstrations do not necessarily provide evidence of empathic or vicarious affective arousal. Much the same effects have been obtained when children are simply told about the choices or preferences of others (Bandura & Mischel, 1965; Duncker, 1938).

The importance of the simple transmission of information, as a determinant of the behavioral effects of social observation, is clearly indicated in the findings of numerous other experiments with both children and adults, in which various kinds of simple verbal or motor learning are shown to be enhanced by prior observation of outcomes which indicate the correct and incorrect responses of another person (Bruning, 1965; Kanfer & Marston, 1963a; Lewis & Duncan, 1958; Marston, 1966). The problem in the interpretation of all of these studies arises primarily from the difficulty of making the inference that empathic or vicarious experience occurs during the period of observation, in the absence of any overt behavioral index of the affective value of the observed social stimuli. This difficulty is also apparent in the conflicting results of experiments with both children and adults on the question of whether the mere observation of another person's aggression will strengthen or reduce the observer's aggressive dispositions (Bandura et al., 1963a; Berkowitz & Geen, 1966; Feshbach, 1961; Rosenbaum & deCharms, 1960; Wheeler & Caggiula, 1967). Comparisons among these results suggest that the observation of aggression may have generalized motivational effects which are inversely related to the amount of affective arousal which the observer brings into the observation situation. The results also suggest that the subsequent aggressive behavior of the observer is quite sensitive to other social cues in the situation which provide information about the appropriateness or permissibility of the behavior. A general conclusion that one can draw from all of these studies is that the empathic or vicarious affective value of social stimuli might be examined more effectively by using the stimuli as outcomes which are contingent on the observer's overt performance of an act. It would then be possible to demonstrate the reinforcing or suppressive effects of the stimuli, even though they had no directly positive or aversive consequences for the observer.

Altruistic and sympathetic acts provide what are perhaps the most interesting examples of the role of empathic and vicarious experience in the acquisition and maintenance of internalized control over social behavior. An act may be described as altruistic when its choice, in preference to an alternative act, is at least partially determined by expected consequences which will benefit another person rather than the actor. The absence of any reinforcing consequences for the actor is a commonly assumed criterion for the altruistic component of social behavior (see, for example, Durkheim, 1951, pp. 217–240). From the point of view of a concept of internalization, however, it is necessary to assume that altruistic acts are reinforced through the affective value of their outcomes for others, despite the fact that they may have no directly positive consequences for the actor (or that they may even have directly aversive consequences). The reinforcing outcomes of an altruistic act may be contained in its concretely visible consequences for others, or in the actor's cognitive representation and evaluation of such consequences, when the actor is able to respond to the perceived or cognized consequences with empathic or vicarious changes of affective state. Empathic or vicarious control of behavior is in fact a prerequisite of the truly altruistic act. And since altruistic behavior must have some independence of any directly beneficial consequences for the actor, it may always be said to be under some degree of internalized control.

It has been demonstrated in a number of studies that children have some disposition to share valued resources with their peers, and also to extend aid when their peers are under distress (Fischer, 1963; Handlon & Gross, 1959; Hartshorne, May & Maller, 1929; Lenrow, 1965; Murphy, 1937; Rosenhan & White, 1967; Ugurel-Semin, 1952; Wright, 1942). Similar dispositions are apparent in the actions of adults who are exposed to social situations in which they have the opportunity to behave in such a way as to produce desirable consequences for another person (Berkowitz & Daniels, 1964; Berkowitz & Friedman, 1967; Goranson & Berkowitz, 1966; Schopler & Matthews, 1965). Some experiments also have been conducted as attempts to demonstrate the same kinds of dispositions in other primates (Mason, 1959; Masserman, Wechkin & Terris, 1964; Miller et al., 1963; Nissen & Crawford, 1936). None of these studies is directly addressed to the question of how children or animals originally acquire the kind of responsiveness to social stimuli which would make such dispositions altruistic. Moreover, with the exception of the studies which have been reported by Lenrow (1965), and by Rosenhan and White (1967), it is difficult to determine the extent to which the behavior that is observed in these studies is under the control of altruistic expectations. It frequently appears that the behavior is either reinforced by explicit rewards or elicited by the expectation of direct social approval, or that it represents a cooperative effort to produce a mutual exchange of positive outcomes for both self and other. Recent experiments on the cooperative behavior of monkeys in feeding situations (Boren, 1966; Horel, Treichler & Meyer, 1963) provide especially interesting examples of the difficulty of maintaining such behavior when it is no longer instrumental to the mutual exchange of food. In the case of experiments which have focused on reactions to the distress of a peer (for example, the experiments with monkeys which are reported by Masserman et al., 1964, and by Miller et al., 1963), the altruistic character of the observed behavior also remains indeterminate, because it is possible that the subjects might have been acting to avoid their own experience of aversive stimulation. A comparison of two closely related experiments with rats (Lavery & Foley, 1963; Rice & Gainer, 1962) is particularly instructive in making the point that acts which reduce the distress of a peer need not be empathically motivated, but may rather be directed to the reduction of stimulation that is experienced as being directly aversive.

One possible way of demonstrating the learning of altruistic behavior is suggested by a recent experiment in which six- to eight-year-old girls and a female socializing agent were used (Aronfreed & Paskal, 1965). The experiment was designed to first attach the child's empathic positive affect to expressive cues which conveyed the pleasurable affective state of the agent, and to then establish the altruistic value of an overt act that the child could use instrumentally to produce the agent's expressive cues. During the initial socialization paradigms, the agent sat very close to each child, and demonstrated the operation of a choice-box which was automated to dispense a small candy as the outcome of operating one lever and a red light as the outcome of operating another lever. Each outcome was programmed to a 60 per cent probability schedule, so that its occurrence would not be predictable on an individual trial. The child simply watched while the agent varied her choices over twenty demonstration trials. The agent showed no reaction during the trials on which her choices produced no candy. But when the red light was activated on the remaining trials, the agent showed one of three patterns of response which represented variations in the contingencies between her expressive affective cues and her behavior toward the child. The contingencies were designed to support the inference that the subsequent reinforcement value of the expressive cues was attributable to social conditioning of the child's empathic experience. In the basic experimental paradigm, the agent smiled, stared at the red light, and exclaimed *"There's the light!"* in a pleased and excited tone of voice. Immediately following these expressive cues, the agent gave the child a firm hug, and simultaneously turned toward the child with a very broad direct smile. This procedure exposed the child repeatedly to a close temporal association between the agent's expressive cues of pleasurable affect and her own direct experience of the agent's apparently spontaneous physical affection. In contrast, the children in one control paradigm were exposed only to the agent's expressive cues, and the children in another control paradigm were exposed only to the agent's affection.

The effects of the three paradigms were then immediately tested with a common performance task, during which the child herself operated the choice-box over a great many trials. The agent now sat across from the child, facing the rear of the box, with her gaze fixed on another red light that was visible only to her (although the child was told of its presence). The red light on the front of the box, which had been visible to the child during the initial socialization paradigms, was now deactivated on a pretext. The child was told that she could keep all of the candy that came out of the box (but that she was not to eat it immediately). During this task, the agent showed no reaction when the child's choices produced candy. But whenever the child chose to operate the lever which produced the red light, the agent would smile at the light and exclaim *"There's the light!"* thus producing the same expressive cues which had been used to convey her pleasure in the initial paradigms. The child was placed, then, in a situation where her empathic and altruistic dispositions could be tested by her repeated choices between an act that produced candy for herself and an act that produced only observably pleasurable consequences for another person.

The majority of the children who had been exposed to the basic social conditioning paradigm, in which the agent's expressive affective cues had occurred in close contiguity with their own direct experience of the agent's affection, actually chose to produce the light for the agent more frequently than they chose to produce candy for themselves. Their behavior presented a marked contrast to that of the children in either of the two control groups, whose earlier exposure to the red light had been associated only with the agent's expressive cues or only with the agent's physical affection. Children from both of the control paradigms showed significantly higher frequencies of choice of the candy-producing lever than did children from the conditioning paradigm. The behavioral differences among the groups, during the performance test for altruism, may be attributed to the empathic value which the agent's expressive cues of positive affect had acquired for the conditioning group. Since the agent's expressive affective cues were not contingent on the children's overt acts during the initial paradigms, but were made contingent on overt choices for all groups during the test, the experimental effect cannot easily be attributed to the children's perception of the cues as evidence of direct social approval of their choices.

There are some interesting similarities and differences between a concept of sympathy and a concept of altruism. Some efforts to define sympathy have postulated complex affective and cognitive dispositions which correspond to what have been defined here as empathic and vicarious experience (see, for example, Allport, 1954, or McDougall, 1908, pp. 150–179). Such broad definitions give little attention to the nature and origin of sympathetic behavior as a specific reaction to the observed or anticipated distress of another person. Empathic or vicarious experience must be inferred as a prerequisite of sympathetic behavior, since an act is truly sympathetic only to the extent that it is motivated by the actor's affective response to another person's actual or potential distress. Thus, in those experiments in which animals are shown to perform actions which relieve the distress of another animal (for example, Miller et al., 1963, or Rice & Gainer, 1962), the previously cited limitations on their demonstration of altruism are equally applicable to their demonstration of sympathetic behavior—that is, the performing animal might well experience the observed distress cues as aversive events which directly impinge upon itself.

The affective base for a concept of sympathetic behavior is less broad than the corresponding base for a concept of altruistic behavior, because sympathetic behavior always has the aversive affective determinant of empathic or vicarious distress. The conditions of reinforcement for sympathetic behavior are, however, less restrictive than those for altruistic behavior. A person's sympathetic behavior may be altruistic to the extent that its expected reinforcing consequences are limited to the reduction of empathic or vicarious distress which the person will experience when another person is relieved or protected from distress. Recent experiments with college students (Buss, 1966; Schopler & Bateson, 1965) appear to demonstrate such altruistic components in sympathetic behavior. But even though sympathy itself requires the capacity for empathic or vicarious experience of distress, overt sympathetic behavior is also often controlled by a person's anticipation of direct social reward or of subsequent reciprocity from another person. Observational studies of children's behavior (Isaacs, 1933; Murphy, 1937) illustrate that sympathetic behavior is not always altruistic. Children will often aid or show solicitude toward their peers because they anticipate social approval or the mutual benefits of cooperation in a shared difficulty. The internalized status of a sympathetic act may therefore vary in accordance with the extent to which its motivation and reinforcement are independent of external outcomes which are directly experienced by the actor.

The socialization of sympathetic behavior requires two basic components. First, the child must acquire empathic or vicarious affective reactions to cues which indicate the distressful experience of another person. Secondly, the child must acquire specific forms of overt behavior which are instrumental to the reduction of the other person's distress. Overt sympathetic acts may be established to some extent through the effects of external social reinforcement in shaping and narrowing the child's earlier and more generalized dispositions (for example, its dispositions toward the expression of affection or toward cooperative actions). The external reinforcing event may be the elimination of the observable cues of another person's distress, which results in the reduction of the child's own empathic or vicarious distress. Or the external reinforcement may take the form of social approval or other rewarding outcomes which are directly experienced by the child. In either case, distress-reduction or other potentially reinforcing changes of affective state may become directly attached to the intrinsic cognitive correlates of the child's sympathetic acts, so that the maintenance of the acts is no longer dependent on their observable external consequences. After the child has had some opportunity for concrete observation of other people's experience of distress and relief of distress, then the affective changes which motivate and reinforce its sympathetic behavior may come under the more internalized control of its cognitive representation of social stimuli which were formerly directly observable.

The shaping of sympathetic behavior by reinforcing social outcomes is not the only form of learning through which the behavior can acquire internalized value. The apparently early initiation and rapid acquisition of sympathetic behavior (Murphy, 1937) suggest, in fact, that the more effective source of its learning is the young child's imitative disposition to reproduce those observed sympathetic acts of socializing agents which have been associated with its experience of relief of distress. The prototypical paradigm for this kind of imitative learning may be that in which the child's own directly experienced distress is reduced by the actions of a potential model. However, the observed sympathetic behavior of a model may acquire distress-reducing value for the child even when it is directed to another person, if the child is capable of responding empathically or vicariously to the other person's experience of relief of distress. Either of these opportunities for observational learning may attach a potentially reinforcing affective value, which corresponds to reduction of distress, to the child's cognitive representation of the model's behavior, and therefore to the intrinsic cognitive correlates of its own emerging repertoire of sympathetic acts. The child can then reduce the empathic or vicarious distress which it experiences, in response to the perceived distress of another person, by reproducing the model's sympathetic behavior. And since the cognitive representations which are correlated to the child's imitative performance of a sympathetic act have already acquired some internalized affective value, through the process of observational learning, the reinforcement of the act will be at least partially independent of its immediately observable consequences. It is also possible that the child's sympathetic behavioral dispositions can acquire some generalized intrinsic value through observational learning that does not necessarily produce imitation of the same actions which it has observed in the behavior of a model. Lenrow (1965) has found that the verbal expression of sympathy among both children and adults, and the performance of concrete sympathetic acts by children, are facilitated by actual or role-played previous experience as the recipient of sympathetic behavior under conditions of distress.

An Illustrative Experiment

Both the conditioning of empathic experience and imitative learning can be illustrated by a recent experiment on the acquisition of sympathetic behavior, in which seven- and eight-year-old girls were exposed to socialization by a female experimental agent (Aronfreed & Paskal, 1966). Each of five different experimental groups was exposed to a sequence of three distinct and immediately successive phases of socialization. During each phase, the child classified twelve small toy replicas of real objects in accordance with whether she thought each toy most appropriate for a house, a dog, or a school. The toys were changed between phases. The child indicated her classification by pushing one of three levers on a choice-box. Since the middle lever was used for the dog category, and the toys were selected to make its use inappropriate, it was ordinarily chosen very infrequently or not at all. This procedure made it possible to treat choices of the middle lever as an index of sympathetic behavior during the test (third) phase of the experimental sequence.

The prototype for the empathic and imitative components in the learning of sympathetic behavior was the first of the five experimental sequences. It may be used as the reference point for describing the design of the three phases within all of the sequences. The first phase was designed to condition the child's empathic distress to the cues of distress which were being emitted by the experimental agent. The conditioning was effected by introducing the necessary temporal contiguity between the agent's cues and the child's own direct experience of distressful stimulation. Both the child and the agent wore earphones, on the pretext of monitoring noise from within the choice-box. Among the twelve trials for the classification of toys, there were six on which the child heard a highly aversive loud noise through her earphones during the intertrial interval that followed her choice. The occurrence of the noise, which lasted for seven seconds, was unpredictable and not contingent on the child's classification. Three seconds before the onset of the noise, the agent began to show distress by placing her head in her hands (the child had been told previously that the noise in the agent's earphones would be even louder). The agent's distress cue was continued until the noise terminated.

The second phase was designed to establish the distress-reducing value of the agent's sympathetic actions toward the child, when the agent herself wore no earphones and was no longer under distress. The agent now had the role of a potential model for sympathetic behavior. She used another choice-box to indicate her own classification of each toy after the child had classified it. She also told the child that she might be able, while she was using the second choice-box, to turn off the noise that the child would still hear occasionally through her earphones. The agent began to indicate her classification of the toy on each trial by poising her hand, for a few seconds, over the levers on her box. On six of the twelve trials, she chose either the house or the school lever (these were obviously the only correct choices for almost all of the toys). On the remaining six trials, the child began to hear the highly aversive noise through her earphones at this point. The agent moved fairly quickly to push the middle lever on her box, and this action terminated the noise. The agent thus clearly gave up the opportunity to make a correct classification in order to reduce the child's distress.

The third phase was designed to test whether the child had acquired an imitative disposition to reproduce the observed sympathetic acts of the model, and also to examine the function of a third person's distress cues in eliciting the child's sympathetic behavior. This test phase was constructed so that the empathic aversive value of observed distress cues could be demonstrated by making their elimination a reinforcing event that was contingent on the child's overt behavior, rather than having to rely only on a demonstration that the child's behavior was affected by exposure to the cues. Another girl was now introduced as a new subject, although she had in fact been trained as a dummy to emit distress cues during the primary subject's test phase. On each trial, the dummy classified each toy first, and the subject had the agent's earlier role of then showing her classification on the second choice-box. The dummy wore earphones, but the subject did not. On six of the twelve trials, the dummy and subject simply made their successive choices. On the remaining six trials, the dummy placed her head in her hands at the point where the subject was about to make her choice. If the subject made the sympathetic choice of the middle lever, the dummy would immediately terminate her distress cue. But if the subject made a nonsympathetic, task-oriented choice, the dummy would not raise her head until five seconds after the subject had completed her choice.

The remaining four experimental sequences were essentially permutations of controls on the three socialization phases which are described above for the first sequence. The second sequence differed from the first only in that the agent's distress cues during the first phase were not paired with the aversive noise that the child heard. The noise occurred at the same six intervals, but the distress cues were emitted only during the noiseless intervals which followed the remaining six trials. This design eliminated the temporal contiguities which would be required to produce conditioning of empathic distress. The third sequence also replicated the first, except that the noise which the child heard during the second phase was sharply reduced to a very mild intensity, so that the agent's sympathetic behavior would acquire only minimal distress-reducing value and would be less effective in establishing the child's imitative disposition. The fourth and fifth sequences were identical to the first, with the exception that two levels of reduction were introduced, during the third (test) phase, in the social stimuli which were presumably required to elicit and reinforce the child's sympathetic behavior. In the fourth sequence, the dummy wore the earphones, but she emitted no distress cues. In the fifth sequence, she did not even wear earphones.

During the first two phases of all of the sequences, the children were highly task-oriented. They used the middle lever on the choice-box (the dog classification) typically only once or twice. During the third phase, however, the children in the basic first sequence showed a marked preference for the middle lever. Half of them chose it on six or more trials. Almost all of the remainder of these children showed lesser but quite sizeable increments in their choices of the middle lever. In all of the other four sequences, the children generally continued to show a strong task-orientation during this test for sympathetic behavior. The frequency distributions of their choices of the middle lever were quite similar to the corresponding distributions for the first two phases. When children from all of the sequences were compared with respect to the shifts in the frequencies of their choices of the middle lever, between the first two phases and the test phase, there was a powerful and highly reliable difference between the effect of the first sequence and the effect of any other sequence.

In addition to the general support which these experimental results give to the conception of the learning of sympathetic behavior which was outlined earlier, there are a number of other useful inferences which can be drawn about the acquisition of imitative and empathic dispositions. For example, the failure of the second sequence to produce very much sympathetic behavior indicated the importance of establishing empathic distress, through the contingencies of a conditioning paradigm, during the first phase of socialization. Apparently, sheer information about the experience of another person was not sufficient to elicit the children's imitation of the previously observed behavior of a sympathetic model. Imitation seems to be dependent on some reinstatement of the affective conditions under which a model's behavior has acquired value for the child. Secondly, the fact that the third sequence produced little sympathetic behavior indicated that the children's disposition to imitate the model was not merely determined by observation of the model's actions, even though these actions were directed to their own welfare, or by knowledge that reproducing the actions would reduce another person's distress. During the second phase of the third sequence, the experimental agent's sympathetic actions toward the child terminated only a mild noise, so that they would acquire only minimal potential imitative value for reduction of the child's later empathic distress during the test phase (in contrast to the first sequence, where the noise heard by the child during the second phase continued to be highly aversive). It appears, therefore, that a component of the reinforcement value of imitative behavior is determined by the changes of affective state which the child has experienced in association with its observation of a model. The relative ineffectiveness of the fourth and fifth sequences in producing sympathetic behavior demonstrated the specific function of distress cues as elicitors of the children's sympathetic behavior during the third (test) phase. The role of external social stimulus control in the imitation that was shown by children from the first sequence was also confirmed by the fact that their choices of the middle lever were almost entirely confined to the six trials on which the dummy emitted distress cues. It is clear that the children in the first sequence were not showing merely a generalized disposition to reproduce the previously observed actions of another person.

The most striking ancillary finding of this experiment appeared in the sympathetic behavior of children from the fourth sequence, in which the dummy wore earphones but emitted no distress cues. During the test phase, these children showed discernible increments in their choice of the middle lever, despite their fairly strong task-orientation. The frequency of their choices was, in fact, closer to the frequency for children from the first sequence than were the frequencies for children from any of the other control sequences. Moreover, they chose the middle lever significantly more often than did children from the fifth sequence, in which the dummy wore no earphones. Since their behavior was independent of any exposure to distress cues, and was also not reinforced by the externally observable termination of such cues, it seems probable that their sympathetic behavior was controlled by their cognitive representations of the distress-reducing (or distress-avoiding) consequences of their actions for another child who was wearing the earphones. Their sympathetic acts seemed, then, to have acquired a certain amount of intrinsic value which was independent of concrete external outcomes.

The role of the intrinsic representational value of imitation was also suggested by the absence of sympathetic behavior in the third sequence. Children in this sequence did have an opportunity to reduce empathic distress by terminating the external distress cues of another person during the test phase. But they had observed the model's sympathetic behavior, during the second phase, under conditions in which it would not acquire much intrinsic value (because the children had experienced only minimal distress). Finally, some additional information about the function of cognitive representations was obtained from introspective reports which the children gave during a verbal inquiry that followed the experimental session directly. Almost all of the children perceived the dummy's distress cues as indicators of loud noise in her earphones. In many cases, however, the children's reports did not reveal a clear recognition that the dummy's apparent distress could have been relieved by their choice of the middle lever. Among children in the first sequence, reported awareness of this contingency was a very reliable predictor of maximal sympathetic behavior. Among children in all of the other sequences, reported awareness of the contingency was unrelated to their behavior.

STUDIES OF THE EFFECTS
OF NATURALISTIC SOCIALIZATION

There is a very substantial body of surveys which attempts to relate various indices of children's internalized control over their behavior to the child-rearing practices of their parents. Some of the findings of these surveys have been sufficiently consistent to warrant theoretical attention as rough confirmations of inferences which can be drawn more firmly from experimental studies of the internalization process. The value of these findings for an understanding of the mechanisms of internalization is limited, however, not only by the usual constraints on the inferences which can be drawn from correlations, but also by the fact that the correlations represent the effects of unknown interactions of different types of learning. Nevertheless, the kinds of child-rearing variations which have been studied most extensively sometimes lend themselves quite readily to analysis in terms of concepts of learning, particularly in cases where paradigms of direct training appear to be applicable.

There is little reason to think that any index of internalization is consistently related to the care or treatment of the young infant, or to pacing processes such as weaning or toilet training (W. Allinsmith, 1960; Burton et al., 1961; Grinder, 1962; Sears et al., 1965, Ch. 6; Whiting & Child, 1953, Ch. 11). There is some evidence, however, that the learning processes which underlie internalization may be dependent on a certain minimum of nurturance (warmth, affection, etc.) in the general climate of child-rearing. A number of investigators (Bandura & Walters, 1959; Bronfenbrenner, 1961; Sears et al., 1957, Ch. 10) have reported relationships which indicate that children's control over their aggressive behavior, their responsibility in achievement tasks, and their reactions to their own transgressions, are all characterized by a relatively low degree of internalization when the children have been exposed to extreme parental rejection or punitiveness. There are also suggestions, in cross-cultural comparisons of entire societies, that very severe early socialization is positively associated with the incidence of theft and with the absence of self-blame for illness (Bacon, Child & Barry, 1963; Whiting & Child, 1953, Ch. 11).

A great many writers have taken the view that children acquire a very broad and generalized disposition to internalize control of their social conduct, and that the wide range of variation in parental nurturance is a uniformly critical determinant of this disposition (Ausubel, 1955; Bowlby, 1947; Bronfenbrenner, 1960; Sears et al., 1957, Ch. 10; Sears et al., 1965; Whiting & Child, 1953, Ch. 11). These formulations of an identification process bear some resemblance to a view that was originally put forth by Freud (1933)—that the motivation to reproduce the properties of a "love object" was a major source of the child's identification with its parents (though Freud actually emphasized the punitive and threatening aspects of the parents as the more significant source of the child's conscience). The most explicit formulations are couched in behavioristic concepts of learning (Mowrer, 1960b, Ch. 3; Sears et al., 1957, Ch. 10; Whiting & Child, 1953, Ch. 11). It is assumed that many stimulus attributes of the mother, and of other socializing agents, may acquire positive affective value for the child because of their association with its experience of care, affection, and approval. The child is then presumed to be motivated to reproduce many of the attributes of its nurturant models, particularly when their affectionate presence is absent or withdrawn, so as to provide itself with reinforcement through the positive value that has become intrinsically attached to the attributes. This replicative disposition is thought to apply not only to the behavioral attributes of socializing agents, but also to the child's acquisition of the cognitive schemata which are transmitted in their evaluative reactions to its behavior. The disposition is also apparently considered to extend to the behavioral and cognitive features of the punitive actions of socializing agents.

There are in fact very severe limitations on the view that the magnitude or extensiveness of parental nurturance is a uniformly functional determinant of the strength of a broad disposition which the child acquires toward the internalized control of its behavior. In many surveys, no consistent association has been found between parental nurturance and various indices of the child's internalized control over its behavior (Grinder, 1962; Heinecke, 1953; Sears et al., 1965, Ch. 6; Whiting & Child, 1953, Ch. 11). The reports of other studies (Bronfenbrenner, 1961; Burton et al., 1961; Sears et al., 1957, Ch. 10) suggest restricted positive relationships between parental affection and certain forms of social behavior which are under some degree of internalized control by the child. The studies which are reported by Bronfenbrenner (1961) and by Burton et al. (1961) also indicate, however, that very nurturant parents have children who show less responsibility and more cheating than children whose parents are more modal in their nurturance. The same type of relationship is implied in the finding by Whiting and Child (1953, Ch. 11) of a limited amount of positive cross-cultural relationship between overall severity of early socialization and the tendency of members of a society to blame themselves for illness (note the interesting contrast to the corollary finding by the same investigators that self-blame for illness was distinctly uncharacteristic of societies in which early socialization was extremely severe).

This entire pattern of findings, when taken together with the findings from studies of delinquent groups (Bandura & Walters, 1959; Glueck & Glueck, 1950; McCord, McCord & Howard, 1963), points quite firmly to the inference that positive correlations between the nurturance of parents and indices of internalized behavioral control in their children are generated entirely by the effects of extreme parental rejection or punitiveness. Close inspection of the data from the relevant studies clearly indicates that the correlations are apparent only when parents who give very little nurturance to their children are separated from all other parents. Supportive evidence for the same inference comes from studies of patterns of socialization which would tend to dilute the strength of the child's affective ties to a specific agent of nurturance. For example, there tends to be less self-blame for illness among societies with an extended family structure than among societies with a nuclear family structure (Whiting, 1959). And children who have been raised in institutional and concentration camp settings have remarkably poor control over their aggressive behavior (Freud & Dann, 1951; Goldfarb, 1945). It would seem, then, that a certain minimum intensity of social attachment to a nurturant figure is required to produce effective internalization of the child's control over conduct. Beyond the requirement of this minimal threshold, however, internalization cannot be regarded as a generalized, continuous function of parental nurturance. Internalization appears to be modulated by only a restricted range of variation in nurturance, around the point at which a strong positive attachment is formed between child and socializing agent.

It is not difficult to understand why some minimum of nurturance from socializing agents might be prerequisite to the child's acquisition of any substantial degree of internalized control over its behavior. The lack of nurturant treatment would interfere with the establishment of the positive or aversive value of a great variety of social stimuli which are transmitted through the behavior of others. These stimuli acquire much of their affective value through contingencies which first relate them to the more primary nurturant functions of the child's caretaking agents. Without a background of sustained nurturant treatment, they may acquire only a very limited value for control of the child's behavior. A deficit in the child's experience of nurturance might result, for example, in the attachment of little positive value to the behavior of parents as social models, and therefore in a curtailment of the child's imitative disposition to adopt their behavioral and cognitive controls. The consequences of deprivation of nurturance can perhaps be postulated even more clearly, however, for the disruption of the effectiveness of direct training in producing internalization through the positive or aversive outcomes of the child's overt behavior. The nurturance of parents is an important determinant of their rewarding and punitive power. If they have been generally affectionless or indiscriminately punitive, then there is very little basis for the establishment of the value of their resources for positive reinforcement and control of the child's behavior. Conversely, they may be unable to make effective use of withdrawal of affection, which may be the most effective component of any form of punishment in producing aversive control over the child's behavior. This component of punishment may then not induce sufficient affection as a medium of punishment if the child has become adapted to a high level of aversive stimulation from the parents. Punishment may then not induce sufficient discriminant anxiety to motivate the child's internalization of behavioral suppression or corrective reactions to transgression. The absence of loss of affection as a medium of punishment may also orient the child toward other components of punishment, such as physical pain or verbal attack, which would be less likely to permit the child's anxiety to become independent of external surveillance or threat (Aronfreed, 1961). For reasons which are similar to those outlined above, a certain minimum of nurturant treatment would also be required to establish the child's empathic or vicarious reactions to social cues which indicate the pleasurable or distressful consequences of its actions for other people.

The crucial role of a minimal threshold of parental nurturance in fostering internalization does not imply that nurturance beyond such a threshold has no further influence on the socialization process. The findings of a number of experimental and correlational studies indicate that the dispositions of children to reproduce certain aspects of the behavior of social models, or to perceive their own attributes as being similar to those of a model, are fostered by the model's nurturance (Bandura & Huston, 1961; Mussen & Distler, 1959; Mussen & Parker, 1965; Mussen & Rutherford, 1963; Sears, 1953). There is also evidence which suggests that the effectiveness of punishment, in the induction of some forms of internalized aversive control over the child's behavior, may be partially determined by the level of nurturance that the child experiences from the punitive agent. Nurturance does not appear to have this effect in some of the recent experiments which have used verbal punishment to induce self-criticism in children (Aronfreed, 1964; Aronfreed et al., 1963). Nor is the effect apparent in experiments which have used punishment training to induce internalized behavioral suppression in dogs (Black, Solomon & Whiting, 1954; Freedman, 1958). But other investigators have reported that children show more evidence of internalized suppression, or of self-criticism based on the previous criticism of a socializing agent, when they have been punished by a nurturant agent than they do when they have been punished by a relatively neutral agent (Grusec, 1966; Mischel & Grusec, 1966; Parke & Walters, 1967).

There are many reasons to expect that the effectiveness of socializing agents in transmitting both social reward and punishment would be sensitive to a wide range of variation in their nurturant attributes. For example, the child's attentiveness to specific features of a socializing agent's positive or aversive reactions to its behavior may be directly influenced by its past experience of the probability of nurturant interaction with the agent. Or the child's expectation of nurturance may control its overt performance of behavior that was originally acquired through mechanisms of learning which were not in themselves sensitive to its experience of nurturance. In the case of aversive learning, there is the further important consideration that the level of nurturance would establish a context in which punishment would acquire salience and magnitude by contrast, and that the amount of contrast would determine the child's experience of withdrawal of affection (see, for example, Grusec, 1966, and Sears et al., 1957, Ch. 10). But it is inconceivable that all of the internalized products of socialization could be derived from a generalized disposition of the child to reproduce the attributes of socializing agents, which is in turn a singular function of the amount of nurturance that the child has experienced. Such a conception would provide no specification of the distinct mechanisms of internalization for a great variety of different forms of social behavior. Nor would it specify the differential probabilities of occurrence of these forms of behavior in particular stimulus situations. An overly generalized view of the function of nurturance in socialization is especially discrepant with the very large role of punishment and anxiety in establishing the child's internalized aversive control over its behavior, since the punitive behavior of parents is necessarily distinct from their nurturant or affectionate presence. A much more complete account of internalization can be made under the assumption that the nurturance of parents conditions their effectiveness as socializing agents only to the extent that it determines the acquired affective value of many more specific aspects of their behavior, which are crucial to the power of their control over the child's behavior. Under such an assumption, discrete mechanisms of internalization would be attributable to a variety of contingencies and parameters of learning, into which nurturance would enter only as one determinant of the resources of a socializing agent for inducing changes of affective state in the child.

Nurturance and social attachment would have an early and lasting influence on the effectiveness with which parents and other socializing agents can transmit rewarding consequences of the child's behavior. Common observation suggests that direct training through positive social reinforcement is a powerful determinant of certain socially valued forms of conduct—such as, for example, sharing, honesty, and responsibility—which seem to require sustained external support before they come under the control of the child's own internalized monitors. The rudiments of these forms of conduct often occur with fairly high frequency in the behavior of the very young child. They therefore have the advantage of an early history of selective reinforcement. For example, young children often hold out or pass things to their care-taking agents. They may also bring or pick up things which another person may want. And they sometimes actively direct their affection toward other people. Parents and others will tend to reinforce these forerunners of sharing or altruistic behavior. Likewise, certain frequently reinforced early rudiments of honesty can be seen in the child's accurate discrimination between those objects which it may use or touch and those which it may not, or in its verbal self-report on its activities.

In general, child-rearing surveys have not provided very much information about the internalized behavioral consequences of direct parental rewards in the socialization of the child. In a number of studies, the frequency or magnitude of parental reward that is given specifically for independence have been found to be positively correlated with various indices of achievement motivation or performance (Crandall, Preston & Rabson, 1960; McClelland, 1955; Rosen & D'Andrade, 1959; Winterbottom, 1958). In contrast, the more general disposition of parents to reward the child with verbal approval or affection does not appear to show a consistent direction in its relationship to children's honesty or responsibility (Bronfenbrenner, 1961; Burton et al., 1961; Grinder, 1962; Sears et al., 1965, Ch. 6). The contrast between the two sets of findings may be attributable in part to differences between the areas of behavior in the extent to which the effects of positive reinforcement are dependent on the complementary role of punishment. Punishment may be used more intensively on conduct that is relevant to honesty or responsibility than it is in the area of achievement. Some more consistent evidence for the effect of reward on the child's internalized positive control of conduct can be found in the recent studies of Mischel and his co-workers (Mischel, 1966; Mischel & Gilligan, 1964; Mischel & Staub, 1965) on children's regulation of the timing and magnitude of their own rewards. These studies indicate that the ability to delay reward may be a function of the child's past history of social reinforcement for tolerance of delay.

More evidence is available on the child's internalization of aversive control over its behavior through the direct training medium of parental punishment. The parents' use of punishment is ordinarily assessed in the context of a broader variety of external controls over the child's behavior, which are collectively gathered under the heading of discipline. The most common practice is to divide the disciplinary habits of parents into two categories. "Psychological" or "love-oriented" discipline has withdrawal of affection as one of its prototypes, and so includes ignoring or isolating the child, as well as more explicit indicators of rejection, disappointment, or coldness. This first category of discipline is also usually defined to include reasoning, explanation, and verbal disapproval or evaluation of the child's actions. Inquiry into the child's motivation for its actions, and encouragement of its self-corrective reactions, are also sometimes included. The second category of discipline consists of more concrete reactions, which usually result in the direct application of aversive stimulation to the child. It includes physical punishment and direct verbal assaults such as "bawling-out" and "screaming." Ridicule or public shaming are also sometimes included in the second category.

The significant general properties of these two categories of discipline can be usefully summarized, with reference to their impact on the child, when they are respectively subordinated to the concepts of *induction* and *sensitization* (Aronfreed, 1961). These concepts are addressed to the different types of contingencies of learning which are nested in the two broad categories of discipline. The learning contingencies determine the child's internal or external orientation in its management of the anxiety that becomes attached to its potential or committed transgressions. The less directly punitive forms of discipline tend to induce in the child a set of resources which can both intrinsically mediate the child's anxiety and be instrumental in the reduction of anxiety. For example, the anxiety that is elicited in a child by a parent's withdrawal of affection is much less dependent on the parent's continued presence or physical proximity, and is therefore more likely to become internalized, than is the anxiety that can be elicited by physical punishment or by other kinds of increments of concrete noxious stimulation. The effectiveness of social stimulus changes which convey withdrawal of affection is in fact often determined by physical separation from the parent's affectionate presence. Correspondingly, the parent who uses controlled verbal evaluation of the child's actions, as a medium of discipline, expands the child's own cognitive resources for internalized control of its behavior. And if the child is made to focus on the intentions which precede its actions, or is reinforced for self-correction of its behavior, then it is more likely to exercise active control over its own behavior on subsequent occasions, in order to reduce the anxiety that has become associated with incipient or committed transgressions. Induction types of discipline have in common, then, that they tend to make the child's control of its behavior independent of external contingencies. In contrast, disciplinary habits of direct physical and verbal attack may be characterized as sensitization because they tend merely to sensitize the child to the anticipation of punishment. Sensitization discipline reinforces the child for attention to the potential punitive responses of others. But it does not allow the anxiety-reducing value of the child's behavioral suppression, or of its reactions to transgression, to become easily divorced from the control of changes in the external social cues which signal or represent punitive consequences.

Relationships between parental discipline and the child's internalized control of behavior have been found in a number of surveys. The consistency of the findings is most striking for children's reactions to their committed transgressions. The children of parents whose disciplinary habits fall predominantly in the induction category show more internalization in their reactions to transgression than do the children of parents whose disciplinary habits fall predominantly in the sensitization category (W. Allinsmith, 1960; Aronfreed, 1961; Burton et al., 1961; Heinecke, 1953; Hoffman & Saltzstein, 1967; Mac-Kinnon, 1938; Sears et al., 1957, Ch. 10; Whiting & Child, 1953, Ch. 11). The evidence is less consistent on the relationship between parental discipline and the effectiveness of the child's internalized suppression of socially prohibited behavior. A relationship which is parallel to that found for reactions to committed transgressions is fairly clear in surveys which have assessed the child's control over aggressive behavior (B. Allinsmith, 1960; Bandura & Walters, 1959; Glueck & Glueck, 1950; Sears et al., 1957, Ch. 7; Sears, Whiting, Nowlis & Sears, 1953). The findings have been more ambiguous, however, where honesty or obedience have been used as indices of internalization (W. Allinsmith, 1960; Grinder, 1962; Sears et al., 1965, Ch. 6). MacKinnon (1938) did find a substantial positive relationship between the honesty of college students and their parents' use of "psychological" discipline. But Burton et al. (1961) have reported a study of young children in which the findings seem opposite in direction. The inconsistency among these findings may be partially attributable to the fact that recent surveys assess children's cheating or disobedience in situations where a standard of conformity is explicitly conveyed to the child by an external agent, and where there is consequently too high a probability that the child's behavior will be sensitive to its perception of external surveillance or risk of punishment.

The reported relationships between parental discipline and internalized behavioral suppression present a particularly interesting problem of interpretation in the case of the child's control of aggressive behavior. In addition to the studies which are cited above, there are a number of other studies which indicate that the children of parents who use the more physical and direct methods of punishment are themselves more physically aggressive in their relationships with their peers (Becker, Peterson, Luria, Shoemaker & Hellmer, 1962; Eron, Walder, Toigo & Lefkowitz, 1963; Lefkowitz, Walder & Eron, 1963) or in their behavior toward dolls (Levin & Sears, 1956). This entire body of findings is often interpreted as evidence that punishment which is "severe" or intense in magnitude will not be effective in producing internalized suppressive control over aggression. But such an inference is inconsistent with the general literature on punishment learning (Church, 1963; Solomon, 1964). It is also inconsistent with the findings of experiments which clearly demonstrate that children will show more internalized suppression of punished behavior after intense punishment than they will after mild punishment, provided that they can discriminate between punished and nonpunished acts (Aronfreed & Leff, 1963; Parke & Walters, 1967). There is in fact no reason to suppose that physical or direct forms of punishment are more painful or aversive in magnitude to the child than are the forms of punishment which have been placed here in the category of induction discipline. It is quite possible, on the contrary, that withdrawal of affection, which parents often make the focus of induction discipline, may be the most aversive component in the child's experience of any kind of punishment. A more plausible account of why the more "severe" forms of punishment seem to produce poorer internalized control of direct aggression may be found in the different conditions of learning which are embedded in the conceptual distinction between induction and sensitization discipline.

More direct forms of punishment may induce less internalized control of aggression simply because they are more effective in sensitizing the child to external risk of punishment than they are in providing the child with affective and cognitive monitors which are intrinsically associated with its own behavior. This interpretation of the relationship between parental discipline and the child's control of aggression has the advantage of being more broadly applicable to other indices of children's internalized behavioral control, outside of the area of aggression, which are also predictably related to the parents' use of induction or sensitization discipline. It has sometimes been suggested that more direct forms of punishment actually serve as a model for the child's own physical aggression (Bandura & Walters, 1959; Bandura & Walters, 1963b; Miller & Swanson et al., 1960; Sears et al., 1957, Ch. 7). Although it is certainly true that the child's aggressive motivations and behavior may be influenced by its observation of the aggression of other people (Bandura & Walters, 1963a), it is by no means clear as to just how children's typical aggressive actions toward their peers would follow from their observation of the aggression that is evident in their parents' discipline. Moreover, aggression in the context of discipline is not only observed by the child. It is also directed at and experienced by the child. Whatever disposition the child might have to imitate the aggression could therefore hardly be expected to simply negate the aversive and suppressive effects which the aggression would have as a punitive reaction to the child's own aggressive behavior. Since the more aggressive types of discipline are often found to be associated with other kinds of evidence of minimal internalization in the child's control of its conduct—for example, in the child's reactions to its own committed transgressions—it seems more economical to attribute their effects on the child's control of aggression to the same properties of sensitization to external punishment which appear to account for the more general weakness of internal monitors in children who are primarily exposed to such discipline.

The usefulness of the broad distinction between induction and sensitization patterns of discipline can be sharpened somewhat if we look more closely at certain specific components of the punishment learning situation. For example, the findings of a number of studies suggest that the use of reasoning or explanation by parents is in itself positively correlated with evidence of internalized suppression or reactions to transgression in the behavior of their children (W. Allinsmith, 1960; Bandura & Walters, 1959; Burton et al., 1961; Sears et al., 1957, Ch. 10; Sears, et al., 1965, Ch. 6). The findings of other studies indicate that the children of parents whose disciplinary habits are induction-oriented tend to show a more complex and abstract orientation toward principles of conscience, when they are asked to verbally express and apply their evaluative standards to specific actions, than do the children of parents whose disciplinary habits are sensitization-oriented (Hoffman & Saltzstein, 1967; Kohlberg, 1969). Both of these sets of findings would support the inference that the verbal context of induction discipline gives the child representational and evaluative cognitive equipment which tends to free its behavior from the control of concrete indicators of rewarding and punitive consequences.

The contingencies under which withdrawal of affection is often experienced by children may also make a special contribution to the more effective internalization that is produced by induction discipline. Although loss of affection may be the most generally effective component of any form of punishment, parents who prolong their withdrawal of affection, or focus their child's attention on it, may also regulate their punitive reactions in ways which give the child some control over their behavior and its own anxiety. For example, they may tend to reinstate their affection only after the child has activated its own resources to evaluate, arrest, or correct its transgressions. In contrast, sensitization discipline would tend to make external punishment or absence of punishment, rather than any act of the child, the event that marks the resolution of a transgression. The results of one survey (Aronfreed, 1961) have shown that children's internalized self-corrective dispositions, in reacting to their own transgressions, are positively associated with their mothers' use of induction discipline; whereas their dispositions to perceive the resolution of transgression in external punitive events are associated with their mothers' use of sensitization discipline. Some findings from the recent study by Hoffman and Saltzstein (1967) more specifically suggest that withdrawal of affection in itself is not as effective in producing internalization of the child's corrective reactions to its transgressions as are the parents' attempts to induce the child to reinstate their affection by exercising active control over its conduct.

There are also some other important differences between the temporal contingencies which characterize induction and sensitization discipline. The central place of reinstatement of affection, as a reinforcement contingency within induction discipline, would tend to maintain the cognitive and affective salience of a transgression for the child, and to elicit anxiety of greater and more uncertain duration than the anxiety that would be elicited by more direct and quickly terminated punishments. A more prolonged and variable period of anxiety would increase the probability that the child would actively attempt to reduce the anxiety rather than wait upon external events. Moreover, parents who use a preponderance of induction discipline may also be more inclined to punish their children long after the occurrence of a transgression that was not immediately known to them. In contrast, sensitization discipline tends to expose the child to aversive stimulation that is more narrowly focused in time. And parents who are disposed to use sensitization discipline may be more likely to react concretely only to transgressions which occur in their immediate presence. Sensitization discipline might therefore have the effect of sharply limiting the length of time during which the child would continue to experience anxiety after its commission of a transgression that was not under direct surveillance.

REFERENCES

ALLEN, V. L., & CRUTCHFIELD, R. S. Generalization of experimentally induced conformity. *Journal of Abnormal and Social Psychology,* 1963, 67, 326–333.

ALLINSMITH, BEVERLY B. Directness with which anger is expressed. In D. R. Miller, G. E. Swanson, et al., *Inner conflict and defense.* New York: Holt, 1960. Pp. 315–336.

ALLINSMITH, W. The learning of moral standards. In D. R. Miller, G. E. Swanson, et al., *Inner conflict and defense.* New York: Holt, 1960. Pp. 141–176.

ALLPORT, F. H. *Social psychology.* Cambridge, Mass.: Houghton Mifflin, The Riverside Press, 1924.

ALLPORT, G. W. The historical background of modern social psychology. In G. Lindzey (Ed.), *Handbook of social psychology.* Vol. 1. Cambridge, Mass.: Addison-Wesley, 1954. Pp. 3–56.

AMSEL, A., & WARD, J. S. Frustration and persistence: Resistance to discrimination following prior experience with the discriminanda. *Psychological Monographs,* 1965, 79, No. 4 (Whole No. 597).

ARGYLE, M. Social pressure in public and private situations. *Journal of Abnormal and Social Psychology,* 1957, 54, 172–175.

ARONFREED, J. The nature, variety, and social patterning of moral responses to transgression. *Journal of Abnormal and Social Psychology,* 1961, 63, 223–240.

ARONFREED, J. The effects of experimental socialization paradigms upon two moral responses to transgression. *Journal of Abnormal and Social Psychology,* 1963, 66, 437–448.

ARONFREED, J. The origin of self-criticism. *Psychological Review,* 1964, 71, 193–218.

ARONFREED, J. The internalization of social control through punishment: Experimental studies of the role of conditioning and the second signal system in the development of conscience. *Proceedings of the XVIIIth International Congress of Psychology.* Moscow, USSR, August, 1966.

ARONFREED, J. *Conduct and conscience: The socialization of internalized control over behavior.* New York: Academic Press, 1968, in press.

ARONFREED, J., CUTICK, R. A., & FAGEN, S. A. Cognitive structure, punishment, and nurturance in the experimental induction of self-criticism. *Child Development,* 1963, 34, 281–294.

ARONFREED, J., & LEFF, R. The effects of intensity of punishment and complexity of discrimination upon the learning of internalized suppression. Unpublished manuscript. University of Pennsylvania, 1963.

ARONFREED, J., & PASKAL, VIVIAN. Altruism, empathy, and the conditioning of positive affect. Unpublished manuscript. University of Pennsylvania, 1965.

ARONFREED, J., & PASKAL, VIVIAN. The development of sympathetic behavior in children: An experimental test of a two-phase hypothesis. Unpublished manuscript. University of Pennsylvania, 1966.

ARONFREED, J., & REBER, A. Internalized behavioral suppression and the timing of social punishment. *Journal of Personality and Social Psychology,* 1965, 1, 3–16.

ASCH, S. E. Studies of independence and conformity: I. A minority of one against a unanimous majority. *Psychological Monographs,* 1956, 70, No. 9 (Whole No. 416).

AUSUBEL, D. P. Relationships between shame and guilt in the socializing process. *Psychological Review,* 1955, 62, 378–390.

AZRIN, N. H., & LINDSLEY, O. R. The reinforcement of cooperation between children. *Journal of Abnormal and Social Psychology,* 1956, 52, 100–102.

BACON, MARGARET K., CHILD, I. L., & BARRY, H., III. A cross-cultural study of some correlates of crime. *Journal of Abnormal and Social Psychology,* 1963, 66, 291–300.

BAER, D. M., & SHERMAN, J. A. Reinforcement control of generalized imitation in young children. *Journal of Experimental Child Psychology,* 1964, 1, 37–49.

BANDURA, A. Social learning through imitation. In M. R. Jones (Ed.), *Nebraska symposium on motivation.* Vol. X. Lincoln, Neb.: Univer. of Nebraska Press, 1962. Pp. 211–269.

BANDURA, A. Influence of models' reinforcement contingencies on the acquisition of imitative responses. *Journal of Personality and Social Psychology,* 1965, 1, 589–595. (a)

BANDURA, A. Vicarious processes: A case of no-trial learning. In L. Berkowitz (Ed.), *Advances in experimental social psychology.* Vol. II. New York: Academic Press, 1965. Pp. 1–55. (b)

BANDURA, A., GRUSEC, JOAN E., & MENLOVE, FRANCES L. Observational learning as a function of symbolization and incentive set. *Child Development,* 1966, 37, 499–506.

BANDURA, A., GRUSEC, JOAN E., & MENLOVE, FRANCES L. Vicarious extinction of avoidance behavior. *Journal of Personality and Social Psychology,* 1967, 5, 16–23.

BANDURA, A., & HUSTON, ALETHA C. Identification as a process of incidental learning. *Journal of Abnormal and Social Psychology,* 1961, 63, 311–318.

BANDURA, A., & KUPERS, CAROL J. The transmission of patterns of self-reinforcement through modeling. *Journal of Abnormal and Social Psychology,* 1964, 69, 1–9.

BANDURA, A., & McDONALD, F. J. The influence of social reinforcement and the behavior of models in shaping children's moral judgments. *Journal of Abnormal and Social Psychology,* 1963, 67, 274–281.

BANDURA, A., & MISCHEL, W. Modification of self-imposed delay of reward through exposure to live and symbolic models. *Journal of Personality and Social Psychology,* 1965, 2, 698–705.

BANDURA, A., & ROSENTHAL, T. L. Vicarious classical conditioning as a function of arousal level. *Journal of Personality and Social Psychology,* 1966, 3, 54–62.

BANDURA, A., ROSS, DOROTHEA, & ROSS, SHEILA A. Transmission of aggression through imitation of aggressive models. *Journal of Abnormal and Social Psychology,* 1961, 63, 575–582.

BANDURA, A., ROSS, DOROTHEA, & ROSS, SHEILA A. Imitation of film-mediated aggressive models. *Journal of Abnormal and Social Psychology,* 1963, 66, 3–11. (a)

BANDURA, A., ROSS, DOROTHEA, & ROSS, SHEILA A. A comparative test of the status envy, social power, and secondary reinforcement theories of identificatory learning. *Journal of Abnormal and Social Psychology,* 1963, 67, 527–534. (b)

BANDURA, A., ROSS, DOROTHEA, & ROSS, SHEILA A. Vicarious reinforcement and imitative learning. *Journal of Abnormal and Social Psychology,* 1963, 67, 601–607. (c)

BANDURA, A., & WALTERS, R. H. *Adolescent aggression.* New York: Ronald, 1959.

BANDURA, A., & WALTERS, R. H. *Social learning and personality development.* New York: Holt, Rinehart & Winston, 1963. (a)

BANDURA, A., & WALTERS, R. H. Aggression. In H. W. Stevenson (Ed.), *Yearbook of the National Society for the Study of Education.* Part I. *Child psychology.* Chicago: Univer. of Chicago Press, 1963. Pp. 364–415. (b)

BANDURA, A., & WHALEN, CAROL K. The influence of antecedent reinforcement and divergent modeling cues on patterns of self-reward. *Journal of Personality and Social Psychology,* 1966, 3, 373–382.

BAYROFF, A. G., & LARD, KATHERINE E. Experimental social behavior of animals. III. Imitational learning of white rats. *Journal of Comparative Psychology,* 1944, 37, 165–171.

BECK, R. C. On secondary reinforcement and shock termination. *Psychological Bulletin,* 1961, 58, 28–45.

BECKER, W. C., PETERSON, D. R., LURIA, ZELLA, SHOEMAKER, D. J., & HELLMER, L. A. Relations of factors derived from parent-interview ratings to behavior problems of five-year-olds. *Child Development,* 1962, 33, 509–535.

BERGER, S. M. Conditioning through vicarious instigation. *Psychological Review,* 1962, 69, 450–466.

BERKOWITZ, L., & DANIELS, LOUISE R. Affecting the salience of the social responsibility norm: Effects of past help on the response to dependency relationships. *Journal of Abnormal and Social Psychology,* 1964, 68, 275–281.

BERKOWITZ, L., & FRIEDMAN, P. Some social class differences in helping behavior. *Journal of Personality and Social Psychology,* 1967, 5, 217–225.

BERKOWITZ, L., & GEEN, R. G. Film violence and the cue properties of available targets. *Journal of Personality and Social Psychology,* 1966, 3, 525–530.

BETTELHEIM, B. Individual and mass behavior in extreme situations. *Journal of Abnormal and Social Psychology,* 1943, 38, 417–452.

BLACK, A. H., SOLOMON, R. L., & WHITING, J. W. M. Resistance to temptation as a function of antecedent dependency relationships in puppies. *American Psychologist,* 1954, 9, 579. (Abstract)

BOEHM, LEONORE. The development of conscience: A comparison of American children of different mental and socioeconomic levels. *Child Development,* 1962, 33, 575–590.

BOREN, J. J. An experimental social relation between two monkeys. *Journal of the Experimental Analysis of Behavior,* 1966, 9, 691–700.

BOWLBY, J. *Forty-four juvenile thieves: Their characters and home life.* London: Baldiere, Tindall, & Cox, 1947.

BROGDEN, H. E. A factor analysis of 40 character traits. *Psychological Monographs,* 1940, 52, No. 3 (Whole No. 234).

BRONFENBRENNER, U. Freudian theories of identification and their derivatives. *Child Development,* 1960, 31, 15–40.

BRONFENBRENNER, U. Some familial antecedents of responsibility and leadership in adolescents. In L. Petrullo & B. M. Bass (Eds.), *Leadership and interpersonal behavior.* New York: Holt, Rinehart & Winston, 1961. Pp. 239–272.

BROWN, J. S. A behavioral analysis of masochism. *Journal of Experimental Research in Personality,* 1965, 1, 65–70.

BROWN, J. S., MARTIN, R. C., & MORROW, M. W. Self-punitive behavior in the rat: Facilitative effects of punishment on resistance to extinction. *Journal of Comparative and Physiological Psychology,* 1964, 57, 127–133.

BRUNING, J. L. Direct and vicarious effects of a shift in magnitude of reward on performance. *Journal of Personality and Social Psychology,* 1965, 2, 278–282.

BURTON, R. V., MACCOBY, ELEANOR E., & ALLINSMITH, W. Antecedents of resistance to temptation in four-year-old children. *Child Development,* 1961, 32, 689–710.

BUSS, A. H. Instrumentality of aggression, feedback, and frustration as determinants of physical aggression. *Journal of Personality and Social Psychology,* 1966, 3, 153–162.

CAIRNS, R. B. Attachment behavior of mammals. *Psychological Review,* 1966, 73, 409–426.

CAIRNS, R. B., & JOHNSON, D. L. The development of interspecies social attachments. *Psychonomic Science,* 1965, 2, 337–338.

CAMPBELL, B. A., SMITH, N. F., & MISANIN, J. R. Effects of punishment on extinction of avoidance behavior: Avoidance-avoidance conflict or vicious circle behavior. *Journal of Comparative and Physiological Psychology,* 1966, 62, 495–498.

CHURCH, R. M. Transmission of learned behavior between rats. *Journal of Abnormal and Social Psychology,* 1957, 54, 163–165.

CHURCH, R. M. Emotional reactions of rats to the pain of others. *Journal of Comparative and Physiological Psychology,* 1959, 52, 132–134.

CHURCH, R. M. The varied effects of punishment on behavior. *Psychological Review,* 1963, 70, 369–402.

CRANDALL, V., PRESTON, ANNE, & RABSON, ALICE. Maternal reactions and the development of independence and achievement behavior in young children. *Child Development,* 1960, 31, 243–251.

DENENBERG, V. H., HUDGENS, G. A., & ZARROW, M. X. Mice reared with rats: Modification of behavior by early experience with another species. *Science,* 1964, 143, 380–381.

DiLOLLO, V., & BERGER, S. M. Effects of apparent pain in others on observer's reaction time. *Journal of Personality and Social Psychology,* 1965, 2, 573–575.

DINSMOOR, J. A., & CLAYTON, MARILYN H. A conditioned reinforcer maintained by temporal association with the termination of shock. *Journal of the Experimental Analysis of Behavior,* 1966, 9, 547–552.

DUNCKER, K. Experimental modification of children's food preferences through social suggestion. *Journal of Abnormal and Social Psychology,* 1938, 33, 489–507.

DURKHEIM, E. *Suicide.* Glencoe, Ill.: Free Press, 1951.

ENDLER, N. S. Conformity as a function of different reinforcement schedules. *Journal of Personality and Social Psychology,* 1966, 4, 175–180.

ERON, L. D., WALDER, L. O., TOIGO, R., & LEFKOWITZ, M. M. Social class, parental punishment for aggression, and child aggression. *Child Development,* 1963, 34, 849–867.

ESTES, W. K. An experimental study of punishment. *Psychological Monographs,* 1944, 57, No. 3 (Whole No. 263).

FARBER, I. E. Response fixation under anxiety and non-anxiety conditions. *Journal of Experimental Psychology,* 1948, 38, 111–131.

FERSTER, C. B., & SKINNER, B. F. *Schedules of reinforcement.* New York: Appleton-Century-Crofts, 1957.

FESHBACH, S. The stimulating versus cathartic effects of a vicarious aggressive activity. *Journal of Abnormal and Social Psychology,* 1961, 63, 381–385.

FISCHER, W. F. Sharing in preschool children as a function of amount and type of reinforcement. *Genetic Psychology Monographs,* 1963, 68, 215–245.

FREEDMAN, D. G. Constitutional and environmental interactions in rearing of four breeds of dogs. *Science,* 1958, 127, 585–586.

FREUD, ANNA, & DANN, SOPHIE. An experiment in group upbringing. In *The psychoanalytic study of the child.* Vol. VI. New York: Intern. Univer. Press, 1951. Pp. 127–168.

FREUD, S. *New introductory lectures in psychoanalysis.* New York: Norton, 1933.

GERARD, H. B. Conformity and commitment to the group. *Journal of Abnormal and Social Psychology,* 1964, 68, 209–211.

GLUECK, S., & GLUECK, ELEANOR. *Unravelling juvenile delinquency.* New York: Commonwealth Fund, 1950.

GOLDFARB, W. Psychological privation in infancy and subsequent adjustment. *American Journal of Orthopsychiatry,* 1945, 15, 247–255.

GORANSON, R. E., & BERKOWITZ, L. Reciprocity and responsibility reactions to prior help. *Journal of Personality and Social Psychology,* 1966, 3, 227–232.

GRINDER, R. E. Parental child rearing practices, conscience, and resistance to temptation of sixth-grade children. *Child Development,* 1962, 33, 803–820.

GRINDER, R. E. Relations between behavioral and cognitive dimensions of conscience in middle childhood. *Child Development,* 1964, 35, 881–891.

GRUSEC, JOAN. Some antecedents of self-criticism. *Journal of Personality and Social Psychology,* 1966, 4, 244–252.

GRUSEC, JOAN, & MISCHEL, W. Model's characteristics as determinants of social learning. *Journal of Personality and Social Psychology,* 1966, 4, 211–215.

GWINN, G. T. The effects of punishment on acts motivated by fear. *Journal of Experimental Psychology,* 1949, 39, 260–269.

HANDLON, BRITOMAR J., & GROSS, PATRICIA. The development of sharing behavior. *Journal of Abnormal and Social Psychology,* 1959, 59, 425–428.

HANER, C. F., & WHITNEY, E. R. Empathic conditioning and its relation to anxiety level. *American Psychologist,* 1960, 15, 493. (Abstract)

HARLOW, H. F., & HARLOW, MARGARET K. The affectional systems. In A. M. Schrier, H. F. Harlow, & F. Stollnitz (Eds.), *Behavior of nonhuman primates: Modern research trends.* Vol. II. New York: Academic Press, 1965. Pp. 287–334.

HARTSHORNE, H., & MAY, M. A. *Studies in the nature of character.* Vol. I. *Studies in deceit.* New York: Macmillan, 1928.

HARTSHORNE, H., MAY, M. A., & MALLER, J. B. *Studies in the nature of character.* Vol. II. *Studies in service and self-control.* New York: Macmillan, 1929.

HEINECKE, C. M. Some antecedents and correlates of guilt and fear in young boys. Unpublished doctoral dissertation, Harvard University, 1953.

HICKS, D. J. Imitation and retention of film-mediated aggressive peer and adult models. *Journal of Personality and Social Psychology,* 1965, 2, 97–100.

HILL, W. F. Learning theory and the acquisition of values. *Psychological Review,* 1960, 67, 317–331.

HOFFMAN, M. L. Child-rearing practices and moral development: Generalizations from empirical research. *Child Development,* 1963, 34, 295–318.

HOFFMAN, M. L. *Early processes in moral development.* Chicago: Aldine, 1968, in press.

HOFFMAN, M. L., & SALTZSTEIN, H. D. Parent discipline and the child's moral development. *Journal of Personality and Social Psychology,* 1967, 5, 45–57.

HOLT, E. B. *Animal drive and the learning process.* Vol. I. New York: Holt, 1931.

HOREL, J. A., TREICHLER, F. R., & MEYER, D. R. Coercive behavior in the rhesus monkey. *Journal of Comparative and Physiological Psychology,* 1963, 56, 208–210.

HUMPHREY, G. Imitation and the conditioned reflex. *Pedagogical Seminary,* 1921, 28, 1–21.

HUMPHREY, G. The conditioned reflex and the elementary social reaction. *Journal of Abnormal and Social Psychology,* 1922, 17, 113–119.

ISAACS, SUSAN. *Social development in young children.* London, Routledge, 1933.

JACOBS, R. C., & CAMPBELL, D. T. The perpetuation of an arbitrary tradition through several generations of a laboratory micro-culture. *Journal of Abnormal and Social Psychology,* 1961, 62, 649–658.

JENKINS, W. O. A temporal gradient of derived reinforcement. *American Journal of Psychology,* 1950, 63, 237–243.

JONES, MARY C. Elimination of fears in children. *Journal of Experimental Psychology,* 1924, 7, 382–390.

KAMIN, L. J. The delay-of-punishment gradient. *Journal of Comparative and Physiological Psychology,* 1959, 52, 434–436.

KANFER, F. H. Vicarious human reinforcements: A glimpse into the black box. In L. Krasner & L. P. Ullman (Eds.), *Research in behavior modification: New developments and implications.* New York: Holt, Rinehart & Winston, 1965. Pp. 244–267.

KANFER, F. H., BRADLEY, MARCIA M., & MARSTON, A. R. Self-reinforcement as a function of degree of learning. *Psychological Reports,* 1962, 10, 885–886.

KANFER, F. H., & MARSTON, A. R. Human reinforcement: Vicarious and direct. *Journal of Experimental Psychology,* 1963, 65, 292–296. (a)

KANFER, F. H., & MARSTON, A. R. Determinants of self-reinforcement in human learning. *Journal of Experimental Psychology,* 1963, 66, 245–254. (b)

KELLEY, H. H., THIBAUT, J. W., RADLOFF, R., & MUNDY, D. The development of cooperation in the "minimal social situation." *Psychological Monographs,* 1962, 76, No. 19 (Whole No. 538).

KELMAN, H. C. Compliance, identification, and internalization: Three processes in attitude change. *Journal of Conflict Resolution,* 1958, 2, 51–60.

KIMBRELL, D. L., & BLAKE, R. R. Motivational factors in the violation of a prohibition. *Journal of Abnormal and Social Psychology,* 1958, 56, 132–133.

KOBASIGAWA, A. Observation of failure in another person as a determinant of amplitude and speed of a simple motor response. *Journal of Personality and Social Psychology,* 1965, 1, 626–630.

KOHLBERG, L. The development of children's orientations toward a moral order. I. Sequence in the development of moral thought. *Vita Humana,* 1963, 6, 11–33.

KOHLBERG, L. Development of moral character and moral ideology. In M. L. Hoffman & Lois W. Hoffman (Eds.), *Review of child development research.* Vol. I. New York: Russell Sage Foundation, 1964. Pp. 383–431.

KOHLBERG, L. *Stage and sequence: The developmental approach to moralization.* (Tentative title) New York: Holt, Rinehart & Winston, 1969 (in press).

KUO, Z. Y. Studies on the basic factors in animal fighting: VII. Inter-species coexistence in mammals. *Journal of Genetic Psychology,* 1960, 97, 211–225.

LAVERY, J. J., & FOLEY, P. J. Altruism or arousal in the rat? *Science,* 1963, 140, 172–173.

LAZARUS, R. S., SPEISMAN, J. C., MORDKOFF, A. M., & DAVISON, L. A. A laboratory study of psychological stress produced by a motion picture film. *Psychological Monographs,* 1962, 76, No. 34 (Whole No. 553).

LEFKOWITZ, M., BLAKE, R. R., & MOUTON, JANE S. Status factors in pedestrian violation of traffic signals. *Journal of Abnormal and Social Psychology,* 1955, 51, 704–705.

LEFKOWITZ, M. M., WALDER, L. O., & ERON, L. D. Punishment, identification, and aggression. *Merrill-Palmer Quarterly,* 1963, 9, 159–174.

LENROW, P. B. Studies of sympathy. In S. S. Tomkins & C. E. Izard (Eds.), *Affect, cognition, and personality: Empirical studies.* New York: Springer, 1965. Pp. 264–294.

LERNER, E. *Constraint areas and the moral judgment of children.* Menasha, Wisc.: George Banta Publ. Co., 1937.

LEVIN, H., & SEARS, R. R. Identification with parents as a determinant of doll play aggression. *Child Development,* 1956, 27, 136–153.

LEWIS, D. J., & DUNCAN, C. P. Vicarious experience and partial reinforcement. *Journal of Abnormal and Social Psychology,* 1958, 57, 321–326.

LOGAN, F., OLMSTED, D. L., ROSNER, B. S., SCHWARTZ, R. D., & STEVENS, C. M. *Behavior theory and social science.* New Haven: Yale Univer. Press, 1955.

LOVAAS, O. I., FREITAG, G., KINDER, M. I., RUBENSTEIN, B. D., SCHAEFFER, B., & SIMMONS, J. G. Establishment of social reinforcers in two schizophrenic children on the basis of food. *Journal of Experimental Child Psychology,* 1966, 4, 109–125.

MACCOBY, ELEANOR E. Role-taking in childhood and its consequences for social learning. *Child Development,* 1959, 30, 239–252.

MACKINNON, D. W. Violation of prohibitions. In H. A. Murray, et al., *Explorations in personality.* New York: Oxford Univer. Press, 1938. Pp. 491–501.

MACRAE, D., JR. A test of Piaget's theories of moral development. *Journal of Abnormal and Social Psychology,* 1954, 49, 14–18.

MAIER, N. R. F. *Frustration: The study of behavior without a goal.* New York: McGraw-Hill, 1949.

MARSTON, A. R. Imitation, self-reinforcement, and reinforcement of another person. *Journal of Personality and Social Psychology,* 1965, 2, 255–261.

MARSTON, A. R. Determinants of the effects of vicarious reinforcement. *Journal of Experimental Psychology,* 1966, 71, 550–558.

MARSTON, A. R., & KANFER, F. H. Human reinforcement: Experimenter and subject controlled. *Journal of Experimental Psychology,* 1963, 66, 91–94.

MASON, W. A. Development of communication between young rhesus monkeys. *Science,* 1959, 130, 712–713.

MASSERMAN, J. H., WECHKIN, S., & TERRIS, W., JR. "Altruistic" behavior in rhesus monkeys. *American Journal of Psychiatry,* 1964, 121, 584–585.

McCLELLAND, D. C. Some social consequences of achievement motivation. In M. R. Jones (Ed.), *Nebraska symposium on motivation.* Vol. III. Lincoln, Neb.: Univer. of Nebraska Press, 1955. Pp. 41–65.

McCORD, JOAN, McCORD, W., & HOWARD, A. Family interaction as antecedent to the direction of male aggressiveness. *Journal of Abnormal and Social Psychology,* 1963, 66, 239–242.

McDOUGALL, W. *An introduction to social psychology.* London: Methuen, 1908.

MEDINNUS, G. R. Behavioral and cognitive measures of conscience development. *Journal of Genetic Psychology,* 1966, 109, 147–150.

MILGRAM, S. Behavioral study of obedience. *Journal of Abnormal and Social Psychology,* 1963, 67, 371–378.

MILGRAM, S. Group pressure and action against a person. *Journal of Abnormal and Social Psychology,* 1964, 69, 137–143.

MILLER, D. R., SWANSON, G. E., et al. *Inner conflict and defense.* New York: Holt, 1960.

MILLER, N. Acquisition of avoidance dispositions by social learning. *Journal of Abnormal and Social Psychology,* 1961, 63, 12–19.

MILLER, N. E. Liberalization of basic S-R concepts: Extensions to conflict behavior, motivation, and social learning. In S. Koch (Ed.), *Psychology: A study of a science.* Vol. II. *General systematic formulations, learning, and special processes.* New York: McGraw-Hill, 1959. Pp. 196–292.

MILLER, N. E., & DOLLARD, J. *Social learning and imitation.* New Haven: Yale Univer. Press, 1941.

MILLER, R. E., BANKS, J. H., & OGAWA, N. Role of facial expression in "cooperative-avoidance conditioning" in monkeys. *Journal of Abnormal and Social Psychology,* 1963, 67, 24–30.

MISCHEL, W. Theory and research on the antecedents of self-imposed delay of reward. In B. A. Maher (Ed.), *Progress in experimental personality research.* Vol. III. New York: Academic Press, 1966. Pp. 85–132.

MISCHEL, W., & GILLIGAN, CAROL. Delay of gratification, motivation for the prohibited gratification, and responses to temptation. *Journal of Abnormal and Social Psychology,* 1964, 69, 411–417.

MISCHEL, W., & GRUSEC, JOAN. Determinants of the rehearsal and transmission of neutral and aversive behaviors. *Journal of Personality and Social Psychology,* 1966, 3, 197–205.

MISCHEL, W., & LIEBERT, R. M. Effects of discrepancies between observed and imposed reward criteria on their acquisition and transmission. *Journal of Personality and Social Psychology,* 1966, 3, 45–53.

MISCHEL, W., & STAUB, E. The effects of expectancy on working and waiting for larger rewards. *Journal of Personality and Social Psychology,* 1965, 2, 625–633.

MOWRER, O. H. *Learning theory and personality dynamics.* New York: Ronald, 1950.

MOWRER, O. H. *Learning theory and behavior.* New York: Wiley, 1960. (a)

MOWRER, O. H. *Learning theory and the symbolic processes.* New York: Wiley, 1960. (b)

MURPHY, LOIS B. *Social behavior and child personality: An exploratory study of some roots of sympathy.* New York: Columbia Univer. Press, 1937.

MUSSEN, P., & DISTLER, L. M. Masculinity, identification, and father-son relationships. *Journal of Abnormal and Social Psychology,* 1959, 59, 350–356.

MUSSEN, P., & PARKER, ANN L. Mother nurturance and girls' incidental imitative learning. *Journal of Personality and Social Psychology,* 1965, 2, 94–97.

MUSSEN, P., & RUTHERFORD, E. Parent-child relations and parental personality in relation to young children's sex role preferences. *Child Development,* 1963, 34, 589–608.

MYERS, J. L. Secondary reinforcement: A review of recent experimentation. *Psychological Bulletin,* 1958, 55, 284–301.

NEWCOMB, T. M. *Social psychology.* New York: Dryden, 1950.

NISSEN, H. W., & CRAWFORD, M. P. A preliminary study of food-sharing behavior in young chimpanzees. *Journal of Comparative Psychology,* 1936, 22, 383–419.

O'Connell, E. J., Jr. The effect of cooperative and competitive set on the learning of imitation and nonimitation. *Journal of Experimental Social Psychology,* 1965, 1, 172–183.

Parke, R. D., & Walters, R. H. Some factors influencing the efficacy of punishment training for inducing response inhibition. *Monographs of the Society for Research in Child Development,* 1967, 32, No. 1 (Serial No. 109).

Parsons, T., Bales, R. F., et al. *Family, socialization and interaction process.* Glencoe, Ill.: Free Press, 1955.

Penney, R. Children's escape performance as a function of schedules of delay of reinforcement. *Journal of Experimental Psychology,* 1967, 73, 109–112.

Piaget, J. *The moral judgment of the child.* Glencoe, Ill.: Free Press, 1948.

Piaget, J. *Play, dreams, and imitation in childhood.* New York: Norton, 1951.

Rescorla, R. A., & LoLordo, V. M. Inhibition of avoidance behavior. *Journal of Comparative and Physiological Psychology,* 1965, 59, 406–412.

Rice, G. E., & Gainer, Priscilla. "Altruism" in the albino rat. *Journal of Comparative and Physiological Psychology,* 1962, 55, 123–125.

Rosen, B., & D'Andrade, R. The psychosexual origins of achievement motivation. *Sociometry,* 1959, 22, 185–218.

Rosenbaum, M. E., & deCharms, R. Direct and vicarious reduction of hostility. *Journal of Abnormal and Social Psychology,* 1960, 60, 105–111.

Rosenhan, D., & White, G. M. Observation and rehearsal as determinants of prosocial behavior. *Journal of Personality and Social Psychology,* 1967, 5, 424–431.

Rotter, J. B. Generalized expectancies for internal vs. external control of reinforcement. *Psychological Monographs,* 1966, 80, No. 1 (Whole No. 609).

Schachter, S. The interaction of cognitive and physiological determinants of emotional state. In L. Berkowitz (Ed.), *Advances in experimental social psychology.* Vol. I. New York: Academic Press, 1964. Pp. 49–80.

Schein, E. H. Reaction patterns to severe, chronic stress in American Army prisoners of war of the Chinese. *Journal of Social Issues,* 1957, 13, 21–30.

Schopler, J., & Bateson, N. The power of dependence. *Journal of Personality and Social Psychology,* 1965, 2, 247–254.

Schopler, J., & Matthews, Marjorie W. The influence of the perceived causal locus of partner's dependence on the use of interpersonal power. *Journal of Personality and Social Psychology,* 1965, 2, 609–612.

Sears, P. S. Child-rearing factors related to playing of sex-typed roles. *American Psychologist,* 1953, 8, 431. (Abstract)

Sears, R. R., Maccoby, Eleanor E., & Levin, H. *Patterns of child rearing.* Evanston, Ill.: Row, Peterson, 1957.

Sears, R. R., Rau, Lucy, & Alpert, R. *Identification and child training.* Stanford, Calif.: Stanford Univer. Press, 1965.

Sears, R. R., Whiting, J. W. M., Nowlis, V., & Sears, P. S. Some child-rearing antecedents of aggression and dependency in young children. *Genetic Psychology Monographs,* 1953, 47, 135–234.

Sgan, Mabel L. Social reinforcement, socioeconomic status, and susceptibility to experimenter influence. *Journal of Personality and Social Psychology,* 1967, 5, 202–210.

Sheffield, F. D. Theoretical considerations in the learning of complex sequential tasks from demonstration and practice. In A. A. Lumsdaine (Ed.), *Student response in programmed instruction: A symposium.* Washington, D.C.: National Academy of Sciences–National Research Council, 1961. Pp. 13–32.

SIDMAN, M. On the persistence of avoidance behavior. *Journal of Abnormal and Social Psychology,* 1955, 50, 217–220.

SIDOWSKI, J. B., WYCKOFF, B., & TABORY, L. The influence of reinforcement and punishment in a minimal social situation. *Journal of Abnormal and Social Psychology,* 1956, 52, 115–119.

SKINNER, B. F. *Science and human behavior.* New York: Macmillan, 1953.

SOLOMON, R. L. Punishment. *American Psychologist,* 1964, 19, 239–253.

SOLOMON, R. L., & BRUSH, ELINOR S. Experimentally derived conceptions of anxiety and aversion. In M. R. Jones (Ed.), *Nebraska symposium on motivation.* Vol. IV. Lincoln, Neb.: Univer. of Nebraska Press, 1956. Pp. 212–305.

SOLOMON, R. L., KAMIN, L. J., & WYNNE, L. C. Traumatic avoidance learning: The outcomes of several extinction procedures with dogs. *Journal of Abnormal and Social Psychology,* 1953, 48, 291–302.

SOLOMON, R. L., & TURNER, LUCILLE H. Discriminative classical conditioning in dogs can later control discriminative avoidance responses in the normal state. *Psychological Review,* 1962, 69, 202–219.

SOLOMON, R. L., & WYNNE, L. C. Traumatic avoidance learning: The principles of anxiety conservation and partial irreversibility. *Psychological Review,* 1954, 61, 353–385.

STEIN, ALETHA H., & WRIGHT, J. C. Imitative learning under conditions of nurturance and nurturance withdrawal. *Child Development,* 1964, 35, 927–938.

STEIN, L. Secondary reinforcement established with subcortical stimulation. *Science,* 1958, 127, 466–467.

STEVENSON, H. W. Social reinforcement of children's behavior. In L. P. Lipsitt & C. C. Spiker (Eds.), *Advances in child development and behavior.* Vol. II. New York: Academic Press, 1965. Pp. 97–126.

STONE, W. F. Autokinetic norms: An experimental analysis. *Journal of Personality and Social Psychology,* 1967, 5, 76–81.

TERMAN, L. M., ET AL. *Genetic studies of genius.* Vol. I. *Mental and physical traits of a thousand gifted children.* Stanford, Calif.: Stanford Univer. Press, 1925.

THIBAUT, J. W., & KELLEY, H. H. *The social psychology of groups.* New York: Wiley, 1959.

TURNER, W. D. Altruism and its measurement in children. *Journal of Abnormal and Social Psychology,* 1948, 43, 502–516.

UGUREL-SEMIN, R. Moral behavior and moral judgment of children. *Journal of Abnormal and Social Psychology,* 1952, 47, 463–474.

VYGOTSKY, L. S. *Thought and language.* Cambridge, Mass.: M.I.T. Press, 1962.

WALTERS, R. H. Delay of reinforcement gradients in children's learning. *Psychonomic Science,* 1964, 1, 307–308.

WALTERS, R. H., BOWEN, NORMA V., & PARKE, R. D. Influence of looking behavior of a social model on subsequent looking behavior of observers of the model. *Perceptual and Motor Skills,* 1964, 18, 469–483.

WALTERS, R. H., & DEMKOW, LILLIAN. Timing of punishment as a determinant of response inhibition. *Child Development,* 1963, 34, 207–214.

WALTERS, R. H., LEAT, MARION, & MEZEI, L. Inhibition and disinhibition of responses through empathetic learning. *Canadian Journal of Psychology,* 1963, 17, 235–243.

WALTERS, R. H., & PARKE, R. D. Influence of response consequences to a social model on resistance to deviation. *Journal of Experimental Child Psychology,* 1964, 1, 269–280.

WALTERS, R. H., & PARKE, R. D. The influence of punishment and related disciplinary techniques on the social behavior of children: Theory and experimental findings. In B. A. Maher (Ed.), *Progress in experimental personality research.* Volume IV. New York: Academic Press, 1967. Pp. 179–228.

WALTERS, R. H., PARKE, R. D., & CANE, VALERIE. Timing of punishment and the observation of consequences to others as determinants of response inhibition. *Journal of Experimental Child Psychology,* 1965, 2, 10–30.

WEINGOLD, H. P., & WEBSTER, R. L. Effects of punishment on a cooperative behavior in children. *Child Development,* 1964, 35, 1211–1216.

WHEELER, L., & CAGGIULA, A. R. The contagion of aggression. *Journal of Experimental Social Psychology,* 1967, 2, 1–10.

WHITING, J. W. M. Sorcery, sin, and the superego: Some cross-cultural mechanisms of social control. In M. R. Jones (Ed.), *Nebraska symposium on motivation.* Vol. VII. Lincoln, Neb.: Univer. of Nebraska Press, 1959. Pp. 174–195.

WHITING, J. W. M., & CHILD, I. L. *Child training and personality.* New Haven: Yale Univer. Press, 1953.

WIKE, E. L. (Ed.). *Secondary reinforcement: Selected experiments.* New York: Harper & Row, 1966.

WINTERBOTTOM, MARIAN R. The relation of need for achievement to learning experiences in independence and mastery. In J. W. Atkinson (Ed.), *Motives in fantasy, action, and society.* Princeton, N.J.: Van Nostrand, 1958. Pp. 453–478.

WOLFE, J. B. Effectiveness of token rewards for chimpanzees. *Comparative Psychology Monographs,* 1936, 12, 1–72.

WRIGHT, BEATRICE A. Altruism in children and the perceived conduct of others. *Journal of Abnormal and Social Psychology,* 1942, 37, 218–233.

ZAJONC, R. B. Social facilitation. *Science,* 1965, 149, 269–274.

ZIMMERMAN, D. W. Durable secondary reinforcement. *Psychological Review,* 1957, 64, 373–383.

CHAPTER **5**

A Cognitive Theory
Of Socialization

Alfred L. Baldwin

New York University

The purpose of this chapter is to discuss the possible contributions of a cognitive theory to the study of socialization. Part I of the chapter will be devoted to a discussion of cognitive theory, while Part II will be concerned with the problems of socialization from the point of view of cognitive theory.

A theory of socialization must be based upon a theory of behavior and a theory of learning. If the task of the theory of socialization is to explain how the child becomes an individual who fits into his society, who shares its beliefs and values, who has acquired and uses skills that are important for the maintenance of the society, then a theory of socialization is one large portion of a general theory of human behavior and learning. In addition to describing a theory of behavior and learning, a theory of socialization must, in addition, show how the conditions specified by the theory as necessary for attainment of a socialized state are actually realized in any particular society. If the theory says, for example, that conscience is acquired through imitation of a role model, it must also show that children in the society do, in fact, imitate role models. An adequate theory cannot merely suggest hypothetical events in the life of a child that would produce socialization, but must also demonstrate that such events actually occur.

While in principle, only a part of the child's acquisition of adult behavior and personality characteristics is strictly socialization, socialization permeates so completely the child's growth and development that it is almost impossible to separate socialization from child development in general. Maturation must, for example, play a role in the development of the child, but the socialization practices of a society are, themselves, adapted to maturational factors. Thus learning to walk probably reflects important maturational elements, but society's demand that children walk is adapted to the fact that children cannot learn to walk in the first three months of life and many kinds of socialization of independence depend upon the expectation that children of four and five are able to locomote.

Not only does maturation enter into child development, but some of the skills and knowledge that are common to people in a society may well be acquirable without social tuition—learning to avoid walking off cliffs, for example. But the socialization of the child may involve social tuition of such risks in the physical world even if it is not strictly necessary, and also the socialization practices of a society tacitly assume that some necessary learnings are acquired through contact with the inanimate world. Thus it is expected that the child will have acquired such knowledge and experience even if no specifically relevant child-rearing practices exist.

Thus it seems unfeasible to consider socialization as just a part of the child's learning in childhood; rather it is a factor in the child's growth and development that cannot be segregated from other developmental influences in the sense of being *the* explanation of some aspects of the child's behavior, while playing no role in other aspects of development.

In the light of these preliminary considerations, this chapter will first describe the general nature of a cognitive theory of behavior, at least this author's conception of it, and will also attempt the broad outline of a theory of cognitive learning. We take for granted that socialization plays a role in all aspects of this development of the child, but we will not attempt any specific allocation of its influence.

Then in part two of the chapter, we will show some examples of cultural coding of environmental stimuli that are reflected in people's cognitive representations; we will point to some specifically social examples of information-seeking behavior; and we will discuss briefly how the common beliefs of society's members about child behavior and learning influence the child-rearing practices of the society.

PART I—A COGNITIVE THEORY OF BEHAVIOR AND LEARNING

Preview

In this section, the author's version of a cognitive theory of behavior and learning will be briefly summarized. The following sections will then discuss some aspects of the theory more fully.

1. A cognitive theory of behavior assumes that the first stage in the chain of events initiated by the stimulus situation and resulting in the behavioral act is the construction of a cognitive representation of the distal environment. The later events in the chain are instigated, modified and guided by this cognitive representation. The cognitive representation thus acts as the effective environment which arouses motives and emotions, and guides overt behavior toward its target or goal.

2. This cognitive representation changes in character as the child grows up.

    a. In the very young child the cognitive representation is relatively narrow and focused upon some momentarily salient aspect of the immediately perceptible environment; it is strongly dependent upon the momentary state of the child, such as his drive state, his emotional state, his specific orientation, and upon the ongoing action of the moment.

    b. With learning and maturity, the cognitive representation becomes a relatively *broad integrated representation* of the environment including many features that are not directly perceptible, although from a strictly informational point of view, the cognitive representation is not enriched since it cannot contain more information than the proximal stimulus situation. It is a coding of the proximal stimuli although the term "coding" suggests a too-restricted view of the process by which the cognitive representation is constructed.

    c. With learning and maturity, the cognitive representation separates the self and the environment. The individual himself is represented as behaving in the external environment. The individual himself gradually comes to be portrayed as acting, feeling and wanting, and as having various properties such as abilities, traits and values.

    d. With learning and maturity, the cognitive representation of the environment becomes relatively *neutralized* to the emotional and motivational state of the organism. It guides the expression of various emotions and the satisfaction of various motives, but the representation itself is a relatively neutral rendering of the properties of the external environment.

    e. With learning and maturity, the cognitive representation becomes coded in a more complex fashion reflecting the acquisition of language, cultural labels, etc. The individual becomes capable of double coding in the sense that he relates a label to its referent without confusing it with its referent.

    f. All of these changes represent trends. They are never completely finished (neutralization, for example). Furthermore, they do not apply to all behavior; some behavior continues to be mediated by the simpler mechanisms even while other behavior is mediated by the later-developing mechanisms. By and large, thoughtful, planned voluntary behavior reflects the operation of the more complex mechanisms while dreams, motor skills, automatized habits, impulses, and involuntary expressive behavior each in its own way reflects the operation of earlier, though not less, adaptive mechanisms.

    g. In general higher level mechanisms control lower level ones if they come into conflict. It is this fact that justifies the label "higher" and "lower," not some abstract value system, nor even differences in degrees of adaptiveness.

3. The acquisition of the content of the cognitive representation follows in general the principles of learning: contiguity, generalization, reinforcement, and repetition. With cognitive growth these principles operate under specific restraints; for example, an event is much more reinforcing to an action if it is cognized as the result of the act than if it is seen as an accidental contiguity.

4. Cognitive acquisition is furthered by specific kinds of information-getting behavior such as orienting responses, visual scanning, exploratory behavior and the like. The effectiveness of such behavior depends upon its making contiguities, similarities, repetitions, and reinforcements cognitively clearer than they would otherwise be. These information-getting behaviors change with age and learning and show effects of socialization.

5. Some of this information-getting behavior is motivated by cognitive unclearness or confusion (epistemic motivation). In this case the information-seeking behavior can itself become cognitively guided as, for example, the scientific method.

What is a Cognitive Theory?

Let us consider some of the features of a cognitive theory. It seems necessary for anybody beginning a chapter on cognitive theory to attempt to define it with some care. The term "cognitive theory" did not originate as a self-description by the people whose theories have been labeled cognitive. It is, instead, a descriptive term, applied to a variety of psychological theories on an intuitive basis, but without a very clear definition. At the same time, cognitive functions have been investigated by a number of people who are not considered cognitive theorists by themselves or by other people.

Various people have attempted to provide definitions of cognitive theory, one of the most recent being by Van de Geer and Jaspens in the *Annual Review of Psychology*, 1966. The present definition is generally in agreement with theirs.

The author defines cognitive theory as a theory of human behavior which postulates a general cognitive mechanism as the initial step in the chain of events leading from the stimulus to the response. The assumption behind cognitive theory is that stimuli are received and processed to extract the information that they contain. This information is in some way integrated into a cognitive representation of the environment in which the individual himself is represented. The cognitive representation might alternatively be called a belief about the content of the environment.

The essential point is that the information thus received, coordinated and integrated into some kind of a representation provides the effective stimulus for the instigation and guidance of goal-directed behavior. If such a cognitive representation does exist, one of its adaptive functions is that the same cognitive representation may elicit a variety of motivations depending upon the state of the organism, and may guide a variety of behavior sequences directed toward different targets. In other words, the individual cognizes his environment in much the same way whether he is hungry and utilizes this information about the environment to find food; whether he is bored and utilizes this information to find entertainment; or whether he is motivated to go to work and utilizes the cognitive representation of the environment to guide him to his office.

There is, of course, evidence that the state of the organism does, to some extent, modify the cognitive representation of the environment; but if it is hypothesized that motivations determine the cognitive picture to any great extent, much of the advantage of a cognitive theory is lost. It is important that it describe an information extraction process that is *relatively* neutral to the individual's motivation, and thus can serve to guide a variety of quite different goal-directed behaviors. The neutralization of such cognitive functions is, in fact, one aspect of cognitive socialization.

In many ways, a cognitive theory is an attempt to refine naive psychological beliefs. In everyday life people tacitly assume that other human beings directly perceive some features of the environment and that they cognize some aspects of the environment that are not directly perceivable. Furthermore, things which are not cognitively represented (i.e., unknown) are assumed not to influence behavior. Naive psychology also tacitly assumes that the cognitive representation is a conscious phenomenal experience. It is this feature of naive psychology that has contributed to the beliefs that cognitive theories are inherently mentalistic. While some psychologists' cognitive theories have espoused the notion of a phenomenal experience, it is entirely possible for a cognitive theory to be behavioristic.

The cognitive representation may be conceived as a hypothetical construct whose justification depends upon its fruitfulness in predicting and interpreting overt behavior.

Cognitive theories do not, however, include all theories which postulate an intervening mechanism between stimulus and response. Specifically, psychoanalytic theory contains an elaborate set of hypotheses about the nature of consciousness and the factors that determine access to consciousness. In psychoanalytic theory, however, the consciousness is described more as a sequence of thoughts than an integrated cognitive representation of the environment. There is no inherent conflict between psychoanalytic theory and cognitive theory. The two could be readily bridged. It happens that psychoanalytic theory has been more concerned with the psychodynamics of access to consciousness than with a description of cognitive processes.

Modern S-R (stimulus-response) theory also contains various hypotheses about intervening mediating responses. These intervening responses have some of the same advantages as a cognitive representation does. Miller, in his discussion of the liberalization of the S-R point of view (1959), points to the efficiency of an intervening mediating response which can be elicited by a variety of different stimulus conditions and can be connected to a variety of different responses. It simplifies the mechanism that would be otherwise necessary to connect every stimulus with every response directly. It is just this efficiency which makes a cognitive theory attractive. Many of the intervening responses hypothesized by S-R theorists are, however, not representations of the external environment; rather they are internalized actions such as words or eating movements, or emotional responses such as fear.

Among S-R theorists, Berlyne (1965) hypothesizes a structure of intervening mediating responses which does function as a representation of the external world. His "situational" thoughts represent the external world, and his "transformational" thoughts represent the individual's beliefs about what behavior can transform one situation into another. Thus, it would be quite appropriate to call Berlyne a cognitive theorist. This label, of course, does not make him any less of an S-R theorist. He believes these intervening responses have all the characteristics of responses in S-R theory: they can be attached to stimuli, they serve as stimuli to responses, show generalization, and they are presumably learned through reinforcement.

Berlyne illustrates the fact that there is no inherent contradiction between a cognitive theorist and a S-R theorist, despite the fact that historically the two have frequently been opposed. Theorists representing the two schools have frequently been in clear opposition in their explanations of some particular phenomena, but the opposition is not inherent in the basic assumptions of the two theoretical points of view. Thus, Berlyne is attempting to describe a cognitive representation in S-R terms.

Surprisingly enough, many cognitive theorists have not been concerned with actual cognitive processes. Thus, Lewin, who certainly was a cognitive theorist, largely ignored the processes by which the external environment leads to a particular cognitive structure. He was concerned with the dynamics of cognitive structures and their relation to need systems, but he was quite properly accused of being both post-perceptual and pre-behavioral in his theorizing. His and others' lack of concern with cognitive processes may represent a persistence of certain naive psychological assumptions in scientific theories of psychology. Thus, in everyday life, perception is tacitly assumed to be a direct registration of the environment. Naive psychology contains few hypotheses about its mechanism. In fact, it seems as if in naive psychology the accuracy of cognition is assumed to be highest where the process is most direct and least explicit. The direct eye-witness report of a crime is frequently given greater credence by a jury than a more logical rational reconstruction of a crime based upon circumstantial evidence.

Certainly, any cognitive theory of behavior that pretends to be adequate must contain a theory of actual cognitive processes. Even though cognitive theorists have not been especially concerned with cognitive processes, other psychologists have been. Psychologists are gradually building a considerable body of theory and fact about the nature of perception and information processing. While both perception and information processing could be incorporated into some theory that did not postulate a cognitive representation, they are obviously central to a cognitive theory. It seems likely that many investigators of perceptual processes and cognitive function would accept the central postulate of cognitive theory as stated at the beginning of this section.

What Considerations Justify a Cognitive Theory?

The advantage of a cognitive theory lies, as indicated earlier, in the fact that the postulation of a general cognitive mechanism simplifies the explanation of the relationship between the external stimulus and the behavior of the organism. It is, in principle, entirely possible to write behavioral laws which directly relate the proximal stimuli as they impose on the sensory surfaces of the body, the organismic states as they are measured or inferred, and the motor responses of the individual. Furthermore, if these relationships were simple, such a formulation of psychological laws would have a great deal to recommend it. There are many reasons, however, why such laws are extremely difficult to discover and complicated to describe.

The main reason for this complication is that the human organism like all other biological organisms is adapted to its environment. It has, through phylogenetic development, evolved a number of behavior mechanisms, including its capacity for learning, which makes it adaptive to complicated environments. In addition, the learning process itself increases the organism's adaptability to the environment. The objects to which the organism is adapted are, of course, actual environmental objects. They are the potential dangers, the potential sources of food, clothing, shelter. And other people in the environment are sources of blame and praise, hostility and beneficence. It is only reasonable, therefore, that a human being's adaptive behavior can be most simply described in terms of the impact of environmental objects upon him and his impact upon these external environmental objects.

It is entirely possible for a mechanism which is adapted to environmental objects to operate by way of very simple stimulus-response relationships. Thus, for example, the herring-gull chick is well-adapted to obtaining food during the time it is a fledgling by pecking at the beak of the mother gull as she stands over the nest. As Tinbergen and his colleagues have shown (Tinbergen & Perdeck, 1950), the mechanism for this response is very simple to describe: the releaser stimulus is a segregated red area against a yellow ground. In the gull chick's environment this simple behavior mechanism leads to its effectively obtaining food under most circumstances.

It is, therefore, not a logical inference from the fact of environmental adaptation that the organism must have some integrated environmental representation to which it responds. In the case of mature human behavior, however, since it must be adapted to a wide variety of rapidly changing circumstances, a general cognitive mechanism which represents the distal objects of the environment in a reasonably accurate form would obviously be of great functional value. Similarly, some kind of guided behavior involving a cognitive feed-back mechanism is of clear functional value.

Since the adaptive value of behavioral acts stems from their maintenance of certain invariant relationships with environmental objects, it is reasonable that psychological laws couched in terms of these objects are probably simpler than laws couched in terms of the proximal stimuli and the motor responses of the organism. This seems particularly true when we recognize by how many different and alternative channels of communication any particular environmental object may impinge on the organism. Thus the approach of a fire truck to my apartment building may be signalled by visual cues, by auditory cues, by a telephone message from someone who sees it, or a variety of other channels. It is apparent that a general cognitive mechanism which provided an internal representation of distal environmental objects has the advantage that many psychological laws of behavior, learning, reinforcement, motivation and emotional response can be expressed in relatively simple terms.

The weakness of this argument, of course, is that the complexity of the mediating process between the distal stimuli and the cognitive representation is not avoided by merely assuming a cognitive representation. The problem of explaining how an accurate cognitive representation of the distal environment is produced contains the same problems of sorting out which proximal stimuli relate to what distal objects as would a theory which attempted to relate overt behavior directly to proximal stimuli. There is thus no necessary advantage in a cognitive theory. But the division of the behavioral mechanism into two steps —first, the construction of a cognitive representation, and second, the execution of a behavior sequence—may indeed divide the problems of psychological explanation into two meaningful and manageable chunks; whereas, the attempt to directly relate proximal stimuli to motor responses requires that all the problems be solved in a single transformation, so to speak.

In addition, it is a good strategy to devise psychological mechanisms which correspond to the adaptive problems of the organism. Psychology has been neglectful of the facts of adaptive behavior, probably because adaptive mechanisms have frequently been described teleologically and thus have circumvented the essential explanatory problem. But on the other hand, behavioristic and objective psychology, in its effort to achieve a genuinely causal rather than teleological explanation of behavior, has often lost sight of the essential adaptive function of causal mechanisms such as reinforcement learning or generalization or habituation.

This, then, is the argument for searching for a general cognitive mechanism in human behavior. It would have great functional value and simplify psychological explanations if it did exist; an engineer designing an organism would find it very useful to invent a cognition-like mechanism. These are not logical arguments that it does exist, but they are persuasive arguments for hypothesizing a general cognitive mechanism in order to test its fit to actual empirical facts. The major problem of cognitive theory is, however, not to justify its possible value, but to explain how a general cognitive mechanism could function.

What is the Nature of the Cognitive Representation?

In the history of cognitive theories, the cognitive representation has sometimes been called a cognitive map, thus tacitly restricting the cognitive representation to something like a geometric model. The historical reason is probably that Tolman (1932) was directly concerned with rats in mazes and that Lewin (1936) seriously attempted to describe all behavior as a locomotion in a geometrical space. This is not the place to assess the fruitfulness of that strategy (see Baldwin, 1967), but it seems unduly restrictive.

In the most general sense, a cognitive representation is a coding of the information in the environment, but it must be a coding that indicates the structure of the environment, i.e., the relationships among items as well as the items themselves. It is not limited to the information immediately available; it obviously draws upon memory as when I recall I left my briefcase in the office and thus am able to go get it, and it surely depends on memory in many other ways. But this does not modify the fact that it is a coding of the environment and may include any kind of coding: visual, verbal, or strategies and plans for action.

The cognitive representation also embodies beliefs about the environment that are cultural conventions. The coding itself, if verbal, is one such convention. But in addition, the cognitive representation may contain other people with hostile or benevolent intentions; acts labelled with value judgments; or moral obligations. In fact, it can be viewed, if one likes, as a representation projected onto the environment to meet the necessities of adaptive behavior and cultural conformity rather than as an accurate picture of the external environment. Depending upon one's epistemological beliefs, one might hold a variety of positions about the reality status of the distal objects so represented. But no specific assumption of realism is necessarily required in order for a cognitive representation to be a useful theory of behavior.

Finally, the cognitive representation may double code the environment, whenever there is genuine symbolic behavior. A person hearing a verbal description does not confuse the words with what they refer to. A visual image is not ordinarily confused with a visual perception. The cognitive representation, generally speaking, is internal but projected onto the environment so that the individual perceives the environment not his perception of it. His behavior is felt to be guided by the environment, not a cognitive map of it. But much cognitive activity involves verbal labels, logical thought, and arithmetic operations, where the labels represent the objects but are distinct from them.

Age Changes in Cognitive Representations

The argument that has just been advanced in justification of a cognitive theory of behavior is much more appropriate when we consider the thoughtfully planned goal-directed behavior of adults than if we look at the behavior of very young children, or the behavior of people under extreme stress or even the relaxed pleasurable activity of the person having fun. The concept of an information extraction process leading to a cognitive representation makes best sense for cognitively guided behavior.

A major problem for a cognitive theory is, therefore, how to conceptualize other sorts of behavior. One possibility is to distinguish between cognitively guided behavior and non-cognitively guided behavior, or to distinguish between sensorimotor behavior and behavior based on mental representations (Piaget, 1952); or like Bruner (1964) to distinguish between enactive, iconic and symbolic understandings; or with Freud, to distinguish primary and secondary process thinking. Werner (1957) is also struggling with the same problem in his description of orthogenetic laws, although he does not label the mechanisms at a specific level.

In this section we will capitalize on the suggestions of these theorists but attempt some integration of them. Instead of assuming that a cognitive representation is itself an acquisition of the child during the general preschool period, we will assume that even the neonate has a cognitive representation. But we will try to encompass the general facts of cognitive development by postulating various changes in the character of the cognitive representation.

The cognitive representations of the very young child are assumed to have the following features that distinguish them from the mature cognitive representations of the adult in his most rational moments:

1. They are relatively narrow and limited to what is immediately perceptible rather than being a broad integration of perceptual data, past experience, and tacit assumptions about the external world.

2. Not only is the cognitive representation of the young child inherently limited, but it is also undifferentiated in the sense that the self and the environment are not differentiated. Thus the young baby does not cognize his own actions as a figure against an environmental background. Rather, he experiences some amalgam of the action and its environmental feedback. The hypothesis that for young children and lower animals objects are "things of action" has been suggested by several people and emphasized by Werner (1948). The same idea seems inherent in Bruner's description of an enactive representation (1964). We have tried to capture this feature of the infant's behavior by the assumption that he fails to differentiate cognitively the self from the environment. That hypothesis itself has, of course, been suggested in psychoanalytic theory, in Piaget (1952), in Werner (1957), and others.

3. The cognitive representation of the young child is assumed to be highly dependent upon the momentary state of the organism. Not only is it inherently limited to the immediately perceptible, but it may be further narrowed by the child's drive state, or affect, by salient external stimuli, or by his ongoing action, or the direction of his orientation. Thus a high drive may restrict the child's cognition to a goal object; salient stimuli may capture the child's attention and

prevent his seeing other aspects of the stimulus field; and if the child is engaged in goal-directed behavior, his cognition may be narrowly focused upon
the target to the exclusion of other aspects of the environment. This postulate
is intended to capture some of the psychoanalytic hypotheses about the primary
process as well as many common sense observations about children's short-
sightedness, impulsiveness and absentmindedness.

With age, maturity and experience, the character of the cognitive representation gradually changes. It comes to include parts of the environment that
are not immediately perceptible but these extensions of the cognitive representation are meshed into the perceptible. The cognitive representation takes the
form of a portrayal of the individual himself acting, feeling, and thinking as a
figure against a representation of the environment. It becomes neutralized,
relatively speaking, to drive states and affect, and escapes the narrowed focus
on the object that is the center of attention.

In addition, of course, cognitive representations come to reflect the child's
knowledge about the world; and his acquisition of cultural beliefs.

Furthermore, with the acquisition of language and other cultural cues, his
cognitive representation becomes more complex and symbolic. By the time the
child is in school, his understanding of many phenomena in verbal or some
other form is incorporated into his cognition. Yet at the same time he is clear
about the distinction between the verbal label and its referent. In a sense his
cognition is doubly coded: it contains a representation of the environment and
also a symbolic description of it. Some people believe the acquisition of this
type of conceptual thinking marks the actual beginning of cognitive representation. This type of thinking is found in the "stage of concrete operations" for
Piaget and it marks the beginning of verbal mediation and the "two-step process" as described by various S-R theorists.

Cognitive Theory of Learning

Thus far we have been concerned with the description of a cognitive representation as a coding of environmental information, and a description of its
change with age. These age changes are presumably the results of both maturation and learning.

In this section, we turn to a cognitive theory of learning. Since all socialization represents learning, a cognitive theory of the socialization process must
include a theory of learning. Much of the discussion in this section is frankly
speculative, in the sense that there is relatively little empirical data to substan-
tiate many of the distinctions that are drawn. On the other hand, the distinctions follow logically from the basic premise of a cognitive theory. The basic
distinction is between the acquisition of cognitive representation and the acquisition of behavior that is guided or instigated by these cognitive representations.

Just as cognitive representations change with age, so we assume that learning changes with age.

In a general sense, we hypothesize that learning in its earliest form corresponds more or less closely to the conventional description of learning in S-R terms. As the child develops, we believe the same general factors—contiguity, reinforcement, generalization, and repetition—operate but in a more precise and differentiated way.

Even in accounting for learning in very young children, the assumptions of S-R theory may be too general. To illustrate this qualification, Miller (1959), in his article on the liberalization of the S-R theory, points to a basic assumption that every behavior which can be attached to any stimulus by means of reinforcement must, by definition, be attachable to every other stimulus—provided that the other stimulus can be attached to some response by a process of reinforcement. In other words, S-R theory as it is currently described assumes that every learnable response can be connected to every stimulus that is capable of eliciting a response. As Miller, himself, says, this is a very strong assumption; one that has not been empirically demonstrated, and very possibly it is not true. In the behavior of animals, some responses seem to be more readily connected to some stimuli than to others, and it seems quite possible that in the study of infant behavior, we will also find that there is not a completely unconstrained acquisition of any response to any stimulus. Nevertheless, the usefulness of the principles of reinforcement, generalization, secondary drives, etc., are hardly debatable.

However, when the child's cognitive representation begins to show some organization, we believe that this organization affects profoundly the learning process.

One distinction inherent in a cognitive theory is the distinction between response acquisition and the acquisition of cognitive relationships. The first accounts for the learning of behavioral responses to a situation; the second accounts for the acquisition of such beliefs as that A causes B, that C is equivalent to D, or that E implies F.

We assume that the raw data for the acquisition of cognitive structure and for the learning of adaptive responses depend upon the existence of consistent contiguities and similarities between events in the environment. Thus the scientific proof of a causal relation depends ultimately on observing that the effect consistently follows the cause. The sophistication of science lies in observing this consistency even if the effect is apparently remote from the cause, in tracing the causal chain that connects the two, and in demonstrating a causal relation by setting up situations where alternative causes are held constant.

The scientific method, we assume, represents cognitive learning in its most mature highly-developed form. The task of a cognitive theory of learning is to show how it develops.

There is evidence to suggest that behavior can be learned with a minimum of cognitive structure. When the frequency of personal pronouns is increased during a conversation by making some response of the experimenter, like a head nod, contingent on the occurrence of the desired behavior, some people seem to have no awareness that they have learned anything or of the contingency between the behavior and the reinforcement. The evidence for lack of awareness is not thoroughly substantiated, but it seems possible that such learning can occur.

Cognitive learning, on the contrary, requires that pairing of the stimuli or the contiguity between the response and the reinforcement be cognitively related to each other. Our hypothesis is that such a cognitive relation will enhance the acquisition process. It is still the repeated contiguity of the response and the reinforcement that produces the behavior change, but any factors that organize the stimulus field so that the relation between the behavior and the reinforcement is made more cognitively clear will facilitate learning.

There are a variety of factors that organize the cognitive field. One set of these are the unit-forming factors described by Wertheimer (1923). Actually, these factors are very similar to the factors that contribute to learning, viz., contiguity, repetition, similarity, etc. There are also other kinds of organizing factors, e.g., temporal proximity under certain conditions leads to the perception of causality. This is a refinement of the general unit-forming factors, and should be particularly important in making the relation between an act and its reinforcement clear. On the other hand, it is possible for contiguities not to lead to inclusion in the same perceptual unit if other factors segregate them. Under these conditions, our hypothesis is that the contiguity will be less effective in producing learning.

With later cognitive growth, many other factors enter into the establishment of a cognitive relation. In one informal discrimination experiment, for example, the key stimulus was, in one case, a tiny square in the corner of the correct card. In another condition, it was a tiny irregular patch that looked like an accidental splatter of ink. The discrimination was made much more difficult by making the relevant stimulus look "accidental" rather than intentional.

In general, therefore, cognitive learning is the establishment of a belief that two events have a particular relationship. As the child grows older, he is capable of understanding and discriminating complicated relationships, and various subtle factors interact to make a relationship apparent. While the basic factors are still contiguity and similarity, the simple principles of conditioning become refined and modified under the influence of cognitive organization.

Cognitive learning is S-S (stimulus-stimulus) learning as has been pointed out many times. Even the subject's own behavior is viewed as a stimulus that is related to other stimuli contingent upon it. As it happens, observational learning has been discussed and investigated by several people, particularly Bandura and Walters (1963).

Bandura particularly has accumulated a variety of empirical data showing that behavior can be acquired by the individual through imitation and that reinforcements of other people's behavior can also teach the observer to behave in the reinforced fashion. This entire set of findings is quite consistent with the notion of cognitive learning. The fact that observed contingencies in other people's actions can be utilized in the service of different motives suggests that learning through observation is cognitively mediated. In one of Bandura's experiments, one child saw another being rewarded for one kind of behavior and punished for another. In a free-play situation, he tended to behave in the fashion that had been reinforced in the other child's behavior. On the other hand, when he was asked to perform the acts for which the other person had been punished he could do so. What had been acquired through observation was a cognitive structure in which certain acts lead to reinforcement and others lead to punishment. The children tended to perform the acts in a free-play situation which they judged were rewarded; but they were quite able to perform the acts that had been punished if these were requested.

The simplest form of observational learning, imitation, is not an easily explained phenomenon. In some cases imitation may merely consist of observing a combination of acts and then being able to perform them. But imitation occurs early in life and it is not always cognitively mediated.

Information Getting and Information Seeking

The achievement of a cognitive representation is not solely a matter of interpreting incoming data; it also depends upon various sorts of activities that gather new information, and integrate into a single cognitive representation data that may have been gathered sequentially.

Information gathering may take numerous forms. Some of the types of information gathering that have been recently investigated are the orienting response which reflects alertness, and also a pointing of the receptors in the direction of the alerting stimulus. Attention is a more internalized sort of information gathering which not only focuses upon certain aspects of the sensory stimuli, but also cuts out other features of the incoming stimulation. By paying attention to specific features of the environment, the individual may easily discover relationships which would escape a more random and wandering survey. At the same time, concentration on some feature may blind the individual to relationships which would be more obvious if he would relax and just look.

Information-getting behavior may also take the form of overt exploration, trial and error, experimentation and the like. The more sophisticated forms of experimentation consist in setting up a situation where specific information can be obtained. According to Piaget (Inhelder & Piaget, 1958), this is one of the achievements of the period of formal operations.

Finally, information gathering may be social. The child may ask questions, and even within that realm there are good questions and useless ones. Some people have acquired the ability to utilize other people effectively in getting information by asking good questions. While question asking is the most obvious form of social information gathering, there are other sorts as well. The child who expresses his ideas freely puts himself in the position of having his beliefs confirmed or corrected while the shy withdrawn child may never test his beliefs in a social context.

Thus, there are many kinds of information gathering. Much of it occurs without the individual particularly trying to seek information. The information-gathering function of behavior may be incidental to the more specific goal of the behavior. But it is also true that information seeking may be a deliberate action. It is presumably motivated by cognitive unclearness or ignorance. Berlyne (1965) speaks of this as epistemic motivation and he would see the same motivation underlying such acts as thinking and reasoning to bring about cognitive clarity.

We assume that all of these types of information gathering and seeking develop as the child grows older, partly under the impact of maturation, partly through contact with reality, and partly through explicit socialization pressures. The child is taught to look carefully before crossing the street, he may be taught or discouraged from asking questions when he does not know; in school he is specifically educated in a repertoire of information-gathering behavior— perhaps most obviously, reading. The development of such behavior interacts with other aspects of cognitive growth. Information gathering results in a more complete cognitive representation, but also it depends upon a certain reflectiveness in the child and a certain interest in truth for its own sake.

PART II—THE STUDY OF SOCIALIZATION

From the point of view of cognitive theory, one of the most important and interesting research questions is the role of socialization in the development of the cognitive representations as described in the previous part.

There are cultural uniformities in the processes of thinking, in beliefs about causality, in the assumptions about space, time, number, and order. Unfortunately, there are not enough comparative cultural studies of these beliefs and their acquisition to make clear the role of society in the acquisition of such beliefs, nor are there clear findings about the child-rearing antecedents of the understanding of these concepts of the inanimate world.

Some people have certainly viewed this kind of intellectual development as primarily maturational. Piaget and his colleagues at Geneva (Inhelder & Piaget, 1958) maintain that while the experiences of the child certainly contribute to his understanding and stimulate growth processes, the crucial factor is a kind of spontaneous equilibration of thought processes that is instigated by the conflicts inherent in the relatively disorganized thought processes of the preschool child. The result of this equilibration is the attainment of the stage of concrete operations. The essential feature of that achievement, according to Piaget, is the organization of these thought processes into coherent groupings, marked by reversibility. Piaget does not view such cognitive functions as conservation, seriation, etc., as beliefs that are taught to the child or even learned by the child. Instead they are the natural outcomes of an equilibration process.

The role of clearly identifiable cultural elements in conservation of quantity is shown in Greenfield's study (1966) of conservation in Sengalese children. In the first place, it turned out that there was no way to translate the phrase, "Is the water in the two glasses really equal or do they just look equal?" The distinction between appearance and reality could not be conveyed to the children.

A more striking difference between Sengalese and American children was in the role of "action-magic." One of the reasons American children use to support the belief in the conservation of quantity is that the experimenter just poured the water from one glass into another. The tacit meaning seems to be, "All you did was just pour it, you didn't change it in any way." In Senegal, an apparently similar argument was made by 20 per cent of the children but in support of non-conservation: "There's more in this glass because you poured it." Greenfield hypothesizes that the experimenter was attributed the power to change the quantity just by pouring it. Therefore, she repeated the experiment asking the child to pour the water. The amount of conservation increased and the experience also contributed to the maintenance of conservation on later tests.

Thus it is clear that while conservation may represent an equilibration process, the elements which go into the conflict situation and which may prevent conservation show cultural variability.

The concepts of the inanimate world are often not viewed as a consequence of socialization because we assume that they are correct. The only way that people can differ from the cultural consensus is to be wrong. This argument is not entirely valid, but it is probably true that properties of the physical world do lead to certain beliefs.

It is more interesting to examine people's concepts of interpersonal relations because here it seems clear that they reflect a cultural consensus. Naive psychology has frequently been disconfirmed by empirical research. Yet in making interpersonal judgments, there is a clear logic, a clear theory that shows many similarities to problem solving in mathematical situations.

The development of concepts of interpersonal relations has been investigated by the Baldwins (Baldwin & Baldwin, 1967). One of their investigations, for example, is concerned with children's concepts of kindness and how the concept changes with age.

The basic assumption underlying their research is that "naive psychology" as it has been described by Heider (1958), and as it is elucidated by their own investigations, represents a set of tacit beliefs about human behavior. It can, at least in some cases, be expressed in a formal elegant theoretical system. The basic theory underlying the Baldwins' research is diagrammatically represented in Figure 5.1. A_1 and A_2 represent two alternative acts that a person P might perform, and C_1 and C_9 represent a variety of consequences. The dotted lines connecting A_1 with C_1, C_3, C_5, and C_8 exemplify the fact that this particular act has a number of consequences; and the dotted lines connecting A_2 with C_3, C_5, C_7, and C_9 represent the various consequences of that act. Some consequences are common to the two acts, C_3 and C_5; whereas A_1 is the only act which leads to C_1 and C_8, and A_2 is the only act which leads to C_7 and to C_9.

Naive psychology begins with the assumption that the behavior is intentional. The person must know some of the consequences of his act before he can perform it intentionally. Therefore, the more credit he will get, if they are valued, and the more blame if they are disvalued. And the more their achievement will lead to the attribution to him of the ability to achieve them and the more his failure to achieve them will result in judgments of inability. The psychological consequences of an act on other people—credit, blame, anger, or

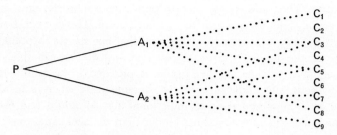

FIGURE 5.1.   Diagram of consequences of two alternative acts.

fear—are predicated on the assumption that the individual knew the consequences at the time he performed the act. There are, to be sure, degrees of
knowledge of consequences; some acts have consequences that could not possibly have been recognized by the individual; others are consequences that he
perhaps didn't anticipate, but readily could have; whereas others are consequences that he did recognize fairly clearly. These differences in the extent to
which the consequences are judged to be cognitively clear to the person obviously affect other people's responses to his action; but the details of this relationship have not been thoroughly explored and will not be discussed any
further in this chapter. The situations the Baldwins present to their subjects
state clearly that the consequences are either known or unknown.

Secondly, the attribution of intention to the person depends upon what
consequences the two alternative acts have in common and in what respect they
differ. Only the consequences which are different for the two acts are the basis
for attribution of intention. If the consequences of all of a person's alternatives
are identical, he cannot help causing those consequences, and thus his behavior
offers an observer no basis for a judgment of intention.

Assuming, however, that the two alternative acts do have some different
consequences, the task of the observer is to decide which consequences of the
individual's action were intended and which were not. It is quite possible for a
person to be aware of some consequence of his action, and to perform an act
that brings about that consequence without intending to do so. That particular
result of the act is incidental to his intention and not the reason for the behavior. Thus, whenever a performed act has more than one consequence the
observer may entertain the hypothesis that either consequence or both were
intentional. How the observer decides among these hypotheses is by no means
clear, but one factor seems to be supported by the experimental data. If the
subject is asked to judge the strength of the intention to benefit another person
or kindness of an act, the existence of an alternative motivation leads the observer of the behavior to judge it as less kind. For example, if an act benefits
both the actor and another person, whereas its alternative would harm both the
other person and the self, the observer of the behavior consistently judges it as
less kind, than if self-interested motivation were not a possible interpretation
of the choice.

In the experiment on judgments of kindness, the subject is presented with ten pairs of pictures. The child in the picture performs exactly the same act in both pictures and this act always benefits another person. The context, however, varies between the two pictures in such a way that one specific hypothesis about the nature of the judgmental process can be tested. For example, in one picture the act that benefits another person is pictured to be accidental, and performed without any knowledge of its consequences; whereas in the other picture the act is represented as an intentional act. All adults and even most five-year-olds judge the intentional act kinder than the accidental one.

In other pairs of pictures, the contrast is the presence or absence of an alternative motivation. In one picture, for example, a child spontaneously gives his baby brother some toys while in the other picture he performs the same act after his mother tells him to. In the second picture, an alternative motivation, obedience to the mother, is provided as a possible reason for the behavior. The first one is seen as kinder than the second presumably because the motivation to benefit the baby brother is more unambiguous.

In other pictures, the alternative motivation is some sort of moral obligation. For example, one pair contrasts benefitting a person to whom the child owes a favor versus benefitting a person to whom no favor is owed. Various obligations are represented in different pairs: the obligation to benefit an invited guest, the obligation to return a favor, and the obligation to help someone who is in serious trouble.

For adults, any alternative motivation seems to make the act less kind; kindness is clearest where it appears as a pure expression of the desire to benefit another person. For children, it seems that kindness is less differentiated from conformity to obligation. Some kindergartners, for example, say helping your brother when mother tells you to is kinder than doing it on your own. Ninety-seven per cent of the 4th graders say it is kinder to help a boy out of serious trouble than to help him out of a minor jam, but 72 per cent of an adult sample say the reverse—arguing that one ought to help people in real trouble but helping them out of an unimportant difficulty is real kindness.

Thus it appears that younger children may fail to discriminate between the desire to benefit another person and conformity to a moral obligation, but that is not the whole story. Some children—perhaps all children at some age—say it is kinder when one conforms to the obligation and benefits the other person. They answer opposite to adults and justify their response by the opposite reasoning of adults.

In summary, we have reported on two aspects of the socialization of the individual's cognitive representation. It would be very pleasant if we could report on the socialization of many other aspects of cognitive development: the development of selective attention, the acquisition of all sorts of information gathering and selection, the acquisition of epistemic motivation, as well as the process by which the content of cultural beliefs is instilled. Unfortunately, there is little empirical research even on age changes in these various cognitive functions, let alone research on the actual socialization process.

Socialization and Naive Psychology

The final topic of this chapter is a brief discussion of the hypothesis that the socialization practices of a society reflect the culture's implicit or explicit psychological hypotheses about how children function and what influences will modify that function.

Some child-rearing practices of a society are quite deliberate—i.e., child-rearing is a manifest function of the behavior. Such practices as putting pepper on the mother's breast during weaning, explaining to the child why he is being punished, or making the child confess his crime before he is forgiven all, imply some belief that the procedure will modify the child's behavior in the desired direction.

Other child-rearing practices are more a matter of the mother's doing what seems natural to her. Thus the mother who spanks the child for breaking her dishes may or may not be guided by a belief that spanking is an efficacious way of changing behavior. She may merely be expressing her anger at the child. Such actions may, of course, be influential on the child's development, whether they are explicitly educational or not.

Even these spontaneous social actions of adults toward children reflect many implicit psychological beliefs about children. Thus, the mother in our society is less likely to become angry when a two-month-old wails for a long period than if a four-year-old does the same thing. The four-year-old "knows better" or "should be able to say what is the matter." Similarly, parents may be more modest about their sexual behavior in front of a six-year-old than a six-month-old, because from their point of view, the six-month-old doesn't know what the behavior means.

It is important, therefore, to know the naive psychological theory of a society in order to understand its socialization practices. Heider (1958) has described many features of the naive psychology of Western cultures. Baldwin (1967) has summarized Heider and tried to extend his description of naive psychology to include beliefs about child behavior and child development.

One important feature of naive psychology is that it is a cognitive theory in the sense the term was defined at the beginning of this chapter. Baldwin's analysis of it suggests that regarding children it may be rather extreme. Whereas in this chapter, the cognitive representations of young children are viewed as quite different in character from the cognitive representations of adults, in everyday life, one of the main differences which people recognize between children and adults is a matter of how well-informed they are. The basic processes of learning and perception are assumed to be much the same for children and adults, but the adult has much more knowledge. Certainly we seem to assume in naive psychology that both children and adults receive information, and then act on the basis of it. The basic cognitive assumption is reflected in the fact that the major mechanism of the naive psychology of learning how to behave is learning what the consequences of one's actions are. These consequences may be directly experienced; in fact, adults reward and punish children to help them learn behavior that does not have obvious intrinsic rewards and punishments. But the cognitive assumption also leads to the belief that children can be verbally instructed and can acquire behavior patterns in that way.

Naive psychology does not, however, picture children as entirely cool and collected. It is commonly believed that children are impulsive and may not use their information to guide behavior. Thus one socialization task is defined as teaching the child to look before he leaps, and to stop and think before acting seems to be commonly believed to be more efficacious at this point than mere instruction.

Cognitive learning is not the only mechanism of learning involved in naive psychology. Both in the acquiring of new behavioral skills and in automatizing a desirable habit, people believe in the efficacy of drill and practice. There are many adages in our society pointing to the need to try again, apparently on the assumption that practice brings improvement.

Finally, there is some recognition of a maturational process, in that people generally feel that a child can be too young to be able to learn some particular information or skill. Explicit attempts to teach the child are usually withheld until the child reaches the "proper" age; and the child is given some time in which to acquire the socialized form of the behavior. In fact, the child is not held legally responsible for his behavior until he has become an adult.

The importance of these tacit psychological beliefs for the understanding of socialization of the child is that they may be empirically justifiable or they may not be. To the extent that the culturally common beliefs about children do not describe how children actually function, the child's behavior and development are likely to be adversely affected. On the other hand, the socialization practices are relatively well-adapted as evidenced by the fact that they have functioned.

These matters are vital to understand in the present period of emphasis upon innovation in education. It is almost certainly true that some of the inefficiency in education and some of the maladjustment in our society is a result of the fact that naive psychology is in error at places. It is important, therefore, to explore the problems carefully and empirically. On the other hand, innovations, even if they are empirically based, should be initiated cautiously if one wants to avoid upsetting the "balance of nature." There may be ways to effectively toilet train at six months, or teach the child to read at two years. These possibilities should be entertained, and it is certainly true that much of the resistance to such innovations is not empirically founded. But in other fields, we have seen the occasionally disastrous side effects of empirically based innovations, like thalidomide, because of too little attention to the ramifications of change. The fact that some child-rearing practice is solidly built into our culture should make us cautious about changing it, but should not discourage us from considering its bad consequences and the possibility of improvement.

SUMMARY

This chapter of cognitive theories of socialization has turned out to be more on cognitive theory than on socialization, largely because so little empirical work on socialization has been guided by cognitive theory. We have presented, however, a cognitive theory of behavior and of learning that is specifically directed toward the understanding of cognitive processes in children and the problems of cognitive socialization.

This was followed by a discussion of the socialization of some cognitive functions and ended with a discussion of the naive psychology of socializing agents in our society. This naive psychology is also a cognitive theory, although not identical to the relatively refined version presented earlier. Even if a cognitive theory of behavior eventually is found to be unproductive, it is still important to describe the tacit psychological beliefs of socializers.

REFERENCES

BALDWIN, A. L. *Theories of child development*. New York: Wiley, 1967.

BALDWIN, A. L., & BALDWIN, CLARA P. The development of children's concepts of kindness. Unpublished manuscript, New York Univer., 1967.

BANDURA, A., & WALTERS, R. H. *Social learning and personality development*. New York: Holt, Rinehart & Winston, 1963.

BERLYNE, D. E. *Structure and direction in thinking*. New York: Wiley, 1965.

BRUNER, J. S. Course of cognitive growth. *American Psychologist*, 1964, 19, 1–15.

GREENFIELD, PATRICIA M. On culture and conservation. In J. S. Bruner et al., *Studies in cognitive growth*. New York: Wiley, 1966. Chapter 11, pp. 225–256.

HEIDER, F. *The psychology of interpersonal relations*. New York: Wiley, 1958.

INHELDER, B., & PIAGET, J. *Growth of logical thinking from childhood to adolescence*. New York: Basic Books, 1958.

LEWIN, K. *Principles of topological psychology*. New York: McGraw-Hill, 1936.

MILLER, N. E. Liberalization of basic S-R concepts: Extension to conflict behavior, motivation and social learning. In S. Koch (Ed.), *Psychology: A study of science*. Vol. 2. New York: McGraw-Hill, 1959. Pp. 196–292.

PIAGET, J. *The origins of intelligence in children*. New York: International Universities Press, 1952.

TINBERGEN, N., & PERDECK, A. C. On the stimulus situation releasing the begging response in the newly hatched herring-gull chick. *Behavior*, 1950, 3, 1–38.

TOLMAN, E. C. *Purposive behavior in men and animals*. New York: Century, 1932.

VAN DE GEER, J. P., & JASPARS, J. F. M. Cognitive functions. In P. R. Farnsworth (Ed.), *Annual review of psychology*, 1966, 17, 145–176.

WERNER, H. *Comparative psychology of mental development*. (Rev. Ed.) Chicago: Follett, 1948.

WERNER, H. The concept of development from a comparative and organismic point of view. In Dale Harris, *The concepts of development: An issue in the study of human behavior*. Minneapolis: Univer. of Minnesota Press, 1957.

WERTHEIMER, M. Untersuchungen zur Lehre von der Gestalt. II *Psychologische Forschung*, 1923, 4, 301–350.

CHAPTER 6

Stage And Sequence:
The Cognitive-Developmental
Approach To Socialization

Lawrence Kohlberg

Harvard University

For a number of years, I have been engaged in research on moral and psychosexual development, guided not by a theory, but by an approach labeled
"cognitive-developmental." The label "cognitive-developmental" refers to a set
of assumptions and research strategies common to a variety of specific theories
of social and cognitive development, including the theories of J. M. Baldwin
(1906), J. Dewey (1930), G. H. Mead (1934), Piaget (1948), Loevinger (1966),
and myself (Kohlberg, 1966b, 1968, 1969).

In this chapter, we shall attempt first to present and justify the general
assumptions of the cognitive-developmental approach. Next we shall consider
their application to the phenomena of moral socialization, contrasting our approach with social learning and psychoanalytic approaches. Finally, we shall
consider processes of imitation and identification from our point of view, since
these processes are held to be basic in cognitive-developmental theories as well
as in social-learning and psychoanalytic theories of social development.

I. THEORIES OF COGNITIVE DEVELOPMENT
AND THE ORIGINS OF MENTAL STRUCTURE

Before considering the application of cognitive-developmental theories to
socialization, we shall outline the basic characteristics of these theories in the
cognitive area. Cognitive-developmental theories presuppose the assumptions
listed in A. L. Baldwin's chapter on cognitive theory in this volume, but share a
number of basic further assumptions as well. Baldwin defines as "cognitive"

Much of the author's research reported here has been supported by N.I.C.H.D. Grant
HD 02469-01. The first half of the chapter is a revision of a paper prepared for the Social
Science Research Council, Committee on Socialization and Social Structure, Conference on
Moral Development, Arden House, November, 1963, supported by MH 4160 of N.I.M.H.

theories which postulate a representational or coding process intervening between stimulus and response. This representation is applicable to a variety of proximal stimuli and may elicit a variety of responses depending upon "non-cognitive" motivational and situational factors. In Baldwin's version of cognitive theory, it is assumed that such representations are learned, but that such learning does not depend upon making an overt response to any of the stimulus elements in the environment being learned, nor does it depend upon any definite reinforcement for learning (though such reinforcement may be necessary for performance as opposed to learning). As Baldwin points out, his conception of cognitive theory embraces most theories giving attention to cognitive phenomena including mentalistic-associationistic theories of cognition like psychoanalysis as well as behavioristic-associationistic theories like S-R mediation theories. Drawing examples from this volume, Aronfreed's and Bandura's social-learning theories recognize cognitive principles of learning in Baldwin's sense, although Gewirtz's does not.

In contrast to associationistic theories of cognitive learning, cognitive-developmental theories make the following assumptions:

1. Basic development involves basic transformations of cognitive *structure* which cannot be defined or explained by the parameters of associationistic learning (contiguity, repetition, reinforcement, etc.), and which must be explained by parameters of organizational wholes or systems of internal relations.

2. Development of cognitive structure is the result of processes of *interaction* between the structure of the organism and the structure of the environment, rather than being the direct result of maturation or the direct result of learning (in the sense of a direct shaping of the organism's responses to accord with environmental structures).

3. Cognitive structures are always structures (schemata) of *action*. While cognitive activities move from the sensorimotor to the symbolic to verbal-propositional modes, the organization of these modes is always an organization of actions upon objects.

4. The direction of development of cognitive structure is toward greater *equilibrium* in this organism-environment interaction, i.e., of greater balance or *reciprocity* between the action of the organism upon the (perceived) object (or situation) and the action of the (perceived) object upon the organism. This balance in interaction, rather than a static correspondence of a concept to an object, represents "truth," "logic," "knowledge," or "adaptation" in their general forms. This balance is reflected in the underlying *stability* (conservation) of a cognitive act under apparent transformation, with development representing a widened system of transformations maintaining such *conservation*.

The assumptions just listed are assumptions which hold for cognitive development in general, i.e., for the development of ways of thinking about both physical and social objects. Their application to social development is made more concrete by the following additional assumptions about social-emotional development, assumptions whose explanation is left to our section on moral development.

5. Affective development and functioning, and cognitive development and functioning are not distinct realms. "Affective" and "cognitive" development are *parallel;* they represent different perspectives and contexts in defining structural change.

6. There is a fundamental unity of personality organization and development termed the ego, or the self. While there are various strands of social development (psychosexual development, moral development, etc.), these strands are united by their common reference to a *single concept of self* in a *single social world.* Social development is, in essence, the restructuring of the (1) concept of self, (2) in its relationship to concepts of other people, (3) conceived as being in a common social world with social standards. In addition to the unity of level of social development due to general cognitive development (the *g* factor in mental maturity tests), there is a further unity of development due to a common factor of ego maturity.

7. All the basic processes involved in "physical" cognitions, and in stimulating developmental changes in these cognitions, are also basic to social development. In addition, however, social cognition always involves *role-taking,* i.e., awareness that the other is in some way like the self, and that the other knows or is responsive to the self in a system of complementary expectations. Accordingly developmental changes in the social self reflect parallel changes in conceptions of the social world.

8. The direction of social or ego development is also toward an equilibrium or *reciprocity* between the self's actions and those of others toward the self. In its generalized form this equilibrium is the end point or definer of morality, conceived as principles of justice, i.e., of reciprocity or equality. In its individualized form it defines relationships of "love," i.e., of mutuality and reciprocal intimacy. The social analogy to logical and physical conservations is the maintenance of an *ego-identity* throughout the transformations of various role relationships. (A concrete early developing example discussed later is the child's belief in his own unchangeable gender identity, which develops at the same age as physical conservations.)

The statement listed first presupposes a distinction between behavior changes or learning in general and *changes in mental structure.* Structure refers to the general characteristics of shape, pattern or organization of response rather than to the rate or intensity of response or its pairing with particular stimuli. Cognitive structure refers to rules for processing information or for connecting experienced events. Cognition (as most clearly reflected in thinking) means putting things together or relating events, and this relating is an active connecting process, not a passive connecting of events through external association and repetition. In part this means that connections are formed by selective and active processes of attention, information-gathering strategies, motivated thinking, etc. More basically, it means that the process of relating particular events depends upon prior general modes of relating developed by the organism. The most general modes of relating are termed "categories of experience." These categories are modes of relating applicable to any experienced event, and include the relations of causality, substantiality, space, time, quantity and logic (the latter referring to relations of inclusion or implication between classes or propositions).

The awareness that the child's behavior has a cognitive structure or organizational pattern of its own which needs description independently of the degree of its correspondence to the adult culture is as old as Rousseau, but this awareness had only recently pervaded the actual study of cognitive development. Two examples of the revolution resulting from defining the structure of the child's mind in its own terms may be cited. The first is that of Piaget (1928), whose first psychological effort was to classify types of wrong answers on the Binet test. By moving beyond an analysis of intellectual development in terms of number of right answers to an analysis in terms of differences in structure, Piaget transformed the study of cognitive development. The second example comes from the study of children's language (Chomsky, 1968) based for a generation on counting frequency and correctness of nouns and verbs as defined by conventional adult grammar. In the last decade, psychologists have approached children's grammar with the methods of structural linguistics, as if the child's language were that of an exotic tribe with its own structure. While the implications of the Piagetian revolution in cognition and the Chomskian revolution in language are far from clear, they have made the conception of mental structure a reality accepted even by associationistic theories of cognition (cf. Berlyne, 1965), though not by most associationistic theories of social learning.

Our second statement suggested that cognitive-developmental theories are "interactional," i.e., they assume that basic mental structure is the product of the patterning of the interaction between the organism and the environment rather than directly reflecting either innate patterns in the organism or patterns of events (stimulus contingencies) in the environment. The distinction between theories stressing the innate and theories stressing the acquired has often been thought of as a contrast in quantitative emphasis on hereditary biological factors as opposed to environmental stimulation factors in causing individual differences. When the problem is posed in such a fashion, one can be led to nothing but a piously eclectic "interactionism" which asserts that all concrete behavior is quantitatively affected empirically by both hereditary and environmental factors. The theoretical issues are quite different, however. They are issues as to the location of the principles producing basic mental structure within or without the organism.

It is evident that general questions as to the origins and development of mental structure are not the same as questions as to the origins of individual differences in behavior. As an example, while the fact that one six-year-old child may pass all the six-year items on the Binet test and another fail them all might be attributed purely to hereditary differences in general intelligence, the patterns of behavior involved in the child's actual Binet performance (e.g., knowing the word "envelope") may be purely culturally learned behavior. Because many American psychologists have been peculiarly concerned with individual differences rather than developmental universals, and because they have failed to understand the distinction between behavior differences in general and behavior structure, they have frequently misinterpreted European theories of development. As an example, some American writers have misinterpreted Piaget's stages as "maturational" and have thought that he claimed intelligence is unaffected by environment. Others (like J. McV. Hunt, 1961, 1963) have correctly interpreted Piaget's stages as being based on the assumption of organism-environment interactions, but take this assumption as indicating that individual differences in intellectual performance are less hereditary than was long believed. In fact, there is nothing in Piaget's theory which suggests that individual differences in speed of development through his stages are not primarily due to hereditary factors.

Distinctions between environmental, maturational and interactional theories of the origins of mental structure, then, are not distinctions based upon quantitative assumptions about the role of heredity in the formation of individual differences. In terms of quantitative role, maturational or nativistic theories, like those of Lorenz (1965), or Gesell (1954), recognize the importance of environmental stimulation in modifying genetically grounded behavior patterns. In a similar sense, associationistic-learning theorists like Pavlov (1928) or Hull (1943) recognize the quantitative role of hereditary traits of temperament and ability in causing individual differences in personality and in rate and type of learning. The difference between the two types of theories is not in the recognition of both innate and environmental causal factors in development but in which set of factors is seen as the source of basic patterning.

The contrast between the *modifying* and *structuring* roles awarded to experience becomes clear with regard to the issue of critical periods. Most research on the effects of experience upon development has postulated "critical periods" in which the individual is especially sensitive to environmental influence in a given domain. Yet this notion of extreme quantitative sensitivity depends upon a maturational or nativistic theory.

The existence of a fixed time period, during which a certain amount of stimulation is required to avoid irreversible developmental deficits, presupposes an innate process of growth with an inner time schedule and an inner pattern which can be arrested or distorted by deficits of stimulation.

In the nativistic view, stimulation may be needed to elicit, support, and maintain behavior patterns but the stimulation does not create these patterns, which are given by templates in the genotype. In fact, learning or environmental influence itself is seen as basically patterned by genetically determined structures. Learning occurs in certain interstices or open places in the genetic pattern, and the structuring of what is learned is given by these patterns (Lorenz, 1965). As an example, ethological "imprinting" or Freudian "libidinal fixation" represents a type of learning, a determination of response by environmental stimulation. However, the "learning" involved represents a specific sensitivity or open spot in a genetically patterned social-sexual response. As another example, an insect or bird may learn a specific "map" of the geography of its home place, but ethologists view this map as structured by an innate organization of space in general (Lorenz, 1965).

In dealing with developmental changes, nativistic theories such as Gesell's (1954) have stressed the notion of unfolding maturational stages. The patterning of these age-specific behavioral forms, their order and timing, is believed to be wired into the organism. The organism grows as a whole so that the effort to teach or force early maturation in one area will either be ineffective or will disrupt the child's total pattern and equilibrium of growth.

In contrast to nativistic theories, learning theories may allow for genetic factors in personality and in ease of learning of a complex response, but they assume that the basic structure of complex responses results from the structure of the child's environment. Both specific concepts and general cognitive structures, like the categories of space, time, and causality, are believed to be the reflections of structures existing outside the child, structurings given by the physical and social world.

Almost of necessity, the view that structure of the external world is the source of the child's cognitive structure has led to an account of the development of structure in associationistic terms. From John Locke to J. B. Watson and B. F. Skinner (Kessen, 1965), environmentalists have viewed the structure of behavior as the result of the association of discrete stimuli with one another, with responses of the child and with experiences of pleasure and pain.

We have contrasted the maturationist assumption that basic mental structure results from an innate patterning with the learning theory assumption that basic mental structure is the result of the patterning or association of events in the outside world. In contrast, the cognitive-developmental assumption is that basic mental structure is the result of an interaction between certain organismic structuring tendencies and the structure of the outside world, rather than reflecting either one directly.

This interaction leads to cognitive *stages* which represent the *transformations* of simple early cognitive structures as these are applied to (or assimilate) the external world, and as they are accommodated to or restructured by the external world in the course of being applied to it.

The core of the cognitive-developmental position, then, is the doctrine of cognitive stages. Cognitive stages have the following general characteristics (Piaget, 1960):

1. Stages imply distinct or *qualitative* differences in children's modes of thinking or of solving the same problem at different ages.

2. These different modes of thought form an *invariant sequence,* order, or succession in individual development. While cultural factors may speed up, slow down, or stop development, they do not change its sequence.

3. Each of these different and sequential modes of thought forms a *"structured whole."* A given stage-response on a task does not just represent a specific

response determined by knowledge and familiarity with that task or tasks similar to it. Rather it represents an underlying thought-organization, e.g., "the level of concrete operations," which determines responses to tasks which are not manifestly similar. According to Piaget, at the stage of concrete operations, the child has a general tendency to maintain that a physical object conserves its properties on various physical dimensions in spite of apparent perceptual changes. This tendency is structural, it is not a specific belief about a specific object. The implication is that both conservation and other aspects of logical operations should appear as a logically and empirically related cluster of responses in development.

4. Cognitive stages are *hierarchical integrations.* Stages form an order of increasingly differentiated and integrated structures to fulfill a common function. The general adaptational functions of cognitive structures are always the same (for Piaget the maintenance of an equilibrium between the organism and the environment, defined as a balance of assimilation and accommodation). Accordingly higher stages displace (or rather reintegrate) the structures found at lower stages. As an example, formal operational thought includes all the structural features of concrete operational thought but at a new level of organization. Concrete operational thought or even sensorimotor thought does not disappear when formal thought arises, but continues to be used in concrete situations where it is adequate or when efforts at solution by formal thought have failed. However, there is a hierarchical preference within the individual, i.e., a disposition to prefer a solution of a problem at the highest level available to him. It is this disposition which partially accounts for the consistency postulated as our third criterion. "Hierarchical" and structural cognitive stages may be contrasted with "embryo-logical," motivational, or content stages (Loevinger, 1966). The latter represent new interests or functions rather than new structures for old functions, e.g., anal interests are not transformations of oral interests, they are new interests. While to some extent higher psychosexual stages are believed to typically include and dominate lower stages (e.g., genital interests dominate or include pregenital interests), this integration is not a necessary feature of the higher stage (e.g., lower stage interests may be totally repressed or be in conflict with higher stage interests).

The question of whether cognitive stages "exist" in the sense just defined is an empirically testable question. It has been held by B. Kaplan (1966) and others that stages are theoretical constructions, and that their theoretical value holds independently of whether or not they define empirical sequences in ontogeny. One cannot hold this to be true for embryological stages because there is no clear logical reason why an "anal" content is higher than an oral content. In the case of structural stages, however, their conceptual definition is based on a hierarchy of differentiation and integration. Every theoretical set of structural stages is defined in such a way that a higher stage is more differentiated and integrated than a lower stage. In this sense, a set of structural stages forms a valid hierarchy regardless of whether or not they define an ontogenetic sequence.

In spite of this fact, it is extremely important to test whether a set of theoretical stages does meet the empirical criteria just listed. If a logical developmental hierarchy of levels did not define an empirical sequence, the hierarchy would neither tell us much about the process of development nor justify our notion that the sequence is interactional in nature. If an empirical sequence were not found, one would argue that the "stages" simply constituted alternative types of organization of varying complexity, each of which might develop independently of the other. In such a case, the "stages" could represent alternative expressions of maturation or they could equally well represent alternative cultures to which the child is exposed. It would hardly be surprising to find that adult physical concepts are more complex, more differentiated and integrated in educated Western culture than in a jungle tribe. The fact that the Western and tribal patterns can be ordered at different levels of structural organization, however, would tell us little about ontogenesis in either culture, and would leave open the possibility that it was simply a process of learning cultural content.

In contrast, if structural stages do define general ontogenetic sequences, then an interactional type of theory of developmental process must be used to explain ontogeny. If the child goes through qualitatively different stages of thought, his basic modes of organizing experience cannot be the direct result of adult teaching, or they would be copies of adult thought from the start. If the child's cognitive responses differed from the adult's only in revealing less information and less complication of structure, it would be possible to view them as incomplete learnings of the external structure of the world, whether that structure is defined in terms of the adult culture or in terms of the laws of the physical world. If the child's responses indicate a different structure or organization than the adult's, rather than a less complete one, and if this structure is similar in all children, it is extremely difficult to view the child's mental structure as a direct learning of the external structure. Furthermore, if the adult's mental structure depends upon sequential transformations of the child's mental structure, it too cannot directly reflect the current structure of the outer cultural or physical world.

If stages cannot be accounted for by direct learning of the structure of the outer world, neither can they be explained as the result of innate patterning. If children have their own logic, adult logic or mental structure cannot be derived from innate neurological patterning because such patterning should hold also in childhood. It is hardly plausible to view a whole succession of logics as an evolutionary and functional program of innate wiring.

It has just been claimed that it is implausible to view a succession of cognitive stages as innate. This claim is based on an epistemological assumption, the assumption that there is a reality to which psychology may and must refer, i.e., that cognition or knowing must be studied in relation to an object known. The claim does not hold for postural or other stages which are not directly defined by reference to an outer reality. The invariant sequences found in motor development (Shirley, 1933) may well be directly wired into the nervous system. The fact that the postural-motor development of chimpanzees and man proceed through the same sequence suggests such a maturational base (Riesen and Kinder, 1952). The existence of invariant sequence in cognition is quite a different matter, however, since cognitions are defined by reference to a world. One cannot speak of the development of a child's conception of an animal without assuming that the child has had experiences with animals. Things become somewhat more complicated when we are dealing with the development of categories, i.e., the most general modes of relating objects such as causality, substance, space, time, quantity, and logic. These categories differ from more specific concepts, e.g., the concept of "animal," in that they are not defined by specific objects to which they refer but by modes of relating any object to any other object. Every experienced event is located in space and time, implies or causes other events, etc. Because these categories or structures are independent of specific experiences with specific objects, it has been plausible for philosophers like Kant to assume that they are innate molds into which specific experiences are fitted. If structures or categories like space and time are Kantian innate forms, it is difficult to understand how these structures could undergo transformation in development, however.

The interactional account assumes that structural change in these categories depends upon experience, then. The effects of experience, however, are not conceived of as learning in the ordinary sense in which learning implies training by pairing of specific objects and specific responses, by instruction, by modeling, or by specific practice of responses. Indeed, the effects of training are determined by the child's cognitive categories rather than the reverse. If two events which follow one another in time are cognitively connected in the child's mind, it implies that he relates them by means of a category such as causality, e.g., he perceives his operant behavior as causing the reinforcer to occur. A program of reinforcement, then, cannot directly change the child's causal structures since it is assimilated to it.

An understanding of the effect of experience upon cognitive stages presupposes three types of conceptual analysis customarily omitted in discussions of learning.

In the first place, it depends on analysis of universal structural features of the environment. While depending on structural and functional invariants of the nervous system, cognitive stages also depend upon universal structures of experience for their shape. Stages of physical concepts depend upon a universal structure of experience in the physical world, a structure which underlies the diversity of physical arrangements in which men live and which underlies the diversities of formal physical theories held in various cultures at various periods.

In the second place, understanding cognitive stages depends upon a logical analysis of orderings inherent in given concepts. The invariance of sequence in the development of a concept or category is not dependent upon a prepatterned unfolding of neural patterns; it must depend upon a logical analysis of the concept itself. As an example, Piaget (1947) postulates a sequence of spaces or geometries moving from the topological to the projective to the Euclidean. This sequence is plausible in terms of a logical analysis of the mathematical structures involved.

In the third place, an understanding of sequential stages depends upon analysis of the relation of the structure of a specific experience of the child to the behavior structure. Piaget (1964) has termed such an analysis an "equilibration" rather than a "learning" analysis. Such an analysis employs such notions as "optimal match," "cognitive conflict," "assimilation," and "accommodation." Whatever terms are used, such analyses focus upon discrepancies between the child's action system or expectancies and the experienced events, and hypothesize some moderate or optimal degree of discrepancy as constituting the most effective experience for structural change in the organism.

In summary, an interactional conception of stages differs from a maturational one in that it assumes that experience is necessary for the stages to take the shape they do as well as assuming that generally more or richer stimulation will lead to faster advances through the series involved. It proposes that an understanding of the role of experience requires: (1) analyses of universal features of experienced objects (physical or social), (2) analysis of logical sequences of differentiation and integration in concepts of such objects, and (3) analysis of structural relations between experience-inputs and the relevant behavior organizations. While these three modes of analysis are foreign to the habits of associationistic-learning theorists, they are not totally incompatible in principle with them. While associationistic concepts are clumsy to apply to universal objects of experience or to the logical structures of concepts and to the problem of match, it can be done, as Berlyne (1961, 1965) has demonstrated. As yet, such associationistic analyses have not led to the formulation of new hypotheses going beyond translations of cognitive-developmental concepts into a different language.

The preceding presentation of the cognitive-developmental approach has been rather abstract. Accordingly it may be useful to present an empirical example of a cognitive-stage sequence and elaborate why it requires an interactional theory of process for its explanation. The dream concept, studied by Piaget (1928), Pinard and Laurendeau (1964), and myself (Kohlberg, 1966a) presents a simple example. The dream is a good example of an object or experience with which the child is familiar from an early age, but which is restructured in markedly different ways in later development. One of the general categories of experience is that of substantiality or reality. Any experience must be defined as either subjective or objective. As the child's structuring of this category develops, his experience of the dream changes. According to Piaget, the young child thinks of the dream as a set of real events, rather than as a mental imagining. This represents the young child's "realism," his failure to differentiate the subjective appearance from objective reality components of his experience.

Table 6.1 indicates the actual steps of development which are found in children's beliefs about dreams. The first step (achieved by about 4 years, 10

TABLE 6.1

SEQUENCE IN DEVELOPMENT OF DREAM CONCEPT IN AMERICAN AND ATAYAL CHILDREN

Step	Scale Pattern Types						
	0	1	2	3	4	5	6
1. *Not Real*—Recognizes that objects or actions in the dream are not real or are not really there in the room.	−	+	+	+	+	+	+
2. *Invisible* — Recognizes that other people cannot see his dream.	−	−	+	+	+	+	+
3. *Internal Origin*—Recognizes that the dream *comes from* inside him.	−	−	−	+	+	+	+
4. *Internal Location*—Recognizes that the dream *goes on* inside him.	−	−	−	−	+	+	+
5. *Immaterial* — Recognizes that the dream is not a material substance but is a thought.	−	−	−	−	−	+	+
6. *Self-caused*—Recognizes that dreams are not caused by God or other agencies but are caused by the self's thought processes.	−	−	−	−	−	−	+
Median age of American children in given pattern or stage (Range=4 to 8)	4,6	4,10	5,0	5,4	6,4	6,5	7,10
Median age of Atayal of given pattern. (Range=7 to 18)	8	8	10	16	12	11	
No. of American children fitting scale types=72; not fitting=18.							
No. of Atayal children fitting scale types=12; not fitting=3.							

months by American middle-class children) is the recognition that dreams are not real events; the next step (achieved soon thereafter), that dreams cannot be seen by others. By age six, children are clearly aware that dreams take place inside them and by seven, they are clearly aware that dreams are thoughts caused by themselves.

The concept of stages implies an invariant order or sequence of development. Cultural and environmental factors or innate capabilities may make one child or group of children reach a given step of development at a much earlier point of time than another child. All children, however, should still go through the same order of steps, regardless of environmental teaching or lack of teaching.

Table 6.1 shows a series of patterns of pluses or minuses called Guttman scale types, suggesting that the steps we have mentioned form an invariant order or sequence in development. If there is an invariant order in development, then children who have passed a more difficult step in the sequence, indicated by a plus, should also have passed all the easier steps in the sequence and get pluses on all the easier items. This means that all children should fit one of the patterns on Table 6.1. For instance, all children who pass or get a plus on Step 3, recognizing the dream's internal origin, should also pass Step 2 and Step 1. The fact that only 18 out of 90 children do not fit one of these patterns is evidence for the existence of invariant sequence in the development of the dream concept. (This is more precisely indicated by a coefficient of reproducibility of .96 and an index of consistency of .83, calculated following Green [1956].)

The importance of this issue of sequence becomes apparent when we ask, "How does the child move from a view of dreams as real to a view of dreams as subjective or mental?" The simplest answer to this question is that the older child has learned the cultural definition of words like "dream" and "real." The child is frequently told by parents that his dreams are not real, that he shouldn't be upset by them, that dreams are in your mind, etc. In the learning view, this verbal teaching eventually leads the child from ignorance to knowledge of the culture's definition of the dream. It is a little hard for this verbal-learning view to account for invariant sequence in the development of the dream concept since it seems unlikely that children are taught Step 3 later than Step 2 or Step 1.

The issue of sequence becomes more critical when sequence can be examined in cultures with different adult cognitive beliefs than our own (Kohlberg, 1966a). The Atayal, a Malaysian aboriginal group on Formosa, believe in the reality of dreams. Most adult Atayal interviewed on the dream equated the soul, the dream, and ghosts. Dreams, like ghosts, are neither thoughts nor things; dreams are caused by ghosts and during the dream the soul leaves the body and experiences things in far places.

Interviews of Atayal boys and young men of various ages indicated a very interesting pattern of age development. The youngest Atayal boys were much like the youngest American boys in their responses. Up until the age of eleven, the Atayal boys seemed to develop toward a subjective conception of the dream through much the same steps as American children, though more slowly. As the table shows, the Atayal boys' answers fell into the same sequential scale pattern as the American boys. This suggests that the Atayal children tend to develop naturally toward a subjective concept of the dream up to age 11, even though their elders do not believe dreams are subjective and hence are giving them no teaching to this effect. Both the youngest child's conception of the dream as real and the school age child's view of the dream as subjective are their own, they are products of the general state of the child's cognitive development, rather than the learning of adult teachings (though the adolescent's later "regression" to concepts like those held by the younger children does represent such direct cultural learning).

The apparent invariant universal sequence in the development of the dream concept in the absence of adult cultural support cannot be interpreted as being the direct result of maturational unfolding, since the culture can "reverse" it by specific training, a reversal presumably very difficult to teach for maturational postural-motor sequences. A maturational interpretation is also contradicted by the fact that the Atayal children go through the same sequence more slowly than do their Taiwanese and American age-mates, presumably because the Atayal exist in a somewhat cognitively impoverished general culture, i.e., they have less

general experience. In this regard the Atayal children are like culturally deprived American slum Negro children who also appear to go through the dream
sequence more slowly than middle-class Negro controls, even when the two
groups are matched on psychometric intelligence (Kohn, 1969).

The culturally universal invariants of sequence found in the dream concept can be adequately understood through a logical analysis of the stages themselves. The steps represent progressive differentiations of the subjective and objective which logically could not have a different order. The first step involves a
differentiation of the *unreality* of the psychic event or dream image. The next
step the differentiation of the *internality* of the psychic event from the externality
of the physical event. A still later step is the differentiation of the *immateriality*
of the psychic event from the materiality of other physical events. This sequence
corresponds to the logical tree in Figure 6.1.

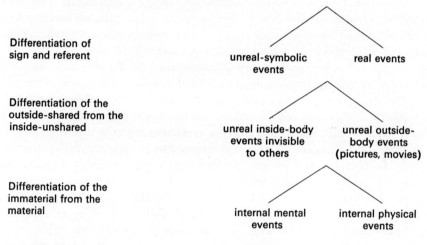

Differentiation of
sign and referent

                    unreal-symbolic   real events
                          events

Differentiation of the
outside-shared from the
inside-unshared

             unreal inside-body   unreal outside-
             events invisible   body events
               to others   (pictures, movies)

Differentiation of the
immaterial from the
material

              internal mental   internal physical
               events   events

FIGURE 6.1.

It is apparent that the differentiation of the immaterial from the material
presupposes the inside-outside distinction since all immaterial events are inside
the body (but not vice versa). It is also apparent that internality (location of
the dream experience inside the body) presupposes unreality (recognition that
the dream is not a real object) since a real object could hardly be in the body.
The observed sequence, then, is one which corresponds to an inner logic of the
concept of reality itself.

It is apparent that dreams are universal features of the child's experience.
It is also apparent that a considerable degree of conflict between the dream
experience and the waking experience of reality is a universal feature of experience. This experienced conflict or disequilibrium is presumably the "motor" for
movement through the sequence in the absence of adult teaching, though the

discrepancies and matches in experience in this area have not been clearly specified.

The data on Atayal dream "regression" introduce a useful additional clarification of the nature of the cognitive-developmental approach. The approach is not a theory about the process by which *all* behavior change occurs, as "learning theories" are. It is rather a program of analysis. Some behavior changes are "structural" and "directed" as evidenced by proceeding through sequential stages while other behavior changes are not. This is the first question for empirical investigation since it determines any further theorizing about processes of development of the phenomena. Behavior changes which are universal, progressive, and irreversible require a different analysis than do reversible situation-specific learnings. While a cognitive-developmental approach may attempt to account for reversible situational learning (as we do in discussing imitative learning), it may also be satisfied with associationistic accounts of situational learning. As an example Turiel's (1969) cognitive-developmental interpretation accounts for Atayal children's "regressive" learning of the adult culture's ideology as a reversible content-learning fitting associationistic notions of social training, modeling and reinforcement; a learning that is superimposed upon the structural development of subjective-objective differentiation. In Turiel's view, only this latter type of change requires an interactional equilibration theory of process.

The Atayal example, however, also suggests that a third "regressive" type of behavior change may require elaboration by cognitive-developmental theory. Turiel assumes that the Atayal's dream regression is not a true regression in structure, but is a content learning superimposed on a mature cognitive structure and hence does not require special theoretical principles for its explanation. While the Atayal example is an extremely ambiguous case of regression, it is obvious that true regression does occur. As is described elsewhere (Kohlberg, 1969), Piaget's cognitive tasks are passed at markedly lower levels by schizophrenic and brain-damaged subjects than by mental age normal controls. While longitudinal studies have not been carried out, we can assume that where brain damage or the onset of schizophrenia occurred in late childhood, actual regression (rather than failure of development) has occurred. It is obvious that processes accounting for such regressive change are distinct from those producing either progressive sequential change or those producing reversible specific learnings. We may simply decide to exclude such regressive processes from our analysis on the grounds that they are outside the psychological system which assumes an intact nervous system and are not required to account for the effects of a blow on the head. Or we may decide that a developmental theory must include a systematic analysis of regression, along the lines outlined by Kramer (1968) and by Langer (1967).

The need to include an account of regression in a cognitive-developmental theory is suggested by some additional data from the Atayal study. The Atayal's learning of the adult dream ideology did not appear to be a smooth and painless superimposition of social content on an underlying cognitive structure. Rather it appeared to engender complications and conflict in the adolescents' cognitive responses. Atayal children acquired the conservation of mass of a ball of clay at the usual age (7-8). Nevertheless, at age 11-15, the age of dream "regression," they partially "lost" conservation. The loss did not seem to be a genuine regression, but an uncertainty about trusting their own judgment, i.e., there was an increase in "don't know" responses. Apparently, adolescent confrontation with adult magical beliefs led them to be uncertain of other naturally developing physical beliefs, even when the latter were not in direct conflict with the adult ideology. The findings on the Atayal, then, seem loosely compatible with experimental findings by Langer (1967) suggesting that some forms of cognitive conflict lead to progressive change while others lead to regressive change. The eventual goal of a cognitive-developmental theory, then, is a specification of the types of discrepancies in experience which lead to forward movement, to backward movement, and to "fixation" or to lack of movement.

II. THE PROBLEM OF STRUCTURE IN SOCIALIZATION—THE FAILURE OF NATURALISTIC STUDIES

Before elaborating on the application of the cognitive-developmental approach just outlined to the socialization field, we need to briefly consider the more popular alternatives, the psychosexual-maturational and associationistic-learning approaches to socialization.

For the past generation, socialization research has consisted primarily of naturalistic cross-sectional studies correlating individual and cultural differences in parental practices with differences in children's motivational behavior. The theoretical framework guiding most of this research has represented varying balances of reinforcement learning theory (primarily of a Hullian variety), Freudian psychosexual theory, and anthropological culturology. A clear statement of the theoretical framework, with special focus on the psychosexual-maturational, is provided in D. R. Miller's chapter in this volume; an earlier statement is provided by Child (1954).

In the last few years, widespread dissatisfaction with the approach has been expressed by many researchers, including many of those most active in its development. This dissatisfaction has arisen because the correlations found in the studies have been low in magnitude and inconsistently replicated from one study to the next. As a result, neither clear, practical, nor theoretical conclusions can be drawn from the findings. In this section, we shall briefly document the problematic nature of the findings in one sample area, moral development. We shall then go on to consider the reasons for these difficulties, arguing that while part of the difficulties have arisen because of specific defects of theory and of measurement methodology, these defects are incidental to an unfeasible definition of the whole problem of socialization research. In particular we shall argue that studies correlating individual differences in child-rearing practices with individual differences in cross-sectional traits cannot in themselves help answer the problems of the development of universal personality structures to which such theories as psychoanalysis are basically addressed. Our critique, then, is similar to that advanced in the previous section in which we noted confusions introduced by American misinterpretation of Piaget's theory of the development of cognitive structure as a theory about the quantitative influence of various factors upon individual differences in cognitive traits.

My own pessimism about the naturalistic studies of socialization came as the result of engaging in comprehensive reviews of the socialization of moral Kohlberg, 1963a) and psychosexual (Kohlberg, 1966b) behaviors.

With regard to morality, the hypothetical personality structure focused upon has usually been termed "conscience" or "superego." This "structure" has been studied as behavior through measures of "resistance to temptation" (failure to deviate from cultural standards under conditions of low surveillance) and as affect through measures of guilt (self-critical or self-primitive symbolic response after deviation from such cultural standards). Conscience or superego as studied has been loosely similar, then, to common-sense concepts of moral character (conceived as a set of virtues like honesty, service and self-control) such as were used by Hartshorne and May (1928-30) and the socialization studies have often employed "moral character" measures as measures of "conscience."

The socialization studies, then, have attempted to relate childhood and adolescent measures of individual differences in "conscience strength" to:

1. Early experiences of restraint or gratification of oral, anal and sexual drives;
2. Amount and method of moral discipline;
3. Parent attitudes and power structures relevant to various theories of identification.

In general, no correlations have been found between parental modes of handling infantile drives and later moral behaviors or attitudes.

With regard to reward, no relations have been found between amount of reward and moral variables in twenty different studies of moral socialization. With regard to physical punishment, two studies find a positive correlation between *high* physical punishment and *high* moral resistance to temptation. Two studies find *no* correlation between physical punishment and resistance to temptation. Two studies find *high* punishment correlated with *high* delinquency, i.e., with *low* resistance to temptation. Three studies find *high* punishment correlated with *low* projective guilt (low morality). Three studies find *no* correlation between punishment and guilt. One is tempted to interpret these findings as representing a pattern of correlations randomly distributed around a base of zero.

With regard to psychological punishment, findings are more consistent. While only one of six studies found any relation between psychological discipline and moral behavior (resistance to temptation), a majority of studies (eight out of twelve) found a relation between psychological punishment and "guilt," usually defined as making confessional and self-critical responses. In most of these studies, "psychological discipline" has included both parental "love-withdrawal" and parental "induction" in Aronfreed's (1961) sense of verbal elaboration of the bad nature and consequences of the act for other people and for the self. When "induction" is distinguished from "love-withdrawal," it is found to correlate with both verbal "guilt" and internalized moral judgment in preadolescents (Aronfreed, 1961; Hoffman & Saltzstein, 1967), while "love-withdrawal" is not. Thus it appears that the findings on "love-withdrawal" are probably an artifact of combining love-withdrawal with "induction," which is why the relations are found in some studies but not others. Induction, however, is not punishment in the ordinary sense of the term, since it is difficult to view it, as one can love-withdrawal, as the infliction of psychological pain on the child. Rather it appears to be a cognitive stimulation of a moral awareness of the consequences of the child's action for other people. That this is the case is suggested by the fact that induction is also related to internalized moral judgment, which in turn is related to age and intelligence.

In summary, neither early parental handling of basic drives nor amount of various types of discipline have been found to directly correlate with moral attitudes or behavior in the studies surveyed.

With regard to parent attitudes, some consistent findings appear but their theoretical interpretation is unclear. In particular they give no clear support for the notion that early identifications are central to a moral orientation. Investigators concerned with identification have focused especially upon dimensions of parental power and nurturance. With regard to power, no clear relation with moral variables has been found. As an example, three studies report a positive correlation between paternal power and the boy's conscience, three report a negative correlation, and three report no correlation. With regard to affection, the findings are more consistent. Eight studies report a positive correlation of maternal warmth and conscience, one reports a negative correlation (among girls only), and four report no correlation. These findings, while weak, are consistent with a "developmental-identification" theory of conscience. However, a detailed examination of these findings does not support such an interpretation (Kohlberg, 1963a, 1964; Aronfreed, 1969). The common notions that if children like their parents, they will be accepting of their admonitions and that "bad children come from bad homes" are adequate to account for these findings. In other words, both the findings on inductive discipline and the findings on parental warmth suggest that children living in a positive social climate will be more willing to learn, and more accepting of, social norms than children living in a hostile or frightening climate. The finding does not seem to be specific to a moral structure but is a general tendency in the social attitude field (W. Becker, 1964). The same correlations with parental warmth and acceptance are found for the learning of achievement standards, for instance. In general, the clearer and the more consistent the findings in the moral area, the more obviously they fit a common-sense interpretation. As an example, perhaps the clearest set of findings in the family and personality literature is that delinquents come from bad homes compared to social-class controls. The badness of these homes is nonspecific, and interpretation in terms of single theoretically meaningful variables used to define these homes as bad (e.g., low warmth, use of physical punishment, frequency of divorce) fails to hold up because the interpretation or variable does not explain much variance in the normal population.

Furthermore, the more clear findings are generally ones relating current parent attitudes to current child attitudes, rather than relating early childhood experience to later personality structure. Correlations such as those mentioned on warmth and inductive discipline are clearest when they are taken as between current parent attitudes and adolescent or preadolescent attitudes. Positive relations between parental warmth and moral attitudes have not been found at the preschool-kindergarten level (Sears, Rau & Alpert, 1965; Burton, Maccoby & Allinsmith, 1961) nor does kindergarten parental warmth predict to preadolescent moral attitudes.

Our survey indicates that socialization studies of morality have yielded few empirically powerful predictors of moral behavior. Where powerful predictors have been found (as in the Glueck studies [Glueck & Glueck, 1950] of delinquency), these predictors shed little light on any theory of socialization process. One line of reasoning as to why the studies of socialization have failed is embodied in the writings of social learning revisionists, such as Aronfreed, Bandura, and Gewirtz in this volume, who once engaged in child-rearing studies of the type described. In their view, this failure is partly methodological and partly theoretical. On the methodological side, the assessment of behavior by verbal interview and test methods and the use of a correlational methodology cannot be expected to lead to the firm conclusions found through experimental manipulations of social behavior. On the theoretical side, guidance of naturalistic studies by Freudian (and Hullian) hypothetical constructs concerning internal states (e.g., "identification," "guilt") with vague surplus meaning, has led to the inability of researchers to agree on appropriate measures of these states, or to derive unambiguous predictions from the theories involved.

The cogency of these critiques is indicated by the quite powerful results obtained in their experimental studies of socialization, reported in the chapters by Aronfreed, Bandura, and Gewirtz. As an example, Aronfreed is able to show that all children learn to at least minimally "resist the temptation" to take an attractive toy because of experimental punishment (disapproval and candy withdrawal) but that degree of resistance is regularly related to the timing of punishment. These extremely clear experimental results are not supported by the naturalistic studies, which do not show amount of punishment or timing of punishment (Burton et al., 1961) related to resistance to temptation. From the perspective of the experimenter, one can cogently argue "so much the worse" for the naturalistic studies. Findings based on a clear methodology are not invalidated by lack of support from a muddy methodology. More basically, however, the theory behind the social-learning experiments does not imply any predictions as to the effects of early parental reinforcement upon later social behavior. Reinforcement-learning theories are not theories of structural change, i.e., they do not assert that childhood learnings are irreversible or that they should determine later behavior in different situations. It is part of the routine strategy of many social-learning experiments to demonstrate reversibility of the learned performance, i.e., to show that the learned behavior extinguishes under nonreinforcement. Social-learning theories do not claim extensive transfer of learning, i.e., they do not claim that reinforcement learning creates generalized traits of personality manifested in many situations. The experimental studies of socialization are, in effect, cogent demonstrations of the irrelevance of early home reinforcement parameters for later behavior. Insofar as Aronfreed demonstrates "resistance to temptation" behavior is largely determined by the experimental manipulation in a given situation and not by individual differences in traits of conscience, he demonstrates the irrelevance of early childhood learnings to the behaviors in question. It can be argued, then, that the failure of social-learning theory to receive support from naturalistic as well as experimental studies is not only due to the measurement problems and the absence of controls in the naturalistic studies but to the fact that they were misconceived as applications of the theories of learning used in them. An appropriate naturalistic study of social learning would not relate individual differences in parental practices of a global nature to individual differences in later global personality traits. Instead, it would relate trial-by-trial changes in children's situational behavior to the trial-by-trial training inputs of the parents.

Our discussion of the social-learning critique of the naturalistic studies has emphasized that the problems to which the naturalistic studies were addressed are not those to which social-learning theories are addressed. The original assumptions of the naturalistic studies were those shared by psychoanalytic and neo-psychoanalytic theories of personality development, i.e., theories which assumed the existence of relatively irreversible structural changes in generalized personality organization. The problems addressed by the studies were those of the ways in which early experiences formed fixed personality structures, and have used the term "socialization" to refer to the establishment of such enduring personality structures as were compatible with the demands of the child's culture.

The studies, then, assumed that early childhood represented a "critical period," i.e., a period of age-specific irreversible changes in personality. They have also assumed that the social processes and influences (primarily parental) forming personality in this period were different than the general processes of reversible social learning or social influence found in adult behavior. This assumption is most clear in the psychoanalytic theory, which assumes that structural change seldom occurs in adulthood, and that such structural change as does occur in adulthood rests on transference of infantile attitudes. These notions of childhood as a critical period have derived primarily from psychoanalytic conceptions of maturational sequences of basic drives. While psychoanalysis has stressed maturational content rather than cognitive structure, and has conceived of sequences as maturational rather than interactional, it agrees with the cognitive-developmental approach in analyzing behavior change as a process of development, i.e., as a directed process of structural change exemplified in culturally universal sequential stages. Because it is maturational, psychoanalytic theory is even more clear than cognitive-developmental theory in distinguishing between the causes of forward movement (which is maturational) and the causes of fixation or of backward movement (which represent environmentally induced strains or frustrations).

It is evident that insofar as the naturalistic studies were based on psychosexual theory, these studies should have started by empirically establishing the natural age-developmental trends postulated by psychosexual theory, since psychosexual theory describes socialization in terms of fixations, regressions, or inhibitions in such developmental trends. Almost none of the myriad studies of socialization have actually attempted to do this. Instead most have "bootstrapped" this essential first phase of the task. Insofar as they have been psychoanalytically oriented, they have (1) theoretically assumed (rather than observed) psychosexual stages, (2) theoretically assumed that some behavior measure was in fact a valid measure of some aspect of psychosexual development, and have then gone on to (3) hypothesize some relation of a child-rearing practice to individual differences in the behavior measure at a given age. The "bootstrapping" strategy has assumed that if the predicted correlation between child-rearing practices and the variable was found, that this would confirm (1) the postulated psychosexual sequences, (2) the validity of the measures employed, and (3) the postulated relation between the child-rearing practice and fixation of the psychosexual sequences. Obviously this research strategy is unworkable as the results of the studies have demonstrated.

From one point of view the strategy might be considered one in which psychosexual stages are considered postulates useful in discovering some reliable and powerful relations between early experience and later personality. From another perspective, the strategy might be conceived as one of testing the validity of psychosexual theory. From either point of view, the strategy has failed. With regard to the first point of view, very few reliable and powerful empirical correlations have been obtained which would aid in predicting the behavior of any individual or group of children. From the second point of view, the bootstrapping approach cannot be said to be testing psychoanalytic theory. If it had worked, it might have provided some support for the theory, but its failure is not evidence against the theory which cannot be said to be "tested" by such studies.

The objection to the bootstrapping approach is not so much that it was methodologically inappropriate to the difficult problem of socialization as that it was based on a misconception of psychoanalytic theory. We noted that Piaget's (1964) theory of the *development* of cognitive structures found in every human has been frequently misinterpreted by Americans as a theory of the origins of individual differences in intellectual abilities or traits, leading some Americans to view his interactionism as genetic maturationism and others to view his interactionism as a doctrine of the environmental determination of IQ difference. We have noted that theories of reinforcement learning have also sometimes been misinterpreted as theories designed to account for stable individual differences in personality traits, whereas these theories do not postulate personality traits in the first place. Learning theories are statements of laws or functional relations holding for all men, not theories designed to make statements about individual differences. It is an equally American misinterpretation to view psychoanalytic theory as directly relevant to an understanding of individual differences in personality traits. In part, psychoanalytic theory is a theory of laws of mental functioning in all humans. In part, it is a theory of a development and maturation. In part, it is a theory of psychopathology. It has never claimed, however, to be a theory designed to predict adult individual differences or traits from specific childhood experiences; a task Freud (1938) claimed was impossible.

While Freud had special reasons for viewing the problem of the prediction of individual differences as unresolvable, a little thought leads to the recognition that there is no general theoretical question as to the origin of individual differences nor any conceivable general answer to such a question. While American researchers will always be obsessed with the problem of the prediction of individual differences, this problem is no more likely to lead to conceptual advance in social science than is meteorological prediction likely to lead to general advance in physical science. This contention may perhaps be clarified by pointing to certain extreme examples of "meteorological" studies of child-rearing antecedents of student activism. Of what theoretical significance could it be to examine the child-rearing antecedents to participation in a transitory social movement in the United States? It certainly can contribute nothing to the understanding of personality development or socialization defined outside of the culture of the American college of the 1960's. It is of equally little sociological or practical significance. One might be practically interested in the current values and personality integration of student activists, but hardly in the childhood correlates of activism. If this criticism is accepted, one must ask whether a study of the child-rearing correlates of variations in American middle-class five-year-old boys' performance on some cheating tasks in the year 1965 is likely to be of conceptual interest, since the correlations are unlikely to hold true in another society, in another moral task, at another year or in another historical period, as the lack of replicability of the conscience studies suggests.

We have stated that the conceptually interesting problems of socialization are not the problems of accounting for the natural correlates of individual differences in behavior traits. Indeed, some understanding of the inconsistencies of the naturalistic studies arises when it is recognized that socialization seldom gives rise to traits as usually conceived. With regard to "resistance to temptation" or "moral internalization" no findings have been reported suggesting fundamental revisions of Hartshorne and May's (1928-30) conclusions as to the situational specificity and longitudinal instability of moral character, as is discussed in detail elsewhere (Kohlberg, 1964; Sears et al., 1965; Grim, Kohlberg & White, 1968).

Correlations between tests of resistance to temptation are low, and test-retest stability of these measures is low (correlations between cheating tests typically range between 0 and 40, six-month test-retest coefficients range between 30 and 60).

An example of the failure of resistance to temptation tests to represent conscience structure comes from a study by Lehrer (1967). Lehrer made use of Grinder's (1964) ray gun test of resistance to temptation. Grinder reports that a large majority (about 80 per cent) of sixth-grade children cheat for a prize badge on this test. Lehrer decided to improve the circuitry and the instructions involved in the test to control for certain minor factors that might discourage cheating. Rather than making cheating more likely, her improvements led to less than 25 per cent of the sixth-graders cheating. Probably the increased size and computer-like appearance of the gun led the children to believe it had score-keeping powers. Obviously the behavior of the 55 per cent of children who cheat on one machine but not the other is not determined by features of conscience strength.

Long ago MacKinnon (1938) suggested that conscience or superego was only one factor in actual moral behavior, such as the decision to cheat. A clearer index of conscience would be provided by assessments of guilt, a more stable or general tendency. While guilt was the moral force in personality, actual moral decisions depended on the interaction between guilt and other factors in the personality and in the situation. This plausible view led socialization analysts to proliferate projective measures of guilt and to relate them to child-rearing practices. There has been little agreement on what constitutes guilt in projective responses to transgression stories, however. The chief disagreement has been between those who view guilt as a conscious cognitive moral judgment (i.e., statements that an actor feels bad and blames himself after transgressions) and those who view it as unconscious anxiety and self-punitive tendencies (projections of harm, punishment, catastrophe and self-injury after transgression). Needless to say, the two are empirically unrelated. Furthermore, when the latter conception of guilt is employed, varying indices of guilt do not correlate well with one another and little story-to-story generality or test-retest stability of guilt is found (studies reviewed in Kohlberg, 1963a). Not surprisingly, then, little consistency from study to study has been found as to child-rearing antecedents of guilt (studies reviewed in Kohlberg, 1963a).

Consistencies between studies of child-rearing antecedents of conscience presuppose that the measures of conscience in one situation relate to measures in another, and that measures of conscience at one age correlate with measures at another. While no longitudinal studies of child-rearing correlates of conscience have been carried out, a study of aggression has (Sears, 1961). Sears found that child-rearing correlates of aggression in children age 5 failed to correlate with aggression to these same children at age 12. This is hardly surprising in light of the fact that measures of aggression at age 5 failed to predict aggression at age 12. Given a similar longitudinal instability in "conscience strength," the lack of consistency in findings on its child-rearing correlates is not surprising.

III. AN EXAMPLE OF SOCIAL DEVELOPMENT
DEFINED IN COGNITIVE-STRUCTURAL TERMS—
MORAL STAGES

At first, the disappointing results summarized in the previous section suggest that all social behavior is reversible situation-specific behavior to be studied by such methods and concepts as those used by social-learning theorists. However, we shall now try to show that there are stages or directed structural age-changes in the area of social-personality development just as there are in the cognitive area. In Section V we shall go on to argue that these structural changes are not explainable in terms of the methods and concepts of social learning. In this section, we shall attempt to show that these structural-developmental changes can provide definitions of individual differences free of the problems which have confounded the naturalistic socialization studies in the sense that they generate situationally general and longitudinally stable measures which relate meaningfully to social-environmental inputs. Our argument will be based on findings in a specific area, morality. However, we shall argue that success in this area is only a special case of the potential success arising from definitions of social development in cognitive-structural terms.

In spite of its obviousness, our focus upon situational generality and longitudinal predictability as a prerequisite for the meaningful study of socialization deserves some elaboration. The bulk of thinking about socialization is thinking about personality and culture, conceived as patterns or structures abstractable from the raw data of the myriad social behaviors in which individuals engage. The legitimate abstraction of a concept of personality from such raw data depends on the ability to predict behavior from one situation or time period to the next from the personality concept in question, i.e., it depends upon the demonstration of its situational generality and longitudinal continuity.

In the previous section we pointed out that the ordinary personality "traits" focused upon in naturalistic studies of socialization are not stable in development. The ordering of individuals on motivated traits like dependency, aggression, affiliation, anxiety, need-achievement, and conscience-strength either predicts very little or not at all to later ordering on these same traits, if the two orderings are separated by many years (Kagan & Moss, 1962; MacFarlane, Allen & Honzik, 1954; Sears, 1961; Emmerich, 1964). The personality traits outside the cognitive domain which have proved most stable are those of little interest to socialization theory, e.g., traits of temperament like introversion-extroversion and activity-passivity (Kagan & Moss, 1962; Emmerich, 1964). These traits are uninteresting to socialization theory because their stable components seem to be largely innate (Gottesman, 1963) rather than to be the products of socialization, because they are traits of style rather than content of social action, and because they do not predict the general adjustment of the individual to his culture (La Crosse & Kohlberg, 1969).

The study of socialization in terms of personality formation under the assumption of trait stability, then, is unjustified. Most theories of personality formation do not assume trait stability, however. They assume rather that personality undergoes radical transformations in development but that there is continuity in the individual's development through these transformations. In other words, they conceptualize personality development as an orderly sequence of change, with the individual's location at a later point in the sequence being related to location at an earlier point in the sequence. In the words of John Dewey (1930), "Psychology is concerned with life-careers, with behavior as it is characterized by changes taking place in an activity that is serial and continuous, in reference to changes in an environment which is continuous while changing in detail."

While Dewey assumed that behavior is determined by the current ongoing situation in which the person is engaged, the situation is as that person defines it. This definition, in turn, is a result of sensitivities developing out of earlier situations, e.g., "One and the same environmental change becomes a thousand different actual stimuli under different conditions of ongoing or serial behavior" (Dewey, 1930).

In this view, early experience determines the choice of one or another path or sequence of development. It does not lead to the stamping in or fixation of traits carried from situation to situation throughout life. As stated by John Anderson (1957), "The young organism is fluid, subsequent development can go in any one of many directions. But once a choice is made and direction is set, cumulative and irreversible changes take place."

While continuity in personality development may be defined in terms of a number of alternative sequences available to different individuals in different social settings, most developmental theories of personality have employed some notion of a single, universal sequence of personality stages (S. Freud, 1938; Gesell, 1954; Erikson, 1950; Piaget, 1928). Such stage theories view the child's social behavior as reflections of age-typical world views and coping mechanisms rather than as reflections of fixed character traits. As the child moves from stage to stage, developmental theorists expect his behavior to change radically but to be predictable in terms of knowledge of his prior location in the stage sequence and of the intervening experiences stimulating or retarding movement to the next stage.

If continuity in personality development is to be found, then, stage theories hold that personality must be defined in terms of location in regular sequences of age development. The first and grossest implication of this view is that personality description must be phrased in age-developmental terms. In most studies of socialization, concepts of age-development have been theoretically assumed and empirically ignored. We have noted this in psychoanalytically oriented studies which continue to define individual differences with "superego strength" measures theoretically assumed to be related to psychosexual age-development in spite of the fact that these measures do not relate empirically to age-development. It is also true in more learning-theory oriented studies of socialization, which define socialization as *learned conformity* to the standards of the group, and ignore the relations of such conformity to age-development. Usually these studies assume that social age-development generally coincides with "socialization."

In Child's (1954) definition socialization is "the process by which an individual, born with behavior potentialities of an enormously wide range, is led to develop actual behavior confined within the narrower range of what is customary for him according to the standards of his group." The socialization conception of moral development is implied in its definition in terms of strength of resistance to temptation and strength of guilt. "Resistance to temptation" means amount of conformity to cultural moral rules, "guilt" means degree of conformity to these rules after deviation in the form of culturally expected forms of reparation for deviance. In the psychosexual field, socialization has been defined as increased conformity of attitudes to cultural norms for masculine or feminine roles, usually as measured by M-F tests.

While it has seemed plausible to equate "moral development" or "psychosexual development" with degree of conformity to the culture, it turns out that conformity does not in fact define trends of age-development. In the area of morality, the dimension of increased "resistance to temptation" as experimentally measured (honesty in old-fashioned terms) does not seem to define a trend of age-development at all. Sears et al. (1965) did not find an increase in experimental honesty from age 4 to 6 ; Grinder (1964) did not find an increase from 7 to 11; and Hartshorne and May (1928-30) did not find an increase from 11 to 14. In the psychosexual area, "internalization" or "identification," i.e., sex-typed preference and choice, does not increase regularly or clearly with age after 7 (Kohlberg, 1966b). The lack of longitudinal stability in measures of "conscience strength," then, becomes more intelligible when it is recognized that the child's moral maturity, in an age-developmental sense, does not predict to his performance on these measures. In some sense, we know that the average adult is morally different from the average four-year-old. Measures which fail to capture this difference must completely fail to capture whatever continuities exist in development.

The fact that degree of conformity measures fail to capture age-development is only a special case of the fact that polar traits in the personality area are seldom either age-developmental or longitudinally stable. By polar traits are meant traits defined by a quantitative ordering of individuals on a single dimension (such as aggression, dependency, etc., e.g., Loevinger, 1966). Most developmental theories of personality assume that such "traits" are differential balancings of conflicting forces and that these balancings differ at different points in the life cycle as new developmental tasks are focused upon. Developmental theories assume that a certain minimal level of certain polar traits must be present for solution of a developmental task, but further increase on the variable is no sign of increased maturity. As an example, achieving a certain level of conformity may become a "milestone" representing the formation of conscience in various theories. Further development, however, may lead to a relaxation of conformity with assurance that impulse control has been achieved, or it may lead to an apparent non-conformity as autonomous and individual principles of values are developed. As an example, guilt has typically been measured by number and intensity of self-blaming and reparative reactions to stories about deviation from conventional norms for children (e.g., opening some boxes hidden by one's mother, cheating in a race, etc.). Age-developmental studies indicate that almost no direct or conscious guilt is expressed to such stories of conventional deviation by children under eight, that the majority of children age 11-12 express some guilt, and that there is no age increase in amount or intensity of guilt after this age (evidence reviewed in Kohlberg, 1969). Ratings of intensity of guilt, then, may group at the low to moderate end both the immature who have not achieved a minimal level of conformity and the mature who have transcended such conformity and have a humorously detached sense that they do not have to show what good boys they are in obeying mother in such stories. If one were interested in using projective "guilt" as an index of moral maturity, one would simply note the qualitative presence of conventional guilt reactions to some transgression story as an indication of having passed one of a number of milestones in moral development, rather than constructing a polar trait of guilt intensity.

While the study of age-development can go a certain distance using moderate levels of polar traits as milestones, the developmentalist holds that satisfactory definition or measurement of age-development requires definition of changes in the shape, pattern, or organization of responses. The developmentalist holds that a closer look at changes over time indicates regularities representing basic changes in the shape of responses rather than changes in their strength. This is, of course, the implication of an account of development in terms of stages. Stage notions are essentially ideal-typological constructs designed to represent different psychological organizations at varying points in development. The stage doctrine hypothesizes that these qualitatively different types of organization are sequential, and hence that the individual's developmental status is predictable or cumulative in the sense of continuity of position on an ordinal scale.

In what has been said so far, there is little divergence between the views of psychoanalytic, neo-psychoanalytic and cognitive-developmental approaches to personality. The cognitive-developmental approach diverges from the others, however, in stressing that directed sequences of changes in behavior organization or shape always have a strong cognitive component. On the logical side, our approach claims that social development is cognitively based because any description of shape or pattern of a structure of social responses necessarily entails some cognitive dimensions. Description of the organization of the child's social responses entails a description of the way in which he perceives, or conceives, the social world and the way in which he conceives himself. Even "depth" psychologies recognize that there are no affects divorced from cognitive structure. While social psychology for a long time attempted to measure attitudes as pure intensities, the birth of a theoretical social psychology of attitudes (e.g., various cognitive balance theories) has come from the recognition that the affect component of attitudes is largely shaped and changed by the cognitive organization of these attitudes.

On the empirical side the cognitive-developmental approach derives from the fact that most marked and clear changes in the psychological development of the child are cognitive, in the mental-age or IQ sense. The influence of intelligence on children's social attitudes and behavior is such that it has a greater number of social-behavior correlates than any other observed aspect of personality (Cattell, 1957). In terms of prediction Anderson (1960) summarizes his longitudinal study of adjustment as follows:

> We were surprised at the emergence of the intelligence factor in a variety of our instruments (family attitudes, responsibility and maturity, adjustment) in spite of our attempts to minimize intelligence in selecting our personality measures. Next we were surprised that for prediction over a long time, the intelligence quotient seems to carry a heavy predictive load in most of our measures of outcomes. It should be noted that in a number of studies, adjustment at both the child and the adult level, whenever intelligence is included, emerges as a more significant factor than personality measures.

It is apparent that the power of IQ to predict social behavior and adjustment springs from numerous sources, including the social and school success experiences associated with brightness. However, a large part of the predictive power of IQ derives from the fact that more rapid cognitive development is associated with more rapid social development. This interpretation of IQ effects has been thoroughly documented in the area of sex-role attitudes. An example of this fact comes from a semilongitudinal study of the sex-role attitudes of bright and average boys and girls (Kohlberg & Zigler, 1967). In the first place, this study indicated significant IQ effects in performance on seven tests of sex-role attitudes (some experimental-behavioral, some verbal, some projective doll-play). In the second place, the study indicated that while there were marked and similar developmental trends for both bright and average children, these trends were largely determined by mental as opposed to chronological age. Parallel curves of age-development were obtained for both groups with the curves being about two years advanced for the bright children (who were about two years advanced in mental age). As an example, bright boys would shift from a preference for adult females to a preference for adult males on experimental and doll-play tests at about age 4 whereas the average boys would make the shift about age 6. The same findings held in a study of retarded and average lower-class Negro boys, half father-absent, half father-present (unpublished study by C. Smith, summarized in Kohlberg, 1966b). The average boys made the shift to the male at age 5-6, the retarded boys at age 7-8. Clearly, then, sex-role age-developmental trends are mediated by cognitive development.

Turning to morality, "resistance to temptation" has a moderate but clearly documented correlation with IQ.[1] These findings are not too helpful, however, since resistance to temptation does not define any dimension of age-development of morality. We shall now attempt to show that more "cognitive" dimensions of moral judgment do define moral age-development, and that once moral judgment development is understood, the development of moral action and moral affect becomes much more intelligible and predictable. The assertion that moral judgment undergoes regular age-development and that this development is in some sense cognitive has seldom been questioned since the work of Hartshorne and May (1928-30) and Piaget (1948). However, extreme proponents of the cultural relativism of values must logically question both these contentions, as Bronfenbrenner (1962) has recently done. Bronfenbrenner has claimed that class, sex, and culture are more important determinants of Piaget-type moral judgment than is age-development. Examination of this claim may usefully clarify the sense in which moral judgment is said to have a cognitive-developmental component. One sense of the assertion that moral judgment development is cognitive is that it involves an increase in the child's knowledge of the content of conventional standards and values of his group. This is indeed the nature of moral judgment as measured by conventional "moral knowledge" tests like those of Hartshorne and May (1928-30). In this sense, it is plausible to assert that insofar as the content of standards and value labels differs by class, sex, and culture, so will the development of moral judgment. In another sense, however, moral judgments change in cognitive form with development. As an example, it is generally recognized that conceptions and sentiments of justice ("giving each his due") are based on conceptions of reciprocity and of equality. Reciprocity and equality are, however, cognitive as well as moral forms. Piaget (1947) has done a number of studies suggesting that the awareness of logical reciprocity (e.g., recognition that I am my brother's brother) develops with the formation of concrete operations at age 6-7. Our studies (Kohlberg, 1969) indicate that use of reciprocity as a moral reason first appears at the same age.

Another example of cognitive form in moral judgment is the consideration of intentions as opposed to physical consequences in judging the badness of action. According to Piaget (1948), the development of moral intentionality corresponds to the more general cognitive differentiation of objective and subjective, physical and mental, discussed in Section I. Accordingly, it is not surprising to find that in every culture, in every social class, in every sex group, and in every subculture studied (Switzerland, United States, Belgium, Chinese, Malaysian-aboriginal, Mexican, Israel, Hopi, Zuni, Sioux, Papago) age trends toward increased intentionality are found. It is also not surprising to find this trend is always correlated with intelligence or mental development in all groups where intelligence measures have been available. Finally, it is not surprising to find that such cultural or subcultural differences as exist are explainable as due

---

[1] All findings on moral development discussed are documented and referenced in Kohlberg, 1969 ; some are to be found in Kohlberg, 1963a, 1964; so they will not be referenced in this chapter.

to the amount of social and cognitive stimulation provided by the culture in question.

As an example, in all nations studied, there are social-class differences in the direction of earlier intentionality for the middle class. These are not class differences in values, but class differences in the cognitive and social stimulation of development. In each class, the older and more intelligent children are more intentional. If the "retardation" of the lower-class child were to be explained as due to a different adult subcultural value system, the older and brighter lower-class children would have to be more "retarded" than the younger and duller lower-class children, since they should have learned the lower-class value system better. Intentionality, then, is an example of a culturally universal developmental trend, which is universal and regular in its development because it has a "cognitive form" base in the differentiation of the physical and the mental.

In contrast, however, a number of the dimensions of moral judgment studied by Piaget are really matters of content rather than cognitive form. An example is the dimension of responsiveness to peer, as opposed to adult, expectations. While Piaget (1948) hypothesizes this dimension as part of his autonomous stage, his rationale for deriving this from a consideration of cognitive form is vague and unconvincing. There is nothing more cognitively mature to preferring a peer than an adult. It is not surprising to find, then, that this dimension does not vary regularly with chronological and mental age, that what age trends exist are absent in some national groups (e.g., the Swiss), and that in general this dimension is sensitive to a wide variety of cultural and subcultural influences which cannot be analyzed in rate of development terms.

In summary, then, universal and regular age trends of development may be found in moral judgment, and these have a formal-cognitive base. Many aspects of moral judgment do not have such a cognitive base, but these aspects do not define universal and regular trends of moral development.

Using the Piaget (1948) material, we have indicated that there are "natural" culturally universal trends of age-development in moral judgment with a cognitive-formal base. Age trends, however, are not in themselves sufficient to define stages with the properties discussed in our first section. While Piaget attempted to define two stages of moral judgment (the heteronomous and the autonomous), extensive empirical study and logical analysis indicate that his moral stages have not met the criteria of stage he proposes (summarized in our first section), as his cognitive stages do.

Taking cognizance of Piaget's notions as well as those of others such as Hobhouse (1906), J. M. Baldwin (1906), Peck and Havighurst (1960), and McDougall (1908), I have attempted to define stages of moral judgment which would meet these criteria. A summary characterization of the stages is presented in Table 6.2. The relations of the stages to those of other writers is indicated by Table 6.3.

The stages were defined in terms of free responses to ten hypothetical moral dilemmas, one of which is presented subsequently in Table 6.5. Stage definition

TABLE 6.2

CLASSIFICATION OF MORAL JUDGMENT INTO LEVELS AND STAGES OF
DEVELOPMENT

Levels	Basis of Moral Judgment	Stages of Development
I	Moral value resides in external, quasi-physical happenings, in bad acts, or in quasi-physical needs rather than in persons and standards.	Stage 1: Obedience and punishment orientation. Egocentric deference to superior power or prestige, or a trouble-avoiding set. Objective responsibility.
		Stage 2: Naively egoistic orientation. Right action is that instrumentally satisfying the self's needs and occasionally others'. Awareness of relativism of value to each actor's needs and perspective. Naive egalitarianism and orientation to exchange and reciprocity.
II	Moral value resides in performing good or right roles, in maintaining the conventional order and the expectancies of others.	Stage 3: Good-boy orientation. Orientation to approval and to pleasing and helping others. Conformity to stereotypical images of majority or natural role behavior, and judgment by intentions.
		Stage 4: Authority and social-order maintaining orientation. Orientation to "doing duty" and to showing respect for authority and maintaining the given social order for its own sake. Regard for earned expectations of others.
III	Moral value resides in conformity by the self to shared or shareable standards, rights, or duties.	Stage 5: Contractual legalistic orientation. Recognition of an arbitrary element or starting point in rules or expectations for the sake of agreement. Duty defined in terms of contract, general avoidance of violation of the will or rights of others, and majority will and welfare.
		Stage 6: Conscience or principle orientation. Orientation not only to actually ordained social rules but to principles of choice involving appeal to logical universality and consistency. Orientation to conscience as a directing agent and to mutual respect and trust.

Source: Kohlberg, 1967, p. 171.

is based on a subsumption of a moral judgment under one of twenty-five aspects of moral judgment listed in Table 6.4.

These aspects represent basic moral concepts believed to be present in any society. As an example, "10, punishment" is a culturally universal concept entering into moral judgment as is "19, rights of property" or "23, contract." Each of these concepts is differently defined and used at each of the six stages. Definition or usage of concepts at each stage can logically be claimed to represent a differentiation and integration of the concept as it is used at the preceding

TABLE 6.3

Author	Amoral	1. Fearful–Dependent	2. Opportunistic	3. Conforming to Persons	4. Conforming to Rule	5,6. Principled–Autonomous
Moral Stages						
McDougall (1908)	1. instinctive		2. reward and punishment	3. anticipation of praise and blame		4. regulation by an internal ideal
J. M. Baldwin (1906)		1. adualistic	2. intellectual		3. ideal	
L. Hobhouse (1906)	1. instinctive	2. obligation as magical taboo		3. obligation as ideals of personal virtue	4. obligation as rules of society	5. rational ethical principles
Piaget (1948)	1. premoral	2. heteronomous obedience to adult authority	3. autonomous—reciprocity and equality oriented			4. autonomous—ideal reciprocity and equality
Peck and Havighurst (1960)	1. amoral		2. expedient	3. conforming	4. irrational-conscientious	5. rational-altruistic
Kohlberg (1958)		1. obedience & punishment oriented	2. instrumental egoism and exchange	3. good-boy approval oriented	4. authority, rule and social order oriented	5. social contract legalist orientation 6. moral principle orientation
Ego or Character Types						
Fromm (1955) Riesman (1950)		1. receptive, tradition-directed	2. exploitative, anomic	3. marketing, other-directed	4. hoarding, inner-directed	5. productive, autonomous
C. Sullivan, Grant and Grant (1957)		I_2 passive—demanding	I_3 conformist (exploitative)	I_3 conformist (cooperative)	I_4 authoritarian—guilty	I_6 self-consistent I_7 integrative
Harvey, Hunt & Shroeder (1961)		1. absolutistic—evaluative	2. self-differentiating	3. empathic		4. integrated—independent
Loevinger (1966)	1. presocial	2. impulse-ridden, fearful	3. expedient	4. conformist	5. conscientious	6. autonomous 7. integrated

stage. An example of the six stages of definition of one aspect of moral judgment is presented in Table 6.5. This table indicates how the aspect of intentionality studied by Piaget (1948) has been defined in terms of each of the six qualitative

TABLE 6.4

CODED ASPECTS OF DEVELOPING MORAL JUDGMENT

Code	Description	Aspects
I. Value	Locus of value —modes of attributing (moral) value to acts, persons, or events. Modes of assessing value consequences in a situation.	1. Considering motives in judging action. 2. Considering consequences in judging action. 3. Subjectivity vs. objectivity of values assessed. 4. Relation of obligation to wish. 5. Identification with actor or victims in judging the action. 6. Status of actor and victim as changing the moral worth of actions.
II. Choice	Mechanisms of resolving or denying awareness of conflicts.	7. Limiting actor's responsibility for consequences by shifting responsibility onto others. 8. Reliance on discussion and compromise, mainly unrealistically. 9. Distorting situation so that conforming behavior is seen as always maximizing the interests of the actor or of others involved.
III. Sanctions and Motives	The dominant motives and sanctions for moral or deviant action.	10. Punishment or negative reactions. 11. Disruption of an interpersonal relationship. 12. A concern by actor for welfare, for positive state of the other. 13. Self-condemnation.
IV. Rules	The ways in which rules are conceptualized, applied, and generalized. The basis of the validity of a rule.	14. Definition of an act as deviant. (Definition of moral rules and norms.) 15. Generality and consistency of rules. 16. Waiving rules for personal relations (particularism).
V. Rights and Authority	Basis and limits of control over persons and property.	17. Non-motivational attributes ascribed to authority (knowledge, etc.). (Motivational attributes considered under III above.) 18. Extent or scope of authority's rights. Rights of liberty. 19. Rights of possession or property.

Code	Description	Aspects
VI. Positive Justice	Reciprocity and equality.	20. Exchange and reciprocity as a motive for role conformity. 21. Reciprocity as a motive to deviate (e.g., revenge). 22. Distributive justice. Equality and impartiality. 23. Concepts of maintaining partner's expectations as a motive for conformity. Contract and trust.
VII. Punitive Justice	Standards and functions of punishment.	24. Punitive tendencies or expectations. (a) Notions of equating punishment and crime. 25. Functions or purpose of punishment.

Source: Kohlberg, 1967, pp. 172-173.

stages. To document the way in which form of moral judgment is distinct from action content, Table 6.5 presents standardized arguments (Rest, 1968) at each stage of intentionality both for and against stealing the drug in the dilemma involved. Table 6.5 also indicates the sense in which each stage of orientation to intentions entails a differentiation not made at the preceding stage.

TABLE 6.5

SIX STAGES OF ORIENTATION TO INTENTIONS AND CONSEQUENCES (ASPECTS 1 AND 2) IN RESPONSE TO A MORAL DILEMMA

In Europe, a woman was near death from cancer. One drug might save her, a form of radium that a druggist in the same town had recently discovered. The druggist was charging $2,000, ten times what the drug cost him to make. The sick woman's husband, Heinz, went to everyone he knew to borrow the money, but he could only get together about half of what it cost. He told the druggist that his wife was dying and asked him to sell it cheaper or let him pay later. But the druggist said, "No." The husband got desperate and broke into the man's store to steal the drug for his wife. Should the husband have done that? Why?

Stage 1.   Motives and need-consequences of act are ignored in judging badness because of focus upon irrelevant physical form of the act (e.g., size of the lie), or of the consequences of the act (e.g., amount of physical damage).

Pro —He should steal the drug. It isn't really bad to take it. It isn't like he didn't ask to pay for it first. The drug he'd take is only worth $200, he's not really taking a $2,000 drug.

Con —He shouldn't steal the drug, it's a big crime. He didn't get permission, he used force and broke and entered. He did a lot of damage, stealing a very expensive drug and breaking up the store, too.

Stage 2.   Judgment ignores label or physical consequences of the act because of the instrumental value of the act in serving a need, or because the act doesn't do harm in terms of the need of another. (Differentiates the human need-value of the act from its physical form or consequences.)

Pro —It's all right to steal the drug because she needs it and he wants her to live. It isn't that he wants to steal, but it's the way he has to use to get the drug to save her.

Con —He shouldn't steal it. The druggist isn't wrong or bad, he just wants to make a profit. That's what you're in business for, to make money.

TABLE 6.5 (continued)

Stage 3. Action evaluated according to the type of motive or person likely to perform the act. An act is not bad if it is an expression of a "nice" or altruistic motive or person and it is not good if it is the expression of a "mean" or selfish motive or person. Circumstances may excuse or justify deviant action. (Differentiates good motives to which an act is instrumental from human but selfish need to which it is instrumental.)

> Pro —He should steal the drug. He was only doing something that was natural for a good husband to do. You can't blame him for doing something out of love for his wife, you'd blame him if he didn't love his wife enough to save her.

> Con —He shouldn't steal. If his wife dies, he can't be blamed. It isn't because he's heartless or that he doesn't love her enough to do everything that he legally can. The druggist is the selfish or heartless one.

Stage 4. An act is always or categorically wrong, regardless of motives or circumstances, if it violates a rule and does foreseeable harm to others. (Differentiates action out of a sense of obligation to rule from action for generally "nice" or natural motives.)

> Pro —You should steal it. If you did nothing you'd be letting your wife die, it's your responsibility if she dies. You have to take it with the idea of paying the druggist.

> Con —It is a natural thing for Heinz to want to save his wife but it's still always wrong to steal. He still knows he's stealing and taking a valuable drug from the man who made it.

Stage 5. A formal statement that though circumstances or motive modify disapproval, as a general rule the means do not justify the ends. While circumstances justify deviant acts to some extent they do not make it right or lead to suspension of moral categories. (Differentiates moral blame because of the intent behind breaking the rule from the legal or principled necessity not to make exceptions to rules.)

> Pro —The law wasn't set up for these circumstances. Taking the drug in this situation isn't really right, but it's justified to do it.

> Con —You can't completely blame someone for stealing but extreme circumstances don't really justify taking the law in your own hands. You can't have everyone stealing whenever they get desperate. The end may be good, but the ends don't justify the means.

Stage 6. Good motives don't make an act right (or not wrong); but if an act follows from a decision to follow general self-chosen principles, it can't be wrong. It may be actually right to deviate from the rules, but only under circumstances forcing a choice between deviation from the rules and concrete violation of a moral principle. (Differentiates good motives of following a moral principle from natural motives as following a rule. Recognizes that moral principles don't allow exceptions any more than do legal rules.)

> Pro —This is a situation which forces him to choose between stealing and letting his wife die. In a situation where the choice must be made, it is morally right to steal. He has to act in terms of the principle of preserving and respecting life.

> Con —Heinz is faced with the decision of whether to consider the other people who need the drug just as badly as his wife. Heinz ought to act not according to his particular feelings toward his wife, but considering the value of all the lives involved.

Source: Rest, 1968.

While it is not surprising to consider concepts of intentionality developing along cognitive-formal dimensions, it may surprise the reader to find that motives for moral action (Aspects 10 and 13 of Table 6.4) also have a cognitive-formal element. Table 6.6 presents the definition of moral motives characteristic of each stage, in a form similar to that of Table 6.5. It should be recalled that we are still dealing with concepts, here concepts of motives manifestly relevant to the concepts of intentions involved in the previous table. As Table 6.6 indicates, each stage involves a differentiation not present at the preceding stage.

The definition of the stages is not dependent on responses to a particular set of materials, however, but is based on a system for scoring any moral judgment

TABLE 6.6

MOTIVES FOR ENGAGING IN MORAL ACTION
(ASPECTS 10 AND 13)

Stage 1. Action is motivated by avoidance of punishment and "conscience" is irrational fear of punishment.

    Pro—If you let your wife die, you will get in trouble. You'll be blamed for not spending the money to save her and there'll be an investigation of you and the druggist for your wife's death.

    Con—You shouldn't steal the drug because you'll be caught and sent to jail if you do. If you do get away, your conscience would bother you thinking how the police would catch up with you at any minute.

Stage 2. Action motivated by desire for reward or benefit. Possible guilt reactions are ignored and punishment viewed in a pragmatic manner. (Differentiates own fear, pleasure, or pain from punishment-consequences.)

    Pro—If you do happen to get caught you could give the drug back and you wouldn't get much of a sentence. It wouldn't bother you much to serve a little jail term, if you have your wife when you get out.

    Con—He may not get much of a jail term if he steals the drug, but his wife will probably die before he gets out so it won't do him much good. If his wife dies, he shouldn't blame himself, it wasn't his fault she has cancer.

Stage 3. Action motivated by anticipation of disapproval of others, actual or imagined-hypothetical (e.g., guilt). (Differentiation of disapproval from punishment, fear, and pain.)

    Pro—No one will think you're bad if you steal the drug but your family will think you're an inhuman husband if you don't. If you let your wife die, you'll never be able to look anybody in the face again.

    Con—It isn't just the druggist who will think you're a criminal, everyone else will too. After you steal it, you'll feel bad thinking how you've brought dishonor on your family and yourself; you won't be able to face anyone again.

Stage 4. Action motivated by anticipation of dishonor, i.e., institutionalized blame for failure of duty, and by guilt over concrete harm done to others. (Differentiates formal dishonor from informal disapproval. Differentiates guilt for bad consequences from disapproval.)

    Pro—If you have any sense of honor, you won't let your wife die because you're afraid to do the only thing that will save her. You'll always feel guilty that you caused her death if you don't do your duty to her.

    Con—You're desperate and you may not know you're doing wrong when you steal the drug. But you'll know you did wrong after you're punished and sent to jail. You'll always feel guilty for your dishonesty and lawbreaking.

TABLE 6.6 (continued)

Stage 5. Concern about maintaining respect of equals and of the community (assuming their respect is based on reason rather than emotions). Concern about own self-respect, i.e., to avoid judging self as irrational, inconsistent, nonpurposive. (Discriminates between institutionalized blame and community disrespect or self-disrespect.)

> Pro —You'd lose other people's respect, not gain it, if you don't steal. If you let your wife die, it would be out of fear, not out of reasoning it out. So you'd just lose self-respect and probably the respect of others too.

> Con —You would lose your standing and respect in the community and violate the law. You'd lose respect for yourself if you're carried away by emotion and forget the long-range point of view.

Stage 6. Concern about self-condemnation for violating one's own principles. (Differentiates between community respect and self-respect. Differentiates between self-respect for general achieving rationality and self-respect for maintaining moral principles.)

> Pro —If you don't steal the drug and let your wife die, you'd always condemn yourself for it afterward. You wouldn't be blamed and you would have lived up to the outside rule of the law but you wouldn't have lived up to your own standards of conscience.

> Con —If you stole the drug, you wouldn't be blamed by other people but you'd condemn yourself because you wouldn't have lived up to your own conscience and standards of honesty.

Source: Rest, 1968.

unit or sentence in any context. As an example, Table 6.7 indicates some statements by Adolf Eichmann which were scored by stage and aspect with good interjudge agreement, using general definitions of each stage at each aspect, such as those provided by Tables 6.4 and 6.5 for two aspects.

While the evidence is far from complete, all the evidence to date suggests that the stages do meet the criteria of stages proposed in our first section. This evidence comes from studies conducted in Taiwan, Great Britain, Mexico, Turkey and the United States. In addition to middle- and lower-class urban boys, the studies have included preliterate or semi-literate villagers in Turkey, Mexico (a Mayan group) and Taiwan (an Atayal group).

Figures 6.2 and 6.3 suggest the cultural universality of the sequence of stages which we have found. Figure 6.2 presents the age trends for middle-class urban boys in the U.S., Taiwan and Mexico. At age 10 in each country, the order of use of each stage is the same as the order of its difficulty or maturity. In the U.S., by age 16 the order is the reverse, from the highest to the lowest, except that Stage 6 is still little used. At age 13, Stage 3, the good-boy middle stage is most used. The results in Mexico and Taiwan are the same, except that development is a little slower. The most conspicuous feature is that Stage 5 thinking is much more salient in the U.S. than it is in Mexico or Taiwan at age 16. Nevertheless, it is present in the other countries, so we know that it is not purely an American democratic construct. The second figure (6.3) indicates results from two isolated villages, one in Yucatan, one in Turkey. The similarity of pattern in the two villages is striking. While conventional moral thought (Stages 3 and 4) increases

TABLE 6.7

SCORING OF MORAL JUDGMENTS OF EICHMANN FOR DEVELOPMENTAL STAGE

Moral Judgments	Score*
In actual fact, I was merely a little cog in the machinery that carried out the directives of the German Reich.	1/7
I am neither a murderer nor a mass-murderer. I am a man of average character, with good qualities and many faults.	3/1
Yet what is there to "admit"? I carried out my orders. It would be as pointless to blame me for the whole final solution of the Jewish problem as to blame the official in charge of the railroads over which the Jewish transports traveled.	1/7
Where would we have been if everyone had thought things out in those days? You can do that today in the "new" German army. But with us an order was an order.	1/15
If I had sabotaged the order of the one-time Fuhrer of the German Reich, Adolf Hitler, I would have been not only a scoundrel but a despicable pig like those who broke their military oath to join the ranks of the anti-Hitler criminals in the conspiracy of July 20, 1944.	1/1
I would like to stress again, however, that my department never gave a single annihilation order. We were responsible only for deportation.	2/7
My interest was only in the number of transport trains I had to provide. Whether they were bank directors or mental cases, the people who were loaded on these trains meant nothing to me.	2/3
It was really none of my business.	2/7
But to sum it all up, I must say that I regret nothing. Adolf Hitler may have been wrong all down the line, but one thing is beyond dispute: the man was able to work his way up from lance corporal in the German army to Fuhrer of a people of almost eighty million.	1/6
I never met him personally, but his success alone proves to me that I should subordinate myself to this man. He was somehow so supremely capable that the people recognized him. And so with that justification I recognized him joyfully, and I still defend him.	1/17
I must say truthfully, that if we had killed all the ten million Jews that Himmler's statisticians originally listed in 1933, I would say, "Good, we have destroyed an enemy."	2/21
But here I do not mean wiping them out entirely. That would not be proper —and we carried on a proper war.	1/1

* The first code number in this column refers to Stages 1-6 (see Table 6.2); the second number refers to the aspect of morality involved (see Table 6.4).
Source: Kohlberg, 1967, p. 177.

steadily from age 10 to 16, at 16 it still has not achieved a clear ascendency over premoral thought (Stages 1 and 2). Stages 5 and 6 are totally absent in this group. Trends for lower-class urban groups are intermediate in rate of development between those for the middle-class and the village boys.

While the age trends of Figures 6.2 and 6.3 indicate that some modes of thought are generally more difficult or advanced than other modes of thought, they do not demonstrate that attainment of each mode of thought is prerequisite to the attainment of the next higher in a hypothetical sequence.

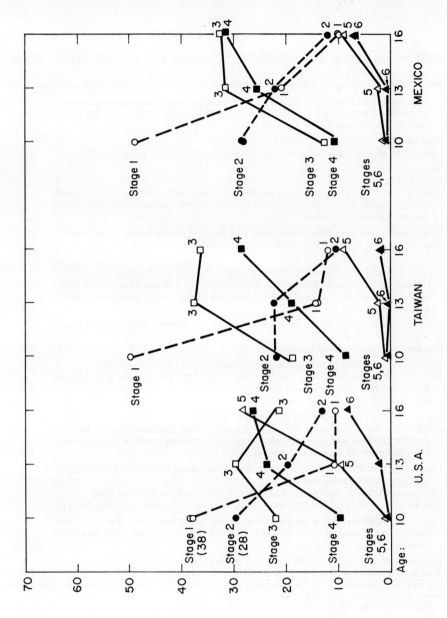

FIGURE 6.2. Age trends in moral judgment in middle class urban boys in three nations.

The importance of the sequentiality issue may be brought out from two points of view. With regard to the definition of moral development, it is not at all clear that Stages 5 and 6 should be used to define developmental end points in morality. Figure 6.2 indicates that Stage 4 is the dominant stage of most adults.

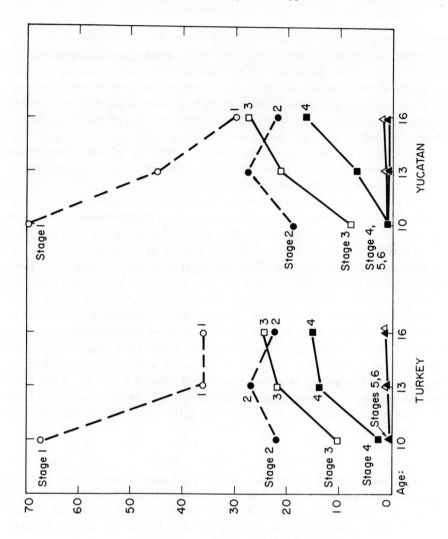

Percentage of Total Moral Statements

FIGURE 6.3. Age trends in moral judgment in isolated village boys in two nations.

It is possible to view Stages 4, 5, and 6 as alternative types of mature response rather than as a sequence. Indeed, this is the view of some writers who view conventional-authoritarian (Stage 4) adult character types as opposed to humanistic (Stages 5 and 6) character types as representing alternative channels of personality crystallization. If Stages 5 and 6 persons can be shown to have gone through Stage 4 while Stage 4 persons have not gone through Stages 5 and 6, it can be argued that the stage hierarchy constitutes more than a value judgment by the investigator.

Our age trends indicate that large groups of moral concepts and ways of thought only attain meaning at successively advanced ages and require the extensive background of social experience and cognitive growth represented by the age factor. From usual views of the moralization process, these age changes in modes of moral thought would simply be interpreted as successive acquisitions or internalizations of cultural moral concepts. Our six types of thought would represent six patterns of verbal morality in the adult culture which are successively absorbed as the child grows more verbally sophisticated. The age order involved might simply represent the order in which the culture presented the various concepts involved, or might simply reflect that greater mental age is required to learn the higher type of concept.

In contrast, we have advocated the developmental interpretation that these types of thought represent structures emerging from the interaction of the child with his social environment, rather than directly reflecting external structures given by the child's culture. Awareness of the basic prohibitions and commands of the culture, as well as some behavioral "internalization" of them, exists from the first of our stages and does not define their succession. Movement from stage to stage represents rather the way in which these prohibitions, as well as much wider aspects of the social structure, are taken up into the child's organization of a moral order. This order may be based upon power and external compulsion (Stage 1), upon a system of exchanges and need satisfactions (Stage 2), upon the maintenance of legitimate expectations (Stages 3 and 4), or upon ideals or general logical principles of social organization (Stages 5 and 6). While these successive bases of a moral order do spring from the child's awareness of the external social world, they also represent active processes of organizing or ordering this world.

Because the higher types of moral thought integrate and replace, rather than add to the lower modes of thought, the Guttman (1954) scaling technique used for the dream concept in our first section is not appropriate for our material, based on the usage of the stages in free responses. It does become appropriate, however, if we measure children's comprehension of each stage instead of their use of it. Rest (1968) has asked S's to recapitulate in different words statements at each stage of the sort presented in Tables 6.5 and 6.6. In general, subjects can correctly recapitulate statements at all stages below or at their own level, correctly recapitulate some, but not all statements at one stage above their own, and fail to correctly recapitulate statements two or more stages above their own (Rest, 1968; Rest, Turiel & Kohlberg, 1969). Even where this is not the case, e.g., where an S can recapitulate a statement two stages above his own, his comprehension still fits a Guttman scale pattern, i.e., he will comprehend all the statements below the plus-two statement including the statement one above his own.

While the pattern of actual usage of stages does not fit a cumulative model, it does fit a non-cumulative model of sequence. The profile of usage of other stages in relation to the child's modal stage is presented in Figure 6.4. This figure indicates that on the average, 50 per cent of a child's moral judgments fit a

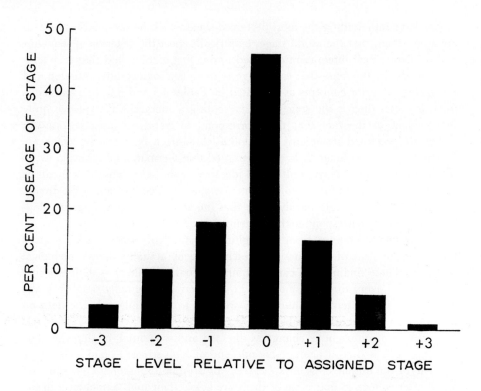

FIGURE 6.4. Profile of stage usage.

single stage. The remainder are distributed around this mode in decreasing fashion as one moves successively farther on the ordinal scale from the modal stage. An individual's response profile, then, typically represents a pattern composed of the dominant stage he is in, a stage he is leaving but still uses somewhat and a stage he is moving into but which has not yet "crystallized."

The pattern of usage of different stages becomes intelligible when it is recalled that, in a certain sense, all the lower stages are available or at least comprehensible to the S. The pattern of usage, then, is dictated by a hierarchical preference for the highest stage a subject can produce. While S's have difficulty comprehending stages above their own, and do not have difficulty with stages below their own, they prefer higher stages to the lower stages. If they can comprehend a statement two stages above their own, they prefer it to a statement one above. If they comprehend statements one stage but not two above their own, they prefer them to statements either two above or one below their own. If hypothetical statements at their own stage are presented to S's, and they have not yet produced statements of their own, the S's tend to prefer the one above to their own level statement.

It appears, then, that patterns of actual usage of stages are dictated by two opposed sequential orders, one of preference and one of ease, with an individual modal stage representing the most preferred stage which he can readily use. It is apparent, then, that the moral stages empirically meet the criterion of sequence and of hierarchical integration discussed in our first section, and that they logically meet it in the sense that each stage represents a logical differentiation and integration of prior concepts as indicated in Tables 6.5 and 6.6. In some sense, then, one can discuss the stages as representing a hierarchical sequence quite independent of the fact that they correspond to trends of age-development. Table 6.7 presented statements by Adolf Eichmann, a Nazi leader, which are largely Stage 1 and Stage 2. It can be argued that German adolescents grew up into a Stage 1 and 2 Nazi adult moral ideology in the same sense that it can be argued that Atayal children grow up into a Stage 1 or 2 conception of the dream. In such a case, we would hardly argue that the actual sequence of age-development would fully correspond to the sequence just described.

Preliminary findings from a longitudinal study of American boys speak directly to the issue of the extent to which ontogeny actually follows the logical sequence. These findings are based on 50 boys, half middle class, half working class, studied every three years over a 12-year period. Originally ranging in age from 10 to 16, on terminal study they were 22 to 28. While only the data on development after age 16 has been fully analyzed (Kramer, 1968), the findings fit a picture of ontogenetic change as directed and sequential, or stepwise. The one exception is that at one age period (end of high school to mid-college) 20 per cent of the middle-class boys "regress," or drop in total score. They come up again after college so that none of them are below their high-school level in the late twenties and almost all are above that level. No such temporary "regression" occurs in the non-college or lower-class population. The only cases of "regression" found in the lower-class sample were among six delinquents followed longitudinally. For three of these, reform school and jail had an actual "regressive" effect on morality.

The findings on regression are cited to clarify the meaning of sequence in the study of ontogeny suggested in connection with the Atayal dream concept. The claim of the theory is that the "normal" course of social experience leads to progression through the sequence. Special forms of experience, like jail, may have a "regressive" effect. If one finds "regression" because of college experience, one must analyze the college experience in terms different from those appropriate for earlier or later sequential movement, as Kramer (1968) has done using "cognitive conflict" concepts.

In addition to sequence, stages must meet the criterion of consistency implied by the notion of a "structured whole." On the logical side, consistency is found in the fact that twenty-five distinct aspects of moral judgment may be logically defined from the core concepts of the six stages. On the empirical side, both consistency across aspects and consistency across verbal situations are to be found. Such consistency is indicated, first, by the fact that an average of 50 per cent of a subject's moral judgments fit a single stage. Second, such consistency is indicated by fairly high correlations in moral levels from one story to another. The highest such correlation is .75, the lowest .31, the median .51. Third, it is indicated by the fact that these correlations between situations are not specific, i.e., there is a general moral level factor. A general first moral level factor accounts for most of covariations from situation to situation (Kohlberg, 1958, 1969).

While the stage conception implies that stages constitute "structured wholes," the stage notion also suggests that (1) age should lead to increasing consolidation or equilibrium in a given stage, and (2) that higher stages eventually represent better or more equilibrated structures than lower stages (Turiel, 1969). As children move into adulthood, then, those who remain primarily at Stages 1 and 2 crystallize into purer types, an extreme being some delinquents with an explicit Stage 2 con-man ideology. Subjects moving into the higher stages (4, 5 and 6) stabilize more slowly than the lower stage subjects, but by the middle twenties have become the purest types of all (Turiel, 1969; Kramer, 1968).

We have reported a variety of evidence suggesting that moral stages fit all the criteria of stages in the social domain. Our earlier discussion claimed that if this were the case, we should be able to solve the problem of longitudinal predictability which has frustrated so much of socialization research. Preliminary longitudinal findings indicate that this is the case. The correlation between moral maturity scores at age 16 and in the mid-twenties was .78 ($n = 24$).[2] While only a very small sample ($n = 8$) of middle-class 13-year-olds have reached the mid-twenties, the correlation between moral maturity at age 13 and in the mid-twenties was equally high (r between age 13 and age 24 $= .92$; r between age 16 and age 24 $= .88$). It is clear, then, that a study of environmental determinants of moral level at 13 can have long-range meaning. The degree of predictability achieved suggests the potential fruitfulness of defining social behavior in terms of developmental sequence instead of in terms of traits for socialization research.

IV. RELATIONS BETWEEN COGNITION, AFFECT AND CONDUCT IN SOCIAL DEVELOPMENT

We have seen that moral judgment stages provide a definition of continuity through transformations of development necessary before the naturalistic study of socialization can begin. We shall now consider how these "cognitively" defined stages of judgment illuminate "non-cognitive" moral development in the spheres of affect and of action. This sentence is, however, a misstatement of both Piaget's and our position, which is not the position that cognition determines affect and behavior, but that the *development* of cognition and the development of affect have a common structural base. Rather than saying, as we did earlier, that "regular age-developmental trends in moral judgment have a formal-cognitive

---

[2] Because of shakeup and "regression" in college, the correlations between moral maturity at age 16 and in college were much lower ($r = .24$). As previously noted the regressors all "straightened out" by the mid-twenties (Kramer, 1968).

base," we should have said that "age-developmental trends in moral judgment have a formal-structural base parallel to the structural base of cognitive development." While the notion of cognitive-affective parallelism is not abstruse, it has been difficult for American psychologists to grasp. The doctrine has, however, entered the American research literature as it has been independently elaborated by Werner (1948) and his followers (Witkin, 1969). A structural dimension of development, such as "differentiation," is considered to characterize all aspects of the personality—the social emotional, the perceptual, and the intellective. As measured by age-developmental perceptual tasks, "differentiation" is quite highly correlated with standard psychometric intelligence measures as well as with a variety of social attitudes and traits. Harvey et al. (1961) also elaborated a "structural parallelism" view of personality development in terms of increased structural differentiation and integration of conceptions of self and others, implying both cognitive and attitudinal correlates.

In Piaget's (1952a) view, both types of thought and types of valuing or of feeling are schemata which develop a set of general structural characteristics which represent successive forms of psychological equilibrium. The equilibrium of affective and interpersonal schemata involves many of the same basic structural features as the equilibrium of cognitive schemata. It is generally believed that justice (portrayed as balancing the scales) is a form of equilibrium between conflicting interpersonal claims, so Piaget (1948) holds that "In contrast to a given rule imposed upon the child from outside, the rule of justice is an imminent condition of social relationships or a law governing their equilibrium." In Piaget's view logic is also not a learned cultural rule imposed from the outside, but a law governing the equilibrium between ideas rather than between persons. Both violation of logic and violation of justice may arouse strong affects. The strong affective component of the sense of justice is not inconsistent with its structural base. As was already stated, the structure of reciprocity is both a cognitive structure and a structural component of the sense of justice.

What is being asserted, then, is not that moral judgment stages are cognitive but that the existence of moral stages implies that moral development has a basic structural component. While motives and affects are involved in moral development, the development of these motives and affects is largely mediated by changes in thought patterns.

Among the implications of this statement are the following:

1. There should be an empirical correlation between moral judgment maturity and non-moral aspects of cognitive development.

2. Moral judgment stages or sequences are to be described in cognitive-structural terms even in regard to "affective" aspects of moral judgment, like guilt, empathy, etc.

3. There should be an empirical correlation between maturity on "affective" and cognitive aspects of morality, even if affective maturity is assessed by projective test or interview methods not explicitly focused on moral judgment.

4. The way in which moral judgment influences action should also be characterizable in cognitive-structural terms.

5. The socioenvironmental influences favorable to moral judgment development should be influences characterizable in cognitive-structural terms, for example, in terms of role-taking opportunities.

With regard to the first point, correlations between group IQ tests and moral judgment level at age 12 range from .30 to .50 in various studies. These correlations indicate that moral maturity has a cognitive base but is not simply general verbal intelligence applied to moral problems. This fact is indicated by the existence of a general moral level factor found among our situations after correlations due to intelligence are controlled for. The relation of moral judgment to intellective development is suggested by the fact that our stage definitions assume that Piagetian concrete operations are necessary for conventional (Stage 3 and 4) morality and that formal operations are necessary for principled (Stage 5 and 6) morality. Some crude and preliminary evidence that this is the case comes from a finding that moral judgment maturity and a crude test of formal operations correlated .44 with tested verbal intelligence. The Piagetian rationale just advanced, as well as other considerations, suggests that cognitive maturity is a necessary, but not a sufficient, condition for moral judgment maturity. While formal operations may be necessary for principled morality, one may be a theoretical physicist and yet not make moral judgments at the principled level. In fact, a curvilinear relation between IQ and moral maturity is found. In the below-average range, a linear correlation ($r = .53$) is found between IQ and moral maturity, whereas no relationship ($r = .16$) is found between the two measures in the above-average group. In other words, children below average in IQ are almost all below average in moral maturity. Children above average in IQ are equally likely to be low or high in moral maturity. The theories just proposed suggest not only a nonlinear relation between IQ and moral maturity but a decline in the correlation between the two with age. Moral judgment continues to develop until age 25 (Kramer, 1968), although only for half the middle-class population, whereas general intellectual maturity does not. While bright children attain formal operations earlier than duller children, most of the dull children eventually attain them. The duller children, then, tend to develop more slowly in moral judgment but may develop longer. IQ is then a better indicator of early rate of development than it is of terminal status, which is more determined by social experience.

The second point (that affective aspects of moral development are to be described in cognitive-structural terms) was partially documented by our indicating how our stages defined moral affects in Table 6.6 just as they defined "cognitive" dimensions like intentionality in Table 6.5. Table 6.6 indicates that each "higher" affect involves a cognitive differentiation not made by the next "lower" affect.

Table 6.6 assigns guilt over deviation from conventional rules leading to injury to others to Stage 4 (guilt over violation of internal principles was assigned to Stage 6). Stage 4 guilt implies differentiating concern about one's responsibility according to rules from Stage 3, "shame" or concern about the diffuse disapproval of others. Stage 3 concern about disapproval is, in turn, a differentiation of Stage

1 and 2 concerns about overt reward and punishment characteristic of lower stages.

In a certain sense, the cognitive-structural component of guilt would be obvious if it had not been ignored in psychoanalytic theory. Guilt in its most precise sense is moral self-judgment, and it presupposes the formation of internal or mature standards of moral judgment. Psychoanalysts have assumed the early formation of internalized guilt, of self-punishment and self-criticism tendencies, and have generally assumed that this formation occurs in the early latency period, ages 5 to 7, as a reaction to the Oedipus complex. In fact, however, researchers who have used story completion tests of guilt reactions do not find open self-criticism and self-punishment tendencies appearing in response to transgression stories until preadolescence or late childhood. When asked, children under seven almost never say a deviant child who escaped punishment would feel bad. While young children do not show conscious guilt, they do project unrealistic punishment into incomplete stories of transgression. Psychoanalytically oriented researchers have assumed such punishment concerns reflect the child's unconscious guilt, projected out into the world because it is unconscious. In fact, no satisfactory evidence has been accumulated for thinking this is true, since punishment concerns do not correlate positively with other behaviors which might represent moral internalization. Both the punishment concerns of Stage 1 and the guilt of Stage 4 or Stage 6 represent anxiety about deviating from the rules, structured in different ways. In some sense, the feeling in the pit of one's stomach is the same whether it is dread of external events or dread of one's own self-judgment. The difference between the two is that in one case the bad feeling is interpreted by the child as fear of external sanctioning forces while in the other case, it is interpreted by the child as produced by the self's own moral judgments. When the child reaches adolescence, he tends to reject fear as a basis for conformity. If he is a member of a delinquent gang he will deny the anxiety in the pit of his stomach because it is chicken to fear the cops. If he has developed more mature modes of moral judgment, he will link the same dread in the pit of his stomach to his own self-judgments and say, "I could never do that, I'd hate myself if I did." The difference between the two is a cognitive-structural difference, not a difference in intensity or type of affect. The difference is a real one, however, since intense fear of punishment does not predict to resistance to temptation, whereas self-critical guilt does.

We have already noted that projective-test studies indicate that self-critical guilt appears at about the same age as conventional moral judgment. The coincidence in the age of appearance of projective guilt and of "mature" or conventional moral judgment suggests that the two should be correlated among individual children of a given age. (As stated, this was the third implication of the structural parallelism interpretation of our stages.) The clearest findings of correlation are those reported by Ruma and Mosher (1967). Ruma and Mosher decided they could avoid the many problems of measuring imaginary guilt by assessing guilt about real behavior through use of a population of thirty-six delinquent boys. Measures of guilt were based on responses to a set of interview questions as to how the boy felt during and after his delinquent acts (assault or theft). The primary measure was the sum of weighted scores for responses expressing negative self-judgment and remorse (2) as opposed to responses expressing concern about punishment (1) or lack of concern (0). The correlation between this measure and a moral maturity score based on stage-weighted ratings of response to each of six of our conflict situations was .47 ($p < .01$). This correlation was independent of age, IQ, or social-class effects. They also found a correlation of .31 ($p < .05$) between the life-situation guilt measure and the Mosher guilt scale, "...a sentence completion measure of guilt using referents suggested by the psychoanalytic conception of guilt" (Ruma & Mosher, 1967). The correlation of moral judgment maturity and the Mosher guilt scale was .55. Maturity of moral judgment ideology, then, related somewhat better to two measures of guilt—one real-life, one projective—than they do to each other.

With regard to moral emotion, then, our point of view is that the "cognitive" definition of the moral situation directly determines the moral emotion which the situation arouses. This point of view has been generally held by the "symbolic interactionist" school of social psychology, which has stressed that socially communicated symbolic definitions determine the actual felt attitudes and emotions experienced by the individual in given situations. The empirical findings supporting this general point of view are cumulative and striking, and constitute much of the core content of many social-psychology textbooks. One striking line of evidence is that on the effects of drugs on behavior. Naturalistic studies by sociologists clearly suggest that pleasurable marijuana experiences and marijuana "addiction" are contingent on learning the "appropriate" symbolic definitions of the experience (H. Becker, 1963). Experimental studies indicate that while autonomic stimulants elicit generalized arousal, whether such arousal is experienced as anger, elation, or some other emotion is contingent on the social definition of the situation attendant on administration of the drugs (Schachter, 1964).

In our view, the basic way in which "affect" is socialized is not so much by punishment and reward as it is by communication of definitions of situations which elicit socially appropriate affect. In addition, our approach points to certain fundamental and "natural" cognitive bases of moral emotion, and views cultural definitions as representing only certain selective emphases and elaborations of these bases. The utilitarians were almost certainly correct in emphasizing that the central basis of moral emotion is the apprehension of the results of human action for the pain and harm (or joy and welfare) to human (or quasi-human) beings. Our studies of moral judgment in a variety of Western and non-Western cultures indicates that the overwhelming focus of moral choice and feeling is such personal welfare consequences. The child's whole social life is based on "empathy," i.e., on the awareness of other selves with thoughts and feelings like the self. The analyses of the development of the self by Baldwin (1906) and G. H. Mead (1934) have clearly indicated that the self-concept is largely a concept of a shared self, of a self like other selves. The child cannot have a self-conscious self without having concepts of other selves. Perceived harm to others is as immediately, if not as intensely, apprehended as is harm to the self. Empathy does not have to be taught to the child or conditioned; it is a primary phenomenon. What development and socialization achieve is the organization of empathic phenomena into consistent sympathetic and moral concerns, not the creation of empathy as such.

Our view of the way in which moral values influence action is generally similar. We noted in our second section that socialization studies of "resistance to temptation" had provided few solid findings because "resistance to temptation" is largely situation-specific, as Hartshorne and May (1928-30) demonstrated. While low correlations between cheating in one situation and cheating in another are to be found, these correlations are not due to internalized moral values or standards in the usual sense. These correlations are largely due to nonmoral "ego strength" factors of IQ and attention, and the correlations between cheating tests disappear when these ego factors are controlled (Grim et al., 1968). Attention, measured as standard deviation of reaction time, has been found to correlate in the 50's and 60's with scores on cheating tests. Moral "values" or attitudes conceived as affective quanta in the usual social attitude sense do not predict directly to behavior in conflict situations. Half a dozen studies show no positive correlation between high school or college students' verbal expression of the value of honesty or the badness of cheating, and actual honesty in experimental situations. Undoubtedly part of this failure of correlation is due to "deceptive" self-report tendencies. The same desire leading to a desire to cheat to get a good score leads to an over-espousal of conventional moral values. However, the problem is deeper than this, since affect-intensity projective measures of guilt fail to predict resistance to temptation unless they include the cognitive-structural self-critical components already discussed. The real problem is that general intensity measures of espousal of moral attitudes have little relation to the forces determining behavior in concrete conflict situations.

When cognitive and developmental measures of moral judgments and attitudes are used, better results are obtained. While Hartshorne and May (1928-30) found only low correlations between these tests of conventional moral knowledge ($r = .30$) and experimental measures of honesty, the correlations were at least positive and significant. When my transcultural measure of moral maturity is employed, better results are obtained. In one study, correlations of moral judgment maturity with teachers' ratings of moral conscientiousness were .46, and with teacher ratings of fair-mindedness with peers were .54. In another study the correlation of moral maturity with peer ratings of moral character was .58. These correlations are not too clear in meaning since moral judgment is a clear age-developmental variable, whereas ratings of moral character are not. Clearer relations of judgment and action come if particular stages of moral judgment are related to theoretically meaningful types of moral decisions.

As an example, in the ordinary experimental cheating situations, the critical issue is whether to follow the norm when the conventional expectations of the adult and the group about not cheating are not upheld. The experimenter explicitly leaves the child unsupervised in a situation where supervision is expected. Not only does the experimenter indicate he does not care whether cheating goes on, he almost suggests its possibility (since he needs cheaters for his study). While the conventional child thinks "cheating is bad" and cares about supporting the authority's expectations, he has no real reason not to cheat if he is tempted, if the authorities don't care and if others are doing it. In contrast, a principled (Stage 5 or 6) subject defines the issue as one involving maintaining an implicit contract with the adult and reflects that the general inequality or taking advantage implied by cheating is still true regardless of the ambiguity of social expectations in the situation. As a result, it is not surprising to find that principled subjects are considerably less likely to cheat than conventional or premoral subjects. In a college group only 11 per cent of the principled students cheated as compared to 42 per cent of the conventional subjects. In a sixth grade group, only 20 per cent of the principled children cheated as compared to 67 per cent of the conventional children and 83 per cent of the premoral children.

In the studies mentioned, the critical break was between the principled and the conventional subjects. Another break occurs where the subject is faced with disobeying the rules formulated by an authority figure who is seen as violating the rights of another individual. An example is the Milgram (1963) obedience situation. In this situation the experimenter orders the subject to give an increasingly severe electric shock to a stooge "learner" who has agreed to participate in a nonsense-syllable learning experiment. In this study, only the Stage 6 subjects would be expected to question the authority's moral right to ask them to inflict pain on another. Stage 5, "social contract" subjects, would tend to feel the victim's voluntary participation with foreknowledge released them from responsibility to him while their agreement to participate committed them to comply. As expected, 75 per cent of a small group (6) of Stage 6 subjects quit as compared to only 13 per cent of the remaining 24 subjects at lower moral stages. Some replication of this result comes from preliminary findings of a study of the Berkeley students who did and did not participate in the original free speech sit-in. As expected, 80 per cent of the Stage 6 subjects sat in, as compared to 10 per cent of the conventional and 50 per cent of the Stage 5 subjects. A similar majority of the Stage 2 subjects also sat in, for different though predictable reasons (Haan, Smith & Block, 1969).

The studies just cited help to clarify the relative role of cognitive definitions and of affect-intensity in determining moral choice. We have seen that cognitive definitions determined cheating behavior whereas attitude-strength measures did not. In the Milgram (1963) situation, Stage 6 cognitive definitions determined choice but a projective measure of sympathy did not. High-empathy subjects were no more likely to quit than low-empathy subjects. In the Berkeley situation, Stage 6 subjects also chose to disobey authorities in the name of individual rights, but without concern for individual rights involving empathy for a concrete victim, supporting the interpretation that the Stage 6 decision to resist was not based on a quantitative affective base. Some tentative findings suggest that amount of empathy was influential in the conventional level subjects' decisions, though not in the principled's subjects' decision. Indeed the Stage 5 subjects were the most prone to say they wanted to quit but did not, i.e., they were restrained by contractual principles in spite of their empathic feelings. This interpretation of the affective and situational influence in the Milgram moral decision is similar to that just advanced for the cheating decision. When affectively or situationally strongly tempted, conventional subjects will cheat. Similarly, when empathy leads to strong "temptation" to violate the rules and authority of the experimenter, conventional subjects will quit (or when fear of the authority leads to strong temptation to violate conventional rules against hurting others, conventional subjects will comply).

The interpretation just advanced suggests that quantitative affective-situational forces are less determining of moral decisions at the principled than at the conventional level. This interpretation coincides with another cognitive-developmental interpretation as to the relation of moral judgment to moral action. It was noted that the "cognitive" traits of IQ and attention correlated with measures of honesty, even though honesty is not directly an age-developmental or a cognitive-developmental trait. Drawing upon Williams James' (1890) doctrine of the will as attention, our interpretation holds that IQ, and especially attention, enter into moral decisions as non-moral tendencies of "strength of will" or "ego strength" (Grim et al., 1968). In part, the moral neutrality of "ego strength" is indicated by the fact that attentive children simply are not tempted and hence need make no moral decision to resist temptation. Attentive children are not only more likely to resist temptation, but attentive non-cheaters are more likely to say that they did not think of cheating after temptation than are inattentive non-cheaters (Krebs, 1967). In part the moral neutrality of "ego strength" or "will" is also indicated by the fact that while "strong-willed" conventional subjects cheat less, "strong-willed" premoral subjects cheat more (Krebs, 1967). Among conventional Stage 4 children, only 33 per cent of the "strong-willed" (high IQ, high attention) cheated as compared to 100 per cent of the "weak-willed" (low IQ, low attention). In contrast among the Stage 2 "instrumental egoists," 87 per cent of the "strong-willed" children cheated whereas only 33 per cent of the "weak-willed" children cheated. Presumably the weak-willed Stage 2 children were tempted (distracted and suggested) into violating their amoral "principles." At the principled level, however, resistance to temptation is less contingent on "strength of will," and hence is also less contingent on situational-affective forces of a sort irrelevant to their moral principles. All of the children at the principled stage were low on attention, yet only 20 per cent cheated.

In summary, then, while moral judgment maturity is only one of many predictors of action in moral conflict situations, it can be a quite powerful and meaningful predictor of action where it gives rise to distinctive ways of defining concrete situational rights and duties in socially ambiguous situations. The causal role of moral judgment appears to be due to its contribution to a "cognitive" definition of the situation rather than because strong attitudinal or affective expressions of moral values activate behavior. To a certain extent, it is no more surprising to find that cognitive moral principles determine choice of conflicting social actions than it is to find that cognitive scientific principles determine choice of conflicting actions on physical objects. Moral principles are essentially believed by their holders to define social "laws" or realities just as physical principles are felt to define physical laws or realities. This is true less in the abstract than in the concrete definition of the situation. While the "value of trust and contract" sounds like an empty abstraction, the principled subject's awareness that the experimenter in the cheating situation trusts him is concrete and real and is an awareness missing at lower stages.

In terms of implication for research strategy, the findings suggest that situational action is not usually a direct mirror of structural-developmental change. Once structural-developmental change has been assessed by more cognitive methods, however, it is possible to define structural-developmental changes in situational behavior, e.g., consistent non-cheating becomes a "milestone" behavior for Stage 5. Whether the milestones are reached first in action (consistent non-cheating) or in judgment (Stage 5) is an open empirical question.

V. CONCEPTUALIZING SOCIAL ENVIRONMENT IN TERMS OF ROLE-TAKING OPPORTUNITIES AND STRUCTURAL MATCH

We stated in Section I that an understanding of hierarchical interactional stages depends upon analyses of (1) universal structural features of the environment, (2) the order of differentiations inherent in given concepts, and (3) relations between the structure of specific experiences and the child's behavior structures, defined in terms of conflict and match. The universal structural features of the environment relevant to moral stages are partly those of the general physical environment since moral stages presuppose cognitive stages. At the first moral stage, the regularities of the physical and the social environment are confused and the basis of conformity to social laws is not much different than the basis of conformity to physical laws. More fundamentally, however, there are universal structures of the social environment which are basic to moral development. All societies have many of the same basic institutions, institutions of family, economy, social stratification, law, and government. In spite of great diversity in the detailed definition of these institutions, they have certain transcultural functional meanings. As an example, while the detailed prescriptions of law vary from nation to nation, the form of "law" and the functional value of its importance and regular maintenance are much the same in all nations with formal law.

In addition to common institutions, however, all societies are alike in the sheer fact of having institutions, i.e., in having systems of defined complementary role expectations. In cognitive-developmental or "symbolic-interactional" theories of society, the primary meaning of the word "social" is the distinctively human structuring of action and thought by role-taking, by the tendency to react to the other as someone like the self and by the tendency to react to the self's behavior in the role of the other (Mead, 1934; Baldwin, 1906; J. Piaget, 1948). There are two subsidiary meanings of "social," the first that of affectional attachment, the second that of imitation. Both human love and human identification, however, presuppose the more general sociality of symbolic communication and role-taking. Before one can love the other or can model his attitudes, one must take his role through communicative processes (Mead, 1934; Kohlberg, 1966b). The structure of society and morality is a structure of interaction between the self and other selves who are like the self, but who are not the self. The area of the conflicting claims of selves is the area of morality, or of moral conflict, and the modes of role-taking in such conflict situations represent the varying structures of moral judgment and choice defining our various stages. Role-taking itself represents a process extending beyond the sphere of morality or of conflicting claims. Moral role-taking itself may have many affective flavors, as our discussion of attitudes of empathy, guilt, disapproval, and respect suggested. Basically, however, all these forms imply a common structure of equality and reciprocity between selves with expectations about one another. Our moral stages represent successive forms of reciprocity, each more differentiated and universalized than the preceding form.

We have discussed the logical ordering of the stages in terms of the differentiation of twenty-five specific moral categories or aspects. However, we take as primary the categories of reciprocity and equality, e.g., the categories of justice, as these are used to define social expectations and rules. The most primitive form of reciprocity is that based on power and punishment, i.e., the reciprocity of obedience and freedom from punishment. Next (Stage 2) comes literal exchange. Then comes a recognition (Stage 3) that familial and other positive social relations are systems of reciprocity based upon gratitude and the reciprocal maintenance of expectations by two social partners. At Stage 4, this develops into a notion of social order in which expectations are earned by work and conformity, and in which one must keep one's word and one's bargain. At Stage 5, the notion of social order becomes a notion of flexible social contract or agreement between free and equal individuals, still a form of reciprocity (and equality). At Stage 6, moral principles are formulated as universal principles of reciprocal role-taking, e.g., the Golden Rule or the categorical imperative "So act as you would act after considering how everyone should act if they were in the situation." In other words, at the conventional level, the social order is felt to embody the structures of reciprocity defining "justice," whereas at the principled level the social order is derived from principles of justice which it serves. Principles of justice or moral principles are themselves essentially principles of role-taking, i.e., they essentially state "act so as to take account of everyone's perspective on the moral conflict situation" (Mead, 1934). At the principled level, then, obligation is to the principles of justice lying behind the social order rather than to the order itself, and these principles are principles of universalized reciprocity or role-taking.

If moral development is fundamentally a process of the restructuring of modes of role-taking, then the fundamental social inputs stimulating moral development may be termed "role-taking opportunities." The first prerequisite for role-taking is participation in a group or institution. Participation is partially a matter of sheer amount of interaction and communication in the group, since communication presupposes role-taking. In addition, the centrality of the individual in the communication and decision-making structure of the group enhances role-taking opportunities. The more the individual is responsible for the decision of the group, and for his own actions in their consequences for the group, the more must he take the roles of others in it. It has sometimes been held that the subordinate takes the role of the superior more than vice versa (Brim, 1958). If true, this is true only at the level of the dyad. The group leader must role-take all the subordinate's roles and be aware of their relations to one another, while the subordinate is only required to take the role of the leader. It is likely that leadership positions require not only more complex or organized role-taking but more affectively neutral objective and "rules and justice" forms of role-taking, since the leader must mediate conflicts within the group, as Parsons and Bales (1955) have claimed is the case for the "father" or "instrumental leader" role. While leadership roles might be expected to require more role-taking than follower roles, it is also likely that "democratic leadership" requires more role-taking than "autocratic leadership" on the part of both leader and follower, since the group leader must be more sensitive to the members' attitudes, and the members will engage in more communication with the leader and have more responsibility for the group decision, as Lippett and White's (1943) studies suggest.

For the developing child, there is presumably a rough sequence of groups or institutions in which he participates. The first, the family, has received the most attention in socialization theories. From our point of view, however, (1) family participation is not unique or critically necessary for moral development, and (2) the dimensions on which it stimulates moral development are primarily general dimensions by which other primary groups stimulate moral development., i.e., the dimensions of creation of role-taking opportunities. With regard to the first point, there is no evidence that the family is a uniquely necessary setting for normal moral development. An ordinary orphanage is a poor setting in terms of role-taking opportunities so it is not surprising to find institutionalized retardates more retarded in moral judgment development than control retardates living with their families. On the same Piaget (1948) measures on which institutionalized children are more backward than children in families, however, kibbutz children are equal to city children living in families. In general kibbutz children are "normal" in moral development in spite of marked reduction in amount of interaction with their parents. In Section II, we pointed out that bad families contribute heavily to delinquency, and it may be noted that delinquency is associated with a low level of moral judgment development. The fact that bad families lead to moral arrest and moral pathology does not imply, however, that a good family is necessary for moral development. While parental rejection and use of physical punishment are both negatively correlated with moral internalization and moral stage-development measures, this again is indicative of the negative rather than the positive influence of the family. Extremely high warmth and complete absence of punishment do not seem to be particularly facilitating of moral development. With regard to the second point, the positive dimensions of family interaction contributing to moral development seem understandable in terms of role-taking opportunities. Hostility and punishment obviously do not facilitate the child's taking of his parents' role. Peck and Havighurst (1960) report that ratings of maturity of moral character are related to ratings of common participation in the family, to confidence sharing, to sharing in family decisions, and to awarding responsibility to the child, a cluster well summarized under the rubric of "role-taking opportunities." As cited earlier, Hoffman and Saltzstein (1967) found "inductive discipline" associated with moral internalization. Inductive discipline, i.e., pointing out to the child the consequences of his action to others and his own responsibility for it, would seem to represent a form of creating moral role-taking opportunities.

With regard to my own measure of moral maturity, a study by Holstein (1968) indicates that parental provision of role-taking opportunities in moral discussion is a powerful predictor of moral judgment at age 13. Holstein taped discussions over revealed differences in moral opinions on hypothetical situations between mother, father and child for 52 suburban middle-class families. Parents who encouraged their child to participate in the discussion (i.e., who were rated as "taking the child's opinion seriously and discussing it") tended to have relatively mature or conventional-level (Stage 3 or 4) children. Seventy per cent of the encouraging parents had conventional children, while only 40 per cent of the non-encouraging parents had conventional children. Amount of paternal and maternal interaction with the child (play, discussion, affection) was also related to the child's moral level.

The second group in which the child participates is the peer group. While psychoanalysts have taken the family as a critical and unique source of moral role-taking (e.g., identification), Piaget (1948) has viewed the peer group as a unique source of role-taking opportunities for the child. According to Piaget, the child's unilateral respect for his parents, and his egocentric confusion of his own perspective with that of his parents, prevents him from engaging in the role-taking based on mutual respect necessary for moral development. While the empirical findings support the notion that peer-group participation is correlated with moral development, it does not suggest that such participation plays a critical or unique role for moral development. Peer-group isolates matched for social class and IQ with children highly chosen by their classmates tend to be quite markedly slower in moral development than the leaders. This slowness, however, is not particularly manifested as an arrest at Stage 1, more or less equivalent to Piaget's heteronomous stage. In particular, peer-group participation is not especially facilitative of development on the moral dimensions focused upon by Piaget, as opposed to other dimensions of moral development. Indeed no differences have been found on measures of intentionality between sociometric stars and isolates, or between kibbutz (peer-group centered) and city children. In summary, then, while peer-group participation appears to be stimulating of moral development, its influence seems better conceptualized in terms of providing general role-taking opportunities rather than as having very specific and unique forms of influence.

A third type of participation presumed important for moral development is that of participation in the secondary institutions of law, government and, perhaps, of work. One index of differential opportunities for participation in the social structures of government and of work or economy is that of socioeconomic status. It is abundantly clear that the lower class cannot and does not feel as much sense of power in, and responsibility for, the institutions of government and economy as does the middle class. This, in turn, tends to generate less of a disposition to view these institutions from a generalized, flexible and organized perspective based on various roles as vantage points. The law and the government are perceived quite differently by the child if he feels a sense of potential participation in the social order than if he does not. The effect of such a sense of participation upon development of moral judgments related to the law is suggested by the following responses of sixteen-year-olds to the question, "Should someone obey a law if he doesn't think it is a good law?" A lower-class boy replies, "Yes, a law is a law and you can't do nothing about it. You have to obey it, you should. That's what it's there for." (For him the law is simply a constraining thing that is there. The very fact that he has no hand in it, that "you can't do nothing about it," means that it should be obeyed—Stage 1.)

An upper middle-class boy of the same IQ replies, "The law's the law but I think people themselves can tell what's right or wrong. I suppose the laws are made by many different groups of people with different ideas. But if you don't believe in a law, you should try to get it changed, you shouldn't disobey it." (Here the laws are seen as the product of various legitimate ideological and interest groups varying in their beliefs as to the best decision in policy matters. The role of law-obeyer is seen from the perspective of the democratic policy-maker—Stage 5.)

Studies of moral judgment development in Taiwan, Mexico, the United States (where class groups were matched on IQ), and Turkey indicate that middle-class and lower-class urban males go through the same stages and that the lower class is more retarded in development than the middle class. Retardation is more marked when the lower class is more impoverished (Mexico, Turkey) than where it is more stable economically (United States, Taiwan). Development of Negro slum groups is more like that found in Mexico than that found in the stable upper lower-class American group.

To some extent, differences between peasant village and urban groups may also be viewed as representing differential opportunities for role-taking and participation in secondary institutions. The Mexican, Turkish, and Taiwanese villager grows up with a sense of participation in the village, but little in the more remote political, economic, and legal system. To a considerable extent, age progressions of development are similar to those of the lower-class urban males except for a total, rather than relative, failure to attain the more generalized stages of moral principle, and except for less tendency toward adult fixation at a morally alienated (Stage 2) level.

These findings contrast with many sociological notions as to how group memberships determine moral development. It is often thought that the child gets some of his basic moral values from his family, some from the peer group, and others from his social-class group, and that these basic values tend to conflict with one another. Instead of participation in various groups causing conflicting developmental trends in morality, it appears that participation in various groups converges in stimulating the development of basic moral values, which are not transmitted by one particular group as opposed to another. The child lives in a total social world in which perceptions of the law, of the peer group, and of parental teachings all influence one another. While various people and groups make conflicting *immediate demands* upon the child, they do not seem to present the child with basically conflicting or different stimulation for *general moral* development.

The examples of role-taking opportunities just elaborated are essentially specifications of the general belief that the more the social stimulation, the faster the rate of moral development. These theories do not account for specific transitions from stage to stage or to eventual fixation at a particular stage. Such explanation requires theories of structural conflict and structural match, extensively elaborated in the moral domain by Turiel (1969). The problem posed by stage theory is that the stimulus inputs received by the child are usually either assimilated to his own level or are not perceived as stimuli at all. As an example, a Stage 2 delinquent is offered "role-taking opportunities" by an understanding psychotherapist, but these opportunities are perceived as opportunities to "con a sucker" and do not stimulate development beyond Stage 2. In the Rest studies (Rest, 1968; Rest et al., 1969), it was found that there was a strong tendency to assimilate higher level moral judgments to the subject's own level or one below it. The problem of moral change would appear to be one of presenting stimuli which are both sufficiently incongruous as to stimulate conflict in the child's existing stage schemata and sufficiently congruous as to be assimilable with some accommodative effort.

With regard to the assimilation of moral judgments made by others, the "match" notions just presented suggest that there would be maximal assimilation of moral judgments one level above the subject's own. The rationale for this was made clear in the discussion of the Rest studies of the hierarchy of comprehension and preference for the six stages (see p. 379 ff.). To test this "match" hypothesis, Turiel (1966) divided sixth-grade children (themselves equally divided by pretests among Stages 2, 3 and 4) randomly to one of three treatment groups. The treatments consisted of exposure to advice by an adult E on two hypothetical moral conflict situations. The first treatment group received advice one stage above their own, the second two stages above their own and the third one stage below their own. The children were post-tested one month later on both the pretest and the treatment situations. Turiel found a significant increase in usage of thinking one stage above in the plus-one treatment group. He found no significant increase in usage of thinking two stages above in the plus-two treatment group. He found an increase in usage of thinking one stage below in the minus-one group, but this increase was significantly less than the increase of plus-one thinking in the plus-one treatment group.

Turiel's laboratory study has received naturalistic validation from Blatt's (1969) program of classroom discussions of moral dilemmas held once a week for three months at the sixth-grade level. Blatt's procedure was to elucidate the arguments of the Stage 3 children as against the Stage 2 children on hypothetical moral conflicts, then to pit the Stage 3's against the Stage 4's, and finally to himself present Stage 5 arguments. The effect of this procedure was to raise 45 per cent of the children up one stage (as compared to 8 per cent in a control group), and 10 per cent up two stages. A majority of the Stage 2 subjects moved to Stage 3, a majority of the Stage 3 subjects to Stage 4. There was very little movement from Stage 4 to the Stage 5 level presented by the teacher.

One reason the Blatt study induced more change than the Turiel study was because the discussions were carried on over a greater time period. The Blatt procedure also differed in inducing greater conflict through disagreement. Presumably a sense of contradiction and discrepancy at one's own stage is necessary for reorganization at the next stage. A series of studies by Turiel (1969) are systematically exploring the role of such cognitive-conflict parameters in moral judgment change.

Findings on "match" in parent influences on moral development are still ambiguous. No relationship has been found between the moral level of fathers and of their children (Kramer, 1968; Holstein, 1968). A clear relationship between mother's level and the level of her child (of either sex) has been found by Holstein. While 50 per cent of 41 mothers at a conventional level had premoral (Stage 1 or 2) children, none of 12 principled mothers had children at this low level. From a direct transmission or social learning point of view, there is no reason why conventional mothers should be less effective in transmitting (their own) conventional moral ideology to their children than principled mothers. The one-above hypothesis also does not account for the superiority of principled mothers in stimulating movement from the premoral to the conventional level. It may be that it is the match of the principled mothers' action, not their judgment, which is crucial to this effect.

The problem of "match" is not only a problem of the assimilation of moral statements by others but a problem of the assimilation of their actions. With regard to actions, the slum child may well interpret the behavior of policemen, teachers, and gang buddies as being based on his own Stage 2 individual behavior and exchange conceptions. It may be that if the boy also has a bad family, in the Gluecks' (Glueck & Glueck, 1950) sense, there is no model of altruistic Stage 3 action to generate either conflict in his Stage 2 schema or any Stage 3 moral material to be assimilated. The problem of match is also a problem of assimilation of the child's own behavior to his moral ideology. Freedman (1965) has stressed the accommodation of moral attitudes to actual behavior in the service of reduction of cognitive dissonance, where moral attitudes are defined in the "non-predictive" sense discussed earlier. Our developmental conception is one in which cognitive balance is not so simple and in which cognitive dissonance can lead to reorganization upward or downward. However, no work has yet been done on moral behavior—moral ideology relations—from this perspective.

In summary, then, a theory of "match" in morality should account for the effect of inputs of moral judgment and moral action at particular stages. In its broadest sense the match problem is the problem of the fit of the individual's ideology to his world. Stage 2 "fits" a slum or jail world, Stage 4 fits the traditional army world, Stage 5 fits the academic and bureaucratic worlds. In this regard, the changes of "world" characterizing adult socialization may require the same types of theoretical analysis as those of childhood.

VI. EXPERIMENTAL STUDIES OF SOCIAL LEARNING AND STRUCTURAL-DEVELOPMENTAL CHANGE

In Section II, we suggested that the major rationale for conducting naturalistic studies of socialization rested on the assumption that personality development involved structural change and that the effects of early experience upon behavior are relatively permanent, irreversible and different in kind than are the effects of experience upon behavior change in adulthood. We noted that theories of socialization based on general learning theories typically do not make such assumptions about structural change. It is not surprising, then, to find that socialization theorists oriented to general principles of learning have turned away from naturalistic studies to studies involving the experimental modification of situational behavior. It is also not surprising to find that these studies have shown social-learning principles to be powerful predictors of behavior, while the naturalistic studies have not. The discrepancy between the degree of support for social-learning theory coming from experimental and from naturalistic findings may be explained on two grounds. The first is that the long-run effects of natural socialization inputs upon structural change require different principles of explanation than are applicable to short-run situational change. The second is that there is no such thing as long-run structural change, and the short-run situational changes explained by social-learning theories cancel each other out so as not to yield long-range predictions at the trans-situational and longitudinal level explored by the naturalistic studies of personality. Because the methodological ambiguities of the naturalistic studies are great, most social-learning theorists have not taken a clear position on this issue, but have tended to dismiss the findings of the naturalistic studies as too weak methodologically to require detailed explanation.

With regard to the actual experimental studies, some seem designed with the assumption that there is no such thing as structural change in development. Others seem to be asserting that some behavior changes have more "structural" properties than other behavior changes, but that these changes, too, are explicable by the general principles of learning. As discussed earlier, the empirically minimal properties of structural change are a considerable degree of stability or irreversibility of the change (e.g., resistance to extinction or counter-conditioning) and a considerable degree of generalization of the change to situations not manifestly similar to the situations in which change was initially induced.

The simplest type of study based on the first assumption is one showing that conditioning can change or mimic behavior having a label the same as that employed in a structural theory. An example is Azrin and Lindsley's (1956) study of the "learning of cooperation." Cooperation is thought of by Piaget and others as a natural and relatively irreversible developmental trend resulting from the child's differentiation of his own "egocentric" perspective from that of others. Parten and Newhall (1943) provide considerable support for this "structural" view of cooperation since they find regular relationships of naturalistically observed cooperation to chronological and mental age, and considerable day-by-day or situational stability to the child's level of cooperation. Azrin and Lindsley conducted a training study inducing "cooperation," apparently to demonstrate that cooperation was a product of operant learning. Their operational definition of cooperation was the matching of one child's placement of a stylus to the other's placement, such matching being a contingency for receiving a candy. Needless to say, the children's rate of stylus matching increased after reinforcement and extinguished after non-reinforcement. The reversibility of the learning of the response, then, indicated that no structural change was induced. No transfer of training was tested, nor was there any definition of what the term "cooperation" might mean in terms of some generalization dimension. ("Sharing" of the reinforcer was not even involved as a learning dimension in the study, from the outset the children shared.) The study, then, leads only to the conclusion that children will adjust the placement of a stylus in such a way as to receive a reinforcer, but this finding does not appear to have any theoretical significance for the problem of structural change in development.[3]

A second type of social-learning approach to developmental structure is

---

[3] The positive side of these studies emerges where the behavior studied is of obvious practical significance. Thus Baer and his coworkers (Baer, Peterson & Sherman, 1967) demonstrate that specific problem behaviors of preschool children are amenable to replacement with more positive behavior by operant techniques. In light of the tendencies of teachers to inappropriately define annoying behavior as representing pathological personality structures and to respond accordingly, these studies have obvious usefulness. However, except in their impact upon the evaluation of the child by others, the Baer manipulations are presumably as structurally irrelevant to the child's personality development as are the Azrin and Lindsley (1956) induction of changed stylus behaviors in their children.

exemplified by Bandura and MacDonald's (1963) experimental induction of changes in Piagetian moral judgment. It is not quite clear whether the intent of the study was to explain structural change in social-learning terms or to demonstrate that Piaget's (1948) behavior definitions did not have any structural component.

The first intent would imply that Piaget had correctly identified a response with some structural properties but had employed a faulty "maturational" theory to explain its development, which could be better explained by social-learning processes. The second intent would imply that Piaget had incorrectly attributed structural properties to his moral stage measures, either because his methods were poor or because moral judgment responses have no structural properties. Piaget (1948) himself believed that his moral judgment stages are structural in the sense that (1) they represent "structural wholes," i.e., a constellation of traits indicative of global heteronomous or autonomous attitudes toward rules, and (2) that they constitute a relatively irreversible sequence. According to Piaget, one index of the child's stage location is that of his judgment in terms of intentions or consequence when the two conflict, e.g., judging it is worse to break ten cups while washing the dishes than one cup while stealing candy. Bandura and MacDonald (1963) tested second grade children on a series of these items and found some were "at the autonomous stage" (judged in terms of intentions) while some were "at the heteronomous stage." Children at each stage were then exposed to reinforced models emitting the opposite type of judgment. Bandura and MacDonald found substantial learning of the opposite type response. Not only was a "higher stage" readily learned, but it generalized to some new items. Learning was about equal whether it was "progressive" or "regressive." The apparent conclusion to be drawn from the study is that intentionality is learned by ordinary reversible social-learning mechanisms, and that the age trends in intentionality found by Piaget correspond to a learning of the adult cultural norms.

The findings from a number of other studies warn us against accepting these conclusions at face value. Some of these findings come from experimental studies of the training of conservation (reviewed in Sigel & Hooper, 1968; Kohlberg, 1968). Almost all of these studies have given great attention to the issue of whether the behavior changes induced by training are "structural" or not. "Structural change" has been assessed by:

1. the degree of generality or transfer of conservation (e.g., conservation of liquid to conservation of solids to conservation of number);
2. the degree of irreversibility of conservation in the face of training or trick demonstrations designed to induce non-conservation.

While the findings are somewhat conflicting, the following conclusions emerge (Kohlberg, 1968):

1. "Naturally" developed concepts of conservation are quite generalized (i.e., there is a general "conservation factor" in conservation tests).
2. Naturally developed concepts of conservation are quite irreversible.

3. Conservation is difficult to teach by ordinary learning methods to children at an appropriate readiness "age" and almost impossible at younger ages.
4. When taught by some methods, conservation shows some generality and irreversibility. In this it deviates from the specificity and extinguishability of most social-learning study changes. At the same time, however, taught conservation is far less generalized and irreversible than natural conservation.

In light of these findings, the ready reversibility of moral judgment responses in the Bandura and MacDonald (1963) study is suspicious. How are the discrepancies between the ease of learning or unlearning of Piaget's (1948) moral judgment and the difficulty of learning Piaget's (1947) conservation to be accounted for? One answer would be that cognitive tasks (e.g., conservation) do involve structural development but that social or moral tasks do not, but simply involve the learning of cultural values. A second answer would be that morality is an area of structural development, but that Piaget's concepts and methods for defining structure are not as adequate in the moral field as are his concepts and methods in the area of logical operations.

A number of facts point to the validity of the second rather than the first conclusion.[4] Our review of the findings with our own moral stages indicated that they did have structural properties. Our review also indicated that the studies of Turiel (1966) and of Rest et al. (1969) yielded quite different results than those of the Bandura and MacDonald study. "Social learning" of the stage above the child's own was much greater than learning of the stage below the child's own. The discrepancy, however, was one of preference and assimilation not of cognitive learning, since children recalled the one-below arguments better than the one-above arguments.

The Turiel studies (1966, 1969), then, suggest that moral judgment is an area of structural development, but that Piaget's concepts and methods are not good measures of structure in this area. The Kohlberg (1969) assessment method involved classifying open-ended responses into one of six stage categories, whereas Piaget's (1948) assessment involved asking children to choose between two prepackaged alternatives, e.g., "Was John who broke one cup or Charles who broke ten cups worse?" This facilitates children's social learning of the content of the "right answer" without necessarily implying development of awareness of the structure underlying the right answer. Furthermore the Piaget stories do not reveal awareness or unawareness of intentions in moral judgment, but simply how much these are weighted against consequences. Age-developmental studies indicate an awareness of the modifying role of intention among almost all children of the age of the Bandura and MacDonald subjects. Some limitation of the role of intention, as opposed to consequence, is involved even in

---

[4] The points made here are elaborated and documented in the discussions of replications of the Bandura and MacDonald (1963) study made by Crowley (1968) and Cowen, Langer, Heavenrich and Nathanson (1968).

judgment of adults, who consider it worse to kill someone in a car accident by negligence than to purposefully and malevolently insult someone. Accordingly, the shifts in the Bandura and MacDonald study do not represent an actual learning or "unlearning" of a basic concept of intentions, but a learning to weigh them more or less heavily as opposed to consequence. Piaget asserts that awareness of intention is "structural" in the sense that it represents advance on one of eleven dimensions defining the autonomous stage of moral judgment. However, empirical studies reviewed elsewhere (Kohlberg, 1963a, 1969) indicate that children of a given age who are mature on Piaget's tests of intentionality are not more mature on the other Piaget dimensions of the morally autonomous stage, i.e., there is no general Piaget moral stage factor (while there is a general moral stage factor in the various Kohlberg situations and dimensions).

In summary, then, Piaget's definitions of moral judgment responses do not meet the naturalistic criteria of structural stages and hence social-learning manipulations of these responses do not indicate that moral judgment is not structural nor do they indicate that social-learning operations can account for structural development. A hypothetical comparison may clarify the basic point. Bandura and MacDonald's (1963) intent was analogous to operant manipulations of a behavior, such as guilt-strength, which is considered structural in psychoanalytic theory. The theoretical futility of such efforts is self-evident, since the psychoanalyst always says the behavior changed is not structural, and is not what they would term "real guilt," regardless of the outcome of the study. In the moral judgment case, however, the issue of the structural nature of the variable is an empirically definable matter, not an issue of what Piaget's theory might be assumed to say, and this line of experimentation can eventually lead to some conclusions.

Our comparison of the Turiel and the Bandura and MacDonald studies indicates, then, that prior naturalistic study of structural aspects of development is required before experimental manipulations can lead to conclusions about structural development. The contrast between the intent of the Bandura and MacDonald study and that of the experimental studies of conservation is enlightening. The conservation studies assume the existence of structural development and manipulate inputs in order to accelerate such development. The purpose of such studies is to allow us to conceptualize the conditions for cognitive structural change, not to reduce explanations of structural change to explanations developed for other purposes. It is hard to believe that experimental studies of socialization will not take on the same intent soon.

The Bandura and MacDonald (1963) study suggests an additional positive goal for studies manipulating developmental responses besides the goal of accelerating development common to the conservation studies. While Piaget's measures of intentionality are not direct assessments of "structural" stages, they do reflect some natural or cross-culturally universal trends of development. Age trends toward intentionality have been found in every literate culture studied (Switzerland, Belgium, Britain, Israel, United States, Taiwan) as well as in all but one preliterate or semi-literate culture studied (Atayal, Hopi, Zuni, Papago, Mayan, Sioux) (Kohlberg, 1969). Accordingly, the social learning processes exemplified by the Bandura and MacDonald "backward" manipulations are not only distinguishable from the processes naturally leading to the development of intentionality, but they are in partial conflict with them. The same statement may be made about the Turiel (1966) study which did induce some learning in the one-below condition. This type of learning may not be unusual in actual social life. An extreme natural example offered earlier was the Atayal adolescent's social learning of "regressive" dream beliefs. Perhaps another, more artificial, example is provided by the Milgram (1963) obedience study in which the subjects may "learn" from an authority that it is right to shock people in certain situations.

In our discussion of the Atayal dream concept, we suggested that the "social learning" of such regressive beliefs was not smoothly superimposed upon the child's previous cognitive structure, but engendered conflict and doubt in the child or to his other "natural" beliefs. A study by Cowen et al. (1968) suggests that the regressive learning in the Bandura and MacDonald study involved some such conflict and that this learning had somewhat different properties than progressive learning. In one part of their study, Cowen et al. replicated the Bandura and MacDonald findings. Their study also involved a more extensive test of the generality and stability of the learning involved. Such tests indicated that the downward learning was less stable over time than the upward learning as expressed in the decline of use of the model's downward moral reasons (consequences) in a two-week delayed post-test for the regressive group, in contrast to no such decline in retention of the model's reasons in the upward-learning group. This discrepancy between upward and downward reasoning was especially marked for new, as opposed to retest, items. In addition, the authors note that for both learning groups almost all learning took place in the first two trials, that learning seldom went above the 60 per cent criterion, and that the children seemed extremely confused and uncertain as to their reasons after the learning trials. Rather than smooth change following the general laws of learning, the children seemed to have been confronted with the fact that a social authority contradicted their own notions. Their long-range response to this contradiction varied according to whether the authority espoused a view above or below the child's own. In summary, then, the study of the effects of social influence upon responses at various developmental levels may contribute an understanding to that vast border line of socialization in which both cultural learning processes and cognitive-structural processes influence one another.

VII. SOCIAL-LEARNING STUDIES
AND THE CONCEPT OF INTERNALIZATION

The social-learning studies considered so far have been primarily efforts to deny, rather than to explain, structural-developmental change. The work of Aronfreed and others, however, represents a positive effort to explain structural-developmental change within the general principles of associationistic theories of social learning. As Aronfreed's discussion in this volume suggests, structural-developmental change is usually defined by social-learning theorists as "internalization." According to Aronfreed,

> The young child's behavior is initially highly dependent on its experience of external events which are transmitted through the presence and activity of its socializing agents. But its behavior gradually comes to be governed, to a considerable extent, by internal monitors which appear to carry many of the functions of the external controls originally required to establish the behavior (Aronfreed, 1969, p. 263).

The concept of internalization is an attractive one since it seems to define basic structural-developmental changes in a way amenable to experimental investigation. As an example, Aronfreed finds that mild experimental punishment will lead children to resist touching attractive toys even in the absence of an adult monitor, and that this punishment is more effective if it is closely timed to follow onset of the touching act. Aronfreed interprets this effect as the result of classical conditioning of anxiety directly to internal proprioceptive cues of incipient action (as opposed to the conditioning of anxiety to external cues of punishment). Such an experimental induction of internalization seems analogous to the basic processes of natural socialization designed to produce reliable conformity in the absence of sanctions. It also seems analogous to the natural developmental trend in children toward increased self-government, self-control or ego strength. When the analogy to self-control is considered carefully, however, it becomes clear that the child conditioned to feel anxiety over kinesthetic cues of incipient action has no more made a gain in self-control than has the dog conditioned in a similar fashion or the child whose conditioned anxiety represents a phobia. Self-control implies control and inhibition of action by an organized self or ego with cognitive representations of itself and the world, and with an intelligent flexibility as to the cues and conditions of inhibition or release of action. Insofar as inhibition of action is determined rigidly by the paradigms of classical conditioning, it indicates the absence of self-control in the usual sense.

If internalization as experimentally studied has not represented the formation of new structural mechanisms of self-control, neither has it represented structural-developmental change itself. As Aronfreed notes, there is little evidence that experimental inductions of resistance to temptation have the situationally general and irreversible character of structural-developmental change. The sheer fact that a child will follow instructions without someone in the room is itself no evidence that something more than reversible situational learning has been induced. It is clear, then, that experimental inductions of "internalization" cannot be considered to represent the induction of structural-developmental change in the absence of direct evidence of situational generality and irreversibility of such learning.

We have claimed that the experimental studies of internalization have not actually studied either the acquisition of new mechanisms of self-control or the formation of irreversible trans-situational learning, and hence do not really shed light on any process of "internalization" distinct from the general processes of reversible situation-specific learning. In this regard, they are no different than the naturalistic studies of internalization discussed earlier. The experimental studies have operationally defined internalization as degree of conformity to the experimenter's instructional or modeling behavior. As indicated earlier, naturalistic studies of moral internalization have also defined it in conformity terms, i.e., as behavioral, affective, or cognitive conformity to the moral standards of the child's culture. As another example, sex-role "internalization" has been studied in terms of "masculinity-femininity," or "sex-role identification," i.e., in terms of tests of conformity to statistically modal responses of males as opposed to females in the child's culture (studies and measures reviewed in Kohlberg, 1966b).

In our earlier discussion, we noted that these naturalistic measures of moral internalization did not seem to represent measures of structural change any more than did the measures used in experimental studies of internalization like Aronfreed's. The naturalistic measures also appeared to be situation specific and longitudinally unstable (i.e., reversible). The same is more or less true of measures of "sex-role internalization" (evidence reviewed in Kohlberg, 1966b). In essence, we argued that conformity definitions of response were inadequate to define structural change in development because they ignored sequential changes in the shape or patterning of responses.

We must ask, then, in what sense the internalization concept is useful in the definition of structural-developmental change. It is evident that natural moral development is grossly defined by a trend toward an increasingly internal orientation to norms. Our moral stages, as defined by the aspect of sanctions in Table 6.6, clearly represent increasing interiorized orientations to moral norms moving from a concern for sanctions to a concern for praise and blame to a concern for internal principles. This stage conception of internalization is similar to that stated by McDougall (1908) in the first textbook of social psychology:

> The fundamental problem of social psychology is the moralization of the individual into the society into which he is born as an amoral and egoistic infant. There are successive stages, each of which must be traversed by every individual before he can attain the next higher: (1) the stage in which the operation of the instinctive impulses is modified by the influence of rewards and punishments, (2) the stage in which conduct is controlled in the main by anticipation of social praise and blame, (3) the highest stage in which conduct is regulated by an ideal that enables a man to act in the way that seems to him right regardless of the praise or blame of his immediate social environment.

There are certain fundamental differences in this stage concept of moral internalization and the conformity concept, however. In the first place while "internality" is an essential component of McDougall's idea of mature morality, this internality is not defined relative to degree of conformity to a cultural standard, as in a resistance-to-temptation study. Rather it is defined in terms of an "ideal enabling a man to act in a way that seems to him right regardless of praise or blame." This ideal hardly needs to be an internalized cultural standard. When Luther said, "Here I stand, I can do no other," he represented McDougall's highest stage but he was not conforming to an internalized cultural standard of any recognizable sort, since the ideal was self-formulated. In practice, then, the developmentalist is arguing that we can tell whether the norm an individual is following is "moral" or "internal" by looking at the way in which the individual formulates the norm, i.e., its form, and without reference to a specific external cultural standard. A cultural norm, common especially in the lower class, is "stay out of trouble." It is clear that such a norm cannot be held as a moral ideal by an individual regardless of the processes of "norm-internalization" to which the individual is exposed. Our own position is that the only fully internal norm is a moral principle, and that a moral principle (our Stage 6) is definable according to a set of formal attributes which are culturally universal.

The first point brought out by the stage conception, then, is that internality is merely part of the conception of a moral orientation rather than being a general socialization dimension definable without reference to the concept of a moral orientation. The distinction between moral principles and other cultural standards is just that one is not expected to have as fully an internalized orientation to other cultural standards. Moral principles are categorical imperatives, all other standards are hypothetical imperatives contingent on the individual's aims in the situation. The young child may first require admonition and punishment to brush his teeth and eventually brush his teeth without sanctions. In the adult, such an "internalized" orientation of the norm of toothbrushing is quite different from an internalized orientation to a moral norm. If the adult forgets his toothbrush when travelling, he feels no obligation to brush his teeth nor any guilt for failing to do so. He will justify his toothbrushing instrumentally and selfishly (it prevents cavities and keeps his teeth clean) rather than because of respect for the rule or principle of toothbrushing. In sum, then, moral internalization in the sense of development of moral principles cannot be equated with some general dimension of social-norm learning.

The meaning of internalization in the moral domain also makes clear a second point implied by the stage position, which is that internalization must imply cognitive as well as affective correlates. The man in the street knows that a dog or an infant can be trained to refrain from eating meat powder when hungry even in the absence of surveillance by the socializing agent but refuses to consider such conformity "moral." Likewise, the dog's deviance is not considered immoral nor does it arouse moral indignation, because the dog is not considered moral. The dog is neither moral nor immoral "because he doesn't know right from wrong." When the dog has "internalized" the rule to refrain from eating meat powder, it is not because he is "acting in terms of an ideal that seems to him right regardless of praise or blame," but because he has not correctly discriminated the occasions where punishment is likely from those where it is not. The animal or infant has no concept of a rule which is guiding his behavior but instead is responding to cues in the physical or social situation to which he has been aversively conditioned. Children acquire conceptions of rules by age 5-6, but it is not until adolescence that children cognitively formulate moral principles in McDougall's sense of ideals guiding the self's behavior regardless of external social or authoritative support.

In summary, then, there is a sense in which socialization agents hold as their goal the development of internalized moral standards in the young and there is also a sense in which the development of internalized moral standards is a "natural" trend regardless of the specific expectations and practices of socialization agents. Neither the expectations of socialization agents nor the natural trends of development are well defined by a conformity conception of internalization, however. This is apparent in the case of Western adults who do not define moral internalization as behavioral conformity to the cultural code, but rather as the development of a morality of principle which is above actual conformity to cultural expectations. The existence of such parental expectations for socialization "above the culture" must in turn arise from parental recognition of partly natural or autonomous developmental trends in the formation of an internal morality.

Socialization analyses have tended to take an ethnographic description of the content of adult cultural expectations as defining the end point and direction of the socialization process, apart from natural age trends. It is obvious that there is some gross match between trends of age-development and adult expectations in any culture, or the culture would hardly be transmitted. This gross correspondence, however, may as much represent the shaping of adult expectations by developmental realities as the shaping of developmental progressions by adult expectations. There is, we believe, common meaning to the image of maturity guiding socialization in any culture, an image largely reflecting universal and natural trends of social development. In our contemporary culture this core of common meaning is generally called "ego maturity" or "ego strength." There are a large number of competencies expected of adults in our culture which psychologists include in this rubric. The most general of these capacities are those for love, work, and morality. There can be little question that middle-class American socialization expectations are more centrally oriented to the development of such basic capacities than they are to the teaching of detailed conformity to the set of specific and culturally arbitrary definitions of behavior in specific roles defined by the ethnographer or the sociologist. It seems likely that there are culturally universal or near-universal values suggested by the words "love," "work," and "morality," and that these values recognize natural developmental trends and progressions. The development of moral capacities (as well as capacities to work and to love) involves an orientation to internal norms, but this development cannot be defined as a direct internalization of external cultural norms.

If the student of socialization ignores these maturity components of social development in favor of simpler conformity or internalization concepts he will not only fail to describe "natural development" correctly but he will fail to describe the aims and expectations of socialization agents correctly. As a result he will fail to understand the socialization process insofar as this process is essentially a matching (or mismatching) of the developmental expectations of the parent and the developing capacities of the child.

VIII. IMITATION AS A FUNDAMENTAL PROCESS IN SOCIAL DEVELOPMENT: BALDWIN'S THEORY

In the preceding sections, we have argued that the enduring products of socialization must be conceived of in terms of cognitive-structural changes with "natural" courses or sequences of development rather than in terms of the learning of culture patterns. These changes are results of the general processes of cognitive development as these restructure conceptions of the social self, the social world, and the relations between the two. While cognitive, these processes responsible for social development are theoretically different from those responsible for development of physical concepts because they require role-taking. Since persons and institutions are "known" through role-taking, social-structural influences on cognitive-structural aspects of social development may be best conceived in terms of variations in the amount, kind and structure of role-taking opportunities.

In order to tie our conceptions of role-taking to notions of socialization "processes" (of motivation and learning), we shall now elaborate a cognitive-developmental account of processes of imitation and identification. As we indicated earlier, role-taking is a broader term than imitation, but in our opinion all role-taking has imitative components or roots. At the adult level, however, we do not overtly imitate, we "role-take."

In our earlier discussion of the Bandura and MacDonald (1963) study of modeling of moral judgment, we indicated some of the ways in which imitation did not help explain structural development. Is there a sense in which it does? J. M. Baldwin (1906) and Piaget (1951) have postulated that imitation is a natural and active tendency in the human infant, and that this tendency is necessary to account for the infant's cognitive and social development.

One sense in which Baldwin and Piaget have claimed that imitation was an explanatory principle of development is the sense in which they equate imitation with a basic functional tendency they call "accommodation." As stated by Baldwin, "Reaction of the imitative type is the original form of mental accommodation to the environment" (1906, p. 528). We will not elaborate this difficult conception here beyond suggesting some of its intuitive rationale. It is clear that imitation involves a cognitive copying process. There is a sense in which any cognition is a copy of a part of the environment, since an image or symbol has a relation of "likeness to" an environmental object or structure. In Baldwin's and Piaget's view, representation or imagery then implies a distinctive active copying tendency, since they believe all images and representations are forms of action, not passive redintegration of sensations (as introspective associationism and psychoanalysis claimed).

Whatever one's views as to the role of imitation in the development of cognitive representation, there can be little question that imitation is an extremely basic mechanism in the formation of social knowledge. Struck by such phenomena as sociodramatic play, there is hardly a writer concerned with the problem of how the child comes to know his society who has not been struck by the place of the child's imitative or role-taking tendencies in the growth of such knowledge.

Baldwin's view that the child's knowledge of society develops at first through imitation seems to be saying little more than the social-learning truism that the child's knowledge of society grows through the observational learning of the behavior of others (learning, which translated into performance, is termed "imitation"). The more distinctive feature of Baldwin's view is that such imitation provides the structure of the child's social relationships, i.e., of his self as it relates to other selves. In the social-learning view of imitation, it is a matter of little moment whether a response is learned by imitation or by reinforced trial and error since it functions in the same way once learned. In contrast, Baldwin argues that imitation is important because it determines the structure of the child's self-concept, and of his concepts of others, a structure, in turn, determining the use of the behavior pattern learned through imitation.

According to Baldwin,

> the growth of the individual's self-thought, upon which his social development depends, is secured all the way through by a twofold exercise of the imitative function. He reaches his subjective understanding of the social copy by imitation, and then he confirms his interpretations by another imitative act by which he ejectively leads his self-thought into the persons of others (1906, p. 527).

Baldwin's central claim (made also by Mead [1934]) is that the child's self-concept and his concept of other selves necessarily grow in one-to-one correspondence. The child cannot observationally learn the behavior pattern of another without putting it in the manifold of possible ways of acting open to the self. Once it becomes something the self might do, when others do it, they, too, are ascribed the subjective attitudes connected with the self's performance of the act.

As stated by Baldwin,

> What the person thinks as himself is a pole or terminus and the other pole is the thought he has of the other person, the "alter." What he calls himself now is in large measure an incorporation of elements that at another period he called another. Last year I thought of my friend, W., as someone with skill on a bicycle. This year I have learned to ride and have imitatively taken the elements formerly recognized in W's personality over to myself. All the things I hope to learn to become are, now, before I acquire them, possible elements of my thought of others.

> But we should note that when I think of the other, I must construe

him as a person in terms of what I think of myself, the only person whom I know in the intimate way called "subjective." My thought of my friend is not exhausted by the movements of bicycling, nor by any collection of such acts. Back of it all there is the attribution of the very fact of subjectivity which I have myself. I constantly enrich the actions which were at first his alone, and then became mine by imitation of him, with the meaning, the subjective value, my appropriation of them has enabled me to make (1906, pp. 13-18).

According to Baldwin, then, there are two intertwined mechanisms of society, of sharing. The first is imitation of the other, the second is "ejection," i.e., empathy or "projection" of one's own subjective feelings into the other. Imitation of the other not only leads to a changed self-concept (e.g., a self who rides the bicycle), but it leads to a changed concept of the other because the activity (bicycle-riding) has a new meaning after it is done by the self, and this meaning is read back as part of the other.

The basic starting point of any analysis of the growth of social knowledge, then, must be the fact that all social knowledge implies an act of sharing, of taking the viewpoint of another self or group of selves. This fact is paralleled on the active side by the fact that all social bonds, ties, or relationships involve components of sharing. The word "social" essentially means "shared." The motivational problem usually proposed to socialization theory is the question of why the "selfish" or impulsive infant develops into a social being, i.e., one who wants to share activities with others, to share goods with others, to be a member of a common group, to maintain shared norms, and to pursue shared goals. The answer of developmental theory is that the self is itself born out of the social or sharing process, and therefore, motives for self-realization or self-enhancement are not basically "selfish" in the perjorative sense, but require sharing. Developmental theory, then, presents a radically different picture of the birth of social motives than do all other theories. Other theories have assumed that social motives are either instinctive or result from the association of socializing agents and their behavior with gratification and anxiety to the child. In contrast, developmental theories assume a primary motivation for competence and self-actualization which is organized through an ego or self whose structure is social or shared.

Two basic psychological mechanisms of sharing have been proposed by developmental theory, "role-taking" and imitation. Baldwin (1906) and Mead (1934) engaged in extensive written debate as to the relative priority of the two mechanisms in social development. Baldwin viewed similarity of self and other as directly striven for through imitation, whereas Mead viewed it as the indirect result of role-taking involved in communicative acts. The child's attitude, he thought, became like that of the other because both respond alike to a common symbol or gesture. Because the child has responded in the past to the other's gesture, when he makes the gesture himself, he calls out in himself implicitly the response he calls out in the other. Mead further points out that much sociality, much mutual role-taking, occurs through cooperative interaction in which each individual's role is different, in which roles are complementary rather than similar. Nevertheless, the study of infancy indicates that similarity to others is directly striven for, and that such striving or imitation precedes, rather than follows, the development of linguistic communication. Accordingly, it seems to us that Mead's conceptions must be embedded in a broader developmental account of the self which includes early imitative behavior and the matrix of infant cognitive development out of which the self emerges.

Like Mead, Baldwin was struck by the fact that the younger child's social interaction is structured in terms of dyadic complementary roles, and that young children tend to play out both sides of these complementary roles as a mechanism of self-development. As stated by Mead,

> The child plays that he is offering himself something, and he buys it; he gives himself a letter and takes it away; he addresses himself as a parent, as a teacher; he arrests himself as a policeman. He has a set of stimuli which call out in himself the sort of response they call out in others. A certain organized structure arises in him and in his other which replies to it, and these carry on the conversation of gestures between themselves (1934, pp. 150-151).

According to Baldwin also, the basic unit of the self is a bipolar self-other relationship, with a resulting tendency to play out the role of the other, i.e., the child either has an "imitative" or an "ejective" attitude toward another person. When the child is imitating or learning from the other, his attitude is one of "accommodation," i.e., his behavior is being structured by the structure of the behavior of the other. It is a matter of little import whether the child's action is structured by the other in the form of spontaneous imitation or in the form of instruction or command. A modeling is taken as an implicit command, and an explicit command can always be modeled (i.e., "Do it this way," accompanied by a demonstration). In either case, the structure of the activity belongs to both parties, but it is being passed on from the active to the passive one. The central focus is upon a novel structure which the active agent has which the passive agent does not.

In contrast, the active or assimilative self is one which knows what it is doing, and which ejects its own past attitudes into the other. Whether the child is active or passive, there is a focus upon an activity of one person with an attitude of accommodation to it in the other. The attitude of the child practicing something he has already learned through imitation or compliance, then, is always different than the attitude he held in the process of learning it. In learning an activity associated with the superior power or competence of the adult, the child's attitude is accommodatory and, in that sense, inconsistent with the prestigeful activity being learned. Accordingly, the child tends to turn around and practice the activity on, or before the eyes of, some other person whom he can impress, into whom he can "eject" the admiration or submissiveness he felt when learning the act.

The actual "ejective" phase of self-development appears to first develop in the second year of life. At that age, the child seems to attribute feelings to others and to show things to, and communicate with, others. At the end of the second year, a "negativistic crisis" (Ausubel, 1957) typically occurs. This is a phase in which self and other are sharply differentiated and the difference between copying the self and copying (or obeying) the other are sharply distinguished. An example of the counter-imitation of this era is a $2\frac{1}{2}$-year-old's consistent response of "Not goodbye," when someone said "Goodbye" to him.[5]

Interestingly, however, it is just at this age of "independence" that the child acquires a need for an audience, a need reflected in "look at me" or attention-seeking behavior. Indeed, it is striking to notice that "look at me" behavior often is a phase of imitative acts at this developmental level. The father takes a big jump, the same $2\frac{1}{2}$-year-old imitates, and then demands that the father look at him just as he looked at the father in imitating. Imitation immediately placed the child in the model's role, and led him to eject into the adult his own capacity for admiration.

Thus Baldwin would account for the "show-and-tell" behavior of the 3-4-year-old as the reverse form of the sharing involved in the initial imitative act. Imitation, then, generates social sharing at both the learning and the practicing phase. Seeking to act competently almost always requires another person for the imitative young child. First, the child needs another self as a model of what to do. Second, because he has learned from a model, he needs to practice what he has learned on another self, e.g., to be a model to another.

Much of the show-and-tell behavior of the preschool child shades over into "private" or "egocentric" speech (Kohlberg, Yaeger & Hjertholm, 1968) which accounts for about a third of the preschool child's verbal output. Mead would explain such speech by the need to tell another person what one is doing in order to establish its meaning for the self, a meaning which requires "taking the role of the other" toward the self's activity. According to Mead, the self needs an audience to be a self, to establish the meaning and value of its own action. Eventually, this audience becomes an internal and abstract "generalized other," but first it is the concrete other of the egocentric dialogue.

In spite of these differences in emphasis, Baldwin and Mead would agree that the preschool child's need to show and tell others about his activities reflects the egocentric "ejection" of the subjective component of the bipolar self upon another to establish the meaning of the self's activity, an interpretation far different from the usual "dependency motive" interpretations of attention-seeking.

An experiment by Emmerich and Kohlberg (1953) provides some crude support for Baldwin's analysis in that it suggests the bipolarity of the imitative and the audience-seeking and egocentric-speech tendencies in the child. The study is discussed further in Section XIII in that it indicated both of two experi-

---

[5] This negativism about imitation and obedience is paralleled by a negativism about receiving help, the insistence on "doing it oneself." A typical expression was the same child's insistence that a coat be put back on him so he could take it off himself after it had been removed by a helpful adult.

mental conditions, prior negative criticism by an adult E and prior helpfulness, equally led to high imitation by kindergarten children in contrast to a no-interaction condition. These conditions which led to high imitation were, however, the exact opposite of those which led to high audience-seeking and egocentric speech. The "no prior interaction" condition elicited the most such speech in contrast to both of the conditions eliciting imitation. This negative association between the situations eliciting imitation and those elicting social speech was reflected in negative correlations between situational change scores in the two types of social behavior. Children who went down in social speech (compared to a pretest baseline) were high in imitation, those who went up in such speech were low in imitation $(r = -.34)$. This negative association between the situational conditions eliciting imitation and the conditions eliciting audience-seeking speech does not mean that children who imitate do not engage in social speech. In fact the two go together as developmental or personality dispositions, as Baldwin's analysis (as well as others) suggests. The correlation between pretest audiencing speech and subsequent imitation was .45. The negative association was rather between the occasions for audiencing and imitative behavior as bipolar tendencies, not between the two of them as general social dispositions.

Age-developmental studies suggest that look-at-me attention-seeking precedes the seeking of approval from others. It is clear that the child who shows off to the adult the act he has just learned from him will not seek the adult's approval. As the child matures, he recognizes that imitation of the act does not make him as competent as the model, and that performance of one competent act still leaves the adult a generally superior performer. As the child acquires a stable sense of the superiority of the older model, "look at me" after imitation becomes the request for approval, "did I do it right?" Baldwin's (1906) account, then, suggests that much of the need for approval is born from the fact that most of the child's accomplishments are imitative. Almost everything the young child strives to do or accomplish is something he sees another person do first and which he learns, in part, imitatively. The young child's accomplishments, his talking, walking, dressing himself, toileting, etc., are all activities that he sees others do and knows they can do. Because they are his models for activity, their approval of his performance counts.[6]

Following Baldwin, then, we may propose that the motivational basis of social reinforcement is to be found in the child's imitative tendencies, his tendencies to engage in shared activities. The child's "look at me" behavior is not so much a search for adult response as it is a search for confirmation of social or imitative learning. Insofar as the desire for approval arises developmentally out of "look at

---

[6] The interpretation just advanced reverses social-learning accounts of the relations between imitation and social approval. Gewirtz (1969) notes, like Baldwin, that almost every behavior which socialization requires is a behavior children see others do first. Accordingly, says Gewirtz, when a child is rewarded for a step in socialization, he is also being rewarded for imitating, and so a generalized habit of imitating is born. In a subsequent section, we consider this argument in more detail.

me" behavior, it, too, is not a sign of some more concrete reward which the child seeks. As we elaborate in a subsequent section, the child's dependence on social reinforcement is heaviest at the developmental stage where he is concerned with "doing things right" but has no clear internal cognitive standards of what is right and so must rely on the approval of authorities to define "right" behavior. The child's initial desires to perform competently, to succeed, rest on intrinsic competence motivation. The infant struggles to master a task without the least concern for adult reward for performing the task, and without the least concern for the adult's judgment as to whether or not he is doing it right. Social development up until age 6-7 is not a matter of internalizing "extrinsic" social reinforcement into intrinsic competence motivation; rather it is a process of growing sensitivity to external social definers of standards of competence, and in that sense an increased sensitivity to "extrinsic" social reinforcement. This increased sensitivity, in turn, is the result of a growing sense of dependence upon having a social model of performance. The tendency to imitate, to seek a model of performance, itself rests primarily upon intrinsic competence motivation, upon the "need" to act or function. The child's fundamental motive in imitation is expressed in the familiar cry, "what can I do?" Relying on models to do something interesting and effective, he comes to feel increasingly that he must rely also on them to tell him "how he is doing." In this view, competence motivation engenders imitation which engenders social dependency through an increased sense of discrepancy between the child's own activities and the norms embodied in the activities of his models.

In Baldwin's account, the development of the imitative process into social dependency, the need for approval, is also part of the development of imitation into "identification," into the combination of attachment, admiration, and desire for normative guidance which forms a focus of the child's attitude toward his parents. Identification as discussed by Baldwin is a constellation of attitudes similar to that termed "satellization" by Ausubel (1957). Ausubel distinguishes between an imitative "incorporatory" attitude and a "satellizing" attitude. An incorporative child is a general imitator, he is always ready and eager to imitate any interesting or prestigeful model, because such imitation is a primitive form of self-aggrandizement, of getting something the model has or sharing his prestige. In contrast, the satellizing child is loyal to his past modelings of his parents and to their expectations, and will pass up the opportunity to copy the new prestigeful response of the model. In fact, Ausubel et al. (1954) predicted and found that "imitative" or "suggestible" copying of the preferences of a prestigeful model was negatively correlated with satellizing attitudes toward parents.

The distinctions between an "incorporatory" and a "satellizing" attitude are suggested by the following examples:

Incorporatory — Boy, aged 4, to male adult interviewer, "You're twice as big so you have twice as much brains. I'm going to knock your brains out, and then they'll go in my brains and I'll be twice as smart."

Satellizing — Boy, aged 12, asked about his father: "I'd like to be like my father because I think of him as nice and I was brought up by him and learned the things he taught me so I could be a good boy because he always taught me to be good."

Boy, aged 15: "I try to do things for my parents, they've always done things for you. I try to do everything my mother says, I try to please her. Like she wants me to be a doctor and I want to, too, and she's helping me to get up there."

It is clear that the examples cited illustrate different cognitive and moral levels of thought. Since the four-year-old's thinking is concrete and physicalistic, becoming like another involves a transfer of body contents.[7] In contrast, the older boy's conceptions are based on psychological likenesses through processes of teaching and conformity to expectations. Furthermore, the admired quality of the model has shifted from power and smartness to moral goodness.

These identification statements are "moral" in a double sense. First, the content of what is to be shared with, or learned from, the parent is a moral content. The parent both models and expects the good. The boy wants to be like the model in the ways expected by the model. Second, the reasons for identifying with the parent are moral. The boy wants to be like the parent because the parent is good, and the boy wants to be good. More specifically, however, to become good is to give something to the parent to whom one owes something, because what the parent wants is for the child to be good.

As we discuss later, the development of such "moral identifications" presupposes the development of moral thought already discussed. At the same time, however, Baldwin (1906) points out that these identifications rest on a sense of a shared self built up because the child feels he shares with the adult everything that he has learned from him. This sense of a normative shared self Baldwin terms "the ideal self" and equates it with moral conscience. As we have seen, Baldwin says that the bipolar self involves an active, assertive, controlling self and a passive, submissive, imitative self. The child may be either as occasion arises. With a younger child or a parent in a permissive mood, the child himself defines what is to be done and the other is merely an object to be manipulated, an agent in terms of whom the action may be carried out. With an older person or in a novel situation, the child expects to be the object in terms of which action determined by the other is carried out.

Whether the self determining the child's action is the other (the adult) or the child himself that is "selfish," it is a bipolar self, not a shared or sharing self. The act of adjusting to or obeying the adult need not imply an experience of self-control and unselfishness by the child since the self controlling the child and demanding sacrifice of his wishes is not his own self. Though the child's action may be determined by the dominating self of the other, still that other self is conceived by the child in its own image as a basically impulsive or need-gratifying self (insofar as motives are assigned to it at all). The experience of unselfish

---

[7] In our opinion, it is the concrete bodily nature of the young child's thought and the resulting magical and destructive notion of becoming like another by physical possession which makes early identification "incorporative," rather than such identification being the result of the child's domination by oral libido.

obligation requires that the two selves be identified or unified with one another, an integration which is not achieved by motives to imitate or obey in themselves.

How does such a concept of a shared self which wants to be good and to conform to rule arise? The experience required, says Baldwin, is one in which the child perceives the parent as putting pressure on the child to conform to something outside the parent. Such an experience is not bipolar since the parent wants the child to be like himself vis-a-vis his attitude toward the rule. The parent's self is seen as simultaneously commanding (the child) and obeying (the rule). Thus initiating action and conforming are seen as both parts of the same self, a self-controlling self.

Such conformity to a third force might simply be perceived by the child as indicating that a third person dominates the parent as the parent dominates the child. However, the fact that such pressure to conform goes on in the absence of the third person or authority tends to give rise to the concept of a generally conforming self. In addition, the fact that the conformity is shared in the family or group gives rise to a sense of a common self which the child is to become.

Originally such a general or ideal self is largely in the image of the parents. It is ideal to the child, it is what he is to become, but it is largely realized in the parents. This does not mean that there is no differentiation of parents from the rule; the parents are seen as obeying the rule. It does mean that the image of a good, conforming self which obeys the rules tends to be in the parent's image.[8]

In summary, Baldwin holds that in the years three to eight, the child develops from seeing interaction as governed by bipolar self-other relations to seeing it as governed by rules. These rules are shared by both members of the self-other dyad. As "ejected" into others in the course of action, they are what Mead (1934) termed "the generalized other," the common rules and attitudes shared by the group. As these rules are felt as governing the self, but as being imperfectly known and followed by the self, they are the "ideal self." The sense of the rule-following self, "the ideal self," is more personal and more closely equated with the parent than is the system of rules themselves, "the generalized other."

Baldwin's concepts imply that as the child develops a sense of himself as a "good boy" governed by shared rules, his relations to others are increasingly dominated by a sense of himself as a "good boy" whose relations of sharing with others (especially those close to him) are based on this common "goodness," this common "ideal self." His non-moral forms of self-aspiration (his desire to be a powerful, strong, clever self) are neither ideal nor a basis for sharing, and in that sense are not an "ideal self." Given the formation of an ideal self, then, it determines forms of social relationship as well as regulating moral behavior.

---

[8] By experience of conflict between models and by perception of their failure to incarnate the rule, the self which is the child's model becomes recognized as abstract and impersonal and is embodied as conscience, according to Baldwin (1906). In this sense, however, a morality of principle is still based on identification, but an identification with a set of principles (or a principled self) rather than another person.

As an example of the role of the ideal self in social relations, one might cite the state of "being in love" as conventionally (or romantically) defined. All psychological analyses of love, including the psychoanalytic, agree that it involves a relationship of identification (or sharing between selves) involving idealization of the other, and a sense of being governed by an unselfish or sacrificial concern for the love object. In other words it involves a sense of sharing based on the ideal self, not the concrete self.[9]

In spite of the obvious scope and suggestiveness of Baldwin's and Mead's theories of the role of imitation and role-taking in the function of the social self, these theories have been almost completely neglected by research child psychologists. The remainder of this chapter will attempt to elaborate these concepts, to compare them with more familiar psychoanalytic or social-learning concepts, and to document them in terms of research findings.

IX. GENERAL COMPARISON OF COGNITIVE-DEVELOPMENTAL, PSYCHOANALYTIC AND SOCIAL-LEARNING CONCEPTS OF IDENTIFICATION

It is apparent that Baldwin's cognitive-developmental view of moral development and identification has similarities to the psychoanalytic view in which moral "internalization" is the result of a process of parental "identification," i.e., a motivated transfer of norms outside the self-system into the boundaries of the self-system, a process located in the years four to eight by both Baldwin (1906) and Freud (1938).

In the cognitive-developmental account, however, the notion of "moral internalization" does not imply a simple and literal transfer, incorporation, or internalization of something outside the ego to something inside. Assimilation of the "outside" to "inside" depends upon the structural reorganization of the external norm and upon structural reorganization of the self assimilating the norm. At the earlier stages of valuing (Stage 1), cultural standards and values are oriented to as labels of good and bad external physical events and actions (e.g., punishment and other bad happenings) and the self's pursuit of values lies in the avoidance of "bad" physical events and objects. By Stage 3, cultural standards are conceived of as "internal" in the sense that they are defined as internal psychological dispositions or virtues in the self and moral expectations

---

[9] The role of "ideal self" identifications in social relations is clearest at the "good boy–good girl" stage of morality. It is not surprising to find that girls achieve good girl (Stage 3) morality earlier than boys and persist in it longer, so that most adult Stage 3 persons are female (Kohlberg, 1969). Girls move to this position faster (and perhaps stay there longer) because they are forced to differentiate the prestige of goodness from the prestige of power in defining their own roles. In any case, girls focus upon a "good girl" ideal-self morality and this focus is associated with an emphasis on love relationships of the sort described, often prefigured in an idealized relation to the father, first found in girls at age 7-8, rather than in the "Oedipal" (3-5) period (Kohlberg, 1965, 1966b).

(and virtues) in others, and the self is defined as "someone trying to be a good person." At this conventional level, however, values are still seen as depending upon some actual social relations of sharing, upon a concrete social order with actual shared expectancies. The standard is contingent upon its being held and maintained by others, and upon approval and disapproval by others. Only at the stage of principle, rather than at the stage of identification with authority, are norms oriented to as fully internal, in the sense of resting upon a basis of self-selection (and ideal universality or the capacity to be shared) rather than upon actual sharedness.

The cognitive-developmental view holds that the development of morally relevant identifications is a relatively advanced phase of development of the imitative process, and accordingly, that a theory of identification with parents must be part of a much broader account of the development of imitative processes in general. Psychoanalytic theories of parent identification are obviously unsuitable to deal with the bread-and-butter phenomena of imitation which constitute the basis of much of the child's ordinary situational and reversible social learning. As Bandura points out in this volume,

> According to the (neo-psychoanalytic) theories of identification reviewed, in order to get a boy to emulate a baseball player such as Mickey Mantle, it would be necessary for the youngster to develop an intense attachment to the brawny model who would then withhold affectional responsivity. Or the youngster would have to develop strong incestuous desires towards Mrs. Mantle and hostile rivalrous feelings toward the slugger (p. 233).

Of course, psychoanalytic theories of identification were not designed to account for such phenomena of imitation, and presuppose a sharp distinction between identification as a process of structural change in the personality and ordinary imitation. Occasionally psychoanalytic writers use examples of the child's daily imitations as exemplifying principles of identification (e.g., Anna Freud's [1946] child who plays dentist out of "identification with the aggressor"), but in so doing run the risk of the absurdities Bandura mentions. Essentially, psychoanalytic identification theory has no detailed way of dealing with daily imitation and presupposes a theoretical discontinuity between processes of imitation and processes of identification.

In the research literature (Kohlberg, 1963a), it has been customary to distinguish between identification (as structural change) and imitation according to the following empirical criteria of structure:

1. In identification, modeling is generalized and trans-situational. A variety of behaviors and roles are reproduced in a variety of situations. In imitation, modeling is of specific behaviors in specific situations.

2. In identification, modeling is persistent and occurs in the absence of the model.

3. In identification, performance of the modeled behavior appears to be

motivated intrinsically. It persists in the absence of any obvious reinforcement to which it is instrumental.

4. In identification, performance of the modeled behavior is relatively
   irreversible or non-extinguishable even when it is non-reinforced or
   punished.

In research practice, these distinctions between identification and imitation
have been assumed rather than observed, in the sense that a paper and pencil
measure of similarity between the child's self-concept and his concept of his
parent is assumed to have the structural properties mentioned, while an experimental measure of imitation of a strange experimenter is assumed not to have
these properties. Given the fact that distinctions between identification and
imitation have been assumed rather than studied, it is fair to say, as Bandura does
in this volume, that a review of the research literature gives no support for the
notion of two distinct realms or processes of modeling, one of "deep" identification and the other of superficial imitation. Bandura, as well as Aronfreed and
Gewirtz, argue that the distinctions between imitation and identification are not
distinctions between processes but rather represent a continuum of stimulus,
response, and reinforcement generalization of processes of imitative learning
which have the same basic social-learning antecedents whether they are situation-
specific or whether they appear to be generalized and functionally autonomous.

The cognitive-developmental approach would agree with these writers in
seeking theoretical continuity between the two and in rejecting general theories
of identification which cannot directly handle the phenomena of imitation. The
developmentalist diverges from the social-learning analyst in holding that while
many of the *functions* and causal antecedents of imitation and identification are
continuous, the cognitive-*structure* characteristics of phenomena of imitation and
identification are different and discontinuous.[10] In considerable part, the differences customarily implied by the terms "imitation" and "identification" are
differences in the developmental level of structure implied by the two terms. In
distinguishing between continuity of function and discontinuity of structure, the
developmentalist is employing a familiar strategy. Stages of morality, stages of
intelligence, etc., all imply a continuity of function (e.g., moral value-judgment)
together with a discontinuity of the structures (moral stages) fulfilling those
functions. Piaget (1951) has attempted to employ this strategy to define the
early stages of imitation. In Piaget's view imitation is defined functionally

---

[10] It is evident that either the psychoanalytic or the cognitive-developmental conceptions of identification-internalization presuppose a self-concept or ego with boundaries. Since
associationistic social learning postulates no self-system, the concept of identification cannot
be meaningful within it. In Aronfreed's (1969) treatment, "internalization" refers to the
operation of a variety of learning mechanisms (some cognitive, some simple conditioning)
which can lead to relatively permanent response-patterns, but does not presuppose an ego
or identification processes. The cognitive-developmental theory assumes, like psychoanalysis,
that the ego's judgment of perceived similarity between self and other are basic structural
components of attitudes of identification, but, unlike psychoanalysis, assumes these are
conscious cognitive judgments.

(primacy of accommodation over assimilation) in a continuous fashion, but each new stage of intelligence or cognition leads to new stages of imitation.

The cognitive-developmental view of identification differs from the psychoanalytic in the following regards:

1. Identification is viewed as a cognitive-structural stage of more general imitative or social-sharing processes.
2. Accordingly it is not uniquely dependent upon particular motives and ties only present in the early parent-child relationship.
3. Identifications are not totally fixed, irreversible, or "internalized." Identifications are "solutions" to developmental tasks which may change in object or nature with new developmental tasks.

It was said that the cognitive-developmental account distinguishes identification (generalized enduring modeling and perception of a portion of the self as shared with the parents) from imitation, but makes the distinction relative and one of developmental structure, rather than of dichotomous processes. In the cognitive-developmental account, however, enduring tendencies to model are only one component of a larger constellation of attitudes termed "identification" or "satellization." The constellation includes the following components:

a) tendencies to imitate the parent or other model,
b) emotional dependency and attachment to the parent,
c) tendency to conform to the parent's normative expectations,
d) perceived similarity to the parent,
e) idealization of the parent or of his competence and virtue,
f) vicarious self-esteem derived from the parent's competence or status,
g) ability to derive self-esteem from the parent's approval and so to forego other sources of prestige or competence, with associated security of self-esteem, moderate level of aspiration, etc.

This constellation is believed to develop more or less gradually in the "latency" years (4-10) in most (but not all) "normal" children, and to wane or decline with the growth of independence in adolescence. Accordingly the constellation is a major component in the definition of a later childhood stage of ego development in the theories of Baldwin, Ausubel, Loevinger and myself.[11]

The existence of such a constellation of attitudes has received considerable support from the research literature. Correlations between affectional attachment responses (wanting to be with the parent), imitation responses, perceived similarity responses, and awarding of authority and competence are consistently reported in the literature and are all related to parental nurturance (evidence reviewed in Kohlberg, 1966b). These attitudes toward parents (though not

---

[11] The major alternative focus for defining this era of social development has been Piaget's (1948) and H. S. Sullivan's (1953) focus upon development of "Stage 2" peer attitudes of egalitarian competition, cooperation, and exchange as opposed to the development of "Stage 3" attitudes of identification, approval-seeking, loyalty, and gratitude toward parents. I have argued that both develop in this era, but that there is typically a hierarchical and unified (rather than conflicting) relation between these two foci of development.

specifically to the same-sex parent) are also correlated with acceptance of the conventional moral code or of parental moral expectations, and to self-report measures of adjustment (evidence reviewed in Kohlberg, 1963a, 1966b). Furthermore, it seems fairly clear that whatever major "positive" or "socialized" contribution to development is made by identification dispositions is based on this constellation. While perceived similarity and affectional reactions to parents are jointly tied to acceptance of the moral code and to self-rated adjustment, measures of dispositions to play adult or same-sex role are not (evidence reviewed in Kohlberg, 1963a, 1966b). In other words, it is not so much that moral content is internalized by identification as it is that the identifying attitude is a "moral" attitude of conformity to shared expectations.

We have referred to satellizing or developmental identification as a constellation of attitudes of attachment, imitation, and conformity to the expectations of the model. This is because definite causal priorities are not definitely implied by a cognitive-developmental identification theory. Insofar as these three attitudes are linked in other theories, such causal sequences are assumed. Anaclitic identification theory (Sears, 1957) assumes a sequence in which (1) parental nurturance (and nurturance withdrawal) causes (2) identification (modeling) which causes (3) the internalization of parental moral expectations. While single causal sequences are oversimplified, the developmental view stresses that the desire to model the adult leads to attachment and social dependency, rather than the reverse, a theme taken up at length in Section XIV.

The cognitive-developmental concept that imitative attitudes support and stimulate a dependency relationship is quite different in its implication than are psychoanalytic theories of identification which suppose that it is primarily a form of substitution for the relationship to the other person by acting upon the self in the role of the other. As a relationship of sharing with another person, developmental identification is not as fixed, "internalized," or self-directed as is implied by psychoanalytic concepts. In its moral implications, satellizing identification leads to a "semi-internalized" conformity to expectations and concern about disapproval based on a sense of sharing these expectations, not to an "internalized" self-critical and self-punitive "superego." (As noted previously, it is linked to a conventional rather than a fully internalized moral orientation.) Furthermore, satellizing identifications are not the unilateral cause of the formation of conventional "good boy" morality. In actuality, the structure of these identifications partially presupposes conventional moral concepts and attitudes. Such identifications, however, support conventional morality, give it specific content, and deepen its affective significance. A somewhat superficial analogy may be drawn between relations to parents and relations to a personal god in moral development. Children of varying religions (Catholic, Protestant, Jewish, Muslim, Buddhist, atheist) go through the same sequence of moral stages. As they pass through these stages, religious relations are redefined. (As an example a Stage 2 Protestant boy says, "The best rule is to be a good Christian. You be good to God and He'll be good to you." Of being a "good son" he also says, "If you do things for your father, he'll do things for you.") Attitudes toward God, in turn, support moral attitudes, particularly at the conventional levels of morality. This is because they give the child the feeling that someone besides himself really cares that he is good, i.e., that he has someone with whom to share his moral expectations of himself. Similarly, once relations to parents have been defined in moral-identificatory terms, they tend to support moral attitudes because they provide a matrix of generalized support and care about the child's being good. While "society" or other authorities expect the child to "be good," the child is only one of many for everyone but his parents.[12]

From the cognitive-developmental viewpoint, then, it is impossible to conceive of such basic and near-universal features of personality development as morality as being directly caused by parent identification. There are too many developmental and cultural forces tending to produce "normal" morality to see these attitudes as contingent on special unique relationships to parents. As we elaborate later, the role-taking opportunities required for moral development need not be specifically familial nor need they imply identification in any specific sense. Accordingly, our view is that identifications do not cause moral (or sex-role) internalization but develop in parallel with them, and help to support moral or sex-role attitudes. Cognitive-developmental changes in conceptions of moral rules and social-sex roles are causative forces in the formation of parent identifications as much or more than the reverse. The research evidence supporting the cognitive-developmental (as opposed to the psychoanalytic) conception of the role of identification in psychosexual and moral development will be briefly considered at the end of this chapter, after a consideration of the imitative process and its development.

X. COGNITIVE-STRUCTURAL STAGES OF IMITATION-IDENTIFICATION

A discussion of stages in the cognitive organization of imitation, must start by noting that all imitations, including its early forms, are cognitive, as Aronfreed's and Bandura's chapters very convincingly argue. Bandura's studies demonstrate no-trial observational learning and storage by preschoolers of complex new behavior patterns of models. Developmental studies such as Piaget's (1951) document the same characteristics as are true of later infant imitation. It is evident that such acquisition and the resulting generalized and autonomous

---

[12] It may be the loss of this support of the parent's special concern about the child's being good which leads to "regression" to instrumental hedonism on leaving home in some of the college-age population (Kramer, 1968). Decline in attitudes of identification with parents, as well as decline in religious attitudes, appears to characterize both regression to preconventional morality and progression to principled morality in a college population (Haan et al., 1969). If no one else one cares about cares whether the self is good, one tends to fall back upon self-chosen goals and standards, whether these are amoral or morally principled. In the latter case, one cares about the principle, however, rather than about "being a good self."

enactment of an absent model's behavior presupposes what Aronfreed (1969) terms a "cognitive template" and Bandura (1969) "an image" guiding imitation. Such a "cognitive template" is involved in much or most of the ordinary phenomena of infant imitation, such as is involved in language learning.[13]

The cognitive prerequisites of imitative behavior are further suggested by the fact that it is difficult or impossible to teach highly *generalized* imitation by instrumental-learning procedures to most lower animals like rats (Solomon & Coles, 1954). In contrast, cognitively higher animals, e.g., primates, readily display generalized imitative behavior and imitative learning (Warden & Jackson, 1935).

While some associationistic (or social-learning) theories of imitation, like those of Aronfreed (1969) and Bandura (1969), recognize the cognitive skill components in imitation acquisition, they fail to recognize stages of imitation, i.e., radical reorganizations of the imitative act due to changes in its cognitive structure. With regard to infancy, Piaget's (1951) observations have led him to define the following stages of imitation:

1. *Pseudo-imitation because of lack of differentiation between stimuli produced by self and other (Intelligence Stage 2)* (1-3 months). Stimuli made by other which are similar to those the child makes himself and which provide feedback to prolong the child's own circular reactions will prolong or elicit the child's response, e.g., crying by another child will prolong or trigger the child's own crying.

2. *Pseudo-imitation to make an interesting spectacle last (Intelligence Stage 3)* (3-7 months). The child will employ a schema already in his repertoire to maintain a like schema of action modeled by the adult. If the adult imitates what the child is doing (putting out his tongue), the child will repeat his own act to "make" the adult continue in this interesting activity.

3. *Imitation of new models (Intelligence Stage 4)* (7-10 months). The child will imitate a visually perceived movement by the adult for which he has only kinesthetic or auditory but not visual feedback, e.g., matching a visually perceived mouth movement of the adult. He will also imitate new schemas by trying out various known schemata which gradually become closer to the model. No effort is made to reproduce models too remote from his own schema, but some novelty in the modeled activity is required.

---

[13] In the Piaget (1951) framework an image of action is a rather late-developing (age 1) representational schema, one that itself presupposes imitation for its genesis. Before imitation involves copying novel responses, Piaget terms it "pseudo-imitation." A discussion of whether or not imitation is "cognitive" presupposes some distinction between "genuine" and pseudo-imitation (Gilmore, 1967). One condition for defining genuine imitation is that the subject has attended to cues of similarity and difference between his behavior and the model's. A second is that the behavior pattern is actually acquired from observation of the model rather than being learned in other ways. Much of what has been studied experimentally as "imitative learning" is not imitation in this sense, but is simply the gradual increase of performance of similar responses under reinforcement, without real specification of the conditions of original acquisition of the responses.

4. *Imitation of unfamiliar models (Intelligence Stage 5)* (10-18 months). The child will imitate visually perceived new movements of parts of the body not visible to it. Imitation of the new is systematic experimental groping toward the new model as in active imitation of new speech sounds not in the child's repertoire.

5. *Deferred imitation (and playful "making believe" one is another) (Intelligence Stage 6)* (after 18 months). Imitates a new action when the model is no longer present. As an example, the child imitates a temper tantrum of another child, not at the time, but the next day (the imitator never having had a temper tantrum herself).

Piaget's observations of these five stages of imitation are sufficiently accurate to generate a test of infant development which is stage-sequential in the sense of defining a cumulative Guttman scale (Hunt & Uzgiris, 1967). Among other dimensions characterizing this developmental scale are the dimensions of increased situational generality, independence of the presence of the model, and independence of an overt eliciting stimulus customarily used in distinguishing between imitation and identification. At the first stages of imitation the infant simply repeats specific responses made by another which are already in his repertoire and which are modeled before his eyes. At Piaget's final stages of sensorimotor imitation (by age 2) the child will play at being an absent person in the sense of deliberately enacting a set of behaviors characterizing another person. This is the first developmental approximation of identification-like behavior.

From the Piaget point of view sensorimotor cognitive organization is more or less completely developed by age 2 but the processes of cognitive organization characterizing maturity at the sensorimotor level must be repeated again at the symbolic-conceptual level, a process completed (at the level of concrete concepts) at about age 7-8 with attainment of the logic of classes, relations, and number. With regard to identification, the final stage of sensorimotor imitation launches the child into the beginnings of identification, i.e., the symbolic equations of the self with another (rather than the equations of an act of the self with an act of the other). From the Piaget point of view, the psychoanalytic descriptions of identification fantasies involving "magical" or logically impossible transformations of identity belong to this symbolic but prelogical era of thought (2-5). Early in this period the child first "fantasies," enacting roles other than his own, and then gradually learns (or develops) a firm sense of the limits of his own identity, i.e., that he can't change sex or age-status, that he can't take his father's place, etc. Associated with (1) clear establishment of the limits of his physical identity is the growth of (2) selectively modeling persons similar in identity, (3) selectively modeling in terms of attributes of admired models which can be shared because they are teachable psychological skills and virtues rather than physical attributes and symbols, and (4) awareness that possible sharing is through exhibiting the model's norms of goodness with regard to the child's own role activities rather than directly imitating the grown-up role activities.

These trends were illustrated by the quotations explaining Baldwin's theory and Ausubel's concept of "satellization." They all imply a trend to structure imitative processes in terms of conceptions of structured roles, i.e., of categories of persons in defined relations to one another with normatively defined functions. These role conceptions themselves depend upon "concrete operations," i.e., the logic of classes and relations.

The developmental trends in cognitive structuring of modeling and identity concepts in the years 4 to 8 just enumerated have formed the basis of a general theory of psychosexual development in these years which I have propounded (Kohlberg, 1966b). The theory explains a large number of age-developmental trends and sequences which seem to occur regardless of any vicissitudes of particular parent-relations. The theory may be summarized as follows:

1. The concrete, physicalistic, and symbolic nature of the child's thought and interests leads him to conceive of interpersonal relationships in terms of body actions and to define social roles in terms of physical characteristics and differences. The elaboration of the physical bases of sex-role concepts in the concrete thought of the child leads to a core of common meaning of these concepts, regardless of cultural and family variations in sex-role definition.

2. Accordingly, there are "natural" developmental trends or sequences in sex-role attitudes, trends not directly structured by cultural teaching, which are the products of cognitive development. Because of the universal physical dimensions of sex-role concepts and because of culturally universal developmental transformations in modes of conceptualizing, it is plausible to expect some relatively invariant developmental trends in sex-role concepts and attitudes.

3. The fact that sex-role concepts have physical dimensions suggests that the formation of a sex-role identity is in large part the comprehension and acceptance of a physical reality rather than a process primarily determined by sexual fantasies, social reinforcement, or identification with models. The child's basic sex-role identity is largely the result of self-categorization as a male or female made early in development. While dependent on social labeling, this categorization is basically a cognitive reality judgment rather than a product of social rewards, parental identifications, or sexual fantasies. The reality judgments, "I really am and will always be a boy" or "I really am and will always be a girl," are judgments with a regular course of age-development relatively independent of the vicissitudes of social labeling and reinforcement. This course of age-development is dependent upon complex modes of cognitive organization and development. The stabilization of sex-role identity implied in the judgment, "I really am and will always be a boy," is dependent upon the types of cognitive reorganization discussed by Piaget (1947) as "conservation of the identity of physical objects" and is not completed until age 6-7 at the time that other forms of physical conservation are fully stabilized.

4. The motivational forces implied in such reality judgments are general "drive-neutral" motives of effectance, or competence, which orient the child both toward cognitive adaptation to a structured reality and toward the maintenance of self-esteem. Accordingly sex-typed preferences in activities and

social relationships (masculinity-femininity) are largely the product of such reality judgments of sex identity. The boy, having labeled himself as male, goes on to value masculine modes because of the general tendency to value positively objects and acts consistent with one's conceived identity.

5. To a large extent, the value of social reinforcers to the child is determined by his sex identity rather than the reverse. As opposed to a social-learning sequence, "The boy wants rewards, the boy is rewarded by boy things, therefore, he wants to be a boy," a cognitive theory assumes a sequence, "The boy asserts he is a boy. He then wants to do boy things; therefore, the opportunity to do boy things and the presence of masculine models is rewarding."

6. The tendency to value positively and imitate self-like objects tends to radiate out in the child's development in the form of imitation and liking for the same-sex parent. The boy's preferential attachment to the father as against the mother proceeds from, rather than causes, basic sex-role identity and basic tendencies to imitate the father preferentially. It depends not only upon a prior stable gender identity (point 3 above) and masculine values (point 4 above), but upon the formation of abstract cognitive categories of likeness involved in the boy's inclusion of his father in a category of "we males."

7. The effect of father-identification (in the case of boys) is, then, not to cause the child to desire and ascribe to generalized sex-role stereotypes and a basic gender identity, but to aid in defining the masculine role in more individualistic terms related to the father's particular role definitions. This does not make the boy more "masculine" but it may serve to make the boy more conforming to parental expectations. In particular it may lead the child to define his masculine role aspirations in more "moral" and more achievement-oriented terms as opposed to the more physicalistic power terms found in the young child's sex-role imagery. Same-sex parent identification is less cause than consequence of natural trends of self-categorization and sex-role stereotyping. Its developmental function is primarily to channel relatively crude sex-role aspirations and stereotypes into culturally conforming and "moral" role aspirations.

The fact that the developmental changes in imitation and identification just discusssed are cognitive-structural has been well documented. Piaget (1951) and Hunt and Uzgiris (1967) document point-to-point relationships between stages of imitation and general stages of sensorimotor intelligence. The cognitive nature of stabilization of gender identity, of same-sex modeling and same-sex attachment behavior has been documented by showing its relatively invariant relationships to mental age as opposed to other factors (Kohlberg & Zigler, 1967). The formation of normative "good boy" identifications with parents is correlated with maturity of moral judgment (in turn, correlated with mental age), so it, too, is in considerable part a cognitive-structural development.

We have just sketched some of the age-developmental cognitive-structural changes through which the imitative process proceeds. These changes are paralleled by clear developmental changes in sheer amount of imitation in experimental situations. During the age of 2-3 there is a well-documented "negativistic" period (Ausubel, 1957). In the period from 3-5 there is a regular increase in conformity to suggestion or instruction, which is accompanied by an increase in imitativeness (Kohlberg & Zigler, 1967). In a study discussed further in Section XII, Kuhn and Langer (1968) found only 20 per cent of 3-year-olds imitated an adult E in a "neutral" experimental condition (children told they could do what they wanted) in which 80 per cent of 4-year-olds imitated. Indeed the 3-year-olds imitated as much (20 per cent) under a condition where they were told *not* to imitate as they did in a neutral condition.

From the period of 5-8 there is a regular decline in imitativeness of an adult model under "neutral" experimental conditions, (Kohlberg & Zigler, 1967) so that 8-year-olds superficially appear much like the 3-year-olds in disposition to imitate. The trends mentioned are again largely a function of cognitive maturity, of mental rather than chronological age. In the 3-4 period where imitation is developmentally increasing, bright children imitate more than average children, whereas bright children imitate less in the 6-8 period when imitation is declining (Kohlberg & Zigler, 1967). Similar findings are reported by others comparing retarded and average school-age children.

As we document further in Section XII, this curvilinear trend partly reflects changes in definitions of what is good or right or conforming behavior in ill-defined situations. The 4–5-year-old takes the adult's example as his cue to what he wants the child to do, the 6–7-year-old child is aware that "copying someone else's work isn't good," "you should do your own work," etc. When a group of twelve 4-year-olds were asked about copying, none said it was bad, whereas a majority of a group of twenty-four 6-year-olds did (Kohlberg, unpublished interview data). This in turn reflects a growing orientation to stable normative patterns of an "ideal self." According to our viewpoint, this developmental decline in imitativeness does not reflect the disappearance of the modeling process, but rather its transformation into more structured identifications with normative models as reflected in "good boy" concepts. The findings of Ausubel et al. (1954, that *low* imitation in school-age children was correlated with *high* identification with parents or high satellizing attitudes supports this interpretation.

In summary, then, the developmental trends in modeling processes in the years 3 to 8 broadly summarized by Baldwin (1906) under the name of "the formation of an ideal self" and by Ausubel as "satellization" have a detailed cognitive-structural base in the general development of concepts of roles and rules in this period discussed by Piaget (1947). While much of the particular content and intensity of these identifications is given by individual family experience, much is also universally derived from the common basic meanings of age and sex-roles at a given cognitive stage.

XI. THE MOTIVATION FOR IMITATION IS INTRINSIC—EFFECTANCE AND INTEREST AS DETERMINING IMITATION

While few would question that early imitation entails cognitive patterning and skill components, cognitive-developmental theories also hold a "cognitive" theory of the motivation of imitation, a theory of the same sort as that involved in explaining curiosity, and exploratory and mastery behavior. The conditions leading to such behaviors are best conceived along the lines of Piaget's (1952b) notions of assimilation, White's (1959) notion of competence or effectance motivation, and Hunt's (1963) notions of information-processing motivation.

Effectance theories of motivation have always been difficult to grasp because they do not assume any "pushes," "drive states," "needs" or other definite sources of activity. They assume that one does not need to ask for specific deficit states to explain why the organism is active, any more or (perhaps) less than one needs to ask for specific states to explain why the organism is at rest. Like operant analyses, it assumes a motivational analysis is one of (a) the conditions under which this, as opposed to that, activity occurs, and (b) of the directed quality of the action. This directed quality, it believes, cannot be defined in terms of goals or end states which are distinct from the activities or the behavior structures seeking them (or from the situation in which the organism finds itself), but must be defined in terms of forms of relation between the action and its results (or between the act and the object), forms suggested by words like "mastery." It is this refusal to separate the act and the "reinforcer" which discriminates theories of effectance motivation not only from drive theory but from driveless accounts of motivation in terms of external reinforcement. The general rationale for effectance concepts of motivation is most lucidly presented by White (1959). In terming an effectance concept of the motive for imitation "cognitive," we do so because effectance concepts are most clearly required for cognitive activities, which are very hard to account for in terms of "drives" or "reinforcers." It is almost impossible to discuss the "energetic" and the patterning or "structural" characteristics of cognitive activities independently of one another. The "motivational" characteristics of an object arousing curiosity and the activities upon the object terminating curiosity are defined by the relation of the cognitive-structural characteristics of the object to the cognitive-structural characteristics of the child's behavior patterns, relations definable in terms of structural match or balance. If an object fits a schema or behavior structure, but does not fit it too well, it arouses exploratory or mastery behavior, as has been documented repeatedly since the days Baldwin (1895) first formulated the notion of "assimilation" and "schema." The assumption that the motivation of imitative behavior is best explained by effectance theory, then, is the assertion that the primary conditions which arouse imitation are a moderate degree of mismatch between the child's behavior structure and the behavior of the model (or later between the behavior structure of the child and the structure of the situation as this mismatch may be reduced by imitating the model), and the conditions which terminate it are a better state of match, balance, or "mastery" between the child's behavior and the model's (or between the child's behavior and the situation).

We shall attempt to elaborate the foregoing view of the motivation for imitation by working from some facts. The first fact is that much imitation appears to be intrinsically motivated, in the sense of having no obvious external reinforcer for which the imitative act is instrumental or contingent. Much apparently non-reinforced imitation is discussed by Bandura (1969) under the heading of "vicarious reinforcement," since none of his studies involve directly reinforcing the child for imitating. One cannot, however, explain his findings of imitation of nurturant or powerful models in terms of vicarious reinforcement, since power leads to imitation but consumption of resources does not (Bandura, Ross & Ross, 1963c). Furthermore, Bandura gets a high level of imitation in his control groups exposed to his non-nurturant or powerless models.

As an example, in one study Bandura and Huston (1961) had an adult make nurturant responses to one group of preschool children while the children played with toys, while ignoring a second group. The adult then made various irrelevant non-aggressive (e.g., marching) and aggressive gestures (knocking down a rubber doll) while performing a simple task which the child then performed. In the nurturant condition, almost all the children imitated the adult (100 per cent on aggression, 65 per cent on marching). What is also striking, however, is that in the control condition, a great deal of imitation occurred also (80 per cent on aggression, 25 per cent on marching). The imitation in the control group is not to be attributed to socially learned generalized imitativeness of young children. The discrepancy between the 100–80 per cent aggression and the 65–25 per cent marching makes that clear enough. Even the 65–25 per cent of children marching is high, however, compared to the findings from other studies. Anyone who (like the author, Kohlberg & Zigler, 1967) has attempted to get preschool children to imitate an experimental model will realize it is not that easy. Bandura's success in eliciting imitation is due to the interesting and zany things he has his adult models do. An adult goose-stepping around the room shouting "March, march, march!" or pummeling a Bobo doll is clearly a fascinating spectacle to the child. If the adult is not crazy and seems at all encouraging ("nurturant") the child is likely to follow suit.

If preschool children often like to imitate interesting behaviors with no extrinsic reinforcement consequences, infants are even clearer in this desire. This is demonstrated by the standard results achievable with infant tests of imitation, such as those developed by Valentine (1942), and by Hunt and Uzgiris (1967) following Piaget (1951). A stranger elicits these imitative behaviors one by one without following them with any clear reinforcement. Yet the tests work regardless of the prior social reinforcement history of the infant but cannot be made to work with nonimitative species. Any observer of these imitation tests with infants will note two qualitative characteristics of early imitation which further bespeak its basic independence of extrinsic reinforcers. First, it customarily occurs in a play context, rather than in the context of being a means to some external goal. Second, early imitation clearly displays a joy in the reproduction of irrelevant details of the model's action. There seems to be a desire to exactly replicate for its own sake, rather than simply to match to some degree of similarity associated with reinforcement. In other words, the similarity sought is not as a discriminative cue associated with reinforcement, as in a "matching to sample" response, but is sought without regard to a criterion of similarity.

Because early imitation often appears to be intrinsically motivated, because it is species-specific or characteristic of some gregarious species (e.g., primates), and because it is so universal within the species, it has often been taken to be instinctive. There are certain telling characteristics of imitation, however, which do not fit our usual concepts of instinct. The first characteristic is the flexibility of the behavior patterning or structuring of imitative acts. The behavior patterns referred to by the word "imitation" are far from fixed; there is no specific patterned action which is imitative nor is there any fixed specific releaser stimulus for imitative behavior. The characteristic of imitation is the absorption of new behavior patterns from the environment. Our characterization of early imitation as cognitive is itself a statement that its patterning is not instinctive or innate. Not only is imitation flexible and cognitive rather than being instinctively fixed and blind, but its forms change with cognitive-structural growth. The second "non-instinctual" characteristic of imitation is the flexibility of the motivational conditions for the performance of imitative acts. Instinctive behaviors are repeatedly performed, with durations of exhaustion followed by periods of readier elicitation. In contrast, imitative behavior is exploratory and playful rather than being repetitive and compulsive. While there is an emphasis on exact reproduction of the model, this reproduction is not repeated in the same way over long periods of time. Typically, the child imitates a behavior only as long as it is novel and interesting, and then he goes on to imitate something else. This characteristic "seeking of novelty" in the conditions eliciting imitative behavior is as inconsistent with an instinct notion as it is with the operant notion that an imitative act will be repeated as long as it is followed by some extrinsic reinforcer.

The reasons we have just advanced for rejecting the idea that imitation is instinctive are also reasons why we are led to reject Aronfreed's (1969) affect-conditioning theory of the motivational conditions for imitative behavior. As opposed to social reinforcement theories, the cognitive-developmental approach agrees with Aronfreed that the (motivational) "foundations of imitative learning appear to lie in the conditions of the child's observations (of the model) rather than in the modification of the child's overtly emitted behavior by positive or aversive external outcomes" (p. 280). However, it does not appear plausible to define the "conditions of observation" leading to imitation as a contiguity between the behavior of the model and a strong affective state in the child. In the first place, the infant frequently imitates the behaviors of adults who are not emotionally important to him, as the construction of a baby test of imitation by a strange examiner indicates. Second, when he does imitate, the behaviors imitated are often not those immediately associated with affectively significant events, as baby tests of imitation of gestures with little affective charge document. Third, the affect-conditioning model suggests a repetitive or compulsive character to imitative behavior which is quite different from that usually found. As noted, behaviors tend to be imitated or reproduced only as long as they are novel.

Having rejected instinct, reinforcement, and classical conditioning accounts of the motivation for early imitation, what positive account of the conditions for imitation may be given? We may start with the simple generalization that the one common condition of stimuli that are imitated is that they are interesting. One simple cue to interest value is attention, so that anything which leads an action to be attended to may be sufficient to lead to its being imitated. Many of the dimensions of interest or attention have been catalogued by Berlyne (1961) under such headings as complexity, novelty, etc. The statement that the motivational conditions for imitation are cognitive, then, implies that they are not found in fixed intraorganismic needs, but in "objective" dimensions of the stimulus which make it interesting. These dimensions or conditions are not located purely in the stimulus, however, since they also include its match to the child's behavior structure, as is implied by dimensions like "novelty," or by the dimension of similarity of the model to the self (e.g., that it is a person being imitated). In general, if a person does something interesting, the infant tries to assimilate it to his own behavior capabilities; he tries to see if he can do it too. If the behavior is not interesting or if the child, through repetition, is sure he can do it, he is unlikely to imitate the behavior.

One way of looking at Piaget's (1951) stages of imitation is as a series of progressions in the kinds of events which elicit imitation. Following Baldwin's (1895) fundamental insights, Piaget defined imitation and its development in terms of the growing complexity of "circular reactions."

The fundamental unit of directed behavior in infancy is a circular reaction, that is, a patterned action which produces feedback stimuli which are the natural elicitors of the act in question. The first and simplest circular reactions are those innately wired to produce such a reaction (sucking which itself produces the tactile pressure on the mouth which naturally elicits sucking, or clenching the fist which produces the pressure on the child's palm naturally eliciting further clenching). These behaviors, then, naturally lead to cycles of repetition, and soon generate integrations in which activities in one modality (waving the hand) lead to sensory feedback in another modality (the spectacle of a moving hand) which leads to repetition of the activity in the first modality, repetitions with functional value (developing eye-hand coordination). This is termed "primary circular reaction," and is in turn followed by a stage of "secondary circular reaction" (the feedback from the act is from its effect in moving an external object), "tertiary circular reaction," etc. These progressive complications of the circular reaction define Piaget's (1952b) stages of sensorimotor intelligence. As stages of circular reaction, they define an active tendency to repeat any behavior pattern with a "circular" feedback stimulation output.[14] Postulating an active tendency

---

[14] This active tendency toward repetition is in a sense like the Freudian (1938) "repetition compulsion" without the instinctual underpinnings.

toward repetition, it was Baldwin's (1895) further genius to see that the basis for the child's imitating another was no different than the basis for imitating himself. If a child by accident performed a behavior leading to an interesting result, he would desire to repeat it. To do so, he must copy his own behavior. The situation is no different if another performs the interesting behavior. Insofar as repetition rests upon accommodation to, or copying of, a model or stimulus pattern, then, it is imitation. Expressed in slightly different terms, almost anything which might lead the child to repeat a novel behavior pattern he emitted could lead him to repeat the behavior pattern of another. A specification of the motivational conditions for imitation, then, does not imply a special imitative motive, but derives from the conditions leading to the reproduction of any interesting behavior pattern.

We have so far discussed the interest value of the act to be imitated in terms of dimensions of the structure of the act itself, such as its complexity and novelty. A large part of the interest value of many imitated actions, however, rests upon the effects of the act upon other objects. When the infant repeats one of his own acts which has interesting consequences, an operant analysis will claim that the consequences serve as a "reinforcer" for the act. As already mentioned, however, exploratory or playful acts do not appear to be under the stable control of definite reinforcers. An interesting light, sound, or movement resulting from a playful act soon ceases to be interesting, and ceases to function to maintain the behavior. Furthermore, while the effect of the child's actions maintains his behavior, the relation between behavior and effect does not look Skinnerian under close scrutiny. Close observation of infant learning suggests that the goal state is not defined directly by either external or internal stimuli ("reinforcers"), but is defined by a *relation* of mastery between the act and its effects. In other words, the effects of the child's behavior are only reinforcing if they are caused by the self's action, while the self's action is only satisfying if it leads to effects, to mastery. As an example (Piaget, 1952b), the infant's kicks start a toy bird swinging and the child delightedly kicks "to make the bird swing." One cannot call the external event itself (swinging of the bird) a reinforcer of kicking, since it is not the external event which is the "reinforcer," but its relation to the act of kicking, a relation of causality or mastery. If the adult makes the bird swing, this leads to renewal of the kicking to reestablish the connection. It is quite difficult for reinforcement theory to explain why the infant kicks when he is already being reinforced for lying still. Furthermore, as mentioned, the swinging of the bird is not a stable reinforcer; the infant soon loses interest when he has assimilated it (established its relation to his own behavior).

This example (Piaget's infant kicking to make the bird swing) is used by Piaget as an example of a "secondary circular reaction." It may also be described as an assimilation of an interesting event. Basically, early imitation of another is also assimilation of an interesting event. This interest may be generated either by the form of the model's act, or by its striking consequences. This simple formulation in terms of assimilation of the interesting is most clearly applicable to infant imitation. However, it is also applicable to much preschool imitation, as was mentioned earlier in connection with Bandura's studies.

XII. SOCIAL REINFORCEMENT AND IMITATION AS A FORM OF NORMATIVE CONFORMITY

In this volume, Gewirtz suggests that imitation is a generalized response based on reinforcement for making responses similar to those of others. He notes that while adults may not systematically intend to reward and support imitative behavior, almost all the socialization demands of the adult involve expecting the child to make responses or develop skills like those already displayed by other people, by older members of the group. Accordingly, Gewirtz says, any reward for socialization achievement is also a reward for imitating. In our discussion of Baldwin, we observed that he, too, notes the omnipresent connection between the child's social achievements and his imitative tendencies, but uses this connection between achievement and imitation to explain approval-seeking (i.e., social reinforcement effects), rather than deriving imitation from it. Baldwin's approach rests on the theory that both early imitation and early mastery of basic skills are motivated by intrinsic competence or effectance tendencies. Children in orphanages try to walk, talk, etc., as well as try to imitate with a minimum of social reinforcement. According to the cognitive-developmental interpretation, the fact that the child's achievements are imitative engenders a concern for social approval, as the child comes first to need another self (or an audience) as confirmation of his achievement and then to systematically ascribe superior competence to the adult model or audience. In other words, "intrinsically" motivated imitation should come under the control of social reinforcers increasingly with age-development (up to about age 5-6), rather than originating from such reinforcement.

There are three points to the interpretation we have just advanced. The first is that the ordinary social reinforcement effects upon imitation (or any other task) behavior in the child are based upon the child's "primary competence motivation," upon his generalized desire for task success. This intrinsic desire for success is mediated by external social definitions through social reinforcement. But the desire for success is not the desire for the concrete reinforcers administered. By this we mean that it is more correct to say that the child wants to secure rewards or approval as a sign that he has performed the task competently rather than to say that the child wants to perform competently in order to obtain situational rewards or approval. The role of reinforcers is primarily that of cognitively redefining success in terms of social standards rather than through directly strengthening an associated response.

The second point of our interpretation is that there is an age increase in the child's concern about external social definitions of correct performance, in his "need" for approval, up until about age 6-7. The third (and most questionable) point is that this development is mediated by the imitative process itself, in addition to being mediated by the child's growing awareness of the limits of his own competence. While the second point receives some documentation from social learning studies (Stevenson, 1965), this documentation is sketchy, because of the indifference of most research students of social reinforcement to developmental variables. The third point has not been considered at all in research studies.

Accordingly, the remainder of this section will attempt to document the first point. It carries the following implications:

a) Social reinforcement affects children's imitation primarily because it has informational value, i.e., because the reward is perceived as indicating that the child's response is correct or in accordance with a standard in the mind of a person more competent than the self. A schedule of social reinforcement functions primarily as a long-winded instruction or definition of the right answer; it does not function like a food pellet to a rat. If the situation is one in which a social reinforcer does not symbolize a judgment of normative conformity, the social reinforcer ceases to function.

b) One or no-trial extinction of imitation "learned" under social reinforcement will occur under conditions where the child is given relevant information that the situation or rules are "new" or changed.

c) In some cases, social reinforcement functions as the equivalent of a direct instruction to imitate. Where more subtle mediation of imitation by the desire for task success appears, it is primarily in situations in which the definition of the rules of the game are ambiguous.

d) The preschool child's general cognitive ambiguity about the rules of the game encourages both imitation and susceptibility to reinforcement which does not appear to be "normative" or instructional to the adult. Because young children have few clear cognitively defined standards or information concerning correct performance, they do not clearly discriminate between correct performance and being rewarded, and hence are more likely to appear to be governed by extrinsic and arbitrary social reinforcement contingencies.

The first implication is that the effectiveness of social reinforcers is contingent on the child's interpretation of them as a symbol of a competent judgment, of correct performance. To illustrate, a social-learning analyst actually installed in a preschool a machine which emitted a tape-recorded vocalization, "That's good," after a bar was pressed, under various schedules of reinforcement. After an initial amused run on the machine, clearly motivated by the desire for novelty, the machine lay dormant, its reinforcing power spent. Obviously, "That's good" did not stand for a social judgment. Another illustration is suggested by Bandura's studies of "vicarious reinforcement." Models receiving social reinforcement were imitated in the Bandura and MacDonald's (1963) study of the modeling of moral judgment. However, in another study adult models who were given concrete social "rewards" (candy, ice cream, etc.) were not imitated more than those who were not rewarded. The most likely interpretation is that the non-imitated models did not receive their rewards in a way in which they could be viewed as indicating correct performance.

The fact that the effectiveness of social reinforcement depends upon a normative context has been obscured by the preschool child's readiness to assume a normative context, a "rule" on which the reward is based, where none exists. As an example, in a study (Kohlberg, 1969) children were told a story in which a boy faithfully watched his baby brother and was punished by his mother on her return (or abandoned the baby but was rewarded by the mother on her return). Most 4-year-olds (though knowing obedient baby-sitting was "good") said the punished boy was bad for obediently baby-sitting. Most 5-year-olds said the boy's baby-sitting was good but he was a bad boy because "he must have done something bad to get punished" and went through a variety of cognitive contortions to balance the act and the sanction. By age 7, about half of the children were able to completely disentangle "goodness" or the rule from reinforcement and to say the child was good and there must be something foolish or bad about the mother to punish him (still maintaining cognitive balance but of a more differentiated justice-balance sort). This demonstration of the extent to which "arbitrary" social reinforcement carries a normative meaning for the preschool and kindergarten child suggests that a very arbitrary social reinforcement schedule will still owe much of its power to its ability to define the child's act as good or bad (or as successful or unsuccessful). When concrete reward and punishment are still equated with being good or bad, the value of physical or social rewards administered by an authority is as much due to their assumed connection with competent and correct performance as is the value of correct performance due to its association with physical reinforcers. Furthermore, it is the informational value of reinforcement as defining correct performance which probably leads to any durable generalized effects it might have. Accordingly, the effects of arbitrary and concrete reinforcement would be expected to have more enduring effects at an age where they are confused with the normative, and in a situation where the normative is ambiguous.[15]

An experimental example of this point is provided by a study of Bandura, Ross and Ross (1963b), who found children were much more likely to imitate the aggressive behavior of Rocky, the bully, if Rocky was successful in beating up his victim and taking his toys than if he was defeated. In the successful condition, 60 per cent of the children said that they would like to be like Rocky "because he was a fighter, he got good toys." While not attributing virtue to Rocky, they said his victim was "a crybaby, didn't share, was mean, dumb, etc." This is hardly surprising when it is found that most children of this age (4-6) not only say that the "good guys win" but explain that you can tell who are the "good guys" in TV shows because they win (Kohlberg, 1965). Bandura (1969) accounts for this

---

[15] To illustrate, children aged 9 to 16 were asked if they would "change their mind" about a moral judgment question for 50 cents in the Kohlberg (1958, 1969) study. Moral Stage 1 subjects tended to say, "Yes, because you know the answer, you have the answers in the back of the book (from which the questions were read)." Stage 2 subjects tended to say, "I'd take the 50 cents and tell you I'd changed my mind." Children above Stage 2 tended to say they would not change their minds.

cognitive balancing as *ex post facto* verbal cognitive dissonance reduction, i.e., rationalization for imitation the children want to do anyhow for vicarious rewards. In contrast, our interpretation makes it causative and postulates that Bandura would not get this "vicarious reinforcement effect" with children over seven who are more able to differentiate goodness from arbitrary success.

We have claimed that more enduring effects of social reinforcement are contingent on their normative-informational components. One cannot doubt that a concrete reward or prize engenders more immediate incentive to perform than a mere verbal acknowledgment that the child's response is correct. The effect of a concrete reward as an added incentive may lead to more or faster learning as well as performance. However, there is little reason to think that a concrete reward engenders a longer-range disposition than does a sign of social approval, given that either reinforcer leads to any learning or behavior change. While the child may perform more eagerly to get a physical prize than to be told he is right, long-range maintenance of the behavior depends on the cognitive stability of the child's definition of the behavior as "good" or "right." The effects of reward depend for their stability on either the expectation of future reward or on the redefinition of successful or good behavior. As already mentioned, the two tend to be equated by young children, who only form generalized expectations of reward if they think the behavior is generally considered good by adults. The child understands that whether or not he gets candy for a performance is highly specific to the situation and the adult, and that the more generalized component of his learning is that of whether the act is good or bad.

An example of the cognitive flexibility or reversibility of imitative learning under concrete reward is provided by a study of Turiel and Guinsburg (1968). The situation used by Turiel was the "conventional" Miller and Dollard (1941) instrumental imitation situation in which the child watches a model find candy under one of two boxes. When the child was told that the E had put two candies under one box, he engaged in "no-trial imitation." When he was told that the E had put one piece of candy under each box, he engaged in "no-trial" counter-imitation (went to the other box). If the child imitated for many rewarded trials under the imitation-reward condition, he would nevertheless immediately stop imitating as soon as he was told the second candy had been placed under the alternative box. The point is, of course, that prior rewards for imitation, direct or vicarious, are irrelevant where the situation can be directly defined cognitively. Past rewarded imitation will only be maintained where it is appropriate to the situational "rules of the game" or where "the rules of the game" are cognitively ambiguous.

In summary, we have claimed that the more durable effects of social reinforcement in young children (aged 3-8) are the result of the informational value of such reinforcement in normatively defining the "successful" or "right" response. Only from such a perspective do studies of "vicarious reinforcement" effects, such as those of Bandura (1969) and his colleagues on imitation, make sense. The concept of vicarious reinforcement presupposes cognitive processes of observational learning and is objected to on these and other grounds by Gewirtz (1969). While presupposing cognitive processes, vicarious reinforcement concepts assume these processes are irrational. Such an irrational cognitive component is implicit not only in theories of vicarious reinforcement, but in Whiting's (1960) "status envy" theory that identification is based on the desire to consume the resources possessed or consumed by the model.

In general, it is not "rational" to believe that doing what the model does will lead to getting the rewards the model gets. Turiel's study (Turiel & Guinsburg, 1968) clearly indicates that if you provide the child with information that allows him to infer that he will not get the reward the model received, the child will not imitate. The only conditions under which "vicarious reinforcement" will lead to modeling with some persistence are the conditions in which vicarious reinforcement is taken by the child as indicating that the model made the "right" or successful response. This, in turn, is contingent upon the normative context of the situation, and upon the prior beliefs about the good held by the child. Where the child's normative standards are confused and externalized, a rather arbitrary reinforcement pattern will still be interpreted normatively.

The fact that vicarious social reinforcement has a "normative" rather than a "pellet" effect on modeling is indicated by the studies on the imitation of the self-administration of rewards (Bandura & Kupers, 1964; Bandura & Whalen, 1966; Bandura, Grusic & Menlove, 1967). These studies indicate that the child will imitate a model's self-denial in giving himself physical rewards for performance in a game that a model has imposed upon himself, but that this imitation is partly contingent on perceiving the model rewarded for his self-denial. Bandura's interpretation, in terms of vicarious reinforcement, supposes that the child through no-trial observational learning foregoes the unlimited and concrete reinforcers he could give himself for the sake of the "pie in the sky" of the limited and "vicarious" reinforcement of the model. In fact, the reinforcement effect only makes sense as defining the normatively correct pattern of reward for the game, i.e., as indicating that the model is following the rules.

We have discussed the fact that much imitation is motivated by the desire to succeed by following "the rules of the game," and that much of the effect of social reinforcement upon imitation depends upon this desire, rather than upon a past reinforcement history or upon fixed needs. The major "motivational" conditions determining experimental imitation, then, are the rules of the game of the task situation as this is determined by the conditions of instruction on the one hand, and the cognitive-developmental status of the child on the other. This conclusion is very convincingly documented in a study by Kuhn and Langer (1968). In this study, preschool children were exposed to an adult model who performed three acts (putting marbles in a bowl, putting them in a circle, and building with blocks). The children were then given one of seven instructions ranging from 1. explicit instruction to imitate a stressed act of the model ("While I'm gone you put the marbles in the bowl just like I did. I'll have a prize for you when I come back."), to 4. "neutral" condition ("You can do anything you want while I'm gone. I'll have a prize for you when I come back."), to 7. instructions not to imitate the stressed act ("When I'm gone, be sure not to do what I did. When I come back, I'll have a prize for you.").

The results for the stressed act indicated that the "neutral" condition was treated like an instruction to imitate. Under the "explicit" instructions (Conditions 1-3), 100 per cent of a group of 4-year-olds imitated the stressed act. In the "neutral" condition, 80 per cent of the children imitated the stressed act. Essentially, none of the children imitated the stressed act under the negative instruction condition. With regard to "incidental imitation" (i.e., imitation of the two acts of the experimenter not mentioned in the instructions), the results were equally clear. In the neutral condition, 80 per cent of the children engaged in incidental imitation. In the next most neutral condition ("You don't have to put the marbles in the bowl like I did."), there was 50 per cent imitation. In all other conditions of instruction, there was no substantial incidental imitation (less than 20 per cent imitated) even where the children were instructed to imitate the stressed act. These results clearly indicate that the children only engaged in incidental imitation when they were puzzled as to what they were supposed to do. If they knew what to do, whether told positively (imitate the stressed act) or negatively (don't imitate the stressed act), they did not engage in incidental imitation.

It is unlikely that this tendency of 80 per cent of 4-year-olds to incidentally imitate in the neutral condition was due to any generalized disposition to imitate based on prior social reinforcement for imitating. If such were the case, one would expect the children to incidentally imitate when they were told to directly imitate, since this indicated that the situation was one of reinforcement for imitation. Furthermore, one would expect more individual variation than occurred. The individual differences found were purely cognitive-developmental. Most 3-year-olds failed to imitate directly (20 per cent) in the neutral condition (as noted earlier) and they also failed to imitate indirectly in this or any other condition. In other words, they had not yet developed a conception that "when in doubt, do what the model does."[16]

In the Kuhn and Langer (1968) study, almost all of the variance in imitative behavior was accounted for, a rare feat in experimental social psychology. Almost all the variation can be accounted for in terms of variation in the cognitive ambiguity of the instructions and the cognitive maturity of the child, variation which cannot be explained by drive or reinforcement concepts of motivation and habit.

The Kuhn and Langer study indicates how one kind of cognitive ambiguity, that of the definition of the task, determines amount of imitation. The study suggests a continuity between the determinants of childhood imitation (e.g., ambiguity in task definition) and those studied by social psychologists of adult-

---

[16] That the age effect in question is primarily a function of cognitive maturity is suggested by the Kohlberg and Zigler (1967) study in which all age differences in imitation were largely mental rather than chronological age effects.

hood interested in the conditions of conformity to group norms as mediated by the behaviors or judgments of others. In other contexts, the child's cognitive uncertainty as to his capacity to succeed in the task, independently, is an equally powerful determinant of imitation. This is demonstrated by a study of Turnure and Zigler (1964). Normal children, aged 8, were given two measures of imitation, the Miller and Dollard (1941) measure of looking for a toy under the same box as a child stooge, and Emmerich and Kohlberg's (1953) measures of making sticker designs like those of an adult *E*. Before the imitation tasks, the children were given some prior tasks. Half were told by the *E* that they were doing well on the tasks (success), half that they did poorly (failure). After the success condition, none of the children imitated at all in either task, after the failure condition a slight majority imitated on both tasks. Obviously individual differences irrelevant in the success condition (since no one imitated) determined the split between imitators and non-imitators in the failure condition. These individual differences, however, themselves seem largely individual differences in expectations of task success. Turnure and Zigler (1964) ran a retarded group of the same mental age[17] through their experimental procedures. About half of the retarded children imitated under the success condition, while 90 per cent imitated under the failure condition. Turnure and Zigler present evidence suggesting that this greater proneness to imitate is due to a history of experiences of failure and uncertainty about independent task performance. Accepting this interpretation, it would appear that Turnure and Zigler have predicted and accounted for all the variance in their dependent variable, imitation, by one independent variable (success-failure expectation) since they were able to predict variability from 0 per cent imitation in one group to 90 per cent imitation in another.

Like the Kuhn and Langer (1968) study, the Turnure and Zigler study indicates that most of the variance in many experimental imitation studies is determined by the child's desire to successfully perform the task, as this is mediated by varying definitions of task success. The fact that failure experiences in a prior task generate imitation in a subsequent task is not derivable from an operant analysis, but requires an explanation in terms of the cognitive redefinition of the self's capacities in the task situation.

Like the other studies discussed in this section, the Turnure and Zigler (1964) study indicates that most of the variations in amount of imitative behavior in experimental situations with rules (tasks or games) is to be explained in terms of variations in the normative value of the model, i.e., in the extent to which the experimental situation defines the model behavior as indicating the "right answer" for the child to give to the task, and in the extent to which it defines the child's independent or imitative behavior as likely to yield the right answer

---

[17] By using a mental age control, the study presumably eliminates a further source of the greater imitativeness of retardates relative to controls of the same chronological age, the earlier discussed tendency of less cognitively mature children to imitate more.

to the situation. This interpretation encompasses the experimental findings on the effects of prior task reinforcement (Turnure and Zigler, 1964) as well as the effects of direct and vicarious reinforcement upon imitative behavior. Taken together with the findings on the interest value of the model's act discussed previously, this interpretation accounts for the bulk of the reported experimental findings on imitation in young children.[18] The remaining findings, those on the status characteristics of the model in relation to those of the child, are taken up in the next section.

XIII. STATUS OF THE MODEL AND THE CHILD: COMPETENCE AND SIMILARITY AS DETERMINANTS OF IMITATION

We have considered so far the motivational conditions for imitation as they reside in the interest-value of the act and in the appropriateness of imitative behavior to the situation (its social reinforcement parameters). We shall now consider the conditions of imitation as they reside in the personality or status of the model, i.e., in the quality of his relationships to the child, to other persons, or to the larger social structure. A consideration of the status conditions of imitation takes us closer to the concerns of traditional psychoanalytic and neopsychoanalytic theories of identification, e.g., theories which invoke the model's love withdrawal, his aggressiveness, his power, his possession of envied resources, etc., as major determinants of the child's modeling.

Almost all of the theories of identification just listed have assumed a strong deficit-state motivation for identification, i.e., either the model's infliction of pain-anxiety (identification with the aggressor, A. Freud, 1946; Sarnoff, 1951), the model's withdrawal of love (anaclitic identification, A. Freud, 1946; Sears, 1957), or the model's control or withholding of someone or something else desperately wanted by the child (status envy identification, Whiting, 1960). The reason for this focus on strong deficit states becomes clearer if it is recognized, as Whiting (1967) has pointed out, that these theories are really designed to account for illogical fantasy identifications, such as identification with the opposite-sex role. The theories more or less assume some magical thought processes involved in identification, i.e., a magical equation of self and other. One may term such equations magical since they are "incorporative," i.e., they involve the notion of "being the other" or "absorbing him," not becoming like another person distinct from the self through approximating his behavior. In other words, they assume that the reason for identification is either to do away with another causing the self pain (defensive identification), or to "be the other" so that the self can love

---

[18] The studies which suggest more mechanistic Skinnerian interpretations of imitation learning have been conducted with grossly retarded (Baer et al., 1967), or autistic children (Lovaas, 1967) who have not reached preschool cognitive maturity and do not seem to display the "natural" imitativeness discussed in the previous section, which was said to increase with such cognitive maturity.

or hate itself as it has the other from whom one is separated. The processes involved in identification have been assumed to be illogical in another sense, the sense of being equations of the self with others whom one cannot "really" become, or like whom it is maladaptive to become. Finally the processes involved have been assumed to be illogical in the sense of leading to self-other equations of a painful or self-punishing sort, e.g., in the creation of a "superego."

The two notions of strong deficit state and magical thought process are interlocked, since presumably some strong deficit state must be a motivator for magical cognitive processes. In other words, psychoanalytic and neo-psychoanalytic theory has assumed that identification is illogical, i.e., a defense, and hence must be a reaction to an intense pain experience or a negative drive state. The defensive character of identification is assumed not only by its illogical character, but by its presumed fixity, rigidity, or persistence in the face of situational inappropriateness.

As we discuss in more detail subsequently, while psychoanalytic and neo-psychoanalytic identification theories were designed to account for the pathological and the structurally fixed, actual research applications of the theories have been to the phenomena of ordinary imitation or to self-conscious perception of similarity to one's parents or one's parents' sex-role. Neither of these sets of phenomena reveal anything rigidly fixed since perceived similarity measures of identification are not fixed or longitudinally stable (the boy who is heavily father-identified one year is not the next, Kohlberg, 1965). Also, neither of these sets of phenomena involve anything directly illogical or pathological since there is nothing, per se, more illogical or pathological about thinking one has values or personal traits like the father than the mother.[19] With regard to sex role, the process by which a child acquires an identification with his own role is not the process by which he acquires an "illogical" or "pathological" identification with the opposite-sex role, as our cognitive-developmental theory stressed. Since studies of sex-typing in preschool and school children include few children with definite opposite-sex identification, but only children more and less "mature" in development of a logical or conforming identity, these studies also are irrelevant to distress-defense theories of identification.

In light of what has been said, it is not surprising to find that reviews of the findings of research studies of imitation and perceived similarity provide little support for the neo-psychoanalytic theories mentioned (Kohlberg, 1963a ; Bandura, 1969). More specifically they suggest the following qualifications about these theories:

1. *Anaclitic theory.* While prior nurturance (and perhaps nurturance-withdrawal) are correlates of imitation-identification in a number of studies, they are not stronger determinants than a number of others.

---

[19] There is no positive correlation between measures of perceived similarity with the opposite-sex parent and measures of "maladjustment" or "neuroticism" in women and only a slight one in men.

As elaborated earlier, "positive atmosphere" effects seem to best fit these findings, e.g., that the instructions and examples of liked persons are more readily assimilated than those of disliked persons.

2. *Identification with the aggressor.* Few studies have found any "identification with the aggressor" effects. The few studies finding such effects can be best interpreted in terms of the concept that "the aggressor" is perceived as powerful, competent and sex-appropriate (masculine). In any case, the theory does not account for general-power competence effects.

3. *Status envy theory.* Bandura et al. (1963c) found that the experimental owner of resources was imitated, not the consumer of the resources. Admiration of the power of the "owner" rather than envy of the consumer was presumably, therefore, the determinant of imitation.

As theorists concerned with identification have focused more specifically on the phenomena of childhood imitation, sex-typing, and perceived similarity to parents, they have increasingly converged on a notion of power as the central status attribute in modeling. This central focus is to be found in the theories of Brim (1958), Kagan (1958), Maccoby (1959), Parsons and Bales (1955), and Mussen and Rutherford (1963). In contrast to neo-psychoanalytic theories, these theories do not assume identification to be an incorporation of the other, but view it as a process of role-playing, i.e., of enacting the role of the other. The theories assume that roles are packages of behavior performed by classes of persons, so that playing the other's role does not imply magically equating the body or identity of the self with the other, nor does it imply that one plays the other's role in order to "magically" give oneself what the other gives or to magically do away with the other. The most elaborated of these theories (Brim, 1958; Maccoby, 1959) start from G. H. Mead's (1934) analysis of the bipolar or complementary role-taking process. In interacting with another, the child must implicitly take the other's role. Under certain circumstances, covert role-taking will lead to overt role-playing. In some cases, the absence of the other will make playing his role realistic or appropriate. As an example, it is sometimes found that on the death of a father, the widow or son will not only take over the father's functions but will play out stylistically and interpersonally the particular role of the father, a role they had long taken implicitly in interacting with him. In other cases, the role of the other will be played out as fantasy, a playing out which may promote competence in the child's playing of his own role with the other (Maccoby, 1959). From this perspective, it is logical to assume that the basic conditions for taking and playing the role of the other are that the consequences of interaction with the other are important to the child. If the other person controls resources on which the child depends, and access to these resources is contingent on playing a certain role to the other or in correctly anticipating the other's role, then the child should "identify with" or play out the other's role under appropriate "free" conditions. It is evident this type of analysis of identification as role-playing or role-practice is fitted to deal with the child's selective enactment of familiar roles (other than his own) in an unstructured situation, such as family doll-play. It is not, however, a theory of general conditions under which a child will learn a behavior or attitude of a model or wish to be like another person, including conditions in which he had not had a history of complementary role interaction with that person.

When one considers the general characteristics of models which elicit imitation, it becomes apparent that power is too narrow a term for the attributes of favored models. As Bandura's (1969) Mickey Mantle example suggests, any form of competence by a model in any (or no) direct relationship to the child may elicit imitation. While power is one index of competence, it is only one of many. As long as this is true, boys will continue to prefer to be like big league ball players or inventive scientists to being like generals or senators or bankers. The cognitive-developmental theory, then, would propose that there are as many qualities of an emulated model as there are perceived forms of competence. In addition to sheer perceived competence, the perception of similarity to, or relevance of, the model to the self is the other major status determinant of imitation-identification.

The statement just made is, in effect, a direct derivative of the notions of the primary competence motivation for imitation discussed in previous sections. The motive for imitating is not a peculiar or special one, as identification theories have assumed. The reason for imitating is to do the competent, "smart," right, or effective thing. Insofar as the model's status is an index of his competence, it tends also to be an index of the competence or "rightness" of his action. Insofar as this is the case, one need not assume that the enactment of the model's behavior is instrumental to some further equation of the self and the model, and hence need not assume that this equation involves magical thinking. The assumption is rather that the power and competence of the model leads the child to see the specific act modeled as competent (or "big boy") and so makes it gratifying to perform, because he likes to perform competent acts, which make him feel more competent. It does not assume that the child's modeling indicates the desire to introject the model, to magically share his powers, or to act toward the self as the model has.

We have discussed so far the status determinants of imitation in a way which would account for an adult's tendency to copy the tennis style of a tennis star, or the writing style of a Freud. The account, however, raises a number of issues about the development of concepts of competence and their relations to modeling. Piaget and Baldwin discuss early infant motivation in terms of assimilation of the interesting and circular reaction. As the infant's cognitive structuring of the self and the world progresses, the assimilation of the interesting becomes a definite motive to master, to be competent, to demonstrate power or control over events. Such a development presupposes a differentiation between the self (as a locus of agency) and the other (as a locus of agency), a sense of causal relation, and a differentiation of what the self causes from what others cause. These differentiations in concepts of objectivity and causality develop in sequential order and are completed by the end of the second year of life (Piaget, 1954). At this point, the desire for mastery is reflected in the need to do things oneself. A typical incident is a two-year-old's frustration at putting on his coat, followed by a temper tantrum if his mother tries to help him. The temper tantrum indicates that the child clearly differentiates what he can cause from what others can do, and as a result only what he can do leads to a sense of "mastery."

We have pointed to the cognitive development of a self-other differentiation in causality as transforming effectance motivation, the assimilation of the interesting, into a definite desire for power and control over things and people. At first it would seem that such competence strivings would lead only to independent and negativistic rather than imitative behavior. It is clear, however, that such a striving for power and control is a precondition to perceiving superior power and control in a model, and imitating as a result. At an early stage of lack of differentiation of self and world, the child may not imitate the adult's act which generates interesting consequences (swinging the birds) because he will "believe" that he generated those consequences himself. At a later stage, however, he will imitate the adult to gain the assurance that he, too, can generate those consequences. At the stage of negativism, the child makes an even sharper differentiation of what he can do and what the other can do. Before this period it is typical that the child feels satisfied if the act is completed with the aid of the mother or someone else like the self.[20] At the negativistic stage insistence on independence in the performance of an act is independence in performing an act "imitatively" learned from others. In our example, "putting on the coat myself" is still an imitation of the mother's care-taking act. So "independence," "doing things oneself," is still an expression of competence motivation which generates further imitation.

The negativistic crisis, then, heralds the clear awareness that there is something more competent and powerful in being the model than in imitating. This first leads to the "look-at-me behavior," the need to turn around the imitator-imitated roles described in connection with Baldwin's (1906) theory. It also leads to an increasing selectivity of models on the grounds of relative power and competence. With growing awareness of relative competence and power, the child will award some generalized capacity or power to adults or others regardless of the particular consequences of the adult's specific act. At this point the child takes "on faith" the fact that the adult's act is a demonstration of power and competence and imitates it in order to make sure that he, too, can do the "grown up" or "big boy" thing being modeled.

The cognitive-structural developments in the differentiation of the competence of self and other just discussed are largely responsible for the growing

---

[20] It is this undifferentiated feeling of mastery which psychoanalysis termed "primary identification with the mother" and "feelings of omnipotence" and which Ausubel (1957) terms "executive dependency associated with volitional independency." The lack of differentiation of causal agency, however, is actually not limited to the mother, as these terms suggest.

generalized imitativeness of adult models found in the years 3 to 6, and discussed in Section X. In the period from 5 to 8, there is further cognitive development in concepts of competence which leads to selective imitation of good and skillful, as opposed to older and more powerful, models and to a selective modeling of good and skillful behavior by the model (as opposed to other aspects of his behavior). These trends were discussed in Section X, and related to the development of concrete-operational conceptualization of role relations and attributes. In terms of concepts of competence, we shall merely stress here that the change is from physicalistic to psychological-normative notions of the relative competence of individuals. During the earlier (3-5) period, the child assimilates the superior skill and virtue of individuals to their age-status, which is defined in terms of physical size and strength. An earlier quoted example was the boy who discussed the adult's task skill as a product of "bigger body, bigger brain." Children under five do not tend to be able to distinguish age from size, and assume that physically growing up automatically leads to possessing adult competence, just as their own growing up has led them to no longer be that worst of all categories, "babies." By the early school years, the child has discriminated physical attributes of competence (being big and strong, and owning things) from "psychological" attributes of competence ("being smart," "knowing things," "doing things right," "being good") which represent the fitness of behavior to a normatively defined role with a status in a social order (Kohlberg, 1965, 1969). Associated with this differentiation is a more refined and disciplined imitation of the "good" and "smart" way of doing things of the model rather than a simple sharing of the activity.

Associated with this differentiation of competence from age-size is a growing differentiation of the competences appropriate to males and females. At the preschool level, sex differences are more or less equated with age differences. Insofar as the sexes are different, it is because males are physically bigger and stronger than females, just as grown-ups are bigger and stronger than children (Kohlberg, 1966b). As an example, four-year-old Philip told his mother, "When you grow up to be a Daddy, you can have a bicycle too (like Daddy's)." As "virtues" or forms of competence are discriminated from age-size, these virtues become increasingly sex-typed. In the years from 4 to 7, girls develop a clear perception that feminine competence and status are based on being "attractive" and "nice," rather than on being powerful, aggressive, and fearless. (Boys come to make grossly similar distinctions, in learning to differentiate the qualities of the "good guys" and the "bad guys," both of whom are alike in physical attributes.)

There are, then, major developmental shifts in status-dimensions of the model leading to imitation. These shifts are not due to the formation of new motives for imitation, but are due to cognitive-structural transformations in conceptions of role-competence. These cognitive changes lead to a rechanneling of primary competence motivation into varying channels of selective imitation. A single example may clarify the point. Psychological discussions of "ownership of resources" have a simple cash meaning in the world of the American child. When asked, "who is the best one in the family," a majority of 24 middle- and lower-class six-year-old boys and girls replied "the father," and give as the single most frequent reason "because he makes the money" (Kohlberg, 1965). In contrast, a minority of four-year-old children choose father as "best," and none give "making money" as a reason for choice of "best one in the family." The response that father is the best one in the family forms the highest step in an age-developmental cumulative Guttman scale of appreciation of the father's cash function which includes the following items or the following order of increased maturity:[21]

1. Father chosen as the one most needed to buy things in the store.
2. Father chosen as most needed in the family in general.
3. Father chosen as best one in the family.

This development in awareness of economic functions of the father closely parallels the following logical development of a general understanding of economic roles which is stage sequential (Guttman scaleable) and is closely linked to Piaget's (1947) stages of logical development (Strauss, 1954; Danziger, 1958):

1. *Preconceptual* (Age 3-4). Money is not recognized as a symbol of value different from other objects and it is not understood that money is exchanged in purchase and sale transactions. Money is not recognized as necessary for gaining all objects from stores, i.e., as necessary for having food.

2. *Intermediate* (Age 4-5). Children recognize that money transfer is required in stores, but do not recognize that the transfer is an exchange of equal economic value. The exchange of work or job for salary is not understood, nor is the scarcity of money understood. Money is thought to come from a store or the bank without any exchange or input required. The mother is as much or more the supplier of money and goods than the father because she goes to the bank and gets the money, and goes to the store and buys the food.

3. *Concrete operational* (Age 6-8). Children recognize money transactions as involving a logical relation of reversible, reciprocal, and equal exchange of values. They understand that the storekeeper must pay money to others for his goods, they understand the work-salary exchange, and the scarcity or "conservation" of money. Accordingly, the child recognizes the need and importance of the father's work-role ("otherwise the family will die or starve").

The logical and sequential nature of the development of the valuing of the father's economic function indicates that it is not a cultural learning of the male-dominant and materialistic values of the American culture, but is a natural cognitive development (in families with a sexual division of labor in economic

---

[21] Obviously, the scale is derived from children in intact families with non-working mothers.

roles). This cognitive development in definitions of family power and prestige, in turn, is a determinant of modeling. At age 4-5, physicalistic sex stereotypes are critical in differentiating mother and father roles (Kohlberg, 1965, 1966b). While fathers are perceived as bigger, stronger, and more aggressive than mothers by age 4-5, social power and prestige are not clearly typed in favor of the father until 6-7 (Emmerich, 1961; Kohlberg, 1965). This, in turn, is linked to the father's economic and work functions, as already discussed.

The developmental tendency to award greater authority to the father-role leads in turn to a developmental increase in modeling the father in the ages (4-7) mentioned. This tendency is true for girls as well as boys.[22]

To close the cognitive-developmental circle, bright children are advanced on all the trends mentioned, including the trend for boys and girls to increasingly orient to the father as a model.

The fundamental assertion of the present section has been that the general characteristic of the model's status leading to imitation is his role-appropriate competence as this is perceived by the child, and that this perception undergoes cognitive-developmental transformations. While this generalization is so prosaic as to scarcely require documentation, it does cast light on the findings of studies of social-power effects on imitation which are otherwise puzzling. In particular, these studies indicate the following points:

a) Interpersonal power over the child is only an aspect of general competence which is the determining status attribute for modeling.

b) The import of power for the child's modeling is contingent upon whether power is a role-appropriate form of competence, an issue determined by the child's sex-role stereotypes.

With regard to the first point, Van Manen (1967) found that adolescent children's value-similarity to the father was not correlated with the father's dominance over the boy or the father's dominance over the mother. The boy's identification, however, was correlated with the father's external occupational competence (job success and satisfaction as perceived by father, mother, and in part, "objectively"). Sixty-six per cent of the children of the 80 fathers dissatisfied with their jobs were low in value agreement with their fathers, as compared to only 7 per cent of the children of the remaining 225 fathers.

With regard to the second point, paternal dominance over the spouse (Hetherington, 1965; Hetherington & Frankie, 1967) has been found to correlate markedly and clearly with boys' same-sex parent imitation-identification as measured in a quasi-experimental setting. These same studies indicated that there was no relationship between maternal dominance and girls' same-sex parent identification. Dominance is a form of competence in fathers because it is role-appropriate (as perceived by children) but it is not a form of competence in mothers.

---

[22] In the case of the girls this modeling is not part of a global desire to be like the father, but is due to the notion that he knows the right way to do things better than the mother, is smarter, etc.

These findings clarify various puzzles in social-learning experiments on imitation. As an example, among 16 experimental groupings in the Bandura et al. (1963c) study of control of resources, the single highest modeling effect was that found for boys to imitate a male adult who was ignored by a female adult who dispensed rewards to the boy subject. The rewards were candies, cookies, etc., typically dispensed by "mother figures." The boys in this condition tended to criticize the lady dispenser and sympathize with the ignored male (e.g., "She doesn't share much, she's greedy. John played bravely even though she didn't share."). Even in preschool, when feminine power violates sex stereotypes of feminine givingness and when masculine impotence coincides with masculine "virtue" and "bravery," it seems to be sex-typed virtue and not bare power which leads to imitation

In addition to the role appropriateness of the model's competence, a cognitive-developmental theory would stress that the relevance of the model's role to the child's own is a major determinant of imitation. A major determinant of relevance is the degree of similarity between the child and the model. At an adult level, this has been documented by Stotland and his colleagues (Stotland, Zander & Natsoulas, 1961). At the childhood level, and at the level of gross sameness of role, it is so basic as to have been ignored. We noted that at the earliest stage of imitation, the child only "imitates" the behavior of others which is already in his repertoire, i.e., the infant's repetition of other's actions and his repetition of his own actions are indistinguishable. At later stages, novel behavior of others is repeated, but with an increasing sensitivity to the like-self quality necessary for another to serve as model. While the infant may imitate physical things and animals, this is presumably because the boundaries of self as animate and human are not clearly distinguished from the not-self as inanimate or non-human. In any case, by age 5, prolonged imitation of the non-human is considered pathological. By age 5, the sameness of sex of child and model has also become a most basic determinant of modeling, as discussed previously. After age 5, there is also a fairly steady increase of imitation of peers, as compared to an adult, in spite of recognition of the superior competence of adults[23] (Kohlberg & Zigler, 1967). The importance of similarity as a determinant of modeling is not only highly important by age 6, but it is a focus of generalized awareness. In one study (Kohlberg, 1965, 1966b) children aged 4 to 8 were shown animal pictures in sets composed of four animals of the same species, two of which were of the same color. The child was then asked, "Which animals do the same (specified) activity?" and "Which animals like each other?" Over 70 per cent of the responses of children 5 and over named the same-colored animals for both these sets of questions, although four-year-olds did not choose the same-colored animals beyond the level of chance (33 per cent). This growing self-consciousness about

---

[23] This tendency is, of course, task-relative. In an instructional setting with a right answer, adults are preferentially imitated; in a value-preference situation, peers are preferentially imitated.

similarity is suggested by the response of a seven-year-old boy after his four-year-old brother had just expressed a preference for a male baby-sitter. When the younger boy was asked why he wanted a boy, his older brother intervened to say, "because he's a boy, himself, of course."

While similarity is a major determinant of imitation, it is only one of many determinants of the model's relevance to the child's imitation. The concept of similarity is itself a cognitive-classificatory development of the concrete-operational period. Before the period of categorical-classificatory thought, feelings of "likeness" may be based as much on proximity, familiarity, and dependency as upon similarity in role, status, or attribute. As an example, it is not until about age 6 that the boy preferentially imitates his father even though he preferentially orients to boys as opposed to girls at an earlier age (Kohlberg, 1966b). Before this, the young boy tends to feel his mother is most like him because feelings of social closeness at young ages are based more on association than upon judgments of similarity. As conceptual relations between persons become based on attributes of similarity and class membership, so do definitions of social ties.

As an example, when children were asked to put family dolls together with the ordinary concept-formation instruction ("Put the ones together that go together"), it was not until age 5 that a majority of children grouped the dolls on the basis of similarity (boys together, mothers together, etc.). Before this, dolls were primarily grouped associatively ("the boy and girl go together because they play together"). At age 5-6, then, categorization (object-sorting) and generalized preference in imitation (same-color animals choose each other) develop together. With age and IQ controlled, significant correlations were found between object-sorting classification, same-color choice on the animal test, and doll-play imitation of the same-sex parent, indicating the cognitive roots of a growing same-sex orientation of imitation.

Of the determinants of relevance other than similarity, prior interaction with the model is perhaps most important. Many of the effects of prior experimenter nurturance or reward upon the child's imitation may be understood in these terms. As an example, a study by Emmerich and Kohlberg (1953) involved three groups of kindergarten children. In the first or nurturance group, children were given help and praise by the experimenter in a puzzle task; in the second or conflict group, children were given help but blamed and criticized in the task; and in a third group the children were ignored by the experimenter during their work on the puzzle. The experimenter then joined the child in a sticker-kit design-making session in which the child's tendency to copy the experimenter's designs could be measured. The results were a significantly lower amount of imitation for the children who had been ignored (0.4 imitative designs) than for either of the other two conditions (3.0 and 3.2 imitative acts respectively). There were no differences between the children who were nurtured and those who were criticized and blamed.

What seemed to count was the mere fact of interaction, whether that interaction was negative or positive. Thus, an interpretation of the nurturance condition as causing responses like the E's to acquire secondary reinforcement value seemed ruled out. In both conditions of high interaction, it seemed that the experimenter's helping and evaluating activity defined him as someone who was a relevant norm-setter for shared activities in the situation. Whether help and evaluation of the child were positive or negative, the experimenter defined himself as an evaluator, guide and participant in the child's activities. If the experimenter fairly explicitly defines himself as a norm-setter in shared activities with the child, it seems obvious that he is more likely to be imitated than if he does not.

In summary, then, the findings on selective imitation of models may be best explained in terms of the child's perception of the models' competence and of their relevance to his own role. The age-development of selective preference for models may be explained in terms of the cognitive development of the child's concepts of role competence, and in his conceptions of dimensions of relevance such as similarity.

XIV. THE DEVELOPMENT OF
SOCIAL DEPENDENCY AND ATTACHMENT

In Sections VIII and IX, we sketched a conception of identification in which imitation was one component of a cluster of attitudes of perceived similarity, dependency, attachment, approval-seeking, and moral conformity toward the parent. We said that all the correlational studies supported the existence of such a cluster of attitudes toward parents. We questioned the neo-psychoanalytic sequence designed to account for these correlations and pointed out that Baldwin's (1906) theory suggested that under at least some conditions, this sequence might be turned on its head. The alternative sequences proposed are as shown in Figure 6.5.

Examples of the cognitive-developmental sequence appear in the formation

Neo-Psychoanalytic	Cognitive-Developmental
1. Child's dependency based on care-taking and affection.	1. Child's imitation of competent and interesting behavior of adult.
2. Imitation as a substitute for parental nurturance.	2. Desire for normative conformity, i.e., a sense of shared standards for behavior, desires to imitate.
3. Internal normative conformity in order to maintain self-approval based on 2.	3. Dependency, i.e., persistent sense of need for guidance and approval by the model.

FIGURE 6.5.

of adolescent or adult relations of dependency-identification, where these have no basis in extensive prior interaction and care, and where there is no sexual basis for the relation. A familiar case to the reader is the identification of a student with a same-sex teacher. Such relations are based on the competence and interest value of the teacher's behavior generating (or joining with a prior) desire to be like, or to be in a role like, the teacher, which in turn generates a need to share his normative attitudes and obtain his guidance, approval, etc. This sequence, familiar enough in young adulthood, is also apparent in childhood relations to older same-sex figures. The seven-year-old boy quoted earlier, who explained that his younger brother wanted a male baby-sitter "because he was a boy himself" went on to say that he (the seven-year-old) wanted a male baby-sitter because "a girl can't teach me anything."

The sequence just described also best fits the available evidence on the development of the boy's orientation to the father in the years from 4 to 8 (Kohlberg, 1966b). The development of the boy's attachment and identification with the father is of particular interest because it is the first strong attachment which cannot be explained in terms of the physical caretaking or social instinct theories so frequently introduced in discussions of the mother-child tie. The existence of the shift has been documented in studies with various social classes and ethnic groups, using various measures which all show preschool boys as somewhat female-oriented in doll-play and experimental tests of social dependency toward adults and parent figures, and show a shift to male-oriented preference at about age 6 (Kohlberg, 1966b). While all identification theories postulate such a mother-father shift for the boy, none provide a very adequate mechanism for it. It does not seem that the shift could be a result of the fact that the father actually becomes the primary nurturer and rewarder in these years while the mother ceases to be, while the psychoanalytic account in terms of castration anxiety raises many difficulties in accounting for a positive shift in dependency.

The cognitive-developmental explanation of a developmental shift in the boy's orientation to his parents is straightforward. The theory would claim that the child learns to sex-type himself and his activities during the second and third year. By the age of 3 to 4 the boy knows quite well he is a boy and prefers "boy things" to "girl things" simply because he likes himself and that which is familiar or similar to himself. Up to this point in his development, he has remained mother-oriented, however. Tending now to prefer masculine activities, he seeks a model for these activities. Thus he is led to select his father rather than his mother as a model. Imitation in turn leads to emotional dependency upon the father. The sequence can be diagramed as shown in Figure 6.6.

The existence of such a sequence was confirmed in a semi-longitudinal study of boys aged 4 to 8 (Kohlberg, 1966b; Kohlberg & Zigler, 1967). Like other studies, this study indicated that there was a clear preference[24] for appropriately

---

[24] "Clear" male preference on these tests denotes over 60 per cent of the choices or responses of the age group went to the male object or figure.

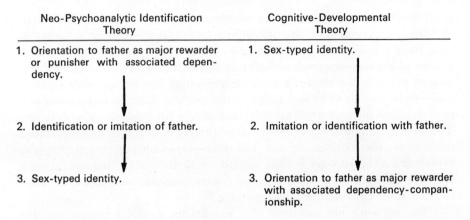

FIGURE 6.6.

sex-typed objects and activities by age 3 (on Brown's [1956] IT Scale and the Sears et al. [1965] Pictures Test), a clear preference for imitating the male figure by age 5 (on Hartup's [1962] measure of imitating the doll father as against the doll mother and on the measure of imitating a male E more than a female E), and a clear preference for orienting social dependency to the male at age 6 (on Ammons & Ammons [1949] measure of relative choice of father and mother doll as agent of nurturance and on a measure of amount and "dependency" of talk to a male, as opposed to a female, E).

The age at which an individual child advanced through this sequence varied considerably. One of the major determinants of speed of movement was cognitive maturity. As a group bright boys, aged 4 (mental age 6), displayed male preference in dependency and imitation as well as in sex-typing whereas average boys did not display male dependency preference until age 6[25] (Kohlberg & Zigler, 1967). Regardless of the boy's speed in moving through the sequence, however, he moved through it in the same order, i.e., the tests mentioned defined a cumulative Guttman scale. All but 3 of 48 boys fell into one of the four scale-type groups (passes all preference tests, passes sex-typing and imitation but not dependency tests, passes sex-typing tests only, fails all tests).

The existence of such a sequence and its relation to cognitive maturity is extremely difficult to explain in terms of any other theory of identification. All the usual theories that might account for the measured shifts from mother to father between the ages of 4 and 6 seem to be ruled out by a study by C. Smith (unpublished, summarized in Kohlberg, 1966b). Half of the subjects of the study, all Negro boys, came from father-absent homes, half from father-present

---

[25] Bright boys go through the sequence faster than average boys because: (a) they cognitively stabilize a gender identity faster (as in the "conservation of sex-role" test), (b) they become aware of general relations of similarity faster, i.e., become aware that they and their fathers are both male sooner (as in the concept-formation test), and (c) become aware of the competence of male adults sooner (as in awareness of the father's economic role).

homes. These groups in turn were equally divided by age (5 and 7) and by IQ (average and mildly retarded). The boys were administered the same tests as in the Kohlberg and Zigler (1967) study. The age trends for both father-absent and father-present Negro boys of average IQ were quite similar to those found in an average IQ middle-class white population. By age 7 almost all boys had 100 per cent masculine choice on the IT Scale and a clear majority were father, as opposed to mother, oriented on the identification measures. At age 5 identification choice was mixed (about 50 per cent) and masculine sex-typing was incomplete. Clear IQ effects were found in both father-absent and father-present groups, similar to those found in middle-class children (Kohlberg & Zigler, 1967). Mildly retarded boys aged 7 were more like their mental age counterparts (the average IQ boys aged 5) than they were like their chronological age counterparts (the average IQ boys aged 7). In sum, general cognitive and social development is leading the father-absent boys to develop attitudes of "identification" toward non-existent fathers which are grossly similar to those father-present boys develop toward their own fathers.

These findings indicate that the age-developmental trend toward father identification cannot be explained by any of the usual theories, such as anaclitic theory (an actual increase in nurturance and reward by the father), imitation theory (fear of retaliation by the father for sexualized attachment to the mother), social reinforcement theory (mother shifts to rewarding the boys for imitating the father). All these theories assume a present and active father.[26]

In the case of the boy's identification with the father (or with a teacher) we have stressed a definite sequence in which a similar identity precedes imitation, which precedes dependency-attachment. We have done so to stress the fact that the element of the identification-cluster which appears to be the developmentally simplest and earliest in the child, social dependency (the need for proximity, help, and response), is not, in general, the first and prior element in the formation of human bonds.[27] The case of the development of the boy's identification with the father in the years 4 to 8 is artificial, however, since the cognitive-development requirements of this particular development slow its component down into a definite sequential order. Where developing cognitive abstractions are not involved in slowing down the steps in identification, its different components tend to develop more or less simultaneously.[28]

---

[26] The fact that these theories do not explain sex-typed preference or the child's sense of gender identity goes without saying, since such a sex-typed identity is established before, or in the absence of, a preferential identification with the father and even in the absence of a father at all.

[27] To recur to the earlier example, the student who displays early help-seeking or instrumental dependency to a teacher is most unlikely to form any social or stable attachment, unlike the student who follows the identification sequence.

[28] As an example, girls, too, seem to increase, though less markedly, in father identification in the 4 to 7 period, partly because of increased awareness of the prestige or competence of the father's role. In this development, there seems to be no particular sequence in the relative increase of imitation and dependency components of identification.

We have stressed the boy-father identification to establish the fact that: (1) the formation of human social bonds or attachments requires components of past shared-identity (similarity) and of the disposition to share and learn new behavior patterns (imitation), and (2) therefore, the motivational determinants of attachment are in large part those discussed already as determinants of imitation. These considerations allow us to sketch out briefly a general cognitive-developmental theory of attachment which contrasts markedly with social learning, psychoanalytic, and ethological theories of attachment. (A comprehensive survey of these theories and the relevant research data is provided by Maccoby, 1969.)

Our theory holds that the motivation of social attachment, like the motivation of imitation, must be primarily defined in terms of effectance or competence motivation. The interest value of the activities of the other, his competence and social value, the relevance of his competence to the self's own action, and the general degree of similarity or like-mindedness of the self and other are all major determinants of dependency or attachment as we have shown they are for imitation-identification. All these conditions have repeatedly been found to be important by social psychologists concerned with studying adult affiliation, friendship formation, marriage, and leader-follower relations.

As studied by social psychology, a social attachment or bond is conceived of as a relationship of sharing, communication, and cooperation (or reciprocity) between selves recognizing each other as other selves. In contrast, all popular child psychological theories have denied that experience of, and desire for, sharing and communication between selves are the primary components of a human social bond. Their model of the child's attachment to others has been based on a model of an attachment to a physical object, or to a physical source of physical pleasure or pain. The "physical object" concept of social attachment is equally basic to Freudian (1938) theory (cathexis of the physical body of the other), to secondary drive and reinforcement theory (presence and response of the other is associated with care-taking reinforcement and so becomes a secondary reinforcer, i.e., the presence of the bottle or the breast is desired because it is associated with hunger reduction), and to ethological "social instinct" theory which implies that clinging responses are imprinted on the body of the mother as the baby chick is imprinted on a physical decoy (Bowlby, 1958; Harlow, 1959).

If, in contrast to physical theories, one takes the desire for a social bond with another *social self* as the primary "motive" for attachment, then this desire derives from the same motivational sources as that involved in the child's own strivings for stimulation, for activity, mastery, and for self-esteem. Social motivation is motivation for shared stimulation, for shared activity, and shared competence and self-esteem. Social dependency implies dependency upon another person as a source for such activity, and for the self's competence or esteem. The basic nature of competence motivation, however, is the same whether self or the other is perceived as the primary agent producing the desired stimulation, activity, or competence, i.e., whether the goal is "independent mastery," social mastery (dominance), or social dependence. The differences between the two are differences in the cognitive structures of the self-other relationships involved.[29]

In our discussion of Baldwin's theory of the bipolar social self (Section VIII), we indicated the exact sense in which the same desire to master an activity or situation would at one time lead the child to imitative following, at another to dominating "showing off," at a third to independent "doing it myself." We cited research showing that imitation and "verbal dependence" were tendencies correlated with one another and with brightness and active mastery in preschool children. The research showed that while these tendencies were positively correlated in children, they were negatively correlated in situations, some situations being appropriate for imitation, others for verbal dependency, others for independent mastery. These situational definitions were in turn related to the cognitive-developmental status and self-concept of the child. The polarity between active mastery and passive dependence is, then, not a polarity between two motives but a polarity of social-situational and self-definition. (A generally passive-dependent child is not one with a stronger motive for a social bond; if he were, he would engage in more of the independent behavior which would win him social approval.)

The more physicalistic models have found favor in considering early attachment, because of the physical dependency of the infant and his apparent similarity to infants in lower species with more definite or rigid instincts. It is clear, however, that there is no such definite attachment to the mother in the infant before the age of six months, i.e., there are no separation reactions before this period (Yarrow, 1964; Schaffer & Emerson, 1964). This casts suspicion on mechanistic imprinting or conditioning accounts which are plausible for the early forming attachments of lower species.

Human (and perhaps primate) attachments, even in the first two years of life, reflect the fact that they are attachments to another self or center of consciousness and activity like the self, i.e., that they are "identifications."

This fact of human attachment implies the following characteristics:

1. *Attachment involves similarity to the other.* Attachment is only to another person, not toward physical objects. The distinctive sign of instinctual imprinting in lower species is that a decoy object may be imprinted. In baby monkeys, there may be an attachment to a blanket or cloth figure, but it is not a social attachment,

---

[29]An account of social ties in terms of competence motivation and resulting desires for sharing does not deny the importance of sex, aggression, and anxiety in human relations. It does deny that drives provide the basic source of human social attachment. Were human attachments dependent upon instinctual drives, they would have the unstable periodicity, the promiscuity of arousing objects, the narcissistic quality which drives typically have, not only in mammals but in humans. Even the most attached male is capable of fantasy sexual arousal by someone to whom he is not attached, and is capable of sexual drive reduction in nonsocial onanistic ways. Sexual lust is anchored by a social attachment of sharing which makes it love; without such sharing, it is not a cause of attachment. As dryly stated by Kinsey et al. (1953), "In a socio-sexual relationship, the sexual partners may respond to each other and to the responses made by each other. For this reason, most persons find socio-sexual relationships more satisfactory than solitary sexual activities."

as the Harlows (Harlow & Harlow, 1962) discovered. Whether "contact-comfort" blankets or oral drive-reducing bottles are involved, neither creates a social attachment.

2. *Attachment involves love or altruism toward the other,* an attitude not felt toward bottles or cloth mothers. Altruism, of course, presupposes the "ejective" consciousness of the feelings and wishes of the other, i.e., empathy or sympathy.

3. *Attachment and altruism presuppose self-love.* The striving to satisfy another self presupposes the capacity or disposition to satisfy one's own self. Common sense assumes that the self (as body and center of activity) is loved intrinsically, not instrumentally (i.e., not because the body or the body's activities are followed by reinforcement or drive reduction). It is this nucleus of self-love which is involved, also, in organizing attachment to others.

4. *Attachment involves a defined possessive bond or relation linking the self and the other.* This is most clear when the bond is least "selfishly" possessive, as in the parent's attachment to his child. The difference between the attachment of the parent and that of the nurse or foster mother to the child illustrates this component.

5. *Attachment presupposes the desire for esteem in the eyes of the other or for reciprocal attachment.* In other words, it presupposes self-esteem motivation and the need for social approval, again presupposing ejective consciousness.

To summarize, a human social bond presupposes a relation to another self, a relation which involves various types of sharing and of identification between the self and the other.

We have stressed the cognitive structures and self-esteem motivations found prerequisite for post-infant human attachment by social psychology. The rudiments of these prerequisites are also evident in primate and infant attachments. With regard to mammalian attachments, it is striking that the social species are also (a) the more cognitive species, (b) the more imitative species, and (c) the more playful (primary competence motivated) species. The fact that these attributes are primary to monkey sociality is suggested by the Harlows' (Harlow & Harlow, 1962) studies of monkey socialization. First the studies indicate that monkey attachment is neither the result of drive reduction nor of imprinting in any mechanistic sense. Associations of a wire "mother" with hunger-satisfaction do not lead to attachment to the wire "mother" or to anything else. Cloth "mothers" will be clung to by baby monkeys for "contact comfort" in quasi-instinctual fashion, but this does not generate later social attachment either to the cloth "mother" or to other monkeys any more than does experience with wire mothers. The fact that satisfaction of contact-comfort needs and early "imprinting" of these needs on a cloth mother does not generate any forms of social behavior in the monkey is indicated by the absence of social behavior or attachment in adult monkeys to either their cloth "mothers" or to other monkeys. If contact comfort does not generate social attachment by "imprinting" mechanisms neither does sheer visual exposure to other monkeys (in other cages) generate attachment or lead to social "imprinting," though it does lead to prepatterned responses.

What Harlow has found to be sufficient for the formation of monkey attachments and for "normal" adult social and sexual behavior is social inter-action with peers in play. What elements of play interaction are important has not been specified, though it is clear the elements are more than body contact, visual exposure, and drive reduction. It is very likely that it is the social quality of the interaction that is important, where "social" is taken as reciprocity or sharing of behavior. In general, even simple social play and games have the character of either complementarity-reciprocity (I do this, then you do that, then I do this) or of imitation (I do this, and you do this, too). In either case there is a shared pattern of behavior, since reciprocal play is a sort of reciprocal imitation ("you follow me, then I follow you"). One cannot claim that such sharing creates "the ejective consciousness" in the monkey, but the contrast between films of mother monkeys without childhood social experience and those who have had such experience suggests something like "ejective consciousness" in the normal monkey mothers. The socially deprived monkey mothers simply treat their infants as disturbing physical things, in marked contrast to the normal monkey mothers.

Turning to the human data, the widespread notion that a specifically maternal early caretaking relationship is essential for basic social development has borne up poorly under careful research scrutiny (Yarrow, 1964). Where early maternal deprivation has a deleterious effect on social development, it is part of a more general "package" of insufficient stimulation, cognitive as well as social, leading to retardation rather than irreversible "damage," and leading to cognitive, as well as emotional retardation (Casler, 1961; Dennis & Najarian, 1957). While adolescents and adults with long histories of social deprivation, of mistreatment, and of transfer from institution or foster home to foster home seem deficient in a capacity for social attachment, there is no clear evidence that these effects are due to infant deprivation, rather than to later negative influences in their life. In particular, insofar as deprivation or institutionalization have deep social effects, it seems to be due to the absence of stable and pleasurable social interaction, rather than a lack of maternal caretaking which produces weakened social ties. A. Freud and Dann's (1951) report of the deep identifications and attachments between young children which developed in a Nazi concentration camp without maternal caretaking suggest, at a deeper human level, the normal social attachments which peer interaction and sharing cause at the monkey level in Harlow's (1959) studies.[30]

---

[30] Insofar as early social environments cause schizoid and autistic withdrawals from social interaction which are not genetic, the effect appears not to be a sheer deprivation effect so much as an effect of nonresponsive and nonreciprocal mothering. As White (1963) suggests, it is the feeling of noncontrol, incompetence, of not having a predictable and recip-rocal effect on the human environment which is probably the experiential agent in the autistic child's focus upon things, not people, as objects for interaction.

We have pointed out that the evidence suggests that positive social attachments develop out of intrinsic motivation to engage in social interaction and the intrinsic pleasure of social interaction, regardless of specific body instincts and drives. We have also said that the evidence suggests that this aspect of ego development has a natural developmental course and robustness in early life, so that, like other aspects of ego development, it is responsive to a much wider variety of functionally equivalent types of social stimulation than is suggested by doctrines of "mother love." We shall now trace a few of the steps in the development of social attachment implied by this account.

As was the case for stages of imitation, age-developmental progressions of attachment are generated by cognitive-structural changes. In the infant period, this is indicated by the work of Decarie (1965). Decarie found (a) close age parallels between Piaget progressions in physical object concepts and social object-relations or psychoanalytic ego-stages, and (b) correlations between the two such that infants advanced on one scale were advanced on the other. For various reasons, it is more plausible to assume that cognitive advance is the more basic or causal factor in this parallelism, though there is some reason to think that the cognitive advance is reflected earlier in the social-object world than in the physical-object world. In the preschool period, this is suggested by my own work on father-attachment just summarized. Our sketch of the age-development of attachment stresses the following strands in cognitive-developmental theories of ego-development:

1. The Piagetian development of the concept of the mother as a permanent, causally independent but familiar object (completed by age 2).
2. The development of the child's conception of the parent (or older sibling) as having a mind, intelligence or will different than, and superior to, the child's own mentality or will, but one which he can share through processes of learning, conformity, and winning affection (completed by age 6-7). This development is termed "satellization" by Ausubel (1957), formation of "ideal self" by Baldwin (1906). The cognitive developments involve (a) the ability to make comparative judgments of competence, (b) the differentiation of the child's own mind and perspective from that of others, (c) development of conceptions of shared ascribed social identities of sex, age and kinship, and (d) the development of conceptions of shared rules.
3. The development of conceptions of reciprocity, of choice, of shared but relative self-chosen and individual values and identities (completed in adolescence) ; and the development of intimacy, friendship and love as discussed by Erikson (1950) and Sullivan (1953).

It is obvious that our account assumes that intense and stable attachment (love) is a mature end-point of ego-development, not a primitive tendency. A careful analysis of the research on age differences in response to separation and object-loss (Branstetter, 1969) supports this assumption.

As was the case for imitation, we must commence our account by noting that social objects are first responded to more than physical objects because they are much more interesting. It is evident that other people are especially interesting to infants and that this interest is due primarily to the fact that people look familiar and yet they are complex stimulus objects constantly engaging in interesting activities having some relationship to the infant's own activities. While some of the most interesting things done by social objects are to care for the needs of the infant, these activities fall into a much larger class of interesting activities.[31] The fact that the motivational conditions for early social responses are general information-processing conditions is suggested by recent findings on the determinants of attention and smiling to human-face schemata, e.g., "stimuli that resemble the infant's schema will maintain his attention with the greatest intensity. Stimuli that very closely match or have no relation to his schema will hold his attention for a much shorter time" (Kagan, 1968). In addition, however, the sudden recognition of the familiar (whether faces or other configurations) elicits smiling, because it leads to a rapid assimilation of an uncertain experience (Piaget, 1952b).[32] In this sense, the child's early social smile is functionally continuous with much of his later smiling and laughter at funny stimuli, i.e., stimuli which are first incongruous but suddenly "fall into place" in a somewhat unexpected way, as all theories of humor emphasize.

We have stressed the role of assimilation of the familiar and interesting in one positive social response, the smile. Failure to assimilate the unfamiliar and incongruous seems to be responsible for another early "attachment" response, the 8-12-month reaction of "stranger anxiety" (Morgan & Ricciutti, 1968). Before the appearance of stranger anxiety, all human faces tend to be assimilated to the familiar "mother" schema. The clear failure to fit the schema seems to induce stranger anxiety. After "normal" stranger anxiety has subsided in development (e.g., after 1 year) the donning of a mask by the mother will elicit a similar reaction of anxious response to incongruity in the apparently familiar (though the sheer presentation of a mask will not).[33] We do not yet know enough either about the infant's schema development or about the general conditions of schema-stimulus match to specify what is the optimal amount of incongruity to

---

[31] Wolff (1965) notes that attentiveness to external stimuli in very young infants was lowest when the infant was hungry or otherwise viscerally excited. The account which follows assumes that the infant's "social responses" are part of this broad attentiveness to the outside world, rather than that the child attends to the outside world only when something external meshes with a visceral drive-state.

[32] The notion that smiling to human faces is due to an association with feeding satisfaction has been disproved. Association of face-schema with bottle feeding reduced, rather than increased, smiling to a schema of the face in orphanage infants (because it made it overly familiar) (Wilson, 1962). The notion that the human face constitutes a specific "innate releasing mechanism" for an instinctive smiling response also seems untenable, since a large variety of complex stimuli will elicit smiling (Wilson, 1962).

[33] Just as smiling to a face has been reviewed as involving an innate releasing mechanism, stranger anxiety has been viewed as an innate "flight" response terminating the period of "imprinting" or attachment (Schaffer, 1966). Not only does the onset of stranger anxiety not terminate the potential for attachment, but it disappears in a way instinctive flight responses do not.

produce pleasurable attention and what is an overload of incongruity producing distress. However, the burgeoning work on infancy clearly suggests that early "social" responses will be understood in terms of the broad picture of assimilative reactions to patterned stimuli rather than in terms of specific prepatterned, maturationally unfolding responses to innate releasing stimuli for "attachment" or "flight," or by histories of conditioning (Ricciutti, 1968).

The implication of what has been said so far is that the infant's "social attachment" responses in the first eight months are simply part of his responsiveness to patterned external stimulation, rather than being genuinely "social" or forming the necessary groundwork of later human ties. We have claimed that preference for his parent over a stranger, so-called "stranger anxiety," is a negative response to the unfamiliar. In this regard it seems no more "social" than his anxiety about being placed in a strange room as opposed to a familiar room. Ainsworth (1963, 1964) suggests that it forms part of a sequential pattern of attachment behaviors, but neither her work nor that of Decarie (1965) has succeeded in arriving at a sequential or cumulative scale of social or mother "object relations" which clearly indicates any patterning not due to the sequential patterning of infants' responses to physical objects based on general Piagetian principles of cognitive development. The stages of the infant's construction of permanent independent physical objects have close parallels in the child's growth of awareness of the permanence and independence of social objects like the mother, as Decarie (1965) has documented. The age at which the child first shows stranger-anxiety and separation responses is the age (6-9 months) at which he first shows awareness of the permanence of physical objects (Decarie, 1965; Schaffer and Emerson, 1964). It is obvious that the permanent existence of the mother is a precondition to missing her. The open question is whether there are steps in the formation of a mother attachment which indicate something more than the child's general cognitive growth in response to external objects whether physical or social. If not, there is no reason to assume that early experience should have a basic effect on capacities for later social attachment unless early deprivation or trauma were so extreme as to retard responsiveness to external stimuli and cognitive development in general.

We have claimed that the 9-month response to the socially unfamiliar is in itself not "social" since it is no different from the child's response to the unfamiliar in general. The child's early separation responses may represent something more specifically social than this, however. The fact of object constancy indicates the beginning of a growth of selfness, a discrimination between the self and outer objects. While the mother must be recognized in some sense as an outer object to be missed when she is not present, she is also more self-like than other outer objects, as psychoanalytic theories of infancy have always stressed.

In a certain sense, the mother may be a part of the child to be missed as a part of his body might be missed. Separation and stranger anxiety, then, may not only be a reaction to an unfamiliar situation, but to the change or loss of a more or less permanent self. While a mother-infant identification may not be responsible for separation reactions in the first year of life, it seems clearly involved in reactions in the second year of life. By the second year of life, there is a self-other differentiation at the level of bodies but not of minds and wills. While "ejective consciousness" is established in the second year of life, the child's confusion between his own perspective on objects or mental reactions and those of others (termed egocentrism by Piaget [1947]) continues in quite gross form until age 5-7. Before the two-year-old's "negativistic crisis" signals awareness of a differentiation of wills and agencies, the child feels no sense of incompetence or weakness in either imitating others, obeying others (i.e., in being the agent of another's will), or in being helped by others (i.e., in the other being an agent of his will). In the second year of life, then, there is a sense in which the psychoanalytic notion of a primary identification or undifferentiated symbiotic bond with the mother is an accurate characterization of social relationships.[34]

Insofar as this is the case, this tie is not social; it involves neither acts of sharing nor love for the other nor the desire for love. This is brought out in Ausubel's (1952, 1957) account of the development of identification-attachment. According to Ausubel, in this undifferentiated phase, the infant conceives of the caretaker as a mere extension of his own wishes and actions, as an executive arm. Accordingly the infant's dependency upon the parent is essentially an instrumental or executive dependency rather than a volitional dependency, i.e., it is not a willingness to subordinate his actions to the wishes or responses of the parent. It does not imply any orientation to the psychic state of the mother, i.e., no desire to share psychic states, no altruism about her state, and no concern about being loved (as a psychic state in the other, important for self-esteem). Ausubel believes that growing cognitive differentiation of self and other and growing awareness of the superior power of the parents precipitates a third-year negativistic crisis typically resolved by accepting a satellite role in the family. The satellizing child gives up a sense of self-esteem based on his own power and achievement (and a controlling executive dependency over the mother which extends his sense of power to what he can get the mother to do) for a sense of vicarious self-esteem as the result of vicarious sharing of parental superiorities and as the result of being loved and being positively evaluated by parents and others. Both identification and volitional dependency are motivated by needs for self-esteem in a satellite role. The need to be loved does not precede identification but is contemporaneous with it in a total process of cognitively realistic ego devaluation where love, acceptance and attractive adult role models are available.

Ausubel's crisis-oriented typological account is useful as a dramatic sketch of the development of identification, compressing into a single conflict and a

---

[34] Bowlby (1958) and others have exaggerated the specificity and depth of the symbiotic clinging attachment to the mother in the second year of life, however. A recent carefully controlled study of the reactions of infants (age 1½ to 3) to hospitalization involved comparisons of mother-absent, "substitute-mother" volunteers, and rooming-in groups. While many of the mother-absent infants showed intense distress, there were no differences between the real and substitute-mother groups in distress reactions (Branstetter, 1969).

single relationship a process of social development going on in the first eight years of life. The account is limited, not only by condensing too much development into the resolution of a single crisis, but by its neglect of the positive experiences of, and motives for, sharing. Shared goals, shared norms and shared esteem are derived by Ausubel from a clash which leads the child to give up a unilateral primary "egoistic" will and sense of competence or self-esteem for a unilateral "derived" sense of goals and sense of self-esteem, rather than from more positive, unconflicted and egalitarian experiences of sharing.

In particular, both Ausubel and the psychoanalytic accounts of second-year sociality stress a negative mother-child symbiosis expressed in a physical clinging and a demandingness which results from the child's seeing the mother as a physical extension of himself. In addition, however, the child in the second year of life clearly takes a delight in sharing through imitation, reciprocal play and communication (e.g., pointing things out to the other). It is this type of experience, rather than clinging, which clearly indicates that other people are people to the infant, not security blankets or "cloth mothers" to be clung to in unfamiliar situations. The bridge between the physical and the social is suggested by the infant's response to his own mirror-image (Dixon, 1957). The eight-month-old child's interest in his mirror "twin" is based largely on the fact that his mirror twin "imitates" him. The infant acts repetitively to get the mirror twin to "imitate" his movements. According to Dixon, however, the infant is far more interested in his real twin than in his "mirror twin," and this interest is largely connected with simple imitative games in which each takes turns imitating and eliciting imitaton from the other.

Social objects early become a special focus of attention and recognition because they do more interesting things. They become differentiated from physical things because a major vehicle for interacting with them is to imitate them rather than to manipulate them. Social objects not only do interesting things, but these interesting activities may be shared and made one's own by imitation or by reciprocal interaction. By the second year of life, most children are tagalongs behind their older siblings, following siblings more than they follow their mothers. They tag along because what their older siblings do is interesting, more interesting than the parent's sedate activities. They follow along, not to watch, but to imitate and participate in these activities. The motivation for this "tagging-along" is effectance motivation, the motivation behind the perennial question, "What is there to do?" and the satisfaction of the motive is through imitation of the interesting. In large part, then, the child is dependent upon the other as a model for his own activities, and the motivation for this dependence is the motivation for imitation we have discussed before. It is also clear that the two-year-old is not attached to the older brother he slavishly imitates in the sense that he is to his mother; when in a state of insecurity or need, the two-year-old quickly turns to his mother, not his brother. We argued earlier, however, that sheer physical need for the presence and services of the other does not in itself generate social bonds because it does not involve a motive to share between self and other or to be guided by the response of the other. It is an open question whether the child's symbiotic relation to his mother constitutes a more basic or favorable base than do his relations to peers and other adults for the cultivation of a desire to share, and a "satellizing" renunciation of nonshared wishes and sources of self-esteem for shared ones which is basic to the formation of later stable social bonds.[35]

The ego-development theories of Baldwin (1906), Piaget (1948), Ausubel (1957), and Loevinger (1966) suggest that the child's further development of social ties and his development of moral attitudes become different sides of the same coin. M. Blatt (unpublished research) has found that children's conceptions of love and friendship go through stages parallel to my moral judgment stages. It is not until the onset of Stage 3, "good boy" morality, at age 6-7 that the child expresses the desire to be liked independently of being given rewards; expresses the desire to do something for someone he likes; feels being a friend of, or being liked by, someone prestigeful gives him derived self-esteem; or thinks that he likes his parent or friend, even though they are momentarily frustrating him. At this point, the child's social tie to his parent becomes the satellizing moral identification previously discussed. The development of attachment and love past satellization to intimacy must be left for subsequent treatment.

XV. IDENTIFICATION AND PSYCHOPATHOLOGY

We have claimed that specific identifications with specific parent figures may: (a) speed up (or slow down) development in natural moral or psychosexual sequences,[36] and (b) may give particular stages of development specific content and affective significance. The child's stage of development in turn colors or gives specific significance to the child's relationships to his parents. We have claimed, however, that specific identifications with specific parent figures are neither necessary nor sufficient conditions for normal moral or psychosexual development.

The need to explain general trends of both moral and sex-role development in terms independent of specific parent-child ties or identification is indicated by research findings reviewed elsewhere (Kohlberg, 1963a, 1964, 1966b).

1. Children and young adults are no more like their parents in level of morality or of masculinity-femininity than they are like a random parental indi-

---

[35] It must be stressed that psychoanalytic, ethological, or S-R theories basing later dependency or attachments on mother-infant relations in the first two years are not as yet based on any substantial research findings. The facts are more to the contrary. As a single example from many, Kagan and Moss (1962) found a correlation of only .33 between affectional dependency in the first three years of life and at ages 6-9, and a similar correlation of .33 between anxiety at loss of nurturance across the same periods.

[36] As an example, if the child's family world fits a Stage 1 conception that the right thing is to avoid punishment and to be obedient, he is likely to remain at that stage longer than others, though not to remain there forever. At age 13, parental use of physical punishment correlates significantly with Stage 1 thinking. Nevertheless, almost all Stage 1 3-year-olds eventually move out of Stage 1, after leaving home if not before (Kohlberg, 1969).

vidual of the same social class. All reported studies indicate no correlation between the masculinity-femininity of the child and the masculinity-femininity of their same-sex parents (Terman & Miles, 1936; Mussen & Rutherford, 1963; Angrilli, 1960). There is no significant correlation between the stage or level of moral maturity (as defined by my methods) of male adolescents or young adults and that of their fathers (Holstein, 1968; Kramer, 1968). While "principled" mothers are more likely to have "conventional" children than less-advanced mothers, this is not due to identification mechanisms. If it were, conventional mothers should have more conventional-level children than principled mothers (Holstein, 1968).

2. Measures of identification (perceived similarity) with the same-sex parent do not clearly and consistently relate to moral and sex-role maturity or to moral and sex-role "internalization" (i.e., to acceptance of conventional moral and sex-role attitudes and standards). With regard to sex role, measures of girls' femininity tend to correlate with measures of identification with the opposite-sex parent rather than the same-sex parent. Measures of boys' masculinity correlate with measures of identification with the same-sex parent at most, but not all, age periods. With regard to morality, low significant correlations are found between parent identification measures and acceptance of the conventional moral code. These are not sex-specific, e.g., measured identification with the same-sex parent is not more clearly related to moral attitudes than is identification with the opposite-sex parent. These correlations may be best explained along the lines of the findings on warmth and liking, e.g., that if the child likes his parent, he tends to agree with him and learn more from him as reflected in both moral attitude measures and perceived similarity measures.

3. There is no generalized "identification-internalization factor" in children's personality. Measures of moral and of sex-role attitudes or development are not correlated with one another. Measures of identification do not correlate well with one another. Measures of identification at one age do not predict to measures of identification at another age.

4. The presence of a same-sex parent is not necessary for normal moral or psychosexual development. Children in the kibbutz and children from father-absent households are little different from children of intact families in all measured or observed aspects of "normality" or development of sex-role, as well as of moral, attitudes and behavior.[37]

There is a widespread misunderstanding of the research findings as indicating "the importance of the father for the development of the boy's sex-role

---

[37] Differences appear where intactness of the family represents the general "badness" or deviance of the parents and the environment as in the Gluecks' (Glueck & Glueck, 1950) studies of delinquency in which divorce, parent-conflict, criminality and neglect of children form part of a bad-environment package. Where some control of these correlates of a single-parent household is attained in a research design, the actual presence of a specific parent does not appear salient. One study, however, that of Hoffman and Saltzstein (1967), does report more internalized moral judgment and guilt in father-present boys than in a sample of father-absent boys matched for IQ and social class (Hoffman, 1969).

identity." In fact, no study has shown any marked differences between father-absent and father-present boys with regard to measures of masculine-feminine attitudes (Terman & Miles, 1936; Barclay & Cusumano, 1965; C. Smith summarized in Kohlberg, 1966b). A naturalistic longitudinal study by McCord, McCord and Thurber (1962) indicated no difference between father-absent and father-present families in incidence of effeminacy or homosexuality in boys.

While these findings clearly contradict any theory that claims that particular identifications or good parent relations are necessary for normal social development, there are some findings suggesting that bad parent relations are retarding or disrupting of such development. As an example, McCord et al. (1962) found intact families with strong marital conflict produced "effeminate" boys more frequently than either the conflict-free or the father-absent families. Hetherington (1965) and Hetherington and Frankie (1967) also find the sons of extremely submissive fathers to be low on sex-typing and on father imitation compared to the sons of high dominant fathers. The sons of dominant fathers appeared to be no different from a random population, or even from C. Smith's father-absent population, however (Kohlberg, 1966b). In other words, while markedly bad, deviant, or conflictful mother-father relations produce disturbances in sex-role attitudes, exposure to a "good" or conforming mother-father interaction is neither necessary for normal sex-role development (since it does not favor father-present over father-absent boys) nor does it even favor normal sex-role development (since highly masculine and dominant fathers are no more likely to have masculine sons than are fathers in the middle range).

In the moral area, the findings of the Gluecks (Glueck & Glueck, 1950) clearly indicate that delinquent boys are much more likely to come from markedly "bad" families, according to any criterion of "badness." But again, a specific relation to a specific good parent is neither necessary nor sufficient for normal or advanced moral development, since father absence, father's moral level, and use of "good" child-rearing techniques, however defined, do not predict to such maturity (Kohlberg, 1969).

The contrast between the relatively clear findings on effects of deviantly bad parents and the lack of findings on the effects of parent absence (or of normal variations in child-rearing practices) upon socialization is theoretically important for several reasons.[38] Limiting ourselves to identification theory, we pointed out that psychoanalytic identification theory (especially identification with the aggressor notions) was designed to account for illogical, pathological, or deviant identifications. We pointed out that a theory as to why boys want to be boys is not a theory as to why a boy wants to be a girl in some generalized sense; nor is an explanation of why boys want to be good in general, an explanation of why a particular boy seems to want to be bad or sees himself as bad in some generalized

---

[38] The practical implications of this conclusion imply a revolution in current social work and mental health services for children now addressed to helping the child under the presupposition of preserving his relation to a "bad" but intact family.

sense. While we cannot conclude that boys low in masculinity or delinquent boys have formed a definite deviant "opposite-sex" or "bad" identification modeled on a parent, it is at least possible that some of the effects of bad families are due to this mechanism.

There is at present, little definite reason to view "opposite-sex identification" as a valuable explanation of sexual psychopathology, since homosexuals are not clearly more "opposite-sex identified" than heterosexuals (Kohlberg, 1966b). With regard to some forms of moral psychopathology, however, deviant parental identifications seem more directly relevant. Freud's (1938) reasoning that pathological feelings of being blamed by others (paranoia) and of self-blame (depression) require a notion of fixed self-blaming structure, somewhat ego-alien but at the same time internalized within the psyche and based on identification, still seems convincing. Self-criticism and self-punishment by definition require identification in the broad sense of taking the role of the other, and severe forms of self-punishment and self-blame must be modeled in some sense on parental reactions in young childhood since the parent is ordinarily the only agent who engages in intensive punishment and blaming activities. Explanations of pathological guilt (i.e., guilt in the absence of serious transgression of self-accepted standards) suggest a base in idiosyncratic family and childhood experience, explanations of normal guilt (guilt over transgressions of self-accepted moral standards) do not.

Unfortunately, it is premature to attempt explanations of psychopathological identifications because there are almost no data concerning them except clinical case studies. The research literature is irrelevant to such questions except under the dubious assumption that measures of developmental lag in sexual or moral attitudes, or low scores on verbal measures of conformity to conventional moral or sex-role standards reflect pathological identifications (e.g., that a low score on an M-F test is a measure of a cross-sex identification of an illogical or pathological sort). A consideration of theories of psychopathological identification requires the kind of developmental and longitudinal data on psychopathology not now available. The analysis of such data may provide more of an integration of psychoanalytic and cognitive-developmental concepts than this chapter has suggested.

REFERENCES

AINSWORTH, M. D. Development of infant-mother interaction among the Ganda. In B. Foss (Ed.), *Determinants of infant behavior*. Vol. II. London: Methuen, 1963.

AINSWORTH, M. D. Patterns of attachment behavior shown by the infant in interaction with his mother. *Merrill-Palmer Quarterly*, 1964, 10, 51-58.

AMMONS, R., & AMMONS, H. Parent preference in young children's doll-play interviews. *Journal of Abnormal and Social Psychology*, 1949, 44, 490-505.

ANDERSON, J. Development. In D. Harris (Ed.), *The concept of development*. Minneapolis: Univer. of Minnesota Press, 1957.

ANDERSON, J. The prediction of adjustment over time. In I. Iscoe & H. Stevenson (Eds.), *Personality development in children*. Austin: Univer. of Texas Press, 1960.

ANGRILLI, A. F. The psychosexual identification of preschool boys. *Journal of Genetic Psychology*, 1960, 97, 329-340.

ARONFREED, J. The nature, variety, and social patterning of moral responses to transgression. *Journal of Abnormal and Social Psychology*, 1961, 63, 223-241.

ARONFREED, J. The concept of internalization. In D. A. Goslin (Ed.), *Handbook of socialization theory and research*. Chicago: Rand McNally, 1969. Chapter 4.

AUSUBEL, D. P. *Ego development and the personality disorders*. New York: Grune & Stratton, 1952.

AUSUBEL, D. P. *Theory and problems of child development*. New York: Grune & Stratton, 1957.

AUSUBEL, D. P., ET AL. Perceived parent attitudes as determinants of children's ego structure. *Child Development*, 1954, 25, 173-183.

AZRIN, N., & LINDSLEY, O. R. The reinforcement of cooperation between children. *Journal of Abnormal and Social Psychology*, 1956, 52, 100-102.

BAER, D., PETERSON, R., & SHERMAN, J. The development of generalized imitation by programming similarity between child and model as discriminative for reinforcement. *Journal of Experimental Analysis of Behavior*, 1967, 10, 405-416.

BALDWIN, J. M. *Mental development in the child and the race*. New York: Macmillan, 1895.

BALDWIN, J. M. *Social and ethical interpretations in mental development*. New York: Macmillan, 1906.

BALDWIN, J. M. *Thoughts and things or genetic logic*. 3 Vols. New York: Macmillan, 1906-11.

BALDWIN, J. M. *Genetic theory of reality*. New York: Putnam's, 1915.

BANDURA, A. Social-learning theory of identificatory processes. In D. A. Goslin (Ed.), *Handbook of socialization theory and research*. Chicago: Rand McNally, 1969. Chapter 3.

BANDURA, A., GRUSIC, JOAN, & MENLOVE, FRANCES. Some social determinants of self-monitoring systems. *Journal of Personality and Social Psychology*, 1967, 5, 449-455.

BANDURA, A., & HUSTON, A. C. Identification as a process of incidental learning. *Journal of Abnormal and Social Psychology*, 1961, 63, 311-319.

BANDURA, A., & KUPERS, CAROL. Transmission of patterns of self-reinforcement through modeling. *Journal of Abnormal and Social Psychology*, 1964, 69, 1-9.

BANDURA, A., & MACDONALD, F. The influence of social reinforcement and the behavior of models in shaping children's moral judgment. *Journal of Abnormal and Social Psychology*, 1963, 67, 274-281.

BANDURA, A., ROSS, D., & ROSS, S. Transmission of aggression through imitation of aggressive models. *Journal of Abnormal and Social Psychology*, 1963, 66, 3-11. (a)

BANDURA, A., ROSS, D., & ROSS, S. A comparative test of the status envy, social power and secondary reinforcement theories of identificatory learning. *Journal of Abnormal and Social Psychology*, 1963, 67, 527-534. (b)

BANDURA, A., ROSS, D., & ROSS, S. Vicarious reinforcement and imitative learning. *Journal of Abnormal and Social Psychology*, 1963, 67, 601-607. (c)

BANDURA, A., & WHALEN, CAROL. The influence of antecedent reinforcement and divergent modeling cues on patterns of self-reward. *Journal of Personality and Social Psychology*, 1966, 3, 373-382.

BARCLAY, A., & CUSUMANO, D. Effects of father absence upon field-dependent behavior. Paper delivered at meeting of the American Psychological Association, September, 1965.

BECKER, H. *Outsiders: Studies in the sociology of deviance.* New York: Free Press, 1963.

BECKER, W. Consequences of different kinds of parental discipline. In M. Hoffman & L. Hoffman (Eds.), *Review of child development research.* Vol. 1. New York: Russell Sage Foundation, 1964.

BERLYNE, D. *Conflict arousal and curiosity.* New York: McGraw-Hill, 1961.

BERLYNE, D. *Structure and direction in thinking.* New York: Wiley, 1965.

BLATT, M. The effects of classroom discussion programs upon children's level of moral judgment. Unpublished doctoral dissertation, Univer. of Chicago, 1969.

BOWLBY, J. The nature of the child's tie to his mother. *International Journal of Psychoanalysis,* 1958, 39, 350-373.

BRANSTETTER, E. Separation reactions in hospitalized children with and without substitute mothers. Unpublished doctoral dissertation, Univer. of Chicago, 1969.

BRIM, O. G., JR. Family structures and sex-role learning by children. *Sociometry,* 1958, 21, 1-6.

BRONFENBRENNER, U. The role of age, sex, class, and culture in studies of moral development. *Religious Education,* 1962, 57, 3-17.

BROWN, D. G. Sex-role preference in young children. *Psychological Monographs,* 1956, 70, No. 14.

BURTON, R. V., MACCOBY, ELEANOR, & ALLINSMITH, W. Antecedents of resistance to temptation in four-year-old children. *Child Development,* 1961, 22, 689-710.

CASLER, L. Maternal deprivation: A critical review of the literature. *Monograph of the Society for Research in Child Development,* 1961, No. 26.

CATTELL, R. B. *Personality and motivation: Structure and measurement.* Yonkers, N.Y.: World Book, 1957.

CHILD, I. Socialization. In G. Lindzey (Ed.), *Handbook of social psychology.* Cambridge: Addison-Wesley, 1954.

CHOMSKY, N. Language and the mind. *Psychology Today,* 1968, 1 (9), 48-51, 66-68.

COWEN, P., LANGER, J., HEAVENRICH, J., & NATHANSON, M. Has social learning theory refuted Piaget's theory of moral development? Unpublished manuscript, 1968.

CROWLEY, P. M. Effect of training upon objectivity of moral judgment in grade-school children. *Journal of Personality and Social Psychology,* 1968, 8, 228-233.

DANZIGER, K. The development of children's economic concepts. *Journal of Genetic Psychology,* 1958, 47, 231-240.

DECARIE, THERESE G. *Intelligence and affectivity in early childhood.* New York: International Universities Press, 1965.

DENNIS, W., & NAJARIAN, P. Infant development under environmental handicap. *Psychological Monographs,* 1957, 71, No. 7 (Whole No. 436).

DEWEY, J. Experience and conduct. In C. Murchison (Ed.), *Psychologies of 1930.* Worcester: Clark Univer. Press, 1930.

DIXON, J. C. Development of self-recognition. *Journal of Genetic Psychology,* 1957, 91, 251-256.

EMMERICH, W. Family role concepts of children ages six to ten. *Child Development,* 1961, 32, 609-624.

EMMERICH, W. Continuity and stability in early social development. *Child Development,* 1964, 35, 311-333.

EMMERICH, W., & KOHLBERG, L. Imitation and attention-seeking in young children under conditions of nurturance, frustration, and conflict. Unpublished mimeographed paper, Univer. of Chicago, 1953.

ERIKSON, E. *Childhood and society.* New York: Norton, 1950.

FREEDMAN, J. L. Long-term behavioral effects of cognitive dissonance. *Journal of Experimental Social Psychology,* 1965, 1, 145-155.

FREUD, ANNA. *The ego and the mechanisms of defense.* New York: International Universities Press, 1946.

FREUD, ANNA, & DANN, SOPHIE. An experiment in group upbringing. In R. Eissler et al. (Eds.), *The psychoanalytic study of the child.* Vol. 6. New York: International Universities Press, 1951.

FREUD, S. *The basic writings of Sigmund Freud.* New York: Modern Library, 1938.

FROMM, E. *Man for himself.* New York: Rinehart & Co., 1955.

GESELL, A. The ontogenesis of infant behavior. In L. Carmichael (Ed.), *Manual of child psychology.* New York: Wiley, 1954.

GEWIRTZ, J. L. Mechanisms of social learning: Some roles of stimulation and behavior in early human development. In D. A. Goslin (Ed.), *Handbook of socialization theory and research.* Chicago: Rand McNally, 1969. Chapter 2.

GILMORE, B. Toward an understanding of imitation. Unpublished manuscript, Waterloo Univer., 1967.

GLUECK, S., & GLUECK, E. *Unraveling juvenile delinquency.* New York: Commonwealth Fund, 1950.

GOTTESMAN, I. Heritability of personality: A demonstration. *Psychological Monographs,* 1963, 77, No. 9.

GREEN, B. A method of scalogram analysis using summary statistics. *Psychometrika,* 1956, 21, 79-88.

GRIM, P., KOHLBERG, L., & WHITE, S. Some relationships between conscience and attentional processes. *Journal of Personality and Social Psychology,* 1968, 8, 239-253.

GRINDER, R. Relations between behavioral and cognitive dimensions of conscience in middle childhood. *Child Development,* 1964, 35, 881-893.

GUTTMAN, L. The basis for scalogram analysis. In S. A. Stougger et al., *Measurement and prediction.* Princeton: Princeton Univer. Press, 1954.

HAAN, N., SMITH, M. B., & BLOCK, J. The moral reasoning of young adults: Political-social behavior, family background and personality correlates. *Journal of Personality and Social Psychology,* **1969 (in press).**

HARLOW, H. Love in infant monkeys. *Scientific American,* 1959, 200, 68-74.

HARLOW, H., & HARLOW, MARGARET. Social deprivation in monkeys. *Scientific American,* 1962, 207 (5), 136-146.

HARTSHORNE, H., & MAY, M. A. *Studies in the nature of character.* Columbia Univer., Teachers College. Vol. 1: *Studies in deceit.* Vol. 2: *Studies in service and self-control.* Vol. 3: *Studies in organization of character.* New York: Macmillan, 1928-30.

HARTUP, W. W. Some correlates of parental imitation in young children. *Child Development,* 1962, 33, 85-97.

HARVEY, O. J., HUNT, D., & SCHROEDER, D. *Conceptual systems.* New York: Wiley, 1961.

HETHERINGTON, E. MAVIS. A developmental study of the effects of sex of the dominant parent on sex-role preference, identification and imitation in children. *Journal of Personality and Social Psychology,* 1965, 2, 143-153.

HETHERINGTON, E. MAVIS, & FRANKIE, G. Effects of parental dominance, warmth and conflict on imitation in children. *Journal of Personality and Social Psychology,* 1967, 6, 119-125.

HOBHOUSE, L. T. *Morals in evolution.* London: Chapman & Hall, 1906.

HOFFMAN, M. Moral development. In P. Mussen (Ed.), *Manual of child psychology.* New York: Wiley, 1969.

HOFFMAN, M., & SALTZSTEIN, H. Parent discipline and the child's moral development. *Journal of Personality and Social Psychology,* 1967, 5, 45-57.

HOLSTEIN, CONSTANCE. Parental determinants of the development of moral judgment. Unpublished doctoral dissertation, Univer. of California, Berkeley, 1968.

HULL, C. *Principles of behavior.* New York: Appleton-Century, 1943.

HUNT, J. McV. *Intelligence and experience.* New York: Ronald Press, 1961.

HUNT, J. McV. Motivation inherent in information processing and action. In O. J. Harvey (Ed.), *Interaction.* New York: Ronald, 1963.

HUNT, J. McV., & UZGIRIS, I. An ordinal scale of infant development. Unpublished manuscript, Univer. of Illinois, Urbana, 1967.

JAMES, W. *Principles of psychology.* New York: Holt, 1890.

KAGAN, J. The concept of identification. *Psychological Review,* 1958, 65, 296-305.

KAGAN, J. The many faces of response. *Psychology Today,* 1968, 1, No. 8, 22-27.

KAGAN, J., & MOSS, H. *Birth to maturity.* New York: Wiley, 1962.

KAPLAN, B. The study of language in psychiatry. In S. Arieti (Ed.), *American handbook of psychiatry.* Vol. 3. New York: Basic Books, 1966.

KESSEN, W. (Ed.) *The child.* New York: Wiley, 1965.

KINSEY, A., ET AL. *Sexual behavior in the human female.* Philadelphia: W. B. Sanders, 1953.

KOHLBERG, L. The development of modes of moral thinking and choice in the years ten to sixteen. Unpublished doctoral dissertation, Univer. of Chicago, 1958.

KOHLBERG, L. Moral development and identification. In H. Stevenson (Ed.), Child psychology. *62nd Yearbook of the National Society for the Study of Education.* Chicago: Univer. of Chicago Press, 1963. (a)

KOHLBERG, L. The development of children's orientations toward a moral order: 1. Sequence in the development of moral thought. *Vita Humana,* 1963, 6, 11-33. (b)

KOHLBERG, L. Stages in conceptions of the physical and social world. Unpublished monograph, 1963. (c)

KOHLBERG, L. Development of moral character and ideology. In M. L. Hoffman (Ed.), *Review of child development research.* Vol. 1. New York: Russell Sage Foundation, 1964.

KOHLBERG, L. Psychosexual development, a cognitive-developmental approach. Unpublished mimeographed manuscript, Univer. of Chicago, 1965.

KOHLBERG, L. Cognitive stages and preschool education. *Human Development,* 1966, 9, 5-17. (a)

KOHLBERG, L. A cognitive developmental analysis of children's sex-role concepts and attitudes. In E. Maccoby (Ed.), *The development of sex differences.* Stanford, Calif.: Stanford Univer. Press, 1966. (b)

KOHLBERG, L. Moral and religious education and the public schools: A developmental view. In T. Sizer (Ed.), *Religion and public education.* Boston: Houghton-Mifflin, 1967.

KOHLBERG, L. Preschool education: A cognitive-developmental approach. *Child Development,* 1968 (in press).

KOHLBERG, L. *Stages in the development of moral thought and action.* New York: Holt, Rinehart & Winston, 1969.

KOHLBERG, L., YAEGER, J., & HJERTHOLM, E. The development of private speech: Four studies and a review of theory. *Child Development,* 1968 (in press).

KOHLBERG, L., & ZIGLER, E. The impact of cognitive maturity on sex-role attitudes in the years four to eight. *Genetic Psychology Monograph,* 1967, 75, 89-165.

KOHN, N. Performance of Negro children of varying social class background on Piagetian tasks. Unpublished doctoral dissertation, Univer. of Chicago, 1969.

KRAMER, R. Moral development in young adulthood. Unpublished doctoral dissertation, Univer. of Chicago, 1968.

KREBS, R. L. Some relationships between moral judgment, attention and resistance to temptation. Unpublished doctoral dissertation, Univer. of Chicago, 1967.

KUHN, D., & LANGER, J. Cognitive-developmental determinants of imitation. Unpublished manuscript, 1968.

LACROSSE, J., & KOHLBERG, L. The predictability of adult mental health from childhood behavior and status. In B. Wolman (Ed.), *Handbook of psychopathology.* New York: McGraw-Hill, 1969.

LANGER, J. Disequilibrium as a source of cognitive development. Paper delivered at the meeting of the Society for Research on Child Development, New York, March 21, 1967.

LEHRER, L. Sex differences in moral behavior and attitudes. Unpublished doctoral dissertation, Univer. of Chicago, 1967.

LIPPETT, R., & WHITE, R. The effects of social climates. In R. Barker, J. Kounin & H. Wright (Eds.), *Child behavior and development.* New York: McGraw-Hill, 1943.

LOEVINGER, J. The meaning and measurement of ego development. *American Psychologist,* 1966, 21, 195-217.

LORENZ, K. *Evolution and the modification of behavior.* Chicago: Univer. of Chicago Press, 1965.

LOVAAS, O. I. A program for the establishment of speech in psychotic children. In J. Wing (Ed.), *Childhood autism.* Oxford: Pergamon Press, 1967.

MACCOBY, ELEANOR. Role-taking in childhood and its consequences for early learning. *Child Development,* 1959, 30, 239-252.

MACCOBY, ELEANOR. Social attachment. In P. Mussen (Ed.), *Manual of child psychology.* New York: Wiley, 1969 (in press).

MACFARLANE, J., ALLEN, L., & HONZIK, N. *A developmental study of behavior problems of normal children between 21 months and four years.* Berkeley: Univer. of California Press, 1954.

MACKINNON, D. W. Violation of prohibitions. In H. A. Murray (Ed.), *Explorations in personality.* New York: Oxford Univer. Press, 1938. Pp. 491-501.

MCCORD, J., MCCORD, JOAN, & THURBER, EMILY. Some effects of paternal absence on male children. *Journal of Abnormal and Social Psychology,* 1962, 64, 361-369.

MCDOUGALL, W. *An introduction to social psychology.* London: Methuen, 1908.

MEAD, G. H. *Mind, self, and society.* Chicago: Univer. of Chicago Press, 1934.

MILGRAM, S. Behavioral study of obedience. *Journal of Abnormal and Social Psychology,* 1963, 67, 371-378.

MILLER, N., & DOLLARD, J. *Social learning and imitation.* New Haven: Yale Univer. Press, 1941.

MORGAN, G., & RICCIUTTI, H. Infant's responses to shapes during the first year. In B. M. Foss (Ed.), *Determinants of infant behavior.* Vol. 4. London: Methuen, 1968.

MUSSEN, P., & RUTHERFORD, E. Parent-child relations and parental personality in relation to young children's sex-role preferences. *Child Development,* 1963, 34, 589-607.

PARSONS, T., & BALES, R. F. *Family, socialization and interaction process.* Glencoe, Ill.: Free Press, 1955.

PARTEN, M., & NEWHALL, S. M. The development of social behavior in children. In R. Barker, J. Kounin & H. Wright (Eds.), *Child behavior and development*. New York: McGraw-Hill, 1943.

PAVLOV, I. P. *Lectures on conditioned reflexes*. New York: Liveright, 1928.

PECK, R. F., & HAVIGHURST, R. J. *The psychology of character development*. New York: Wiley, 1960.

PIAGET, J. *The child's conception of the world*. New York: Harcourt, Brace, 1928.

PIAGET, J. *The psychology of intelligence*. London: Routledge, Kegan Paul, 1947.

PIAGET, J. *The moral judgment of the child*. Glencoe, Ill.: Free Press, 1948. (Originally published in 1932)

PIAGET, J. *Play, dreams, and imitation in childhood*. New York: Norton, 1951.

PIAGET, J. *Les relations entre l'affectivitie et l'intelligence dans le development mental de l'enfant*. Le course de Sorbonne psychologie. Paris: Centre de Documentation Universitaire, 1952. (Mimeographed) (a)

PIAGET, J. *The origins of intelligence in children*. New York: International Universities Press, 1952. (b)

PIAGET, J. *The construction of reality in the child*. New York: Basic Books, 1954.

PIAGET, J. The general problems of the psychobiological development of the child. In J. M. Tanner & B. Inhelder (Eds.), *Discussions on child development: Proceedings of the World Health Organization study group on the psychobiological development of the child*. Vol. IV. New York: International Universities Press, 1960. Pp. 3-27.

PIAGET, J. Cognitive development in children. In R. Ripple & V. Rockcastle (Eds.), *Piaget rediscovered: A report on cognitive studies in curriculum development*. Ithaca, N. Y.: Cornell Univ. School of Education, 1964.

PIAGET, J. *On the development of memory and identity*. Worcester, Mass.: Clark Univer. Press, 1968.

PINARD, A., & LAURENDEAU, M. *Causal thinking in children*. New York: International Universities Press, 1964.

REST, J. Developmental hierarchy in preference and comprehension of moral judgment. Unpublished doctoral dissertation, Univer. of Chicago, 1968.

REST, J., TURIEL, E., & KOHLBERG, L. Relations between level of moral judgment and preference and comprehension of the moral judgment of others. *Journal of Personality*, 1969.

RICCIUTTI, H. Social and emotional behavior in infancy: Some developmental issues and problems. *Merrill-Palmer Quarterly*, 1968, 14, 82-100.

RIESEN, A., & KINDER, E. *The postural development of infant chimpanzees*. New Haven: Yale Univer. Press, 1952.

RIESMAN, D. *The lonely crowd*. New Haven: Yale Univer. Press, 1950.

RUMA, E., & MOSHER, P. Relationship between moral judgment and guilt in delinquent boys. *Journal of Abnormal Psychology*, 1967, 72, 122-127.

SARNOFF, I. Identification with the aggressor: Some personality correlates of anti-Semitism among Jews. *Journal of Personality*, 1951, 20, 199-218.

SCHACHTER, S. The interaction of cognitive and physiological determinants of emotional state. In L. Berkowitz (Ed.), *Advances in social psychology*. Vol. I. New York: Academic Press, 1964.

SCHAFFER, H. R. The onset of fear of stranger and the incongruity hypothesis. *Journal of Child Psychology and Psychiatry*, 1966, 7, 95-106.

SCHAFFER, H. R., & EMERSON, P. E. The development of social attachment in infancy. *Monograph of the Society for Research in Child Development*, 1964, 29, Serial No. 94. Pp. 1-77.

SEARS, R. R. Identification as a form of behavior development. In D. B. Harris (Ed.), *The concept of development.* Minneapolis: Univer. of Minnesota Press, 1957.

SEARS, R. R. Relations of early socialization experience to aggression in middle childhood. *Journal of Abnormal and Social Psychology,* 1961, 63, 466-493.

SEARS, R. R., RAU, L., & ALPERT, R. *Identification and child-rearing.* Stanford, Calif.: Stanford Univer. Press, 1965.

SHIRLEY, MARY. *The first two years.* 2 vols. Minneapolis: Univer. of Minnesota Press, 1933.

SIGEL, I., & HOOPER, F. (Eds.) *Logical thinking in children: Research based on Piaget's theory.* New York: Rinehart & Winston, 1968.

SOLOMON, R., & COLES, R. A case of failure of generalization of imitation learning across drives and across situations. *Journal of Abnormal and Social Psychology,* 1954, 49, 7-13.

STEVENSON, H. Social reinforcement of children's behavior. In C. Spiker (Ed.), *Advances in child development.* Vol. II. New York: Academic Press, 1965.

STOTLAND, E., ZANDER, A., & NATSOULAS, T. Generalization of interpersonal similarity. *Journal of Abnormal and Social Psychology,* 1961, 62, 250-258.

STRAUSS, A. The learning of social roles and rules as twin processes. *Child Development,* 1954, 25, 192-208.

SULLIVAN, C., GRANT, M. Q., & GRANT, J. D. The development of interpersonal maturity: Application to delinquency. *Psychiatry,* 1957, 20, 373-385.

SULLIVAN, H. S. *An interpersonal theory of psychiatry.* New York: Norton, 1953.

TERMAN, L. M., & MILES, C. C. *Sex and personality studies in masculinity and femininity.* New York: McGraw-Hill, 1936.

TURIEL, E. An experimental test of the sequentiality of developmental stages in the child's moral judgment. *Journal of Personality and Social Psychology,* 1966, 3, 611-618.

TURIEL, E. Developmental processes in the child's moral thinking. In P. Mussen, J. Langer & M. Covington (Eds.), *New directions in developmental psychology.* New York: Holt, Rinehart & Winston, 1969.

TURIEL, E., & GUINSBURG, G. The cognitive conditions for imitation without reinforcement. Unpublished manuscript, 1968.

TURNURE, J., & ZIGLER, E. Outer directedness in the problem solving of normal and retarded children. *Journal of Abnormal and Social Psychology,* 1964, 69, 427-436.

VALENTINE, C. W. *The psychology of early childhood.* London: Methuen, 1942.

VAN MANEN, GLORIA. An interpersonal theory of deviance: A test of general theory. Unpublished doctoral dissertation, Univer. of Chicago, 1967.

WARDEN, C., & JACKSON, T. Imitative behavior in the rhesus monkey. *Journal of Genetic Psychology,* 1935, 46, 103-125.

WERNER, H. *The comparative psychology of mental development.* Chicago: Wilcox & Follett, 1948.

WHITE, R. Motivation reconsidered: The concept of competence. *Psychological Review,* 1959, 66, 297-333.

WHITE, R. Ego and reality in psychoanalytic theory. *Psychological Issues,* Vol. III, No. 3. New York: International Universities Press, 1963.

WHITING, J. W. M. Resource mediation and learning by identification. In I. Iscoe & H. W. Stevenson (Eds.), *Personality development in children.* Austin, Tex.: Univer. of Texas Press, 1960. Pp. 112-126.

WHITING, J. W. M. The concept of identification. Paper delivered at the meeting of the Society for Research in Child Development, New York, March 21, 1967.

WILSON, J. An experimental investigation of the development of smiling. Unpublished doctoral dissertation, Univer. of Chicago, 1962.

WITKIN, H. A. Social influences in the development of cognitive style. In D. A. Goslin (Ed.), *Handbook of socialization theory and research*. Chicago: Rand McNally, 1969. Chapter 14.

WOLFF, P. H. The development of attention in young infants. New York Academy of Sciences, *Transactions*, 1965, 118, 783-866.

YARROW, L. J. Separation from parents during early childhood. In M. L. Hoffman & L. W. Hoffman (Eds.), *Review of child development research*. New York: Russell Sage Foundation, 1964. Pp. 89-136.

CHAPTER 7

Psychoanalytic Theory
Of Development: A Re-Evaluation

Daniel R. Miller

University of Michigan

Although psychoanalysis has been part of the academic scene for more than half a century, its fruitfulness as a theory of socialization is still a matter of considerable debate among social scientists. It is even difficult for specialists to agree on the phrasing of basic premises and on the techniques of testing validity because of fundamental differences in philosophy of science. This chapter presents a formulation of the theory that has gradually coalesced as the writer tried to make it meaningful in a course for graduate students in sociology, social psychology, and psychology. The formulation reflects the cross-fertilization of different disciplinary viewpoints, and has benefited considerably from the flexibility of an audience not handicapped *a priori* by commitment to the positions of particular philosophic or clinical groups, and ever ready to question the ambiguous or confusing principle.

As incipient social scientists, students find it easiest to grasp the principles of psychoanalytic theory when they are analyzed separately with respect to assumptions about biological endowment, perception, learning, and socialization. It is in terms of these topics that the material of this chapter is organized. Each section starts with some basic assumptions which are sometimes hard to formulate because their sources are scattered throughout the psychoanalytic literature. The examination of some common misunderstandings, and a translation of principles into the current terminology of social science follow. This recasting of theory reveals the necessity for certain revisions, foremost among which is its reconceptualization in interpersonal terms. Some possible changes are suggested which center about the concept of identity.

The outlining of psychoanalytic theory for a class highlights the fact that, although the system is often viewed as being outside the mainstream of academic thought, it provides detailed positions with respect to all of the issues of concern to academic specialists in developmental theory. It proposes a series of stages, specifies the adult's practices associated with each, postulates the maturation and timing of the child's capacities, and proposes some relationships between experiences at each stage and the child's motivation, perception, and learning. The theory is original in its linking of early parental practices in socializing the infant's bodily functions with later attributes of personality. Among the better-known examples are the presumed associations between the mother's methods of feeding and the child's passivity, toilet training and his expression of aggression, the parents' reactions to sexual curiosity and his later relationships with the opposite sex. Also original are the complex analyses of subjective states, both conscious and unconscious, which are used to explain the differential reactions of children to the same objective events. Careful descriptions are provided of concepts and principles, which, like those of other fallible systems, vary considerably in clarity and probable validity. Since the assessment of validity is an empirical matter, and there are so many principles, the theory deserves more than the blanket endorsements or condemnations that it sometimes receives at the hands of some of its adherents and detractors.

The complications entailed in assessing psychoanalytic theory objectively necessitate a final section on the special attributes that will always make it a more loaded topic than most of the ones studied by academicians. As will be shown, it is an oversimplification to dismiss the critical reactions solely or primarily as personal resistances. Throughout the chapter, it will be assumed that the reader is acquainted with the basic principles of the theory as presented by Fenichel (1945), Klein (1948), and Munroe (1955).

BIOLOGICAL ENDOWMENT

In its assumption about inherent functions, psychoanalytic theory places most emphasis on the maturing of potentials at various stages, and on a homeostatic model of motivation. Various senses and acts mature and become socially salient at different times, a fact that helps to define the so-called psychosexual stages. A stage can be said to exist, however, only when a socializing agent initiates a new type of consistent activity that is intended to modify the child's behavior. The activity may be necessitated by the child's initiation of a new kind of behavior, such as attacks on siblings or masturbation, but it need not be. The parents may decide to modify an ongoing pattern such as the child's toilet habits, or his dependence on adults. In fact, many new functions mature without becoming the objects of socialization. For example, genital manipulation begins toward the end of the first year, but since the adults make no issue of the practice, there is no new stage. In short, while the activity initiated by the adult is sometimes aimed at curbing some recently matured behavior, that behavior does not define a stage unless the adult does something about it.

Motivational assumptions are fundamental in explaining how the experiences in each stage enable the child to acquire the judgment and skills that he will need as an adult. Freud postulates two basic instincts, Eros and Thanatos, which provide the energy for the mental apparatus and are the sources of other motives. Stimulation, which is presumed to release these energies from the Id, is considered as being inherently unpleasant because it builds up tension, thus creating a homeostatic imbalance. The child is inherently inclined to keep active until the tension is released and equilibrium re-established. Drives are dispositions to engage in the activities that reduce specific sources of tension and restore the initial balance.

The unfortunate translation of "treib" as "instinct" connotes to some readers that the maturing reactions are conceived as fully-formed, complex processes, like the insect's nest-building or the stickleback's courtship. In actuality, clinical descriptions of infants convey a gradual unfolding of potentials which are molded by social experience into myriad forms. Even vision, which used to be viewed primarily as a maturing function, develops normally only if the infant has continual contacts with adults. Without adequate social stimulation not even the axes of the eyes become aligned (Spitz, 1945).

Not only was Freud averse to postulating fully-formed instincts; he was, in fact, exceptionally parsimonious in compiling his list of unlearned characteristics. This parsimony, combined with a model of motivation that is concentrated on sources of tension beyond the individual's control, probably accounts for the impression one gets from much of the psychoanalytic literature that the child is a passive product of his social milieu (White, 1963). Explanation of the child's changes over time are focused primarily on various aspects of his parents' practices, such as type of weaning, timing of toilet training, and amount of maternal warmth. The parsimony probably accounts for the relative neglect of dispositions to initiate behavior, particularly in the absence of physical emergencies. In much of the literature on development, such propensities are overlooked or derived from erotic and aggressive motives. Except for the references to subjective experience, the resulting explanations are sometimes surprisingly similar to those offered by most animal psychologists and sociologists, and quite different from those offered by psychologists interested in perception or by psychoanalysts such as Bernfeld (1929), Ferenczi (1950), and Klein (1948), whose assumptions about the early availability of complex perceptual skills tend to be ignored or rejected by their more orthodox colleagues.

In much of the recent literature in developmental psychology, intrinsic pleasure has been attributed to an activity entailing initiative and given such labels as play, manipulation, exploration, and the expression of curiosity. Once the child's explorations of new sensations and objects are viewed as intrinsically gratifying, they can serve as bases for deriving many other types of initiative. It is obvious that other inherent dispositions will have to be postulated in order to explain how the child comes to respond to social pressures by such complex processes as judging, agreeing, rejecting, and striking out on his own.

PERCEPTION

Like other perceptual theories the psychoanalytic one begins with the assumption that, at birth, the child has no information about his world. He knows nothing about objects, not even about the existence of himself or his mother; he is uninformed about the effects of physical laws like gravity; he cannot act with reference to distance, or time, or conservation of volume. All this knowledge must be acquired. It is so voluminous that much of it is ordered in terms of complexity and learned in stages. The process is a lengthy one. At sixteen months, a child has not yet included some organs in his image of his body; a year later he thinks the moon is following him when he moves around; many more years must pass before his sense of time is fully developed. Even in adulthood he will be trying to improve his sensitivity to the ways others are feeling.

So close is the neonate's initial world to a tabula rasa that he does not know the difference between real events and imagined ones. The process entailed in his learning to tell them apart is used to explain the origins of individual differences in later reactions to conflict, particularly predilections for different defense mechanisms, conceptions of people, and ability to handle stress.

In all theories of perceptual development it is taken for granted that the child is born with a capacity for imagery; that experiences leave sensory traces which he can re-experience in the appropriate circumstances. In psychoanalytic theory the earliest experiences are depicted as intense ones that presumably leave deep traces. The infant is at the mercy of urgent frequent drives like hunger and pain, which are experienced vividly when redintegrated. In other words, once the infant has been hungry and then fed, he has memory traces of the feeding, which he pictures the next time he becomes hungry. Since he has no concept of reality, he cannot, at first, tell the difference between the "hallucinatory wish-fulfillment" that is a memory of being fed and the image of the actual event. The discrimination has to be learned.

The results vary depending on the conditions under which they are acquired. One of those conditions is the length of the interval between initial hunger pangs and the ingestion of milk. The delay can vary from the time required to prepare a bottle to very long periods for the neglected child. The hungry infant first cries. After a while, he stops and makes sucking movements like those he uses when he is nursing. It is assumed that the memory traces of previous feedings are activated at this time. If he is not fed he resumes his crying.

If the mother's timing is relatively consistent and the delays not long, she can be optimistic about her baby learning to discriminate between the two kinds of imagery without much difficulty. There are a number of reasons. First, images of the actual ingestion of food are usually more vivid than hallucinatory ones, which are, after all, only traces of the originals. Second, although recalled and actual feedings are pleasurable, the latter is assumed to be the more gratifying. Next, contiguity of the two types of imagery is assured by prompt feeding, which helps to highlight their differences. Fourth, hallucinated events are followed by hunger and further wish-fulfilling fantasies, while the real events are followed by a satiety that terminates the chain of hunger-associated images. Finally, if the feedings occur promptly, the ratio of realistic to hallucinated images is higher than if feedings are delayed and the child experiences a chain of experiences consisting of crying and recalled images. Promptness, then, insures maximal reinforcement of the realistic images.

If the mother neglects her baby or is inconsistent in her feedings, he remains hungry for relatively long periods, during which he cries and then yields to a fantasy of sucking. This is succeeded by further crying when the actual hunger pangs become more intense. The alternation of crying and fantasy presumably continues until he is finally fed. Assuming the description is correct, there are a number of reasons for predicting that this child will take a longer time to discriminate reality from fantasy than the one who is fed more promptly. The fantasy of sucking is followed by images of the real event less often, so he has less opportunity to compare their qualities. Since he is deprived of food for longer periods, his wish-fulfilling imagery probably becomes increasingly vivid with the intensification of the hunger pangs, and less easily differentiated from the real experience. Compared to the child who is fed promptly, the deprived one also obtains more experience with getting gratification from the numerous and intense wish-fulfilling fantasies, which provide some solace when he is overwhelmed by hunger. It may consequently be presumed that even when he learns to tell the two images apart, his discrimination will not be as good as that of the consistently fed child, and he will be more inclined to resort to wish-fulfilling fantasy as a means of reducing his discomfort.

These speculations illustrate a number of the basic psychoanalytic assumptions about perception. First, subjective experience is viewed as a basic key to behavior. In the explanation of the hungry child's series of disturbed and contented reactions, for example, it is assumed that he cannot tell reality from fantasy and that he is experiencing wish-fulfilling feedings. Second, principles of learning are used to explain how the actual and subjective experiences contribute to the creation of internal structures. It is presumed that the two regimens of feeding differ in their reinforcement of the wish-fulfilling imagery, and, ultimately, in their reinforcement of denial. Structures like defense are invoked to explain autonomous characteristics which cause two children to react differently to the same type of situation. In some instances, it is only by knowing how an event is experienced by a person that its meanings and effects on him can be interpreted by the observer. Given two mothers who gently urge their sons to wash their faces every morning and night, one son reacts warmly to the gentleness and conforms in a short time, while the other experiences the request as coercive pressure to repeat meaningless acts. His subsequent predilection for placating authorities by compulsive ritual mirrors his incorrect interpretation and insensitivity to her gentle methods and good intentions. Once subjective interpretation is taken into account in explaining behavior, the child can no longer be regarded solely as a product of external stimulation.

Like physical performance, perception is assumed to vary qualitatively as a function of sets of skills acquired in different stages. At first, events are experienced in terms of the concrete pleasant and unpleasant feelings resulting from specified actions with parts of objects, since it takes time to discriminate entire objects. According to the theory the infant experiences his mother in terms of those of her features which are most associated with satisfying his needs: her face, her breast, her hands. She next becomes a total physical being, but perceived as having what adults conceive as limitless powers. In time he becomes aware of her limitations, but is still inclined to idealize her. In further stages, he evades her influence, denigrates her, and finally makes a realistic assessment of what she is like.

He never forgets any of his different conceptions. Each stage lasts long enough to reinforce its style of perception in a large variety of contexts. Yet the qualitative differences between experiences characteristic of various stages make it impossible to integrate them as part of the same experience. The child cannot simultaneously conceive of his mother as a part-object and complete object, or as having both limitless and limited powers. As he matures, then, he learns to "split" (Klein, 1948) perceptual categories into sets, each corresponding to one of the stages. In later years he responds to any incident in terms of all the sets, and often in incompatible ways. If he is hurt, for example, an infantile part of him seeks solace, the part that is baby becomes enraged, the boy in him denies the pain, and the adult in him tries to understand the difficulty so he can do something practical about it. When the reactions are incompatible, the adult is sometimes able to act only if he has some means of selecting some and suppressing others. One of the commonest means of reducing the number of alternatives is to resort to a defense mechanism that creates unawareness of the alogical impulses that were acquired in the earliest stages of development.

Certain of the foregoing assumptions help to clarify some of the frequent misunderstandings of the theory of castration fear which sometimes lead to its being characterized as unreasonable or as being too improbable to merit study. What follows is an attempt to describe the premises and the thinking underlying the theory, and to show that it contains a number of testable hypotheses that are worth investigating. Whether or not they are supported by evidence is a separate matter.

On what basis does Freud postulate universal castration fears? The answer to this question can be traced to a group of premises. One is the sudden maturation of sexual sensitivity. Some time in the fourth or fifth year, boys reach a new stage of sexual maturity in which they reveal intense sexual excitement and a strong interest in the structure and functioning of the genitals of both sexes. It is at this time that children begin to stimulate their genitals, follow adults to the bathroom and bedroom, and play "doctor games."

According to another premise there is an inherent, usually latent, sexual component in all relationships. The relationships between parents and children are not exempt because they are kin or belong to different generations. On the contrary, the constant, intimate contact heightens the mutual sexual attraction. Because of the mother's long experience in denying her incestuous desires, she becomes disgusted when her son is sexually aroused. Since he has not yet been trained in the aversion of his desires, he is not inhibited about manifesting his excitement and exploring its causes.

The crucial assumptions about the origins of castration fear pertain to the meaning the boy gives to his mother's behavior. Since the events take place when he is nearing the end of the anal stage, he is presumably still struggling to control his aggressive impulses, which he projects to her. In other words, the closest thing in his experience to her manifestations of disapproval is the tempestuous rage that often overwhelms him. His discrimination of others' emotions still being very poor, he interprets her negative reactions as signs that she is feeling that way about him. His exaggeration of her hostility thus causes him to become excessively frightened, resistant, or angry when she tries to restrict his sexual activity.

The theory thus emphasizes the child's perceptions in explaining his behavior. His version of events is presumed to be "unrealistic," and representative of the view of the world typical at his stage of development. To the extent that the resultant conflict reinforces his projection the defense remains part of his repertory of perceptual responses.

Still further misinterpretations are assumed, which result from lack of experience with certain physical and social principles. According to the theory, the obvious discomfort suffered by adults when the boy masturbates convinces him that this activity is hurting them and that they are bound to retaliate. But why should he think they will hurt his genitals rather than some other organs? The answer presumes the validity of the talion principle, according to which the attacks on others by means of a particular organ lead to the expectation that they will retaliate by punishing the offending organ. To the child, such a punishment seems quite likely in the physical and social world as he knows it. At first he assumes that all bodies are like his—until he sees a little girl being bathed or diapered. Is it not reasonable for him to conclude that she was once like him, that the adults have altered her, and they can do it to him? His conception of their methods, as described in psychoanalytic theory, may seem farfetched to some readers unless they keep in mind how primitive a young child's conception of causality can be, and how strong is his inclination to project his aggression to his parents. To picture his idea of the alteration, one need only see the panic created in a little boy by the joking gesture of removing his nose and pretending that one's thumb is the amputated organ, or the relief that greets the magical reconnection of the nose. He obviously believes that an adult can remove and replace the organ at will.

The best method of summarizing the assumptions underlying the theory of castration fears is to list some of the most frequent criticisms. It is objected that the theory does not account adequately for the origins of what is depicted as a strong, lifelong fear. Few parents punish their children for sexual expression or even think of doing so, and almost no adults ever threaten their children with castration. Few children report fears of castration, and fewer adults remember having such fears. In short, the whole idea seems far-fetched to some people because it is so remote from children's actual experiences. Even if it were shown that they do develop such irrational impressions, this would still be ignored by some positivists, who, being peripheralists, treat the child as a black box and ignore his subjective experiences as they would other epiphenomena.

The answers have the common theme that the criticisms are based on misunderstandings of premises. It is conceded, for example, that few parents either punish their children for sexual expression or threaten castration. Contrary to the implications of this point, however, it is assumed in psychoanalytic theory that aversions can be reinforced by strong, even unconscious, parental emotional reactions, and do not necessarily require deliberate punishment. The mother's involuntary disgust can serve as a stronger deterrent than spanking. Next, the psychoanalyst is not surprised if people cannot report unpleasant feelings which are incompatible with their everyday conceptions of themselves. Though they are forgotten, he points out, they may still be manifested in action.

That the child thinks in nonlogical ways is easy to visualize, and has been corroborated in many studies. Psychoanalytic theory adds further assumptions about the kind of nonlogical thinking created by the child's projections and his conceptions of his parents' limitless powers.

It is the incompatibility of these misperceptions with the adult's logical ways of thinking that accounts for their gradually becoming unconscious and, possibly, for the common impression that they are improbable. Improbability is a prejudgment of an empirical issue. The history of science provides many instances of improbable sounding hypotheses that were prematurely dismissed, some even in the face of confirming evidence.

LEARNING

Many of the principles of psychoanalytic theory pertain to the learning of responses significant in genetic development. Sometimes the processes are specified; more often they are implied. Occasionally they are used to explain the origins of internal structures that create differential responses to social situations. In this section some of the principles of learning implicit in psychoanalytic theory are summarized in the current language of the experimental psychologist. Although alien to Freud's writing this terminology is more helpful than his more intuitively defined concepts in making explicit some of his underlying assumptions.

Reinforcement.   Starting with inherent tendencies to seek pleasure and to avoid pain, Freud postulates that both are attained by the reduction of tension. Specific acts and objects which reduce tension are reinforced by the resultant pleasure or reduction of discomfort, and become the goals of future efforts to reestablish equilibrium. As noted earlier, wishful images, the traces of tension-reducing events, can be reinforced like acts and later redintegrated.

At each stage the child learns a group of skills which are presumably necessary to, or components of, the more complex skills of the next stage. The contents of socialization are thus ordered in terms of increasing complexity. At any point in time, the parents are guided in their methods of instruction and standards of accomplishment by their conceptions of the maturational process and the acquisitions of previous stages. In the first period, the mother establishes a feeding regimen; the infant must learn to ingest food and to retain it. In subsequent periods, the parents educate the child to employ acceptable expressions of locomotion, exploration, aggression, and sexuality, and habits of cleanliness and elimination.

In explaining how stimuli become associated in a family, Freud invokes what would now be called primary reinforcement. According to current language, when an unconditioned stimulus, which has innate affective value, is paired with a conditioned stimulus, which is neutral, the latter gradually acquires the properties of the former to elicit affect. In other words, when the taste of milk, which is innately pleasurable, is paired with soothing maternal sounds, which initially have no meaning to the baby, the sounds soon make the baby feel good even in the absence of food. When paired with feeding, the views of the mother's face or of the bottle soon become new sources of gratification. Once the mother's voice produces contentment, it can serve, in turn, as a secondary reinforcer, which gives pleasure to other stimuli, such as the color of her hair. The pairing of a primary reinforcer, like feeding, with crying, strengthens the baby's tendency to cry as a means of avoiding hunger. Similarly, the pairing of a secondary reinforcer, like maternal expression of affection, with cuddling, reinforces the latter.

Freud would certainly have approved the concept of generalized reinforcer (Skinner, 1953), a special type of secondary reinforcement that is strongly motivating because it is frequently associated with a number of primary reinforcers. Maternal affection, for example, which is associated with feeding, protection from sources of anxiety, absence of physical punishment, and pleasant physical manipulation, is a goal which all infants strive to attain.

Why does one react so strongly by means that were reinforced mostly in childhood, and which, in many cases, might be expected to be extinguished over the years? A fundamental assumption, implied more often than stated, is that learning is permanent; that memory traces do not dissipate with disuse. "No experience in human development is ever cast aside or obliterated ..." (Segal, 1964). Traces of the earliest events have a special impact because they are learned when the infant is most modifiable, and serve as the foundation for skills learned in later stages. In other words, the child must differentiate real from unreal before he can acquire a body image, he needs a body image before he has a concept of internal and external events, he must differentiate between such events before he can distinguish between self and others, and so forth.

Traces of early events may appear to be forgotten for a number of reasons. Awareness may have been altered by one of the defense mechanisms or because of competition with stronger traces. Sometimes early events cannot be verbalized either because they were not originally labelled, their perception was originally blurred by anxiety, or they were experienced in terms of alogical categories that have no counterparts in the concepts used by adults (Schachtel, 1959).

In the language of learning, the child acquires three products from each stage. They are a family of stimuli pertinent to the adults' goals for the child, a family of responses, and a mediating set of internal structures of the type described in cognitive systems of learning. A family of stimuli is a group all of which can elicit the same response; the mother's voice, the white bottle, or being cuddled, can all elicit sucking. A family of responses is viewed here as a set of alternatives, like Hull's habit-forming hierarchy (1937), all leading to the same goal. Because of differential reinforcement, responses in a family are hierarchically ordered; when one is blocked, a substitute is very likely to be chosen from one of the most preferred alternatives and not likely to be chosen from one of the least preferred alternatives.

When one response in a family is reinforced, the others all tend to be evoked under the same conditions. During the anal stage, training in sphincter control can be described as reinforcing a family of responses sharing the common goal of expressing anger and containing such members as constipation, stubbornness, stinginess, and passive resistance. If the adults elicit the child's anger and stubborn resistance by a new requirement that he always be in bed at a particular time, he is likely to express any of the total family originally reinforced by toilet training in the new context.

The reinforcement of responses as members of the same family is not necessarily planned by adults, but is often a fortuitous result of the timing and context of a socialization practice. Overeating when passivity cannot be expressed, or being compulsively late when anger is blocked make no logical sense, except to the social scientist who observes that they are paired countless times under conditions that reinforce the connections. Similarly, though training in ritualistic and repetitive acts and in passive compliance are furthest from the minds of adults, they can reinforce such reactions by early, inflexible, and rigidly timed training in cleanliness or sphincter control. Because of the presence of many reinforcers, the child acquires far more than either he or his parents realize.

Conflict. Socialization in the different stages of development interests the psychoanalyst because of the light it throws on the resolution of inner conflict. His professional concern with symptoms leads him to concentrate on conflicts between impulses to approach and avoid the same object. The patient typically wants to engage in a morally proscribed act, but also wants to avoid it because of its undesirable consequences for the object or the anticipation of guilt. Most conflicts pertain to the control of impulses like sex and aggression, the expression of which is subject to complex social regulation. Symptoms are viewed as socially undesirable compromises, or derivatives of the forbidden impulse and the moral standard.

Arousal means increase in tension. Once aroused, a forbidden impulse must be expressed in some form. But it need not be direct. If the impulse is to hurt an adult, the child has available the many forms of expression that he learned in the different developmental stages. Among the possibilities are complaining to a sibling, having attacks of diarrhea, overeating, or going to sleep. A primary task of the theory is to explain the reasons why people with the same conflict develop different derivatives.

The selection is certainly influenced by the differential reinforcement of various alternatives, which determines their order in the hierarchy of preference. In accounts of individual predilections for various symptoms, great emphasis is placed on the conditions of learning, such as the timing, flexibility, and harshness of weaning or toilet training. It is assumed, for example, that when toilet training is too harsh, the child has difficulty in learning to control his sphincter muscles, that he is frustrated and often angry with the parents. His parents' discomfort when he loses sphincter control reinforces this response as a means of expressing aggression against them.

In the resolution of a conflict, the derivatives tend to be chosen from within the same family, and not at random from all possibilities. This is primarily because of the qualitative differences between the families learned in different stages. Within a stage all the responses require approximately the same degrees of effort and skill, and a child at that level of development can gratify himself by shifting from one response to another and still meet the adults' standards. A baby naturally changes from crying to eating to cuddling, all simple responses that provide him and his mother with satisfactions appropriate to their relationship. He is neither able, nor is he expected to act like older children, who take initiative or explore sexuality. Many of the reactions of different stages tend, in fact, to be incompatible; one cannot simultaneously be passive and independent, or rebellious and conforming.

The hierarchization of levels is explained partially on the basis of fixation. Because the skills of each level are built on the skills of earlier levels, difficulties at any stage of development interfere with learning at subsequent stages. The child usually traverses them without mishap, but he does not do as well as he might have if he had not had the original difficulties. He is said to be fixated at the level at which he can behave most adequately. When he is unable to resolve conflicts in a mature manner he regresses to that level. If it is one in which a clear body image is not yet developed, regression will be manifested in confusions of internal with external events and of self with other.

The extent of the regression is also affected by the degree of skill required to function at each level, the social desirability of the different levels, and the intensity of the conflict. As the child progresses from earlier to later psychosexual stages, he finds that the tasks are increasingly difficult to perform, but that the social rewards increase. A conflict is readily obliterated by a primitive response such as going to sleep, but the child's obliviousness of the conflict may create social difficulties. A more complex set of skills, like those used to work things out with an antagonist, requires the expenditure of much more effort, but ultimately earns greater social rewards.

In the psychoanalytic theory of conflict, the choices of alternative objects or acts within the families of a particular stage are explained in terms of what the learning theorist thinks of as generalization. In the case of stimulus generalization, a response that has been learned on presentation of a particular stimulus may also be evoked by other similar stimuli not used in the training. Freud (1924) uses this principle to explain how a phobia resulted when a boy transferred his conflict from his father to horses. Father and horse were similar in that both were large and strong and had light skins. Both also had dark areas around the mouth and eyes: the father had a beard and glasses and the horse had a black snout and blinders.

Displacement along such dimensions is obviously irrational, and is contingent on regression to stages when discriminations easily made by adults have not yet been learned by the child. Displacements can also take place along other dimensions which are organized in terms of similar meanings. A boy can displace fear of the father, for example, to fear of other authority figures. The kinds of meaning vary with the stage of development. As the child matures (Reiss, 1946), the bases of generalization shift from similar sounds to opposite meanings to synonyms. These stages parallel the neologisms, the hostile interpretations, and the rational thinking that are postulated in the different psychoanalytic stages.

Displacement of acts depends on response generalization, in which the stimulus that was originally paired with a particular response also evokes other, similar responses without training. According to psychoanalytic theory, training in the use of an organ generalizes; the same mode of behavior is transferred to other zones of the body, other objects, and even the use of concepts (Fenichel, 1945). Once reinforced, the retention of feces can generalize so that the child rebelliously retains food in his mouth when forced to eat. The retention may later be extended to financial activities, philately, and inexpressiveness.

AGE GRADING

Learning theory is designed to account for changes in the individual's behavior. It explains *how* new, enduring individual traits are acquired, not *what* is acquired. In the literature on social learning, the actual contents that are acquired—the skills, values, and information—are usually dismissed by the abstraction "responses." In contrast, systems for analyzing socialization are designed to account for the survival of the society, and to differentiate stages primarily in terms of their contents. Their organization is then related to the maturational process and the family's place in the community and society. Age grading is a procedure employed in all societies as a basis for organizing the process of socialization. A short outline of age grading reveals that psychoanalytic theory represents a special conception of socialization.

Every new generation must learn to perform at least the minimal roles necessary to perpetuate the basic norms and structure of the society. To attain this goal, and thus assure continuity despite births and deaths, the society devises procedures for socializing each new generation. It transmits the cultural heritage by creating in every person the potentials for taking all the roles he will have to assume during his lifetime. Age differences constitute a primary basis for allocating roles and defining standards of performance because the goals of socialization are so complex and the person's capacities differ with his stage of maturation. Every society, therefore, has its "recognized division of the life of the individual as he passes from infancy to old age" (Radcliffe-Brown, 1929). The division produces a sequence of age grades or spans, each defined in relation to the achievements of past grades and the anticipated activities of future ones.

In the early age grades the child must learn to perform a diffuse group of acts requiring skills that he will need in the later stages of development. Some examples are obeying adults, using self-control despite frustration, and regulating behavior in light of the group's norms. These are acquired as he participates in relationships, within which the roles are allocated on the basis of age. As he engages in some common endeavor with a parent or relative, he learns about the behavior required and the rights of a person not only in his age grade but also in that of an adult. Successful participation in reciprocal activities also reinforces sensitivity to the other person's motives, and enhances the ability to behave in a constructive, complementary manner. In time, the child internalizes the norms for different age grades, judges his adequacy in the light of those norms, and adjusts his behavior accordingly, even in the absence of observers. He also comes to expect others to treat him in a manner appropriate to a person of his age, sex, and position in society.

Psychoanalytic theory can be viewed as a special system of age grading, the primary object of which is to explain the origins of symptoms. To this end, the theory postulates a normal sequence of stages within each of which the child learns the skills he will later apply to the resolution of inner conflict. Deviations from the experiences typical of normal development in each stage are used to explain potentials for various disorders.

The socialization of sex and aggression is described in detail for all stages because these needs are frequent components of the stable, insoluble conflicts that are accompanied by continuing anxiety and pathology. The development of perception is emphasized because it is a basic ingredient in the analysis of defense mechanisms, which are primary determinants of symptom formation. In common with other systems of age grading, psychoanalytic theory also describes the learning of physical, cognitive, and social skills that have most consequence for people's relationships with one another.

Cross-cultural differences in socialization and age grading. The appraisal of psychoanalytic theory requires separate consideration of three features: the postulated universality of stages; the connections between parents' techniques and children's personalities; the theory's fruitfulness in raising issues critical to socialization. The fact that Freud's experience was largely limited to patients from the middle and upper class in central Europe makes it seem improbable that he developed universal principles that are relevant to socialization of people without symptoms, of the working classes in central Europe, or of the citizens of western European or American countries, not to mention members of societies with polygynous or matrilineal structures. It also seems unlikely, in view of the myriad practices both within and between societies, that some universal issues arise at roughly the same stage of maturation in all societies and require similar kinds of socialization. Such probabilistic arguments are frequently raised in criticisms of the theory. Their appeal is easily conveyed by some illustrations of the many differences in prescribed and proscribed activities, agents of socialization, differentiation of norms by sex and age, sanctions and rewards, timing and duration of training, and sequence of number or age grades.

Within American society, norms about the expression of aggression in the middle and working class differ for the same sex and age; timing and harshness of weaning also differ in the two social classes; there are fewer age grades in rural than in urban areas; discipline is harsher for children in Catholic families than for children in Protestant families; many methods of socialization are initiated earlier and are accompanied by clearer sanctions when the fathers work in entrepreneurial rather than bureaucratic organizations. The still greater variations in methods and agents of socialization used in different societies are associated with additional variables such as those pertaining to kinship, geography, and economics. The same skill may be taught by a father in one society, a maternal uncle in a second, and members of the extended family in a third, depending on the responsibilities of kin; duration of breast feeding, and its associated physical intimacy with the mother, tends to be longest where there is a dearth of protein in the diet; standards for expressing aggression differ, depending on whether the society is peaceful or warlike, nomadic or agricultural. In general, the more complex the society, the longer is the period of training, the more numerous, differentiated, and changing are the age grades, and the greater is the probability of discontinuity (Benedict, 1938) from one grade to another.

Despite the unpromising sample from which psychoanalytic theory was derived, a strong case can be made for the probable universality of some of the proposed stages. Though the issues of socialization treated in the theory are far from exhaustive, some of them seem the inevitable lot of the family in every society. The oral stage is initiated by a universal need: the neonate is too helpless to obtain food for himself. He cannot even ingest it properly. Feeding is, therefore, essential to his survival, a fact that gives it far greater urgency than other parental responsibilities such as keeping the child clean or warm. In every society, then, his feeding must be a central feature of his relationship with his mother in the initial grade. Studies of the traits he acquires in that relationship, such as passivity and the experiencing of his world in oral terms, reveal that they generalize and are related to behavior in later years (Blum & Miller, 1952; Child, 1954; Whiting & Child, 1953).

There are equally convincing reasons for assuming that the phallic period depicts another universal stage in socialization. Survival of society, however, not of the child, is the reason why each new generation must learn an aversion to incestuous relationships. Freud outlines the process for one group in his account of the Oedipus complex. He may not have taken into account all the possible variations of acts and objects that are defined as incestuous in certain underdeveloped countries, but his estimate of the significance of the issue for socialization is now buttressed by evidence that training in the incest taboo is found in all human societies and even in some of the higher orders of mammals and birds (Aberle et al., 1963).

Though most specialists are convinced that the incest taboo is a necessary condition for the survival of family and community, they are in disagreement about the ways in which it insures the society's continuity across the genera-tions. They take it for granted that training is necessary because of the inherent desire by members of the opposite sex to engage in sexual relationships regard-less of age or kinship. Some specialists also stress that unlimited sexual expres-sion, particularly before adolescence, would interfere with many kinds of social endeavor, particularly educational activities in the family. Hence society must restrict the expression of the drive in general, particularly with incestuous ob-jects. According to the more popular theories, the incest taboo guarantees the community's survival by guaranteeing exogamous mating, by minimizing the probability of lethal genes, and helping parents to retain the power necessary to educate the young (Aberle et al., 1963).

Even if the incest taboo is universal, this does not validate a second as-sumption of psychoanalytic theory, that the sexual drive reaches a peak of in-tensity at a particular stage of maturation. The assumption is supported by some evidence, but there is not much of it. If the sexual drive does mature at a particular stage, its regulation probably becomes a matter of focal concern in the relationships between parents and offspring in the age grade that starts at that time. If development is more irregular, the socialization of sexual expres-sion can become part of a number of stages, depending on when the drive is manifested and when the parents take cognizance of it.

The survival of neither the child nor the society is entailed in the sociali-zation of the anal sphincter. Although hygienic considerations make the train-ing a universal necessity, it lacks the urgency of the socialization of gastro-intestinal and of genital functions. Hence the task can be initiated at any time and its prominence in familial relationships can vary considerably. No evidence has been produced in support of the claim that anal sensitivity matures at a particular stage of development. In fact, the considerable variations in timing and method of training in various societies convey the impression that the child's anal maturation has much less bearing on the adults' methods than their ability or willingness to tolerate dirt. Unlike oral and genital functions, then, the anal one is probably not the focus of relationships at the same stage of de-velopment in every social group, and the socialization is probably not associated with the learning of the same family of skills in different societies.

According to the conception of the anal stage, the traits of obstinacy, or-derliness, and parsimony are significantly related to one another and to the parents' style of toilet training. Tests of the anticipated associations between traits reveal that they vary with the group's sex, generation, and culture (Barnes, 1952; Hetherington & Brackbill, 1963; Rapaport, 1955). However, neither timing, severity, nor style of toilet training are significantly associated with the configuration of "anal" traits (Bernstein, 1955; Beloff, 1957; Erikson,

1945). The theory of anality obviously needs to be modified. Freud probably overgeneralized the conclusions he derived from a special group for whom training in sphincter control initiated a hostile struggle for dominance between parent and child. Data from other groups make it apparent that aggression is the primary issue of socialization, that resistance of attempts to control defecation is a possible, but not necessary, instrument the child can employ in his battle with his parents.

To carry out its functions every society must inculcate in its members the desire to express aggression within the limits set by a group. When the child becomes mature enough to endanger others or himself by such acts as biting his mother, striking siblings, or entering dangerous settings, the adults must teach him the norms governing the expression of initiative and aggression. The teaching is a lengthy process because he is reluctant to relinquish his pleasure in novel or destructive activities. Anal socialization can become one subject of contention if it is begun very early, when the child cannot yet sit up and he cannot understand the reasons for the training. Under such conditions, the scheduling and necessary restrictions of physical movement can elicit considerable anxiety and hostility. In most societies, toilet training occurs later, when the child understands the reasons and is able to comply easily with his parents' requests.

Even when training is late, however, stubbornness and orderliness can still be reinforced by struggles over activities like washing and going to bed on time. The latter are not inherently "anal," even though they can be members, along with anal retention or expulsion, of a family of responses that is reinforced by the socialization of aggression. In American groups, children's so-called anal traits are not significantly associated with toilet training, but are significantly similar to the same traits in the parents (Beloff, 1957; Hetherington & Brackbill, 1963). This suggests that the child can become stubborn or orderly or stingy primarily because he identifies with his parents as disciplinarians, not necessarily because his methods of resisting their anal training are reinforced by his pleasure in fighting with them.

Generalizing from the foregoing, one can postulate that the more the survival of the society or the individual depends on the child's acquiring certain skills, and the more narrow the time span in which the skills must be learned, the greater is the likelihood that the socialization will reinforce universal families of stimuli and responses. Conversely, the less contingent the survival of the society or individual is on the inculcation of particular skills, or the broader the time span in which the necessary skills can be acquired, the less the commonality in the families of stimuli and responses. In the extreme case of pleasure in physical destruction, which threatens both the community and the child, and which arises in a narrow span of time because of physical maturation, considerable overlap can be expected universally in the activities of socializing adults, and, consequently, in the families of stimuli and responses. In the case of defecation, the child obviously needs some training, but since the function threatens the integrity of neither the society nor himself and can be modified within a broad span of time, the socialization can be accomplished by many agents and methods, and with children varying so much in maturity that little, if any, overlap need be expected in the families of stimuli and of responses learned in different social groups.

When anal training begins very early, the baby's reactions to the incomprehensible, unwelcome restriction can be reinforced in association with oral responses. Passivity, emphasis on oral pleasures, and omnipotence, which are typical of this age grade in every society, may be then integrated in a family that also includes such anal traits as ritualistic style, diarrhea, and unquestioned obedience. If the training is too early and too burdensome, an inclination, when under stress, to retreat into fantasy may also be reinforced as a member of the family. At a given age grade, then, different societies can reinforce identical or overlapping families of response, or may reinforce only a common response, such as control of the anal sphincter.

RELATIONSHIPS AND IDENTITY

The current formulation of psychoanalytic theory represents only a beginning, and it is tempting to speculate on directions in which it can be extended. One of the obvious gaps in the current theory stems from its concentration on the first years of life, on the apparent assumption that they hold the keys to all that occurs later. This emphasis can be traced to Freud's great success in explaining pathology by relating symptoms to the early socialization of physical functions. Like the British philosophical empiricists, whom he knew well, Freud was impressed by the extent to which experience is defined by the observer's characteristics, particularly his physical senses and bodily structure, and attempted to concentrate the developmental theory to their socialization. Though the resultant system paid rich dividends, it lacks some of the parameters needed to explain socialization in the later age grades, when the person can think abstractly and symbolically. This deficiency is remedied in the models proposed by Bion (1963) for analyzing the development of cognition, and by Erikson (1950, 1959) for analyzing the development of social behavior. Bion specifically describes the emergence of logical thinking and creativity, and Erikson is concerned with abstract reactions such as trust.

The task of describing the later age grades highlights another difficulty in the current theory, the fact that it is concentrated on intrapersonal issues. Often overlooked, even in sociological writings, is the fact that both partners in a relationship have to be socialized to live with one another. Not only must the three-year-old learn to control his aggression more than he did in the previous age grade; his mother must also learn to act differently than she did when he was more passive and dependent. Difficulties in the age grade can be caused by problems of either partner in the relationship or by their inability to develop a working pattern of interaction with one another.

An appreciation of the import of interpersonal patterns for socialization is revealed in much of the clinical literature, particularly in the description of the

Oedipal period. What is lacking is a standard terminology that takes the reciprocality of relationships into account. Increased interest in such terminology, and in interpersonal principles, has been spurred recently by the clinical evidence that many symptoms help to maintain the stability of familial relationships. Often the official patient is less disturbed than another family member, whose pathology flares up when the patient begins to improve. Hence, any change in the status quo is resisted by the total family. In explaining such phenomena most investigators begin with a picture of the family as a miniature social system in which responsibilities are allocated in terms of age and sex, and behavior judged in the light of common values.

Many examples of familial patterns are reported in the literature. Relationships after childbirth have been described (Benedek, 1938) as an exchange of resources in which the mother, who is recovering from the physical changes of the birth process, can be sufficiently nurturant to the ever-demanding infant only if the husband is sufficiently supporting in his contacts with her. Some pathological relationships are described which stem from the deprivations for mother and child created by the father's attempts to mother the infant instead of supporting his wife. In some accounts of schizophrenia (Bateson et al., 1956), the symptoms are analyzed in terms of inconsistent messages to approach and to retreat, which are given to a person who can neither escape from the situation nor comment on the inconsistencies. The conflicting messages are used by their sender as a means of maintaining power. Still another explanation of pathology (Miller & Westman, 1966) links it to the development of an identity which, by its compatibility with those of the other family members, enables them to obtain a mutually acceptable expression of illegitimate impulses. Still other viewpoints have been recently summarized by Bell and Vogel (1960) and by Handel (1967). Some of the systems that have been proposed for classifying different aspects of relationships are summarized by Miller (1963).

Despite their differences in theory, most investigators tend to think of relationships as interactions between selves, and communications about them. Common to the sociological term "looking glass self" (Cooley, 1902) and the psychoanalytic term "projective identification" (Klein, 1948; Segal, 1964) are the assumptions that we are all inclined to see ourselves as we are seen by others and that we see others by projecting ourselves. Such formulations are founded on the faith that behavior is determined largely by conceptions of the identities of objects, particularly of people. Conceptions of objects and their interrelationships constitute the internal society. Organized around the identity of self, the internal society provides a frame of reference for understanding and judging the meaning of interpersonal events. According to Klein (1948), it is by projecting parts of his internal society to others and then putting himself in their places that each person is able to picture how they are reacting.

Socialization can be viewed as a process in which identities of self and others are developed in the various age grades. The concept of identity connotes, for example, that every male learns not to be a boy in general but rather the boy who is the son of his particular father and mother and the brother of his sister.

In the normal family, he has learned to participate in relationships which permit the attainment of the family's goals in a manner that satisfies the needs of its members. All relationships obviously vary with the structure of the family, which is affected, in turn, by its position in the community and society.

At each stage of development the self is identified in accordance with the meanings and values of some group, such as the family or peers or teachers. At first the group is important because it can enforce conformity to its standards by punishments and rewards. Later it is incorporated as part of one's internal society, at which time conformity depends on internal pressures of shame and guilt in addition to the fear of discovery. Level of self-esteem fluctuates with the discrepancies between behavior and the norms of one's external and internal groups.

During each stage, then, every person derives conceptions of his group, the rules governing behavior, and the identities of self and others. He also acquires the skills that enable him to work productively in complementary relationships with others in his group.

The conception of self has the advantage of formulating motives and values in the terms in which they are experienced. The concept also helps the researcher to integrate the enduring dispositions of individuals with the properties of relationships, and to view both in terms of the societal context in which they are taking place. The self thus provides a bridge between psychological and social phenomena.

ON OBJECTIVITY AND THE EVALUATION OF PSYCHOANALYTIC THEORY

There are some special characteristics of psychoanalytic theory which lead to frequent misunderstandings, even of principles that are accepted without criticism when they are included as parts of other systems. Modern readers often have difficulties with the type of discourse, which reflects a mid-European, clinical tradition. The style of some of the writing is best understood when viewed in the context of a time when both the romantic philosophers and Darwin had great status. Although empirical work was respected, there was much less concern than at present with the rigorous definition of terms, objective measurement, or the creation of tight, miniature systems. As practicing clinicians, psychoanalysts still follow the medical practice of reporting the intensive observation of small numbers of cases. Principles are espoused by leaders of schools, from some of which members are expelled for theoretical deviations. Since the public's acceptance of theories affects their exponents' financial welfare and their ability to recruit trainees, disagreements between schools develop political overtones that interfere with the objective assessment of evidence. Such characteristics give dated or unscientific airs to some of the psychoanalytic writing. Though they sometimes lead to misunderstandings, they are not relevant to the validity of the theory.

Probably the greatest source of misunderstanding is the relativistic psychoanalytic position, one with which a Kant or a Heisenberg would readily sympathize, which postulates that the average person, who has been socialized in the perceptual styles of his culture, is thereby handicapped in his understanding of the socialization of those very styles. In particular, according to the assumption, his training in the distortion or obliteration of certain impulses interferes with his understanding of the ways in which children learn to express those impulses. Without the special experience of being a patient in psychoanalysis, runs the argument, he cannot expect to understand certain aspects of the theory. Such a claim often frustrates even the friendly reader, who thinks he can follow the writings of psychoanalysts, not to mention the skeptical one who can pick many examples of principles which require no special training to understand.

Very confusing to the layman are the emotional attacks on the theory made by some self-styled scientists, and some of the equally emotional rejoinders by psychoanalysts. Psychoanalytic writing has become a special target for the neo-positivist (Farmer, 1967), who believes that the methods of classical mechanics are needed to provide theoretical order in the social sciences. In line with this bias, the positivist often uses quantification as an end in itself, performs mathematical analyses on miniature theoretical systems which are presumably derived from observation, and favors a social determinism based on the behavioristic reduction of man to S-R mechanisms. Often he is justifiably critical of reification by some psychoanalysts of concepts like "identification" and "ego." He is also on strong ground when he points to the ignorance some psychoanalysts display about findings relevant to their theory that are reported in the journals of other professions, and when he objects to pronouncements about a variety of subjects based solely on extrapolations of psychoanalytic theory.

The positivist is naively identifying his faith in a particular philosophy of science with universal truth when he takes the psychoanalysts to task because they do not measure unconscious reactions directly or because their methods are not quantified. Personal vindictiveness rather than parochialism appears to motivate his virulent criticism of principles he has misinterpreted and whose meaning he has not taken the trouble to check (Hook, 1960), or his comparisons of the theory to the "demonology of the dark ages" (Bandura & Walters, 1963). Such accusations seem to focus on the publications of some psychoanalysts, whose predilection for needless jargon and jejune writing is a far cry from the crystalline clarity and profundity of Freud's papers. The biased critic is, unfortunately, all too ready to judge a total system by the inferior product of some of its supporters.

Hostile rejoinders are not surprising when a small group of innovators is strongly criticized by those in power. Freud was not hesitant to make scathing references to ". . . so-called scientific opponents . . . whose sole claim to be heard rests on their impartiality—which they have preserved by keeping from the facts" (Freud, 1949, p. 180). Psychoanalysts are being ". . . put in the pillory and exposed to the ill-treatment of the mob," he complained, "as though they have offended a political opponent in the Middle Ages" (Freud, 1949, p. 177). Once both sides become vindictive, their positions become increasingly extreme, and the route is open to increased mutual misunderstandings. Despite this problem, the continuing production of imaginative studies, both experimental and clinical, reveals that the system of psychoanalytic developmental principles is viable in that investigators in many disciplines are intrigued by its contents and are finding these principles amenable to empirical testing.

REFERENCES

ABERLE, D. F., ET AL. The incest taboo and the mating pattern of animals. *American Anthropologist,* 1963, 65, 253–265.

BARNES, C. A. A statistical study of Freudian theory of levels of psychosexual development. *Genetic Psychology Monographs,* 1952, 45, 105–175.

BANDURA, A., & WALTERS, R. H. *Social learning and personality development.* New York: Holt, Rinehart & Winston, 1963.

BATESON, G., JACKSON, D., HALEY, J., & WEAKLAND, J. Toward a theory of schizophrenia. *Behavioral Science,* 1956, 1, 251–264.

BELL, N. W., & VOGEL, E. F. (Eds.) *A modern introduction to the family.* New York: Free Press, 1960.

BELOFF, H. The structure and origin of anal character. *Genetic Psychology Monographs,* 1957, 55, 141–172.

BENEDEK, T. Adaptation to reality in early infancy. *Psychoanalytic Quarterly,* 1938, 7, 200–215.

BENEDICT, R. Continuities and discontinuities in cultural conditioning. *Psychiatry,* 1938, 1, 161–167.

BERNFELD, S. *The psychology of the infant.* New York: Brentano's, 1929.

BERNSTEIN, A. Some relations between techniques of feeding and training during infancy and certain behavior in childhood. *Genetic Psychology Monographs,* 1955, 51, 3–44.

BION, W. *Elements of psychoanalysis.* London: Heineman, 1963.

BLUM, G. S., & MILLER, D. R. Exploring the psychoanalytic theory of the oral character. *Journal of Personality,* 1952, 31, 278–304.

CHILD, I. L. Socialization. In G. Lindzey (Ed.), *Handbook of social psychology.* Vol. 2. Cambridge, Mass.: Addison-Wesley, 1954. Pp. 655–692.

COOLEY, C. H. *Human nature and the social order.* New York: Scribners, 1902.

ERIKSON, E. H. Childhood and tradition in two American Indian tribes. *Psychoanalytic Study of the Child,* 1945, 1, 319–350.

ERIKSON, E. H. *Childhood and society.* New York: Norton, 1950.

ERIKSON, E. H. Identity and the life cycle. In *Psychological issues.* Vol. 1. New York: International Universities Press, 1959.

FARMER, M. The positivist movement and the development of English sociology. *Sociological Review,* 1967, 15, 5–20.

FENICHEL, O. *The psychoanalytic theory of neurosis.* New York: Norton, 1945.

FERENCZI, S. Stages in the development of a sense of reality. In *Sex in psychoanalysis.* New York: Brunner, 1950.

FREUD, S. Analysis of a phobia in a five-year-old boy. *Collected papers.* Vol. 3. London: Hogarth, 1924. Pp. 149–295.

FREUD, S. *New introductory lectures on psychoanalysis.* London: Hogarth, 1949.

HANDEL, G. (Ed.) *The psychosocial interior of the family.* Chicago: Aldine, 1967.

HETHERINGTON, E. M., & BRACKBILL, Y. Etiology and covariation of obstinacy, orderliness, and parsimony in young children. *Child Development,* 1963, 34, 919–943.

HOOK, S. (Ed.) *Psychoanalysis, scientific method, and philosophy.* London: Evergreen, 1960.

HULL, C. L. Mind, mechanism and adaptive behavior. *Psychological Review,* 1937, 44, 1–32.

KLEIN, M. *Contributions to psychoanalysis.* London: Hogarth, 1948.

MILLER, D. R. The study of social relationships. In S. Koch (Ed.), *Psychology: A study of a science.* Vol. 5. New York: McGraw-Hill, 1963. Pp. 639–737.

MILLER, D. R., & WESTMAN, J. C. Family teamwork and psychotherapy. *Family Process,* 1966, 5, 49–59.

MUNROE, R. *Schools of psychoanalytic thought.* New York: Dryden Press, 1955.

RADCLIFFE-BROWN, A. R. Age organization terminology. *Man,* 1929, No. 13.

RAPAPORT, G. M. A study of the psychoanalytic theory of the anal character. Unpublished doctoral dissertation, Northwestern Univer., 1955.

REISS, B. F. Genetic changes in semantic conditioning. *Journal of Experimental Psychology,* 1946, 36, 143–152.

SCHACHTEL, E. G. *Metamorphosis.* New York: Basic Books, 1959.

SEGAL, H. *Introduction to the work of Melanie Klein.* London: Heineman, 1964.

SKINNER, B. F. *Science and human behavior.* New York: Macmillan, 1953.

SPITZ, R. Hospitalism. In *The psychoanalytic study of the child.* Vol. 1. New York: International Universities Press, 1945. Pp. 53–74.

WHITE, R. Ego and reality in psychoanalytic theory. *Psychological issues.* Vol. 3. New York: International Universities Press, 1963.

WHITING, J. W. M., & CHILD, I. L. *Child training and personality.* New Haven: Yale Univer. Press, 1953.

CHAPTER **8**

Culture, Personality, And Socialization: An Evolutionary View

Robert A. LeVine

University of Chicago

In the behavioral sciences as well as biology, the Darwinian model remains our most plausible means of conceptualizing the interaction between organisms and environments. Much of the theorizing relevant to culture and personality has been based on the assumption that individual behavior is adaptive with respect to the social and physical environments of the individual, and that socialization of the child is pre-adaptation of growing individuals to their future environments by incorporating into their early learning the fruits of experience of earlier generations of adapting adults. In one form or another, this view is taken as axiomatic by psychologically minded anthropologists and sociologists and socially minded psychologists and psychoanalysts. It was as characteristic of theoretical statements of forty years ago as it is today. For example, W. I. Thomas, one of the originators of the culture and personality field, asserted, "The human personality is both a continually producing factor and a continually produced result of social evolution," (Thomas & Znaniecki, 1927, Vol. II: 1831) and went on to state:

The whole process of development of the personality ... includes the following parallel and interdependent process:

(1) Determination of the character on the ground of the temperament;

(2) Constitution of a life-organization which permits a more or less complete objective expression of the various attitudes included in the character;

(3) Adaptation of the character to social demands put upon the personality;

(4) Adaptation of individual life-organization to social organization (Thomas & Znaniecki, 1927, Vol. II: 1863).

From the viewpoint of research priorities and strategy, the assumption of personality-culture adaptation implies that there is great value in studying comparatively the environmental characteristics of social and cultural systems in relation to distributions of individual behavioral dispositions within populations, as in what Inkeles (1959) calls correlations between a state (i.e., a global or integrative characteristic of an environmental system) and a rate (i.e., an index of behavior aggregating individual responses for a population). Although, as Inkeles (1963) points out, Durkheim's (1951) classic study of suicide, first published in 1895, was such an investigation, the field of culture and personality is still far from having a comprehensive body of generalizations validated by research and systematically related by theory.

The future of culture and personality study as a science of Darwinian ancestry may be foreseen by examining some of its more prodigious cousins in the comparative fields of human biology, e.g., population genetics, human ecology and demography, and epidemiology.[1] In those fields, sufficient consensus has been achieved concerning the measurement of relevant individual characteristics, the means by which they are transmitted, and the definition of population units, that investigators have been able to generate substantial bodies of accepted generalizations, and mathematical formulations concerning the complex interaction of variables and the dynamics of stability and change. In culture and personality we have to solve a myriad of methodological problems before making this kind of progress, but it could be useful at this stage to attempt a more detailed application of the Darwinian model to our own subject matter. Campbell (1966) has outlined the general conditions for such applications:

> The most exciting current contribution of Darwin is in his model for the achievement of purposive or ends-guided processes through a mechanism involving blind, stupid, unforesightful elements. In recent years, the cyberneticist Ashby (1952), Pringle (1951), and others have pointed out anew the formal parallel between natural selection in organic evolution and trial-and-error learning. The common analogy has also been recognized in many other loci, as in embryonic growth, wound healing, crystal formation, development of science, radar, echo-location, vision, creative thinking, etc. . . . The three essentials are these:
>
> 1. The occurrence of variations: heterogeneous, haphazard, "blind," "chance," "random," but in any event variable. (The mutation process in organic evolution, and exploratory responses in learning.)
>
> 2. Consistent selection criteria: selective elimination, selective propagation, selective retention, of certain types of variations. (Differential survival of certain mutants in organic evolution, differential reinforcement of certain responses in learning.)
>
> 3. A mechanism for the preservation, duplication, or propagation of the positively selected variants (the rigid duplication process of the chromosome-gene system in plants and animals, memory in learning).

---

[1] See Alland (1967) for an application of the Darwinian model to culture as studied by anthropologists.

Given these conditions, an evolution in the direction of better fit to the selective system becomes inevitable (Campbell, 1966, pp. 26–27).

The primary purpose of this chapter is to attempt a preliminary application of this model to the interaction of culture and personality, with special reference to the process of socialization. It is necessary first of all to review the concepts of socialization extant in the behavioral sciences.

CONCEPTS OF SOCIALIZATION

Three different views of the process of socialization, corresponding roughly to the disciplinary orientations of cultural anthropology, personality psychology, and sociology, have dominated behavioral science theory and research. Socialization has been seen as enculturation or the intergenerational transmission of culture, as the acquisition of impulse control, and as role-training or training for social participation. Each view has taken a simple form in which a single set of factors has been emphasized to the exclusion of others, often with a naive assumption that its operation was self-evident, and one or more complex forms in which account was taken of interacting and limiting factors with a greater attempt to spell out the mechanisms involved.

1. Socialization as enculturation.   From the viewpoint of anthropologists who regard themselves as cultural relativists and cultural determinists (particularly of the configurational school), a basic problem of human life is the preservation and continuity of distinctive patterns of culture, their transmission from generation to generation. Some of them have preferred the term enculturation to socialization because it explicitly brings to mind the notion of acquiring, incorporating, or internalizing culture. Indeed, in the simpler form of this view, enculturation is seen as an automatic process of absorption, in which the child as tabula rasa acquires culture simply by exposure to it over time. Since his entire environment is culturally determined, and since the innate equipment of children everywhere is the same and is favorable to the acquisition of culture patterns, children absorb culture in every aspect of their experience. This pervasive absorptive process may be studied in many areas of cultural life, but it is conceived of holistically and can be presumed to take place, at least in an intact and stable culture. Apart from "enculturation," which never gained a universal currency, the process has been termed education, cultural transmission, and cultural conditioning, although the last, as Hallowell (1954) has pointed out, was not used in the technical sense of behavioristic learning theory. In its earlier conceptualization by anthropologists of the Boas school including Benedict (1938), no particular learning mechanisms were regarded as specific to the process of cultural acquisition, since the child was seen as internalizing culture through instruction, observation and imitation, reward and punishment only as parts of his exposure to the total culture and its patterns.

The more complex forms of this viewpoint involve some attempt to conceptualize the mechanisms involved. Mead (e.g., 1964) and her co-workers have looked at enculturation in the terms of communication and information theory. Child-rearing is seen as a process of communicating culture, encoded as messages implicitly and explicitly in behavior, to the child. In this translation of the configurational view into the language of a more precise theoretical system, essential aspects of the earlier formulation have been retained: its conception of the child as a passive receiver of culture; its holism, i.e., the assumption that a stable culture provides mutually consistent content in the apparently diverse environment of messages to which children are normally exposed; and the insistence that specific cause-effect relations cannot be meaningfully isolated from the overall mutually reinforcing patterns of communicative events.

A considerably more complex view of the enculturative process can be found in works by students of cognitive development such as Bruner, Olver, Greenfield et al., (1966) and Kohlberg (1966). In this view, it is acknowledged that children acquire cultural beliefs and categories of thought, but within the limits set by sequences of cognitive development common to all humans. The study of enculturation becomes the study of interaction between cultural beliefs transmitted to the child through teaching and social experience, on the one hand, and universal stages of cognitive development, on the other.

2. Socialization as the acquisition of impulse control. Psychologists and psychoanalysts of the drive-theory persuasion conceive of humans as born with drives that are potentially disruptive to social life, and see the problem of socialization in terms of taming disruptive impulses and channeling them into socially useful forms. The broadest and perhaps earliest concept of socialization is that in which the socialized individual, whose impulse life is harnessed, regulated, and controlled in accordance with the fundamental requirements for social order, is contrasted with the unsocialized child, whose selfish pursuit of drive satisfaction could bring harm to others and to the fabric of society unless checked and channeled by those who raise him. Feral children allegedly raised apart from human contact are offered as examples of the unsocialized individual in physical maturity, a non-social human.

The simple form of this concept of socialization is presented by Freud in *Civilization and Its Discontents* (1930). There the conflict between the biological drives of individuals and the requisites of social organization[2] is stated in its most emphatic form. According to Freud, social organization requires that the sexual drive be sublimated into aim-inhibited forms allowing group formation and fellow-feeling without possessiveness, and that the aggressive drive, being such a threat to social order, be turned inward in the form of an aggressively self-policing superego. The cost of harnessing the sexual drive is the repression of incestuous wishes, a major source of neurotic symptoms, and the cost of re-

---

[2] Although the German *kultur* has been translated "civilization," it is clear throughout that by this term Freud is referring to what contemporary social scientists call "social organization." Hence, I use the latter term.

pressing aggression is the neurotic sense of guilt. Social organization thus exists, benefits, and advances through attenuating one drive and reversing the other, causing immense suffering to many individuals. The details of the socialization process are spelled out in Freud's other works. He sees few genuine compatibilities between society and the individual, and hardly any ways in which social and cultural life serve the individual's needs rather than the reverse. The one-sided character of his view makes it simpler than later concepts derived from the drive-theory position.

Among the more complex views of socialization as the acquisition of impulse control is the ego-psychology position developed within the mainstream of psychoanalytic thought by Hartmann (1958) and others. In this position, as opposed to Freud's, there is room for neutralized drive energy, which can be discharged in forms not disruptive to the social organization, and a conflict-free sphere and secondary autonomy in the ego, in which the forces of biology and society are not pitted against one another. Socialization of the child is seen as including the development of adaptive capacities that will serve himself as well as the social organization.

The psychoanalytic behaviorism of Miller and Dollard (1941) and Whiting and Child (1953) is the complex version of this basic orientation that has had the greatest influence on socialization research. In this view, the child's primary (innate) drives form the basis for his later social adjustment by acting as reinforcers for socially valued habits and for secondary (acquired) drives that reinforce the acquisition of a wide variety of positive social behavior patterns, including the internalization of models for appropriate behavior in social roles. The emphasis is on the effects of drive-reduction as social reinforcement, and on a simultaneous gain for the individual and the organization of social life. While harnessing the potentially disruptive impulses of the child is seen as a primary goal of the socialization process, it is not regarded as its only goal; and while Freudian concepts such as displacement and the sense of guilt are retained, they are interpreted in terms of their positive functions for social order. Whiting and Child's discussion (1953, pp. 218–262) of the origins of guilt, stressing the part that guilt plays in social control rather than the suffering it causes the individual, is a particularly good illustration of this departure from the Freud of *Civilization and Its Discontents*. Even so, the acquisition of socially functional impulse control is viewed as leaving the individual with anxious preoccupations that find cultural expression in magic, religion, and other forms of collective fantasy and ritual.

3. Socialization as role training.   The third major concept of socialization is that of training the child for participation in society, a participation that is seen as occurring on terms set "by society" rather than on the individual's own terms. The emphasis is on the social purpose of socialization, a process conceived of as designed to achieve the conformity of individuals to social norms and rules. Although there is some resemblance to the Freudian formulation, this sociological view differs in stressing positive social prescriptions rather than proscriptions or prohibitions, and in seeing no necessary conflict between conformity and individual satisfaction.

In the simpler form of this conceptualization, it is taken for granted that the purpose of child training is social conformity, that the content of the training is dictated by social norms, and that conformity is so routinely and automatically achieved for the majority of individuals that the process producing it is hardly worth studying. If one knows the norms and sanctions of the social structure, according to this Durkheimian view, one can predict the aggregate social behavior of individuals without attention to the details of learning and other modes of acquisition. Adequate socialization is a given of the normal operation of a social system; where it does *not* occur, i.e., in deviant behavior, it is necessary to raise questions of how and why, but not otherwise.

In role theory terms, social structure consists of institutionalized roles antedating any particular generation of individuals. If the structure is to survive, persons must be found to fill these roles. Socialization of the child is a necessary but by no means a sufficient method of attaining this goal. Most mature persons have been adequately socialized to be responsive to societal demands and incentives, but the problem remains of placing them in positions where they will contribute most effectively to the maintenance of the social system.

The processes of recruitment and selection are the means society has of solving this problem. In recruitment, the social structure finds institutionalized procedures for attracting and channelling persons to valued roles, and selection (differential recruitment) operates to match individual skills with role requirements, i.e., to put square pegs in square holes. Individuals are thought of as they would be in the personnel office of a firm, as manpower with pre-existing capacities for filling pre-existing positions. It is the firm which sets the criteria for job performance, establishes incentives for optimal performance, selects applicants on the basis of capacities appropriate to different jobs, and provides on-the-job training where needed. In this simple personnel office view, which has considerable currency among sociologists, the successful or unsuccessful operation of the social system is traced to strengths and weaknesses in the institutional system of social placement, social sanctions, and role structures rather than to characteristics of the individuals filling the roles.

In the more complex forms of this conceptualization, the compatibility of early socialization with later role demands is seen as problematic rather than assumed. Conformity is not taken for granted but regarded as an adaptive accomplishment to be explained in terms of complex mechanisms integrating individual behavioral dispositions with the needs of the social structure. In the formulation of Parsons (1949), Parsons and Shils (1951), Inkeles and Levinson (1954) and Spiro (1961), personality and social structure are conceived of as separate systems with their respective requirements for system-maintenance, consisting of drive-reduction in one form or another on the personality side, and role demands on the side of the social system. These requirements do not necessarily take similar behavioral forms but must be brought into some minimum degree of compatibility to insure the survival and stability of society. In other words, whatever its role demands, the social system must allow individuals sufficient satisfaction of their intrapsychic needs; and whatever their press for satisfaction, individuals must perform appropriately in their social roles; when these conditions are not met, change toward a more stable situation must occur. Inkeles and Levinson (1954) conceptualize this in terms of functional congruence and noncongruence between the personality and sociocultural system; Spiro (1961) discusses it in terms of the problem of social conformity.

In contrast to the simpler Durkheimian view, these complex theoretical positions assign a central place to socialization processes. Parsons (1949) distinguishes between primary socialization, which occurs early in life and lays down the basic structure of the personality system, and secondary socialization, a more specialized role-training oriented to institutional requirements of the social system. In addition, however, Parsons (1964), Brim (1966) and others have shown that even primary socialization is socially structured experience, and that the psychoanalytic theory of object relations and identification can be translated into the language of role and social structure through the medium of G. H. Mead's interactionist view of the self.

The model of socialization resulting from these theoretical discussions is that of the social system operating in two major *indirect* ways to influence the early experience of individuals: (a) through family structure, which determines the nature of the child's earliest interpersonal experience (leaving a normative residue), but which in turn is affected by the wider social system with which it is integrated; and (b) through parental mediation (Inkeles 1955, 1966), in which parents deliberately train their children for successful adaptation to a changing social order. This model spells out some of the mechanisms by which the personality system of the individual as laid down early in life is made amenable to the demands of the social system. Although admitting mutual influence between personality and social system, it strongly emphasizes the influence of the latter on the former, and underplays the costs of social conformity in individual frustration and conflict. (Spiro, 1961; and Whiting et al., 1966, explicitly include factors of "psychological cost" in similar functional models of personality–social structure relations.)

Although theories of this sociological-functionalist persuasion have made their strongest efforts to reconcile role theory with psychoanalytic views of personality, behavioristic psychology is more obviously compatible with their position, particularly the parental mediation hypothesis. As Parsons (1949) recognized some time ago, the conceptualizations of sanctions (+ and −) in the social system, and values (+ and −) in the cultural system, are analogous to positive and negative reinforcement in stimulus-response theories of learning. In parental mediation, as pointed out by LeVine, Klein and Owen (1967), the sanctions and values of the sociocultural order are translated by parents into rewards and punishments, or encouragement and discouragement, for childhood behavior that has relevance to adult role performance. The social learning position of Bandura and Walters (1963), stressing response-reinforcement as opposed to acquired drives, is quite congenial to this sociological position. The shaping of children's behavior in the direction of cultural values and norms has been recognized by anthropologists for many years although without explicit knowledge of the law of effect (see LeVine, 1963), and the Hullian anthropologists of the 1930's and 1940's (e.g., Murdock, Gillin, Whiting) combined reinforcement notions from psychology with functionalist concepts from anthropology and sociology. If the image of parents reinforcing responses that are eufunctional in a social or cultural system makes such a plausible convergence of ideas from different disciplines, it may be because both "reinforcement" and "social function" are intellectually descended from the Darwinian model of selective survival and adaptive fit that has so strongly influenced the way we think about man.

These three directions of thought about socialization have been presented as divergent views on the subject, but it is clear that they are not necessarily incompatible with each other. At the most common-sense level, children do absorb their culture through diverse exposures and communication, they do have their impulse life harnessed and channelled, and they do receive training for social participation. The authors of the more complex forms of the positions reviewed above have attempted in more sophisticated language to do justice theoretically to this variety of tasks and consequences of socialization within their respective theoretical frameworks. They all see early experience as leaving permanent residues on the individual, they all view socialization as socially purposive to some degree, and most envision some version of adaptation as integrating individual development and societal goals. These common elements suggest the possibility of developing a comprehensive view of the socialization process by the more explicit application of the Darwinian model that has proved so fruitful in other fields.

APPLICABILITY OF
THE VARIATION-SELECTION MODEL
TO CULTURE AND PERSONALITY

To explore the applicability of the variation-selection model outlined by Campbell, we must lay bare three assumptions concerning personality, the sociocultural system, and adaptation.

1. Distribution of personality traits, like the distributions of genetic and other biological traits, are statistical characteristics of populations, aggregated from measurements taken on individuals and exhibiting considerable interindividual variation, which can be expressed for comparative purposes by measures of central tendency (e.g., mean, median) and by population frequencies (i.e., per cent of population exhibiting the trait). There is no contradiction in assuming both intra-population variability and cross-population differences in central tendency; many normally distributed biological traits (e.g., adult stature) show significant variation across human populations. While many of the personality traits of greatest interest in comparative studies are likely to be normally distributed within populations, others may be discrete traits of very

frequent or very rare occurrence (cf. LeVine, 1966c). It is expected that some personality traits will vary significantly across intra-population groups defined by sex, age, occupation, status, and other aspects of differential social participation and differential exposure to cultural influences.

2. A sociocultural system, as a selective environment interacting with individual behavior, is a structure of institutional demands and opportunities. The demands are for conformity to norms of role performance, and entail punishment for failure to conform as well as social rewards for conformity; the opportunities are socially acceptable pathways for individuals to gain satisfaction of subjectively experienced needs. Each institution makes demands of *and* offers opportunities to, individuals, although some institutions tend to be structured around demands, others around opportunities (as in Kardiner's distinction between primary and secondary institutions and Whiting's concept of maintenance system and projective system). Certain personality traits are more compatible with successful conformity to certain norms and with certain pathways for satisfaction. Individuals differing on such traits will perform differently in their social roles and in taking advantage of opportunities, and will experience correspondingly differing degrees of reinforcement from their sociocultural environment.

3. The individuals in a given population are not necessarily aware of the evolved adaptations between personality and institution in which they participate. This needs to be emphasized because the purposive, profit-and-loss language of a theory of selection and adaptation seems to imply the operation of conscious, rational choice by individuals of the means required for the best environmental "payoff." It should be remembered, however, that this evolutionary model is borrowed from fields in which consciousness and purposive foresight are out of the question. As Campbell says,

> It is through such a process of selective cumulation of the unlikely that the extremely improbable and marvelous combinations found in plants and animals become, in fact, highly probable. As understood by present-day biologists, the elegantly engineered and complexly coordinated animals have been developed through this uncoordinated, unforesightful, unplanned, elementaristic process (Campbell, 1966, p. 27).

In the context of human culture, it is unlikely that members of a society are aware of the broader adaptive functions of customs assuring their survival, e.g., of the parts that dispersion of settlement and intergroup warfare play in maintaining the man/land ratio within a particular subsistence level.[3] This seems true as well of cultural adaptations to high infant mortality rates. For example, Whiting (1965) suggests that the prolonged taboo on post-partum sexual activity of women operates to insure the survival of infants in populations with low-protein diets by allowing the infants a longer period of breast feeding. If one asks a woman in such a population (as I have) why she is re-

---

[3] See Alland (1967, pp. 221–223) for discussion of this point.

fraining from sexual activity, she will offer reasons of morality or the belief that breast milk is poisoned by the husband's seminal ejaculation during coitus. Whatever reason she offers, she is unaware of the nutritional inadequacy of her customary diet, although this may well have acted as the selective pressure favoring a longer post-partum sexual taboo. Adaptations of this sort seem to develop so gradually that their survival advantages over previous customs are not noticeable to any given generation of individuals even though each may be responding subliminally to selective pressures. Furthermore, as soon as the practice becomes institutionalized, it is surrounded with a protective covering of normative pressures and associated non-empirical beliefs which increase its incentive values and thereby insure its performance more securely than any rational calculation of survival chances would. Each individual then sees the custom as having immediate value for his social adaptation (i.e., conformity to norms) and for other immediate personal concerns that he has (often ideologized or rationalized in moral or religious terms), but he may remain unaware of the custom's relevance to individual and group survival. Thus a bifurcation develops between the manifest and latent functions of the custom.

Humans are nonetheless the only animals that *can* become aware of and consciously direct their adaptive behavior. It is thus safest to assume that humans *need not* be aware of more than a fraction of the adaptive values of individual behavioral dispositions, but that they *can become* conscious of a wider range of such values, with important consequences for socialization of the child that are discussed below.

Having stated these assumptions, we can proceed to apply the Darwinian model to culture-personality relations. First we must ask whether or not our subject matter meets the three conditions stated by Campbell to be essential for such an application: the occurrence of unplanned variations, consistent selection criteria, and a mechanism for the preservation and duplication of positively selected variants. The first is to be found in personality characteristics, as conceptualized of in the psychology of individual differences. Personality characteristics in this sense are certainly variable, not only within a population as a whole but even among the children of a single set of parents. This variation is generally thought of as produced by the interaction of genetic constitution and early experience in complex ways that are not yet adequately understood, but in which uncontrolled or "accidental" factors such as innate reaction levels, sibling position, parents' personality and infantile traumata are critical. Thus there is unplanned variation in abundance.

Consistent selection criteria are provided by the sociocultural system in its normative aspect, which includes positive and negative standards of behavior (e.g., ideal personality types and rules of personal conduct as well as criteria for successful role performance), a system of comparative social evaluation (in which the standards are publicly and invidiously applied to persons and personality characteristics), and a system of allocation and enforcement (in which rewards and punishments are differentially distributed to persons in accordance with the evaluations of them and their behavior).

The cognitive activity of socializing agents preserves positively selected variants, and deliberate socialization acts toward duplicating them in the next generation. Every adult individual perceives the environment around him and notices to some degree the evaluative and distributive operations of the socio-cultural system. From observation of individual instances of conformity and nonconformity, positive and negative evaluation, success and failure, social reward and punishment—in a process equivalent to the vicarious trial-and-error or observational learning of reinforcement theorists—he draws conclusions about which behavioral dispositions are favored and which disfavored. These inductive conclusions become part of his cognitive structure, joining the attitudes, beliefs and values already there, and becoming consistent with them to some degree. From this cognitive structure as repeatedly modified by social perception and his own normative experience, comes his definition of the situation in which he sees his children growing up and his prescriptions and proscriptions for their adaptive performance. This is his ground plan for the deliberate socialization of his children, guiding their training toward certain goals and away from others. Thus the socializing agent's beliefs and values concerning various personality characteristics and their outcomes are shaped by his perceptual experience as a participant observer in a normative environment and serve in turn to dictate the direction in which he shapes his children's behavior. The adult in his role as parent or socializing agent performs the function of feedback from selective experience that is performed by reproduction in population genetics and by memory in trial-and-error learning.[4]

The image of culture-personality relations constructed by exploring the applicability of Campbell's three conditions for the evolutionary model is of course grossly oversimplified. Indeed, even in population genetics and trial-and-error learning, matters are by no means as simple as the bare statement of the variation-selection system seems to imply. The simplification of primary interest here concerns the duplication of positively selected variants. The truth is that there is much slippage between the preserved information about selective pressures and what subsequently becomes manifest in observable form. In genetics, what is encoded in the genes (the genotype) is not fully expressed in the phenotype of anatomical structure unless environmental factors (e.g., nutrition) are facilitating; in trial-and-error learning, complex processes of remembering, including forms of inhibition, intervene between memory and performance and prevent much that is stored in the memory from being expressed in behavior. The counterpart in socialization is that the explicit goals of socializing agents are frequently not realized in the behavior of those they train, first because the socializers are at best imperfect psychological engineers (they do not command the necessary but as yet ill-known laws of behavior acquisition),

---

[4] In the more differentiated societies the storage and selective propagation of information about the environment is institutionally specialized and performed by schools, libraries, religious and political organizations, rather than by ordinary parents. Here as elsewhere in the chapter parents are used as illustrative of the category of socializing agents rather than exhaustive of it.

and second because they must operate within the limits set by their trainees' pre-existing behavioral dispositions, acquired genetically and through "accidental" events of early experience over which the socializing agents have little conscious control. Recognition of this slippage between environmental information and subsequent performance brings to our attention two major sets of variables related to socialization: the conscious aims, concepts, and knowledge of the socializers with respect to the process of socialization, and the relation between unplanned and deliberate influences in the child's behavioral development.

The cognitive structures of the socializers mediate between selective pressures in the environment and the socialization process to which the child is subjected. The intelligence and cognitive complexity of the parent, his conceptual and verbal apparatus (including ideological formulations), the information about the environment that is available to him—all of these are thus determinants of how environmental experience in the adult world is transformed into training experience for childern. This can be illustrated by three hypothetical societies:

In the first society, a nonliterate agricultural group, the emphasis during the first two or three years of life is on feeding and indulging the child so that he will live despite a high infant mortality rate; parents do not think of shaping his behavior during this time. Their concept of socialization is of a training that is postponed until the child is old enough to understand and be useful. When that time comes, their primary goals are concrete and straightforward: to teach the child to submit to legitimate authority (probably requiring physical punishment because the child is introduced to external controls fairly late in development) and to teach him to participate responsibly in the economy (beginning early and with simple task performance); they are sometimes summarized by the parents as obedience or respect. These goals have proved valuable for social adaptation for many generations; there is no serious thought of changing them, and their correctness and necessity are perceived as absolute by adults in the society, who have never contemplated any alternatives. Socialization is rarely discussed in abstract language but usually in terms of concrete social and economic situations.

The second group is a Protestant sect in Western Europe or America, in the 17th–19th centuries. For adult members of the group the world is defined by the scriptures as interpreted by their founder and other leaders in written works and oral instruction. These teachings, internally consistent and forming a deductive system of thought, present a single ultimate goal of conduct—salvation—and detail the ways in which salvation is to be achieved. Alternate forms of behavior are explicitly considered and frequently condemned as idolatry, sin, satanism, and popishness, leading to damnation, the opposite of salvation. Members of the group are taught to see every act as having moral and religious significance, leading toward or away from salvation. This applies with great force to the raising of their children. Child rearing practically from birth onwards is prescribed by religious leaders and designed to foster qualities such as self-control and self-reliance which help provide the individual with the means for his own salvation. Even the feeding, sleeping arrangements, and tending of infants are infused with moral considerations, and parents apply abstract terms derived from religious teachings to their concrete behavior as socializers and to their children's behavior. They have explicit non-empirical beliefs, religiously based, concerning the relation between parental acts and their behavioral consequences in the child. In a word, socialization of the child has become *ideologized,* i.e., made part of an abstract set of ideas concerning what happens and ought to happen in real behavior.

The parents of this hypothetical Protestant sect differ cognitively from those of the hypothetical nonliterate society in a number of important ways. Most basically perhaps, the Protestant parents view the conduct of infants, children and parents in abstract terms, seeing each behavioral event as an instance of a general dispositional quality, which has as much reality for them as the concrete social and economic situation has for the nonliterate parent. The latter is less accustomed to applying abstract labels to his parental behavior, and he is therefore considerably less aware of what he does as a socializer. Self-awareness is another feature distinguishing the thought of the Protestant parent from that of the nonliterate. The latter, having relatively little experience in generalizing about or applying general labels to his parental behavior, is also inexperienced in considering alternative patterns of behavior and defining his own contrastively against them. In his phenomenal absolutism (see Segall, Campbell & Herskovits, 1966), he tends to see his own behavior as automatic and stemming necessarily from the universal situation of child and parent; the categories in his thought for other ways are neither salient nor elaborated. The Protestant parent has a salient and elaborated conceptual category—the sinful ways of the non-believer—and he has been trained to define his own behavior contrastively, in terms of polar opposites. Thus his self-awareness as a socializer, although limited to poles of good and evil, is greater than the less differentiated view of the nonliterate parent. A third difference lies in the coherence or unity of the two cognitive structures: the Protestant parent operates within an explicit ideology that has the appearance of a deductive system in which diverse prescriptions are unified by their derivation from a single set of axiomatic premises. The nonliterate parent's concept of his child-training program gains some unity from its simplicity, but his actual child-training practices, being less verbalized and less self-consciously performed, are likely to be less forced toward mutual consistency. Such a parent notices inconsistencies less and is less bothered by them than a parent guided by an explicit ideology. Thus the parents in the two groups differ in the abstractness, contrastive self-awareness, and coherence of the cognitive structures by which they mediate between their environment and the ways they prepare their children to meet it.

The third group is a cluster of university-educated families in contemporary America. The ways in which parents there think about their child training resembles in some ways both of the other groups. Like the nonliterate parents, they are concerned about the health and economic future of their children, and they have inherited from the Protestant cultural ancestry of America much of the ideology of self-control and self-reliance (though shorn of some of its religious axioms) that characterized the Protestant sect. There are two important ways, however, in which they differ drastically from the other two groups. First, the American parents assume that the sociocultural criteria for evaluating behavior change from generation to generation and that their children will be judged by somewhat different standards as adults than those by which the parents were judged. Hence they search for information from the environment concerning the new selective pressures to which their chilrden will have to adapt in the future; in so doing, the parents enter into a more deliberate interaction with social and cultural system, self-consciously acting as mediators of environmental feedback to their children. (As Riesman, 1950, has pointed out, sometimes the children in such subcultures are in closer touch with new trends and may transmit environmental information to their parents who, recognizing the power of change, alter their socialization accordingly.) Second, the parents in this third group believe that science, rather than religion or tradition, can tell them how to produce in their children desirable behavioral dispositions. Hence they seek advice from and are responsive to pediatricians, educators, child psychologists, and other "experts" on child rearing concerning the best ways to produce intelligence, emotional stability, and other adaptive qualities in their children. Since "expert" advice is not based on a substantial body of validated generalizations, the opinions of scientists, practitioners, and quasi-scientific journalists and writers fluctuate, and parental beliefs and practices follow these fluctuations.

From this perspective, the concepts of child rearing and training held by these American parents represent an attempt to *rationalize* the process of socialization by consciously gearing both its ends and means to information feedback from a changing environment. In this attempt, the goals of socialization can be altered according to shifts in selective pressures favoring certain personal qualities and discouraging others, and the means are alterable as new information is received concerning what methods the experts believe to be optimal for the fostering of adaptive personal qualities. This type of cognitive structure has much more flexibility and self-awareness than that of the Protestant sect members, and a great deal less coherence, because of its openness to diverse and changing sources of prescriptions for behavior.

Although parental socialization concepts in all three societies are adapted to selective pressures operative in their respective sociocultural systems, the major differences lie in the parents' awareness of their adaptation and of what they have adapted to, the abstractness and generality of their thinking about it, the sense of conscious choice among alternative practices, and their responsiveness to environmental change. Since the cognitive structure of the parent determines in great measure how and to what extent he translates his selective environment into training experiences for the child, it can be seen that the nature of socialization as a process mediating between adult experience and child training is dependent on whether the parent's concepts of socialization are abstract or concrete, differentiated or undifferentiated, verbalized or unreflective, ideologized or rationalized, absolute or relativistic, deductive or pragmatic, rigid or flexible, coherent or disunified. Cultures vary widely on dimensions of parental cognition. It is consequently untenable to think of socialization as a uniform mechanism for the propagation of positively selected variants, operating identically in all populations as genetic reproduction does. We need a more complex view that takes account of cultural variation.

These considerations of cross-cultural variability in parental cognition bring us back to the relation between unplanned and deliberate aspects of socialization. The variation-selection model as Campbell presents it places great weight on the unplanned, haphazard or unforesightful quality of the variation that is acted upon by selection criteria in such a way as to effect differential propagation of variants. But in human affairs the dividing line between the unplanned and the deliberate is not constant; it varies with the cognitive differentiation, purposiveness, and environmental information of individuals.

This is even true for the genetics of populations. Humans, being the only species with consciousness of the means by which innate characteristics are transmitted, are in a unique position to create a more efficient, tightly controlled system of selective propagation than could occur through natural selection. Selective breeding in animal husbandry is an example of this that antedates Mendelian genetics. Eugenicists have argued that human breeding should not be left to the haphazard vagaries of personal choice but that existing scientific knowledge be used to extend purposive control over human reproduction by formulating general policies of selection that harness mating practices more tightly to societal goals. Although the mutation process that generates haphazard variation could not be controlled with present knowledge, the adoption of eugenic proposals would certainly reduce heterogeneity and push back the line between the deliberate and the unplanned in mating behavior.

So it is with socialization, except that the counterparts to eugenic proposals have been adopted by numerous groups, most conspicuously nonconformist religious sects, utopian communities, and totalitarian societies. In those groups an effort is made to remove child training from the sphere of individual choice and make it part of a grand design conceived by the leaders and centrally administered for the entire community. As in eugenics, the aim is to reduce haphazard and possible deleterious variation in the interests of achieving societal goals. One way of doing this is to make the grand design or ideology part of each parent's cognitive map and to instruct him in the ways he can contribute to achievement of the common goals by shaping his child's behavior. This parental collaboration is necessary but not sufficient; in fact, such groups tend to remove much of the child-training function from parents and the family altogether and assign a larger part of it to bureaucratically organized educational institutions whose policies can be more easily and efficiently controlled by the central administration in accordance with the grand design. The desirability of such an arrangement was foreseen by Plato in *The Republic* and realized in its most extreme form in the Israeli kibbutz described by Spiro

(1957, 1958), where even infant care is bureaucratically organized, with children in group residences under specialized non-familial caretakers from the first year of life, and with a myriad of environmental details being dictated and standardized by ideological considerations. Such arrangements do not alter the individual variation generated by differences in genetic constitution and traumatic accidents, but they do make the conditions of early life more uniform and could conceivably diminish the effects of sibling position on personality. It is in any event doubtful that such centrally planned socialization could be as successful as intended because humans have less complete knowledge of behavior acquisition processes than they do of genetic transmission. It must nevertheless be admitted that these planned societies have reduced sources of intrapopulation heterogeneity and pushed back the line between the deliberate and the unplanned in socialization so as to minimize the latter realm.

Cases of maximally planned child training illustrate, by their extreme contrast with the more usual situation in which families are left to train their own children as they see fit, the variability in location of the boundary between deliberate and unplanned aspects of socialization, but this variability is by no means limited to extreme cases. Families influenced by different religious and political value systems differ significantly in how they see fit to train their children (see Whiting et al., 1966), and some of these value systems involve tighter and more conscious control over the details of socialization than others. In their comparison of Zuni Indians, Texans and Mormons in New Mexico, Whiting et al. (1966) show that the value systems of the three communities emphasize different types of behavior as particularly important to socialize (aggression among the Zuni, dependence among the Texans, sexuality among the Mormons), with a correspondingly greater degree of conscious attention and explicit normative regulation in their respective focal areas of behavior. Thus what is relatively unregulated and unplanned in one group is the object of intensely deliberate socialization in another. Their study of groups occupying the same physical environment stresses the area of proscriptive control, but Barry, Child and Bacon's (1959) cross-cultural study of subsistence economy and child rearing (showing an emphasis on obedience and responsibility in agricultural and pastoral societies and self-reliance and achievement in hunting and gathering societies) suggests that a certain *prescriptive* area of socialization may be isolated for greater conscious elaboration as well. Where religious ideology plays a part, as in Zborowski's (1949) example of the emphasis on booklearning in the socialization of Eastern European Jewish boys, the amount of deliberate planning of prescribed child-training routines is likely to be even greater. Thus the boundary between unplanned and deliberate aspects of socialization varies widely across cultural groups and across different areas of child behavior within a culture.

A further complication concerning the factor of conscious planning in socialization is the tendency of parents to justify, rationalize and explain their practices on ideological or pragmatic grounds of a purposive nature that are unrelated to the historical causes for their adoption. Outside of artificially created systems like those of utopian communities where the discontinuity with past socialization can be historically documented, the observer is tempted to take the *post facto* explanations of parents as representing the ideological origins of their practices. This is extremely unreliable unless independent evidence shows that the belief preceded the practice for, as Whiting and Whiting (1959) have argued, beliefs are frequently constructed to reduce the cognitive dissonance between a child-training practice (caused by ecological or structural pressures) and incompatible ideals in the culture. We are likely to find, for example, that where many persons live in one household, children will be carefully trained not to fight, presumably to prevent disruption of the household solidarity needed to maintain cooperation in economic and other tasks. The ubiquity of this relation between household size and severity of aggression training cross-culturally (see Whiting et al., 1966; Minturn & Lambert, 1964) confirms this functional explanation and suggests as a plausible possibility that large households came first and required suppression of overt hostility for their maintenance. But explicit recognition of this adaptation by parents would require verbalizing the very hostility the household members are trying to suppress. Thus there is cognitive dissonance between the parent's awareness of the adaptation and his cultural ideals of interpersonal behavior; the dissonance is reduced by adopting the cultural explanation that anger will make a child ill, or that fighting will offend the gods or disrupt the harmony of the universe. Apart from their role in reducing dissonance, such beliefs relate an adaptive practice to an existing cognitive structure in the parent, viz., the religious, ethical, or cosmological system in which he already believes, and hence he can more readily assimilate them and less easily forget or neglect them. From the outside observer's point of view, this state of affairs means parents will present their child-training practices as the deliberate application of general ideological principles when they were in fact developed under the pressure of unmentioned ecological and social-structural factors. One generation's practical necessities become the next generation's exalted ideals.

This confounding of the deliberate and the unplanned (but adaptive), which we encountered earlier in this chapter in the case of the post-partum taboo on sexual intercourse, brings us back to the familiar phenomenon of the multi-functional nature of customs well imbedded in the culture and the fact that some functions are manifest and others latent. An evolutionary viewpoint easily encompasses the idea that those customs having multiple functions are more likely to survive and that certain functions will be more visible and obvious than others of no less importance. Although the phenomenon is comprehensible in the broader theoretical framework, it nevertheless often presents a serious problem for the empirical understanding of which environmental stimuli the parent is responding to. Does he give his infant toys to play with because of a conscious or preconscious goal of intellectual enrichment geared to ultimate educational and economic success, or because he simply enjoys seeing the child enjoy himself, with this vicarious enjoyment pattern having been unconsciously selected for in generations of worldly success through cognitive enrichment?

The answers to such questions, or their re-formulation in answerable form, cannot be simple, and no adequate answer can fail to take account of the cognitive complexity and variability of human cultures.

To summarize: In discussing the applicability of the variation-selection model to culture-personality relations we have found that Campbell's highly generalized statement of it, in a form as applicable to radar, embryonic growth, and creative thinking as it is to organic evolution and trial-and-error learning, is oversimplified for our present subject matter. The slippage between available selective information and subsequent propagation, inherent in other applications of the variation-selection paradigm, is of critical importance in the study of culture and personality because it is not constant across human populations but varies widely, making it difficult to construct a single working model of environmental feedback and duplication for all societies. The major sources of variation are the cognitive structures (their complexity, purposiveness and responsiveness to environmental change) of the socializing agents who stand between the adult environment and the reinforcement schedules of their children. Variations in the purposive ideologization and rationalization of child-training concepts across populations make it impossible to draw a universal boundary between deliberate and unplanned elements in the socialization process, and the blurring is compounded by *post facto* cultural explanations that make unplanned adaptive practices appear to have developed from pre-ordained policies. Even in the most planned societies, genetic constitution and accidents of early experience generate a core of haphazard heterogeneity in personality characteristics, but heterogeneity appears to be greater in less planned societies, with adaptation probably occurring through a closer analogue to natural selection in the latter case. Thus, strict application of the generalized variation-selection model will not do, and we must seek a more complex and variable evolutionary framework for culture-personality adaptation.

AN EVOLUTIONARY MODEL: BASIC CONCEPTS

The attempt to construct an evolutionary model of personality-culture relations analogous to those that have proved fruitful in the comparative population studies of biology was originally based on the assumption that, like those more advanced fields, our subject matter concerns statistical distributions of individual characteristics and the selective operation of environments. Intergenerational transmission of characteristics, selective pressures on individuals and populations, processes of adaptive equilibrium and adaptive change, are additional foci of common concern. In the last section we found that a widely applicable conceptualization of evolution, the variation-selection model, needs to be modified to encompass the peculiar features of human population-environment relations in general and personality-culture relations in particular, features stemming from the important but variable roles of consciousness, purposiveness, and cognitive complexity in human adaptation. The present section presents the first part of an evolutionary model designed especially for relations between personality and the sociocultural system. In this first part the focus is on the processes of personality development and socialization, and the basic concepts are personality genotype, personality phenotype, and deliberate socialization.

1. *The personality genotype.* This refers to a set of enduring individual behavioral dispositions that may or may not find socially acceptable expression in the customary (or institutionalized) behavior of a population. Its major characteristics are early acquisition (through the interaction of constitution and early experience), resistance to elimination in subsequent experience, and capacity for inhibition, generalization, and other transformations under the impact of experiential pressures. It acts as a set of constraints on later learning and on the adaptive flexibility of the individual.

Three broad classes of dispositions comprise the personality genotype:

(a) Basic, probably genetically determined, parameters of individual functioning, such as general activity level and thresholds for perceiving, discriminating, and reacting to simuli (e.g., arousal and irritability thresholds). These dispositions set gross limits on the quantities of behavioral output and stimulus input characteristic of one individual as compared to another.

(b) Intense, unconscious, and often conflicting wishes and fears concerning mental representations of human objects, and defenses against the conflicts. These motivational dispositions, which account for the generalizable goals of psychobiological drives such as sexuality and aggression, take the form of largely unconscious fantasies representing the self and significant others in emotional terms, and they supply direction and symbolic content to interpersonal behavior and perception when environmental demands are slack or ambiguous.

(c) Fundamental adaptive functions which monitor and regulate response to stimuli coming from the external environment and from internal needs. These include a basic perceptual organization (e.g., self-other differentiation, reality-testing), a drive organization (e.g., capacities for stable effective responses to human objects including the self), and the functions of information processing (perceptual discrimination, memory, thinking, learning), control (e.g., delay of gratification, moral restraints), and synthesis (ability to mediate between drives, controls, and environmental demands).

The personality genotype is complexly formed but has at least the following sources: (a) genetic constitution; (b) patterns of stimulation, gratification, frustration and attachment to caretakers in infancy; (c) patterns of childhood separation (temporary and permanent) and perceptions of threatened separation from love objects causing fear and hatred of others in the immediate environment, and giving rise to intra-psychic conflicts, their representation in unconscious fantasies, defenses against the conflicts, and identifications with objects perceived as lost; (d) traumatic experiences, i.e., the influx of greater stimulation than the child can master, causing developmental arrest or regression and the subsequent formation of a repressed motivational complex.

These influences act to form the personality genotype as an organization of motives, cognitions, and adaptive habits during the first five or six years of life, but many of their separate effects are manifested in infancy and early child-hood as individual differences in activity or passivity, irritability, dependence, hostility, sociability, inhibitions, imitativeness, masculinity-femininity, and other observable (phenotypic) behaviors. Determinants acting earlier form con-straints on subsequent development. For example, genetic differences in per-ceptual thresholds may determine whether or not a given amount of stimula-tion will be traumatic. In like manner, if we take as given that self-other differentiation and capacity for delay of gratification, in their most developed forms, are contingent on optimal frustration during a critical period of infancy, then it follows that infants who do not experience optimal frustration at that time will develop defects in cognitive and control functions that will affect the way they perceive and experience separation and potential traumata during childhood. A proper understanding of the development of the personality genotype would include a telescoping series of developmental contraints as one form (among many) of interaction between innate and environmental, and earlier and later, determinants. In its final form the personality genotype is itself an organized set of constraints on the later development of the individual.

The above mentioned sources of the personality genotype are, with the exception of genetic constitution, social stimuli impinging on the infant and child and are parts of larger patterns of social interaction that are in turn as-pects of social structure. The events in infant care and child life that lead to attachments, aversions, separations, traumata, and their complex psychological residues can be seen as simple outgrowths of social structure and therefore as varying concomitantly with structural variations across populations. For exam-ple, the number of nuclear families sharing a courtyard and cooperating in do-mestic tasks may determine the likelihood of multiple mothering for infants. The presence, absence, or frequency of polygyny and its associated rules of husband-wife relations may determine the time interval between births and therefore the average age at which children experience the birth of the next sibling. The clustering or dispersal of residences in local communities, and the density of settlement, may determine the availability of children from outside the family as playmates. The degree of mother's participation in occupational roles such as cultivator and trader may determine the amount of time she has available to attend to her children and the likelihood of her using supplemen-tary caretakers. The marriage pattern, particularly the frequency of legitimized unions, may determine the number of households in which fathers are avail-able as objects for love, hate, and identification; and the rate of divorce or con-jugal separation may determine the number of children who become separated from one or both parents. In these (and many other) cases, abrupt or recurrent events having an impact on the child's experience, and consequently on his personality development, are unplanned and usually unconscious by-products of variations in the structure of family, community and occupation.

The relations between social structure and typical patterns of childhood experience pose two important problems: Are such relations accidental, evolved through an adaptive variation-selection process, or the product of purposive social policy? Do they reduce variation among the personality genotypes of a population?

In dealing with the first of these problems we return briefly to the question of consciousness and purpose discussed in the preceding section. At the most superficial level, an answer is easy. Adults respond to the coercive pressures of their social and economic environment—e.g., the need to grow food or find a job in the face of potential scarcity, the need to cluster and cooperate for mutual defense against invaders—and they create living arrangements designed first and foremost to solve these practical problems of survival. Child rearing must be adjusted accordingly, fitted into a pattern of family and community life already fashioned for other purposes. From this point of view the resultant patterns of childhood experience are accidental consequences of socioeconomic adaptation. But there are limits inherent in the raising of children: each generation must survive the high mortality period of infancy and early childhood characteristic of most human populations until recently (and of many today), and they must be capable of carrying on basic subsistence tasks as their elders decline in vigor. If these conditions are not met the population will not survive, no matter how successful their mode of production or defense.

It seems altogether plausible that some populations have at times reacted to ecological shifts with new structural arrangements that failed to meet these conditions—e.g., an organization of work in which infants and children were neglected physically and emotionally, with a consequent rise in infant mortality and decline in the educability of children for their occupational roles. There would then have to be a modification in the new structure to allow better child care, or the population would be threatened with demographic and economic collapse and eventually disappear or become absorbed into neighboring populations that have better adapted child-care practices. In other words, selection would operate, across both historical and inter-population variation, to eliminate structural variants incompatible with the basic conditions for child care and to propagate structural variants that do meet the conditions. If this has indeed happened in human history, we would be justified in stating that customary patterns of childhood experience are not entirely accidental by-products of social structure but have adaptively evolved through haphazard variation and selective retention. To put it more accurately, *limits* on the impact of social structure on childhood experience have probably been evolved through variation-selection. Within these broad limits, i.e., so long as structural arrangements do not endanger the survival or occupational trainability of children, social structures are free to vary in accordance with ecological demands and to alter the shape of childhood experience in a non-purposive way.

A further qualification on the proposition that childhood experience is an accidental by-product of social structure is required for those populations, discussed in the preceding section, in which the basic conditions of infant and child care are self-consciously planned to achieve developmental goals dictated by a general ideology. The analogy with eugenics is an apposite one here, for eugenicists desire central and selective control over what is normally a rather

haphazard process. Societies that have consciously organized the social experience of the infant and child in accordance with ideological goals are not as
hard to find as those that have adopted eugenic policies, but they are the exceptions that prove the rule. The rule, i.e., the normal state of affairs in most
human societies, is that infant and child care is conducted in multi-functional
social units (such as the family) by persons having other tasks and responsibilities, so that child rearing takes place in a social context largely established for
other purposes. Although mothers in some societies seek for ideological reasons
to stimulate, gratify or frustrate their infants and children more than their
counterparts elsewhere, no more than a fraction of the significant social-
emotional experience in early life can be attributed to purposive manipulation.
This fraction may or may not be extremely influential in personality development; present evidence does not allow us to say with any certainty. What we
can say, however, is that the effects of early influences on the complex structure
of motives, cognitive patterns, and capacities here called the personality genotype, are still so imperfectly known, even by scientific investigators of child
development, that manipulative *intent* on the part of parents is no guarantee
of success.

It is inherently difficult to discover what the pre-verbal child perceives
and experiences and what parts of his environment are particularly significant
to him, and this lack of feedback from him reduces the advantage that self-
conscious manipulation of early environment has over unconsciously evolved
practices in achieving long-range developmental goals. (In this regard, the
emphasis that modern parents, with their self-consciously manipulative intent,
put on the early development of speech in the child should be especially noted.)
Thus, though populations vary widely in the extent to which they aspire to
manipulate the pre-verbal environment of the child, and though sociocultural
evolution seems to have set limits on the range of child-rearing possibilities, the
social-structural sources of influence on development of the personality genotype are predominantly unplanned consequences of small group interaction patterns. In their social roles (as husband, wife, kinsman, producer, consumer,
etc.) and social behavior, parents are unwittingly generating an environment
that profoundly affects the emotional development of their children.

The other question posed by relations between social structure and childhood experience is whether or not the structural determination of childhood
environments tends to homogenize the early experiences that form personality
genotypes in a population. In general, social structure operates to make social
behavior more uniform. When an aspect of behavior comes under normative
regulation, it may no longer be varied freely without being stigmatized as deviant and punished by social sanctions. In the absence of normative regulation
of family life, characteristics like legitimized marriage, divorce, polygyny, birth
spacing, father absence, might be randomly distributed among humans. The
fact is they are not randomly distributed; there are sharp discontinuities across
human populations in norms of marriage and family life, and the frequency
distribution curves for relevant behavioral characteristics are distinctly different

in different populations. Most frequently, such curves are either *J*-curves in which a large majority conform to a norm (e.g., legitimized marriage among middle-class Americans) or bell-shaped curves in which variation is normally distributed around a population mean that represents a normative ideal (e.g., family size among middle-class Americans). There may be no variation among population members in their recognition of a normative ideal, but there is always variation in the incidence of actual social behavior patterns. So, in a population universally regarding polygynous marriage as ideal, there will be some men who remain monogamists because of poverty, causing variation in the social experience of their children. Thus conformity to social norms does not in practice mean uniformity of childhood social environment.

The timing of structurally patterned events in a family also creates variations in childhood experience. For example, the oldest children in a polygynous family may spend their first few years of life in a monogamous unit, whereas those born after their father has several wives are exposed to a very different environment. The developmental cycle through which domestic groups pass in many societies (cf., Goody, 1962; and Gray & Gulliver, 1964) diversifies the experience of children in the "same" family. A population may have a high divorce rate, but any particular divorce, occurring at different points in the lives of the several children of the union, is likely to affect them differently. Thus, potentially traumatic events, and separations, though caused by widespread patterns of family structure, are likely to have a differential effect even on children in the same family. Environmental differences among siblings is even greater where norms select first or last children (or sons) for special treatment, as in primogeniture or the practice of keeping the last child home. When we consider the pre-existing genetic variations among siblings with which these environmental variables interact, we can see that the number of combinations and permutations among factors influencing the personality genotype is very great indeed. Structural determinants narrow the range of variation but they do not eliminate it. Thus, we might expect a given trauma or separation experience to be "characteristic" (i.e., more frequent) of one population as opposed to another but not uniform within it.

We can summarize this presentation of the personality genotype by stating that it is an enduring organization of drives, cognitions and adaptive capacities, is formed early in life, varies widely across individuals and (in frequency and central tendency) between populations, and acts as a series of constraints on later development and learning. Many of the formative influences on the personality genotype can be seen as indirect outcomes or by-products of social structure, to which certain survival-oriented limits have probably evolved, and which necessarily narrow the range of genotype dispositions in a population sharing a social-structural environment. These formative influences are nevertheless in most societies sufficiently variable in their impact on individual experience and sufficiently free of manipulative intent to be considered unplanned and non-normative sources of personality variation.

The dispositions comprising the personality genotype are by definition latent and do not always find socially acceptable expression. It is as generalizable constraints on later learning and performance that their influence is manifested. The constraints stemming from the drive residues of infancy and childhood (as shaped by patterns of stimulation, attachment, and separation) act as internal motivational pressures for gratification, provide a symbolic interpretation of later social experience, and give direction and content to free choice behavior (as in interpersonal relations and fantasy). The constraints resulting from early ego development act as limits on the complexity and intensity of stimuli (external and internal) to which the individual can respond effectively, and therefore constitute thresholds of perceptual discrimination and stress tolerance.

2. The personality phenotype. This refers to the observable regularities of behavior characterizing an adult functioning in the variety of settings comprising his environment. The personality phenotype of an individual includes his patterns of performance in social roles, in formal and informal settings, in interaction and alone, in coercive and free-choice situations, under stressful and relaxed conditions, in verbalization and actual behavior. It includes his conscious attitudes, values, and groups, his skills, competence and knowledge, and his preferences and tastes in recreational and hedonistic activities. If the individual is functioning normally, his phenotypic personality is a stable organization of traits that affords him satisfaction of his perceived needs, enables him to meet social demands and take advantage of sociocultural opportunities, and protects him from excessive anxiety.

The phenotype is not independent of the genotype; it *is* the personality genotype modified by prolonged normative experience, first through the deliberate socialization of the parents, later through direct participation in the wider social system. The phenotypic personality develops within the constraints of the genotype and, when formed, allows unconscious motivational components of the latter normatively regulated expression in overt behavior. The most noticeable expressions in phenotypic behavior are idiosyncratic mannerisms, inhibitions, and other facets of distinctive behavioral style. These character traits, as they are called by psychoanalysts, are fixed, stabilized expressions of defenses against unconscious impulses, and they frequently incorporate into their content some of the original impulse that is being defended against.

It is a fact of social perception that we notice and sense the unconscious motivation of character traits when they are distinctively idiosyncratic and approach the limits of social acceptability, but we are generally incapable of seeing them in members of our own population when the behavior patterns involved are very common and completely acceptable. In the latter case, it takes a foreigner to point out to us the arbitrary, irrational and perhaps compulsive quality of the behavior and make us realize that what we had seen as "natural," "normal," "rational," or "adaptive," because of its familiarity and normative acceptability, might be as unconscious in origin and defensive in function as an idiosyncratic mannerism. (For a general discussion of the "phenomenal absolutism" underlying culture-bound perception, see Segall et al., 1966; for the use of outsiders' judgments in group personality assessment, see LeVine, 1966b.) The point is that it is not only idiosyncratic character traits that are defensive expressions of genotypic conflicts but also character traits widespread in the population; this is what Fromm (1941) and others have referred to as "social character." In the present perspective, social character refers to all character traits positively valued and relatively frequent in a population, and includes non-defensive (conflict-free) dispositions of the personality genotype that become enduring features of social behavior.

One of the most important integrating characteristics of the personality phenotype is a self-concept, an internal mental representation of the self that includes boundaries between, and identities with, the self and other individuals, groups, and ideologies. In his functioning as a member of society, the individual uses this enduring self-concept to monitor his own behavior and to determine the extent to which each of his behavior patterns is ego-syntonic, i.e., consistent with his image of himself. This self-concept, having been produced in part through normative social experience, represents social norms as it selects among possible behaviors (in a manner analogous to other forms of variation and selection) those that are consistent with the socially acceptable image that the individual wants to present to the world. In the category of unacceptable are behaviors seen as immoral, impolite, childish, stupid, crazy (or their nearest equivalents in other cultures); these are viewed as ego-dystonic, except under especially permissive conditions, and are eliminated in favor of more acceptable behaviors. When the individual loses the capacity to suppress certain behavior that he himself regards as unacceptable in one of those senses, i.e., is unable to keep his behavior ego-syntonic, then he develops a neurotic or psychotic symptom. When he alters his self-concept so as to include the defensive contents of a neurotic symptom (e.g., develops a rationalized inhibition out of a phobia), he has developed a neurotic character trait.

The distinction between genotypic and phenotypic personality contains elements of familiar behavioral science polarities—unconscious versus conscious, latent versus manifest, subjective versus objective, general versus specialized—but two other elements require further emphasis. First, the phenotypic personality is responsive to contemporaneous environmental pressures—in the form of real, threatened, or promised social rewards, punishments, incentives—whereas the genotype is the relatively unchanging "internal environment" of the personality, responsive only to its own past, and can be used for or against adaptation without altering its direction and content. In their phenotypic expression, genotypic dispositions may be suppressed and disguised for purposes of social adaptation and conformity but are not thereby eliminated.

Second, the personality genotype is inherently more variable and heterogeneous in a population than is the phenotype; the former reflects individual constitution and experience, whereas the latter reflects the normative consensus of society. Insofar as populations have intact, functioning social structures, there must be such a consensus represented in the phenotypic personalities of its members, no matter how diverse their underlying genotypic dispositions. In measuring these dispositions, the closer the investigator comes to what is explicitly prescribed by norms, the more agreement and homogeneity he finds in a population, whereas the closer he comes to normatively permissive areas of behavior—in which "free," i.e., genotypically expressive, choice is possible—the more heterogeneity of response within a population. This has been less clear than it might be because terms like "values" have been used to cover dispositions varying widely in their degree of normative prescriptiveness; hence some (usually sociological) investigators, measuring individuals' perceptions or expectations of norms, find populations homogeneous on "values," while other (usually psychological) investigators measuring personal interests and tastes find a heterogeneity of "values." It is in the nature of genotype-phenotype relations, as conceptualized here, that one will be more variable than the other unless a radical breakdown in social consensus has occurred.

3. Deliberate socialization.   This refers to the intentions and actions of the parents (or substitutes) in training the child. In this process there are several factors: the child and his presocialized behavior, the goals of the parents, the means they use to achieve their goals, and the consequences of applying these means.

The argument can be anticipated briefly as follows: Parents use reward, punishment, and instruction to shape the child's behavior, already genotypically influenced, in the direction of social norms; the typical result is a phenotypic personality involving both preparedness for adaptation to the adult environment and unsatisfied needs stemming from conflicts between personality genotype and normative demands. The model of training is that of behavioristic response-reinforcement theory, with the added assumptions that the major formative influences on the child's personality are ordinarily outside parental control and have acted before deliberate parental training, and that parental reinforcement schedules, whether or not effective, have unintended motivational consequences of great importance for personality-culture interaction.

(a) The child. No matter how early parents begin deliberate training, they find neither a tabula rasa nor a passive receiving instrument in their child. Even the infant is an active organism, striving and exploring within the constraints of his constitutional dispositions and developmental immaturity. Parental training must deal with the child's unprovoked behavioral output, and it must be geared to his perceptual thresholds and his tolerance limits for particular types of stimulation. Some active infants seem intractable to their parents; others are resistant to manipulation in more passive ways, and parents may find the difficulties so great that they postpone training to a later age. With the exception of the most self-consciously manipulative modern and ideologized parents, most parents in most societies postpone the first onset of serious behavioral manipulation until the child can talk, and begin more intensive training in useful skills when the child has "sense," usually about five or six years of

age. (In some societies there are clear-cut phases of this type, while in others, the intensity of training is gradually increased.)

The child's behavioral development goes on regardless of whether or not anyone is attempting to manipulate it and to produce desirable habits. Maturational processes make new forms of behavior possible, and the child is continuously interacting with his environment, experiencing gratification and frustration, suffering trauma and separation, acquiring attachments and avoidances, observing the behavior of others, spontaneously imitating what he sees, developing pleasant and frightening fantasies and increasingly differentiated patterns of thought and action. Anyone who has observed two- and three-year-old children in a society where socialization in any serious purposive sense begins later than that, has seen behavior patterns of personal and cultural distinctiveness, obvious precursors of adult behavioral styles. These are early phenotypic expressions of the personality genotype, preceding the onset of manipulative training. The point is that whenever the parent begins deliberate training of his child, be it at two or six years of age, he confronts not a completely unformed mass of clay ready to be shaped, but a set of genotypic dispositions that already give the child's behavior shape and purpose of its own not necessarily consistent with the parents' purposes. The parent, unlike the animal experimenter, cannot dispose of his subject and obtain a more tractable one; he must render the child tractable and amenable to training by persistent effort, by increasing reward and punishment as seems necessary, and by finding within the child dispositional allies that can be harnessed to the parent's goals. The personality genotype of the child sets the stage for impending conflict in the socialization process. And since each child in a family has a different personality genotype, each poses its parents a different set of training problems.

(b) Parental goals. The parent (assisted by other socializing agents and agencies) has the task of directing the behavioral, i.e., phenotypic, development of the child toward normative, socially valued goals. Insofar as he performs this task, the parent is acting as the feedback mechanism, mediator of environmental information to his child, implicitly communicating messages about discrepancies between the child's current behavior and environmental norms of behavior as he attempts to eliminate those discrepancies through training. More immediately, however, the parent's training program is determined by his phenomenal field, a field in which environmental information is only one of several forces and may be muted in its effect on parental behavior.

The phenomenal field of the parent is his view of the child training situation as influenced by factors internal and external to that situation. In such a field of forces, a number of determinants contribute (positively and negatively) to a few resultant outcomes. The outcomes in this case are decisions concerning child training; the determinants are all the sources of pressure, constraint, belief and value that influence his training decisions. Some of these sources are in the parent's personality, some are in the social system in which he participates, and some are in the behavior of the child with whom he interacts. Research into parental phenomenal fields has been fragmentary and incomplete, so that we do not have a clear picture of how the diverse forces combine, or what their valences are, or how they are assigned valences that account for their relative contributions to the resultant decisions. We do have some idea of the range of forces involved. Brim (1959) has referred to this complexity:

> With respect to the six types of causes of parent behavior considered here, one recognizes that the individual operates or behaves in his parent role as part of a social system. The parent engages in behavior vis-a-vis the child in interaction situations which are regulated by social norms or rules as to what is appropriate and inappropriate. As an individual, the parent is also restricted by repressed and unconscious motives which work to determine his behavior in parent role performance in ways unknown to him. Moreover, the pressures of time and the demands of the conflicting social situations involved in a large family as well as restrictions placed upon behavior by the absence of certain economic goods, whether these be living space, the absence of toys, or more generally, the simple absence of money, all work to limit the rational and self-controlled performance of the role (Brim, 1959, p. 55).

Some of the influences on child training decisions are enduring parameters of the parent's personality: his intelligence, his internalized moral and social values (reflecting in part normative information from the environment in which he grew up), his preferences, sensitivities and aversions derived from unconscious genotypic dispositions. Other influences originate in relatively permanent aspects of his life situation: e.g., concepts of competence based on his own occupational experience, concepts of his social and economic environment based on the breadth of his experience (including travel), the structure of housing and settlement in which he is raising his child, and traditional folk beliefs concerning child training (ethno-education). Still other influences are long-term but recurrent pressures generated by the life situation: work fatigue, marital adjustment, other family relationships. Then there are influences that change with the development of the family, including the number of other children and their ages, the parent's amount of experience as a trainer of children, and the generalizations he has drawn from observing the effects of his previous child training. Finally, there are the immediate, but not necessarily recurrent or developmental, pressures such as short-run economic necessity (e.g., giving one parent less time to spend with the child or making the child's early occupational maturity seem more important), current child-care fashions, and other potentially relevant persuasive communications to which the parent is exposed (e.g., through the mass media). All of these interact with the child as perceived by the parent, who may or may not attempt to tailor his training program to what he sees as this particular child's individual characteristics. The complexity of this interaction can be illustrated by the case of the parent whose first male child, being particularly demanding, reactivates in the parent jealousy from his own early experience with a younger brother, and who therefore is particularly punitive in training this child, affecting the entire training process with this inappropriate emotion.

These influences on the parent's definition of the child-training situation operate, as Brim suggests, to limit his role as a simple mediator of environmental norms; they act as a filter through which environmental information must pass if it is to affect the training of the child. The parent lacking in the ability to think abstractly may see no connection between environmental events and his child's behavior; the ignorant or provincial parent may be simply unaware of the broader environmental context of his life, the parent engaged in marital conflict may not pay attention to external events and norms; the parent dominated by unconscious wishes and fears may misperceive environmental cues or inaccurately transform them into child-training practices. If a parent is under intense pressure to adjust to difficult domestic or economic conditions, these may come to dominate his thinking to such an extent that he thinks only of his child's adaptation to similar conditions, neglecting other realistic goals. The parent, then, is often not a smoothly operating child-preparation machine. Given all these, and many other, possibilities for faulty transmission between adult performance criteria and child-training goals, one might wonder if parents are able to perform this function at all and if so, how. They are able to do so in relatively stable societies because the more enduring influences on their phenomenal fields are not independent of contemporaneous environmental information concerning future adaptation of their child; i.e., the parents' internalized values and life experience and their current life pressures approximate the child's future environment well enough to act as adaptive guides to training even in the absence of accurate and conscious parental transmission of environmental information; child training is thus overdetermined. In rapidly changing societies or immigration situations, however, discontinuities between past, present, and future environments force parents to attune themselves to the environment and seek from it novel information about adult performance criteria or see their children suffer the effects of serious maladaptation as adults (see Inkeles, 1955; Miller & Swanson, 1958). It should be no surprise, then, that rapidly changing societies provide our best examples of parents attempting to rationalize their child training in terms of feedback from the environment, as well as our most familiar instances of maladaptation in rural immigrants to the city who fail to change their child-training goals rapidly enough to provide their children the competence they need for economic viability and mobility in urban industrial society (see Inkeles, 1966).

Despite the complex determination of parental phenomenal fields, and the equally complex variations in the filtration they provide for environmental information, the theoretical model of parental mediation is a simple one. Parents want their children to be able to meet societal demands and to take advantage of such opportunities for personal success or fulfillment (social, economic, political) as the sociocultural system offers. These are their most general training objectives. To attain them, the parents must anticipate what demands and opportunities the child will face in adulthood, through generalization of their own direct and vicarious experience as participant observers in a sociocultural system approximating that of the future adult, or through a self-conscious search for new information about social norms and payoffs, or through both. This information about the normative environment as the parent sees it gives him a view of what he is preparing the child for, and can be translated into criteria for evaluating behavior patterns manifested by the child. Although there can be a good deal of slippage between the objective sociocultural environment and evaluative decisions made by the parent, parental mediation is at least theoretically self-correcting in that, in situations where the parent's own past experience is not an adequate guide for the child, the social payoffs for adaptation and penalties for maladaptation increase in value and hence in salience for parents, increasing the pressure on them to notice discrepancies between their children's behavior and societal norms.

One set of conclusions the parent draws from participant observation in his normative environment concerns the kinds of personality traits and types that lead to respectable, righteous, and pragmatically successful adult behavior. He sees persons varying in personality characteristics receive varying amounts of endorsement or resistance from the sociocultural system, and he aggregates these instances and arrives at inductive generalizations concerning personality ideals which, if compatible with other parts of his cognitive structure, will act as a guide to the qualities he will attempt to reinforce and eliminate in his child. Elsewhere (LeVine, 1966a), I have argued this in detail for self-reliant achievement and sycophantic obedience as ideals of personality derived from status systems in which differing behavior patterns (occupational performance and political loyalty, respectively) led to upward mobility.

(c) *Parental means.* To give normative shape to the child's behavior, the parent has a number of means at his disposal. First is his power to reward and punish the child, based not only on control of resources seen by the child as necessary or desirable to his welfare but also on the child's emotional attachment to and dependence on the parent. No less important is his knowledge of adaptive skills in which to instruct the willing child. Since the parent, especially in the more differentiated societies, does not himself command all skills he wants his child to learn, he delegates part of the training task to specialists— schools, tutors, and institutionalized apprenticeship. Although he certainly uses reinforcement procedures, the parent is not simply an administrator of rewards and punishments, but an executive of sorts, making decisions about what kind of training is needed, who should give it to the child, and what level of performance the child should reach.

The role of verbal and behavioral feedback is critical in distinguishing the processes of deliberate socialization from the unplanned acquisition of behavioral dispositions through early experience. In deliberate socialization, the parent is specific enough in his goals and the child developed enough in his responses that it is possible for the trainer to gauge his immediate success or failure in attaining a training goal, and then modify the quantity or quality of his reinforcement accordingly. The feedback permits establishment of a self-correcting system of training, with parental training being varied in response to the child's performance until the desired performance is achieved, a highly efficient way of shaping behavior. As mentioned before, parents who seek to extend purposive manipulation into the early life of the child are particularly concerned that their children acquire language skills as early as possible so that they can obtain verbal feedback from the child as to the effectiveness of their training procedures. But feedback from non-verbal behavior also enables the parent to adjust his training to the child's performance and improves his ability to obtain desired results. Feedback is also essential in parental decisions concerning non-parental training: e.g., a parent who sees his child doing badly in school may decide that special tutoring is required to insure the child's admission to a higher school later on. The ultimate in self-regulation is achieved if the child acts on the basis of his own feedback to correct his mistakes and improve his performance, which children do when they have internalized adult standards of performance.

Through these conditioning processes the child acquires a range of adaptive skills which, along with earlier patterns of social behavior, become habitualized in a normative direction. It must be emphasized, however, that deliberate socialization operates predominantly on overt behavior, i.e., on the behavioral phenotype, and modifies only the overt expressions of the personality genotype—suppressing some genotypic tendencies, permitting restricted expression of others, disguising some for socially sanctioned behavior, and using others for adaptive purposes. The resultant character structure is thus based on but not reducible to the personality genotype which, in the process of deliberate socialization, has its first but far from last encounter with the normative pressures of the sociocultural environment.

(d) Consequences. Socialization has intended and unintended products. Its intended products are skills and inhibitions; skills for adaptive performance, inhibitions of genotypic tendencies incompatible with conformity to normative demands. Unintended products include the various motivational side-effects of suppressing or attenuating genotypic tendencies.

The cross-cultural evidence taken as a whole indicates how extremely effective deliberate socialization is in producing adaptive skills in growing individuals. At the level of skills related to subsistence activity and dominant cultural values, the old idea that "culture" can turn the child into anything "it" wants seems to receive strong support: In groups to whom waterways are importantly involved in subsistence, children learn to swim early and well (Mead, 1930); in some agricultural groups, six-year-old children can cultivate fields (LeVine & LeVine, 1963); children of political elites learn respect behavior when they are tiny (Read, 1959); etc. The evidence concerning the acquisition of skills in children so strongly suggests their enormous malleability that it is virtually taken for granted that if pressures are exerted in a given aspect of training, the majority of children in a population will comply with appropriate learning even if the tasks are complex.

Concerning inhibitions, the matter is more complex. At one level, this type of socialization is highly effective, too, in producing compliance with social constraints, i.e., overt conformity to social prohibitions. There is little question that if enough negative pressure is brought to bear in the socialization process, highly motivated behaviors such as sexuality and aggression can be suppressed so thoroughly in most of the population that they look almost non-existent to the casual observer. But suppression is not elimination, and while phenotypic expressions can be brought into line with even strict cultural prohibitions, the underlying genotypic dispositions, both motivational and cognitive, cannot be "stamped out" or "extinguished." Indeed, Whiting and Child (1953) have argued that the inhibition of a motive through socialization actually *increases* its strength, although altering its direction in favor of objects dissimilar to those that were culturally prohibited (displacement).

The impossibility of eliminating common genotypic motives through socialization of the child is frequently encountered in studies of particular cultures. For example, in my own work (LeVine, 1959) I found that the Gusii, although known for their sexual prudishness among the peoples of Western Kenya, and although maintaining strict sexual prohibitions in many areas of life, had a very high frequency of rape by local and cross-cultural standards. Gusii socialization of sex, being strict and repressive concerning public manifestations of sexuality but relatively permissive concerning sexual feelings and clandestine sexual acts, was predicated on the existence of enforcement procedures (feuding) which had broken down (at the inter-clan level) during British colonial administration. At the time of my field work, the strict sex-training practices, although still effective in maintaining conformity to intra-clan prohibitions, did nothing to prevent inter-clan sex offenses and could even be seen as promoting rape by raising the average level of male sexual frustration and making females resistant to heterosexual advances. Hence the paradox of an ethnic group notorious for both its prudery and its sex crimes. Whiting et al. (1966) present another example in the case of the Zuni Indians, whose well-known emphasis on harmony and peaceful solidarity is belied by their intense and frequent malicious intrigues over witchcraft. The authors argue that the strict socialization of aggression in Zuni children is necessitated by the crowded housing conditions in which they are raised but that the aggressive motivation finds an outlet in witchcraft beliefs and clandestine intrigues.

In both of these ethnographic instances, socialization of the child brings about overt conformity to prohibitive standards in one arena of social life but leads to unintended consequences based on genotypic dispositions in other arenas. The social system "pays" for social control in visible, primary group relations with a certain amount of disruption and strain behind the scenes or beyond the confines of the primary group. This social "cost" factor appears to be present wherever social norms require suppression of motives in socialization of the child. Parents are then put in the position of unwittingly fostering deviant behavior as they consciously attempt to build into their children the inhibitions that will enable them to conform to institutional demands, although quite possibly institutional functioning gains more from the conformity than it loses in the deviant behavior (as an evolutionary model would require for a stable system). Where socialization of the child's impulse life is so thorough that he becomes a virtually self-policing individual, it may be, as Freud proposed, that the cost is paid not by the social system but by the individual, who turns his socially unacceptable impulses against himself and suffers self-hatred, painful neurotic symptoms, and crippling inhibitions. This latter situation may be optimal for institutional functioning unless the incidence of psychopathology and discontent become so great as to exact their own toll from the social system.

As the foregoing discussion suggests, adaptation of the individual to his sociocultural environment begins in the process of child socialization but is not successfully completed there, partly because the parent is an imperfect mediator of environmental pressures and often cannot anticipate them accurately, and partly because deliberate socialization can have unintended consequences that are maladaptive. This means that adaptation must be a continuing process in adult life, although many of the basic patterns of adaptive behavior are established in the training of the child. But there are, as we have seen, limits to the modification of individual behavior in the interests of adaptation to institutional environment, limits stemming from the personality genotype as a highly resistant organization of motives and cognitive dispositions. The genotypic tendencies can be suppressed, disguised, and diverted but they are hardly ever eliminated in socialization through the life cycle. They seek expression in overt behavior, and no social system is so prescriptive and coercive as to prevent such expressions; there are always loopholes in normative prescriptions for role performance, and areas for choice and alternative possibilities. Therefore the sociocultural environment must bend at points before these inflexibilities of the personality system, and adaptation is achieved through compromise. Institutionalized forms of adaptation (e.g., social conformity) between personality and sociocultural systems can be seen as *compromise formations*[5] in which constraints and demands of both the personality genotype and the normative environment are represented. They have evolved from the interaction of environmental pressures and genotypic pressures operating over time. Although movement is toward a steady state in which the more pressing demands of both sides are adequately satisfied, many particular institutionalized adaptations are "bad" compromises, in which one side or another is overrepresented. The stability of bad compromise formations depends on whether they co-exist in a system with

---

[5] The term *compromise formation* is derived from the Freudian conceptualization of neurotic symptom formulation, in which expression of the forbidden impulse and expression of the defense against the impulse are combined in a disguised and displaced form, as they are also in dreams according to psychoanalytic theory (see Fenichel, 1945). A detailed account of institutionalized compromise formations (e.g., willing conformity, coerced conformity with motivational displacement, normative pluralism) will be presented in a subsequent paper, but one methodological point belongs here, viz., the natural confounding of individual disposition and situational demand in all evolved patterns of behavior is present also in institutional adaptations of personality and culture, making it inevitable that in observation of adaptive social behavior we are usually observing an expressive compromise rather than a simple response to internal or external stimuli.

other adaptive compromises that compensate their imbalance adequately. When the steady state of optimal functioning is reached, then we expect change only when the institutional environment changes in scope or in the content of its normative demands or opportunities, or when the personality genotype characteristic of the population undergoes a change. The forms of institutionalized adaptation, and the processes of stability and change, constitute the second part of this evolutionary model and are beyond the scope of the present chapter.

CONCLUSIONS

On the basis of this first part of an evolutionary model of culture-personality relations, it is possible to locate those points at which processes analogous to the Darwinian mechanisms of variation and selection seem to be operating, and to identify relevant problems for empirical research.

There are four processes discussed so far to which the variation-selection model could plausibly be fitted:

1. *The adaptation of early child-care customs to ecological pressures.* Since infants must survive a period of high mortality and be able to acquire basic subsistence skills in order for a population to survive, it is reasonable to assume that the infant-care customs of stable or growing populations are a product of an evolutionary process in which poorly adapted populations failed to survive, were absorbed into better adapted populations, or radically changed their customs of infant care. This process was discussed as evolving limits on the extent to which the structure of primary groups in which children are raised could be altered in accordance with the requirements of the wider social structure. It may be, however, that this process makes more positive contributions to personality-environment adaptation. For example, Nimkoff and Middleton (1960) have shown that families in hunting and gathering societies are smaller than in agricultural societies, and we know from studies within our own culture (see Clausen, 1966) that smaller families produce children different in certain behavioral dimensions (e.g., higher on achievement even with social class held constant). This accords with the finding of Barry, Child and Bacon (1959) that parents in hunting and gathering societies emphasize self-reliance and achievement in child training, but it does not necessarily support their assumption that it is the deliberate socialization of the parents that produces requisite amounts of these dispositions in their children to maintain the subsistence economy.

Could it be that children raised in small families have early experiences that equip them with genotypic dispositions making them easier to train in self-reliance and achievement? In other words, could it be that the greater potential for self-reliance and achievement of children raised in small families helped give small families a selective advantage in hunting and gathering groups? Or perhaps more reasonably, could it be that the greater potential for obedience and responsibility of children raised in large families contributed to the selective advantage of large domestic groups once the food-producing revolution had occurred? These are difficult problems to research, but they raise the possibility that the structure of the primary groups in which children are raised might be more tightly adapted to ecological pressures than is readily apparent, with the personality outcome of early primary group experience being a factor in the evolution of more adaptive forms. Although the mechanisms involved are far from clear, this type of evolutionary conceptualization, closer to the original Darwinian model, is a challenging source of rival hypotheses for theorists who tend to assign conscious parental mediation and deliberate socialization the central role in the adaptation of child rearing.

2. *The initial adaptation of genotypically varying personalities to normative pressures through deliberate socialization.* In this process, the distribution of personality genotypes provides the unplanned variation, and the parent's values and decisions concerning child training constitute the consistent selective criteria. The variation-selection model fits at the level of the population, in which normatively agreeing parents act selectively on the randomly varying personality genotypes of their children, and at the level of the parent-child dyad, in which the child's behavioral output, at first haphazardly compatible and incompatible with parental goals, is shaped toward greater compatibility by the differential reinforcement of the parent. To a degree not adequately documented and undoubtedly variable cross-culturally, the parent acts as an agent of society and in response to its changing norms, so that child training helps prepare the child for future normative environments. This preparation cannot be completed in childhood because child training cannot anticipate in all their specificity the micro- and macro-environments to which the future adult will adapt. So this is initial adaptation, in which the child develops some skills and inhibitory controls that will facilitate his subsequent adaptive behavior.

3. *The secondary adaptations of individual personality to normative environments through selective social behavior.* This has to do with differing genotype-phenotype relations within the personality of the individual as he occupies differing normative environments (social roles) successively or simultaneously. The personality genotype is a continual source of impulses, wishes, and ideas that constitute unplanned variation from the viewpoint of performance in social roles. The individual has in the self-image that is central to his phenotypic social character a set of criteria for selecting among these genotypic impulses those that are consistent with his normatively shaped self-image. Furthermore, each role or other ecological niche he occupies provides its own criteria for evaluating and administering rewards and punishments for behavior of varying degrees of compatibility with his genotypic dispositions. Operating within the limits set by his own (perhaps temporarily) stabilized self-image, he responds to the demand characteristics of the micro-environment, experiencing or anticipating reward and punishment for genotypically derived behaviors until some of the underlying dispositions are selected for expression in overt be-

havior, others for suppression, displacement, or disguise, in a stabilized adaptation to the niche. On a similarly experimental basis he selectively regulates the amount and kind of genotypic expression in the various environmental niches that comprise his life situation, until a total life adaptation is reached. If he moves from one role or status position to another or otherwise alters his life situation, the selective process will be repeated.

4. *The adaptation of aggregate personality characteristics of populations to normative environments through the selective pressure of social sanctions.* This refers to the means by which the frequency distributions of phenotypic character traits in a population come to fit the society-wide normative ideals of role performance or at least to be skewed in that direction compared to societies with other normative ideals. The details of this will be included in the second part of the evolutionary model and can be dealt with only briefly in this chapter. Phenotypic character traits, although normatively influenced and shaped, are still highly variable in a population because they are imbedded in different personality structures, with varying genotypic capacities for approximating ideal role performance. Some persons have genotypic personality traits that are favored by the normative environment in which they function; in consequence they manifest greater talent, skill and fluency in role performance, are able to take greater advantage of opportunities, and achieve greater success and other social rewards. Other persons, though able to acquire normatively sanctioned character traits through socialization and subsequent secondary adaptation, have a harder time conforming and performing in roles because their genotypic dispositions are less compatible with environmental demands and opportunities; in consequence they do not manifest excellence in role performance, are less able to gain success and social rewards, or are more likely to engage in deviant behavior and incur negative sanctions. This variation in social competence (see Inkeles, 1966) is constantly being acted upon by social sanctions, with the effect of differentially distributing social rewards and punishments (success and failure, upward and downward mobility, honor and stigma, prestige and disgrace, etc.) in accordance with demonstrated level of competence on a more or less permanent basis. In addition, however, the operation of this selective procedure is highly visible to actors in the social system, particularly in societies in which status mobility is possible, so that knowledge of which character traits are associated with competence and incompetence becomes widespread in the population and affects the deliberate socialization of children. In other words there is feedback from the selective pressure of social sanctions on adults to parental training of children, inducing parents to train their children to meet operative standards of competence. Over time, this feedback, if consistent, results in the production through socialization of a higher frequency of persons with character traits labeled as competent until some stable state is reached. In societies where relatively little mobility is possible, stability may have been reached such a long time ago that the feedback is hardly necessary since parents' internalized norms are an adequate guide to socially ap-

proved competence without redundant observation of environmental selection. This conception of personality-environment adaptation is applied to relations between status-mobility systems and frequency of achievement motivation in research on three Nigerian ethnic groups by LeVine (1966a).

It is thus clear that the Darwinian variation-selection model provides a plausible conceptualization of culture-personality relations in adaptive terms, so long as one identifies those junctures in social and psychological functioning at which unplanned variation and cumulative selection can reasonably be thought to operate. Rather than a single adaptive process bringing personality and sociocultural environment into some kind of fit, there are variation and selection mechanisms operating at numerous levels, not all of them mentioned here, toward stable integration of individual dispositions and social norms. The fact that human adaptation of this kind is not attained through a single, fixed mechanism probably permits greater flexibility and efficiency of adaptation and more rapid adjustment to environmental change.

In terms of research implications, its permission of greater cross-population variability in responsiveness to environmental feedback and in tightness of conscious control over selection assigns a central role to the purposive behavior of parents and other socializing agents. It is parents who decide how to organize relations between environments and children, and we need to know much more about the cognitive and other bases for their decisions before we can understand how these relations are organized in culturally differing populations.

From the present theoretical perspective, then, the most urgent objective for empirical research on socialization is to understand the relation between the planned and unplanned aspects of social learning, how this relation varies across societies, and the kinds of adaptations that are made possible with varying degrees of conscious linkage between environmental feedback and deliberate socialization. In their central position as socializing agents, parents are able to act on their perceptions of the child's personality and the environment's demands and opportunities to create the basis for adaptive fit between personality and culture; it is essential that we investigate more intensively what these perceptions are and how parents organize their perceptions to arrive at training decisions.

REFERENCES

ALLAND, A. *Evolution and human behavior.* Garden City: Natural History Press, 1967.

ASHBY, W. R. *Design for a brain.* New York: Wiley, 1952.

BANDURA, A., & WALTERS, R. *Social learning and personality development.* New York: Holt, Rinehart & Winston, 1963.

BARRY, H. H., III, CHILD, I. L., & BACON, M. K. Relation of child training to subsistence economy. *American Anthropologist,* 1959, 61, 51–63.

BENEDICT, RUTH. Continuities and discontinuities in cultural conditioning. *Psychiatry,* 1938, 1, 161–167.

BRIM, O. G., JR. *Education for child rearing.* New York: Russell Sage Foundation, 1959.

BRIM, O. G., JR. Socialization through the life cycle. In O. G. Brim, Jr. & S. Wheeler, *Socialization after childhood.* New York: Wiley, 1966.

BRUNER, J. S., OLVER, ROSE R., GREENFIELD, PATRICIA, ET AL. *Studies in cognitive growth.* New York: Wiley, 1966.

CAMPBELL, D. T. Variation and selective-retention in sociocultural evolution. In H. R. Barringer, G. I. Blanksten & R. W. Mack (Eds.), *Social change in developing areas: A re-interpretation of evolutionary theory.* Cambridge, Mass.: Schenkman, 1966.

CLAUSEN, J. A. Family structure, socialization, and personality. In Lois W. Hoffman & M. L. Hoffman (Eds.), *Review of child development research.* Vol. 2. New York: Russell Sage Foundation, 1966.

DURKHEIM, E. *Suicide.* Glencoe, Ill.: The Free Press, 1951.

FENICHEL, O. *The psychoanalytic theory of neurosis.* New York: Norton, 1945.

FREUD, S. Civilization and its discontents. In J. Strechey (Ed.), *The complete psychological writings of Sigmund Freud.* (Std. Ed.) London: Hogarth, 1930.

FROMM, E. *Escape from freedom.* New York: Farrar & Rinehart, 1941.

GOODY, J. (Ed.) *The developmental cycle in domestic groups.* Cambridge: Cambridge Univer. Press, 1962.

GRAY, R., & GULLIVER, P. *The family estate in Africa.* London: Routledge & Kegan Paul, 1964.

HALLOWELL, A. I. Psychology and anthropology. In J. P. Gillin (Ed.), *Toward a science of social man.* New York: Macmillan, 1954.

HARTMANN, H. *Ego psychology and the problem of adaptation.* New York: International Universities Press, 1958.

INKELES, A. Social change and social character: The role of parental mediation. *Journal of Social Issues,* 1955, 11, 12–23.

INKELES, A. Personality and social structure. In R. K. Merton, L. Brown & L. S. Cottrell, Jr. (Eds.), *Sociology today.* New York: Basic Books, 1959.

INKELES, A. Sociology and psychology. In S. Koch (Ed.), *Psychology: Study of a science.* Vol. VI. New York: McGraw-Hill, 1963.

INKELES, A. Social structure and the socialization of competence. *Harvard Educational Review,* 1966, 36, 265–283.

INKELES, A., & LEVINSON, D. J. National character. In G. Lindzey (Ed.), *The handbook of social psychology.* Vol. II. Cambridge, Mass.: Addison-Wesley, 1954.

KOHLBERG, L. A. Cognitive stages and preschool education. *Human Development,* 1966, 9, 5–17.

LEVINE, R. A. Gusii sex offenses: A study in social control. *American Anthropologist,* 1959, 61, 965–990.

LEVINE, R. A. Behaviorism in psychological anthropology. In J. M. Wepman & R. W. Heine (Eds.), *Concepts of personality.* Chicago: Aldine, 1963.

LEVINE, R. A. *Dreams and deeds: Achievement motivation in Nigeria.* Chicago: Univer. of Chicago Press, 1966. (a)

LEVINE, R. A. Outsiders' judgments: An ethnographic approach to group differences in personality. *Southwestern Journal of Anthropology,* 1966, 22, 101–116. (b)

LEVINE, R. A. Toward a psychology of populations: The cross-cultural study of personality. *Human Development,* 1966, 9, 30–46. (c)

LeVine, R. A., Klein, Nancy, & Owen, Constance. Father-child relationships and changing life-styles in Ibadan, Nigeria. In H. Miner (Ed.), *The city in modern Africa.* New York: Praeger, 1967.

LeVine, R. A., & LeVine, Barbara B. Nyansongo: A Gusii community in Kenya. In Beatrice Whiting (Ed.), *Six cultures: Studies of child rearing.* New York: Wiley, 1963. (Published separately. New York: Wiley, 1966)

Mead, Margaret. *Growing up in New Guinea.* New York: Morrow, 1930.

Mead, Margaret. *Continuities in cultural evolution.* New Haven: Yale Univer. Press, 1964.

Miller, D., & Swanson, G. *The changing American parent.* New York: Wiley, 1958.

Miller, N., & Dollard, J. *Social learning and initiation.* New Haven: Yale Univer. Press, 1941.

Minturn, L., & Lambert, W. E. *Mothers of six cultures.* New York: Wiley, 1964.

Nimkoff, M. F., & Middleton, R. Types of family and types of economy. *American Journal of Sociology,* 1960, 66, 215–225.

Parsons, T. *The social system.* Glencoe, Ill.: The Free Press, 1949.

Parsons, T. *Social structure and personality.* New York: The Free Press, 1964.

Parsons, T., & Shils, E. (Eds.) *Toward a general theory of action.* Cambridge, Mass.: Harvard Univer. Press, 1951.

Pringle, J. W. S. On the parallel between learning and evolution. *Behavior,* 1951, 3, 175–250.

Read, Margaret. *Children of their fathers: Growing up among the Ngoni of Nyasaland.* New Haven: Yale Univer. Press, 1959.

Riesman, D. *The lonely crowd.* New Haven: Yale Univer. Press, 1950.

Segall, M., Campbell, D. T., & Herskovits, M. J. *The influence of culture on visual perception.* Indianapolis: Bobbs-Merrill, 1966.

Spiro, M. E. *Kibbutz: Venture in utopia.* Cambridge, Mass.: Harvard Univer. Press, 1957.

Spiro, M. E. *Children of the kibbutz.* Cambridge, Mass.: Harvard Univer. Press, 1958.

Spiro, M. E. Social systems, personality and functional analysis. In B. Kaplan (Ed.), *Studying personality cross-culturally.* Evanston: Row Peterson, 1961.

Thomas, W. I., & Znaniecki, F. *The Polish peasant in Europe and America.* Chicago: Univer. of Chicago Press, 1927.

Whiting, J. W. M. Effects of climate on certain cultural practices. In W. H. Goodenough (Ed.), *Explorations in cultural anthropology.* New York: McGraw-Hill, 1965.

Whiting, J. W. M., & Child, I. L. *Child training and personality.* New Haven: Yale Univer. Press, 1953.

Whiting, J. W. M., & Whiting, Beatrice B. Contributions of anthropology to methods of studying child rearing. In P. Mussen (Ed.), *Handbook of research methods in child development.* New York: Wiley, 1959.

Whiting, J. W. M., et al. The learning of values. In E. Z. Vogt & E. Albert (Eds.), *Peoples of Rimrock.* Cambridge, Mass.: Harvard Univer. Press, 1966.

Zborowski, M. The place of book-learning in traditional Jewish culture. *Harvard Educational Review,* 1949, 19, 87–109.

CHAPTER **9**

Interpersonal Interaction
And The Development Of The Self

Leonard S. Cottrell, Jr.

University of North Carolina

Probably very few people reared in Western middle class culture have not read or had quoted to them Polonius' parting advice to Laertes as the latter was departing for France. One of the most familiar parts of the father's farewell counsel is:

> This above all: to thine own self be true,
> And it must follow, as night the day,
> Thou canst not then be false to any man.
>
> *Hamlet,* Act I, Sc. 3.

The validity of this statement is no doubt widely accepted without question, but it can be regarded as a highly interesting hypothesis that social psychologists have somehow overlooked. If we were to undertake a research design to test the hypothesis, one of the first problems we would encounter is that of making clear what we mean by the term "thine own self." Here again, what has seemed so obvious—everyone surely knows what his "own self" is— becomes problematical when we attempt to make its meaning explicit and precise. Perhaps this is why so many people regard the social psychologist as a boring fellow who is always ponderously making problems of what everyone else knows to be simple fact.

Be that as it may, we are taking the position in this chapter that Laertes, even as you and I, would be hard put to state explicitly what his father referred to as "thine own self." Even more taxing would be to account for having an "own self," though for Laertes this would not be so difficult since he would be certain that whatever his self was, it came as part of his nature. We, for our part, could not be so comfortable in accepting the self as given. The aim of this chapter is to clarify what is denoted by the term "self" and to suggest how it emerges, develops and functions. Such suggestions could hopefully be sources of explicit hypotheses for empirical testing.

BASIC PROCESSES

At this point we must present a somewhat simplified description of what, in the frame of reference of this discussion, will be regarded as the fundamental process out of which the self emerges. Let us assume two persons, A and B, who are involved in some activity in which their behavior is interdependent. That is, the acts of A are responses to those of B and in turn serve to evoke ensuing acts of B, and vice versa with B. If this interaction is repeated some, as yet unspecified, number of times, two results seem to occur. In the first place, each of the participants learns, i.e., can reproduce, a series of acts representing his part of the interact. This is so obvious and familiar in the experience of everyone that no formal proof is called for. Somewhat less obvious, but held here also to occur, is that each of the participants learns the action sequence that constitutes the part of the other in the interact *as he has perceived that action sequence.* An interesting and somewhat mystifying aspect of this second result is that the learning of the acts of the other may, and usually does, take place without overt practice. In other words, the acts of the other may be incorporated in incipient or latent behavioral mobilizations that appear in overt manifestations only when the situational context is so structured that A, for example, finds himself in the position of B, whereupon he behaves as B did when A was acting his own position. Thus a father in teaching his four-year-old daughter to play the first few bars of "Three Blind Mice" on her toy piano held her hand and guided her fingers to strike each note with the comment, "Now you hit this one, then this one, then this one, etc." This little interact had occurred only a few times when he later observed his daughter to be holding her right hand with her left and guiding her index finger while telling herself, "Now you hit this one, then this one, etc." She was not yet striking the correct notes in the correct sequence, but she was reproducing a substantial portion of the father's role, as well as of her own in the little interact.[1] Another child of six who lived on a farm where playmates were scarce was observed in solitary play to reproduce a considerable part of the community in the parts she played. She was frequently taken by her mother on various calls upon neighbors. In her play she acted out her mother's role and the roles of the various neighbors visited, reproducing characteristic conversation content, tone of voice, posture, gesture, etc.

One can, without difficulty, assemble an unlimited number of anecdotes similar to those cited above, especially after attention has been focused on such occurrences. It is surprising, therefore, that more formal and systematic testing of the proposition is reported so infrequently in the literature,[2] especially since the process involved is of such crucial importance in the personality development, socialization and social integration.

---

[1] For additional illustrations, see Cottrell, 1942a.

[2] See Ofshe (1966). This research is not directed specifically at the development of self-systems, but does illustrate the feasibility of experimental testing of interactive propositions.

The question is not whether or not participants in interaction incorporate into their own response systems the actions of one another. The weight of evidence and observation seems to support the assumption that this is a basic and pervasive tendency. More fruitful questions for research have to do with making explicit the conditions, organic, psychological, and sociological, that determine the extent and accuracy with which the process takes place (Ofshe, 1966; Turner, 1956). In any case, we are dealing with a kind of response that seems to be well-grounded in the constitution of the human organism and is probably derived from the survival value of the capacity to anticipate oncoming acts and stimulate an adaptive response or mobilization and readiness. The process is what George Herbert Mead first described as "taking the role of the other." Other terms such as empathic response, identification, internalization, have been used in varying degrees of approximation in describing the phenomenon. Whatever the terms used, the essential thing to keep in mind is that something takes place whereby an interacting system is imported in some form into the neuromuscular system of the individual participant and he becomes within himself an arena in which the interacting parts are represented. Moreover, under appropriate external conditions, any one of the parts may be enacted overtly by the individual. Again we must emphasize that he enacts the parts as he has perceived and experienced them in the previous interaction.

It can readily be seen that the phenomena discussed here are not only rich in interest and significance for understanding personal and social behavior, but extremely difficult to study with present research procedures. The usual biological or psychological experimental studies of an individual's organic or behavioral responses, as complicated as these are at times, are relatively simple in contrast to studies of overt interaction, to say nothing of the process of importation of the interactional processes into the subjective arena.

It is encouraging and of the greatest significance that conventionally trained "learning psychologists" are now addressing themselves to the problems raised forty years ago by social behaviorists like George Herbert Mead. The work of Albert Bandura and his collaborators represents the most advanced efforts by learning psychologists to grapple experimentally with problems relevant to the processes and products of social interaction. His brilliant experimentation is reported in this volume,[3] and the reader who has some

---

[3] See Bandura (1969). Bandura is not primarily concerned with the emergence of the self-system as here conceived. However, it will be clear that his work on problems of "social learning" is highly relevant to more adequate conceptualization as well as empirical work on the self. The quality of his work is such that one may be forgiven for presuming to voice the wish that he had been more familiar with the work of George H. Mead and of those who derive their theoretical orientations from him.

Bandura's work suffers the limitations inherent in what Robert R. Sears (1951) has called a "monadic" as opposed to a "dyadic" form of conceptualization in psychology. Indeed most of the work cited by Ruth Wylie (1961) in her useful summary of work on the self-concept has the same limitation. Wylie's own excellent analysis and interpretation would undoubtedly have been more penetrating and suggestive had she been better acquainted with the long-standing interactive tradition in American social psychology as

sophistication in the phenomena of interactional behavior will readily see how close Bandura has come to a long-standing theoretical position in social psychology deriving from the work of Mead (1913).

Experimentation by Bandura and others cited by him (see his references) strongly supports what he refers to as identificatory learning and what we have referred to above as a basic process. I stated propositions concerning this process in 1942 (Cottrell, 1942a). These propositions will require substantial revision in the light of work like Bandura's and work toward which his is clearly leading. However, they will serve to illustrate certain conceptual positions which need to be more adequately incorporated in the kind of work the social-learning psychologists are doing.

This is not the place to undertake an extensive critique of the social-learning psychologists represented in Bandura's work. It will be sufficient for our present interest to suggest certain inadequacies of the conceptualization that, if corrected, would bring this research to bear more crucially on the social-interactionists' assumptions and hypotheses.

In the first place, the interactionist's position represented in this chapter requires that when A and B have been involved in an interact directly or vicariously, adequate examination of the results would reveal that each has incorporated the component roles of the *whole act*. This is hypothesized whether we are dealing with a dyad or a greater number of participants. That is to say, if A is involved in an interact with B, C, and D, appropriate testing should reveal that he has covertly "learned"—acquired the action patterns of B', C', and D' (Cottrell, 1942a, Propositions I–III). To be sure, the complexity becomes too much if the social act involves more than a very limited number of "others." However, multi-person social acts tend themselves to become "simplified" into interactions among collective entities which are perceived, experienced, reacted to and incorporated by the actor as "generalized" others, yielding self-other incorporated interacts of the type $A \leftrightarrows G'$.

While Bandura's findings are generally consistent with the whole act incorporation hypothesis, his use of a modified conventional learning theory

---

represented in the work of William James (1890), James M. Baldwin (1895), John Dewey (1916), Charles H. Cooley (1902), George H. Mead (1913) and Ellsworth Faris (1937).

Illustrative of more recent writers, those who in varying degrees draw on this tradition are: Herbert Blumer (1939), Robert E. L. Faris (1952), Alfred R. Lindesmith and Anselm Strauss (1956), Erving Goffman (1959, 1961), Ralph H. Turner (1956), Nelson N. Foote (1951), Manford H. Kuhn (Kuhn & McPartland, 1954), Orville G. Brim (1960), Harry Stack Sullivan (1940), Norman Cameron (1947), Omar K. Moore (1958), Walter Coutu (1949), Jacob L. Moreno (1945), Tamotsu Shibutani (1961), and Eugene Weinstein (1966).

Broadly representative of the range of conceptualizations of the self in contemporary psychology that stem from essentially monadic models are those by: Gordon W. Allport (1938, 1960), Erik Erikson (1950), D. O. Hebb (1960), Ernest Hilgard (1949), Carl Rogers (1951), Theodore Sarbin (1952), Muzafer Sherif and Hadley Cantril (1947). Some of these, e.g., Sarbin, and Sherif and Cantril, represent a fairly close approach to dyadic models.

paradigm with its focus on the individual learning of specific acts presented by a "model" with appropriate rewards and punishments does not lead readily to a more comprehensive perspective that includes the assumptions stated above.

In the second place, and closely related to the previous comment, Bandura's conceptualization does not appear to provide sufficient grounds for adequate specification of the situational fields in which the learning takes place and is reproduced. It is not clear in much of the reported experimentation that the subject is actually involved in an interact directly or vicariously. Furthermore, while the subject is usually presented with a "stimulus," ostensibly evocative of the learning situation, it is far from clear that such a stimulus includes not only the situational structure including the subject and models, but the positioning of the subject in the role of the model whose behavior he was supposed to have "learned." Some of the experimentation approximated these conditions, but much more sophisticated handling of situational structure and positioning is called for.

Third and finally, the conceptualizations as seen in the work on identificatory learning do not provide an adequate basis for discrimination between what is "learned" or incorporated from the "other" and thus becomes the property of the learner but not experienced as part of his identity or self, and what does become assimilated to one or another of his identities. The first of these forms provides the organism with expectancy postures to which the acts of the self are oriented. The second form becomes a constituent of the identity that requires validating responses of others present in the external world, or internally represented, to support.

Precise specifications of situational and subjective determinants of the form the identificatory learning takes is a major problem in the field of the self. This of course has not been a problem explicitly addressed by the investigators like Bandura, but their work will undoubtedly become increasingly relevant to it.

EMERGENCE OF THE SELF

We can consider the relevance of the "role-taking" process for the emergence of what is experienced as the self. Assuming that the human interactant does in fact acquire the responses of the other to his own acts in such a way that he can respond to himself as he has perceived the other to respond, then it is clear that this is one way he can become an object to himself. Indeed, from the general point of view represented here, one can perceive his actions and their meanings only from the response standpoint of another involved in the interact. We literally do not "know what we are doing," nor even what or who we are except in terms of the responses of others that give meaning to our acts and define us to ourselves. A crucial experimental test of this position is not possible within the framework of our standards regarding the value and inviolability of the person. Approximations can be made through the accidental failures in the careers of individuals, and through observation of the differences in self-perceptions that are correlated with known differences in the responses provided by various interactional fields. Thus far this has been done only in a sporadic and unsystematic manner, but the evidence is consistent with the general position. Thus until a conceptualization with more face validity and evidentiary support is presented, we shall proceed on the assumption that what we experience as self is a reflexive product of social interaction.

At this point it is well to remind ourselves of two things. One is that we are dealing with actual behavior, both in the overt interaction in which A and B are involved and in the covert incipient act mobilizations that represent the overt acts when imported into the organisms of the participants. It is not always easy to remember that so-called internalized interacts are not "merely words" but are basically behavioral mobilizations, incipient to be sure, but act organizations nonetheless. The covert behavioral mobilizations and their relations to interactive events and to symbolic stimuli constitute a highly important field of research not yet adequately developed. A promising lead was opened up by Edmund E. Jacobson as early as 1932 when he conducted experimental studies of muscular tension accompanying "imaginative behavior." While a great deal of electromyographic work has been done since then, the suggestions this work had for the study of overt and covert processes in interactive and reflexive behavior have not been followed up. Of special significance in the development of this field is the work of Ralph F. Hefferline and his students. His investigations are giving exciting content to his statement in 1962: "In my opinion the region under the skin, where covert behavior, both operant and respondent, takes place, is psychology's new frontier, and this environment needs to be coordinated with the external environment by whatever means can be contrived in order that a scientific account of the stimulus control of the organism may be completed" (Hefferline, 1962, p. 134).

A second observation, which at first appears to contradict what we have just stated, is that most interaction, both overt and covert, involves so many act mobilizations at such a rapid rate that the organism could probably not manage to actually produce all of them fast enough, even incipiently, nor provide the energy to do so. In any case, we do know that the bulk of our interchanges take place by means of "shorthand" signals variously termed gestures, signs, and symbols. These devices, standing for action, permit rapid interchanges with minimal overt action or covert mobilization. However, when the connection between gestures and actions they indicate becomes so attenuated that the user is unable to produce the acts when necessary, then actual communication becomes ambiguous and frequently meaningless.

These devices, and especially the vocal gesture, not only make rapid and efficient interaction possible but greatly enhance the capability of the individual to respond to his own impulses, attitudes, and overt acts with the acts of the other through the use of that other's gestures that signalize his responding attitudes and overt acts.

When an actor's incipient or overt acts evoke within his own reactive system the responses of others to those acts, he experiences an essential element in what is referred to as a self. So far as we know, this is the only way a self is achieved. This is an enormously important achievement. Jumping ahead of our story and setting aside for the moment all the complications and problems that the concept presents, we see the self-system as having basic functions in the personality. One such function is serving as a monitoring, direction-maintaining, and decision-reference system. We shall find that a knowledge of the self-systems of the person takes us a long way toward understanding and predicting his behavior (Cottrell, 1933; Burgess & Cottrell, 1939; Cottrell, 1941). Another basic function is to provide the person with that "sense of being" without which human life appears intolerable. The much discussed "search for identity" is essentially a search for a satisfying and well-supported self-system. We shall return to a discussion of the functions of the self-system, but enough has been said to indicate how important it is to gain an under-standing of what the self-system is, how it develops, as well as the problems that confront it.

STRUCTURE OF THE SELF

The self should be conceived of as not a "thing" but a process. This statement is problematic at best, but the intent of it is to discourage images of the concept that picture it as a fixed entity like a ball or a "little man." Use has been made of such expressions as "self-other system" or "self-system" in an effort to keep in mind that what we are dealing with is a process, the experience of which is referred to as an entity, the self. To be sure, a process can be and is legitimately and usefully referred to as an entity. The atom is essentially a process, an energy system; so is the solar system. And yet it is useful for many purposes to refer to these processes as entities. So it is with the self. The articulated system of behaviors in which are linked the act mobilizations of the actor and the evoked act mobilizations experienced as anticipated responses of objective others or as previously incorporated acts of others that constitute the "inner forum" of the person and which responses are assumed by the person towards his own act or tendency is obviously a dynamic process. The whole complex can also be referred to as an entity, the self or self-system, but the reality and nature of the behavioral process must always be comprehended in any attempt to analyze the phenomena. Thus if a student says, "I would lose all respect for myself if I should cheat on an examination," his statement makes sense and for ordinary conversation can be left as it is. But if we want to make clear the operations that underlie such a statement, we must conceive it in the following manner: The incipient act to cheat on an examination present in the student evokes incipient mobilizations of derogating and rejecting responses he has incorporated through taking the role of significant reference others in their responses to similar behavior, either his own or that of an observed other who has cheated. Note that up to this point the student could have said, "I would lose the respect of certain others if I cheated." He would in such a case be using the role-taking process to anticipate the acts of others. But he says, *"I* would lose respect for *myself*." This points to the fact that the responses of the defining others have somehow been adopted as his own, sometimes referred to as identification. An interesting question for research is what determines when incorporated responses are kept at the "they" position and when adopted as ego's own? At any rate, we can see that what is experienced as self is a complex dynamic process. Incidentally, the illustration just given represents one of the simpler of the self-other processes. As the work of Bandura (1969) shows, these processes are apparently too complex to be handled by the simpler forms of stimulus-response and learning theories and derivative research designs.

Another aspect of the self-system which makes it difficult to study, especially by so-called "objective" methods, is its subjective or "mentalistic" character. The way the person perceives the responses of others to his own actions, the way he perceives himself from the response perspectives thus provided, and the reference others he takes into account in responding to his attitudes and actions are not subject to direct observation except by the actor himself. An observer can only see overt behavior or instrument recordings of certain aspects of covert behavior and listen to words of the actor and from these manifestations inferentially construct the subject's self-system. To be sure, these inferences can provide the basis for quite accurate predictions as to how the subject will report his self-perceptions, his expectations of specified others, and his definitions of situations. If this were not so, even in everyday life, ordered social life would not be possible since most of our activities depend upon reasonably valid perceptions of, and expected responses from, other participants in our life situations. Indeed it is largely in terms of consensually validated self-systems, sometimes referred to as identities, that we "live, move and have our being." Much of our activity and striving, perhaps most of it, is directed toward establishing and maintaining social contexts supportive of desired identities, or toward changing contexts that impose unwanted identities.

The term "identity," as used in this discussion, refers to a special self-other system. Much of the time the term is used to refer to what might be called culturally defined categories or stereotypes such as lawyer, policeman, artist, woman, college student, welfare client, etc., for which there are more or less uniform mutual systems of expected behavior. But the term is also accurately used to refer to less conventionally defined self-systems, such as "good sport," "con artist," "hen-pecked husband," "easy touch." There are also highly idiosyncratic self-systems that may be referred to as identities, though this is a much less common use of the term. In any case, the basic process is the same, and an identity exists only through the appropriate defining responses of reference others. Furthermore, it should be clear that an identity name or category such as Negro, student, lawyer, parent, "good sport," or "spoil sport" has no intrinsic content or meaning. Their meaning is found in their reference to specified contexts of expectations and responses of the relevant others to the actor so categorized. As can be seen, the term is synonymous with self-other system.

There is much talk these days about the "search for an identity," especially by adolescents and youths. This search appears to lead frequently to rather insulated, individual efforts to probe the psyche to find the "real self," to look for "kicks" and to get "experience." Little or no attention seems to be given to the necessity for establishing a stable social context in which an identity can be defined and supported through the responses of relevant others. In this connection, it is interesting to note that, quite unwittingly, some of this search has resulted in the emergence of a subculture which supports a recognized identity called "hippie" or some other similar term. Once an identity is established, those who are so identified go to great lengths to maintain a context of responding others that supports it. This appears to be true of any established self-system. We shall have occasion later to refer to the apparent motivating force of self-systems.

It is not easy to regard as plausible the assertion that all self-systems, even ones that appear to an observer or even to the person himself to be negative in value, tend to maintain themselves. However it is not difficult to find, for example, in a person with a well-developed self-other pattern of being rejected or inferior, tendencies to select situations or manipulate situations so that they confirm the self-perception—all the while the person complaining of his ill fortune. These and similar tendencies have been variously labeled by clinicians as the result of the "need to fail" or the "masochistic" needs, or the "death wish." In a self-other conceptual framework, no special impulse or instinctive need is required beyond perhaps the "need to be" in whatever terms such being may have been established. The strategies and tactics of maintenance of the ostensibly "punishing" self-other patterns appear to be largely "unconscious." Those involved in maintenance of "rewarding" patterns are more frequently conscious, though by no means always so. In his chapter on "The Development of Interpersonal Competence," Eugene Weinstein (1969) points out the well-nigh universal tendency of persons to manipulate others to evoke responses that validate a desired identity. He proposes a systematic analysis of the strategies and techniques used and the capabilities needed to be successful at "altercasting," as he terms the process. Such knowledge can then presumably be used in deliberately developing such competence in the management of interpersonal relations. His provocative statement raises many fascinating problems not only intrinsic to the processes studied, but more general ones such as the nature of social life and the emergent self-other structures among a population of interactants, all highly competent in altercasting.

SOME PROBLEMS OF THE SELF

The conceptualization of human behavior in terms of self-other systems poses some interesting problems. Since the processes involved are complex at best, we have tried to avoid introducing the complications until the basic model has been set forth. However, the problems cannot be avoided any longer, and indeed in some ways, they are more interesting than the basic processes we have been discussing.

Ambiguity of communication and "distortion" of self-perception.   Assuming the validity of the proposition that the self emerges and is perceived by the individual only through the responses of reference others whose role he takes toward his own acts, then it follows that congruence between the perception others have of the actor and that which he has of himself depends primarily on the accuracy of the actor's perception and reproduction of those responses. There are an indefinite number and variety of factors that affect the accuracy of an actor's perception and reproduction of the responses of others to his own actions. We can only touch upon a few general conditions here (Weinstein, 1969, will be especially helpful). First, there is the obvious factor of concealment. Reference others can and do knowingly speak and act in ways that reflect to the person a perception of himself that does not coincide with the way he is perceived by these others. Actually, it is very difficult to "put on an act" or "maintain a front" at variance with more genuine reactions and not have the discrepancy perceived by the target person, especially where the interaction is prolonged and relatively intimate. A parent who is fundamentally hostile to his child, but who tries to cover up by a compensatory role of the loving parent, almost uniformly produces behavior of the child that reflects the underlying hostility of the parent. In less intensive contacts it is possible to sustain a game of pretense that all but deceives the participants themselves. In any case, it may be hypothesized that distortions of self-perceptions are frequent products of more or less conscious efforts to disguise responses.

Aside from deliberate concealment is the distortion resulting from the ambiguity in the meaning of gestures and acts. This is a frequent condition when members of differing subcultures interact. Even in the intimate interpersonal interactions of the family, what appear as minor differences in family relations and upbringing can produce ambiguities and misinterpretations of behavior between husband and wife, and the gap between generations will produce failures in communication between parents and children.

Another source of distortion in interaction is a deficiency in empathic capability. The sources of such deficiencies have not been systematically studied, but it is likely that both constitutional and experiential factors will be found to affect the role-taking ability and hence the development of self-perceptions.[4]

A fourth source is the tendency to project established self-other patterns on new situational fields. For example, a person whose self-other system has been developed in situations where he has characteristically been the recipient of accepting and friendly responses from the defining others will frequently be

---

[4] Empathic behavior has long been a matter of interest and speculation. There is wide agreement that whatever is denoted by the term is of central significance in theoretical and practical understanding of the processes of interaction and communication. Relative to its importance, it is still an undeveloped area of theoretical and empirical inquiry (see Cottrell & Dymond, 1949, pp. 705–712; Katz, 1963).

found to perceive new and undefined situations as accepting and friendly whether in fact they are or not. Of course, it is true that his perceptions and consequent behavior will frequently induce accepting and friendly responses and thus confirm his "behavioral prophecy." This also seems to be true even when the relationship resulting from such projections appears to be punishing the actor. What determines the rigidity and flexibility of previously established self-other systems has not been adequately studied, but it is clear that there is a considerable range of variability in this respect.

Other factors that produce ambiguities and errors in self-perception could be mentioned, but most will be found to be subsumed under one or another of those indicated above.

Multiple self-systems, conflict and consistency.   It hardly needs to be demonstrated to members of a complex urban industrial society that they frequently appear both to themselves and to others to be rather different persons in different situations. Or, to put it somewhat more precisely, a person participating in a series of life situations requiring different roles and composed of reference others who present different expectations will operate with correspondingly different perceptions of himself. Some students of behavior, e.g., William James (1890), have gone so far as to state that a person has a somewhat different self for every social relationship in which he participates. With certain reservations and modifications this statement is borne out in everyday experience as well as in systematic research.[5] Certainly this would be a logical result, assuming the self-system emerges in the manner outlined in this chapter and assuming that the person participates in interactive contexts that are different in their demands and expectations and are relatively insulated from one another. Conflict within the personality can profitably be conceptualized as conflict between self-other systems incorporated from incompatible life situations. The experience of conflict, of course, does not appear unless intra- or interpersonal conditions exist which evoke the contradictory self-other systems simultaneously. Not all self-systems inhabiting a personality are conflicting. Many may be different but not inconsistent or contradictory.

Actually, we are not faced with the task of demonstrating that multiple self-systems do occur, or that behavior of the person can be construed in these terms. Rather, the more interesting and significant tasks are those of exploring the implications of multi-self phenomena. How are the component self-systems organized into a single personality structure? How are conflicts dealt with? How does such a complex of behavior systems gain consistency and coherence?

---

[5] In the chapter by Weinstein (1969), it is suggested that some persons are skillful at quickly establishing ephemeral definitions of situations and special positioning in those situations to achieve confirmation of a desired identity which itself may be quite temporary and used as a means of achieving a given purpose. This claim suggests a very promising line of empirical inquiry that should yield important information on conditions of rigid and fluid self-other systems.

Is there a "real" or "central" self? How does it emerge? And how does it function? These are some of the significant problems of conceptualization and empirical research.

Management of conflict and achievement of consistency. All personality systems are subject to some degree and form of conflict and every theory of personality has its own conceptualization of the nature and management of conflict. It is not claimed here that all intrapersonal conflict can be comprehended within the conceptualization of the personality as a population of self-other systems, but a substantial part of it can be. In the intrapersonal relations among different self-other systems, two kinds of conflict can be distinguished with respect to their origin. The first type of conflict derives from the conditions that (a) any social act requires the participation of differently functioning parts; and (b) each of the participant persons incorporates in his response system the roles of the participant others. To illustrate how this type of conflict can emerge, let us take a court trial and focus our attention on the judge, the prosecuting attorney, and the defense attorney. Through their practice they have each assimilated the self-other patterns appropriate for each of the parts. Indeed as the trial process proceeds, each participant is assumed to be covertly "taking the role of the other" and thereby anticipating his actions. However, as long as each is clear as to his proper identity, there is no conflict as to what his part of the act is. On the other hand, in some circumstances, say when the defense attorney is performing poorly in the view of one or both of the others, there will often be some tendency toward supplying that role. The judge, for example, may and frequently does slip from the position of impartial adjudication and perform functions of one or another of the attorneys. In such an instance, he would experience a conflict between two components within his personality. Here we have a system of roles or self-other patterns that are different but not inconsistent, and produce conflict only when the same person is stimulated to act in two or more capacities simultaneously.

In the ordinary course of events, conflicts of the first type mentioned do not occur because situations are sufficiently clearly defined and the acts and expectations of others are sufficiently compelling to keep the actor in his appropriate identity.[6] Where situations and roles are weakly or ambiguously structured or defined, uncertainty and conflict result, e.g., the ambiguous situation confronted by persons in transitional and marginal positions such as adolescence, partially assimilated migrants, and persons in process of changing status.

A second type of conflict occurs when self-other systems appropriate to different situations are simultaneously evoked, and where performance in one role calls for acts that violate the requirements of the other. Continuing with our court room scene, let us suppose that the defendant is a close kinsman of

---

[6] See propositions bearing on this point in Cottrell, 1942b.

the judge. The latter would have to disqualify himself because the demands and expectations of him vis-a-vis a close relative would be in sharp conflict with those appropriate to the role of impartial judge.[7] In this instance, conflict is avoided by moving out of the situation. Unfortunately, many of our conflicts arising out of overlapping situations cannot be so readily resolved, though we do resolve some by just this device of keeping situations apart that call for incompatible self-other systems. Compartmentalization and insulation of situations calling for incompatible self-other systems is accomplished by various means: (1) spatial and temporal separations; and (2) cultural definitions, conventions and similar symbolic differentiations.

A somewhat different way of reducing conflict is by differential commitment to and evaluation of the roles one must enact in his different life situations. Thus, one may be a severe and demanding teacher or critic, or a hard-driving, unfeeling executive, but maintain that actually he is a mild, indulgent, friendly soul who is required by his job to act quite against his "real" inclinations. The harsher and sterner selves may in fact be no less real, but may represent less commitment and be valued less than his more friendly self. He can thus moderate the felt conflict to some extent. He may, of course, be practicing self-deception, but as long as he can maintain unawareness of the deception, he experiences a blunting of the contradictions.[8]

Thus far we have suggested that reductions of conflict among self-other patterns may be accomplished by clear unambiguous definitions of the situation and by the insulation of situations evoking incompatible self-other patterns in the same person. A third type of device has been suggested for reducing at least felt conflict, namely by misperceiving or remaining "unconscious" of those self-systems that are incompatible with the systems being enacted. Thus far, conceptualization of the processes that affect awareness of self-systems and their relations in the personality has not gone beyond the assumption that the mechanisms of repression formulated in psychoanalytic theory are adequate. We cannot explore this problem here, but there is need to take a fresh look at the phenomena of unconscious behavior from the standpoint of social-interaction theory.[9]

A fourth suggested means of achieving unity and coherence and minimizing conflict among the component systems is through a basic striving for consistency

---

[7] Helpful here is Robert K. Merton's distinction between what he calls role-sets and status-sets (1964; Merton & Barber, 1963).

[8] Weinstein (1969) has translated some of these conflict-management devices into more deliberate, manipulative tactics.

[9] Thus far no satisfactory conceptualization of unconscious behavior in terms of social-interaction theory has been developed. An early attempt by W. I. Thomas in 1927 was not satisfactory (see Thomas, 1966). The formulation by C. Wright Mills (1963) was clearly more interactional and closer to what is required. A more explicit attempt to utilize a Meadian model of the self is presently being made by Charles Varela in a study he proposes to submit as his doctoral dissertation to the Sociology Department of New York University in 1968. Varela is exploring the possibilities of equating unconscious acts with acts of the "I" that have no available implicit "other" or "me" responses as Mead uses those terms.

(Lecky, 1951). This principle of consistency is assumed to be intrinsic in the nature of the organism or imposed by the requirements of survival in a world evoking conflicting alternative responses. But this conceptualization is inadequate unless it can give explicit answers to the question: Consistency with what? It also needs to be explicit about the processes whereby consistency is achieved. Proponents on one or another variant of the principle of consistency rarely, if ever, give answers to these questions.

If the problem of consistency is phrased in terms of the self-other conceptualization rather than in terms of an assumed general intrinsic tendency, it becomes somewhat more amenable to empirical investigation and manipulation. To explore this claim, we shall need to use the concept "generalized other" which was introduced many years ago by George Herbert Mead (1913) in his lectures on the nature of the self. The concept refers to the apparent tendency of participants in a group to go beyond acquiring specific self-other patterns representing their interactions with various members of the group and to construct generalized others representing the expectations of the group as a whole vis-a-vis the actor and to perceive and react to his own acts from the perspective of this collective image. Thus a member of a baseball team will acquire specific self-other patterns derived from his interaction with specific other players; but he will also develop a team-as-a-whole image, not necessarily assignable to any one member. To be sure, this generalized other may for some players be embodied in some team member or some figure in baseball's Hall of Fame who personifies the "ideal player." For other players, the generalized other may be less clearly personified. There is some evidence that individuals vary considerably in the degree to which their generalized others are personalized.[10] This kind of variation suggests an interesting hypothesis that the more clearly personalized the generalized other, the stronger will be its effect on behavior. This hypothesis is given some plausibility by the fact that the self is an emergent of interpersonal processes. This suggests that expectations and demands attributed to a significant "other" should be responded to more readily than to disembodied rules, laws, norms, etc. In this connection it is interesting to note the tendency of many religions to embody their values and requirements in a person, e.g., Christ, Buddha, Mohammed.

The relevance of the concept of the generalized other for the problem of achieving consistency in behavior should by now be reasonably clear. The player on the baseball team who is confronted by the various contingencies of the game is not only acting to meet specific expectations of the players involved in a specific maneuver but is scrutinizing and commenting upon his acts and guiding his future actions from the perspective of the generalized other that represents the collective goals and the general standards and expectations of the group. Hence, insofar as the requirements of the generalized other are clear, the specific activities of the player will tend to exhibit consistency and coherence as

---

[10] Charles W. Estus (1966) finds this to be the case in the religious experience of the subjects he studied.

long as he is functioning in the situations defined by this membership on the team. Even if he deliberately or unintentionally deviates from the expectations of the generalized other, he will nevertheless perceive and evaluate such deviant behavior from the response perspective of that other.

Up to this point we have illustrated the application of the self-other conceptualization to the problem of consistency within a single context, namely, the baseball game. At first blush this illustration might appear to be irrelevant since the problem of consistency is not so much one of the consistency within a single context as one of consistency among the self-other systems derived from several contexts whose generalized others require not merely different but contradictory or incompatible behavior. This is especially, though not exclusively, true of urban industrial societies. As we have indicated previously in discussing conflict, there are various adaptations to this condition, one of which is the insulation of situations requiring contradictory behavior. But this is not always possible and is apparently becoming less so as we become increasingly aware of how behavior in one context has repercussions in another. The processes of impingement of different situational identities is most evident in the life activities of persons whose careers are largely in the public eye, e.g., political officials, school teachers, and clergymen. But all persons in a complex and heterogeneous society are confronted with situations calling for identities requiring behavior that is disparate if not contradictory. Corporate business is concerned about family life, political opinions, religious habits, and social life of its management personnel. Government as well as private corporations have been progressively inquiring into areas long regarded as private and establishing increasingly detailed dossiers. The church militant is seeking to make religious standards more effective guides to behavior in a wide range of secular situations. Perhaps the increasing concern about the invasion of privacy is symptomatic of how drastically that privacy has already been invaded. And we mean by privacy, after all, the integrity of the barriers that we wish to maintain between our different arenas of activity and their cognate selves.

Whatever the validity of these impressionistic observations, it is frequently claimed that there is an increasing urgency in the search for what is variously described as one's real self or one's true identity or essential being or basic values, goals or standards around which to develop order and consistency in one's life. The distribution of the population with respect to this alleged need, as well as with respect to alternate forms of adaptation to a world of unstable and conflicting demands and expectations, is itself an interesting and significant empirical question, especially when the degrees of conflict and forms of adaptation are correlated with personal and social conditions in which they occur.

Our interest here, however, is to see whether or not we can make a useful formulation of the problem in terms of the self-other conceptualization. If, then, we continue to conceive of the personality as confronted with the problem of achieving consistency in a population of self-other systems derived from the various interactive contexts in which the person participates, we are led rather readily to suggest as one solution the construction of what we can call a cardinal or central self-other system to which the other selves are subordinated in the sense that pressure of some kind is put upon those sub-systems to become consistent with the expectations and demands of the central self-other system.

But is this merely playing games with words, or do people actually function in such a way that we can regard this as a possible interpretation? In considering this question, we might ponder the behavior involved in such statements as, "A gentleman would under no circumstances do such an such," or "As a Christian I must always ... etc.," or "The loyal citizen of ——————— will always conduct himself ... etc." Among other possible interpretations each of these statements can be construed as indicative of the existence of a general self-other system that monitors and controls behavior in specific situations. Charles Estus (1966) made a study in which he attempted to delineate the various self-systems exhibited by his subjects and to discover whether or not their reports provided evidence of the functioning of a central self-other system that appeared to monitor and control the sub-self-systems. His method was that of an exhaustive series of interviews with thirty subjects in a single community. While a few of his subjects did not appear to have a central system (and this fact itself is of great interest), the majority reported behavior that was interpreted as evidence of such a structure. It will be remembered that in our preceding discussion of intrapersonal conflict we suggested that some proportion of persons in any sample would probably be found to function in more or less insulated situations of conflicting expectations without appearing to require any resolution of the potential strain.

The nature of the other in the allegedly central self-other system is of great interest. Estus reports considerable variation: for some there was a vividly clear image of a sacred figure—God, or Christ; for others there was the image of a concrete person from previous experience, such as a parent, teacher, "saintly character," who embodied the "touchstone requirements." In other cases there was a collective symbol, such as "the Church;" in still others there was some not too well-defined image of the "middle-class standards." It is interesting to note the rather explicit reports of dialogue with the central other where this was perceived in personal terms as compared with a less clear-cut interaction with an impersonal image. In the latter case there is some suggestion that the person either carried on a dialogue with an imagined interlocutor who personalized the impersonal expectations or himself took the role and presented the demands and expectations to which he then responded in the capacity of the particular subself being scrutinized. Estus concluded from his observations that the structure and functioning of a central self-other system is an essential of what people refer to as religious experience regardless of the nature of the central self-other, and that religious behavior can be fruitfully studied in the self-other framework.

Though not appearing in any of the cases reported by Estus, the possibility of the other in the central system being perceived as one's own "better self" should be taken into account in further explorations. This is apparently the "ego ideal" in Freudian terms. If we return for a moment to the other in the central systems reported by Estus, we can point out that regardless of the perception of that other, its role must be taken by the person himself toward the acts or intentions identified as his own. In other words, the acts of the putative other are still acts of the same organism whose acts are being reacted to by the putative other. Hence, when a person says "I am proud of myself" or "I am disgusted with myself," he may, and usually does, believe that the internal interaction represents only himself, when as a matter of fact, it involves incorporated actions of some reference other whose role the actor has taken in responding to something he has done. It is not unreasonable to venture the guess that most internal commentary on one's behavior would show upon scrutiny that the commentator is the enacted role of some identifiable reference other. Indeed we should reiterate the basic position taken in this concept of the self, namely, that we can perceive, evaluate, and otherwise react to ourselves only through the acts of others who respond or have responded in the past to us, and whose role we have taken for ourselves as objects.

On the other hand, our conceptualization must make provision for the instances in which the origins of the "other" part of the self-other system are no longer identifiable and the person appears to experience a truly self-self dialogue and is convinced he experiences a self without the mediation of some other. In this case, we would have to assume that the person has identified so closely with certain others in his past that these others no longer exist as objects for him. However, this self operates as an other in the interaction with the person's other selves, so that the basic interactional model of the self still obtains. It is not unlikely that empirical studies will show the central self-other system of many mature persons to be of this apparent self-self character. Laertes' "own self" to which Polonius admonishes him to be true is undoubtedly one or another of what we have called the cardinal or central self-other systems which will be watching his performance as a gentleman, soldier, student, and young man on adventure bent. In any case, the functioning of the various types of monitoring self-other systems and the conditions under which the various types emerge is an extremely important area for empirical studies. The results should have profound implications for the way we approach problems of developing personalities capable of functioning in a changing, conflictful, and frequently anomic world.

Flexibility and rigidity.   From one perspective the conceptualization here represented appears to emphasize the variability of personality and the apparent ease with which it can change. From an opposite position, the mechanical rigidity of behavior appears to be the predominant feature. Observation of behavior using any conceptual framework will demonstrate wide differences among persons as to the range of behavioral characteristics, as well as the readiness with which they change their behavior patterns. Moreover, in exploring the observed variability and flexibility, such conceptualizations are confronted with the necessity for identifying and assessing the relative weight to assign situational and intrapersonal determinants. It will not be possible to give extensive consideration here to the way this problem can be approached within the self-other framework. Some brief indications of our approach must suffice.

In the first place, this approach requires linking observed behavior with the nature of the situations in which it occurs, as well as the position occupied by the subject in those situations. It is hypothesized that variations in observed behavioral characteristics will be found to reflect variations in the structure of situational fields in which the person participates and/or variations in the action position he occupies in these situations. To this hypothesis must be added the condition: as the subject perceives or defines the situations and his position in them. This latter condition points immediately to the fact that this approach recognizes intrapersonal components in the determination of behavior. What they are and how they operate will be discussed later.

When a person is observed to vary in behavior in certain crucial respects, it will be assumed that he is functioning in differently structured situational contexts or in different role positions in similarly structured fields. The task, then, is to analyze the structures of the situations and the self-other or role patterns that compose them and the location of the subject in these contexts. But what is frequently forgotten is that the observer's definition of the situational field may differ from that of the subject whose behavior he is seeking to understand. He must, therefore, have some means of determining the way the subject is perceiving himself and others and their expectations.

How one determines the way another perceives a situational field and himself in it is a critical area of methodology almost completely neglected in the literature and instruction of so-called behavioral science. Most authorities in methodology regard the procedures required by this field of observation as intuitive art not amenable to objectification and communication. They are certainly justified in this opinion because those who claim it as a legitimate part of the methodological equipment of behavioral scientists have done little to objectify and communicate the procedures that are alleged to yield the required information. It is of course quite possible that these procedures are in fact intuitive and cannot be objectified and taught systematically. However, resignation to this conclusion should be postponed until a thoroughgoing attempt is made to refute it. At the moment we can hardly go beyond the general statement that the procedure is a combination of what for a lack of a better term has been called empathy or role-taking and the use of perceptions so derived for successive inferences upon which predictions are made, which are in turn checked against further observation (Cooley, 1926; Cottrell, 1941; Cottrell & Dymond, 1949, pp. 355–359; Katz, 1963). Actually we are constantly using such procedures in our common, everyday efforts to "understand" other people, and to anticipate their behavior in on-going social activity.

Another frequently overlooked consideration is that situations that may appear as different in content, e.g., a family situation versus a work situation, may be structurally similar, or the reverse may be true. Thus, work and home situations, though differing in content of activity, may both be strictly authoritarian and the person may be authoritative in one and subordinate in the other, or in one or the other structural positions in both, and so on through the various contingencies.

It is clear from our discussion so far that, quite apart from the complications introduced by intrapersonal factors, the description, systematic analysis and classification of situational fields calls for increased effort. It is much easier to seek for explanatory processes within the person than it is to study the complex interactions of their life situations. This, no doubt, accounts for a good deal of our reluctance to depart from conceptualizations that place major emphasis on intrapersonal processes. But the construction of more adequate behavioral theory awaits a sophistication in dealing with situational contexts and their dynamics that matches what has been achieved in intrapersonal theory. In any case, enough has been said to suggest that explanation of change and stability in behavior patterns must take fully into account the situational determinants.

As will be seen in the following discussion, what appear to be intrapersonal factors affecting persistence and change in self-other behavior, cannot actually be considered in isolation from situational contexts. But for practical as well as theoretical purposes, we can treat them as though such a separation is possible.

We can start with the proposition that once self-other patterns are acquired or "learned" they persist, but with varying tendencies or "pressures" to be enacted. Social-learning theorists like Bandura will quite properly point out that this proposition leaves aside the important question of what determines whether a self-other pattern is learned or not. Furthermore, the proposition appears to ignore the fact that learned responses can be and are extinguished. These are obviously not trivial objections, but we shall set them aside for the moment and come back to them later.

It will help make concrete the problems we are discussing if we can present a brief description of a case with which I had some professional contact some years ago.

Otto B., a fifteen-year-old boy, was brought to the juvenile court by his parents who charged that he was "incorrigible." He had dropped out of school, was roaming the streets, refused to come home, and frequently "went on the road" and was picked up and returned many times by the police. The parents complained that he was beyond their control, defied and cursed them when they tried to discipline him, and said they wanted to send him to the state school for delinquent boys where he would be under strict discipline. They were persuaded to let a probation officer try to handle the case informally and work with the boy to see what could be done short of an institutional commitment.

The probation officer who had excellent relations with a local child guidance clinic undertook an intensive program of family investigation and personal supervision of the boy. Of special interest are his findings:

(1) The father and mother were German born and had migrated as adolescents to a large city in the U.S. where they settled in a German neighborhood.

(2) Mr. B., the father, was a skilled worker when he married Mrs. B. and they remained in the German community for some time.

(3) At the time of the complaint there were 5 children: a married daughter age 22, a son age 20, a daughter age 17, Otto age 15, and a daughter age 13.

(4) Five years previous to the complaint, the family had moved from the rather closely-knit German community to a culturally heterogeneous community near the plant where Mr. B. was employed as a foreman.

(5) The parents reported no problems with the older children. In the previous community they were known as model children, and it was not until Otto began associating with children in the new neighborhood that they began to have trouble with him.

(6) The father was a very strict disciplinarian and allowed no questioning of his authority. None of the three older children showed signs of serious rebellion. Apparently the families in the German neighborhood gave support to the authoritarian patterns of the father. As Otto began to act in the manner of the children in the new neighborhood who were less rigorously controlled, the father became progressively harsher in his efforts to discipline his son. The stronger the father's measures, the more hostile and rebellious Otto became. In reporting his efforts the father described very severe treatment indeed—beatings with broomsticks, choking, putting pepper in the boy's eyes, and other punishments that at one point led neighbors to consider complaining to the police. The mother was softer in attitude and tried unsuccessfully to buffer the relationship between father and son, but was submissive to the father and could only counsel her son to be obedient and "stay out of trouble." The older children felt the father was justified in trying to "keep Otto from turning into a bum."

(7) Confronted by increasing truancy from home and school, unmanageable behavior at home, and involvement in some thefts, the parents appealed to the juvenile court for help.

Otto was described as an attractive, well-developed boy who talked quite readily about his difficulties. He wanted to quit school and get a job and live away from home. He was extremely hostile to his father, being unable to discuss their relations without weeping. He was also very resentful of his older siblings who sided with his father. He appeared fond of his mother, but gave no evidence of hope for support and security from her. He gave more signs of genuine affection for his younger sister who showed him some sympathy and covertly gave him aid and comfort, such as letting him into the house when his father had locked him out, giving him money from her allowance, saving food for him, and the like. He in his turn was protective of her in the neighborhood as well as in the home.

Efforts to reach some working accommodation at home meeting no success, all parties agreed that Otto should live with an uncle, a younger brother of his mother who had himself come through considerable conflict with his own parents, who had become a successful draftsman, and married and had two sons age 10 and 8. The uncle was considerably more lenient in his manner and dealt with Otto by friendly kidding. It also helped that he was an ardent fisherman and would take Otto on numerous fishing trips which were eagerly looked forward to by the boy.

Otto was placed in an unskilled job but walked out of it after a reprimand by his supervisor. This same sequence was repeated several times, and it became apparent that any exercise of authority evoked in Otto a very defiant reaction which usually lost him his job. In the meantime he was discovering that good jobs demanded skills he did not have, and he finally agreed to go to a vocational high school for training in his uncle's field and to work part-time in his uncle's shop.

Except for very few occasional visits to see his mother when his father was not at home, and somewhat more frequent exchange of visits with his younger sister, Otto had no further contact with his family.

The case was closed after the boy had completed a year-and-a-half of his vocational training. He seemed quite settled in his vocational aims, was getting good grades in his courses, was doing well in his uncle's office, was well liked by his uncle's wife and children, and had established several friendships with young people he met through his younger sister. It was felt that he would do well in situations in which he was not threatened by strict authoritarian treatment, but that he was likely "to blow his top" in such situations. He admitted he had this risk and agreed to try not "to start fighting his old man" whenever someone started "ordering him around."

Some years after this case was closed, a young mother came to the clinic with her two-and-a-half-year-old son for advice on how to deal with what she described as behavior difficulties she was having with him. It early became apparent that she was more concerned about the father's treatment of the child than she was about the child's own behavior. Moreover, she was apprehensive over the increasing tension between her and her husband over his disciplinary actions. She described him as extremely harsh and strict and reported that he frequently struck the child hard enough to bruise him when the child did not respond to the father's directions. Her name was Mrs. Otto B.

Renewed explorations with Otto concerning his various relationships yielded substantial support to the following tentative findings:

(1) He had a well-developed self-other pattern of defiant child–harsh authoritarian father. In situations where superordinate persons asserted authority he tended to rebel. In the situation where he was confronted by the negativistic behavior of his infant son he found he had learned quite well the harsh-father end of the self-other system.

(2) His relations with his wife—the characteristics he reported that made him fond of her, were strongly reminiscent of his relations with his younger sister.

(3) Less firmly established, but clear enough to be of interest, was the pattern of relations he appeared to be establishing with two apprentice

draftsmen in his place of employment. The good-natured kidding and kindly-advisor relations displayed to them was not unlike the way his uncle had treated Otto.

(4) It seemed clear that Otto was quite unaware of the resemblances noted above, and indeed was quite surprised to discover how much of his hated father he had absorbed.

While it must be recognized that these observations undoubtedly reflect a selective conceptual bias, they can at least serve to illustrate and to suggest certain propositions that can be subjected to more rigorous and controlled testing.

In the first place, it would appear that a self-other pattern is extremely hard to modify as long as the person is locked into the kind of situation in which the pattern emerged. Presumably Otto and his father could by dint of Herculean effort or by being "rewarded" sufficiently have modified their pattern of interaction, but the prospects appeared very slight indeed.

Second, neither the pattern of the punished and defiant son nor that of the harsh punishing father appeared to have been "rewarded" in the ordinary sense of that term. They were nevertheless very thoroughly learned and readily reproduced in the appropriate situational contexts—in the home, in the employment situation, and in Otto's rendition of the role of father. This would suggest that self-other patterns are learned in any situation where the person is a participant in a significant interact (begging the question of what is a "significant interact" for the time being). Obviously there is some discrepancy between this proposition and some, but not all of, the findings of Bandura and similarly oriented investigators. Efforts to reconcile the discrepancies should lead to important advances in the theory of processes and products of social interaction.

Third, a self-other pattern learned in one situation will tend to be evoked in other situations of similar structure. This condition includes the requirement that the respondent occupy one or another of the action positions defined by the self-other pattern. Otto reacted to situations of authority, e.g., job situations, in the pattern derived at home with himself as the rebellious subordinate. However, he took the superordinate role in his own nuclear family where the structure was one in which the subordinate role was pre-empted by his own son. Here again the question of whether or not the pattern carried over is one which has been "rewarded" is moot. The possibility that an apparently punished pattern may in fact have been rewarding in some un-conscious manner must of course be recognized. But this too must be tested, lest we fall into unprofitable tautologies.

A fourth proposition not clearly illustrated by our case, but needing mention at this point, is as follows. Well-established self-other patterns tend to operate selectively in two ways: (1) by leading the person to "select" relationships in which the pattern is readily enacted; and (2) by being projected on to ambiguous, not rigidly structured situations that can be structured to permit the pattern to be expressed. The physical resemblance between young Mrs. B.

and Otto's favorite sister and the relationships revealed in her descriptions of her own past, strongly suggest that certainly Otto's choice of her and very probably hers of him was far from accidental. In the case of Otto's performance as a father, it could be said that several alternative patterns could have been chosen to define the relationship. However, Otto unwittingly projected his own pattern on an only partially structured situation.

A fifth proposition, again only partially illustrated by our case, is that a previously established self-other pattern that is projected on to new situations, will evoke responses from others called for by that pattern, and hence structure the situation so as to support and validate it. A person with pattern expectations of being rejected or attacked, or loved and accepted will frequently perform in such a way as to evoke responses confirmatory of his "working hypothesis."

In considering the fourth and fifth propositions stated above, it will be of interest to refer to Eugene Weinstein's chapter on interpersonal competence. It will be seen that the processes we here allege to take place more or less unwittingly in the "natural" state of affairs are also capable of being used deliberately and manipulatively by the person to evoke responses in relevant others that support a desired identity in him.

From propositions four and five, we may suggest a sixth, namely, that self-other patterns established earlier in the developmental history of the person, will appear more persistently than later-established ones. Earlier patterns are more likely to operate to select subsequent situations confirmatory of the earlier pattern or to be projected upon and to shape later, less structured situations to evoke validating responses required by the earlier pattern. These earlier patterns are therefore likely to appear more general in the sense of being operative in a wider range of situations than are later ones which are more likely to be situation specific. Here again, empirical work will have to be directed to the problem of persistence of what may appear to an observer as unrewarding or punishing patterns.

This latter continuing problem suggests one further explanatory suggestion that should be fully explored. The self, as a person perceives and knows it, is according to our conceptualization experienced by the person only through his taking the role of his reference others in responding to himself. This is the way he becomes an object to himself. The being he knows therefore lives in the responses of others externally present and/or internalized. It may well be that the "need" to preserve this sense of being is a source of a strong motivation to maintain the interactive systems through which this being exists even when these systems appear to be self-frustrating.

CHANGING SELF-OTHER SYSTEMS

The foregoing discussion has been directed to suggested conditions associated with persistence of self-other systems. It is clear that some degree of persistence and stability is intrinsic in the processes by which self-other systems emerge. It can also be observed in passing that some degree of stability is a functional necessity for the mutual predictability required in a stable social structure. As impressive as are the conditions making for stability and persistence in the self-system, it is nevertheless true that change is no less intrinsic in the process. A cautionary parenthetical comment should be entered here that might best be expressed by the suggestion that we use the terms "apparent persistence" and "apparent change." When Otto B. was allowed to live with his maternal uncle, to the probation officer he was a "changed person." The uncle's manner of interacting, using genial companionship seasoned with control through good-natured kidding and other similar responses, evoked a very different response from that evoked by the boy's father. Yet Otto apparently never got rid of the old pattern which appeared when he was confronted by a domineering supervisor and when he was confronted by the infant negativism of his son.

Otto did manifest a different (changed?) self-other pattern of interaction with an adult responsible for him and indeed developed a corresponding difference in his self-perception and expectation of others, e.g., his manner of handling subordinate associates in his place of employment which was reminiscent of the pattern developed in the Otto-uncle situation. But so far as our information went, the Otto-father pattern was not significantly modified. To ask if this was a case of change or not may seem to be quibbling, but it does pose a very interesting empirical problem for study.

Leaving aside for the moment the issues raised by our caution, we can offer the general proposition that the self-system changes when the defining responses of its reference others change. Here, as always, we must urge care in identifying the reference others. What appear to an observer to be the objectively present reference others may not be at all. A person's perception of himself may be derived from internalized others whose defining responses are completely contradictory to those of the ostensibly real others in the situation. The audience may heap genuine praise on the performer, whose inner audience tells him he was a dismal flop—or vice versa. These considerations suggest another neglected field of investigation, namely the complex relations between internal and external "others"—the conditions under which they merge or remain insulated.

Leaving aside complicating problems and caveats, we can say that in general, changing situational fields produce changes in self-other systems. For present practical purposes, we can include here changes that occur when the person moves from one type of situational field to another, e.g., one with an authoritarian to another with an egalitarian structure; when the "same" situation changes its structure, e.g., a person who rejected finds himself accepted by the "same" others; and, when the same situational field remains stable but the person's position or role in it is changed, e.g., changes in status positions. These kinds of situational changes can be seen in micro- as well as macro-systems, and the systematic analysis of the relation between the situational and the correlative intrapersonal changes is a major area of theoretical as well as practical concern to the social psychologist. It is in the study of these processes of change that the conceptualizations of investigators like Bandura and

Weinstein become most clearly relevant. And it is in this area also that the need for much clearer and more sophisticated concepts for the analysis of situational fields is pressing. This need becomes especially acute as social psychologists address themselves to study problems of rapidly changing societies.

Biological changes induce changes in the self-system. The changes so induced are rarely directly produced but occur through the changes in the person's position in his life situations as they are induced by changes in his organism, e.g., the changes in responses and expectations of others through the age grades of the individual (Cottrell, 1942b). Even if some organic change, glandular for example, directly causes changes in the behavior of the person, this change in behavior would have to induce changes in the defining responses of reference others for it to become part of the person's perception and definition of himself.

But change of the self-other systems is not only induced by changes in the objective situation or of position in situations. There are endogenous changes conceived as arising in the interaction among the self-systems that constitute the personality. Our theoretical position leads us to perceive thinking as internal dialogue, mental conflict as conflict of self-systems, daydreaming and reverie as playful subjective manipulations of situations and roles in them, prayer and meditation as in part an examination of self-systems from the perspective and expectations of the cardinal or central or ultimate other. Clearly, all of these processes open up wide opportunities or reconstructing definitions of identity and of imagined situations required to validate it. Such reconstructions may and do lead to overt behavior in the direction of modifying the external world to conform to the new definition of the situation emerging from the intrapersonal processes.

Enough has been said to indicate that it is as necessary for the student of the self to assume change as it is to assume stability in the processes and products of interaction. Even in the most stabilized social relationships, each encounter contains some element of novelty.

SUMMARY

The purpose of this chapter has been to outline the main features of a conceptualization that has been implicit in a tradition of long standing in social psychology, but which has never been fully implemented in appropriate research strategies and designs. Psychology has not yet accomplished the shift from a monadic to a dyadic form of conceptualization of its problems. Happily a shift is under way as seen in works we have cited; and while I predicted (Cottrell & Gallagher, 1940) a development in this direction would take place in the 1950's, it is coming in the 1960's and it should be greatly accelerated in the 1970's. We may be reasonably confident that conceptualizations and research designs will show increasing sophistication concerning the structure and dynamics of interactive situational fields, the covert behavioral and symbolic incorporation of these fields of activity in the response systems of the participants, and the perception and understanding of intrapersonal as well as overt behavior of the person in these terms. As this development takes place, socialization will be a term that will gain far more explicit and precise meaning than it now has.

REFERENCES

ALLPORT, G. W. *Personality: A psychological interpretation.* New York: Holt, 1938.

ALLPORT, G. W. *Personality and social encounter: Selected essays.* Boston: Beacon Press, 1960.

BALDWIN, J. M. *Mental development in the child and the race.* New York: Macmillan, 1895.

BANDURA, A. Social-learning theory of identificatory processes. In D. A. Goslin (Ed.), *Handbook of socialization theory and research.* Chicago: Rand McNally, 1969. Chapter 3.

BLUMER, H. Social and individual disorganization. *American Journal of Sociology,* 1939, 42, 871–877.

BRIM, O. G., JR. Personality development as role learning. In I. Iscoe & H. Stevenson (Eds.), *Personality development in children.* Austin: Univer. of Texas Press, 1960.

BURGESS, E. W., & COTTRELL, L. S., JR. *Predicting success or failure in marriage.* New York: Prentice-Hall, 1939. Pp. 172–217, 290–312.

CAMERON, N. A. *The psychology of behavior disorders: A biosocial interpretation.* Boston: Houghton Mifflin, 1947.

COOLEY, C. H. *Human nature and the social order.* New York: Scribners, 1902.

COOLEY, C. H. The roots of social knowledge. *American Journal of Sociology,* 1926, 32, 59–79. Republished in C. H. Cooley, *Sociological theory and social research.* New York: Holt, 1930. Chap. 9.

COTTRELL, L. S., JR. Roles and marital adjustment. *Publications of the American Sociological Society,* 1933, 27, 107–115.

COTTRELL, L. S., JR. The case study method in prediction. *Sociometry,* 1941, 4, 358-370.

COTTRELL, L. S., JR. Analysis of situational fields in social psychology. *American Sociological Review,* 1942, 7, 370–382. (a)

COTTRELL, L. S., JR. The adjustment of the individual to his age and sex roles. *American Sociological Review,* 1942, 7, 617-620. (b)

COTTRELL, L. S., JR., & DYMOND, ROSALIND F. The empathic responses: A neglected field for research. *Psychiatry,* 1949, 12, 355-359, 705-712.

COTTRELL, L. S., JR., & GALLAGHER, RUTH. *Developments in social psychology 1930–1940.* Beacon, N.Y.: Beacon Press, 1940.

COUTU, W. *Emergent human nature: A symbolic field interpretation.* New York: Knopf, 1949.

DEWEY, J. *Democracy and education: An introduction to the philosophy of education.* New York: Macmillan, 1916.

ERIKSON, E. *Childhood and society.* New York: Norton, 1950.

ESTUS, C. Selected factors in the decision making of members of religious organizations. Doctoral dissertation, Department of Sociology, New York University, 1966.

FARIS, E. *The nature of human nature: And other essays in social psychology.* New York: McGraw-Hill, 1937.

FARIS, R. E. L. *Social psychology.* New York: Ronald Press, 1952.

FOOTE, N. N. Identification as a basis for a theory of motivation. *American Sociological Review,* 1951, 16, 14–21.

GOFFMAN, E. The moral career of the mental patient. *Psychiatry,* 1959, 22, 123–142.

GOFFMAN, E. *Encounters: Two studies in the sociology of interaction.* Indianapolis: Bobbs-Merrill, 1961.

HEBB, D. O. The American revolution. *American Psychologist,* 1960, 15, 735–745.

HEFFERLINE, R. F. Learning theory and clinical psychology—an eventual symbiosis? In A. J. Bachrach (Ed.), *Experimental foundations of clinical psychology.* New York: Basic Books, 1962. Pp. 97–138.

HILGARD, E. Human motives and the concept of the self. *American Psychologist,* 1949, 4, 374–382.

JACOBSON, E. E. Electrophysiology of mental activities. *American Journal of Psychology,* 1932, 44, 677–694.

JAMES, W. *The principles of psychology.* New York: Holt, 1890.

KATZ, R. L. *Empathy, its nature and uses.* New York: Free Press of Glencoe, 1963.

KUHN, M. H., & McPARTLAND, T. S. An empirical investigation of self-attitudes. *American Sociological Review,* 1954, 19, 68–78.

LECKY, P. *Self consistency: A theory of personality.* New York: Island Press, 1951.

LINDESMITH, A. R., & STRAUSS, A. L. *Social psychology.* New York: Dryden Press, 1956.

MEAD, G. H. The social self. *Journal of Philosophy,* 1913, 10, 374–380. For a more extended treatment see the stenographic report of his lectures at the University of Chicago published under *Mind, self and society.* Chicago: Univer. of Chicago Press, 1934.

MERTON, R. K. The role-set: Problems in sociological theory. In L. A. Coser & B. Rosenberg (Eds.), *Sociological theory: A book of readings.* New York: Macmillan, 1964.

MERTON, R. K., & BARBER, ELINOR. Sociological ambivalence. In E. A. Tiryakian (Ed.), *Sociological theory, values and sociocultural change.* New York: Free Press of Glencoe, 1963.

MILLS, C. W. *Power, politics and people.* I. L. Horowitz (Ed.). New York: Oxford Univer. Press, 1963.

MOORE, O. K. Problem solving and the perception of persons. In R. Tagiuri & L. Petrullo (Eds.), *Person perception and interpersonal behavior.* Stanford, Calif.: Stanford Univer. Press, 1958.

MORENO, J. L. *Psychodrama and the psychopathology of interpersonal relations.* New York: Beacon House, 1945.

OFSHE, R. Effect of interaction in interpersonal communication. Unpublished master's thesis, Department of Sociology, Queens College of City Univer. of New York, 1966.

ROGERS, C. *Client-centered therapy: Its current practice, implications, and theory.* Boston: Houghton Mifflin, 1951.

SARBIN, T. R. A preface to a psychological analysis of the self. *Psychological Review,* 1952, 59, 11–22.

SEARS, R. R. A theoretical framework for personality and social behavior. *American Psychologist,* 1951, 61, 478–480.

SHERIF, M., & CANTRIL, H. *The psychology of ego involvements.* New York: Wiley, 1947.

SHIBUTANI, T. *Society and personality: An interactionist approach to social psychology.* Englewood Cliffs, N.J.: Prentice-Hall, 1961.

SULLIVAN, H. S. Some conceptions of modern psychiatry. *Psychiatry,* 1940, 3, 1–117.

THOMAS, W. I. *Social organization and social personality.* M. Janowitz (Ed.). Chicago: Univer. of Chicago Press, 1966.

TURNER, R. H. Role-taking, role-standpoint, and reference-group behavior. *American Journal of Sociology,* 1956, 61, 316–328.

VARELA, C. An interactional theory of the unconscious (tentative title). Doctoral dissertation in preparation, Department of Sociology, New York Univer., 1968.

WEINSTEIN, E. Toward a theory of interpersonal tactics. In C. Backman & P. Secord (Eds.), *Problems in social psychology.* New York: McGraw-Hill, 1966.

WEINSTEIN, E. The development of interpersonal competence. In D. A. Goslin (Ed.), *Handbook of socialization theory and research.* Chicago: Rand McNally, 1969. Chapter 17.

WYLIE, RUTH C. *The self concept: A critical survey of pertinent research literature.* Lincoln, Nebr.: Univer. of Nebraska Press, 1961.

CHAPTER **10**

Some Principles
For The Design Of
Clarifying Educational Environments

Omar Khayyam Moore and Alan Ross Anderson

University of Pittsburgh

When the ordinary typewriter was an exciting novelty, Mark Twain, who was an early typewriter buff, called it a "curiosity-breeding little joker"—and so it was, then. The *talking typewriter,* invented by Moore and Kobler (Moore & Kobler, 1963; Kobler & Moore, 1966), is a contemporary novelty which also elicits a good deal of curiosity. There have been numerous popular articles about it, and most of those who have played with it find it fascinating. Unfortunately, the interest generated by this machine does not carry over, necessarily, to the theoretical ideas which lie behind it. We say "unfortunately" for good reason. The machine itself is less important than the principles which guided its construction. The talking typewriter is merely one of a large number of possible inventions which can be made, we think, using this same theoretical context as a guide.

Our main purpose in this chapter is to explain and to illustrate a set of principles, four in number, for designing learning environments within which even very young children can acquire complex symbolic skills with relative ease. We intend to show, as we go along, that these principles for designing *clarifying* educational environments (where by a "clarifying educational environment" we mean an educational environment aimed to make the student [subject? victim?] *clear* about what he is doing, and more generally, what is going on) are systematically related to both a theoretical analysis of human culture and an interpretation of the socialization process, i.e., that process whereby a human infant, beginning life as a biological *individual,* becomes a *person*—and whose infantile *behavior* is gradually transformed into adult *conduct.*

In order to understand these "design principles," we must first explain the

Most of the theoretical work reported here was supported by the Office of Naval Research, Group Psychology Branch, Contract #SAR/Nonr-609(16). With respect to applications, the major source of support has been the Carnegie Corporation of New York. The cost of developing the "talking typewriter" (Edison Responsive Environment) was borne exclusively by the McGraw-Edison Company of Elgin, Illinois.

theoretical system out of which they emerged. We will then go on to a statement of the principles themselves, and finally we will consider, in some detail, an illustrative application of these principles to the problem of designing an actual learning environment. At this point, we will have come full circle—the talking typewriter will appear in a meaningful context as one part of a learning environment.

It will also be obvious that the talking typewriter is itself fundamentally a "social science invention." Because it *is* a social science invention, it is difficult to use it or similar devices intelligently without an appreciation of the social scientific ideas on which it is based.

Finally, before turning to our first task, that of sketching out the theoretical system upon which the set of principles is founded, we wish to acknowledge the contributions to our thinking of George Herbert Mead (1932, 1934, 1936, 1938),[1] the father of the symbolic interactionist position in social psychology, and Georg Simmel (English translation, 1959), the originator of the school of "formal" sociology. We regard these men as central figures in the creation of the kind of sociology which can yield applications both at the level of mechanical inventions and social inventions. It may seem strange to some that we believe that Mead and Simmel have ideas which lend themselves to applications. Mead and his followers often have been criticized for spawning ideas which lacked testable consequences—to say nothing of applications; and to the best of our knowledge we are the only ones who have seriously entertained the thought that Simmel was within a light year of a practical application. We hope to show here that leading ideas taken from these two men can be reshaped into working principles for designing educational environments.

THEORETICAL BACKGROUND[2]

Folk Models

We think that it is a mistake to regard the ordinary human being as an *a*theoretical or a *non*theoretical or even an *anti*theoretical creature. Some contemporary behavioral scientists seem to assume that the ordinary man, a citizen in good standing in whatever community he lives, is woefully lacking in intellectual resources to guide him in managing his affairs. He is credited only with some folk sayings and proverbs, some practical knowledge, some skill at rule-of-thumb reasoning, some tradition-based explanations—and that is about it.

---

[1]From time to time we will try to acknowledge our indebtedness to various authors, but a complete list of those authors to whom we feel indebted would be impossible for either of us to provide.

[2]Since this section is mainly a summary of our own ideas, some worked out jointly, some separately, we have felt free to paraphrase our own papers without specific references. However, anyone who wishes to go more deeply into these ideas should read A. R. Anderson and Moore, 1959, 1962, 1966; Moore, 1957, 1958, 1961, 1964, 1965a, 1965b, 1968; Moore and A. R. Anderson, 1960a, 1960b, 1960c, 1962a, 1962b, 1968.

In a contrary vein, we suggest a different view of "man." We think that early in human history, probably at about the time men developed natural languages, they also created models of the most important features of their relations with the environment.[3] These were relatively abstract models which collectively covered relations holding between (1) man and nature—insofar as nature is not random; (2) man and the random or chancy elements in experience; (3) man in his interactional relations with others like himself; and (4) man and the normative aspects of group living. Cultural structures falling within these four classes of models were created in early history by many unsung Edisons and Einsteins (perhaps it would be more appropriate to say that they were created by the unsung Meads and Simmels of prehistory). Consequently, there does not exist a society, however "primitive," that does not have cultural objects falling within these four categories of models. It is convenient to have a name for all four classes of models, a name that suggests their origin early in human history. We call them "folk models."

Every society, as far back as we have any evidence, has *puzzles* which, we suggest, stand in an abstract way for nonaleatory man-nature relations. Every society has some *games of chance*. According to our view of the matter, games of chance are abstract models of the aleatory aspects of existence. Every society has *games of strategy* in the sense of von Neumann (1928; von Neumann & Morgenstern, 1947). These games capture some of the peculiar features of interactional relations among men, relations in which no party to an encounter controls all of the relevant variables upon which the final outcome depends, though each controls some of these variables and each participant must take some account of the potential actions of others involved in the situation if he is to behave intelligently. Every society has *aesthetic entities,* i.e., art forms which we claim give people the opportunity to make normative judgments about and evaluations of their experience. All societies make use of these folk models in the socialization of the young and for the re-creation, or recreational enjoyment, of those who are older. Simple forms of these models are internalized in childhood and more complex versions of them sustain us in adulthood.

It should be pointed out that until mathematicians had made formal analyses of the structure of some of these folk models, their depth and subtlety were not appreciated fully. Of the four classes of folk models distinguished above, two have received adequate formal treatment, specifically, the various mathematical theories of probability have all games of chance as models, and the various mathematical theories of games of strategy have all games of strategy as models.

---

[3] In common with many contemporary philosophers, we acquire a certain sick feeling when hearing talk about "man," or even worse, "Man." When one reads translations of Aristotle, and finds that "Man is a rational animal," one has the idea that something deep is going on, but obvious parallels ("Whale is a large animal," "Mouse is a small animal") make the locution seem as ludicrous as it is.

We nevertheless defer to a tradition, with the understanding that when we use the term "man" we are referring to human beings, and that, in consequence, all the appropriate verbs should be in the plural.

The formal analysis of puzzles is not in as satisfactory a state as are games of chance and games of strategy; however, we have suggested that the methods of natural deduction may help clarify the structure of puzzles.[4] When it comes to aesthetic entities, everyone is at sea and it is not known whether mathematical analyses of aesthetic objects, should such analyses prove possible, would result in *only one* or *more than one* distinct class of models. It is well to remember that until the work of von Neumann (1928) no one was in a position to make a mathematically rigorous distinction even between games of chance and games of strategy—so we should be careful about making the assumption that aesthetic objects would yield to but one overall formal theory. Regardless of this, the mathematical research into the structure of folk models has made it perfectly obvious to us that early man was not a simple-minded clod. It required inventors of genius to create these intricate objects, but even a child can begin to play with most of them. Not much in the way of technical expertise was needed to fashion the equipment used in connection with folk models: bits of wood, or stone, would do for the "pieces" used in most board games; a primitive technology was no bar to the creation of conceptually complex cultural entities.

Historically speaking, man not only invented and developed these fascinating folk models, he also devised suitable techniques for seeing to it that they were mastered by the ordinary citizen. If we think of these models as constituting the basic theoretical arm of a society's culture, then it is quite important that everyone, or virtually everyone, learns them. To put it another way, if folk models are abstract schemata which help orient us toward a wide variety of problems, then we should get them down pat. With respect to their inculcation, observe that, in general, they are learned, but not taught. What is taught are the "rules of the game," and once the rules are understood, each participant is largely on his own, except when the models are perverted by professionalism.

In every society there are social norms which distinguish between serious matters on the one hand, and fun and games on the other. Usually, specific times and places are set aside for the enjoyment of folk models. Also, the stakes for winning or losing are kept at some nominal value insofar as profit and loss enter. In addition, there are norms which regulate expressions of feeling and emotion with reference to using folk models. During the course of playing with a model, one is permitted to experience a fairly wide range of feelings and emotions, but extremes are excluded. These models serve, as it were, as a school for emotional expression—this is a kind of "school" in which boredom is unlikely and uncontrolled emotional frenzy is forbidden. All in all, the set of norms governing the use of folk models, and the models themselves, have proved so successful that

---

[4]A good simple treatment of natural deduction is contained in Fitch's text in symbolic logic (1952). Experimentation on human higher-order problem solving which takes into consideration natural deduction is rare. However, some of our colleagues have attempted to take this into consideration, see Carpenter, Moore, Snyder and Lisansky (1961). The preparation for an approach to natural deduction in terms of experimental techniques was worked out largely by Scarvia B. Anderson and Moore in a series of studies beginning in 1952 (S. B. Anderson, 1955, 1956, 1957; Moore & S. B. Anderson, 1954a, 1954b, 1954c).

people have to be prohibited from playing with them too much, despite the conceptual depth of the materials with which they deal. If we think of the models as teaching devices, then they are instructional with respect to relatively universal features of man's environment—they are abstract symbolic maps of human experience. We also can see that they "teach" in ways that satisfy the following conditions:

1. They are "cut off," in some suitable sense, from the more serious sides of the society's activity, that is to say, they are cut off from immediate problems of welfare and survival. For example, if a child is learning the intricacies of social interaction, the activity in which he is experiencing or practicing the interaction must allow him to make many mistakes without endangering the lives or futures of those around him, to say nothing of his own safety. Similarly, such rewards as he receives from the activity must not be too expensive to those around him, or again, the activity would have just those serious consequences which these models, as teaching devices, must avoid.

2. But in spite of the fact that the teaching devices must avoid serious consequences, some motivation must be built into them, or else the learner may lose interest. If we rely on the distinction between activities that are intrinsically rewarding, and those that are rewarding only as a means, or extrinsically rewarding, we may say that the rewards in the learner's activities must be intrinsic or inherent in the activity itself. We call such activities "autotelic": they contain their own goals and sources of motivation.

3. And finally, these teaching devices, if they are to be theoretically relevant to the problems which are likely to be encountered outside the context of an autotelic environment, indeed must be models of serious activities.

Thus far we envisage a situation like this: Every society makes up abstract symbolic models of its most serious recurrent problems. Despite the complex structure of these models, everywhere they are learned with pleasure by ordinary people. Every society has social norms governing the use of its folk models and these norms have the effect of making the models autotelic, so even though the models are models of serious matters, they must be treated playfully.

The notion that materials, in the sense of the contents of everyday life, are somehow abstracted from the stream of living and reappear as the play forms of sociability is a distinctively Simmelian idea—we borrowed it from him. It is he who argues that:

> Actual forces, needs, impulses of life produce the forms of our behavior that are suitable for play. These forms, however, become independent contents and stimuli within play itself or, rather, *as* play. There are, for instance, the hunt; the gain by ruse; the proving of physical and intellectual strength; competition; and the dependence on chance and on the favor or powers that cannot be influenced (Simmel, 1959, p. 42).

And he goes on to say that:

> To the person who really enjoys it [play], its attraction rather lies in the dynamics and hazards of the sociologically significant forms of activity themselves. The more profound, double sense of "social game" is that not only the game is played in a society (as its external medium) but that, with its help, people actually "play" "society" (Simmel, 1959, p. 50).

What Simmel did not do was to carry through a mathematical analysis of his cherished "play forms" of human association. He did see the need for such a formal analysis; in fact, he called for the creation of a kind of "social geometry" which would be up to characterizing the structure of play forms. He did not see that probability theory does the trick for games of chance, and, of course, the work of von Neumann (1928) on games of strategy did not come along until ten years after Simmel's death. And we all are still waiting for an intellectual giant the size of von Neumann to do a satisfactory mathematical analysis of aesthetic play forms. Nonetheless, the basic program for "formal" sociology, as envisaged by Simmel, is being carried out and we like to think of ourselves as helping a little.

It should be remarked that the possibilities for developing an appropriate "social geometry" are not limited to analyzing folk models. For example, normative systems are of obvious importance in interpreting human interaction. Prior to the past decade, very little had been done toward developing a mathematical analysis of such systems. It was partly in response to our sense of the need for a program of formal sociology in this area that we undertook studies in what is now called "deontic logic." This topic has been treated by a vast number of investigators since von Wright's seminal essay of 1951, and the improvement in our own understanding of the basic ideas involved can be seen by comparing the analysis we offered in 1957 (A. R. Anderson & Moore, 1957) with a 1967 version (A. R. Anderson, 1967).[5]

Another problem area which has significance for "formal" sociology is the mathematical treatment of the notion of relevance. Human affairs are conducted within universes of discourse in which some standards of relevance are presupposed, but the study of "relevant implication" was a neglected area in mathematical logic, so efforts were made to create the required formal machinery.[6] Interestingly enough, the improvement in our understanding of problems in deontic logic came about mainly because of this apparently unrelated work on the logic of relevance. This was one of those "unexpected" bonuses which we come to "expect" from what seems, on the surface, to be merely remote abstract consideration.

---

[5]Though the interest in deontic logic is our common concern, most of the relevant work under this project has been done by A. R. Anderson (1956a, 1956b, 1958a, 1958b, 1959a, 1962). For a reference to von Wright's essay, and a reasonably complete bibliography as of 1966, see the reprinted version of A. R. Anderson, 1956a.

[6]Again, the logic of relevant inference and entailment is of common concern. In this case the work has been done by A. R. Anderson (1957, 1959b, 1963); A. R. Anderson and Belnap (1958, 1959a, 1959b, 1959c, 1961a, 1961b, 1963); A. R. Anderson, Belnap and Wallace (1960); Belnap (1959a, 1959b, 1960a, 1960b, 1960c, 1960d, 1967); and Belnap and Wallace (1961); building their work on an important paper of Ackermann (1956).

Another area of investigation should be mentioned which also fits into the program of "formal" sociology. It turned out that there were almost no mathematical analyses of the logical structure of questions and answers. Yet surely here, if anywhere, is a distinctively human preoccupation, namely, the asking and answering of questions. The formal treatment of questions and answers is called "erotetic logic," a term introduced in 1955 by Mary and Arthur Prior (1955). It is being pursued by our colleague, Nuel D. Belnap, Jr. (among others), whose *An Analysis of Questions* (1963) provides a substantial treatment of this topic with bibliographical references.

Personality

Turning now from folk models *qua* cultural objects to some of their implications for personality, there is another possibility with reference to them that Simmel did not pursue. If our folk models and his play forms have the theoretical importance we attribute to them, then they should be of help in analyzing the structure of human personality. We have given some thought to this matter and our considerations have led us in the direction of the work of George Herbert Mead. As a heuristic gamble, we were willing to assume that the major functional components of human personality, and the organization of these components, reflect the structure of the folk models. By taking this view of human personality, we were led to ask whether each of the four kinds of folk models corresponds to a characteristic attitude or perspective that a person might take toward his world. It is our thesis that each class of models does so correspond, and that the models build upon one another in a particular order.

In capsule form, our position is:

1. Puzzles emphasize a sense of agency. We call this the "agent perspective." This is the outlook that perhaps Cooley (1902) had in mind when he spoke of "the joy of being a cause."

2. Games of chance emphasize a sense of patienthood, i.e., being the recipient of consequences over which we have virtually no control. We call this the "patient perspective."

3. Games of strategy presuppose an agent-patient perspective, but emphasize what we call the "reciprocal perspective." In Meadian terminology this would seem to be the perspective of a "significant other." For example, in playing bridge there is room for meaningful acts of agency and we are sometimes patient to all manner of outrageous happenings, some due to chance, some due to our opponent, some due to our partner, and even a few of our own doing. But the heart of the game (as von Neumann [1928] showed with beautiful precision) lies in the possible interrelations between the two opposing teams, each of which must take the other into account. This means that a genuine game of strategy, such as bridge, does not reduce mathematically into either the form of a puzzle or the form of a game of chance. This means, also, that a person who is looking at the world from the standpoint of the reciprocal perspective does not see another human being as merely puzzling or unpre-

dictable, but rather he sees him as someone who is capable of looking at him as he looks at the other.

4. Aesthetic entities emphasize a sense of assessing, evaluating or judging. This perspective presupposes *significant others* in interaction, i.e., it presupposes entities that behave in terms of the other three perspectives. We call this judgmental stance the "referee's perspective." The point of view of a judge in a bridge tournament (or any given player when he looks at his own play or the play of others as if he were the judge) is not that of any player *qua* player, nor is it some sort of average or consensus of the players' viewpoints. The referee's concern ranges over the whole game—his viewpoint presupposes that there are players with their reciprocal perspectives. With reference to Mead's analysis of personality, we think that the concept of the referee's perspective is a plausible explication of his concept of the "generalized other."

We made the point in connection with the reciprocal perspective that it did not collapse, logically speaking, into either of the two perspectives upon which it builds, namely, the agent and the patient perspectives. The reason we said this is that the mathematical structure of games of strategy is not reducible to either puzzles or games of chance. We want to make a similar argument now about the referee's perspective—it does not reduce to or collapse into any or all of the other three perspectives. Our reason for being confident about this is that the mathematics of the referee's perspective, insofar as it is deontic or normative, does not reduce to ordinary extensional logic, nor to the logic of possibility, nor to the logic of probability. The referee's perspective is a logically distinct realm. We realize that not everyone would find this line of reasoning convincing—and perhaps it should not be relied on too heavily—but we remember that not long ago there were those who thought it very unlikely that deontic logic could be set up on a solid footing, namely, on a basis which would not immediately collapse into the standard extensional systems.

A human being who has been socialized in the sense of Mead, i.e., an individual who has acquired a social self, should be able to take any of the four perspectives mentioned above. What is more, he should be able to handle them one by one, in pairs, in triples and in one superordinate quadruple—depending, of course, on the nature of the problem with which he is confronted. We say that his social self is constituted, in part, by the organization of these perspectives. A social self is neither something that anyone is born with, nor does it come about automatically through the processes of physiological maturation; rather, it is an achievement in learning which we think is guided in part by autotelic folk models.

We agree with the general Meadian analysis about how the social self, as an organization of perspectives, emerges out of a matrix of social processes—and how it, in turn, may affect these same processes. We appreciate particularly the suggestions Mead makes concerning the process whereby the interplay among human beings begins with a "conversation of gestures" and leads on to symbolic interaction. This interaction takes place through the use of "significant symbols"

—these symbols being defined in terms of a common universe of discourse. This universe of discourse, in turn, gains its relevance by virtue of its systematic relations to the set of social processes out of which the social interaction arises. For us, among the most significant of what Mead calls "significant symbols" are the symbolic complexes which we have dubbed "folk models." Of course, natural languages as systems of significant symbols are of prime importance, too. We agree completely with Mead about this.

Mead was well aware of the importance of play and of games as part of the process whereby a social self is acquired. In fact, he made a distinction between playing and taking part in a game to drive home his point that the development of the human personality takes place in a series of interrelated phases. A young child may *play* in the sense of taking the role of a series of significant others, but until he grasps the structure of the rules which make a game a game—that is until he can govern his ongoing conduct in the light of what we call the referee's perspective, or in Mead's terminology, the "generalized other"—the child is only *playing* and not *gaming*. And, to the extent that he is not up to handling games, he is only partially socialized. Clearly, it is compatible with the Meadian position to assume that conduct which flows from a mature social self would involve the use of each of the perspectives in the solution of challenging problems. It is convenient to think of each perspective as a part of the social self. As has been made clear above, we think that there are at least four such parts of a socialized human being: agent, patient, reciprocator, and referee.

Information Processing

Any problem worthy of the full talents of an adult human being requires that he carry out a great deal of information processing with respect to it. Obviously, this information processing is subject to some kind of control. The question is "What kind?" In terms of an engineering analysis, there are two major kinds of control systems that we can consider: those of the *open-loop* variety and those of the *closed-loop* variety.

An open-loop control system is one which exercises its control in a way that is independent of the output of the system. Open-loop systems, generally speaking, are not bothered by problems of instability.

A closed-loop control system is one in which the control is somehow dependent upon the system's output (or some symbolic representation of that output).

Closed-loop systems tend to suffer from various forms of instability. As was remarked before, human beings must have some sort of a control system to govern their information processing. Judging from the tendency of human beings to become unstable, we guess that the human control system is of the closed-loop variety. As a matter of fact, we assume a great deal more than that—we posit that the four perspectives constitute a subsystem which functions as part of an overall control system governing information processing.

It may seem to some that our brief discussion above about control systems is very remote from a Meadian analysis. We do not think that this is the case at all. Mead attempted to formulate a number of ideas which, in retrospect, can be recognized as brilliant anticipations of concepts which later received explicit treatment along the lines that he suggested. The Meadian notion of an attitude or perspective is a case in point. Let us listen to Mead a bit as he tried to tell his students and colleagues what he meant by an attitude.

> Present results, however, suggest the organization of the act in terms of attitudes. There is an organization of the various parts of the nervous system that are going to be responsible for acts, an organization which represents not only that which is immediately taking place, but also the later stages that are to take place. If one approaches a distant object he approaches it with reference to what he is going to do when he arrives there. If one is approaching a hammer he is muscularly all ready to seize the handle of the hammer. The later stages of the act are present in the early stages—not simply in the sense that they are all ready to go off, but in the sense that they serve to control the process itself. They determine how we are going to approach the object, and the steps in our early manipulation of it. We can recognize, then, that the innervation of certain groups of cells in the central nervous system can already initiate in advance the later stages of the act. The act as a whole can be there determining the process (Mead, 1934, p. 11).

When Mead advanced this analysis of an attitude, his remarks were interpreted by many to be sheer teleological nonsense. Now, we understand these ideas much better—he is saying that ongoing human activity is subject to a closed-loop control system. No contemporary engineer would regard this as metaphysics (in the ba-a-ad sense).[7]

Information Processing for Human Beings

We posit a control system which governs information processing that is sufficiently reflexive to allow a human being to stand back from himself in order to view himself as an object. What is more, this control system must allow him to see himself from the standpoint of any of the perspectives while he is planning or executing actions. This hypothetical control system must make provision for the fact that we can and do soliloquize. It must both permit and control internal dialogues such as: "I would like to do X, but I am not sure that it would make me happy. My father approves, but he doesn't understand. My mother doesn't approve and she does understand. It's illegal, but my friends say it is good." We all go round and round like this, looking at the world in terms of what we can do, what might happen to us, what our friends and enemies think, and what the referee might say. Sometimes these considerations get out of hand and we become bogged down in repetitious and viciously circular chains of reasoning. Sometimes we fail to consider a problem from some important perspective.

---

[7]We are well aware that "metaphysics" has an honorific sense, stemming from Aristotle's attempt to figure out how the universe ticks, and a pejorative sense, stemming from the logical empiricist rejection of theology and its sister-disciplines (e.g., Mariology). A good bit of what we are trying to convey in this chapter is probably metaphysics, in what we *hope* is a "good" sense.

The upshot is: we *assume* that a fully socialized human being, in a state of good emotional health, would have a control system which permits him to consider himself in a reflexive way from the standpoints which are represented abstractly in cultural terms by the four autotelic folk models.

Order of Mastering Perspectives

If the social self consists in part, at least, of an organization of perspectives, and if these perspectives are learned, then the question can be raised as to whether they are acquired in some particular order. Is the socialization process some sort of ordered sequence? We believe so and our analysis of human developmental phases follows our interpretation of Mead quite closely. We assume that the agent and patient perspectives are the first to develop—they are "twin born" to use Mead's expression. The notion of an agent is linked to that of a patient—but it may take an infant some time to discover that this is so; there are indeed studies which indicate that it takes a while for new-born infants to begin to understand the difference between their own bodies and their environment. But even if the agent-patient pair are twin-born, we still think of this pair as one term in a relation with the reciprocal perspective. Finally, the complete development of personality involves the pair-wise combination of the complex term agent-patient-reciprocal with the referee perspective. As was remarked earlier, the building up of this system into its most complex form does not mean that all parts need be involved in the solution of all problems; the system is sufficiently flexible, if its development goes well, so that the "parts" can be used one at a time, or in various combinations. As one can see, this is a fairly complex system even without further complications; there are some, on which we would now like to comment.

Complications Concerning Kind-Heartedness

Up to the present point, this summary of our position about human personality has made only passing reference to feeling and emotion. Are we to imagine that human beings are engaged mainly in the processing of information *sans* an involvement with affect? This would be an odd view of human nature, though the Meadian system tends to be odd in just this way. Mead had little to say about feeling and emotion. At the very least, we believe that it is essential to posit a *system* of feeling and emotion, and to make some assumptions about this system. This obviously is a complex topic. Here we will mention only a few of our assumptions—some which will help us later in the task of formulating principles for designing educational environments.

1. Each perspective is directly connected to the system of feeling and emotion so that the control system gets a "reading" from the system of feeling and emotion about reactions to plans and the execution of plans, or, more generally, about ongoing activity. This means that we can have, but need not have, "mixed feelings and emotions." For example, a

mountaineer, in thinking about rappelling down a cliff, may feel elation as an agent, anxiety as a patient, shame at the possibility of showing fear in front of his climbing companions (in a reciprocal sense), and guilt for rappelling at all since he is a family man and knows he should not take such risks—his own (kind-hearted) referee perspective says he is out of bounds.

2. The system of feeling and emotion is so organized that, under some circumstances, at least, it is possible to change the scale of feeling and emotion without necessarily altering its relative proportions. For example, in playing a game of chess, we can run through a wide gamut of emotions in, as it were, "attenuated" form—we can experience token amounts of anxiety, fear, etc., without literally panicking. Of course, the system of feeling and emotion may get out of control as in some kinds of mental illness—the scale of intensity may be shifted in the direction of gross exaggeration, on the one hand, or flatness of affect, on the other.

3. We not only have feelings and emotions, but each individual, in a reflexive way, can learn about his own reactions. The possibility of gaining some reasonable self-control with respect to affect, depends upon learning to recognize, differentiate and generalize about this vital aspect of ourselves; in other words, feeling and emotion can be schooled—and the use of autotelic folk models is normally part of this educational process.

Interlude

Someone who has followed the heuristic ideas presented above about human culture and the socialization process might be tempted to ask the following question: "If you regard these autotelic folk models so highly as guides to action, if they, indeed, represent abstractly so many salient features of human existence, and if they provide a basis for the structure of human personality, then do we need scientific models as opposed to folk models?" Our answer is that we do need scientific models. Folk models have served man well during most of his history, but there is something radically wrong with them with respect to their present theoretical relevance—something has happened which has rendered them worse than obsolete.

So long as the ordinary man lived out his life within the context of a static social framework, these models matched his world; the models themselves are essentially static entities. For instance, in any play of the game of chess, the rules —that is, the boundary conditions—remain constant. There may be plenty of lively action going on within this stable frame of reference and the participants may feel a wide range of emotions, but the rules are both fixed and inviolable in a normative sense. If you are working a puzzle, say a jigsaw puzzle, the picture to be completed does not change as you work on the puzzle, and the pieces preserve constancy of size and shape. If you go to see a play two nights in a row, it remains the same play with trivial variations; the actors do not change their lines because you have seen it before, though you may appreciate it more thoroughly on seeing it the second time. The basic point we are attempting to make is that folk models mirror the static quality of unchanging or imperceptibly changing societies. The folk models in this respect are like the Newtonian conceptions of space and time—both presuppose a frame of reference which is invariant with respect to all that goes on within it.

Today we live in a new world, a world in acceleration, a dynamic fluid world. In the 1940's the major industrial societies underwent a massive acceleration in technological development. This increase in the rate of technological change was so large, as far as its social consequences are concerned, as to amount to a difference in kind rather than one of degree.[8] Because of this, we, along with many others, have come to divide technological history into two main periods—the primitive, from the dawn of human history to the 1940's, and the modern, from the 1940's on. In order to make this case we draw graphs of technological functions, plotting, on a time scale of 10,000 years, such things as the speed of travel, the force of explosives, the size of objects which can be manipulated with precision, the number of people who can be included simultaneously within one communication network. The curves for these and many other technological functions bend sharply upward at about this time and they are now heading off the graph. Of course, there are some who are unhappy with the notion of pinpointing this acceleration in the decade of the 40's. They prefer to think in terms of a series of accelerations, each jolt larger than its predecessor. The time span for this series is taken to be the first half of the twentieth century. In any case, we agree with those who see a radical change.

Many aspects of this radical change in technological capability have become matters of grave concern. For example, most reasonably well-informed people understand that because the first fission device multiplied the explosive force of previous weapons a thousandfold, and a few years later a fusion device multiplied explosive force a million times, mankind now is in a position to do something it could never do before—to wit, it can commit suicide. All of this boggles the mind, but the aspect of the matter to which we want to draw attention here is the significance of the new technology for the socialization process.

We think that one important result of this technological leap is that we are in transition from what we have called a "performance" society to a "learning" society. In a performance society it is reasonable to assume that one will practice in adulthood skills which were acquired in youth. That, of course, has been the traditional educational pattern for human beings, and it is reflected in our linguistic conventions. We say that a medical student, for instance, learns medicine and the doctor *practices* it. There is also the *practice* of law, and in general, adults

---

[8]We yield to none in insisting on our inability to make the difference between "kind" and "degree" clear, and this is not the place to try to go into the matter. But it does seem apparent that the difference between two chicken eggs of a slightly different size is a difference of degree, whereas the differences between either of the two eggs or a behemoth is of rather more startling proportions; the latter we think of as a difference in kind.

have been the *practitioners* of the skills which they learned as apprentices. In contrast, in a learning society, it is not reasonable to assume that one will practice in adulthood the skills which were acquired as a youth. Instead, we can expect to have several distinct careers within the course of one lifetime. Or, if we stay within one occupational field, it can be taken for granted that it will be fundamentally transformed several times. In a learning society, education is a continuing process—learning must go on and on and on. Anyone who either stops or is somehow prevented from further learning is reduced thereby to the status of an impotent bystander.

We assume that the shift from a *performance* to a *learning* society calls for a thoroughgoing transformation of our educational institutions—their administration, their curricula, and their methods of instruction. Education must give priority to the acquisition of a flexible set of highly abstract conceptual tools. An appropriate theoretical apparatus would range not only over the physical and biological sciences, but over the subject matter of the behavioral and social sciences as well. What is required is the inculcation of a deep, dynamic, conceptual grasp of fundamental matters—mere technical virtuosity within a fixed frame of reference is not only insufficient, but it can be a positive barrier to growth. Only symbolic skills of the highest abstractness, the greatest generality, are of utility in coping with radical change. This brings us back to the folk models which are inculcated in childhood. If they "teach" a conception of the world which is incompatible with a civilization in acceleration, then we have the challenge of creating new models appropriate for these changed and changing circumstances—we need models that are fundamentally dynamic.

In the next section of this chapter we will present some very general principles for designing educational environments. It will be apparent at once that we have tried to learn some lessons from the thousands of years of human experience with autotelic folk models, but as was indicated above, we do not think that it is wise to be bound to them in any exclusive sense. The usual kinds of autotelic folk models could get along very nicely with sticks and stones on their physical side; however, dynamic models for a learning society seem to require the imaginative use of a much more subtle technology.

PRINCIPLES FOR
DESIGNING CLARIFYING ENVIRONMENTS[9]

Our task now is to state and explain a set of four principles for designing educational environments. Any environment which satisfies all four of these principles will be said to be a "clarifying environment."

It will be seen that the first three principles to be treated are directly related

---

[9]It should be made clear that though this chapter is in a certain sense a joint venture, the experimental and sociological part of the work belongs entirely to Moore. There is no particular point in trying to disentangle our contributions to what goes on here, beyond noting that the present chapter represents the results, some of which have been reported elsewhere, of about ten years of collaboration. Formulation and application of the principles to follow are the results of Moore's work.

to the notion of a folk model. The fourth principle seeks to make provision for the fact that we live in a world undergoing dynamic change.

1. Perspectives Principle. One environment is more conducive to learning than another if it both permits and facilitates the taking of more perspectives toward whatever is to be learned.

2. Autotelic Principle. One environment is more conducive to learning than another if the activities carried on within it are more autotelic.

3. Productive Principle. One environment is more conducive to learning than another if what is to be learned within it is more productive.

4. Personalization Principle. One environment is more conducive to learning than another if it: (1) is more responsive to the learner's activities, and (2) permits and facilitates the learner's taking a more reflexive view of himself as a learner.

The statement of the foregoing four[10] principles is sufficiently cryptic to make even a phrenologist happy. In spite of this fact, we believe they make some sense; and we forthwith proceed to try to explain the sense we think they make.

Perspectives Principle

The perspectives to which this principle refer are, of course, the four discussed in the previous section, namely, agent, patient, reciprocator and referee. This principle assumes, *ceteris paribus,* that learning is more rapid and deeper if the learner can approach whatever is to be learned:

  (a) from all four of the perspectives rather than from just three, from three rather than from just two, and from two rather than from only one; and
  (b) in all combinations of these perspectives—hence, an environment that permits and facilitates fewer combinations is weaker from a learning standpoint than one that makes provision for more combinations.

Another aspect of environmental flexibility with respect to the assumption of perspectives has to do with the attitude the learner brings to the environment each time he enters it. Imagine a learner who, one day, is filled with a sense of agency—he is in no mood, for instance, to be patient to anything or anybody. An environment will be more powerful from a learning standpoint if it lets him start off with whatever perspective he brings to it, and then allows him to shift at will.

As a parenthetical remark about shifting from one perspective to another, we think that young children do not have what is sometimes called a short "attention span," but they do have a relatively short and unstable "perspective span." This is one reason why there is little use in trying to deliver a lecture to a young child—he is not up to assuming the stance of a patient for very long at a

---

[10]C. S. Peirce observed somewhere that he had a "certain partiality for the number *three* in philosophy." From what follows, the reader will observe that *we* have a partiality to its successor. On the other hand, even Peirce occasionally gave way to *four* (1868).

time. But he can stay with the same topic or subject matter if he is permitted to run through a rather wide range of perspectives in whatever order he pleases.

When experts in education maintain that formal schooling is unsuitable for the very young child, the use of the word "formal" denotes the typical classroom situation in which most acts of agency are allocated to the teacher, the referee's role is also assigned primarily to the teacher, and the assumption of the reciprocal perspective in the form of interacting with peer-group members is forbidden through rules which are against note passing and which impose silence. About all that is left to the child is to be patient to the acts of agency of the teacher. This undoubtedly is an unsuitable learning situation for most young children—and the perspectives principle says that it is not as conducive to learning as a wide variety of alternative arrangements.

Another way to get the flavor of the perspectives principle is to pose the question as to why amusement parks amuse the young, but pall so rapidly. Think about the merry-go-round, the roller coaster, the fun-house with its surprises, etc. —it is apparent that what all of these "amusements" have in common is the rapid, involuntary shift in viewpoint within the context of one basic perspective; specifically, each exploits some facet of patienthood. Any environment which tends to confine people to one basic perspective is apt to become boring rather quickly. Of course, the symbolic level of amusement-park entertainment is relatively low, too, although it is high in its appeal to simple feelings and emotions. Consequently, a few trips to an amusement park go a long way.

Clearly, the theater is a more subtle form of entertainment; with it the shifts in perspectives are largely symbolic in character, rather than grossly physical. However, like the amusement park, the theater shares a weakness. Both force us to be spectators—patient to what goes on. An amusement-park ride hauls us through a predetermined course without any opportunity for changes due to our own acts of agency; similarly, plays run their predetermined courses. Though the patient perspective is salient at the amusement park and the theater, the referee's stance comes into the picture, too, as we assess and evaluate what goes on. There is also the vicarious opportunity to place ourselves in the roles of others, as, for instance, when we witness the screams and squirmings of others on a roller-coaster ride.

It should be noted that these and related forms of amusement are changing. Recent innovations in motion pictures permit the audience to vote from time to time on how they want things to come out. This is a step, though a crude one, in allowing for the agent perspective in entertainment. Some new amusement-park rides give a few controls to the passengers. Also, turning our attention for the moment to "cultural" entertainment, the traditional museum seems to be on its way out—more and more displays are subject to some sort of control by the visitor. So, we see the amusement park, the theater (at least motion pictures), and the museum moving away from the boredom inherent in a confining perspective. They are coming closer to satisfying the perspectives principle, which (to repeat) says that "one environment is more conducive to learning than another if it both permits and facilitates the taking of more perspectives toward whatever is to be learned."

Autotelic Principle

For an environment to be autotelic it must protect its denizens against serious consequences so that the goings on within it can be enjoyed for their own sake. The most obvious form of protection is physical. There are sports which come perilously close to violating their own autotelic norms because of physical risks —mountaineering is one. When a mountaineer is asked why he climbs, the fact that this question arose indicates something is amiss. People do not go about asking bowlers, chess players, and tennis players, to take one mixed bag of players, for deep reasons to justify their activities. Mountaineers, like racing-car drivers, are always trying to prove that their sport only appears to be dangerous—they argue that it is not hazardous for those who are properly trained.

When it comes to designing educational environments, especially those concerned with the acquisition of intellectual skills, almost everyone is pretty well agreed to keep physical risk out. True, there are some advocates of corporal punishment; and we should remember that there is the occasional fanatic, such as a teacher we once knew who thought that the only way to do mathematics was in an ice cold room. He began each class by throwing open the windows, even on bitterly cold days, which gave a kind of chilly introduction to algebra.

It is relatively easy to keep physical risks out of educational environments though there may always be the school-yard bully who punishes the scholar for his scholarship, and today, big-city schools increasingly require policemen to maintain order. Even so, it is more difficult to keep psychological and social risks out of an educational environment. If a student feels, while taking an exam, that he may disgrace himself and blight his future by failing to make a mark high enough to get into some special program, or if he feels that learning is simply a means of staying on a gravy train with stops only for prizes, honors, and scholarships on the way to success, then the whole learning environment is shot through with high psychological and social risks. For a learning environment to be autotelic, it must be cut off from just such risks.

Granted the nature of our present public and private school systems, and their relation to the broader society, it is doubtful that, at this time, more than a small fraction of the school day could be made autotelic. As a matter of fact, it is very difficult to arrange matters so that even a preschool child can have as much as thirty minutes a day that is really his, in the sense that none of the significant adults in his life is in a position to manipulate him, and where the things to be learned in the environment have a chance to speak persuasively to him in their own tongue.

Most contemporary education is nonautotelic; in fact, it prides itself on its nonautotelic status—school counselors carefully explain the financial and social rewards of further schooling. Through public service announcements, officials plead with dropouts to come back, and again, the basic argument given for returning to school is for rewards—financial and social. We never have heard a public service announcement which said something like, "Come back to school. Algebra is better than ever!"

The school day is so crammed full of activities that are planned to lead directly to the goal of at least one college degree, that a student seldom has the leisure to follow out the implications of an interesting problem, should he have the social misfortune of becoming intrigued by something truly puzzling. If a highly competent student works very hard, he may win a little extra time in which he can entertain a few ideas without having to cash them in at a science fair or some other parody of independent thinking.

Not only is the educational system largely nonautotelic in character, but the traditional folk models are in danger of being swept away. Little-league baseball replaces vacant-lot baseball. Amateur athletics in general seem to be turning into quasi-professional activities. On the more intellectual side our puzzles have been incorporated into the structure of tests—all current tests of ability are really a series of short puzzles.

Regardless of all of this, the autotelic principle states that the best way to learn really difficult things is to be placed in an environment in which you can try things out, make a fool of yourself, guess outrageously, or play it close to the vest—all without serious consequences. The autotelic principle does not say that once the difficult task of acquiring a complex symbolic skill is well underway, it is then not appropriate to test yourself in a wide variety of serious competitions. It is a common misunderstanding of the notion of an autotelic environment to assume that *all* activities should be made autotelic. Not so. The whole distinction requires a *difference* between a time for playfulness and a time for earnest efforts with real risks.

Productive Principle

Our statement of the productive principle is enigmatic at this point because we have not yet clarified the term "productive," though we have made implicit use of the concept of "productivity" in our prior discussion of folk models. So let us be explicit now.

We will say that one cultural object (a cultural object is something that is socially transmissible through learning) is more productive than another cultural object if it has properties which permit the learner either to *deduce* things about it, granted a partial presentation of it in the first instance, or *make probable inferences* (Peirce, 1955) about it, again assuming only a partial exposure to it.

Some examples may help. A perfect instance of a productive cultural object is a mathematical system. We can give the learner some axioms, some formation and transformation rules, and then he is at liberty to deduce theorems on his own. The logical structure of the system is what makes it productive. However, we are not always in a position to deal with such beautifully articulated structures. A case in point is the periodic table of elements. Its structure is productive on the basis of *probable inference* as opposed to *deductive inference*. Our evidence for productivity in this case is that empty cells in the table have been filled in with elements having the predicted properties. But compare the periodic table with an alphabetical arrangement of the same elements. The latter is less productive than the former by a country mile. In order to be more precise about all of this we would need a general theory of "probable inference" as well as a theory of "deducibility." We hope that a crude characterization of productiveness will be sufficient for our present purposes.

Turning back to the principle itself, it says, again *ceteris paribus,* that of two versions of something to be learned, we should choose the one which is more productive; this frees the learner to reason things out for himself and it also frees him from depending upon authority.[11]

Folk models, taken collectively, are good examples of productive cultural objects. To illustrate, once the simple rules for playing chess are mastered, it is not necessary to consult anyone in order to go on playing chess. It is true that one may be playing badly, but the structure of the rules for playing are sufficiently productive to guarantee that it is bad chess and not bad checkers that is being played.

Now that we have cleared things up a bit, someone might wonder why anyone would bother to state the productive principle as a principle for designing educational environments. Surely, people would not select the less productive of two versions of something to be learned. Yes, they would! The example above concerning the periodic table did not just pop into our heads. We observed, not long ago, a science teacher who had his students learn the atomic numbers and the atomic weights of the elements *in alphabetic order.* This is a tough task, and only a few of the children could manage it. Doubtless, you say, this is a rare aberration. Again, we beg to disagree. Let us take, as our case in point, the teaching of reading in the United States.

As everyone knows, or is supposed to know, there are two contrasting kinds of orthographic systems. On the one hand, there is the ideographic sort in which knowing some "words" give almost no clues as to how to handle the next written word. The Chinese system of writing is of this kind ; it is barely productive at all.[12] On the other hand, there are many systems of writing which are alphabetic. Once the learner has cracked the code which relates the written and spoken versions of the language to each other, he can write anything he can say, or he can read anything that has been written. (The only things sacrificed by not referring to authority are the niceties of spelling and punctuation, but the phonetics carry the meaning.) Such alphabetic systems of writing are productive cultural objects, even, we should point out, in the case of a child of our acquaintance who spelled the word for eyes as "is." Given our usual spelling habits, this looks at best like an imaginative leap at an attempt to spell "eyes," but as Moore has pointed out

---

[11]Though we do not know exactly how to characterize "productivity," we can give at least one clear example. The "natural deduction" methods of Gentzen, Jaskowski, Fitch (see Fitch, 1952, for references), and others are "productive" in that they help the student figure out what is going on. By contrast Nicod's single axiom for the propositional calculus prompted Irving Copi to quote Dr. Johnson's alleged remark about a woman preaching: it is "like a dog's walking on his hind legs. It is not done well; but you are surprised to find it done at all."

[12]There is some *slight* productivity in the fact that such characters as those for *tree, grove,* and *forest* have a reasonable connection: a tree looks like 木, a grove like 林, and a forest like 森. Similarly the character 口 means (among other things) *mouth, entrance, opening, hole.* But whoever would have guessed that 龜 meant "turtle?"

elsewhere (1963), English orthography has more coherence than it is given credit for. However, many of the standard textbooks for teaching beginning reading used in our country today treat written English as if it were Chinese.

Personalization Principle

This principle, unlike the others, has two distinct parts: the idea is that the environment must be both (1) responsive to the learner's activities, and (2) helpful in letting him learn to take a reflexive view of himself. The explanation comes in two pieces.

1. The responsive *condition.* The notion of a responsive environment is a complex one, but the intuitive idea is straightforward enough. It is the antithesis of an environment that answers a question that was never asked,[13] or, positively stated, it is an environment that encourages the learner first to find a question, then find an answer. The requirements imposed upon an environment in order to qualify it as "responsive" are:

(a) It permits the learner to explore freely, thus giving him a chance to discover a problem.

(b) It informs the learner immediately about the consequences of his actions. (How immediate is "immediate" will be discussed later.)

(c) It is self-pacing, i.e., events happen within the environment at a rate largely determined by the learner. (The notion that the rate is *largely* determined by the learner and not *wholly* determined by him is important. For example, some hyperactive children rush at their problems so much that the consequences of their actions are blurred—there must be provision for slowing down the learner under some circumstances; also, there are occasions when he should be speeded up. Nonetheless, it is basically self-pacing.)

(d) It permits the learner to make full use of his capacity for discovering relations of various kinds. (No one knows what anyone's full capacity for making discoveries is, but if we hand the learner a solution we certainly know we are not drawing upon his capacity.)

(e) It is so structured that the learner is likely to make a series of interconnected discoveries about the physical, cultural or social world. (What this amounts to depends, of course, upon what kinds of relations are being "taught" within the environment.)

The conditions for responsiveness taken together define a situation in which a premium is placed on the making of fresh deductions and inductions, as opposed to having things explained didactically. It encourages the learner to ask questions, and the environment will respond in relevant ways; but these ways

---

[13]We are all familiar with situations where we are given information we did not want to have. Our earlier discussion indicates our belief that many school children are in this situation (as we both were), and we suppose that the adult analogue is wading through all that dreary stuff about soap, while waiting for the eleven o'clock news on TV.

may not always be simple or predictable. For a learner to make discoveries, there must be some gaps or discontinuities in his experience that he feels he must bridge. One way that such discontinuities can be built into a responsive environment is to make provision for changing the "rules of the game" without the learner knowing, at first, that they have been changed. However, it will not do to change the rules quixotically—the new set of rules should build upon the old, displacing them only in part. Such changes allow the learner to discover that something has gone wrong—old solutions will no longer do—he must change in order to cope with change. In other words, if you want a learner to make a series of interconnected discoveries, you will have to see to it that he encounters difficulties that are problematic for *him*. When he reaches a solution, at least part of that solution should be transferable to the solution of the next perplexity.

Finally, though a responsive environment does respond, its response has an integrity of its own. It is incorrect to think of a responsive environment as one which simply yields to whatever the learner wants to do—there are constraints. To take a trivial example, if the question is how to spell the word "cat," the environment permits the learner to attempt to spell it K-A-T—there is no rule against trying this, but he will not succeed that way, where by "succeeding," we mean *both* getting a satisfactory response from the environment, *and* learning the sort of thing the environment was devised to help him learn. Without the latter condition the environment would not be informative.

2. The reflexive condition. One environment is more reflexive than another if it makes it easier for the learner to see himself as a social object. We previously made the point, the Meadian point, that the acquisition of the social self is an achievement in learning. Unfortunately, some of us are underachievers. One reason, we think, for our ineptitude in fashioning ourselves is that it is hard to see what we are doing—we lack an appropriate mirror. The reflexiveness which is characteristic of maturity is sometimes so late in coming that we are unable to make major alterations in ourselves. "The reflexive condition" is fairly heavy terminology; all we mean is that if an environment is so structured that the learner not only can learn whatever is to be learned, but also can learn about himself *qua* learner, he will be in a better position to undertake whatever task comes next. It facilitates future learning to see our own learning career both retrospectively and prospectively. It is a normal thing for human beings to make up hypotheses about themselves, and it is important that these hypotheses do not harden into dogma on the basis of grossly inadequate information.

We find it not at all surprising that athletic coaches have made more use of reflexive devices in instruction than have classroom teachers. This does not surprise us because of our confidence in play forms. It is in the realm of sports that motion pictures of learning and practice have come into wide usage. Coaches go over games with their players, spotting weaknesses, strengths, etc.— they do not forget their opponents, either. Of course, motion pictures used reflexively have limitations, but surely coaches have taken a step in the right direction.

The four principles presented above, perspectives, autotelic, productive, and personalization, are offered as heuristic guides[14] for constructing educational environments. Undoubtedly, they are vague and ambiguous; the critical question is whether they are so deficient as to be useless. We do not think that they are totally without merit. In the next section we offer an application of the principles to show what can be made of them.

AN APPLICATION OF THE FOUR PRINCIPLES

Imagine that for some unaccountable reason you were given the problem of designing an educational environment for preschool children. Imagine also that this environment is to be one in which the children learn to read their natural language. What would you do?

One of us has taken upon himself the task of building several such environments, beginning with the very simple, and gradually working up to larger, more complex ones. This evolution of environments was marked by a gradual increase in the sophistication of the technology which went into them. The four principles we have discussed were used in designing both the overall structure of these environments and the technology used within them. We would like to make it clear, incidentally, as a methodological point, that the ideas came first, and the applications (both in logic and behavioral science) came afterwards. However, our understanding of the principles and the clarity with which we saw their relevance increased with the experience of actually constructing learning environments.

Let us go over each principle to see what it "tells" us to do.

Perspectives Principle—Application

If the children who come to the environment are to learn to read, we should ask what sort of an activity reading is. In the simplest terms, reading involves the decoding of a message which was previously encoded.[15] Leaving aside the special case where the reader decodes his own material, as a reader we are patient to the symbolic consequences of someone else's activity. We read what the writer wrote. This is banal, all right, but it does point to a one-sided emphasis in reading that the principle seeks to avoid. Is there some way to allow the learner to stand in the relation of agent as well as patient to reading material?

---

[14]Some people might prefer that we convert the principles into empirical propositions and then proceed to test their truth. We would caution that they would require a much more rigorous formulation if they were to be treated as anything more than heuristic guidelines. The difficulty in such reformulations is that the principles make use of a number of concepts which are not very well understood mathematically. So, for the moment, let us take them as guides, and *only* as such.

[15]Here we are simply going to bypass the usual hornet's nest of questions about the logical and ontological status of "information" about "type-token" distinctions and the like. We will also fail to discuss the question as to whether speech is encoded writing, or writing is encoded speech ; not that these are unimportant issues, but this is not the place to discuss them.

First, the perspectives principle urges that we think about this. An answer comes readily. Reading should be treated as part of a correlative process. Specifically, the decoding and encoding of messages, that is, reading and writing, should be developed together. Reading emphasizes patienthood and writing emphasizes agency. Once one begins to look around for correlative processes which give the learner an opportunity to take more perspectives toward his task, other combinations come easily to mind. For instance, what about listening and speaking? Obviously, listening stands to reading as writing stands to speaking. The first pair, reading and listening, is on the side of patienthood; the other pair is on the side of agency.

Thus we are being led by the perspectives principle to widen our definition of the learner's task. Originally, we thought of him as learning to read, now we see him as learning to handle a four-fold set of linguistic processes: reading, writing, listening, speaking. With regard to this set, the learner's redefined task is to communicate more effectively rather than simply to read.

Up to this point we have drawn on only two of the four basic perspectives, agent and patient, but the reciprocal perspective suggests something else. As will be recalled, to take the reciprocal perspective is to look at our own behavior from the standpoint of someone else. What implications does this have for reading?

If we are reading something, we may want to know who wrote it. We may want to know why he wrote it. We may wish to understand the context out of which the message comes. It would seem that we should begin to learn very early to distinguish among various sources of messages if we are to put ourselves in the frame of reference of the sender. Some messages come from ourselves, that is, we are decoding what we have previously encoded. Some messages come from persons whom we know, and some messages come from strangers. This, of course, is looking at the sources of messages from the standpoint of the pair of perspectives, patient-reciprocal. If we think of writing, or more broadly, of preparing a message, again we need to know whether the message is being done for our own later use, for the use of others whom we know (and whose peculiarities we may wish to take into account) or for strangers. From this standpoint the perspectives pair which is involved is agent-reciprocal.

In designing our educational environment according to the reciprocal perspective, the learner should be led to distinguish among the various possible targets for his messages, and he should be led to discriminate among the various possible sources of messages which come to him. If, for instance, all of the reading material in the educational environment is prepared by anonymous outside experts, then how will the learner have any chance to make the discriminations about which we have been talking? It will not do, either, for all the material to come from the learner himself or from those he knows. Perhaps an illustration may make our meaning plain. In one of our laboratories some of the children were taking dictation at three and four years of age. The children had a chance to learn to distinguish between themselves and others as "dictators." One little boy, who took dictation quite well, his own and others, would at first refuse to recognize himself if he had botched his recording. One moment he would say,

"That little boy doesn't speak right," and in the next breath he would take credit for something well done.

Taking the reciprocal perspective seriously encourages us to design the environment so that the learner can come to make clearer distinctions between himself and other people, both in the encoding and decoding of messages. Concretely, this means that the environment must make explicit provision in terms of time, place, and equipment for the learner to produce material (a) for his own exclusive use, (b) for those he knows, and (c) for general consumption, as well as to receive information (a) from himself, (b) from those he knows, and (c) from total strangers, e.g., Mark Twain.

It should be remembered, in terms of either the Meadian or our own theoretical position, that to say the learner should come to make clearer distinctions between himself and other people, does not presuppose that his "self" is a pre-formed finished product. Quite to the contrary, learning to make such distinctions is part of the process whereby the learner develops a sense of self-identity or, in general, a more adequate self.

This account helps us take care of agents, patients, and reciprocators, or so we believe; now how about referees? Clearly, encoding and decoding messages has to be done in accordance with some set of rules, otherwise the messages would be meaningless or garbled. The rules of a natural language and its written counterpart are so difficult to formulate that linguistics has not yet succeeded in adequately characterizing the formal structure of any natural language. Therefore, it is impossible for us to teach the learner the rules of the game in an explicit didactic way.

How are we to handle this? How are we to encourage the learner to view his own acts of communication and those of others from the standpoint of a set of common ground rules? We could, of course, bring in a teacher who would tell the student such things as, "Read more clearly," or "That is an improperly constructed sentence." To have a teacher behave in this fashion would provide a referee, a very authoritative referee, but the perspectives principle says that the learner is to be encouraged to take the referee's perspective *himself* in evaluating his own and other's on-going activities. In order to get him to assume this stance, what seems to be required is to have breaches of the common rules of communication become problems for the learner. The example above of the little boy who took dictation is to the point. When this boy originally either told a story or read a story (which was being recorded), there was always a strong tendency to criticize him for speaking unclearly, garbling words, and so on. However, his inadequacies became problems *to him* when he attempted to decipher his own speech. Since the environment was arranged so that he easily could re-do sections of his own recordings, and compare his messages with messages from others, he had the opportunity of assessing and evaluating the adequacy and appropriateness of his own communication.

The idea of making rule violations a genuine problem to the learner as a step toward getting him to take the referee's perspective seems sound enough, but it does not go to the heart of the problem—it might result only in the learner's taking a rule-oriented view of what just happened to become problematic to him. He needs to be placed in a position where he can oversee the whole communication process as it goes on within the environment. To put it another way, he needs to be put in a position that is *super*ordinate to the component processes of communication: reading, writing, listening and speaking (all of which are being carried out in terms of an appropriate variety of message sources and targets).

The referee's perspective suggests, then, that we create a superordinate task which will use the subordinate communications skills as means to accomplish it. The overall task which was set up in several environments was that of publishing a newspaper. (It will be made clear below, when we treat the autotelic principle, that the publishing of a newspaper goes on in what is called a "transfer room," rather than in the autotelic environment per se. Newspaper publishing is not treated as a purely autotelic matter in this transfer room.) This is a task in which the participants not only can use their communication skills, but they have to establish standards for what is published. If the children are permitted to work out their own criteria for interest, relevance, and clarity for the intended audience, they must oversee the whole operation as an umpire would.

To get the first newspaper started, two highly competent children, who had been in this special educational environment for three years and who could read, write, type, and take dictation, were selected as editors. When they were five-years-old they began to publish their own newspaper with some initial assistance from adults. By the time they were seven, another group of five-year-olds was ready to start its newspaper. So, instead of having adults help in establishing another newspaper, the two senior editors were asked to select two editors for the paper-to-be, and then to explain to them what the job of editor amounted to. The experienced editors were none too sanguine about the feasibility of explaining anything to children so young, but they agreed to try. They had the satisfaction of knowing that the children with whom they would be dealing were of their own choosing.

A convenient way to get some feel for how the children behave in terms of the referee's perspective is to follow one of their discussions. Given below is a transcript of part of an editors' conference. The cast consists of a seven-year-old girl, Venn, co-editor of the first newspaper; a seven-year-old boy, Jeffrey, co-editor of the first newspaper; Pam, newly appointed five-year-old girl, co-editor of the new newspaper; Larry, four-year-old boy, co-editor of the new newspaper. The extent to which four able children can deal meaningfully with the problems of deciding what is "fit to print" (apologies to the *New York Times*) is indicated in an extended quotation below. But first, a parenthetical remark.

Four children are serving as editors. Explicit provision must be made in the environment for rotating this role, otherwise the opportunity to see what goes on from the editor's desk would be a restricted one. Plainly enough, some children are prepared to be editors at first and others will come along later. Some may not be up to the job at all, in which case they should be given a chance to rise as high as they can. Also, it is important for former editors to serve as contributors who have to put up with editors. One practical way to rotate the role of editor is to have different editors for different issues. We shall now "listen in" on a conversation the children had on the subject.

> Venn: Jeffrey and I have chosen you two to be the editors of the first-grade newspaper. My first question is, Would you like to be the editors of the first-grade newspaper?
>
> Larry and Pam (in unison): Yessssssss!!!
>
> Venn: Well—one of—the editor is the boss of the newspaper and you are going to be the boss, so, one of the ways to get an article is, you can tell a child—
>
> Larry: What's a child?
>
> Venn: You can tell a child, give a child an idea—
>
> Larry: But what's a child?
>
> Venn: You're a child—
>
> Larry: Oh—
>
> Venn: . . . give a child an idea and he can think about it for a while, or a child can think up his own idea. He'll type that once he gets it, and then he will give it to you. If there are too many errors, give it back. If it's O.K.—its O.K. But if there's a few errors, correct them. But if there's too many errors—you can't just—
>
> Larry: Correct them?
>
> Venn: . . . correct them or it would be more—
>
> Larry: Could Pam help me, then, correct them?
>
> Venn: Yes—if there's too many you shouldn't correct them because if you did correct them, you might be correcting too many and it would be more of your article than theirs. Once you get a lot of this material, like riddles, poems, jokes, cartoons and—
>
> Jeffrey: And comics—
>
> Venn: . . . and comics, you can choose the ones that—you can both decide the ones that are most interesting and the ones that aren't you leave out, then you type them on stencils—and then when you get all the stencils you run them off on the mimeograph machine. Now, a mimeograph machine is this thing right there.
>
> Larry: How do you work it?
>
> Venn: You'll find out. After you mimeograph it, you collate it. And then staple it, and then it is ready to give out. And—Pam? Do you have any questions? Pam—
>
> Pam: Well, what if all of them are not too good—what do you do really?
>
> Larry (at the same time Jeffrey is talking): You correct all of them—
>
> Jeffrey: You give them back and make them start all over again on a different one.
>
> Venn: As you would if they were wrong, you would send them back—
>
> Pam: Ahhhh—
>
> Venn: Before, if they were wrong as we told you—
>
> Larry: All of them?
>
> Pam: Why?

Venn: Because—

Larry: If we get tired then we couldn't be the editors if we got too tired, right?

Venn: Editors—if you are going to be an editor, editors don't get tired.

Larry: But erasing all those things, right? they will—

Jeffrey: On stencils you don't erase—special kind of correcting fluid—

Venn: Stencils are made out of wax.

Larry: I think I've used them before—

Venn: No, Larry—

Larry: But I think I've seen them run once.

Pam: I think he has seen them once, but I'm not quite sure cause I haven't seen them once.

God may allow himself the luxury of resting on the seventh day, but this privilege evidently is not for editors—"Editors don't get tired." It isn't too often that we have a chance to listen to young children discuss a difficult problem. We find their viewpoints fascinating; leaving aside the little exchange about "What's a child?" the rest is really quite subtle. By the way, the recording of the conference indicates that Venn slurred the word "child" when she first used it—it sounded like "chile." Larry misunderstood her. Also, he may have been surprised by a child using the word "child" because adults generally are the ones who use this term.

It is interesting to contrast the views of the experienced children with the inexperienced youngsters. For little Larry, the main problem he saw in correcting errors was the time and effort it might take—he wanted to be certain he had Pam's help in this. Venn and Jeffrey knew that the sheer physical act of correcting errors, for instance on a stencil, was trivial. As experienced editors their point was the delicate one having to do with human relations and the integrity of other people's work. Venn said it quite well—"If there's too many [errors] you shouldn't correct them because if you did correct them, you might be correcting too many, and it would be *more of your article than theirs*." Evidently, Venn and Jeffrey feel that at some point an editor would become the contributor if he "corrected" the article too much. The same sort of point was brought up by Pam when she said, "Well, what if all of them are not too good—what do you do, really?" Venn replies that it is the same problem as correcting too many errors. Jeffrey and Venn agree, give it back and have them start over.

It seems to us that all of the editors, especially the experienced ones, are too confident of the "rightness" of their judgments. There is still an absolutistic streak in their attitude toward what it means to be the referee. None of them, at that time, ever had had to put up with an unreasonable editor.[16] It would be intriguing to know whether they would evolve some mechanism whereby contributors who felt they had been unfairly or improperly judged would have some court of appeal. (We did not get to find out because the grant under which we were working ran out the next year.) In any case, the perspectives principle

---

[16]It may come as a surprise to the reader, as it did to us, that the concept of an "unreasonable editor" can be made mathematically precise, as Dana Scott (1956) pointed out.

urges us to create opportunities for the learners to get an overview of their environment and to learn to make assessments and evaluations of a normative kind.

Autotelic Principle—Application

The most obvious application of this principle is to the physical safety of the children. Since they are permitted to explore the environment freely and much of what they do is self-determined, it is imperative to examine every aspect of the environment for hazards. Naturally enough, the safety of the children is of first importance, but the environment needs some protection, too. We use the somewhat awkward expression "childproofing the environment" to cover both aspects of this relation—we want the children to be safe, but we do *not* want them to ruin the environment. This is much easier said than done. It has taken as much as three months of engineering time to work out solutions for some seemingly simple problems. For example, the automatic carriage return on the ordinary electric typewriter is dangerous because a tiny child could have his fingers hurt if he is unlucky enough to have them in the wrong place when the carriage snaps back. We designed a clear plastic shield to prevent this from happening. This sounds easy to do, but it takes a good deal of thought to come up with a practical shield which the operator can remove quickly but the child cannot. Most educational environments are not troubled by the safety factor because the children are not given sufficient freedom to get into serious difficulties and the environments are relatively bare.

An autotelic environment must afford the learner more than physical safety —he must be free from various kinds of social pressures. At the very least, this means privacy vis-a-vis the authority figures in his life. We can remember very well explaining the autotelic principle to an architect who was to design an autotelic environment for a public school. He seemed to understand what was wanted and in about two weeks he came back with beautiful colored drawings showing an open park-like area which was sprinkled with clear plastic bubbles, each bubble slightly larger than a phone booth, and each bubble containing a child who could see everything around him, and who could be seen by anyone who chanced by. This is not quite the idea.

As most of us can recall from our own childhood, play means *both* not having to do something *and* not having to do it in the presence of authorities. The demand for privacy during playtime seems to require children to disappear into cracks between buildings, or cellars, caves, tree houses and other uncomfortable places. They seem to care little about comfort if its sacrifice will purchase some freedom. So the idea is to make a place into which children can disappear during (autotelic) playtime—a place where they cannot be followed by those whom they may be trying to avoid.

There is an indefinitely large number of architectural arrangements which would do for this purpose so long as whatever structure is used is protected by norms which prevent a bossy older sister, a domineering mother, an anxious father, or a meddling grandparent from coming in. Sometimes we have used air-conditioned, windowless, prefabricated buildings as the shell for such environments. Inside there is compartmentalization—there are sound-proofed booths for individuals and larger rooms for groups. Sometimes, rather than constructing a separate building for the environment, we have used space within an existing structure. In either case, the heart of the matter is to delineate clearly the protective boundary of the environment so that even a two-year-old will be led to recognize the distinction between being in it and being out of it. This distinction can be conveyed physically in many ways and we try to use as many *differences* as we can, partly because some children, mentally retarded ones, for example, need all the help they can get to make this distinction. We have used differences in color, texture, temperature, and so on, very freely to define the environmental boundary.

Even if the architecture of the environment spells privacy for the learner, the social norms which define the environment as autotelic must be made clear to him. We have found that most children are more likely to believe what other children say than they are to believe adults when it comes to the question of freedom. Therefore, we rely on children to explain the rules of the environment to newcomers. The rules are simple enough—the problem is to make them credible. The first rule is, you do not have to come here at all. The second rule is, you may leave when you wish. The third rule is, you do not need to explain your comings and goings. These are the basic explicit rules. There are some implicit rules which bind the staff and which may or may not be of direct concern to the learner. The prime implicit rule is that the behavior of the learner in the environment is a private matter for the staff. The learner himself may talk about it in any way he pleases and to whom he pleases. What all this means is that parents, for example, are not allowed to watch their own children, nor do they get reports which would enable them to follow their child's progress in the environment. The children are not graded. Of course, if the staff sees a serious medical, educational or social problem developing, this is promptly brought to the parent's attention. The point is *not* to neglect measles, or hysteria; it is rather to give the tykes a little time off every day, when they can enjoy learning something without being under the nose of Mommy, or Daddy, or Big Brother.

After a child has been coming to a well-run autotelic environment for some time, he will have learned some things which he may wish to practice. In several of our educational ventures we have designed a kind of half-way station between the world outside the autotelic environment and the autotelic environment per se. We call this a "transfer room" (a concept to which we referred earlier). It is physically and normatively distinct from the basic autotelic environment. It is in the transfer room, for example, that the children publish a newspaper. They begin such activities only after they have learned how to read, type, etc. In the transfer room they practice these skills within the context of some superordinate task. The normative rules for the transfer room might best be described as permissive rather than autotelic. For instance, several groups of youngsters not only published a newspaper but they sold it. The newspaper itself with its signed articles gave parents and others a pretty good idea of what their children were doing and thinking. By definition, a newspaper is not private, but public. The children used the newspaper to gain approval and to express criticism. In brief, there are many kinds of extrinsic rewards and punishments associated with this activity. We think that the transfer room is a valuable adjunct to an autotelic environment if there is any reason to believe that the world outside that environment does not provide adequate opportunities for the learners to apply their skills. An appropriately designed transfer room and suitable transfer-room activities allow for the "transfer" of what is learned within an autotelic environment to problems outside its boundary.

Sometimes the question is asked as to why the children should trust the adults in the autotelic environment to be autotelic toward them if children are assumed to be somewhat distrustful of adults in general. We, of course, do not assume that all children are distrustful of adults. We do assume, however, that most children two years of age and older have discovered that questions such as "Would you like to wash your hands?" are best translated as the imperative "Wash your hands!" We find that children only gradually come to trust the adult staff who manage the environment. It helps to create this trust if the staff avoids taking nonautotelic roles with the children outside the environment. An instructive mistake will show what is to be avoided. In one educational experiment the director reported to us that his children did not behave at all as he would have expected—they did not seem to explore very much, they frequently refused to come to the laboratory, they stayed for relatively short periods of time—evidently something had gone wrong. It turned out that this project director used his laboratory staff in two conflicting roles. Some of them served as part-time bus monitors. As bus monitors they had to discipline the children in a variety of ways to assure the safe operation of the bus. Then these same people would appear in the laboratory as staff members who are carefully instructed not to reward or punish the children. Quite understandably these preschool children were confused. Older, more sophisticated children might have been willing to accept the thesis that one person can wear two hats, but it was asking too much of this particular group. When this was pointed out, the director changed his job assignments appropriately and within a few weeks the behavior of the children became more relaxed, refusal rates went down, and length of stays increased.

It seems to us that the autotelic principle gives some general guidance in constructing the physical side of an educational environment and in formulating its rules and procedures. When we first began to experiment with autotelic environments we held our breath lest the children really would not come back unless they were given candy, gold stars, etc., on the one hand, and threats and punishments, on the other. These environments were not built for a day, a week, or even a month—we hoped the children would find them fascinating for years! We now know that such attractive environments can be built and that the children will come to them for an indefinitely long period of time. If suitable transfer rooms and transfer-room activities are provided, the children can develop exceedingly high levels of skill and they take considerable pride in their accomplishments. An article by a teenager written for a high school newspaper conveys some sense of the way the children felt about their experience in one laboratory. This piece was written by Nancy Jordon, an assistant editor of her paper.

READING LAB PRODUCES PAPER

The first grade in connection with the reading lab puts out its own newspaper. We felt it might be to our advantage to interview the Staff. We walked in a little apprehensively wondering just what to ask and how to approach our competitors. They seemed to regard us with awe and a little hesitation as to our true intentions. But they were a rather talkative group and it didn't take very long for each to willingly expositate on his contributions and prove an individual superiority.

Everyone Contributes

The paper is compiled solely by the children and they seem to regard any assistance as an infringement upon their skill. Everyone in the class is a contributing reporter who types up his own story and then several others type up the sheets for the newspaper itself and run them off on the thermo-fax machine, an instrument whose complexities are clearer to the first-grade than they are to us. We were also proudly told by one interested, lively little girl, "I could type when I was two years old!"

A boy standing nearby not to be outdone added "I learned to type four years ago." Since they are both only six and we are sixteen and hardly able to pluck out a few lines with one finger, we began to feel slightly inferior.

Satisfies Literary Needs

The stories are typed in the lab and one of the editors assured me that everybody in the class "liked" to participate in this sort of literary self-expression. Some of the others appeared more dubious but all were extremely fond of typing and genuinely enjoyed this program.

The development of the paper was adequately expressed in a rather concise sentence by the editors, "Well one day Mrs. Coogan told us a surprise and we were the editors."

Mrs. Coogan helps to correct the articles and when questioned how they knew the spelling of such a variety of words, the response was naturally that they were fully acquainted with the use of the dictionary. They all seemed to think reading and correcting articles was fun or anyway the finding of other people's mistakes. We complimented them on their paper and someone quickly apologized "I saw a little mistake but we decided to skip it."

Sacred Document

By accident a copy of their paper was dropped, a hush fell over the room. Two or three children quickly retrieved the journal with stricken faces for they had an intense pride in their achievement and were not ready to see a product of such hard effort mutilated or destroyed in any way.

We asked for any final comments; first we received a blank stare but then someone kindly volunteered "Well I was just thinking if you wanted to use my riddle . . ." Another boy with a rather dream-like expression said, "I have something to say . . . I was at the beach and . . ." As we left we overheard one boy say to a friend, "We were having a meeting!" and with the aptness of childhood logic the other's reply was "Who cares, that's stupid!"

Productive Principle—Application

The guidance which this principle gives us with respect to reading is quite straightforward. It invites us to consider very carefully the structure of what is to be learned. If children are to read, they must break the code that relates the spoken language to the written language (the spoken part having been learned already in an autotelic way; mothers do not send their babies to the Sorbonne for lectures—the babies learn to speak because *they* find it fun to communicate in some more sophisticated way than crying). For present purposes we will confine ourselves to the English language as an example, but the reader will see that many of our considerations would carry over to any language with a similar orthography, i.e., a system of symbols designed to mirror speech. Among such we mention Greek, Hebrew, Russian, Arabic, German, Latin—all of which have had, at one time or another, distinctive *alphabets:* conventional squiggles on paper intended to indicate the sounds made in the course of talking (a writing system quite different from that of the Chinese, mentioned above).

If we ask ourselves whether our present English alphabet is better than some alternative versions of it, we can see at once that it leaves a good deal to be desired. Too few symbols are trying to do too much work. This produces unnecessary ambiguity, which in turn produces confusion for the learner.

Sir James Pitman (1965), the grandson of Sir Isaac Pitman, inventor of the system of shorthand which bears his name, developed an alphabet consisting of forty-four symbols, more than enough to represent the forty phonemes of English. This system is intended to be used as an initial teaching alphabet (i.t.a.) after which the learner is expected to switch over to the conventional alphabet. There is no question about it, Pitman's system is more productive than the conventional alphabet. It is being used on an experimental basis in our country now. We have not used it largely because the typewriters employed in our work have the standard keyboard. Now some typewriter companies are offering the Pitman symbols.

Besides the question of productivity, there are some other issues which arise with respect to Pitman's system. What happens if some children do not switch easily to the conventional system? Might not some people welcome a group of second-class readers (those who never switched) as targets for exploitation? There are many other issues of this kind which come up when the question is one of adopting or not adopting an innovation on a mass basis. Here, all that we wish to note is that the productivity principle alerts us to alternatives, some of which are clearly superior to the conventional system.

Personalization Principle—Application

Responsive condition. In applying the responsive condition to the learning of basic communication skills, we will concentrate here on the design of responsive environment equipment. Equipment is not the whole story, but it will be recalled that one of the requirements imposed on an environment in order to qualify it as responsive is that it should permit the learner to explore. We mean that he should be able to explore the entire environment, not just the equipment it may contain.

Suppose we wish to design a machine which will help a child learn to "read." Following our prior application of the perspectives principle, we place reading within the context of the four-fold set of linguistic skills: speaking-listening; writing-reading. We have mentioned five conditions for responsiveness, and we will now attempt to design our machine so that it will satisfy these conditions.

a. *It permits the learner to explore.* It seems simple enough to say that the learner should be free to explore and presumably what he is free to explore is our hypothetical machine. Does this mean that he should be free to take the machine apart? Leaving aside the complication that he might hurt himself—a contingency forbidden by our prior application of the autotelic principle—the idea is not to explore the machine as such. Rather, what we want him to do is to explore something else using the machine as a tool or means for exploration. True, he will have to learn something about the machine in order to use it as a tool, but most of the machine's characteristics *qua* machine are irrelevant to the task of enhancing communication skills.

What in the world is it, then, that the learner is to explore? We have agreed to confine ourselves to English, for present purposes. The English orthographic system, as we all know, consists of more than the upper and lower case alphabets —it also has various punctuation marks. What is more, all of these symbols must be used in accordance with certain conventions, such as proceeding from left to right, from top to bottom, and with various kinds of juxtaposition. It is this complex system of English orthography that we want to open up for exploration.

The learner should find it easy to produce any part of it at will; it should be convenient to expose him to it; and whatever is done with it should exemplify its various conventions. Our task, then, as clarified by the responsive condition, is to design a machine which the learner can use to explore this system. When the matter is looked at in this light, it is quite apparent that clever inventors have anticipated us, in part. There already exists an inexpensive, reliable orthographic machine—it is called a "typewriter." It has both the upper and lower case alphabets, standard punctuation, and its mode of operation exemplifies the basic orthographic conventions—its carriage goes from right to left so that the writing proceeds in the approved left to right fashion (of course, some typewriters go "backwards," e.g., Arabic typewriters, which are just right for Arabs), the carriage return and the line feed give us the required top to bottom movement, and the appropriate combined use of the space bar, tab, margin settings and carriage return provides for the many conventions pertaining to juxtaposition.

The typewriter is patently the kind of machine that we want but it is inadequate in certain respects. As long as we stay with reading and writing it does well enough, but it makes no provision for speaking and listening. If we are to tie our four linguistic processes together, then the capabilities of the type-writer must be extended. It needs a voice so that the learner can begin his exploration of the complex relations holding between the spoken and written forms of English. It also needs some of the attributes of dictation equipment, that is, it needs a recording-reproducing component. It needs all of these capabilities if the system to be explored is not just English orthography, but English orthography combined with spoken English. The "talking typewriter," which we promised to place in perspective, represents a first step toward the construction of an adequate responsive machine to be used as a part of an overall *clarifying* environment in which the learners have the opportunity to acquire basic com-munication skills.

Returning for the moment to the topic of English orthography, let us think a little bit about the keyboard of our "orthographic machine." The responsive condition urges that we use a full keyboard so that the learner can explore freely the alphabets and punctuation.

Although we know that there are conflicting views about exposing the full standard keyboard to the learner, we still believe that this is a useful way of introducing children to the kind of thing they find in books. We have, indeed, had encounters with prominent and highly respected authorities who object strenuously to this idea. We recall vividly long discussions with them about excep-tional children, their feeling being that a retarded child would be overwhelmed by a full keyboard. They wanted to cover the keyboard, except for perhaps two or three letters at first, and when their "subjects" had learned these letters, they could move on to others. Finally, after the alphabet was mastered, they conceded that it might be advisable to teach a few punctuation marks.

Their argument has a plausible ring to it—also, it surely is an empirical matter to determine how much of a system a learner should be exposed to initially. Nevertheless, the responsive condition suggests that we allow free exploration. Why? The basic answer is that we presuppose that *the what* of what is to be learned constitutes a system and not a random or miscellaneous collection of things. This is certainly true of language both in its written and spoken forms and their interrelations. Language is a system. If language is presented in such a way that its systemic properties are hidden or obscured, the learner may fail to master it. The more stupid the learner, the more essential it is to make these systemic properties evident. With respect to orthography the punctuation marks are the basic "traffic" signs which govern the flow of the symbols of the linguistic code, e.g., stop, go, caution. The distinction between upper and lower case letters is also part of this system of traffic signs. We asked these authorities whether they thought these symbolic traffic signs were most needed by the gifted or the re-tarded. They thought that the gifted had less need for explicit well-marked sym-bolic highways. Agreed! But it was precisely the retarded who were to be deprived of the opportunity to come in close contact with periods, commas, question marks, exclamation points, and other aids!

In designing the keyboard for the talking typewriter, provision was made for an overlay to cover the keys so that they can be exposed selectively. We made this provision because we knew that for some research purposes, the total keyboard would be too much or somehow irrelevant. Nevertheless, free exploration means *free exploration of a system*. On the negative side, it can serve as a warning that restricted exploration entails the risk of the learner not coming to grips with whatever it is he is to master.

b. *It informs the learner immediately about the consequences of his actions.* This condition, like the one above, is related to the notion of a system. We really do not mean that the learner is to be informed about *all* the consequences of his actions—this would be an impossible requirement. What we mean is that the consequences of the learner's actions which are *directly relevant* to the linguistic system which he is learning are to be reported back to him. For example, it is relevant to the relation holding between English orthography and English speech that the written C-A-T is pronounced as we generally say it. Hence, if the learner writes C-A-T he should hear it as well as see it. This connection should be as close as possible—we can easily obtain a verbal response from the machine in a little less than 1/10th of a second, and for many purposes this is fast enough.

There is a deeper point here, though, than the one having to do merely with the machine's speed of response, namely, it has to do with making it manifest to the learner that the pronunciation of the word *cat* is a consequence of his having typed C-A-T. After hitting the final "T" he might strike another key. How does he know that the verbal consequence had nothing to do with his final action? He cannot be certain unless the machine is designed so that for varying periods of time we can block or stop all machine actions except those that are consequential vis-a-vis certain actions of the learner. In our simple-minded illustration here, we need to provide for the blocking of the keyboard until the pronunciation of "cat" is completed, otherwise the learner will find it very difficult to trace the consequences of his own actions. The selective blocking of various machine functions at certain times, depending, of course, on what the learner has done, will help make it evident to him that some things are system-relevant consequences of his actions, and certain other things are not. From an engineering standpoint, this blocking of machine functions is again one of those things which is much easier said than done. This condition which we place upon a responsive environment may simplify things for the learner but it leads to nightmarish engineering problems if the system handled by the equipment is at all complex.

The talking typewriter as a responsive-environments device has within it explicit provision for the blocking of machine functions so that the learner can find out more easily what follows from what.

c. *It is self-pacing.* Many instructional systems are not at all self-pacing, for example, educational TV. Self-pacing devices must have controls for the learner himself. The concept of self-pacing should go beyond the mere slowing down or speeding up of a process. It should include controls suitable for bringing about both the repetition of sequences and scanning ahead. The controls for office dictation equipment are a good example of what is wanted—with a touch of a finger the operator can stop, repeat, go forward normally, and speed forward or backward. It is this kind of flexibility that gives practical reality to the notion of self-pacing. We will want to include appropriate self-pacing controls in our machine—they should be at least as flexible as those built into standard dictation equipment.

d. *It permits the learner to make full use of his capacity for discovering relations.* It is easier to say what this condition does not mean than to state its positive attributes. The trouble is, we know so little about human capacities. However, we can be reasonably certain that our machine is not drawing upon these capacities if the learner is told what to do, how to do it, and what to think about what he has done.

The notion of discovery carries the connotation of obtaining the sight or knowledge of something for the first time. Many present-day machines falling under the general educational classification of "computer-aided instruction" are quite frankly for drill, not discovery. Drill undoubtedly has its place in education; no one could possibly learn to spell or play a musical instrument without it, but drill is not what we are talking about when it comes to the notion of a responsive environment.

It is very hard to decide how far one can go in making things clear to the learner without spoiling his chance of making a discovery. Let us return to the keyboard of our hypothetical machine. Imagine that we place a light under each key. Now, suppose that whatever key should be struck next, say, for the spelling of *Mississippi,* lights up. The subject probably would notice this very quickly—a small discovery in itself. The trouble with this discovery, at least as far as spelling is concerned, is that it eliminates the need for any further discoveries. A pigeon could learn to peck only the lighted key and he could get along just fine without learning anything about English orthography. We have placed three fringe lights on the keyboard of the talking typewriter: one for upper case, one for lower case and one for space bar. These lights (which can be turned off or made to blink) are not there to tell the learner what to do next, as was true in the case of the pigeon example, but to signal the major states of the system for which there are virtually no visual clues provided otherwise by the system.

There are many other clues which we can build into our keyboard without eliminating the need for further discoveries. For example, since the learner will eventually be able to type and it is convenient to use standard typing conventions, we can color code his fingers to match a color coding of the keys. This means that by striking the right keys with the right fingers he will be learning "correct fingering." To give him a clue about the proper domain of keys for each hand a noticeable pressure difference can be made between the left- and right-hand keys. This clue can help him orient his hands.

Notice that the clues that we have mentioned, namely, the left-hand–right-hand pressure difference, the matched color-coding of keys and fingers, and the fringe lights, serve to help the learner to master the machine. They neither give away secrets about the mysteries of orthography nor do they obviate the need to make discoveries about them.

    e. *It is so structured that the learner is likely to make a series of interconnected discoveries.* What is emphasized in this condition is the idea of interconnectedness among discoveries. We want the learner to be put in a position where he can use the results of one discovery for making the next, and so on. In effect, if you think of him as playing a kind of game with the machine, then it must be possible to change at least some of the rules quickly, and turn the situation into a new game.

    This condition suggests that the machine's supervisor, as opposed to the user of the machine, must have a set of remote controls. Let us imagine that some learner is playing happily with the individual characters of the orthographic system. However, suppose also that there are signs that he has just about mastered these characters in the sense that he can accurately match the visual to the auditory, and vice versa. Before long he will tire of this. If the supervisor must stop the learner while he changes the machine, then this is a clumsy interruption—it tells the learner to expect something. If, instead, the supervisor can throw some switches at a remote station, the learner will suddenly find himself confronted with a new problem. It will be up to him to notice that something has gone wrong and to work out a new pattern of play. If the new game bears no relation to the old, then the results of learning will not be cumulative, so we have to decide what of the old should be carried over into the new situation.

    In the case of English orthography it is a straightforward matter to use letters to make words, words to make sentences, sentences to make paragraphs and from there to many different kinds of higher-order entities. Games can be played at each level and the transition from level to level can be turned into a new opportunity for discovery. So our machine must be flexible enough to handle a series of interconnected language games.

    As was remarked before, it is best if the transition from game to game can be controlled from a remote station. In the talking typewriter provision has been made for just such a series of remote control transitions. At the simplest level the mechanical system can handle games with individual characters of the orthography up to games at the level of paragraphs and stories.

    From what has been said about the application of the responsive condition it should be perfectly evident that there are an indefinitely large number of different machines which could satisfy the various requirements for "responsiveness." It should be equally clear that the human personality can serve as a "responsive instrument," too.

    There is one danger to which we would like to call your attention concerning all of this, namely, there is the risk of assuming that since a particular machine *can* be used as part of a responsive environment that it necessarily *will* be so used. The talking typewriter is a case in point. It can be a useful part of a responsive environment if it is properly programmed. However, it can be programmed so that it negates each and every condition for responsiveness. It can

(a) limit exploration, (b) mislead the learner about the consequences of his actions, (c) force someone else's gait on the learner, (d) make it unnecessary for the learner to make discoveries, and (e) make it difficult for the learner to build upon his insights.

Reflexive condition. There is a good deal being said these days about individualized instruction. There are those who maintain that one of the principal contributions which advanced technology can make to education is through the exploitation of the capacities of computers to treat each learner as a class of one. Each learner can be branched off in ways that are appropriate for him—there is to be an educational "prescription" written for each student. In principle, no two students need have the same prescription.

We are very much in favor of such individualization, but there are further distinctions to be made. Let us suggest, in terms of the reflexive condition, that what is wanted is a personalized, as opposed to a merely individualized, instructional milieu. According to the reflexive condition the educational environment should be so constructed that it is convenient for the learner to acquire a historical knowledge of himself as he develops over time. He should come to see himself as having a career as a learner. The various perspectives which he can assume as agent, patient, reciprocal other and referee should come to be seen as parts of a personality system, namely, his own personality.

Concretely, how are we to go about designing reflexiveness into our environment so that the learner will come to see himself developmentally? One of the first things that comes to mind, because of its use in sports, is to exploit the resources of sound-color motion picture photography. The same films which the investigator may want as part of his documentation of laboratory procedures and results can be shared with the learners. In one laboratory, for instance, we constructed a learning booth with an automatic photographic system for the making of high quality 16mm sound-color motion pictures. Learners were then shown films of themselves in various phases of their learning experiences. Their interest, as you might expect, was extremely high. There is no question in our minds that this was an enlightening experience for them. But this is only one step in the right direction. Are we simply to try for complete photographic coverage? Are we to show learners everything that they do? Clearly, this would be both uneconomic and *self*-defeating. This would lead toward vicious circularity with learners watching themselves watching themselves, and so on. Of course, the high cost of film making would keep this reflexive process from becoming absurd. However, on the positive side, we need some direction with respect to the appropriate use of reflexive techniques.

Let us remind ourselves of our goal as it is defined by the reflexive condition. We want the learner to see himself develop over time, to see his own personality as a whole. This means that he needs to see himself in perspective. You will recall that in our previous discussion of the perspectives principles, we stipulated that the learner should find it convenient to engage in acts of agency, to be patient to events, to see himself through the eyes of others, and to evaluate his conduct from the standpoint of a referee. Now, in terms of the reflexive condition, he should be encouraged to see himself learning to do these same things. Therefore, if we are, for instance, using photographic techniques, we need to sample his behavior as an agent, as a patient, etc.

To be specific about this, imagine that we have 1,000 feet of sound-color motion pictures of a learner. Assume that in accordance with the reflexive condition we want to help him develop a sense of history about himself. So, let us place the learner in the position of a film editor. Let us ask him to select 250 out of the 1,000 feet for his own film library. Next, let us have the laboratory staff select 250 feet from this same 1,000. Next, let some significant person in the learner's life select 250 feet from the 1,000. (We have to be careful here so as not to violate the autotelic principle.) Let all of these selections be made independently—each "editor" is to act without knowledge of the others. Further, let both the filming and the editorial work continue over some reasonably long period of time so that the learner has had an opportunity to develop and increase his degree of skill and sophistication. Let us make one further assumption—we shall stipulate that each editor who selected from the basic film stock operated under the instruction to produce a film that is characteristic of the learner. We have now reached the point for the learner and the other editors to be patient to the consequences of the others' acts of agency. The learner will have the opportunity to see himself as others see him. We then can make it possible for him to make a new set of selections, that is, to make a new film, one that takes into account what others noticed about him. He may want to go back to the original footage and look for aspects of himself which everyone has neglected.

All of the foregoing may sound hopelessly expensive and time consuming but with the advent of video tape and convenient editing devices this is not so impractical. In any case, in discussing the reflexive condition, as in the discussion of each of the other principles, the basic idea has been to illuminate possibilities. A clearer understanding of what is possible and desirable will undoubtedly have an effect on the development of appropriate technology.

CONCLUSION

Now that the reader has been hauled through this chapter, kicking and screaming for all we know, what is it that he is supposed to have gotten from this panoramic view of our position, besides intellectual indigestion? For one thing, we hope that we have made good on our promise to show the talking typewriter for what it is, namely, a social science invention. We hope the reader agrees that there is scientific continuity holding between the contributions of Mead and Simmel and our own efforts. Our most important aim, however, has been to make plausible the contention that it is our general theoretical or heuristic orientation which led to the formulation of principles for the design of *clarifying* environments, and to the illustrative applications of these principles. If we have accomplished this, then our main goal has been reached.

We yield to no one (for the second time in this chapter) in feeling dissatisfied with the lack of formal rigor which pervades our whole enterprise. But, being perennial optimists, despite all the commonsensical grounds for pessimism, we trust that we will become more sure-footed as we proceed.

REFERENCES

ACKERMANN, W. Begründung einer strengen Implikation. *Journal of Symbolic Logic,* 1956, 21, 113-128.

ANDERSON, A. R. *The formal analysis of normative systems.* Technical Report #2, Contract #SAR/Nonr-609(16). New Haven, Conn.: Office of Naval Research, Group Psychology Branch, 1956. (a) Also in N. Rescher (Ed.), *Logic of action and decision.* Pittsburgh: Univer. of Pittsburgh Press, 1967.

ANDERSON, A. R. Review of Prior and Feys. *Journal of Symbolic Logic,* 1956, 21, 379. (b)

ANDERSON, A. R. Review of Wilhelm Ackermann, Begründung einer strengen Implikation. *Journal of Symbolic Logic,* 1957, 22, 327-328.

ANDERSON, A. R. A reduction of deontic logic to alethic modal logic. *Mind,* 1958, 67 n.s., 100-103. (a)

ANDERSON, A. R. The logic of norms. *Logique et Analyse,* 1958, 1 n.s., 84–91. (b)

ANDERSON, A. R. On the logic of "commitment." *Philosophical Studies,* 1959, 10, 23-27. (a)

ANDERSON, A. R. *Completeness theorems for the systems E of entailment and EQ of entailment with quantification.* Technical Report #6, Contract #SAR/Nonr-609 (16). New Haven, Conn.: Office of Naval Research, Group Psychology Branch, 1959. (b) Reprinted in *Zeitschrift fur mathematische Logik und Grundlagen der Mathematik,* 1960, 6, 201–216.

ANDERSON, A. R. Reply to Mr. Rescher. *Philosophical Studies,* 1962, 13, 6-8.

ANDERSON, A. R. Some open problems concerning the system E of entailment. *Acta Philosophica Fennica* (Helsinki), 1963, fasc. 16.

ANDERSON, A. R. Some nasty problems in the formal logic of ethics. *Nous,* 1967, 6, 345-360.

ANDERSON, A. R., & BELNAP, N. D., JR. A modification of Ackermann's "rigorous implication." (Abstract) *Journal of Symbolic Logic,* 1958, 23, 457-458.

ANDERSON, A. R., & BELNAP, N. D. JR. A simple proof of Gödel's completeness theorem. (Abstract) *Journal of Symbolic Logic,* 1959, 24, 320–321. (a)

ANDERSON, A. R., & BELNAP, N. D., JR. Modalities in Ackermann's "rigorous implication." *Journal of Symbolic Logic,* 1959, 24, 107-111. (b)

ANDERSON, A. R., & BELNAP, N. D., JR. A simple treatment of truth functions. *Journal of Symbolic Logic,* 1959, 24, 301-302. (c)

ANDERSON, A. R., & BELNAP, N. D., JR. Enthymemes. *Journal of Philosophy,* 1961, 58, 713-723. (a)

ANDERSON, A. R., & BELNAP, N. D., JR. The pure calculus of entailment. *Journal of Symbolic Logic,* 1961, 27, 19-52. (b)

ANDERSON, A. R., & BELNAP, N. D., JR. Tautological entailments. *Philosophical Studies,* 1961, 13, 9-24. (c)

ANDERSON, A. R., & BELNAP, N. D., JR. *First degree entailments.* Technical Report #10, Contract #SAR/Nonr-609(16). New Haven, Conn.: Office of Naval Research, Group Psychology Branch, 1963. Also in *Mathematische Annalen,* 1963, 149, 302-319.

ANDERSON, A. R., BELNAP, N. D., JR., & WALLACE, J. R. Independent axiom schemata for the pure theory of entailment. *Zeitschrift fur mathematische Logik und Grundlagen der Mathematik,* 1960, 6, 93–95.

ANDERSON, A. R., & MOORE, O. K. The formal analysis of normative concepts. *American Sociological Review,* 1957, 22, 1-17. Also in B. J. Biddle & E. Thomas (Eds.), *Social role: Readings in theory and applications.* New York: Wiley, 1966.

ANDERSON, A. R., & MOORE, O. K. *Autotelic folk models.* Technical Report #8, Contract #SAR/Nonr-609(16). New Haven, Conn.: Office of Naval Research, Group Psychology Branch, 1959. Also in *Sociological Quarterly,* 1960, 1, 203-216.

ANDERSON, A. R., & MOORE, O. K. Toward a formal analysis of cultural objects. *Synthese,* 1962, 14, 144-170. Also in M. W. Wartofsky (Ed.), *Boston studies in the philosophy of science, 1961/1962.* Dordrecht, Holland: D. Reidel, 1963.

ANDERSON, A. R., & MOORE, O. K. Models and explanations in the behavioral sciences. In G. J. DiRenzo (Ed.), *Concepts, theory, and explanation in the behavioral sciences.* New York: Random House, 1966.

ANDERSON, S. B. Shift in problem solving. *Naval Research Memorandum, Report #458.* Washington, D. C., 1955.

ANDERSON, S. B. Analysis of responses in a task drawn from the calculus of propositions. *Naval Research Laboratory Memorandum, Report #608.* Washington, D.C., 1956.

ANDERSON, S. B. Problem solving in multiple-goal situations. *Journal of Experimental Psychology,* 1957, 54, 297-303.

BELNAP, N. D., JR. Pure rigorous implication as a *"Sequenzenkalkül."* (Abstract) *Journal of Symbolic Logic,* 1959, 24, 282–283. (a)

BELNAP, N. D., JR. Tautological entailments. (Abstract) *Journal of Symbolic Logic,* 1959, 24, 316. (b)

BELNAP, N. D., JR. *A formal analysis of entailment.* Technical Report #7, Contract #SAR/Nonr-609(16). New Haven, Conn.: Office of Naval Research, Group Psychology Branch, 1960. (a)

BELNAP, N. D., JR. Entailment and relevance. *Journal of Symbolic Logic,* 1960, 25, 144-146. (b)

BELNAP, N. D., JR. First degree formulas. (Abstract) *Journal of Symbolic Logic,* 1960, 25, 388-389. (c)

BELNAP, N. D., JR. EQ and the first order functional calculus. *Zeitschrift fur mathematische Logik und Grundlagen der Mathematik,* 1960, 6, 217–218. (d)

BELNAP, N. D., JR. *An analysis of questions: Preliminary report.* Santa Monica, Calif.: System Development Corporation, 1963.

BELNAP, N. D., JR. Intensional models for first degree formulas. *Journal of Symbolic Logic,* 1967, 32, 1–22.

BELNAP, N. D. JR., & WALLACE, J. R. *A decision procedure for the system $E_{\bar{I}}$ of entailment with negation.* Technical Report #11, Contract #SAR/Nonr-609(16). New Haven, Conn.: Office of Naval Research, Group Psychology Branch, 1961.

CARPENTER, J. A., MOORE, O. K., SNYDER, C. R., & LISANSKY, E. S. Alcohol and higher-order problem solving. *Quarterly Journal of Studies on Alcohol,* 1961, 22, 183–222.

COOLEY, C. H. *Human nature and the social order.* New York: Scribners, 1902 (1922, 1930). P. 217.

FITCH, F. B. *Symbolic logic.* New York: Ronald, 1952.

KOBLER, R., & MOORE, O. K. *Educational system and apparatus.* U.S. Patent #3,281,959. 27 figures, 51 claims granted, 12 references. Also granted in many foreign countries, 1966.

MEAD, G. H. *The philosophy of the present.* LaSalle, Ill.: The Open Court, 1932.

MEAD, G. H. *Mind, self and society.* Chicago: Univer. of Chicago Press, 1934.

MEAD, G. H. *Movements of thought in the nineteenth century.* Chicago: Univer. of Chicago Press, 1936.

MEAD, G. H. *The philosophy of the act.* Chicago: Univer. of Chicago Press, 1938.

MOORE, O. K. Divination—a new perspective. *American Anthropologist,* 1957, 59, 69-74. Also in W. A. Lessa & E. Z. Vogt (Eds.), *Reader in comparative religion: An anthropological approach.* (2nd Ed.) New York: Harper & Row, 1965.

MOORE, O. K. Problem solving and the perception of persons. In R. Tagiuri & L. Petrullo (Eds.), *Person perception and interpersonal behavior.* Palo Alto, Calif.: Stanford Univer. Press, 1958. Pp. 131-150.

MOORE, O. K. Orthographic symbols and the preschool child—a new approach. In E. P. Torrence (Ed.), *Creativity: 1960 proceedings of the third conference on gifted children.* Minneapolis: Univer. of Minnesota, Center for Continuation Study, 1961. Pp. 91–101.

MOORE, O. K. *Autotelic responsive environments and exceptional children.* Report issued by The Responsive Environments Foundation, Inc., Hamden, Conn., 1963. Also in J. Hellmuth (Ed.), *The special child in century 21.* Seattle: Special Child Publications of the Sequin School, Inc., 1964; and O. J. Harvey (Ed.), *Experience, structure and adaptability.* New York: Springer, 1966.

MOORE, O. K. Technology and behavior. In *Proceedings of the 1964 invitational conference on testing problems.* Princeton: Educational Testing Service, 1964. Pp. 58-68.

MOORE, O. K. From tools to interactional machines. *New approaches to individualizing instruction.* Report of a conference to mark the dedication of Ben D. Wood Hall, May 11, 1965. Princeton, N. J.: Educational Testing Service, 1965. (a) Also in J. W. Childs (Ed.), *Instructional technology: Readings.* New York: Holt, Rinehart & Winston, 1968 (in press).

MOORE, O. K. Autotelic responsive environments and the deaf. *American Annals for the Deaf,* 1965, 110, 604-614. (b)

MOORE, O. K. On responsive environments. *New directions in individualizing instruction.* Proceedings of the Abington Conference, 1967. Abington, Penna.: The Abington Conference, 1968.

MOORE, O. K., & ANDERSON, A. R. *Early reading and writing, part 1: Skills.* 16 mm. color and sound motion picture. Pittsburgh: Basic Education, Inc., 1960. (a)

MOORE, O. K., & ANDERSON, A. R. *Early reading and writing, part 2: Teaching methods.* 16 mm. color and sound motion picture. Pittsburgh: Basic Education, Inc., 1960. (b)

MOORE, O. K., & ANDERSON, A. R. *Early reading and writing, part 3: Development.* 16 mm. color and sound motion picture. Pittsburgh: Basic Education, Inc., 1960. (c)

MOORE, O. K., & ANDERSON, A. R. Some puzzling aspects of social interaction. *Review of Metaphysics,* 1962, 15, 409–433. (a) Also in J. H. Criswell, H. Solomon & P. Suppes (Eds.), *Mathematical methods in small group processes.* Stanford, Calif.: Stanford Univer. Press, 1962. Pp. 232–249.

MOORE, O. K., & ANDERSON, A. R. The structure of personality. *Review of Metaphysics,* 1962, 16, 212-236. (b) Also in O. J. Harvey (Ed.), *Motivation and social interaction.* New York: Ronald Press, 1963.

MOORE, O. K., & ANDERSON, A. R. The responsive environments project. In R. D. Hess & R. M. Baer (Eds.), *Early education*. Chicago: Aldine, 1968.

MOORE, O. K., & ANDERSON, S. B. Modern logic and tasks for experiments on problem solving behavior. *Journal of Psychology,* 1954, 38, 151-160. (a)

MOORE, O. K., & ANDERSON, S. B. Search behavior in individual and group problem solving. *American Sociological Review,* 1954, 19, 702-714. (b)

MOORE, O. K., & ANDERSON, S. B. Experimental study of problem solving. *Report of Naval Research Laboratory Progress,* 1954, August, 15-22. (c)

MOORE, O. K., & KOBLER, R. *Educational apparatus for children.* U.S. Patent #3,112,569. 6 figures, 13 claims granted, 6 references. Also granted in many foreign countries, 1963.

PEIRCE, C. S. Some consequences of four incapacities. *Journal of Speculative Philosophy,* 1868.

PEIRCE, C. S. *Philosophical writings of Peirce.* New York: Dover, 1955.

PITMAN, J. Man—the communicating animal, par (verbal) excellence. In A. C. Eurick (Ed.), *New approaches to individualizing instruction.* Princeton: Educational Testing Service, 1965. Pp. 49-60.

PRIOR, MARY, & PRIOR, A. Erotetic logic. *Philosophical Review,* 1955, 64, 43-59.

SCOTT, D. A short recursively unsolvable problem. *Journal of Symbolic Logic,* 1956, 21, 111-112.

SIMMEL, G. *Georg Simmel, 1858-1918: A collection of essays.* K. H. Wolff (Ed.). Columbus: The Ohio State Univer. Press, 1959.

VON NEUMANN, J. Zur Theorie der Gesellschaftsspiele. *Mathematische Annalen,* 1928, 100, 295-320. Reprinted in A. H. Taub (Ed.), *Collected works.* Vol. 6. New York: Pergamon, 1961.

VON NEUMANN, J., & MORGENSTERN, O. *Theory of games and economic behavior.* Princeton: Princeton Univer. Press, 1947.

CHAPTER **11**

Social Structure And Socialization

Alex Inkeles

Harvard University

Social structure impinges on, and in many ways determines socialization. In its turn, socialization may have substantial effects on social structure. This relationship is not necessarily one of discrete interactions, but may take the form of cycles or other sequences prolonged over substantial periods of historical time. We do not deal here with exchange between two self-contained and more or less independent systems of action, but rather with a part-whole relationship, a substructure of socialization being one of the functional requisites of any social system (Levy, 1952). Understanding this relationship is further complicated by the fact that the part is not entirely subsumed under the whole, but rather includes elements dependent on still other systems.

Like a distressingly large number of other social science terms, "socialization" applies to an exceedingly large range of phenomena. It simultaneously describes a process, or input, external to the person, the individual's experience of the process, and the end product or output. In its broadest conception, socialization refers to the sum total of past experiences an individual has had which, in turn, may be expected to play some role in shaping his future social behavior. From the perspective of different disciplines one would, of course, take a stronger interest in some of these early experiences, and be concerned more with certain later behaviors, than others. Encounters unique to a given person, yielding decidedly idiosyncratic behavior, may be of great significance to the clinical psychologist, but they have little interest for the anthropologist, whose concern is more with shared and culturally patterned experiences. Some practices which are widely diffused and personally important to many people, let us say the trimming of the Christmas tree, may be prime data for the anthropologist, but will meet relative indifference on the part of the sociologist because these experiences do not in major degree shape one's selection of or performance in importantly differentiated social roles.

From the sociological point of view, socialization refers to the process whereby individuals acquire the personal system properties—the knowledge, skills, attitudes, values, needs and motivations, cognitive, affective and conative patterns—which shape their adaptation to the physical and sociocultural setting in which they live (see Inkeles, 1966b). The critical test of the success of the socialization process lies in the ability of the individual to perform well in the statuses—that is, to play the roles—in which he may later find himself. The subtlety and complexity of the problem of socialization stems, in good part, from the diversity of these statuses and from the uncertainty as to the roles which may be associated with them.

Some of the statuses a person will acquire are definitely known and more or less invariant. His sex and age group, usually his religion and ethnicity, fall in this category. Socialization to the roles appropriate to such statuses may, therefore, be relatively less problematic. Other positions the person will later occupy may be much less definite. Thus, it may at the outset be quite uncertain whether a man will be chief or follower, doctor or boot black, married or single. Some of the statuses a man can find himself in as an adult may not even have existed when he was a boy, as for example the airplane or space pilot. Some roles a man plays he may largely have invented or created himself as in the case of Young Man Luther (Erikson, 1958). The problems of socialization will therefore be markedly different in societies with more complex status differentiation than in those of more simple structure, and will be much more perplexing in those societies which assign individuals to their statuses predominantly on an ascriptive basis as against those which leave the attainment of most status positions more open to achievement or to accident.

Whatever the degree of rigidity or flexibility in their usual pattern of allocating individuals to status positions, societies will also vary in the degree to which they are experiencing stability or undergoing rapid change. When rapid change is experienced by a society, the established system for assigning individuals to recognized statuses may break down. Wholly new statuses may come into existence, sometimes in large numbers and requiring many status incumbents. An outstanding example would be the shift in the modern Euro-American nations from a predominantly rural resident, agriculturally employed, labor force to an overwhelmingly urban resident, industrially employed, population. Quite substantial strain may thus be put on the existing system of socialization, and many individuals may find themselves inadequately socialized to the demands of the roles they are now called on to play. Late or adult socialization, and other forms of re-socialization, may therefore be required. Even if such measures are adopted, many individuals may feel themselves dislocated, unfit or inadequately prepared for the tasks facing them in the statuses they have acquired or to which they have been assigned. In turn, the society or major institutional units within it, may find the discharge of their social responsibility for production, security, governance or whatever, impaired by the inadequate role performance of the individuals they have recruited or have had assigned to them.

To fashion a very simple analogy, then, we may say that the problem of socialization is rather like that of putting on a play. Under the simplest of circumstances the script is fixed and has been handed down unchanged through generations. There are very few parts to play, and it is well-known exactly who will play which part, so that firm preparation may be made long in advance. Everyone knows all the parts very well, so that interaction among the actors is smooth and satisfying. Since the play has been played many times before, all the props and necessary accouterments are in ample supply and well-tried. The performance runs smoothly and continuously. This presumably is the condition which prevailed in relatively stable and isolated pre-literate or "primitive" societies before their encounter with modern "civilization."

At the other pole we have the style of play which is more like a modern "happening." In this case there is no specification as to exactly how many "actors" there are, and their "parts" are only vaguely defined. Indeed, there may be no fixed script at all. The play may never have been put on in quite this form before, so that the interplay of the actors is uncertain and difficult, and neither the other players nor the audience can do much to influence the course of the action in the "right" direction. New parts are being added all the time, and old ones cut out. No one is too firmly assigned to any given part, and the actors often improvise their roles as they go along. This more extreme, and perhaps limiting, case highlights the point that socialization, or training for role performance, would be quite a different task for the directors, the actors, and the audience in this more unstructured social drama than would be the case in the more traditional pattern. Of course, no society and very few organizations could for very long endure in a state so fluid as to approximate the model of a happening. Nevertheless, due to the rapidity and extensiveness of social change, many parts of the world in the mid-twentieth century more nearly approximate the happening than they do the fixed and frozen drama of the traditional model of socialization.

Every individual, as we encounter him, is the outcome, the "product," in a sense, of a given socialization process. This outcome, "successful" or "unsuccessful" from the perspective of a particular social system in a given time and place, will, in fact, depend on a series of inputs. Most apparent, it will depend on the original genetic potential of the individual and the degree to which climate, alimentation, nurturance and other factors have permitted the realization of that potential. The outcome will also have been influenced, in part, by the personality of the individuals with whom the socializee has been in significant contact, such as relatives, teachers, friends, co-workers, and bosses. Finally, the result of socialization will be shaped by certain more or less fixed or regular aspects of the network of social relations in which the individual lives. It is these regular, recurrent, or socially structured aspects of the individual's experience which are of particular interest to the sociologist as "inputs" in the socialization process. Similarly, on the "output" side the sociologist is concerned mainly with those actions of the individual which play some part in the maintenance and change of those patterned and recurrent modes of social interaction which provided the systematic property of the concept of social structure.

The complexity of both social structure and socialization is such that we cannot hope to deal with the impact of the former on the latter without considerable differentiation of the elements of both. For socialization we shall adopt the conventional division of the life cycle into periods of infancy and childhood, youth and adolescence, the middle years, and old age. Each period may be conceived as focused on some issue central to that stage of personal development, thereby rendering certain aspects of social structure more relevant as influences on the socialization process.

For each period we will identify and discuss four main elements in the socialization matrix: the main socialization *issue,* that is, the typical life condition or social demand which dominates the attention of socializee and socializers and becomes the characteristic or defining aspect of any given stage of individual bio-social development; the *agents* of socialization, those individuals and social units or organizations which typically play the greatest role in the socialization process in the several stages of development; the *objectives* which these agents set as the goals for successful socialization in each period, that is, the qualities they wish to inculcate and the conditions under which they prefer to train the socializee; and the main *task* facing the socializee, that is, the problem to be solved or the skill learned as it confronts the socializee from his internal personal perspective.

Several broad aspects of social structure may be considered of likely relevance to the socialization process at any stage of the life cycle, and may therefore serve us as a checklist to insure systematic coverage. The dimensions we will consider are:

1. ecological: here we note the size, density, physical distribution, and social composition of the population; its relationship to its resource base, and to surrounding populations.

2. economic: this has special reference to the social forms for defining, producing and distributing goods and services. The type and amount of material resources available in a given society are also important. Economic and ecological elements may be intimately related.

3. political: the political subsystem encompasses the structure of power: its distribution, forms, and application, along with the institutional arrangements for generating, legitimating and exercising it.

4. system of values: economic and political institutions of course embody values, but many important values which guide socialization efforts are not most visible or effective in their more institutionalized forms. In addition, a large part of socialization consists in the simple effort to inculcate values.

These four dimensions are not all of the same type. The ecological concerns primarily the population; the system of values mainly expresses what is sometimes called culture; and the economic and political dimensions have reference mainly to institutions. These latter dimensions of social structure may, however, also be understood as referring not so much to concrete institutions as to functions which must be fulfilled. Our four aspects of social structure are, therefore, not exhaustive. Others might well be selected, either to enlarge this list or to reflect a different perspective. We might have included or substituted other dimensions of social structure such as the system of stratification, or the modes of social control and the patterns of deviance; or other institutional complexes such as the kinship organization, the family, the school, or the work unit. Our objective here, however, is not to provide a catalogue of social institutions. Rather it is to present a mode of analysis, which can serve to *illustrate* the relations between selected elements of social structure and the socialization process. We mean to provide a model which can easily be carried over for use in the analysis of socialization issues as they arise in other institutions and social structures.

The elements of social structure are not mutually exclusive, but interpenetrate in a complex web of relations constituting the total sociocultural system. The degree of consistency or coherence among the socialization pressures generated in each of the realms of social structure, presents special problems for analysis. For example, socialization to the demands of the economic system may require the traits of aggressiveness, including the objective of eliminating your competitors; secrecy, as in the preservation of trade secrets; and the minimization of charitable impulses in favor of the maximization of profits. By contrast, the effective functioning of the political system may require individuals to display tolerance for opposition and especially for defeated opponents; to disclose fully and publicly all relevant facts at one's disposal; and to assign priority to humane and welfare goals over other considerations. Where there are such discordances among the role requirements of different elements of the same society, the agents of socialization face difficult choices of emphasis, just as, in time, the socializee will face difficult choices both in selecting his own course of action and in reconciling the action in one role subsystem with that in another.

There are, in addition, major complications which arise from the problem of levels of complexity in social structure. In the economic subsystem of modern society, for example, the elements of structure will range from a unit relatively as simple and concrete as the role of industrial worker, through institutions such as the factory, and networks of institutions such as "an industry," to something so large and complex as "the economic system of the United States." There may be a tendency for certain qualities to be widely diffused across all the levels of any given subsystem of society, thus rendering the same personal attributes adaptive throughout. It is often the case, however, that the performances typically required at different levels of the *same* subsystem are less alike than those for comparable levels of *different* subsystems. Both the assembly line worker and the factory manager or entrepreneur may require a strict sense of time to fulfill their obligations. But for effective performance of his role the entrepreneur will also need high achievement aspirations, initiative and autonomy in far greater degree than is required of the ordinary worker. For his part, the production line worker job may require manual dexterity, or interpersonal skills in handling his relations with supervising personnel and fellow workers, which in nature or degree are quite different from the skills appropriate to management roles. Whether these appropriate special qualities are developed during early life or through later training "on the job," different socialization practices clearly will be required to equip men to perform these different roles which are nominally part of the "same" societal subsystem.

We cannot here systematically review the problem of socialization as it presents itself at each of the levels in each realm or subsystem of society. Rather, we must restrict ourselves to illustrations which can serve as models of a mode of analysis appropriate to the complexity of the social structure of large scale societies.

INFANCY AND EARLY CHILDHOOD

These two periods of the life cycle are distinctive enough to warrant separate treatment, but for reasons of economy we treat them together. The central *issue* of this period is the infant's helplessness, his utter dependence on adults for sustenance in life. The main *objective* of the socialization agents, apart from keeping the child alive, is to move him on the next stage of his development. The main *task* of the child is to master control of his body, to adjust it to rhythms and other modes of action acceptable to the adults around him, and to secure himself against the most obvious physical dangers of his environment. Problems of physical mastery and control occupy a great deal of everyone's attention, socializer and socializee alike, not only in toilet training, but in bringing the child to the point where he can walk, talk, feed and dress himself, and learn to stay out of the most obvious and immediate dangers such as fire and water.

Probably the single most important acquisition of this period, however, is language, the control of which is only partly a matter of physical development. Language is the critical symbol system which will mediate the greater part of all later experience. Indeed, the other processes of physical training also have significance far beyond their immediate and obvious purpose, since they inevitably affect the psychic qualities of the child as well. The simplest and most efficient way to keep a child out of danger might be physical restraint, and beyond that would be to issue constant and fearful warning cries as he moved about. While this would keep him out of danger, it would also greatly restrict his exploratory behavior and encourage passivity and timidity. A society which requires its males to be assertive and fearless, as for example in hunting big game, could hardly afford paying that price in order to keep its children out of trouble around the campgrounds.

Taking into account the roles girls will later play, parents almost everywhere seem to train them more vigorously in obedience, responsibility and nurturance, whereas boys are more socialized to be achieving, self-reliant, and independent. Where the conditions of life seem to require the utmost of males in this respect—as in cultures herding large animals—the emphasis on these "manly" qualities is generally heightened. It is interesting to note, however, that in societies in which self-reliance is maximally adaptive, the mode is often not strictness of early training, but rather the giving of great freedom to young boys. Apparently spending a good deal of time away from home in the company of other boys in autonomous gangs is recognized in many societies as likely to be the most effective method for early inculcation of independence, self-reliance, and the drive for achievement (see Aberle, 1961).

Ecological.   The direct impact of ecological patterns on infant socialization practices has not been much studied. The world is experiencing increasing densities of population both because of absolute population growth and the ubiquitous spread of urbanism. Freedom to explore one's environment over a wider range, and to do so less under the immediate surveillance of adults, would seem to be greater in rural settings, although this might be less true of an Indian peasant village, with its extremely high density, than of an American urban slum. The shift to smaller families, and to physical separation of the nuclear conjugal family from extended kinship groups, should bring greater concentration and perhaps intensity of interaction between socializing agents and the child. Instead of passing from hand to hand and encountering one face after another, the child is limited, the greater part of the time, to interaction with the mother, and perhaps to one or two siblings. If the mother is inadequate to the task of child-rearing, the consequences will obviously be more serious than in environments in which there are many parent surrogates who can step in to supplement the mother's efforts. Barring this contingency of an inadequate mother, however, the intense pattern of interaction of mother and child is likely to lead to precosity and early development of speech and perhaps motor skills.

Little truly systematic research has been done comparing socialization in rural as against urban families. Studies in France indicate there are indeed important differences which rest, in part, on the dissimilarity in occupation and in part on the ecology of rural versus urban life. The greater isolation and family centeredness of rural life means a slow social awakening for the rural children, greater fear of strangers, and slower development of imagination and language skills. By contrast, both the responsibilities early assigned to them, and their contact with animals and nature, seem to yield the rural children early and highly developed sensory motor functioning (Lanneau & Mabrieu, 1957).

The movement from countryside to city typical of the first part of the twentieth century has in mid-century been followed by a new movement from the city to the suburbs. From an ecological point of view, however, we should note that in suburban living the physical separation of the father's place of work, and hence his absence from the home, is even more marked than in the city. The physical separation of each family homestead from every other is also notable. In addition the suburbs, at least in the United States, are characterized by higher degrees of homogeneity in their ethnic, religious, and socioeconomic composition than are most cities. As yet, however, we do not know what effect, if any, these and other ecological consequences of suburbanization will have on infant and child socialization.

Economic. In systems in which scarcity of food or shelter is acute, the helplessness of the child may lead to the extinction of all but the most hardy. In certain districts of East Pakistan, for example, when there are food shortages it is expected that the distribution will be arranged to insure the survival and effectiveness of the male head of the household. Even barring such extreme circumstances, the resources generally available in any given society will obviously influence the conditions of socialization of the child. These effects will, in part, be mediated by the system of stratification. McClelland (1961) argues that the increased wealth of the more ambitious and rising classes of society leads them to acquire servants to whom they turn over the rearing of their children, with a consequent reduction in the children's need for achievement (*n ach*) and subsequent decline in their entrepreneurial effectiveness.

The most direct effects of the economic order on the conditions and patterns of infant socialization are related to the work and production patterns characteristic for a given society. If young women are expected to work in the fields during child-bearing years, as among the Tanala as described by Kardiner (1939), the prospect is increased for relative neglect of children who must either be left at home unsupervised or brought to the fields. The nature of the father's employment will greatly affect the degree to which children grow up in a father-absent home. Certain occupations such as fishing or itinerant selling, or the lack of local employment opportunities, may require long periods of absence by the father. Indeed, the fathers may be away almost all the time, and the children grow up in what is, in effect, a female-headed household more or less exclusively subject to the socialization efforts of women. This condition is extremely common among American Negro families, and in the famous Moynihan Report it was identified as perhaps the most critical problem of the American Negro family (see Rainwater & Yancey, 1967). One popular psychoanalytically oriented theory holds that in the father-absent home the young boy develops too close an identification with the mother. Fear of this feminine identity later leads to a reaction formation, characterized by over-assertion of masculine traits, which in slum conditions easily finds expression in male delinquency. Evidence in support of this hypothesis drawn from American cities is not substantial, although research on non-literate societies seems to support the theory (see Whiting, 1965; Bacon, Child & Barry, 1963).

The nature of a man's experience on the job may also produce effects carried over into the home and expressed in his treatment of his children. Miller and Swanson (1960) made an important contribution in their investigation of the consequences for child training—in systems of expressive behavior, styles of punishment, and cognitive modes—as these may depend on whether the father is employed in a bureaucratic (mass) or entrepreneurial (small scale) setting. They reasoned, for example, that middle class "bureaucrats"—meaning mainly people working for large scale organizations—are currently faced by diminishing needs to internalize traditional standards, and hence would less often emphasize defenses such as turning on the self and reversal. By contrast, the working-class men in these bureaucratic atmospheres, faced by work ever more simple and routine, were expected to resort increasingly to the defense of denial and to the cultivation of leisure activities.

Miller and Swanson were far from successful in accurately rating the quality of the occupational setting of their subjects as "entrepreneurial" or "bureaucratic," although the bulk of their evidence supports the theoretical importance of the distinction they introduced. Further support for the idea that the quality of the father's work setting will significantly influence his child-rearing efforts was provided by McKinley (1964), who obtained fairly precise measures, separately for the middle and working class, of the degree to which the father was closely supervised on the job. He found, in both social strata, that fathers who were more closely supervised—as against those with more autonomy on the job—tended to be more punitive in the treatment of their sons. These relationships apparently are quite general. Thus, Pearlin and Kohn (1966) demonstrated that in Italy as well as the United States the closeness of supervision, the amount of self-reliance required on a job, and the extent to which it involves working with people or things all seem to influence the values which fathers emphasize in their child-rearing.

An ever increasing proportion of the population is employed by large, often vast, corporate enterprises, and the labor force within them is believed to be experiencing increasingly common conditions of work. Along with ever rising personal income, the equalizing effects of social welfare legislation, and of benefits providing more widespread leisure, these changes in the occupational structure may in time bring about a high degree of homogenization in the work and work-related life experience of all members of the labor force. If it is correct that differentiated work conditions for the breadwinner yield differentials in their respective child-rearing practices, it should follow that homogeneity in work and work-related conditions will in time increase the homogeneity of socialization practices.

Political. Just as in the control of economic resources, so in the command of power the dominance of the adult over the infant is virtually absolute. With increasing motility the child can escape surveillance, restraint and punishment, but only to very limited degrees. The forms in which parental power is exercised are believed to play a major role in determining the patterns of political action later to characterize the adult. Fromm (1941) early explored this relationship in the development of authoritarianism in the German family, and his work influenced the classic study of *The Authoritarian Personality* (Adorno, 1950). Erikson (1950) has interpreted the structure of power relationships in the American family as a training ground in compromise particularly suited to the pattern of political life in the United States.

Just how far the political system as a whole, and the parent's position in it, influence the forms and content of the socialization of his children is not well documented. The research of McKinley, and Miller and Swanson cited above, would suggest a model of direct carry-over—the more authoritarian, or democratic, the larger political milieu in which the parent participates, the more authoritarian, or democratic, his treatment of his own children. There is room, however, for a predictive model based on the anticipation of a reaction in the home against the predominant pressures of the political system outside it.

The value system. Limits on the child's grasp of language and relevant experience make the direct and explicit inculcation of values of minor importance in infancy and early childhood. The indirect influence of cultural values in shaping socialization practices is, however, enormous, and the child's acquaintance with the values implicit in various socialization practices may be more important than the manifest content he learns from these activities.

Feeding schedules, for example, should be understood not exclusively in terms of nurturance or in relation to the cycle of hunger pains in the infant, but also as expressing, and presumably communicating to the child, some of the emphasis his culture places on the ordering of events in strict accord with a clock-paced schedule. Such an orientation to time, if it exists, will, of course, be communicated to the child not through one infant-care discipline alone, but through several. The orientation to time will thus be expressed not only in feeding schedules, but in toilet training, play and sleeping arrangements, procedures for dress, and in numerous other ways. Similarly, the handling of the child and the procedures adopted for or imposed on his care will express his society's values concerning orderliness and abstemiousness, aggressiveness, expressive behavior, striving, intellect and so on through the register of culturally important value themes.

Of course, the values being thus expressed and inculcated in the child will not exist in a social vacuum. The value system of any culture has a certain integrity and autonomy which permits it to persist relatively intact over time, but it must inevitably reflect the influence of conditions in the social structure in which the values are operative. Thus, in an emerging industrial society we may well expect the value of timeliness to be fostered and reinforced as an element in child rearing. In a society in which the scientific and technical mode of action is predominant, the values expressed in child rearing may come to be greatly influenced by the diffusion of the opinion of "experts." This will be especially marked in the segments of the population more highly educated and more inclined to follow the latest scientific advice. Thus, Urie Bronfenbrenner (1958) notes that in the United States over a quarter-century, from 1930 to 1955, American mothers became consistently more flexible with regard to infant feeding and weaning. Most notable, however, was the extent of the shift of the middle-class mother from great strictness to much greater permissiveness with regard to both feeding and toilet training. These changes, according to Bronfenbrenner, "show a striking correspondence to the changes in practices advocated in successive editions of the U.S. Children's Bureau bulletins and similar sources of expert opinion." Furthermore, the changes seemed most marked "in those segments of society which have the most ready access to the agents or agencies of change."

LATE CHILDHOOD AND ADOLESCENCE

In this period changes in physical and mental capacity—as for example, sex and aggression—stemming from the maturational process, interact with changes in society's response to and expectations about the individual as a potential member of society. The capacity of the individual to adjust to these changes, and the flexibility of the society in adapting to the impact of these adjustments, presents the central *issue* of this stage of the life cycle. The individual increasingly takes on roles which foreshadow, are directly supplemental to, or already fall within the realm of adult roles. The acquisition of such roles is, however, uneven. In our society, for example, adolescents are able to assume adult economic roles long before they are permitted to assume comparable roles in the political realm. The *task* of the adolescent is to manage the changes in himself, and the changing expectation of society towards him, without too vigorously disrupting the patterns of adult control and dominance. The *objective* of the socializers is to move the adolescent as effectively as possible toward the eventual assumption of adult roles by getting him to give up earlier gratifications and to train for new obligations. At the same time, society is often not yet ready to grant the adolescent full responsibility or authority. Substantial strain may result from the discrepancy between the adolescent's sense of his capacity, and his awareness of his increased responsibility, on the one hand, and his still sharply circumscribed autonomy and authority, on the other.

From a structural point of view the central feature of this period is the gradual replacement of the family and adult kin by other *agents* and *agencies* of socialization: schools, teachers, peer groups, tribal or political authorities, local heroes, religious specialists, actors and other public figures, and so on. So far as the content of socialization is concerned, problems of physical management, while far from irrelevant, become decidedly secondary to others such as: the acquisition of values; learning specific adult relevant skills, especially those connected with earning a living; managing mature heterosexual relations; and manifesting increased readiness to accept responsibilities relevant to adult status such as marriage and parenthood.

Ecology.   The age structure of a population can never make its effect felt entirely independently of the society's cultural and institutional framework, but within those limits it may greatly influence the extent to which other youths rather than adults socialize the adolescent. The post-war baby boom in the United States, for example, may not be entirely unrelated to the problems of controlling the human wave tactics adopted by adolescent crowds in various American cities and resorts. The role of other youths, as against adults, as agents of socialization will also be affected by the degree of age grading in a society, especially with regard to residence. When the youth population is diffused in small numbers in families, or comparable settings, which are heterogeneous in age composition, the role of adults in the socialization process can be very much greater. Even within the home, the proportion of youths versus adults may influence the opportunities for adult control, the bases of solidarity in opposition to parental desires, and the prospects for introducing new role models.

Economics.   Within the constraints imposed by the system of power and the structure of values, the system of resource allocation can greatly influence the socialization process in adolescence. Where adults, and especially the father, more or less totally control access to a livelihood through control of scarce resources such as land, hunting rights, and special artisan skills, then the influence of the father and other adults as socialization agents and as models to be emulated will be proportionately great. At the other pole, an open labor market permitting youth to earn independently, the availability of an abundance of material goods, and certain values concerning youth and its rights, have combined in many of the advanced industrial countries to free adolescents from adult economic control and increased the importance as socializing agents of peers, mass media, youth leaders, and others outside the family and extended kin network (see Coleman, 1961).

In modern technologically based societies the socialization experience of adolescents has also been deeply affected by the patterns of occupational recruitment and practice characteristic of an industrial order. When farming and crafts were the main occupations, a young man was socialized to his occupational role by working with his father or by being apprenticed to an artisan. Even the professions, such as law and medicine, socialized their members through an apprenticeship system. Except in rare cases, this system has been replaced by training in specialized schools for the professions and for most nonprofessional but technical occupations. Consequently, socialization to occupations is now much more the responsibility of formal, more impersonal, specialized agencies. In certain ways this has widened access to these desirable occupational positions, since acceptance for training is decided by objective criteria in more or less open competition. In other ways, however, it means more restricted access, because young people must fairly early decide on the career they will follow, and get on the right "track." It is no longer possible for a young Abe Lincoln to come out of the backcountry with only a few years of schooling, and that mostly self-instruction, and apprentice himself to a local lawyer as the start of a career in law.

Politics.   As in the case of goods and services, the pattern of socialization depends on the distribution of resources—in this case, power. Where young people, in their own right or through youth groups, are able effectively to represent their "interests" in the political arena, the forms and content of socialization will be different from the case where youths are politically dependent and subordinate. The issue has recently been dramatized throughout the world by the role of the Red Guards youth groups in Communist China. Under conditions of very rapid change, or under the stimulus of revolutionary leadership, the values and action patterns of the older generation may become unacceptable, and the youth may act independently of established traditions or use established political arrangements to introduce new social policies. At this stage anomalies in social structure may be glaring, as exemplified in the requirement that 18-year-olds in the United States serve in the army even though they are not entitled to vote.

Values.   Late childhood and early adolescence are the prime periods for the formal inculcation of social values. In good part the indoctrination is specific, explicit, and didactic. Teachers, wise men, sages, oracles, and every other adult, if prepared to, practice telling the young the principles of right living. Folk sayings, proverbs, fairy tales, and a variety of exhortatory literature will spread the doctrine of the particular culture: Love thy neighbor, or, the only good *whoever* is a dead *whoever;* turn the other cheek, or, an eye for an eye; a man should try to get all he can, or, moderation in all things. The values taught will usually cover all things—they will define the goals of life, specify the legitimate paths to their attainment, elaborate the rewards, judge the deviant, abstractly resolve conflicts, and even suggest the appropriate compensations for failure.

The adolescent cannot, however, be expected automatically and passively to accept the values disseminated by society and by the adults with whom he is most intimately in contact. Indeed, if those values are not consistent, and often they are not, the adolescent is forced to choose between them, or he may be forced into passivity and inaction in order to avoid violating the norms of one or another of his mentors. In a more critical culture, and in a more self-conscious age, adolescents may also become acutely aware of the contrast between the values expressed by adults and those implicit in their actual behavior. The sensitive adolescent may, then, reject the formally espoused values, or act mainly in accord with what he judges to be the covert values. In either case, conflict with adults and representatives of adult society is likely to result.

In times of rapid social change, furthermore, adults may become uncertain as to the validity and appropriateness of the existing values as standards to guide the rearing of youth. A study of child-rearing values in three generations of Soviet Russian families showed marked shifts in the values each generation of parents deemed appropriate for raising their children. In guiding their children's preferences in the occupational realm, for example, those who raised them in the Tsarist period give greatest emphasis to material rewards (41 per cent) and to tradition, i.e., following in father's footsteps (35 per cent). These value emphases declined markedly among the parents who raised their children in the Revolutionary era. Among them there was an understandable sensitivity to the political implications of having a child hold any given job. By the time the generation of parents which would raise its children after World War II came forward, there was a total transformation in the relative standing of the value emphases in socializing the child's occupational aspirations. In this new generation of parents, encouraging the child to seek a job assuring "self-expression" emerged as the overwhelmingly dominant emphasis (62 per cent), whereas "rewards" and "tradition" as themes now were emphasized by a mere 24 per cent *combined* (Inkeles, 1955).

ADULT YEARS AND OLD AGE

Trusting that the fuller account of the interaction of socialization and the social structure in infancy, childhood, and adolescence will suffice to exemplify the recommended mode of analysis, I will restrict myself to a much briefer statement concerning the adult years and old age. This account is necessarily a simplified analysis, which neglects important variation in different cultures, strata, and historical epochs. Instead, the picture given is that appropriate mainly to large scale industrial societies.

In adulthood the main *issue* is the degree to which the individual accepts, and the quality of his performance in, the whole panoply of roles which accompany the statuses of adulthood such as husband, father, earner of a living, member of a religious community, warrior, citizen of a polity, and so on.

The *task* of the socializee is to "fit in," "to take hold," in the large set of new statuses into which he is now thrust. What in adolescence may be a forgivable relapse, indicating that one is not quite yet ready but must try again, becomes in adulthood a serious failure which is not easily forgiven and may not admit of repeated trials. The adolescent must "put off childish things," renounce adolescent indulgences, and accept serious adult responsibilities. In contrast to earlier periods, the content to be learned shifts from general dispositions, such as reliability which is applicable to a wide variety of roles, to highly specific skills and responsibilities especially relevant to more specialized roles. The agents of socialization shift markedly. Kin and others whose role is personally or professionally protective, such as teachers, are replaced by formal, impersonal, organizational agencies which less "treat" and more "handle" and "process" the individual. Peers continue to be important, but they can less be selected by preference. Instead, they come more to be "built into" one's situation, having been previously recruited by others, as in the work gang. These more impersonal and professional agents of socialization tend to have highly specific and delimited objectives in their efforts to socialize the adult socializee. They teach one to drive, to do a certain job, to follow a certain path, without necessarily having any concern with our performance in related tasks, without the obligation to show strong interest in our future roles, and generally without profound consideration of the relation of these new roles to our general social and emotional adjustment.

In old age there is an analogue to the main *issue* of infancy and early childhood, in that adjustment to physical changes comes again to oblige us to acquire new skills and change established habits. The older person must, of course, accommodate not only to actual transformations in his physical capacity, but to changes in the expectation of others with regard to a person of his age. A main part of the older individual's *task* is to learn to renounce or abandon previously held positions, and especially the power, prestige, and economic rewards associated with them. The learning of entirely, or largely, new roles may be also required, such as dealing with total leisure. Except insofar as old people are confined in specialized institutions, the more formal and bureaucratic agencies of socialization become relatively unimportant as progressive withdrawal from the standard roles of the middle years occurs. Again as in adolescence, one's peers become very important socializing agents, and in a peculiar reversal, so do one's own children and other juniors and subordinates whom one earlier had socialized. The *objective* of the socializers tends to be short term, in the nature of the case, not so much to teach specific skills as to encourage acceptance of a new status. New skills, however, are not unimportant as an area of concern, as older men may learn to garden, work in pottery, paint and otherwise acquire skills which are appropriate to full-time leisure.

This sketch of individual socialization through the life cycle, brief, unsystematic and necessarily very incomplete, may yet serve to highlight a number of general issues which are critical in defining the influence of social structure on socialization. We may note the following seven main points:

1. Effective socialization is a pre-condition of organized social life. Every social organization must be prepared to do some socialization of its constituent members, partly to teach ways of acting distinctive to its needs and new to the socializee, and partly to reinforce established patterns, thus insuring minimal drift away from expectations and norms. Every social organization, even a dyad, is, therefore, to some degree an agent, or "producer" of socialization. Most organizations have other, more specific, functions to perform, however, such as production, consumption, policing, and the like. Therefore, they must inevitably rely on other social units to provide the basic socialization of their ultimate constituents or members. Each social unit is, therefore, also a "consumer" of the products of prior socialization by other social agencies. The family is clearly the prime and most ubiquitous agency serving this function of general socialization. Where formal schooling exists, it generally is second in importance in fulfilling the function of general socialization.

2. The concentration of attention on the family as a socialization setting may be justified on the grounds that its impact is prior to that of other efforts, and presumably comes at a time when the individual is most malleable. From a sociological perspective, however, much of the research on infant and child socialization is too exclusively concerned with problems in the mastery of basic disciplines such as toilet training, control of aggression, and understanding and speaking the native language. Child-rearing research has relatively neglected to study the acquisition of other skills relevant to social functioning such as competition, cooperation and sharing, mutual support, observance of group rules and the like. Even within its accepted frame of reference, child socialization research has considered as major independent variables mainly the in-built maturational potentials of the child, and the personality and child-rearing techniques particular to a given parent. Social class and ethnic differences in child rearing have been carefully noted, but not systematically and theoretically

integrated as an element in research design. The significance of gross occupational differences has been somewhat studied, but in very modest degree relative to research which does not systematically take account of this basic attribute.

Other aspects of social structure which may impinge on the parent-child relation have been studied hardly at all. Although the observation of everyday life makes it apparent that much of what each parent does to the child is guided by reference to some image of "what he must be like to get on in life and the 'world' later," we know very little of what these images are, where parents get them, and how successfully they translate them into action in their socialization practices. Ethnic and regional differences, the styles of child rearing in homes of parents of varying political persuasion, and the effects which social conditions such as depression and war have on the modes and content of infant and early child socialization have been little studied.

3. Despite the massive importance of the earliest years in the development of the individual, we must recognize that socialization is a process that goes on continuously throughout the life cycle. By the age of four the brain may have attained 90 per cent of its potential weight, but at that age the individual, as a member of society, has probably acquired not much more than 10 per cent of the repertoire of social roles he will later play in life. We can be easily misled by the assertion that in the development of our general intelligence, 50 per cent takes place between conception and age 4, and 30 per cent more between ages 4 and 8. Social development, admittedly harder to measure, must be recognized as mainly occurring at later ages. A child may at age 11 know 50 per cent of all the words he will know, but so far as other forms of socially relevant knowledge are concerned, virtually all his learning and development are still ahead of him. Realistic vocational interests, for example, seem to develop mainly in the period between 14 and 20. Certainly at age 4, whatever may be the weight of his brain, almost everything an individual is to learn of team work, of sports, of politics, of large scale organization and bureaucracy, of earning a living, of war, and of heterosexual love is yet to come.

Not only do new socialization problems and issues come to the fore as the individual moves through the life cycle, but the processes of social change may transform his situation within a short space of time and require of him profound new learning within the space of a single phase of the life history. Major economic changes such as depression, radical political changes such as war and revolution, and technological innovation are among the more dramatic instances, yet in dynamic industrial societies less dramatic but cumulatively substantial processes of culture change requiring individual adaptation have become endemic.

4. Recognizing the life-long continuity of socialization requires us to acknowledge the importance of social units other than the nuclear family as socializing agencies. The school is generally so recognized, but largely with regard to the content of the formal instruction which it dispenses. Inadequate attention has been paid to its role as a training ground in dealing with peers, as the

child's first introduction to formal authority and bureaucratic organization, and as inculcator of cultural values, not necessarily explicitly taught but latent in the forms and content of teaching (see Dreeben, 1967). The factory and office, the government bureaucracy, the church, the hospital, the political party, the army, are examples of but a few of the agencies which both set expectations as to what is adequate socialization and themselves engage in various forms of socialization (see Inkeles, 1966b). These formal agencies, furthermore, may include much less formally organized subunits, each of which also sets standards and socializes both new and old members. These subunits include the office or shop work group, the army platoon or crew, and the neighborhood community. Still other relatively enduring social units quite outside any formal organization also play important roles in socialization, such as the neighborhood gang, and the circle of friends.

5. The complexity of social structure, even within nominally "simple" societies, predetermines a necessary complexity of the socialization experience of the individual. The fact that any individual learns to live in society and meet its myriad demands is no less awesome than that any child learns to understand and use a language. Some results of socialization, of course, are appropriate to participation in all or a great variety of the statuses an individual will occupy. The most obvious of these is knowledge of a language. The predisposition to conform to social rules has been cited as perhaps the single most important quality a person must learn in any society. Certain qualities which suffuse the culture and permeate the social structure—for example, tendencies toward dominance or submission, or emotional expressiveness—may be adaptive in a wide variety of situations. Ultimately, however, specific roles come down to fairly specific behaviors, and the number of those which must be learned by the individual in the course of his socialization is very great. Just how great this repertory of potential behavior is in the average individual has not been systematically studied.

6. The integration of the individual as a psychic or personality system and the integration of society as a social system set limits on the variability of socialization within any given sociocultural system. If the socialization demands of different parts of the social system are too disparate, individuals may be subject to unendurable pressure or conflict. This is certainly one element contributing to what the anthropologists have noted as the "strain toward consistency" in cultures. If the individuals whom the system must integrate in coordinated social action have been too diversely socialized, then, as in Yeats' "Second Coming," the falcon cannot see the falconer, the center cannot hold, and things fall apart.

7. Although socialization is one of the most important mechanisms giving society stability and continuity, it may also serve as a major vehicle for change. Some individuals, indeed whole segments of a population, may be socialized to play the role of creative, innovative, change-inducing catalysts. The entrepreneur in economic development represents this tendency, and McClelland (1961) argues it requires specific socialization of a strong need for achievement.

When structural change has taken place due to major innovations in economic and political forms, in the extreme case through revolution, sustaining the revolution and adapting people to it both in the adult and the upcoming generation depend on socialization to new role demands. Unless it can successfully effect this re-socialization, no major process of social change can hope to endure.

REFERENCES

ABERLE, D. F. Culture and socialization. In F. L. K. Hsu, *Psychological anthropology.* Homewood, Ill.: Dorsey Press, 1961.

ADORNO, T. W., ET AL. *The authoritarian personality.* New York: Harper, 1950.

BACON, MARGARET K., CHILD, I. L., & BARRY, H., III. A cross-cultural study of correlates of crime. *Journal of Abnormal and Social Psychology,* 1963, 66 (3).

BRONFENBRENNER, U. Socialization and social class through time and space. In Eleanor E. Maccoby, T. M. Newcomb & E. L. Hartley (Eds.), *Readings in social psychology.* New York: Henry Holt, 1958.

COLEMAN, J. S., ET AL. *The adolescent society: The social life of the teenager and its impact on education.* Glencoe, Ill.: Free Press, 1961.

DREEBEN, R. The contribution of schooling to the learning of norms. *Harvard Educational Review,* 1967, 37 (2).

ERIKSON, E. H. *Childhood and society.* New York: Norton, 1950.

ERIKSON, E. H. *Young man Luther: A study in psychoanalysis and history.* New York: Norton, 1958.

FROMM, E. *Escape from freedom.* New York: Farrar & Rinehart, 1941.

INKELES, A. Social change and social character: The role of parental mediation. *Journal of Social Issues,* 1955, 11, 12–23.

INKELES, A. The modernization of man. In M. Weiner (Ed.), *Modernization.* New York: Basic Books, 1966. (a)

INKELES, A. Social structure and the socialization of competence. *Harvard Educational Review,* 1966, 36 (3). (b)

KARDINER, A. *The individual and his society: The psychodynamics of primitive social organization.* New York: Columbia Univer. Press, 1939.

LANNEAU, G., & MABRIEU, P. Enquête sur l'éducation en milieu rural et en milieu urbain. *Enfance,* 1957, 4 (Sept.–Oct.), 465–485.

LEVY, M. J. *The structure of society.* Princeton: Princeton Univer. Press, 1952.

McCLELLAND, D. C. *The achieving society.* Princeton, N. J.: D. Van Nostrand, 1961.

McKINLEY, D. G. *Social class and family life.* New York: Free Press of Glencoe, 1964.

MILLER, D. R., & SWANSON, G. E. *Inner conflict and defense.* New York: Holt, Rinehart, 1960.

PEARLIN, L. I., & KOHN, M. L. Social class, occupation, and parental values: A cross-national study. *American Sociological Review,* 1966, 31.

RAINWATER, L., & YANCEY, W. L. *The Moynihan report and the politics of controversy: A trans-action social science and public policy report.* Cambridge: M.I.T. Press, 1967.

WHITING, BEATRICE B. Sex identity conflict and physical violence: A comparative study. *American Anthropologist,* 1965, 67 (6), Part 2.

CHAPTER **12**

Culture And Cognitive Growth

Patricia Marks Greenfield and
Jerome S. Bruner

Harvard University

We shall ask, in the pages that follow, what it means, intellectually, to grow up in one cultural milieu and not another. It is, of course, a form of the old question of how heredity and environment relate: How, in this case, does intellectual development depend upon external influences; in what respects is it a series of unfolding maturational states? But the question is now in qualitative terms. The older debate on heredity versus environment was without a possible solution. For there is no psychological phenomenon without a biologically given organism nor one that takes place outside an environment. But we can, nevertheless, study the intersect in growth of biological background and cultural milieu with the more modest aim of learning what kinds of cultural difference make an intellectual difference at what points in development and how it comes about in some particular way.

It is not a new idea that cultural variation yields variation in modes of thought. It is a persistent theme in anthropology (for example, Boas, 1938; Mead, 1946; Whorf, 1956). Psychologists have also interested themselves in cultural influences on cognitive development. However, the methods used have rarely been equal to the task at hand. Anthropology's most recent and most promising approach, ethnoscience, explores qualitative cognitive variation by exploring the native terminology used for a particular objectively definable domain such as plants or disease or kinship (Sturtevant, 1964). Ethnoscience is limited as a method for investigating cognitive processes precisely because it does not deal with *processes* at all but with intellectual *products* as embodied in language. Like the older anthropological strategy of inferring living cognitive processes from static cultural products such as myth, ritual and social life (e.g., Durkheim & Mauss, 1963; Lévi-Strauss, 1962), ethnoscience infers the mind of the language user from the lexicon he uses. When we know the culturally

This article was supported in part by a grant from the Carnegie Corporation of New York, No. B-3004 and a contract from the United States Office of Education, No. 4–10–136, to Harvard University, Center for Cognitive Studies. Also by a pre-doctoral fellowship from the Public Health Service, No. 5–F1–MH–15, 200–02, to Patricia Marks Greenfield.

standard system for kinship or disease classification we still do not know how the system developed or how it is used in novel situations. It is a bit like studying the growth of logic and thought in children of our own society through an analysis of grammar or logic in the books found in the library. It may help to define the idealized version of logical thought in the culture to do this. But it can tell little about the processes involved. In this respect, it is somewhat like some contemporary efforts to found psycholinguistics on the assumption that the rules underlying grammatical competence are the same as the laws that govern the production of grammatical sentences by native speakers. The laws governing the production of sentences may or may not be the same as the rules of grammar that are used to describe the correct combinations in the language.

In the 1930's and 40's psychologists carried IQ tests around the world. They had learned little more than that "natives" fared worse than standardization groups at home when projective tests came into vogue in the 50's (Lindzey, 1961), and cross-cultural attention shifted from intellect to affect. Again, the intrinsic value of intelligence tests was limited, abroad as at home, by the fact that the IQ is not a *process,* but the product of many complex cognitive processes that other methods would have to unravel—and a product closely geared to school achievement in Western European culture at that. An ideological factor further complicated this work. As Strodtbeck (1964) points out, you can "prove" the power of heredity if you assume your test is "culture-free" (for example, Porteus' maze); whereas differences are due to environmental factors on the assumption of a "culturally relative" test. The assumption in a particular study probably reflected personal bias more than any other factor. Later the absurdity of this distinction, parallel to that of choosing between heredity and environment, became evident.

The point of view animating the present discussion is that intelligence is to a great extent the internalization of "tools" provided by a given culture. Thus, "culture-free" means "intelligence-free." Such a view of cognitive development has been put forth elsewhere (Bruner, 1964). Here we shall examine it by comparing intellectual development in cultures with radically different technologies.

One of the most interesting and oldest lines of cross-cultural work in cognition is through the study of sensation and perception. More than one intelligence tester noted that performance tests often seemed to put foreigners at as much of a disadvantage as verbal tests and was forced to conclude that perceptual as well as verbal habits could vary radically from culture to culture (Cryns, 1964; Jahoda, 1956; Wintringer, 1955). If this were so then the study of perception could be fundamental in understanding any psychological process involving a response to the outside world.

The classical work on perception was done by the Cambridge Anthropological Expedition to the Torres Straits in 1901–1905. A famous and intriguing finding was that of Rivers (1905) concerning the lesser susceptibility of the Murray Islanders to the Müller-Lyer illusions. The Todas of India yield a similar finding. This result has been interpreted to mean that the Todas, un-accustomed to inferring three dimensions from two dimensional displays, were less subject to the illusion; for as soon as three dimensional stimulus materials were used, cultural differences disappeared (Bonte, 1962).

This work—suggesting the effect of *particular* cultural conditions such as the absence of pictures—has been followed up with studies of illusions in new places (e.g., Allport and Pettigrew in South Africa, 1957) and by carefully controlled experimentation with line drawings. The latter studies have shown the interpretation of Rivers' work to be a correct one (Hudson, 1960). The effects obtained appear to depend upon perceptual *inference;* members of different cultures differ in the inferences they draw from perceptual cues, not in the cues they are *able* to distinguish. Such an interpretation suggests the value of studying more directly the way in which the cues are assimilated to different schemata in different cultures with the effect of producing large cultural differences. It is conceivable that one can also find differences in the cues most likely to be used in organizing percepts, given sufficiently complex stimulus fields. This is to say that, given complex input, the principles of selectivity will vary from culture to culture. This was certainly the point of the Cambridge studies under Rivers and of the careful observations of Bogoras in his work among the Chukchee (1904).

Our own cross-cultural work has followed other lines, lines of more recent historical development. We have asked first the naive question: Where in a culture should one find differences in the processes of thought? The anthro-pological linguists (e.g., Whorf, 1956) suggested a concrete answer; where there are language differences there may (or should?) be cognitive differences. Our results have led us away from the parallelism of Whorf toward the in-strumentalism that is more typical of Vygotsky (1961) and Luria (1961). Language as a tool and a constraint on cognitive development will be discussed below in more detail.

We, like most others who work on development, were strongly influenced by Piaget. But although Piaget has given us our richest picture of cognitive development, it is one that is based almost entirely on experiments in which age alone is varied. While he admits that environmental influences play a role, the admission is *pro forma,* and inventive experiments remain confined to Western European children, usually middle-class children at that. Where Piaget's work has been extended to non-Western societies, the emphasis has been almost en-tirely quantitative. Such work has been confined largely to timetable studies, to the time "lag" in the development of "foreign" children in contrast to chil-dren in Geneva or Pittsburgh or London (Flavell, 1963). A series of experi-ments carried out by the Harvard Center for Cognitive Studies has explored the role of culturally transmitted technologies in intellectual growth by the use of instructional techniques and cross-cultural studies (Bruner, Olver, Green-field et al., 1966). By comparing children of different ages in extremely different cultures we can ask the developmental question in its most radical form. We are not the only ones to have gone abroad with such an intention, and we shall also use the work of others in specifying the impact of culture on growth.

We shall, in what follows, focus on two kinds of cultural constraints operating in development: value orientation and language. They seem fruitful for organizing our findings and illustrating the problems involved.

VALUE COMPLEXES AND COGNITIVE GROWTH

Let us, in the interest of specificity, limit our discussion of value orientations to the cognitive implications of one particular value contrast: collective *versus* individualistic orientation. Kluckhohn (Kluckhohn & Strodtbeck, 1961), in her studies of basic value orientations, attests to the fundamental nature of such a "decision" about orientation, commenting upon its importance for individual coping as well as for social solidarity. This value contrast represents more than alternate ways of seeing how things ought to be. Rather it reflects a contrast in how things *are*—a matter of world view about origins and existence and not merely a normative matter.

We begin with a series of studies carried out by Greenfield (Bruner et al., 1966) in Senegal, the westernmost tip of former French West Africa in 1963–1964. These studies explored two main areas of cognitive development: concept formation and conservation in the classic Piagetian sense. The two areas complement each other nicely, for much of intellectual growth can be summarized as the development of equivalence or conservation, the equivalence rule of concepts being more "internal" and that of conservation more "external" in orientation. The subjects in both sets of experiments were all Wolof, members of the country's dominant ethnic group. The children were constituted into nine groups, better to discern the effect of cultural differences—three degrees of urbanization and education were represented, with three age levels within each.

The cultural milieu of our first group, rural unschooled children and adults, had neither schools nor urban influence. Although their traditional Wolof village had an elementary school, they had never attended it. The three age groups were: six- and seven-year-olds, eight- and nine-year-olds, and eleven- to thirteen-year-olds. There was also a group of adults.

The second major group—the bush school children—attended school in the same village or in a nearby village. This group was partitioned among first graders, third graders, and sixth graders, corresponding as closely as possible to the three age levels of the unschooled groups.

The third major group comprised city school children. These children lived in Dakar, Senegal's cosmopolitan capital and, like the second group, included first, third, and sixth graders. All the children were interrogated in Wolof, although French was the official language of instruction.

Returning now to the question of collective and individualistic orientations, we find that they have cognitive manifestations so basic as to render certain experimental procedures possible or impossible. In both the conservation and the concept experiments, the children were asked to give reasons for their answers. With both American and European children this type of question is usually put something like this: "Why do you say (or think) that thus and such is true?" Specifically, in a conservation problem, a child might be asked: "Why do you say that this glass has more water than this one?" But this type of question would meet with uncomprehending silence when addressed to the unschooled children. If, however, the same question were changed in form to "Why *is* thus and such true?" it could often be answered quite easily. It would seem that the unschooled Wolof children lack Western self-consciousness: they do not distinguish between their own thought or statement about something and the thing itself. Thought and the object of thought seem to be one. Consequently, the idea of explaining a *statement* is meaningless; it is the external event that is to be explained. We might expect from all this that the relativistic notion that events can vary according to point of view may be absent to a greater degree than in Western culture. This expectation is confirmed in Greenfield's concept formation studies, where the unschooled children can group a given set of objects or pictures according to only one attribute although there are several other possible bases of classification. Let it be noted that the Wolof *schoolchildren* do not differ essentially from Western children in this respect. It appears that school tends to give them something akin to Western self-consciousness, for they can answer questions implying a distinction between their own psychological reactions and external events; and, as they advance in school, they become increasingly capable of categorizing the same stimuli according to several different criteria or "points of view."

Piaget has proposed that intellectual growth begins with an egocentric stage, based on the inability to make a distinction between internal and external (Piaget, 1930). This stage is then followed by a more developed egocentrism in which inner and outer are distinguished but confused. When inner psychological phenomena are attributed to inanimate features of the external environment, we have "animism;" when psychological processes are given characteristics of the inanimate, external world, we speak of "realism." These two tendencies are supposed to be complementary and universal forms of childish thought. Their mutual presence indicates a preliminary distinction between inner and outer.

In contrast to this formulation, we should like to propose that in traditional, collectively-oriented societies this distinction *never* gets made, that the world stays on one level of reality, and that this level is *realistic* rather than *animistic*. Animism, we realize, has often been considered the characteristic of "primitive" thought par excellence. We rather suspect it is only the "powerful," well-cared for, competent child who sees the world in the pattern of his own feelings, and not the malnourished child of many traditional subsistence cultures like the Wolof. Kardiner (1965), too, has made this point with respect to the psychoanalytic conception of the "omnipotence of thought," noting that it is only where the child's every whim is satisfied that he is led to believe his thought omnipotent. Our claim is more severe. It is that animism does not develop where there is no support given for individualistic orientation. The argument would be that the child is not cognizant of his own psychological properties, does not differentiate these from properties of the physical world, and is therefore not cognizant of any psychological properties—far be it from him to attribute such properties to *inanimate* objects. In place of the cultivation of individual subjectivity, there is instead a reinforcing of the idea of "reality," "people-in-a-world-as-a-unity."

Consider the following evidence in support of this point. In an equivalence experiment done in the United States by Olver and Hornsby (Bruner et al., 1966), children were shown an assortment of pictures and asked to put the similar ones together. They were then asked the reasons for their groupings. Children as they grow older form groups increasingly by the rule of super-ordinate grouping (those things go together that share a common attribute). The earlier pattern is more complexive in the sense that things go together because they fit into a story together or whatnot. The transition from the earlier to the later mode of grouping is handled by "egocentrism." Things are alike by virtue of the relationship that "I" or "you" have to them, or the action taken toward them by "I" or "you." This is the picture in the United States. But Reich (Bruner et al., 1966), using parallel techniques with Eskimo children in Anchorage, Alaska, finds that they do not express the function of things in terms of personal interaction with them nearly so often as do the American children of European descent. The Eskimo value system stresses self-reliance, but strongly suppresses any expression of individualism as an attitude toward life. The Eskimos are a subsistence culture that requires group action in its major forms of activity—sealing, caribou hunting, stone weir fishing. Eskimo children develop their superordinate structures without the intervention of the kind of egocentrism we observed in European children. Thus, such egocentrism cannot be a universal stage, not even in the development of superordination. Instead, it appears clearly relative to cultural conditions and values.

It should be clear by now that the kind of implicit egocentrism where one cannot distinguish different personal viewpoints, the kind that we have been calling *realism,* is strikingly different from the type that explicitly relates everything to oneself. Indeed, an explicit concept of self implies some sort of idea of not-self, for every concept must be defined as much by what it excludes as by what it includes. Or, to use Piaget's terminology, we could say equally well that an undifferentiated egocentrism that ends in realism is diametrically opposed to the kind that ends in "artificialism," the tendency to see all physical phenomena as made by and for men. This tendency is closely related to animism. It is the artificialistic type of egocentrism that appears in Olver and Hornsby's experiments and is probably typical of individualistically-oriented industrial societies.

Unself-conscious realism was clear at yet another point in the Senegalese experiments. Here, too, one sensed its origin in the absence of control over the inanimate world characteristic of indigenous societies. In the classic experiment on the conservation of a continuous quantity (Piaget, 1952), one of two identical beakers was filled with water to a certain level. The Wolof child poured an equal amount in the second beaker. Then the experimenter poured the water from one beaker into a longer, thinner beaker, causing the water level to rise. The child was then asked if the two beakers contained the same amount of water or if one had more than the other and why. He was then asked for a reason. A type of reason in support of non-conservation judgments appeared that we had not seen before among American children (Bruner et al., 1966), although Piaget (1952) reports one example in a Swiss four-year-old. This was the "magical" action reason: the child would say, "It's not the same" because "you poured it." The shift from equality to "inequality" was being resolved and justified by recourse to the experimenter's action. A natural phenomena was being explained by attributing special "magical" powers to intervening human agents. More likely, as Kohler (1937) points out, this as well as other cases of magical causation are made possible by realism in which animate and inanimate phenomena occupy a single plane of reality. That is, the child in the conservation experiment is faced with the following sequence of events: (1) water a certain way, (2) experimenter's action, (3) water changed. When the child says the amount is not the same because the experimenter poured it, he is basing his causal inference on contiguity—the usual procedure even in our society. But under ordinary circumstances, we would accept an explanation in terms of contiguous physical events *or* contiguous social events, but not a causal chain that included *both* kinds of event. Thus, "magic" only exists from the perspective of a dualistic ontology.

Note well that school suppresses this mode of thinking with astonishing absoluteness. There is not one instance of such reasoning among either bush or city Senegalese children who have been in school seven months or longer. Once again school seems to promote the self-consciousness born of a distinction between human processes and physical phenomena.

We can argue that just as soon as the child is endowed with control in the situation, his realism and magical reasoning will disappear. And so it turned out to be. The experiment was done again; everything remained basically the same with one exception: this time the child did *all* the pouring himself. Would he find yet another "magical" explanation for the seeming inequality of the water? Or, indeed, would he be as likely to believe that the water in the two beakers was uneven? We would reason that he would not. For while the child would be perfectly willing to attribute "realistic" powers to an authority figure like the experimenter, the child would not attribute any special powers to himself for his experience had taught him that he had none.

Our suspicion was well confirmed by the results. Among the younger children, two-thirds of the group who transferred the water themselves achieved conservation, in contrast to only one-quarter of the children who had only watched the experimenter pour. Among the older children, the contrast was equally dramatic: eight in ten of those who did the pouring themselves, as compared with slightly less than half of the others, achieved conservation. When the child poured himself, his reasons were dramatically different from those given when an adult was pouring. Magical-action virtually disappears when the unschooled children themselves pour. What emerges instead are identity reasons—reference to the initial state of the system. The child who pours on his own now uses his initial equalizing operation as the basis for his justification of conservation: "They were equal at the beginning."

Price-Williams' (1961) study of conservation among Tiv children in Nigeria lends further weight to the point. He found that all of the Tiv children had achieved conservation of both continuous and discrete quantity by age eight, in sharp contrast to our upper limit of 50 per cent with much older Senegalese children. The description given by Price-Williams of the children's behavior during the experiments indicates that Tiv culture is quite different from Wolof in promoting an active manipulative approach to the physical world. He describes the children's behavior like this: "These children would spontaneously actually perform the operation themselves. . . . Furthermore, they would reverse the sequence of operations, by, for example, pouring back the earth from the second container to the first" (Price-Williams, 1961, p. 302). Such self-initiated action was *never* observed among unschooled Wolof children and may well be the key to the great disparity between the two cultures in spontaneous conservation results.

It may be that a collective, rather than individual, value orientation develops where the individual lacks power over the physical world. Lacking personal power, he has no notion of personal importance. In terms of his cognitive categories, now, he will be less likely to set himself apart from others and the physical world, he will be less self-conscious at the same time that he places less value on himself. Thus, mastery over the physical world and individualistic self-consciousness will appear together in a culture, in contrast to a collective orientation and a realistic world view in which people's attitudes and actions are not placed in separate conceptual pigeonholes from physical events.

This formulation is commonsensical; absence of personal mastery over the world is consonant with a collective orientation. And, indeed, we have observed empirically that the very same Wolof children who lack self-consciousness when questioned about their "thoughts" also seem to be hindered by a lack of experience in manipulating the physical world when they approach a problem relating to the conservation of quantity across transformations in its appearance.

Is there, however, developmental reason for this dichotomy between individual mastery and a collective or social value orientation? How does each come about? Is there a point in child-rearing at which a choice is made? Rabain-Zempléni (1965) has studied the fundamental ways in which the Wolof child (in his traditional bush setting) relates to the world of animate and inanimate things around him from the time of his weaning (age two) to his integration into a peer group (age four). Her findings confirm the preceding interpretation of later intellectual development among Wolof children and elucidate in a most dramatic fashion the antecedents of these developments in terms of child training practice and infant experience. Her work suggests that there is a developmental reason for the dichotomy between physical mastery and a collective orientation and that it appears at the very beginning of life. We learn that:

> In a general way, motor manifestations of the child are, from the first year of life, not treated as productions existing for themselves in their capacity of exercising nascent functions, but already are interpreted as signifying a desire on the part of the child oriented in relation to some person (Rabain-Zempléni, 1965, p. 17, *our translation*).

So it seems as if adult members of a family evaluate and interpret the child's emergent motor activity either in terms of the relation of this activity to the people around him or in terms of motor competence per se, depending on the culture to which they belong. The child's attention must therefore be turned toward one or the other of these facets of physical activity. If, as in the Wolof case, the child's activity is not evaluated per se but in terms of its relation to group members, then one would expect both less mastery of physical acts and less differentiation of the physical from the social, that is, a "realistic" world view. Thus, adult interpretation of the child's first actions would seem to be paradigmatic for the choice between an individualistic and a collective orientation; for a social interpretation of an act not only relates the actor to the group but also relates the group, including actor, to physical events. When, on the other hand, acts are given an interpretation in terms of motoric competence, other people are irrelevant, and the act is separated, moreover, from the motivations, intentions, and desires of the actor himself.

Let us return once more to the Wolof to trace a more complete developmental sequence in a collectively oriented culture. Rabain-Zempléni's naturalistic observations confirm our hypothesis, derived from the conservation behavior of the unschooled children, that Wolof children lack manipulatory experience, for she notes that manipulation of objects is an occasional and secondary activity for the child from two to four and that, furthermore, the Wolof child's "self image does not have to rest in the same way as in Europe on the power which he has over objects, but rather on that which he has over other bodies" (p. 13). She also notes that verbal interchanges between children and adults often concern the relations which are supposed to exist between people but rarely concern explanations of natural phenomena.

At the same time as the Wolof child's manipulation of the physical, inanimate world fails to be encouraged in isolation from social relations, the personal desires and intentions which would isolate him from the group are also discouraged. Thus, a collective orientation does not arise simply as a by-product of individual powerlessness vis-a-vis the inanimate world, but is systematically encouraged as socialization progresses. Western society recognizes individual intention and desire as a positive function of age. According to Rabain-Zempléni, Wolof society does the reverse: the newborn child is treated as a person full of personal desire and intention; after he reaches the age of two, the adults in his milieu increasingly subordinate his desires to the ends of the group; he becomes less and less an individual, more and more a member of a collectivity.

When the social and physical constitute but a single level of reality, neither type of explanation should take precedence. To us who give precedence to physicalistic explanations, however, it may often appear that traditional peoples emphasize the social. This impression may be exaggerated by the fact that they often have greater knowledge about the social than the physical realm. Since a social explanation is considered perfectly adequate, we would not expect such people to press on for a physical account.

Gay and Cole's (1967; Gay, 1965) research among the Kpelle of Liberia furnish many other indications of the way in which people-as-causative-agents can play an extraordinary role in the traditional structure of knowledge. In school, facts are true because the teacher says them, and so there is often no attempt at understanding other reasons why or proving the fact for oneself. This same observation has been noted many places in Africa, for example, by Lapp[1] in Cameroun. His experience was similar to ours in this respect, for he found that the way to combat this tendency in teaching natural sciences was to have the students rather than the teacher do the demonstrations.

One other example from Cole and Gay. Among the Kpelle, arguments are won when they are unanswerable. Again, the ultimate criterion is social—does the other person have a comeback?—rather than "objective" or external. What is being argued about takes a back seat to the arguers.

Most intriguing is Rabain-Zempléni's observation that in the natural situation of sharing a quantity among several persons, a situation not too different from the second half of the conservation experiment where a quantity is divided among six beakers, more attention is paid to which person receives the substance at what point in the distribution than to the amount received. It is like their conservation explanations: more attention is focused on the person pouring— the social aspect of the situation—than on the purely physical aspect, the amount of water.

What is most interesting is the fact that, on a broader cultural level, this very same quality has been recognized by the poets of *négritude* or the African Personality as setting off black from white. Lilyan Kesteloof (1962) in her book on Aimé Césaire, the originator of the concept of *négritude*, contrasts its elements with the "valeurs-clef" of Western civilization. In opposition to "l'Individualisme (pour la vie sociale)" of European cultures she places "solida-rité, née de la cohésion du clan primitif" (p. 84). Leopold Sédar Senghor, poet and President of Senegal, defines *négritude* in more psychological terms as "participation du sujet à l'objet, participation de l'homme aux forces cosmiques, communion de l'homme avec tous les autres hommes" (Monteil, 1964, p. 31).

This complex, moreover, is held to be found in all African societies and to stem from common cultural features. The strong element of collective or social values is particularly clear in the modern concept of African socialism

---

[1] Personal communication from D. Lapp in 1965.

which, unlike Western socialism, is supposed to be a mere modernization of existing ideals and social conditions rather than a radical revolution.

We have come far afield from intellectual development, but what is so intriguing about these world views and ideologies is that they should be so strongly reflected in the details of cognitive growth. Bear in mind, however, that the distinctions we are proposing are not all-or-none, although they have been so presented for the sake of clarity. Our evidence, furthermore, is thus far all from Africa. It is interesting that many different ethnic groups should seem to have so much in common, but on the other hand, we do not really know to what extent this social or collective orientation may be typical of all nonindustrial, traditional, or, perhaps, oral cultures. It is not certain that it is even a valid description for every African society. Finally, although we started out talking about the ramifications of a social or collective orientation, we do not really know what causes what in the whole complex of features that we have ended up discussing.

LANGUAGE AND COGNITIVE GROWTH

Our second cultural constraint is language. What does it mean intellectually to speak one language rather than another? What does it mean to write a language as well as to speak it?

Language at the highest level of generality can be divided into two components, a semantic and a syntactic. Most experiments attempting to relate language to thought have emphasized the semantic side in the style of Benjamin Lee Whorf (1956). Here the linguistic variable is the *richness* of the lexicon that a language has available to represent a given domain. Implicitly, but not explicitly, these experiments deal with the vocabulary of any one language *at a single level of generality*—its words rather than any structural relation among them.

A second kind of semantic linguistic variable is more structural. It deals with the *number of levels of generality* that can be encoded by the lexicon of a given language for a particular domain. We shall be interested in the relation of both these kinds of semantic variable to concept formation.

Finally, there are the syntactic properties of language to relate to the logical structure of thought. Hitherto, the cross-cultural study of the relation between syntax and thought has been sorely neglected, although a recent paper (McNeill, 1965) suggests that there is reason to believe that the lexical encoding of events is but a special (and perhaps trivial) case of grammatical encoding. Sapir (1921) may have been the earliest to think explicitly and clearly about the manner in which syntax can shape thought.

In the view of linguistic relativity inspired by Whorf, language is seen as a system of related categories that both incorporates and perpetuates a particular world view. On the lexical level, every language codes certain domains of experience in more detail than others. It has been suggested that when a given language symbolizes a phenomenon in a single word, it is readily available as a classifying principle to speakers of that language. Although any familiar experience can be coded in any language through the simple expedient of a paraphrase, experiences that *must* be expressed in this way are supposed to be less available to speakers of the language (Brown, 1958). Some experiments have focused on this sort of difference between languages. Others have focused on the fact that grammatical considerations force certain classificatory dimensions on speakers of a given language (e.g., time for speakers of English, shape for speakers of Navaho) and derive the hypothesis that the dimensions thus emphasized should be more available for cognitive use in categorization, discrimination, etc., to speakers of that language than for speakers of another language without such obligatory distinctions.

Why have experiments generated by these ideas yielded such diverse and confusing results? Under what conditions (if any) can a relatively rich or poor lexicon defined only by *number* of terms affect nonlinguistic cognitive activity? These are the issues that concern us in this section.

Now, hypotheses about the effect of "numerical richness" can be based on a comparison of different languages with respect to the same domain or a comparison of different areas within a single language. Research has for the most part yielded ambiguous or negative results for studies of the first kind (interlingual) while a good number of the intralingual studies have confirmed the "richness" hypothesis. A close look reveals, however, that these two types of research differ in other ways than their results. The intracultural studies have used as their cognitive measure some memory task such as recognition of the identity of denoted stimuli earlier encountered. One classic experiment, done by Brown and Lenneberg (1954), showed, for example, that ease in *naming* colors made recognizing them easier when they appeared in a larger array. The cross-cultural studies, on the other hand, have usually dealt with judgments of *similarity* among *several* stimuli rather than with the *identity* of a *single* stimulus over time. A classic experiment was done by Carroll and Casagrande (1958), in which children were asked which of two stimuli (e.g., a yellow block and a blue rope) would go best with a third item which was like one of the pair on color and like the other in shape. The subjects were Navaho-dominant and English-dominant Navaho children and white children from three to ten years of age. The Navaho-dominant children were expected to be more sensitive to form than the other groups, because Navaho has an obligatory distinction in its verbs: the *form* of an object dictates the verb of handling. The Navaho-dominant Indian children did indeed classify by form more frequently than did the English-dominant ones, but, alas, the white children who knew *no* Navaho used form most frequently of all! Other experiments have found much the same kind of anomaly (e.g., Doob, 1960; Maclay, 1958).

McNeill (1965), in reviewing this literature, concludes that language does not influence perception but only memory. He proposes that a perceptual representation consists of both a schema—the linguistic label—and a correction —the visual image, but with time the correction and its label tend to be lost, thus accounting for the influence of language on memory.[2] The implication is that the cross-cultural studies mentioned above were unsuccessful because they dealt with present perceptual processes. Indeed, the one unambiguously successful cross-cultural study (Lenneberg & Roberts, 1956) involved a memory task. Before evaluating this formulation, consider one of our own experiments (Bruner et al., 1966). Children were presented with pictures in sets of three. They were asked to choose the two out of each three that were most alike and to give a reason for their choice. In each of the triads, two pictures were similar in color, two were similar in form, and two were similar in the function of the object pictured. French or Wolof was the language of our subjects who took part in the experiment in a manner presently to be related.

But consider first the Wolof and French lexicons available for dealing with the task. Only words at a single level of generality—the most specific—will be considered at this point. In Wolof, it is impossible to make explicit the three color groupings possible in the experiment without the supplementary aid of French words. Specifically, in the last set of three pictures, the French word *bleu* (blue) must be used if one is to specify the basis of grouping by naming the color, for there is no single word for this color in Wolof. In the second set, color-grouping involves contrasting a pair of predominantly orange pictures with a predominantly red one. The Wolof language codes both colors with a single word (*honka*), so that verbalizing the basis of the grouping by means of the Wolof word could not be as satisfactory as using the French word *orange,* for it would not contrast the pair with the third member of the set. For the first set of three pictures, Wolof does almost as well with coding the relevant colors as French, although yellow, the color involved in forming the color pair, is not as codable by Wolof according to the criterion (suggested by Brown, 1958) of agreement between speakers of the language. In fact, the same word is sometimes used to name both yellow and orange, the "contrasting" color of the third picture in the triad.

Let us pass over a comparison of the coding of shapes by the French and Wolof languages, for the relative strength of the two languages is much less clear, and this comparison is not necessary for present purposes. With regard to functional grouping, both easily find ways of saying, "These things are to eat, to wear, to ride in." One cannot say that Wolof is superior to French in this regard, but unlike the color case, it is not clearly inferior in its ability to code at least those aspects of function demanded by the functional groups in this experiment.

On lexical grounds, then, one would at very least expect that monolingual Wolofs would be less color-oriented and more functionally oriented in the content of their groupings than bilinguals, and that both of these groups would

---

[2] The expression "tend to get lost" is advisable, for it is sometimes the case that the correction is not lost but magnified, producing exaggeration in memory—the familiar opposition between "levelling" and "sharpening" introduced long ago by Bartlett (1932) and the Gestalt theorists (e.g., Koffka, 1935).

form fewer color and more functional groups than monolingual French children, in a forced-choice situation, where one type of attribute must be used at the expense of others.

The results, however, were unambiguously contrary to these expectations. The Wolof monolinguals, that is, the unschooled bush Wolofs, could use nothing but color as a grouping principle even when given a chance to make second choice groupings. The other groups of children, in sharp contrast, used color less and less with age and increasingly turned to the other types of attribute. Obviously, the lack of color words does *not* stop monolingual Wolofs from grouping by color.

But does it make their color discriminations less accurate? In asking this question, our experiment becomes in one respect like the intracultural tests of the Whorfian hypothesis described above; the task now involves the accuracy of color discriminations. It is no longer a matter of choice between color or form as bases of grouping. It is quite a straightforward matter to identify errors in color discrimination that can be directly related to lexical structuring. For example, the second set of pictures consists of two predominantly orange pictures and one predominantly red one. The orange colors are in fact identical. An error was counted when a child who claimed to be grouping according to color would select one orange and one red picture as being *most* similar. This choice was clearly wrong from an objective point of view, for he could have chosen the two orange ones that were of identical color. If such errors of discrimination are due to lexical coding, Wolof monolinguals should make them most frequently, Wolof bilinguals next most frequently, and French monolinguals not at all. The results are exactly as predicted. At every age, bilinguals make fewer errors of this kind than Wolof monolinguals, and the French bilingual children make no such errors at all.

These errors, by absolute standards, are infrequent, even in those groups of children where they occur most often. There are never more than three color discrimination errors in any single group (comprising about twenty children). These relatively rare mistakes are not a major conceptual feature in the total context of Wolof equivalence grouping. We begin to wonder whether the lexical features of language should be assigned as large a role in thought as has been claimed by Whorf and even others who have spoken of covariation rather than determinism.

Of great theoretical interest is the fact that these perceptual errors decrease with age until at last they are completely eliminated in all groups. It appears that age brings increasingly accurate perceptual discriminations. This would appear to be a universal trend, even when the lexicon of a culture hinders rather than facilitates such discrimination. We may conclude that with age the constraints of reality increasingly overcome language if they are opposed.

Is it, as McNeill[3] suggests, that such findings prove merely that people learn to see? Clearly language influences perception and not just memory, at least during childhood. As early as 1915, Peters (cited in Smith, 1943) experi-

---

[3] In a personal communication from D. McNeill in 1966.

mentally produced color matching errors in children through teaching them an artificial vocabulary in which certain colors were lexically indistinguishable. Later, when the children were taught these lexical distinctions, the corresponding perceptual discriminations also appeared. Even earlier, Tucker (1911) observed this same situation naturally and intraculturally; he found that children would group together different colored wools called by the same name. Lenneberg, on the other hand, confirms the notion that this influence of lexicon on perception diminishes with age; for he finds that the absence of certain terminological color distinctions adversely affects color memory in Zuni adults (Lenneberg & Roberts, 1956) and present color perception in Wolof *children* but does not affect present perception in Zuni adults (Lenneberg, 1961). Even adults, however, may fall back on language to aid perception when conditions become particularly difficult, as, for example, when all the relevant stimuli are present but spatially separated (Bruner, Postman & Rodrigues, 1951). Indeed, in terms of the eye movements necessary to visual perception, spatial separation may be translated into a mild form of temporal separation.

McNeill's hypothesis about language affecting only the memory pattern is plainly false. Yet his notions of schema plus correction may still hold. In fact, Ranken (1963) shows that *linguistic coding* in the form of assigning names can help when it is a matter of ordering shapes relative to one another *where it is not necessary to remember their exact form,* but that it can hinder performance in tasks where the precise image of the same stimuli must be utilized (as in a mental jigsaw puzzle). We interpret this outcome to mean that the label helps where a general schema suffices for the cognitive task in question, but that it produces deceptive vagueness where the task actually involves both schema and correction, i.e., an exact image.

A schema can operate *only* when called into play; language affects cognition *only* if a linguistic coding occurs, that is, only if the stimulus is given a verbal representation. It is possible that these conditions prevail only when a task is difficult to perform by means *other* than linguistic coding. But that is a moot point much in need of further investigation. Perhaps, too, different cultures vary in their tendency to use such linguistic encoding. Unschooled Wolof children in our experiment, for instance, showed a much stronger tendency to use ostensive, as opposed to verbal, reasons for their groupings. That is, they would "explain" their grouping choice by pointing to the common pictorial elements. Such ostensive definition may have counteracted the detrimental effects of an inexact vocabulary by bypassing language altogether. We do well to remember, in assessing cross-cultural studies, that most cultures are nontechnically traditional, less verbally oriented than our own.

In summary, it appears from our own and other work that linguistic encoding of the stimuli relevant to a given problem situation can affect the ordering of stimuli by providing a formula for relating them across time (Brown & Lenneberg, 1954; Van de Geer & Frijda, 1961; Lantz, 1963; Lantz & Stefflre, 1964; Koen, 1965) or space, as our Wolof results and the Bruner, Postman and Rodrigues (1951) experiments show. The influence of encoding becomes stronger as cognitive conditions become more difficult, making an ikonic approach to the problem increasingly ineffective and a symbolic approach more crucial. Such conditions are produced as the situation becomes less "simultaneous" and more a matter of memory and as the number of stimuli to be dealt with simultaneously approaches 7 ± 2, the limit of immediate perception and memory (Miller, 1956; Brown & Lenneberg, 1954). These generalizations about the conditions under which linguistic encoding will affect other cognitive operations must be further qualified. They hold only if a linguistic representation is available to the person in question and has been activated.

Whether or not the linguistic effect will be positive or negative depends on the fit between linguistic representation and situation. If linguistic encoding is *inappropriate* to the task at hand, either because the labels do not encode all the necessary information (the mental jigsaw puzzle in Ranken's experiment), or because the labels cut the domain in places other than those the task demands, linguistic organization can have an adverse affect on task performance (e.g., Lenneberg & Roberts, 1956). Whether or not a label encodes all the necessary information depends not only on the task but also on the array of stimuli. A given label becomes ineffective in distinguishing a given stimulus if it must be discriminated from others to which the name could also apply (Lantz & Stefflre, 1964).

We began by considering the part that a lexicon plays in determining the content of equivalence groupings. We have emerged with the conclusion that factors other than lexicon determine the bases or dimensions of equivalence but that a specific lexicon may influence the "band width" of the individual categories that constitute the dimension. In the end, we have seen that the equivalence of two spatially separated stimuli is affected similarly by lexical conditions as that of two temporally separated stimuli. Thus, "equivalence" and recognition have much in common.

Let us turn now from the role of labels per se to the role of a set of hierarchically organized labels, that is, to the role of lexical richness defined in structural terms. There has been much controversy about the role of superordinate words in conceptual thought. The Wolof language, in contrast to French (and to English), has neither the word "color" nor the word "shape." It is clear from the results reported above that the lack of the word "color" does not hinder color groupings from being formed. Does the absence of the general word, however, mean that the Wolofs have no general concept of color? If not, is there much consequence in this seemingly grievous deficit?

Consider Figure 12.1. It is one possible representation of the hierarchical structure of the first set of three pictures used in the present experiment.

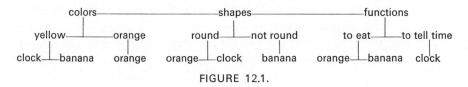

FIGURE 12.1.

If this hierarchical organization corresponds to the type of structure generated by the subject to deal with the task, then his use of the superordinate words "color" or "shape" should indicate that the person is operating at the top of the hierarchy and has access to the entire hierarchy. One would predict, then, that he would be able to supply more than one kind of attribute if pressed. For he is plainly contrasting, say, *color* with *shape* or with *use*. By the same reasoning, his exclusive use of shape names or color names alone (e.g., "round," "yellow") would mean that he was operating one level lower in the hierarchy. He would be "cut off" from the top of the hierarchy and its connections with other branches. He would therefore be less likely to operate in branches other than the one in which he found himself. A concept (a consciously or explicitly recognized concept) is defined as much by what it excludes as by what it includes, by its contrast class. The concept of color per se comes into being through contrast with an opposing idea. An opposing concept to color per se cannot be a specific color: just as "round" is related only to other shapes, so "yellow" relates only to other colors.

If this reasoning is correct, then one would expect that, if a subject ever used an abstract word like "color" or "shape," he would also vary his choice of grouping attributes when asked to make a first and second choice of pairs for each of the three sets of pictures. But if he used only a concrete word like "red," then one would expect him to form nothing but color groupings in all six tasks. Our results do indeed indicate that there is a significant association between use of superordinate words like "color" and "shape" and the number of different types of attribute used for grouping. And this relationship holds when all other factors such as knowledge of French and school grade are held constant. Thus, if a Wolof child uses a superordinate word, his chances of grouping by a variety of attributes are twice as great as those of a child who utilizes no superordinate vocabulary. Recall that when a Wolof child uses the word "color," it is a French word that he is introducing into a Wolof linguistic context.

Although all our experimentation was carried out in Wolof, we also ran additional sixth grade Wolof groups in French in order to assess the effect of using one language or another when all other factors are held constant. The relationship between use of superordinate words and variety of attribute used is weakest under this condition. But before interpreting this finding, consider one further observation. The experiment was also carried out in French with French children in the sixth grade. It is in this experiment that the strongest relationship is found. If a French child uses an abstract "top-of-the-hierarchy" label, he is almost certain to vary his basis of grouping at least once. So we must conclude that access to the pure conceptual hierarchy as diagrammed is indicated by the use of abstract terms *only if* the linguistic terms have been thoroughly mastered in all their semantic implications. Our results indicate that such is the case under normal conditions of spontaneous use in the context of one's native language. But when the Wolof children are interrogated in French, their use of superordinate language seems to have a forced character and indicates little about hierarchical structure and where they are in that structure.

The reasons for color preference among the Wolof are too complicated to discuss here. What needs emphasis is that the basis of equivalence is not an either/or phenomenon, as so much experimentation has assumed. It is, rather, a matter of adding new bases to old and of *integrating them in a hierarchically organized structure*. Everybody is more or less limited in the range of classificatory bases available to him. It is not that one person uses color, the other shape. Rather, one can use color, the other can use shape *and* color. It is the structure of the lexicon and not simply its list of terms that is crucial.

Superordinate class words are not just a luxury for people who do not have to deal with concrete phenomena, as Roger Brown (1958) hypothesizes. In a way quite different from that envisaged by Whorf in the lexical version of his hypothesis, we seem to have found an important correspondence between linguistic and conceptual structure. But it relates not to words in isolation but to their depth of hierarchical imbedding both in the language and in thought. This correspondence has to do not with quantitative richness of vocabulary in different domains or with "accessibility" but with the presence or absence of higher order words that can be used to integrate different domains of words and objects into hierarchical structures. No matter how rich the vocabulary available to describe a given domain, it is of limited use as an instrument of thought if it is not organized into a hierarchy that can be activated as a whole.

Consider now the grammatical aspect of language. In previous work (Vygotsky, 1961; Bruner et al., 1966) the structure of equivalence groupings was found to become increasingly superordinate with age and less complexive and thematic. Superordinate structure is not the same as the use of a general or superordinate word. The attribute that organizes a superordinate group may be general or specific, but it must be explicitly stated to be shared by every member of the group in question. Thus, "they are all the same color" would have the same structural status as "they are all red." In terms of this structural criterion, all the children studied in Senegal conform to the usual development trend. Although the grouping *choices* of our unschooled Wolof group got increasingly systematic with age, their explanations showed a somewhat different form. Instead of explicitly connecting the common attribute to every member of their groupings in the manner described above, they would explain their grouping with a single word, saying, for example, nothing more than "red." What may we make of this?

Consider the matter in purely grammatical terms. For perhaps we can find a connection between conceptual organization and grammatical rules. Let us posit, first, three stages of symbolic reference. The first is the ostensive mode: mere pointing at the object of reference. The second, the labeling mode, consists of nothing more than a verbal tag. This tag replaces or accompanies the operation of pointing. The third mode is sentential. Here the label is integrated into a complete sentence. In the present experiment, these three modes were defined as follows, and the definitions applied to grouping reasons: (1) pointing—no verbal response; (2) labeling—label only; no *verb* in utterance, for example, "red"; (3) sentential placement—complete sentence, for example, "this is red."

Among French monolinguals, pointing is nonexistent even among first graders. Pointing, however, occupies a definite position in the reasoning of all the youngest Wolof groups, especially the unschooled, but disappears in all the groups with advancing age. The other differences set the unschooled children apart from all the school children. In the unschooled groups, labeling, the simple paradigmatic mode, increases with age. But the use of sentential placement does not increase with age but remains at a constantly low level. In all the school groups, both Wolof-French bilingual and French monolingual, the ostensive mode gives way to sentential placement with age and increased schooling. There is, let it be noted, virtually no difference on any criterion between the oldest French monolinguals and the oldest Wolof-French bilinguals *when the experiment is run in French*. The superiority is slightly on the side of the French when the experiment is carried out in the native language of each group. The contrast that is most dramatic is between Wolof children in school speaking French and those not in school speaking Wolof, with virtually no overlap in the distributions. Some 97 per cent of the 11- to 13-year-old Wolof monolinguals (the unschooled Wolof children) use the labeling mode; 90 per cent of the Wolof sixth graders doing the experiment in French use the sentential mode.

These results using grammatical criteria reveal larger differences between the groups who know French and those who do not than those using the earlier, more semantic verbal measure of grouping structure. Is there, however, any direct relation between grammatical and conceptual structure? A child can frame an explicit superordinate structure in either the labeling or sentential modes. This superordinate structure can be of a general or itemized type. An example of a general superordinate language structure in the labeling mode would be "These—round." Expressed sententially, this structure would be "These (or "They") are round." An itemized superordinate in labeling form might be "This—round; this—round." An example of the same structure expressed in the sentential mode would be "This (or "It") is round; this (or "it") is round." Obviously, a limitless variety of nonsuperordinate structures may be expressed either as labels or as complete sentences. It is valid, then, to ask whether the use of a particular mode of reference is associated with a particular conceptual structure. The answer is a strong affirmative for both schooled and unschooled Wolof children. When a school child frames a reason in the sentential mode, the probability that he will form a superordinate structure of either the itemized or general type is on the average almost three times as great as when he uses simple labeling. For an unschooled child, this same probability of a superordinate structure is almost six times as great when his reasons are sentences rather than labels.

For a school child, moreover, the probability that a superordinate structure will be in a general (rather than itemized) form is more than four times as great when a grouping reason is expressed in the sentential mode. In the unschooled groups, the number of reasons falling into these categories is very small. If, however, all four unschooled groups are combined, the relationship does hold: superordinate reasons expressed as labels take the general form about half as often as do those expressed as complete sentences.

We are led to the hypothesis that school is operating on grouping operations through the training embodied in the written language. This hypothesis has a good theoretical basis. The written language, as Vygotsky (1961) points out, provides an occasion in which one must deploy language out of the immediate context of reference. Writing virtually forces a remoteness of reference on the language user. Consequently, he cannot use simple pointing as an aid, nor can he count on labeling that depends on the present context to make clear what his label refers to. Writing, then, is training in the use of linguistic contexts that are independent of the immediate referents. Thus, the embedding of a label in a sentence structure indicates that it is less tied to its situational context and more related to its linguistic context. The implications of this fact for manipulability are great; linguistic contexts can be turned upside down more easily than real ones can. Indeed, the linguistic independence of context achieved by certain grammatical modes appears to favor the development of the more self-contained superordinate structure used by the school children.

Note the recurrence of a theme that has been running through all of our results: it is always the schooling variable that makes qualitative differences in directions of growth. Wolof children who have been to school are more different intellectually from unschooled children living in the same bush village than they are from city children in the same country or from Mexico City, Anchorage, Alaska or Brookline, Massachusetts (Bruner et al., 1966). Similar results demonstrating the huge impact of school have emerged from the Belgian Congo (Cryns, 1962) and South Africa (Biesheuvel, 1949; and personal communication from W. H. O. Schmidt, 1965).

How, then, do school and language interrelate? We may hypothesize that it is the fact of being a *written* language that makes French such a powerful factor in the cognitive growth of the children we have studied. For all of the semantic and syntactic features that we have discussed in relation to concept formation—a rich vocabulary that is hierarchically organized, syntactical embedding of labels, etc.—become necessary when one must communicate *out of the context* of immediate reference. And it is precisely in this respect that written language differs from spoken. But school itself provides the same opportunity to use language out of context—even spoken language—for, to a very high degree, what one talks about are things not immediately present.

SCHOOL, LANGUAGE, AND INDIVIDUALISM

In the last section, the final emphasis was on the role of school in establishing context-independent modes of thinking through the separation of the written word from the thing it stands for and the separation of school from life. How exactly does this process relate to the decline of a "realistic" world view and the correlative rise in self-consciousness discussed in the section before? Realism, as a world view, can characterize a person's concept of language and words, as well as his concept of thought in general. When a word is considered to be as "real" as the thing for which it stands, the psychological attitude (and philosophical position) is called nominal or verbal realism. School separates word and thing and destroys verbal realism by presenting for the first time a situation where words are systematically and continually "there" without their referents. The rules of the "Original Word Game," described by Brown (1958) in which the tutor acts as though things are but signs of their names, are for the first time systematically and thoroughly broken. That is, the sequence object-name no longer is invariant. When names, or symbols in general, no longer inhere in their referents, they must go somewhere; and the logical place is the psyche of the language user. Thus, the separation of word and thing demands a notion that words are in people's heads, not in their referents. (This point has been well made by Ogden and Richards, 1930.) The concepts "thinker" and "thought processes" thus become important in the shedding of nominal realism. Meaning is seen to vary with the particular speaker, and the notion of psychological relativity is born. Implicit in this notion is the distinctness of oneself and one's own point of view. Thus, the individual must conceptually separate himself from the group; he must become self-conscious, aware of having a particular slant on things, a certain individuality.

The destruction of nominal or verbal realism may thus be the wedge that ultimately fragments the unitary solidarity of a "realistic" world view. Once thought has been dissociated from its objects, the stage is set for symbolic processes to run ahead of concrete fact, for thought to be in terms of possibility rather than actuality. At this point, symbolic representation can go beyond the capacities of an ikonic system, to use Bruner's (1964) terms, and the way is open for Piaget's stage of formal operations, where the real becomes but a subset of the possible (Inhelder & Piaget, 1958). So school and the written language may have a privileged position in the shift from a collective to an individualistic orientation chronicled above.

CULTURE AND BIOLOGICAL GROWTH

Lest it be thought that we espouse a view of complete cultural determinism, which we do not, we conclude with some remarks on the interaction of cultural constraints and universal biological maturation.

Because the doctrine that ontogeny recapitulates phylogeny was given too literal a form in biology, a more sophisticated consideration of the relation between phylogeny and ontogeny was also given up. Species-specific behavior does not appear out of the blue. It has evolutionary history, and that history reflects itself in the early growth of the young. We are primates, and our primate heritage affects our growth. All cultures must work on the stuff of the biological organism, specifically on man's primate constraints.

One of the huge discontinuities in man's evolution was his capacity for language and symbolism, and this only gradually achieves realization through training. Sapir (1921) may have been quite right in pointing out that no human language can be shown to be more sophisticated than any other and that the speech used by the member of the Academy is no more complex than that of a Hottentot. But again it was Sapir who pointed out that it is in extracting from our use of language the powerful tools for organizing thought that peoples differ from each other. The intellectual nurturing that makes it possible eventually to use language as a tool of thought requires long years and complex training.

It is here that the difference comes. If that intellectual training is not forthcoming, if language is not freely employed in its pragmatic function of guiding thought and action, then one finds forms of intellectual functioning that are adequate for concrete tasks, but not so for matters involving abstract conception. As Werner (1948) pointed out, "Development among primitive people is characterized on the one hand by precocity and, on the other, by a relatively early arrest of the process of intellectual growth" (p. 27). His remark is telling with respect to the difference we find between school children and those who have not been to school. The latter stabilize earlier and do not go on to new levels of operation. The same "early arrest" characterizes the differences between "culturally-deprived" and other American children (e.g., Deutsch, 1965).

In short, some environments "push" cognitive growth better, earlier, and longer than others. What does not seem to happen is that different cultures produce completely divergent and unrelated modes of thought. The reason for this must be the constraint of our biological heritage.[4] That heritage makes it possible for man to reach a form of intellectual maturity that is capable of elaborating a highly technical society. Less demanding societies—less demanding intellectually—do not produce so much symbolic embedding and elaboration of first ways of looking and thinking. Whether one wishes to "judge" these differences on some universal human scale as favoring an intellectually more evolved man is a matter of one's values. But however one judges, let it be clear that a decision *not* to aid the intellectual maturation of those who live in less technically developed societies can not be premised on the careless claim that it makes little difference. If this chapter shows anything, it is that it makes a huge difference to the intellectual life of a child simply that he was in school.

REFERENCES

ALLPORT, G. W., & PETTIGREW, T. F. Cultural influence on the perception of movement: The trapezoidal illusion among Zulus. *Journal of Abnormal and Social Psychology*, 1957, 55, 104–113.

---

[4] This constraint is, however, somewhat variable in that widespread malnutrition can affect the neurological and mental functions of large groups of people (Biesheuvel, 1943, 1949, 1956, 1963).

BARTLETT, F. C. *Remembering.* Cambridge, England: Cambridge Univer. Press, 1932.

BIESHEUVEL, S. *African intelligence.* Johannesburg: South African Institute of Race Relations, 1943.

BIESHEUVEL, S. Psychological tests and their application to non-European peoples. In *The Yearbook of Education.* London: Evans, 1949. Pp. 87–126.

BIESHEUVEL, S. Aspects of Africa. *The Listener,* 1956, 55, 447–449.

BIESHEUVEL, S. *The human resources of the Republic of South Africa and their development.* Johannesburg: Witwatersrand Univer. Press, 1963.

BOAS, F. *The mind of primitive man.* New York: Macmillan, 1938.

BOGORAS, W. G. *The Chukchee.* New York: G. E. Stechert, 1904–1909. Part 1, *Material culture,* 1904; Part 3, *Social organization,* 1909.

BONTE, M. The reaction of two African societies to the Müller-Lyer illusion. *Journal of Social Psychology,* 1962, 58, 265–268.

BROWN, R. *Words and things.* Glencoe, Ill.: Free Press, 1958.

BROWN, R., & LENNEBERG, E. H. A study in language and cognition. *Journal of Abnormal and Social Psychology,* 1954, 49, 454–462. Reprinted in S. Saporta (Ed.), *Psycholinguistics: A book of readings.* New York: Holt, Rinehart & Winston, 1961. Pp. 480–492.

BRUNER, J. S. The course of cognitive growth. *American Psychologist,* 1964, 19, 1-15.

BRUNER, J. S., OLVER, ROSE R., GREENFIELD, PATRICIA M., ET AL. *Studies in cognitive growth.* New York: Wiley, 1966.

BRUNER, J. S., POSTMAN, L., & RODRIGUES, J. Expectation and the perception of color. *American Journal of Psychology,* 1951, 64, 216–227.

CARROLL, J. B., & CASAGRANDE, J. B. The function of language classifications in behavior. In Eleanor Maccoby, T. M. Newcomb & E. L. Hartley (Eds.), *Readings in social psychology.* New York: Holt, 1958. Pp. 18–31.

CRYNS, A. G. J. African intelligence: A critical survey of cross-cultural intelligence research in Africa south of the Sahara. *Journal of Social Psychology,* 1964, 57, 283–301.

DEUTSCH, M. The role of social class in language development and cognition. *American Journal of Orthopsychiatry,* 1965, 35, 78–88.

DOOB, L. W. The effect of codability upon the afferent and efferent functioning of language. *Journal of Social Psychology,* 1960, 52, 3–15.

DURKHEIM, E., & MAUSS, M. *Primitive classification.* Chicago: Univer. of Chicago Press, 1963.

FLAVELL, J. *The developmental psychology of Jean Piaget.* Princeton, N. J.: Van Nostrand, 1963.

GAY, J. H. Education and mathematics among the Kpelle of Liberia. Paper read at Commission Interunions de l'Enseignement des Sciences, Dakar, January, 1965.

GAY, J. H., & COLE, M. *The new mathematics and an old culture: A study of learning among the Kpelle.* New York: Holt, Rinehart & Winston, 1967.

HUDSON, W. Pictorial depth perception in subcultural groups in Africa. *Journal of Social Psychology,* 1960, 52, 183–208.

INHELDER, B., & PIAGET, J. *Growth of logical thinking from childhood to adolescence.* New York: Basic Books, 1958.

JAHODA, J. Assessment of abstract behaviour in a non-Western culture. *Journal of Abnormal and Social Psychology,* 1956, 53, 237–243.

KARDINER, A. Lecture at Harvard University, Cambridge, Mass., April, 1965.

KESTELOOF, LILYAN. *Aimé Césaire.* Paris: Editions Presse Seghers, 1962.

KLUCKHOHN, FLORENCE R., & STRODTBECK, F. L. *Variations in value orientations.* Evanston, Ill.: Row, Peterson, 1961.

KOEN, F. The codability of complex stimuli: Three modes of representation. Unpublished paper, Univer. of Michigan, Ann Arbor, Mich., 1965.

KOFFKA, K. *Principles of Gestalt psychology.* New York: Harcourt, Brace, 1935.

KOHLER, W. Psychological remarks on some questions of anthropology. *American Journal of Psychology,* 1937, 58, 271–288. Reprinted in Mary Henle (Ed.), *Documents of Gestalt psychology.* Berkeley, Calif.: Univer. of California Press, 1961. Pp. 203–221.

LANTZ, DOROTHY L. Color naming and color recognition: A study in the psychology of language. Unpublished doctoral dissertation, Harvard Univer., 1963.

LANTZ, DOROTHY L., & STEFFLRE, V. Language and cognition revisited. *Journal of Abnormal and Social Psychology,* 1964, 69, 472–481.

LENNEBERG, E. H. Color naming, color recognition, color discrimination: A reappraisal. *Perceptual and Motor Skills,* 1961, 12, 375–382.

LENNEBERG, E. H., & ROBERTS, J. M. The language of experience: A study in methodology. *International Journal of American Living,* Supplement, 1956, 22 (Memoir 13).

LÉVI-STRAUSS, C. *La Pensée sauvage.* Paris: Plon, 1962.

LINDZEY, G. *Projective techniques and cross-cultural research.* New York: Appleton-Century-Crofts, 1961.

LURIA, A. R. *The role of speech in regulation of normal and abnormal behavior.* New York: Liveright, 1961.

MACLAY, H. An experimental study of language and non-linguistic behavior. *Southwestern Journal of Anthropology,* 1958, 14, 220–229.

McNEILL, D. Anthropological psycholinguistics. Unpublished paper, Harvard Univer., 1965.

MEAD, MARGARET. Research on primitive children. In L. Carmichael (Ed.), *Manual of child psychology.* New York: Wiley, 1946. Pp. 735–789.

MILLER, G. A. The magical number 7, plus or minus 2: Some limits on our capacity for processing information. *Psychological Review,* 1956, 63, 81–97.

MONTEIL, V. *L'Islam noir.* Paris: Editions du Seuil, 1964.

OGDEN, C. K., & RICHARDS, I. A. *The meaning of meaning.* (3rd Rev. Ed.) New York: Harcourt, Brace, 1930.

PIAGET, J. *The child's conception of physical causality.* London: Kegan Paul, 1930.

PIAGET, J. *The child's conception of number.* New York: Humanities Press, 1952.

PRICE-WILLIAMS, D. R. A study concerning concepts of conservation of quantities among primitive children. *Acta Psychologica,* Amsterdam, 1961, 18, 297–305.

RABAIN-ZEMPLÉNI, JACQUELINE. Quelques réfléxions sur les modes fondamentaux de relations chez l'enfant wolof du sevrage à l'intégration dans la classe d'âge. Paris: Association Universitaire pour le Développement de l'Enseignement et de la culture en Afrique et à Madagascar, 1965.

RANKEN, H. B. Language and thinking: Positive and negative effects of naming. *Science,* 1963, 141, 48–50.

RIVERS, W. H. R. Observations on the senses of the Todas. *British Journal of Psychology,* 1905, 1, 322–396.

SAPIR, E. *Language: An introduction to the study of speech.* New York: Harcourt, Brace, 1921.

SMITH, H. C. Age differences in color discrimination. *Journal of General Psychology,* 1943, 29, 191–226.

STRODTBECK, F. L. Considerations of meta-method in cross-cultural studies. In A. K. Romney & R. G. D'Andrade (Eds.), *Trans-cultural studies in cognition. American Anthropologist,* Special Publication, 1964, 66, 223–229.

STURTEVANT, W. C. Studies in ethnoscience. In A. K. Romney & R. G. D'Andrade (Eds.), Trans-cultural studies in cognition. *American Anthropologist,* Special Publication, 1964, 66, 99–131.

TUCKER, A. W. Observations on the color vision of school children. *British Journal of Psychology,* 1911, 4, 33–43.

VAN DE GEER, J. P., & FRIJDA, N. H. Codability and recognition: An experiment with facial expressions. *Acta Psychologica,* Amsterdam, 1961, 18, 360–367.

VYGOTSKY, L. S. *Thought and language.* New York: MIT Press and Wiley, 1961.

WERNER, H. *Comparative psychology of mental development.* Chicago: Follett, 1948.

WHORF, B. L. *Language, thought, and reality.* J. B. Carroll (Ed.) Cambridge, Mass.: Technology Press, 1956.

WINTRINGER, J. Considérations sur l'intelligence du Noir africain. *Revue de Psychologie des Peuples,* 1955, 10, 37–55.

PART II
CONTENT OF SOCIALIZATION

CHAPTER **13**

The Acquisition Of Language

James J. Jenkins

University of Minnesota

There is wide agreement that the socialization of the child is enormously facilitated by, or even largely dependent upon, his comprehension of language.
Thus, language learning (or, more generally, language development) has
ranked high in importance as a topic in social psychology. Indeed, the recent
Social Psychology by Brown (1965) devotes almost one-seventh of its pages to
the topic of language acquisition and the role of language in social behavior.

Similarly, those psychologists who are concerned with developing a psychology of language have recognized from the very infancy of the field that
language development was a key problem that demanded adequate description
and explanation. Blumenthal (1968) in reviewing the early research in psycholinguistics, selects the acquisition of language as the most intensively studied
problem and points out that the theoretical issues involved are crucial to one's
entire position in the field.

It is obvious that having a psychology of language and having a theory of
language development are both intimately related to what one thinks language
is. One could suppose, for example, as Wundt did in his classic works (1900,
1901), that the "total idea" of a sentence was primary and that the "idea" was
reduced to the elements of speech by a process of analysis. Alternatively, one
could, along with Paul (1886), suppose that the word-concept was primary
and that a synthetic process was required to build a sentence up from the isolated elements. One could, in accord with the writings of behaviorists like Watson (1925), focus attention on language as speech and treat it as a motor-skill
system. Or one could with the neo-behaviorist, Skinner (1957) deal with the
"utterance" as the functional unit and treat whole language sequences as unitary instrumental acts.

Language, more clearly than any other subject matter area, shows the

Preparation of this paper was supported in part by grants to the University of Minnesota, Center for Research in Human Learning, from the National Science Foundation
(GS 1761), the National Institute of Child Health and Human Development (PO
1-HD-01136) and the Graduate School of the University of Minnesota.

critical interaction of the nature of the subject matter and the nature of the appropriate psychology. Language is obviously multi-leveled and many-dimensional. It can be viewed as being organized in an endless variety of ways. The particular way one takes it, largely determines the kind of psychology that one develops as being appropriate for it. Conversely, if one is wedded to a particular kind of psychology, that fact alone may determine what he thinks language must be.

As an illustration, consider the following: A fundamental polarity with regard to language is with respect to the nativist-empiricist position. Students of language have held positions varying from the radical view that any isolated normal child will develop a language of his own to the equally radical view that language learning is simply a matter of automatic learning processes shared by men and lower animals alike. The first position argues that the child generates language naturally as a result of being human, and the second argues that the child speaks because that activity happens to be something that is rewarded in the kind of culture we have designed. The first sees a radical discontinuity between lower animals and men; the second sees only quantitative differences in the number of associations which can be readily formed.

These views are clearly the product of the times at which men worked and reflect changes in both psychology and linguistics and their interactions (see Fodor, 1966). The science of linguistics came into great intellectual prominence (as philology and historical linguistics) shortly before the birth of psychology an an independent discipline. The early experimental psychologists had a picture of language as a system that was gradually changing over time but preserving important and powerful internal relationships. Because the only language family that had been studied in detail was Indo-European, there were massive sets of common features that seemed to be the constants of language. Psychologists such as Wundt felt that language preserved important aspects of the functioning of the human mind that could not be captured by any other form of investigation.

With the study of the languages of the American Indians in their apparent wild diversity, however, the supposed "universal" nature of the Indo-European languages was ripped to shreds (see Boas, 1911). Languages were discovered which appeared to be radically different from any kinds previously known and the pendulum of scientific thought began to swing in the other direction. Perhaps it was possible for a language to take any form whatsoever; perhaps all languages were completely arbitrary and any set of conventions or rules could be employed. Perhaps the consistency of Western thought itself was due to the homogeneity of languages rather than to a common understanding of the world. Perhaps, as Sapir (1929, 1939) and Whorf (1956) argued, language determined the nature of the mind instead of vice versa.

It is not hard to see that the first point of view is readily compatible with a psychology that stresses the nature of the mind and of thought as "given" or innate and that the second is compatible with a psychology that stresses the role of environment and the plastic nature of the mind. The relationship is not absolute, of course. One *can* be an environmentalist under the first system and a nativist under the second, but one's belief about language is one of the powerful pressures that finally determines one's total psychological position, or conversely, is determined by it.

But such general issues are not at all the only ways that one's notion of language affects one's psychology. At a much more specific level, the analysis of language determines the kind of psychology one writes for it. There is no end of variation here but four examples will suggest the range of views that have been popular in the last forty years concerning the acquisition of language. Roughly characterized, the four models are: language as words; language as strings of words or classes; language as utterances; language as a structural system.

Each of these views stresses some aspect of language that is salient in the course of language development and each furnishes an "explanation" of such development. In a pedagogical sense each is valuable in calling attention to its own class of phenomena and that is useful even if the position itself must be abandoned later for a more inclusive system.

LANGUAGE AS WORDS

One fact about language that seems obvious to all of us is that language is made up of words. This must have been obvious to the ancients as well, since there appear to have been many systems of writing based on some sort of characterization for every word (sign writing, pictograms, ideograms, etc.) long before the alphabetic system (based on a small number of sounds) was developed (for discussion, see Brown, 1958). For a variety of reasons, word-based systems of writing are hard to learn and difficult to use and with a few notable exceptions (such as Chinese) they have been replaced by the more efficient alphabetic systems. Yet, their widespread existence confirms the saliency of "wordiness" of language. Every child seems to discover that "things" have names and goes through a period in which "What is it?" is a constant question and a name (a word) is the standard response. We recognize the status of words today by marking them with blank spaces on either side when we write them and we find it difficult to read material in which this convention has not been followed:

Removingspacessometimesdeletescuesthatareusedbyreaders.

Fal ses pac eso fte ncr eat edi ffi cul tie sfo rth ere ade r.

For these reasons and many more the word has been a frequent candidate for the unit of analysis of language.

If one thinks of language as consisting of words, its acquisition presents no formidable problem. One merely has to show how a child learns words. This can be viewed in two ways: first, as the motor skill that is involved in saying words and, second, as the process of getting the words attached to meanings. The traditional analysis of this problem rests on a fairly straightforward combination of instrumental learning and classical conditioning.

According to this view, the child begins to acquire language by making noises almost at random, making the full range of possible vocal tract sounds. As he approaches the kinds of sounds actually used in the language of his parents and nurses, he receives explicit reward and reinforcement from the parents who are eager to hear him talk and can be counted on to hear him say words and give him attention and praise if there is any excuse at all ("Listen, dear, he said, 'Da-Da'."). Further, the closer he gets to the language sounds, the more he receives secondary reinforcement, accruing to the noises themselves; that is, as he approximates the sounds made by the people who provide him with primary reinforcement in the form of food, comforts, etc., those noises serve as reinforcements. Thus, we see the parents "shaping" vocal behavior by their reinforcing activities and the child "shaping" himself as the noises become closer and closer to those of the language and, hence, more secondarily reinforcing. In this fashion it is supposed the child learns to make the sounds and sound sequences that are important in the language. The same forces lead him to "drop out" the "foreign" and unusual sounds that he made at an early age. (For detailed accounts see Irwin & Chen, 1946; Miller & Dollard, 1941; Mowrer, 1950, 1954; Osgood, 1953; Osgood & Sebeok, 1954.)

While this view offers an account of the imitations of language and provides the child with the necessary skills to talk, it is clear that this procedure does not in itself provide the sounds and sound sequences with meaning. The traditional view with respect to meaning focuses on reference and is usually solved by simple association or an appeal to classical conditioning. The child learns behavior that is appropriate to objects in the world. He learns to hold and suck on a bottle; hold, squeeze, grasp and throw a ball, etc. Now (as represented in the famous paradigm used by Floyd Allport, 1924) when the ball is presented to the child, it serves as the unconditioned stimulus for all the relevant responses to ball. If, at the same time, the parent says "ball," this will play the role of the conditioned stimulus and, as a result of classical conditioning, the word "ball" will be associated with the responses appropriate to the object, ball. If the child has learned to imitate as suggested above (or if there is a circular auditory-oral reflex as Allport hypothesized), he will say some approximation of "ball" on hearing the world "ball" and thus, again by simple association, will learn to label objects correctly. Therefore, simple Pavlovian conditioning with a few assists from instrumental conditioning accounts for both the development of *understanding* of language (words associated with objects and words associated with appropriate responses) and the ability to *use* language correctly (objects elicit the right words).

The only other kind of meaning that is considered is "emotional meaning" which is also subsumed under the conditioning paradigm. Words, or the objects they represent, are experienced under pleasant or unpleasant conditions and the responses to the conditions are associated to the words and objects by classical conditioning. Thus if a child's mother does not like spiders and he is around his mother when she is frightened by a spider, it is likely that the emotional state of the child will be one of distress because his mother is disturbed and that this distress will become associated with the sight of the spider and the words that the mother speaks, "Look out for the spider!" "Oh! There's a spider!" etc. The child thus will wind up with the same fears and biases as his parents and will associate the same emotional responses to many people and institutions (see Osgood, 1953; Osgood, Suci & Tannenbaum, 1957; Staats & Staats, 1957). Other accounts of learning what words mean put more stress on conceptual categories and hypotheses but are not too far from the associative account (Brown, 1958, furnishes a good example).

The further development of language is easy to chart once it has started. McCarthy (1930, 1954) has summarized a great deal of the data on language growth in her reviews of children's language. If one counts the number of words the child knows, this shows steady growth virtually throughout the entire life span. If one counts the number of words per sentence, this increases over the early years and stabilizes at about adolescence. Comparable figures are available for the number of words spoken per day, the average length of written sentences, the number and proportion of simple sentences used, the number and proportion of complex sentences used, etc.

For this view of language the questions of growth are mainly solved by charting number of units at each age level. The description of the growth is the expected resultant of the variables earlier enumerated and, once the growth has been simply described, the task is pretty much over. The view has been especially important in calling attention to vocabulary limitations of children and the importance of word-frequency considerations. In both these respects the impact of this model on education has been very considerable. It has been the custom, ever since Thorndike's early work on word counts, to devise reading materials for school children on the basis of frequency of usage data and vocabulary size restrictions (see Thorndike & Lorge, 1944). Thus, a typical grade school "reader" has been carefully crafted to introduce new words at some given rate and in order of frequency of usage for the most part so that the child will learn the most useful materials as rapidly as possible. In similar fashion the number of words per sentence is carefully monitored and increases steadily over the training years.

Vocabulary measures themselves constitute an interesting literature (see Miller, 1951; Jersild & Ritzman, 1938; Young, 1941). Most people know more words than they use in their everyday speech so it is customary to speak of a passive (recognition) vocabulary and an active (speaking) vocabulary. It is also plain that different words are used by the same person when he speaks and when he writes so one might further divide them into writing and speaking vocabularies. Further reflection suggests that this is not the end. One uses different vocabularies with his friends, his church group, his maiden aunt, his professional colleagues, etc. Special vocabularies may grow up in relation to hobbies, crafts, trades, professions, political, social, fraternal, economic groups, etc.

This observation of multiple vocabularies has two consequences. We expect on the one hand that the behavior of the individual will change in relevant ways as he moves from one group to another. On the other hand we expect that the vocabularies that one knows will reflect and indicate the situations in which he uses language. In addition, one's general vocabulary varies with intelligence and is the single best predicter of scholastic success. Thus, this aspect of language justifies its measurement by serving useful practical predictive purposes. (Tyler, 1965, discusses its relation to intelligence, age and sex differences.)

Word-frequency counts have been found to index many interesting relationships that hold for samples of written language. In addition, word frequencies enter into many psychological activities involving perception, learning, recall and problem solving. Miller (1951) offers the most complete single account of word frequency phenomena but other interesting materials will be found in Zipf (1935, 1949), Pierce (1961) and Cherry (1957). The major phenomena can be characterized under two headings: Zipf's law and frequency as a psychological facilitator.

Zipf's law refers to a set of relationships found to hold for many diverse counts of language (ranging from Joyce's *Ulysses* to a compilation of newspaper stories). In the simplest and best known form it states that the frequency of usage of a word multiplied by its rank order yields a constant for any given large-sized text. This means that if one makes a word count and then orders the words in accord with their frequency, the relationship of those frequencies will form an orderly series. If the frequency of the first word is 5,000, the frequency of the second should be 2,500, the frequency of the third should be 1,666, etc., down to the five-thousandth word which should have a frequency of only one. Zipf interprets these and other phenomena in terms of a model which treats with the tension between listeners and speakers as each tries to follow the "law of least effort" but other writers have attempted more statistically sophisticated explanations (see Mandelbrot, 1953; Howes, 1964).

Word frequencies enter into psychological experimentation largely as indices which predict the ease or difficulty of using a particular word in experimentation. All other things being equal, a more frequent word will be seen more readily in a brief visual exposure (Howes & Solomon, 1951), will be heard more clearly through masking noise (Rosenzweig & Postman, 1958), will be more readily guessed with negligible cues (Goldiamond & Hawkins, 1958), will be more easily learned (Underwood & Schulz, 1960) and will have a higher probability as an association (Howes, 1957).

All of these phenomena studied in children and adults and found in adult writing give supporting evidence to those who maintain that much of what is important about language is to be found in treating it as a collection of words and that these important units are strong contributors to all language phenomena.

LANGUAGE AS STRINGS OF WORDS

While the study of language as consisting of words is both interesting and rewarding, it is clear that we have not "explained language" with that simple conception. The second thing that "everybody knows" about language is that the words are ordered or combined in sequences and that the exact pattern of the sequence is of critical importance. "Brutus killed Caesar" has radically different meaning from "Caesar killed Brutus." "The little girl rode on a horse" is a clear and unambiguous sentence in English but an alphabetical assembly of the same words is just a list, "a, girl, horse, little, on, rode, the." Ordering by word length is no help, "a, on, the, girl, rode, horse, little" and inverting the original order is just nonsense, "Horse a on rode girl little the." Clearly, what a collection of words means may be dependent on the ordering of the words, as in the first example, and whether a string of words has any meaning whatsoever may depend on the ordering, as in the second example. In general, if one takes a sentence of ten words or so and starts putting the words in all possible orders (there are 3,628,800 possible orders for ten words), only a handful will be found that make English sentences and even they may not say anything reasonable. A collection of words must be ordered properly to form an instance of language.

This view takes on, then, the responsibility of accounting for not only words but the ordering of words in sentences as they are spoken and as they are understood. There are two general approaches to this problem. One is to take the tack that humans engage in probability learning and that words are probabilistically linked together in productive arrangements. The other approach asserts that the words that are learned are learned as members of classes and that certain sequences of classes form permissible sequences. Both of these approaches are readily related to the general American associationistic tradition. Both of them promise rigorous solutions of the ordering problems without invoking mysterious "structures." Both draw attention to interesting language phenomena. Finally, they may easily be fused in a joint model, which can be characterized as the probabilistic linking of classes of words, the words themselves having varying probabilities of membership in the classes.

The view that this task can be taken on with the usual tools of the psychological tradition is of some importance and is vigorously disputed. In a classic paper, Lashley (1951) set the problem of serial order with confidence that it could not be solved within the simple associationist tradition. Miller (1951) however, treats with a variety of efforts to evaluate sequence effects in language and language-like materials, without supposing new devices; Osgood and Sebeok (1954) tie the traditional psychological tools together with Information Theory, the new statistic of the 1950's, and offer the package to solve the problem. Many psychological writings of the late 1950's and early 1960's discussing order effects in language and language learning (e.g., Deese, 1961; Jenkins, 1965; Jenkins & Palermo, 1964; Braine, 1963a, 1963b; Brown & Berko, 1960) are predicated on the assumption that the task can be thus undertaken.

It was early seen (Osgood & Sebeok, 1954) that the tools of psychology were well adapted to the linguistics of the period. What Hockett (1961) has called the "item and arrangement grammar" is ideally designed for a "class and class-sequence" psychological explanation. If the item and arrangement grammar will account for the structure of everything that counts as language, then the only task is to make the psychological class and class-sequence mechanism plausible because the two systems are formally the same and the class-sequence machinery can do exactly what the item and arrangement grammar can do. The linguists and psychologists found one another's accounts of language and one another's philosophies of science readily compatible. Both were behavioristic, operationalistic and positivistic. Both believed that they were completely objective and that solutions to complex problems were found by attacking the lowest order elements first and proceeding upward steadily and inexorably. Maclay (1964) has characterized the relation of the fields in the early 1950's as "marked by an air of interdisciplinary celebration."

Persuasive evidence for the point of view of probability chains is readily obtained with almost any sort of sequential language task. If, for example, one is asked to complete the following sentence: "The little———is playing in the yard," it is apparent that the choice of words to fill this blank is quite limited. The most obvious choices are all singular animate nouns (e.g., dog, cat, squirrel, boy, girl, child), and the most popular choices are in practice more likely to be limited to singular, animate, human nouns.

The same kind of constraint is found for letters within words, to take another example. Thus, if we have a three-letter word, we can investigate the degree of constraint at each position. The sequence "s–p" offers only four possibilities (sap, sip, sop, sup) ; the sequence "sa–" has at least nine possible endings (sad, sag, sam, san, sap, sas, sat, saw, say) ; and the sequence "–ap" has eleven permissible beginnings (cap, fap, gap, jap, lap, map, nap, pap, rap, sap, tap and possibly bap and zap). This suggests that vowels carry less information than consonants (which is generally true) and that different positions are differentially constrained.

Experimentation in the area leads to two very general, reasonable conclusions: The more context there is, the narrower is the choice at any one point. The fewer members of the class there are, the more restricted is the choice.

The account of the acquisition of language here is easily imagined. It begins exactly like the single word model sketched before. Then, when single words are well learned and related to objects and events in the world, the emphasis shifts to permissible or useful word sequences and the learning of many such sequences. As the sequences become learned, words are associated to the words that precede and that follow them, essentially as a chain, A-B-C-D, for example. As many linguistic chains are learned, overlapping chains are encountered. Chains that overlap create interfering or conflicting associations. If, for example, one has learned A-B-C-D and A-B-C-E, then the sequence A-B-C will give rise simultaneously to both the terms D and E. This event (their simultaneous arousal) is sufficient to cause the association of D and E, even if they have never occurred together in overt discourse. This means that words that can occur at the same place in a string of words will become related to each other as class members.

This kind of indirect association, usually called *mediated association,* assures the development of classes that are required by the adult grammar. Indeed, it can be seen that it is a kind of ideal solution if one permits classes of different strength. The words that most overlap in terms of similar contexts will be the most tightly bound together and those that overlap rarely will be least tightly bound. Thus, one can explain the high strength of the association of the words *boy* and *girl* on the grounds that these two words must occur in many of the same sentences at very high rates. They are not only grammatically equivalent but also semantically very similar (they share the features: young, animate, human, small, noisy, etc.). Thus, mediated associations lead to classes or clusters of words that serve both grammatical and semantic purposes.

We can give this sketch some realistic support by looking at the utterances of children when they begin speaking two-word sentences. Virtually all investigators of children at this stage (about 18 months to two years) report essentially the same phenomena. Brown and Fraser (1963), Braine (1963b) and Miller and Ervin (1964) report the use of two-word sentences involving some kind of "pivot word" or "operator" and a class of other words that are in general substitutable under the other pivots or operators. The pivot words are never used together though the content class members sometimes are. Thus one may get "Where bear." "Where doll." "Where box." "Where train." etc.; and the corresponding utterances "Fix bear." "Fix doll." "Fix box." "Fix train." etc. If a new "pivot word" or "operator" appears such as "there" or "gimme," we are not at all surprised to see all (or a good proportion) of the content class used in this frame as appropriate conditions arise.

One may think of these classes as protoclasses which undergo progressive refinement into finer and finer subdivision as the child's language skills increase and as new demands are made for linguistic accuracy. Animate and inanimate classes, for example, may be early differentiated as different operators are found to be appropriate to one and not the other.

While the device of mediated association for the production of classes may not appear at first to be particularly powerful, it can be made to do a great deal of semantic and grammatical work. It also has the advantage of fitting data from classic psychological situations which had been puzzling earlier. For example, word associations have been collected by psychologists for clinical and experimental reasons for almost 100 years. Within the theories of association, however, it remained a curiosity that the stimulus word and the response word in word association tended to be for the same part of speech for adults, though they were commonly of succeeding parts of speech for children (see Woodworth, 1938; and Woodworth and Schlosberg, 1954, for a discussion). This shift is now nicely expressed as a consequence of increasing linguistic sophistication with age. Similarly, Jenkins and Russell (1960) and Jenkins and Palermo (1965) report changes in word associations for given age groups over the last fifty years. These shifts are in the same directions as the shift observed with increasing age. The writers attribute the shift to the increasing exposure to language as a result of the advent of modern communications, increased schooling, higher literacy, etc.

More specific and to the point, there is direct experimental reason to believe that the mechanism postulated above does work in the manner described and that it is closely related to children's language development. The most systematic study of the effects of mediated association was performed by Horton and Kjeldergaard (1961). The one most pertinent to the present discussion is McNeill's. McNeill (1963) performed an experiment in which nonsense terms were embedded in strings of sentences which subjects were required to learn. The nonsense words were arranged so that identical sequences led to different nonsense terms as indicated: ".....nonsense term 1..........nonsense term X....."; ".....nonsense term 1..........nonsense term Y..." As learning of the sentences progressed, the subjects were given association tests involving the nonsense terms. At the beginning of learning, the terms elicited one another randomly; with some learning, the early term in a sequence (nonsense term 1) was found to elicit its appropriate sequential nonsense terms (X and Y). Finally, when the sentences were well learned, the nonsense terms occupying the same positions began to elicit each other (X elicits Y as a response). This is exactly in accord with the theoretical expectation, of course.

In the natural setting Brown and Berko (1960) gave association tests and tests measuring grammatical development to preschool children and children in the early grades. They found, as did Ervin (1961), that associations change from sequential word pairings (*dark-night*) to "same part of speech" pairings (*dark-light*) as children grow older. They also discovered that the change in the kind of word association given was correlated with the ability to make grammatical use of new words introduced in a linguistic context. In short, the marginal conditions that should have been found, if the associative origin of classes were true, were in fact observed.

In a very general sense this theory of speech classes arising through the automatic operations of associations has a theory of meaning accompanying it. The meaning of any particular word is, of course, still determined by the combination of instrumental and Pavlovian conditioning as it was above, but only at the beginning of language development. As soon as word-to-word associations begin to appear, a "network theory" of meaning begins to emerge. (This has been developed in its most elaborate form by Deese, 1965.) The meaning of a word is now not only the primary experiences that may have accompanied it but also involves in some fashion the meanings of the words that are associated with it. Thus, an enormous richness is developed and the meaning of terms is greatly enhanced. In this way it may be argued that associations are not only guides to the structure of language but also guides to meaning and thought, a point that had long been argued by many clinicians.

The interesting relationships found to hold for word association phenomena in language and in many other psychological activities have strengthened the view that this is an important way to look at language. Word association data display an orderly structure in themselves (see Deese, 1962, 1965). The distribution of word association responses by frequencies is much like Zipf's law, treated above. The most popular response to a stimulus has a very high frequency, the next most popular falls off rapidly, etc., in most cases preserving something very much like the Zipf-type relationship (Skinner, 1937). Word associations can be used to show organization of verbal materials in learning and free recall and a host of studies have explored such associative organization as a function of many measures and conditions (see Cofer, 1965, for review). Word associations have been used in many studies of perception, learning and transfer to demonstrate the ease with which behavior may be modified when associative connections are present to facilitate the new behavior (see Jenkins, 1963, for a discussion).

Overall, there is a wealth of information on the phenomena of association, the emergence of associates in classes as a result of mediated association, the facilitation of behavior through associative chains and classes and the like. In addition, it is easy to show the effects of highly determined versus weakly determined sequences in perception and other tasks. (The classic study is Miller & Selfridge, 1950.) The formulation has its greatest difficulty, however, in giving a reasonable account of the assembly problem; namely, the sequencing of classes. No one has elaborated any view beyond some general form of "probabilistic learning" for the formation of the permissible sequences of classes of words. Further, the problem of class sequences does not yield in any simple manner to known psychological mechanisms. It is an easy task to show in the laboratory that animals can learn chains of behaviors of great length and complexity. But so far, this has been done only for chains of specific items rather than classes. A rat can be induced to build up a behavior sequence that consists of pulling a chain, getting a marble, rolling it across a track, pushing it up a ramp and dropping it in a hole. Such demonstrations are common and are usually constructed by beginning at the goal and working backwards (e.g., the marble is lodged on the edge of the hole and the rat is rewarded for any movement towards it, then for any movement that knocks it in, then for moving it a quarter inch so it falls in the hole, etc.). It is *not* easy to show how these behaviors and all their variants can be assembled in other chains for other purposes. Further, there is no evidence that language sequences are built up in this fashion (back-to-front in minute steps) even for particular sequences.

The more one examines this problem the more difficult it becomes. If there is no mechanism that specifies how sequences are to be formed, perhaps one could begin with a list of the permissible sequences and watch for their occurrence or study their development. But there is no list of the permissible sequences, nor is it clear that children either hear or produce an abundance of permissible sequences as they develop language. Braine (1963a, 1963b) tried to circumvent this difficulty by holding that children associate terms with positions in sentences and that they manifest "contextual generalization" which gets them to "similar" positions in other sentences. A rejoinder by Bever, Fodor and Weksel (1965a) disputed that even this general kind of move could solve the sequencing problem and argued that there were too many different sentence forms and that children must learn an underlying grammar rather than a surface grammar anyway. The argument is fairly instructive (see also Braine,

1965; and Bever, Fodor & Weksel, 1965b) but the problem is set rather than solved.

Support for some kind of contextual generalization can be found in experiments such as Werner and Kaplan's (1952) but the generalization may be the result of linguistic development rather than the predecessor of it. Similarly, studies showing that children are sensitive to the semantics and syntactics of form classes, such as those of Brown and Berko (Berko, 1958; Brown, 1957; and Brown & Berko, 1960), tell us that the child has indeed detected the correlations that are present but they do not serve to tell us how he has detected them. While writers sometimes appeal to semantic factors in language learning (Jenkins & Palermo, 1964), and, indeed, they surely must play a role, there has been no explication of that role that is sufficiently explicit to test.

Thus, while classes may be generated by associative processes and semantic correlates may be established, neither of these suffices to account for the phenomena which generated the view being considered, the impressive facts of ordering in language.

LANGUAGE AS UTTERANCE

The orientations toward language given above have appealed to simple notions of what one knows about language; namely, that it is composed of words and that it has important ordering properties. A different approach is possible and has been recommended by the famous psychologist, B. F. Skinner. In his book *Verbal Behavior* (1957) Skinner argues that one should come to language as to any other behavior and ask what the functional units are, rather than assuming that they are immediately given in one's prior conception of the nature of language. His contention is that language is of special psychological interest in that it happens to be behavior which is reinforced only by other beings; it does not produce any reinforcement or serve any biological function apart from its effect on someone else.

The questions for Skinner are concerned with the functional stimuli for verbal utterances, the functional classes of the responses evidenced by the speaker, and the reinforcements that are applied to increase the probability of given classes of behaviors in the presence of given stimuli. Language enters in not only on the stimulus side and the response side but also as a powerful source of reinforcements. It is firmly asserted that the behavior of the organism is at all times a resultant of his past history and current circumstances and that the task of the psychologist is to make clear how these variables control the behavior. The ultimate test for Skinner is the prediction and control of functional units of behavior, not the accounting for behavior as it happens to be described by someone else (e.g., the linguist). He suggests that one keep in mind "specific engineering tasks" such as teaching, giving instructions, supplying information and doing therapy to make sure that one is considering the kinds of processes and relationships which are truly productive; that is, those that will help us achieve these goals effectively.

Verbal behavior is seen as being importantly divided into two great functional classes—*mands* and *tacts*. Mands are verbal behaviors which function to obtain some specific reinforcement for the organism and are under the general control of the states of deprivation or needs of the organism. Examples might be: "Please pass the salt," "Water!" "Got any cigarettes?" "Can I have something to eat?" etc. (The word comes from com*mand*, de*mand*, etc.) Tacts are verbal behaviors which say something about the state of the world. Examples might be: "It's raining outside," "Here comes the postman," "There's bread in the cupboard," etc. (The word comes from con*tact*, suggesting contact with the world.)

It is readily seen that mands work for the speaker and are successful to the extent that they bring about the desired reward. Thus, mands are "shaped" like any other instrumental acts and are maintained in strength by reinforcement. When a mand stops working in a given situation, it will be extinguished. (A child will "fuss" to get its mother's attention as long as she provides it in response to that behavior. If she stops, the child eventually stops too.)

It is more difficult to see how tacts work since they are not in any obvious sense to the speaker's advantage. They do, however, provide the listener with some information. Skinner argues that the reporting of tacts is maintained by the interested listener through a program of *generalized reinforcement*. The listener cannot always use food or any other single reward as a reinforcer because the tact may be needed when the speaker is not hungry. Thus, a generalized reinforcer like praise, smiling, thanks, etc., is substituted. This presumably has its reinforcing power through the mechanism of secondary reinforcement and because its wide generality and constant association with primary reinforcement does not "wear out" as a reinforcer.

To these two major categories of verbal behavior Skinner adds a number of useful minor categories. *Echoic* responses are those which echo language just heard. Such responses can be reinforced in a general manner to produce imitation of verbal behavior itself as a response. This obviously is an important asset to the acquisition of new items of language behavior. *Textual* responses are those of reading either out loud or silently and represent important skills to acquire and powerful mechanisms for governing subsequent behavior, both verbal and otherwise. *Intraverbal* responses are associations between verbal items and other verbal items. At this point Skinner includes all of the word association behaviors studied above as raw material on which the organism can work in the process of "composing" new utterances. In addition, he regards almost all academic knowledge as a process of building up appropriate sets of intraverbal responses. Finally, as a special class of intraverbals, Skinner discusses *autoclitics* or, more simply, verbal behavior about one's own verbal behavior. For example, one may say, "I guess . . .," "I think . . .," "I'm sure . . ." as indications about the degree of strength he means to assign to whatever sentence it is that follows the phrase.

One of the great virtues of Skinner's approach is that it keeps the investigator focused on the task that language is supposed to be doing. His view calls attention especially to the role of the audience in creating a stimulus situation controlling language and in providing reinforcements that further shape language behavior.

The Skinnerian view obviously holds that reinforcement plays the key role in the development of language. It does not concern itself with problems such as the development of classes and sequences other than to point out that every time the speaker more closely approximates the language of his community, his likelihood of reinforcement increases and the time delay before reinforcement decreases. Therefore, it is a fair conclusion that language behavior approaches the normative language by some sort of successive approximation. It is idle to speculate on the particular physiological machinery involved, just as it is idle to speculate on the particular musculature involved when a rat depresses a lever in a Skinner box. The only things that count are the conditions which set the contingencies for reinforcement. If the Skinner box is set up appropriately, an experimenter can put a rat in it and come back in a few hours with the certainty that the rat will be pressing the bar lawfully and at a prescribed rate. If one objects that the experimenter will not know whether the rat is pressing with his left or right paw, the experimenter's answer is that he wasn't asked to control that behavior. If it is decided to control that, he can do it in exactly the same way with a little more elaborate machinery. But, he will argue, the principles are exactly the same. Nothing new is added or subtracted, only the conditions have been altered appropriately. To return to language he will not attempt to describe the machinery involved in language acquisition, but if there is some piece of language behavior that is of interest and if it is indeed a functional piece, he will show you how to control it.

Most of the experimentation that has been done within the Skinnerian framework has been oriented toward two problems: showing that generalized reinforcers actually do work and showing that various pieces of verbal behavior can be increased and decreased in frequency as a result of reinforcement. Many experiments have done both at once. Such experiments on reinforcement have generally taken the following form: The subjects are given a verbal task, such as saying words, making sentences, or choosing phrases. The experimenter monitors their work until he establishes a base rate for the behavior in which he is interested (for example, using the first person pronouns, "I" and "we"). Then the experimenter begins reinforcing the subject by saying "good" or "umm-hmm" when the subject says a sentence with "I" or "we" in it. Usually during this period, the rate of the response increases over the base-line value. Finally, the experimenter stops reinforcing the behavior and the rate usually drops.

These experiments have been criticized on the grounds that many subjects "know" what is going on and are trying to do what the experimenter wants them to do. There is an extensive literature on the question of whether the subject's "awareness" is important in this kind of manipulation of his behavior. In the course of the controversy it turned out that "awareness" was very poorly defined and that many investigators had very different ideas about what they meant by it: awareness that the experimenter was saying something; aware-ness of its function; aware of what conditions were involved in determining when the experimenter said it; aware of the connection between the experi-menter's "reinforcer" and the subject's behavior; awareness of the purpose of the experiment? The general problem is treated in Eriksen (1962). Krasner (1958) and Salzinger (1959) have reviewed the experimental literature on the effects of reinforcement on verbal behavior and Speilberger (1965) and Dul-aney (1962) have given thoughtful critiques of the meaning of the awareness problem and its implications for psychological research and theory.

Application of the theory to normal children or strict experimental tests of it are difficult in the naturalistic situation. With children suffering from pathological deficits such as infantile autism, however, dramatic results have sometimes been obtained (see Lovaas, Berberich, Perloff & Schaeffer, 1966, for example).

Skinner's approach has been most severely criticized by Chomsky (1959) in an extensive attack on its goals, methods, procedures and claims.

LANGUAGE AS A RULE SYSTEM

The final orientation to be described here argues (as Skinner does) that simple notions about language being made up of words and orderings are a poor base for a psychology of language. It disagrees sharply with Skinner, however, about what to do about it. While Skinner goes into laboratory psychology in a search for a solution, this position turns to modern linguistics in search of a more ade-quate description of the nature and structure of language. As a result of its findings there, it argues that associationistic psychology is not adequate to ac-count for the complexity that language behavior is shown to have.

This movement toward a deep linguistic conception of language is recent and as yet it is not well-integrated into the psychological framework. The lin-guists, themselves in the midst of a theoretical revolution, are presenting new concepts and ideas for the psychologists to consider as well as powerful argu-ments that the presently accepted psychological machinery is not enough to ex-plain language behavior (see Chomsky, 1957, 1959, 1965).

This position argues that language is infinitely variable; that is, there is no limit to the number of sentences in English either as to length or as to variety. This means that the assumptions of the earlier models are incorrect. In respect to the view of language as words, the new view points out (as we did) that a sentence is not a word heap. Extending the argument, it points out that the second model rests on the assumption that some set number of sentence frames will be sufficient to describe the sentences of a language. This is flatly denied. It is argued instead that what is learned is not words or particular sentence orders but rather *productive rules* that enable the speaker to produce the infinite vari-ety of sentences that he produces and to understand the infinite variety of sen-tences that he hears (see Miller & Chomsky, 1963; Miller, Galanter & Pribram, 1960).

The argument here is one of great generality for psychology. It applies over all areas in which complex behaviors and skills are involved. In its simplest form it is easy to see and appreciate. Consider teaching multiplication to grade school students. We do not try to teach the products of all numbers multiplied by all other numbers. We break the task into a series of steps which require only a small amount of sheer memory work (the products of all combinations of pairs of digits from 0 through 9) and the acquisition of a set of rules about what to do when we get more than single digits to multiply. Most of us have learned these procedures so well that we have forgotten the extensive rules that we mastered. ("Place the two numbers one above the other so that the right-hand digits are directly above each other. Start with the furthest right digit in the lower figure. Get the product of this digit with the right-hand most digit of the upper row. If the product is a single digit, write it in the first available row beneath the lower digit in the same column as the lower digit. If the product is two digits, write the right-hand member of the two digit number in the place described and 'carry' the left-hand digit . . . etc.") The virtue of this abstract approach (as opposed to learning all the products of all the possible numbers) is that the rule system will apply to and give a correct result for any set of numbers that one has the patience to compute. The rules are *recursive;* they can be applied again and again until the problem is complete. The complete memorization procedure, on the other hand, would take most of one's life to learn even a reasonable level (say, all the digit pairs up to $1,000 \times 1,000$), and one would always face the hazard of running into a problem for which one had never learned the answer. Thus, our whole educational system has elected to learn a *computing technique* rather than to learn all the items of information that would be required in the super-large multiplication table.

While this example may seem far-fetched since no one in this age would think of trying to memorize all possible number pairs, there is a sense in which the psychologist's proposals about language learning have been nearly equivalent to the massive memorization procedure. For this reason a strong pressure is now felt toward a rule-based examination of language. It is not supposed, of course, that the rules for language are learned as single particular grammatical rules or that people even know that they "know" the rules. It *is* supposed that much of language is "computed" rather than "stored" and that this is what accounts for our tremendous capacity to utter novel but appropriate sentences and to understand new sentences when we hear them.

The attempt to specify the nature of the rules of language is instructive with respect to the kinds of models that psychologists have tried to employ. On the one end, as we have seen, language has been treated as a set of words. This implies unitary meanings and some form of compounding within the sentence. At the other extreme we have the sentence (or some larger collection) as a unit which is to be understood as a single whole. Both of these approaches attempt to discover and settle on "the right level" of analysis, the right unit size, etc. But the rules of language as the linguist sees them do not argue for a single level or a single kind of relationship or a single kind of unit. The rules of language are, instead, sets of nested and interlocking rules showing how the various levels interact in the complete structure of language.

While we cannot compress a course in linguistics into a few pages, we can indicate the direction that the linguistic analysis takes (see Chomsky, 1967, for a brief statement). First, it is noted that language behavior is segmented and that the segments are identifiable and classifiable; that is, we can say "this segment is like that segment" *with respect to some level of analysis*. Thus, at the level of "sound units" we can say that the *p* in "pa" is like the *p* in "pea" and both of them are like the *p* in "pooh." This level is called the *phonemic* level. It is important to note that the segments that we are calling *p* may have quite different properties physically and acoustically. In experiments with synthetic speech it can be shown that the noise that makes the *p* sound at the beginning of "pea" does not sound like *p* when it is put in front of the *"ah"* vowel. In fact, it is heard as *"ka"*! The constancy that we hear as a single type of speech sound may have a highly variable physical base. We treat these speech sounds as if they were the same at the beginning, middle and end of words; as if they were separable and commutable. Physically they are not. The important point is that there is an abstract level of linguistic analysis at which these are identical elements, separable from context, commutable, etc.

Above the phonemic level we encounter meaningful sequences called *morphemes*. The problem of specifying meaningful units that are represented in strings of phonemes is not a simple matter. For a string like "boy" we may want to talk about a referent and try to establish a relationship between this string and some class of items in the world. But for a string like "maybe" it is not reasonable to talk about a referent at all. Other strings like "if" and "to" (as in "he has to go") frustrate any simple analysis.

Above the morphemic level there are collections of *syntactic units* which have new unities of their own; that is, they stand in certain specifiable relationships to each other that are not indicated either by their sounds or by their meanings. Thus, we can say that "the girl" and "a man" are similar in a fashion that does not depend on the fact that they overlap in sound or that they are both human and animate, but rather depends on the fact that they can both be subjects or objects of certain kinds of sentences or can take given roles in noun phrases, prepositional phrases, etc. In short, at some level of abstraction these segments can be seen as instances of "the same thing."

Beyond this level we can see that two segments like "the boy hit the ball" and "the dressmaker cut out the pattern" are similar to each other in some fashion that neither sentence shares with "the machine was assembled by the man." And we also know that the first two sentences can be changed to make them like the third (e.g., "the ball was hit by the boy") and vice versa ("the man assembled the machine").

This kind of analysis can be extended in either direction. On the one extreme, it can be shown that the units of sound can be regarded as composed of bundles of distinctive features (voicing, nasality, etc.) and on the other extreme, it can be shown that whole sets of sentences are systematically interrelated. At this point all we need to establish, however, is that verbal utterances can be divided into segments and that these segments may be regarded as being at different abstract levels. The problem in giving a complete description of language lies in specifying what the levels are, what rules apply at each level, and how the levels and rules interrelate.

It is obvious that the levels of language are not independent of each other, yet it is important to note that they are not completely dependent either. If one "spells out" a text in the phonemic alphabet, it is obvious that there are special constraints on what combinations can appear at the beginning, middle or end of a word (e.g., no English word starts with *ft* but this combination can occur in medial or final positions). If one did not consider both levels of analysis (morphemic and phonemic) at the same time, one would miss these constraints, or having seen certain statistical regularities, one would fail to see the source of the regularities. But much of the higher levels is not represented in the lower levels. For example, the semantic similarity of "man" and "boy" is not reflected at all in the phonemic level. In general, higher levels constrain and modify events at lower levels in very specific ways. Aside from these specific constraints, however, the lower levels may vary freely according to their own rules. What this combination of dependence and independence means for the psychologist is that attempts to confine the analysis of language to any particular level will encounter phenomena which they *cannot* explain.

The approach of the linguist is not by any means that of the psychologist but the linguist's work may be used for a description of the sentences in the language that the psychologist has to explain. The linguist tells us, for example, that a sentence may be adequately described by giving a list of the rules that would have to be used to generate that sentence if it were produced by a special grammatical machine. In overview, the machine would generate an underlying structure by special rules, called phrase structure rules, would transform that structure by certain formally specified transformational rules to produce a terminal structure and then would "spell out" the terminal string with the proper phonemic rules. A complete description of a sentence would begin with deep generative rules, would pass through transformations and would finally be put in phonemic notation. There is no assertion that this is what a speaker does or that a hearer "unpacks" a sentence by reversing this in some way. All that is asserted is that this much machinery is needed to specify what a sentence is and to describe it. If that is so, the argument goes, then the psychological account must be at least that complex, for it must explain that much in the way of segmentation and rule structure.

This argument has sometimes been scorned by saying that it leads to absurdities: explaining how a dog can catch a ball would involve showing that the dog knew how to compute differential equations. This occasions merriment on the side of the animal trainers who know that one trains and rewards a dog for the act of ball-catching, one does not try to teach him mathematics. It is met with solemn agreement by the new theorists who say that real understanding of the dog's ability to catch a ball entails precisely that kind of account because that is exactly what physics tells us the skill requires. It appears that different ends are sought and the antagonists have different goals in mind. "Explanation" to the first group consists of a procedure for getting the animal to perform the act. "Explanation" for the second group consists of understanding how the animal can do the act at all.

Most of the research which has been motivated by systematic linguistic considerations has been aimed at highly technical targets (e.g., speech synthesis as in Cooper, Liberman, Lisker & Gaitenby, 1963; and Liberman, Cooper, Harris & MacNeilage, 1963) or has been of the nature of a "demonstration" of linguistic effects on psychological functions. One group of investigators demonstrated that the phrase structure analysis of a sentence corresponds to interesting perceptual phenomena (Fodor & Bever, 1965; Garrett, Bever & Fodor, 1966). Johnson (1965) found that phrase structure marks discontinuities in sentence learning. Miller (1962) studied psychological relations between sentences involving different transformations. Clifton and Odom (1966) provided experiments of their own and an effective summary of such research. Gough (1965), Slobin (1966a) and Wason (1965) have all studied sentence comprehension and evaluation. A host of such experiments are being performed currently.

Very little is known about the acquisition of the rules of language. Given the rate at which language is acquired and the flexibility of the child with respect to his ability to learn any human language readily, it is conjectured that the child has some powerful mechanisms that must determine his choice of behavioral rules when he is exposed to language samples. Current formulations are shifting rapidly to more serious consideration of innate components and much less stress on traditional learning (see especially Smith & Miller, 1966; Lenneberg, 1967). There is little evidence that a child is carefully tutored or "shaped" as psychologists have sometimes stressed. Indeed, McNeill (1966) presents an example (taken from a tape recording of an actual exchange) that humorously taunts the whole notion: Child: "Nobody don't like me." Mother: "No, say 'nobody likes me'." Child: "Nobody don't like me." ... (Eight repetitions of this dialogue.) Mother: "No, now listen carefully; say '*nobody likes me*'." Child: "Oh! Nobody don't likes me."

What *is* apparent and well documented is that the child is very systematic in his approach to language. It may be that he moves from one system to another, testing, changing, testing, trying again, or it may be that he chooses one system and progressively differentiates it into finer and finer portions; but the evidence that he is doing *something* systematic is overwhelming. The kind of thinking presented in the examples under the mediational approach, of course, shows such systematicness and can be appealed to here. More broadly, however, there is evidence that the child is struggling with a system for generating language at every stage and in very complex ways. Linguists who have listened to their children have provided some persuasive accounts (e.g., Velten, 1943; Weir, 1962).

There seems to be agreement from several sources that the first "grammars" of children are the "pivot-open" grammars described by Braine (1963b), Miller and Ervin (1964) and Brown and Fraser (1963) mentioned earlier. It will be recalled that the child seems to develop two classes of words, *pivots* (P), which are widely applied to many situations and objects (examples are words like "fix," "where," "that," "here," "see"), and an *open* (O) class of things, events, actions, etc., that the pivots may be applied to. Membership in the open class expands rapidly (hence the name), while the pivots seem to be a limited set. For a given child, utterances may consist of P + O, O alone, or O + O. If a new word comes into the lexicon, it may readily be used with several P class members. It is not known whether this is a necessary stage for the development of child language or even if every child goes through some such stage. In either event the complexity of a child's language grows rapidly and a variety of complex language behaviors are observed that we are not sure how to describe, much less account for.

An interesting example of sweeping change is provided by Ervin's longitudinal study of the language development of a few children. She got tape recordings on a weekly basis and tested the children frequently. Ervin (1964) found a rather startling demonstration of the effects of systematicness. The first verbs that children ordinarily acquire tend to be irregular verbs. They usually learn these correctly in several tenses, e.g., *take-took, run-ran, come-came,* etc. When the regular verbs begin to appear, the child almost immediately regularizes the irregular verbs. In spite of the fact that the child "had them right" and practiced them many times, he now begins to produce "errors" like *take-taked, run-runned, come-comed,* etc. (We might note he has neither heard nor been reinforced for these.) Clearly, in this case the systematicness overcomes the concrete examples and the practice. Later, the child has to re-learn the irregularity he once knew.

As researchers look at language acquisition further along they see evidence of more complex development of systematicness in the more complicated levels of syntax. Brown and Bellugi (1964) conclude that they must appeal to "the induction of latent structure" and that this is outside the scope of current learning theory.

Current work with children stresses careful observation and recording. But these must be supplemented by probing and testing to make the developmental patterns clear. A pattern of investigation that has recently appeared is one of concern for a particular phenomenon like the appearance and mastery of questions or negatives and the study of this aspect longitudinally.

Bellugi (1967), for example, has conducted a very careful study of the development of negation in three children who were studied longitudinally over a major part of their language development. She found good evidence for "stages" of development of the children with respect to their abilities to employ the full range of negations which English makes possible. The stages can be roughly characterized as follows:

Period A: (Children attach a negative element to a sentence nucleus.) "No flag," "no the sun shining," "no go back," "don't wear shirt."

Period B: (The negative element is now positioned internally in the sentence and has several forms like *no, not, don't, can't.*) "I don't see top to that," "he can't go," "don't want me pull it?" "why not he take bath?" "why we didn't?"

Period C: (Auxiliary verbs appear along with their transformational rules —number and tense agreement are problems to be worked out.) "Mommy, they not wet," "the sun is not too bright," "it's not big enough," "that not go in here," "I don't like some," "you don't want some supper," "why I can't put them on?"

Later periods are much less clear and Bellugi treats them as having to do with problems of special rules in English since the children seem to have mastered the fundamental questions of negation in sentence combination, embedding, etc. Persistent problems have to do with certain verb forms which are irregular or permit optional treatment of the negative (e.g., *I think he isn't going* and the form, *I don't think he's going.* The children construct the first form but not the second). A second problem has to do with indefinites (some, none, any, somebody, nobody, anybody, etc.) where the children fail to recognize restrictions on the amount of negation permitted (e.g., "I can't do nothing with no string," "you're not gonna have no friends," "nobody won't recognize us"). A third problem has to do with "tag sentences" usually appended to sentences to ask negative questions. Presumably the difficulty here has to do with the rules of agreement which govern such tags. The child's errors suggest that he has the general form but not quite the right rules—"you are a poor lady, weren't you?" "you 'posed to cut out the lines, don't you?" "I have a lot of Ursula's toys, don't we?"

Through these developments, Bellugi sees the constant organization and reorganization of the child's rule structures, each change making some constructions possible but creating errors in other places where the rules are not sufficient. A new mastery in one area (such as auxiliary verbs) creates new problems in another area, where and how to create a negative with the auxiliaries. Getting the declarative-negative still leaves the problem of the question-negative to be solved and the errors in word order show the child struggling with the two sets of transformations at the same time with only partial success.

The important thing about the success of studies like Bellugi's is that they show consistent parallels from one child to another (see also Menyuk, 1963, 1964). This consistency argues that there is a ground plan for the development of rule structures for us to study. It may even suggest that there is a universal plan which transcends the particular language being learned. That suggestion is not supportable at the present time, but there are hints in the study of Russian and Japanese children that there may be impressive constancies when we know how to analyze them (see Slobin, 1966b; and McNeill, 1966).[1]

---

[1] Recent reviews of interest to readers following the literature in the area are Diebold, 1965; and Ervin-Tripp and Slobin, 1966. Books of readings include Bever and Weksel, 1968; Fodor and Katz, 1964; Jakobovits and Miron, 1967; Lyons and Wales, 1966; and Saporta, 1961.

To date the new approach to the psychology of language seems to be producing interesting new approaches to language acquisition by suggesting that "what-is-learned" is a quite different thing than the proponents of simpler models of language ever considered. Thus, this model has stimulated new approaches to research and has demanded that psychologists give thought to new mechanisms that can explain the complex systematic learnings that are becoming so well-documented in the course of language development.

REFERENCES

ALLPORT, F. H. *Social Psychology.* Boston: Houghton Mifflin, 1924.

BELLUGI, U. The acquisition of the system of negation in children's speech. Unpublished Ph.D. thesis, Harvard Univer., 1967.

BERKO, J. The child's learning of English morphology. *Word,* 1958, 14, 150–177.

BEVER, T. G., FODOR, J. A., & WEKSEL, W. On the acquisition of syntax: A critique of "Contextual Generalization." *Psychological Review,* 1965, 72, 467–482. (a)

BEVER, T. G., FODOR, J. A., & WEKSEL, W. Is linguistics empirical? *Psychological Review,* 1965, 72, 493–500. (b)

BEVER, T. G., & WEKSEL, W. (Eds.) *The structure and psychology of language.* New York: Holt, Rinehart & Winston, 1968.

BLUMENTHAL, A. L. Early psycholinguistic research. A review in T. G. Bever & W. Weksel (Eds.), *The structure and psychology of language.* New York: Holt, Rinehart & Winston, 1968.

BOAS, F. (Ed.) *Handbook of American Indian languages.* Part I. Washington, D.C.: Smithsonian, 1911.

BRAINE, M. D. S. On learning the grammatical order of words. *Psychological Review,* 1963, 70, 323–348. (a)

BRAINE, M. D. S. The ontogeny of English phrase structure: The first phase. *Language,* 1963, 39, 1–13. (b)

BRAINE, M. D. S. On the basis of phrase structure: A reply to Bever, Fodor and Weksel. *Psychological Review,* 1965, 72, 483–492.

BROWN, R. W. Linguistic determinism and the part of speech. *Journal of Abnormal and Social Psychology,* 1957, 55, 1–5.

BROWN, R. W. *Words and things.* Glencoe, Ill.: Free Press, 1958.

BROWN, R. W. *Social psychology.* New York: Free Press, 1965.

BROWN, R. W., & BELLUGI, U. Three processes in the child's acquisition of syntax. *Harvard Educational Review,* 1964, 34, 133–151.

BROWN, R. W., & BERKO, J. Word association and the acquisition of grammar. *Child Development,* 1960, 31, 1–14.

BROWN, R. W., & FRASER, C. The acquisition of syntax. In C. N. Cofer & B. S. Musgrave (Eds.), *Verbal behavior and learning.* New York: McGraw-Hill, 1963.

CHERRY, C. *On human communication.* Cambridge, Mass.: M.I.T. Press, 1957.

CHOMSKY, N. *Syntactic structures.* The Hague, the Netherlands: Mouton, 1957.

CHOMSKY, N. A review of *Verbal behavior* by B. F. Skinner. *Language,* 1959, 35, 26–58.

CHOMSKY, N. *Aspects of the theory of syntax.* Cambridge, Mass.: M.I.T. Press, 1965.

CHOMSKY, N. The formal nature of language. In E. H. Lenneberg, *Biological foundations of language.* New York: Wiley, 1967.

CLIFTON, C., JR., & ODOM, P. Similarity relations among certain English sentence constructions. *Psychological Monographs,* 1966, 80 (5, Whole No. 613). P. 35.

COFER, C. N. On some factors in the organizational characteristics of free recall. *American Psychologist,* 1965, 20, 261–272.

COOPER, F. S., LIBERMAN, A. M., LISKER, L., & GAITENBY, J. H. Speech synthesis by rules. In C. G. M. Fant (Ed.), *Proceedings of the speech communication seminar.* Speech Transmission Laboratories, Royal Institute of Technology, Stockholm, 1963.

DEESE, J. From the isolated verbal unit to connected discourse. In C. N. Cofer (Ed.), *Verbal learning and verbal behavior.* New York: McGraw-Hill, 1961.

DEESE, J. On the structure of associative meaning. *Psychological Review,* 1962, 69, 161–175.

DEESE, J. *The structure of associations in language and thought.* Baltimore: Johns Hopkins Univer. Press, 1965.

DIEBOLD, A. R., JR. A survey of psycholinguistic research, 1954–1964. In C. E. Osgood & T. A. Sebeok (Eds.), *Psycholinguistics: A survey of theory and research problems.* Bloomington, Ind.: Indiana University Press, 1965.

DULANEY, D. E. The place of hypotheses and intentions: An analysis of verbal control in verbal conditioning. *Journal of Personality,* 1962, 30 (Suppl.), 102–129.

ERIKSEN, C. W. (Ed.) *Behavior and awareness.* Durham: Duke University Press, 1962. Pp. 73–101.

ERVIN, S. M. Changes with age in the verbal determinants of word-association. *American Journal of Psychology,* 1961, 74, 361–372.

ERVIN, S. M. Imitations and structural change in children's language. In E. H. Lenneberg (Ed.), *New directions in the study of language.* Cambridge, Mass.: M.I.T. Press, 1964.

ERVIN-TRIPP, S. M., & SLOBIN, D. I. Psycholinguistics. *Annual Review of Psychology,* 1966, 17, 435–474.

FODOR, J. A. Current trends in cognitive psychology. Address given at the Center for Research in Human Learning, University of Minnesota, July 6, 1966. (Mimeographed)

FODOR, J. A., & BEVER, T. G. The psychological reality of linguistic segments. *Journal of Verbal Learning and Verbal Behavior,* 1965, 4, 414–420.

FODOR, J. A., & KATZ, J. J. (Eds.) *The structure of language: Readings in the philosophy of language.* Englewood Cliffs, N. J.: Prentice-Hall, 1964.

GARRETT, M., BEVER, T. G., & FODOR, J. A. The active use of grammar in speech perception. *Perception and Psychophysics,* 1966, 1, 30–32.

GOLDIAMOND, I., & HAWKINS, W. F. Vexierversuch: The log relationship between word-frequency and recognition obtained in the absence of stimulus words. *Journal of Experimental Psychology,* 1958, 56, 457–463.

GOUGH, P. B. Grammatical transformations and speed of understanding. *Journal of Verbal Learning and Verbal Behavior,* 1965, 4, 107–111.

HOCKETT, C. F. Grammar for the hearer. In R. Jakobson (Ed.), *Structure of language and its mathematical aspects.* Proceedings of the 12th Symposium in Applied Mathematics. Providence, R. I.: American Mathematical Society, 1961. Pp. 220–236.

HORTON, D. L., & KJELDERGAARD, P. M. An experimental analysis of associative factors in mediated generalization. *Psychological Monographs,* 1961, 75 (11, Whole No. 515).

HOWES, D. H. On the relation between the probability of a word as an association and in general linguistic usage. *Journal of Abnormal and Social Psychology,* 1957, 54, 75–85.

HOWES, D. H. Application of the word-frequency concept to aphasia. In A. V. S. DEREUCK & M. O'CONNOR (Eds.), *Disorders of language.* London: Churchill, 1964. Pp. 47–75.

HOWES, D. H., & SOLOMON, R. L. Visual duration threshold as a function of word probability. *Journal of Experimental Psychology,* 1951, 41, 401–410.

IRWIN, O. C., & CHEN, H. P. Development of speech during infancy. *Journal of Experimental Psychology,* 1946, 36, 431–436.

JAKOBOVITS, L. A., & MIRON, M. S. *Readings in the psychology of language.* Englewood Cliffs, N.J.: Prentice-Hall, 1967.

JENKINS, J. J. Mediated association: Paradigms and situations. In C. N. Cofer & B. S. Musgrave (Eds.), *Verbal behavior and learning.* New York: McGraw-Hill, 1963. Pp. 210–245.

JENKINS, J. J. Mediation theory and grammatical behavior. In S. Rosenberg (Ed.), *Directions in psycholinguistics.* New York: Macmillan, 1965. Pp. 66–96.

JENKINS, J. J., & PALERMO, D. S. Mediation processes and the acquisition of linguistic structure. In U. Bellugi & R. Brown (Eds.), The acquisition of language. *Monographs of Social Research and Child Development,* 1964, 29 (1, Serial No. 92).

JENKINS, J. J., & PALERMO, D. S. Further data on changes in word-association norms. *Journal of Personality and Social Psychology,* 1965, 1, 303–309.

JENKINS, J. J., & RUSSELL, W. A. Systematic changes in word-association norms, 1910–1952. *Journal of Abnormal and Social Psychology,* 1960, 60, 293–304.

JERSILD, A. T., & RITZMAN, R. Aspects of language development: The growth of loquacity and vocabulary. *Child Development,* 1938, 9, 243–259.

JOHNSON, N. F. Linguistic models and functional units of language behavior. In S. Rosenberg (Ed.), *Directions in psycholinguistics.* New York: Macmillan, 1965. Pp. 29–65.

KRASNER, L. Studies of the conditioning of verbal behavior. *Psychological Bulletin,* 1958, 55, 148–170.

LASHLEY, K. S. The problem of serial order in behavior. In L. A. Jeffress (Ed.), *Cerebral mechanisms in behavior: The Hixon symposium.* New York: Wiley, 1951. Pp. 112–136.

LENNEBERG, E. H. *Biological foundations of language.* New York: Wiley, 1967.

LIBERMAN, A. M., COOPER, F. S., HARRIS, K. S., & MACNEILAGE, P. F. A motor theory of speech perception. In C. G. M. Fant (Ed.), *Proceedings of the speech communications seminar.* Speech Transmission Laboratories, Royal Institute of Technology, Stockholm, 1963.

LOVAAS, O. I., BERBERICH, J. P., PERLOFF, B. F., & SCHAEFFER, B. Acquisition of imitative speech by schizophrenic children. *Science,* 1966, 151, 705–707.

LYONS, J., & WALES, R. J. (Eds.) *Psycholinguistics papers.* Edinburgh: Edinburgh Univer. Press, 1966.

MACLAY, H. Linguistics and language behavior. *Journal of Communication,* 1964, 14, 66–73.

MANDELBROT, B. An informational theory of the structure of language based upon the theory of statistical matching of messages and coding. In W. Jackson (Ed.), *Proceedings of a symposium on applications of communication theory.* London: Butterworth, 1953.

MCCARTHY, D. *The language development of the preschool child.* Minneapolis: Univer. of Minnesota Press, 1930.

McCarthy, D. Language development in children. In L. Carmichael (Ed.), *Manual of child psychology.* New York: Wiley, 1954. Pp. 492–630.

McNeill, D. The origin of associations within the same grammatical class. *Journal of Verbal Learning and Verbal Behavior,* 1963, 2, 346–351.

McNeill, D. Developmental psycholinguistics. In F. Smith & G. A. Miller (Eds.), *The genesis of language.* Cambridge, Mass.: M.I.T. Press, 1966.

Menyuk, P. A. A preliminary evaluation of grammatical capacity in children. *Journal of Verbal Learning and Verbal Behavior,* 1963, 2, 429–439.

Menyuk, P. A. Alteration of rules in children's grammar. *Journal of Verbal Learning and Verbal Behavior,* 1964, 3, 480–488.

Miller, G. A. *Language and communication.* New York: McGraw-Hill, 1951.

Miller, G. A. Some psychological studies of grammar. *American Psychologist,* 1962, 17, 748–762.

Miller, G. A., & Chomsky, N. Finitary models of language users. In R. D. Luce, R. Bush & E. Galanter (Eds.), *Handbook of mathematical psychology.* Vol. II. New York: Wiley, 1963.

Miller, G. A., Galanter, E., & Pribram, K. H. *Plans and the structure of behavior.* New York: Holt, 1960.

Miller, G. A., & Selfridge, J. A. Verbal context and the recall of meaningful material. *American Journal of Psychology,* 1950, 63, 176–185.

Miller, N. E., & Dollard, J. *Social learning and imitation.* New Haven: Yale Univer. Press, 1941.

Miller, W., & Ervin, S. The development of grammar in child language. In U. Bellugi & R. Brown (Eds.), The acquisition of language. *Monographs of Social Research and Child Development,* 1964, 29 (1, Serial No. 92).

Mowrer, O. H. *Learning theory and personality dynamics.* New York: Ronald Press, 1950.

Mowrer, O. H. The psychologist looks at language. *American Psychologist,* 1954, 9, 660–694.

Osgood, C. E. *Method and theory in experimental psychology.* New York: Oxford Univer. Press, 1953.

Osgood, C. E., & Sebeok, T. A. Psycholinguistics: A survey of theory and research problems. *International Journal of American Linguistics,* 1954, 20 (4, Mem. 10). P. 203.

Osgood, C. E., Suci, G. J., & Tannenbaum, P. H. *The measurement of meaning.* Urbana: Univer. of Illinois Press, 1957.

Paul, H. *Prinzipien der Sprachgeschichte.* Halle: Neimayer, 1886. (2nd Ed.) English translation by H. Strong, 1889.

Pierce, J. R. *Symbols, signals and noise.* New York: Harper, 1961.

Rosenzweig, M. R., & Postman, L. Frequency of usage and the perception of words. *Science,* 1958, 127, 263–266.

Salzinger, K. Experimental manipulation of verbal behavior. *Journal of General Psychology,* 1959, 61, 65–94.

Sapir, E. The status of linguistics as a science. *Language,* 1929, 5, 207–214.

Sapir, E. *Language.* New York: Harcourt, Brace, 1939.

Saporta, S. (Ed.) *Psycholinguistics: A book of readings.* New York: Holt, 1961.

Skinner, B. F. The distribution of associated words. *Psychological Records,* 1937, 1, 71–76.

Skinner, B. F. *Verbal behavior.* New York: Appleton-Century-Crofts, 1957.

SLOBIN, D. I. Grammatical transformations and sentence comprehension in childhood and adulthood. *Journal of Verbal Learning and Verbal Behavior,* 1966, 5, 219–227. (a)

SLOBIN, D. I. The acquisition of Russian as a native language. In F. Smith & G. A. Miller (Eds.), *The genesis of language: A psycholinguistic approach.* Cambridge, Mass.: M.I.T. Press, 1966. (b)

SMITH, F., & MILLER, G. A. (Eds.) *The genesis of language: A psycholinguistic approach.* Cambridge, Mass.: M.I.T. Press, 1966.

SPIELBERGER, C. D. Theoretical and epistemological issues in verbal conditioning. In S. Rosenberg (Ed.), *Directions in psycholinguistics.* New York: Macmillan, 1965. Pp. 149–200.

STAATS, C. K., & STAATS, A. W. Meaning established by classical conditioning. *Journal of Experimental Psychology,* 1957, 54, 74–80.

THORNDIKE, E. L., & LORGE, I. *The teacher's word book of 30,000 words.* New York: Teachers College, Columbia Univer., 1944.

TYLER, L. *The psychology of human differences.* (3rd Ed.) New York: Appleton-Century-Crofts, 1965.

UNDERWOOD, B. J., & SCHULZ, R. W. *Meaningfulness and verbal learning.* Philadelphia: Lippincott, 1960.

VELTON, H. V. The growth of phonemic and lexical patterns in infant language. *Language,* 1943, 19, 281–292.

WASON, P. C. The contexts of plausible denial. *Journal of Verbal Learning and Verbal Behavior,* 1965, 4, 7–11.

WATSON, J. B. *Behaviorism.* New York: The People's Institute, 1925.

WEIR, R. H. *Language in the crib.* The Hague, the Netherlands: Mouton, 1962.

WERNER, H., & KAPLAN, E. The acquisition of word meanings: A developmental study. *Social Research and Child Development Monographs,* 1952, 15 (51), 84.

WHORF, B. L. *Language, thought and reality.* J. B. Carroll (Ed.) Cambridge, Mass.: M.I.T. Press, 1956.

WOODWORTH, R. S. *Experimental psychology.* New York: Holt, 1938.

WOODWORTH, R. S., & SCHLOSBERG, H. *Experimental psychology.* (Rev. Ed.) New York: Holt, 1954.

WUNDT, W. *Volkerpsychologie.* Vol. I. *Die Sprache.* Leipzig: Engelmann, 1900.

WUNDT, W. *Sprachgeschichte und Sprachpsychologie.* Leipzig: Engelmann, 1901.

YOUNG, F. M. An analysis of certain variables in a developmental study of language. *Genetic Psychology Monographs,* 1941, 23 (1).

ZIPF, G. K. *The psycho-biology of language.* Boston: Houghton Mifflin, 1935.

ZIPF, G. K. *Human behavior and the principle of least effort.* Cambridge, Mass.: Addison-Wesley, 1949.

CHAPTER **14**

Social Influences In The
Development Of Cognitive Style

Herman A. Witkin

State University of New York, Downstate Medical Center

In seeking out the social influences that help shape a child's cognitive development a first and obvious place to look is the cognitive environment in which
he grows up. Fruitful research into the sources of a child's cognitive make-up
has taken the form of examining the relation between a child's cognitive characteristics and the opportunities for their development and the values attached
to their achievement, both in the family and in the broader social environment. Bing (1963), for example, was able to show that mothers of children
high in verbal competence provided them with considerable verbal stimulation in early childhood, made story books available to them, and encouraged
their participation in conversation at family meals.

One contribution of the recent extensive work on cognitive style is the
suggestion that in seeking the sources of a child's cognitive make-up it may
be profitable to look as well at places in the socialization process that appear
quite distant from the cognitive sphere. The view of cognition that has come
from the cognitive style work is that cognitive functioning is embedded in
a personal life and its development is embedded in a personal history. Whatever affects a child's development as a person may therefore in some degree
help shape his cognitive make-up. As an illustration of the value of "looking
at distant places" in the socialization process for the origins of cognitive characteristics, we have found in our own work (Witkin, Dyk, Faterson, Goodenough & Karp, 1962; Dyk & Witkin, 1965) that the age-appropriateness of
the mother's physical care of her child (taken as one sign of her attitude toward
his functioning independently) is associated with the degree of his analytical
competence in such laboratory perceptual tasks as the rod-and-frame test.

Conversely, cognitive styles may provide a useful medium through which
to examine the role of socialization in psychological development. The self-

The work described in this paper was supported by a grant (M-628) from the
United States Public Health Service, National Institutes of Health.

consistent modes of functioning we call cognitive styles are manifestations, in the cognitive sphere, of still broader dimensions of personal functioning, evident in similar form in many areas of the individual's psychological activity. Cognitive styles thus speak on more than cognition. Studying the role of socialization in the development of cognitive styles becomes then a means of studying the way in which broad psychological dimensions develop in response to social forces.

There is also a more specific methodological advantage in studying salient psychological dimensions through their manifestations in the cognitive sphere. Cognitive functions can be assessed by controlled laboratory procedures and so serve as discernible "tracer elements" for identifying and evaluating these broad dimensions. A useful strategy in developmental research has been to select specific "end points" in development and then to assess the role of particular developmental forces in their determination. A common difficulty in the application of this strategy has been the identification of end points which are both salient and measurable. Cognitive styles are good candidates for such end points.

This chapter will illustrate these concepts by considering some studies of social influences affecting the development of one intensively studied cognitive style—the global-articulated dimension of cognitive functioning. The studies fall into three main areas: mother-child relations, cross-cultural comparisons and sex differences. Before considering these studies it is necessary to characterize the global-articulated cognitive style and its connection to forms of functioning in other psychological areas. A sketch of our view of the development of this cognitive style in relation to development in other psychological areas will help justify the strategy followed in these studies of "looking at distant places" in the socialization process for origins of cognitive style. This view has been spelled out in detail elsewhere (Witkin et al., 1962) and may be summarized here.

Briefly, we consider an articulated cognitive style to be an indicator of a high level of differentiation in the cognitive area; its development during growth proceeds in close, mutual interrelation with the development of differentiation in other areas, manifested in other identifiable indicators.

With regard to the cognitive area, perceptual organization early in development is apt to depend greatly on structural properties of the stimulus field. With structured fields, perception of a part of the field is likely to be strongly dominated by the overall organization of the field; fields that lack inherent structure are likely to be apprehended as relatively unorganized. As the child's interaction with the world about him grows, stimulus objects within it acquire meaning and functional significance. This helps make for greater discreteness of parts of the field in experience and contributes to organizations of the field in addition to that indicated by geometrical-structural arrangements. Perception may be considered articulated, in contrast to global, if the person is able to perceive items as discrete from background when the field is structured (analysis), and to impose structure on a field, and so perceive it as organized, when the field has relatively little inherent structure (structuring). Movement toward articulation during growth occurs not only in experience of an immediately present stimulus configuration—i.e., perception—but also in experience of symbolic material—i.e., thinking. Articulated experience is indicative of developed differentiation.

Differentiation of the self may also be conceived in terms of articulation. Very early in life, we may imagine, the child experiences himself and the environment as a more or less amorphous, continuous body-field matrix. Boundaries are later formed between body and the world outside and some awareness developed of the parts of the body and their interrelatedness. Whereas the child's early conception of his body is thus relatively global, later it is more articulated—that is, the body is experienced as having definite limits or boundaries, and the parts within as discrete yet formed into a definite structure. An articulated body concept is indicative of progress toward differentiation. Developed self-differentiation also shows itself in awareness of needs, feelings and attributes which the person identifies as his own and as distinct from those of others, in other words a sense of separate identity. Sense of separate identity implies experience of the self as segregated and structured, that is, as articulated. An important factor in the development of self-differentiation is the movement away from the initial inevitable state of unity with the mother toward some degree of separation. In the course of this evolving relation with the mother and other people the child identifies and internalizes particular values and standards (internal frames of reference).

Developed differentiation also shows itself in the presence of structured, specialized defenses and controls for channeling of impulse and expenditure of energy. This is in contrast to what we find in the relatively undifferentiated state, early in life, when impulse, if accumulated, is likely to flood the organism and find expression in diffuse, system-wide reactions. Some of the known systems of defense may be considered to reflect less developed differentiation than others. Massive repression and primitive denial, for example, because they involve a relatively indiscriminate turning away from perception of stimuli and from memory for past experiences, represent relatively nonspecific ways of functioning, compared to such mechanisms as intellectualization and isolation. In the areas of defenses and controls the tendency to use structured, specialized defenses may be considered an indication of developed differentiation.

As noted, the various indicators of developed differentiation are not conceived as separate achievements in isolated channels of growth, but rather as diverse expressions of an underlying process of development toward greater psychological complexity. Extensive research (Witkin et al., 1962) has in fact shown that these various indicators of developed differentiation tend to "go together" in the same person. Brief speculation about the ways in which development in the various psychological areas considered are linked during development makes plausible the finding of an association, in the same person, of characteristics of more developed or less developed differentiation. The experienced world, body and self emerge from an initial continuous body-field matrix; and the further crystallization of experience within the body-self "segment" and the field "segment" proceeds in such a way during development that greater articulation in one area is likely to depend upon and foster the achievement of articulation in the other. For example, the achievement of a segregated structured self provides internal frames of reference for viewing, interpreting and dealing with the world from the position of an autonomous agent, enjoying an existence apart from the field, rather than fused with it. This in turn is likely to aid in the development of an articulated way of experiencing the world. At the same time, a tendency for experience to be articulated, as it registers from moment to moment, is likely to contribute to articulation of the self. Considering the development of defenses in relation to the development of articulated experience and self-differentiation, structured controls make possible the regulation of attention which in turn is important if the ability to analyze and structure experience is to develop. Again, continued easy spilling over of impulse through failure to develop structured controls may hamper the development of self-differentiation. If standards taken over from parents are not assimilated during growth, and remain as raw intruding proscriptions, the achievement of a segregated structured self is made exceedingly difficult.

To the extent that an articulated cognitive style is an outcome of an underlying process of differentiation of the psychological system as a whole, it follows that any of the social influences that affect progress toward differentiation may be profitably examined for determinants of development along the global-articulated dimension. Of the social influences likely to affect differentiation, the studies to be reviewed have focused mainly on the influences which may hamper or foster separate, autonomous functioning. Included among these influences have been, first of all, the extent of opportunity and encouragement the child receives while growing up to achieve separation, particularly from the mother—in other words, to move toward self-differentiation. Another social influence considered in these studies, closely related to encouragement of separation, and, like it, affecting development toward autonomous functioning, is the manner of dealing with the child's expression of impulse. Imparting standards for internalization, which become the child's own, and within limits, allowing impulse expression so the child may learn to identify his impulses and to cope with them, are calculated to help the development of autonomous functioning. Some of the studies have also considered characteristics of the mother herself which may aid or hinder her part in the separation process, as well as in imparting standards for internalization and in regulating the child's impulse expression.

These highly interrelated factors—handling of separation, regulation of impulse expression, and characteristics of mother as a person affecting her part in these processes—constitute a "socialization cluster" which influences a child's progress toward separate autonomous functioning. The sections that follow report studies in which development of an articulated cognitive style (and, in some instances, of associated characteristics of developed differentiation as well) has been examined in relation to this socialization cluster. Though the studies to be reviewed have done more to sketch in connections between the socialization cluster and cognitive style than to work out the processes underlying these connections, their findings already lend considerable support to the hypothesis that a mode of socialization which fosters separate functioning is associated with achievement of an articulated cognitive style.

A. STUDIES OF MOTHER-CHILD INTERACTIONS AND OF "MOTHER-AS-A-PERSON"

Studies in this area have been conducted both in our laboratory (Witkin et al., 1962; Dyk & Witkin, 1965) and elsewhere (Seder, 1957; Corah, 1965; Barclay & Cusumano, 1965). Our own studies have focused on the socialization cluster with particular reference to the mother's role. Although his relation to his mother is only one "front" in the developing child's struggle for achievement of autonomous functioning, the mother's typically extensive and strong involvement with the child in our culture undoubtedly makes this a main "front." The studies have been both cross-sectional and longitudinal and have evolved toward more precise specification of the processes of mother-child interaction early in life which may contribute to the development of differentiation, and thereby to an articulated cognitive style.

1. Mother-Child Interactions from the Mother's Viewpoint

The first of this progression of studies explored patterns of relation to the family, particularly to the mother, of ten-year-old boys who presented a picture of greater or more limited differentiation. Degree of differentiation was assessed in various areas of the child's functioning.

To determine whether his experience of the field was relatively global or articulated, we evaluated both his perceptual and intellectual functioning, and considered the analytical and structuring aspects of articulation. For the analytical aspect, in perception, we used our tests of field dependence: the rod-and-frame test, the body-adjustment test and the embedded-figures test. In the first of these tests, the subject, seated in a completely darkened room, must adjust a luminous rod, contained within a tilted frame, to a position he perceives as upright. The body-adjustment test is similar except that the subject, seated in a tilted room, must adjust his own body to the upright. Finally, the task in the embedded-figures test is to locate a previously seen simple figure within a complex figure designed to embed it. Performance in each test reflects the extent to which perception of an item (rod, body, or geometric figure) is dictated by the organized context of which it is a part, or extent of field dependence.

To evaluate analytical functioning in intellectual activity we used scores for three subtests of the WISC (Wechsler Intelligence Scale for Children) subtests (Block Design, Object Assembly and Picture Completion) which have been found to load the same factor as tests of field dependence and other tests of analytical ability (Goodenough & Karp, 1961; Karp, 1963). The structuring aspect of articulation was evaluated by means of the Rorschach for which a special rating scale was devised to evaluate the extent to which the child's percepts reflected an attempt to impose structure on the amorphous ink blots. Articulation of experience was also assessed from the quality of the child's account, on interview, of everyday events and activities, of himself and other people, and of the world in which he lives.

With regard to level of differentiation in other areas of functioning, articulation of body concept was assessed from the child's human figure drawings, rated according to degree of articulation of his figures; and his sense of separate identity was judged particularly from his relation to the adult examiner while taking a test (e.g., whether he sought guidance from the examiner as to how to proceed or was able to define his own role in relation to the task; whether or not he had confidence in his ability to perform the task). Finally, to evaluate differentiation in the area of defenses, projective tests were used to determine the extent of the child's tendency to use structured, specialized defenses.

In this first study, interviews with mothers seemed the most appropriate way to begin exploration of aspects of mother-child interactions relevant to the development of differentiation. The interviews, conducted in the home, examined mother-child relations fairly comprehensively, and the overall ratings made of the interviews were anchored to specific indicators or clues. These indicators fell into three categories, together reflecting the socialization cluster:

(1) Indicators relevant to evaluating separation from mother. This included five indicators which, stated in terms of discouragement of separation, were:

    (a) Physical care of child is inappropriate to his age.

    (b) Through fears and anxieties for or ties to her child, mother markedly limits his activities and his going into the community.

    (c) Mother regards child as delicate, in need of special attention or protection, or as irresponsible.

    (d) Mother does not accept masculine role for child.

    (e) Mother limits curiosity, stresses conformity.

(2) Indicator relevant to evaluating control of aggressive, assertive behavior. This indicator was: maternal control is not in the direction of a child's achieving mature goals, or becoming responsible; or is consistently directed against child's asserting himself. Patterns which led to the judgment "indicator present," included: submissive, indulgent maternal behavior; administration of discipline in arbitrary fashion, "on impulse," and the use of irrational threats to control aggression; maternal wavering between indulgent and coercive behavior. A mother's inability to set limits for her child, and to offer him and help him absorb a clear set of values interferes with the child's development of controls.

(3) Indicators relevant to evaluating personal characteristics of the mother. Characteristics chosen for consideration were those relevant to the mother's part in the separation process and the impulse-regulation process. The two indicators were:

    (a) Mother in rearing child does not have assurance in herself. Lack of self-assurance hampers a mother's ability to define her role as a mother and thereby her ability to help her child define his own role as a separate person. Lack of self-assurance is also likely to make it difficult for a mother to set and maintain limits, thus hurting the child's achievement of self-regulation.

    (b) Mother does not have a feeling of self-realization in her own life. We considered that a mother who herself has a sense of self-realization would be better able to allow her child to separate from her and develop as an individual.

Using these specific indicators as guides, ratings were made of the mother-child interaction as to whether in its total impact it had tended to foster the child's development of differentiation (IFD—interactions fostering differentiation) or to interfere with the development of differentiation (IID—interactions interfering with differentiation). These ratings of IID or IFD showed a pattern of significant correlations with measures of differentiation of the children. Boys whose mothers were judged to have interacted with them in ways that fostered differentiation tended to have an articulated cognitive style, an articulated body concept, a developed sense of separate identity, and specialized structured defenses. Although the very character of the interview procedure and the use of global ratings in this first study prevented separate assessment of the components of the socialization cluster, these results indicated that the socialization processes implied by the cluster are relevant to development of a more global or more articulated cognitive style. Some of the subsequent studies, as will be seen, focused more specifically on individual components of the socialization cluster, taken separately.

The findings of this first study were confirmed in two further studies in our laboratory and additional validation has come from independent studies by Seder (1957), Dawson (1963, 1967) and Berry (1966a, 1966b). These independent studies are of particular value in their confirmation since they used methods and populations quite different from our own. Seder gave questionnaires to mothers to obtain information about child-rearing practices; and the children in her study were from a suburb of Boston. Dawson also used questionnaires, given to the subjects themselves, to obtain information about child-rearing practices, and his subjects were from the Temne and Mende tribes of Sierra Leone, Africa, cultural groups radically different from the one we studied. Berry also studied the Temne, and the Eskimo as well; he too used questionnaires filled out by his subjects.

In Seder's study, for example, the questionnaire sought information about specific child-rearing practices and the answers obtained from each question were rated separately. This contrasts to the situation in the kind of "free" interview we used, where independent assessment of information about a particular area (as child-rearing practices) is impossible since it is intertwined with information about other areas (as characteristics of the mother or the child himself). Among Seder's specific results we find, for example, that field-dependent boys were not allowed to set their own standards but were pressed toward standards and goals set by their parents; were severely punished for aggressive, assertive behavior; were punished according to parents' whims and moods; were generally disciplined in an "authoritarian manner;" and were protected from attacks from other children by their mothers, who also settled their disputes for them. One of the salient features of the picture for field-independent boys was that their fathers were more often the mediators of discipline. In line with this last result (and with our own observation that mothers judged on interview to have interfered with development of differentiation in their children complained of nonparticipation of fathers in rearing their children), Barclay and Cusumano (1965) have recently reported that boys from fatherless homes tended to be field dependent; and Bieri (1960) found that women who identified with their fathers tended to be field independent; for men the result was in the same direction, but did not reach significance.

The findings of the Dawson and Berry studies will be considered in a later section.

Studies we did which followed the home-interview investigation sought to specify further the nature of the mother-child interaction contributing to more differentiated or less differentiated functioning in the child, and thereby to an articulated or global cognitive style, and to examine components of the socialization cluster separately from each other. In one further line of work mother-child interactions were explored from the standpoint of the child; in another, characteristics of the mother-as-a-person were studied through tests of differentiation. The studies in both areas used methods which, as compared to the interview procedure, delimited the information entering into the assessments made.

2. Mother-Child Interactions from the Child's Viewpoint

We hypothesized that a mother who, as those judged from interviews to have interfered with the development of differentiation in their children, lacks self-assurance in dealing with her child, limits his activities and responsibilities because of her own fears and anxieties, does not accept a masculine role for him, and discourages self-assertion, would be experienced by the child as non-supportive. On the other hand, mothers who deal with their sons in the contrasting ways found among those judged to have fostered differentiation would more likely be experienced by their children as supportive.

An evaluation of views held by children of their parents was made in one study through their projections of parental role in TAT stories. TAT stories containing parental figures were rated in terms of whether the parent was portrayed in an essentially supportive or non-supportive role, and a total score was then computed for each child for "mother" stories, "father" stories and both kinds combined. In a first study, and in two subsequent validation studies, these scores showed a pattern of significant correlations with scores for tests of perceptual field dependence. Field-dependent children tended to see both mothers and fathers as nonsupportive.

It is impressive that the characterizations of parental role by children in their TAT stories, though often taking the exaggerated and caricatured form which the fantasy setting of the TAT allows, were consistent with impressions derived from interviews with mothers. Significant correlations were found between children's TAT ratings and ratings of mothers' interactions with their children made from the home interview data. There is thus congruence in the aspects of parent-child interaction relevant to development of the global-articulated cognitive style revealed by these two different approaches, each assessing the parent-child relation from the viewpoint of one of the members of the interacting pair. The TAT approach, it is worth noting, allows us to specify the information used in making judgments more precisely than does the interview approach. In the TAT method of assessing the child's view of the parent-child relation, the data obtained are relatively delimited and no factual information is obtained about the other member in the interaction. The interview method, used to assess the relation from the mother's viewpoint, elicits a wide range of information, including factual data about the child himself, beyond what the mother reports about the interaction.

3. Personal Characteristics of Mother

A second line of inquiry suggested by the home-interview studies was into characteristics of mothers relevant to their role in the child's development of differentiation, including his cognitive style. These new studies also had the methodological objective of identifying more specifically and separately the factors that went into ratings of interviews with mothers.

The impressions of mothers that emerged from the interviews with them suggested that entering into the IID-IFD classification was the mother's own level of development with respect to articulation of experience, sense of separate identity and impulse control. For example, mothers rated IID seemed to lack definition of their roles as wives and mothers, clarity as to how to implement their goals, developed controls, and awareness of their children as separate persons. It seemed altogether plausible that mothers with these qualities, suggestive of limited differentiation, would be handicapped in helping their children separate from them. These impressions led us to studies of the mother's own level of differentiation with the specific expectations that, first, extent of the mother's own level of differentiation would be related to IID-IFD ratings, and second, that more differentiated children would be likely to have more differentiated mothers. Assessment of differentiation of mothers was made by two of the techniques used to evaluate this dimension in children: the figure-drawing test and the embedded-figures test. Comparison of mother's scores on these tests with IID-IFD ratings of home interviews and with children's measures of differentiation in various areas of functioning partially confirmed both expectations.

4. Studies of Special Groups of Children

A check on the concept that impeding the process of separation during early development will hinder progress toward articulated cognitive functioning has now been made by the study of groups in which special circumstances make separation "naturally" difficult.

The blind are one such group. Because they cannot see, their dependence on others—and particularly on the mother—in all kinds of activities is inevitably intensified. Examples may be found at every hand to illustrate the magnitude of the difference between blind and sighted children in the extent to which dependence on others is realistically required. For instance, in assessing degree of autonomy in our sighted children, we gave attention to such specifics as the age at which the child began to go to school unescorted and to ride a bicycle on trafficky streets. An attempt to apply criteria of this kind to the blind quickly reveals the extent of their enforced dependency. The blind child realistically needs guidance in finding his way around until a relatively advanced age; and bicycle riding is hardly possible for him.

In undertaking the study of the blind we expected that because of the realistic pressures toward dependency to which they are subject while growing up, the process of separation would tend to be hampered and the blind would therefore be more global in their cognitive functioning than their sighted peers.[1] At the same time, we expected to find individual differences in cognitive style and in other characteristics of differentiation among the blind as we have among the sighted, and for similar reasons. Though all parents of blind children are forced to deal with the same common obstacles to achievement of separate functioning which blindness presents, they are likely to handle the separation problem differently; and the blind children themselves are apt to be different in their starting make-up in ways that may affect the separation process.

The study of the blind (Witkin, Birnbaum, Lomonaco, Lehr & Herman, 1968), which used tactile and auditory tests of field dependence, confirmed the expectation of both less developed articulation and a wide range of individual differences along the global-articulated dimension in the blind. Ratings of clay models of the human figure, evaluated for sophistication of body con-

---

[1] Intensification and prolongation of dependence, with its negative consequences for separation, is of course not the only ground for expecting less developed articulation in the blind. Another factor of obvious importance likely to contribute to the same outcome is the greater ease of articulating a field through vision, which makes possible apprehension of the field and its parts at once together.

cept in the same way we evaluate figure drawings for this quality, related significantly to measures of field dependence. As in the sighted, articulated experience of stimulus configurations tends to go with an articulated body concept.

Further studies are now needed in which mother-child interactions of blind children, particularly in the area of separation, are examined in relation to their cognitive style, paralleling the studies already done with sighted children. The deficit suffered by the blind child, and the special developmental tasks it generates, offer unusual opportunities for focused studies of the relation between socialization and cognitive style.

5. A "Telescoped" Longitudinal Study

The studies considered thus far have implicated the socialization cluster as a factor in the child's development along the global-articulated cognitive dimension. At the same time, because all the studies were cross-sectional, they leave open the large issue of cause-effect relations. Moreover, these studies share the limitation of all cross-sectional studies that they can do little to expose the processes at work during development which have as their outcome the particular connections observed. Elucidation of process is best achieved through longitudinal studies which start with separate observation of mother and infant and which follow their continuous interaction after they are brought together. A further advantage of a longitudinal study started in infancy is that it permits examination of interaction processes at the very outset and at different stages of development. Attempts at reconstruction of the early picture through cross-sectional studies conducted at later stages present the inevitable problems inherent in the use of retrospective data.

Balancing the advantages of longitudinal studies for an understanding of developmental processes are the many well-known practical difficulties they present. Longitudinal studies are most likely to pay off, even against these difficulties, if they start with focused questions and specific hypotheses. Cross-sectional studies, done beforehand, are one source of questions and hypotheses to be pursued in longitudinal studies. After the cross-sectional studies described had been completed, it was clear that for the further working out of the role of socialization processes in the development of cognitive style a longitudinal study was needed; the cross-sectional studies already done offered many specific leads for such a study as to "*what* to look for," "*why* to look for it," and, to an extent, "*how* to go about looking for it."

In a study of a group of boys we followed from ages 10 through 24, we found striking relative stability over this long age span in measures of cognitive style and articulation of body concept. A recent study by Wender, Pedersen and Waldrop (1966) found differences in children at age 2½ which related to differences in cognitive style at age 6. Children who were field independent at age 6 showed at age 2½ a high degree of autonomous involvement in play, lower response to physical contact, less frequent attention-seeking behavior and less orality. Moreover, in another longitudinal group the differences found at age 2½ were related in turn to specific differences in the first 24 hours of life.[2] Children who at 2½ years of age showed the characteristics associated with later development of field independence, in infancy showed vigorous and smooth sucking, strong response to interruption of sucking, slow rate of falling asleep and mild response to body contact. Thus, later differences among children in cognitive style go with differences already discernible at the outset of life. Finally, several studies have shown, as did the study of Wender et al., that individual differences in the global-articulated cognitive style are evident quite early in life. Konstadt and Forman (1965), Goodenough and Eagle (1963), and Eagle and Goodenough[3] found such differences at age 5; and Banta[4] has observed differences as early as age 3.

The results of these studies give promise, on several grounds, that a longitudinal study of the origins of cognitive style is worthwhile and is likely to prove productive. First, identification of continuities, important in longitudinal work, is clearly possible. Second, the dimension with which we are concerned figures in the stream of development early and late, reflecting its continuous importance. Third, because the end-point of formed cognitive styles toward which a longitudinal study would lead is "in" quite early in development, there is the great practical advantage that the longitudinal study can be of short duration, ending perhaps when the children are as young as 3 years of age. Fourth, cognitive styles show marked relative stability during the growth years; to have such a stable developmental end-point is critical in longitudinal studies. Finally, cognitive style—and through it, level of differentiation—may be assessed by objective laboratory procedures.

We have taken still another kind of preparatory step toward a longitudinal study, aimed again at making the study more efficient by having specific hypotheses at the start. This has been to conduct a hypotheses-seeking "telescoped" longitudinal study. A number of the children who had been studied in infancy by Escalona et al., (1952) were tested by us for level of differentiation when they were 6 to 9 years old. On the basis of test performance at these later ages a group of 12 highly differentiated children and a group of 12 relatively undifferentiated children were selected from the total group of 72 tested. My colleague, Ruth Dyk, has made an intensive study of the infancy records of these two groups of children in order to identify differences between them in characteristics of the infants themselves and in characteristics of mother-infant interactions. Choices of characteristics to examine were guided by suggestions from the cross-sectional studies described, and additional characteristics were suggested by the infancy records themselves. At the time the study of the infancy records was made, our knowledge of early manifestations or pre-

---

[2] Personal communication from Dr. Richard Bell.

[3] Personal communication from Drs. Carol Eagle and Donald Goodenough.

[4] Personal communication from Dr. Thomas Banta.

cursors of differentiation was limited, and, as noted, the study had as its goal the generation of hypotheses for a later focused longitudinal study. In view of these considerations, the study of the infancy records was made with knowledge of the infant's later level of differentiation.

The differences in mother-infant interactions apparent in the infancy records of the later more differentiated and less differentiated children are particularly relevant to the issues of this chapter. Evidence on mother-infant interactions was sought particularly in accounts of the mother's manner of comforting her infant when the infant was distressed. I would like to enumerate some of the features of the mother's interaction which were associated with a later global way of experiencing in the child, on the one hand, or an articulated way of experiencing, on the other. Thus, in the group of later less differentiated infants, when delay in comforting occurred, it was typically associated with the mother's lack of perception of distress in the infant or indifference to his distress because of her own mood at the time; or a disregard of the infant's special need of the moment because of her fixed adherence to some child-rearing rule (as scheduled feeding) to which she was committed in advance. When mothers of infants in this group reacted very quickly to distress it often reflected their own anxiety. Mothers of this group also tended to be nonspecific in their response to the infant's distress, repeatedly applying the same comforting technique. One of these mothers repeatedly put her infant to her breast at any indication of his distress, even at times when the observers noted specific signs of satiation, such as spitting; another of these mothers always picked up her baby when he cried. Nonspecificity in comforting also occurred because the mother's own anxieties and wishes prevented her accurate differentiation of signs of distress.

These characteristically global perceptions and global methods of responding on the part of the mother, we may imagine, do not give the growing child the kind of differentiated feed-back to his actions and feelings, nor the kind of specificity and variety in experience necessary if his experience both of the environment and of himself is to have specificity and shadings of meaning which articulation implies.

In another area of experience, experience of the body, mothers' typical manner of interacting with infants who later turned out to be relatively undifferentiated did not seem conducive to achievement of an articulated body concept. Handling of the baby's body was lacking in sensitivity ("handling the baby all in one piece," as one record put it) ; in some cases it was minimal in amount, providing limited opportunity for exploration of the mother's body and differential "feeling" of its own body; or when close body contact was maintained it seemed calculated to gratify the mother more than the baby, a motive which is likely to work against separation. These characteristics of body-to-body contact between mother and infant in the later limitedly differentiated children not only fail to provide the kinds of bodily experiences needed for achievement of an articulated concept of the body, but they also seem likely to work against differentiation of self from nonself. With regard to the patterns of mother-infant interactions described, the later highly differentiated group presented a contrasting picture.

These and other leads obtained from the "telescoped" longitudinal study will be checked in a systematic longitudinal study about to be undertaken in our laboratory. This new study will have the highly focused character which we had anticipated the preparatory "telescoped" study would give it. It is to be hoped that our objective of elucidating *processes* of socialization in cognitive development will be advanced by this new study.

B. CROSS-CULTURAL STUDIES

Our own studies have been done with families in a large metropolis (New York City), predominantly middle-class and Jewish. Seder (1957), as we have seen, obtained results similar to ours with families from a suburb of Boston, suggesting that the relations we observed between socialization and cognitive style are not limited to the particular kind of group we studied. The possibility is raised by the apparent generality of this relation that groups differing in aspects of the socialization cluster we have found relevant to the development of differentiation will also differ in the cognitive style predominant among its members. One way of checking this possibility is through cross-cultural studies which select for comparison societies known to be widely different with regard to the socialization cluster. Two such studies have been done, one by Dawson (1963, 1967), the other by Berry (1966a, 1966b). In another study (Dershowitz, 1966) a comparison has been made of two subcultural groups within the United States.

Dawson, in his study of the Temne and Mende of Sierra Leone, found in both tribes that subjects exposed to strict, dominant maternal control tended to be field dependent. In addition to relating cognitive style to socialization emphases within each tribe, Dawson also compared the two tribes with regard to predominant cognitive style. On the basis of the socialization cluster found in Seder's study and in our own work to be associated with a more global or articulated cognitive style, Dawson predicted that Temne tribe members would be more field dependent than members of the Mende tribe. Dawson's analysis of child-rearing practices in the two tribes was based upon both descriptions given in the general anthropological literature and results of questionnaires filled out by tribal members themselves. The analysis showed that, in the area of separation, Temne parents, compared to Mende parents, are less encouraging of assumption of responsibility in their children and place greater stress on authority. There was also evidence of greater maternal dominance among the Temne. In the area of controls and imparting standards, Temne parents are more severe in discipline, using physical punishment rather than deprivation, and less consistent in child-rearing. They are also more prone to uncontrollable rage. This socialization cluster is similar in many aspects to the one associated with a global cognitive style in American families. Dawson found, as predicted, that the Temne as a group were significantly more field dependent than the Mende.

The second cross-cultural study of cognitive style, done by Berry, again examined two cultures extremely different in the socialization cluster: These groups were again the Temne, and the Eskimo of Baffin Island. The Eskimo, in contrast to the Temne, allow their children extreme freedom and rarely use corporal punishment (Hrdlicka, 1941). These characterizations from anthropological studies were confirmed by self-ratings Berry obtained from tribal members in his study. In keeping with expectations from the socialization cluster identified in the American studies, Berry found the Eskimo to be strikingly more field independent than the Temne.

Finally, Dershowitz compared two American groups considered to differ in the socialization cluster we have been considering, and therefore expected to differ in the global-articulated cognitive style and related characteristics of differentiation. One group consisted of highly orthodox Jewish boys from families predominantly of East European origin, the other of matched white Protestant boys. In the kind of orthodox Jewish families from which Dershowitz drew his sample, the primary concern of the father is with scholarly pursuits. In contrast to this non-worldly emphasis in the father's role, to the mother is left responsibility for tasks of everyday living. It is thus upon the mother that the child leans in matters related to the physical world. It is to her that his body "belongs." Typical of these mothers' relations to their sons is great solicitude for their sons' welfare and well-being, joined with a strong feeling of self-sacrifice for their children. The outcome of this family pattern is strong maternal domination over male children, with the father almost an absentee as far as the son's physical and emotional being is concerned. When Jewish boys of such family background were compared to white Protestant boys, the Jewish boys, as expected, were significantly more global in their cognitive functioning and gave evidence of a strikingly more global concept of their bodies. When these orthodox Jewish boys and Protestant boys were in turn compared to a third group of boys drawn from more assimilated Jewish families, this third group occupied an intermediate position in their performance in tests of differentiation.

The results of the Dawson, Berry and Dershowitz studies suggest that the global-articulated cognitive style may be a very useful variable in cross-cultural studies of socialization. This cognitive style may be conceived as the end-product of particular socialization processes, and so may be used for comparison of socialization emphases in different cultures. It has the additional methodological advantage for cross-cultural research that it may be assessed by objective language-free tests applicable to different cultural settings.

C. SEX DIFFERENCES

Sex differences in cognitive style have been observed in a wide variety of groups, and there is some evidence of congruent sex differences in differentiation in other psychological areas as well. To this point these sex differences have not been specifically studied in relation to the socialization process. It seems likely, however, that the socialization cluster identified as important for the development of more differentiated or less differentiated functioning enters into the development of sex differences as well, though it surely does not fully account for these sex differences.

In the cognitive area, boys and men tend to be more field independent than girls and women. Though this difference is small, compared to the range of individual differences within each sex, it is very pervasive. The observation of greater field independence in men has been made in groups of widely different backgrounds within the United States, as well as in groups in France (Andrieux, 1955; Bennett, 1956), Holland (Wit, 1955), Italy,[5] Israel,[6] Japan (Kato, 1965), Hong Kong,[7] and Sierra Leone, Africa (Dawson, 1963, 1967; Berry, 1966a, 1966b). Further, within each sex, extent of field dependence has been related to scores on masculinity-femininity scales (Miller, 1953; Crutchfield, Woodworth & Albrecht, 1958; Fink, 1959). Moreover, sex differences in field dependence have been observed over a wide age range, although they may not exist below the age of 8 (Crudden, 1941; Goodenough & Eagle, 1963) or in geriatric groups (Schwartz & Karp, 1967).

Paralleling this pervasive sex difference in perception, men have been found to show more articulated functioning in intellectual activities as well. (See, for example, Guetzkow, 1951; Sweeney, 1953; Milton, 1957.)

With regard to sex differences in differentiation elsewhere than in the cognitive area, our own work has not been directed toward investigation of this issue. Examination of the literature on sex differences suggests, however, that some of the well-documented sex differences that have been observed may be interpreted as reflecting a tendency for men to show greater differentiation than women in areas other than the cognitive. The evidence is especially suggestive in the area we have called "sense of separate identity," which implies more articulated experience of the self. (For a review of the evidence on sex differences in behavior indicative of a developed sense of separate identity see Witkin et al., 1962.)

The tendency for men to show greater articulation in their cognitive functioning than women is clearly evident in quite varied social groups. Its pervasiveness is certainly consistent with the possibility that this sex difference is rooted in genetic and/or constitutional differences between men and women. Equally plausible, however, is the possibility that this sex difference is so pervasive because the socialization processes applied to boys and girls in different cultures share important common characteristics. This may well be true for components of the socialization cluster with which we have been concerned: separation, impulse expression, and characteristics of mother as a person.

---

[5] Personal communication from Sheldon Korchin.

[6] Personal communication from Marvin Rothman.

[7] Personal communication from Robert Goodnow.

Moreover, even if biological differences between the sexes are in fact a source of sex differences in cognitive style, these biological differences may very well exert their influence through strongly fostering different child-rearing practices and social roles for the two sexes, even under widely different cultural conditions, and it is these differences in child-rearing and social role which in turn shape the development of cognitive style and related characteristics of differentiation.

In the absence of directly relevant research on the problem, we can only speculate about the ways in which the socialization cluster may operate differentially for boys and girls, throughout a wide range of cultures, so as to have the observed sex differences as an outcome. Though our studies to this point have focused on mother-*son* interactions, we have formed the impression in the course of our work that in the subculture from which our subjects came, mothers, in their relations with their daughters, were often likely to emphasize the kinds of child-rearing procedures we found in boys to be associated with the development of a global cognitive style and other indications of limited differentiation. For example, some mothers who had daughters in addition to the son taking part in our study, placed greater stress on social training for their daughters than for their sons, but were more accepting of assertiveness and encouraging of achievement (as in school) for their sons. Consistent with this observation is the impression that for boys our society places positive value on characteristics associated with developed differentiation and for girls it places positive value on characteristics associated with limited differentiation. A review of the relevant evidence by Tyler (1965) suggests, moreover, that in American culture there is the commonly held view that men are independent and women are dependent. Even among children, boys held in esteem by their fellows are likely to be independent whereas popular girls are likely to be dependent (Tuddenham, 1951, 1952). Studies by Carden (1958) and Iscoe and Carden (1961) have linked these cultural emphases to cognitive style by showing, through sociometric assessments, that girls prefer other girls with a relatively global cognitive style, whereas boys prefer boys with an articulated style. Our sex-role stereotypes, which even young children learn to value positively, thus include characteristics subsumed under differentiation. Pressure on growing children to comply with these stereotypes may accordingly contribute to the pervasive sex differences in cognitive style that have been observed, and to differences in extent of differentiation more generally.

What has been said about American culture may apply to non-Western societies as well. A survey of a large number of cultures, illiterate for the most part, has shown that men characteristically engage in activities in which self-reliance and achievement are stressed, as combat and work (Barry, Bacon & Child, 1957). In these cultures, the tasks of child-rearing and running the home are most often assigned to women. Congruent with these differences in social assignments, training for boys most often emphasizes independence. Thus, at least with regard to the separation component of the socialization cluster, the emphases in mother-child interaction found in association with the development of a global cognitive style seem more evident in the raising of girls than of boys in a wide range of cultural settings.

A check on these concepts may be made through cross-cultural studies in which sex differences in cognitive style are explored in relation to sex differences in socialization.

CONCLUSION

In overview, development of the global-articulated cognitive style is part of a larger process of development toward greater differentiation. It is for this reason that the cluster of social factors influential in determining progress toward differentiation has proved to be important for development of an articulated cognitive style. While much remains to be done in working out the processes by which the operation of this socialization cluster influences the development of cognitive style, the linkages established in the work already done point the way which further research on these developmental processes may take.

REFERENCES

ANDRIEUX, C. Contribution a l'etude des differences entre hommes et femmes dans la perception spatiale. *L'annee Psychologique,* 1955, 55, 41–60.

BARCLAY, A., & CUSUMANO, D. R. Father absence, cross-sex identity and field dependent behavior in male adolescents. Paper presented at the Annual Meeting of the American Psychological Association, 1965.

BARRY, H., BACON, MARGARET, & CHILD, I. A class-cultural survey of sex differences and socialization. *Journal of Abnormal and Social Psychology,* 1957, 55 (3).

BENNETT, D. H. Perception of the upright in relation to body image. *Journal of Mental Science,* 1956, 102, 487–506.

BERRY, J. W. A study of Temne and Eskimo visual perception. Preliminary report. Paper read before the Edinburgh University Psychology Society, 1966. (a)

BERRY, J. W. Temne and Eskimo perceptual skills. *International Journal of Psychology,* 1966, 1, 207–229. (b)

BIERI, J. Parental identification, acceptance of authority and within-sex differences in cognitive behavior. *Journal of Abnormal and Social Psychology,* 1960, 60, 76–79.

BING, ELIZABETH S. Effect of childrearing practices on development of differential cognitive abilities. *Child Development,* 1963, 34, 631–648.

CARDEN, JOYCE A. Field dependence, anxiety, and sociometric status in children. Unpublished master's thesis, Univer. of Texas, 1958.

CORAH, NORMAN L. Effects of the visual field upon perception of change in spatial orientation. *Journal of Experimental Psychology,* 1965, 70, 598–601.

CRUDDEN, C. H. Form abstraction by children. *Journal of Genetic Psychology,* 1941, 58, 113–129.

CRUTCHFIELD, R. S., WOODWORTH, D. G., & ALBRECHT, RUTH E. Perceptual performance and the effective person. Lackland AFB, Texas, *Personnel Laboratory Report,* 1958, WADC-TN-58-60. ASTIA Doc. No. AD151039.

DAWSON, J. L. M. Psychological effects of social change in a West African community. Unpublished doctor's dissertation, Univer. of Oxford, 1963.

DAWSON, J. L. M. Cultural and physiological influences upon spatial-perceptual processes in West Africa. Parts I and II. *International Journal of Psychology,* 1967, 2, 115–128; 171–185.

DERSHOWITZ, Z. Influences of cultural patterns on the thinking of children in certain ethnic groups: A study of the effect of Jewish subcultures on the field-dependence–independence dimension of cognition. Unpublished doctor's dissertation, New York Univer., 1966.

DYK, RUTH B., & WITKIN, H. A. Family experiences related to development of differentiation in children. *Child Development,* 1965, 30, 21–55.

ESCALONA, SIBYLLE, LEITCH, MARY, ET AL. Early phases of personality development: A non-normative study in infant behavior. *Monograph of the Society for Research in Child Development,* 1952, 17 (1).

FINK, D. M. Sex differences in perceptual tasks in relation to selected personality variables. Unpublished doctor's dissertation, Rutgers Univer., 1959.

GOODENOUGH, D. R., & EAGLE, CAROL J. A modification of the embedded-figures test for use with young children. *Journal of Genetic Psychology,* 1963, 103, 67–74.

GOODENOUGH, D. R., & KARP, S. A. Field dependence and intellectual functioning. *Journal of Abnormal and Social Psychology,* 1961, 63, 241–246.

GUETZKOW, H. An analysis of the operation of set in problem-solving behavior. *Journal of Genetic Psychology,* 1951, 45, 219–244.

HRDLICKA, A. The eskimo child. *Smithsonian Institute Report,* 1941, 562–577.

ISCOE, I., & CARDEN, JOYCE A. Field dependence, manifest anxiety, and sociometric status in children. *Journal of Consulting Psychology,* 1961, 25, 184.

KARP, S. A. Field dependence and overcoming embeddedness. *Journal of Consulting Psychology,* 1963, 27, 294–302.

KATO, N. The validity and reliability of new rod frame test. *Japanese Psychological Research,* 1965, 7 (3), 120–125.

KONSTADT, NORMA, & FORMAN, ELAINE. Field dependence and external directedness. *Journal of Personality and Social Psychology,* 1965, 1, 490–493.

MILLER, ANN S. An investigation of some hypothetical relationships of rigidity and strength and speed of perceptual closure. Unpublished doctor's dissertation, Univer. of California, 1953.

MILTON, G. A. The effects of sex-role identification upon problem solving skill. *Journal of Abnormal and Social Psychology,* 1957, 55, 208–212.

SCHWARTZ, D., & KARP, S. A. Field dependence in a geriatric population. *Perceptual and Motor Skills,* 1967, 24, 495–504.

SEDER, JUDITH A. The origin of differences in extent of independence in children: Developmental factors in perceptual field dependence. Unpublished bachelor's thesis, Radcliffe College, 1957.

SWEENEY, E. J. Sex differences in problem solving. *Technical Report* No. 1, Dep't. of Psychology, Stanford Univer., 1953.

TUDDENHAM, R. D. Studies in reputation: III. Correlates of popularity among elementary school children. *Journal of Educational Psychology,* 1951, 42, 257–276.

TUDDENHAM, R. D. Studies in reputation: I. Sex and grade differences in school children's evaluations of their peers. *Psychological Monographs,* 1952, 66 (Whole No. 333).

TYLER, LEONA E. *The psychology of human differences.* (3rd Ed.) New York: Appleton-Century-Crofts, 1965.

WENDER, P. H., PEDERSEN, F. A., & WALDROP, MARY F. A longitudinal study of early social behavior and cognitive development. *American Journal of Orthopsychiatry,* 1966, 319–320.

WIT, O. C. Sex differences in perception. Unpublished master's thesis, Univer. of Utrecht, 1955.

WITKIN, H. A., BIRNBAUM, J., LOMONACO, S., LEHR, S., & HERMAN, J. L. Cognitive patterning in congenitally totally blind children. *Child Development,* 1968, in press.

WITKIN, H. A., DYK, RUTH B., FATERSON, HANNA F., GOODENOUGH, D. R., & KARP, S. A. *Psychological differentiation.* New York: Wiley, 1962.

CHAPTER **15**

Early Sex-Role Development

Paul H. Mussen

University of California, Berkeley

It is a banal truth that the individual's sex role is the most salient of his many social roles. No other social role directs more of his overt behavior, emotional reactions, cognitive functioning, covert attitudes and general psychological and social adjustment. Linton observed that "the division of the society's members into age-sex categories is perhaps the feature of greatest importance for establishing participation of the individual in culture" (Linton, 1945, p. 63).

Nor is the ascription of any role more fundamental for the maintenance and continuity of society. Activities, tasks, characteristics and attitudes are assigned differentially to men and women in all cultures. But, as Margaret Mead (1935) demonstrated so effectively in her now-classic study of three New Guinea tribes, there are marked differences among cultures in the specific activities and personality characteristics ascribed to males and females, and in the degrees of differentiation between the two sex roles. Among the Arapesh, both men and women are cooperative, unaggressive, responsive to the needs of others—characteristics typically associated with the feminine role in Western culture. In marked contrast, the Mundugumor would be regarded as "masculine" by our cultural standards, for both men and women tend to be ruthless, aggressive, severe, and unresponsive. Neither of these tribes put any emphasis on the contrast between the sexes. In the third tribe, the Tchambuli, the personality characteristics of the two sexes are the reverse of what is usual in our own culture. Tchambuli women are dominant, impersonal and managing; the men are less responsible and emotionally dependent (Mead, 1935).

Although each culture has its own definitions of male and female roles and characteristics, there are some impressive cross-cultural regularities, some core concepts of masculinity and femininity (d'Andrade, 1966). For example, the majority of societies around the world organize their social institutions around males, and in most cultures men are more aggressive and dominating, have greater authority and are more deferred to than women. They are generally assigned the physically strenuous, dangerous tasks and those requiring long periods of travel. Women, on the other hand, generally carry out established routines, ministering to the needs of others, cooking, and carrying water. The husband-father role is *instrumental,* i.e., task-oriented and emotion-inhibited in nearly all cultures, and the wife-mother role is customarily more *expressive,* i.e., emotional, nurturant, and responsible (Parsons, 1955).

These almost universal sex differences are apparent among children. Systematic ethnographic observations indicate that boys in most cultures are much more likely to engage in conflict and overt aggression, and girls are more likely to be affectionate, cooperative, responsive, sociable, and succorant (d'Andrade, 1966).

These cross-cultural regularities in sex differences might be interpreted to mean that male and female roles and personality characteristics are biological "givens." Indeed they are, to some extent, based upon biological factors such as the male's superior strength and endurance. But there are a few cultures, such as the Tchambuli, in which the usual sex-role assignments do not apply or may even be reversed. Moreover, in most cultures, there are some biologically normal individuals whose behavior and characteristics are like those of the opposite, rather than their own, sex. From these facts, it must be concluded that, by and large, sex-role differences do not stem directly from biological factors. Being born a boy does not mean that the individual will *automatically* become masculine in the sense of acquiring masculine behavior, affective responses, characteristics, and cognitive responses.

The term sex-typing refers to the process by which the individual develops the attributes (behavior, personality characteristics, emotional responses, attitudes, and beliefs) defined as appropriate for his sex in his own culture. "This process is the link between the ascriptive act by the society (namely the parents, at first) and the role performance by the child. ... There is nothing automatic about the connection between ascription and role adoption; sex-typing is a ... complex process" (R. R. Sears, 1965, p. 133). Sex-typed or sex-appropriate behavior, reactions, characteristics, beliefs and attitudes—overt as well as covert —are the *products* (or outcomes, derivatives, or consequents) of this complex process.

Although there is a substantial body of research and theory on sex-typing, our understanding of the process is far from complete. The primary purpose of this chapter is to review the major explanatory hypotheses related to this process—those dealing with the fundamental antecedents and underlying mechanisms—and relevant empirical data. The discussion is largely confined to the early phases of sex-typing; first, because the first few years are of critical importance in this process and, secondly, because most of the theories link the process to the child's earliest *social,* particularly familial, experiences. Undoubtedly the sex-typing process is influenced in critical ways by extra-familial relationships (with peers, teachers and others in the community), and by experiences of later childhood and adolescence. These have not as frequently been the foci of theory or research and hence we will make no attempt to deal with them systematically in this chapter.

Theories of sex-typing can best be understood in the context of current knowledge of developmental trends in sex-role acquisition and the stability of sex-typed characteristics. A brief, very much summarized account of the pertinent findings follows.

DEVELOPMENTAL TRENDS
IN SEX-ROLE DEVELOPMENT

Methodological Problems

The major problems in research on sex-typing are related to the selection of criteria, i.e., the assessment of sex-role development. Many investigations make use of tests of masculinity and femininity. For example, in one test for young children the subject is presented with a line of fourteen toys, seven that appeal to girls (e.g., dolls, cribs, dishes) and seven that appeal to boys (e.g., knives, boats, racing cars). He is instructed to rank in order of preference the toys he would like to play with (Rabban, 1950). In another test, the child is first shown a sexless stick figure, IT, and then given groups of pictures of masculine and feminine toys, activities, objects, and clothes. He is asked to designate, in order, the objects and activities IT prefers, the assumption being that the choices attributed to IT reflect the child's own preferences. Older children, adolescents, or adults are asked to indicate their agreement or disagreement with statements indicative of masculine and feminine attitudes or interests (e.g., I enjoy participating in active sports).

All these tests may be scored from complete masculinity to complete femininity. The rationale underlying the scoring is empirical: objects or items presented (or agreement with statements) are chosen significantly more frequently by members of one sex than by the other. Does the subject choose toys and activities typically chosen by boys? Does he respond to questions (or agree with statements) in characteristically masculine ways?

In other studies, behavioral manifestations of sex-typed characteristics in natural settings or in structured situations have been used as indices of sex-role development. These have included frequency of aggressive (masculine) behavior or dependent (feminine) behavior on the playground or in specially devised doll-play situations (P. Sears, 1951). In one recent intensive study of nursery school children, conducted by Sears, Rau and Alpert (1965), measures of "gender role" included behavioral observations, observer's ratings of each subject's masculinity or femininity and an area usage score—the amount of time the child was observed in a nursery school area predominantly used by members of his own sex. In addition, doll-play sessions yielded several measures relevant to sex role (e.g., the extent to which male and female dolls were used as agents of sex-typed activities).

Since all these tests or observations presumably reflect generalized characteristics of masculinity or femininity, the derived scores or ratings should be correlated positively with each other. Unfortunately, however, the correlations are generally low. Masculine interests are correlated with masculine personality characteristics (as rated by observers) among adolescents (Mussen, 1961), but most studies have failed to demonstrate strong relationships. Thus, the inter-correlations among the five nursery school and assessment measures used in the Sears, Rau and Alpert study, ranged from 0 to .71 for girls, with a median of .36, while the median for boys was only .15. On the basis of these intercorrela-tions the authors concluded that the products of sex-typing are not well inte-grated at nursery school age but there is a "higher integration of femininity than of masculinity" (Sears et al., 1965, p. 180).

The generally low intercorrelations among the measures may make it dif-ficult to interpret the results of studies of sex-typing. The findings of one study may not support (or may even contradict) those of another, not because the conclusions based on one set of data are faulty, but rather, because the studies used vastly different, uncorrelated operational measures of sex-typing.

Trends in Sex-Typing

What is known about developmental trends in sex-typing? Apparently the process begins very early—though not by means of instinctive, innate, constitu-tional, or automatic mechanisms. Dramatic evidence for this statement is found in research on hermaphrodites or pseudohermaphrodites, individuals born with genital anomalies that make their physical sex ambiguous. Parents or physi-cians generally assign a sex role to such individuals in early infancy, and the child ordinarily begins to assume the behavior and characteristics appropriate to this role. This assignment may subsequently be shown to be contradictory to the individual's biological (chromosomal, gonadal or hormonal) sex. Even under these circumstances, however, sex-typed characteristics and reactions congruent with the initial label or sex-role assignment, including affectional orientation toward the "opposite" sex, are maintained. Moreover, attempts to reassign sex in accordance with the predominant physical attributes are usually unsuccessful and may result in severe psychological stress, unless the change is made *before the child is two years old* (Hampson, 1965).

Clearly, then, the very first years are of crucial importance for sex-role development. Once established, the individual's sex role appears to be fixed and irreversible. In this sense, the first two years seem to constitute a critical period in sex-typing.

A number of relevant empirical studies of normal children's sex-typing of interests, activities and attitudes also show that the process develops rapidly in the early years. According to these studies, generally employing the kinds of techniques of sex-role assessment described earlier, by the age of three or four, boys express clear-cut preferences for masculine activities, toys and objects (Brown, 1957; Hartup & Zook, 1960; Kagan & Moss, 1962; Rabban, 1950). Sex-typed behavior becomes progressively more firmly established with age thereafter (Rabban, 1950).

In general, boys show earlier and sharper awareness of sex-appropriate behavior and interests. Age trends for sex-typed preferences for girls are some-what more variable and less clear-cut. While most girls adopt patterns of be-havior, interests and activities that are congruent with the feminine stereotypes, many girls between the ages of three and ten show rather strong preferences for masculine games, activities and objects (Brown, 1957; Hartup & Zook, 1960). Very few boys of this age prefer feminine activities and young boys have stronger preferences for masculine toys than girls for feminine toys. For both sexes, age trends in preference for peers of the same sex roughly parallel those for sex-typed preferences for objects and activities. Almost all boys prefer other boys as friends during the early school years, and many girls of this age prefer their male peers. Furthermore, a substantial number of girls wish they were boys or "daddies" but very few boys want to be girls or "mommies" (Brown, 1957). This may be a reflection of the girl's incipient awareness of the relative devaluation of the female role in the culture.

Subgroups within our own culture differ in degree and timing of sex-typing. Boys and girls of the lower class become aware of their appropriate sex-role patterns earlier than their middle-class peers and their preferences conform more closely to the male and female stereotypes. Thus, lower-class boys reached a stable, high level of sex-appropriate choices by the time they were five, while middle-class boys did not do so until they were six. Analogously, lower-class girls made definite sex-appropriate choices by the age of six, but middle-class girls had not reached this level even by the age of eight (Rabban, 1950). Perhaps this is due to the clearer differentiation between adult masculine and feminine roles in the lower class, and the lower-class mothers' more energetic and consistent encouragement of appropriate sex-typing.

Stability of Sex-Typing

Are these early developed sex-typed characteristics stable and continuous over time? Is the highly masculine young boy likely to become a highly masculine adolescent or adult, and the highly feminine nursery school girl a highly feminine woman? The answers to these questions require longitudinal study. Unfortunately, there are very few such studies and data are consequently rel-atively sparse. What little evidence we have, however, suggests that the answers are affirmative. For example, Kagan and Moss (1962) studied the relationship between the childhood and adult characteristics of the subjects in the Fels Research Institute's longitudinal population. Their subjects, intensively observed at four developmental periods during childhood, were rated on such characteristics as aggression, passivity, dependency, achievement motivation, anxiety, heterosexual behavior and sex-typed activities. Adult status on each characteristic was assessed from intensive interviews when the subjects were between twenty and thirty years of age.

Traits congruent with appropriate sex-typing were found to be relatively stable from childhood to maturity. For example, girls high in passivity and dependence during childhood manifested these characteristics as adults, although passive dependent boys were not likely to retain these characteristics. Analogously, for males, high levels of aggression and heterosexual behavior in childhood predicted anger arousal and strong sexual orientation in adulthood. This prediction did not hold for females. It was concluded that "behavioral stability depended on congruence with sex-role standards" (Kagan, 1964, p. 155).

In this same population, the tendency to act in sex-appropriate ways was highly stable from early childhood to adulthood for both sexes (Kagan & Moss, 1962). These findings are consistent with some others based on other longitudinal data that showed that aggressive adolescent boys become aggressive, easily angered, men. Among these boys, the ones with appropriate sex-typed patterns of interest and behavior were likely to become masculine, "instrumental" adults—self-sufficient but lacking in sociability and introspection. Those who were more feminine in interest patterns during adolescence became more emotionally expressive men, less self-sufficient, more dependent, more sociable and interested in others (Mussen, 1961).

To summarize, there is substantial evidence that sex-typing begins very early and becomes crystallized during the first few years of the child's life. Once sex-typed characteristics are strongly established, they tend to be maintained over a considerable span of time.

What are the factors underlying this remarkably rapid course of growth and development and the stability of sex-typing? The corpus of theory relating to the process outweighs the available solid, systematic data. Attention in the following section will therefore be centered on theories, but, wherever possible, pertinent research findings will be cited.

THEORIES OF SEX-ROLE DEVELOPMENT

Three general types of explanatory hypotheses about sex-role development may be differentiated. The first, a social-learning theory of sex-typing, emphasizes factors such as tuition (teaching), reward and punishment, generalization and imitation, in the development and strengthening of sex-typed behavior. The second type of hypothesis, which is related to the first—particularly to the concept of imitation learning—views sex-typing as a product of *identification*. According to the third explanatory hypothesis, recently proposed and elaborated by Kohlberg (1966), sex-typing is a natural concomitant of cognitive development and maturation, emerging quite independently of specific training and learning experiences.

Social-Learning Theory

Social-learning theory explanations of sex-typing are the most traditional, best-known and probably the most widely accepted. Moreover, some of the basic principles of learning, such as those concerned with the effects of reward and punishment, are universally included in the folk wisdom about child-training.

Most experts in the field of socialization speak of the child's "learning a sex role" which is taught to him by the agents of socialization, most particularly by his family. "Many agencies share in teaching a child the expected behavior of his sex, but the family is pre-eminent" (Elkin, 1960, p. 53). Sex-role training is seen as beginning at birth, with the use of blue blankets for boy infants and pink ones for girls; the roles are "drilled in" intensively and continuously throughout childhood.

In their explanation of sex-typing, social-learning theorists invoke well-known, experimentally verified principles of learning. The factors that are central are differential and selective rewards and punishments, generalization, mediation, modeling and vicarious learning.

Stated in the simplest terms, social-learning theory holds that sex-appropriate responses are rewarded (reinforced) by parents and others, and hence are repeated (increased in frequency). Sex-inappropriate behavior, on the other hand, is likely to be punished and hence to diminish in strength and frequency, i.e., to become extinguished.

On a common-sense basis, this argument seems irrefutable. Moreover, there is abundant experimental evidence showing that, even within the first few weeks of life, infants can learn to make specific responses to specific stimuli. For example, they can learn to turn their heads, smile, and vocalize in response to the approach of others, if these responses are frequently rewarded (Rheingold, 1956).

Is there evidence that the theory is applicable to the very early learning of sex-typed responses? Certainly, parents are keenly aware of the cultural definition of sex-role behavior, and it may be inferred that they reward their children's sex-appropriate responses and punish those that are inappropriate. Moreover, children feel that their parents want them to adopt sex-appropriate behavior (Fauls & Smith, 1956).

Middle-class fathers freely admit that they would be concerned if their sons showed a lack of responsibility and initiative, inadequate school performance, insufficient aggression or too much passivity, ineptitude in athletics, over-conformity, excitability, too much crying or other childish behavior (Aberle & Naegele, 1952). Presumably these fathers would punish their sons for manifesting such characteristics and would reward them for the opposite kinds of behavior. But this could not be done during infancy, for such characteristics would not be apparent until later on. Yet, as noted earlier, sex-typing begins very early in the child's life. If social-learning theory is applicable, there must be rewards for sex-typed behavior beginning in the first year or two. The argument may be compelling, but firm supportive data are lacking. In fact, there is very little evidence that infant boys and girls receive any significant differential treatment by either, or both, parents. Thus, in their comprehensive study of child-training practices, Sears, Maccoby and Levin (1957) found no sex differences in most aspects of feeding or toilet training, or surprisingly, in training for modesty and the inhibition of sex play. Mothers were somewhat more indulgent and warmer toward their infant daughters than toward their infant sons, however.

More rigorous and detailed observation and analysis of infant-parent interactions might reveal that parents do reward and punish their sons and daughters differently, especially for responses related to sex-typing. So far, however, such data are not available.

Direct rewards appear to be effective in fostering sex-appropriate behavior later in childhood. Even here, however, the evidence, although consistent with social-learning theory, is not impressive. In an excellent summary of the social-learning point of view as applied to the sex-typing of aggression and dependency, Mischel says:

> The greater incidence of dependent behaviors for girls than boys, and the reverse situation with respect to physically aggressive behavior, seems directly applicable in social-learning terms. Dependent behaviors are less rewarded for males, physically aggressive behaviors are less rewarded for females in our culture and consequently there are mean differences between the sexes in the frequency of such behaviors after the first few years of life.
>
> Unfortunately, present evidence that the sexes are indeed treated differentially by their parents with respect to the above behaviors is far from firm and much more detailed investigations are needed of the differential reward patterns and modeling procedures used by mothers, fathers and other models with boys and girls in the natural setting. The current empirical evidence is equivocal, although consistent with a social-learning view (adapted from Mischel, 1966, p. 75).

For example, among the middle-class preschool and kindergarten boys and girls studied by Sears et al.,

> aggression was the area of child behavior in which the greatest sex distinctions were made by parents. Boys were allowed more aggression in their dealings with other children in the neighborhood, and were more frequently encouraged to fight back if another child started a fight (Sears et al., 1957, p. 403).

A number of mothers apparently felt that being "boylike" implied being aggressive, especially in self-defense, with playmates. As social-learning theory would predict, since they are rewarded for aggressive behavior, boys manifest greater physical aggression and more negativistic behavior.

Girls, on the other hand, receive more praise for "good" behavior (obedience, conformity, sweetness and non-aggressiveness). They are more often subjected to punishment and withdrawal of love for aggression and disobedience. And, as learning theory would predict, girls are, in fact, more obedient and conforming in their relationships with others.

Unfortunately, the data of this study came exclusively from maternal interviews and hence may be biased. There are no definitive studies relating reliable and objective observations of parental rewards and punishments to children's sex-typed behavior.

Other evidence consistent with the social-learning point of view comes from a cross-cultural study involving 110 cultures. In the vast majority of cultures surveyed, sex differences in child-training practices seemed clearly designed to produce sex-typed characteristics. Girls in most cultures are subjected to greater pressures (rewards and punishments) that lead to the development of nurturance, obedience and responsibility and boys all over the world are more trained to achieve and to be self-reliant. In other words, patterns of child-rearing practices seem to be oriented toward molding the prescribed adult sex-appropriate characteristics, thus minimizing what Benedict termed "discontinuities in cultural conditioning" (Barry, Bacon & Child, 1957).

Generalization.   Of course, social-learning theorists do not argue in favor of the simplistic notion that direct rewards and punishment are the only sources of the development of sex-typed responses. Other important principles of learning are also central in their explanations of the development and maintenance of sex-typed behavior. There is, for example, the principle of generalization, which states that when a response has been learned to one stimulus, it is likely to occur in response to other, similar stimuli. The greater the degree of similarity between the original stimuli and those in a new situation, the greater the likelihood that the response will occur. Applied to the learning of sex-typed behavior, this principle would assert that if the boy is rewarded for expression of aggression toward other children in his own backyard, he is likely to behave aggressively in his interactions with children in other situations such as nursery school. Similarly, the little girl's compliance or obedience, rewarded by her mother, is likely to generalize to her relationships with other adults, such as teachers.

Certain broad patterns of behavior, attitudes, and characteristics that are related to later sex-typing may be established early in childhood as a consequence of parental rewards and punishments. This was demonstrated in the recent study of Sears et al. (1965) in which many child-rearing variables were correlated with measures of sex-typing. They discovered two clusters of child-rearing variables that were associated with sex role. One was related to permissiveness with respect to sex play, and the other to disciplinary methods and aggression. Sex permissiveness was correlated with masculinity and non-permissiveness with femininity *for both sexes.*

> ...the more freedom these children had for sexual play (i.e., the more permissive the parents were), the more masculine (or non-feminine) they became. This would occasion no surprise if we had been measuring the child's active sex play itself, but the measures showing this effect are quite detached from such overt sexuality. The choice of toys and occupations, in particular, seemed distant from sex behavior. Whatever the mechanism by which encouragement or discouragement of active sexual behavior was translated into the liking or disliking of other gender role

activities, there is little doubt that discouragement produced a passive, non-masculine quality in a boy's behavior and a passive femininity in the girls' (Sears et al., 1965, p. 190).

Severity of socialization during nursery school—i.e., strong demands for good table manners, severe toilet training, maternal punishment for aggression and high use of physical punishment—also tends to femininize children of both sexes.

These masculine and feminine responses manifested by these children in nursery school may be interpreted as generalizations of behavior learned at home. In relatively relaxed, permissive homes, a child of either sex is rewarded for exploring, experimenting, seeking outgoing activity, and aggression, i.e., for displaying essentially stereotyped masculine behavior and qualities. These responses become stronger and are likely to generalize. In nursery school and test situations, these generalized responses will be manifested in his preference for energetic, adventurous, masculine games and activities. In a restrictive milieu, on the other hand, the child is rewarded for—and learns—obedience, passivity, and the inhibition of strong overt reactions, responses that are generally considered feminine. These reactions and characteristics, established in the home, generalize to other situations, and are reflected in an orientation toward feminine interests and activities.

As the child's cognitive development progresses, he forms concepts, and attaches labels to objects and events. These labels may then serve as the bases for further generalization, i.e., all stimuli with the same label may elicit the same reactions. This is called *verbal mediation*, or *mediated generalization*.

It is easy to see how mediated generalization facilitates development and crystallization of sex-typing. The boy's social learning experiences are likely to result in associations between terms such as "good boy," "boys' games" and "that shows you're strong" and parental approval and reward. Consequently, responses and activities having these labels become attractive to the boy and he is likely to learn them. Analogously, for boys, labels such as "sissy," "girlish," "nice" are likely to be linked with parental disapproval (punishment) and interests, activities and behaviors labeled in these ways will be avoided.

Imitation. Recently Bandura and other social-learning theorists have dealt systematically with the enormously potent influence of imitation—also called observational learning, vicarious learning, and modeling—on behavior development. The major conclusion of a vast amount of research is that simply by observing a model's behavior, the child may acquire responses, including sex-typed ones, that were not previously included in his behavioral repertoire. This may be true even if the child does not perform imitative responses, or receive reinforcement at the time he is observing the model. For example, in several studies, Bandura and his colleagues have shown that after exposure to aggressive models children will imitate many novel aggressive responses (Bandura, 1966; Bandura, Ross & Ross, 1961; Bandura & Walters, 1963).

It is impossible to determine how much of the child's repertoire of sex-typed responses develops as a result of the imitation of models. But there is little doubt that from very early childhood onward, children learn by imitating models, either because they are instructed to do so, or because they simply "want to." If the child's imitative behavior is rewarded frequently "a secondary tendency to match [imitate] may be developed and the process of imitation becomes the derived drive of imitativeness" (Miller & Dollard, 1941, p. 10).

The questions of why and how the process of imitation develops remain unanswered. But clearly, once imitation begins, it becomes a highly significant means of acquiring new responses. Many of the child's sex-typed responses may develop simply through imitation of his like-sexed parent's behavior.

A note of caution must be sounded. On the basis of their recent research, summarized above, Sears et al. (1965) rejected the imitation hypothesis as an explanation for the acquisition of sex-typed behavior, concluding that it is "deceptively simple." Bandura's research had shown that powerful and nurturant models were more likely to be imitated than models lacking these characteristics. But the study of Sears et al. yielded no data supportive of a "modeling" hypothesis which stated that "if the father is more nurturant and more powerful than the mother, the child will use him as the more-to-be-imitated model, and will thus be more masculine" (Sears et al., 1965, p. 187).

Nor were there any significant correlations between their parental power and nurturant scales and measures of sex role for either sex. The investigators attributed this negative finding to the fact that the responses imitated in the Bandura studies were simple and easily recognized, while Sears et al. were concerned with the emulation of "that very complex quality of gender role exemplified in parental behavior" (Sears et al., 1965, p. 186).

Identification

The acquisition and development of many complicated sex-typed patterns of behavior, personality characteristics, motives and attitudes do not yield readily to analysis in terms of social-learning theory. Many such responses appear to develop spontaneously, without direct training or reward and without the child intending to learn. A more subtle process, identification, has been hypothesized to account for such developments.

> . . . sex-typing has been interpreted by non-psychoanalytic theorists as an instance of primary identification. Gender roles are very broad and very subtle. It would be difficult to imagine that any kind of direct tuition could provide for the learning of such elaborate behavioral, attitudinal, and manneristic patterns as are subsumed under the rubrics of masculinity and femininity (Sears et al., 1965, p. 171).

The concept of identification originated within the framework of psychoanalytic theory. Freud defined it as the process which "endeavors to mold a person's own ego after the fashion of one that has been taken as a model" (Freud, 1921, p. 62).

Because of its extensive, explanatory powers, the concept also appeals to many non-psychoanalytic theorists. Learning theorists conceptualize identification as "learned drive" or "motive" to be like a model (e.g., parents). The child's identification with his parents is seen in his attempts to duplicate or emulate their ways of behaving, thinking, and feeling and to adopt their ideals, attitudes and opinions.

Clearly, imitation and identification are concepts that have much in common and it is frankly difficult to make precise or rigorous differentiations between them. In fact, Bandura and Walters deny that such a differentiation is possible:

> ... observational learning is generally labeled "imitation" in experimental psychology and "identification" in theories of personality. Both concepts, however, encompass the same behavioral phenomena, namely the tendency for a person to reproduce the actions, attitudes, or emotional responses exhibited by models (Bandura & Walters, 1963, p. 89).

These theorists prefer to use the term "imitation" to refer to "the occurrence of any matching responses" (Bandura & Walters, 1963, p. 90).

Although this argument has considerable merit, most students of socialization—and of sex-typing in particular—find the concept "identification" a very useful one. It is generally used to denote a particular kind of imitation: the spontaneous duplication of a model's complex, integrated pattern of behavior (rather than simple, discrete responses), without specific training or direct reward but based on an intimate relationship between the identifier and the model. Phenomenologically—from the child's viewpoint—identification is manifested by the belief that he possesses some of the model's attributes and feelings (Kagan, 1958).

> If a six-year-old boy is identified with his father, he necessarily regards himself as possessing some of his father's characteristics, one of which is maleness or masculinity. Moreover, if a child is identified with a model, he will behave, to some extent, as if events that occur to the model are occurring to him. If a child is identified with his father, he shares vicariously in the latter's victories and defeats; in his happiness and in his sorrow; in his strengths and in his weaknesses (Kagan, 1964, p. 146).

The outcomes or products of the process are assumed to be relatively stable and enduring and highly resistant to change. Broad, pervasive aspects of personality and character, such as inner control or conscience, and sex-typing are presumably assimilated or absorbed by means of identification. Obviously identification with the like-sexed parent enhances the child's sex-typing considerably. As Kagan points out,

> The boy with a masculine father gains two products from an identification with him—the vicarious power and strength that facilitate future attempts to master sex-typed skills, and the continued exposure to sex-typed be-

havior. This exposure facilitates the acquisition of sex-typed responses (Kagan, 1964, p. 148).

Three major hypotheses about the origins and development of identification have been proposed: defensive identification, the original psychoanalytic hypothesis; the developmental identification hypothesis, based essentially on the principles of learning; and the role-playing hypothesis, derived from sociological conceptualizations.

Defensive identification.   The original, psychoanalytic formulation of defensive identification linked the process to the resolution of the Oedipus complex. The young boy, having libidinous feelings toward the mother, begins to see his father as a competitor for the mother's love and attention and, therefore, as an object of antagonism, envy and hostility—"a rival who stands in his way and whom he would like to push aside" (Freud, 1949, p. 91).

But the boy soon begins to fear that his father will castrate him in retaliation for his envy and hostility, as well as for his sexual strivings toward the mother. This fear, together with the boy's realization that he cannot succeed in this struggle, lead to the resolution of the Oedipus complex. Instead of competing with his father and feeling hostile and jealous, the boy *identifies* with him. Identification in a sense *replaces* the Oedipal conflict. It is as though the boy said, "if I *am* him, he can't hurt me."

Identification then serves the functions of reducing the boy's fear of the father and permitting him to enjoy the mother's love vicariously. (If he *is* the father, he possesses the mother's love.) Such identification has also been labeled "aggressive identification," and "identification with the aggressor" (A. Freud, 1946; Bronfenbrenner, 1960; Mowrer, 1950, pp. 573–616).

Two recent theorists, Kagan (1958) and Whiting (1960), also suggest that envy (though not exclusively of a sexual kind) is a central factor in the development of identification. The child envies a broad range of the model's powers and capabilities as well as his efficient control and enjoyment of resources. The child covertly practices the roles of the model so that, at least in fantasy, he is like the envied model, controlling and consuming the valued resources he lacks in reality. Underlying the child's development and maintenance of identification is a desire "to experience or obtain positive goal states that he perceived that the model demands" (Kagan, 1958, p. 298).

The classical psychoanalytic hypothesis that identification is motivated by fear of castration clearly cannot explain the girl's identification with her mother. To explain this, Freud postulated the mechanism of anaclitic identification, rooted in the girl's love and attachment as well as her need to insure the continuation of her dependency relationship with the mother. Fear of the loss of the mother's love, and the frustration and deprivation this would entail, motivate the girl to identify with her mother.

Developmental identification.   The hypothesis of developmental identification, which is related to the concept of anaclitic identification, maintains

that love and affection for the model are the principal factors instigating identification. If the child has pleasant, nurturant, rewarding interactions with
the parent, that parent's behavior—his activities, speech, and mannerisms—
acquire positive value or, in learning theory terms, secondary reward value.
The child, being dependent on the nurturant parent, feels frustrated when
he is absent. But by performing some of the acts ordinarily performed by that
parent, the child is able to provide himself with some of the rewarding feelings
originally associated with the parent's presence. Developmental identification,
manifested in the child's imitation of the parent's behavior, is motivated by
the child's desire to "reproduce bits of the beloved and longed-for parent"
(Mowrer, 1950, p. 615).

Developmental identification can readily explain the girl's identification
with her mother, but accounting for the boy's father-identification is theoretically more troublesome. Since the mother is the primary source of nurturance
and affection for all infants, both boys and girls should at first identify with
her. To identify with his father, the little boy must, in some way, "abandon
the mother as a personal model and shift his loyalties and ambitions to his
father" (Mowrer, 1950, p. 607).

Mowrer has suggested that the infant's first identification with his mother
is undifferentiated, i.e., it is with the mother as an adult human being, not
specifically as a man or a woman. After the child becomes aware of sex
differences,

> the father, who has played a somewhat subsidiary role up to this point,
> normally comes forward as the boy's special mentor, as his proctor, guide,
> and model in matters which will help the boy eventually to achieve full
> adult status in society, not only as a human being, but also in the unique
> status of a *man* (Mowrer, 1950, p. 608).

This shift to father-identification is based on affection and love for the
father. This usually occurs at the age of three or four, when

> the good father tends to "take [his son] on," to accept responsibility for
> him in a way that he does not do for his little girls. The boy becomes *my
> boy, my son;* the father permits the child to accompany him in his work,
> if possible, and otherwise creates special opportunities for excursions and
> experiences which the mother could not well provide. The father, in other
> words, begins to open up for the child a glimpse into "man's world"
> (Mowrer, 1950, p. 610).

Role theory and identification. For role theorists, identification is
equated with "role-playing," e.g., identification with the father is synonymous
with "playing the father's role." The child's role-playing is purposive because
it provides practice for significant adult behavior (Maccoby, 1959).

Two factors determine the extent of the child's role-playing or the strength
of his identification: (1) frequency and intensity (or intimacy) of the child's
interaction with the model; and (2) the model's power over the child, i.e.,
his control of resources that are valuable to the child (Maccoby, 1959). From

the child's point of view, the model's power may involve both giving nurturance and reward (the major determinants of developmental identification) and the ability to threaten and punish (of paramount importance in producing defensive identification) (Mussen & Distler, 1959).

Studies of identification and sex-typing.   Identification with the like-sexed parent is often regarded as a *sine qua non* of appropriate sex-typing. Whether or not such a sweeping generalization is valid, there is evidence that *lack* of such identification has deleterious effects on sex-typing. For example, three- and four-year-old boys reared without fathers in their homes are retarded in acquiring typically masculine aggressive patterns of behavior, presumably because they did not have masculine models available (Sears, Pintler & Sears, 1946). Such boys also have difficulties establishing relationships with their peers, perhaps because of their inadequate development of the masculine skills and orientations necessary for successful peer interactions (Lynn & Sawrey, 1958).

Homosexuality.   More dramatic, and perhaps more relevant, evidence comes from investigations of the backgrounds of homosexuals, individuals who have not acquired the most essential attribute of adequate sex-typing, sexual orientation (object choice) toward the opposite sex. Clinical evidence suggests that the male homosexual is overly attached to his mother, identifying with her rather than with his father (Bieber et al., 1962). This may be due to rejection by the father, together with acceptance by the mother, or perceptions of the mother as the more dominant and powerful parent. If either of these conditions obtains, the boy does not shift from early identification with his mother, remains excessively dependent on her, and does not identify with his father or other adult males. If he maintains his identification with the mother, he will, as a consequence, assume her sex-object choice.

"If mother (like women in general) is sexually oriented toward men, and if the boy's strongest personal alignment remains with her, then he too, as a consequence of his persistent mother-identification, will tend to be sexually oriented toward men" (Mowrer, 1950, p. 612).

In order to test the Freudian hypothesis that male homosexuals show stronger identification with their mothers and less identification with their fathers, Chang and Block (1960) assessed the identification patterns of twenty overt homosexual male adults and a matched group of twenty men who were not homosexuals. Their data supported the hypothesis, showing clearly that overt male homosexuals were relatively more strongly identified with their mothers than with their fathers. In brief, failure to identify with the like-sexed parent seems to be an antecedent of homosexuality or inappropriateness of sex-object choice.

Sex-typing of nursery school children.   Measures of sex-typing have been used as indices of identification in a number of systematic studies involving normal children from intact families. In one study designed to test the relative truth values of the developmental, defensive and role-playing hypotheses of identification, boys' masculinity scores were related to their perceptions of their fathers (Mussen & Distler, 1959). The questions underlying the study were: Do highly masculine boys view their fathers as nurturant and rewarding, as the developmental hypothesis would predict; as punitive and threatening, in accordance with the defensive identification hypothesis; or, as powerful controllers of resources (rewards and punishment), as role theory would hold? Thirty-eight five-year-old boys were given the IT Scale, a projective test of sex-role preference (Brown, 1956) and the ten most masculine boys and the ten least masculine were selected for further study. These twenty boys completed a series of incomplete, semi-structured doll-play stories, that revealed their perceptions of their parents. As would be predicted from the developmental identification hypothesis, the highly masculine boys significantly more frequently portrayed their fathers as nurturant and rewarding. There was also some slight support for the defensive identification hypothesis, however, with highly masculine boys perceiving their fathers as more punitive.

These boys also scored higher than the boys low in masculinity in *father power,* a score reflecting both the extent of the child's interaction with his father and the degree to which the latter has power over him, i.e., controls rewards and punishments. This last finding may be regarded as evidence in support of the role theory of identification. It may *be concluded that this study, designed to evaluate the three theories, yielded some support for all of them. The evidence for the developmental hypothesis is the most clear-cut and impressive, however.

Interviews with the mothers of the boys generally corroborated the doll-play findings. The fathers of the highly masculine boys were reported to be warmer and more affectionate toward their sons and more interested in them. These results, too, may be interpreted as supportive of the developmental and role-theory hypotheses of identification, but they provide no support for the defensive identification hypothesis.

In a replication and extension of this study, the IT Test was administered to five- and six-year-old boys and girls who completed the same incomplete stories in doll-play (Mussen & Rutherford, 1963). In addition, each mother was interviewed intensively and both parents answered personality questionnaires and a "play and games list" dealing with the parent's encouragement or discouragement of the child's participation in certain typical sex-typed activities.

The study yielded further evidence for the developmental identification hypothesis as applied to both sexes. Appropriate sex-typing among boys was again found to be related to perceptions of fathers as warm, nurturant, and rewarding. The findings for girls paralleled those for the boys. Highly feminine, appropriately sex-typed girls described their mothers in doll-play as significantly warmer, more nurturant, affectionate and gratifying than the other girls did. The data from maternal interviews buttressed these findings, mothers of highly feminine girls reporting more interest in their daughters and warmer relationships with them. None of the evidence fitted the defensive identification model.

Other factors were also found to be conducive to the young girl's feminization. Mothers' self-acceptance and fathers' masculinity of interests and orientation, as well as the fathers' encouragement of their daughters' participation in feminine activities, were associated with high degrees of femininity in the girls.

It must also be noted that not all investigations of identification and sex-typing have yielded positive results. Sears et al. (1965) found no significant correlations between their scales of parental nurturance and power, on the one hand, and their measures of their nursery school subjects' sex-role behavior. Judging from their data,

> There is no evidence that the feminine girls' mothers were warm or set high standards (except for table manners) or used love-oriented discipline, or specified themselves as models. The masculine boys' parents, in the home, were not warm, nor did they use love-oriented discipline or refer to themselves as models ... the primary identification theory as an explanation of gender role is poor (Sears et al., 1965, p. 194).

It is difficult to determine exactly why these results are so vastly different from those obtained in the studies reviewed above, but a number of possible reasons may be suggested. For one thing, the subjects of the Sears et al. study were at least a year younger than the subjects of the other studies and perhaps their patterns of identification were not yet well-enough crystallized. Moreover, they were all from highly intelligent, well-educated families where sex roles may be less clearly differentiated than they are in lower-middle class, more poorly educated families from which the subjects of the other studies came. Most importantly, different operations were used in assessing sex-typing: preferences for obvious, easily recognized masculine and feminine activities and objects in the IT Test versus actual choices of objects and activities plus more subtle, more complex qualities of sex role in the Sears et al. study (1965). In any case, the findings of the latter study make it clear that, at least during the nursery school period, developmental identification does not seem to be a complete and adequate explanation of sex-typing.

Cognitive-Developmental Theory of Sex-Typing

A theoretical interpretation of the acquisition of sex-typed behavior and attitudes that contrasts sharply with learning theory identification interpretations has recently been proposed by Kohlberg (1966). The theory is linked to two prominent recent developments in psychology: the renaissance of cognitive developmental theory, stimulated by the work of Piaget and his followers, and the new stress on motives such as curiosity, mastery, exploration, competence and effectance.

Kohlberg's intriguing theory is based on the assumption that the basic patterning of sexual attitudes is to be found neither in biological instincts nor in arbitrary cultural norms, but in universal aspects of "the child's cognitive organization of his social world along sex-role dimensions" (Kohlberg, 1966, p. 82). The development of sex-typing is conceived as an aspect of cognitive growth which involves basic, qualitative changes with age in the child's modes of thinking and concomitantly, in his perceptions of the physical and social world, including his sense of self, and of his sex role. Learning, particularly observational learning, plays some role in sex-role acquisition, but the most significant factor is the child's *cognitive activity*—his active selection and organization (structuring) of his perceptions, knowledge and understanding.

The child's initial conception of sex role stems from

> important, "natural" components of patterning; i.e., aspects of sex-role attitudes which are universal across cultures and family structures and which appear relatively early in the child's development. This patterning of sex-role attitudes is essentially "cognitive" in that it is rooted in the child's conceptions of physical things, the bodies of himself and of others, as he relates body concepts to his conceptions of a social order which makes functional use of sex categories in quite culturally universal ways. Rather than biological instinct, it is the child's cognitive organization of social role concepts around universal physical dimensions that accounts for the existence of universals in sex-role attitudes (adapted from Kohlberg, 1966, p. 82).

Sex-typing is initiated by the very early sex *labeling* of the child which begins with hearing and learning the words "boy" and "girl." By the age of two or three, children know their own self-labels, and in the next couple of years, they label others according to conventional cues. The child regards his sex-identification as an "abstract self-concept" which, when stabilized, is practically fixed and irreversible, "maintained by a motivated adaptation to physical-social reality and by the need to preserve a stable and positive self-image" (Kohlberg, 1966, p. 88). The child's basic sexual self-concept (his self-categorization as "boy" or "girl") becomes the major organizer and determinant of many of his activities, values, and attitudes. The boy in effect says, "I am a boy, therefore I want to do boy things, therefore the opportunity to do boy things (and to gain approval for doing them) is rewarding" (Kohlberg, 1966, p. 89).

The child's sex self-concept or gender identity becomes stabilized at about five or six years of age, at the same time that the child begins to understand the principle of conservation—the fact that physical properties such as mass, number and weight are stable and invariant. With further cognitive development, he acquires a number of cross-cultural stereotypes of masculine and feminine behavior—of males as active, dominant, powerful and aggressive, and females as more nurturant. These are not derived from parental behavior or direct tuition, but rather, stem from universal perceived sex differences in bodily structure and capacities.

Once established, basic sex-role concepts generate new sex-typed values and attitudes. Kohlberg postulates five mechanisms by which sex-role concepts become directly translated into masculine-feminine values:

(1) The first, an expression of Piaget's notion of *assimilation,* is the child's "tendency to respond to new activities and interests that are consistent with old ones" (Kohlberg, 1966, p. 112). By the age of two, there are clear-cut sex differences in interests, activities and personality characteristics. New objects or activities consistent with established interests and preferences are assimilated, while discrepant ones are not.

(2) Children make value judgments consistent with their self-concepts of sex role. The three-year-old has a "naive or egocentric tendency to value anything associated with or like himself" as best (Kohlberg, 1966, p. 113), and hence values and seeks objects and activities that are representative of his own sex.

(3) Young children tend to associate positive, self-enhancing values with sex-role stereotypes and these values are motivating. For example, masculinity is associated with values of strength, competence, and power, and for the boy, acquiring this stereotype produces a motivation to enact a masculine role, to conform to the stereotype. According to Kohlberg, this is true regardless of the rewards associated with the role.

(4) The child perceives his gender role as normative and hence generates judgments that conformity is morally right and deviations are morally wrong.

(5) Modeling or identification is the fifth mechanism, but Kohlberg's analysis of the process is strikingly different from the psychoanalytic or learning interpretations discussed earlier. Sex-typing is not conceived as a *product* of identification; quite the contrary, identification is a consequence of sex-typing. Boys model themselves after males because they already have masculine interests and values; "for the boy with masculine interests and values, the activities of a male model are more interesting and hence more modeled" (Kohlberg, 1966, p. 129).

Once the modeling process begins, it continues, with widespread effects. The child begins to imitate not only individually admired acts; but he wants to be like the model in general and hence needs a continuing relationship to him to attain this goal (Kohlberg, 1966, p. 134).

> In summary, then, the boy's general competence motivation leads him to prefer and imitate masculine roles and models on a twofold base, first because they are "like self" and second because the boy awards superior prestige, power and competence to such roles. These tendencies lead him to develop preferential imitation and approval seeking from the father, but only after a delay period. This delay period occurs because cognitive growth is required before the father's role is categorized in terms of "we males," and before the father's occupational and familial role is perceived as more prestigeful than the mother's in terms of economic, occupational, and instrumental functions. During this period, the boy's identi-

fication with the father tends to be assimilated to general stereotypes of the masculine role having little to do with the father's individual role and personality (adapted from Kohlberg, 1966, p. 136).

Since the cognitive-developmental theory of sex-typing was proposed very recently, there have not yet been direct tests of specific hypotheses derived from theory and adequate evaluation is not possible. Nevertheless, Kohlberg's presentation is intriguing, thoughtful, stimulating, and plausible. It cites relevant, supportive evidence and emphasizes a number of important problems neglected by other theories of sex-typing.

The stress on early sex labeling, underplayed in other theories, seems warranted in view of facts reviewed earlier. Most importantly, Kohlberg's stress on the critical roles of cognitive growth and changes in cognitive organization seem a much needed antidote for the neglect of these phenomena in traditional learning theory and psychoanalytic hypotheses about identification and sex-typing. His arguments in these matters are compelling. There is little doubt that the child's cognitive abilities—his perceptions and understanding of his environment—strongly influence the development of sex-role behavior. Unfortunately, however, the mechanisms underlying cognitive development have not been carefully specified or adequately analyzed, changes being attributed to "natural" (i.e., unexplained) events.

The theory is a descriptive-developmental one and is not primarily concerned with antecedent-consequent relationships in sex-typing. As a result, it gives less adequate attention to individual differences in degrees of sex-typing, i.e., within-sex differences in strength of sex-typed responses. Kohlberg views these fundamentally as the outcomes of differences in level or rate of cognitive development. This hardly seems a satisfactory explanation, however, for in any group of boys of the same age and of equal intelligence, there are wide variations in degrees of masculinity of interests, attitudes and behavior. Kohlberg acknowledges that "a family climate of warmth, expressiveness, security . . . and high social participation" may facilitate sex-typing because it "allows for the exploration and integration of the new and the problematic" in development (Kohlberg, 1966, p. 156). But in general his theory underemphasizes the potency of reinforcement of sex-typed responses, modeling, and identification in the sex-typing process.

A SYNTHESIS AND POINT OF VIEW
ON SEX-ROLE DEVELOPMENT

As this review demonstrates, there is a variety of theories of sex-typing and acquisition of sex role. Each undoubtedly contains some truth and each has some empirical support. Yet none of the theories by itself is able to account for all the observed phenomena and all the data on the acquisition of sex-typed behavior.

A comprehensive theory of sex-role development—if such is possible—will have to incorporate aspects of all three theories, and in addition, include some factors not explicitly handled in any of them. Furthermore, such a theory must explain individual differences in sex-typing as well as general age developmental trends in the process.

It may be hypothesized that normally, for most children, learning, identification and cognitive organization all contribute to the development and growth of sex-typing and sex-role acquisition. It seems likely that learning is of paramount importance in the very early phases of sex-role development and that identification and cognitive growth play vital, facilitating roles later on. That is, the first established components of sex role are probably learned by means of reinforcement and imitation. Certainly specific and discrete sex-typed responses can be trained and learned in this way, and, probably more importantly, so can broad, pervasive sex-typed personality characteristics, attitudes and approaches—products of generalizations from specific responses—which, once formed, generalize to many situations.

If children between the ages of one and four were reared in a highly controlled, laboratory setting (God forbid), their training—and consequently their learning—could probably be programmed in such a way as to produce stereotypical sex-appropriate behavior, profoundly reversed sex roles, or something in between. Undesirable as this would be from other points of view, it would be theoretically possible for the child to acquire the overt aspects (and probably some of the covert attributes) of sex-role behavior in this way, without forming an identification relationship with a like-sexed adult.

But happily, reinforcement learning is not ordinarily the only process involved in sex-role development. In the course of growing up, most children form affectionate relationships with their parents, identify with them, and take them as behavior models.

The sequence of critical events in sex-role development, as we view it, is labeling, tuition (training), and identification. Obviously, training is not entirely superseded by identification when the latter process begins. Rather, training and learning continue with broader, more striking consequences after the child has identified with his parents.

As Kohlberg suggests, labeling the child properly initiates the process of sex-typing. But the simple act of labeling is not sufficient to set the process in operation. The assigned label must be salient for the child and must be regarded as positive, valuable, and rewarding. The fifteen-month-old child who is appropriately labeled, but is at the same time restricted, given no freedom for self-expression and made to feel inadequate, will not be highly motivated to act in sex-appropriate ways. In order to be effective (i.e., to promote sex-typing), labeling must occur within a context of a "sense of autonomy" (Erikson, 1950), i.e., feelings of self-reliance, worthiness, and adequacy. If the label is applied with signs of love and affection, with clear indications of acceptance and approval, it will be associated with positive feelings (rewards). Under these circumstances, the boy will like to hear himself called a boy and he will be motivated to perform more "boy" activities. In other words, the label becomes an incentive for acquiring more sex-typed behavior. What is important, then, is not only the label itself, but its associations and the context within which it is assigned.

Parents have two major tasks in promoting their child's sex-typing. The first is *tuition*, i.e., teaching the child appropriate sex-typed responses through rewards and punishments, and guiding his behavior, directing it into the proper channels. The second is *providing a model* of the proper general attitudes and personality characteristics for the child to emulate.

Fortunately, most parents can perform these tasks without great difficulty because they themselves have absorbed and incorporated sex-appropriate responses, characteristics, and attitudes and they have clear conceptions of appropriate masculine and feminine behaviors. They expect different responses from their sons and daughters and, from early childhood on, properly reward and encourage sex-appropriate responses (or intimations that the child is trying to behave in sex-appropriate ways), including early imitation of sex-appropriate models. Sex-inappropriate behavior, and attempts to imitate opposite-sex responses, are punished and discouraged.

But parents do not wait passively for the occurrence of sex-typed responses that they reward. They participate in their child's sex-typing more actively, guiding his activities by providing him with sex-appropriate objects and toys and then rewarding with approval his interest and his manipulations of these. Thus many little girls of two are presented with dolls and carriages and rewarded for their play with these toys. Through these experiences they acquire many sex-typed responses, become more keenly aware of, and evaluate highly, the kinds of activities that are sex-appropriate (Hartley, 1964).

As his sex-appropriate responses and characteristics become progressively strengthened as a consequence of reinforcement, the child's cognitive abilities increase. His perceptions, understanding and interpretation of the world become more mature, adult-like and realistic. His concepts of his own sex role become more comprehensive and accurate, and in turn, lead to further channelization of his behavior, ready assimilation of sex-appropriate responses, and rejection of the inappropriate.

The principle of conservation or invariance is applicable to conceptions of sex role, too. When he has acquired the principle, the child is more aware of the essentially constant, invariant components of masculine and feminine roles as well as of those which, though often associated with one of these roles, are not necessary components. Thus, the more mature cognitive organizations facilitate the selection of behaviors to be emulated, imitated, and thus acquired.

Identification with the parent of the same sex plays an analogous, and critical, facilitating role in sex-typing. Undoubtedly superficial, overt sex-typed characteristics (e.g., aggression) can be acquired and strengthened without any substantial identifications. Boys whose fathers do not live at home may learn masculine responses and may take on other male models or identificands. Social pressures soon convince the child that his rewards come from sex-appropriate responses and from emulation of models of his own sex.

Yet, some profound and subtle aspects of masculinity and femininity would not develop without identification with the like-sexed parent. Both clinical case studies and systematic investigations make it clear that such identification is an important antecedent of the formation of heterosexual orientation, probably the most important single component of sex role (Chang & Block, 1960), and of general, pervasive sex-typed interests and attitudes (Mussen, 1961; Payne & Mussen, 1956). In brief, identification with his like-sexed parent directs the child in the development of a broad range of new, subtle, and highly significant aspects of sex role—role behaviors not readily acquired through simple reinforcement learning.

In addition, the tendency to imitate the like-sexed parent may also generalize. The boy who finds emulation of his father rewarding is motivated to imitate other male models (including some more masculine than his father) and thus further to enhance the sex-typing process.

There are, of course, in both sexes, a wide range of individual differences in degrees of sex-typing achieved, i.e., in the closeness of fit between the individual's behavior and stereotyped sex-typed patterns of behavior. The boy who is closely identified with his "all-American" father is likely to possess all the characteristics and behaviors that comprise the stereotyped masculine pattern. In contrast, the son of a relatively effeminate man will lack many of these characteristics and patterns if he is strongly identified with his father.

Does the level of sex-role development affect general psychological or social adjustment? There are no data to answer this question adequately, but clinical experience suggests that the factors of paramount importance are the individual's acceptance of the behaviors and characteristics, and his confidence that these fulfill adequately, if not completely, the cultural prescriptions for members of his sex. It may be hypothesized further, that such self-acceptance and confidence are characteristic of individuals whose sex-role development is rooted in substantial identification with his like-sexed parent.

REFERENCES

ABERLE, D. F., & NAEGELE, K. D. Middle class fathers' occupational role and attitudes toward children. *American Journal of Orthopsychiatry*, 1952, 22, 366–378.

BANDURA, A. Social learning through imitation. In M. R. Jones (Ed.), *Nebraska symposium on motivation*, 1962. Lincoln: Univer. of Nebraska Press, 1962.

BANDURA, A. Vicarious processes: A case of no-trial learning. In L. Berkowitz (Ed.), *Advances in experimental social psychology*. Vol. II. New York: Academic Press, 1966.

BANDURA, A., ROSS, DOROTHEA, & ROSS, SHEILA. Transmission of aggression through imitation of aggressive models. *Journal of Abnormal and Social Psychology*, 1961, 63, 575–582.

BANDURA, A., & WALTERS, R. H. *Social learning and personality development*. New York: Holt, Rinehart and Winston, 1963.

BARRY, H., BACON, M., & CHILD, I. L. A cross-cultural survey of some sex differences in socialization. *Journal of Abnormal and Social Psychology*, 1957, 55, 327–332.

BIEBER, I., DAIN, H. J., DINCE, P. R., DRELLICH, M. G., GRAND, H. G., GUNDLACH, R. H., KREMER, M. W., RIFKIN, A. H., WILBUR, C. B., & BIEBER, T. B. *Homosexuality.* New York: Basic Books, 1962.

BRONFENBRENNER, U. Freudian theories of identification and their derivatives. *Child Development,* 1960, 31, 15–40.

BROWN, D. G. Sex-role preference in young children. *Psychological Monographs,* 1956, 70, 1–19. No. 14.

BROWN, D. G. Masculinity-femininity development in children. *Journal of Consulting Psychology,* 1957, 21, 197–202.

CHANG, J., & BLOCK, J. A study of identification in male homosexuals. *Journal of Consulting Psychology,* 1960, 24, 307–310.

D'ANDRADE, R. Cross-cultural studies of sex differences in behavior. In Eleanor Maccoby (Ed.), *The development of sex differences.* Stanford, Calif.: Stanford Univer. Press, 1966.

ELKIN, F. *The child and society.* New York: Random House, 1960.

ERIKSON, E. H. *Childhood and society.* New York: Norton, 1950.

FAULS, L. B., & SMITH, W. D. Sex role learning of five-year-olds. *Journal of Genetic Psychology,* 1956, 89, 105–117.

FOSTER, J. C. Play activities of children in the first six grades. *Child Development,* 1930, 1, 248–254.

FREUD, ANNA. *The ego and the mechanisms of defense.* New York: International Universities Press, 1946.

FREUD, S. *Group psychology and the analysis of the ego.* London: Hogarth Press, 1921.

FREUD, S. *An outline of psychoanalysis.* New York: Norton, 1949.

HAMPSON, J. L. Determinants of psychosexual orientation. In F. A. Beach (Ed.), *Sex and behavior.* New York: Wiley, 1965. Pp. 108–132.

HARTLEY, RUTH. A developmental view of female sex-role definition and identification. *Merrill-Palmer Quarterly,* 1964, 10, 3–16.

HARTUP, W. W., & ZOOK, E. A. Sex-role preferences in three- and four-year-old children. *Journal of Consulting Psychology,* 1960, 24, 420–426.

JONES, M. C. The later careers of boys who were early or late maturing. *Child Development,* 1957, 28, 113–128.

JONES, M. C., & MUSSEN, P. H. Self conceptions, motivations, and interpersonal attitudes of early and late maturing girls. *Child Development,* 1958, 29, 491–501.

KAGAN, J. The child's perception of the parent. *Journal of Abnormal and Social Psychology,* 1956, 53, 257–258.

KAGAN, J. The concept of identification. *Psychological Review,* 1958, 65, 296–305.

KAGAN, J. Acquisition and significance of sex typing and sex role identity. In Hoffman & Hoffman (Eds.), *Review of child development research,* Vol. I. New York: Russell Sage Foundation, 1964.

KAGAN, J., & LEMKIN, J. The child's differential perception of parental attributes. *Journal of Abnormal and Social Psychology,* 1960, 61, 446–447.

KAGAN, J., & MOSS, H. A. *Birth to maturity.* New York: Wiley, 1962.

KOHLBERG, L. A cognitive-developmental analysis of children's sex-role concepts and attitudes. In Eleanor Maccoby (Ed.), *The development of sex differences.* Stanford, Calif.: Stanford Univer. Press, 1966.

LANSKY, L. M., CRANDALL, V. J., KAGAN, J., & BAKER, C. T. Sex differences in aggression and its correlates in middle class adolescents. *Child Development,* 1961, 32, 45–58.

LINTON, R. *The cultural background of personality.* New York: Appleton-Century-Crofts, 1945.

LYNN, D. B., & SAWREY, W. L. The effects of father absence on Norwegian boys and girls. *Journal of Abnormal and Social Psychology,* 1958, 59, 258–262.

MACCOBY, ELEANOR. Role-taking in childhood and its consequences for social learning. *Child Development,* 1959, 30, 239–252.

MEAD, MARGARET. *Sex and temperament in three primitive societies.* New York: Morrow, 1935.

MILLER, N. E., & DOLLARD, J. *Social learning and imitation.* New Haven: Yale Univer. Press, 1941.

MISCHEL, W. A social learning view of sex differences in behavior. In Eleanor Maccoby (Ed.), *The development of sex differences.* Stanford, Calif.: Stanford Univer. Press, 1966.

MOWRER, O. H. *Learning theory and personality dynamics.* New York: Ronald Press, 1950.

MUSSEN, P. H. Some antecedents and consequents of masculine sex-typing in adolescent boys. *Psychological Monographs,* 1961, 75, 1–24. No. 2.

MUSSEN, P. H., & DISTLER, L. Masculinity, identification, and father-son relationships. *Journal of Abnormal and Social Psychology,* 1959, 59, 350–356.

MUSSEN, P. H., & JONES, M. C. Self-conceptions, motivations and interpersonal attitudes of late and early maturing boys. *Child Development,* 1957, 28, 243–256.

MUSSEN, P. H., & JONES, M. C. The behavior inferred motivations of late and early maturing boys. *Child Development,* 1958, 29, 61–67.

MUSSEN, P. H., & RUTHERFORD, E. Parent-child relations and parental personality in relation to young children's sex-role preferences. *Child Development,* 1963, 34, 589–607.

PARSONS, T. Family structures and the socialization of the child. In T. Parsons & R. F. Bales (Eds.), *Family, socialization and interaction process.* Glencoe, Ill.: Free Press, 1955.

PAYNE, D. E., & MUSSEN, P. H. Parent-child relations and father identification among adolescent boys. *Journal of Abnormal and Social Psychology,* 1956, 52, 358–362.

RABBAN, M. Sex-role identification in young children in two diverse social groups. *Genetic Psychology Monographs,* 1950, 42, 81–158.

RHEINGOLD, HARRIET. The modification of social responsiveness in institutional babies. *Monograph of Social Research and Child Development,* 1956, 21. No. 2.

SEARS, P. S. Doll play aggression in normal young children: Influence of sex, age, sibling status, father's absence. *Psychological Monographs,* 1951, 65. No. 6.

SEARS, R. R. Identification as a form of behavioral development. In D. B. Harris (Ed.), *The concept of development.* Minneapolis: Univer. of Minnesota Press, 1957. Pp. 149–161.

SEARS, R. R. Development of gender role. In F. A. Beach (Ed.), *Sex and behavior.* New York: Wiley, 1965. Pp. 133–163.

SEARS, R. R., MACCOBY, ELEANOR, & LEVIN, H. *Patterns of child rearing.* Evanston, Ill.: Row, Peterson, 1957.

SEARS, R. R., PINTLER, M. H., & SEARS, P. S. Effect of father separation on preschool children's doll play aggression. *Child Development,* 1946, 17, 219–243.

SEARS, R. R., RAU, LUCY, & ALPERT, R. *Identification and child rearing.* Stanford, Calif.: Stanford Univer. Press, 1965.

WHITING, J. W. M. Resource mediation and learning by identification. In I. Iscoe & W. Stevenson (Eds.), *Personality development in children.* Austin, Texas: Univer. of Texas Press, 1960. Pp. 112–126.

CHAPTER **16**

On Psychosexual Development

William Simon and John H. Gagnon

*Institute for Juvenile Research and
State University of New York, Stony Brook*

Erik Erikson (1963) has observed that, prior to Freud, "sexology" (a wretched and discredited term) tended to see sexuality as suddenly appearing with the onset of adolescence. From Erikson's point of view, Freud's discovery of infantile and childhood expressions of sexuality was a crucial part of his contribution. Libido—the generation of psychosexual energies—was now viewed as a fundamental element of the human experience from its very inception, at the latest beginning with birth and possibly prior to birth. Libido was conceived as something essential to the organism, representing a kind of biological constant with which forms of social life at all levels of sociocultural organization and development, as well as personality structure at each point in the life cycle, had to cope.

In Freud's view, the human infant and child behaved in ways that were intrinsically sexual and that remained in effective and influential continuity with later forms of psychosexual development (Freud, 1953; Chodoff, 1966). Implicit in this view was the assumption that the relation between available sexual energies and emergent motives and attachments would be complex—but direct. In some aspects of psychoanalytic thinking, both adolescent and adult sexuality were viewed as being in some measure re-enactments of sexual commitments developed, learned, or acquired during infancy and childhood.

This view presents both an epistemological and sociolinguistic problem. Freud's language was the language of adult sexual experience imposed upon the "apparent" behavior and "assumed" responses, feelings, and cognitions of infants and children. Acts and feelings are defined as sexual, not because of the actor's sense of the experience, but because of the meanings attached to those acts by adult observers or interpreters whose only available language is that of adult sexual experience (Schachtel, 1959). However, the assumptions implicit in the adult terminology with which such behaviors are perceived and considered must be approached with caution. The dilemma arises from the

A revised version of a paper presented at the National Institute of Child Health and Human Development Conference on Social Aspects of Socialization, December 8, 1967. This research was supported by United States Public Health Service Grant HD02257.

problem of distinguishing between the sources of labeling specific actions, gestures, or bodily movements as sexual. For the infant playing with his penis, the activity is not sexual in the sense of adult masturbation, but merely diffusely pleasurable in the same manner as are many other activities. The external observer imputes to the child the complex set of states that are generally associated with physically homologous adult activities. It is only through the processes of maturing and learning these adult labels that the child comes to masturbate in the fullest sense of the word. It is in the process of converting external labels into internal capacities for naming that the activities become more precisely defined and linked to a structure of sociocultural expectations and needs that define what is sexual. To suggest that infant or childhood genital play is prototypical of or determines adult patterns is to credit the biological organism with more "natural" wisdom than we normally do in areas where the biological and the sociocultural intersect. Undeniably, sexuality is rooted in biological processes, capacities, and possibly even needs. But admitting this in no way provides for a greater degree of biological determinism than is true of other areas of corresponding intersection. Indeed, the reverse may be true: the sexual area may be precisely that realm wherein the superordinate position of the sociocultural over the biological level is most complete.

It is important to note here that the very diffuse quality of most of preadolescent experience poses a number of major problems, one of which is the extreme difficulty in getting accurate data. Part of the problem centers on a kind of faulty recall which is not rooted merely in inaccurate memories. This is a source of error pointed out in the existentialist insight that rather than the past determining the character of the present, it is possible that the present significantly reshapes the past, as we reconstruct our autobiographies in an effort to bring them into greater congruence with our present identities, roles, situations, and available vocabularies. The other part of the problem results from attempting to gather data from children who when interviewed are ill-equipped to report upon their own internal states or from adults who are asked to report on periods of life when complex vocabularies did not exist for them. The problem is attempting to determine what is being felt or thought when confronted with organisms whose restricted language skills may preclude certain feelings or thoughts.

Essential to the perspective of this chapter is the assumption that with the beginnings of adolescence—and with the increasing acknowledgement by the surrounding social world of an individual's sexual capacity—many novel factors come into play, and that an over-emphasis upon a search for continuity with infant and childhood experiences may be dangerously misleading. In particular, it may be a costly mistake to be overimpressed with preadolescent behaviors that appear to be manifestly sexual. In general, it is possible that much of the power of sexuality may be a function of the fact it has frequently been defined as powerful or dangerous. But this overenriched conception of sexual behavior (to the degree that it occurs) must largely follow upon considerable training in an adult language which includes an overdetermined conception of sexuality.

Thus it does not necessarily follow that the untrained infant or child will respond as powerfully or as complexly to his own behaviors that appear to be sexual to an adult observer as will that observer.

Of all the experiences of the preadolescent, it would appear that the most influential in the determination of later psychosexual development is that large and complex cluster of elements that come under the heading of sex-role learning. It is perhaps better to label this process "gender-role" learning, underscoring thereby its indirect link to sexuality in many, if not most, of its aspects. In other words, we may find that the development of an emerging sense of self is significant in the determination of later sexual commitment or capacities, but that this sense of self *does not* itself derive, in most cases, from preadolescent sexual or even near-sexual experiences.

For the purposes of this chapter, we reject the unproven assumption of the "power" of the psychosexual drive as a fixed biological attribute. We feel there is little evidence to suggest that such a "drive" need find expression in specific sexual acts or categories of sexual acts. More importantly, we reject the even more dubious assumption that sexual capacities or experiences tend to translate immediately into a kind of universal knowing or wisdom; the assumption that sexuality possesses a magical ability that allows biological drives to seek direct expression in psychosocial and social areas in ways that we do not expect in other biologically rooted behaviors. This assumption can be seen in the psychoanalytic literature, for example, in which the child who views the "primal scene" is seen on some primitive level as intuiting its sexual character. Also, the term latency, in its usage by psychoanalytic theorists, suggests a period of integration by the child of prior intrinsically sexual experiences and reactions which reduces adolescence, on this level, to a mere management or organization on a manifest level of the commitments and styles already prefigured, if not preformed, in infancy and childhood experiences.

In contradistinction to this tradition, this chapter adopts the view that the point at which the individual begins to respond in intrinsically sexual ways, particularly in terms of socially available or defined outlets and objects, is a time during which something occurs which is discontinuous with previous "sexual experience" (whatever that might mean). Further, at this point in the developmental process, both seemingly sexual and seemingly nonsexual elements "contest" for influence in complex ways which in no respect assure a priority for those elements that are apparently sexual in character.

The prevailing image of the sexual component in human experience is that of a fairly intense, high-pressure drive (except, perhaps, during later stages of the life cycle) that constrains the individual to seek sexual gratification either directly or indirectly. This is clearly present in the Freudian tradition. A similar position is observable in more sociological writings. This is apparent, for example, in the thinking of Kingsley Davis for whom sex is also a high-intensity, societal constant that must be properly channeled lest it find expression in behaviors which threaten the maintenance of collective life (Davis, 1961; Durkheim, 1951).

Our sense of the available data suggests a somewhat different picture of human sexuality, one of generally lower levels of intensity or, at least, greater variability in intensity. More clearly evident among females than males (see below), there are numerous social situations or roles where reduction and even elimination of sexual activity is managed by greatly disparate populations with little evidence of direct corollary or compensatory intensification in other spheres of life (Gagnon & Simon, 1968a). It is possible that, given the historical nature of human societies, we are victim to the needs of earlier social orders. For earlier societies it may not have been a matter of having to constrain severely the powerful sexual impulse in order to maintain social stability (particularly in family life), but rather a matter of having to invent an importance for sexuality not only to insure high levels of reproductive activity but also to provide a socially available reward that might be placed at the service of many social ends. A part of the legacy of Freud is that we have all become relatively adept at seeking out the sexual ingredient in many forms of nonsexual behavior and symbolism. What we are suggesting is in essence the now three-decade old insight of Kenneth Burke (1935) to the effect that it is entirely plausible to examine sexual behavior for its capacity to express and serve nonsexual motives.

For us, then, sexual behavior is socially scripted behavior and not the masked or rationalized expression of some primordial drive. The individual learns to be sexual as he or she learns sexual scripts, scripts that invest actors and situations with erotic content. One can easily conceive of numerous social situations in which all or almost all the ingredients of sexuality are present, but which remain nonsexual in that not even sexual arousal occurs (Simon & Gagnon, 1967a). Thus combining such elements as desire, privacy, and a physically attractive alter of the appropriate sex, the probability of something sexual occurring will, under normal circumstances, remain exceedingly small until either one or both actors organize these elements into an appropriate script. The very concern with foreplay in sexual behavior suggests something of this order. From one point of view, foreplay might be defined as progressive physical excitement or what the authors (Gagnon & Simon, 1968b) have elsewhere referred to as the "rubbing of two sticks in order to get a fire going" model. From another point of view, this activity may be defined as a method of eroticizing the body and the activity, as a method for transforming mute, inarticulate gestures and motions into a sociosexual drama.

Lastly, in these introductory comments we might continue to belabor the issue of sociocultural dominance by making some preparatory distinctions, distinctions that we would have to make in any event. Psychosexual development, while a universal component in the human experience, certainly does not occur with universal modalities. Even ignoring the striking forms of cross-cultural variability (Ford & Beach, 1951), we can observe striking differences within our own population, differences that, given the relatively low level of thinking and the sparsity of research in the area, appear to require not a description of psychosexual development, but descriptions of different developmental processes characterizing different segments of the population. The most evident of these are the large number of important differences between observable male and female patterns of sexual behavior (Maccoby, 1966). This particular difference may in some respects be partly attributable to the role played by the biological substratum (Hamburg & Lunde, 1966; Young, Goy & Phoenix, 1964). We have to account not only for the gross physiological differences and the different roles in the reproductive process that follow from these physiological differences, but must also consider differences in hormonal functions at particular ages. Yet, while our knowledge of many of the salient physiological and physiochemical processes involved is far from complete, there is still little immediate justification for asserting a direct causal link between these processes and specific differential patterns of sexual development observed in our society. The recent work of Masters and Johnson (1966), for example, clearly points to far greater orgasmic capacities on the part of females than males; however, their concept of orgasm as a physiological process would hardly be a basis for accurately predicting rates of sexual behavior. Similarly, within each sex, important distinctions must be made for various socioeconomic status groups whose patterns of sexual development will vary considerably, more impressively for males than for females (Kinsey, 1948). And with reference to socioeconomic status differences, the link to the biological level appears even more tenuous, unless one is willing to invoke the relatively unfashionable conceptual equipment of Social Darwinism. These differences, then, not only suggest the importance of the sociocultural elements and social structure, but also stand as a warning against too uncritical an acceptance of unqualified generalizations about psychosexual development.

CHILDHOOD

Obviously Erikson is correct in agreeing with Freud: we do not become fully sexual all at once. There is significant continuity with the past; nevertheless, continuity is not causality. Even in infancy experiences can occur that will strongly influence later sexual development. However, such experiences will, in all likelihood, be influential not because of their essentially sexual character, but because of their general influential character; that is, they probably influence many more things than just sexual development. It is also possible to talk about the kinds of experience that give rise to fixation, but such experience is probably as unusual as it is traumatic and can hardly be the basis for general theories. One has difficulty conceiving of situations in infancy—or even early childhood—that can be linked to psychosexual development on a level more specific than that of potentiation.

In infancy and in the interrelationships that are part of infant care, we can locate many of the pre-verbal experiences that are preparation for the development of verbal capacities which, in turn, will bind the child to the social world. In this period we can locate some of the experiences—perhaps only sensations—that will help bring about a sense of the body and its capacities for pleasure and discomfort, and we can also locate the experiences that will influence the child's ability to relate to other bodies. The key term remains potentiation: it is possible that through these primitive experiences, ranges are being established, but these ranges are sufficiently broad and overlapping that little can follow by way of specification except through the dubious route of tortured reconstruction. Moreover, if these are profoundly significant experiences to the child—and they may well be—they stand not as expressions of biological necessity nor the inherent wisdom of the body, but as expressions of the earliest forms of social learning (Gewirtz, 1961).

Unlike the period of infancy, where at best we are confronted with a universe of unnamed gestures, it is possible to conceive of activity in childhood that appears to be explicitly sexual to the observer. About half of all adults report having engaged in some form of "sex play" as children (Kinsey, 1948, 1953). And conceding a certain role to faulty recall or repression, the proportion having behaved this way may be as much as half again as large. The crucial and almost impossible question remains: What does it mean to the child? It is likely that some part of the adult definition of the activity is realized by the participants, but one suspects—as in much of childhood role-playing—that their sense of the adult meaning is fragmentary and ill-formed. It is clear that some learning about the adult world's judgments of the sexual occurs as is indicated by the fact that a high proportion of adults recall that they were concerned, while engaging in childhood sex play, over the possibility of being "found out." However, it may not be the content of sex play activity—as if they were responding to their nascent sexuality—but the mystery that enchants the child (Freud, 1964). Stated differently, the child may be assimilating external bits of information about sex for which, at the time, there are no real internal correlates.

For some small number of persons sexual activity does occur during preadolescence. Probably the largest group are those who become involved as objects of adult-initiated behavior. But for most of them, little seemingly follows. Lacking appropriate sexual scripts the experience remains unassimilated, except perhaps for those who derive a "meaning" of the experience from a subsequent clinical situation. For some it is equally clear that a severe reaction does follow from falling "victim" to the sexuality of some adult figure, but here it is debatable whether this reaction follows from the sexual act itself or from the social act, the tone, and the intensity of the reactions by others (Gagnon, 1965). In short, relatively few preadolescents become truly sexual, that is, become sexually active. For preadolescent females more often than males, this sexual activity is not immediately related to internal states—capacities for sexual arousal or sexual gratification—but to an instrumental use of sexuality to achieve nonsexual goals and gratifications. This "seductive" preadolescent female, for all her statistical rarity, may represent a significant adumbration of a more general pattern of psychosexual development: a process wherein a commitment to sociosexuality precedes a commitment to sexuality. Among sexually active preadolescent males, behavior appears to be more intrinsically sexual and is associated with a high frequency of subsequent deviant adaptations, most often homosexual (Gebhard et al., 1965).

Of considerable importance is the internalization of values—or the images that powerfully stand for values—that may not be directly or exclusively referential to sexual matters. These values or value images will constitute aspects in the construction of sexual scripts giving rise to senses of the evil, the extraordinary, and the erotic. Despite our present capacity as a society to generate high levels of public discourse about sexual matters, it is probably not unreasonable to assert that learning about sex in our society is learning about guilt; conversely, learning how to manage sexuality constitutes learning how to manage guilt. An important source of guilt is the imputation by adults of sexual capacities or qualities in children that the children may not have, but that result in—however imperfectly—children learning to act as if they had such capacities or qualities. For example, at what age do girls learn to sit with their knees together, and when do they learn that the upper part of the torso must be hidden, and what of a sexual nature do they learn from all this? Childhood learning of major themes which establish sex or gender role identities is of critical importance. Much of what appears under the heading of sex-role learning involves elements that are remote to sexual experience or that become involved with sexuality only after the latter has become salient (Sears, 1965). Here the meanings and postures of masculinity and femininity are rehearsed and assimilated in many nonsexual ways. Here, also, the qualities of aggression, deference, and dominance needs, which Maslow (1939, 1942)—however imperfect his data—persuasively argues are strongly implicated in the organization of sexual styles, are initially rehearsed, experimented with, and assimilated.

Kagan and Moss (1962) report similar findings: aggressive behavior is a relatively stable aspect of male development and dependency is a similar characteristic in female development. Significant appearances of aggressive behavior by females tended to occur most often among females from well-educated families, families that tended to be more tolerant of deviation from sex-role standards. They also find, of particular interest, that ". . . interest in masculine activities for age 6 to 10 was a better predictor of adult sexuality than was heterosexual activity between 6 and 14." Curiously, they also report that "it was impossible to predict the character of adult sexuality in women from their preadolescent and early adolescent behavior." This the authors attribute to a random factor, that of an imbalance of sex ratios in the local high school and, more significantly, to the fact that "erotic activity is more anxiety-arousing for females than for males" and that "the traditional ego ideal for women dictates inhibition of sexual impulses."

This concept of the importance of early sex-role learning for male children may be viewed in two ways. From one perspective elements of masculine-role learning may be seen as immediately responsive to—if not expressive of—an internal sexual capacity. From another perspective, we might consider elements of masculine identification merely as a more appropriate context within which the mediation of the sexual impulse—which becomes more salient with puberty —and the socially available sexual scripts can occur. Our bias, of course, is towards the latter.

The failure of sex-role learning to be effectively predictive of adult sexual activities, noted by Kagan and Moss, also may lead to alternative interpretations. Again, from one perspective, where sexuality is viewed as a biological constant for both women and men, one can point to the components of female-role learning that facilitate the successful repression of sexual impulses. The other perspective or interpretation suggests differences in the process not of handling sexuality, but of learning how to be sexual, differences between men and women that will have consequences for both what is done sexually as well as when it is done. Our thinking, once again, tends towards the latter. This position is supported by some recent work of the present authors (Simon & Gagnon, 1967b, 1967c) on female homosexuals, where it is observed that patterns of sexual career management (e.g., the timing of entry into actual sexual behavior, entry into forms of sociosexual behavior, onset and frequency of masturbation, number of partners, reports of feelings of sexual deprivation, etc.) were for lesbians almost identical with those of heterosexual women. Considering what was assumed to be the greater salience of sexuality for the lesbian—her commitment to sexuality being the basis for her entry into a highly alienative role—this seemed to be a surprising outcome. What was concluded was that the crucial operating factor was something that both heterosexual and homosexual women share: the components of sex-role learning that occur before sexuality itself becomes significant.

Social class differences also appear to be significant, although both in the work of Kinsey (1948, 1953) and that of Kagan and Moss they appear as more important factors for males than for females. Some part of this is due to aspects of sex-role learning which vary by social class. Differences in the legitimacy of expressing aggression or perhaps merely differences in modes of expressing aggression come immediately to mind (Sears, 1965; Biller & Borstelmann, 1967). Another difference is the degree to which sex-role models display a capacity for *heterosociality*. The frequently noted pattern of the sexual segregation of social life among working-class and lower-class populations may make the structuring of later sexual activity, particularly during adolescence, actually less complicated (Rainwater, 1966; Simon & Gagnon, 1966). Another aspect of social class differences is the tolerance for deviation from traditional attitudes regarding appropriate sex-role performances. Clearly, tolerance for such deviance is positively associated with social class position, and it may well stand in a highly complex and interactive relationship to capacities for heterosocial activities.

We have touched here upon only a few of the potentially large number of factors that should be related to important social class differences and to the processes of psychosexual development. In general, even during this relatively early period of life, complex elements of the ego begin to take form, including the crude outlines of what might be called a repertoire of gratifications. It seems rather naive to conceive of sexuality as a constant pressure upon this process, a pressure that has a particular necessity all its own. For us, this crucial period of childhood has significance not because of what happens of a sexual nature, but because of the nonsexual developments that will provide the names and the judgments that will condition subsequent encounters with sexuality.

ADOLESCENCE

Adolescence is a period with ill-defined beginning and end points. There is variation in its general definition, still greater variability in the application of these definitions, and the situation is additionally complicated by the variability of developmental rates of specific individuals. However ill-defined this period may be, the beginning of adolescence marks the time when society, as such, first acknowledges the sexual capacity of the individual. His or her training in the postures and the rhetoric of the sexual experience will now begin to accelerate. Most importantly, the adolescent will start to view others in his or her immediate environment—in particular, peers, but also some adults—as sexual actors and will find confirmation of this view in the definitions of others toward these actors.

As has already been indicated, for a number of individuals sexual activity begins prior to adolescence, or some portion of children begin engaging in adolescent sexual behavior before they are defined as adolescents. Thus, Kinsey (1948, 1953) reports that by age 12 about a tenth of his female sample and a fifth of his male sample had already experienced orgasm through masturbation. (There is some evidence that early entry into sexual activity is associated with alienative adjustments in later life, but this may not be a function of sexual experience per se so much as the consequence of having fallen out of the more modal socialization patterns and, as a result, having to run greater risks of not receiving appropriate forms of social support.) But this is still an atypical preface to adolescence. For the vast majority, aside from relatively casual childhood sex play and the behaviors that post-Freudians view as masked sexuality, movement into sexual experience which the actor defines and accepts as such begins with the passage into adolescence. Even for persons with prior sexual experience, the newly-acquired definition of their social status as adolescents qualitatively alters the meaning of both current and prior sexual activity; they must now integrate such meanings in more complex ways, ways that are related to both larger spheres of social life and greater senses of self. For example, it is not uncommon during the transitional period between childhood and adolescence for both males and females to report arousal and orgasm while engaging in many kinds of physical activity that are not manifestly sexual— climbing trees, sliding down bannisters, or other forms of activity where there is genital contact—without it being defined as sexual by the adolescent (Kinsey, 1948). Indeed, in many such cases there may not even follow subsequent self-explorations in order to achieve some repetition of what was, in all likelihood, a pleasurable experience.

The onset of adolescent sexual development, which really represents the beginning of what will be an adult commitment to sexuality, will be somewhat disjunctive with past experience in most cases. As we have suggested, not only are future experiences to occur in much more complex situations, but also for the first time the more explicit social implications of sexual activity will further complicate matters (Reiss, 1960). The need to manage sexuality, following from a growing sense of having a sexual status, will derive not only from the intrinsic attractions of the sexual experiences for some, but from the increasingly important role sexuality will play in the conduct of both heterosocial and homosocial relationships.

The onset of adolescence demands a separate consideration on our part of the developmental process for males and females. The one thing both genders will share at this point is the reinforcement of their competence in their new sexual status by the occurrence of a dramatic biological event: for males the discovery of the ability to ejaculate, for females the onset of menstruation. This difference can be made evident in the simplest way by pointing to the separate modal routes into sexual experience. For males the organizing event that initiates a sexual commitment is the biological event of puberty; within two years of puberty all but a relatively few males have their commitment to sexuality reinforced by the experience of orgasm, almost universally brought about by masturbation (Kinsey, 1948). The corresponding organizing event for females is not a biological but a social event: the arrival at an age that suggests a certain proximity to marriage. In contrast to male masturbation rates, we find that only two-thirds of a female population will report ever having masturbated (and then, characteristically, with much lower frequency), and cumulatively we have to go into the latter part of the third decade of life (the twenties) before a proportion is reached which is comparable to that reached by males at age 16 (Kinsey, 1948, 1953). Indeed, it is significant that about half of the females who masturbate will do so only after having their sexuality reinforced by the experience of orgasm in some sociosexual situation. This contrast between males and females, which we will elaborate below, once again points to a distinction between the developmental process for males and that for females: the movement from sexuality to sociosexuality characteristic of males is reversed for females.

When we turn to a more detailed view of the adolescent male experience, despite the fact that we have up to now worked very hard to establish the dominance of the sociocultural or social-psychological over the biological sphere, we must now briefly reverse course. There is some evidence that the early impulse to sexual expression—again initially through masturbation—is linked to high hormonal inputs during the period of puberty, producing an organism that, to state it in its simplest terms, is easily "turned on" (Kinsey, 1948). It is not uncommon for young male adolescents to report frequent erections during this period, often without the provocation of erotic preoccupations. This obviously focuses considerable attention on the genitalia. Yet, however powerful the biological origins of the propensity for the young adolescent male to masturbate, the meaning and the organization of the activity tend to occur in terms of social and psychological factors.

On one level masturbation is a guilt and anxiety provoking activity for most adolescent males. And despite changes in the rhetoric of public and semi-public discourse on the topic—a shift from a rhetoric of mental and physical destructiveness to one of vaguely inappropriate or nonsocial behavior—this is not likely to change in the foreseeable future. It may be this very element, however, that permits the sexual experience to generate an intensity of affect that may often be attributed to the powers of sexual capacity itself. This guilt and anxiety does not follow simply from the general societal disapproval of this activity. Rather it appears to derive from several sources, one of which is the difficulty encountered in presenting a sexual self to members of the immediate family, particularly parents, where the sentimental and the erotic still remain ill-defined. Another source of guilt and anxiety stems from the fact that arousal and excitement in sexual activity increasingly derives from vicarious organization of sociosexual activity—fantasies involving doing sexual "things" to others or having others do sexual "things" to oneself—or from the assimilation and rehearsal of available sexual scripts, many of which involve engaging in proscribed activities or relationships. An additional source of guilt or anxiety centers on the general sanction against masturbatory behavior, an activity which few males are willing to admit to after the period of early adolescence.

Despite guilt and anxiety, which may consequently become part of the more general commitment to sexuality for many men, masturbation remains an extremely positive and gratifying experience, as it constitutes for most males through the middle of adolescence the major source of sexual outlet and is engaged in fairly frequently during this period. This form of introduction to sexuality tends to give rise to a capacity for detached sexual activity, activity where the only sustaining motive is sexual; this may actually be the hallmark of male sexuality in our society.

Of the three sources of guilt and anxiety alluded to above, the first, the problem of managing both sexuality and an attachment to family members, is probably common across social class lines. The other two sources should display marked social class differences. The second, the problem of managing a fairly elaborate and exotic fantasy life, should most typically be a problem for higher social class levels. On lower class levels there is a less frequent use of fantasy during masturbation, and this in turn may be linked to a generalized lack of training and competence in the manipulation of symbolic materials (Kinsey, 1948). Higher social class male adolescents are presumably trained for such competence. Masturbation accompanied by fantasy should in turn reinforce the manipulation of symbolic materials. If we de-emphasize the physical component in the masturbatory act, it can be conceptualized as an activity in which the actor is, in effect, training himself to invest symbols with affect and to derive gratification from the manipulation of symbols. Successfully doing this results in what is classically the best reward or reinforcer in learning theory terms: it is the immediate, specific, and pleasurable experience of orgasm. It may well be that this behavior—which is something females tend not to engage in—plays a role in the processes by which middle-class males catch up with females in measures of achievement and creativity and then, by the end of adolescence, move out in front. This is, of course, merely a wild hypothesis—the Dr. Krankeit (sic) hypothesis (Kenton, 1958). This primary reliance upon masturbation with fantasy should also have a number of consequences beyond the capacity for a relatively detached sexual performance. One such consequence is a tendency to eroticize large parts of the world, as well as an ability to respond to a wide array of visual and auditory *stimuli*. Moreover, to the extent that Wilhelm Reich (1942) is correct in his assertion that the scripting for masturbatory fantasies has a non- and possibly anti-coital character, we might also expect both a capacity and a need for fairly elaborate forms of sexual activity. Further, in so far as the masturbatory fantasy focuses upon relationships and activities essentially preparatory to the coital act, the masturbatory experience should also reinforce an already developing capacity for sustaining heterosocial activity.

The third source of guilt and anxiety, essentially the unmanliness of masturbation, should be more typically a concern of lower social class male adolescents. Among these lower-class male adolescents the general pattern of sexual segregation of social life and the relatively narrower range of rewarding social experiences available to them should combine to constrain the adolescent to move into heterosexual relationships sooner than does his middle-class counterpart. The first condition, the sexual segregation of social life, should make it easier for him to gravitate toward a world of casual, if not exploitative, sexual relations; it is easier for him than for the middle-class adolescent to learn that he does not have to love everything he desires. The second condition—the more limited available social rewards and particularly rewards deriving from activities that will be validated by his peers—should lead to an exaggerated concern for masculinity-enhancing behavior leading, in turn, to displays of physical prowess, successful staging of aggressive behaviors, and visible sexual success. The three—physical prowess, aggressive behavior, and sexual success—are, of course, not unrelated and frequently are mutually reinforcing.

Available data suggest, in line with the above, that one of the differences between lower-class and middle-class male adolescents is the phasing of entry into heterosexual forms of sociosexuality or the phasing of movement from masturbation to coital behavior (Kinsey, 1948). In a sense, the lower-class male is the first to reach "sexual maturity" as defined by those working in an essentially Freudian tradition. That is, these lower-class males are generally the first to become exclusively heterosexual and exclusively genital in orientation. One consequence, however, is that while their sexual activity is almost exclusively heterosexual, it also tends to be more homosocial in character. The audience to which the lower-class male's sexual activity is directed will tend not to be his female partner, but rather it will be more referential to his male peers (Simon & Gagnon, 1966). Middle-class adolescent males, who will initiate coital activity at a significantly later time, will not be exempt from a need and tendency for homosocial components in their sexual lives, but the complexity of their fantasies as well as their social training in an environment less sexually segregated—a world in which distinctions between masculine and feminine roles are not as clearly drawn—will facilitate an easier withdrawal from homosocial commitments. This difference between the social classes will obviously have important consequences for the management of stable adult relations, a point which we will consider below.

One characteristic that will tend to be common to the male experience during adolescence is that while this stage provides extensive opportunity for developing a sexual commitment in one form or other, there is little training in the management of affectively-charged relations with females. The imagery and rhetoric of romantic involvement is abundantly present in the society, and it is not unlikely that a great deal of this is absorbed by the male adolescent, but it is not likely to be significantly tied to a sexual commitment. To the degree that it is related to sexuality, the connection may be quite inhibiting, as is suggested by the still operative "bad girl–good girl" distinction. This is important to keep in mind as we turn now to a consideration of the female side of this story.

The pattern of female development during adolescence is so resistant to social class variation that one is tempted to seek explanation in something as relatively immutable as the biological level (Kinsey, 1953). However, we will resist this temptation. The female, to be sure, is not provided with the same biologically-rooted incentive to begin an active sexual commitment; but, by the same token, little evidence exists that there is either a social or a biological inhibitor to the development of such a commitment. In simplest terms, the physical equipment for the generation of sexual pleasure is clearly present by puberty and before (Kinsey, 1953), but it tends not to be used by many adolescent females on any social class level. Masturbation rates are fairly low (and those who do masturbate do so fairly infrequently), arousal from explicitly sexual materials and situations is an infrequent occurrence, and there are exceedingly few reports of a self-conscious feeling of sexual deprivation during this period. Explanations for this low level of female sexual activity or interest are numerous on both functional and historical grounds. The basic element in all of these is the idea that females in our society are not encouraged to be sexual, and, indeed, it is possible that they are strongly discouraged from being sexual. As Rheingold (1964) describes this: where men have only to fear sexual failure, women have to fear failure and success simultaneously. Or, as several people have observed, while the category "bad boy" has many descriptive sub-categories, the category "bad girl" tends almost exclusively to describe sexual delinquencies. Clearly, it is both difficult and dangerous for a female to become too committed or too sexually active during adolescence.

Whether this extended period of relative sexual inactivity represents the outcome of successful repression of an elementary sexual urge or merely represents a failure to have an opportunity to learn how to be sexual, is an important question for consideration. The alternative answers have different implications for how we view the later development of a sexual commitment during late adolescence or postadolescence. The "repression answer" suggests that we approach later activity in terms of processes of de-inhibition by which the female learns to find, in varying degrees, modes of more direct expression of internally experienced feelings. It also requires a quest for the sexually determined aspects of nonsexual behavior. The "learning answer" suggests that women create or invent a capacity for sexual behavior, learning how to be aroused and learning how to be responsive. The latter approach also implies greater flexibility in overall adjustments; unlike the repression view, it makes sexuality something other than a constant that is likely to "break loose" at any point in strange or costly ways. In addition, the learning approach lessens the power of the sexual component as a variable; all at once, there is no necessarily healthy or pathological component to a particular style of sexual activity. Lastly, the appeal for us of this approach is somewhat subjective: it tends to seem less like a projection of male sexuality.

The absence of intrinsically sexual activity by adolsecent females does not mean that sexual learning and training fail to occur. Curiously, women who are, as a group, far less sexually active than men, receive far more training in self-consciously conceiving of themselves as being sexual on the object level. This is particularly true for recent age cohorts. On the level of the cosmetic self, females begin relatively early in adolescence to define attractiveness in at least partially sexual terms. One suspects that the same instrumental approach that marked our preadolescent "seductress" now characterizes larger proportions of adolescent females. Parsons' (1954) language of the wife "using" sex to bind the husband to the familial unit, for all its harsh sound, may be quite accurate. In more general terms, the development of a sexual role appears to involve a need to assign to that role services other than pleasure.

To complete this picture of a lack of symmetry between the sexes, the female appears to be trained in precisely that area for which males during adolescence are least trained and for which they are least expected to display a capacity: intense, affect-laden relationships and the rhetoric of romantic love. When sexual arousal is reported by females during this period, it is more often reported as a response to representations of romantic love than as a response to erotic representations.

The movement into later adolescence and the concomitant increase in opportunities for sociosexual activity can be described as a situation in which males—committed to sexuality and relatively untrained in the rhetoric of romantic love—interact with females who are committed to romantic love and relatively untrained in sexuality. Dating and courtship may well be considered processes in which persons train members of the opposite sex in the meaning and content of their respective commitments. And while data in this area are deficient in many regards, the data that are available suggest the exchange system does not often work smoothly. Thus, as is partly suggested by Ehrmann's (1959) work and partly by our own present studies of college students, it is not uncommon to find, ironically, that the male suitor frequently becomes emotionally involved with his partner and correspondingly less interested in engaging in sexual activity with her, and that the female, whose appreciation of the genuineness of her suitor's affection allows her to feel that sexual activity is now both legitimate and desirable, becomes more interested in engaging in sexual activity with him. Data from the authors' recent study of college students, now under analysis, demonstrate that this difference in commitment is exemplified in several ways. One such item, dealing with the number of times individual respondents had intercourse with their first partner, shows the mode for males around one to three times, while the mode for females is at ten times or more. Clearly, for females, initial intercourse becomes possible only in relatively stable relationships or relationships involving rather strong bonds.

On a theoretical level, we find the male experience conforming to the general Freudian expectation with males moving from a predominantly sexual commitment to an ability to form cathectic attachments in loving relationships. In effect, this movement is reversed for females with cathectic attachments being, in many cases, a necessary precondition for coital activity. It is not surprising, perhaps, that Freud had great difficulty approaching female sexuality. This "error" in conceptualizing female sexuality—of seeing it either as being similar to male sexuality or as a mirrored image—may derive from the fact that so much of the theory construction in this area was done by males. In Freud's case, we also have to consider the very conception of sexuality that was essential to most of Victorian Europe—it was an elemental beast that had to be curbed.

In addition, it is particularly important to consider social class differences among females, if only as a way of assessing the possibility of a biological factor producing the above-discussed outcome. As we have already indicated, there are very few such differences, far fewer than may be observed among males. One, however, is particularly relevant to this question—the age of first intercourse. This varies inversely with social class and is strongly associated with similar class differences in age of first marriage (Kinsey, 1953). There is no evident basis for associating such social class differences with biological differences. A second difference, perhaps linked only indirectly to social class, is educational achievement. For this variable a single cutting point appears to separate two distinct populations: women who have attended graduate or professional schools and all other women. The former tend to be the most "successful" sexually—at least if one is willing to accept as a measure of success the relatively crude indicator of the proportion of sexual acts that culminate in orgasm. One possible interpretation of this finding derives from Maslow's (1939, 1942) work: women who survive the academic process and go on for additional training are more likely to be more aggressive and/or have strong dominance needs, and both characteristics are associated with heightened sexual commitments. Another somewhat more general interpretation would argue that in a society which still strongly encourages women to form primary allegiances to roles as wives and mothers, the decision to go on to graduate school represents something of a deviant adaptation. This adaptation represents, in turn, a failure of, or alienation from, modal female socialization processes. And, in effect, it is faulted socialization which produces both the academic or professional commitment and the sexual commitment.

For both males and females, progressively greater involvement with socio-sexuality may be one of the factors that marks the end of adolescence. This is a transition about which little is really known, particularly with reference to noncollege populations. Work currently under way by the authors supported by the National Institute of Child Health and Human Development, is attempt-ing to deal with this problem. Our present feeling about the place of sexuality in the management of this transition is that it plays a significant role. First, on a somewhat superficial level, progressive involvement in sociosexuality is im-portant in family formation or in the entry into roles and role obligations that are more explicitly adult in character. But, perhaps on a more fundamental level, it is possible that sociosexual activity is the one aspect of identity experi-mentation that we associate particularly with later adolescence, a period in which the psychosocial moratorium that Erikson describes as protecting the adolescent during this period of crises and experimentation fails to operate (Erikson, 1963; Reiss, 1960). This may be partly due to the fact that the society has some difficulty protecting the adolescent from the consequences of that part of his behavior it is not prepared to admit he is engaging in. More importantly, it may be due to the fact that we have, at all age levels, great problems in talking about sexual feelings and experiences in personal terms which, in turn, make it extremely difficult to get social support for our experi-ments with our sexual selves (the term "pluralistic ignorance" is perhaps no-where more applicable than in the sexual area). It may be that these experi-ments with sexual capacities and identities rank among the first unprotected tests of competence and the quest for a basis for self-acceptance. We suspect that success or failure in the management of sexual identity may have conse-quences in many more areas of personality development than merely the sexual sphere.

ADULTHOOD

All but very few persons in our society ultimately marry. The management of sexual commitments within a marital relationship characterizes the larger part of postadolescent experience in our society. Once again, it is important to underscore the real poverty of data on this topic. Sexual adjustment presum-ably plays an important role in overall marital adjustment. This judgment largely derives from studies of broken marriages or marriages that are in trouble, and we really have very little sense of the degree to which sexual problems in troubled or dissolved marriages exceed those found in marriages which remain intact. It is possible that we have assumed an important role for sexuality and the management of sexuality in the maintenance of marital bonds because we have assumed sex itself to be an important part of most people's lives. This may not be true. Particularly after the formation of the marital unit, it is quite possible that sex declines in salience. It may stand as less important than alternative modes of gratification, or the weight of alter-native gratifications may minimize the effects of sexual dissatisfaction. It is also possible that individuals learn to derive sexual gratification from non- or only partially sexual activities. This is not to suggest support for the concept of sublimation, but rather to point out that in the processes that follow marriage, newly learned alternative patterns of gratification may substitue for the sexual.

The main determinant of adult rates of sexual activity in our society is the level of male commitment. While interest in intercourse is highest for males during the early years of marriage, a corresponding peak in coital interest occurs much later in marriage for females (who require longer periods of time to either become de-inhibited or to learn to be sexual—depending upon your point of view). Nonetheless, coital rates in marriage decline steadily through marriage (Kinsey, 1953). This decline, it should be noted, can only be partly attributed to declines in biological capacity on the part of the male. The decrease may derive from many things. In many cases the problem is one of relating sexually to a person whose roles have become complicated by the addition of maternal functions (Freud, 1949). For lower-class males, there is a problem of not receiving homosocial support for marital intercourse, to which we might also add the disadvantage of being less trained in the use of auxiliary materials to heighten sexual interest (Simon & Gagnon, 1966). For middle-class males, the decline is less steep, owing perhaps to their ability to find sexual stimulation from auxiliary sources—literature, movies, etc. Also operative is a greater capacity for invoking and responding to fantasy. It should be noted that for about 30 per cent of college-educated males, masturbation continues as a regular source of sexual outlet in marriage and during periods when a wife is available (Kinsey, 1948). To this we might add an additional but unknown proportion who do not physically engage in masturbation but for whom the source of sexual excitement is not just coital activity alone but also the fantasy elements which accompany coital activity. But even for the middle-class male, sexual activity declines in degrees that cannot exclusively be accounted for by changes in the organism. Perhaps it is simply that the conditions under which we learn to be sexual in our society make it extremely difficult to maintain high levels of sexual performance with a single partner over long periods of time. This may remain relatively unimportant in the maintenance of the family unit or even the individual's sense of his own well-being because of the relative unimportance of sexual dissatisfaction or the relatively greater significance of other areas of life.

About half of all ever-married males and a quarter of all ever-married females will engage in extramarital sexual activity at one time or another. For females there is some suggestion of a secular trend toward increases in extramarital activity from the beginning of this century to the early fifties. This is linked to a corresponding generational rise in rates of orgasm during this same period (Kinsey, 1948, 1953). It is possible that the very nature of female sexuality may be undergoing change. Our current data will hopefully shed some light on this. For males there are strong social class differences, with lower-class males accounting for most of the extramarital activity, particularly during the early years of marriage. This may be a direct reflection of their earlier mode of assimilation of the sexual commitment. As we previously observed, it is difficult for lower-class males to receive homosocial validation from marital sexual activity (unless, of course, it culminates in conception); this is not the case for extramarital activity for which there is abundant homosocial validation.

In general, it is our feeling that sexuality and sexual activity are by and large derivative functions even during adulthood. There are only a few periods in the life cycle at which there are high rates of sexual activity and/or sexual activity that is complicated by passion and high intensity of affective investment. These are usually adolescence in the male, the early and romantic years of marriage for both men and women, and the highly charged extramarital experiences that can be called affairs. Most of the time sex is really a relatively docile beast, and it is only the rare individual who through the processes of self-invention or alienation from the normal course of socialization is prepared to risk occupation, present comfort, wife and children, or the future for the chancy joys of sexual pleasure.

From this point of view it might be more proper to suggest that, contrary to the Freudian point of view that sex manifests itself in some form in other types of conduct or that other conduct is symbolic of sexual conflict, reports of sexual conflict may in fact stand for difficulties in the more conventional zones of life. Thus, the married couple who come for counseling because of a sexual problem may be merely reporting the conventional rhetoric of the society about what they think the sources of a marital difficulty ought to be. Ovesey (1950) reports that homosexual dreams (overtly homosexual, not merely symbolic) of heterosexual men really relate to occupational problems and that the submissiveness required occupationally appears in the convenient symbolism of the "purported" femininity of homosexual relations. Indeed, many forms of both heterosexual and homosexual acting-out seem to be related to stress reactions to other life situations rather than having specifically sexual motivations. Thus, studies of sex offenders often are overly concerned with the sexual life of the offender when this may merely be the symptom of disorders of other kinds.

CONCLUSION

It is only a fairly recent development in the history of man that he could begin to conceive of the possibility of social change, that he could begin to understand that his time and place did not represent the embodiment of some eternal principle or necessity, but was only a point in an on-going, dynamic process. For many it is still more difficult to conceive of the possibility of the nature of man himself changing, and particularly changing in significant ways (Van den Berg, 1964). Much of this conservative view of man still permeates contemporary behavioral science. Thus, for many social theories, a view of man as a static bundle of universal needs supplies the necessary stability not available elsewhere in the flux of social life. A conception of man as having relatively constant sexual needs is a necessary part of this point of view. As a contrast to this conservative view, we have attempted to offer a description of sexual development as a variable sociocultural invention, an invention that in itself explains little and requires much explanation.

REFERENCES

BILLER, H. B., & BORSTELMANN, L. J. Masculine development: An integrative review. *Merrill Palmer Quarterly,* 1967, 13, 253–294.

BURKE, K. *Permanence and change.* New York: New Republic, Inc., 1935.

CHODOFF, P. Critique of Freud's theory of infantile sexuality. *American Journal of Psychiatry,* 1966, 123, 507–518.

DAVIS, K. Sexual behavior. In R. K. Merton & R. Nesbitt, *Contemporary social problems.* (2nd Ed.) New York: Harcourt-Brace, 1961.

DURKHEIM, E. *Suicide.* Glencoe: The Free Press, 1951.

EHRMANN, W. *Premarital dating behavior.* New York: Holt, 1959.

ERIKSON, E. H. *Childhood and society.* (2nd Ed.) New York: Norton, 1963.

FORD, C. F., & BEACH, F. A. *Patterns of sexual behavior.* New York: Harper, 1951.

FREUD, S. The most prevalent form of degradation in erotic life. *Collected papers,* Vol. 4. London: Hogarth, 1949.

FREUD, S. Three essays on sexuality. *Complete psychological works.* (Std. Ed.) Vol. VII. London: Hogarth, 1953. Pp. 135–245.

FREUD, S. Analysis terminable and interminable. *Complete psychological works.* (Std. Ed.) Vol. XXIII. London: Hogarth, 1964. Pp. 216–253.

GAGNON, J. H. Female child victims of sex offenses. *Social Problems,* 1965, 13, 176–192.

GAGNON, J. H., & SIMON, W. The social meaning of prison homosexuality. *Federal Probation,* 1968. (a)

GAGNON, J. H., & SIMON, W. Sex education and human development. In P. J. Fink (Ed.), *Human sexual function and dysfunction.* Philadelphia: F. A. Davis, 1968. (b)

GEBHARD, P. H., ET AL. *Sex offenders.* New York: Harper & Row, 1965.

GEWIRTZ, J. L. A learning analysis of the effects of normal stimulation, privation, and deprivation in the acquisition of social motivation and attachment. In B. M. Foss (Ed.), *Determinants of infant behavior.* New York: Wiley, 1961. Pp. 213–290.

HAMBURG, D. A., & LUNDE, D. T. Sex hormones in the development of sex differences in human behavior. In E. Maccoby (Ed.), *The development of sex differences.* Stanford: Stanford Univer. Press, 1966. Pp. 1–24.

KAGAN, J., & MOSS, H. A. *Birth to maturity.* New York: Wiley, 1962.

KENTON, M. (pseud. of Southern, T. & Hoffenburg, M.) *Candy.* Paris: The Olympia Press, 1958.

KINSEY, A. C., ET AL. *Sexual behavior in the human male.* Philadelphia: Saunders, 1948.

KINSEY, A. C., ET AL. *Sexual behavior in the human female.* Philadelphia: Saunders, 1953.

MACCOBY, E. (Ed.) *The development of sex differences.* Stanford: Stanford Univer. Press, 1966.

MASLOW, A. H. Dominance, personality, and social behavior in women. *Journal of Social Psychology,* 1939, 10, 3–39.

MASLOW, A. H. Self esteem (dominance feeling) and sexuality in women. *Journal of Social Psychology,* 1942, 16, 259–294.

MASTERS, W. H., & JOHNSON, V. E. *Human sexual response.* Boston: Little, Brown and Co., 1966.

OVESEY, L. The homosexual conflict: An adaptational analysis. *Psychiatry,* 1950, 17, 243–250.

PARSONS, T. The kinship system of the contemporary United States. In *Essays in sociological theory.* (Rev. Ed.) New York: The Free Press, 1954.

RAINWATER, L. The crucible of identity: The Negro lower class family. *Daedalus,* 1966, 95, 172–216.

REICH, W. The function of the orgasm. In *The discovery of the Orgone.* Vol. I. New York: Orgone Institute Press, 1942.

REISS, A. J., JR. Sex offenses: The marginal status of the adolescent. *Law and Contemporary Problems,* 1960, 25, No. 2.

RHEINGOLD, J. C. *The fear of being a woman.* New York: Grune & Stratton, 1964.

SCHACHTEL, E. *Metamorphosis.* New York: Basic Books, 1959.

SEARS, R. R. Development of gender role. In F. A. Beach (Ed.), *Sex and behavior.* New York: Wiley, 1965. Pp. 133–163.

SIMON, W., & GAGNON, J. H. Heterosexuality and homosociality: A dilemma of the lower class family. 1966. (Mimeographed)

SIMON, W., & GAGNON, J. H. Pornography, raging menace or paper tiger? *Trans-Action,* 1967, 4, 8, 41–48. (a)

SIMON, W., & GAGNON, J. H. The lesbians: A preliminary overview. In J. H. Gagnon & W. Simon (Eds.), *Sexual deviance.* New York: Harper & Row, 1967. (b)

SIMON, W., & GAGNON, J. H. Femininity in the lesbian community. *Social Problems,* 1967, 15, 212–221. (c)

VAN DEN BERG, J. H. *The changing nature of man.* New York: Dell, 1964.

YOUNG, W. R., GOY, R., & PHOENIX, C. Hormones and sexual behavior. *Science,* 1964, 143, 212–218.

CHAPTER **17**

The Development
Of Interpersonal Competence

Eugene A. Weinstein

State University of New York, Stony Brook

If the sociologist's principal abstraction, social structure, has any concrete expression, it is to be found in myriad everyday social encounters. The operation of the larger system is dependent upon the successful functioning of the microscopic and episodic action systems generated in these encounters. And these, in turn, require that participants are able to effectively pursue their personal goals. In the long run, if social structure is to be stable, individuals must be successful in achieving personal purposes (Weinstein, 1966).

But just how, in the concrete, are personal purposes pursued? Sociological social psychology has largely ignored this problem. Instead, people are assumed to develop purposes consonant with the requirements of the social system in which they find themselves, and learn a set of culturally given rules for pursuing them. This side of a Huxleian Utopia, life is not quite like that. Normative scripts embodied in role expectations are far from complete, and often are tangential to issues of central concern to us. Nor is role reciprocity automatic; it well may be the product of extensive and quite subtle negotiations with others whose purposes are not complementary to ours.

Acquiring the interpersonal skills necessary to engage in such negotiations is central to the socialization process. In a very real sense it *is* socialization.[1] For, if the process is defined as equipping individuals to function as participating members of society, no set of skills (except the prerequisite linguistic ones) is as essential to participating in society as the skills enabling people to get others to think, feel, or do what they want them to.

This skill or set of abilities allowing the individual to shape the responses he gets from others is what Foote and Cottrell (1955) mean by interpersonal competence. Foote and Cottrell go on to analyze competence into what they

---

[1] There is, of course, a less imperialistic formulation in which socialization for interpersonal competence is seen as a special case of the more general issue of socialization for competence per se. See Smith, 1965.

regard to be its constituent elements: autonomy, creativity, empathy, health, intelligence, and judgment. Cogent arguments are presented justifying the inclusion of each dimension but these are based mainly on logical appeals to the nature of personality development. Their case does not follow directly from any explicit set of propositions about the nature of the interactive process and the requirements it makes of participants.

The present discussion of interpersonal competence will attempt to go beyond Foote and Cottrell's by taking the interactive process as its starting point. A conceptual model will be presented, and from this model, essential components of competence will be derived. Each of the components will then be analyzed in terms of its development, with current research knowledge of the socialization antecedents of the component reviewed. Before embarking on this enterprise, it might be wise to note that there will be a good deal more conceptualizing and speculating than presenting of research findings. This is a matter of necessity, rather than choice. For, central as the problem of interpersonal control is to social theory, there is precious little research telling us how people acquire the abilities necessary to exercise control over others.

A CONCEPTUAL FRAME
FOR INTERPERSONAL COMPETENCE

There are currently two major modes of approach to interaction extant in the social psychological literature. One focuses principally upon goals and sees interaction as the exchange of rewards and costs. Little attention is specifically paid to how the exchanges actually take place. There is bargaining but no bargaining process. While something of a caricature, the exchange oriented models of Thibaut and Kelley (1959), and Homans (1961) fit this pattern, with Blau (1964) being a little more sensitive to the concrete mechanics of exchange.

The second approach is not so much concerned with the purposes of participants in interaction as it is with the character of interchange between the actors and the episode of interaction in which they are engaged. Of prime concern to this second approach, articulated in the work of Goffman (1959, 1961) and Garfinkle (1964), are the processes by which the parties guide and draw inferences about their current situation, and the rules, both spoken and implicit, which serve to structure their interaction. In the present analysis both schools are drawn upon, with the second taking logical primacy. Much of what follows is a formalization of Goffman, with concepts introduced to make more explicit the personal purposes of the participants.

This analysis is based upon the following set of interconnected concepts:

Interpersonal task: that response or set of responses of alter which ego is attempting to elicit. Contained in the set are covert as well as overt tasks so that ego may be trying to get alter to think or feel something as well as do something ("Lend me five dollars" versus "Think I'm intelligent."). It is assumed that in a given encounter, an actor has a set of interpersonal tasks, each having a theoretically specifiable reward value for him.

Interpersonal competence: the ability to accomplish interpersonal tasks. This is no more than saying that interpersonal competence boils down to the ability to manipulate others' responses. As such the concept is value free. We may wish to manipulate alter's responsive behavior for our own personal ends. Or our purpose in controlling the responses alter makes may be to enhance his own development as in the case of psychotherapy. Competence is relative to the actor's purposes.

Further, by defining interpersonal competence in terms of the actor's aims, we avoid the necessity of settling by fiat the issue of the generality of competence. It could be the case that competence is a role-specific or even a relationship-specific capacity. Or, allowing for some interrole variability, competence could be a kind of *g*-type stable trait. How much is specific and how much general becomes an empirical question.

Lines of action: those activities of ego directed toward alter's perception designed to elicit the task response from alter. Caution must be used in interpreting the word "designed." No assumption of conscious and deliberative planning for manipulation is necessary to this framework (or is it apt to be empirically accurate, either). While a good many of the things we do to affect the behavior of others may be the result of rational reflection, we may be unaware of many of the tactics we use. Nor are we necessarily aware of the interpersonal tasks our behavior serves.

Encounter: any contact between persons involving an interpersonal task on the part of at least one participant.

Situation: all stimuli present in an encounter at any given time which are potentially meaningful (i.e., possess symbolic content) for one or more of the participants. Encounters do not take place in a vacuum but are embedded in situations, or what is equivalent to a Lewinian field. Recognition is given in the definition to the possibility that the field may differ for each of the participants in a single encounter.

Defining the situation: the process of selecting and organizing stimuli in the situation into a coherent whole. This concept is presented as a kind of shorthand summary of all the internal processes mediating between the impinging of situational stimuli and the selection and evocation of responsive lines of action. Its end product is the actor's *definition of the situation:* his best guess as to the nature of the reality with which he is currently engaged; his answer to the question, "What's going on here?" It is from this definition of the situation that inferences concerning alter's probable behavior, alter's expectations of ego's behavior, and appropriate norms are drawn. In other words, it is from his definition of the situation that ego's interpersonal tasks are formulated and lines of action to pursue them are selected.

Projected definition of the situation: lines of action directed at selectively influencing alter's definition of the situation. Since alter's interpersonal tasks, and hence the lines of action used to pursue them, flow from his definition of the situation, the problem of interpersonal control becomes the problem of successfully affecting the way alter defines the situation. Lines of action will be constructed so as to selectively modify the symbolic content of the situation *as perceived by alter*. From ego's perspective, the ones selected are likeliest to influence alter's definition of the situation in a manner which increases the probability of the desired task response being chosen by alter. Thus, if ego is successful, what was an interpersonal task for him will become a line of action for alter.

The effects of ego's acts on alter's definition of the situation are not necessarily those ego predicts. Alter's definition of the situation is not only a function of the cues available to him but also the nature of alter's mediating processes. A variety of concepts has been used to denote the organization of such processes including apperceptive mass, frame of reference, adaptation level, plans, etc. All involve the interpenetration of current and past experience, namely the process of investing stimuli with meaning. The internalized network of categories that serve the central mediating function shall be referred to as the actor's system of meanings. Here "meaning" is used in its broadest sense to include not only physical perceptual aspects, but also connotative ones such as values and affective tone. Thus ego must take into account both the content of his own lines of action, and alter's system of meanings in attempting to increase the likelihood of eliciting the task response.

Working consensus: following Goffman's (1959, p. 9) usage, a tacit agreement as to whose claims to what issues will be temporarily honored. It is an agreement about what reality is to be, the definition of the situation jointly subscribed to (although not necessarily believed in) by the participants in the encounter.

Each line of action modifies somewhat the symbolic content of the situation. And, as situations change, so may their definitions by the several participants. Yet situations are not in complete flux. The working consensus operates to provide boundaries to the moment-to-moment changes in definitions of the situation as well as boundaries to the kinds of tasks which are pursuable and the lines of action usable to pursue them within any encounter. In this respect, it can be argued that the stabilizing function of the working consensus makes it a prerequisite for the maintenance of interaction.

Situational identity: the locus of all situationally relevant attributes imputed to the actor. Thus defined, the concept both includes and is broader than the traditional sociological notion of role. While being in the role of doctor or mother may be a crucial aspect of one's situational identity, there are other aspects which often assume great importance. When do sociologists talk about the injured party, the beholden, the more virtuous than the other, or the helpful (or helpless) roles? Yet these identities are an integral part of a great deal of everyday interaction.

At first blush, the kinds of things subsumed under situational identity may appear to be too diverse for systematic analysis. The examples include aspects which are structurally given, or are part of the history of the relations between parties, or are characteristic of their interchange in the current encounter, or which are derivative from the situational context in which the encounter takes place. What they have in common is the tendency, in social perception, to make the individual the locus of what he has done, what has happened to him, and the situation in which his action is located. These are all part of who he is, as far as he is viewed by and responded to by others.

Agreement about situational identities is at the core of the working consensus. There can be no working consensus nor can interaction long be maintained if there is not substantial agreement as to who everyone is. Thus, who one is can be critically important in the pursuit of interpersonal tasks. Many of the claims one person makes on another and the lines of action used to present those claims are legitimized on the basis of normative expectations regarding the behavior of particular kinds of people.

But situational identities are also important as loci of rewards and costs in themselves. There are many occasions when an actor's purpose is to see himself as being a certain kind of person and receive confirmation for that valued identity in the responses of others. As Berne (1964) notes, this process can be a mutual or "transactional" one in which the relationship takes on the quality of a structured game. This is not to deny that one might have highly specific objectives in an encounter such as "touching" the other for a five dollar loan. However, the identity one has to assume in order to get the five dollars will constitute an important set of costs for him. It is only in the most impersonal encounters that the situational identities of the parties are not a principal nexus of rewards and costs. Often, they are precisely and completely that.

Identity bargaining: lines of action directed at establishing certain situational identities for the participants as terms of the working consensus (see Weinstein & Deutschberger, 1964). A working consensus, especially as it bears upon who the participants are and will be, may not be established directly but may be the result of negotiation, and even subsequent renegotiation. An actor may, in his projected definition of the situation, call attention to aspects of himself that serve to establish his identity. This is the *self presentation* about which Goffman (1959) is so eloquent. Or, the actor may attempt to assign an identity to another or withhold one from him by making it contingent on some specific line of action. This approach to the allocation of situational identities is referred to as *altercasting* (Weinstein & Deutschberger, 1963).

Skill at establishing and maintaining desired identities, both for one's self and for others, is pivotal in being interpersonally competent. This skill is dependent in turn upon three other variables. First, the individual must be able to take the role of the other accurately; he must be able to correctly predict the impact that various lines of action will have on alter's definition of the situation. This is what is meant by empathy if we strip the concept of its affective overtones. Second, the individual must possess a large and varied repertoire of lines of action. Third, the individual must possess the intra-personal resources to be capable of employing effective tactics in situations where they are appropriate.

SOCIALIZATION FOR EMPATHY

The discussion of socialization for empathy will first consider the capacities underlying empathy. Next, a theoretical description of its beginnings and subsequent development is presented. Finally, the activities of socializing agents which promote the development of empathy are examined.

There is a good deal of literature on the measurement of empathy, personality correlates of empathy, and the way empathy functions in social relationships, as for example, in marriage. But there is little research available on empathy as a dependent variable, on its causes and development. What follows, then, is mainly a set of presumptions. To the extent they are empirically testable, they form the outlines of a sorely needed research program on the development of empathy.

Capacities underlying Empathy. Some contribution to empathy comes from constitutional capacities operating in interaction with socializing experiences. Chief among them is intelligence. Empathy, as we have defined it, requires the actor to assess accurately the other's definition of the situation. Since these definitions are a function of alter's system of meanings, empathy depends upon the accuracy with which these meanings are mapped. And the ability to map meanings requires, in turn, the symbolic skill which will allow the actor to entertain multiple perspectives simultaneously, an ability often defined as a central component of intelligence. This is one of the rare cases in which there is empirical substantiation for hypotheses about empathy. Consistent positive correlations between measures of role-taking accuracy and IQ are to be found in the research literature on correlates of person perception.[2]

A second capacity underlying empathic ability is cue sensitivity. Out of the total configuration of stimuli available in the situation, one must be able to focus on those which have inferential relevance for the way the other is internally structuring reality. Lack of normal development of sensory modalities would inhibit cue sensitivity and hence empathy. It would be expected, for example, that the deaf would exhibit lower levels of empathy, particularly in a culture as verbally oriented as ours.

Some capacity for selective focusing is learned, of course. Sensitivity to verbal productions is socially conditioned in the very process of language acquisition. A similar process is involved in learning the culturally defined meanings of common gestures, facial expressions, and voice inflections. But accurate role-taking involves more than cognizance of common cultural meanings since

---

[2] For a review of the correlates of accuracy in person perception, including intelligence, see Allport, 1961.

not all people have the same cultural background or interpret cultural meanings in the same way. Heightened cue sensitivity is necessary for recognition and discrimination of subtle differences in meaning between individuals and for the same individual in differing situations.

Cue sensitivity, especially at the more refined levels of discrimination capacity, involves more than sensory acuity. People differ in their attentiveness to stimuli. This derives in part from constitutional differences in dimensions such as reactivity to stimulation, observable almost from birth. Heightened attentiveness to stimuli may serve to compensate for some of the deficiencies inherent in the focusing process in which irrelevant stimuli are screened out in perception. It is possible to over-generalize incoming data, excluding cues that are relevant precisely because of their discrepancy with dominant themes put forth in the overt performance of the other. This is particularly the case when focus is placed exclusively on verbal aspects of the other's behavior. As we noted previously, the meanings projected by the other are designed to be assimilated directly in a way that is consistent with his purposes. Such a projected definition of the situation may be substantially different from the one he holds internally. Words are the most direct and most easily falsified cues to one's meanings so that a good deal of inaccuracy can result from listening only to what is said. Persons with high empathic capacity can "listen" to feelings and moods as well as to words. Readings of the former come from subtle inflectional, postural, or physiognomic cues which become especially salient as awareness of discrepancy between them and what is being said develops. Following this line of reasoning, one might expect an association of empathy with the cognitive style of perceptual vigilance as opposed to perceptual defense.

The genesis of Empathy.   The earliest roots of empathy are to be found in precisely the same process as Piaget (1950) sees in the development of sensorimotor intelligence. This is the emerging capacity to distinguish self from non-self. In the initial stages, the child makes overt responses to stimuli. He then becomes aware of his own responses and begins to respond to them. These secondary responses facilitate discrimination of self from non-self and form the base for the development of empathy. Take the situation in which a new baby comes into the household of a child who is still mainly preverbal, perhaps twelve months old. It is quite common for the child to be upset, perhaps even cry the first time or so he hears the new baby cry. But he soon becomes cognizant that it is not he that hurts, and it is not uncommon for the one-year-old to laugh with relief upon making this discovery. In the process, he also learns something else, admittedly at a very crude and rudimentary level. He learns that others have affective responses separate from but akin to his own. By the age of three, most children respond in ways that show their recognition of the meaning of affect-connected cues as separate from their own feelings at the time (Murphy, 1937). The clearest illustration is found in responses to distress on the part of others, the expression of sympathy. These responses can take a number of forms. In reaction to an upset child young children may offer expressions of comfort, seek help from an adult for the upset child, or even punish the cause of the distress as when one child attacks another. Whatever the form it takes, the response of sympathy is predicated on taking the role of the other.

The sympathy example illustrates the earliest mode of inference to the role of the other. Cues from the other are recognized as similar to cues from one's own behavior and the generalization is made to the kinds of feelings in one's self ordinarily associated with such cues. But empathy extends beyond the mere recognition of affective states. The real payoff for taking the role of the other is to anticipate his behavior, for only through anticipation is effective control possible in the long run. Anticipation requires the development of conceptual facility far beyond the recognition of cues in the responses of the other. One must be able to reconstruct the situation as it impinges upon the other; the other's responses serve to validate the reconstruction. The question is how the process of inferring the role of the other develops.

The principal mode of inference underlying early sympathetic behavior is generalization from self to other based upon recognition of the other's response. Logically similar to this mode, but at a more advanced conceptual level is *projective role-taking*. Generalization is made, not only from the response of the other but from a perception of the situation as it impinges on the other. One attempts to take the role of the other by projecting one's self into his perspective: "If I were confronted by this set of circumstances, how would I respond?"

The accuracy of this mode of inference depends on how clearly the circumstances (including our own acts) impinging on the other are perceived and on how correct is the assessment of their meaning to him. Since, in projective role-taking this assessment is based on a projection of one's own meanings, accuracy probably depends in part upon the similarity in meanings between the role-taker and the one whose role is being taken. This leads us to the prediction that empathy would be higher among individuals having undergone similar socialization experiences. Since socializing experiences, and hence meanings, tend to cluster within social categories, one would predict greater empathy within such social categories as age, sex, ethnic group, rural vs. urban background, etc., than across them.

The inherent limitations to projective role-taking are clear; not everyone has the same meanings as we do. The connotative aspects of words can vary substantially, particularly in their evaluative aspects. Take for example, the differences in connotation of the term "socialist" to a Laborite M.P. and a Birchite congressman. If he is insensitive to the possibility of such differences, the projective role-taker can only raise his arms in bewilderment when others respond in ways which flow logically from perspectives different from his own.

Recognition that others can have different ways of looking at the world comes fairly early. A major source is contact with peers and with adult authority figures outside of the family, schoolteachers, ministers, doctors, etc. The child learns that certain perspectives, certain modes of evaluation, are associated with particular social positions. So schoolteachers are particularly concerned with orderliness, doctors with not making a fuss, grownups with being obeyed, other children with the rules of play. Such learning becomes generalized to a mode of role-taking that one might call *positional role-taking*. Meanings are recognized as being associated with the particular social niche occupied by the other.

Positional role-taking, as a mode of inference, is learned as an inherent part of the process of role-learning. Learning to be a patient to a doctor, a student to a teacher, a child to an adult, a chum to another child, means learning expectations for both one's own role and those reciprocal to it. The learning process is posited to follow the model outlined by Mead (1934). Role expectations are first associated with specific representatives of a social position. Later, as social contacts broaden, they are generalized into positional stereotypes. Role-taking then involves evoking the stereotypic role expectations associated with a particular social position. The ability to use this kind of role-taking is part of the standard equipment of the standard actor in standard social systems. To the extent his stereotypes fall within the boundaries of cultural consensus regarding role expectations, the actor is equipped to participate adequately in the role networks of which he is a part.

While positional role-taking may be adequate for most social relationships, particularly those which are impersonal in nature, it too has limitations as a sole mode of inference. Not all doctors, teachers, lawyers, women, or lower-class people hold the same meanings; stereotypes break down as the characteristics of a particular instance move away from the central tendency. Furthermore, positional stereotypes have limited usefulness in close, highly personalized relationships. Some necessary refinement of positional stereotypes takes place with the development of *personality stereotyping* as a mode of role-taking.

Personality stereotyping involves placing the other into a particular personality category. Placement is based on the recognition of one or two features held by the perceiver to be central to the category. Generalization then takes place so that the full "syndrome" of traits and associated meanings is attributed to the other. The other is expected to act consistently with the "syndrome." The personality categories learned in commonplace socialization strike a familiar ring; "nice guy," "touchy," "bastard," "smart aleck," are a sample. In a sense these too could be called role labels, but they refer more to styles of role performance than to positional location. Later, one finds an occupational world peopled by representatives of stereotypes like "back-stabber," "operator," or "patsy." Such stereotypes can improve predictive accuracy beyond that available from the positional expectations alone.

A large vocabulary of refined personality stereotypes can lead to high levels of role-taking accuracy upon fairly short acquaintance. There are apocryphal stories of men who can size someone up "just by the way he shakes hands or looks you in the eye." While cues like these may have some predictive validity, the skillful role-taker is chary of becoming so committed to their implications that he overlooks negative evidence.

The willingness to abandon stereotypes and base role-taking on direct experience with a specific other is *individuation;* the other's system of meanings is mapped on the basis of his responses. Projective role-taking is often the starting point for individuation. Negative instances, responses which are not consistent with the meanings imputed to the other, provide the clues for differentiation, providing, of course, that one has the capacity to recognize them and attribute them to differences in meaning rather than to the other's recalcitrance or ill will. Take, for example, offering to help another. Suppose the other responds by forcefully, even aggressively, refusing the offer. One might be perplexed and feel, "but I was only trying to be helpful." If this occurs again, with the same negative response from the other, it should become clear that receiving help does not mean the same thing to him as it does to you. It is likely to mean to him that his adequacy is being questioned.

But discrepancies are not always recognized for what they imply. Any long term relationship offers the potential for individuation and high levels of empathy; it does not guarantee this will take place. Among the principal barriers to empathy, regardless of the mode of inference, are the meanings one holds for one's self. Much of our behavior is motivated by the desire to see ourselves as behaving in a certain kind of way, as being a certain kind of person. Consensual validation is sought in the responses of the other. Thus we are prone to demand that the other hold meanings for our behavior consonant with our ideal concept of ourselves. This might be called *autistic projection* as distinguished from projective role-taking. In autistic projection, we do not necessarily assume that our acts mean to the other what they would mean to us; rather we assume they *should* mean to the other what we need them to mean. The other's meanings only become salient when his responses do not meet our requirements. Projective role-taking can be highly accurate if we are free to see our own behavior as it would appear to us if it were coming from another person: "If I were in his shoes, how would my behavior look to me?" The standards we hold for the kind of person we are often lead to distortions in our conception of what our behavior is actually like. Autistic distortions are most likely to occur in close relationships since the other's conception of us is apt to have more impact on our own self-concept under those conditions.

To what extent do these types constitute a developmental sequence? Murphy's (1937) early work on sympathy indicates that the rudiments of projective role-taking occur quite early, by the age of three. Baldwin's (1965) work on the attribution of intent suggests a good deal of autism in the early years. Children at various ages are asked to evaluate the intent of an actor choosing between two different courses of action. Each choice is characterized by a pattern of consequences (positive or negative) for the chooser and for the subject. Young children tend to disregard the consequences of a choice for the chooser, looking only at how the choice will affect them. For example, they may equate all situations having negative consequences for themselves as indicating intent to harm when adults would consider the possibility of legitimate self-interest of the chooser and differentiate such situations from cases involving active negative intent toward the subject. The "errors" of the young children come from considering only consequences to self rather than taking the role of the other.

Positional stereotyping probably begins to develop as the child moves from home to school, with personality stereotyping coming somewhat later as the child develops both conceptual skill and a vocabulary of types. Individuation is likely to develop last in the sequence. However, the types should not be regarded as sequentially emergent. One type does not become perfected and the next begin to arise from it. Rather, the beginnings of all the types, with the possible exception of individuation, occur by the early school years, with overlapping development after that.

Promoting Empathic Development

We have already noted that language-learning and role-learning carry along with them the development of empathic capacity. But beyond such culturally standard training, are there particular socialization practices which facilitate or inhibit accuracy in role-taking?

It may be assumed that exposing the child to a breadth and variety of social relationships facilitates the development of general role-taking accuracy. The larger the number of roles encountered by the child, the more he has opportunity to develop an effective vocabulary of positional stereotypes. Projective role-taking is also facilitated. One of the best ways to improve the capacity to take a given role is to have played it one's self. The greater the variety of social situations encountered by the child, the more will be his firsthand acquaintance with the exigencies of role behavior in such situations. It should be noted that opportunities for breadth in social relationships are not exclusively a matter of parental encouragement. In a very real way, such opportunities are part of the child's life chances and heavily affected by his social class origins. Lower-class children are less likely to have the experiences which will facilitate role-taking accuracy, especially with those outside of their class. One can speculate about the implications this has for their developing the interpersonal skills necessary for upward mobility.

Effective development of projective role-taking is dependent upon several parental practices. Foote and Cottrell (1955, p. 75) suggest that intimate communicative relations are probably essential. This involves making affective responses, both positive and negative, clear to the child so that he can get a more accurate sense of the impact of his acts.

> Striking the child in anger at something he has done and in other ways reacting to his acts so that he discovers that "parents too are human," is more in the direction of reciprocity and communication than the detached and impersonal application of rules of punishment and reward (Foote & Cottrell, 1955, p. 85).

Parents can actively promote an orientation toward projective role-taking. The child can be encouraged to consider the impact of his acts on others by having his attention called to how he would feel or react if he were confronted by similar circumstances. These lessons can come out of episodes in the relationship with the parent or indirectly, when the parent points out the reasons for another's behavior. Still less direct are disciplinary practices which focus on the reasons for behavior rather than the act alone. In all these cases, the child is learning to be sensitive to motivation and that others have purposes and feelings as well as he. If the lessons are one-sided, if the child is simply asked, "How would you feel?" and then only when he has misbehaved, their effectiveness will be limited. The parent can serve as a role model, pointing out instances in which her acts are being shaped by the probable effects on others including the child, himself. (This last point does *not* include the ubiquitous, "I'm doing this for your own good.")

Some socialization practices may be expected to inhibit role-taking accuracy to the extent that they are conducive to autistic projection. Particularly important are those which lead to the development of standards for the self which are vulnerable to recurrent possibilities for invalidation. The parents of a fairly bright child may do him a disservice by constantly emphasizing his brilliance and their expectations for extraordinary achievement. Constantly faced with these standards, others become evaluators rather than people with feelings and motives. Highly authoritarian child-rearing patterns are likely to lead to autistic projection. They are associated with rigidity in super-ego development. Rigid super-ego standards for self-performance are met not by questioning one's own performances, but by attacking the validity of others' responses when they fail to confirm these standards.

Authoritarianism may inhibit role-taking accuracy in a second way. One likely consequence of authoritarian child-rearing is an intolerance for ambiguity. In later life this is likely to lead to an overcommitment to ambiguity-resolving stereotypes, particularly positional stereotypes. This commitment is bolstered by a sense of moral imperative so when a doctor behaves in a way different from the stereotype, the stereotype is not questioned, but the doctor's integrity is.

ACQUIRING A REPERTOIRE OF TACTICS

Interpersonal competence is the ability to control the responses of others. Controlling others starts with the beginning of life, although it is clear the infant is not conscious that his behavior is affecting the responses of others toward him. His primary tactic in getting what he needs from others is simply to communicate the need. He cries. One cannot assume that infants know they are communicating. Just at what point in the developmental process the child can cry voluntarily is unclear. It is at that point, however, that crying becomes the first interpersonal tactic. Psychoanalysis offers other instances of preverbal attempts at interpersonal control. Oral hostility in relation to weaning and oral retention as resistance to toilet training are two of the most commonly cited patterns.

As self-consciousness depends upon the development of language, so does the development of more self-conscious use of interpersonal tactics. Their genesis can be seen in the distinction Lindesmith and Strauss (1956) draw between speech for one's self and speech for others.

> For some time after he has begun to speak, the child makes little distinction between words that he addresses to himself and those that he addresses to others. After a time, however, he learns to adapt his remarks to the exigencies of the social situation. He becomes aware of the responses of others to the remarks he makes, and therefore begins to adapt them to the requirements of intelligible communication.

It is, however, more than intelligible communication that is at issue. Take, for example, a two-year-old child who, in playing with his cup of milk, spills it. His mother responds angrily, perhaps slapping his hand and telling him it is naughty to play with milk. The next night, when reaching for some food, he accidentally knocks over his milk and begins to cry. But his mother does not reprimand him. Instead she says, "That's all right. It was an accident." And so the next night, as he gleefully spills his milk again, he turns beamingly toward his mother and says, "Accident, Mommy." Speech for others not only communicates; it manipulates. Our hypothetical child shows the glimmerings of recognition that how an act is presented will shape the response it receives. This is the prototype of presentation of self (and the beginnings of defenses).

Not only is the distinction implied in "speech for others" learned; it begins to become mandatory as more polished social performances are demanded. Elkin (1958) notes that behaviors "... which may previously have been considered charmingly unself-conscious now are frowned upon as exhibitionist or babyish ..." The child's repertoire develops as he is trained, by parents and others, in the expectations which define the boundaries for his role performances.

Learning what role prescriptions and proscriptions are and how they are met in expressive behavior is fundamental in the development of interpersonal tactics. There is, however, substantial room to maneuver within these normatively given boundaries (see Goode, 1960). The tactics of bargaining and exchange must be learned. One must also acquire techniques for establishing and maintaining situational identities both for one's self and for others (altercasting) as well as learning the more routinized aspects of roles.

Participating effectively in social exchanges depends upon awareness of exchange as an approach to the pursuit of personal goals, the learning of exchange tactics, and the ability to recognize that differing tactics may not be equally effective for all "targets" of interpersonal control. What is effective with peers will not necessarily work with teachers or parents. Radke's work (1964) shows the roots of target differentiation in early family relationships. She finds that preschoolers already are beginning to develop a repertoire of manipulative tactics and they understand that some tactics work better on mothers and others on fathers.

Wood, Weinstein and Parker (1967) carried the exploration of children's interpersonal tactics through the early school years (kindergarten through third grade). Their investigation was based on children's responses to problems of interpersonal control in hypothetical situations involving getting another person to change his mind. The situations involved three different targets of control attempts, mother, best friend, and teacher.

Their findings reveal clear changes in tactic usage as the children advance in age. The modal tactic, used nearly half of the time by children in kindergarten and first grade, but less than one-fourth of the time by second and third graders, was simply asking. In contrast, the modal tactic for third graders (48 per cent) was the use of positive sanctions, offering the other some gift or favor in exchange for changing his mind. This type of tactic comprised only one-eighth of those used by the kindergarten and first-grade children.

Some differentiation in tactic usage by targets was noted. Asking was most common when the situation involved a friend, least common when it involved getting the teacher to change her mind. (There was little consensus as to how to influence the teacher.) Asking was the most common tactic used on mother as well as friend, with positive sanctions second in both cases.

As suggested earlier, communicating needs through crying is the initial interpersonal tactic. Given normal parental practices, it is usually adequate. The common use of asking in the early school years can be regarded as a verbal extension of this pattern. But as the children grow older, asking, and some of its less pleasant forms like begging (a negative sanction?), appear less frequently.

Second and third graders have learned that, even when dealing with friends or mother, more is required than a simple request. It is understood that one is not betraying a friendship or being purposely mean in refusing to honor a request. Compliance thus has a more voluntary character, and more elaborate strategies must be used. These take the form of offers of exchange, whether it be the promise made to mother to be particularly good or the offer of a ride on one's bicycle to a friend. It should be noted that most children were not aware of the reason for the effectiveness of exchange, or at least could not verbalize them when asked why they thought their particular tactic would have the desired effect. While employing tactics having an underlying hedonistic logic, only one-fifth were able to cite recognition of the hedonistic motives of others as the reason for using them. This suggests that early tactics do not flow from conscious planning based upon clearly understood motivational principles but probably reflect imitation and generalization of observed practices and trial and error learning.

A more explicit recognition of hedonism comes quickly enough, however. Its development comes from increasing skill at projective role-taking. It is hastened by the learning of culturally given aphorisms about flattery, fair exchange, and self-interest, aphorisms which serve as axioms in every man's social psychology. And as recognition of hedonism develops, the child becomes more attuned to exchange as a modality in social relationships. He begins to develop tactics necessary for more effective interpersonal bargaining.

Reciprocity in exchange has its foundations early in socialization. The notion of "my turn" is probably familiar to every three-year-old nursery school child. It is from such beginnings that the norm of reciprocity and conceptions of fair exchange evolve (cf., Gouldner, 1960). Probably peers rather than parents have the major influence in the further development of reciprocity and exchange. The authority and rule-based relations in the family are not as conducive to notions of reciprocity among equals as the consensus-based morality of peer culture. And the competition for status in the peer group is likely to have a facilitating effect on the transition from tactics of reciprocity to tactics of advantageous exchange.

Advantageous exchange means maximization of outcome in terms of the balance of rewards and costs for the individual. Maximization, in turn, is likeliest when the other's outcome values for various acts of yours are known to you, but your rewards and costs are not known to him (Thibaut & Kelley, 1959). Peer relations provide a good training ground for learning to conceal one's rewards. Others should not know how important it is to you to have a particular baseball card, or that you have a duplicate of the one you are trading. Being too eager can result in the other's demanding higher payment for the resources under his control so that the ability to keep one's "cool" comes to have tactical value for the child. Smaller children often learn this when they catch on to how older children exploit them. Engaging in bargaining within the peer group, especially the one-upmanship of status bargaining, can begin to sensitize the child to the cues which indicate others' outcome values and the kinds of resources the child can use to trade for what he wants. These are precursors of some of the subtler forms of bargaining for situational identities which make for effective control in later life.

Much of adult interaction centers around establishing and maintaining situational identities. Within any given role, one's situational identity can change from encounter to encounter. And from situational identities flows legitimacy for lines of action and interpersonal tasks. The child learns that the privileges he receives when labelled as a "good boy" are greater than those available to him when he is being identified as a disobedient child. From this he learns that claims to privileges can be legitimized if he can successfully establish the identity of "good boy" in a given encounter with his parents (or promise to maintain that identity in the future). What he can expect to get from others becomes associated with whom he can successfully claim to be. The next step is to learn the cues that are to be given off in establishing an identity. Early attempts are quite direct; he overtly claims to be a good boy. Later, he begins to note the particular acts and demeanor associated with the desired identity and starts to embellish his performances with them as in being especially polite for a period before he asks his mother to be allowed to stay up late. Thus are fashioned the masks he needs to don for effective interpersonal control. As development proceeds, the collection of masks (or parts of them) gets larger, and subtler uses of shading and coloration are learned. Role-modeling plays an increasingly important part in the process as the child becomes aware of the necessity of enhancing the credibility of the masks he wears. Unlike his parents in their relationship to him, the child cannot claim an identity by virtue of authority and have it automatically incorporated as part of the working consensus. His claims are legitimized indirectly by the aptness of his performance so the techniques of prestigious performers are scrutinized, and tried out experimentally, and incorporated when reinforced.[3]

The sanctions employed by others, the teasing, the statements like "big boys don't do that," made as responses to the child's behavior in the role-learning process, provide another kind of learning as well. The child begins to sense that he too can adopt such behavior toward others, directing them to assume roles or play roles in ways which will promote his own goals. These are the roots of altercasting, which later develops into a principal technique of interpersonal control. Personal purposes are pursued through casting others in identities with which the desired behavior is consistent or even prescribed.

Modes of pursuing interpersonal tasks through altercasting are quite varied as are the sanctions used to get the other to assume the identity being projected for him. That certain situational identities are to be valued is stressed early by parents. They make it clear to the child that being "awarded" such identities is contingent on conformity to their expectations. The child quickly begins to turn the tables when he employs such tactics as, "A nice mommy would let her son stay up late to watch the TV special." It is a short step from that tactic to the "If you really loved me, you . . ." universal to courtship in America.

Altercasting can be quite direct as when the individual overtly labels the identity the other is expected to assume in the situation. "Joe, *buddy,* I know you wouldn't mind lending me five dollars." In such cases, the usual implication is that the desired response is required of the other because of his situational identity. For younger children, there is often explicit reference to role prescriptions in the course of pursuing interpersonal tasks. "Joe, you're supposed to let me use your bike because friends are supposed to share" (Weinstein, 1966). Failure to accept the altercast places the encounter in jeopardy, since encounters require the maintenance of a working consensus, which, in turn, requires agreement among the participants as to their respective situational identities.

It is necessary for the child to learn tactics to maintain situational identities, both one's own and those of the other participants. A common tactical problem is dealing with potentially negative implications of specific lines of action for one's own or the other's identity. It is solved by learning techniques for dissociating one's face (or that of the other) from one's actions. This commonly takes the form of "communication about communication." So, when the child refuses to let his friend have a bicycle ride, and says, "My Daddy made me promise I wouldn't let anyone use it," he is affirming two things: first, he is affirming that he is the other's friend; and second, he is affirming that the

---

[3] For a similar treatment of the emergence of situational identities, see McCall and Simmons, 1966.

other's request (and hence the other) is worthy even though he cannot respond to it.

In other forms of communication about communication, the child learns to apologize in advance for acts which may not meet some set of standards as in, "I'm not sure, but I think ..." This is an implicit request to his audience not to evaluate him by the correctness of his statement. The child must also learn that occasions arise in which he is called upon to support the other's social face and must acquire the tactics for doing so. When another child is embarrassed by some faux pas, he might be told, "Don't worry, it could happen to anyone." By implication, the statement informs him that his identity is not being evaluated on the basis of the offending act.

Many of the forms of communication about communication are not learned as tactics nor are they self-consciously employed as such. Rather, they are learned as acts of required tact or politeness. Yet they serve to solve the central problem of interaction—pursuing personal purposes while still keeping the other bound in the relationship. The rules of politeness occupy an important place in the socialization process for this reason. By helping to maintain identities, they serve to preserve encounters. In so doing, they make it easier for people, and the larger social structure, to get their business done.

PERSONAL ORIENTATIONS
AND INTERPERSONAL COMPETENCE

Even if the child can accurately take the role of the other, have some conception of the lines of action most likely to evoke the interpersonal task response, and have those lines of action in his repertoire, he still must be free to use them. It is possible for some people to know how to get what they want and still, because of personality factors, be unable to do so. This last section will consider several personal tendencies which may give or inhibit the freedom to be interpersonally competent.

Rigidity, particularly rule boundedness, is an orientation interfering with interpersonal competence. The "bureaucratic personality" can be conditioned early in life and extend to areas of life quite apart from organizational roles (Merton, 1957). Rule boundedness might develop from overemphasis by parents on prescriptions and proscriptions as the core of role-learning. The child is reinforced for hyperconformity. Deviations are only permitted when they can be legitimized by highly legalistic rationales. In socialization of this type, the child is given little opportunity or encouragement to test limits or explore the boundaries of working consensuses. The generalization he learns is that there is safety within the normatively circumscribed and structured boundaries of roles. The net result is a reluctance to use lines of action not immediately implied by the role. Effectiveness is sacrificed when innovation is called for.

Rigidity in certain aspects of one's self-concept may interfere with competence in a similar way to role rigidity. A person may be loathe to ask another for needed assistance because he cannot afford to see himself in the identity of a supplicant. Or pride in absolute honesty may lead one to misinterpret a request for evaluation by another as calling for objectivity rather than support. The demarcation between rigidity and sincere commitment to values may be more apparent than real. Yet there does seem to be a point at which the self-values served by barring certain lines of action turn out to defeat such a broad range of purposes that they can be regarded as self-defeating in themselves.

At the other pole from these tendencies is the individual who will use any line of action if it appears to promote profitable outcomes for him. For this person, no line of action has cost value due to loss of self-esteem. In its most extreme form this is psychopathy. Somewhat moderated, it falls within the normal range of Machiavellianism as defined by Christie and his associates (Christie & Merton, 1958). The Machiavelle accepts manipulativeness as an orientation toward interaction and suspects others are manipulative too. Being perceived as sincere and unmanipulative may be necessary for one's lines of action to be credible and thus able to affect the other's definition of the situation. So the Machiavelle may find it necessary to conceal his willingness to exploit. If he can do so, there are a number of situations in which the willingness to employ whatever tactics the situation requires serves the Machiavelle in good stead. The empirical evidence seems to suggest that persons high on Machiavellianism are more interpersonally competent (Christie & Geis, forthcoming; Singer, 1964). A touch of psychopathy, then, may be helpful if success in controlling others is the object.

Viewing interaction as the reciprocal attempts of individuals to control each other's behavior means all of us are manipulative. Individual differences are found only in the tactics we are willing to use. If a basically hedonic human nature is assumed, it is not Machiavellianism but its absence which becomes problematic. The argument is that all children start out as Machiavelles (although some are better at it than others). Much of early socialization is directed at repressing these tendencies. The learning of role boundaries and the internalization of moral standards are the means by which natural Machiavellianism is curbed.

This implies that Machiavellian tendencies are the result of "imperfect" socialization. It may be possible that the Machiavelle has been exposed to similar role and moral requirements and accords them some legitimacy while still making them inoperative in much of his behavior. One wonders, then, whether there may be training for Machiavellian attitudes. There is the anecdote about the father who puts his son on the garage roof and urges him to jump, promising to catch him. When the son jumps, the father steps out of the way saying, "That will teach you not to trust anyone." It is unlikely that socialization is often that direct. Incidental learning—hearing of successful misreporting on income tax, or triumphs in office intrigue, or observing the success of manipulative tactics used by sibs and peers—is probably more important. Yet the trust example is well taken since a hallmark of the Machiavelle is his suspiciousness of the motives of others. Seeing others in this way, distrust can serve as a "technique of neutralization" (Sykes & Matza, 1957). Normative proscriptions do not have to be repressed. Instead, manipulative tactics which deviate from them are justified as necessary because of what others can and are willing to do. This is not to argue that distrust is always conducive to competence. The questioning of all motives may lead to inaccurate role-taking at times. It can also cut the individual off from potential sources of rewards by failing to recognize sincere positive feelings.

There are a number of personal orientations which would be expected to affect motivation for interpersonal competence. One would expect persons who are alienated to have low motivation for interpersonal competence. Seeing the world and those in it as unfair and unconcerned except as their own interests are involved promotes the expectation of failure, so why try (cf., McClosky & Schaar, 1965)? An internal locus of control, seeing one's acts as standing in an orderly relationship to the consequences which one receives, would, theoretically, lead to high motivation for interpersonal competence (Roher, Seeman & Liverant, 1962). Ascribing consequences to forces outside one's control and independent of one's activities (external locus of control) tends to be associated with seeing success as unpredictable and hence motivation for achievement through interpersonal control is apt to be reduced. Admittedly, alienation and external locus of control overlap substantially in meaning. They also probably overlap in potential effects on interpersonal competence because they both influence assessments of the probability of failure.

There is a way in which failure affects motivation for interpersonal competence aside from its likelihood of occurrence. The psychological costs of failure may differ considerably from individual to individual. When failure weighs heavily for the individual, many desired responses from others do not become interpersonal tasks. The costs of trying and not succeeding so exceed the costs of deprivation that extremely high success probabilities are needed to overcome this cost threshold level. Failure avoidance rather than success maximization becomes the dominant orientation. It functions to reduce flexibility in the kinds of interpersonal tasks one will risk bargaining for and the kinds of lines of action one will risk using in the bargaining process.[4]

The underlying basis for an orientation toward failure avoidance is likely to be low self-esteem. If we think of self-esteem in quantitative terms, failure for a low self-esteem person will use up a larger proportion of a limited and valued commodity than it will for a person high in self-esteem. For the low self-esteem person, alternatives to a present relationship, while they may be more attractive, are also apt to be seen as less attainable and potentially more costly. Thus he is less likely to use lines of action which would increase his outcomes in a current relationship if they have any risk of disrupting it. Lines of action by others which jeopardize self-esteem are met with high levels of defensiveness. Similarly, his own behavior tends to be presented in studiously correct ways. When exposed to the evaluation of others, he simply cannot afford to be in the wrong.

Much of this syndrome is comparable to what Crowne and Marlowe (1964) call high "need for approval." If popularity with others can be taken as

---

[4] This orientation has been explored in relation to achievement motivation. Cf., Darri, 1964; and Moulton, 1965.

a partial indicator of interpersonal competence, the finding of lower sociometric scores, particularly greater peer rejection, among those high in need for approval offers some substantiation for the line of reasoning taken here (Crowne & Marlowe, 1964, pp. 162–165). Further substantiation is found in Crandall's work (1966) on elementary school children. Children high on her measure of Social Desirability Response Tendency (SDRT, adapted from Crowne and Marlowe's work) are low in self-esteem. Further, their behavior fits the description of failure minimizers. Boys high on her measure were highly suggestable, conventional, inhibited, and controlled. While much concerned with others' evaluations, in free play situations they did not as often seek recognition or approval and avoided achievement activities. High SDRT girls were less aggressive in both physical activities and verbal behavior, and tended to avoid social interaction. Crandall concludes that this behavior pattern seems designed more to avoid disapproval than to gain positive evaluations.

Empirical work on the socialization conditions which produce a failure avoidance orientation to interpersonal relationships is badly needed. In speculating about the sources of failure avoidance, the reinforcement history of the child, particularly in early family relationships, seems important. Parental rejection, to the extent that it leads to low self-acceptance, is involved. However, consistent rejection, in itself, may not produce this outcome. The more likely pattern is one in which the child is reinforced for dependency and yet punished when performances fail to live up to high parental expectations. This may be particularly true when punishments take the form of assigning negative labels to the child. Take the example of the young child who is brought in to pay her respects to company. Mother says, "You look so nice in the new dress I bought you. Dance for Mommy and the company, darling." Upon some coaxing, the child dances and trips in the process. Mother responds by indicating to all, "She's so clumsy, it's really embarrassing." Fostered dependency hooks the child to the mother as a significant source of meanings for the child's self. Yet performances are apt to be met with the mother's projecting negative meanings. The generalization is clear; avoid performances in which you might be evaluated. Safety is sought in those areas of life in which interpersonal standards can be met without strain. But safety has its costs in reduced interpersonal effectiveness.

A BRIEF EPILOGUE

It seems appropriate, at this point, to reiterate the highly speculative nature of what has gone before. These speculations were of two kinds: The *content* of socialization for competence, and the *context* within which such socialization takes place. In sheer volume, speculations about the former exceeded those about the latter. One reason for this is the guidance a conceptual model of interpersonal competence provides in delineating the skills a competent person needs to acquire. No such explicit guidance was available in discussing the process by which the components of competence are acquired. Also, the large body of research literature attesting to the hazards of inferences from socialization experiences to personality outcomes inhibits one's speculative bent. Nevertheless, it seems that concern with the context of socialization for competence has been given short shrift. At the least, it might be well to make more explicit assumptions about socialization for competence that have only been alluded to (or less) in the preceding analysis.

First, socialization *for* competence may be a misnomer. Specific training in role acquisition, the acquisition of norms, and in learning to take the role of others is often directed at enabling the child to behave appropriately, and not necessarily effectively. In the evolution of normative systems, a correlation develops between appropriate and effective behavior but the child may not be self-consciously learning about the correlation as he learns norms. This means that much of interpersonal effectiveness is learned only incidentally. In later life, therefore, we are often unaware of manipulative intent, at least on our own part.

Second, there is an important division of labor between parents and peers in the early socialization process. Basic capacities like empathy and personality orientations conducive to effective interpersonal control are seen as coming primarily from parents. But the refinement of these orientations and their impact in the acquisition and utilization of lines of action seem to be more heavily molded by peer interaction. This is held to be the case because of differences in the kind of interpersonal control that can be exercised by parents and peers over the child's own behavior. There is a way he can learn tactics from peers by observing what they do to him and to other children. He can then apply them in an attempt to control outcomes from them. His outcomes in relation to parents are less subject to his own manipulation. In Thibaut and Kelley's terms (1959), the child is capable of exercising behavior control with peers in a way it is difficult to do with parents who exercise fate control over him.

Finally, there is an implicit learning model underlying what has been said about socialization of interpersonal competence. An extremely important role has been assigned to the same kinds of factors that are involved in social learning theory (Rotter, 1954; Bandura & Walters, 1963). Much of the socialization process depends not on direct training but on incidental learning. Modeling and application, particularly in peer relations, lead to selective reinforcement in shaping the child's repertoire of lines of action. And the role of vicarious reinforcement is held to be crucial. The child becomes both an observer and evaluator of his own behavior. Thus the opportunity to use certain lines of action may have reinforcement value, in itself.

REFERENCES

ALLPORT, G. *Pattern and growth in personality.* New York: Holt, Rinehart and Winston, 1961. Pp. 506–511.

BALDWIN, A. A is happy—B is not. *Child Development,* 1965, 36, 583–600.

BANDURA, A., & WALTERS, R. H. *Social learning and personal development.* New York: Holt, Rinehart and Winston, 1963.

BERNE, E. *Games people play*. New York: Grove Press, 1964.

BLAU, P. *Exchange and power in social life*. New York: Wiley, 1964.

CHRISTIE, R., & GEIS, FLORENCE. *Studies in Machiavellianism*. In press.

CHRISTIE, R., & MERTON, R. Procedures for the sociological study of the value climate of medical schools. *Journal of Medical Education*, 1958, 33, 125–153.

CRANDALL, VIRGINIA. Personality characteristics and social and achievement behaviors associated with children's social desirability response tendencies. *Journal of Personality and Social Psychology*, 1966, 4, 477–486.

CROWNE, D. P., & MARLOWE, D. *The approval motive*. New York: Wiley, 1964.

DARRI, S. K. Level of aspiration as a function of need for achievement and fear of failure. *Dissertation Abstracts*, 1964, 20, 4304.

ELKIN, F. Socialization and the presentation of self. *Marriage and Family Living*, 1958, 20, 321.

FOOTE, N., & COTTRELL, L. S., JR. *Identity and interpersonal competence*. Chicago: Univer. of Chicago Press, 1955.

GARFINKLE, H. The routine grounds of everyday activities. *Social Problems*, 1964, 11, 225–250.

GOFFMAN, E. *The presentation of self in everyday life*. Garden City, N.Y.: Anchor Books, 1959.

GOFFMAN, E. *Encounters*. Indianapolis: Bobbs-Merrill, 1961.

GOODE, W. J. Norm commitment and conformity to role-status obligations. *American Journal of Sociology*, 1960, 66, 246–258.

GOULDNER, A. W. The norm of reciprocity. *American Sociological Review*, 1960, 25, 161–177.

HOMANS, G. C. *Social behavior: Its elementary forms*. New York: Harcourt, Brace and World, 1961.

LINDESMITH, A. R., & STRAUSS, A. L. *Social psychology*. (Rev. Ed.) New York: Dryden Press, 1956. P. 198.

McCALL, G. O., & SIMMONS, J. L. *Identities and interactions*. New York: The Free Press, 1966. Pp. 214–228.

McCLOSKEY, H., & SCHOAR, J. Psychological dimensions of anomy. *American Sociological Review*, 1965, 30, 14–39.

MEAD, G. H. *Mind, self and society*. Chicago: Univer. of Chicago Press, 1934. Pp. 158 ff.

MERTON, R. K. *Social theory and social structure*. (Rev. Ed.) Glencoe: The Free Press, 1957. Pp. 195–206.

MOULTON, R. Effects of success and failure on level of aspiration as related to achievement motives. *Journal of Personality and Social Psychology*, 1965, 1, 399–406.

MURPHY, LOIS B. *Social behavior and child personality*. New York: Columbia University Press, 1937.

PIAGET, J. *The psychology of intelligence*. London: Routledge and Kegan Paul, 1950.

RADKE, M. J. *The relation of parental authority to children's behavior and attitudes*. Univer. of Minnesota, Child Welfare Monographs, 1964. No. 22.

ROHER, J. B., SEEMAN, M., & LIVERANT, S. Internal vs. external control of reinforcement. In N. F. Washburne (Ed.), *Decisions, values and groups*. London: Pergamon Press, 1962. Pp. 473–516.

ROTTER, J. B. *Social learning and clinical psychology*. Englewood Cliffs, N.J.: Prentice-Hall, 1954.

SINGER, J. E. The use of manipulative strategies: Machiavellianism and attractiveness. *Sociometry*, 1964, 27, 120–150.

SMITH, M. B. Socialization for competence. *Social Science Research Council Items,* 1965, 19, 17–22.

SYKES, G., & MATZA, D. Techniques of neutralization. *American Sociological Review,* 1957, 22, 664–669.

THIBAUT, J. W., & KELLEY, H. H. *The social psychology of groups.* New York: Wiley, 1959.

WEINSTEIN, E. Toward a theory of interpersonal tactics. In C. Backman & P. Secord (Eds.), *Problems in social psychology.* New York: McGraw-Hill, 1966. Pp. 394–398.

WEINSTEIN, E., & DEUTSCHBERGER, P. Some dimensions of altercasting. *Sociometry,* 1963, 4, 454–466.

WEINSTEIN, E., & DEUTSCHBERGER, P. Tasks, bargains and identities in social interaction. *Social Forces,* 1964, 42, 451–456.

WOOD, J. R., WEINSTEIN, E., & PARKER, R. Children's interpersonal tactics. *Sociological Inquiry,* 1967, 37, 129–138.

PART III
STAGES OF SOCIALIZATION

CHAPTER 18

The Social And Socializing Infant

Harriet L. Rheingold

University of North Carolina

This chapter will propose that the human infant begins life as a social organism, that while still very young he behaves in a social fashion, and that he socializes others more than he is socialized. These statements are contrary to the generally held notions that the infant is asocial at birth, that he is taught to be social, and that only gradually and by tuition does he acquire the "knowledge, skills, and dispositions that enable him to participate as a more or less effective member of groups and the society."[1]

Such dogmatic proposals require elucidation, but at the outset they require even more a measure of qualification. The statements, for one thing, apply to the infant during the first year or so of life—until the time when effortless locomotion is achieved. Thus, for present purposes a narrow definition of infancy is taken, although the term has sometimes been taken to encompass a longer span of life—even up to the time of speech in the service of needs (Rheingold, 1968). And during the first year of the infant's life, society is not yet concerned with his acquiring such social skills as, for example, cooperation, altruism, or behavior appropriate to his sex.

The proposals, furthermore, apply primarily to infants in modern Western culture. Although they are probably applicable to the human infant in diverse geographical and cultural settings and have been throughout the ages, no attempt will be made here to demonstrate that generality.

The proposals are also limited to the case of the normal infant in the normal environment. Pathological conditions in the infant, in the caretakers, or in the environment would, of course, demand some revision of these statements. The pathological should be considered if there were evidence that it illuminates the course of normal development. In the absence of such evidence,

The preparation of this paper was supported by a Public Health Service research career program award (K6-23620) from the National Institute of Child Health and Human Development.

[1] Quotation from the editor's definition of socialization given to the contributors in presenting the theme of this book.

discussion of the effect of pathological conditions, such as maternal deprivation, seems of little relevance.

Today these proposals may well seem less controversial than they would have a decade or so ago. Students of the development of behavior are beginning to demonstrate the hitherto unremarked competence of the infant organism (Lipsitt, 1967; Papousek, 1967). And, more broadly, the emphasis in psychology today falls more on the behaving organism and less on the impressed organism, more on learning as the result of the organism's own action on the environment and less on learning as the action of the environment on him. An example, of special meaning here, may be seen in the current acceptance of flexible feeding schedules for infants.

To present a complete account, however, it must also be pointed out that the infant's behavior *is* modified by what social encounters he has; in the process he gains knowledge and perfects his skills, and to this extent he too is socialized. Especially important is the attachment he develops to certain persons by means of which they acquire the power to teach him the social ways of his culture. But it will be my contention that in the beginning the power to socialize resides more in him than in these other persons.

In the following presentation, each of the four main proposals will be considered in some detail: that the infant begins life as a social organism, that even early in life he behaves in a social fashion, that he socializes others, and that at the same time he is to some extent socialized by them.

THE NEWBORN IS A SOCIAL ORGANISM

As a member of the class of higher vertebrates that nourish their young with milk secreted by the mammary glands of the mother, the human infant is social by biological origin.

He is thus in contact with other organisms from the moment of birth. At the least, he is a member of a dyad, his mother being the other, but he is, more likely, also a member of a larger group—a family composed of mother and father and, probably, one or more siblings. He is, at the same time, a member of a still larger family group including aunts, uncles, cousins, and grandparents and, similarly, a member of a social class and of a geographical community with a history and a culture. Born at a certain time, he belongs, too, to a generation. He is born, in a word, into an organized society.

In the second instance, more than just contact is involved: the human infant, being one of the most helpless of mammalian infants, is absolutely dependent upon the mature members of his group for his very survival. Left alone, he would perish.

This is not the place to list the newborn's sensitivities and capabilities; a complete and fairly up-to-date catalogue can be found in Peiper (1963). Suffice it for present purposes to say that he can hear, see, smell, taste, and feel heat, cold, and pain. As for his motor capabilities, he can cry, orient his head and mouth to tactile stimulation of his face, suck on a nipple placed in his mouth, and turn his head from side to side when placed prone, but he is not capable of locomotion, nor can he grasp a seen object with his hands.

For these reasons the infant can do little for himself. Nourishment must be brought to him. He must be cleansed of excrement, relieved of air ingested while nursing, and protected from extremes of temperature. His position must be changed frequently to avoid fatigue, and when only a little older he must be provided a measure of visual and auditory stimulation if he is not to fret. He must also be protected from dangers, but such protection goes unnoticed because there are so few dangers in our present day living. All these caretaking operations come to the infant at the hands of people; the mother, the family, the larger group, the whole culture accepts as a primary responsibility the care of the infant. Neglect is a crime and his death a tragedy.

In summary, the human infant is born into a social environment; he can remain alive only in a social environment; and from birth he takes his place in that environment.

THE INFANT BEHAVES
IN A SOCIAL FASHION

From birth the infant possesses the sense modalities that enable him to be sensitive to the stimuli presented by the social objects in his environment. Cribside observation, schedules of developmental progress, and experiments agree that he can see and hear people, smell them, feel their touch and their grasp (see Rheingold, 1966, for a review). If the social object is analyzed as a set of stimuli, it is clear that the human infant is biologically equipped to sense people.

Among the various elements in the infant's environment, people constitute an important class of objects. They are large, prominent, frequently appearing, visually and auditorily complex, moving and active, and they present combinations of stimuli that affect many sensory systems. Furthermore, the objects presenting these stimulus characteristics also minister to the needs of the infant. It is they who feed him, pick him up, hold and carry him, dry, clean, and warm him, and provide him with fresh stimulation. Lastly, they are responsive to him. As they provide stimuli to which he responds, so he provides stimuli to which they respond. A feed-back loop with all its potential for reinforcing behavior is in constant operation.

Not only is the infant sensitive to the stimuli presented by people, he is also responsive to them. Long before he can physically approach people—even within the first month of life—he looks at them and pays them interested attention. The evidence may be seen in the wideness, intentness, and duration of his regard and in the brightening of his face. In the second month of life he follows people as they move into and out of his range. In the third month of life his gaze fastens intently on the eyes of other persons; his face brightens; he smiles, becomes physically active, and even vocalizes. He listens to the voice. His social responses also include the cessation of crying on sight of people, on being talked to, and on being held. He cries, too, when people leave him.

The early development of social responsiveness is still a challenging area for the student of behavior. There may be an unlearned component to the infant's social behavior. Yet the behavior of the infant *is* modifiable by environmental events. It is therefore possible that the infant is responsive to people because they have become associated with the satisfactions resulting from certain caretaking operations. It is also possible that the infant's social behavior has been reinforced by the responses of people to his responses to them. The facts however remain: the human infant is responsive to social stimulation, he prolongs such stimulation, and what is more, he initiates social interaction.

THE INFANT SOCIALIZES OTHERS

The process of socialization, when closely examined, proves always to be a mutual process, affecting the behavior of participants on each side of the equation. In this section I shall draw attention to the infant's side of the equation and attempt to show that he is more than an active partner to the process, that he is in fact the prime mover. To be sure, the parents are already socialized. They, too, began life as social organisms and, growing up, were subjected to social influences. But that particular facet of socialization called parental behavior—caring for the infant in a responsible fashion—is taught to them by the infant. The task here is to speculate on how the parents acquire sensitivity to the stimuli presented by the infant, and how he provides them with the "disposition, skills, and knowledge" that teach them how to behave as parents.

In the pages ahead it may seem at times that the obvious is belabored and the domestic details of the nursery made too explicit. My defense is that overemphasis is required when the customary view of parent-child relationships is to be reversed and that what happens in the nursery, although so commonplace as to escape notice and so familiar as to seem inconsequential, may nevertheless hold answers to important questions.

The birth of the infant profoundly modifies the lives of his parents. The greatest effect is brought about by the birth of the firstborn, and the greatest effect is experienced by the mother. Nonetheless, the birth of a later born infant is not without an effect, and neither the father nor older siblings remain unaffected. What is the nature of these effects upon the caretakers?

The first class of effects may be labeled as physical modifications of their lives. To begin with, the infant requires constant attendance. In a daily round of occurrences he must be fed, diapered, and bathed, to mention but a few of the main caretaking operations. These operations require time and take the place of the other activities that the parents, and particularly the mother, engaged in before the birth of the infant. Milk or other food must be on hand, diapers washed, and clothes cleaned to carry out these elementary operations.

The infant effects a profound change not only in the parents' activities but also in the physical arrangements of their dwellings. Space must be provided for him, as well as some amount of furniture. Even in the home of an only moderately affluent family, the visitor is impressed by the extensiveness of the equipment: crib, Bathinette, playpen, stroller, and high chair, as a minimum. Thus space and funds must be shared.

The disruption of the parents' life formerly devoted only to the satisfying of their own needs is but the observable part of the effect of the infant. The other, and not so readily observable, part is the effect upon their mental lives. These effects may be called psychological or emotional to distinguish them from the physical effects. Here I refer to the concern they feel for the present state and future development of the child; he claims a part of their mental lives. They worry about the wisdom of whatever caretaking operation they are carrying out, weighing its possible long-term effects upon the infant, measuring their caretaking behavior against society's judgment, and comparing it with memories of their own rearing. Times of feeding, quickness of response to the infant's crying, and the use of such soothing devices as the pacifier or rocking are some of the operations that arouse these kinds of concern.

The infant also affects the part of their mental lives that holds their wishes, dreams, and fears about his future appearance, health, intelligence, and personality and about the extent to which he will fulfill their expectations.

Against this background, we may now examine the moment-by-moment effect the infant exerts upon his parents' behavior to show how he socializes them—how he teaches them to assume the role of parents, how he evokes in them the disposition to behave as society expects parents to behave, how he helps them acquire the skills and knowledge that enable them to become effective members of a family and of the community, thus fulfilling their roles as protectors and educators of the young. The specific proposition is that he teaches them what he needs to have them do for him. He makes them behave in a nurturing fashion. As I said elsewhere (Rheingold, 1968, p. 283), ". . . of men and women he makes fathers and mothers."

The main points supporting the proposition are the power of the infant's cry, the stimulating and rewarding effects of his smile, and the reinforcing nature for the caretaker of many routine caretaking operations. None of these are single events; they are frequent and recurrent within a day, and day after day.

The Power of the Cry

The cry of the infant is a social signal: with the cry he communicates with the people in his environment. By means of it he insures his own survival.

The cry calls the adult to the infant's side. It demands attention and cannot be easily ignored. (In fact, to ignore it is a considered act on the part of the hearer.) Man, like other mammals, finds the cry of his infant aversive and its cessation therefore rewarding. Of the greatest importance, and not to be lost sight of, is the observation that the cry originates with the infant; it is he who cries and he who stops crying.

Whatever operation of the caretaker that brought about its cessation is reinforced; that is, the probability of its being used when the infant cries again is increased. Thus, the cry not only summons the mother to his side, but the cessation of the cry instructs her about what will effect the cessation. While for the infant the consequence (caretaker's ministration) may reinforce the cry, for the caretaker, the cessation of the cry reinforces her ministration. Her response to his cry (its nature and timing) modifies the subsequent occurrence of the cry; similarly his response (to cry or to stop crying) modifies her subsequent behavior.

When the parents are not sufficiently perceptive and alert to supply the infant's needs before he becomes distressed, his cry brings them back to the execution of their duties. He requires of them responsible behavior. Helpless though he is, he nevertheless possesses the means of getting others to give him the care he cannot give himself.

The Effect of the Smile

The infant's smile is also effective in socializing his caretakers. Like the cry, it too is a social signal and thus a means of communication. The cry and the smile, however, are independent and mutually exclusive. All investigators of the smile (e.g., Ambrose, 1961; Wolff, 1963) have been impressed by how early it appears, how closely it resembles its mature form, and how minimal are the stimuli that evoke it.

As aversive as the cry is to hear, just so rewarding is the smile to behold. It has a gentling and relaxing effect on the beholder that causes him to smile in turn. Its effect upon the caretaker cannot be exaggerated. Parents universally report that with the smile the baby now becomes "human." With the smile, too, he begins to count as a person, to take his place as an individual in the family group, and to acquire a personality in their eyes. Furthermore, mothers spontaneously confide that the smile of the baby makes his care worthwhile. In short, the infant learns to use the coin of the social realm. As he grows older and becomes more competent and more discriminating, the smile of recognition appears; reserved for the caretaker, it is a gleeful response, accompanied by vocalizations and embraces.

The infant's *vocalizations* as early as three months of age often function as stimuli for the parents' vocalizing. Their answering vocalizations may serve as reinforcers of the infant's vocalizations (Rheingold, Gewirtz & Ross, 1959). Speech soon takes on the form of conversation. It too is a response of the infant that rewards the parent for his attentiveness. Generally, vocalizations are less remarked than the smile and less powerful than the cry in their effect upon the parents' behavior. Still, they spell for the parents the well-being and contentedness of the infant. Since they are the beginnings of speech, more attention should be paid to the transformation of early vocal responses into verbal behavior, especially in the service of social interaction.

The infant thus is helpless only physically, not socially. His smiles and vocalizations to people appear early; he *is* social from a very early age. He has the disposition—even the skills—to be social. His responses to people during the first year of life are predominantly positive. The much publicized "fear" response to strangers turns out on examination to be more fragmentary, more variable, and less common than some of the early literature suggests (Morgan, 1965; Schaffer, 1966). On the few occasions when he cries at the appearance of known persons, it is usually because he requires some caretaking response—if only a change in stimulation—and because he has learned the power of his cry.

The Rewarding Nature of Caretaking

Over and above silencing the cry and evoking the smile (and vocalizations), many caretaking operations seem to be reinforcing in their own right. Proof of this conclusion may be seen in the contented expression of a caretaker as he holds the baby's bottle or strokes his skin. Not only was the caretaker himself once the recipient of these ministrations, but he himself daily experiences the gratifications of eating when hungry, bathing, and covering himself when cold. It may be that as these give him pleasure in the experiencing, so they give him pleasure in the administering.

Thus, to feed, bathe, rock, pat and hold the baby seem to be sources of gratification for the parent, as do such other activities as dressing and covering him, looking at his face, and talking to him. To these should be added also the pleasure of the infant's greeting the parent, recognizing him and turning away from strangers *to* him. Finally, the amount of time spent by a parent just looking at his infant suggests that to watch the activity of a small, active, and lively organism may be reinforcing.

The Infant as Teacher

The infant modulates, tempers, regulates, and refines the caretaker's activities. He produces delicate shades and nuances in these operations to suit his own needs of the moment. By such responses as fretting, sounds of impatience or satisfaction, by facial expressions of pleasure, contentment, or alertness he produces elaborations here and dampening there.

By his behavior he "tells" the parents when he wants to eat, when he will sleep, when he wants to be played with, picked up, or have his position changed. When awake, the infant does not stay content in one place for long. A mother may be observed in a short span of time to turn him over, pick

him up, move him from crib to playpen, set his mobile in motion, start his
music box, wheel him in a carriage, talk to him, turn on the radio or prop
him up in front of the TV, and put a toy in his hand. She does all these
things because with nothing new to look at, with nothing to occupy his hands,
he fusses—that is, before he can crawl to get new stimulation by himself. A
mother's day is spent in keeping the baby from fussing. Trouble ensues only
when the mother out of carelessness ignores his distress signals or out of
design imposes her demands on him.

In these ways, he teaches the parents *how* the caretaking operations should
be performed. He makes them search for and invent new operations. He
teaches them whether a pacifier or a blanket is an acceptable soothing device
for him; more specifically, even, that the pacifier will be more acceptable if
first sweetened by honey, or the blanket, if fuzzy or its binding smooth. From
his behavior they learn what he wants and what he will accept, what produces in him a state of well-being and good nature, and what will keep
him from whining. The caretakers, then, adapt to him and he appears content; they find whatever they do for him satisfying, and thus are reinforced.

A Dimension of Tenderness

The infant also amplifies the dimension of tenderness and compassion characteristic of most *mature* adults. Caring for a helpless organism gives them
an awareness of their own usefulness in the eyes of the world. Their concern
for the infant is generalized to a concern for all living persons, large and
small, here and away.

THE INFANT IS SOCIALIZED

Now that the infant's ability to socialize others has been examined—in considerable detail for purposes of emphasis—it is appropriate for the sake of
completeness to examine the extent to which he is socialized by others. On
the one hand, his parents are no more passive than he is; on the other, his
behavior is as modifiable by their responses as their behavior is by his. The
question to be answered here is how do his experiences with people contribute
to his socialization, as defined earlier. That he possesses the "disposition" to
participate as a member of groups has already been made clear. It is rather
to his knowledge and skills that parents contribute.

In the most general sense, the parents socialize the infant by providing
his environment. Maternal care may be viewed as the source of many important environmental events in the life of the child. It determines the physical
environment, where he will live, and therefore what he will see and hear.
Maternal care also determines what he will be fed, how he will be clothed,
when he will be bathed, and a host of other details of caretaking. Maternal
care, then, is the mediating factor between the young child and the environment.

For the purpose of this chapter, however, the physical environment and the details of physical caretaking are of less consequence than the social environment the parents provide. His experience with the parents, and with the other social objects they introduce to him and permit him to have experience with, provides him with knowledge important for his behavior as a member of society.

In the first instance, he comes to learn the physical and behavioral characteristics of his caretakers and others. Since he is in constant contact with people and is dependent on them, he has the opportunity to learn about them. He learns to differentiate between people and things—they look different, sound different, behave differently, and respond differently. He learns how different people respond to him and how he can modify their responses. He learns what he must do to obtain rewards in the presence of different persons. He learns, thus, to discriminate between the different people in his environment. Such social knowledge he acquires as he acquires all other kinds of knowledge; there appears to be no need to invoke a separate set of laws for social learning.

The social environment he learns becomes, of course, the familiar one, and familiarity as a stimulus property has several consequences of significance for the infant's socialization. Only as a set of stimuli becomes familiar can another set be recognized as unfamiliar. Thus, on the basis of experience with one set of persons the infant gains knowledge by means of which he distinguishes between familiar and unfamilar persons. (For a fuller statement of the process, see Schaffer, 1966.)

Social Attachment

The warmer response he gives familiar persons may be construed as a preference. This preference, built up not only by familiarity but also by mutually reinforcing activities, has been variously labeled as "social attachment," "affectional bond," or "dependency." However labeled, this preference for certain persons endows them with the power to teach the child what he must soon learn about conforming to society's expectations. It confers upon the parents—and the siblings as well—the ability not only to instruct by reward and punishment but to serve as models to be imitated. Thus, the ground is prepared for the growth of subsequent socialization.

Relevance of Habit Training

Habit training might be thought by some to represent the culture's (via the parents) socialization of the infant. By habit training I mean schedules of eating and sleeping, the acceptance of new foods, the termination of breast feeding or bottles, and toilet training. I cannot see that training of this kind should be viewed as socialization in the sense of the term given at the beginning of the chapter. In the first place these accomplishments are more often under the infant's control than the parent's; at the least, habit training of this nature results from a mutual regulation of the infant's and parent's behavior. Second, these accomplishments do not make the infant social or teach him his social roles. Furthermore, a generally relaxed attitude toward these activities prevails in our culture today. For example, it is a common observation that infants often lose interest in breast feeding before the mother is ready to give it up. Sleep takes care of itself as the infant discovers that more interesting events occur by daylight, and toilet training today occurs late and is often postponed.

Although habit training of these sorts may seem of great importance to the parent, during the first year of life its contribution to the infant's socialization is judged to be only minor.

Two other kinds of training may be of greater relevance. Toward the end of the first year, as he becomes capable of reaching what he sees and approaching what he wants, the parents begin to curb his activities by the command, "No-no." The infant learns to obey—more or less consistently—and shows that he remembers. Thus, he may often be observed to reach toward the forbidden object and to draw his hand back before he has touched it or to look at his parent as though to confirm the prohibition. We see in his nascent self-control the beginning of conformity to parental strictures. The other achievement is the capacity to wait. Delay is tolerable, however, because he can be so easily distracted.

More than this, society does not expect of him. He carries no duties or responsibilities for others. Aggressive behavior is still diffuse and poorly directed. Cooperation, sympathy, and altruism come later. Training in behavior appropriate to his sex may have begun, but its forms are still subtle and have not yet been made explicit by students of parental response to infant behavior. Society at any rate has no clear expectations for sex-appropriate behavior in infants so young.

What is important about early achievements is that they are mediated by the behavior of people with whom he has much contact and on whom he depends for care; that is, they are familiar and succoring persons. As he conforms to what they expect and demand of him, he is reinforced by their approval. As social learning, it prepares him for the next phase of socialization.

Looking Ahead

Events in infancy count. They count not because the effect of each is carried forward, whole, intact, and unmodified, but they count because the effect modifies the response to the next event. Thus, with the onset of locomotion, the infant continues to behave as before, active and responsive. Now, though, his mobility meets with restraints imposed by the parent to protect him from dangers and to protect property from him. Now the parents more actively oppose their will to his. The struggle continues through the second year of life as his motor skills become increasingly efficient; it abates only toward the end of the second year as speech comes to serve his needs.

TWO WORDS OF CAUTION

Much in this account has been based on unsystematic observation and may therefore be open to the criticism of personal bias. I have dared to go so far in order to call attention to the infant's social nature and his ability to have an effect upon the behavior of his caretakers. Now that these claims have been made, we can set to work to correct any excesses.

In pondering these matters, it has become increasingly clear to me that our usual methods of studying mother-infant interactions are open to question. Although we can talk about who socializes whom, neither the infant's contribution nor the parent's can be separated when the dyad is studied in real life situations. The child's behavior modifies the parents' behavior, even as his behavior is being modified by theirs. As variables for analysis, they are completely confounded.

Such a situation exists not only in the study of parent-child interaction; psychology meets it in all studies of social behavior. The problem in parent-child interactions can be solved only by the experimental manipulation of the behavior of one or the other of the partners to the interaction. Of the two, the parent's behavior can be the more easily controlled by experimental design. Under naturalistic conditions, specified modifications of parental behavior could be instituted for short periods of time. Or, under laboratory conditions, the experimenter could manipulate one or another of the elements of caretaking. Although little work of this nature has been attempted, it holds the best promise.

SUMMARY

The human infant is born into a social environment upon which he is dependent for survival. Although he is physically helpless during the first few months, he has several effective procedures for insuring that he receives the care he requires. He is socially responsive and he invites social responses from others. By means of his cry and his smile, and to a lesser extent by means of his contented vocalizations, he modifies the caretaking behavior of his parents to suit his needs. They, furthermore, find their caretaking operations reinforcing not only in themselves but also because they result in a diminution of the infant's fretting and in an increase of his social responsiveness.

The infant then may be thought of as a socializer of his parents. He instructs them in the behavior they must display to insure his normal growth and development. He is an effective member of society to the extent that he fashions his caretakers into parents; he organizes a family out of separate individuals.

To correct any overemphasis on the socializing effectiveness of the infant, the socializing effect of the parents on his behavior must also be pointed out. The parents provide the physical, and especially the social, environment that will provide the standard by which the infant will discriminate future events. In this social environment he develops the emotional bond that forms the basis of the parents' ability to instruct him in the ways of his culture.

REFERENCES

AMBROSE, J. A. The development of the smiling response in early infancy. In B. M. Foss (Ed.), *Determinants of infant behaviour*. London: Methuen, 1961. Pp. 179–196.

LIPSITT, L. P. Learning in the human infant. In H. W. Stevenson, E. H. Hess & H. L. Rheingold (Eds.), *Early behavior: Comparative and developmental approaches*. New York: Wiley, 1967.

MORGAN, G. A. *Some determinants of infants' responses to strangers during the first year of life*. Unpublished doctoral dissertation. Cornell University, 1965.

PEIPER, A. *Cerebral function in infancy and childhood*. (Translated by B. Nagler & H. Nagler) New York: Consultants Bureau, 1963.

PAPOUSEK, H. Experimental studies of appetitional behavior in human newborns and infants. In H. W. Stevenson, E. H. Hess & H. L. Rheingold (Eds.), *Early behavior: Comparative and developmental approaches*. New York: Wiley, 1967. Pp. 249–277.

RHEINGOLD, H. L. The development of social behavior in the human infant. In H. W. Stevenson (Ed.), *Concept of development. Monographs of the Society for Research in Child Development*, 1966, 31, No. 5 (Serial No. 107). Pp. 1–17.

RHEINGOLD, H. L. Infancy. *International encyclopedia of the social sciences*. Vol. 7. New York: Crowell-Collier and Macmillan, 1968. Pp. 224–285.

RHEINGOLD, H. L., GEWIRTZ, J. L., & ROSS, H. W. Social conditioning of vocalizations in the infant. *Journal of Comparative and Physiological Psychology*, 1959, 52, 68–73.

SCHAFFER, H. R. The onset of fear of strangers and the incongruity hypothesis. *Journal of Child Psychology and Psychiatry*, 1966, 7, 95–106.

WOLFF, P. H. Observations on the early development of smiling. In B. M. Foss (Ed.), *Determinants of infant behaviour II*. London: Methuen, 1963. Pp. 113–134.

CHAPTER 19

Childhood Socialization

Boyd R. McCandless

Emory University

The emphasis in this chapter is conventional—a developmental description of childhood socialization as developed within the framework of the family. Ancillary aspects of socialization are covered in other chapters of this book. This is helpful in that it gives me a clear mandate for exclusion and inclusion of material, but is also frustrating, in that just as I begin to open up an area, I must close it again for fear of trespass on another author's territory.

The chapter covers nine subtopics, some of them well-buttressed by literature, others of which include less information about childhood socialization. These are: A: Parental Influences. B: Family Social Structure and Socialization—siblings, birth order, and the like. These two topics have been well developed, although the research literature is fuller for birth order than for the other aspects of family structure. C: Influence of the Peer Group is a relatively well-developed topic, as is D: Formal Educational Influences—the School. The literature for this topic is primarily sociometric in nature, and concerns itself with shifts in acceptance and rejection as a function of age and sex. It overlaps with peer groups. Less well documented is E: The Role of Religion. Here, speculatively, we would say that about the only areas of religious group or social life meaningful to children are Sunday School and youth groups. The same lack of information characterizes Topic F: The Role of Formal Organizations—Industrial, Commercial, Governmental. Topic G: This includes the Effects of Urban Environments. Provocative work in this area has come from such authors as Barker and Wright (1954). They contrast the self-confidence and full information provided to children from their midwestern village to the greater social restriction and unknown quality of potential socialization in larger residential areas. Gans (1962) shows that even huge cities contain sub-villages, and documents the culture of an Italian-American urban village. Cloward and Ohlin (1960) analyze environments (typically urban) in terms of the legitimate and illegitimate opportunities they offer children and youth. Among those who have put the Cloward and Ohlin theories to test are Landis and Scarpitti (1965), Short, Rivera and Tennyson (1965), and Tallman

791

(1966). Tallman has provided one of the few experimental tests of the social phenomena that relate to this topic.

Topic H is: Social Class Variations in Socialization Practices. Much work has been done by social psychologists, sociologists, and cultural anthropologists. One of the more meaningful methods of approaching the field is described by Whiting and Child (1953). They speak of five types of human behavior that must be socialized, regardless of the culture: (1) feeding and weaning needs and practices; (2) toileting and elimination needs and practices; (3) sex needs and practices; (4) needs and practices in connection with aggression; and (5) dependency needs and behaviors. Whiting and Child consider each area in terms of the indulgence-strictness a given culture uses, the severity of sanctions about both its occurrence and the form of its occurrence, and the development of anxiety about it. They attempt, with only moderate success, to relate these variables to superstitions about the five areas of socialization.

Topic I, Mass Communication, has received little scientific attention. Thus, while we have many opinions, we have few facts about how it affects childhood socialization. From a layman's point of view, we know that the mass media supply an almost limitless flow of sexual and aggressive stimulation to which the child may respond and to which he must adapt himself. The flow of sexual stimulation makes attempts to repress sex in our culture fruitless, and doubtless exerts a severe strain on the child who strives to suppress unacceptable stimuli and responses. The flow of aggressive stimuli has been shown to be important by modeling theorists, most particularly Bandura and Walters (1963), and imposes on the child, again, a flood of stimuli evocative of hostile and destructive impulses which somehow he must manage in a fashion acceptable to society. As it stands, he seems to pattern himself on the aggressive model, aggressing and destroying as his television model aggresses and destroys.

The author has searched diligently for a model for social theory, and believes he has found it in Erikson's (1956) eight psychosocial stages of man. Each of these stages is thought of by Erikson as a psychosocial crisis, which must be resolved after the fashion of psychoanalytic fixation theory before the next crisis can be undertaken and mastered. The first of the psychosocial crises is Infancy, where the child's crisis is between trust and mistrust. Erikson has charted his eight stages of man in the fashion of the Greek letter, psi. The central arm of the psi extends downward and to the right from the upper left hand corner of his chart at a 45-degree angle. A 90-degree angle is formed by the other two arms of the letter psi, one extending horizontally to the right of the apex of the chart, the other downward vertically. Thus, reading diagonally downward and to the right, we come to the second of the psychosocial crises, corresponding to the second stage of man, Early Childhood, where the psychosocial crisis is between autonomy (self-will, self-determinism) and shame, where the child, as it were, stands naked before his world. Continuing to read the diagonal, we come to the third stage, Play Age, with its crisis between initiative (a proud "beginner of beginnings") and guilt, where the child is immobilized by the too harsh superego. Next comes the crisis between industry (pride in

	Column 1	Column 2	Column 3	Column 4	Column 5
Row 1 Infancy	Trust vs. Mistrust				Unipolarity vs. Premature Self-Differentiation
Row 2 Early Childhood		Autonomy vs. Shame, Doubt			Bipolarity vs. Autism
Row 3 Play Age			Initiative vs. Guilt		Play Identification vs. (Oedipal) Fantasy Identities
Row 4 School Age				Industry vs. Inferiority	Work Identification vs. Identity Foreclosure
Row 5 Adolescence	Time Perspective vs. Time Diffusion	Self-Certainty vs. Identity Consciousness	Role Experimentation vs. Negative Identity	Anticipation of Achievement vs. Work Paralysis	Identity vs. Identity Diffusion

FIGURE 19.1.   A schematic representation of Erikson's eight stages of man, through Stage 5, Adolescence. The chart is read from the upper left corner, vertically downward, diagonally downward, and horizontally. Source: Erikson, 1956, p. 75.

work) and inferiority (the paralysis of school underachievement, for example), which strikes the child at the School Age. Finally, as far as childhood's developmental tasks are concerned, comes the crisis between identity and identity diffusion. The identified child is able to make a confident, happy, self-assured answer to the question, "Who am I," while the unidentified child unhappily does not know.

Erikson makes a set of predictions of an "if-then" nature. *If* the child is handled in such and such a way at such and such a stage, then such and such consequences will follow, leading in turn to such and such events at the time represented by another cell in the chart. *If,* during the stage represented in row 2, column 2, techniques of toilet training and elimination are permissive, exerted after the child has learned postural and symbolic control of himself and his environment, and if they are psychologically or love-oriented and consistent, *then* the child learns to inhibit his impulses to wet and soil, and enters the stage of autonomy self-confident in his mastery of his own body. The alternative is shame, where the child feels himself exposed in his uncleanness to all eyes, a potential victim of a punitive world.

Reading horizontally, along row 1 of Erikson's chart, following the horizontal leg of the Greek letter psi to column 5, we come to the psychosocial crisis of unipolarity versus premature self-differentiation. Unipolarity is the perceptual stage (see Harry Stack Sullivan, 1953) of prototaxis, where the child sees himself at one with his universe. Indeed, he is one with his universe. It is he, he is it. There is no splitting of his infantile ego from the core of this universe—he is its lord and master. In premature self-differentiation, he has split himself off, as Sullivan says, into the good, or relaxed, confident "me," or the anxious, depressed, and fearful *"bad me."*

Similarly, as we read vertically from the apex or upper left hand corner of the chart, we see that trust leads to time perspective in column 1, row 5 of the chart. This follows the vertical arm of the letter psi, which is at right angles to the left arm, and bisected at a 45-degree angle by the center axis of the letter. To organize time, to think and plan ahead, it is obvious that the child must be trusting—otherwise time is uncharted, undependable, and chaotic.

Each cell entry, to Erikson, is bipolar, i.e., no child is *all trusting,* just as no infant is all *mistrust.* The poles of each cell show a small percentage of the hypothetical population at each extreme of trust and mistrust, and the great bulk hovering around the mean at the center of the distribution in a typical bell-shaped curve.

Continuing to read Erikson's chart (Figure 19.1) vertically, but moving to row 5, column 2, we come to self-certainty. This follows autonomy in time: the self-certain child is the one who in earliest childhood was autonomous, the child with high identity consciousness during the Play Age is the one who unsatisfactorily resolved the psychosocial crisis of shame and doubt.

Moving horizontally again, we see that, concurrent with initiative, the child develops a play identification: rejoices in the world of objects and things, which allow him room to exercise his initiative, to create, and to master.

The School Age psychosocial crisis of industry versus inferiority is followed in column 5, row 4 with an identification with the world of work—the time of developing the child's executive department, or his ego, in contrast to identity foreclosure (see cell 5–4, column 5, row 4).

Likewise, reading vertically, initiative precedes the adventures of role experimentation, where the child may play the delinquent one moment, the hero of the Indian wars the next. Guilt is the antecedent of the negative identity, in which the child assumes that since society sees him as bad, as doomed, therefore he is. Industry, in column 4, row 4, logically comes before the anticipation of achievement from honest effort, just as inferiority precedes work paralysis. And each of the rows and columns leads to row 5, column 5, the key to Adolescence, which is *Identity versus Identity Diffusion.*

Each psychosocial crisis is accompanied, at least for middle-class children, by what Erikson calls a psychosocial moratorium. This is the time for the provisional try—a period, short or long, where society, particularly middle-class society, allows the child to experiment, and does not hold him strictly liable for the consequences of his experiments. There are exceptions to this: society offers little by way of a moratorium for the adolescent girl who experiments with sex and becomes pregnant, for example, although even then, if she is from the middle class, she will have more of a chance, more of a way out, than if she comes from the lower class. Today's society allows no psychosocial moratorium, for example, for the high-school dropout. There is no place for him to turn (see, for example, Havighurst et al., 1962, *Growing Up in River City,* a volume, incidentally, that is almost a descriptive model of the social development of middle-class children).

In social development, society sets certain tasks which must be accomplished, usually at fairly clearly specified ages, by its children and adolescents. Erikson's list is one way of looking at developmental tasks. Other lists have been provided for the things children are expected to accomplish and master during infancy, early childhood, the play age, childhood, latency, and adolescence. Most of these lists consider childhood less a time of saltatory transition from one chronological age to another, than of an even flow, at each level of which the mature organism, like the widening river, is expected to encompass more and more territory, do more and more things. Examples are given below:

The list of developmental tasks supplied by Ausubel (1952) is a well-thought-out analysis of the socialization process. Ausubel fits well with Erikson, and anticipates current thinking in two ways: (1) Implicit in his formulation is a general goal of *competence* toward which adequate socialization should be directed. (2) He makes explicit, as few authors do, the point that frustration is neither good, bad, nor indifferent, but simply omnipresent. Rather than evaluating it as good or bad in and of itself, he proposes that it is best studied according to the process and effects of resolving it.

Ausubel, in his 1952 publication, addresses himself primarily to adolescents, but his analysis fits younger children equally well.

A. Socialization must include greater volitional and executive independence. That is, children must be provided with ever-increasing consideration of and respect for their desires, and "given their head" in implementing these desires (subject to certain standards of personal-social safety, social acceptability, and so on).

Specific steps to this end are:

1. Independence in forming goals and making decisions.
2. Assimilating goals and values that are valid *to them,* not simply accepted because of loyalty to parents, peer groups, and so on.
3. Reliance should be progressively removed from parents to other sources of ego support, such as teachers, peer groups.
4. The child's goals and roles should become steadily more realistic (consonant, for example, with his intelligence, dramatic ability, physical strength and coordination).
5. He should be able to endure more intense and prolonged frustration without "shattering"—e.g., losing his own sense of self-worth, giving up his goals, or abandoning his attempts to perform well.
6. Self-critical ability should increase steadily: he should be able to make steadily more accurate assessments of his own performance, such as seeing discrepancies between an objective standard and his efforts to attain it.
7. He should give up his claims to special indulgence ("I am not to blame—I am only a child;" or "I didn't know any better.").

B. For adequate socialization, the child must also move himself out of "second-class citizen" status. He must learn to see his goals as intrinsically worthwhile, and competitive with those, for example, of his parents or teachers. This means that:

1. He should begin to seek and help should be given to him to attain primary status (worthwhileness for his *own* efforts rather than because he is the banker's son).
2. He should increase his own desire to do well for his own personal satisfaction.
3. His self-esteem should increase steadily.

C. Further, he needs to move from what Freud calls the "pleasure principle" to an adjustment whereby he receives his most basic satisfactions from progress toward long-range and high-status goals.

D. Acquisition of moral responsibility is essential for adequate socialization.

The reader will have noted, as he goes through this list (rather freely adapted from Ausubel) that it pertains to children growing up in industrialized, cooperative-competitive, *individually* centered, democratic societies. Such a life plan could be most maladaptive in many societies.

These concepts can also be linked to the more general idea of impulse control, as studied by Mischel (Mischel & Metzner, 1962), and to Erikson's stage of trust (the child who trusts is able to postpone immediate gratification for delayed, but larger, rewards; control of impulsivity increases with chronological age and intelligence, and is correlated with tolerance for ambiguity and assumption of social responsibility). Kagan (e.g., Kagan, Rosman, Day, Albert & Philips, 1964) talks of different intellectual or problem-solving styles. His cognitive style of analysis blends well with Ausubel's criteria for maturity, his impulsive style with immaturity. Parenthetically, it may be that Kagan's impulsive children are those who do not attach great value to the outcomes of the tasks he uses to analyze their behavior. It may be that further study in this interesting area will find that the important variables are how one comes to be impulsive versus deliberate about a given type of task (i.e., how are values and controls learned), rather than whether one is impulsive or deliberative per se.

Maturity, in the sense in which it is discussed here, obviously relates to the dependency-independency dimension of human life. The child must change —must be developed?—from the totally dependent, hedonistic infant who can do nothing for himself to the mature, reasonably self-sufficient organism who manages his own life and gratifies his own needs while leaving room for and making provision for the needs of others. Actually, he must himself learn many roles in which *he* is the gratifier of needs for others.

There are many lists of biological and universal social needs. Among them, for example, are thirst, hunger, comfort-seeking and freedom from pain; and probably activity (or curiosity or the need for exploration), and aggression. Some of these need systems, such as air-hunger, are autonomous: they are satisfied without social dependency or, indeed, interaction. The child breathes independently from birth, or he dies. Others must be satisfied within a social setting, such as hunger, elimination, and aggression. It is these socially conspicuous needs, in all likelihood, that are important in personality and social development.

Bruner (1966) speaks of three general modes of interacting with the environment and, by implication, says the socialized individual must have mastered all three systems. The first concerns the near receptors—the how to do it mechanisms—the hands. Environmental mastery of such things as opposition of thumb and fingers are obvious parts of this system. Next the organism must consolidate its vision and other distance receptors: it must learn how to perceive, coordinate, anticipate. Finally, the fabric of language or symbolic mastery of the environment must be developed. Bruner believes the first of these stages is characteristic of the preschool ages, the second of the elementary school years, and the third reaches its climax at or around adolescence.

The complete dependence of the infant is well exemplified by Piaget (see Hunt, 1961; and Flavell, 1963). Piaget speaks of the sensorimotor stages of development that characterize infants from birth to about two years of age. The first of these shows the young infant (from birth to about one month of age) completely dependent upon his ready-made sensorimotor schemata: i.e., he responds only when stimulation is fed to him. Press on his lips or cheek and he sucks, stimulate the soles of his feet and he flexes them. He is an S-R organism: stimulated, he responds. There is no active groping on the part of the infant—he must be stimulated to respond. Later sensorimotor stages see the child actively feeding back to the environment: seeing the bottle, he makes lip motions as though anticipating sucking, relating to vanished objects, and so on.

How is this early dependence (1) established, and (2) dissipated, as it must be if the organism is to be self-sustaining?

Dependency is established, it is believed, through classical conditioning. As the biological and social needs of infancy are met through parental care-taking, classical conditioned responses are connected with methods of stimulation (feeding, toileting, nurturing curiosity) so that the baby is satisfied and happy and associates parents with this happiness. This leads to his unipolarity —the blending in of all his modes of stimulating and responding happily to his own person. It also leads to a megalomaniacal type of adjustment, in which the child seems to "think" he is the beginning and end of his universe— he is it, it is he!

The most effective ways for parents to establish this complete dependency appear to be according to the laws of learning: immediate, generous, and consistent reward for all the child's demands. Such loving rewards create the atmosphere in which Erikson's psychosocial crises of trust are best established. The trusting infant is the dependent infant.

How is this blissful stage of complete dependency dissipated, as it must be? Through fear—fear of parental support, fear of the loss of love. The megalomaniac infant learns that not all is bliss in his world—he is threatened. The breast is not offered the instant it is wanted. Curiosity is not immediately rewarded by new stimulation. Thus the child learns that he is not the end-all and be-all of the universe, but is subject to forces outside himself. He stands, thereby, not only to lose his primary gains—food, warmth, shelter, stimulation— but the secondary gains of the kindly mother and the doting father, with their smiles, coos, babbles, and other signs of love.

This is the first step in learning that other people are important: they can give, but they can also take away, threatening life itself. This stage is considered by Ausubel to be the stage of satellization: when the child constitutes himself a satellite, a follower, a dependent of the parent (Ausubel, 1954). The child responds to satellization by dependency behaviors—crying, whining, lap-sitting, seeking attention; and by learning dependency alleviators: how to signify to others that they matter to him. The social smile of six weeks may be the first of these signals. These may take social forms, such as asking "please," requesting help, and so on. Their significance is unmistakable: their presence is designed to flatter and please adults so that good things will happen to children. This desire to please adults is greater the greater the power possessed by the adult, and the more positively reinforcing (good to the child) the adult is. Eventually these loving responses are internalized.

The five major areas of power, other than the conventional categories of power in child-rearing, such as power in feeding, are: power in the physical sense, where the parent overwhelms or indicates to the child that he can overwhelm. To the very young child, such power is or obviously can be possessed by parents of either sex. The second area of power is in the area of knowledge, or omniscience: the parent knows all the answers to the child's questions or needs. The third areas of power are influence: social—the power of the circle of acquaintances possessed by the parent—his ability to wield social power; or economic—the importance of the parents' job, the size of their salary or purchasing power. These last two sources of power are much valued by older children, and obvious to children at very young ages (see Wolowitz, 1965). The fourth source of power is virility or generativity, where the parent is seen as fruitful, virile, possessed of the power to propagate himself. It is doubtful whether, outside Freud's thinking about infantile sexuality, this fourth source of power is important to young children, if indeed it is perceived by them at all. A fifth source of power has more to do with how power is exercised than with power itself: it concerns the consistency of parental behavior. If consistent, the parent is powerful—his discipline follows known rules and the child can avoid punishment or censure by bending himself to meet these rules. If inconsistent, there is no point in attempting to please the parent, as such efforts can only be met by frustration, since the exercise of power is confused. The clearly dominant parent seems to exert great control over a child's sex-typing, for example: Moulton, Liberty, Burnstein and Altucher (1966) find their "best socialized" college students (who were strongly identified as males, and controlled from within, i.e., by their own consciences) came from families where, according to the boys' perceptions, the fathers were both clearly dominant and definitely affectionate.

Ausubel's notion of satellization is very close to Freud's conceptualization of identification, in which the infant or child incorporates the image of the parent, first in a dependent fashion, in which modeling is absolute, then in a more independent, automatic-seeming fashion, where the child's identification seems to be as automatic as breathing, and his ease in his identification enables him to seek models outside the parental domain (e.g., Payne & Mussen, 1956). Payne and Mussen find that boys closely identified with their fathers are apparently free to seek masculine models for behavior wherever they wish. The rather effeminate father whose son identifies closely with him does not necessarily have an effeminate son: the boy is free to pattern on surrogate models, such as male teachers, surrogate parents, or uncles.

How does the child regain the independence he must have to live a satisfactory adult life: how does he reach Erikson's stages of initiative, industry, autonomy? Probably through highly selective parental reinforcement, at least in part. The parent may reinforce the dependency behavior, allowing the child to whine or sit on laps or clutch at skirts, while giving more reinforcement to dependency behaviors designed to seek the favor of others, to please, and placate them. The parent also reinforces the child for independence behavior —the seeking of the company and influence of persons other than the parents, particularly peers. The peers in turn reward the child for being independent of his parents through being able to reward him for and by such things as appropriate play behavior. Reinforcement is thought to be more effective when it is partial, so that the child given intermittent reinforcement for behavior designed to manifest independence from the parent is the child most likely to attain that goal (Mednick, 1964).

The child's own executive independence enters here too. The older he is, the bigger and stronger he is, and the more he is able to seek rewards outside the circle of parental influence. As has been said, his peers also reinforce his attempts to be one with them, thus weaning himself from his parents.

The gaining of independence is a saltatory thing. Dependency behavior in boys is not continuous from birth, but rather jumps from one childhood stage to another. What is permissible for the two-year-old is frowned on for the three-year-old. This tendency to push boys remorselessly from dependency to independency appears to be true of all cultures: the little boy is supposed to be independent, full of initiative and enterprise, and is urged toward these latter ends by all means at the disposal of the society. The most dependent boys, as might be expected, are those who are compelled to show much dependency behavior—i.e., to whine and wheedle, which is finally yielded to by the adult, usually the mother, who often shows severe disapproval as she gives in (see Sears, Maccoby & Levin, 1957). Our society has more than one double code: girls and women are expected to be chaste and virtuous sexually, but males are expected to be stalwart, bold, and independent, never giving way to the so-called tender emotions. It may be for such reasons that women, frail though they are, live an average of five or six years longer than boys and men. Kagan and Moss (1960) show the saltatory notion of dependency clearly for the two sexes. High dependency college women are also high in dependency in their elementary school years, but the same thing is not true for Kagan and Moss' males, who show no relation between childhood and adult dependency.

Aggression shows more consistent development from infancy and the preschool years. Ours is a competitive society, and is so recognized. However, aggression is differently channeled at different ages. The little child is allowed to hit and kick and bite, but his older sibling is expected to show verbal aggression only, while by five or six or seven years, verbal aggression must be replaced by the "fighting spirit" and the ethic of competition.

The most aggressive children, at least girls, seem to be produced by mothers who are themselves aggressive, but who are cold and nonpermissive with their daughters. There is, over and above this, a tendency for dominated children and older children to be more aggressive than those who are permissively and democratically reared, or who are younger. Where parents do not allow aggression to be directed against themselves, but urge it toward other children who aggress, the aggressive model tends to be followed. As might be expected, aggression is also shown when parents are extremely permissive to their children. These findings bear out both the displacement and direct modeling theories of aggression, of course, and do not give us any very clear handles by which to manipulate our children. It almost seems that they will be aggressive, regardless of what we do with them, either because of modeling, of displacement, or permission. These might be called the three paths to aggression. The healthiest aggression, however, is probably that directed against the reasonably compliant parent, but the parent who is himself seen as powerful and able to retaliate at will. Here the child can "blow off steam" but at the same time knows the limits of safety.

A. PARENTAL INFLUENCES ON CHILD SOCIALIZATION

As has been suggested earlier in this chapter, parental influences fall logically into two parts: one, sources and types of parental reinforcement, by which we mean loosely the type, severity, consistency, and direction or distribution of parental reward and punishment; and two, parental exercise of power.

First, parents (e.g., Sears et al., 1957) seem to reinforce children according to psychological or physical dimensions, otherwise called reinforcement through love and reinforcement through punishment; or through love-oriented versus thing-oriented techniques.

Withdrawal of love or the threat of it is the paradigm or vehicle for psychological punishment, and seems to be almost uncannily effective as a socializing agent (see, for example, Grusec, 1966). Love "brings the child to heel" and produces self-criticism, while physical punishment is likely to turn him into a rebel. In fact love, ill used, is likely to be too effective, producing an unnatural severity of internalization of conscience or guilt that leaves the child immobilized. A distinction should be made at this time between shame and guilt. Shame is the fear of being caught, or the anticipation of punishment by others. The person caught in minor shoplifting or a social lie is likely to be ashamed. On the other hand, guilt is self-punishment, leading to an individual's refraining from an act or a thought because he anticipates *self*-punishment. It is roughly analogous to conscience, or the Freudian superego, or the juridicial concept of "knowledge of right and wrong." It is not only stronger but more efficient, at least from society's point of view, than shame. Shame requires a moral policeman, as it were, while guilt is self-policing. The "economic" consequences of this are immediately obvious.

A second characterization of parental rewards and punishments on childhood socialization concerns the direction or distribution of application. Learning may occur in either of two ways: because right or correct or good responses are rewarded, or because poor or incorrect or bad responses are punished. Hartup, Moore and Sager (1963) document this process of social reinforcement in terms of the pattern of rewards and punishments that are given, respectively, to boys and girls for sex-appropriate behavior during their preschool and kindergarten years: little boys are punished for playing with girlish toys or indulging in sissy behavior, and are rewarded for playing with masculine toys or indulging in appropriate, male types of behavior. As a consequence, they seem to socialize, or sex-type, early, firmly, and quickly. On the other hand, girls apparently receive little or no punishment for tomboy behavior, but are rewarded for appropriate girlish behavior. The consequence appears to be, and several studies (e.g., Brown, 1958, as well as Hartup et al., 1963) agree on this, that girls sex-type much later in our society than boys. The reason for this, in terms of the economics of the laws of learning (see Mednick, 1964) is that when both rewards and punishments are administered, the child learns not only what he *can* do, but what he *cannot* do: double reinforcement, directionally speaking, is much more informative—extensive—than single-ended reinforcement. While the research evidence is not clear, it seems that a most effective learning occurs when the frequency of reward or positive reinforcement is substantially greater than that of punishment or negative reinforcement (e.g., Mussen & Distler, 1959). Marshall (1965) has provided an excellent review of the effects of reward and punishment.

The next characteristic or dimension of parental reinforcements is well-documented in the general literature on the laws of learning (for example, see Mednick, 1964). Reinforcement, whether it is punishment or reward, will be more effective the sooner it is administered following the response that is to be established; the more consistent it is (i.e., the more likely it is *always* to follow the response) ; and the more generous (in the case of reward) or severe it is. This last law is called amount of reinforcement as it relates to learning, and is more in dispute than the previous two but, within normal limits, it seems to apply to human learning. Type of reinforcement, as has been implied, is also relevant to learning: making the punishment fit the crime, or the reward relevant to the good deed is more than a cliché as far as efficient shaping of behavior is concerned. In complex human learning, however, drive or motivation may be too high. There are suggestions in the literature, most of them coming from animal research, that learning under conditions of intense need may produce responses that are hard to extinguish or replace when they become inappropriate; and that incidental learning (the picking up of possibly useful odds and ends, such as are useful to socially sensitive people) may be reduced when the motivation of the learner is very intense. For example, the child to whom popularity is everything may lose the very goal he seeks because of his inattention to small social niceties, minimal social cues, and so on as he seeks the approval of those in his group whom he perceives as significant.

As has been suggested, a second major arena of child-parent interaction concerns power. The role of power is complex, often blurred, and likely to be confusing to children. A lower lower-class father, for example, is likely to be seen as very powerful physically to both his young and older children. The value of physical power in our culture, however, diminishes as children grow older. The reasons for this are that, by and large, socially valued power is economic and social, rather than physical. The lower-class father, and particularly the minority group father, has little of such power and his children soon come to know it. If, as group data show, the lower-class father combines autocratic control with physical strength, but low "clout" (influence), he and his older children are likely to find themselves on a collision course. The frequency of family disruption when the older children, particularly the boys, are able successfully to compete physically with their aging father, is great. There are few ties of intimacy and warmth to bind the family together—hence it breaks up. The relatively loose family structure of lower-class families may reflect the results of this combination of power and control techniques.

Sociological data also suggest that a model pattern for lower-class men combines physical power with direct sexuality—sexuality relatively unmixed with affection, intersexual mutuality, and respect for their female partners. This provides a socially maladaptive pattern of sex-typing for sons (e.g., the perpetuation of *machismo*—demonstration of virility by random procreation of children with multiple partners—thought to be a major stumbling block for social progress in some American Latin cultures; or the pride that many boys take in widespread promiscuity without psychological intimacy which frequently, within or without a *Hispano* culture, includes pride in illegitimate paternity). Consequences for girls growing up in such a power domain are equally mal-adaptive: to them, the heterosexual-marital role is one of finding the appropriately tough male and submitting to him, typically before marriage in many United States co-cultures. In one junior high school, for example, the most prestigeful girls' club has as its standard for membership illegitimate pregnancy.

When, as often seems to be the case, the male combines physical power and aggression with overt sexuality, but does not stay with the resulting family (or families), disruption of the psychosexual development of the children, probably particularly the boys, is likely to be extreme. In such cases, the mother of necessity assumes the "real" power and her son is left, in effect, a husk as far as maleness is concerned. To prove his maleness, he has no recourse but to the "symptoms" of manhood: a tough, aggressive, frequently delinquent, sexually acting-out pattern that fits him ill for a role in society that is satisfactory either to him or society. Clinical work done with such boys by the author and many of his professional colleagues in the disciplines of counseling and guidance, psychology, psychiatry, social work, and sociology indicates that such boys are confused, lonely, and unhappy, estranged from the world of adults, resentful of yet dependent on women, and deeply frightened about the adequacy of their maleness.

The structure of the society in which they live does little to provide them with assurance or opportunity to demonstrate competence (competence seems more than anything else in our culture to lead to self-esteem which, I believe, is the core of adequate personal-social adjustment). For example, Short et al. (1965) present the contrasting social viewpoints of Negro and white lower- and middle-class teen-agers. The boys who took part in this study perceive their society accurately and, if anything, more optimistically than reality justifies. Among the findings of this provocative study are: Boys, white and Negro, who have joined gangs perceive the illegitimate goals open to them as more frequent and available than the legitimate goals. Lower-class Negro boys who are not gang members see almost as many illegitimate as legitimate opportunities;

whereas for lower-class white boys, non-gang members, the perception of illegitimate opportunities, while relatively high compared with the middle class, is comfortably lower than their perception of legitimate opportunities. For Negro middle-class boys, the ratio of perceived legitimate and illegitimate opportunities is more than two to one; but for middle-class white boys the ratio is almost six to one. In general, Negro boys compared with white boys perceive fewer legitimate and more illegitimate opportunities (sources of power).

One section of Short, Rivera and Tennyson's data is so striking that it should be presented. The tabulation in Table 19.1 shows the total opportunity score (route to "competence" and, thus, self-esteem are adequate synonyms) for the different groups of boys studied. These figures are so dramatic that they need no interpretive comment.

TABLE 19.1

	Total Opportunity Score
Negro gang members	2.1
White gang members	5.0
Negro lower-class, non-gang	7.1
White lower-class, non-gang	12.6
Negro middle-class, non-gang	13.6
White middle-class, non-gang	24.1

Although the data are not as striking as those presented above, middle-class boys, Negro and white, see the adult world as more helpful than do lower-class boys. Interestingly enough, there is no difference in the perception of adult helpfulness between groups of Negro and white lower-class boys; but middle-class white boys perceive a generally more helpful adult world than do Negro middle-class boys. This leads to the suggestion that, the more difficult it is to gain power (as it has been for Negro adults), the less likely is the person to share it or even to use it to help others up the social ladder. Such a suggestion can be stated as a hypothesis, and put to test with possibly useful results.

The data above do not include girls, but there is no reason to think that their pattern would differ dramatically. However, it may well be more positive for Negro girls and women who in today's affluent society are more employable, thus economically powerful, than for Negro boys and men.

This discussion of power and techniques of control also leads to the prediction that ties between adults and children are weaker in the lower socioeconomic than in the middle class. Conversely, it can be predicted that the influence of the peer group will be stronger in the lower than in the middle class: and, in the lower class, relatively greater for boys than girls. These predictions are subject to test and, where relevant evidence has been gathered, it supports them.

Finally, as far as the socialization process is concerned, in our culture a relatively equalitarian balance between father and mother seems to be the optimum on all scores, with a slight tipping of the power balance in favor of the father. Suggestive evidence for this point is provided by Moulton et al. (1966), and Farina (1960). Farina's semi-experimental study shows that, for parents of schizophrenic sons, those whose sons show the poorest pre-illness history and who thus have the poorest prognosis for recovery, the balance of power in the family is toward the mother; parents of non-mentally ill sons are relatively equalitarian; while the balance of power for sons with good pre-illness history and good prognosis for recovery lies toward the father. His study further shows that, in terms of amount of demonstrated parental conflict, parents of non-mentally ill sons show the least, those of sons who are mentally ill but have good histories and prognoses are intermediate, and that conflict is highest between parents whose mentally ill sons have both poor histories and poor prognoses.

The mother's power role is less clear in today's society than the father's. There seems no doubt but what she is seen as equally and perhaps more powerful than the father by young children. She is apparently more likely to use physical discipline on her young son than on her young daughter (perhaps because it is more difficult to control him). This same son goes into a zone of feminine power (almost always) when he enters school, and continues typically in such a feminine world at least until his junior-high-school days. The influence of this on boys' socialization and sex-typing has been scantily explored and demands attention, as the frequency of breakdown of socialization and appropriate sex-typing and identification in today's society is so great as to be alarming. The consensus (by no means based on solid data) is that such breakdown is more frequent for boys and men than for girls and women.

The implications of this feminine world for development of competence and self-esteem for both sexes, but particularly boys, are also grave: there is consensus in the literature, for example, that elementary school teachers assign lower school marks to boys than to girls; and also mark boys as a group lower than their actual standing on objective indices of academic competence. Since the world of school is a major—perhaps the major—arena in which the child tests his competence and thus on the norms of which he bases his self-esteem, it may be that we are producing a nation of boys with shaky self-esteem and fundamental pessimism about their own competence (at least, relatively speaking). The reason for this down-grading of boys is obvious: their female power sources are punishing them for the very things that the society regards as lying at the heart of masculinity: individualism, initiative, energy, divergent (creative) thinking, aggressiveness, and so on. Such traits do not fit neatly into the framework of an orderly classroom. (Almost all forms for employment references for teachers that come to my desk include as a top priority item ability to maintain discipline. By discipline is meant conformity, quietness, neatness— the essential dimensions of a woman's world.)

To include this subsection on the role of power in socialization, Parsons' distinction between instrumental and expressive role-modeling should be noted (see, for example, Johnson, 1963). The instrumental role, in our society, is considered to be masculine: it is the role of testing reality, conforming to facts, living (as it were) in terms of the way things really *are*. It is achievement- and task-oriented. The expressive role is considered to be feminine: it includes comfort-seeking, affiliation, tenderness, solicitude, and nurturance. To cope with a harsh world, both boys and girls need an instrumental model, which is considered to be best provided by the father (and/or male teachers). To make this coping tolerable (or pleasant), the child should also have access to expressive sources which come most appropriately from mothers and/or child-centered, tender woman teachers. Each child, boy or girl, needs to have within him a range of both expressive and instrumental behaviors for his own benefit and the benefit of those with whom he associates.

This leads to the notion of cross-identification, or cross-modeling, where a girl models herself in many ways (socializes) in the same way as her father, and the boy in the same way as his mother. In general, this is probably socially useful, as long as it goes along with established social patterns: it is well for a boy to be cross-modeled if it leads him to an appreciation of art, music, humor, and social give and take, but ill for him to use perfumes or be feminine (passively homosexual) in his sexual behavior. Feminine cross-modeling is likely to make the boy and man more sympathetic with his wife and daughters.

Likewise, cross-modeling, within limits, is good for girls. Girls as well as boys live in a competitive society; marriages are likely to break up, leaving the young wife and mother to fend for herself in a competitive world; widowhood is frequent, with older women typically being left alone for five or six years with such masculine considerations to face as handling the family business, computing income taxes, chauffering herself, and otherwise of necessity acting in ways that are more commonly thought of as masculine rather than feminine. She will be more able to accomplish these developmental tasks if she is cross-modeled, and, like the boy, will undoubtedly be more sympathetic to her husband and her sons if she shares some of their attitudes and interests.

B. FAMILY SOCIAL STRUCTURE
AND SOCIALIZATION—
SIBLINGS, BIRTH ORDER, AND THE LIKE

The research literature in this area is complex, and most of it concerns sibling relations, particularly birth order (most particularly with first borns and only children as compared with later born children). Many references have accumulated in this area.

For example, Sutton-Smith and Rosenberg (1966) find that older children are seen as more bossy, demanding, and likely to be bullies, presumably because they have had the ineradicable early childhood experiences of being the biggest and strongest members of their families. They are seen that way not only by their younger brothers and sisters, but by their playmates (see also Hilton, 1966; and Oberlander & Jenkin, 1966). Younger children, on the other hand, are more often seen as using more subtle influencing techniques: those that characterize the supplicant rather than the master, such as whining, wheedling, sulking, and asking for help. Girls are more likely to model according to good manners, and to use verbal rather than physical techniques of dominance.

Firstborns have also been found to be more dependent, more suggestible, more likely to volunteer to take part in experiments or other volunteer activities, and more likely to be affiliative (i.e., to have their behavior guided by a need to find love) than is true for their younger brothers and sisters.

This area of research has not been a particularly "rich vein." Most studies provide results that would be expected from observation, common sense, and application of a reasonably sophisticated learning theory to the social situation of "first childness." But, from a practical point of view, little help is given in understanding or guiding children by knowing their status within the family. "First childness" is a demographic variable that is mildly helpful in predicting group behavior, but of little value in predicting the individual. It may be of crucial importance for a given child, of none for another.

Speaking generally, we expect first children to be more dependent on authority, more verbal, more conforming, more anxious, perhaps with higher intelligence and school achievement quotients, less aggressive in an acting-out fashion, and so on; but we cannot expect any *specific* first child to behave in this fashion. The first child whose next sibling is 11 months younger than he is in a very different social situation than is the first child whose next sibling is four years younger. The oldest boy with a younger sister is different from the boy with a younger brother, and so on.

Children from families of high density (where the children are closely spaced) have social experiences very different from low family density children. High-density children are more likely to be verbally short-changed, given less adult attention, perhaps less love and affection, experience less care-taking, are earlier put on their own, and so on. The child of an all-boy family has a very different learning experience than the child from the all-girl family. The only brother in a family of girls has experiences radically different from either of the above, and very different experiences if he is, for example, the eldest of four than if he is the youngest of four. One could go on and on with these variations, each of which is undoubtedly of significance for an individual child, but the complexities of which are such that investigators are not likely to come up with any very powerful behavioral-predictor equations.

C. INFLUENCE OF THE PEER GROUP

This has been studied for the most part in a rather non-dynamic, sociometric way. The "why's" have not been investigated, only the "how's." Children, from their earliest social experiences well into the junior-high levels, are unisexual as far as their friendship patterns are concerned, girls tending to select girls as friends, boys boys. They are not as consistent in their patterns of rejection, as girls will reject other girls about as often as boys reject other boys. But their positive groups are, almost without exception, of their own sex. This tendency is so strong that we almost suspect a misfire of social sex-typing when young girls or young boys choose frequently across sex lines in their choices of friends (but not "enemies").

One of the few studies to investigate the "why's" is Staffieri's (1967), which investigated the relation of body build to popularity in boys aged four years through fifth grade. He was interested in investigating social stereotypes. He found consistently for all the ages he studied, even for very young children, that mesomorphs and ectomorphs are overchosen (i.e., receive more positive friendship choices than would be expected by chance). An ectomorph is a thin, wiry little boy, a mesomorph a solid, muscular child, an endomorph a fat boy. The reasons given for choices were very different, however, for ectomorphs and mesomorphs: the ectomorph was consistently described as nervous, jittery, and withdrawn, more vulnerable to hurt, but nonetheless was well-received rather than rejected by his group. He might be characterized as a socially acceptable neurotic, in the sense of the way he is regarded by other children. Mesomorphs have attributed to them all the possible virtues, while endomorphs are characterized as sloppy, mean, and in terms of other adjectives that define socially undesirable persons.

These stereotypes, as mentioned, are formed by the age of four; the children, finally, are aware of their own body builds and the wish to be of a mesomorphic build is typical of small boys. This leads to the suggested conclusion that children perceive themselves as others perceive them, and that it is quite likely that both endomorphs and ectomorphs are self-rejecting, principally because they are so regarded by their social group. Other evidence along this line has been adduced in studies of adolescents and adults (see for example, the self-concept studies of Cortes & Gatti, 1965; and Washburn, 1962).

As has been hinted, the literature on peer influence is profuse, but little of it is dynamic in the explanatory sense. Staffieri's study has been given simply as an illustration of a dynamic approach to the problem.

A few generalizations that may be drawn from the literature are listed below, as are some questions (hypotheses) that may be advanced:

1. The peer group is second only to the parents (including the siblings) in socializing the child. It is probably more powerful in socialization than teachers are.

2. It assumes increasing importance in the *superficialities* of socialization (the descriptive behaviors) with increasing age.

3. Parents and peer group seem to exert almost equal importance by the time children are well into adolescence, at least in the middle class, in rather important life decisions such as whether or not to continue education beyond high school.

4. The peer group is indispensable in role rehearsal (courting behavior, sex-role adoption, dimensions of cooperative and competitive behavior, expression of aggression and dependency, and so on), but the question is open as to whether it is more important even in these overt behavior areas than are

parental models. The peer group may have more influence on the *style* of expression, the family on the *content* of expression.

5. As has been suggested earlier in the discussion of power, the peer group is probably more important in the over-all socialization process of lower- than of middle-class children, and of lower-class boys than of lower-class girls. However, this tentative generalization requires much more study than has been given to it.

6. The peer group supplies important confirmation-disconfirmation of self-judgments of competence and self-esteem, although the foundation of these is probably more influenced by the family.

7. Linearly, at least up to the point of the curve that defines the outstanding sociometric star (the greatly "over-accepted" child), acceptance by peers on a combination of friendship and status variables is perhaps the best single indicator of a child's personal-social adjustment. However, at the "star" end of the distribution, we often find children who are over-striving for acceptance and who seek social acceptance at the cost of other equally or more important aspects of self-social adjustment.

8. Until about adolescence (for girls) and probably into adolescence for boys, the same-sex peer group is the principal arena within which the child develops his peer-influenced socialization. There seems to be relatively little cross-sex influence, although this will vary greatly from school to school and community to community (and child to child, for that matter).

9. Tentatively, we may conclude that at all age levels a sex-integrated peer society better fits children for life in the U.S. culture than does a sex-segregated society. However, the data for this generalization cannot be called hard data, by any means; and I am making a value judgment when I promulgate this generalization. The area is important enough to deserve more study than it has received. Many of my Pakistani-Muslim friends, for example, are appalled by the coeducational pattern, including early dating, that the typical U.S. child experiences. On the other hand, sophisticated observers are alarmed by the social-sexual relations that are standard in sex-segregated schools or other settings for either sex. It can only be concluded that one takes his chances either way.

10. The peer group provides a reference point for self-evaluation of elementary sexuality. Girls compare notes on onset and side effects of menstruation, breast development, co-rehearse courting behavior, and so on; boys rather typically compare ejaculation behavior through social masturbation while at the same time making important value judgments about their own masculinity —e.g., time of onset of sexual maturity, size of penis, status of secondary sex characteristics such as body and facial hair. It seems to make little difference whether girls are moderately early or late in onset of menstruation, although extreme deviations are important. Breast size is a matter of great moment to them. In general, up to a level approaching bovinity, large breasts are considered desirable. However, there are style periods—such as the Twiggy period during which this chapter is being written—that are comforting to flat-chested

girls. For U.S. boys, apparently somewhat independent of ethnicity, large penises, heavy musculature (short of stockiness or the professional-wrestler physique), substantial beards, pubic, chest, belly, arm, leg, but not back, hair are desirable; and early pubescence accords clear and enduring status in the peer group, as well as with teachers and other adults. However, early pubescence for a personally immature boy who cannot yet cope with responsibility and leadership such as are almost automatically assigned to early maturing males may result in serious failure experiences.

Boys much oftener than girls discuss with each other the strategies and techniques of sexual intercourse. Social masturbation (which may have positive mental hygiene effects in our sexually ignorant culture, as well as provide a high risk contingency for youngsters with homosexual predispositions) is common among boys but not girls. Apparently neither boys nor girls share their psychoaffectional sex relations with their peers, except at a rather nonspecific level. Boys are more likely than girls to discuss casual consummatory sex behavior, but neither sex apparently reveals sex behavior occurring in a love context. It is also rare for a homosexual relation that is mixed with affection to be discussed with peers (i.e., boys will discuss social masturbation, but not when they have been emotionally moved toward the other participant or participants). Occasionally (this observation comes from clinical data I have collected) the ban on discussion of homosexual interaction can be very damaging. It is, regrettably, not infrequent for adolescents, male and female, to be approached sexually by like-sex prestige adults. Often they enter an active, guilt-ridden, usually short-lived sexual relation that is buried after its termination, but which leaves lasting doubts about sexual adjustment. I know of many cases that would have been better discussed with peers, among whom there will usually have been some who have been approached by the same prestige figure. Sharing, in such a case, would have been an excellent mental health measure.

It is probable but not certain that sex-social interactions and communication, verbal and behavioral, occur earlier, and are fuller, and franker, and perhaps more useful in lower than in higher socioeconomic circles.

The present complex generalization (Number 10) should be viewed in the context of generalization Number 2, above. These peer interchanges in the sexual-social area are relatively superficial (although often they provide the only functional sex education U.S. youth has). They do not usually extend to deep concerns about sexual adequacy, homo- or bisexual conflicts, inability to achieve genuinely intimate love relations, and so on.

D. FORMAL EDUCATIONAL INFLUENCES— THE SCHOOL

Relevant discussion for this sub-topic is partially covered in the section on peer group influences that immediately precedes this. It is axiomatic that the school provides the peer group for most, but not all, children. Important exceptions who deserve special study are:

1. "Bussed-in" children (i.e., those who are transferred to schools long distances from their home neighborhood). Such children have two peer groups: the neighborhood and the school. This situation becomes increasingly frequent for children with age: the typical elementary-school child goes to a neighborhood school. The school's geographic area increases greatly with junior-high school, and extends still further with secondary school. However, as the child gains his own mobility, his neighborhood becomes less necessary to him, since he can move at will to other neighborhoods.

2. Boarding-school children. The same considerations as listed above apply to them, except that their neighborhood contacts occur only during vacations.

3. Minority group children, particularly submerged minorities. For example, under token integration, the few minority group children in a given school may literally have no *functional* peer group in the school setting. Children who grow up in situations where they are almost the only members of their minority group in the community are likely to have similar experiences. Certain religious groups cut their children off from any but class-contained interaction with their school peers (i.e., forbid afterschool extracurricular activities).

As children in public schools move into the larger junior and senior high school, lower-class children (except for the intellectually adequate boys with outstanding athletic skills) are progressively cut off from the social and extracurricular aspects of school life. Participation in extracurricular activities is rather strongly related to school persistence and achievement, and the tendency to exclude lower-class boys and girls undoubtedly contributes importantly to their low school morale and high drop-out rate.

The schools cannot claim a clean bill of health in developing socialization. Discrimination is rampant on subtle as well as obvious grounds. Pressing socialization needs, such as in the sexual-social area, are all but ignored. Lower-class youngsters, minority group youngsters, non-conforming youngsters, borderline ability youngsters—all are shamefully ignored or even openly discriminated against. The socialization record becomes worse as the child moves from first to twelfth grade.

Children's needs for such conflicting but equally urgent goals as autonomy and dependency are ignored: the school as an institution is remarkably authoritarian and impersonal, progressively so (which is contrary to all logic, particularly as far as autonomy is concerned) the older the child becomes.

From my "in-depth experience" with many, many schools all over the world, I wonder not at the number of socialization failures, but at the number of successes. Socially, the average child succeeds in spite of, not because of, the school. However, it must be added that, if we select the upper one-half to one-third of the population of a given school according to some combined index of grade-getting ability, family social status, social and extracurricular skills, and physical health and appearance, the schools do a good job (or at least, such children thrive in a school setting). However, even selected according to these criteria, minority group children do less well.

E. THE ROLE OF RELIGION

While there is only the most tenuous evidence that religion, in the form of the organized church or synagogue or mosque, accomplishes its stated goal (to make children religious both in spirit and deed, so that behavior across situations is consistent with the tenets of the given religion), there is some evidence that many children find in the youth groups of their religious unit many of the socialization goals they cannot find in their schools.

The basis for this statement is a large sample of autobiographies of adolescents gathered by the author over the years and from most parts of the United States and many parts of the world.

Church (to use the term generically to include synagogues, mosques, temples, and so on) is more likely than school to regard a youngster as being important for *himself* (or perhaps, for his soul—the meaning of the two words actually may not be too different) rather than to value him almost solely in terms of his positive behavioral and social assets. A substantial proportion of my clinical sample (the autobiographies referred to) found within their churches' youth groups an opportunity for social acceptance and rehearsal that their schools did not provide for them. They were accorded a status—a value—not offered by the school, and the contribution to their socialization was usually constructive and often profound. At least, so they report it, and I find no reason to doubt them. Many minority group and low social status children, particularly, find a social setting in their church groups that is partially or completely closed to them in schools. They appreciate it and use it.

However, for this clinical sample, church did not typically extend beyond the social benefits. The ultimate religious goal, stated in the first paragraph of this subsection, was seldom attained. The sample used the church for their own ends, and these were valuable ends. But the church's contribution to more general religiosity, ethics, and morality was minor, at least in the case of this sample. Other than social, the most frequently reported effects of religious affiliation were conflict, guilt, and shame, particularly in the social-sexual area.

The effects of the church deserve much more attention than the relevant social and behavioral sciences have given them. This neglect is probably due to two conditions: the area is a sensitive one in which to do research; and social scientists, like the clinical sample to which reference has been made, are for the most part middle-class people who have as younger people taken their "goodies" from the church and are no longer particularly interested in it, except as rather passive, superficial participators, if that.

Data exist demonstrating that church or church related (i.e., moral) education is quite successful in teaching children the *verbal* distinctions between "right and wrong." They verbalize, from remarkably early ages, all the correct values, but there seems little internalization in the form of conscience, honesty, application of truth, freedom from race prejudice, and so on, that can be directly attributed to church membership. Indeed, several studies exist to show that degree of religiosity is negatively related to some values held to be central in a democratic society. One typical example (O'Reilly & O'Reilly, 1954) reveals that the more religious the student (the study was done with Roman Catholic college students), the more likely he was to be authoritarian and race prejudiced. Kinsey reports that strength of religious affiliation is negatively related to sexual freedom among girls and women. He makes no value judgment about this finding. It is, however, consistent with U.S. cultural and religious standards.

F. THE ROLE OF FORMAL ORGANIZATIONS—
INDUSTRIAL, COMMERCIAL, GOVERNMENTAL

About this topic, as about religion, the social and behavioral sciences have little to tell us. The basic structure of socialization may well be established before formal organizations (with the probable exception of the school) impinge effectively on the child. Exceptions, most likely, are monolithic governments, where political teaching very likely begins in the preschool years. Bronfenbrenner (1962), for example, speculates about the impact of Soviet education on the socialization and character of the child. Certainly, these effects deserve study.

The effects of the opportunities, legitimate and illegitimate, that communities offer children have already been discussed. Other institutional derivatives have been less adequately documented or, where documented, differential effects have not been found: for example, I know of no evidence that Boy Scouts differ from non-Boy Scouts in their social or moral characteristics in any way other than can be accounted for by the fact that boys of higher socioeconomic status are more likely than boys of lower socioeconomic status to be Boy Scouts.

Social class *does* show many relations with behavior, but whether these are due to social class per se or to income, family management and structure, and so on is not clear. The social-class data indicate that in general lower-class children are more honest in admitting delinquent, aggressive, and sexual behavior (or perhaps they do not see so clearly the drift of the questions—also, when anonymity is guaranteed, some of the class differences disappear); that they are less achievement-oriented and more immediate-minded; that they are less likely to work for intangible rewards; that they are, or admit to being, more openly aggressive (although they reject open aggression in their playmates); that they are more closely bound to their peer group and less closely bound by adult standards, and that they are more social in their sexual life (i.e., they are more likely to frown on masturbation, while condoning hetero- or homosexual relations).

Sex differences exist, with lower-class boys being more sexy than middle-class boys, at least by their own admission. In all social classes, social groups seem to be formed more in terms of cliques or snobbish family-status types of groups for girls, more in terms of common interest patterns for boys. This may be because boys can always find status through athletics, while girls depend more for status on family income, education, and so on.

G. THE EFFECTS OF URBAN ENVIRONMENTS

Here again little information has been gathered, other than actuarial. There is no question but what urban children know more people and more types of people, and have to make more complex social adjustments than rural or village children. Barker and Wright (1954) have best documented this in their study of *Midwest and Its Children*. They find that the village is permeable— i.e., children penetrate into all aspects of village life, whereas they are excluded from and are unfamiliar with urban life, except for their immediate family structure. This finding suggests that qualitatively village children may be better informed than urban children, even though the actual variety or quantity of social roles hypothetically open to them is less.

Gans (1962) points out that villages exist within cities and that, in this sense, the metropolitan child may be as isolated from the mainstream of a culture as the rural village child. *De facto* segregation and suburbia also have a provincializing effect. Miel and Kiester's (1967) *The Shortchanged Children of Suburbia* is well worth reading in this context. Representative literature on competence opportunities offered to youth has already been discussed (e.g., Cloward & Ohlin, 1960; Landis & Scarpitti, 1965; Short et al., 1965; and Tallman, 1966). Among this group, Tallman demonstrates experimentally that, given the chance, people will choose legitimate over illegitimate techniques to reach a goal; that they are more likely to cheat when the goal is important to them; and that if they fail to reach it, particularly when they have refused to use illegitimate ways to do so, they devalue it. This last finding has rather profound socialization implications: if a child is prevented from reaching a highly desirable goal, even though he has employed all legitimate techniques, and particularly when he has refused illegitimate techniques, he "gives up."

H. SOCIAL CLASS VARIATIONS
IN SOCIALIZATION PRACTICES

This topic has been construed as overlapping with F above, and has been partially discussed. One additional finding is of interest here: the exposure to violence and restrictiveness so commonly the fate of lower-class children, including their preschool years. Where promiscuity and crime and drunkenness are common, the child is often socialized in an atmosphere of fear ("Be quiet and good and thus stay out of danger") that stifles curiosity and is quite foreign to most middle-class children. The results of this escapism and passivity carry into school life.

As documented by Bernstein (1960), the language environment of lower-class children is likely to differ sharply from that of middle-class children. Adults, for the latter, use language to extend the child's experiences, and to teach him subgoals: how to tie a shoestring at the time the shoestring comes untied, how to say "yes, please," and "no, thank you," and the other social amenities that pave the way for graceful and extensional social and intellectual relations. Often, the only language the lower class child hears is extremely concrete, often inconsistent, and limiting. The following example, from which wide generalizations can be drawn, comes from an observation of a father from the lower socioeconomic classes and his daughter. They were together in the living room, and the three-year-old child was pretending that she was smoking a cigarette. Presently, little finger extended, she pretended to flip the ashes, at which point the father struck her, yelling that this would teach her to be fancy. This anecdote, taken freely from LeShan (1952), illustrates the confusion, the lack of consistent or sensible limits, the mandatory nature of verbal interaction, and the ensuing fear and development of anxiety along with the development of passivity and lack of curiosity that can be produced by harsh, limiting, inconsistent language.

As has been stated, this is likely to produce later social attitudes of withdrawal, passivity, and quiescence that, among other things, militate against adequate adjustment to school or other new situations, particularly those involving abstractions and symbols.

I. MASS COMMUNICATION

The mass media have a unique opportunity, although they seem to be more shaped *by* than shaping *of* contemporary society. As with the role of religion, we have little but actuarial information on the influence of the mass media. We know how many children watch what television program for how many hours a day, but we know little of the influence of the program, or the comic strip, or the newspaper on the child.

Apparently only a minority of children are influenced by the violence so common in television (and presumably movie programs), and these children have already demonstrated undue susceptibility to influence and are already poorly adjusted (Bailyn, 1959). This study done with elementary school boys does not fit well with later studies (see Bandura & Walters, 1963). The Bandura and Walters studies conducted with younger children indicate that exposure to TV violence disinhibits children for some time, particularly in similar situations, in their expression of violent and aggressive behavior.

It has already been noted that the mass media provide a flow of sexual stimulation ranging from very subtle to very open and direct. This flow probably makes it impossible for a child to suppress sex in our culture, particularly after pubescence, when he presumably becomes particularly sensitive to sexual stimulation.

SUMMARY

The structure of this book restricts the present chapter to a rather conventional treatment of childhood socialization, particularly as this is influenced by the family. In my search for a model for socialization, I have adopted Erikson and his model of the eight stages of man, particularly the first five, which take the child through adolescence. Each of these stages is conceived of as a psychosocial crisis, and each must be resolved before the next can be satisfactorily handled by the child. Middle-class society provides a psychosocial moratorium, to protect the child against mistakes that he may make at each of the stages, particularly at adolescence. Lower-class society provides few such safeguards.

Ausubel has described developmental tasks which picture in detail some of the adjustments, particularly with regard to frustration and failure, that the child must make as he undertakes the later psychosocial stages.

In this chapter, I have stressed broad trends and theory more than specific research data. This has brought me to the dependency theory: the child is first totally dependent, later increasingly independent, until in later childhood he fends very successfully for himself as he proceeds through the developmental tasks. The process of acquiring and dissipating dependency through the avenues of parental handling was described, and it was pointed out that in achieving dependency, the child must first master "how to do it"—how to master the world which he can touch with his hands; then his distance receptors; and finally, the abstract symbolic, semantic, linguistic world.

The child is subject to the parents' power, particularly power in the sexual sense, power in the physical sense, power in the influence sense (both social and economic influence), and power in the sense of wisdom. This power cannot be effective unless it is consistently applied.

The saltatory nature of the development of independence in contrast, say, to aggression in our society was pointed out, and the desirability of cross-modeling or cross-identification was discussed, in which the little boy, cross-modeled on his mother, is likely to be more sympathetic with sisters and eventually his wife and daughters. The same thing is true of the little girl cross-identified with her father: she is more able to take her place in a competitive world, as well as be more understanding of husband and sons.

The second half of the chapter discussed (a) Parental Influences on Child Socialization which pointed out that the more rewarding, consistent, and bidirectional—i.e., providing both reward and punishment—the parent is, the more likely he is to be an effective shaper of his child's behavior; (b) Family Social Structure and Socialization where the effects of birth order were discussed, and it was seen that, among other things, firstborn children were likely to be bossy; (c) Influence of the Peer Group, where it was pointed out that we know many of the sociometric "how's," but few of the "why's," and some theories were presented showing the influence of body build on sociometric choice. Formal Educational Influences—the School (d) is influenced by the same factors as the Influence of the Peer Group—in fact, it is composed entirely of the peer group. We know little about the Role of Religion (e) except that religion seems not to have as much influence as it probably should have. The Role of Formal Organizations—Industrial, Commercial, Governmental—(f) again provides little information. The Effects of Urban Environments (g) show that the rural environment or village is more permeable than the larger city, so the child is freer to know of adult organizations. Social Class Variations in Socialization Practices (h) stresses the differences in the type of language and control used with lower- and middle-class children: often violent and restrictive with the former, extensional and encouraging with the latter. Finally, we know little about (i) Mass Communication. More study has been made of how it can be shaped by an appeal to public taste than of how it affects the public welfare.

REFERENCES

ALEXANDER, C. N., JR., & CAMPBELL, E. Q. Peer influences on adolescent aspirations and attainments. *American Sociological Review,* 1964, 29, 568–575.

AUSUBEL, D. P. *Ego development and the personality disorders.* New York: Grune & Stratton, 1952.

AUSUBEL, D. P. *Theory and problems of adolescent development.* New York: Grune & Stratton, 1954.

BANDURA, A., & WALTERS, R. H. *Social learning and personality development.* New York: Holt, Rinehart & Winston, 1963.

BAILYN, LOTTE. Mass media and children: A study of exposure habits and cognitive effects. *Psychological Monographs,* 1959, 73.

BARKER, R. G., & WRIGHT, H. F. *Midwest and its children.* Evanston, Ill.: Row Peterson, 1954.

BERNSTEIN, B. Language and social class. *British Journal of Sociology,* 1960, 11, 271–276.

BROWN, D. G. Sex-role development in a changing culture. *Psychological Bulletin,* 1958, 55, 232–242.

BRONFENBRENNER, U. Soviet method of character education: Some implications for research. *American Psychologist,* 1962, 17, 550–564.

BRUNER, J. S. Education as social invention. *Saturday Review,* 1966, 49, 70–72, 102–103.

CLOWARD, R. A., & OHLIN, L. E. *Delinquency and opportunity.* New York: Free Press of Glencoe, 1960.

CORTES, J. B., & GATTI, F. M. Physique and self-description of temperament. *Journal of Consulting Psychology,* 1965, 29, 432–439.

ERIKSON, E. H. The problem of ego identity. *Journal of the American Psychoanalytic Association,* 1956, 4, 56–121.

FARINA, A. Patterns of role dominance and conflict in parents of schizophrenic patients. *Journal of Abnormal and Social Psychology,* 1960, 61, 31–38.

FLAVELL, J. H. *The developmental psychology of Jean Piaget.* Princeton, N. J..: Van Nostrand, 1963.

GANS, H. *The urban villagers: Group and class, the life of Italiañ-Americans.* New York: Free Press of Glencoe, 1962.

GRUSEC, JOAN. Some antecedents of self-criticism. *Journal of Personality and Social Psychology,* 1966, 4, 244–252.

HARTUP, W. W., MOORE, SHIRLEY G., & SAGER, G. Avoidance of inappropriate sex typing by young children. *Journal of Consulting Psychology,* 1963, 27, 467–473.

HAVIGHURST, R. J., ET AL. *Growing up in River City.* Committee on Human Development, University of Chicago. New York: Wiley, 1962.

HILTON, IRMA. Differences in the behavior of mothers toward their first- and later-born children. Paper read at Fall Meetings, American Psychological Association, 1966.

HUNT, J. McV. *Intelligence and experience.* New York: Ronald Press, 1961.

JOHNSON, MIRIAM M. Sex-role learning and the nuclear family. *Child Development,* 1963, 34, 319–333.

KAGAN, J., & MOSS, H. A. The stability of passive and dependent behavior from childhood through adulthood. *Child Development,* 1960, 31, 577–591.

KAGAN, J., ROSMAN, BERNICE L., DAY, DEBORAH, ALBERT, J., & PHILIPS, W. Information processing in the child: Significance of analytic and reflective attitudes. *Psychological Monographs,* 1964, 78.

LANDIS, J. R., & SCARPITTI, F. R. Perceptions regarding value orientation and legitimate opportunity: Delinquents and non-delinquents. *Social Forces,* 1965, 44, 83–91.

LESHAN, L. L. Time orientation and social class. *Journal of Abnormal and Social Psychology,* 1952, 47, 589–592.

MARSHALL, HELEN H. The effect of punishment on children: A review of the literature and a suggested hypothesis. *Journal of Genetic Psychology,* 1965, 106, 23–33.

MEDNICK, S. *Human learning.* New York: Prentice-Hall, 1964.

MIEL, ALICE, & KIESTER, E., JR. *The shortchanged child of suburbia.* New York: Institute of Human Relations Press, 1967. Pamphlet Series No. 8.

MISCHEL, W., & METZNER, R. Preference for delayed reward as a function of age, intelligence and length of delay interval. *Journal of Abnormal and Social Psychology,* 1962, 64, 425–431.

MOULTON, R. W., LIBERTY, P. G., JR., BURNSTEIN, E., & ALTUCHER, N. Patterning of parental affection and disciplinary dominance as a determinant of guilt and sex typing. *Journal of Personality and Social Psychology,* 1966, 4, 356–363.

MUSSEN, P. H., & DISTLER, L. Masculinity, identification, and father-son relationships. *Journal of Abnormal and Social Psychology,* 1959, 59, 350–356.

OBERLANDER, M., & JENKIN, N. Birth order and academic achievement. Paper read at Fall Meetings, American Psychological Association, 1966.

O'REILLY, C. T., & O'REILLY, E. J. Religious beliefs of Catholic college students and their attitudes toward minorities. *Journal of Abnormal and Social Psychology,* 1954, 49, 378–380.

PAYNE, D. E., & MUSSEN, P. H. Parent-child relations and father identification among adolescent boys. *Journal of Abnormal and Social Psychology,* 1956, 52, 358–362.

SEARS, R. R., MACCOBY, ELEANOR E., & LEVIN, H. *Patterns of child-rearing.* Evanston, Ill.: Row Peterson, 1957.

SHORT, J. F., JR., RIVERA, R., & TENNYSON, R. A. Perceived opportunities, gang membership, and delinquency. *American Sociological Review,* 1965, 30, 56–67.

STAFFIERI, J. R. A study of social stereotype of body image in children. *Journal of Personality and Social Psychology,* 1967, 7, 101–107.

SULLIVAN, H. S. *The collected works of Harry Stack Sullivan, M.D.* New York: Norton, 1953.

SUTTON-SMITH, B., & ROSENBERG, B. G. Sibling consensus on power tactics. Paper read at Fall Meetings, American Psychological Association, 1966.

TALLMAN, I. Adaptation to blocked opportunity: An experimental study. *Sociometry,* 1966, 29, 121–134.

WASHBURN, W. C. The effects of physique and intrafamily tension on self-concept in adolescent males. *Journal of Consulting Psychology,* 1962, 26, 460–466.

WHITING, J. W., & CHILD, I. L. *Child training and personality.* New Haven, Conn.: Yale Univer. Press, 1953.

WOLOWITZ, H. M. Attraction and aversion to power: A psychoanalytic conflict theory of homosexuality in male paranoids. *Journal of Abnormal Psychology,* 1965, 70, 360–370.

CHAPTER **20**

Adolescent Socialization

Ernest Q. Campbell

Vanderbilt University

Some people define adolescence simply as an affliction. Others, probably looking back, follow G. B. Shaw in describing it as such a wonderful time of life that it's a shame to waste it on children. Freudians describe the period as dominated by sexual maturation and the flowering of sexual desire and heterosexual attachments (Blos, 1962, p. 11). Some define the boundaries of the period as set by " . . . from the beginning of puberty to the end of the maturation process" (Van Waters, 1930). Probably a useful perspective is to set the lower limit physiologically (not earlier than the onset of puberty) and the upper limit socially (not later than the assumption of marital and occupational duties). Stated otherwise, adolescence does not begin before one is capable of reproduction and does not extend past entry into wedlock or full-time work. Seen thusly, the title of a popular singer's book of moral advice—Pat Boone, *Twixt Twelve and Twenty*—is not a bad chronological delineation of the period.

From a socialization perspective, it is essential that we define adolescence as a system of rights and duties, a social role, and in order to do so we must set it in a social space. To do this, we need not speak chronologically but in terms of social expectancies. In turn, we are required to specify what particular society we are talking about, and in the present instance, except where otherwise noted for comparative purposes, our focus is on modern American society.

It is important to note that adolescence is a socially created category, as, of course, are all stages in the life cycle (Glick, 1947, 1955, 1957). Childhood is its predecessor and adulthood its termination. Adolescence is a status given defined rights and duties, and assigned a set of expected behaviors. Normally an adolescent is not to be self-supporting or to vote. He cannot go into bars nor buy hard liquor. He is not to marry or to enter parenthood. He cannot be as frivolous as a child or as responsible as an adult. By the same token, it is a vastly variegated period of life, spanning the time from the first pubic hairs to entering military service, from intensive hesitancy toward the opposite sex to involved, semi-

With substantial appreciation to Mrs. John A. Gable for bibliographic and abstracting assistance.

permanent heterosexual attachments, from very limited experience with team sports to athletic scholarships and headlines on sports pages, from bedtimes strictly enforced by mothers to residence in the vast anonymous dormitories of large public universities.

It will be helpful if in the beginning we indicate a general perspective on the social state of adolescence and designate some of the issues that will concern us in this discussion. We will be general before we are specific. Adolescents vary greatly among themselves, and between different social classes and different regions of the country. Much of what we say in this chapter is not as appropriate to rural youth; to youth of the poor, especially those who drop out of school or otherwise assume adult responsibilities early; to minority youth; and to adolescents who, whether for reasons of rejection (social isolation) or choice (personal values, as in studiousness) are socially uninvolved. Thus, the prototype for what we say is the urban, especially the suburban, middle class, though our interpretations should apply, if less specifically, to adolescents throughout modern American society.

Though adolescence is a social role, it has the significant feature of being tied to a limited age span. Thus there is an important sense in which adolescence must be defined chronologically, since structures and norms are keyed in an important way to it: legal and normative definitions of minimum and proper age of marriage are illustrative, as is the fact that the 18-year-old male becomes subject to military draft. A person who is in the 8th grade is supposed to be 13 or 14 years old, and our strong expectation is that the high school graduating class is composed largely of 17-year-olds. Pressures toward automatic promotion of pupils in the public schools reflect this tendency to allot social roles by age. One cannot be licensed to drive a car until he is 16 or so, and those who cannot drive are eliminated from easy access to those major portions of adolescent culture that organize around the automobile. Thus, although it is our intention to discuss adolescent socialization as socialization pertaining to the social role of adolescence rather than as socialization pertaining to a distinct age period, we cannot ignore the major linkages made between age and social expectancies. It is essential, however, that we not link chronological age immutably to the social state of adolescence.

What, then, is supposed to happen during adolescence? How are adolescents supposed to behave and what experiences are they supposed to have? Our answer provides an overview of the concerns of this chapter. First, adolescents are supposed to broaden substantially their range of social contacts and dramatically increase the number of others who are emotionally and normatively relevant to them by becoming less dependent on parents and home and more oriented to peers and to the adult world. Second, adolescents are supposed to experiment with what they are in relation to others in the sense of "trying on" new behaviors and experiences, questioning themselves internally as to what they are and wish to be seen as, working toward integration of past experiences, present performances, and future expectancies, attaining a somewhat coherent, somewhat permanent answer to the question, "Who am I?" Third, adolescents are supposed to be learning to be adults, in the sense of acquiring social skills, selecting internal standards of judgment and conduct, and acquiring through practice in "make-believe" organizational settings (clubs, plays, school newspaper, student activities, etc.) the skills of constraint and presentation needed for success in the adult settings of an industrial, bureaucratized society. Fourth, the adolescent is widely viewed as being simultaneously in a suspended state of supreme frustration and in the middle of the best years of life.

THE STATE AND STATUS OF ADOLESCENCE

Adolescence is the period of tension and peace-making between the dependency of the past and the independence of the future, between demands placed on the actor by an expanding circle of influences and by an increasing awareness of self and need for identity. The period, like all other social roles, has its virtues and its liabilities. The assets of adolescence are those that organize around the facts of physical maturity, energy, strength, and lack of responsibility. The frustrations of adolescents are those that organize around the lack of responsibility and the definition that adolescents, being less than dependable, predictable, and responsible, cannot be trusted with full freedom and citizenship rights.

There is a great deal of anticipatory socialization in almost all stages of the life-cycle, whether in the play of little girls with dolls or in the mock election in a junior high school, whether in technical schools and on-the-job training or in the gradual disengagement of the old in preparation for the role of death. Adolescence particularly is defined as a period of training and preparation for future, i.e., adult roles. Viewed societally, this period is a necessity because of the economic need to keep the young from glutting the job market and because modern technology requires that those entering the labor market be more highly skilled than in the past. Viewed developmentally, this period is a virtue in that adolescents, being old enough to know what they are doing but not saddled with the expectation of being deadly serious about it, can gain an intelligent and realistic sense of self by experimentation with a variety of roles. Physically maturing and intellectually expansive persons, not required or expected to rush into adult responsibilities, can use the time wisely to explore themselves, test their competencies, try new modes of action, discover their limits, catalog their pleasures, and firm up their identities. There is time for uncommitted experimentation where acts are not fully meaningful. We do not expect children to contemplate the question, "Who am I?" because their family circle answers the question for them. Nor do we expect adults to contemplate the question, because they are supposed to know the answer—indeed, prevailing norms suggest that they should seek therapy if they do not know. It may be, then, that one of the best definitions we can give adolescence is that it is that period when the person is intellectually developed enough to be able to ask, "Who am I?", released enough from familial identity to need to ask the question, and free enough of the work-world that he can answer it in broader terms than referring to an occupational activity.

One of the most provocative contemporary facts is that adolescence has been growing at both ends. Physiologically, there is evidence that puberty occurs earlier now than in the past, and various bisexual contacts and behaviors appropriate to provocative sexual experiences (cosmetics, dating, dancing, etc.) occur at earlier ages. At the other end of adolescence the increasing demands for advanced education, and the compatible needs of the labor force to keep untrained personnel out of it, extend the period of dependency in some cases into the mid-20's or later.

There are, then, important ways in which adolescence as a social position is defined by societal needs. If the economy needed many relatively untrained workers, if the population were not growing as rapidly, if every able-bodied person were needed for some immense task such as national defense, what we currently know as adolescence would not exist. On the negative side it is agricultural surpluses, technological advances, and the threat of underemployment, while on the positive side it is a complex economy demanding more highly trained workers, that extend adolescence at the upper age limits. It is because we do not want people to enter the labor market early, want them to be well trained when they do enter it, that we define certain conditions (e.g., school drop-outs) as social problems, create special roles that prove troublesome (e.g., young adults who from a student's status organize social revolt), and fail generally to define sufficiently meaningful activities for persons who are physically and emotionally ready, or believe themselves to be, for more significant activities than they have to do.

Given the expectation that an increasing number of young people must defer adulthood long after they are ready for it, it is necessary to compensate them for deferred gratifications by offering substitute rewards. Since doing so is a very difficult task, being a wasteful use of talent from the society's standpoint and incomplete and unsatisfactory from the adolescent's, we should expect states of intra- and inter-personal tension and anxiety to be commonplace occurrences. How can a meaningful identity develop among those who possess only the shadow of significance and usefulness? Youth in such a state are rather useless: too old to be cuddled and watched over, too young to be productive and dependable. It is a condition to be tolerated by society in anticipation of their future utility. In their immediate state, they are useful principally to each other. Adults manage to make a few of them useful, as high school football heroes and newspaper delivery boys—and, in time of total war, as soldiers. But by and large, they are in limbo, something like a connective tissue that simply holds the generations together.

The child's ripening need for independence leads him psychologically away from his parents and kin, but, unable to establish a state of personal independence (as in work and marriage), he moves instead into the pseudo-independence of the peer group, where he gains the solace of like-situated persons, in the process substituting a dependence on peers for his earlier dependence on parents. Thus, a period that in the abstract has great potential for increasing personal individuation, experimentation, and expansion of borders and boundaries—for permitting individuals to realize their creative potential while free of the routinizing demands of work and family—often has very different effects in reality because the anxieties of freedom create huge conformity pressures regarding details and trivia that become significant.

There is a basic problem in developing commitment among adolescents because society does not need the young and therefore contributes to the trivialization of youth. There is a not unrelated problem of providing youth with disciplined experience, because of ambivalence about youth and consequent uncertainties about how they should be treated. This may be why organized team sports, especially football, are credited by so many as being important character-building devices for youth. They are activities which, once entered into, require discipline and physical effort for success.

Specific to the socialization of adolescents, it is important to note certain emergent properties of the period. Probably, adolescence is the first time that the human being consciously tries to conceptualize himself, consciously works to change himself, and consciously experiments with the presentation of various images of himself before audiences of various others.

Second, adolescence is the period when the human actor becomes *re*-active in his own socialization, which is to say that he plays a more important part compared to childhood in defining what his rights shall be, how he shall be treated, and what he is defined to be.

Third, this period in the life cycle is distinctive because it puts persistent pressures on the adolescent to define an expected future identity: "I'm going to be a cowboy when I grow up" has a substantially different meaning when the 16-year-old says it than when the 6-year-old says it. Questions such as, "What are you going to be when you grow up?" "Where are you going to go to college?" "What grades are you making in school?" "How serious are you about that girl?" and "Do you have a job after school?" have an urgent reality to them that they lacked in earlier years.

Fourth, adolescence introduces the need and theme of unlearning in socialization for the first time; one begins to put away childish things: the reverent adoration of and dependence of parents, concretized conceptions of God, unquestioning obedience to adult standards. Boys no longer define the opposite sex as "dirty ole girls," and girls cease defining the boys as "mean ole things."[1] Elements of what Wheeler (1966) terms disjunctive (as distinct from sequential) socialization are introduced.

Fifth, this is the period when the person must, in a most important sense, come to terms with his dreams, at least by late adolescence; that is, he must make choices, know that he is making them, and know that some of them may be irreversible. He encounters the fact that to be is not to be: he cannot go steady *and* play the field, be in vocational *and* college preparatory curriculums, be a scientist *and* a lawyer, be a member of this clique *and* that clique. Adolescence

---

[1]Margaret Mead (1928) has observed that when, as in Samoa, children observe adults in such adult-type activities as sex and childbirth, the transitions from one life-stage to another are gradual and growth is continuous. This is the same theme that Ruth Benedict (1948) develops; continuity to Benedict means not being taught something one must unlearn later.

is a period in which critically important decisions concerning the future are made, and in which a fuller awareness of one's competence to achieve desired ends is shaped.

Sixth, a personal identity emerges that is determined less severely by those few within one's family and more strongly by friends, peers, teachers, and various specific adults, and conditioned by a new realization that "I" is the continuing entity in the midst of flux. New identities create the fear of losing all that one has had and been, and may explain instabilities in the adolescent's presentation of self as well as explain the ebb and flow of adolescent friendships.

Seventh, adolescence is a period of emergency social growth; the changes in level of expected social skills, and in the diversity and demands of social and interpersonal settings, are much greater between, say, age 13 and 17 than between 34 and 38 or 7 and 11.[2]

Finally, adolescence is a period of major confrontation between values and reality.

Simply to list three sets of influences that largely encompass the socialization agents and experiences of adolescence is to suggest a simplicity that does not exist. Nonetheless, it will be helpful to us to discuss the socialization of the adolescent with reference to the interpersonal influences of parents and peers, the social organization known as the school, and the system of norms and values commonly called youth culture. Useful, yes, but also artificial and at times quite restrictive; for we shall need to say something about continuing relations with parents at the same time that we discuss the substantial influence of youth culture, and when we consider the preparatory, adult-administered, formal structure of the school, we also are aware that the school provides the social setting in which an adolescent-controlled, informal, present-oriented adolescent subculture exists.

Throughout our remaining discussion, we will be preoccupied with a set of questions not unrelated to the "Sturm und Drang" conception of adolescence stated by G. Stanley Hall in 1904. Are adolescents in revolt against their parents? As peers ascend as significant others, do parents recede into irrelevance, and, if so, protesting or acquiescing? Are sharp breaks in attitudes and values as discernible during adolescence as are changes in dress and associations? Is there a youth culture, or an adolescent society, and if so, is it oppositional to the adult society and does it devise boundaries (in language, ritual, etc.) so as to exclude adult influences except on terms set by adolescents? Or, rather, do adolescents continue in compatible, intense relations with their parents, engaged largely in a set of peer associations and activities encouraged and approved by adults? Is adolescence demonstrably more stressful than, say, old age or the early years of marriage?

A starting point for our discussion is provided by two conditions that we regard as beyond dispute: (1) Adolescence *is* a period of increasing freedom from the influence of parents, including both association and evaluation; peers

---

[2]As early as 1937, E. B. Reuter argued both that the prevalence of adolescent disorder is exaggerated and that prevailing tendencies to offer biological explanations of such disorders as exist simply are not tenable.

are correspondingly more important; and (2) Ours *is* an age-graded society, and from this condition flow reasonably coherent behaviors and values among adolescents that permit reference to youth culture and adolescent society. Thus, we do not take their conditions to be problematic; rather, it is our task to discuss the conditions of their being, their major characteristics, and their consequences for the development of the adolescent.

PARENTS, THE HOME, AND THE ADOLESCENT

Children tend to be like their parents. We would be exceedingly surprised were we to discover, in research on any factor whatsoever, that a knowledge of the parents' position or score on the factor did not predict positively to the score or position of the adolescent. This observation, simple as it is, is remarkable in light of fairly prevalent observations concerning adolescent rebellion, rejection of adult authority, alienation, and parent-child conflict which tempt us to conclude that if parents are relevant at all to the behavior and values of youth, they are relevant as negative role models. Yet there is overwhelming evidence of congruity between, illustratively, parents' social class and the social class of the adolescent's date and friends; between parents' frequency of church attendance, or their religious belief systems, and the religious condition of the adolescent; between parents' education and adolescents' educational plans, aspirations, and performance; between the political party preferences and voting behavior of parents and their offspring; and between the racial views of parents and children. The list might be continued indefinitely. Typically, adolescents are distinguished from one another, and by the same variables, as are adults. It seems clear and basic that any observation about the strength and pervasiveness of peer influence and youth culture must be *in addition* to, or supplemental to, the central fact that parents are major shaping influences in the lives of adolescents. We must understand this foundation principle in order to see other influences on the adolescent in proper perspective.

Since everything we know about the behaviors, memberships, and values of individuals confirms a substantial homogamy between parents and their offspring, it seems obvious that verbal rejection of parents and an increasing time-commitment to persons outside the home need not signify either the dissolution of parental influence or the breaking of kin ties. We need look no further than the clear preservation of substantial bonds between the generations to question the significance customarily attached to loyalties to teen peers. This accent rests on failure to understand the complex and subtle relationship between parent and adolescent, and a failure to appreciate the commitment to preserve the relationship that both hold and treasure. This naivete is nowhere more apparent than in Coleman's resting his case for an adolescent society on a finding that nearly as many adolescents would find it harder to take "breaking with your friend" than "your parents' disapproval" (1961, p. 5).

The intellectual tradition that describes adolescence as marked by conflict with, hostility toward, and rejection of parents and other adults flows from observations of the disruptive effects of rapid social change. These changes mean, it is said, that parents have not encountered the conditions adolescents now face and do not understand the behaviors of adolescents in response to these conditions. Correlatively, parents are not good role models for the world the adolescent anticipates; they are, instead, out of touch and inappropriate. If adolescents recapitulated the lives of their parents in a stable societal setting, this conflict of the generations would be much abated. In effect, parents hold values that differ from those of youth, and they can give youth neither the help nor the understanding their circumstances demand. They are, in a word, not modern enough; there is a basic discontinuity between the generations.[3]

From a more psychological viewpoint, a related intellectual tradition defines the necessary pre-adult intrapsychic processes to include increased ego synthesis and coherence of identity. These processes cannot occur under direct parental influence since the traditional relation of the child to his parents is one of dependency and subservience which is antithetical to the processes now necessary. Further, the nature of identity is always affected by the societal setting in which it occurs, and complex society requires identity-formation under conditions of relative autonomy from parents—in contrast to, for example, simple rural farm settings.

This tradition has made its intellectual contribution but now it requires substantial modification. It rests on an assumption that parents are inept in understanding, resistant to change, and hesitant to grant autonomy. While this may describe a generation of parents in a society newly exposed to rapid change, it is exceedingly doubtful that it adequately explains parents in a society that *assumes* change and development. Under circumstances in which, if Condition X exists at the present, the tacit assumption is made that it will be modified in the future, it is entirely problematic whether those who espouse Condition Not-X in the future will come under moral attack. That is, tension between the generations may result not so much from change itself as from unexpected change and unfamiliarity with change.

There are, on the other hand, quite good reasons to expect that a level of conflict between parents and adolescents will occur. Given that increased autonomy and initiative are *desired* states for the adolescent, some degree of parent-child tension should be expected—especially since the conditions under which the adolescent expresses and experiences this autonomy and initiative are not those that directly further the interest of the adults, as might be the case if the adolescent worked in the same work setting as the father and new job tasks and accomplishments were his primary means for showing an increasing competence and independence (Wolf, 1952).[4] Interactionally, the passage out of dependency is a passage into independency, and the actor acquires a new identity for himself

---

[3]This perspective has been encouraged by accounts of various immigrant groups and the revolt by the second generation against the language and customs of the old world.

[4]See also, discussion of these field materials in Endleman, 1967, pp. 82-127.

as others acquire a new conception of him. It is important to note that a *system* of interactions must be changed and a *system* of identities must also be changed. Mutually, old conceptions of self and other must yield to new ones, and all members of the interactional sphere are involved—most especially, perhaps, the parents, since they must make qualitative changes in their modes of relating to the adolescent, shifting from power to companionship and from instructing to advising.

We will appreciate these complex role and identity transformations more if we contrast the family setting to the simple setting of the school. The role expression, "I am a 6th-grade teacher," means that the incumbent knows how to behave in relation to 6th graders, what to expect of them and what to allow them to expect of her; personalities come and go from year to year as students are promoted, but across the years the persons before her are in a known role (6th graders) and, too, *her* identity is constant (6th-grade teacher). Also, the teacher's expectations of her students, and theirs of her, are reasonably role-specific rather than diffuse, and she, by virtue of the continuity of her identity as 6th-grade teacher, is in a strong position for helping students define what being a 6th grader means. Also, as regards any specific set of 6th-grade students, there is no *historical* relationship between teacher and pupil; that is, neither has to forget previous relationships nor modify prior expectations. By contrast, parent and child are, mutually, learning and evolving a relationship that *is* historical, *is* strongly influenced and contaminated by memories of earlier expectations and performances; in addition, they *are* in a relationship concerning which there are immensely strong social and internal pressures that encourage its continuance at a high level of involvement and commitment.

Whatever the extent of stress and conflict between parents and adolescents, we must assess it in proportion to other powerful facts: the strength of their mutual commitment to preserve the relationship, the extent to which the relationship is mutually treasured, and society's interest in preserving familial bonds. Any scholarly effort to describe and dramatize the growth of peer influences, the power of youth culture, the adolescent's struggle for freedom, etc., must eventually come to terms with the fact that family structures endure through the entire period of adolescence—as residential, affectional, and companionship units.[5]

There are, indeed, very significant forces that subdue the intensity of parent-child conflict or reduce its impact when it occurs. The adolescent, compared to the child, can eat more, lift more, run faster, jump higher, recall more, accomplish more. These are very clear signals and present a very cogent, powerful argument to the parent that his quest for autonomy is both natural and necessary.

---

[5]We could not predict from certain accounts of adolescence that parents attend their child's high school graduation and give gifts gladly received, engage mutually and concernedly with the child in selecting a college, are invited to the child's wedding and do in fact attend, exchange visits and Christmas presents across the generations, are welcomed and eager guests in their child's home, fondle and indulge the grandchild, and eventually are mourned upon their death.

Research evidence suggests, indeed, that parents welcome and anticipate such indications of autonomy-readiness.[6] Autonomy is essential, and parents no less than their children realize that any control system obstructing growth into freedom and responsibility will have pathological outcomes in the adolescents' limited competence to perform in adult functions. Indeed, the typical parent should win any direct confrontation with his child that he actually wants to win, since the simple truth is that parents have considerably more resources than the adolescent has: ultimate control over funds, automobile, house keys, use of home for entertainment, financial support for college and other major expenditures, location of residence, etc. They are likely also to be more skilled in manipulative techniques—including the use of various nonrational powers such as appealing to God's will, society's expectations, family tradition and ancestral standards, and the whole aura of sentiments invoked by the social definition that parents are responsible for and interested only in the child's welfare. If then, parents do not make the decisions and, if necessary, require the adolescent's obeisance, it must be because they do not wish to do so.[7] Altogether, it seems reasonable to interpret most parent-adolescent conflict as occurring not because the direction of the adolescent's quest for greater independence is illegitimate but because perfect congruence in the speed and circumstance under which new forms of expression are tolerable is not achieved.[8]

Were parents to maintain rigidly a conception of proper adolescent behavior reflecting the circumstances of their own youth, there undoubtedly would be an immense incidence of conflict between them and their children under modern conditions of rapid societal change. We observe instead that parents, particularly those in urban middle-class settings, value companionship with their children and are strongly motivated to be knowledgeable about the conditions and circumstances of contemporary youth.[9] Many parents are extremely reluctant to establish constraints that appear to handicap the adolescent in his social activities and competition for status and acceptance; they may ask him, or the parents of his friends, what the other children are wearing, how late they can stay up, how much money they are given to spend, when dating is permitted,

---

[6]In a presently unpublished study, I presented parents of high school seniors in ten North Carolina counties with a list of twenty-four possible criticisms of their child or of the relationship between them, and asked the parents to check any and all that apply. The items refer generally to issues of autonomy versus control and closeness versus apartness. The wish for greater independent behavior by the child is expressed very frequently: "I would teach her/him to be more independent than she/he is" is fourth most frequently checked item, for example.

[7]Sam Shepard, district school superintendent in St. Louis, acknowledges this in advising parents concerning their need to see to it that the child does his homework. After assuring parents that the school will give homework every day, he advises them what to do when the child says he has no homework: "The first time, go along with the child and accept his word; the second time, do whatever it is you do in those circumstances when you know that you and not the child are going to prevail."

[8]An unknown incidence of parent-child conflict and tension occurs from the opposite direction, i.e., from the failure and reluctance of the adolescent to "grow up."

[9]This is, indeed, sometimes carried to petty extremes, as in the case of middle-aged women whose purpose in life continues to revolve around the high-school sorority.

etc. Given these pressures toward consensual validation, together with the fact that the adolescent, being human, will follow normal processes of trying to maximize his gains and pleasures, this information exchange probably increases the freedoms available to the adolescent while reducing the amount of adult-type behavior demanded of him. The point to be emphasized is that clashes between the generations are not death struggles. Parents and children are not trying to destroy each other; they are playing the game together, and have the same goals: to secure the capacity of the child for self-direction and self-maintenance, and to preserve a familial network and strong affectional bonds. Note that in groups in which the adolescent's wish for peer acceptance and participation are more intense, parent pressures often increase in the same direction; Douvan and Adelson (1966, p. 320), for example, report that upper-middle class children are the most likely to be responsive to the judgment of the peer group *and* that girls from professional and managerial backgrounds most often report that their parents expect them to be popular and well liked by peers.

Another indication of the fit between parent expectations and adolescent values lies in the substantial amount of coaching in role performance that adolescents receive from their (typically same-sex) parent, in dress, carriage, etiquette, social skills, college selection, entertainment, and athletic development. Indeed, the ready accommodation that parents make to certain adolescent expressive behaviors may encourage their more extreme elaboration, since adolescent slang and other fads lose their symbolic significance and their real function of group identification and boundary drawing when adopted by adults. The halting, modest efforts of adolescents to rebel, gain distinction, show independence, and create distinctive group forms represent an effort to demonstrate, and gain recognition of, a new status and sense of self. More extreme instances of expressive behavior are encouraged by adults who, by imitating adolescent conduct and language, rob them of their meaning and value.

Finally, we should remind ourselves that the special intimacies and commitments of the family bond create conditions that encourage controlled disagreement and the restoration of tolerance and affection. There is a substantial give on both sides, and the avoidance of direct confrontation is valued. Also, the ecology of adolescent behavior functions to reduce the probability of head-on clashes, since a very large proportion of adolescent behavior does not occur under adult surveillance and adolescents do not emit clear signals to parents concerning these (possibly deviant) behaviors; thus ignorance is possible.[10]

The research literature is almost entirely compatible with the conclusions that ties between parents and children remain close throughout the adolescent years; that the positive orientation toward parents does not diminish, and may indeed increase, during adolescence; and that parents and the parent-child relationship both are important influences on the adolescent. Kahl (1953) has shown that high aspirations among "common man" boys occur when parents

---

[10]See Moore and Tumin (1949). Sherif and Sherif (1964) argue that parents simply do not know about much of the questionable behavior of adolescents.

are unsatisfied with their position and encourage their sons to improve on it; they tend not to occur when parents are satisfied and do not stress the advantages of education. Douvan and Adelson (1966, Chapter 5), with a national sample of adolescents, report these findings: more boys name their father, more girls name their mother, as their adult ideal than name any other figure; the proportion of girls regarding parents' rules as right and fair *increases* from ages 12-14 to ages 17-18; and the proportion of girls who want their parents to be less restrictive decreases over the same age period. (These latter two findings suggest that most parent-child conflicts may be concentrated in the *early* years of adolescence.) Dentler and Monroe (1961) found that weak home ties and strained parent-child relations associate positively with patterns of deviant conduct. Rosen (1955), asking Jewish adolescents to name persons whose opinions matter a great deal to them, found more than 90 per cent named one parent or both, and in almost all cases named them *first*. Stone (1960) found that students active in high school organizations and activities more typically had excellent relations with their parents, suggesting that peer group status and close parent-child relations are quite compatible events. Correspondingly, Brittain (1963) found that high-school girls who gave peer-conforming (as against parent-conforming) responses to hypothetical dilemmas had *lower* status among peers, which suggests that positive orientation toward parents is itself a peer value. Epperson (1964) asking pre-adolescent and adolescent respondents whether disapproval of parents, favorite teacher, or best friend would make them most unhappy, found over 80 per cent indicating that parental disapproval would be hardest to bear. Middleton and Putney (1963), studying college students, found that they are more likely to differ with their parents on political matters when parent and offspring are emotionally estranged. Bowerman and Kinch (1959) suggest, in discussing their study of changes in parent-peer orientations between grades 4 and 10, that a lowered orientation toward the family accompanies a normal increase in orientation to peers during adolescence only under conditions of poor adjustment within the family, and thus is not inevitable. The research results also are compatible with the view that parent-child conflict when it occurs is more likely related to trivial matters than to basic issues and values.

Probably, we must restore a degree of balance in closing this section. Some adolescents do engage in, and develop, social systems that adults oppose and decry with great fervor, and available evidence suggests that such adolescent systems may be remarkably resistant to adult intervention.[11] Also, behaviors that are trivial in their ultimate implications for basic values and goals make up a substantial portion of the everyday world even of adults, and we must not denigrate the relevance that conflicts over small matters may have for interpersonal relations or minimize the emotional energy they may absorb. Finally, it is important that we not overemphasize the extent to which parents penetrate the lives of adolescents or adopt their standards to the pressures of the moment. A later section considers

---

[11]For example: Polsky (1962), Short and Strodtbeck (1965), Meyer, Borgatta and Jones (1965), and Smith and Kleine (1966, pp. 424-436, and the bibliography).

the great importance of peers and student cultures to adolescent socialization. Nonetheless, we would not want to confuse episode for pattern, and it does appear that the pervasive, continuing influence of parents as agents of socialization is not expressed best in a conflict mode or negative role-model terms.

PEERS AND YOUTH CULTURE

James S. Coleman in 1961 published *The Adolescent Society,* one of the most significant and competent empirical works produced by American social science. It is now the focus of a considerable controversy, partly because of its overstatement but also on more basic grounds, and a review of its major arguments will help introduce the analysis of peer pressures and youth culture as influences in adolescent socialization.

Coleman reports data gathered in the late 1950's by questionnaire and record-search from the student bodies of ten high schools in the Chicago area ranging in size from 169 to 1,935 students. The task was to describe the adolescent society: its values, its heroes and leaders, the things that determine success and status within it, its associational structures, and their joint effects on the scholastic performance and self-satisfactions of the high school students.

Schools are important institutions in American society not only because they offer formal instruction to the young but also because they are the physical locus for the adolescent society; they are the setting that creates a sufficient demographic density to allow adolescents to build their own social world. A major discovery of Coleman's work is that the presumed *sine qua non* of educational institutions—scholarship—is less valued in adolescent culture than are various other activities, especially athletics for boys and club activities for girls. (Such data lend indirect evidence concerning the strength of adolescent society, since contravalues to formal educational goals survive and flourish in the very setting of the school.)

The adolescent system has meaningful rewards and punishments to bestow, and since this is so, adolescents direct the flow of their energies into activities which maximize the rewards they will receive from the system; the presumption is that the quality of participation in clubs and sports more nearly stretches the potential of the students than do scholarly pursuits, and that especially bright students in particular will understand the reward system and commit their energies appropriately. Findings bear quite directly on the latter point: the smaller the per cent of students in the school who value scholarship, the smaller the difference in standard deviation units between the mean IQ score of the student body and the mean IQ of the students with the highest grades. Best scholars are less well-satisfied with themselves and their status in the system, compared to best athletes, and, considering only those who are *both* scholars and athletes, the vast majority would prefer to be remembered in school as athletic stars rather than as brilliant students. Persons who are members of the leading crowds in these adolescent societies (and presumed to be the normative pace-setters) are especially likely to value athletics and clubs over scholarship. The scholarly student brings glory only to himself (and even must create some of the sense of glory) and follows a lonely pursuit; the club activist and athletic participant engage in inter-personal activities that bring glory and satisfaction to others. Adolescents are said to orient primarily toward this adolescent society, to prefer its pleasures to those given by parents and other adults, and indeed to have only tenuous, often ritualized, ties to the larger institutions of the adult world.

Major responsibilities are placed on the educational system by dominant trends in the modern world: The facts of social change, economic specialization, and technical growth create the need for better informed, more technically skilled young who have been taught by more specialized personnel for longer periods of time than a past age demanded. The consequence is the growth, extension, and elaboration of the public school system, and school becomes the place where during half of his waking hours most months of the year the American adolescent spends his time. It is a setting numerically and interpersonally dominated by age-peers, and provides the shared experiences, common problems, and communication ease from which spring unique perspectives and consensual values. The school grounds are the adolescent's psychological and ecological turf; even if intrapsychic and intrafamilial processes did not make the adolescent's peers attractive to him as comparison points and norm-senders, the physical clustering in schools for such long periods would produce the same high salience of peers. These physical conditions also facilitate the transmission of a culture from one generation of students to the next; each September, a new cohort arrives and is exposed to various informal processes that have the net effect of transmitting system definitions to the novitiates.[12] Coleman describes the total consequences in these words:

> This setting-apart of our children in schools—which take on ever more functions, ever more "extracurricular activities"—for an ever longer period of training has a singular impact on the child of high-school age. He is "cut off" from the rest of society, forced inward toward his own age group, made to carry out his whole social life with others his own age. With his fellows, he comes to constitute a small society, one that has most of its important interactions *within* itself, and maintains only a few threads of connection with the outside adult society. In our modern world of mass communication and rapid diffusion of ideas and knowledge, it is hard to realize that separate subcultures can exist right under the very noses of adults —subcultures with languages all their own, with special symbols, and, most importantly, with value systems that may differ from adults. . . . Society is confronted no longer with a set of *individuals* to be trained toward adulthood, but with distinct social *systems,* which offer a united front to the overtures made by adult society. Thus, the very changes that society is undergoing have spawned something more than was bargained for. They have taken not only job-training out of the parents' hands, but have quite effec-

---

[12]Coleman (1961) does not deal with this indoctrination process nor its consequences, but it presumably is similar to the college-level influences that depress educational goals as reported in Wallace (1966, pp. 65-66).

tively taken away the whole adolescent himself. . . . The elites in the school are not closer to their parents than are the students as a whole, but are pulled slightly farther from parents, closer to fellow-adolescents as a source of approval and disapproval. Thus, those who "set the standard" are more oriented than their followers to the adolescent culture itself. . . . They (adolescents) are still oriented toward fulfilling their parents' desires, but they look very much to their peers for approval as well. Consequently, our society has within its midst a set of small teen-age societies, which focus teen-age interests and attitudes on things far removed from adult responsibilities, and which may develop standards that lead away from those goals established by the larger society (Coleman, 1961, pp. 3, 4, 6, 9).

It is well to note at this point that Coleman does not contend that parents and teachers become irrelevant to adolescents. Indeed, in a footnote to the last part of the quotation above, he quotes a perceptive teen-ager as suggesting that adolescent society is merely an immature adult society which borrows the glamorous and sophisticated part of adult society but scorns the high goals and worthwhile activities of the adult world because these involve responsibilities which the adolescent is not ready to accept (Coleman, 1961, p. 9). To cite other evidence, Coleman reports that about 53 per cent of his respondents selected parents in answering this question, "Which one of these things would be hardest for you to take: your parents' disapproval, your teacher's disapproval, or breaking with your friend?" as against about 43 per cent who selected friend. In commenting on this "rather even split" he observes: "The balance between parents and friends indicates the extent of the state of transition that adolescents experience—leaving one family, but not yet in another, they consequently look both forward to their peers and backward to their parents" (Coleman, 1961, p. 5). Nonetheless, the total emphasis of his report has encouraged many to think of an adolescent world that is immune if not antagonistic to adult values and control. In the terms of politics, these two domains maintain diplomatic relations but view each other with deep suspicion while fighting a sort of cold war.

One additional observation should be made: Coleman's analysis is at the level of the school (or grade in school) as a social system; he is much less concerned with partitioning and differentiation within this system, thus he is little concerned with the influence of smaller substructures in the form of cliques, academic club groups, friends, etc. For example, it remains quite possible that certain socially significant clusterings within the high school are more congruent with adult values and the formal purposes of the school than is indicated in his discussion. His work underplays associational and value diversity within the system.

Despite the attention Coleman's work has received, the idea of a separate social system of adolescence certainly did not originate with him. Indeed, one of the most widely cited *attacks* on the idea of an adolescent society antedates Coleman's work by six years (Elkin & Westley, 1955), and the authors of this critique correctly find support for their position in social stratification studies that demonstrate the continuity of class-related behaviors and values across the generations.[13] Coleman's work itself is directly in the tradition of earlier empirical work by Gordon (1957) which in turn derives from a much older descriptive and theoretical heritage.[14]

Argument over whether there are or are not adolescent societies and youth cultures easily becomes as sterile as the older heredity and environment controversy, as Smith and Kleine (1966, p. 425) observe. The question of whether an adolescent society exists is ultimately a matter of definition. Also, this question is separable analytically from questions of whether this social system (assuming it exists) creates values that are alien to those in some other system, e.g., formal education, parents, or adults in general; of the extent of insulation, hostility, separation, or other devices that maximize intrasystem interaction and restrict contacts across systems; of the degree of value congruence and consensus among participants in the society; of whether participation in and loyalty to the society is characteristic of all, most, or only some adolescents; of whether it is a system that touches the lives of adolescents in a diffuse and pervasive manner, including basic values and central dimensions of the self, or whether instead it deals mostly with occasional matters and general trivia ; of whether participants in other pertinent systems view it with alarm or, at the other extreme, sponsor and encourage it; and of whether its roots lie in confused societal definitions of the adolescent period, in the "storm and stress" of adolescence or an accompanying quest for identity, or in any other postulated source.

If simple *association* and *communication* are the central components of the definition, there is no question that such societies exist; adolescents spend a tremendous amount of time with each other and in conversation with each other. If *interpersonal salience* is the key (by which we mean that adolescents resonate to the expectations of each other, compose a set of reference groups and persons, and are affected by judgments of them made by their peers), again, there can be no issue about adolescent societies except as whether other adolescents are the *only* foci of orientation becomes an issue. The definitional concern and controversy really hinges, then, on two very related issues: whether the "society" has autonomy, and whether it is distinctive. The issue would be meaningless if adolescents in their separate associations merely recapitulated the behaviors and values of adults whenever they could do so appropriately, and the issue would be pretentious if adolescents in employing their peers as reference persons were guided to the same decisions and energy-allocations as had they turned to parents, teachers, or adult neighbors. It is essential, then, as the term is used, to define behaviors and values that are, minimally, distinctive from adult norms and, preferably, oppositional to them; further, the topic is trivial if the issues on which there is opposition are trivial.

---

[13]Elkin and Westley cite particularly Hollingshead (1949) in this regard. And Coleman (1961, p. 94), quite aware of this relevance, includes "Elmtown" among his ten schools and explicitly contends that the ascriptive criteria of family background are unimportant in determining the status system among Elmtown's high-school students.

[14]Examples of the earlier literature include Parsons (1942) and his numerous restatements; K. Davis (1944) ; Tryon (1944) ; and Williams (1960, pp. 77-80).

Though we have contended earlier that parents and adolescents get along remarkably well and that parents are substantial influences throughout the adolescent period, we are prepared now, in apparent contradiction, to take the position that the concept of an adolescent society is a useful description and analytical tool. Its distinctions in comparison to adult society are typically those of relative emphasis, and when it is subversive or substitutive of adult values, these "adult values" most typically represent what *some* adults want *some* of the time. We will not find values wholly absent in adolescent society but wholly present in adult society—or vice versa.[15] The concept does provide us with a handy device for describing some things that make the period of youth relatively distinctive in the life cycle. I will not want my use of the term to connote a subversive system nor one necessarily inappropriate to preparation for adult life.

It will be useful in thinking about the nature of adolescent society relative to parents, adults, schools, and other socializing agencies, to concern ourselves briefly with the conditions that affect the emphasis of this culture. As Scott points out in *Values and Organizations* (1965), the need for socialization and personal change is an inverse function of an organization's success in recruitment, i.e., the more it recruits "our type of person," the less intensive is the necessary re-training. Correlatively, the less should be the discontinuity between the person's past and future when the organization recruits "its type," and finally, to the extent that the social base from which an organization draws its clientele and membership is congruent with the nature of the organization, the less should be the tension between the organization, its recruits, and the client base. These observations suggest that an autonomous, distinctive student culture is least likely to develop in schools where the student body is homogenous, the students know each other in nonschool (e.g., neighborhood) contexts, parents are closely associated with the school and its personnel, and the school's program is in harmony with its environs; and is most likely to develop in schools with opposite characteristics. It follows that the conditions that permit a distinctive student culture are precisely those that maximize the opportunities for school personnel (as an official body) to have a distinctive and autonomous influence on the student, as against merely reinforcing and extending the values and authority of the home and neighborhood. Thus the school as a formal organization is most likely to be an autonomous, distinctive influence under the same conditions as peers are most likely to provide distinctive choice-models for the student.

THE ADOLESCENT SOCIETY AND SOCIALIZATION

To understand the adolescent society in its relevance to socialization, we shall need to bear in mind important differences between the circumstances of the adolescent and those of the child. There are two ways of doing this: one is to

---

[15]But the same observation applies if we contrast Russian to American society, the 1780's to the 1960's, or Yankees in Boston with Negroes in rural Alabama.

describe the widening range of experiences and influences the adolescent encounters; the other is to consider the societal needs and conditions that determine the extent of this widening range. They are in fact closely related and we can consider them together.

Children grow up in families, and the contemporary American family is a remarkably simple structure usually composed of only mother, father, and a small number of children. It often has about as many control agents and norm-senders (parents) as there are control subjects and norm-receivers (children).[16] Relations within the family have the following features: they are age-heterogeneous, ascriptive, particularistic, and diffuse. Societies differ in the extent to which these features govern relations in the various institutional areas, and there are some major spheres of life in every society that are regulated by criteria different from these. In an important work, Eisenstadt (1956) has shown that the transition from childhood to adulthood goes smoothly when the value system of the society heavily emphasizes the principles that regulate family life; otherwise, the transference of identification and the extension of solidarity from family to other sets of relations that are organized by different criteria will be disruptive, and age-homogeneous groups arise at such points to ease the transition. Were occupational and familial role requirements more similar, and in general if the modes of relating in manifold adult social situations were replicative of those experienced in family life, life-cycle transitions would be continuous and gradual, and the need for age-homogeneous groups would not exist.[17] Most particularly, it is the change from the particularistic relations of the family to the universalistic relations of the extended world that occasions difficulty for the personality, basically for two reasons: one, the loss of emotional security provided by the attachments that inhere in particularistic relations; and two, the major change that is required in emotional attitudes toward social objects and in criteria that govern one's relations with them. Adolescent peer groups emerge in the "space" between kinship relations and those governed by achievement criteria, relative specificity of role demand, and universalistic standards of evaluation (Eisenstadt, 1956, pp. 42-51). In addition to acquainting the adolescent with the symbols of identification and standards of evaluation of the larger adult society, age-homogeneous groups provide a setting in which the young person's current dispositions and values are affirmed and in which greater spontaneity in expressive activity is encouraged (Eisenstadt, 1956, p. 166). Peer groups are the bridge between childhood and adulthood when society is complex enough that attainment of full adult status cannot be insured in the family unit (Eisenstadt, 1963, pp. 24-42).

The "classical" statement concerning the sources of intensive conflict be-

---

[16]Granted, these roles can be reversed, with children as the control-agents and norm-senders. But this possibility is not relevant here.

[17]Eisenstadt (1956) observes that the "father" as observed by the child in family settings behaves by standards quite different from those he follows as "male at work." It is in a similar sense that Erikson (1954, p. 57) observes none of the identifications of childhood are with whole people but with different part-aspects (body-parts, habitual activities, and social role) of those by whom they are most directly affected.

tween parents and adolescents, in relation to which a youth culture of given characteristics develops, goes something like this: The givens of age differentiation in
the society, of reduced normative flexibility with increasing age, and the physical,
psychological, and sociological differences between the age groups, establish the
foundations or potential of conflict. The variables that activate this potential and
determine its intensity are the rate of social change, the degree of cultural integration, and the amount of vertical mobility. The setting is complicated further by
the long years of formal education that separate youth from adulthood, theory
from practice, school from life; and by the fact that the adolescent is physically
the equal or superior of adults but socially is subordinated to adults. The authority
of parents, then, is an inherent potential source of conflict, but normally it is bearable because the child lacks knowledge of any other possible structure of interaction, the emotional setting of the family softens the harshness of authority, and
the frequency and intensity of the interaction provide the child with ways of expressing his will within this authority system. However, various contemporary
processes increase the problematic qualities of this authority and make it less
tolerable. These include conflicting norms within the culture, competing authorities such as teachers, the concentration of emotional energies within a small
family, the failure to institutionalize the necessary process by which parental authority atrophies,[18] the definitions of sex in modern society that make parent-child
discourse taboo and lead parents to control by indirect and devious means, and
the emphasis on social mobility that requires many career decisions to be made
during adolescence on which parents' evaluation of future possibilities differs
from that of their child (K. Davis, 1940, 1944).

Youth culture arises with a set of values and perspectives that, given these
tensions, is more satisfying and is experienced as more appropriate by the adolescent. This culture includes the following characteristics: Having a good time is
important, particularly social activities in company with the opposite sex; there
is a strong hedonistic quality. On the male side, extreme emphasis is given to
athletics, and this is a measure of valued masculinity, as sexual attractiveness is a
measure of valued femininity for females. Explicit acceptance of adult-sponsored
interests, expectations, and discipline is negatively valued. Common human elements are emphasized among associates, such as, that a person is valued humanistically for his general demeanor and attractiveness rather than instrumentally for
performance as a competent specialist. Glamour and excitement are sought, and
the luxuriant waste of time is virtuous (Parsons, 1942). Certain major centrifugal
forces operate to secure one's release from this culture as he approaches maturity,
permitting us to speak of self-liquidating features of it (Parsons, 1951, p. 305).
Not only does the adolescent need the psychological security of commonly situated
peers as he moves outward from the family circle, but conditions operative in this
peer setting provide him with needed experiences he is most unlikely to have
received in the family of his childhood. For example, relative to both the family

---

[18]Actually, Deutscher (1962, 1964) concludes that parents readily adapt to "postparental" life and may be disposed to anticipate it.

and the school, the peer group provides a setting in which the power-differential is enormously narrowed (Parsons & Bales, 1955, pp. 108-122). The norm of reciprocity, too, is learned in its fully developed form only in the peer group and not before. This process is valuable for the parents and for their relations with their offspring, since gradually as the child's circle expands and he responds to the evaluative criteria of various others, parents also learn to assess the child not only with reference to familial membership but by reasonably detached, universalistic appraisal of his behavior (Parsons & Bales, 1955, p. 117). The substitution of a lateral for a vertical structure of authority is an essential feature of the adolescent's movement from the associations of the family to those of his fellow youth. Adolescents accept positions of formal authority over their fellows only with great reluctance, especially if this authority is seen as sponsored by adults, and they resist recognition of leadership structures in their informal groups. These attitudes suggest that the model of peer relations is more that of a brotherhood than, say, of a hierarchical arrangement of authority such as a family or a bureaucracy. Parsons has made the following appropriate observation on this point:

> Here it is not without significance that the most prominent class of undergraduate college social clubs are called fraternities and sororities. Members address each other as "brother" and "sister," especially on ceremonial occasions. It is certainly significant that these are symbolized as groups of "siblings" *without* the participation of parent-symbols. The "old grads" are not referred to as "fathers" but are "older brothers." There is, to be sure, sometimes the vaguely benevolent figure of the "house mother," but emphatically never a "house father." In the light of the functions of the youth culture in the process of emancipation from dependence on the conjugal family, particularly the parents, this symbolization is appropriate and significant (1951, pp. 406-407).

Matza (1961) suggests that youth culture has the advantage to society of reducing serious deviancy and the deviant tradition. There are, he says, three major themes in delinquent values, each of which in one way or another involves the celebration of personal prowess: the restless search for excitement, thrills, or kicks; the dreams of quick success, of securing large material awards while avoiding the canons of methodism, security, and routine emphasized by school and work; and aggressive assertion and defense of the self, sometimes called the code of the warrior. Teen-age culture is the conventional version of delinquency, conventional in that it strips away delinquency's most odious features. Teen-age culture emphasizes fun and adventure; it is disdainful of scholastic effort, especially of its visible manifestations; it involves persistent flirtation with boundary areas between propriety and immorality, and tolerates various status offenses such as staying out late, drinking, some sexual explorations, and "conning" parents; and though aggression is substantially tempered, concern with masculine and feminine credentials and recognition is substantial. Teen-age culture, as Matza sees it, is institutionalized "playing at" serious forms of deviance; its great social virtue and contribution is that it offers sufficient inherent satisfactions to attract and maintain the loyalty of many adherents who otherwise would be vulnerable to the appeals of delinquency.

Parents and community representatives do not, of course, analyze either personal or societal needs in everyday discourse in the abstract terms used in this analysis. Yet there is widespread evidence that the adolescent's efforts to gain autonomy and a set of experiences extending beyond the family circle is complemented by adults' acknowledgment that such experiences are necessary preconditions for personal maturity. Therefore, it is easy to exaggerate the degree of discontinuity between the values of the home and those of the peer group. It is easy because the behavior of the adolescent encourages the exaggeration. Telephone conversations, sock colors and heights, pennies in Bass weejuns, shrieks, buttons, slang, old jalopies, and the Beatles suggest that the really meaningful significant others in the adolescent's life space are his fellow adolescents. Too, many of his behaviors suggest the cogency of Mark Twain's famous observation about his judgments of his father: "When I was a boy of fourteen," he said, "my father was so ignorant I could hardly stand to have the old man around. But when I got to be twenty-one, I was astonished at how much the old man had learned in seven years." Yet, it is one thing to observe that adolescents may value certain activities and possessions that certain adult institutions question or oppose, and quite a more difficult task to document that these adolescent values develop and flourish without significant encouragement and appreciation from many adults. It is the drug store owner, the proud father, the striving mother, the man next door, no less than the fellow student who honor Saturday's hero and the beauty queen. Especially in suburban middle-class schools, nothing is more reasonable than to interpret sports, dating, and clubs as para-adult institutions, as practice and preparation for the real thing. Coleman (1961, p. 32) reports, for example, that parents would more likely be proud of their children for making the basketball team than for being made student assistant in a science laboratory.[19]

It is a distinctive feature of the public school system that it provides a demographic mass sufficiently dense to make possible the development and maintenance of an autonomous adolescent social system. The school is, in a real sense, the adolescent's world and they may be more excited about a contest for student body president than adults are about the mayoralty election. But by and large, the adolescent society provides a play-autonomy that adults are content to let prevail precisely because it is nonthreatening and because it is, after all, good practice and good experience. The alternative prospect—of continued close supervision, of contrived and irregular opportunities for self-determination, self-expression, and self-experimentation, of full rather than shared responsibility for the child's socialization—is not an attractive one for parents to contemplate.

---

[19]In my own unpublished study referred to in footnote 6, fathers and mothers, asked whether they would rather have been remembered in school as "brilliant student, star athlete, most popular, or leader in activities," favor the first over the fourth, with the middle two lagging far behind. But, asked how they prefer to have their child remembered in high school, more elect "leader in activities" than elect "brilliant student."

Parents may not be social scientists, but they know full well that the role structure of the modern family is not sufficiently differentiated to provide the range of socialization experiences the adolescent needs in modern society.

Intensive loyalties to a few persons may be thought of as "entangling alliances," they reduce autonomy, encourage particularism, limit mobility, and constrict the range of experience. Indeed, the adolescent who defines a stable, restricted clique, or "goes steady" for extended periods, exchanges family for another interactional setting without adding substantially to the range and diversity of his repertoire of significant others. As associations range wider, one's loyalties become more diffuse, his capacity for "getting along with different kinds of people" increases, and his repertoire of roles is extended. In a word, he is free to respond, and prepared for response, to the occupational demands and opportunities of a mobile, industrial society. Skill in the casual cordiality that marks the business world and the country club is acquired with relative ease when one's life-space is flooded with age-mates toward each of whom one invests a modest, but only modest, degree of positive affect (Schmuck & Lohman, 1965, p. 27). I am describing the modern urban high school, and I am saying that it is a useful, functional mediating institution between the intensive emotional ties of the family, which is a small unit, and the wide-ranging work and social world of adulthood. I am saying also that the peer group loyalties that develop and express themselves on this school stage need not, and typically do not, threaten the emotional bond between adolescent and family. This is so partly because parents expect and desire this growth of extrafamilial involvement (there is more normative consensus among adults about adolescence than we often acknowledge), partly because though adolescents may appear to take their families for granted they rarely seriously desire a permanent rupture or perceive their peers as seriously competitive for their familial loyalties.[20]

The increased differentiation of the adolescent period, the larger number of stimulus-objects to which the adolescent is sensitive, and the expansion of his repertoire of roles, is typically additive rather than substitutive. Adolescence, too, often has been analyzed within a conflict mode which assumes that parents, siblings, and adults become enemies as peers become friends and recording stars become heroes. Loyalty to A is assumed to preclude loyalty to B. This is not a necessary nor even very likely condition, and it is well to observe the powerful influence of parents in the adolescent's selection of peer intimates. (The general principle is that significant others at time I are forces affecting the selection of significant others at time II.) Not only may parents have a direct involvement in who the child selects for his friends, but such values of parents as the child has internalized, and such commitment to parents as he experiences, are independent

---

[20]In a national sample of boys age 14-16, only 29 per cent list acceptance by others among the things boys worry about most, compared to 57 per cent who mention such achievement themes as doing well in school. And the 29 per cent decomposes into 21 per cent mentioning "girls" compared to only 8 per cent mentioning acceptance by peers. Also, almost half (44 per cent) report that they never disagree with parents, and no more than 17 per cent disagree on any specific topic (Survey Research Center, 1955, Table 13, p. 35).

forces in the same direction. All boundary-maintaining systems, such as social class, religion, community, race, and morality, have the effect of reducing the range of choices available to the adolescent, which in effect means that those adolescents most likely to be chosen as friends and associates are precisely those reared in homes substantially similar to the subject's home. In addition, there is theoretical reason to expect that the adolescent, like others, normally selects friends in such a way as to minimize, not magnify, the diversity of expectational systems to which he is exposed.

The rules of the society of adolescents are unwritten and often unspoken. They thus are more subtle, elusive, diffuse, than are the parental "do's" and "don't's" of childhood, or the explicit rules of children's games, and thus they help prepare the adolescent to participate in and be controlled by a larger normative order that is too complex to be reduced to injunctions and legal codes. The activities of adolescents have a normative structure (Moore & Anderson, 1960) that differs from the normative structures of childhood in being less explicit and, contrasted to parents, lacking clearly designated persons of superior status who are the exemplars, proponents, and sanctioning agents of the moral code.

One final observation should be made about the functions served by youth society. There is very substantial emphasis in our attitudes toward the youth period as one of preparation. The time perspective tilts strongly toward the future and the structured activities in which adolescents are required to engage often are defended because they are requisite to some future activities. Adolescents are engaged in activities that are defended far less for their intrinsic worth or gratification than because they are qualificatory to a desired state in adulthood. The emphasis on what Schneider and Lysgaard (1953) term deferred gratification is endemic in the adolescent's life, and although Schneider and Lysgaard see the condition as characterizing the middle class rather than the working and lower classes, our point would be that it is a pervasive feature of the dominant themes communicated by adults to the young of whatever class position. Even current propaganda encouraging young people not to quit school prematurely does not plead the case for the pleasures of the school experience but argues rather that a time will come in the future when one will regret the present personal indulgence of school withdrawal. The emphasis on the preparatory relevance of adolescent experiences carries, too, the definite connotation that the present state is a temporary and transitional one. What is now will not be then, and the really important things come not now but later.

In the midst of such themes of impermanence, preparation, and transition, the activities and values of peer culture have a very solid here-and-now quality about them. Attention orients to the present and the immediate future; conversation flows around what happened last night, who's doing what today, and when the next test is. Though to the detached observer the experiences adolescents create for themselves aid and abet the sense of impermanence and rapid transition —language expressions come and go like magic, recording stars have very brief moments of glory, and yesterday's styles are taboo today—the meaning is quite different to the participants. There is an immediacy about things that gives a power and significance to the present; things are important today. One is living rather than preparing to live, one has being and identity in a system that posts the score and declares the winners now; while French class may be useful if one ever encounters a Frenchman or travels abroad, knowing slang gives validation tonight. Ultimately, French belongs to "them" and is imposed on "us," but the things adolescent culture values are "our" creations, offering useful protection from the implication that the present is a meaningless and worthless state except as it is used to qualify for some desired, remote condition of the future.

SCHOOLS AND ADOLESCENT SOCIALIZATION

Schools have various important relevances to the socialization of adolescents.[21] They are, as we have noted, the physical setting for the youth culture and the various peer groups and cliques that engage the attention of the young. Schools also are charged specifically with the responsibility for preparing the young to function as adults by giving them the skill, attitude, and knowledge bases necessary for good citizenship and economic self-sufficiency. They also are widely recognized as an indispensable vehicle by which those of humble birth improve their station in life, and thus are the means by which lower-class members gain a sufficient acquaintance with middle-class skills that their personal chances of becoming middle class are enhanced. It is in this sense that schools supposedly reduce the power of family and birth as determinative forces in the allocation of privilege. In connection with their essential operation of transmitting the culture, including values as well as information, to the next generation, schools also establish social groups in which the young acquire interpersonal skills; provide personnel in the form of teachers, counselors, and coaches who represent the adult world and are approved to serve as exemplars and role models for students; and have control of substantial sanctioning devices by which to reinforce socially acceptable behavior on the part of children (Goslin, 1965, p. 65). As Goslin remarks (1965, p. 71), the school introduces children, probably for the first time, to institutionalized controls over individual behavior in a formal organization.

Under a system of universal public education, the schools are required to accept and educate all children who apply and meet the quite minimum standards of decorum involved in accepting the school's rules of conduct; in complementary fashion, public law requires that children maintain their enrollment in a school system at least until some minimum age, typically 16, and in point of fact most adolescents continue their education well beyond this minimum age. One way of appreciating the school's potential for socialization lies in a simple reckoning of the amount of time adolescents, certainly those in early and mid-adolescence, spend in school and in activities forced or encouraged by the school. From September until June, children awake five mornings each week and engage them-

---

[21]There is an excellent synthesis of a wide and disparate literature, generally relevant to this section, in Boocock, 1966.

selves instantly in dressing and otherwise preparing for school. They spend 6 to 7 hours daily participating in the formal instructional program of the school, and often remain under school influences after hours while they practice drama or band, attend club meetings, or practice as members of athletic teams. When they return home in the afternoons, it is probable that they must do homework for several hours before retiring for the night. One spends substantially more time in the presence of teachers and classmates than with his parents, sibs, or neighbors. School is where the adolescent spends his time.

It follows that those who run the schools make decisions of momentous significance for the development of the adolescent. They set the curriculum content and requirements that determine the nature and organization of the knowledge presented to students. They purchase equipment and facilities that establish the physical setting within which learning occurs and affect the ease with which teachers undertake to teach. They establish standards by which they seek and employ the instructional staff, and they assign teachers and administrators to particular schools. Finally, and very importantly, they determine who the student's classmates will be by establishing attendance districts and assigning particular students to particular schools. When they are concerned about the extent of differences between one school and another, both professional educators and social reformers historically have focused their attention on the first two of these features: curricula and physical facilities. But from the standpoint of socialization influences, it is the overlooked power of teachers and classmates that gives the school its distinguishing potency.

There is strong evidence that differentiation occurs both within and between schools which has the basic effect of reducing the autonomous influence of the school system on the development of its students. The internal differentiation shows most clearly along curricular lines, with middle-class students taking college preparatory work in large proportions while substantial numbers from working-class backgrounds are enrolled in general and vocational curriculums. Comparing one school with another, the distinction involves segregation of students along social class, racial, and to some extent ethnic lines, and comes about because schools follow geographic lines in their assignment policies. That is, schools have their individual service areas, best expressed in the concept of neighborhood schools. Since people sort themselves residentially along income, race, and ethnic lines, any given urban school tends strongly to be more homogenous than the total community. Given this homogenization of the student body, it is possible, and tempting, for school administrations to assign teachers who are similar in background to the students they teach. This is in fact a common outcome, the best but not the only example of which is the great frequency with which Negro teachers and principals are assigned to schools that are totally or largely Negro in the composition of the student body. The net effects of these practices make for a conservatizing influence from the schools; they "mirror" the adult world as presently constituted and give their clients experiences that tend to perpetuate such arrangements of the present. Whether or not, or the extent to which, these conditions are inevitable is one of the nation's major present concerns, and discussion of this central feature of the schools does not imply its easy remediation.

The significance of this school effect may be dramatized by a brief description of the classmates of the average Negro child compared to those of the average white child in the United States. The average Negro student in the United States, compared to the average white student, is more likely to have classmates

—whose parents are not high-school graduates
—who came from large families
—whose homes are not intact because of the absence of at least one parent
—whose homes lack such material possessions as telephones, vacuum cleaners, and automobiles
—who are Negro
—who have less reading matter in the home, specifically who less often have daily newspapers, encyclopedias, and a large number of books
—who are more likely to drop out of school before graduating
—who, when they graduate, are less likely to continue their education into college
—who are not in a college preparatory curriculum and are not taking those courses ordinarily required for college
—who have never read a college catalog nor talked with a college official about post-high-school plans
—who report low overall grade averages
—whose rates of absence from school are high
—who score low on standard subject matter achievement tests
—who engage in behaviors that distract from concentration and learning, based on principal's reports of disciplinary and behavior problems
—who believe that the fates are against them, as indicated by agreement with the statement, "People like me don't have much of a chance to be successful in life" (Coleman, Campbell et al., 1966).

These items are illustrative rather than exhaustive of the extent to which school administrations manage to create learning environments that differ in quality depending upon the nature of the client population. An important part of a child's learning environment consists of his fellow students, for it is they who provide challenges to achievement or distractions from achievement, who focus attention and energy toward or away from learning: outside the classroom through association and casual discussions, within the classroom by the manner of their response to lesson content and required assignments. One must indeed be remarkably insensitive to the nature of learning to miss this basic point: Those whose nonschool environments are least equipped to provide or support meaningful educational experiences are placed in schools that provide the least stimulating interpersonal environments for learning, whereas those whose home environments most typically provide knowledge and encourage curiosity attend schools that provide interpersonal environments more appropriate to educational tasks. It should be clear that race is merely illustrative of the point; we would make the same observations if we ignored race altogether and compared classmates in suburban with those in inner city schools, or classmates in wealthy urban communities with those in rural Appalachia.

The import is clear: Inasmuch as the level of intellectual activity and educational preparedness of one's classmates creates an environment that either stimulates or depresses one's own intellectual growth, schools often lock students in the environments of their origin and thereby affect the capacity of their graduates to compete for occupational and other economic rewards in adult life. Whereas we have readily recognized the public school system as a major avenue for social mobility and personal advancement, we have largely ignored the ways in which the schools operate as a restraining governor on ambition and performance. The backgrounds that students bring to the school when they first enter it, as shown in their readiness to learn and the educational supportiveness of home and neighborhood, predict powerfully both to the characteristics of their classmates and to the qualifications these students will have when they terminate their exposure to public education.

There are other ways as well in which the formal organization of the schools affects the socialization of youth. To whatever extent uncertainty and anxiety may characterize the life of the adolescent, two major sources of order and regularity are the organization of knowledge that the school provides and the routinization of life that it requires. Certain things are done in certain ways at certain times, and the unseen authority of this management of time must surely have its (unrecognized) stabilizing effects. Even the curriculum, which simply is the division of knowledge into subjects, provides a perceptual structuring; information, rather than random and chaotic knowledge, exists as history and physics and grammar and trigonometry. Similarly, the routines of the day, and the oft repeated rituals of grading, recitation, recess, assembly, bells, and cafeteria lines direct activity and define one's orientation to his environment. In a word, the fact of organization in the school daily confronts the adolescent with an image of order, and assists him in the management and comprehension of time.

We have dwelt earlier on the growth in the adolescent of an orientation toward his peers, and with how, in consequence of this, an age-homogenous group develops that to some extent is resistant to accepting authority from without and to recognizing authority from within; in this sense, the adolescent society is a radical version of democracy. It is peculiar and significant that whereas the school provides the central location for this adolescent system, it is at the same time a constant reminder that authority systems and age-heterogenous relations do in fact continue to exist and to operate. Students may con, co-opt, ignore, attack, dispute, bewail, even prevail against the authority of the school or the wishes of their teachers; they may restrict production, compare notes, cheat, draw boundaries against the intrusion of academic standards. But in spite of all, an ultimate and immediate power is vested in the personages of teachers and principal to interpret policies and issue decrees that are followed though they may cause inconvenience and consternation throughout the student body. These experiences remind adolescents of their ultimate responsibility to an external authority and, by calling attention to the preparatory tasks of the adolescent period, probably have the subtle effect of suggesting the fleeting significance of various peer values and activities. The details of James Dean's biography may seem less compelling after the principal's reminder that college-qualifying examinations will be given a week from tomorrow. Such age-heterogenous relations between teachers and pupils, also, as Eisenstadt (1956, p. 164) suggests, emphasize the great difference in power, and in symbolic and technical competence between adults and adolescents and remind children that there is growth and development yet to be accomplished.

It is useful to concern ourselves for a moment with the characteristics of those adults who stand in complementary role relationships to youth, since they are the tangible personal representations of what adulthood and society are. One of the first things one notes here is how heavily school personnel constitute those adults with whom the adolescent interacts.[22] Teachers are important agents of socialization, then, not only for how much they know but for what they represent. In general, many teachers are status mobile, being of modest if not humble social origins; except possibly in small communities, they are not among the most successful members of the community; again excepting small communities, they may very well not be natives of, nor permanent residents of, the locality served by the school, hence not connected into local kin, neighboring, and power structures; and, while they exceed the general population in intellectual ability, they are below the average of the college-educated portion of the population. Occupationally, they are employees rather than entrepreneurs, and the formal status differences among them are quite narrow, since salary variances are small, and only the three statuses of principal, department head, and teacher are differentiated. Thus it may be suggested that public school faculties are not altogether representative elements of the adult community, that the particular situation of teachers decreases their ability to relate effectively to certain groups of students (those of extremely high and low origins), and that the role demands on teachers pertaining to the treatment of students create a specific rather than a general model of interpersonal relations.

There is also strong evidence that the social class composition of the student body affects the attitudes and work behavior of teachers, and that the class-related characteristics of the individual student affect the teacher's evaluation of and mode of relating to him. The sum of these effects is to make it more difficult for children of lower-class background to relate effectively to the schools and profit maximally from the educational experience. Becker (1952) has observed that the educational performance of children from modest homes makes it more difficult for teachers to feel successful in their work. He indicates further that slum children not only offend the teacher's moral sensibilities, but also by failing to respond to mild reprimands press the teacher into more discipline-maintaining behaviors that are incompatible with her preferred professional image. Principals

---

[22]Excluding parents, the adolescent's interaction with teachers, coaches, and counsellors engages more time and is more diffuse than his relations with any other adults.

in lower-class and minority schools similarly offer a larger and more varied list of complaints about student deportment and activities that interfere with the educational aims of the school (Coleman et al., 1966). Considering the overwhelming evidence that the comportment of middle-class students is substantially more congruent with the academic and moral traditions of the school, it would be rather astounding if the professional socialization of teachers were so complete that their perceptions of students' class position did not influence their mode of relating to students and the aspirations they have for them. For, as Charters points out in a summary article, social class position predicts

> ... grades, achievement and intelligence test scores, retentions at grade level, course failures, truancy, suspensions from school, high school drop-outs, plans for college attendance, and total amount of formal schooling. It predicts academic honors and awards, elective school offices, extent of participation in extra-curricular activities and in social affairs of the school, to say nothing of a variety of indicators of "success" in the informal structure of the student society (Charters, 1963, p. 740).

Though we argue that the teachers' expectations about the students' school performance, based on class, have a subtle self-fulfilling quality about them, there are other ways as well in which social class position affects the socialization experiences provided by the educational system. For a variety of reasons it is more difficult for lower-class students to feel congruent with the school and its purposes; they are more likely to experience school life as an alien world. A view of the school as a useful tool that provides promising interpersonal contacts as well as relevant training is probably much more advanced in the middle class, and it would follow that the utility of the school's program for anticipatory socialization is more advanced too. On the other hand, the disposition to question the utility and relevance of the school is more prevalent in the lower class. Allison Davis (1948) has enhanced our understanding by noting that the lower class child must experience *un*learning if he is to be successful in school, whereas those from the middle class experience continuity and compatibility as between school and nonschool influences. Finally, the costs that schooling exacts in the form of deferred income and other instances of self-discipline are greater proportional to resources in the lower classes.

Insofar as the peer culture and informal social systems of adolescence are concerned, the prevalent literature suggests that the formal educational purposes of the school are subverted by peer norms. This is central to Coleman's interpretation, as we have seen:

> The relative unimportance of academic achievement . . . suggests that the adolescent subcultures in these schools exert a rather strong deterrent to academic achievement. In other words, in these adolescent societies, those who are seen as the "intellectuals," and who come to think of themselves in this way, are not really those of highest intelligence, but are only the ones who are willing to work hard at a relatively unrewarded activity (Coleman, 1961, p. 265).

Observations and research results from other sources are compatible with this view; indeed, the oft-cited idea of "the gentleman's C" forms a part of our folklore about colleges. Bushnell (1965) observes similar phenomena operative at Vassar, and is more explicit than Coleman[23] in stating that in student eyes good grades should not be one's *sole* virtue and they are not worth an intemperate investment of time. Hughes, Becker and Geer (1965), having noted that the amount of time and effort medical students might devote to their studies is theoretically infinite, observe that the student culture provides them with a rationale for the level and direction of their effort; correlatively, this culture provides a collective support sufficiently strong to permit the channeling of energies in directions that are antithetical to faculty will.[24] Wallace (1964, 1966) defines upperclassmen and faculty as separate host groups for entering freshmen at Midwest College and observes a substantial drop in the importance attached to high grades during the course of the freshman year which he attributes to the influence of upperclassmen. That is, the movement in freshman attitudes ". . . was in the direction of greater congruence with the level of importance assigned to getting high grades among their student hosts, and toward greater incongruence with the preference of faculty members in this regard." Newcomb (1943, 1958), to the contrary, was substantially more impressed than these authors by the ability of the faculty to change student values in the direction of prevailing faculty political views, at least in an isolated girls college that had the features of a near-total institution. Also, Turner (1964) noted that peer culture may indeed depress ambition values but that ambitious students may develop considerable dexterity in ritually adhering to peer-culture values while in fact remaining detached from them; this, coupled with the generally positive valuation given academic values in all physical areas covered in his Los Angeles study of ten high schools, permitted individual students to accept the central values of the school while enjoying status and recognition among their peers.

Our discussion thus far may have intimated that the formal system of the school, including its values and its personnel, is a fully integrated, consistent, single-minded entity intent upon imparting the maximum amount of knowledge to all comers to the exclusion of all else. This is a false characterization and should be corrected. There is a substantial compatibility between certain anti- (and non-) intellectual values of the adult community and those commonly observed in peer culture; and if, as Waller (1965) observed, "The culture of the school is a curious melange of the work of young artisans making culture for themselves and old artisans making culture for the young" (p. 108), it is not at all clear that the adults contribute disproportionately to the intellectual portion of this me-

---

[23]In fact, McDill and Coleman (1963) observe that among high-school students college is valued because it connotes adult status, ". . . but scholastic achievement carries the connotation of acquiescence and subordination to adults" (p. 918).

[24]Hughes et al. (1965) believe that Max Weber offered the explanation a half-century ago: "Any group of workingmen possessed of any solidarity whatsoever, and with some common image of themselves and their situation, will not easily yield to any authority full control over the amount of work they do or over the strenuousness of the effort they put forth" (p. 517).

lange. We noted earlier that public school teachers were themselves not among the scholarly elite when they were students, and can hardly represent the best traditions of intellectual inquiry and academic excellence (J. Davis, 1965). Parents, when they observe their teen-age offspring to be indifferent to dating and other forms of sociality, grow concerned and decide that something is wrong. Learning to relax, to have a good time, to get away from it all, not to take things seriously—these appeals occur commonly in advertisements beamed even to *adult* audiences; young people should learn to get along with others, to enjoy the company of others, and popularity is a valued achievement. The mother who complains that her daughter spends too much time on the telephone and receives multiple requests for dates is not nearly so pained as the mother who complains that her daughter reads books endlessly and hardly goes outside the house. Angell, commenting 40 years ago on the recognition the college athlete enjoys, saw clearly that adults no less than peers enjoy his exploits:

> The outstanding athlete is unquestionably the most honored of all students, both by the undergraduates and the general public. So much space is devoted to him in the public press that he attains ten times more notoriety than the most illustrious professor. Among his fellows, his ability is the subject of lengthy and earnest conversation; he is elected to campus honorary societies, is feted, and becomes the recipient of other attentions from his admirers. The fact is simply that he represents achievement in a line of endeavor with which most Americans are heartily in sympathy. And his achievement is obvious, external, to be appreciated by all who care either to witness him in action or to read of his athletic exploits. His light is not, like that of his more intellectual brother, hidden under a bushel of public indifference and lack of understanding (Angell, 1928, pp. 107-108).

In a word, these things that peer cultures do very well indeed—train in sociality, honor athletic prowess, extend heterosexual contact, dampen scholarly excess, and encourage hedonism—are widely appreciated among adults and from this perspective must be viewed as adaptive. It is too much to expect that schools can instill largely alien values—most especially with instructional personnel that is broadly representative of the community in which anti-intellectual values are nurtured.

RELIGION AND THE ADOLESCENT

Adult socialization differs from childhood socialization in its greater emphasis on learning concrete behaviors (e.g., job and marital skills) and its lesser emphasis on learning basic values (e.g., honesty, friendliness, loyalty) (Brim, 1966). Among the major experiences of adolescence is the confrontation between the abstract values taught in childhood and observations of "the way things really are" that expanding experience and intelligence permit. The widespread idealism of youth can be interpreted as an effort to maintain in their personal belief-system, and establish in the world around them, the naive values of childhood in the face of various reality impingements. It is a way of saying that the world should be the way adults said it was, made up of Presidents who never tell lies, officials who never cheat, husbands who love their wives, churchgoers who practice the Gospel, and nations that follow the path of peace. Mixed with the ebullience, enthusiasm, and energy of adolescence, idealism is a way of saying: "Principle should prevail. Compromise is the defeat of principle."[25]

Adolescence is a crisis of faith. An older scholarly tradition explains the phenomena of this age period in terms of developmental psychology and physiology; physical growth and sexual maturity were the keys to moodiness, unpredictability, idealism, religious conversion, peer attachment, and a variegated assortment of other outcomes. It would be foolish of us to assert that the physical changes of adolescence, especially its earlier stages, are trivial. However, we choose to work from a different perspective. We are disposed to emphasize value crises that occur because of increasing contact with a reality that is less fully filtered by parents and the protective world of childhood; the changing conceptions of self that result from vastly wider, more variegated stimuli, most of which are social and only one set of which is physiological; interpersonal tensions that occur because the adolescent and centrally significant others must continue in intense contact while mutually redefining role relationships; and the rapid as well as erratic progressions that characterize the period, as adolescents do in fact survive to enter adulthood.

There is a strong reason to believe that the quality of and changes in the religious beliefs and behaviors of adolescents deserve more attention than they have received from the behavioral sciences. Theological systems are in the business of defining the place of the individual in some total cosmic scheme of things, and religious organizations have a central relevance to the maintenance and transmission of moral and ethical codes—factors that are important to the total socialization process. Religious belief systems provide definitions of the nature of man, of desirable relations between men, and when accepted, satisfy the personal quest for identity, security, and purpose—issues that loom large in the adolescent experience. Religious beliefs and organizations are not, on the other hand, so readily identified with wishes for freedom and autonomy, nor with hedonistic pursuits; in fact, they may be linked in the public eye with adult authority and be unpalatable to adolescents because they are associated with childhood experiences of required church attendance and regular religious indoctrination. Adolescents neither create nor control organized religious institutions and belief structures and consequently will think of them as "ours" only with great difficulty. Church activities for the young fall clearly into the category of adult-sponsored rather than participant-created youth groups.

These latter remarks imply that religious orientations and participation probably decline during adolescence, whereas the former suggest that religious experiences during the period should be quite intense. Congruent with social scientists' greater fascination with deviance than with scrupulosity(Matza, 1964,

---

[25]It is a little noted possibility that the adolescent press for "making values real" may resocialize more calloused adults to take values seriously, and thus have regenerative, restorative effects for basic value systems.

especially pp. 200-201), the amount of information in this area is exceedingly modest whether we refer to empirical studies or to interpretive essays. We rarely acknowledge even the pertinent fact that one of the few *rites de passage* our society has for initiating adolescence is religiously sponsored—Bar Mitzvah in the Jewish faith, Confirmation among Catholics and some Protestant denominations, and the widespread expectation, especially strong in Protestant evangelical groups, that the conversion experience ("joining the church") should occur in early adolescence.[26]

Though the scant attention paid to adolescent religious behavior and value systems limits our discussion, we can at least raise a question concerning the widespread assumption that adolescents are not involved in religious organizations. It is contended that organized religion represents an authority rejected by adolescents, and that where it is not viewed as distasteful it is seen as irrelevant. The empirical data are not at all conclusive, however. The Purdue Opinion Panel, reporting results from its continuing survey of a national sample of youth, fails to show any substantial difference in the church going practices of 12th-grade compared to 9th-grade students; a larger proportion of the former attends more often than once a week *and* less often than once a month. (Nor do they find any increasing difference between parents and youth in religious beliefs; 81 per cent of the 9th graders and 77 per cent of the 12th graders say their beliefs are in accord with both parents [Remmers & Radler, 1957].) Strommen (1963) reporting data from a 1959 national survey of Lutheran youth, finds a very modest drop-off in church attendance when he compares high-school seniors with 10th-grade students: 70 per cent rather than 74 per cent attend church at least once a week. Another national sample, this one reporting participation in church groups rather than attendance at worship services, finds an increase between the ages of 11 to 13 from 10 per cent to 23 per cent (Institute for Social Research, 1960, p. 12). Fichter's data (1954) are not age-specific, but his analysis of religious participation in Easter services, mass, and communion among members of a southern Catholic parish finds youth under 20 firmly involved in these activities while participation declines among those in their 20's and reaches a nadir among those 30-40; the participation curve then turns up among those in their 40's and 50's but does not match the intensity of the teens. Goldsen and associates, analyzing data for around 3,000 students in eleven universities, report about one-fourth attend religious services at least once a week while another one-fourth attend "never or almost never" (Goldsen et al., 1960, p. 157 n). They also find that students who score high on a scale of religious beliefs more often believe that they have lived up to their parents' expectation, which suggests that the church may indeed dampen tendencies toward adolescent revolt. Among YMCA constituents age 18-29, Ross (1950, p. 57) found a decided de-

---

[26]The originating pioneer in the scientific study of adolescence, G. Stanley Hall (1904), devoted an 80-page chapter to adolescent conversion experiences and portions of another chapter to church confirmation. He presents a marvelous array of unsystematic data, some of it compiled through soliciting the views of leading churchmen and evangelists of the day. See especially Chapter 14.

crease in church attendance with increased age: 53 per cent attended at least once a week, 25 per cent less than once a month among those age 18-21, compared to 39 per cent and 33 per cent at age 26-29. Yet Van Dyke and Pierce-Jones (1963), reviewing the literature from 1950 to 1960, report not a single study of religious participation.

Finally, unpublished data (de Bord et al., 1967) from a Nashville survey of 2-child families, both children between the ages of 12 and 18, show a continuing high church-going rate throughout the adolescent period.

Various other indices of religious concern among adolescents might be cited. The empirical data are, in general, so fragmentary that defensible conclusions about adolescent religious behavior, particularly shifts in this behavior as the second decade of life runs its course, cannot be drawn. It seems likely that the various ethnic, faith, regional, class, and rural-urban groups vary considerably in whether or not, and the extent to which, religious participation and orientation change in this age period. Little more can be added except to bemoan the fact that this important area is neglected in socialization research and to express the fear that national policies of church-state separation combined with federal support of research will continue to focus attention on other topics.

CONCLUDING REMARKS

Lengthening periods of training and dependency in complex modern society exacerbate, regarding adolescence, the universal requirement that the meaning of age and age-homogenous groups in the social structure be defined. Youth is a period of expectancy. At some point in the life cycle orientations turn subtly but perceptibly from expectancy toward consolidation and then to memory. Whenever this may happen, it certainly does not happen in adolescence and would be regarded as a major abnormality were it to happen. Ideally, youth would be socialized so as to enjoy and find pleasure in a present status while anticipating and preparing for a future status, and thus striving to pass out of the present one. Societally, there is need to make the status satisfying enough that rebellion does not become a paramount feature and that orientations toward self and toward society do not become perverse. On the other hand, the status must be defined as temporary, one to grow out of: it would be tragic if the rewards should be so nurturant and the demerits so trivial, compared to the anticipated features of an upcoming adult status, that significant energies were directed toward retaining adolescent status indefinitely.

The potential of adolescence lies in acquainting the actor with disparate pressures and in giving him experience with the constant-tension state of a personal world too diverse and complex to permit either complete consistency among and between all his behaviors and values or approval from all sanction-holding others in his environment. It may, indeed, acquaint him with the potential for growth and development provided expressly by his inability to remove dissonance from his values or achieve consensus among all significant others. To find that one can survive the displeasure of others; to enjoy self-fulfilling pleasure in standing alone on occasion; to know the sense of stable self despite the fact that today he is not totally consistent with yesterday—these are necessary lessons to learn. Skilled parents probably teach them inside the home. As the circle and diversity of significant others widens, the social structure of experience explicates this lesson for the growing child.

From this perspective, there is a meaningful sense in which it can be argued that modern society makes adolescence too easy an experience. In the freedom-within-structure terms of Kurt Lewin, we would suggest that in relative proportion the freedom is present but the structure is missing in contemporary urban life. By their reluctance to impose discipline, set limits, make demands, withhold pleasure or impose pain, many parents create life-situations in which their children find it difficult to locate obstacles that challenge their competence and extend their development. Why this should be is beyond the present chapter's scope, but it is a reasonable assumption that popular conceptions of inordinate tension and stress during adolescence lead parents to offer velvety compensations.[27] If, as we assert, parents intentionally dampen the conflict, remove the dissonance, soothe the tension, avoid the clash of wills, forego the arbitrary use of nonrational constraints, and thereby give the period a surrealistic blandness, we then may ask an important question: Is there anything in his experiential world to bring the adolescent to seek his limits, take his lumps, recoup from disaster, search diligently for big answers to big questions through intense concern with religion, ethics, politics, causes, and movements?

We are suggesting that adults make adolescence a vacuum of triviality by too cautiously placing demands and constraints upon it. Adults refuse to be the adolescent's enemy.[28] Douvan and Adelson (1966) comment in a similar vein:

> Some discrepancy of values is sure to be found, since the two generations differ in perspectives, but for the most part, we believe, core values are shared by parents and peers, and conflicts center on peripheral or token issues. This muting of conflict helps produce a fairly untroubled adolescence, in this area at least, and from the point of view of personal adjustment the concordance of values between parents and the peer culture is a desirable thing. But there are other points of view than "good adjustment." An absence of tension between values also tends to produce the bland, docile youngsters who make up the majority in our high schools and colleges, and who forever remain morally and ideologically parochial (p. 84).

Others have suggested that those conditions of development that impose little strain often produce a personality that is stable and integrated but lacking in depth or complexity (e.g., Freedman, 1963). One is led to suggest that G. Stanley

---

[27]The most extreme statement that adolescence is what we define it to be is made in Musgrove (1964). There is, he contends, a psychology of adolescence because psychologists invented it: "The position of youth is only intelligible in terms of the rise since the later 18th century of a psychology of adolescence which has helped to create what it describes" (p. 2). A different but not incompatible view is that indulgence of adolescents results from economic prosperity (see, for example, Blaine, 1966).

[28]Mr. Dooley once observed that good friends are fairly easy to come by, but a really first-class enemy is a treasure to be cherished and protected with one's life (Dunne, 1899, p. 99).

Hall may have been right, but for the wrong reasons, in describing adolescence at the turn of the century as a period of storm and stress. He certainly was not describing an inevitable, intrapsychically determined, biologically given condition of the second decade of life; he may, however, have been a perceptive social observer of an historic period in American life before the nation's succorance of adolescence had progressed to its present moment.

Adolescence is especially important in the socialization process because the object of this process continues in a power-dependent and economic-dependent position but, compared to childhood, has heightened intellectual powers and information which permit articulation and explanation of the demands and expectations he encounters. "Why" questions may be answered in more detail and at higher levels of abstraction. He is better able to understand the forces that shape him and shape his future. The importance of these conscious cognitions emphasizes the importance of adult role-models who guide and advise as much as they control and direct.

In light of this, there are uniquely important problems in the socialization of adolescents during times of rapid change. The aura of change suggests impermanence and a relativistic perspective. If the length of skirts and style of cars so readily change, if men travel to the planets and computers cook dinner, then what, if anything, is or should be permanent? Particularly, this pertains to the search for, and need for, identity. Am I to be as all I see, changing, unstable, impermanent, subject to challenge in the next instant? What, if anything, is it that continues, that remains the continuing me? One suspects that this is the crucial demand placed on the stabilizing institutions in unsettled times, and it provides one definition of the significant, central task in adolescent socialization: To give a sense of and provide the basis for a sense of continuity and order in the self system and the societal system, while preparing persons to respond flexibly and competently to a world that cannot be anticipated.

REFERENCES

ANGELL, R. C. *The campus.* New York: Appleton, 1928.

BECKER, H. S. Social class variations in the teacher-pupil relationship. *Journal of Educational Sociology,* 1952, 25, 451-465.

BENEDICT, RUTH. Continuities and discontinuities in cultural conditioning. In C. Kluckholn & H. A. Murray (Eds.), *Personality in nature, society, and culture.* New York: Knopf, 1948. Pp. 414-423.

BLAINE, G. B., JR. *Youth and the hazards of affluence.* New York: Harper & Row, 1966.

BLOS, P. *On adolescence: A psychoanalytic interpretation.* New York: Free Press of Glencoe, 1962.

BOOCOCK, SARANE S. Toward a sociology of learning: A selective review of existing research. *Sociology of Education,* 1966, 39, 1-45.

BOWERMAN, C. E., & KINCH, J. W. Changes in family and peer orientation of children between the fourth and tenth grades. *Social Forces,* 1959, 37, 206-211.

BRIM, O. G., JR. Socialization through the life cycle. In O. G. Brim, Jr. & S. Wheeler (Eds.), *Socialization after childhood: Two essays.* New York: Wiley, 1966. Pp. 1-49.

BRITTAIN, C. V. Adolescent choices and parent-peer cross pressures. *American Sociological Review,* 1963, 28, 385-390.

BUSHNELL, J. H. Student culture at Vassar. In N. Sanford (Ed.), *The American college.* New York: Wiley, 1965. Pp. 489-514.

CHARTERS, W. W., JR. The social background of teaching. In N. L. Gage (Ed.), *Handbook of research on teaching.* Chicago: Rand McNally, 1963.

COLEMAN, J. S. *The adolescent society.* New York: Free Press of Glencoe, 1961.

COLEMAN, J. S., CAMPBELL, E. Q., ET AL. *Equality of educational opportunity.* Washington: U.S. Government Printing Office, 1966. Pp. 183-202.

DAVIS, A. *Social class influences upon learning.* Cambridge, Mass.: Harvard Univer. Press, 1948.

DAVIS, J. A. *Undergraduate career decisions.* Chicago: Aldine, 1965.

DAVIS, K. The sociology of parent-youth conflict. *American Sociological Review,* 1940, 5, 523-535.

DAVIS, K. Adolescence and the social structure. *Annals of The American Academy of Political and Social Science,* 1944, 236, 8-16.

DE BORD, L., ET AL. Adolescent religious participation in Nashville: A mapping problem. Unpublished paper, Vanderbilt University, 1967.

DENTLER, R. A., & MONROE, L. J. The family and early adolescent conformity and deviance. *Marriage and Family Living,* 1961, 23, 241-247.

DEUTSCHER, I. Socialization for postparental life. In A. M. Rose (Ed.), *Human behavior and social processes.* Boston: Houghton Mifflin, 1962. Pp. 506-525.

DEUTSCHER, I. The quality of postparental life: Definitions of the situation. *Journal of Marriage and the Family,* 1964, 26, 52-59.

DOUVAN, ELIZABETH, & ADELSON, J. *The adolescent experience.* New York: Wiley, 1966.

DUNNE, F. P. *Mr. Dooley in peace and war.* Boston: Small, Maynard & Co., 1899.

EISENSTADT, S. N. *From generation to generation.* Glencoe, Ill.: Free Press, 1956.

EISENSTADT, S. N. Archetypal patterns of youth. In E. H. Erikson (Ed.), *Youth: Change and challenge.* New York: Basic Books, 1963.

ELKIN, F., & WESTLEY, W. A. The myth of adolescent culture. *American Sociological Review,* 1955, 20, 680-684.

ENDLEMAN, R. *Personality and social life.* New York: Random House, 1967.

EPPERSON, D. C. A reassessment of indices of parental influence in "the adolescent society." *American Sociological Review,* 1964, 29, 93-96.

ERIKSON, E. H. *Identity and totality: Psychoanalytic observations on the problems of youth.* Committee on Human Development, University of Chicago. Ann Arbor: Edwards Bros., 1954. Pp. 50-71.

FICHTER, J. H. *Social relations in an urban parish.* Chicago: Univer. of Chicago Press, 1954.

FREEDMAN, M. B. Some theoretical and practical implications of a longitudinal study of college women. *Psychiatry,* 1963, 26, 178-187.

GLICK, P. The family cycle. *American Sociological Review,* 1947, 12, 164-169.

GLICK, P. The life cycle of the family. *Marriage and Family Living,* 1955, 17, 3-9.

GLICK, P. *American families.* New York: Wiley, 1957.

GOLDSEN, ROSE K., ET AL. *What college students think.* Princeton, N.J.: Van Nostrand, 1960.

GORDON, C. W. *The social system of the high school.* Glencoe, Ill.: Free Press, 1957.

GOSLIN, D. A. *The school in contemporary society.* Chicago: Scott, Foresman, 1965.

HALL, G. S. *Adolescence.* New York: Appleton, 1904.

HOLLINGSHEAD, A. B. *Elmtown's youth.* New York: Wiley, 1949.

HUGHES, E. C., BECKER, H. S., & GEER, B. Student culture and academic effort. In N. Sanford (Ed.), *The American college.* New York: Wiley, 1965. Pp. 515-530.

Institute for Social Research. *Becoming adolescents.* Ann Arbor: Univer. of Michigan, 1960. Table 9.

KAHL, J. A. Educational and occupational aspirations of "common-man" boys. *Harvard Educational Review,* 1953, 23, 186-203.

MATZA, D. Subterranean traditions of youth. *The Annals of The American Academy of Political and Social Sciences,* 1961, 338, 102-118.

MATZA, D. Position and behavior patterns of youth. In R. E. L. Faris (Ed.), *Handbook of modern sociology.* Chicago: Rand McNally, 1964. Pp. 191-216.

McDILL, E. L., & COLEMAN, J. S. High school social status, college plans, and academic achievement. *American Sociological Review,* 1963, 28, 905-918.

MEAD, MARGARET. *Coming of age in Samoa.* New York: Morrow, 1928.

MEYER, H. J., BORGATTA, E. F., & JONES, W. C. *Girls at Vocational High.* New York: Russell Sage Foundation, 1965.

MIDDLETON, R., & PUTNEY, S. Political expression of adolescent rebellion. *American Journal of Sociology,* 1963, 68, 527-535.

MOORE, O. K., & ANDERSON, A. R. Autotelic folk models. *Sociological Quarterly,* 1960, 1, 203-216.

MOORE, W. E., & TUMIN, M. M. Some social functions of ignorance. *American Sociological Review,* 1949, 14, 787-795.

MUSGROVE, F. *Youth and the social order.* London: Routledge & Kegan Paul, 1964.

NEWCOMB, T. M. *Personality and social change.* New York: Dryden Press, 1943.

NEWCOMB, T. M. Attitude development as a function of reference groups: The Bennington study. In E. E. Maccoby, T. M. Newcomb & E. L. Hartley (Eds.), *Readings in social psychology.* (3rd Ed.) New York: Holt, Rinehart & Winston, 1958. Pp. 265-275.

PARSONS, T. Age and sex in the social structure of the United States. *American Sociological Review,* 1942, 7, 604-616.

PARSONS, T. *The social system.* Glencoe, Ill.: Free Press, 1951.

PARSONS, T., & BALES, R. F. *Family, socialization and interaction process.* Glencoe, Ill.: Free Press, 1955.

POLSKY, H. W. *Cottage six.* New York: Russell Sage Foundation, 1962.

REMMERS, H. H., & RADLER, D. H. *The American teenager.* Indianapolis: Bobbs-Merrill, 1957.

REUTER, E. B. The sociology of adolescence. *American Journal of Sociology,* 1937, 43, 414-427.

ROSEN, B. C. The reference group approach to the parental factor in attitude and behavior formation. *Social Forces,* 1955, 34, 137-144.

ROSS, M. G. *Religious beliefs of youth.* New York: Association Press, 1950. Table 23.

SCHMUCK, R., & LOHMAN, ANITA. *Peer relations and personality development.* Institute for Social Research. Ann Arbor: Univer. of Michigan, 1965.

SCHNEIDER, L., & LYSGAARD, S. The deferred gratification pattern: A preliminary study. *American Sociological Review,* 1953, 18, 142-149.

SCOTT, W. A. *Values and organizations.* Chicago: Rand McNally, 1965.

SHERIF, M., & SHERIF, C. *Reference groups: Exploration into conformity and deviation of adolescents.* New York: Harper & Row, 1964.

SHORT, J. F., JR., & STRODTBECK, F. L. *Group process and gang delinquency.* Chicago: Univer. of Chicago Press, 1965.

SMITH, L. M., & KLEINE, P. F. The adolescent and his society. *Review of Educational Research*, 1966, 36, 424-436.

STONE, C. L. Some family characteristics of socially active and inactive teenagers. *Coordinator*, 1960, 8, 53-57.

STROMMEN, M. P. *Profiles of church youth*. St. Louis: Concordia Publishing House, 1963.

Survey Research Center. *A study of adolescent boys*. Ann Arbor: Univer. of Michigan, 1955.

TRYON, CAROLINE M. The adolescent peer culture. *Forty-third yearbook of The National Society for the Study of Education*. Chicago: Univer. of Chicago Press, 1944. Pp. 217-239.

TURNER, R. H. *The social context of ambition*. San Francisco: Chandler, 1964.

VAN DYKE, P., II, & PIERCE-JONES, J. The psychology of religion of middle and late adolescence: A review of empirical research, 1950-1960. *Religious Education*, 1963, 58, 529-537.

VAN WATERS, MIRIAM. Adolescence. In *Encyclopedia of Social Sciences*, I. New York: Macmillan, 1930. Pp. 455-459.

WALLACE, W. L. Institutional and life-cycle socialization of college freshmen. *American Journal of Sociology*, 1964, 70, 303-318.

WALLACE, W. L. *Student culture: Social structure and continuity*. Chicago: Aldine, 1966.

WALLER, W. *The sociology of teaching*. New York: Wiley, 1965.

WHEELER, S. The structure of formally organized socialization settings. In O. G. Brim, Jr. & S. Wheeler (Eds.), *Socialization after childhood: Two essays*. New York: Wiley, 1966. Pp. 51-116.

WILLIAMS, R. M., JR. *American society: A sociological interpretation*. New York: Knopf, 1960.

WOLF, CATHERINE. Growing up and its price in three Puerto Rican subcultures. *Psychiatry*, 1952, 15, 401-433.

CHAPTER 21

Occupational Socialization

Wilbert E. Moore

Russell Sage Foundation

Of the many roles or role-constellations that the modern adult is called upon to perform, few exceed in importance the acquisition of requisite skills and attitudes for occupations. In modernized societies, occupation represents a central place in life organization for a vast majority of adult males and a substantial minority of adult females. In temporal terms, occupation is challenged only by the family as the major determinant and locus of behavior; were we to limit our comparison to the waking hours, occupation would appear to be a clear winner. And to the degree that formal education can be viewed as occupational preparation, we need not even exempt children and youths from the salience of occupational matters.

Jobs need not be liked by their incumbents in order to be important. The extent to which work is liberating or repressive of human potentials is the subject of both research and literary opinion. The character of social organization in the contemporary world, however, assures that work will be the principal, normal link between consuming families and the system of economic production. And there is considerable evidence for the view that this is so overwhelmingly normal that individuals and families who fail in at least minimal occupational participation suffer personally and collectively. It almost appears that any job is better than none, though, like most such aphorisms, this one is subject to some modification as one explores the nuances of personal and social expectations.

Occupational socialization appears not to have excited scholarly interest proportional to its importance. One possible reason for relative neglect is that until fairly recently almost all studies of socialization concerned infancy and childhood, whereas occupation, almost by definition, is an adult position in the contemporary world. Of course this does not mean that only adult socialization is involved, for socialization to work roles is properly viewed as a developmental process (Borow, 1966). We shall argue, however, that adult socialization is crucially involved, and for some (certainly growing) portion of the labor force the process continues well into and even through the mature years of life.

Let us start from some orienting assertions, which will form recurrent themes in later discussion. We shall assume:

1) that most occupational incumbents behave approximately according to the normal expectations most of the time;

2) that this assertion remains true (though in an unknown but no doubt reduced degree) when no real and present external sanctions are operative;

3) therefore, we infer that most occupants of work roles have a sufficient degree of internalization of those roles, both cognitively and affectively, that they are likely to perform competently when placed in the appropriate setting of formal expectations.

The agenda for this discussion will include an initial examination of some principal dimensions of the world of work, the characteristics of occupational roles and their settings that are the target of socializing experiences. We shall then proceed to some remarks, also introductory, on socialization with specific regard to occupational selection and performance. This latter focus will be examined thereafter in more detail: the sequences in occupational socialization, the internalization of occupational norms, and modes of reinforcement in a normative order that is neither entirely consistent nor entirely confirmed in behavior.

THE WORLD OF WORK

Work is ambiguous for modern man. In some circumstances work carries a negative sign, as when it is regarded as a painful necessity, to be avoided if possible, in contrast to play, which presumably is always positive. Yet since work is the normal way of securing a livelihood, it, too, is actively sought by those involuntarily unemployed. And at least in most sectors of most economically advanced societies, work has the further merit of confirming the normality of their adult status for most men and many women. Work is even sought by some (actually, nearly all) of those for whom idleness is an economically feasible alternative, and apparently preferred over leisure by some executives and professionals whose level of living would still be very comfortable with substantially less involvement. To cap it all, for some portion of the employed population work appears to be satisfying as well as merely externally rewarding. Thus socialization to the world of work may be for some a kind of conditioning, a reluctant preparation for harsh realities, and for others a kind of commitment to a calling. In view of the ambiguity, we should evince no surprise that the two orientations may operate for the same individuals.

The Meaning of Work and Occupation

Work, though viewed in Judeao-Christian traditions as man's universal, sorry fate, is surprisingly difficult to identify as a distinct form of activity in many societies. And this is most critically the situation in types of societies that are marked by the greatest necessity of gross human muscular activity to sustain life. The difficulty arises from the circumstance that there is no really reliable way of distinguishing work or labor from other presumably useful activities in the absence of sufficient functional specialization to permit a clear demarcation of economic and noneconomic functions. Wherever a monetized labor market exists, work is easily identified as activity that is financially remunerated, either directly or through the sale of products. Otherwise, we are left with the conceptually unsatisfactory alternative of defining work or labor as activity relating to the acquisition, production, or transformation of physical products. This is unsatisfactory precisely because it perforce leaves out of account *services,* and those comprise a major portion of the economic activity of advanced economies.

This small conceptual exercise is introduced because the problem posed is closely linked to another one that is critically relevant to present concerns, that of the concept of occupation. In conjunction, these conceptual problems have both analytical and theoretical importance. Occupation clearly requires specialization of productive tasks, and specialization beyond the ubiquitous differentiation of roles by age and sex within family settings. Otherwise, one's "occupation" would simply be "female adult" (a situation we approach by identifying housewife as an occupation on various official forms).

Now, with some instructive exceptions to be noted shortly, it is precisely in nonliterate and agrarian societies, in which labor may not be clearly identifiable, that task specialization is also likely to be minimal. In other words, having an occupation is not a universal feature of adults, or even male adults, if we use the term at all properly. Aside from the theoretical significance of differentiating societies along this dimension, we derive a tactical lesson: occupational socialization is of very unequal importance across the spectrum of societies, and we should pay scant attention to those outside the "modern" orbit. Occupation, in short, is significant only in situations where there is a more or less formal division of labor, outside the family as a producing unit, and it will normally be linked to a market system of remuneration.

The exceptions to the general lack of occupational specialization in nonliterate and agrarian societies are themselves remarkably general. In virtually every society of which we have any record, problems of health and life are regarded as of such importance, and their solutions sufficiently difficult, that they are beyond the ordinary capacity of the socialized adult (Sigerist, 1951). Rather, these problems are entrusted to specialists who command esoteric knowledge and powers—often a combination of some rational technique with magical manipulation. Commonly, the curer or *shaman* combines the attempt to restore health or preserve life with the strictly religious function of assuring immortality.

These practitioners, prototypes of professionals, often went through long periods of training, although here and there the only requirement for selection has been a vision or other supernatural manifestation of qualification.

The other widely recurrent "occupational" type is the merchant or trader in agrarian societies. Often these people have been ethnically distinct from the local population, and supply goods not locally produced. Where exchange is partly effected in monetary terms, the merchant also commonly serves as a money-lender.

These and other occupational types—for example the priesthood in ancient civilizations or medieval Europe, chiefs or other political officials here and there—are generally *set apart* from the bulk of the population precisely because specialization is uncommon. Although this might be thought to warrant especially careful examination of these occupational prototypes, the transferability of experience to modern settings would be dubious.

In contemporary advanced economies, occupation involves performing a more or less precise *set* of remunerated activities. Even among the lowest-skilled category of worker—the casual laborer—the duties are likely to have a descriptive name, though the performer may not have an enduring relation to them: for example, dishwasher, janitor, ditch digger, sweep-up man, hod carrier. This limiting case is instructive, as it permits clarification of the distinction between a *job* or *position* and an occupation. The occupation of the performer of the tasks just illustrated is *laborer*. Similarly, the occupation of the man who administers a unit in a large corporation is that of *manager,* not, say, "plant superintendent, volatile chemicals, chemical division." This is not to say that there is nothing of interest in socialization for particular jobs and positions. On the contrary, it is only to say that the concept of occupation already represents some degree of generalization: a somewhat homogeneous grouping of very particular jobs and positions. With the rapid increase of specialization there is no absolute assurance that a person having a given occupation can in fact adequately perform every job that falls within that category. Just as occupations multiply apace, so do their subdivisions. This presents problems in socialization, to which we shall return.

Some Significant Occupational Dimensions

The possible ways of distinguishing occupations are many; indeed they may be in effect infinite. However, we shall identify several occupational dimensions that are likely to be especially significant both in occupational choice and in the type of socialization appropriate to performance. No attempt will be made here to work through the interrelations among these occupational dimensions. Many of them do figure in subsequent discussion.

Occupational rank. A first set of dimensions is especially significant in a competitive occupational system, where the rewards of economic participation are unequal. Thus occupations differ in their relative *rank*. One component of occupational rank is that of *skill level*. The simplest operational measure of this dimension is the length of formal training required for qualification. That is likely to be too simple, for skill levels may combine, in differing proportions, cognitive knowledge, "talent" as exemplified in dexterity or analytical ability, and even such seeming personality attributes as dependability (as represented, for example, by the human monitor of highly mechanized systems).

A second component of occupational rank is *prestige*, especially in the broader community and society. Prestige is normally highly correlated with skill, but with some exceptions and with considerable ignorance on the part of the laity of just what is entailed in very technical occupations.

Relative occupational skills and prestige are also normally reflected in *income* differentials. Again the relationship is by no means perfect, even among legitimate or legal occupations, and instances may be found in which it appears that income acts as a bribe to assure the performance of important but distasteful or unprestigeful tasks. Because occupational positions may not be precisely known or their demands precisely understood, say within a residential community, income or its manifest display in consumption may be the principal or sole basis for assigning relative rank—skill or other determinants of rank being merely inferred.

Occupations differ in their desirability in other ways as well, and some of these should be noted. Thus, some occupations offer relatively high *security* of employment for the competent performer, and others, risks either of intermittent unemployment or of outright disappearance of demand for the particular skill combination. Even some relatively highly ranked occupations may offer considerable risks of unemployment: for example, many public offices, or professional athletics. Of course instability of occupational careers may occur both because of changes in actual employment opportunities and from a variety of essentially "personal" circumstances in the lives of participants.

Another range of differences relates to considerations of comfort, cleanliness, and risks to health and life. Again, although it is generally true that dirty and dangerous jobs have a relatively low rank in other respects as well, money may be used as a bribe to get them done, and some (such as piloting spacecraft) may be positively glamorous, partly because of the risk.

Occupations may also be ranked according to the degree of discretion or *autonomy* accorded the performer. There is a vast difference between the factory worker whose tasks are narrow, repetitive, and machine-paced, and the physician in private practice whose judgment in diagnosing and treating a patient's ills is nearly preclusive and final. In bureaucratic organization, autonomy is always somewhat impaired precisely because of the interdependence of the system. Yet discretion is likely to be somewhat associated with hierarchical position, and persons in advisory or problem-solving positions (including repairmen) must be accorded greater latitude than those with more standardized tasks.

Finally, occupations clearly differ not only cross-sectionally but also in temporal perspective. Thus, the differential chances of *mobility* in the strict sense of positional promotion or linked chains of occupational change, as well as in the looser sense of "advancement" (say, in prestige or income) clearly affect the relative desirability of occupations. Some career paths may lead in fact only to dead ends; others may be more properly likened to ladders, and still others to escalators (Moore, 1962, pp. 167–179).

The contexts of work. Some additional dimensions of occupations may give rise to expressions or manifestations of preferential differences, without yielding a reliable scale. This is particularly true of what we may call, for want of a better term, the contexts of work. It appears legitimate to distinguish occupations where the primary focus of attention or activity is on *people,* those that are primarily concerned with *things,* and those that deal mainly with *ideas.* It would be hard to find an occupation that did not have some elements of all three, but illustrations of a predominant focus on one or another come readily to mind.

With the steady bureaucratization of the labor force and the steady rise of "services" as the type of production, dealing with people is a central task for a fairly large proportion of people at work. In some cases the *service* orientation is predominant: professionals dealing with clients, retail clerks and bank tellers, barbers and civil servants. In other cases *authority,* persuasion or influence is paramount: bureaucratic administrators, teachers, and salesmen.

Manual workers are not alone in dealing primarily with things, for this is also characteristic of many engineers, experimental scientists (though, one supposes, somewhat contaminated by ideas), and, in a curious sense, of dentists and surgeons.

Scientists and scholars but also composers and artists, and not a few technical advisers to decision-makers are mainly concerned with ideas. Manipulating either people or things may be almost inconsequential.

The point of discussing these additional occupational differentials is that there is some reason to suppose that the context of work may be an important element in occupational choice and performance, persons of varying personality characteristics finding some types of focus far more congenial than others. Whether such predilections are properly to be viewed as relatively immutable personality differences or are themselves subject to change by occupational socialization raises the fundamental question of selection versus socialization, which will plague us in some subsequent sections.

Normative dimensions of occupations. The rules relating to the proper conduct of an occupation may be rather specific, and some of them must be because of the particular tasks to be performed. Our concern here is more general, namely, the normative orientations that are common to all or most occupations in the contemporary setting of urban-industrial societies.

A first set of norms—essentially a ticket of admission to others—relates to mere *participation in the labor market.* This involves the perception of an adherence to the *contractual* rendering of services in return for wages, salaries, or fees. For at least the male who has completed his formal education, there is a clear obligation to seek work, presumably commensurate with his abilities. The labor market participant, moreover, is also properly *self-interested,* alert to superior opportunities as well as to a fair bargain with his employer, customer, or client. Even for the professional, subject to the norms of service, the quest for superior conditions for performing services is scarcely reprehensible, although some degrees of self-seeking will impair the ideal standards.

A persuasive argument can be made to the effect that the fundamental machine of modern economies is the clock (Moore, 1963a). Certainly the vast majority of people who work are bound by rules of punctuality in starting (and often in stopping) work, and many are held to fairly rigid schedules in the pace, rate, and rhythm of performance. This *temporal ordering* is so general that those who seem relatively free from it, such as some professionals and salesmen working on their own account, are still expected to use time wisely and, on the whole, rather fully.

Some degree of social *interdependence* is intrinsic to the human condition. Yet specialization clearly increases the importance of interdependence and makes its effective realization vastly more complex. Occupational rules specify outright reciprocities and complementarities, and also what we may call "serial" obligations: the worker in a continuous assembly line is dependent on his predecessors; he does not literally reciprocate, but he performs his tasks properly for those dependent on him in turn. When complex organizations are finely integrated, at least in the technical sense of task allocation, over-performance is as disruptive as under-performance. This perception gets right at the point of the norms of interdependence.

Virtually all occupations are supposed to be performed *rationally*. Our concern here is not with tedious debate over the quality of human thought and motivation in terms of personality, but rather with the reality that most occupations are bound by the *norm* of rationality: the sanctioned expectation that tasks will be performed, problems solved, or crises faced by the use of the best available information and logical inferences. Although related to what Inkeles (1966) calls a sense of efficacy as a personality attribute, the norm of rationality is a shared expectation of sensible and even calculating conduct.

At least for wage and salary earners (and they comprise well over four-fifths of the American labor force), employment entails subordination to legitimate *authority*. The power of employers or managers is itself limited by rules of relevance and commonly by other restraints. Although employment itself is contractual, recognition and acceptance of authority is part of the contract. Insubordination constitutes a contractual, and in that sense moral, delict.

People in occupations do things. This banality reminds us that performance is expected to measure up at least to some minimum standards. In fact, it is convenient to distinguish rules or expectations relating to *competence*— having the knowledge or skills requisite to the occupation—and *performance*— the actual use of requisite knowledge and skills in appropriate tasks. And, since not all competent performers will in fact do equally well, it is not surprising that some form of *deference* is given to the good worker (this despite some appropriate cynicism concerning voluntary and sanctioned limits on performance).

This array of general occupational norms has been displayed precisely because they are likely to be taken for granted in highly modernized societies. Yet each is a potential source of some uncertainty and ambiguity in specific situations. And these norms cannot be taken for granted in newly modernizing areas, for they are either lacking or radically different in specific content in tribal or agrarian societies. In other words, these norms are not "normal" in a comparative sense. If indeed they can be pretty much taken for granted among contemporary workers—and that is probably not true for some disadvantaged groups—then the agencies of socialization have been remarkably effective in instilling norms that are in effect precedent to particular occupational rules of conduct.

SOCIALIZATION TO THE WORLD OF WORK

Given the ambiguity and even ambivalence attaching to the meaning of work in modern society, we should expect that the preparation for an occupation will involve either *conditioning* (implying a reluctant adjustment to a harsh reality) or *commitment* (enthusiastic acceptance of pleasurable duties), and almost certainly a mixture of the two in variable proportions. We have no reason to suppose that the conditioning/commitment process is completed in infancy, and, as we shall see, every reason to suppose that such an assumption is nonsense. Our task at this juncture is to lay out, rather briefly, the leading issues and orientations that will then permit, in due course, a rather more careful examination of problems and procedures.

By socialization we shall mean both cognitive learning and at least minimal internalization of appropriate norms. Since our focus is on occupational behavior, our concern will be with the general orienting norms that pervade the world of work and, selectively, with norms rather more specific to occupational categories.

An occupation is a social construct and its performance a social role or set of roles. This is true even if the occupation is technically antisocial (Sutherland, 1937). Indeed, virtually all social action involves norms, although the state of anomie may occur here and there, as in a situation of crisis or other discontinuity. (It is preferable to reserve the term anomie to an objective state of social situations—the condition of normlessness—and not confuse this with individual alienation or action according to inappropriate rules.) At the very minimum, occupational norms must be learned if the worker is to perform satisfactorily.

Any social system can and must survive some merely "external compliance," that is, behavior that is simply responsive to sanctions. This can scarcely be generalized, as some powerful or influential actors in the situation must subscribe to and uphold the norms. Otherwise the normative order could not survive the easy discovery that no one believed in its validity. Thus we are arguing for the necessity of internalization of norms by some—ideally by all—actors in an ongoing system or pattern of action. Several tests of normative socialization are available: compliance with norms—even if contrary to other immediate self-interests—in the absence of sanctions; manifestations of moral outrage at the misbehavior of others; manifestations of guilt following personal misbehavior.

Internalization of norms has the great social advantage of reducing the necessity of surveillance and discipline. This has a special utility in the world of work, as reluctant and discontented workers will perform as nearly as possible at the tolerable minimum of the role range, while the costs of supervising them will be high. It should also be noted that occupations of professional status are granted varying degrees of autonomy in their performance. Unless balanced by self-imposed responsibility, the exercise of professional power would be intolerable and unstable.

For learning, it would appear that any reliable source of information may serve as a more or less effective socializing agency. Yet even cognition must involve affect: the motivation to learn. The concept of conditioning implies a simple, hedonic, pain-and-pleasure principle of affect, but more elaborate and abstract learning is likely to entail subtler rewards and punishments. The family has a primary place in childhood socialization universally, normally supplemented by peer groups. The family provides instruction and admonition, but also adult role models. The peer group often provides childhood play in emulation of adult roles. In tribal and many agrarian societies these structures may provide almost the entire source of learning to be an adult. (I avoid saying "only" for the reason that extra-familial adult role models are also available. Even if age and sex are the sole bases of role differentiation—a limiting case not to be found in nature—the child needs a wider basis of experience than an immediate family can ordinarily provide. But generations are "real" only in the direct lineage of primary families. A community normally affords a relatively even age distribution rather than discontinuous generations. Thus, for example, the first-born's lack of older siblings may be compensated by observation of the older siblings of some of his peers.)

Modern societies have added formal agencies of information and instruction: notably the school, but also books and other printed matter and of course electronic communication. I suggest that to the extent that the relationship of the learner to these agencies approaches affective neutrality, learning may take place but not the internalization of norms. Put more directly, the hypothesis is that normative internalization takes place only in situations marked by strong affectivity in relationships, and some part of the affect must be positive; fear of disapproval or punishment is not to be discounted, however. This is not a very radical idea in view of our knowledge of the importance of response to the expectations of *significant* others, but it does serve to caution against expecting much "character building" to emerge from formal admonition. The capacity of the student in a professional school to recite accurately the appropriate ethical canons may have *no* consequence for his behavior in his professional practice.

The sequence of occupational socialization will plague us repeatedly, for at any given time what appears to be selectivity may simply represent prior socialization. We may note as an aside that psychologists, not surprisingly, normally emphasize personality variables and sociologists situational variables, in accounting, say, for performance differentials. This means that the psychologist has a strong predilection for emphasis on selectivity—the matching of personal traits and occupational requirements—and the sociologist will emphasize the adaptability of performers to the demands of the job. Thus it is something more than neo-Freudian doctrine that leads psychologists to what the sociologists regard as the neglect of adult socialization.

Adult socialization is critical in two notable circumstances relevant to our concerns here. The first is the situation in newly developing countries, where recruits to modern occupations cannot be prepared by their prior experience and attitudes (Moore & Feldman, 1960). The second is the nearly pandemic change in occupational structures *and* of particular occupations in advanced societies. Although the new entrant to the labor force may have the advantage of the general cognitive and normative orientations to the world of work discussed in the first section of this chapter, any early learning of specific occupational skills and norms is almost certain to be partially wrong. Moreover, the change will not stop when he begins his career; continuous socialization is therefore required (Brim & Wheeler, 1966). Even formal education, therefore, is in constant danger of being out of phase with occupational changes. There is, however, a happy congruence of certain features of the school with the *general* normative dimensions of the world of work:

1. The curriculum and study plan as such involve not only major, progressive steps in accomplishments—the "grade" or "form"—but also within the term, the week, and even the day, the child is required to adjust to change in both subject and level of proficiency.

2. The school provides the setting for competitive performance, with presumably commensurate rewards.

3. The introduction of problem solving into the curriculum (usually beyond the two or three most elementary grades) presumably encourages both an adjustment to uncertainty and some measure of creative mastery of that uncertainty (Moore, 1963b, pp. 110–111; on types of problem solving that may begin much earlier, see Goslin, 1967).

Critical Questions

In the following section of this discussion we shall attend to the sequences in occupational socialization, including the troublesome question of selection or socialization and the question of continuous commitment to an occupational career. We shall then examine the processes and degrees of internalization of occupational norms and suggest a theory of occupational socialization congruent with scattered evidence but inviting further inquiry. Finally, seeking to avoid the once-and-for-all-time error previously criticized, we shall examine the modes of reinforcement socially available to buttress frayed consciences and to assuage demoralization.

SEQUENCES IN
OCCUPATIONAL SOCIALIZATION

It is conventional, and therefore by now tedious, to contrast the absolute predictability of adult roles in tribal societies with the necessary openness or uncertainty in modernized societies. The former model is somewhat more exaggerated than the latter, but probably only slightly so. All societies use both *status ascription* and *status achievement,* whatever the prevalent ideal norms; it is impossible to do without these principles (Moore, 1963b, pp. 66–68).

Yet it is fair, because true, to say that one may properly contrast the *ideal* pattern of hereditary social placement in one type of society—in the main, tribal and agrarian social orders—with the *ideal* pattern of uncertain social placement according to the norms of equality of opportunity in modernized social orders. Exceptions abound, and we shall attend to them only when instructive.

Career Choices and Anticipatory Socialization

In the contemporary modernized world (including, perforce, the Soviet Union) the principal sorting mechanism for the adult occupational world has come to be the school—either publicly supported or publicly inspected. (The school's monopoly in the United States is not total, but it appears to be growing. Virtually every job requires at least functional literacy, but entertainers, athletes, unskilled workers—for whom there is a shrinking demand—and even some kinds of small business owners may require little more.) Selective processes of course start before school entrance. One of the major sources of inequality of opportunity is the differential readiness of children to start their education. And the differences persist, or even increase, through the various educational levels (Coleman et al., 1966). Thus many career choices are essentially negative in that the educational qualifications are not met; indeed, if we accept the primacy of environmental influences, we are not dealing with genuine choices but with outcomes.

Small children typically say that they want to have an adult occupation that appears to them glamorous, either out of their local experience, or, more probably these days, from their exposure to television. Maturation consists in part of making more realistic judgments of objective opportunities and personal capacities. The child's fumbling for an identity increasingly includes preparation for a prospective identity.

The nature of occupational choice is still rather poorly known. The process is clearest where, in a sense, there is in fact little choice, as in situations where the son expects to follow his father's occupation. Farming, family-owned business, and several of the professions are strongly "hereditary," though in the case of farming of course most sons go into urban occupations—the point is that virtually no city child chooses farming as a career. In all these instances there is a clear adult role model to follow, and perhaps several, since common occupation is also a strong basis of adult friendships. For other children—and they are in the vast majority—moving toward an adult occupation consists of a complex mixture of narrowing the range of choices (or having them narrowed by poor educational performance); exploration of alternatives by use of information, misinformation, and sheer fantasy; and considerable components of sheer chance. The availability of reliable information is very uneven. (See, for example, Hopke, 1966.) Even where school systems provide vocational or guidance counselors, their information is likely to be out-of-date, and it is not uncommon for them strongly to discourage Negroes or other minority groups from "unrealistic" aspirations. Thus the rare child who has overcome almost overwhelming disadvantages faces still another gatekeeper who directs him to a "vocational" course.

One element of chance in the course of educational careers is the occurrence of unusually influential teachers or perhaps of critical events that open or close opportunities. Although I know of no systematic evidence on the influence of teachers, it is my personal observation that individuals in successful careers—at least in the professions—are able to name several influential teachers, ranging back to elementary school, to recall names, the grade, and the subject matter. With the possible exception of negative nostalgia for a tyrant, other teachers are blurred. If this observation should prove to be correct, it would force amendment to the usual supposition that teachers have little or no effect on attitudes and choices. The occasional teacher may be included as one of the "significant others."

We now come to a paradox. In an urban setting in modernized societies, many of the characteristic attributes or dimensions of occupations lend themselves to anticipatory and gradual, accumulative socialization: monetary payments and the market, specialization, authority, rationality, mobility, and the temporal and spacial separation of work from most other social involvements. Yet it is precisely in these situations, with the necessary openness in the occupational system, increased by changing occupational distributions and the steady appearance of new occupations, that exact childhood socialization to adult occupational roles can be true only for a minority. Inheritance of occupational "categories"—skilled labor, business management—is more extensive than precise occupational succession, but this may add little in the way of necessary skills and norms. Even the professionals (among whom nominal inheritance runs high) must postpone at least their technical learning until late adolescence and early adulthood. And in fields like the academic disciplines or medicine, the training of the young will not be highly replicative of the previous generation's experience. Norms of course may be somewhat less subject to change than are knowledge and practice, but unless the occupational norms are empty but pious generalities, they too will require modifications and additions consistent with new problems and powers.

The educational system may be likened to a succession of ladders, increasingly differentiated in their destinations at higher levels or floors. One problem that arises is that there is little firm footing for the student who gets off, or is pushed off, the ladders prior to the completion of secondary school. He may be able to find steady and perhaps even satisfactory employment, but it is increasingly difficult to do so. For those who do, on-the-job training may inculcate both the skills and the appropriate norms of conduct and performance. (Actually, of course, some of this occurs in nearly every occupation, for it remains true that one learns to do by doing.)

The school is most clearly adapted to preparation for dealing with *ideas,* and thus for occupations with a substantial intellectual content. Dealing with *people* may be learned essentially as a by-product of the circumstance that the school is a social organization. Dealing with *things* may be partially trained through vocational curricula in secondary schools, but in effect "shop" courses serve more nearly as custodial day-care centers for potential delinquents than as genuinely educational enterprises. Thus both as a sorting and as a socializing agency, the school treats these occupational dimensions with a very uneven hand.

For those students who persist to higher educational levels, choices become more frequent as curricula are specialized and differentiated. Some choices become virtually irreversible, either because going back and starting a new course is too costly in time, or because the educational system is not sufficiently flexible to distinguish between an improper choice of route and lack of capacity for any route.

Selection and Socialization

We return, then, briefly to the factors determining both choice and performance in preparing for adult occupational roles. The attempt to decrease the number of failures and misfits by rationalizing the process of choice has had only indifferent success. Standardized tests are available to determine varying aptitudes and interests, and thus to use *selective* criteria for continuing and more specialized *socialization* (Stoker, 1966). Aptitude and ability tests do provide a predictive basis for further academic performance (Goslin, 1963), but that performance in turn has poor predictive power for subsequent careers. There is of course always the possibility that ability tests become self-validating by virtue of their results being known to the person tested or, especially, to subsequent judges. Similarly, occupational interest tests may lead to choices and actions that will validate the advice.

We cannot leave the subject of the educational system without observing that much of the selectivity there practiced is informal and even unconscious. We have earlier commented on the positive influence of particular teachers, but negative selection also occurs. Particularly in elementary grades, displays of originality are commonly discouraged, partly because originality may have a negative correlation with neatness, but mainly because it is a nuisance to the overworked teacher. Schools and teachers differ in this as in other respects, but standardized performance is always easier to administer than is variety.

Continuing Commitment

Let us suppose that the youngster has completed or terminated his formal education and is ready to enter the labor market. By this time he has chosen, or had forced on him, if not a precise occupation at least a somewhat narrow range of alternatives for which he has competence and, possibly, interest. (Let us also for the moment confine our attention to young men, as the ambiguity of position and possible ambivalence of young ladies in the labor force complicates the picture too much.) If and when he secures employment he is likely to require some training—at the minimum, instructions in duties and procedures, the rules of the office and shop, and so on. The question we now pose is whether this ends the matter, and the answer is clearly "No."

The worker must meet minimum levels of competence and performance in order to get and keep his job or, for the self-employed, in order to survive in a competitive market for goods and services. (Sinecures do exist, of course, but they are rare.) If these simply constitute externally imposed conditions, that would end the matter. Note, however, that the uncommitted employee presents the employer with supervisory problems, and the employer will always select the "conscientious worker" if he has a choice.

In the early stages of industrialization the factories and shops are commonly manned by voluntary but reluctant recruits, lacking even the general normative orientations discussed in our first section. Some large but not exactly known proportion of European immigrants to the United States came with no intention of staying, and the same is certainly true of part of the displaced peasants (internal migrants) in Asia, Africa, and Latin America. These workers thus constitute an important source of evidence on adult socialization. Labor commitment, which may remain less than enthusiastic during the entire adult years, nevertheless does occur. It is aided by the intersection of work norms with market norms, those of associations and interest groups, and—particularly in new nations—even with nationalist ideologies (Moore, 1965; Moore & Feldman, 1960).

For the worker whose prior socialization has taken place in the context of "industrial traditions," the question becomes one of the particular occupation, conditions of work, identification of common interests, and the like. Wilensky found in his sample of urban workers only a minority who experienced a "stable career," either by remaining in an occupation or progressing through a sensible sequence of occupations (Wilensky, 1961). Some discontinuities arise from the vicissitudes of the labor market, but some also arise from the voluntary actions of workers, since trial and error in the *honorable* quest for improved opportunities is intrinsic to an open and mobile system. Just as in the educational process, both accident and choice are likely to figure in changing occupations.

The capacity to adapt, to learn new skills, and to adopt new norms is thus a generally desirable set of qualities in the world of work.

Three types of work experience will serve to illustrate the features and problems of continuous commitment.

The first example involves the "submerged sector" of the labor force, variable in size and composition, but sharing the experience of unemployment, intermittent or chronic, or of being paid for menial and unrewarding work. These people are by no means wanting in socialization to the world of work, but their experience can scarcely give them much basis for continuous commitment. Yet it is surely a mistake to view most such individuals as resigned to their fate, particularly if they are relatively young, and certainly a mistake to assume that they set a positive value on deprivation. The "culture of poverty" certainly exists as a set of norms and practices for coping with adversity, but has to be spurious as a set of values that commands allegiance against alternatives. Wilensky (1966) notes that employment is so crucial in modern society for a male's sense of social worth and self-esteem that the common fate of what we have called the submerged sector is virtually total social isolation.

Our second example comprises a major portion of the labor force, those performing tasks in administrative organizations. Indeed, if we include all wage and salary earners as "bureaucratized," they comprise over four-fifths of the entire labor force (Moore, 1966). But let us narrow the field to those organizations that are large enough (say 100 or more total employees) to require several hierarchical levels of administration. One conspicuous feature of such organizations is that job specifications and other procedures are governed by elaborate, specific, and formal rules. Little room for discretion is apparent, though generally discretion increases with rank and reward. But in view of the intrinsic necessity of succession in enduring organizations with mortal (and mobile) inhabitants, some latitude is inevitable. This is true of all role-prescriptive norms.

Now clearly at the minimum the incumbent of an office must learn the appropriate norms in order to perform satisfactorily. Whether he regards them as right or not is a separate question. For some the rules may be simply conditions of employment. Violation is relatively difficult, both because in an interdependent system other people are watching, and because indirect controls are also available—for example, the rules adopted by accountants. Yet higher administrators seek the dedicated subordinate, for commitment tends to be valued in judging men for promotion and other rewards. And since security of employment is commonly granted to administrative staffs in fact if not by rule, an attempt will be made to exclude those who may abuse the privileges of security. Those who see private and public bureaucracies as havens for "organization men" (Whyte, 1956) view socialization to bureaucratic norms as regrettably successful. Merton (1957) in fact identifies ritualistic adherence to rules as a form of social deviation, and so it may be. The question is whether the system tolerates normative innovation for its own good. Argyris (1964) argues that there is an intrinsic conflict between individuals and organizations, which in a sense must be true for all but the pathologically dedicated office-holder, since work organizations are radically limited in purpose or mission compared with the breadth of normal human interests. It does not follow that bureaucratic positions can offer nothing that could command an incumbent's loyalty.

Bureaucratic organizations offer ample opportunities for analysis of the relative weight attached to selection and socialization for those who succeed in a graded career, and for study of ways of handling frustration and even ways of living up to increased and perhaps unsought additional responsibility. It must be supposed that continuous commitment is most difficult for those whose careers have reached "dead ends" well before normal retirement age.

The third example of continuing occupational socialization relates to the learned professions. We shall not stop here to formulate an elaborate definition of the professions. It is generally most sensible to deal with a scale of professionalism, with advanced education and relative autonomy in performance having high scale values. Another professional characteristic, which may be made either definitional or as a generalization about professionals otherwise identified, is commitment to a calling. This means, among other things, loyalty to a collectivity (Goode, 1957) as well as to occupational norms. The professional is expected to meet criteria of competence and performance, and to seek and recognize excellence. And, as earlier noted, it is precisely because professionals enjoy a large measure of autonomy in their exercise of what amounts to a form of power over their clients' welfare that their responsible behavior is, ideally, self-imposed. It is true that other restraints are available: the judgment of peers, disciplinary action by formal associations, law suits by dissatisfied clients. Particularly for the "helping" professions in private practice, however, external controls are likely to be called on only in extreme cases; self-restraint marks the socialized practitioner.

A problem faced by most professionals in the contemporary situation is compliance with the norms of competence, as the knowledge base changes and expands. Valiant resistance to specialization can only result in growing incompetence relative to changing standards set by superior performers. The duty of keeping current is owed not only to clients but also to peers, since poor performance may reflect discredit on the occupation as a whole. The incompetent professional's peers may defend poor performance to the laity and "cover up" for him, but they are likely to admonish him privately not to repeat errors.

In view of the expectation of occupational commitment among professionals, it is not surprising that we encounter some feeling of desertion (if not treason) when a scientist becomes a laboratory administrator, a physician a hospital administrator, or a professor an academic dean. Legal training is apparently more commonly used as a bridge to other occupations, such as politics or business management, and this branching in career lines may be more acceptable to former peers; one suspects, however, at least some ambivalence toward such behavior.

We have been suggesting that for at least part of the labor force occupational socialization does not end with entry into the labor market. This is clearly the case for the occupationally mobile and for those in occupations with changing standards. Whether because of changes in the market for skills or because of changes more or less internal to occupations, we may expect in the future an even greater need for adult adaptability, and in not a few instances outright retraining of a formal kind (Wolfbein, 1966).

INTERNALIZATION
OF OCCUPATIONAL NORMS

So far we have argued that occupations are performed in a social context that is characterized by both general norms, common to the world of work, and more particular rules of conduct applicable to distinct occupations or occupational categories. We have also argued on behalf of the convenience and probability, although not the absolute necessity in every instance, of internalization of these norms by the occupational performer.

Now clearly not all of the norms carry equal moral valence. Some carry high ethical weight, such as the ideal norms of professional loyalty to clients' interests; others may be administrative rules that represent an arbitrary selection among alternatives, simply because some rule is necessary. We shall neglect this end of the scale, as the normative stance here may be more general: acceptance of reasonable rules. We should also expect that distinctive occupational norms of substantial moral content will have a high coincidence with the ranking of the occupation in terms of authority, prestige, and income, though in an increasingly interdependent system the need for assurance of responsible performance becomes very generalized.

Dedication to Ideal Norms

Our discussion of occupational socialization should not be construed too narrowly. For the wage and salary earner four legitimate interests relevant to the world of work may be distinguished: (1) identification with a specific occupation or closely related set of jobs; (2) identification with a more or less distinct status—the basis of industrial unionism, but also of managerial and professional groups; (3) loyalty to an employer at least to the extent that the economic survival and prosperity of the employer is requisite to continued employment and possible advancement; (4) some identification with an entire industry or sector of the economy—steel as opposed to aluminum, private as opposed to public welfare agencies (Moore, 1960). The interesting point about these proper interests is that they are not mutually exclusive, although their claims upon the workman are rarely completely consistent. Thus one requirement of the socialized worker is "balancing off" the possibly divergent claims upon his loyalties.

Specific occupational norms may require us to distinguish ideal and practical norms, a distinction nearly universally valid in patterned social action. Ideal norms constitute standards for approximation. We should have some confidence that they have been internalized if deference is accorded to close approximation and scorn exhibited at serious shortcomings. Despite the reports of fairly widespread indifference and alienation among workers (Wilensky, 1966; Levenstein, 1962), we suggest that respect for workmanship in this sense is also widespread.

Mechanisms of Occupational Socialization

The more or less formal educational systems designed to prepare young adults for the world of work convey with varying degrees of accuracy the formal requirements and formal rules of conduct appropriate to particular occupations. Verbal prescriptions and admonitions are rarely adequate; some form of apprenticeship or on-the-job training is a normal part of occupational socialization. Both in the context of formal training and in the situation of the newly recruited worker, formal precept is supplemented (and at times supplanted) by more knowledgeable associates. Thus in professional schools the less advanced students derive both cognitive and affective cues from those farther along in training (Merton, Reader & Kendall, 1957). The extensive attention to peer groups in the literature often misses the point that their members may not be truly equal. One of the ways in which nominal peers are influential in socialization as *significant others* is that they know and exemplify the norms, and thus are accorded respect as well as liking or affection. This means that peers are less different from adult role models than might at first appear. In both cases it is the expectations of significant others that induce normative compliance and, normally, an actual sharing of attitudes and beliefs. This sharing, whether or not fully articulated, then constitutes an occupational identity, which is collective as well as individual. The individual *belongs*.

A Punishment-Centered Theory of Socialization

The frequency with which initiates to an occupation are put through some form of hazing may be interpreted either as a rather irrational survival of savagery, or possibly as having a definite function in socialization. I suggest the latter is the case. If, instead of hazing, we take the broader notion of suffering, it appears to be a prominent component in the training for all occupations that exhibit strong attention to standards of competence and performance and to identification with the occupation as a collectivity. (Tomkins, 1965, has argued a similar point, his illustrations being the experiences of abolitionists. I owe my particular perception of professional socialization to some comments by Goode, 1957.)

Some professional schools virtually sequester their trainees, setting them apart from normal social activity in what amount to "total institutions"—military academies and some theological schools provide examples (Dornbusch, 1955). Other professional schools approximate such social isolation by the sheer burden of work demanded of students—classes, laboratories, studies, and practice. And despite the possible commitment of the student to his chosen career, at least part of the demands made upon him will be unpleasant and even hazardous to his remaining in good standing.

We thus have some of the ingredients of our proposed theory. The initiate is put through a set of tasks and duties that are difficult, and some are unpleasant. Success is accorded to most of the entrants, but not all; failure is a realistic possibility. These challenging and painful experiences are shared with others, who thus have a sort of fellowship of suffering.

Now if we add the probability that peers and adult role models constitute significant others, and thus that relations with them are marked by some degree of affectivity, we are well on the way to comprehending how an occupational identity gets formed. In short, the theory is that occupational identity and commitment will be proportional to the degree that these conditions are approximated—whether for the individual or for an occupational collectivity.

Although not essential to the theory, some additional and associated features of "punishing socialization" may be noted. Some of the difficult tasks are commonly ritualized and in that sense arbitrary. The medical student bound for a career in psychiatry must memorize the bones of the human body; the law student looking forward to a practice in establishing trusts for wealthy clients must learn endless cases in torts; the doctoral candidate in a university intending to become a statistician must show that he can read French and German as well as have familiarity with outmoded classics; and military training abounds with apparently meaningless tasks. Marks of success, too, are commonly ritualized: awards, election to honorary fraternities, certificates, and diplomas. Yet the punishment does not stop so quickly, at least for occupations high on the scale of professionalism. The medical intern does the medical dirty work around a hospital; the young lawyer does the dirty work around a law firm, or, for that matter, if he attempts to establish an individual practice; the newly minted Ph.D. who enters college teaching does not exactly have to carry senior professors' books, but he does have to teach the courses they do not want. And although greater freedom follows successful survival of trials, the *persistent* possibility of failure is characteristic of most professional and technical occupations. We are suggesting that this is an important ingredient of continuing occupational commitment. Another allegation then follows: that persons who get into positions of absolute security, with no need to expose themselves to risk and uncertainty, in fact become occupationally unproductive. (We have rediscovered Calvinism by a devious route, but there it is.)

Still another feature of occupational socialization—and again we are attending primarily to fairly technical occupations—is the learning of technical language. Note that part of an occupational *patois* will consist of synonyms for words in general usage, and part will refer to objects, ideas, and processes beyond the layman's ken. Aside from facilitating precise technical communication, esoteric language serves to identify and exclude and thus to confirm occupational identity. It appears also to serve a psychological function, a kind of emotional set: now I am thinking technically. (I have found graduate students in sociology appearing disturbed and threatened by discussion of sociological data and principles in ordinary language. One might ask, too severely, what besides vocabulary do they have to hold on to?)

The person who successfully learns the language and skills of a trade, and survives the ordeals that punished him and his fellows will emerge, we are arguing, not only with an internalized occupational commitment but also with an identification with the collectivity, the brotherhood. Yet note that for professional and similar occupations subject to continuing internal specialization and to substantial differences in the style and setting of occupational activities, identification with the occupational collectivity must be increasingly nostalgic: shared suffering and success in the past. Note also that the shared experience need not be entirely simultaneous, as long as the socializing system endures. This circumstance undoubtedly accounts for resistance to major changes in occupational training, for such changes would destroy a bridge across age groups—a bridge increasingly difficult to maintain in technical occupations, where the young, distressingly, know more than their elders. And even if the young are punished no less, and perhaps more, suffering comes in new forms that the older worker did not experience.

Normative Conflicts

Lest we become too impressed with the neatness of occupational socialization that yields conscientious workers in an untroubled world, we should attend to some ambiguities and conflicts in occupational norms.

Medicine offers two classic types of normative conflict, and a host of new ones. The mother-child problem in a difficult childbirth when both cannot be saved is resolved in favor of the child in Catholic doctrine, and in favor of the mother in Protestant and Jewish doctrine. Medical ethics offer no guidance except to save both. Improvements in medical practice, however, make the dilemma increasingly rare. On the other hand, the euthanasia problem is increasingly common, particularly for aged patients. Should those with painful and incurable maladies or who are hopelessly senile be kept alive? Medical ethics say "Yes," but there is no firm consensus in the broader community. More relevant to normative socialization is the greediness of many medical practitioners, and the evidence that spokesmen for the organized profession seem to have been more concerned with medical incomes than with the availability of medical care (Harris, 1966).

Indeed, all of the helping professions in an affluent society may be tempted into serving those best able to pay, and thus abandoning or impairing the service orientation demanded by their professional codes.

Nor is it only professionals, strictly speaking, who face moral dilemmas or temptations to shady or slovenly performance. Should the corporation executive serve stockholder interests, or his own? (They are not always the same.) What are the proper bounds in advertising, or in the manufacture and sale of worthless or harmful products? What are the conscionable limits to restrictions on output (restrictions that in some degree are practiced by *virtually all* occupations)? The circumstance that these questions can be sensibly asked does not bespeak an absence of occupational norms, upheld by honorable workers. The point is that occupations are social constructs, and thus cannot remain isolated from the interests and values of the broader community and society.

Déformation Professionelle

The charming French phrase *déformation professionelle* refers to the possible distortions in character that derive from participation in the world of work—in any occupation. One mild example is the incapacity to divest oneself of occupational concerns in other social contexts: the inveterate "shop talk" of professionals, the businessman who thinks only of business. Yet Wilensky's data confirm a bit of folk wisdom: "If you want a job done, give it to a busy man." It is precisely the hard working and successful portions of the labor force that also become involved in community service and "constructive" recreation. And, conversely, it is those whose jobs are essentially meaningless who find leisure as constituting "time on their hands" (Wilensky, 1966).

The subtler forms of character distortion also merit attention. Rampant and increasing specialization may result in an excessively narrow view not only of the world of work, but of the world generally. Narrow problem solving may inhibit thinking about whether the problem is important. The worker may become overcommitted to occupational norms and practices, resisting even those innovations that would improve his position or make his task easier. And in social situations outside the workplace, popular occupational stereotypes may have some merit: the fussy accountant, argumentative lawyer, didactic teacher, crude and materialistic businessman, inarticulate mechanic or engineer, television-addicted factory worker, and tense and brittle advertising man. It would be surprising if work did not leave its mark, for roles are one thing, but they are played by more or less whole persons.

MODES OF REINFORCEMENT

Just as we have argued that socialization is a continuing and not simply early and terminal process, so we should note that the conscientious performer is rarely isolated from reinforcements. In a sense, internalization of occupational norms is itself a kind of reinforcement, for self-respect may be a powerful restraint on slovenly performance or violation of standards. Additionally, even the relatively autonomous professional is not entirely out of sight of his peers. We have repeatedly used the phrase "expectations of significant others," and that about sums it up. Indifference to the opinions of peers is exceptional and plainly pathological; it is the essence of alienation.

More formal reinforcements also exist. The extremely poor workman finds no market for his services or products. The wage or salary earner is bound by the standards set by his employer, enforced by his supervisor. Occupational associations—particularly among the professions and those seeking professional status—set standards of training and performance, and many provide machinery for formal charges and discipline. Even the government may be used as a disciplinary agent: the damage suit instituted by an aggrieved employer, customer, or client; the removal of a license; perhaps even a charge of criminal misconduct. The rarity of extreme sanctions means either that rules are poorly enforced or that occupational socialization and informal reinforcements serve in most cases. With some possible exceptions—abortion may be one, for the law is more severe than many members of the community would support—the probability is high that socialization works.

REFERENCES

ARGYRIS, C. *Integrating the individual and the organization.* New York: Wiley, 1964.

BOROW, H. Development of occupational motives and roles. In Lois Wladis Hoffman & M. L. Hoffman (Eds.), *Review of child development research,* Vol. II. New York: Russell Sage Foundation, 1966. Pp. 373–422.

BRIM, O. G., JR., & WHEELER, S. *Socialization after childhood.* New York: Wiley, 1966.

COLEMAN, J. S., ET AL. *Equality of educational opportunity.* Washington: U. S. Department of Health, Education, and Welfare, 1966.

DORNBUSCH, S. M. The military academy as an assimilating institution. *Social Forces,* 1955, 33, 316–321.

GOODE, W. J. Community within a community: The professions. *American Sociological Review,* 1957, 22, 194–200.

GOSLIN, D. A. *The search for ability.* New York: Russell Sage Foundation, 1963.

GOSLIN, D. A. The school in a changing society: Notes on the development of strategies for solving educational problems. *American Journal of Orthopsychiatry,* 1967, 37, 843–858.

HARRIS, R. *A sacred trust.* New York: New American Library, 1966.

HOPKE, W. E. (Ed.) *Encyclopedia of careers and vocational guidance.* Vol. I, Planning your career; Vol. II, Careers and occupations. Garden City, N.Y.: Doubleday, 1966.

INKELES, A. The modernization of man. In M. Weiner (Ed.), *Modernization: The dynamics of growth.* New York: Basic Books, 1966. Pp. 138–150.

LEVENSTEIN, A. *Why people work.* New York: Crowell-Collier, 1962.

MERTON, R. K. *Social theory and social structure.* (Rev. Ed.) Glencoe, Ill.: Free Press, 1957.

MERTON, R. K., READER, G., & KENDALL, PATRICIA L. (Eds.) *The student physician.* Cambridge, Mass.: Harvard Univer. Press, 1957.

MOORE, W. E. Notes for a general theory of labor organization. *Industrial and Labor Relations Review,* 1960, 13, 387–397.

MOORE, W. E. *The conduct of the corporation.* New York: Random House, 1962.

MOORE, W. E. *Man, time, and society.* New York: Wiley, 1963. (a)

MOORE, W. E. *Social change.* Englewood Cliffs, N.J.: Prentice-Hall, 1963. (b)

MOORE, W. E. *Industrialization and labor.* New York: Russell & Russell, 1965.

MOORE, W. E. Changes in occupational structures. In N. J. Smelser & S. M. Lipset (Eds.), *Social structure and mobility in economic development*. Chicago: Aldine, 1966.

MOORE, W. E., & FELDMAN, A. S. *Labor commitment and social change in developing areas*. New York: Social Science Council, 1960.

SIGERIST, H. E. *A history of medicine*. Vol. I, Primitive and archaic medicine, Part II, Primitive medicine. New York: Oxford University Press, 1951.

STOKER, H. Using test results in vocational planning. In W. E. Hopke (Ed.), *Encyclopedia of careers and vocational guidance*. Garden City, N.Y.: Doubleday, 1966. Pp. 19–26.

SUTHERLAND, E. H. *The professional thief*. Chicago: Univer. of Chicago Press, 1937.

TOMKINS, S. S. The constructive role of violence and suffering for the individual and for his society. Part 1 of a chapter on The psychology of commitment, in S. S. Tomkins & Carroll E. Izard (Eds.), *Affect, cognition, and personality*. New York: Springer, 1965.

WHYTE, W. H., JR. *The organization man*. New York: Simon & Schuster, 1956.

WILENSKY, H. L. Orderly careers and social participation: The impact of work history on social integration in the middle mass. *American Sociological Review*, 1961, 26, 521–539.

WILENSKY, H. L. Work as a social problem. In H. S. Becker (Ed.), *Social problems: A modern approach*. New York: Wiley, 1966. Chap. 3.

WOLFBEIN, S. L. The future world of work. In W. E. Hopke (Ed.), *Encyclopedia of careers and vocational guidance*. Garden City, N.Y.: Doubleday, 1966. Pp. 37–44.

CHAPTER 22

Socialization For
Marriage And Parenthood

Reuben Hill and Joan Aldous

University of Minnesota

There are good and sufficient reasons for devoting attention in a book on socialization theory to the problem of socialization for marriage and parenthood in America. Americans may not be the most marrying people in the world, as some writers insist, but they can certainly be counted among those most in favor of the institution. Marriedness as a status is highly valued here, with only about three per cent of the marriageable population in the divorced or separated statuses at any one time. Moreover, Americans marry and become parents earliest of all industrialized peoples, fully two years earlier than their neighbors, the Canadians. In addition, Americans are more self-conscious about their marital behavior. A substantial amount of research on marital and parental roles has been done over the years in several academic disciplines and the results have filtered into public print. Other countries do not as yet have as extended coverage of the family, but there is some suggestion that they may be moving toward the American way of married life (Goode, 1963). For these reasons we are focusing on the American setting in this chapter and on its patterns of socialization for marriage and parenthood. Even in the United States, however, as we shall demonstrate time after time, there are gaps in our knowledge, and much of our information does not extend beyond white, middle-class America.

Choosing America as the setting for our discussion, we shall also give primacy, as Americans are increasingly doing, to the marital over the parental dimension. If, at an earlier date, the tasks of parenthood appeared to be virtually coterminous with the family's functions, it is no longer true. The marital career has become salient, clearly differentiated from the parental career. The marital career is lengthening, beginning earlier and persisting longer, at the same time that the parental care functions have been concentrated into a shorter period, due to the "bunching" of childbearing in the early years of marriage and the consequent earlier launching of children into jobs and marriage (Glick, 1957). Moreover, marital companionship and conjugal love have now become the central bonds of family solidarity and stability.

This salience of the marital dimension is new enough in our history to justify the closest attention of socialization scholars. Good descriptive work is required to capture the emergent marriage roles, and the process by which they are learned. By virtue of the recency of their emergence as differentiated family roles they are less likely to be scripted, requiring, therefore, more improvisations in performance. These reasons have prompted us to focus upon the marital dimension in America in this exploratory essay.

We are cognizant of the paucity of empirical research relevant to socialization for the adult roles of spouse and parent, and regard our task more as one of illumination and clarification to open the dialogue for more systematic study rather than to achieve closure about the dimensions we shall describe.

The focus of our attention will be more upon the processes of socialization and resocialization than on the products or outcomes of the processes. We will divide the processes into segments using critical transition points in the pre-marital and immediate post-marital careers, leaving to others the discussion of the child-rearing years. We will further identify and classify, within these phases, the range and variety of relevant socializing situations from informal family and quasi-family settings to formally controlled school situations. The chief concepts utilized are descriptive sensitizers which permit us to see simultaneously *socializee* (ego) and *socializers* (agents and agencies) in *interaction* within the relatively facilitating and confining *settings* in which socialization and resocialization occur. Within this matrix of ego-alter situation, response sets are developed, some of which are activated as self roles appropriate to the position ego occupies at the time; others are anticipatory and are stored as latent roles for later use when ego's position accrues new role expectations, as in marriage.

In brief, taking our cue from Winch (1962), our focus is upon *positional socialization*, that is, socialization into the roles of the marital positions. We shall, thereby, avoid the thorny issues of the development of core personality involved in identification and the process of transmitting deeply rooted response sets from generation to generation. We shall find our task complicated enough in assessing the processes at work which mature and motivate the young to take on the adult statuses of marriage and parenthood.

It may be useful to specify in broad strokes what are the properties of the marriage relation in America for which socialization is needed. The association of marriage is a particularly comprehensive primary group containing two normatively prescribed social positions. Compared with other small groups, the marriage pair is both complicated and simplified by virtue of certain of its properties.

First of all, the marriage pair relationship in this society is simplified by its age similarity which makes husband and wife members of the same generation. The two have a community of experiences common to their generation and similar interests accruing from these experiences. Age similarity also makes for greater symmetry in the power each spouse exercises in decision-making.

All other properties of this small group tend more to complicate than to simplify the task of socialization for role performance. Differences of gender and complications of heterosexuality, at once major sources of attraction drawing the sexes together, are also the basis for the different appraisals of the world which so irritate and alienate the sexes when they are yoked together. The more the wife has been trained to abstain from masculine activities, and the more the husband in his masculinity training has been protected from the values of the world of women, the greater the cleavage between the two in marriage. A second expression of cultural conflict complicating socialization for marriage roles is the phenomenon of marrying outside the parental family, which means that the principals have received their training for marriage in two different parental family settings. Thus, whatever training occurs in the parental family is likely to have to be largely unlearned if incompatible with the model espoused by the spouse's family.

A third complicating feature of this small group is the comprehensiveness and *extreme intimacy* of the marital dyad, the complete communal sharing and lack of outlets for displacement of hostility. The protective barriers which preserve privacy between the sexes tend to be withdrawn in marriage. Secrets are not to be kept from one another. Even the barriers which protect the tender ego from exposure to criticism are expected to fall. The disposition to share is nowhere so elaborated as in the marriage relation.

Finally, the marriage pair is one of the few groups in our society which plans for permanence. It is expected that once the relation has been formally recognized, this small group will seek to build a relationship which can survive personality changes, illness and financial reverses. The husband-wife relation is expected to survive the competitive attractions of professional commitments, demands and dependencies of children, and the variety of entrancing love objects which cross the stage during the marriage span. The marriage group, in sum, has in common all of the recurring requirements of any small group of planning, decision-making, timing and scheduling, and integration of activities to achieve common ends, compounded by this unique feature of the expectation of permanence—a partnership contract without an escape clause.

How does socialization for this unusual set of role requirements take place in American society? In quick preview, we will organize our discussion by stages, beginning with apprenticeship in the parental family with its peculiar contributions and limitations, which, fortunately, may be corrected both by formal study and by observing the marriages of others. This latter corrective occurs simultaneously with exposure to a series of interpersonal situations resembling, in some degree, the tightly knit interdependence of the marriage situation including brother-sister relations, fluctuating "chum" relations and boy-girl crushes, dating and going steady involvements, and the engagement.

But socialization is not all anticipatory in type. It continues after the wedding and honeymoon with much trial and error learning from one another, unlearning and resocialization to cope with the conflicting marriage models brought by the new marrieds from their respective parental families. With the advent of the first child, latent parental roles are not only activated for the first time, but marital roles are once again modified in a continued process of re-socialization. We close the chapter with an examination of the attempts to pro-fessionalize marriage and parenthood by formal training and an assessment of the relative impact these efforts have had on contemporary marital and parental practices.

APPRENTICESHIP
IN THE PARENTAL FAMILY

For good or for ill, socialization for both marriage and parenthood begins in the parental family. In this setting more is "caught" than is formally taught; in-deed, it is less than precise to use the vocabulary of formal education in dis-cussing socialization in the family setting.

Fortunately, perhaps, for the spontaneity of husband-wife relations, parents remain blissfully unaware of themselves as agents of marital socialization. They are much too busy making children conform to their expectations of what a "good child" should be. They tend to ignore the impact of their behavior toward one another as spouses on the imagery of marriage being formed by their children, and they are even less aware of the implications for later marital roles of the cross-sex relations between parent and child of the opposite sex. A possible analogy might be drawn from the situation of the elementary school teacher who is inadvertently engaged in training teachers-to-be while concen-trating consciously on maintaining discipline and focusing on rendering her charges literate. The children acquire, as latent learning, the satisfactions and frustrations of the teaching profession, the hierarchical relations of principal-teachers and teacher-pupils, and the more symmetrical teacher-to-teacher col-league relationship. These observations provide a pre-set about whether it is desirable to aspire to teaching as a status. There is more to these interactions than anticipatory "vocational tasting," however. Children, in mastering the pupil roles, are also perforce learning the reciprocal teacher roles by role-taking, storing them for later retrieval as an apprentice teacher when an adult class-room situation may require their activation.

A fundamental difference between the teacher as unwitting model for teachers-to-be and the parent as unintended model for parents and spouses-to-be is that the average child generalizes his model of the teaching profession from exposure to many different teachers, but is limited to one set of parents from which to glean the norms for his marital and parental roles. Moreover, the normative content of the teacher roles is relatively undifferentiated with respect to gender, whereas the gender norms of both spouses and parents are highly differentiated and complementary, requiring the child to master both sets of roles in order successfully to role-take one while role-playing the other. It is perhaps understandable that the models of marriage developed by many chil-dren show role diffusion and confusion.

. It should also be noted that within the family the parent-child subsystem is intergenerational and many of the norms and mechanisms governing the system are directed toward balancing these unstable intergenerational relations. In contrast, the marital subsystem and the sibling subsystem are generationally homogeneous, with many of their norms and mechanisms directed toward stabilizing intergender relations. Socialization for marriage within the family consists of one generation, the marital subsystem, communicating indirectly and inexplicitly to the next generation with a third subsystem, the parent-child, concerned with issues of respect and optimum distance between the generations, serving as the intergenerational link.

These several subsystems have differentiated objectives and join forces with some conflict and confusion in dealing with the issues of socialization. The two uni-generational subsystems maintain boundaries of separateness while permitting connectedness through the intergenerational parent-child subsystem which becomes the chief vehicle for socialization. The marital subsystem values its privacy (separate sleeping spaces and dressing rooms) and may appear to operate in "closed executive session" on many matters. The sibling subsystem bases its solidarity on its differentiation from the old-fashioned ways of its antecedents and questions what can be learned from a generation already so out-of-date. In a rapidly changing society the gulf between the generations is wide, leaving the two subsystems in a constant state of tension and complicating the mediating tasks of the parent-child subsystem.

Yet despite these structural difficulties the family is the primary socialization agency for training the young in marital and parental roles. Our analysis of the learning process will make use of the paradigm developed by Brim based on a cross-classification of the content of socialization and the requisite characteristics of the individual for satisfactory role performance (Brim & Wheeler, 1966). What ego has to learn with regard to any role can be categorized as either behaviors that indicate he is playing a particular role or the values that provide the rationale for the role behaviors. But to play a role, ego must have knowledge of the values and behaviors constituting the role. He must also be *motivated* to seek these values and behave in the expected fashion, and finally he has to have the *ability* to perform the role behaviors and to internalize the directing values.

The foregoing explanation is an introduction to the forms that socialization for marriage takes in the parental family. The enduring products of early socialization in the family, because they are of the "cold storage" type or anticipatory, are at the level of motivations and value orientations rather than at the level of norms governing day-to-day conduct. The family provides one image of marriage from the repetitive spousal role performances of the parents, insofar as these have been interpretable by children. Less durable, probably, are the behaviors learned from simulated marital roles picked up in self-other interactions with parent and/or siblings of the opposite sex. Let us examine each of these in somewhat greater detail, bringing such research findings to bear as appear to be pertinent.

Motivation to Marry

The value attached to marriage and parenthood, generating the desire to marry and have children, is a lasting product of socialization in the parental family. The research evidence is not entirely satisfactory because the gap is so great between the time when parental indoctrination and/or parental example occurred in childhood and the time in young adulthood when the respondent's degree of commitment to marriage has been elicited by the researcher. Wallin's (1954) study is relevant to the issue. He found marital happiness of parents closely correlated with the attitudes of their college-age offspring toward marriage. Note, however, that it was the less committed male student whose positive evaluation of marriage was most contingent on his parents' marital happiness. Female students in the Wallin study were so unanimously favorable toward marriage that even those from unhappy homes wanted to marry.

Broderick (1965), in a research program with children ranging in age from 10 to 17 years of age, found support for the parental family's effectiveness in motivating children to marry in the high incidence of approval of marriage by children; 67 per cent of 10- to 11-year-old boys and 79 per cent of the girls wanted to get married someday. At later ages the girls and to a lesser extent the boys, by then more experienced in heterosexual relations, were even more affirming of their intentions to get married someday (75 per cent of 17-year-old boys and 94 per cent of the 17-year-old girls). Rose (1955), in comparing college student preferences about marriage with parents' behavior patterns, found preferred age at marriage closely correlated with parents' actual age at marriage. In contrast there was no intergenerational continuity with respect to family size desired or choice of occupation. Rose writes, "Our findings have indicated that children select, consciously or unconsciously, some of the life patterns of their parents as models for their behavior but ignore others."

From these few studies, inadequately designed to confirm or refute the speculations about the impact of early socialization in generating the motivation to marry, we do conclude that the parents' marriage pattern does make a difference in making marriage as a way of life attractive to its offspring, especially for boys whose occupational careers can provide alternative adult roles.

Parental influences on cross-sex choices and progress in courtship. There is also some evidence that parents enter actively into the shaping of values relevant to later marriage in the judgments made about children's friends, dates, and fiances. These lead to proscriptions and actions taken to encourage or forbid future contacts (Bates, 1942; Sussman, 1953). The phenomenon of homogamy in the United States is parentally supported in early childhood in the choice of playmates of the same and opposite sex. It is no accident that children of the same social class, same religious background and same ideological persuasion choose one another as friends, and as young adults choose their marriage partners within the same list of eligibles (Burgess & Wallin, 1943, 1944). Wilson (1953) found conformity to parental standards among college women in ten out of twelve areas, including choice of girl friends, dating and mate selection. The nonconformity having the most negative effects on parent-daughter relations was in the area of mate selection. In other areas of non-conformity, the impact on parent-daughter relations was much less severe. The stake parents have in inculcating standards is high enough in the area of mate selection that families discuss matters of desirable associates in table talk (Bossard, 1943), rendering parental values and standards explicit long before children seriously enter the mate selection game.

A series of articles sparked by Winch (1943) identify still a third impact of socialization in the parental family for marriage. Beginning with the hypothesis that progress in courtship involvement toward marriage would be inhibited by too close attachments to parents (particularly the mother), Winch found by progressive specification and factor analysis of his data that the antecedents of courtship progress were different for males than for females. Kirkpatrick and Caplow (1945) and Komarovsky (1950) elaborated on Winch's basic findings, that progress of men in courtship was related to loosening their attachments to their mothers, whereas for women, courtship behavior was not dependent upon emancipation from either parent. The women could transfer dependence from their parents to their husbands, whereas men had to achieve independence to pursue courtship. Hobart (1958) found an increasing tendency for men as they grew older to be critical of their parents' marital happiness but found emancipation from parents more important than age alone in determining courtship progress. The transition from going steady to engagement represented the turning point in emancipation during courtship.

What do we conclude? As women have long known, men are the problematic element in the marriage relation. Neither their acceptance nor their commitment to the venerable institution can be assumed, and the parental family is important in both. A favorable evaluation of marital happiness of parents makes for a more favorable attitude toward marriage at the abstract level of approving of marriage as a way of life. In adolescence, emancipation from parents, including perhaps a more critical stance toward parental marital patterns, is necessary for young men to become involved and committed to marriage.

Exposure to the marital status and its roles by observation.   The parental family provides the child with his first exposure to the enactment of marital roles. Ego's stance, however, is that of observer rather than of participant in the marital subsystem. Thus his relations to the actors is of the "they-them" type to use Brim's distinction (Brim & Wheeler, 1966). The child is not participating in the relationship. He is neither subject nor object in the interaction relation. Consequently he observes father and mother as subjects, "they," or as objects, "them," in the marital dyad where he always remains an outside observer. Since it involves interaction in which ego is neither subject nor object, it is less likely that the learning about marital roles in this context will become part of his core self-other system.

Little research has been done of this phenomenon of objectifying the parents' marital roles by virtue of the detached observer position occupied by the child, although Mayer's recent provocative paper addresses itself to the alleged superiority of the relatively clear-cut imagery of parental marriage patterns, because of the low visibility of alternative models among the parents of one's peers (Mayer, 1967). There is also some suggestion that individuals have a greater affective investment in the imagery of the parental marriage pattern although the withholding or giving of rewards for subscribing to the parents' pattern would have been at best indirect. Moreover, alternative models, even where visible, are seen fleetingly and superficially as compared with the continuous exposure upon which the imagery of the parental marriage is based.

We have already noted the trend toward giving higher priority to the marital over the parental dimension. If we assume, as a consequence, an increasing accessibility and visibility of the marital subsystem, what "they-them" type learnings might be deduced from observing the marriage of one's parents? We speculate that there are learnings at both the expressive and instrumental levels.

LEARNING AT THE EXPRESSIVE LEVEL

1. The display of unearned and unconditional love between husband and wife provides the observing child with the basis for establishing intimate interpersonal relations outside the family. The "they-me" relations in which the child is involved by virtue of his membership in the parent-child and sibling subsystems of the family often possess a *quid pro quo* quality that contrasts sharply with the uncalculating nature of the marital relationship. Communication of affection between husband and wife and demonstrativeness of affection are audible and visible evidences of the unifying impact of love on the relation. Sex and love are interwoven in the husband-wife relation so that sex gestures take on a symbolic meaning—a kiss means something, a love embrace signals unity, and sex union (although hidden from view) is symbolic of unreserved mutual acceptance.

2. The symmetry of the marriage relation renders visible alternative modes of handling differences in points of view less available in the asymmetrical parent-child relation with the attendant social distance, but parents who want to apprentice their children into constructive conflict need to make the last stage of conflict resolution as accessible to view as their initial irritations.

3. The mechanisms of face-saving, tension-release, resentment disclosure and role modification which are so important for restoring marital equilibrium are learned best in the parental family by observation and modeling. Humor twists, puns, and mirroring the person's feelings are skills of ego protection that parents use to advantage in marriage and should be added to the marriage apprentice repertoire.

LEARNING AT THE INSTRUMENTAL LEVEL

1. Patterns of planning and decision-making often carried out by parents with minimal consultation with children should, if made accessible for obser-

vation, particularly for long-term goals such as budgeting time and expenditures, provide training in judgment and problem solving not usually activated in the parent-child relation.

2. The pattern of mutual consultation in identifying issues and the tendency to use consensus in decision-making provide an invaluable preview of equals coping with the instrumental issues of marriage.

These five examples of expressive and instrumental marital activity may be translated into the reciprocal roles and norms appropriate to the marital positions of husband and wife. The roles of lover, sex partner, confidant, companion, listener, ventilator, tension dispeller, face-saver, and ego builder are found on the expressive side of the ledger. To these may be added the instrumental leadership roles of "idea man," planner, problem solver, policy maker, decision-maker, scheduler, allocator, and evaluator. Many of these roles particularly in the instrumental area are necessary as well for the operation of small *ad hoc* groups. Some of the expressive roles of lover and sex partner, confider and confidant, are uniquely important for the healthy functioning of the marriage pair as a comprehensive dyad. No studies to our knowledge have been undertaken to assess training within the parental family for these highly concrete marital roles. Perhaps this statement of the problem will stimulate such research.

We are forced in searching for relevant studies to consider, rather, the more abstract concepts of marital aptitude or interpersonal competence which have been subjected to research. The marital role performances cited above may be viewed as a set of competences highly relevant to success in marriage. They are nowhere as repetitively and continuously available to children for learning as in the parental family. Terman et al. (1938) termed these competences "aptitudes for marriage" which he assumed to be properties of personality. Foote and Cottrell (1955) identified them as "interpersonal competences" of which empathy (role-taking), creativity, autonomy, and judgment cover particularly well the marital roles delineated above. Children reared in a family in which the marriage is functioning effectively not only observe a viable model in which just such competences are portrayed, but also develop the confidence that success in marriage is achievable.

One of the most puzzling findings from the pioneering study of marital adjustment by Burgess and Cottrell (1939) thirty years ago, since confirmed in several other studies, was the large amount of variance in the couples' marriage adjustment accounted for by the marital happiness of their two sets of parents. A second finding closely related to the marital happiness of parents was equally impressive; namely, the importance of childhood happiness. Longitudinal research would be required to test whether these findings are antecedent-consequent or interdependent relationships. On the surface these findings offer support at a very global level that parental competence in marital relations tends to be transmitted to children to enhance their own prospects of marital success.

Interaction with Parents and Self-Other Learning

In sharp contrast to ego's *detached stance* in learning of the competences utilized in the marital subsystem, he tends to be *fully involved* as a participant in learning roles appropriate to parenthood.[1] Moreover, though the family is an informal socializing agency, his role as student of the values and behaviors his parents are transmitting is clearly prescribed. Here his participation in the interaction results in two kinds of relations. In contrast to the "they-them" pattern of his observation of the marital couple, the child as object of the parent's actions or expectations has a "they-me" relation. When he is subject and the parent is object, the relation becomes an "I-them" type. Beginning as "they-me" and "I-them" relations they are generalized by imaginative internal conversations into "I-me" self-other expectations. Since the child participates in the parent-child subsystem from birth, his learning consists of values and attitudes about himself and others that constitute the very core of his self system as well as particular behaviors and skills.

Socialization for parenthood, as compared to marriage, it seems, is likely to occur under conditions of powerful parent–powerless child interactions with consequently more effective impact on the personality. The child cannot choose to observe rather than to participate. In addition, parents more consciously are attempting to serve as agents of socialization and manipulate their sanctions so as to increase the child's motivation to learn. Moreover, it is likely to occur earlier, including preverbal learnings which make later resocialization more difficult (Brim & Wheeler, 1966, p. 31). The parent-child system also cannot be masked or hidden from the children as the marriage system tends to be, so they can learn from readily apparent role models. Finally, there are opportunities in many families for role rehearsal as older children receive authority at times to serve as parental surrogates for younger siblings. Thus, the manifest roles of the child on which the parent concentrates in bringing about role modifications and the latent roles of the parent which the child learns by imaginative role-taking become highly important constituents of the child's emerging identity. It is, therefore, not surprising that children's play more frequently involves enactment of parent-child roles than husband-wife roles and that young adults are more definite about their own preferences with respect to parental than with respect to marital roles.

Connor, Green and Walters (1958), working with fifty tenth-grade children and their parents, found more agreement than disagreement among parents and children about what "good parents" and "good children" should be. Highest agreement was between mothers and children, next between spouses, and least between father and children, implying greater effectiveness of mothers in the socialization of children for parenthood.

---

[1] We hasten to point out that the son apprenticed to his father never really graduates to become father in his family of orientation. The self-other learning does not involve the internalization of a concrete role type. As Parsons and Bales (1955) have expressed it, "A child can prospectively become a father, but only in another nuclear family; he cannot assume his father's role in this nuclear family."

Emmerich (1961) found evidence in a study of 225 middle-class elementary school children of elaborate differentiation of generational and sex roles in parent-child relations. Children used "power" differences in discriminating parental roles. Parents had high power (control over others), and the father position had higher power than the mother position. With increasing age there was an increasing tendency for children to discriminate male roles by power.

Bath and Lewis (1962) report a convergence of parental and children's attitudes about appropriate parental practices with adolescents as they themselves became adults. This finding, suggesting declining power of the peer group in favor of parental views about parent-adolescent relations, contrasts with the Hobart finding (1958) discussed above of discontinuity in parent-adolescent views about marital roles.

The transmission of parental conceptions about parent-child roles and the activation of latent roles from self-parent interactions in adulthood can be expected to be high in quiet societies with little social change, whereas in urbanizing and industrializing societies, generational discontinuities may be expected (Brim & Wheeler, 1966). Later in this chapter we discuss in greater detail the types of families that maintain continuity from generation to generation even under conditions of rapid social change. The data presented above suggest that continuity of parental roles is altogether more frequent than discontinuity.

Limitations of the parental family as a socializing agent for marriage.
Let us now examine critically some of the limitations of the parental family as a socializing agent for marital roles. The parental family is not ideally equipped for training its members in the concrete roles of marriage. Their performance requires not only the motivation to marry (which the parental family transmits successfully) but knowledge about the marriage situation and how to perform these roles. The parental family is not a repository of such knowledge about marriage nor is it able to provide practical on-the-job training in the skills of marriage.

First of all, we need to recognize that there are very few opportunities even to simulate marital role-playing in the parental family setting. The family script contains no marital parts for children to play. Moreover, the limited visibility of the marital roles and the low degree of institutionalization of these roles makes for vagueness and lack of clarity in role definitions. The situation begs for quasi-marital settings in which to validate marital roles playfully without risking punishment for failure as in child play.[2]

---

[2] It would be profitable to explore the extent to which girls take the opportunity to simulate limited marital roles when the mother of the family is hospitalized or is absent for long periods, serving simultaneously as father's little wife and hostess and as substitute mother to the younger siblings. In the war separation studies, boys were expected to become "the man of the family" including serving as mother's escort (Hill, 1949). Does the incest taboo so inhibit the simulation of spousal roles by children that an emergency situation is required to legitimize it?

A second limitation of the parental family as agent is the uniqueness of the one marriage model provided and in the narrowness of the range of problem solutions developed in one family's history. In very few families is the division of tasks and responsibilities identical. The balance of power and the patterns of planning and decision-making vary from one family to another. But from the socialization experience within the parental family one might infer that there was but one way to operate a marriage. In addition, this one model may prove to be out-of-date by the time the child attempts to activate it in his adulthood. The parental guidelines for marriage should be corrected by the growing child's observations of the marriages of others, of older brothers and sisters, of other relatives and neighbors, and of the age cohort just ahead.

Structural factors setting limitations on socialization in the family of orientation. The limitations of the family of orientation as a setting for learning parent or marital roles are exacerbated by structural factors that affect the complement of family positions with whose incumbents the child interacts, the range of behaviors he observes, and the content of these behaviors. The child gains his knowledge of the behaviors appropriate to the various roles incorporated in the positions of husband-father, wife-mother, son-brother, and daughter-sister by observing role models or through participation in interpersonal situations (Brim, 1960; Goode, 1960). But he lacks the opportunity to take the role of the other or to observe role models if there is a deficit of structure in his family and certain positions are lacking. He is, as a result, culturally deprived with regard to the role performance norms associated with those positions.

The largest body of research having to do with family composition is concerned with father absence and its effects on sex-role learning, a subject having implications for parental and marital socialization. Studies growing out of World War II when men left their families because of military service requirements show how children's knowledge of paternal roles is distorted when the father is gone. Bach, for example, found that lower middle-class school age children whose fathers were in the armed forces displayed an idealized picture of the father in doll-play situations (Bach, 1946). As compared with a control group whose fathers were present, the fantasies of the father-absent group contained fathers who gave and received more affection from their families and more often enjoyed doing things with their families. The fathers were less apt to be demanding and authoritarian. The marital behaviors of these less aggressive, fantasy fathers were also more accommodating. There was more marital discord depicted in the fantasies of the father-present children. In father-absent homes, the children's ideas concerning father-husband roles are heavily influenced, Bach suggests, by the mothers' reports of their husbands. Even children whose mothers spoke to them in highly critical terms of their fathers, however, portrayed fantasy children who were more affectionate to their fathers than was true of children whose mothers gave favorable pictures, though the former's fantasy fathers were more aggressive. Children without fathers, therefore, do not learn from observation or interaction in the home important aspects of the husband-father's role performance. Unless they have learning experiences outside the home that will give them a more realistic knowledge, both boys and girls can be handicapped upon entering marriage. One could speculate that the boys in the Bach sample, if the fathers did not return, would have internalized norms requiring unreasonably high self-control. The girls would expect more affection, support and less conflict from their husbands than they would receive.

Not only are children's conceptions of the paternal role distorted by father-absence, but the behavior of both boys and girls appears to be affected in ways having implications for their future performance of marital roles. Norwegian children whose sailor fathers were gone for long periods of time were less mature than their school-age peers. The girls whose fathers were seldom home were more dependent upon their mothers than girls in complete families. The sailors' wives, in turn, were more protective and demanding of obedience and politeness in their children as opposed to the latter's happiness and self-realization (Tiller, 1958). The sons of the seafarers seemed to be insecure in their sex identity and displayed overly masculine behavior. They had difficulty in getting along with others of their age (Lynn & Sawrey, 1958), something Stolz also found true of preschoolers of both sexes whose fathers had been in service (Stolz et al., 1954). It appears, therefore, that father-absent boys may have difficulty in establishing the peer contacts that would give them the corrective tutelage they need to enter marriage secure in their masculine identity and with a better knowledge of husband-father role requirements. Girls too who have had little opportunity to interact with or to observe their fathers appear to be deficient in their socialization for marriage. Based on their observation of and dependence on mothers who have had to perform both parental roles, these girls will be prepared to play a more dominant role in the marital arrangement than is customarily expected.

A sector of American society where father-absence is common enough that one can seek documentation for the above speculative analysis is among the disorganized Negro families in urban slums of the United States. Here it has been estimated as many as two-thirds of Negro urban poor children will not grow up in families headed by an adult male and female throughout the first eighteen years of their lives (Rainwater, 1966). Research is lacking, however, showing the direct relation of deficit in the network of family positions in the parental home to later difficulties the individual encounters in playing marital or parental roles. Moreover, the available studies are largely concerned with men and not women. Ethnicity and class variable may also be confounded in the studies to be described. Despite these weaknesses, it appears worthwhile to examine the few, relevant studies, because they do provide some support for the argument that the child learns adult family roles from role models in the family of orientation.

There is indication that Negro boys without fathers have difficulty in differentiating sex roles. Five- to 14-year-old youths described themselves in much the same way as did Negro girls of the same ages. Boys from complete homes used many more masculine terms than was true of girls from complete families (D'Andrade, 1962). This finding suggests that Negro boys from father-absent homes may lack adequate knowledge of masculine status of which an important component is the husband-father role. It also appears that men from fatherless homes have less "marital aptitude," a finding consistent with their supposed poorer socialization for husband-father roles. In a small sample of working class Negro men, seven of 21 who came from fatherless homes as compared with four of 21 Negroes matched for age, income, education and region of birth were single or divorced (Pettigrew, 1964). Additional research suggests that the motivation to marry among father-absent boys is less. Of 172 Negro adolescent boys predominantly from unskilled backgrounds, 34 per cent of whom were from fatherless homes, older youths actually showed a decreasing interest in being married. While 71 per cent of the 10- to 11-year-olds expressed a desire to marry, this was true of just 58 per cent of the 16- to 17-year-olds. The figures for the comparable age groups in the sample of 488 white boys were 57 per cent and 77 per cent. Only 12 per cent of these blue collar boys came from fatherless homes.[3] Separate analysis showed children from complete homes to be significantly more positive in their attitudes toward marriage (Broderick, 1965).

The research relevant to the effects of father-absence on marital and parental role learning is meager, but with respect to the absence of other family positions it is largely nonexistent. The large body of research on maternal separation and deprivation has not considered the effects on children's sex-role learning, an area that impinges on socialization for marriage, probably because of the heavy emphasis on cognitive and personality functioning of the child who grows up without a mother.

On the basis of the available research and theory, one can speculate that particularly in the lower classes where marital and parental roles are so clearly differentiated for men and women (Rainwater, 1965), father-absence can be more harmful than mother-absence for the child's socialization into adult family roles. Examining the concepts of knowledge, motivation and ability that Brim has postulated as being essential for role performance (Brim, 1964), it appears that the critical element for boys is motivation. Women have had a greater commitment to family roles throughout their developmental history. From preschool age on, their cultural artifacts and the representatives of the broader society emphasize the centrality of marriage and motherhood for females. There is less emphasis, however, on the male's spouse-parent status. Thus interacting with a man playing husband-father roles would seem to be important for the boy not only to learn the behaviors but to acquire the desire and expectation to occupy the same position.

For girls, the critical element may be knowledge of role expectations. The

---

[3] The percentages on father absence are not reported in the reference source, but come from a personal communication from Broderick.

broad outlines of the skills required for meeting the normative requirements of the woman's family roles can be obtained from agents outside the family, but the little girl appears to be more dependent upon her father's sanctions than her mother's example for learning the feminine behaviors that will enable her to interact more easily with her husband (Johnson, 1963). The boy needing cross-sex reinforcement for his masculine behaviors has a larger number of feminine alternatives outside the family in the case of mother-absence than does the little girl without a father.

This argument is not intended to deny the importance of the wife-mother for the child's learning of marital and parental roles. Her position as instrumental and expressive leader within the family sphere gives her unique influence to motivate her children to acquire knowledge of family roles as well as to delineate their content through her cues and sanctions. She serves as role model for her daughters, and by her role performance indicates to her sons the wife and mother roles their behaviors as husband-father will have to relate to. Obviously, the optimal family situation for the child's socialization into marital and parental roles is one where both parents are present.

The lack of research in the whole area of sib relations (Irish, 1964) means that the effect of having no sibs or only sibs of the same or opposite sex as well as the variation in learning marital and parental roles because of ordinal position is not documented. The absence of an older sib of the same sex, it might be theorized, would be the sib position associated with the most deficiency in knowledge for socialization of adult family roles in contexts where siblings are the socializing agents. Learning from sibs comes not so much from interacting with an alter who is playing a spouse-parent role, but from hearing about and observing a sib's performances in the sequence of stages in heterosexual peer contacts that present contexts outside the family where socialization for marriage occurs. Since much of the younger sib's observations are limited to older sib's preparation for role performance—getting into costume or sharpening interaction skills—the activities of a same-sex sib would be more useful. It also may be easier for adolescents to share confidences with and coach younger sibs of the same sex on the requirements for dating and courtship roles.

But the child who has no sibs of the opposite sex regardless of his ordinal position would also be handicapped. He would lack opportunities in the home for rehearsal with sibs of roles activated by peers of the opposite sex. The advantage sibs enjoy over the cross-sex parent would be their membership in the same generation as ego. There would also be fewer persons of the opposite sex with whom the child interacts or observes to acquire a knowledge of the general behaviors differentiating the sexes which are encompassed in the specific marital and parental role requirements. As far as the latter point is concerned, there is some slight research support (Levinger & Sonnheim, 1965; Toman & Gray, 1961).

Though a deficit in the positions present in the family structure can hamper socialization, so also can an excess of incumbents in the offspring-sibling position. In large family contexts where there are six or more children, Bossard and Boll suggest that parents have little time to give each child undivided attention, and their interpersonal relations with children necessarily center on the maintenance of order (Bossard & Boll, 1956). Unless the child is disturbing others, he is left on his own, and the parents delegate much of his care and discipline to older siblings. Thus the child has less opportunitiy to learn the parents' roles through taking the roles of the other in interaction with them. The knowledge of parental roles he does acquire in this fashion would be most complete with regard to disciplinarian and role-setter with other roles less clear. Along with the narrow range of parental roles activated in parent-child encounters, the lack of opportunity to observe parents interacting as husband and wife handicaps the socialization of children in large families into adult family roles. Parental roles are so demanding that spousal roles assume little importance for man and wife outside the bedroom.

Children in smaller families would engage in more interaction with their parents in which the latter perform as companion, adviser, and confidant as well as social control agents. The children's acquaintance with a wider selection of the parental role repertoire may help to compensate for their lesser opportunity to rehearse the roles. Having fewer siblings, there would be less opportunity to serve as parental surrogates in caring for younger children. The children should, however, have more extensive knowledge of marital roles. Parental requirements are less time-consuming, so they interact as marital partners on occasions when the child can observe them.

In concluding this section on structural factors within the family that set limits on the child's socialization within the family, it is, perhaps, well to add a warning and a disclaimer. The warning is that the difficulties postulated because of deficit in structure or the sheer number of children largely lack empirical support. The feasibility of the argument rests on the reader's judgment of how well it conforms to the role theory and available research from which it derives. The disclaimer exists to serve notice that no claim is being made as to the inevitability of deficiencies in socialization arising from the discussed structural factors. Parents are able to fill in for the absent spouse, and there are persons who can perform as parent substitutes outside the family whether relatives, friends, or community representatives such as teachers. By the very nature of events not everyone who has been well-socialized for marriage will have grown up as the younger sib of a person of the same sex. Parents of large families are not always preoccupied with keeping the family going at the expense of their children and their marital relationship.

It is also true that not all family structural factors affecting adult family socialization were considered. The ages of the parents in the child-rearing years, for example, appear important. If they are over three decades older than the child, generational differences would make them less attractive role models to their children. But this is clear speculation and where there was little foundation in theory or research for an analysis, we have resisted discussing possible factors.

CORRECTIVE OBSERVATIONS
OF MARRIAGES OF OTHERS

Given the limitations of the family as the context for learning parental and marital roles, it is well that the individual even after marriage has opportunities for socialization outside the nuclear family. Through observation and interaction with individuals acting as role models or serving as socialization agents, he becomes acquainted with a wider range of behavior and expectations. The communication media, for example, provide a variety of images of life in other families which the classes and sexes sample differently. The more highly educated, white-collar classes come in contact with a greater portion of the spectrum, because they are more apt to supplement their television viewing and newspaper reading with novels and plays. The working and lower classes tend more to confine their viewing and reading to television and the popular forms of journalism that focus on the image of the consumption-conscious equalitarian family. Since women more than men in the blue-collar classes select the programs, stories and articles that convey this image, the mass media may contribute to marital conflict. Women's knowledge of husband-wife interaction patterns in which the husband adds to his traditional repertoire of roles those of companion and confidant can lead to expectations which men are unprepared and unwilling to fulfill.

Another extrafamilial source of alternate marital and parental behaviors is the age cohort just preceding ego into marriage, and his more precocious age mates. These individuals with whom ego interacts or observes personally can have greater influence as socialization agents than the mass media. In the first instance, ego may consciously play the role of student whether or not he makes the other whom ego is observing or interacting with aware of his role as teacher. As a result the anticipatory socialization is more thorough as ego strives to learn the nuances as well as the readily apparent aspects of the role. He also has more control over the content of the socialization. He can specifically query the person he is using as role model about moot points, a nonexistent possibility with the mass media. One study of married students at a university, living in a student housing unit among other married couples in the same student status, suggests that learning marital roles from observing peers can have positive consequences even after marriage (Riemer, 1951). Their divorce rate was lower than the usual rate for college-educated groups during the first four years of marriage. So potent is this learning that it may well be that some of the difficulties youths experience who marry at culturally defined early stages stem from the lack of opportunity they have had for anticipatory socialization from their peers. Those somewhat older and those in their own age group would not yet have entered the marital state and so could not serve as role models and teachers. Just how isolated early marriers are from socialization opportunities through their generation is a research topic needing investigation.

After the transition point of marriage has been passed, ego can still turn

to extrafamilial agents of socialization. Now, learning instead of being anticipatory can be immediately activated in current role performances, thereby
heightening its value and the individual's motivation to acquire it. Moreover,
it is generally the failures of role performance as judged by spouse and children that send the individual to outsiders, further increasing his desire to learn.

The information applicable to socialization after marriage is largely found
in the research concerned with marital problems. The findings, however, can
be translated into a socialization framework. Marital problems arising from
interpersonal sources can be conceptualized as conflicts in role expectations.
To solve such problems one or both spouses would have to learn different
performance norms and behaviors. When individuals confide their problems
to another, they can be placing this person in the position of agent of socialization as well as cathartic outlet.

Class and sex differences, as is true of the mass media, affect the variety
of persons in the different structural positions to which the individual turns,
the content of the learning sought, and the control the socialization agents are
able to exercise over the individual. Commensurate with the narrower world
of experience of the lower classes—lower classes being used to include both
the stable working class and the irregularly employed poor—the blue-collar
spouse is more limited in the kinds of persons he utilizes as role models. He
more often looks only to relatives precluding an expansion of knowledge much
beyond that learned in the family of orientation, since it is to these individuals
he turns. Mayer found with a middle- and lower-class white sample that while
both groups of wives reported turning first to their husbands with family
problems, middle-class wives then sought assistance from friends and relatives
(Mayer, 1966a). Lower-class wives confided "almost exclusively" in relatives.
They talked to more relatives, but only to *their* relatives and did not include
their in-laws as did the middle-class wives. Thus lower-class wives made use
of a more limited range of alternative sources of knowledge though both
groups restricted their sources to persons of the same sex. Lower-class wives,
however, kept more of their concerns to themselves or revealed them in less
detail. The relatives from whom they sought aid consequently had less information about the type of knowledge the wife needed to improve her role
performance, and would be handicapped in playing the role of socialization
agent.

The lower-class and middle-class women, Mayer found, had different expectations concerning the possibilities of modifying marital interaction, expectations which influenced their utilization of confidants as socialization
agents. The lower-class wives believed that interpersonal difficulties were the
fault of the husband. As a result, they wanted knowledge on how to serve
as agents of socialization in order to change their husbands' behavior. If they
were unsuccessful due to poor training or inability to learn, the wives generally
ceased their socialization attempts as the latter created conflict. Instead, they
attempted to accommodate to their husbands' expectations and behavior with

a minimum change in their own behavior. At this point presumably, they ceased viewing their relatives as role models or agents of socialization and utilized them primarily for purposes of catharsis.

In contrast, the middle-class wives had a less constricted perspective as to the cause of their marital difficulties. Having a sense of control over their life circumstances, they were apt to consider a number of possibilities including themselves and environmental factors as well as their husbands. As a result, they utilized several approaches to handle their marital difficulties, and if one did not prove effective, they tried another based on a different diagnosis of where the problem lay. Thus they could use relatives or friends as role models to supply new behaviors and standards. The wives also could place their confidants in the position of teacher trainers to impart the skills necessary to resocialize their husbands. If neither of these strategies worked, the middle-class women could seek advice on how to manipulate the environment, so as to provide a setting that would encourage more harmonious marital relations.

The greater flexibility of middle-class women in their utilization of confidants as socialization agents is probably associated with the greater emotional investment they have in the marital relationship. They give first priority to their husbands, and this commitment is made easy by the segmented nature of their extrafamilial networks, few of whose members know each other. The openness of the network prevents its functioning as a competing force for the loyalty of the spouse, and its members being unacquainted can not exert concerted pressure to insure that the knowledge one member transmits in his role as socializing agent is acted upon by the middle-class wife.

Lower-class women like their husbands retain strong affective ties outside of marriage with kin and peer associates. Although the evidence is contradictory (Aldous & Straus, 1966), Bott has argued that working-class spouses in contrast to middle-class couples more often are involved in separate closely-knit friendship networks whose members all know each other well, meet together and supply each other's emotional needs (Bott, 1957). Under these circumstances there is also high normative consensus, and the network members exert much influence over each other's behavior. The advice a spouse receives from one network contact generally is respected and supported by another.

The socialization learning acquired in such networks has a traditional orientation with the emphasis on a rigid division of labor, few shared interests and little concern for "successful" sexual relations. Such socialization discourages marital interaction as the solution to marital conflict, a solution requiring little learning of different behaviors on the part of the wife to adjust to the spouse or little effort to socialize the spouse into more congruent patterns. In the rare cases where working-class husband and wife are members of a common tightly-knit network, there is the same phenomenon of the group as a whole enforcing a common orientation toward marital roles. But the common orientation acquired because both spouses are involved in the same clique also emphasizes greater marital closeness (Komarovsky, 1964). Learning different role behaviors under these circumstances would assume greater importance as a means for solving marital problems.

Husbands in the working class, Komarovsky found, appear to have few confidants to whom to turn when they have marital problems. They also experience more self-imposed barriers in seeking help, having internalized the norm that men do not complain about their marital difficulties. When they do, it is to other men. Thus it is only after tentative exploration reveals that a friend also is having problems, that the man will unburden himself. As a result, men's learning different marital roles after marriage would seem to be largely limited to the knowledge they acquire from their wives. Whether middle-class men feel the same reluctance to seek counsel from outsiders and have a similarly limited number of confidants is a question that is largely unanswered in the literature. Although they have higher expectations of marriage than do lower-class men, a factor that would heighten their motivation to do something about interpersonal difficulties, it could be counter-balanced by their greater absorption in occupational concerns. Middle-class men may be able to conform to a norm that forbids discussing failures in marital role performance with third parties by investing more affect in their work. Like lower-class wives, they would be handling marital interaction difficulties by withdrawal but for middle-class men it would be withdrawal to the office not into the circle of kindred as with the women.

For both men and women in the working class, it is the under-30 age group that confides their marital problems to outsiders. Older men become increasingly cut off from kin and peer relations, and older women assume the role of confidant and serve as socialization agents for their younger relatives and friends. There may then be a cut-off point beyond which men and women do not attempt to modify the marital role performance of themselves or their spouses, or at least do not use extrafamilial confidants as socializing agents for this purpose.

If there is such a cut-off point in the middle class, it may come later because of these couples' stronger conviction that they can do something about poor marital relations. Eventually, though, they too may no longer turn to third parties for help. The research on increasing marital disenchantment among middle-class couples over time (Pineo, 1961) suggests that they come to accept the relationship as it exists instead of trying to change it.

But what of the imagery individuals have of other couples' marriages, imagery that affects their own role behavior? Mayer (1966b) queried the middle- and lower-class wives in his research reported earlier about their knowledge of the marriages of the four persons closest to them (the respondents were to exclude the marriages of their parents, their children and their husband). Though lower-class women live in a more constricted sociability setting than do middle-class women, the lower-class wives in the sample knew less about the marriages of close associates than did the middle-class wives. The more the friends of the intimate being discussed by the blue-collar wife were acquainted with one another, the less the respondent was able to report the intimate's marriage problems in depth. The contrary situation existed among the middle-class women. The more closed the friendship network, the more each one knew about the friend with whose marital situation she was most familiar.

There seemed to be several reasons for these findings, reasons that are consistent with and lend support to our previous discussions. As we noted in Mayer's earlier report lower-class wives provide their confidants with less information, keeping more of their marital problem to themselves. This policy seems to stem from their powerlessness, their belief that little can be done by anyone to improve the situation. They also appear to distrust others and do not like to provide them with personal information. Presumably, this would be even more true when the confidant shares some of the same friends. In either case, lower-class women possess less knowledge of the marriages of their associates and less information to pass on to others. If lower-class women possessed interpersonal skills, they would be able to compensate for inadequacies in their communication network by observations and inferences. But they are able to make less use of this strategy than are middle-class women who obtain more information about the marital situation of others indirectly as well as through direct communication with their friends.

Thus lower-class women are doubly handicapped in their attempts to modify their marital roles and those of their husbands so as to develop a better fit. They do not utilize their confidants effectively as socialization agents and their imagery of other people's marriages which might serve as a corrective to their own practices is restricted. If, as Mayer found, a consequence of greater knowledge of other's problems is greater satisfaction with one's own marriage, then one reason for the lower marital satisfaction of blue-collar women (Komarovsky, 1964) may lie in the poverty of their imagery of their associates' marriages.

EXPOSURE TO MARRIAGE-LIKE SITUATIONS IN GROWING UP

In teaching courses in preparation for marriage we have had students, many already married, recall specific situations from childhood in which they experienced intimate pair relationships with other persons. It has been possible for them to identify a number of situations which had real meaning in preparing them for the intimacies of marriage. Some experiences have hurt and maimed the student's capacity to give and receive love, rendering him less marriageable. Others have served to wean him from the confining love of parents to the point of loving members of the opposite sex outside the family. Some of the intimate pair relationships have been with members of the same sex, many with the opposite sex. Most of the relationships which usher the individual toward marriage have been with age mates. Some have been temporary, almost fleeting, others have persisted over several years. All have involved comprehensive dyadic relationships in which the propensity to share and to bridge the separateness of existence brought hints of the emotional interdependence of the marriage relation.

These relationships have all offered the advantages of self-other learning about marriage-relevant roles as against the more objective "they-them" learnings, to be stored now and retrieved later resulting from the child's observations of marriage in the parental family. These several relationships add role content to the manifest repertoire of the spouse-in-becoming. Moreover, they offer also the opportunity to validate in sequence earlier relevant roles learned from self-other interactions. These might be termed the spouse-in-becoming's *pre-marital career*.[4] There is a rough order in the timing of the relationships with one assuming particular salience for marital learning at one period to lapse in importance and be followed by another relationship. Despite their fluctuations as significant socialization vehicles, these relationships continue over time and the roles and the role sequences that they activate constitute the spouse-in-becoming position. The changing role content of this position due to the shifts in role expectations makes up the pre-marital career.

The Brother-Sister Relation

We have already referred to the sibling subsystem within the parental family but have inadequately explored the part it plays in the socialization of its members for marriage. Clausen (1967), in assessing the literature on socialization and ordinal position in the family, sees it as heavy on speculations and light on empirical data. He examined carefully the generalizations about intersibling interaction and personality consequences for different ordinal positions. Some evidence is offered, that an older sibling can be a helpful model for learning sex-appropriate behaviors both at the preschool level (Brim, 1958) and for fourth- through sixth-grade children in two child families (Rosenberg & Sutton-Smith, 1964). Brim demonstrated that a boy with an older brother exhibits more masculine behavior and one with an older sister more feminine behavior than other combinations, arguing that there is added role content internalized from the self-other interactions of the intersibling contacts. Thus, the brother-sister relation appears to offer an early opportunity to enact cross-gender roles within a comprehensive dyadic relationship that are likely to become part of the role repertory of the emergent spouse-to-be.[5]

The brother-sister relation resembles the marriage relationship in its age symmetry, its solidity, its uncircumscribed nature, the propensity to share and support one another in periods of blues and trouble. Because of the incest taboo, the relationship is sexually inhibited but is often deeply affectionate.

---

[4] A career may be viewed as the intercontingency of role sequences which make up the changing role content of a given position. The spouse-in-becoming constitutes such a position and the convergence of role sequences culminating in his marriage would be his premarital career.

[5] The frequent use of sibling terms of "brother" and "sis" by married couples is suggestive of the sibling antecedents in marital role-building.

Particularly where brother and sister are adjacent siblings, reasonably close in age, there often develops a companionship which competes satisfactorily with other attachments into adulthood.

Although the brother-sister relationship is an occasionally fighting relationship, it settles into a calmer tie as the siblings grow older. There is no need to reaffirm their mutual love, no need for protestations of loyalty or fidelity. The relation is characterized by a taken-for-grantedness which is stabilizing, to say the least. As a prototype of marriage, the brother-sister relation offers little hint of the sexual aspects of marriage, offers little variety and spice, but provides a steady sure source of companionship and predictability.

There is some anecdotal evidence also that parents' older siblings of the opposite sex are important models. The mother's brother is often the favorite relative cited by children (Homans & Schneider, 1955) and the husband's sister is perceived by wives as the second most bothersome in-law (Duvall, 1954).

Utilizing the framework applied earlier to socialization for marriage in the parental family, the brother-sister relation offers the first opportunity to the child to validate his gender role in play and to role-take, in an age symmetrical relationship, those aspects of the script of the opposite sex which he has inadequately mastered from his observations of the marital role enactments of his parents. To maintain a viable relationship with the cross-sex sibling, he uses many of the competences of empathy, judgment, and creativity, and the same mechanisms of face-saving and compromise. In this relation, then, the learnings can be put to use at once, and errors of misperception and projection corrected and made part of the child's repertory of manifest roles.

Fluctuating friendships, boy-girl crushes, and solo dating.   Less comprehensive, more fleeting, and sometimes wholly imaginary are the friendship relations which appear in the pre-marital career of the primary school child. The importance of the "chum" has been noted by Sullivan (1953) as a means for the child to disengage himself from the exclusive association of his parents and siblings to achieve affective support, intimacy and complementarity outside the family setting. In this same-sex relation, the child for the first time experiences some of the qualities of the marital relation. If he is fortunate in his friendship choice, there is the same mutual self-disclosure and unconditional acceptance that exists in marriage. The child, thereby, has received learning applicable to the interpersonal demands of serious commitment to someone of the opposite sex.

These early friendships constitute the child's first introduction to alternatives to his family's set of standards for interpersonal conduct. Indeed, the first serious challenge to the parental marriage norms is encountered in the peer contacts of middle childhood. Bowerman and Kinch (1959) with a cross-sectional sample, show a decided drop that begins in the fourth and continues through the tenth grade in the percentage of children preferring association with parents over peers, and preferring parental values to those of peers. Girls disengaged more rapidly from the parental setting than boys.

The work of Broderick and associates in Georgia and Pennsylvania offers excellent descriptive data about the processes of progressive mutual socialization that occur in middle childhood and early adolescence. They describe the role rehearsals and role enactments involved in initiating and sustaining heterosexual relations to the point where stable pre-marital courtships can be undertaken (Broderick & Fowler, 1961; Broderick, 1966).

Among 10- to 11-year-olds in Pennsylvania, Broderick (1966) found the basic social units to be reciprocal friendship pairs or triangles of the same sex with a few less intimate, nonreciprocal cross-sex relationships on the fringes. Although 30 per cent of girls listed among five friends at least one member of the opposite sex, only about three per cent of these were reciprocated cross-sex friendships. Given the usual picture of boys at this age as being violently disinterested in girls, the findings concerning boys are surprising. Roughly three-fifths allegedly had a girl friend, although this was kept so secret that 40 per cent of the girls chosen were not aware of it, and less than 20 per cent reciprocated. About half of both sexes claimed to have been in love at least once, and a small minority (28 per cent) were beginning to date. There was more fantasy and idealizing than realizing of heterosexual love interests at this point in their careers.

The 12- to 13-year-old youths show a narrowing of sociometric cross-sex preferences for friends to 24 per cent for girls and 25 per cent for boys but there is an increase in romantic interests such as enjoying love scenes in movies and going for a walk with a girl from only 8 per cent at 10–11 to 41 per cent two years later.

By 14 to 15 the same sex cliques had begun to open up to the opposite sex. The "secret love" had been replaced with the publicly acknowledged girl friend and steady dating had begun to achieve recognition, especially among girls. Social interaction with the opposite sex had pushed forward on every front.

But it was at 16 to 17 that the clique composition had to be totally restructured to make room for cross-sex pairs. For an important segment of the age cohort, the basic unit of the clique had become not the same sex but the cross-sex pair. For attending movies 80 per cent of boys and 93 per cent of girls favored a cross-sex companion, which indicated a willingness, indeed a preference, for having one's heterosexual activities viewed publicly. Kissing games for fun had disappeared and kissing as symbolic of "something special" was the majority practice (73 per cent of boys, 82 per cent of girls). Almost everyone was either dating or going steady (96 per cent) and roughly a third were currently going steady. Indeed, in examining the movement from 10 to 17 in this community, the process of socialization into sociosexual roles seemed to be functioning smoothly, leading on quite efficiently toward the future stages of courtship, marriage and parenthood.

The implications of the Broderick study for our exploration of socialization into marriage justify a few comments. The processes of socialization appear to be peer initiated and managed, with the more precocious of the age cohorts setting the pace for the majority. There appears to be no sharp break between pre-pubertal attitudes and experiences and those of adolescence. If there is a latency period, as alleged by some analysts, when boys and girls prefer a segregated existence, it does not appear to last beyond age 10 for either sex.

In the period between 10 and 13 the relative isolation of the two sexes is characterized by what appears to be anticipatory rehearsal of the skills and feelings appropriate to the later heterosexual relationships of courtship and marriage. For many this brief period of three years is a point of transition. In the subsequent period of middle adolescence a process of redefinition and mutual socialization by cross-sex groups occurs with group dating as the chief mechanism, moving to solo dating when more experienced. The cross-sex relationships become progressively less idealized thereafter, less secretive and more publicly open, less tragically one way and more reciprocal. And in the process the relationships become for these young actors much more consequential.

Broderick and his associates promise supplementary longitudinal data, validating the crucial transition points of disengagement from parental tutelage to peer socialization, first by same-sex groups and subsequently to the restructured network of cross-sex pairs entering the stage of serious courtship. To date the researches have involved cross-sectional samples and have slighted parents and siblings as co-participants in shaping this phase of the pre-marital career.

Dating and Going Steady

Dating is an American invention of the twentieth century which began in the universities, was picked up by high school students and, as Broderick's findings above indicate, is now practiced by even younger age groups. Waller and Hill (1951) have termed dating "aim-inhibited courtship," because young people can date each other without either of them or their parents assuming that because they date they are seriously interested in each other. They may be, indeed sometimes are, "serious," but just the fact of their dating each other does not commit them in the future. An alternative to dating, widely practiced in the same age groups, is that of "going steady" which may have as little commitment toward marriage as dating. There is frequent reshuffling of "steadies" as they tire of one another.

From the growing literature about the phenomenon of dating, we will limit our discussion to the consequences of dating as socialization of the young for marriage and the phenomenon of going steady as a transition point in that process. Dating and going steady offer opportunities for trying out roles characteristic of the comprehensive marital relation without having to reap the consequences from failure that attend the committed married pair. This is playful interaction rather than "playing for keeps." To be sure, there are hazards in entering into cross-sex relations irresponsibly even under conditions of minimum commitment, and many critics have inveighed against this twentieth century innovation. Some participants have been hurt by dating experiences, some have been exploited, and some of the most successful daters have never learned that marriageability involves something more than being popular. The relationships in dating are often so superficial and circumscribed that couples never transcend the "patter" of their respective "lines."

The more sympathetic critics see dating as excellent preparation for later adult recreation and for the sociability affairs to which middle-class couples turn in pairs for entertainment (relevant, to be sure, to one aspect of marriage), but see in dating limited rehearsal for the more stressful aspects of married living.

Robert A. Lewis (1966) has examined the several factors associated with the development of one crucial marital competence, empathic accuracy, among 114 dating pairs at the University of Minnesota. He offers evidence that the dating relationship may be analogous to the marriage relation since he finds the same close correspondence between high empathy and dating satisfaction which others (Dymond, 1954; Mangus, 1957; Luckey, 1960; and Kotlar, 1961) have reported for marital happiness. Lewis has also confirmed findings of Vernon and Stewart (1957) that empathic accuracy increases by stage of involvement from "just dating," "going steady or pinned" to "engaged." By finer specification, utilizing five stages of involvement, Lewis was able to pinpoint the take-off point at the "going steady" stage when the greatest increase in empathic accuracy occurred. Lewis found depth of acquaintance within one relationship, as measured by length of acquaintance with this partner, level of communication and agreement on basic issues, extent of confiding in partner, and degree of commitment to marriage to be another factor associated with high empathy. Lewis supports our earlier speculation about the socialization learnings from close friendships by showing high empathic accuracy related to a greater number of close friends, more frequent dating experiences, and more frequent going steady experiences.

In sum, the phenomenon of accurate role-taking of the opposite sex so important for marital success appears to be learned in self-other type interactions that are cumulative over several different relationships in the career of the spouse-in-becoming. Such interactions are also cumulative within each relationship by length of acquaintance and degree of commitment. The innovation of dating and going steady as statuses of low interpersonal commitment where the young of both sexes can try out dyadic roles without being held permanently accountable for the outcomes, apparently offers a useful set of socialization experiences. In time they bring about greater commitment[6] as well as improved interpersonal skills required for living within the more responsible and closed comprehensive dyad of the engaged relation.

Engagement as Rehearsal for Marriage

The engagement is the first relationship since beginning to pair off in cross-sex dyads that is publicly recognized as a status within which marital roles may be

---

[6] For a discussion of the involvement process by which couples move from casual dating to formal engagement which we have shortchanged here, see Waller and Hill (1951) and Bolton (1960).

legitimately simulated. Engagement is also the "point of no return" for many couples, the last status in the disengagement from the parental family when the parents still maintain some control and make some demands. Successful disengagement from home becomes almost as important, as a task assignment during this period, as commitment to the new relation.

Because of the wide variation in meaning ascribed to the engagement status in our society, it is hazardous to generalize about its purposes and processes. We identify the start of engagement as the point at which two persons begin to consider themselves seriously as candidates for marriage and take steps to disengage from other competitive commitments. The couple's announcement of the formal engagement and setting the wedding date may follow by several months the beginning of the engagement process and the functions registered in their "private understanding." Precisely when an engagement begins is harder to determine than when it ends. It ends either with the severance of the relation or with some kind of ceremony legitimizing the marriage.

The engagement if treated as a trial or testing period by the couple rather than as a promise-to-marry from which there is no escape, offers an excellent opportunity both for extensive role rehearsals for marriage and for the participation by parents, friends and professionals in socializing the pair for the marital status. A review of some of the functions of the engagement in the middle-class indicates its usefulness:

Exploring family backgrounds and differences.   Because our mate selection market increasingly brings together, in dating and courtship, individuals of diverse backgrounds even though they share the same class and generation, the period of exclusiveness often offers the first opportunity to test the compatibility of their cultural and family backgrounds. Exploration, experimentation and frank discussion are necessary to widen the areas of understanding.

Recovery from courtship insecurities.   It is evident that the engagement is also serving a useful function if it reduces the tension and insecurity brought about by the competition of courtship. The "line" is dropped in engagement, the jockeying for position gradually ceases, and the members relax in the exclusiveness provided them by their friends. They now have some reasonable likelihood of discovering one another as persons.

It is expected that the engagement will tend to set the pair apart from others. Other romantic attachments will be written off. Third parties, including well-wishing parents and relatives, will be put in their place as outsiders. As the relation stabilizes, the tag-ends of ambivalence which arise in all new intimate relations will be tied down securely.

Sharing and planning.   The inviolability of the person and of his property breaks down in engagement as secrets are exchanged, personal experiences and attitudes shared. Such frankness was not acceptable under the circumscribed relations of dating and courtship. During engagement, income and property may become common, joint bank accounts may be experimented with, sharing expenses on dates and working out a program of savings are not unheard of as couples play anticipatory roles in the economic and housekeeping spheres. The exchange of gifts becomes more personal and intimate, and the range of acceptable tokens of appreciation widens noticeably. The leeway in common living allowed by our middle-class society is large for the engaged couple.

Dealing with sex tensions.   The sharing function not infrequently may include sharing a common bed. Roughly, 40 per cent of the engaged couples studied by Burgess and Wallin (1953) dealt with their sex tensions by complete sex union before marriage. The engagement is clearly a transition period in allocating responsibility for dealing with sex tension. In dating and courtship, the rules of the game appear to be those of a contest in which the man seeks to increase the levels of intimacy, and the young woman sets the limits permitted (Ehrmann, 1959). In engagement the boundaries tend to be drawn by both members of the pair, and a beginning is made in mutuality, as each accepts some responsibility for the sex life of the pair. To achieve this rearranging of responsibility, communication about sex increases during the engagement period. Before engagement the buildup to progressively higher levels of intimacy tends to occur through nonverbal gestures resulting in discomfort to some girls. Communication about sex is more difficult when no understanding has yet been achieved. Kirkendall (1961) concludes from his studies of pre-marital sexual intercourse, "Generally speaking, it seems easier to engage in actual intercourse than it is to refer openly to it."

The consequences of sex union before marriage are mixed. There is some evidence of heightened sexuality with wives enjoying the coital experiences of the honeymoon and early weeks of marriage more if they had had previous experience in intercourse (Kanin & Howard, 1958). Carrying the queries on into later periods, Chesser (1957) reported his experienced women having the same sexual advantage in the honeymoon but found their margin over the inexperienced diminishing in the first few months after marriage and disappearing altogether after that.

Whatever advantages in heightened sexuality there may be is counterbalanced by an increase in instability in the relation. Blood (1962) notes that intimacy decreases the momentum toward marriage for the man while increasing the desire to marry for the girl, leading her to cling to a relationship that otherwise is defective. As a consequence, we find greater instability both in the engagement period and later in the marriage if the engagement continues into a marriage. Burgess and Wallin (1953) found twice as many broken engagements where intercourse had occurred and reported that the more frequent the intercourse the greater the number of rings returned. Similarly, marital adjustment is poorer (Terman et al., 1938) and divorce is more likely (Locke, 1951) among those who have engaged in pre-marital intercourse. Whether this same negative relation would hold in today's sexual climate is a research question that needs to be answered.

Orientation to marriage.   The engaged status, when it is admitted explicitly, brings couples into formal socialization settings as candidates for marriage. Ministers are increasingly scheduling conferences with engaged couples before arranging for the wedding. Educators are teaching separate classes for engaged couples treating marital and parental roles. Marriage counseling centers and youth organizations are setting up discussion programs and pre-marital counseling for engaged couples. These agencies use the engagement period to prepare the couple for the first years of marriage and to screen out incompatible couples, if possible, before marriage. The engaged status lends itself nicely to these societal interventions.

In engagement the members of the pair relate to one another more responsibly and less playfully than in their dating phase, and as we have shown from Lewis' research (1966), they are now more communicative and more accurate in their perception of one another. Burgess and Wallin (1953) followed 1,000 engaged couples into marriage and found their engagement adjustment scores highly predictive both of later broken engagements and marital adjustment after three years of marriage. These researchers saw the engagement, in effect, as a dress rehearsal for marriage, pin pointing the areas of disagreement and the points of vulnerability in the relationship.

Although the thirty middle-class engaged couples studied by Rapoport (1964) are few in number and her work is still in the exploratory phase, her findings are most germane to our problem. She posited three intrapersonal and seven interpersonal tasks as salient during the transition from engagement to marriage. The intrapersonal tasks were: (1) making oneself ready to take over the roles of husband and wife; (2) disengaging oneself (or altering the form of commitment) from especially close relationships that compete or interfere with commitment to the forthcoming marital relationship; and (3) accommodating patterns of gratification of pre-marital life to patterns of the forthcoming marital relationship. At this level Rapoport was looking particularly for the extent of movement from self orientation to the development of a couple identity by the end of the engagement period. In the interpersonal realm she was concerned with the "role fit" in initiative-taking and decision-making on a number of issues such as dealing with kinfolk and friends; work and sex roles; family planning; and the plans for the wedding and honeymoon.

Rapoport's engaged couples whom she followed from early in the engagement through the first few months of marriage coped with all ten of the developmental tasks of engagement she had posited reasonably well. The couples proceeded with relatively little help from third parties to undertake the tasks of readying themselves for marriage. They sought to find out what their areas of mutual interest were, to accommodate their activities to these areas, and to discuss their plans for the future. The decision about when to marry was arrived at jointly, with the details of the wedding plans left to the female and the plans for the honeymoon left to the male. As far as the couples' preparedness to take on the roles of husband and wife was concerned, there was a lack of domestic role rehearsal among the women. They were prepared to earn their living but not to perform domestic functions.

With regard to altering close relationships that might compete with the marital relation, all of the women showed problems associated with separating from their parental families, particularly their mothers. On the male side, there were lingering contacts with "old flames" that had to be written off, and occupational pressures in some cases left no time for the fiancee.

Giving up pre-marital gratifications of single life was distinctly more of a male than a female problem. The women were more anxious to get married initially, and the males, although wishing to marry, tended to have a difficult time giving up their all-male activities and gratifications.

The task of establishing a couple identity was one that seemed most uniformly well-achieved by all the couples at a superficial level. All talked in "we" terms and presented themselves publicly to family and friends as a pair. Some seemed to feel almost incomplete without the other, indulged in constant eye contact, checked for corroboration when expressing any opinions.

These couples were most unusual in their sex controls, a characteristic possibly associated with their predominantly Catholic backgrounds. As a matter of principle, all couples in the study postponed sex union until marriage with both members sharing in maintaining the controls on their intimacies. In the engagement phase the anxieties about sex contacts tended to be concentrated among the women, whereas in the honeymoon, after the female's "sexual awakening," the anxieties shifted to the male who worried about being able to satisfy his awakened spouse.

There was some asymmetry in establishing mutually acceptable patterns of communication and of social relationships. The girls were more communicative and more oriented than the young men, on the whole, toward a joint network of relationships. There appeared to be relatively little movement to bring about role modification on these fronts during the engagement.

There was whole-hearted adoption of the norm of joint decision-making. Indeed, their acceptance of the norm of mutual agreement was so strong they tended not to be able to describe how any particular decisions were made; decisions "just happened," sometimes with one taking the initiative, sometimes with the other. In this respect, the couples developed "role fit" reasonably well without appearing to work at matching one another's needs for trading off in using one parental model for one particular issue and another for a second issue as might have been expected.

Rapoport's methodology of following couples longitudinally promises to provide even more provocative data in the future. One misses in these initial vignettes, however, much reference to the participation of parents, friends, and professionals in the socialization of the couple for marriage. Is it a "hands off," "leave-them-alone" policy such as Mayer (1961) reported taken by friends in Jewish-Gentile courtships? There appears to be both searching for information about marriage and building of skills among the couples in what might be termed on-the-job training, but all of this occurred almost totally without supervision or evaluation of progress from more skilled third parties.

A question, inadequately answered by research to date, involves the dynamics of deciding to end the engagement by setting the wedding date, by elopement, or by calling off the engagement. The evidence offered suggests that couples with engagements of less than six months are only somewhat more likely to remain married than those with no engagement at all. Goode's (1956) sample of 425 divorced couples averaged only two months engagement, whereas in the marital success studies by Burgess and Cottrell (1939), and Terman et al. (1938) the couples achieving the highest marital adjustment levels averaged engagements of more than two years. When the engagement brings together two relative strangers, the tasks of achieving a couple identity and a viable partnership ready for the demands of marriage would be more time consuming than for couples who are not so handicapped.

What criteria are used by couples to decide to break the engagement or to set a wedding date? Gerhard Neubeck (1964) in assessing his clinical data from college students sees the decision process ranging from nonconscious, casual, drifting into marriage to informal consideration of alternatives. For the 25 per cent where the wife was pregnant at marriage, the decision may have been precipitated by the pregnancy (Christensen, 1964). For college students, the approaching graduation and economic feasibility of marriage may lead the male to view himself as ready for marriage. For still others, sex tensions may precipitate the decision to marry. We lack firm data which would tell us whether socialization in this last status in the pre-marital career has been effective. Couples should be able to draw upon criteria about which there is some consensus to verify their readiness to take on the responsibilities and stresses of marriage. Unfortunately, these criteria are not as yet provided at any point during their pre-marital careers.

Balancing assets and deficits, the engagement in America proves to be an excellent dress rehearsal for marriage. It provides for more than role simulation, playing at marital roles. There is, in this status, bona fide role-playing of the roles appropriate for the comprehensive dyad entering marriage. The engaged draw on very nearly the totality of their repertoire of latent and manifest role sets to create the combinations appropriate for their marital status-in-becoming.

SOCIALIZATION AFTER MARRIAGE

Our discussion of the array of experiences before marriage relevant to role performance after marriage would lead us to predict the following: high motivation to enter the married status but inadequate knowledge about its requirements, an imagery of the parental marriage pattern stored as latent response sets, and extensive experience in progressively more intimate small dyadic cross-sex groups which incorporate some of the role requirements of marriage.

In most socialization programs there is a terminus of the period of learning, the completion of the acquisition of the desired skills marked by licensing, a graduation ceremony, or other *rite de passage*. Such a *rite de passage* with respect to the marital career involves licensing (a marriage license) and a ceremony. It is hardly accurate, however, to say that the licensing has involved any proof of competence or mastery of the knowledge, skills or abilities required to function effectively in the married status. Neither spouse in his pre-marital socialization has ever played the role of apprentice understudying a skilled performer who would supervise and systematically evaluate ego's marital role performance. Thus the marriage ceremony is often more of a "commencement" than a graduation or terminus of learning. The ceremony authorizes a change of name and the use of the differentiating title of Mrs. for the bride and legitimizes cohabitation to practice the arts of marriage "from this day forward," but the players in the marriage game begin as amateurs.

After examining in some depth the adjustments of a number of newly married couples, Rapoport and Rapoport (1964) have conceptualized "getting married" as a critical transition.

"Getting married" is a critical transition in the careers of the two chief actors, because it constitutes such a sharp change in the role content of the positions each holds, and because it involves the complication of joining their two individual careers into one joint career by the creation of a new comprehensive group. There is discontinuity enough in the two statuses when a moratorium period of transition is introduced. Indeed, Rapoport notes the parallelism with the traumatic crises of sudden onset studied by crisis theorists of the clinical tradition (Lindemann, 1949; Caplan, 1960; and Tyhurst, 1951). She defines this crisis, however, as one of the "normal" but significant transitions from one social status to another over the family's developmental cycle, such as first parenthood, the leave-taking of children which ushers in the post-parental status, and the spouse's dying and the consequent dissolution of the marriage. Thus, "getting married" is a crisis not because it is sudden and unanticipated as are the crises of dismemberment and demoralization which arise from disasters, unemployment of the breadwinner or desertion, but because of the inadequacies of the socialization process in preparing the actors for the roles to be played in marriage. To use Kirkpatrick's terms (1955), the scripts provided the actors are often so inappropriate to the situations encountered that the actors are forced to ad-lib their way through, and later to write their own scripts for dealing with recurring situations.

Rapoport enables us to join crisis theory with family development theory (Hill & Rodgers, 1964) to advantage in conceptualizing this transition period. Before marrying, two spouses-in-becoming have been long term incumbents of child positions in their parental families while simultaneously occupying positions in several nonfamily groups of varying duration. The roles in each of these several positions separately tend to be integrated into *role clusters* which are relatively compatible. For each spouse-in-becoming the combination of role clusters from the positions he holds in the several groups to which he belongs constitutes his *positional set*. The multiple roles in the positional set are substantially less integrated than the individual role clusters causing some internal role conflict when the demands of competing positions collide.

In the transition from the single to the married status, profound changes occur in ego's positional set simultaneously with the positional sets of all the others with whom ego's roles are contingent. Not the least of the others who are affected are the new spouse and both constellations of parents and siblings. Whatever equilibrium existed prior to marriage among these several actors is necessarily upset by the changes in role content (insofar as scripted) demanded by the new change of status. In the period of "getting married" the positional sets of each spouse are changed by dropping some role clusters, that is, by withdrawing from membership in some groups. These might include friendship groups because they are incompatible with one's marriage responsibilities or because they are not shared with the spouse. Role clusters may also be added by joining groups within the young married set, changing thereby not only one's membership but also one's reference groups after marriage.

Perhaps of even more importance is the redefining of each spouse's relationships with both sets of parents and siblings. What changes are made in the role obligations of son as he shifts to married son, of daughter as she shifts from daughter to married daughter, and of siblings to each other as they become married siblings? What reciprocal changes in role obligations of mother and father are made to the new relation of married son or daughter? What room, if any, is there in the parental family's table of organization for the position of son-in-law or sibling-in-law? What script covers the behavior appropriate between the parents and siblings of the bride and the parents and siblings of the groom?

These realignments are among the components of the crisis of transition in "getting married" for which anticipatory socialization has been almost entirely absent and has been to date largely unstudied. Let us remedy the situation by examining the opportunities for mutual socialization and corrective resocialization which appear in the honeymoon and early months of marriage.

The Honeymoon As a Moratorium

The honeymoon is an interlude of varying duration, relatively free of responsibilities, that marks the transition from the single state to the assumption of new familial responsibilities. It is a kind of moratorium on regular social participation provided by society with the expectation that the couple will use this time to prepare themselves for returning to participate in society in their new social roles. At the same time the honeymoon gives others in the couple's social network time to prepare for the new relationship.

Almost unstudied by social scientists, the honeymoon with its sacred inviolability and seclusiveness has been idealized as a tranquil, trouble-free period. Actually the honeymoon, the Rapoports (Rapoport & Rapoport, 1964) report, is far from tranquil. It carries over many of the unfinished tasks of the engagement period and is the scene for much awkwardness and uncertainty in spousal role-playing. The conjugal relation with its all-encompassing demands for intimacy, symbolized by the act of intercourse, creates anxieties ranging from competency concerns to fears of loss of autonomy.

Many couples marry even today without much, if any, previous sex experience together. The first attempts at sexual union are as awkward as any other first attempts at a complex activity requiring the coordination of two participants unused to performing together. Thus Landis (1946) in a study of the length of time some 409 couples took to achieve adjustment in sex areas of marriage found the largest number (47.3 per cent) had difficulties initially in achieving adjustment sexually. It is understandable that sexual intimacies may require a period longer than the usual honeymoon to become more rewarding than anxiety provoking.

Intimacy is probably more of a byproduct than a direct product of purposive action. It is an individual achievement of high order, presupposing, according to Erikson (1950), a well-formed identity, as well as a result of the couple's interaction that newly marrieds tend to expect as a right of marriage but have to work at to achieve. A successful honeymoon in this sense has great value both then and later, when its memory in times of conflict serves to soften antagonism.

The honeymoon usually solves few problems permanently for the pair, but does offer opportunities further to establish their identity as a couple and to make a beginning at developing an authority structure and a mutually acceptable division of labor of some of the instrumental-expressive tasks of early marriage.

A word might be said about the phenomenon of mutual socialization which is characteristic of the honeymoon. This involves a special learner role for which the teacher-learner assignments are not specified (Brim & Wheeler, 1966). Both members enter the status of marriage equally inexperienced unless married before. Hence, neither one more than the other would be justified in assuming the teacher role. The groom has an edge in having made the plans for the honeymoon, but these were facilitating plans and did not include leadership in working out the developmental tasks of this phase of marriage. Moreover, the tasks of the honeymoon are disproportionately in the social-emotional expressive area where the bride may bring greater advance competence. There is, therefore, much trial-and-error learning. Both spouses are so heavily involved neither is able to distance himself from the relation sufficiently to engage in the systematic evaluation necessary to benefit from errors made.

To exacerbate the ambiguity of expectations about leadership on these matters is the lack of any mediator or third party on whom to displace the frustration each is experiencing in attempting to cope with the decisions which need to be made. There is no chance as there was in the engagement period to practice at husband-wife roles without taking the consequences of failure. This is not simulation of marital roles as in early cross-sex situations. This is now "playing for keeps."

Early Months of Marriage

The couple returning from the honeymoon pick up the roles appropriate to the new positions of husband and wife, only a few of which could be activated during the honeymoon proper. A task in the early months of marriage is the need for clarification of the couple's relations with the two sets of parents and siblings. In quiet patrilocal societies the relationship between the husband and his family does not change sharply with marriage but can be traumatic and difficult for the wife who leaves her parental family to live in the family of her husband's parents. In Western societies with their neo-local system of marriage, boundary-maintenance of the conjugal couple with regard to the families of orientation is frequently seen as a problem. Yet research findings do not always show the hypothesized striving for independence and autonomy from the influence of relatives among young couples.[7] There is not only continued visiting after marriage but all manner of exchanges of money, goods, and services including counsel and emotional support between the parents on both sides and their married children (Hill, 1965). Allison Davis (1965) reports for his middle-western couples who have been followed since late adolescence that the relationships between the parental and filial families constitute a genuine social system of participation resembling an extended three generation family. Their relationships go beyond economic aid to include almost weekly intergenerational family dinners, excursions, birthday parties, christenings and frequent telephone conversations fairly equally divided between husband's and wife's parental families.

The findings from a longitudinal study of 48 middle-class couples suggest that the marital couple's functioning is related to their orientation to kindred. In the pilot phase of what promises to be a most informative taxonomy of the adaptations to the first years of marriage Wells Goodrich and his associates (Goodrich, Ryder & Rausch, 1966) have identified a number of modes of responding to the life situations common to the first year of marriage.

The most prominent modality in a factor analysis of 164 variables centers on the continuation of close relations with one of the parental families (often the husband's) and adherence to values of stability and rationality as against change and spontaneity. Closely associated with this modality of continuity of close parental ties is an active social life with friends. The couple's interpersonal relations are characterized by high interest in having children, a somewhat muted sexual relationship and a nonaffective style of husband-wife communication. For these families associations with kin and peers may serve as a substitute for or protection against an intimate marital relation.

In contrast to the first modality, a second involves couples with a high degree of affectivity who have cut themselves off from their families. They seem to have a greater investment in sexuality and at this stage (in the fourth month of marriage) have less interest in the prospects of child care. The spontaneity of this modality appears facilitated by an "openness of structure" as Rausch, Goodrich and Campbell (1963) have termed it allowing couples to work out their problem solutions from a wide range of alternatives or creatively to innovate new solutions, unhampered by the views of family elders.

Other modalities from the factor analysis are built around the adaptations

---

[7] Perhaps the independence strivings are less from one's own parents than from the parents of one's spouse. The interfering relative, after all, is usually identified as an "in-law" (Duvall, 1954).

of individuals whose childhood and adolescence were unhappy. Wives with such troubled backgrounds tend to carry their unresolved problems of adolescence into the marital relationship expressing their conflicts openly. Trouble with the husband's family, sexual inadequacies, difficulty in getting along with friends, and disagreements over housekeeping cluster in the wife's reports. Husbands with such backgrounds of unhappy parent-child relations, in contrast, report no such reenactment of problems in marriage but develop defenses against the overt enactment of conflict. They tend to marry maternal home-centered wives and to invest themselves single-mindedly in matters of occupational ambition. The marriage pattern exemplifies the traditional allocation of roles with husbands expressing less interest in participation in household tasks and their wives expressing less interest in working outside the home. The researchers wonder if the emphasis on role segregation does not serve a defensive function of sanctioning an avoidance of intimacy which might mobilize a marital enactment of the husband's inner conflicts.

A corollary problem of adaptation in early marriage commonly encountered is the battle over which of the two marriage models the spouses have acquired from the two parental families shall have precedence, if either does, in the new marriage. In the economy of problem solving, there is a tendency to bring, first of all, the familiar parental solution to bear. Moreover, at the level of role expectation, the wife will tend to anticipate her husband following the norms to which her mother's husband conformed. It is as if the new couple, although residentially neo-local, had brought the parents with them into their living quarters. In correcting for the incompatibilities engendered by these two marriage models each spouse undertakes to rewrite both his self and other scripts more in line with what he has discovered about the particular spouse he has married in the hope that subsequent performances will find them more nearly in reciprocity.

There is some evidence that those couples who do not succeed in achieving reciprocity of roles attitudinally are prone to divorce. Jacobson's (1952) study of 100 divorced and 100 married couples of the same marital cohort found greater disparity in their conceptions of the appropriate roles for husbands and wives than among his married controls.

Lu (1952) has reported substantially higher marital adjustment scores among newly-married couples in Chicago whose decision-making pattern was equalitarian rather than husband or wife dominated. This relation has also been found for couples whose parental families were husband dominated but who were equalitarian themselves. It would seem that couples do tend to work out their own authority patterns at the expense of discontinuity with the parental pattern (Ingersoll, 1948). We will return again to the issue of continuity of marriage patterns at the close of the chapter.

The couple's development of a predictable authority structure and division of labor in the first months of marriage can rest upon the pre-marital experiences in the engagement and upon the visible patterns of the couple's age peers fully as much as it does upon the competitive imagery of the two parental marriage patterns. It is therefore small wonder that the parental patterns, if in conflict with current majority practice, as in immigrant families, would be set aside for the practices of the couple's peers.

Levinger (1964) brings an additional dimension to bear in his study of the division of labor among recently married couples. He finds a marked tendency, as have others, for specialization between husband and wife to occur with respect to the instrumental tasks of marriage involving the manipulation of objects (repairing things around the house, doing evening dishes, and paying bills). His findings, however, run contrary to the theory enunciated by Parsons and Bales (1955) and tested by Zelditch (1955) for several societies, that it is the wife who will be expected to carry the bulk of the social-emotional tasks in the marriage. Levinger found the performance of social-emotional roles among his young marrieds to be carried out by both husband and wife more or less equally. This was true of such issues as confiding in the other when bothered or upset, trying to discover the other's point of view when a difference of opinion existed and praising the other for something done ego liked. On all these issues husbands were as likely to report and be reported doing these tasks as wives. Levinger also found as great a tendency among his male as his female respondents to rank high in their hierarchy of goals for marriage, marital affection, companionship and happy children.

His explanation for these findings is essentially structural. Since social-emotional behavior is activity that maintains the relations between members, it is ultimately reciprocal and cannot be delegated to persons outside the group. While instrumental task activity activates a subject-object relation, social-emotional activity refers to a subject-subject relation. Since there are only two participants in a marriage, if only one partner engages in social-emotional actions, social interaction breaks down. Where the husband is emotionally absent, the wife's ability to sustain the social-emotional relations is clearly limited. As mother in the larger family subsystem of parents and children, she can play the social-emotional task leader role regardless of her husband's actions; as wife, she cannot.

The Levinger findings carry large implications for the resocialization of the young man for his companionship roles in marriage. The emphasis on the spousal relation is comparatively recent. From his imagery of his parental marriage patterns he may have perceived his mother as carrying the major task of tension management in the family and therefore for the marriage. This perception poorly prepares him for playing the supportive affection-giver to his wife. Unless corrected by the courting relations of his pre-marital career the burden of the resocialization will have to occur during the critical transition of getting married.

Age at marriage is a structural factor, on which there have been numerous studies showing its relationship to marital role performance. It is well established that marriage before 20 is highly vulnerable to divorce and that parental age at marriage is highly correlated with when their children marry (Glick, 1957). Schorr (1966) has recently reviewed the literature establishing the close links between early marriage, premature dropping out of school and lowered employability, pre-marital pregnancy, larger family size than desired, consequent lower income per member, and higher probability of divorce and desertion. Age at marriage, therefore, places constraints on family development, which beg for social attention in the form of young adult socialization before as well as after marriage.

Yet there is some evidence as to positive consequences associated with early marriage. Medalia (1962) has shown for Georgia Tech graduates that those who married while undergraduates had substantially higher scholastic averages than those who remained single until after graduation. This was equally true of those who were 22 or younger upon graduation (who would have married younger than average) against those who were 23 or older at graduation. Controlling for scholastic ability, Jensen and Clark (1958) found a similar superior scholastic adjustment among married undergraduates.

Vincent (1964) in a control study has even been able to demonstrate the benign impact of marriage on those who marry young as well as those who marry at more conventional ages. Administering the California Personality Inventory in 1954 to 517 subjects and again in 1959 to as many as could be located (110 subjects) he divided his after group into those unmarried after five years and those married at 18–20 and at 21–23. The scores for all respondents improved over the five-year period although not significantly for the unmarried. The improvement for the married respondents was more dramatic, with the young marrieds showing the greatest increases. The young marrieds had lower CPI scores before marriage which suggests that marriage may have been an attempt to resolve personal problems and achieve an adult status not granted by parents or the school system. Marriage apparently did have maturing effects increasing dominance, self-control, sociability, and self-acceptance in particular. Additional studies of the phenomena of the consequences of mutual socialization in marriage would be illuminating, since the bulk of the evidence from the analysis of secondary statistics of age at marriage and family instability argues that the responsibilities of marriage are defeating rather than benign in their consequences.

This section on socialization after marriage should not end without an additional note. If there is limited opportunity for role rehearsal of marital roles prior to marriage, marriage itself can serve this function for persons who divorce and later marry another. The first marriage appears for many to serve as a period for trying out and rejecting uncomfortable roles. The next time around, presumably, the individual is a better judge of the mate with whom he can interact satisfactorily while being able himself to give a better performance in his various marital roles. Thus about four-fifths of those who remarry enjoy at least average success, and the rate of remarriage seems to be increasing among men in the higher occupational levels—professionals, proprietors, managers, officials, craftsmen and foremen—men, that is, who set the highest standards for marital performance and are the best marital risks (Bernard, 1956).

Impact of Parenthood as
Adult Socialization after Marriage

For some 90 per cent of married couples (the figure fluctuates with the age group considered) the socialization into marital roles each is undergoing is profoundly affected by their taking on the status of parenthood. Parenthood rather than marriage appears to be the crucial role-transition point that marks the entrance into adult status in our society. Marriage no longer necessarily indicates that the man is performing his occupational role sufficiently well to support a family. Brides, instead of immersing themselves in full-time domesticity, continue to work outside the home to supplement the family income or provide it while husbands are completing their occupational training. In some cases, neither spouse is employed and the couple's economic support comes from parents.

It is with the arrival of the first child that woman's domestic responsibilities defining her socially expected adult roles take on first priority. Her working outside the home becomes problematical, and the role of breadwinner, the major indicator of the male's adult status, devolves upon the husband. Middle-class couples often plan the first pregnancy to coincide with the husband's first full-time job in his chosen occupation. In any case, parenthood more than marriage forces the couple to accept the responsibilities that define the socially expected adult domestic roles.[8]

If parenthood signals maturity to the individual, it also modifies the couple's *raison d'etre*. Both Durkheim and Schmalenbach have argued that the affective commitment that brings husband and wife together in Western societies is an unstable one (Durkheim, 1897; Schmalenbach, 1961). The passionate involvement of two people with each other is a fleeting thing. For the marriage relationship to endure, the sentiment of love must be strengthened by a sense of duty growing out of mutual obligations. Before the coming of children the marriage relationship has a tentative quality. With the advent of parenthood, the trial period is over. The couple is now responsible for a younger generation which represents the continuity of the unit. The social arrangements that husband and wife develop to meet their new responsibilities gives the marriage a stability it lacked before.

The belief that children keep husband and wife together and prevent divorce is a common one. There is some evidence for this belief. Childlessness is higher among divorcing couples, and the larger the number of children, the lower the divorce rate. Yet most authorities agree with Jacobson that divorce

---

[8] Among the unmarried lower-lower class Negro girls in a St. Louis housing project becoming a mother marked maturity (Rainwater, 1966). In some societies marriage depends upon parenthood. The marriage among the Mbuti pygmies, for example, is not considered final until the woman proves her fertility by bearing a child (Turnbull, 1965).

and childlessness are both results of some more fundamental factor in marriage (Jacobson, 1959). Certainly, the transformation in the marital relation that parenthood brings can create strains between husband and wife. The mutual socialization that has gone on between husband and wife has resulted in a web of expectancies and behaviors that give the relationship system-like qualities. The first child as far as the conjugal system is concerned is an intruder. The new parent-child dyadic relations constitute a competing system. The conjugal system instead of being the only component of the family unit becomes a subsystem of the family along with the parent-child subsystem. Man and woman may not yet feel comfortable in their conjugal roles, but they are obligated to add to their repertoire a number of parent roles. Because of the disruption in the established behavior patterns of husband and wife the new parental roles create, LeMasters (1957) characterized the parenthood transition point as one of crisis.

The three-person group as Simmel noted is an unstable relation with tendencies to break into a dyad and an isolate (Simmel, 1964). The neglected husband whose roles as father do not compensate for the loss of wifely attentions is not an uncommon phenomenon (Dyer, 1963). The conjugal subsystem will outlast the parent-child subsystem yet the latter may so eclipse the husband-wife relation during its existence that couples can interact only as parents and not as husband and wife. The responsibilities of parenthood can halt completely the husband's and wife's mutual socialization into a satisfactory marital relation. It is the change in priority of conjugal roles as well as the taken-for-granted quality of the relation brought about by the routinization of interaction over time that middle-class couples fear. For working-class couples, the more stable element in the lower class, both men and women are better prepared to interact as father and mother than in their conjugal roles. There is a segregated pattern of decision-making and task division and less expectation that husband and wife will be companions (Komarovsky, 1964). The tendency is even more pronounced among lower-lower-class couples (Rainwater, 1965). The conjugal system has had such a stunted development that couples may interact more with respect to their children than they ever did about their spousal concerns.

When the demands of conjugal and parent roles conflict, the resulting tension must be settled in some way. In the past parental roles took precedence in the hierarchy of family values to insure that at least some of the children would survive to maturity. Today as then, however, parental role expectations make heavier demands on women than men. This asymmetry in the number of responsibilities each spouse fulfills in parental roles, one can speculate, is responsible for some marital conflict. Wives tied down by family responsibilities resent their husbands' involvement outside the family, and this resentment may be reflected in their resistance to husbands' demands for conjugal intimacies. A longitudinal study of middle-class couples has produced some evidence indicating that in this group parenthood does affect women disproportionately. Disenchantment with marriage among women though appearing later than among men seems to result from parenthood, as occupational commitment has earlier lowered the marital euphoria of men (Pineo, 1961).

The "meta-proscriptions" that exist today to enable couples to handle the competing demands of spouse and children assign a greater importance to the husband-wife relationship. Parental roles still assume priority in daytime hours while children are awake, particularly when the children are younger. Conjugal roles are relegated to night hours when the spouses may be too tired to interact. As children grow older, some studies suggest that husband and wife can give more time to each other. But cross-sectional data show that it is only after children leave home that women's marital satisfaction, waning since the onset of parenthood, begins to pick up (Blood & Wolfe, 1960).

In addition to the contradictory expectations from parental and marital subsystems, there are other reasons for the stressful nature of parenthood. If we are right that parenthood rather than marriage is the indicator of adult status, then the new roles are anxiety provoking. They constitute a test of how well the individual functions as an adult. In addition, the level of anxiety is heightened by the lack of formal or informal training for parenthood. The implicit socialization into parental roles that goes on in the nuclear family through the role-taking the child engages in while interacting with his father or mother is necessarily lacking at the infant stage. Even the role-taking the older child engages in when interacting with his parents would seem to be more effective for acquiring general values rather than the specific skills of parenthood. The cues the parents give through directions, rewards, and punishments focus the child's attention on his own behavior rather than his parents' child-rearing techniques. Actual rehearsal through serving as parental surrogate appears essential for the individual to learn the behaviors associated with parental roles. Yet over a third of the wives and more than half of the husbands in Dyer's middle-class samples were lacking course work or experience with younger siblings or other children (Dyer, 1963).

The tiredness and fatigue, the financial problems, the interruption of routine habits and the increased tension new parents report add to their role-performance problems. When one member of the couple is failing to perform his new roles, the other has difficulty mustering the permissiveness and patience necessary, using Parsons' paradigm of the socialization process, to supply the support that would encourage the deviant (Parsons & Bales, 1955). The interaction balance instead is heavily weighted with criticism rather than rewards when the spouse does try again. Sexual relations could provide a release for the tensions and irritation between husband and wife but this outlet may be restricted by the postpartum moratorium required for the wife's physical recovery, as well as by her fatigue. Thus parenthood may require a longer period of adjustment than did marriage. The new parental roles must be learned and somehow reconciled with pre-existing marital patterns in a context where adult domestic responsibilities can no longer be shirked. It is well that our society places such a high valuation on the achievement of parenthood status within marriage as this valuation may serve to soften some of its attendant trials.

Children as Socializing Agents for Parents

The young intruders whose needs and demands so modify the marital relation can also serve as agents of socialization for their parents.

Paradoxically, the major content of the knowledge parents acquire from children has to do with the parents' performance as socializing agents for these same children. The children, particularly the first child, through their activities outside the family, introduce parents to the formal and informal organizations which function to supplement, counter or support parental efforts to socialize the child. Because the formal education organization has received societal sanction to place the child in the role of learner and to teach him a certain minimum of skills and values, all parents have to take the school efforts into account in their interaction with the child. Lower-class parents may be largely able to nullify school efforts because of the negative attitudes toward education they transmit and the poor study habits their treatment of the child engenders (Gans, 1962), but in their case they lose their children to the peer group.

The child's introduction of his parents to the ways of the peer group, which along with parents and school form the central triumvirate for the socialization of the young, can have great effect on their performance of parental roles. Here too there is a paradox, for when parents are most open to socialization by their children, it appears that the learning the child transmits is most congruent with the parents' customary role performance. Bernstein's distinction between status-oriented and person-oriented families is useful in this connection (Bernstein, 1964). In status-oriented families, the interaction is in terms of the members' age and sex positions. Superior power rests in the parents because of their age, and communication is one-way—from the parents to the child. Prevented from modifying his parents' socialization efforts, the child turns to peers whose activities are often at odds with the values parents are trying to inculcate. When there is a direct clash the parents do not give in, and the child's rebellion generalizes from the issue in question to the parents' authority in other areas. In failing to learn from the child, the parents place their own attempts to train the child in jeopardy. Such families are more often found in the lower class where larger proportions of parents, especially fathers, do not consult with children on decisions involving the children (Elder, 1962). It would also appear that the disjuncture between the first and second generations of immigrant groups or other groups experiencing rapid change stems from the failure of parents to utilize their children as agents of socialization.

Members of the person-oriented family, in contrast, interact on the basis of each other's abilities and capacities. Communication between parents and children is two-way as is socialization. Parents who modify their role in response to children's coaching have greater effectiveness in supervising the child's choice of friends. Parents are also better able to retain their influence over the child when parental and peer expectations of the child clash. These parents respond to suggestions and complaints from the child, but the latter's demands do not require drastic changes in the parents' customary role performances (Bowerman & Kinch, 1959). And as we shall see later, these parents are better able to transmit these less rigid parental role performance norms to their children. Thus by accepting their children as socialization agents, the parents increase their own effectiveness in playing the socializing role.

FORMAL TRAINING
FOR MARRIAGE AND PARENTHOOD

The foregoing discussion has profited from a frame of reference which has viewed the socialization process developmentally over the pre-marital careers of the spouses-in-becoming to the critical role transition of "getting married" which ushers in the post-marital career. We have been sensitized by Brim's paradigm (Brim & Wheeler, 1966) to note, wherever possible for each phase, the inputs of socialization content by the socializing agent with respect to motivation, knowledge and ability, and the relative emphasis on values and behavior. In general, the parental family has proved effective in imparting basic motivations for marriage and parenthood and for sex-role preferences, but it has offered little guidance for obtaining knowledge about or skill in the arts of marriage and parenthood, and opportunities for role rehearsals have been limited.

Subsequent exposure to marriage-like situations over the pre-marital career ranges from same-sex to cross-sex pairs, mostly involving age peers. These experiences have offered ego unsupervised role rehearsals, or simulation of marriage relevant roles, under conditions of low affectivity, resulting in much trial-and-error-type learning. The initially high motivation to marry instilled in the parental family was maintained and even increased over this period; knowledge about sex and the facts of marriage was casually and unsystematically obtained, but it was in the realm of skills in interpersonal relations that the experiences with peers in pre-adolescence and adolescence were most useful.

The critical role transition of "getting married"; namely, the engagement, the honeymoon and the first months of marriage, was characterized by somewhat more systematic search for information to remedy inadequate knowledge about marriage, and extensive practice of the skills required by the new status. In this terminal stage of socialization, the socializees appear to have been left severely alone to socialize one another, with neither one nor the other sufficiently more experienced to take on leadership in the teacher-learner roles. Mutual socialization of one another involved, therefore, trial-and-error learning under conditions of inadequate reinforcement hardly likely to be highly effective. It is not clear from the evidence at hand how much of the imagery of parental marriage models stored as latent roles is activated in the "getting married" phase, necessitating correction through the mechanism of role modification nor is it clear how much of the complex of husband-wife reciprocal roles is produced from script and how much is the product of trial-and-error ad-lib behavior which, if it worked, became incorporated in the pair's role complex. These questions beg carefully designed studies.

Many implications for the organization of systematic programs of family life education can be derived from the foregoing discussion. The evidence would suggest the need for formal preparation for marriage and parenthood for all who wish to marry and have children. Such training would not be just for those deviants whose parental families were inadequate, or who later in their cross-sex contacts demonstrate incompetence, or who still later become pre-maritally pregnant, precociously married and divorced. These deviants are visible reminders of the failure of the social system to socialize its young effectively for marriage and parenthood, and should certainly be reached with programs focussed upon their resocialization.[9] But, the analysis we have undertaken in this chapter argues for a division of labor among informal agencies like the parental family, the peer group, and the couple acting as their own agents in mutual socialization, on the one hand and the formal agencies of school, church and youth agencies on the other hand. All spouses-to-be could thus be reached in a systematic program of training for marriage and parenthood.

The informal agencies examined have been weak in providing knowledge about marriage and parenthood and inadequate in providing systematic supervision and evaluation of the degree of competence developed in the skills and abilities necessary for successful marriage. Programs of reproduction education, of consumer education, and of education in household skills in the schools from kindergarten to university are essentially factual. They impart systematic knowledge about the instrumental task areas of marriage and offer some training in the mastery of instrumental skills. Courses dealing with the family, preparation for marriage, sex education, parent education, and child development are also

---

[9] Programs of resocialization of deviant couples are less frequently group programs using formal educational methods of lectures and discussion although family service agencies have organized just such sessions for clients having common problems. The bulk of the resocialization offered professionally is provided as marriage counseling with both spouses present, if possible. The focus is upon improving the tension management function through improved communication and role modification. A substantial proportion (50–70 per cent) of the case load of the more than 500 family service agencies in the U.S. involves marriage counseling today. Domestic relations courts, public welfare agencies, some business firms, and even universities offer marriage counseling services. The disciplines represented by the 500 members of the American Association of Marriage Counselors, the chief accrediting and standard-setting organization for marriage counseling, include psychology, 26 per cent; social work, 25 per cent; ministry, 15 per cent; education, 8 per cent; medicine, 8 per cent; sociology, 5 per cent; law, 1 per cent; and 12 per cent multi-disciplinary of background.

Training for marriage counseling usually follows clinical training in counseling and psychotherapy as a postdoctoral or postprofessional degree program and includes a minimum of a full academic year of supervised clinical internship in marriage counseling.

For details on the development of marriage counseling, the range of theories drawn upon, and the strategies developed for functioning within the counseling relationship as a social system, see the discussion by Gerald Leslie (1964).

factually oriented to the social-emotional task areas of marriage and parenthood and only occasionally provide training in the skills of interpersonal competence. Unevenly provided in the elementary and secondary schools, but uniformly provided as standard fare in higher education, these programs supplement the informal agencies where they are demonstrably weakest; namely, in providing perspective and systematic knowledge about the phenomena of marriage and parenthood in our society.[10]

Some Consequences of Family Life Education

Attempts at evaluation of family life education have been scanty. There have been virtually no studies of consequences of high school or out-of-school family life programs. Evaluations of college preparation-for-marriage programs published to date run to fewer than twenty studies, and none of them conform adequately to the rigors of experimental design.[11] In contrast Brim's (1959) bibliography of evaluation studies of parent education contains almost seventy items, a limited number of which utilize controls and conform to the requirements of experimental design.

Some kinds of education are relatively easy to evaluate. If one is teaching typewriting, cake baking, or accounting, it is evident without any elaborate evaluation technique whether or not the subject is learned and to what degree the objectives have been attained. But the less tangible and more significant objectives of education like good citizenship, sound health, or successful marriage and parenthood are extremely difficult to evaluate.

There are at least four major methodological factors which enter into the evaluation of formal training courses in relation to the marital performance of the person:

1. How are we to isolate from the whole complex of influences which play upon a marriage the one factor which we are testing, namely, the course?

2. What shall be our operational definition of the course objective of effective marital performance?

3. When should we evaluate our marriage education efforts? At the end of the course, before marriage? After one year of marriage? After five years?

4. Who shall make the evaluation, the student, the teacher, or a third party?

In reviewing the evaluations that have been made of college programs, it is quite apparent that they usually ignore the possibility of self-selection, that

---

[10] For those wishing more detail, an excellent overview of these developments is now available in Kerckhoff (1964).

[11] For more detail and a spirited defense of the effectiveness of marriage courses see the article by Evelyn M. Duvall (1965).

they rely heavily on student testimonials which relate more to student tastes and reactions than to progress toward the course's objectives.[12]

Short-term results.   Most of the evaluations of the marriage preparation courses look directly at the impact of the course during the period in which the students are enrolled. Using before-and-after tests, sometimes with control groups, more often without, a number of measures have been undertaken: measures of knowledge, of attitude change with respect to marriage, sex, and parenthood, and occasionally measures of competence in interpersonal relations.

To demonstrate the amount of learning of factual material is fairly easy with before-and-after information mastery tests (Gillies & Lastrucci, 1954; Moses, 1956), but the relationship of the mastery of factual materials to later marital success is not entirely clear. Moses (1956), in a control group design at Syracuse University, found that the amount of learning of factual material is positively correlated with the degree of commitment to marriage; that is, those who were married or engaged showed greater gains in such mastery than those who were just dating. Pitman (1958) in North Carolina demonstrated that mastery of factual materials was not related to two different types of teaching methods (lectures vs. discussion, but not role-playing), or to size of classes taught. It is well to remember that the factual knowledge tested may be of little relevance to performance of marital roles.

The problem of demonstrating changes in motivation to take on marital roles is somewhat more complex. Gillies and Lastrucci (1954) looked for "changes in attitude in a positive direction toward marriage and family living" using a 50-item sentence completion test. They found changes, all in the expected direction, but were defeated by the phenomenon of self-selection—most of their students were favorably inclined toward marriage before entering the course. Anderson (1953) used a 69-item attitude scale of sex and family life views based on consensus of agreement among recognized leaders in the field of family life education and found a number of significant changes in the predicted direction. Hill (1954) found Puerto Rican students much more volatile in attitude changes during one semester's course work than his North Carolina students, particularly in the areas of family authority patterns, child-rearing practices, and views about governmental services for families. Kerckhoff (1960) reported increased confidence in child-rearing, decreased reliance on experts and increased expectations of children as a consequence of family life courses at Merrill-Palmer. Wherever control groups have been used in family life education evaluations, the experimental family life education groups made greater advances in factual mastery and in attitude change (Walters & Fisher, 1958; Moses, 1956; and Bardis, 1963).

Interesting proposals for evaluation of the therapeutic impact of the functional course have been made by Bee (1952) who suggested utilizing the

---

[12] Kerckhoff (1960) notes in his evaluation of the impact of courses that when their testimonials are arrayed against objective tests students appear to be very poor judges of these matters.

MMPI in a before-and-after analysis to evaluate changes in emotional maturity, the F-test to measure the ideological components of personality, and the projective tests by Murray (TAT) and Rorschach. Gillies and Lastrucci (1954) found no significant changes in the response to the Bell Personality Inventory during the course, and only slightly fewer negative responses to the Mooney Problem Check List, suggesting that the course has less therapeutic than educational impact on the students in attendance. In a better controlled study Wetzel (1962) utilized a control group of students in business administration who were identical in their personality profiles on the Rorschach and the Thurstone Inventory with enrollees at the beginning of the marriage course. He found significant positive changes in the students taking the course compared with the control group, leading to the conclusion that the course aided in modification of psychological blocking and strong affective reactions and brought improvement in ability to relate to others.

One of the most novel evaluative studies which begs replication with more cases is reported by Gillette (1959) who sought to answer three questions: (1) Is it possible to effect changes in interpersonal competence within the framework of a college level course in marriage and the family; (2) What is the relationship between participation in a role-playing experiment within such a course and the internalization of knowledge and attitudes taught in the course; and (3) What are the attitudes of students toward participation in such a role-playing experiment? Gillette compared a randomly selected section of students in the marriage course at the University of North Carolina with which he role-played weekly to improve their autonomy (defined as acting with security as one chooses to act) with a control group in the same course exposed only to tutorial discussion with before-and-after tests on autonomy, attitudes toward issues in marriage and parenthood, and mastery of factual knowledge of the field. He found 60 per cent of the autonomy group made marked progress in autonomy while only 10 per cent of the control group made any progress. The autonomy group made as much progress in attitude changes and mastery of factual materials as the control group. In the final comprehensive examination for the course the students' grades in the autonomy group were distributed in the upper two quartiles of the entire class of over a hundred students. His findings suggest that the group education methods of improving interpersonal competence in quasi-family groups can be usefully applied within the context of the functional marriage education course.

Long-term results.   A more hazardous evaluation procedure involves assessment of the long-run impact of the marriage preparation course—more hazardous because of the many intervening influences which may contaminate the results. A number of indicators of success have been used: percentage married in first five years; percentage divorced, widowed, remarried; percentage "happily married"; percentage who judge the course was helpful in their marriages; and the percentage who show they have been able to apply the findings from other college courses as well as the marriage course in their marriages.

Ellzey (1949), reporting on 1,600 Stephens College respondents who had taken the year-long course in marriage over a ten-year period, found 1,064 married, 96 engaged, 28 with a history of divorce, and 371 still single; 757 rated their marriage "very successful," 264 "successful," and 52 "about as good as average," with 27 identifying it as a failure. There is some correlation between grades received while taking the course and the relative success or failure in marriage as reported by the respondents. This 1946 study had no control group and relied entirely on testimonials concerning the impact of the course which are highly subject to socially desirable answers.

Finck (1956) has followed up 300 former Florida State University marriage course students and a control group of 983 students who didn't take the course. He found that more of the marriage course group were married, that they had more children, used child spacing more, and were more likely to adopt children, but found no significant differences on questions of age at marriage, age differentials between spouses, or proneness to divorce. The results suggest that the differences lie more in the area of motivation but since marriage course students are already strongly committed, the part played by the course is unclear.

The most ambitious study, approaching in part the requirements of experimental design, is a longitudinal study of marital adjustment by Dorothy Dyer (1959) of a group of students who took the marriage course and a carefully matched control group of students at the University of Minnesota. The follow-up on these students was undertaken five years after graduation. Roughly 60 per cent of the experimental group was married compared with 44 per cent of the control group. A significantly higher percentage of the control group was in the less-than-happy categories on the Burgess-Cottrell marital adjustment scale. Finally, in answer to the question "What college courses have contributed to your marriage adjustment?" the experimental group was significantly better at identifying courses in college that had proved helpful to them. Thirty-two per cent of the control group felt no college courses were particularly helpful compared with only 9 per cent of the experimental group. Those who had taken the marriage courses were more specific in their comments and their identification of the help they had received in college toward marriage adjustment. The marriage course had presumably rendered the other work they had taken more salient, enabling them to integrate it into their lives.

This discussion of evaluation of the consequences of family life education suggests the need to make the objectives of family life education much clearer. They have been so lofty it has been almost impossible to evaluate progress or lack of progress with respect to them. There is justification for the belief that specific techniques and factual knowledge can be successfully taught and carried over into marriage. It remains to be seen, of course, whether these are important to the overall success or failure of marriage. The evidence from the attitude changes achieved in the marriage course leads us to the conclusion that persons who have had marriage education are somewhat more realistic in their anticipation of problems and in their general marriage expectations. Marriage education also seems to result in an ability to verbalize somewhat more freely about marriage, its problems, solutions, and nature. Marriage becomes objectified, a vocabulary is learned along with some concepts and principles. The better students, especially, develop an ability to discuss marriage with an emotional detachment[13] and an apparent understanding which many believe to be good because it permits freer marital communication. We have, as yet, to prove that this is conducive to marital success.

Inconclusive though the evaluations of functional marriage education be, the consequences are more dramatic than those reported by Brim (1959) for parent education. The difference is not in the research designs employed because the parent education studies are the more sophisticated, but in the setting and strength of the stimulus variables. In functional marriage courses the setting is one of formal education with consecutive attendance over a longer period of time, with more of the paraphernalia of motivated study such as examinations and course credits and a more professionally trained set of teachers. Moreover, lofty though the objectives of marriage education be, they require change only in the student, not in his parents or in his children. In parent education the criterion variable often involves change in the attitudes or behavior of the children of the participants. Finally, it is possible to undertake functional research with students in the marriage course and feed back information to the instructor to improve instruction. In parent education evaluation is less feasible because the indirect object of the instruction (the child) is not present to provide the feedback.

Limitations of Family Life Education as Formal Socialization

Family life education has not been particularly inventive in reaching families outside of formal school settings, and most individuals, once they become family heads, are inaccessible to formal school programs. Moreover, as presently constituted, formal family life education appears least able to help those who are most in need of socialization into marital and parental roles; namely, lower-class young people. It is in this class that one finds the poorest marital and parental performances as indicated by rates of divorce, desertion and child neglect.

Family life education originated in the interests of college students and their middle-class teachers and clergy. As a consequence the courses that focus on training for marital and parental roles are mainly found in colleges, a setting that automatically eliminates the vast majority of blue-collar youths. In addition, the teaching methods assume a verbal facility and consciousness of interpersonal problems in the student that is largely lacking among the less

---

[13] Goodrich and associates have reported this syndrome accompanied by a lack of spontaneity and a muted sexual relationship in one of their modalities; see our earlier discussion, p. 919.

affluent. Finally, the learning content while relevant to the problems of middle-class college students has less meaning for the high-school drop-out.

College marriage preparation courses are, of course, designed for the middle-class student or the upwardly-mobile middle-class aspirant, but what about the family life education courses in the secondary schools? Do they not reach, one may ask, a major proportion of the non-college-bound youth? It is true that large numbers of lower-class girls, though not boys, are enrolled in such courses as part of the home economics segment of the vocational training curriculum which so many girls not in the college preparation program enter. The high school family living courses, however, tend to concentrate on the home-maker skills of cooking and sewing, the specialties of the instructors with only occasional forays into marital and parental relationships. Too often, moreover, the socialization training offered has a middle-class bias. No one would argue that income management, and dating and courtship are not important topics, but both presuppose certain elements of the standard middle-class life style. In the one case, a stable income of a size that permits allotment decisions is necessary; in the other, a group of eligibles from which to choose a mate, a selection process, and the couple's ability to interact on other than a surface level. More applicable to the concerns of lower-income adolescents would be information about conception and contraception, sexual matters being a prevalent area of ignorance among the less advantaged, or preparation for accommodating marital and parental roles, since a sizable number begin their families before or shortly after marriage. As of now, therefore, formal education for marriage and parenthood is not really designed to meet the socialization needs of non-middle-class people.

Even for the middle-class student, family life courses could increase their effectiveness. Despite a willingness among many instructors to go beyond formal procedures for transmitting knowledge, there is still a lack of supervised role rehearsal through role-playing or evaluation of filmed episodes. Moreover, few teachers work with couples committed to each other who are ready to try out the range of interaction patterns found in marriage. Indeed, most education and counseling services are still rendered to *individuals*, a precious few to *married pairs*, but to date no agency has devised an educational program for training families as groups to cope more effectively with their internal and external problems. We are suggesting the need for programs designed for couples and families. Problems of authority, decision-making, communication, and meeting the emotional needs of members are not issues which can be as profitably mastered in high school and college settings as they can after the individuals are actively engaged in family leadership themselves. Similarly, the trend in the family from active production to consumption requires a basic redefinition of family roles to maximize the enjoyment of the consumption function in family life. In sum, family leadership training is peculiarly difficult to undertake in formal school settings. It is entirely possible that we will have to wait upon basic research on time and role allocation among successful families to make much of a contribution here.

SOCIAL CHANGE AND SOCIALIZATION FOR
MARRIAGE AND PARENTHOOD

"Although no two marriages are ever alike, every society has a clear pattern of how spouses should act and feel toward each other," wrote Linton in 1936. It is doubtful that he would be able to make such a statement today about our own society. The phrase having to do with spousal feelings probably still holds true. There is a definite norm in our own society that individuals marry only when they are in love and that despite the vicissitudes of married life, some sort of positive emotional bond will continue to unite them as the years go on. But the norms no longer clearly specify the components of marital and parental role performance. What seems to have occurred is that norms in this area have become more general, so that a wider range of behavior fits their prescriptions.

With the blurring of traditional sex-role definitions the marital relation is shifting from "closed, defined" interaction patterns to an "open, emergent" structure (Rausch, et al., 1963). No longer, for example, do marital norms enjoin a clear-cut sex-based division of labor and decision-making in which the husband is responsible for matters affecting the family's relations with the broader community leaving internal family affairs to his wife (Blood & Wolfe, 1960). Instead, the operative norms appear to permit a variety of marital organization patterns so long as the latter conform to an equalitarian standard, broadly interpreted, in which each spouse initially has some voice in making the arrangements. Extreme asymmetries in power between husband and wife seem to be diminishing. A somewhat similar condition appears to exist with regard to parental role-performance norms as promulgated by experts. They no longer are confined to the extreme positions on the control and support dimensions of child care, but encompass a comfortable range of middle ground (Caldwell, 1964). Again, there is less asymmetry in the parent-child relationship.

If marital and parental role norms have become less specific, the reasons lie in changes in the broader society. Formerly, when couples grew up in the same local community and had similar family backgrounds the role performance learnings they brought into marriage largely "dovetailed." Starting out with much the same knowledge, the amount of socialization the couple needed after marriage was minimal. Moreover, role performance alternatives less often existed as their associates came from the same community. Since the tasks involved in physical maintenance of the family demanded specific skills of husband and wife, skills that were incorporated in marital and parental role norms, it was fortunate that couples married who held the same role performance norms. The family's existence would have been threatened if the man and woman because of conflicting expectations had been forced to work out the arrangements by which they could function as partners.

Today the family is no longer the production unit for its own consumer needs. Less specific skills are required of the couple to keep the family going.

But the greater geographical mobility of the population brings couples from diverse backgrounds together increasing the need for post-marital socialization. Their knowledge of the range of possible roles is also widened by their contacts with peers whose learnings in the family of orientation differ.

The easing of normative prescriptions has not affected all social groups to the same extent nor in the same aspects of marital and parental role performance. Intimates of the couple may enforce a specific variant of the norms although less concerned third parties in the social network accept only loose conformity. But unless the social network is closely knit, and the intimates transmit the same social norms, the individual being socialized has a number of role alternatives from which to choose.

Men and women have greater opportunity under these conditions to develop the marital and parental relationship most satisfactory to them. At the same time the resultant interaction lacks the conflict-free character that results when individuals conform to predefined, reciprocal role patterns. In addition, to establish a marital organization when the couple has a number of options from which to choose requires a level of interpersonal skills in working out arrangements that many couples do not possess. For this reason, the couples most responsive to the widening of marital and parental role performance alternatives are in the professional, managerial group, the group most affected by raising levels of living and education, and the trend toward person-centered rather than object-centered jobs. These are the couples whose affluence permits them to be concerned about the quality of family relationships, while their education and occupations give them the motivation and interpersonal skills to attempt to develop family roles in harmony with their values.

For all individuals, however, socialization within the parental home has been supplemented by learning from outside agencies that present different images of spousal and parental roles. Thus intergenerational discontinuities occur in role performance in areas where there has been the greatest flux in norms. The allocation of power between husband and wife is one such area in the marital relationship, with disciplinary controls being an analogous area in the parent-child relationship.

The pressures for change emanating from far-reaching societal trends are mediated differently for marriage and parenthood. The existence of an academic discipline with more than a half century's research tradition behind it devoted to the study of children has created a group of concerned experts who have served as change-makers in parental roles. The study of marriage lacks such a tradition partly because adults are better prepared than children both to proscribe study of their behaviors in sensitive areas and to resist proffered advice from students of the family. Since socialization in the family of orientation is less effective for marital than parental roles for reasons discussed in earlier sections, however, individuals have had to do more improvising in their marital relations, and so the basis for more far-reaching changes exists.

One interview study with a representative urban sample of grandparents,

parents, and their married children, where each generation maintained a separate household, has shown marked intergenerational differences in marital role performance. One-third of 84 three-generation lineages maintained the same patterns for dividing marital household tasks over three generations, a figure greater than the continuity in educational achievement—high, middle, or low—relative to others in the same generation found in 20 per cent of the lineages (Aldous & Hill, 1965), but less than the transmission of religious affiliation which occurred in two-thirds of the lineages. In the degree to which the generations conformed to a division of labor based on traditional sex-role task allocation, somewhat more than a fifth ($N = 19$) of the lineages maintained continuity (six lineages showed complete discontinuity with a different arrangement in each generation). This modest continuity of role allocation is somewhat surprising when one considers that discussion of allocation of tasks in the home has not been subject to the equalitarian polemics to the degree to which the allocation of marital authority has. With respect to the pattern of making decisions, 12 of the 80 lineages for which there were data maintained complete continuity, and 14 showed no continuity at all over three generations.

There was also evidence that families have difficulty transmitting patterns that reflect the ability to plan in economic matters. Each family received a planning achievement score based on its tendency to lead, be on a schedule or to fall behind the other families in the sample of its generation in the four areas of durable goods acquisitions, size of residence, income level, and husband's occupational level over the family's life cycle (Hill & Foote, 1967). On the basis of this multi-dimensional indicator, it appeared that of 87 lineages as many three generation lineages ($N = 17$) showed no intergenerational continuity as maintained similar achievement levels. The greatest amount of similarity, fortunately, existed among those scoring high on planning achievement, 12 of 30, compared with 17 for those 57 on schedule or behind. As far as rationality of the families' decision-making processes with respect to a durable goods purchase or residential change was concerned, 6 of the 46 lineages in which these actions were taken used the same patterns of rationality in arriving at their decision, whereas 9 of the 46 lineages showed no continuity.[14]

The greatest similarity in marital role organization arrangements over families representing three generations in time, therefore, existed in the area of marital task division with the least in the areas of decision-making authority and rationality of consumer decisions. The rate of change, however, from generation to generation in marital role performance seems to be decreasing. In every area except economic planning there was greater similarity between parents and their married children than between grandparents and parents,

---

[14] Each family's rationality was compared to the rationality shown by others in the sample of the same generation to control for such possibly confounding factors as number of decisions, types of decisions and income level. The extent of continuity, therefore, took into account the similarity over the generations in level of rationality relative to others of the same generation whether high, middle or low (Aldous, 1963).

with the differences being substantial.[15] If one assumes that the marital organization patterns displayed by the couples at the time they were interviewed for the three-generation study represent their modal behaviors over the period of their marriages, an assumption largely consonant with the findings from cross-sectional studies (Blood & Wolfe, 1960), it would appear that the period of the 1930's was the watershed between the generations. This was the time when the couples in the parents' generation were breaking away from their parental families to establish marriages of their own.

There are two conflicting hypotheses about the types of lineages that will show the greatest degree of intergenerational continuity. One is based on the fact that women more than men are exposed to socialization agencies outside the family as shown by their greater use of confidants and heavier enrollment in family life education courses. Women's greater commitment to family roles also may motivate them to modify and embellish their roles to make their performances more effective. As a result, there should be more discontinuity in marital and parental roles between the generations when the line is linked by daughters. On the other hand, a second hypothesis holds that within the family of orientation, the mother-daughter dyad is more cohesive than is the father-son subsystem (Aldous, 1963). Mother and daughter share common interests and interact more because the daughter's central occupation as an adult will be that of wife and mother, the same as is true of her mother. Since parental roles are less salient for men, fathers are less apt consciously to play the role of socialization agent and the sons are less apt to cast their fathers in this role. As a result, the son's learning of paternal and marital role behaviors from their fathers is a more incidental and less formal process than is true in the mother-daughter relation. One would predict, therefore, more discontinuity between the generations in marital and parental role performances when the relationship is traced through men.

There is some support for both positions from available marital role performance data. The three-generation study discussed above found more continuity of the traditional sex-role division of labor in lines joined by males, though on task allocation a higher proportion of the female lines maintained the same marital pattern, but in neither case are the differences large.[16] In

---

[15] In marital authority patterns 25 of 80 lineages showed parent-child continuity as compared with 14 lineages where the grandparents' pattern was similar to that of their child and his spouse in the parent generation. Comparable figures for the other variables with the parent-child number appering first, the grandparent-parent number next, and the total lineages for which there were data last, are as follows: *Marital Task Division:* 20; 17; 84. *Traditional Sex Role Task Allocation:* 31; 16; 83. *Planning Achievement:* 15; 20; 87. *Rationality in Consumer Decisions:* 15; 6; 46.

[16] The results do not change when continuity is examined over two generations. From this analysis, in addition to examining the two lineage types of grandfather-father-son lineages, the "patrilineages," and the grandmother-mother-daughter lines, the "matrilineages," we can look at parent-married child similarities in the two mixed lineage types of grandmother-mother-married son and grandfather-father-married daughter. We shall add the results involving the married daughter lineages to the matrilineages and the results involving the married son lineages to the patrilineages when we are examining

the area of power allocation, Lovejoy found in a questionnaire study that daughters had moved further than sons from the patterns in their parental families (Lovejoy, 1961). Women were planning to share the traditional feminine decision responsibilities with their husbands and the men were willing to participate. For women the greatest change was in the area of wife working where 87 per cent thought both spouses should share in the decision. In their homes 44 per cent of the mothers had made the decision alone and just 32 per cent of the girls' parents had decided jointly. A comparable change occurred for boys in the area of home decorating where 72 per cent expected to participate with their wives in making decisions. Over half their mothers, 53 per cent, made such decisions alone and in only 14 per cent of their homes did both parents make such decisions. These women college students, however, more often than the men, were planning on joint decision-making patterns in their own homes. The greatest difference appeared in the area of buying a car, clearly a traditional male preserve. Seventy-one per cent of the women believed both spouses should share in the decision. A surprisingly large number of males, 56 per cent, agreed, but a fair proportion, 44 per cent, were loath to surrender this masculine prerogative. Even among the men, however, socialization in the parental family did not "take," assuming parents attempted to transmit the interaction patterns they themselves conformed to, since the men too were planning to play their marital roles differently than they reported their parents had.

A similar sex difference appears in the research relevant to socialization into parental roles. An interview study of mothers and their college student children showed that the daughters as compared with their male peers were more prone to turn against the punitive high-control, low-support child-rearing patterns of their mothers and to accept more permissive, warm role performance norms (Kell & Aldous, 1960). These differences in the extent to which men and women have been influenced by learning counter to parental ways increase the possibilities for marital conflict as well as the need for socialization within marriage. Women appear to be in an ambivalent position. With their broader knowledge of marital and parental role models they have the knowledge as well as the motivation for change. At the same time their higher

---

parent-married child results. On the traditional sex-role task allocation pattern, 4 of 13 of the patrilineages maintained continuity over three generations, but this figure increased to 14 of 33 father-married son two generation lines that showed continuity. For the matrilineages the comparable figure was 8 of 32 lines having intergenerational continuity over three generations, with it increasing to 20 of 50 for the mother-married daughter lines. The marital task division indicator showed 4 of 14 patrilineages maintaining continuity over three generations increasing to 14 of 34 in the father-married son analysis. Comparable three generation figures for the all-female lines were 12 of 32 and 22 of 50 for the mother-married daughter comparison. As would be expected from the over-all results, there was less intergenerational continuity among grandparents and parents than was true of parents and married children. Only in the three generation female lines, and only on the task division variable, was the number of grandparent-parent two generation continuities (9) greater than the number of parent-married child two generation continuities (3).

motivation to set up a workable marital relationship because of their strong commitment to family roles presses them to accommodate to their husbands' more traditional norms.

Interestingly enough, the Kell and Aldous study suggests that as far as women are concerned the greatest mother-child discontinuity in socialization for parental roles came with the generation whose children were born in the 1930's, the same period when there appears to have been the greatest intergenerational change in marital role performance as documented in the three generation study. The women coming to maturity in the fifties were more accepting of maternal ways than their mothers reported themselves to be with respect to their mothers. The thirties seem to have marked the beginning of the period when the middle-class woman learned from extrafamilial sources less restrictive, more supportive parental roles than their mothers had played. Thus Leslie and Johnsen found in their questionnaire research with college-educated women whose childhoods occurred in the early 1930's that they reported themselves to be more permissive in their acceptance of children's sexual curiosity and sex play than their mothers were (Leslie & Johnsen, 1963).

In the area of obedience the results were mixed. The respondents reported themselves as being less accepting of disobedience than were their mothers but much more prone to let their children make decisions. Thus the degree of change appears to be uneven in the various areas of child-rearing as has been shown to be true of marital role performance.

There are several factors affecting the extent to which one generation will depart from the ways of its parents in role performance. One of these is opportunity for socialization outside the parental home. We have already considered in an earlier section how this is affected by variations in confidants and social networks, as well as exposure to the mass media, variations that appear to be associated with class differences as well as sex differences. Where there are class differences in role behaviors, Leslie and Johnsen hypothesized that social mobility should lead to intergenerational discontinuity. They found this to be the case but it was mediated by the grandmothers' positions on the permissive-restrictive continuum in the various child care areas. The socially mobile mothers who came from blue-collar backgrounds were most apt to have changed from parental models when they saw their mothers as being either very permissive or very strict. As noted earlier, a middle range of marital and parental behaviors is increasingly accepted in many groups. The pressure from outsiders, therefore, would be greatest on individuals socialized in families holding extreme positions leading them to accept less discordant standards even if the change leaves them still more restrictive or more permissive than their fellows. And Leslie and Johnsen found it to be true that mothers whose mothers had used a high degree of control were in the strictest group. But all women, even those with comparatively permissive mothers, were more accepting of their children's sexual activities. Since the variation in the mother's degree of permissiveness clustered at the extremely restrictive pole of the continuum, the present generation had very little room to change except to a more permissive position.

Another factor that determines the degree of intergenerational similarity is the amount of post-marital socialization that had occurred. When husband and wife enter marriage with the same role performance standards acquired in their respective families of orientation, there will be little need for post-marital socialization. They can interact on the basis of their role learnings without conflict. Differences in role learnings divide the couple and require change on the part of at least one spouse. Relevant data come from Ingersoll's study of intergenerational changes in conjugal authority patterns as documented in the family histories of 37 working- and middle-class college students (Ingersoll, 1948). In general, couples from homogenous parental authority backgrounds reproduced the same matricentric or patricentric pattern in their own marriage. If the couples experienced different authority patterns growing up, that is, one partner coming from either a father-controlled or mother-controlled family married someone from a parental family having an opposite pattern, the couple through mutual socialization tended to set up an equalitarian relationship and worked out decisions jointly. Here again we see a tendency for change in role performance away from clearly defined standards of who does what toward more interchangeability of role assignments in more symmetrical relationships.

Motivation also plays a part in the child's retention or rejection of his parents' training. Bowerman and Kinch in the study cited earlier found youths more apt to accept parental values than those of their peers when they got along well with their parents and felt understood enough to bring their problems home (Bowerman & Kinch, 1959). Vincent's (1964) follow-up study of high school seniors is relevant here. His respondents five years after high school graduation were more apt to have increased their awareness of the same-sex parent's rewarding and disciplining activities and to report being closer to them when the respondents had taken on parental roles themselves than when they were single or were married and childless. Thus, having children rendered salient to these individuals the child-rearing roles of the parent whose performance was most relevant while the relation they had with the parent was such as to encourage their conformity to the parental model. At least for this sample of lower middle-class adults simply having children appeared to establish the conditions that would encourage intergenerational continuity in parental roles. If this finding holds among other groups, it emphasizes again the greater effectiveness of the family of orientation as a socialization setting for the younger generation's learning parental as contrasted to marital roles.

In the above discussion we have woven together research findings from many studies to support our contention that marital and parental role performance norms have changed. The scattered evidence suggests that couples marrying in the thirties made the decisive break from previous ways of getting along in marriage and rearing children. Their parents who were coming of age and marrying in the first decade of the century were less aware of alternatives to the marital and parental patterns they had acquired in their families of orientation, learnings similar to those of their peers and their marital partners. The present generation of young married couples, even more affected by geographical mobility than their parents of the thirties' generation, and by subsequent economic and educational changes, more often maintain the marital patterns of their parents. Women have seemed readier than men to respond to agents of socialization outside the family. The greatest changes have accordingly occurred in areas where there had been a marked imbalance favoring males, as in the marital authority patterns. Parental behaviors also changed with women again leading the way. Women, however, though moving to less punitive, more supportive maternal roles maintained continuity with the previous generation in their concern about preserving authority over the child. But even here maternal expectations of the child are less rigid, reflecting the movement from extreme asymmetry in family relationships.

CONCLUSIONS

A number of recurrent themes have appeared throughout our discussion of socialization for marital and parental roles. The primary theme that has shaped the analysis has been the postulated shift from parental to marital roles as the central focus in the family life of the individual. Our empirical support for this assertion has been limited to demographic data showing the shortening of the child-rearing period in the family life cycle and a few research studies of marital adjustment and family size preferences. Thus the posited shift remains largely speculative, part of the no-man's-land uncharted by research that characterizes so much of the discussion of socialization for marital and parental roles.

To determine the plausibility of this hypothesis, working-class families constitute a crucial test group. The increased affluence and generally high levels of employment that have characterized the last decade have affected the life style of blue-collar families. Rainwater and Handel (1963) have reported that the greater spatial mobility of these families in their search for better employment opportunities and living accommodations has weakened the separate, closely-knit social networks of kin and peers that husbands and wives possessed. As a result, husbands as well as wives are centering their attention on the nuclear family. Men particularly appear to be more comfortable in the new situation, many interacting with their wives more in parental roles than as marital partners. The couple's common concern with the children serves to postpone their confrontation as husband and wife, roles which neither partner is well socialized to play.

If our thesis is valid, however, marital roles should assume greater importance even while the children are still at home. Cut off from the friendship and kin networks that have transmitted the normative expectations that husbands and wives should lead largely separate existences (except as linked through the children) the wife should be open increasingly to alternative role models. She may be the agent for change as well as the agent of socialization for her husband. He, more involved in his family than with his former associates in the central city, will go along with his wife's teaching and learn the values and behaviors of a marital relation that emphasizes a shared life. This would be the direction of change we hypothesize, and the trend appears to be in that direction.

Rainwater and Handel (1963) found a shift from segregated family roles to joint participation. The husband was more active in family affairs, engaging in decision-making with his wife and assisting her in implementing the decisions. Wives consulted their husbands more and were less apt to see themselves as having to take the major responsibility for family decisions. The couple's joint involvement, we would predict, would in time lead to a focus on their marital roles with the reported greater mutuality in sexual relations generalizing to other areas of the conjugal system. The process and outcome of the hypothesized change in emphasis from parental to marital roles, however, needs systematic examination.

A second theme that has run through the discussion refers to the limitations of the family of orientation as an agent of socialization for marital roles. To be sure, the level of marital satisfaction of the parents appears associated with the motivation of boys to marry, but the child's knowledge about and rehearsal of marital roles largely comes from outside sources. Within the parental family, he can be only an observer not a participant in the marriage subsystem. He does not receive the corrective sanctioning from alter when he tries to play at the role of husband or wife that would occur if he were role-taking in an interaction situation. He is purposely screened from much marital behavior, so that he lacks knowledge as well as role-rehearsal opportunities. It is no accident, we believe, that when children play house, the standard roles are mother, daddy and baby, not husband and wife.

Yet marital discord appears to be transmitted over the generations, suggesting that children learn some marital values and behaviors in unhappy households that ill prepare them for married life. And we have described such possible role-learnings along the instrumental-expressive axis. Researchers need to examine children's conceptions of marital roles to discover the knowledge they do acquire in the parental family.

We have had much to say about changes both in parental and marital roles. The very existence of family life education courses in the schools and marriage counseling and clinical child psychology as professions indicates not only the limitations of the parental family as a socializing agency but also the existence of alternative role performance models. These formal socialization and resocialization agencies are transmitting to the individuals coming under their influence an awareness of alternatives rather than set prescriptions about what behavior is appropriate. Marital and parental roles are sketched within broad guidelines, and the teacher or counselor leaves it to the student or client to work out the marital or parental role complement that seems most satisfactory to him.

Some of the openness of current advice probably stems from the experts' recognition of the marked fluctuation in the role-performance standards that have been advocated over time as well as the lack of agreement as to what constitutes proper role performance. The fluctuations in advice given applies particularly to parent educators whereas the problem of conflicting authorities seems greater among marriage educators. In any case, when experts differ or appear to have changed their minds, couples may seek to resolve the ambiguities by working out the details of their marital and parental role relations by trial and error through mutual socialization.

But we need empirical documentation that the guidelines for marital and parental role-learnings are actually widening leaving the individual couple greater leeway. We have cited in our earlier discussion studies showing intergenerational continuities and discontinuities with the trend away from rigidly defined family roles, but we need more evidence as to the role content areas and the groups most open to norm prescriptions calling for role improvisation under conditions of mutual socialization after marriage.

We also need to discover if the middle-class persons who turn to the formal agencies of socialization have received more or less parental or marital role training in their families of orientation. Who are the persons the family life educators, the marriage counselors and the parent educational people supposedly socialize? It may be that the clientele of the formal agencies represents the first wave of the highly motivated group we mentioned earlier who are in demanding occupations requiring advanced education and in their private lives are setting professional standards of family role performance, standards that require special training.

The themes that have tied together the materials in the chapter have had change as a common dimension. Even the constraints on the parental family as a socializing agency for marital roles have been exacerbated by social change. One way individuals are coping with the problems and opportunities rapid change engenders, we believe, is to hold less rigid family role expectations. Role content acquired in childhood may be outmoded in adulthood, and previous learnings can make for rigidity in performance. Indeed, some readers may well question the desirability of socializing individuals for marital and parental roles prior to marriage while recognizing that training cannot be postponed until a "cram course" after marriage. What is called for is research clarification of the socialization process for marital and parental roles both before and after marriage. Not only would it contribute to our knowledge of an important substantive area, but the results might suggest the points at which social intervention might most profitably occur. The learning of marital and parental roles is too important to be left exclusively to the province of the family. Yet the efforts of the formal socialization agencies have not always been successful. With a firmer empirical basis, the formal agencies would be better prepared to supplement and to encourage the positive activities of the parental family, peers, and other informal agencies currently bearing the brunt of the socialization process, while countering the type of training which has had such negative consequences.

The study of the socialization for adult family roles has theoretical as well as applied contributions to make. Since the process extends into later life, it is a strategic one to examine for similarities and differences in adult and childhood socialization. Other advantages are that the general learning content remains a constant factor over time, and both formal and informal socialization agencies are involved in the process. Thus systematic examination of the phenomenon of socialization for marriage and parenthood should prove a productive area for intrinsic, applied and theoretical reasons. What appears to be lacking is sustained research endeavors to realize this promise. Hopefully this chapter will encourage the necessary effort.

REFERENCES

ALDOUS, JOAN. Family continuity patterns over three generations: Content, degree of transmission and consequences. Unpublished doctoral dissertation, Univer. of Minnesota, 1963.

ALDOUS, JOAN, & HILL, R. Social cohesion, lineage type, and intergenerational transmission. *Social Forces*, 1965, 43, 471–482.

ALDOUS, JOAN, & STRAUS, M. A. Social networks and conjugal roles: A test of Bott's hypothesis. *Social Forces*, 1966, 44, 576–580.

ANDERSON, W. J. A study of the relation between enrollment in a college course in family life and attitude toward courtship and family relations. Unpublished doctoral dissertation, Univer. of Utah, 1953.

BACH, G. R. Father-fantasies and father-typing in father-separated children. *Child Development*, 1946, 17, 63–80.

BARDIS, P. D. Influence of family life education on sex knowledge. *Marriage and Family Living*, 1963, 25, 85–88.

BATES, A. Parental roles in courtship. *Social Forces*, 1942, 20, 483–486.

BATH, J. A., & LEWIS, E. C. Attitudes of young female adults toward some areas of parent-adolescent conflict. *Journal of Genetic Psychology*, 1962, 100, 241–253.

BEE, L. Evaluating education for marriage and family living. *Marriage and Family Living*, 1952, 14, 97–103.

BERNARD, JESSIE. *Remarriage: A study of marriage*. New York: Dryden Press, 1956.

BERNSTEIN, B. Family role systems, communications and socialization. Paper read at Conference on Development of Cross-National Research on the Education of Children and Adolescents, University of Chicago, February, 1964.

BLOOD, R. O., JR. *Marriage*. New York: Free Press, 1962.

BLOOD, R. O., JR., & WOLFE, D. M. *Husbands and wives*. Glencoe, Ill.: Free Press, 1960.

BOLTON, C. D. The development process in love relationships. Unpublished doctoral dissertation, Univer. of Chicago, 1960.

BOSSARD, J. H. S. Family table talk—an area for sociological study. *American Sociological Review*, 1943, 8, 295–301.

BOSSARD, J. H. S., & BOLL, ELEANOR S. *The large family system.* Philadelphia: Univer. of Philadelphia Press, 1956.

BOTT, ELIZABETH. *Family and social network.* London: Tavistock, 1957.

BOWERMAN, C., & KINCH, J. W. Changes in family and peer orientation of children between the fourth and tenth grades. *Social Forces,* 1959, 37, 206–211.

BRIM, O. G., JR. Family structure and sexual learning by children. *Sociometry,* 1958, 21, 1–16.

BRIM, O. G., JR. *Education for child rearing.* New York: Russell Sage Foundation, 1959. Pp. 313–317.

BRIM, O. G., JR. Personality development as role learning. In I. Iscoe & H. Stevenson (Eds.), *Personality development in children.* Austin, Texas: Univer. of Texas Press, 1960. Pp. 127–157.

BRIM, O. G., JR. Socialization through the life cycle. *Social Science Research Council Items,* 1964, 18, 1–5.

BRIM, O. G., JR., & WHEELER, S. *Socialization after childhood: Two essays.* New York: John Wiley, 1966.

BRODERICK, C. B. Social heterosexual development among urban negroes and whites. *Journal of Marriage and the Family,* 1965, 27, 200–203.

BRODERICK, C. B. Socio-sexual development in a suburban community. *Journal of Sex Research,* 1966, 2, 1–24.

BRODERICK, C. B., & FOWLER, S. E. New patterns of relationships between the sexes among preadolescents. *Marriage and Family Living,* 1961, 23, 27–30.

BURGESS, E. W., & COTTRELL, L. S., JR. *Predicting success or failure in marriage.* Englewood Cliffs, N. J.: Prentice-Hall, 1939.

BURGESS, E. W., & WALLIN, P. Homogamy in personal characteristics. *American Journal of Sociology,* 1943, 49, 109–124.

BURGESS, E. W., & WALLIN, P. Homogamy in personal characteristics. *Journal of Abnormal and Social Psychology,* 1944, 29, 475–481.

BURGESS, E. W., & WALLIN, P. *Engagement and marriage.* Philadelphia: Lippincott, 1953.

CALDWELL, BETTYE M. The effects of infant care. In M. L. Hoffman & Lois W. Hoffman (Eds.), *Review of child development research,* Vol. 1. New York: Russell Sage Foundation, 1964. Pp. 9–87.

CAPLAN, G. Patterns of parental response to the crisis of premature birth: A preliminary approach to modifying mental health outcome. *Psychiatry,* 1960, 23, 365–374.

CHESSER, E. *The sexual, marital and family relationships of the English woman.* New York: Roy, 1957.

CHRISTENSEN, H. T. The intrusion of values. In H. T. Christensen (Ed.), *Handbook of marriage and the family.* Chicago: Rand McNally, 1964. Pp. 969–1006.

CLAUSEN, J. A. Family structure, socialization and personality. In Lois W. Hoffman & M. L. Hoffman (Eds.), *Review of child development research.* Vol. 2. New York: Russell Sage Foundation, 1967. Pp. 1–53.

CONNOR, RUTH, GREEN, H. F., & WALTERS, J. Agreement of family members conceptions of "good" parent and child roles. *Social Forces,* 1958, 36, 353–358.

D'ANDRADE, R. G. Father absence and cross-sex identification. Unpublished doctoral dissertation, Harvard Univer., 1962.

DAVIS, A. Changing patterns of socialization in the family. In Iowa State University Center for Agricultural and Economic Development, *Family mobility in our dynamic society.* Ames, Iowa: Iowa State Univer. Press, 1965. Pp. 39–58.

DURKHEIM, E. La prohibition de l'inceste et ses origines. *L'Année Sociologique,* 1897, 1, 1–70.

DUVALL, EVELYN M. *In-laws: Pro and con.* New York: Association Press, 1954.

DUVALL, EVELYN M. How effective are marriage courses? *Journal of Marriage and the Family,* 1965, 27, 176–184.

DYER, DOROTHY T. A comparative study relating marital happiness to university courses helpful to marital adjustment. *Marriage and Family Living,* 1959, 21, 230–233.

DYER, E. D. Parenthood as crisis: A restudy. *Marriage and Family Living,* 1963, 25, 196–201.

DYMOND, R. F. Interpersonal perception and marital happiness. *Canadian Journal of Psychology,* 1954, 8, 164–171.

EHRMANN, W. W. *Premarital dating behavior.* New York: Holt, Rinehart & Winston, 1959.

ELDER, G. H. Structural variations in the child rearing relationship. *Sociometry,* 1962, 25, 241–262.

ELLZEY, W. C. Marriage questionnaire report. *Marriage and Family Living,* 1949, 11, 133–136.

EMMERICH, W. Family role concepts of children ages six to ten. *Child Development,* 1961, 32, 609–624.

ERIKSON, E. H. *Childhood and society.* (2nd ed.) New York: Norton, 1950.

FINCK, G. H. A comparative analysis of the marriages and families of participants in marriage education. *Marriage and Family Living,* 1956, 18, 61–64.

FOOTE, N. N., & COTTRELL, L. S., JR. *Identity and interpersonal competence.* Chicago: Univer. of Chicago Press, 1955.

GANS, H. J. *The urban villagers.* Glencoe, Illinois: Free Press, 1962.

GILLETTE, T. L. Toward a student-centered marriage course. *Marriage and Family Living,* 1959, 21, 150–155.

GILLIES, D. V., & LASTRUCCI, C. L. Validation of the effectiveness of a college marriage course. *Marriage and Family Living,* 1954, 16, 55–59.

GLICK, P. C. *American families.* New York: Wiley, 1957.

GOODE, W. J. *After divorce.* New York: Free Press, 1956.

GOODE, W. J. Norm commitment and conformity to role-status obligations. *American Journal of Sociology,* 1960, 66, 246–258.

GOODE, W. J. *World revolution and family patterns.* New York: Free Press, 1963.

GOODRICH, W., RYDER, R., & RAUSCH, H. L. Patterns of newly wed marriage. *Proceedings of the American Psychiatric Association,* July, 1966.

HILL, R. *Families under stress.* New York: Harper, 1949.

HILL, R. Teaching marriage courses in another culture. Unpublished manuscript, 1954.

HILL, R. Decision making and the family life cycle. In Ethel Shanas & G. F. Streib (Eds.), *Social structure and the family: Generational relations.* Englewood Cliffs, N. J.: Prentice-Hall, 1965. Pp. 113–142.

HILL, R., & FOOTE, N. N. Family development in three generations. Unpublished manuscript, 1967.

HILL, R., & RODGERS, R. H. The developmental approach. In H. T. Christensen (Ed.), *Handbook of marriage and the family.* Chicago: Rand McNally, 1964. Pp. 171–211.

HOBART, C. W. Emancipation from parents and courtship in adolescence. *Pacific Sociological Review,* 1958, 6, 25–29.

HOMANS, G. C., & SCHNEIDER, D. M. *Marriage, authority, and final causes.* New York: Free Press, 1955.

INGERSOLL, HAZEL. A study of the transmission of authority patterns in the family. *Genetic Psychology Monograph,* 1948, 38, 225–303.

IRISH, D. P. Sibling interaction: A neglected aspect in family life research. *Social Forces,* 1964, 42, 279–288.

JACOBSON, H. Conflict of attitudes toward the roles of the husband and wife in marriage. *American Sociological Review,* 1952, 17, 146–150.

JACOBSON, P. H. *American marriage and divorce.* New York: Holt, Rinehart & Winston, 1959.

JENSEN, V., & CLARK, M. Married and unmarried college students. *Personnel and Guidance Journal,* 1958, 37, 123–125.

JOHNSON, MIRIAM M. Sex role learning in the nuclear family. *Child Development,* 1963, 34, 319–333.

KANIN, E., & HOWARD, D. H. Postmarital consequences of premarital sex adjustments. *American Sociological Review,* 1958, 23, 556–562.

KELL, LEONE, & ALDOUS, JOAN. Trends in child care over three generations. *Marriage and Family Living,* 1960, 22, 176–177.

KERCKHOFF, R. Evaluating family life education. *Merrill-Palmer Quarterly,* 1960, 6, 187–191.

KERCKHOFF, R. Family life education in America. In H. T. Christensen (Ed.), *Handbook of marriage and the family.* Chicago: Rand McNally, 1964. Pp. 881–912.

KIRKENDALL, L. A. *Premarital intercourse and interpersonal relationships.* New York: Julian Press, 1961.

KIRKPATRICK, C. *The family.* New York: Ronald Press, 1955.

KIRKPATRICK, C., & CAPLOW, T. Courtship in a group of Minnesota students. *American Journal of Sociology,* 1945, 51, 114–125.

KOMAROVSKY, MIRRA. Functional analysis of sex roles. *American Sociological Review,* 1950, 15, 508–516.

KOMAROVSKY, MIRRA. *Blue collar marriage.* New York: Random House, 1964.

KOTLAR, SALLY. Middle class roles—ideal and perceived in relation to adjustment in marriage. Unpublished doctoral dissertation, Univer. of Southern California, 1961.

LANDIS, J. T. Length of time required to achieve adjustment in marriage. *American Sociological Review,* 1946, 11, 666–677.

LeMASTERS, E. E. Parenthood as crisis. *Marriage and Family Living,* 1957, 19, 352–355.

LESLIE, G. The field of marriage counseling. In H. T. Christensen (Ed.), *Handbook of marriage and the family.* Chicago: Rand McNally, 1964.

LESLIE, G., & JOHNSEN, KATHRYN P. Changed perceptions of the parental role. *American Sociological Review,* 1963, 26, 919–929.

LEVINGER, G. Task and social role specialization of husband and wife behavior in marriage. *Sociometry,* 1964, 27, 433–448.

LEVINGER, G., & SONNHEIM, M. Complementarity in marital adjustment: Reconsidering Toman's family constellation hypothesis. *Journal of Individual Psychology,* 1965, 21, 137–145.

LEWIS, R. A. Empathy and interpersonal perception in dating-pair relationships. Unpublished master's thesis, Univer. of Minnesota, 1966.

LINDEMANN, E. Symptomatology and management of acute grief. *American Journal of Psychiatry,* 1949, 101, 141–148.

LINTON, R. *Study of man.* New York: D. Appleton-Century, 1936.

LOCKE, H. J. *Predicting adjustment in marriage.* New York: Holt, Rinehart & Winston, 1951.

LOVEJOY, D. B. College student conceptions of the roles of the husband and wife in family decision-making. *Family Life Coordinator,* 1961, 9, 43–46.

LU, YI-CHUANG. Marital roles and marriage adjustment. *Sociology and Social Research,* 1952, 36, 364–368.

LUCKEY, ELEANORE B. Marital satisfaction and congruent self-spouse concepts. *Social Forces,* 1960, 39, 153–157.

LYNN, D. B., & SAWREY, W. L. The effects of father-absence on Norwegian boys and girls. *Journal of Abnormal and Social Psychology,* 1958, 59, 258–262.

MANGUS, A. R. Family impacts on mental health. *Marriage and Family Living,* 1957, 19, 256–262.

MAYER, J. E. *Jewish-Gentile courtships.* New York: Free Press, 1961.

MAYER, J. E. *The disclosure of marital problems: An exploratory study of lower and middle class wives.* New York: Community Service Society of New York, 1966. (a)

MAYER, J. E. *Other people's marital problems: The "knowledgeability" of lower and middle class wives.* New York: Community Service Society of New York, 1966. (b)

MAYER, J. E. People's imagery of other's families. *Family Process,* 1967, 6, 27–36.

MEDALIA, N. Z. Marriage and adjustment: In college and out. *Personnel and Guidance Journal,* 1962, 40, 545–550.

MOSES, VIRGINIA M. A study of learning derived from a functional course in marriage and family relationships. *Marriage and Family Living,* 1956, 18, 204–209.

NEUBECK, G. The decision to marry while in college. *Acta Sociologica,* 1964, 8, 56–68.

PARSONS, T., BALES, R. F., ET AL. *Family, socialization and interaction process.* New York: Free Press, 1955.

PETTIGREW, T. F. *Profile of the Negro American.* Princeton, N. J.: D. Van Nostrand, 1964.

PINEO, P. C. Disenchantment in the later years of marriage. *Marriage and Family Living,* 1961, 23, 3–11.

PITMAN, DOROTHY. An evaluation of teaching methods in marriage and family education. Unpublished master's thesis, Univer. of North Carolina, 1958.

RAINWATER, L. *Family design: Marital sexuality, family size and contraception.* Chicago: Aldine, 1965.

RAINWATER, L. Crucible of identity: The Negro lower class family. *Daedalus,* 1966, 95, 172–216.

RAINWATER, L., & HANDEL, G. Changing family roles in the working class. Paper read at American Sociological Association, Los Angeles, 1963.

RAPOPORT, RHONA. The transition from engagement to marriage. *Acta Sociologica,* 1964, 8, 36–55.

RAPOPORT, RHONA, & RAPOPORT, R. New light on the honeymoon. *Human Relations,* 1964, 17, 33–56.

RAUSCH, H. L., GOODRICH, W., & CAMPBELL, J. D. Adaptation to the first years of marriage. *Psychiatry,* 1963, 26, 368–380.

RIEMER, S. Youthful marriages. Paper read at National Council of Family Relations, 1951. Cited by Mary G. Landis, *Building a successful marriage.* Englewood Cliffs, N. J.: Prentice-Hall, 1963.

ROSE, A. Parental models for youth. *Sociology and Social Research,* 1955, 40, 3–9.

ROSENBERG, B. G., & SUTTON-SMITH, B. Ordinal position and sex role identification. *Genetic Psychology Monograph,* 1964, 70, 297–328.

SCHMALENBACH, H. The sociological category of communication. In T. Parsons et al. (Eds.), *Theories of society: Foundation of modern sociological theory,* Vol. 1. New York: Free Press, 1961. Pp. 172–216.

SCHORR, A. *Poor kids*. New York: Basic Books, 1966.

SIMMEL, G. *The sociology of Georg Simmel*. New York: Free Press, 1964.

STOLZ, LOIS M., ET AL. *Father relations of war-born children*. Stanford, Calif.: Stanford University, 1954.

SULLIVAN, H. S. *Conceptions of modern psychiatry*. New York: Norton, 1953.

SUSSMAN, M. B. Parental participation in mate selection and its effects upon family continuity. *Social Forces*, 1953, 32, 76–81.

TERMAN, L. M., ET AL. *Psychological factors in marital happiness*. New York: McGraw-Hill, 1938.

TILLER, P. O. Father absence and personality development of children in sailor families. *Nordisk Psycholis Monographs*, 1958, Serial No. 9. Cited by Lynn, D. B. & Sawrey, W. L. The effects of father-absence on Norwegian boys and girls. *Journal of Abnormal and Social Psychology*, 1958, 59, 258–262.

TOMAN, W., & GRAY, B. Family constellation of normal and disturbed marriages: An empirical study. *Journal of Individual Psychology*, 1961, 17, 93–95.

TURNBULL, C. M. The Mbuti Pygmies of the Congo. In J. L. Gibbs, Jr. (Ed.), *Peoples of Africa*. New York: Holt, Rinehart & Winston, 1965. Pp. 279–318.

TYHURST, J. Individual reactions to community disaster. *American Journal of Psychiatry*, 1951, 107, 764–769.

VERNON, G. M., & STEWART, R. L. Empathy as a process in the dating situation. *American Sociological Review*, 1957, 22, 48–52.

VINCENT, C. E. Socialization data in research on young marriers. *Acta Sociologica*, 1964, 8, 118–128.

WALLER, W., & HILL, R. *The family: A dynamic interpretation*. New York: Dryden, 1951.

WALLIN, P. Marital happiness of parents and their children's attitude to marriage. *American Sociological Review*, 1954, 19, 20–23.

WALTERS, J., & FISHER, CLARA. Changes in the attitudes of young women toward child guidance over a two-year period. *Journal of Educational Research*, 1958, 52, 115–118.

WETZEL, RITA J. The effect of a marriage course on the personality characteristics of students. Unpublished doctoral dissertation, Florida State Univer., 1962.

WILSON, MARGARET S. Do college girls conform to the standards of their parents? *Marriage and Family Living*, 1953, 15, 207–208.

WINCH, R. F. The relationship between courtship behavior and attitudes toward parents among college men. *American Sociological Review*, 1943, 8, 167–174.

WINCH, R. F. *Identification and its familial determinants*. Indianapolis: Bobbs-Merrill, 1962.

ZELDITCH, M., JR. Role differentiation in the nuclear family: A comparative study. In T. Parsons et al., *Family, socialization and interaction process*. New York: Free Press, 1955. Pp. 307–352.

CHAPTER 23

Socialization For
The Middle and Later Years

Matilda White Riley, Anne Foner,
Beth Hess, and Marcia L. Toby

Rutgers—The State University

Mature individuals are widely thought to be unteachable. During childhood they learned basic values, their conceptions of what is good and right and desirable, and during adolescence and young adulthood they completed their formal education. By age 45 they are classified as "older workers," their major child-rearing tasks are completed, and, it is said, they measure time by looking backward rather than forward.

Yet, in fact, individuals proceeding through the middle and later years must continually learn to play new or altered roles and to relinquish old ones. Over the life cycle myriad small adjustments must be made as society continually shifts, new knowledge is developed and as new societal and personal goals evolve. Major adjustments are also required as the occupational role gives way to one of leisure-in-retirement; as the combined roles of spouse-and-parent shift, after the children leave home, to the role of spouse without parental responsibilities, and later to widowhood; as relationships to descendant kin proliferate to grandchildren, great-grandchildren, and numerous in-laws; and as preparation is made for ultimate death. Moreover, with the secular trend toward increased longevity, more and more mature people will be called upon to play a variety of roles in the social structure, and must in some way be socialized to play them. If individuals a century ago had to cope only with

The following persons were kind enough to make valuable criticisms and suggestions on earlier versions of this chapter: Harry C. Bredemeier, John A. Clausen, Richard Cohn, Frank Fasick, Robert K. Merton, Charles Nanry, Talcott Parsons, John W. Riley, Jr., Eleanor Singer, Clarice Stoll, Jackson Toby, and J. Alan Winter.

The chapter draws upon a long-range program of research on aging and the family cycle, to which Marilyn E. Johnson and Mary E. Moore, M. D., have made important contributions. Other members of the research team who have given assistance are: Mildred G. Aurelius, Zelda Cohen, Barbara K. Roth, Sallie S. Smith, and Bernice Starr. The research has been supported in part by research grant HD-00886 from the National Institutes of Health, Public Health Service.

an average lifetime of 40 years, individuals today must be prepared for an average lifetime of 70 years.

How are people socialized for these later phases of life? Is an extrapolation of childhood learning enough to carry them through? And if so, how are basic values implemented, dispositions adapted, early knowledge and skills supplemented to meet the new situations? There are few known answers to these questions. Some theory describes the general process of socialization beyond childhood, but it has not been specified for the later years, nor has it been widely tested. Scattered empirical data suggest certain clues, but most of these findings refer only to our own time and our own society. For this reason, the variable of major interest here, the individual's progress through his life cycle, cannot be easily disentangled from the environing changes in the society; it is difficult to investigate *age* as a possible cause per se, or to determine the potential of the older person for social learning under other sociotemporal conditions.

One theory (Cumming, 1963) that has been central to much recent discussion postulates the concept of *disengagement,* a normal and ineluctable process of mutual withdrawal initiated both by the mature individual and by society. This theory suggests that the individual in middle life, at the very height of engagement, begins to face the inevitability of death and the termination of achievement. According to such a theory, mature individuals are socialized only to relinquish the old, no longer to acquire the new. But is such a tendency to withdraw or to disengage an inevitable concomitant of aging? Or is it a consequence of loss of accustomed roles, of anxieties generated by social pressures?[1] Would older people, if healthy and if provided with socially useful roles, still withdraw?

The scattered evidence suggests that under appropriate circumstances, the motivation to perform can be observed even in advanced old age. Many of the old seem at least as likely as the young to express feelings of adequacy and a sense of satisfaction in various roles (marital, parental, occupational, housekeeping) *as long as* socially approved roles remain available. Thus our examination will focus on the major roles presently open to older people and will indicate that widespread withdrawal might be entirely predictable from the *social* structure—quite apart from any organic or personality changes in the aging *individual* (cf. Kutner, 1962; Rose, 1964). In effect, contemporary socialization is socialization for deviance. Society gets out what it puts in. Thus to treat disengagement as inevitable and desirable is merely to rationalize further inputs of the same kind.

A working model.   This chapter starts, for heuristic purposes, with certain definitions and assumptions as a conceptual model of the socialization process. The basic concepts are drawn mainly from the work of Parsons and his associates, as this organizes the relevant thinking of such earlier scholars as Mead,

---

[1] We shall not deal here with the distinctive character of the early training of today's cohorts of older people as a further possible explanation.

Durkheim, and Freud and as it relates to the present-day thinking of Merton, Cottrell, Brim, Wheeler, Bredemeier and many others. We shall compare this model with empirical research findings[2] on the social learning of individuals past their 30's or 40's, exploring the possible utility of the model, and modifying it in various ways, as a device for ordering and interpreting the data. If, in the present state of the field, these explorations turn out to have value, that value should lie in their revision of existing theories of socialization at all ages so as to give greater stress to societal contributions and societal consequences, and in their implicit suggestions for future research emphasizing the socio-cultural contexts in which the learning of older people takes place.

Our model (to be developed at appropriate points in the discussion) regards socialization beyond infancy as a process occurring, not only *within* the individual being socialized, but also *between* the individual and the more inclusive social systems to which he belongs. Under ideal conditions, the roles he learns are integral parts of the social structure, embodying widely held values, and serving economic, political, and other societal ends. Thus his learning depends only partly upon his own contributions—upon his ability and motivation to learn the role and to perform in it. It depends also upon social contributions —such as educational facilities, the availability of rewards for his performance, the competence of other members of society to let him know what the role expectations are and how nearly he conforms to them, and to approve, disapprove, or otherwise sanction his trial-and-error performances. As the outcome of socialization in such an ideal model, the individual learns new or changed roles and becomes committed to them, meanwhile relinquishing any conflicting prior definitions or commitments. Such an outcome is at once useful to the society and gratifying to the individual. For society, personnel has been trained to man its key roles and perform necessary functions. For the individual, successful role performance has become a personal goal, rewarded both by social approval and by his own sense of self-approval.

How closely does the actual socialization of mature adults approximate such an ideal model? The answer is immediately apparent: not very. Yet what the specific disparities are, and how they arise, is less obvious. Still more obscure is how much of this discrepancy is a necessary consequence of aging and how much simply the consequence of social and environmental conditions peculiar to our immediate time and place. Does the diminishing social participation of the mature individual arise entirely from the physiological and psychological effects of the accumulating years upon his personal capacities? To what extent is it conditioned by the lack of integration into the social structure of later life roles and the paucity of social contributions? Each of these weighty questions claims attention as we try to understand contemporary socialization.

Each section of this chapter will use a part of our conceptual model as an aid to interpreting some of the relevant empirical data, focusing, first, on age as a factor in the contributions that the individual makes to socialization (I) and that society makes to the roles available to him (II); then examining

---

[2] The data reported here are drawn in large part from Riley, Foner et al., 1968.

the nature of individual responses to later life socialization (III) ; and finally, speculating about larger consequences and possibilities (IV). In the main, the discussion will stress the often unrecognized but important place in this process held by society, as it provides the agents and the apparatus for training and as it is, in turn, itself affected by the ways in which its mature members are socialized.

I. INDIVIDUAL CONTRIBUTIONS TO THE PROCESS

The individual's age is one of many personal characteristics which has a bearing on the contributions he is willing and able to make to the socialization process. We shall first indicate the place of the individual's contributions in our conceptual model of the process, and then point to a few of the massive—if often inconclusive—research findings of correlations between age and these contributions.

Certain limitations of the significance of such findings must, however, be noted in advance. First, there are great individual differences among older persons; if some gradually lose their powers, others continue to be active and productive until late in life. Second, much of our knowledge about older persons is culture-bound; in other cultures, such as primitive ones, the elders are reported to have had quite other talents and involvements (Simmons, 1960). Third, many erroneous inferences about aging have been drawn from cross-section comparisons of age cohorts—who differ not only in age, but also in education, income, place of birth, and the historical period through which they have lived. Thus much available research can at best *describe* age differences, not pinpoint aging as a *cause*.

Elements in the Model

The nature of the individual's contributions—juxtaposed against the reciprocal contributions of society—are outlined in Figure 23.1. The individual's age affects each type of contribution: his initial motivation and capacity to learn and to perform in the role (a) ; his willingness to subject himself to the novitiate status and to apply learning strategies (b) ; and his readiness, as the result of socialization, to commit himself (c) to the new norms, rules, definitions, and loyalties (Brim, 1966; Wheeler, 1966). Age also affects the patterned interactions that take place between the individual and the socializing agent (the parent, teacher, or their counterparts in the later life process), as the individual's initial motivations and capacities are transmuted through socialization into the commitments, skills, and knowledge required for successful performance.

Childhood socialization: The basic model. The character of the mature individual's contributions to the process is best understood as a modification of the prototypal model of early socialization. In the classic situation, the

FIGURE 23.1
CONTRIBUTIONS TO THE SOCIALIZATION
OF THE INDIVIDUAL TO A ROLE

Individual Contributions	Societal Contributions
(a) Motivation and capacity to learn and to perform.	(d) Goals and expectations.
(b) Trial-and-error performances.	(e) Facilities, resources, and support for learning.
(c) Responses: learning of skills and commitments (or defenses, deviant adjustments).	(f) Sanctions (positive or negative).

child is helped by the parent (as socializing agent) to learn certain values, norms, and definitions to guide his behavior. This early process depends in part upon an affective (emotionally important) relationship between parent and child, so that the parent is a significant other to the child and his approval is important in motivating and rewarding conformity. Throughout a long series of trial-and-error performances, the child looks for cues of parental approval or disapproval as to how he should behave. In some respects, he tends to imitate the parent, to shape his attitudes and behavior in line with the parent's, thus taking the parent as a role model for his own self-expectations. At the same time, he tries to meet the parent's expectations of him, to adapt his self-expectations so that they will conform, not necessarily to what the parent is, but to what the parent wants the child to be.

Successful outcomes. As the outcome of the ideal process, the child responds in certain ways. Specifically, he acquires knowledge and skills—both in task performance and in human relationships—and also an immediate commitment to perform in the role of child. More generally, he gradually incorporates into his own personality his experiences in this role. He develops an emotional investment in living up to his emergent self-expectations. He internalizes the broad values and definitions underlying the parent's specific demands (the values of achievement or independence, for example), building them into a general set of self-expectations about what he should believe or do or say—developing a conscience (superego or inner forum) of his own. What he learns or fails to learn from childhood socialization serves, then, to structure the contributions he can make to future socialization: the motives, attitudes, and skills he will bring to the roles of adolescence and of later life. (Compare the notion of commitment in Becker, 1960.) And because, ideally, he has learned self-expectations that mesh with societal values, his personal goals *interlock* with societal goals, so that self-approval and social approval act to reinforce one another (cf. Pitts, 1961; Clausen, 1967).

Restructuring of orientations. Major modifications in the familiar model of early learning must be made in any model of later life socialization, since in later life, previously internalized values and definitions must be applied in new roles. A plethora of specialized demands is placed upon the individual in his adult years. He must learn to perform a *multiplicity of roles* (in the church, the community, the occupational structure, as well as in the family), that present the individual with many differing demands. These demands often conflict with his own internalized conceptions of what is good and desirable—and may even conflict with one another (cf. Brim, 1966). Older people must also learn to *relinquish* previous roles for new substitutes, that is, to make *role transfers* (from student to worker, e.g., or from worker to retiree). Here too conflicts may be encountered if the expectations of the substitute role are incompatible with the self-expectations the individual has earlier internalized. (Substitution of a new role, or intensification of an existing one, is implied in role relinquishment in that, up until death, some activity—or inactivity—must always replace the role that has been relinquished.) Ideally, the individual finds means of resolving such conflicts within the structure of his orientations, eliminating dissonance, restoring balance (Heider, 1958; Festinger, 1957; Jackson Toby, 1952; Glass, 1966). In short, successful socialization beyond childhood involves a continual search for the delicate adjustment between the individual's internalized values and definitions and his specific judgments of the behavior and attitudes appropriate to each new role situation. On the one hand, he implements his basic values in the specific situation; on the other, each new situation contributes to his basic value pattern as he generalizes the pattern (or modifies or reinforces it) to cover the new specific applications.

Unsuccessful socialization. In practice, socialization often fails at any age to fit the ideal model. The process is by no means always successful. Strains may arise in the individual's relationship to the socializing agent, or inconsistencies may be discovered in the norms with which conformity is expected. If so, the individual, rather than acquiring the requisite knowledge and commitments, is likely to develop feelings of insecurity and inadequacy, and to resort—Figure 23.1 (c)—to various modes of defense and deviant adjustment (Parsons, 1951; Merton, 1957). He may rationalize, perform compulsively, or (as many older people appear to do) withdraw entirely. Particularly complex are the possibilities of failure when the mature person, unlike the little child who must merely learn a new role, is faced with the dual task of role transfer—of both relinquishing a former role and substituting a new (or redefined) role. Here, he may fail to resolve conflicts imposed by the demands of either the old or the new, developing defenses and deviant adjustments that refer either to the previously internalized norms and definitions or to the new norms and definitions he is expected to adopt.

Research on Aging Individuals

How, then, do older people fit such a model? In what ways does age affect capacities and motivations, trial-and-error performances, and the consequent learning or failure to learn?

A great deal of research points to some assets, but also to many decrements, that accumulate as the individual proceeds through his life course. In particular, the evidence has suggested to a number of scholars that the individual, as he reaches middle age, may begin to withdraw—to reduce both his motivation to learn new roles and his commitment to present ones. The notion of disengagement as a motivated withdrawal, though only tenuously supported by the initial research from which it derived (Cumming & Henry, 1961), has a compelling quality that has provoked many studies and much discussion. Intensive studies by Neugarten (1963), for example, indicate a shift between the 40's and the 60's from active to passive mastery and from outer-world to inner-world orientation. Extensive attitude surveys show a greater fatalism among old than young, a lesser sense of control over the external world (Back & Gergen, 1966). Altogether the weight of evidence suggests that, whether or not older people actively desire to withdraw, there may be processes of constriction, of diminished orientation toward achievement or involvement, that set in with age (see, e.g., Maddox, 1964).

To the extent that aging may indeed interfere with socialization to new roles, inducing withdrawal or other problematical outcomes, the interference is undoubtedly channeled indirectly through the effects of age on the organism, on the accumulation of experience, or on the individual's relative position in the age structure of the society.

Organic factors.   Life cycle changes in the human organism tend to set certain limits to the energies and capacities available for role-learning and role performance in the middle and later years. Just as mortality rates rise with age beyond childhood, so do the rates for chronic diseases and impairments such as heart trouble or deafness. Disability because of poor health increases steadily with age after young adulthood, though even among the elderly only a small minority are so severely handicapped that they cannot carry on their major activity. This increase of disability with age is less pronounced among employed persons—a fact that probably reflects both the better health of those older people who continue to work and the positive effect upon health of sustained work activity.

Decrements in behavior are also associated with aging of the organism— decrements in sensation and perception, in muscular strength, in the ability to react quickly to stimuli and to respond by means of complex sensorimotor coordination. Not all these skills are required for ordinary role performance, however, particularly as much physical labor and many psycho-motor tasks have been taken over by machines. In fact, various studies of job performance show little consistent deterioration with age (Wirtz, 1965).

The background of experience.   The individual brings to each new role, not only his organically based capacities, but also his accumulated stores of previously acquired knowledge and experience. These contributions may, if rigid and restricted, limit his further learning, or foster it if flexible and broad. From his repertoire of internalized role relationships, he may have become narrowly committed to certain norms, people, and ways of doing things (Miller & Swanson, 1958). Or, he may have learned to abstract from his many specific experiences, to develop general value commitments and an extensive inner forum; he may have learned how to use his wider experience to reconcile specific norms with larger value systems and to resolve role conflicts. Indeed, the eldest members may be especially equipped to serve the long-run interest of society insofar as their personal ambitions are no longer at stake and they can afford to take the larger view.

Evidence as to the character and extent of acquisitions from experience is meager. Intelligence tests are available (though less closely correlated with age than with education) which show that scores for information and for verbal and numerical ability tend to increase with advancing age—though scores for other mental abilities decline (Birren, 1963; Botwinick, 1967). And occupational studies report that older workers evince at least as high a degree of responsibility, reliability, reasonableness, interest and conscientiousness as younger ones (Heron & Chown, 1963; Smith, 1952).

Relative position. The individual's capacity and motivation for learning and performance are in part relative—not entirely a function of his own physiology or experience. Since many roles (a job, for example, or a dominant position within the family) are scarce, he must often compete with others who are older or younger than he. Because of rapid social change, marked differences characterize the age strata within the society (cf. Ryder, 1965; Cain, 1964). Educational attainment, for example, declines steadily by age: over 80 per cent of persons in their late 20's, but less than 30 per cent of those 75 or more, have gone beyond the 8th grade. Among people 65 and over, 20 per cent are now (1960) of foreign birth, in contrast with 5 per cent for the country as a whole. And the average income of older families, few of whom share in the generally rising level of wages, is strikingly below that of families in their middle years.

Age differences in education are especially critical because education is closely associated with occupational and cultural concerns, political and economic views, and competence in relationships with family and friends. Indeed, low education is itself associated—and might possibly explain—the very tendencies toward passivity and fatalism that constitute the withdrawal or disengagement of many older people today. Moreover, the individual's early education has implications for his continuing participation in adult education programs in later life (cf. Johnstone & Rivera, 1965), and even for the strategy or attention set necessary for the trial-and-error performances required for further learning—(b) in Figure 23.1—(Birren, 1963). Yet, education is so timed in our society as to set its stamp early upon the individual, concentrated as it is at the start of life rather than uniformly spread over it.

Related to such differences among age categories is the tendency in our society to ascribe certain stereotypes to persons because of their age, quite apart from their actual characteristics as individuals. Thus, because many older persons may be underprivileged, or may withdraw from active role participation, *all* older people may tend to be socially defined as incapable. And older people may often compare themselves with younger segments of the society, rather than using as reference groups their age peers of themselves at an earlier life stage.

Thus many questions remain moot as to the way the maturing individual confronts the special configuration of norms, definitions, and attitudes required for each new role. Has he already acquired the necessary pieces at some earlier point in his role experience? Can he bring these into salience and rearrange them? Can he still learn new pieces to supplement his existing structure? To what extent are his failures due less to his personal inadequacies than to certain shortcomings in the social structure which we shall now examine.

II. SOCIETAL CONTRIBUTIONS
TO THE PROCESS

The individual's age can affect both his own contributions to the socialization process and his access to the performance opportunities and rewards available in particular roles—to the social apparatus whereby learning is inculcated.

Within the social structure, only certain roles are open to persons passing through the middle or later life stages. Social definitions affect the age limits of the student role or the work role, for example. Age-related patterns of marriage and childbearing bound the years within which parents rear their offspring—the wife-mother is in her early 50's, on the average, when her last child is married. Life-expectancy determines the space of the individual's own life, and that of his spouse and friends; among persons aged 65 and over (1960), 19 per cent of the men and 53 per cent of the women are widowed, with the pronounced sex differential due in large part to the greater life expectancy of women. Such age limits are, of course, subject to change over time. The retirement age, now tending to fall below 65, has been declining for many decades. As life expectancy has risen, large proportions of married couples now survive jointly for many years after their last child has left home (Glick & Parke, 1965).

We shall now review the conceptual model once again, this time to emphasize society's part in socialization for new or substitute roles—a part to which less attention has been devoted than to the individual's contributions. We shall then examine some of the contemporary societal contributions to the socialization of older people, using selected roles as case examples.

Elements in the Model

In the ideal model for teaching a new role, society's contributions are complementary to those of the individual—see Figure 23.1, page 955. The primary requirement, as we have seen, is a clear consonance between the goals and norms of the role (d)—the social functions performed by the role—and the dominant values of the society. It is this consonance that assures the individual of positive sanctions for learning (f), that brings his own goals into line with societal goals (provides interlocking of goals), and so gives him a sense of purpose in his performance. Beyond this, the model assumes availability of optimum facilities and resources for teaching the role (e), and the presence of appropriate persons or agencies (socializing agents) who act on behalf of society to transmit its contributions. (These elements have been set forth in application to organizational settings by Wheeler, 1966.)

Childhood socialization: The basic model.   Again the familiar model of childhood socialization suggests modifications requisite for understanding socialization in later life. The parent (as agent for society and as significant other to the child) teaches societal values to the child through the vehicle of his expectations—the ideas and beliefs he expects the child to acquire about what is true, desirable, aesthetically appropriate, or morally right. The process hinges upon reasonably clear societal definitions of norms and goals. Even though the parent—reared in an earlier era and often at a lower socioeconomic level of our upwardly mobile society—may himself be unable as a role model to demonstrate those goals and norms to which he aspires for the child, he can nevertheless transmit them through expectations. In the course of daily interaction (trial-and-error performances or role practice), as the child's acts or expressions of opinion conform to parental expectations, the parent approves or rewards him; and when the child fails to conform, the parent shows disapproval or punishes him. Thus the parent defines the child's behavior as conformist or deviant and administers appropriate sanctions.

Moreover, as this process puts a strain on the child and on the parent-child relationship, ideally the parent demonstrates emotional support for the child and shows love and confidence in him no matter what he does. The parent is also somewhat permissive—strict, but not too strict—in his demands for conformity, understanding the child, and allowing some leeway for practice and experimentation.

Anticipatory socialization.   A good deal of childhood socialization is, of course, the learning in advance of adult roles—not merely deliberate training but also an implicit, often unwitting, role rehearsal—in preparation for the future. Socialization *for* later life roles does not mean that all the learning must occur *during* later life. Anticipatory learning of a not-yet-existent role involves certain departures from the basic model of early learning (Merton & Rossi, 1957). The expectations for filling future adult roles may often be communicated to adolescents by parents, for example, expectations that the adolescent may incorporate into his own self-expectations in the usual way. However, the parents will infrequently themselves constitute the significant others in the future roles; and, since the adolescent cannot yet directly demonstrate either conformity or deviance, at this early stage parents cannot apply full sanctions.

Role networks.   Societal roles are often differentiated in such a way that the network of roles an individual plays may (as through a division of labor) combine to provide the composite of social contributions. As the individual matures and his role networks become increasingly complex, his situation often parallels that of the adolescent where the parents contribute expectations and sanctions for the learning of achievement and independence, the school provides opportunity for the acquisition of knowledge, while the peers supply emotional support and release the strains attendant upon learning (Riley & Cohn, 1958).

Reciprocal socialization.   Another aspect of socialization of unquestionable importance for later life roles—though it has received little attention—derives from the reciprocal character of the process itself: as the socializing agent interacts with the individual he is training, he himself may thereby learn new or modified norms and attitudes—rather than merely reinforcing old ones. As the parent socializes the child, he almost certainly as a consequence both teaches certain things to himself and also learns from the growing child (cf. Lipset et al., 1954). For example, teaching independence to the offspring *ipso facto* reinforces the value of independence in the parent, thus preparing him for autonomy in his own future roles as older parent or grandparent. Training the child to adapt to a changing world or a higher status may require the parent himself to seek new understandings (from the mass media, e.g., or from friends). The parent who influences his offspring toward upward mobility may in turn learn from the offspring certain norms of this new and higher status. So too, the parent who helps his child to apply family norms outside the family (such as honesty in testing situations in school) may have to revise his expectations in line with the child's reports of revised norms applied to new situations.

In such fashion the reciprocal relationship between parent and offspring may play a part in socializing the parent himself during his middle years. Or one spouse, in socializing his mate, may come to learn his own role better. Or, to take a different example, the dying spouse or elderly parent may, through his preparation for death, prepare the bereaved in advance to face his own demise and to accept the finitude of mortal existence.

Role relinquishment.   Societal contributions are made also (though these are little understood) to the adult learning of role relinquishment (Bredemeier & Stephenson, 1962; and cf. Van Gennep, 1960). Learning the role of adult initially involves renouncing that of dependent child. Learning the role of retirement involves renouncing that of work. Or, at the end of the life cycle, preparation for death requires relinquishment of all worldly roles. Although we shall need to examine the process through further examples, the societal inputs appear to be the reverse of those for role acquisition. In effect, society replaces its positive contributions (as in Figure 23.1 above) with negative ones:

the expectations for role performance (d) lose their consonance with the dominant values of the society; and, with the consequent diminution of social utility, social approval also dwindles (f); while facilities and resources (e), if available at all, support conformity, not to the old, but to the altered expectations. Now the individual must learn to give up those contributions he formerly received: the specific opportunities to act out his internalized values; his relationships to significant other people in the role system; and the specific rewards.

In the ideal model, then, the dual process of *role transfer* is facilitated by a combination of such negative mechanisms which aid individuals in relinquishing previous roles and those positive mechanisms needed for the acquisition of new ones.

Research on Roles for Older People

How closely does the actual process of socialization correspond to such an ideal model? To what extent are positive functions, facilities, and rewards invested in the new roles which mature adults must learn to acquire? To what extent, and how, are negative contributions introduced into the former roles that must now be vacated? This aspect of socialization has been little studied. Moreover, the several roles open to older people differ markedly in the contributions made by society to the socialization process (see Figure 23.1 above): in the clarity and social utility of their goals (d); in the opportunities and support provided (e) to persons learning to play or to relinquish them; in the approval or status (c) with which performance is rewarded. Later life roles vary also in the availability of socializing agents—appropriate persons or groups to convey the expectations, sanctions, and support. We shall first outline some of the contributions possible, then examine a few selected examples in further detail.

Contributions to role acquisition.   The nature of the acquisition process depends upon whether the role to be learned is (1) a simple substitute for the individual's previous role, whether it (2) differs from it in degree, or (3) differs in kind (cf. Benedict, 1938). Not all of the roles encountered in adulthood are new to the individual, requiring major new socialization. Many are, rather, *direct substitutes* for roles learned previously—involving little basic change in expectations or sanctions. Thus, individuals forced out of short-lived occupations (professional athletes, dancers, actors) may utilize their own training by becoming teachers or coaches; or they may shift to another occupation (as into business) which, though new in many details of skill and implementation, is nevertheless compatible with the same underlying norms of achievement. Or people who move to new communities, though they must work out a fresh set of relationships, may still carry over from their former community life the same basic norms and relational skills.

Certain other roles in the structure merely become *intensified* (redefined or increasingly salient) for the individual in later life, as these roles take over activities or satisfactions from a relinquished role. Thus, as the individual loses one role (e.g., of parent or of worker), another existing role (of spouse, friend, member of church or community) may take on enhanced importance in supplying him not only with human relationships and emotional support, but also with activities to be performed and with a structure for his free time (Moore, 1963). Here, too, little new socialization may be required, though the expectations and sanctions of several previous roles must often be fused into the ones remaining.

The distinctly *new* types of roles available to mature adults (those for which major socialization is required) are widely varied, ranging from parent-in-law and grandparent to retiree, widow, and (for some 4 per cent of the population 65 and over) inmate of an institution (cf. Brim, 1967). The type and extent of societal contributions also vary from one role to another. For certain new roles, the societal function is evident, the norms institutionalized, and the expectations and sanctions largely positive—as when women in their middle years enter the work force. For other new roles, however, the expectation-sanction system is far from positive, since the functions are less clearly valued or constitute reductions in the functions of the relinquished roles. For instance, the grandparent (like the parent of an adult child) is permitted to dispense certain services and material supports, and to engage in certain expressive activities; yet is prohibited by the norm of independence from encroaching upon the parental responsibilities of his young adult offspring or interfering with their authority. It is no longer his function to socialize or control either the young adults or their little children.

To the extent that some new roles fail to present goals that are valued by society, there can be no clear expectations of constructive performance, facilities and resources for training are likely to be in short supply, and rewards tend to become minimal or even negative. Under these conditions, the individual is given little incentive to learn, and societal inputs appear to fall far short of the model of optimum socialization.

Contributions to role relinquishment.   Among the roles to be surrendered in middle and later life are two of the most important and socially valued, as women complete the rearing of their children and men retire from work. In these instances (though not necessarily in the case of preparation for widowhood, to cite a different example), role rehearsal for relinquishment appears to start far in advance of the role's termination. *Expectations* of full performance are gradually reduced over the years, and the individual begins to receive negative *sanctions* (or meets with indifference) for those very performances for which he had previously been rewarded. The parent of the young child, for example, begins to practice relinquishment of his child-rearing function long before the offspring becomes an adult—as the growing child becomes increasingly independent, has phases of "rejecting" the parent, and surrounds himself with supportive peers. Or the worker in his middle years—long before retirement—may be bypassed for promotion, no longer consulted or esteemed, *merely* because of his age. Even when his competence has not declined, the worker may lose prestige or other rewards because of pressure of younger workers for his job, or because of the relative excellence of the more recently trained in comparison with him.

As an aid to further understanding of the processes of role relinquishment and the transfer to new roles within the contemporary situation of older people, we shall now examine the extreme examples of loss of the roles of worker and spouse. We shall investigate societal contributions—(d), (e) and (f) in Figure 23.1 above—and shall also look for clues to the individual's responses to the process—(c) in Figure 23.1—as these will be further discussed in Section III.

Acquisition of the Role of Retiree

How, and to what extent, does the social structure contribute to socialization for the retirement role? We shall consider, first, the process of teaching the new role (or roles) of retirement itself, and then turn to the mechanisms for relinquishing the previous role of work.

Goals and expectations. No positively valued goal has yet been assigned to the retirement role. Burgess calls it a "roleless role." Thus there are no clear and widely shared expectations as to what role occupants are to do. Norms inferred from studies of actual behavior show individual retirees pursuing varied *ad hoc*, short-run goals, derived largely from previous free-time interests and activities. There is indication of much *passivity*. Participation in political roles, while widely maintained, is rarely extended. A good deal of time is spent in just taking it easy. Although there is, to be sure, an expectation of continued self-maintenance—care of health and home—a degree of economic dependence is legitimated (as through Social Security, Medicare, and financial assistance programs), as is increased dependence upon relatives in cases of illness or decrepitude. By and large, the socially defined positive criterion of successful performance in retirement is limited to immediate personal gratification, which tends to become an end in itself. The negative criterion is that the retiree not intrude upon the active members of society.

Sanctions. Such goallessness is bound up, of course, with the ineffectiveness of sanctions in facilitating socialization. Without clarity in the norms, specific performances cannot be defined as either conformist or deviant; nor can appropriate rewards or punishment be meted out. Without clear congruence between the functions of role activities and the values of the society, social sanctions tend to be indifferent or negative, rather than positive. Thus, although status for past achievements may be accorded to the elder who merely rests on his laurels for a short period before his death, continuing esteem is rarely elicited by protracted idleness over many years.

Hence two major requirements for socialization, according to the model (Figure 23.1), fail to be met. There are few clear expectations (d), and few positive incentives (f). There is little to give the retired person a sense of usefulness, in a society where usefulness is valued.

Facilities and support. At the same time, there appear to be incipient facilities and supports (e) to aid acceptance of this ambiguous role. Direct teaching is limited, of course, by the confusion in the norms. Yet resources for transmitting certain clear expectations (regarding finances, health, housing, food preparation) are now available in occasional retirement planning programs introduced by companies or unions. The teaching of expectations for leisure may be increasingly facilitated, and the leisure role rehearsed, as adult offspring influence their retired parents, as retired husbands and their wives bring together their differing role experiences, or as the mass media supply information about manners and customs. Older people do not generally serve as role models for one another (Rosow, 1967), although presently retired parents may act as models for their middle-aged offspring, some as positive models but many, because of their unenviable position, as negative ones.

Far more widely available than such sources of indoctrination are potential sources of emotional support and permissiveness to aid adjustment to retirement. Expert help is furnished by ministers, social workers, doctors, psychotherapists. Tension release is offered through entertainment programs on television and radio. Expressive activity is fostered by old age centers and informal friendship groups. And above all, the solidarity of the family supports the attempts of the retired individual to reconcile discrepant or conflicting role expectations: the family permits a degree of childlike or idiosyncratic behavior in their elders (whom they at the same time isolate from outside sanctions).

Some individual responses. The outcome of present socialization for the retirement role is difficult to gauge, since there can be no objective criteria of conformity or of successful resolution of conflict. Subjective studies of "adjustment" or "morale," however, show suggestive results. Many individuals report satisfactory adjustment; for example, in a 1965 poll, 61 per cent of the retired said that retirement had fulfilled their expectations for a good life (Harris, 1965). Perhaps such adjustment arises from widespread motivation of individuals 65 or more to withdraw; perhaps it is facilitated by family and other supports; or perhaps it results from sturdy individuals simply making the best of their lot. Nevertheless, studies of retired persons also show that the lowering of income often leads to a sense of economic deprivation (Thompson & Streib, 1958); and retired persons are more likely to show low morale than others of the same age who are still working (Streib, 1956; Kutner et al., 1956). Such discrepancies are no doubt related to the fact that the learning of a new role (such as retiree) cannot be understood without the counterpart process of relinquishing the previous role (work)—a matter to which we shall now turn.

Relinquishing the Work Role

How does the social situation act upon men to socialize them to loss of the work role? When the process of relinquishing the work role is compared with the juvenile process of preparing to acquire this role, the direction of all the usual societal contributions clearly appears to change. The *expectations* to perform change to expectations to cease performance. *Facilities* to aid the learning and continuance of performance change to facilities for training in relinquishment. Workmates who formerly *supported* role activity must now support the discarding of it. The positive *rewards* are now withdrawn—not merely wages, but more importantly, the approval of valued achievement (as well as the opportunity to relate to work associates).

Institutionalization of retirement.   One important feature of these altered contributions is the set of symbolic structures that surround them. Retirement, as withdrawal from the occupational role, is institutionalized: it is *expected* (d). Despite the great value attached to work in general, for the older man abdication of it is the "right" thing to do. The institutional arrangements are often embodied in impersonal contracts covering such matters as seniority, term of office, retirement age, or pension plans; and the pension itself, as Goffman has suggested, becomes a formal reward for waiving the right to work (Goffman, 1962). Thus, whatever sense of failure the individual may feel relative to his self-expectations, whatever loss of capacity he may sustain, however much he may resent the barrier to his continued search for success, he can nevertheless legitimately attribute his occupational withdrawal to society. Retirement as an institution protects him from personal guilt.

Anticipatory socialization.   A second important characteristic of socialization for relinquishing the work role is the degree of advance preparation. Reinforcing the institutionalization of retirement, which tends to emphasize the positive aspects of terminating the job, much anticipatory socialization stresses the negative aspects of the job itself.

Thus, while the individual is growing older, the work role itself often deteriorates around him. *Expectations* of performance may rise—with technical advance and the entrance of more recently trained workers—to new levels apparently unattainable by him. Or, as he nears the apex of the work force hierarchy, the remaining opportunities dwindle. At the same time, *sanctions* become ambiguous. Role inadequacy may be ascribed to the worker just because of his age: he may be passed by for promotion or his services subtly undervalued, so that he himself begins to develop anxieties about his own capacity. Decreasing rewards are thus accompanied by increasing feelings of dissatisfaction and frustration. A number of *facilities* and mechanisms contribute to this process of advance socialization. Many older workers, despite seniority protections, experience a series of job losses and changes, often with consequent downgrading. Retraining programs seem largely inaccessible to the old.

Some insightful clues to the nature of role rehearsal for retirement are afforded by a study of managers in a large corporation (Goldner, 1965) where demotion has become a normal aspect of the subculture. Company superiors and co-workers communicate expectations of possible failure, and those already demoted serve as warnings to the others. While such mechanisms operate to prepare men for leveling off or declining successes, other mechanisms hold the workers to their jobs until the time of retirement by cloaking these demotions in ambiguity or providing vague criteria for advancement.

Some individual responses.   The study indicated a variety of ways in which individual managers might adapt to anticipatory socialization of this kind. Some may counter threats of demotion by emphasizing the personal hardships suffered by those higher up or the price one must pay for moving up the career ladder. Some may shift their sphere of involvement—to community or family activities, for example—in order to compensate for defeats in work. Others may lose self-respect, evading encounters with former associates who may know of the demotion. Thus various defenses and preparations for occupational withdrawal begin to appear far in advance of the retirement age.

Widowhood

Another important example of socialization for role transfer occurs in the case of widowhood, when an individual must relinquish the role of spouse and adjust to a state of marital singleness. (Note that the age of onset of widowhood has been steadily postponed over the last decades, so that widowhood is typically associated not only with women, but also with the aged.) Various studies suggest the nature of societal contributions, as well as some types of individual response.

Relinquishment of the conjugal role.   As in relinquishment of the work role, giving up the former conjugal role may be accompanied by a general tendency for societal inputs to become negative rather than positive. The individual, when widowed, is now *expected* (save for the later eventuality of possible remarriage) to learn to abdicate his earlier functions—looking after the physical and emotional needs of the spouse or (for the male) supporting his wife. The available *facilities and resources* are no longer devoted to successful performance of the marital role, but to renouncing it. Although there may often be little advance socialization prior to actual bereavement (J. Riley, 1968), husband and wife may sometimes prepare one another, and there may have been relevant role rehearsal on the occasion of earlier losses (e.g., of parents or other objects of affection). Former *rewards* are now withdrawn as the individual is deprived of the love and companionship of many years. Moreover, the subtle social approval accorded to the married state tends to be replaced with pity or indifference.

There is one notable difference, however, between the rewards foregone in relinquishing the marital role and those lost with the work role. The major loss in widowhood is the relationship to a significant other person; in retirement, it is the opportunity to act out an internalized value. Thus bereavement is not a threat to the self-image in the same sense as retirement. It results neither from the individual's failure, nor from his loss of capacity to perform the functions of the role (cf. Cumming, 1963). Hence, bereavement may, for many individuals, be the easier to sustain. (Newcomb, 1961, has suggested that, at least in adolescence, individuals with complete freedom of choice are more likely to shift their friends than their values.)

Bereavement. Intense socialization for the transfer from old to new occurs during the period immediately following the death of the spouse. Here the *expectations* emphasize recovery from grief and resumption of activities; the *sanctions* are structured to reward return to normal functioning; strong emotional *supports* are afforded and permissiveness allows—even prescribes—the demonstration of grief (Parsons & Bales, 1953).

Much of this support takes the form of ritual, of symbolic declaration of solidarity between the bereaved and the kin and community to which the deceased belonged (Durkheim, 1951; Parsons & Lidz, 1967). Various agents are available to aid the socialization at this point—doctors, ministers, social workers, lawyers, insurance agents, funeral directors (although the norms are not always clear, and the preparation of the agents themselves is sometimes confused). Relatives and friends stand by, although, for the aged widow whose parents are dead and whose children may have grown apart, *close* kin are sometimes absent. The assistance available during the mourning period is often curtailed soon after the initial shock. A British survey portrays the subsequent period of desolation and physiological stress, in which the widowed person is typically left alone, with little further attention or emotional support from the external world (Gorer, 1965).

Learning the role of widow. How adequately, following bereavement, does the social structure facilitate socialization to the new role?

In regard to *expectations,* the widow is expected to resume her previous level of activity, *not* to withdraw from role participation. Yet the goals of such activity seem to be a truncated version of the earlier goals and are no longer clearly integrated into the structure of societal goals. The major function remaining from the former spousal role is that of home maintenance (housekeeping or gardening), as most older people up to the stages of decrepitude continue to inhabit and operate their own homes. But this function is now focused, not on a significant other person, but on the self. The independence norm tends to inhibit substituting for the lost relationship any major responsibility for other kinfolk. Thus the widowed old person—except under the special condition of illness or disability—typically lives (often entirely alone) near his children but not with them (Shanas, 1962; Townsend, 1957). The grandparent who would usurp the parental prerogatives of authority and responsibility may even be denied warm relationships with grandchildren and harmonious ones with adult offspring.

Major emotional *support* for learning and performing the new role is often provided by friends as well as relatives, although the financial support of widows is notoriously small (Epstein, 1964). Older people gravitate toward friendships among age peers (Rosow, 1967), and the widowed tend to have higher friendship participation in communities where many other widows are also present (Blau, 1961). As in earlier periods of role transfer, such as adolescence, it is through peer support that individuals often seek reassurance, release from stress, and a renewed sense of identity.

Has there been socialization for widowhood *in advance?* For the required independence, the answer seems to be yes. Independence training in many forms has been recurrent throughout much of earlier life, especially in the middle class where independence training for occupational achievement is often stressed. Yet, for the solitary aspect of this new status, the preparation is less obvious. Perhaps the prior period of husband-wife relationship has itself served as a degree of preparation. Durkheim suggested long ago that suicide rates among the widowed are apparently lowest under those societal conditions where suicide rates for the married are also low—implying, perhaps, the development within certain marriages of the requisite sense of security and autonomy (Durkheim, 1951 translation).

Sanctions for performance in the widow role per se seem largely confined to the indifference accorded to solitary aged individuals. At the same time, certain positive rewards accrue from the independence which elicits respect from the community and also leaves the individual free—much as the retired worker is free—either to develop new goals and new activities, or to resort to inactivity and aimlessness.

In sum, societal contributions for transfer to widowhood, as for transfer to retirement, appear generally inadequate in terms of our model. While negative pressures foster withdrawal from the previous role, there are few positive incentives for involvement in the new one. The losses meted out to the individual appear to outweigh the gains.

Some individual responses.   For the individual, the outcome tends to be, at least initially, traumatic. Grief reactions at the time of bereavement are typically intense, often including somatic distress, preoccupation with the image of the deceased, hostile reactions, or feelings of guilt (Lindemann, 1965). Despondency may decrease over the subsequent years (Kutner et al., 1956), requiring, according to Freud, an extended period of reality testing to demonstrate that the loved object no longer exists. Yet the extreme sense of desolation does not invariably decrease over the years; studies comparing widowed with married persons show, on the average, that the former have fewer contacts with their children, greater unhappiness, higher rates of suicide and of death (e.g., Gurin, Verhoff & Feld, 1960).

These examples suggest that the social structure is presently more conducive to the relinquishment of key roles than to the learning of whatever new roles are available to older people. When an older person effects the transfer from an old to a new role, he appears not to display the eagerness with which many younger persons transfer into the work role, for example, or into the role of parent. The older person's transfer is often the result of enforced relinquishment, or of the imbalance between uncertain rewards in the new role and increasing punishments (or threats of punishment) in the old (cf. Homans, 1961). In effect, withdrawal from many past involvements—without full opportunity for replacement—seems to be socially imposed upon the aging individual.

III. SOME VARIATIONS
IN INDIVIDUAL RESPONSE

Let us now turn to a more careful scrutiny of the connections between such societal contributions and the nature of the individual's responses to the socialization process. If withdrawal is a predominant response of older people to required role transfers (given negative contributions to encourage relinquishment, without adequate positive contributions to enhance new learning), what other types of response is the individual likely to make? And which types occur most frequently when people of various ages—not just the aged—are confronted with a similar dilemma?

Further Specification of the Model

Implicit in the foregoing examples, but not yet clarified in our conceptual model, is the range of reactions of older people under the impact of contemporary socialization—see (c) in Figure 23.1, page 955. Let us turn to a paradigm that specifies these reactions in further detail.

Certain assumptions will simplify our presentation of this paradigm. Since the individual's responses to a required role transfer (such as retirement) depend upon his own internalized values and upon the values built into the norms of the two roles, the one he must vacate and the one he will enter, we shall assume (1) that the role to be relinquished (e.g., work) is based upon a central societal value (achievement), and (2) that the modal individual has originally learned norms and definitions consistent with such a value. A moment's reflection will show that, given these assumptions, if the new role, too, is governed by a norm compatible with societal values, the new role will thereby provide continuity for the individual between his internalized norms and those he must now adopt; and *per contra,* if the new norm is incompatible, the new role will provide discontinuity as the examples will show. Three ideal-typical courses (cf. Parsons & Shils, 1951) appear, then, to be open to the individual faced with such a role transfer—see Figure 23.2.

FIGURE 23.2
SOME ALTERNATIVE INDIVIDUAL RESPONSES
TO A REQUIRED ROLE TRANSFER

A. *Substitution* of a new role consonant with his internalized norms.

B. *Restructuring of his orientations* (norms or role definitions) so as to resolve the dissonance between the new role and his internalized norms.

C. *Defense mechanisms and deviant adjustments* to handle the unresolved dissonance.

Substitution.   First (Type A), he can substitute a new (or redefined) role compatible with his established values and attitudes. If widowed, he may remarry. If required to give up the occupational role for retirement, for example, his first option is to find a substitute activity that fits his internalized norm of achievement—such as (short of another full-time job) a part-time job, turning a hobby into a serious enterprise, helping his children or friends at their jobs, or making home repairs. Precisely what constitutes a substitute depends (since we are here discussing the individual's responses) upon the individual's own definitions. As long as he succeeds in finding a substitute, no internal conflict arises. The expectations of his new role will be consonant with his existing self-expectations.

Restructuring of orientations.   If the individual fails to find such substitute roles, however, the new expectations he must learn will be in conflict with his self-expectations. As a retired person, for example, he may elect to spend his time in aimless or self-gratificatory activity that directly negates his urge to continue with disciplined, goal-directed occupations. Since the conflict may engender feelings of guilt and inadequacy, a second course is for him to restructure his orientations so as to reduce the dissonance (Type B). On the one hand, he may *redefine* as achievement those leisure activities that are available to him—babysitting with grandchildren, housekeeping, keeping up with neighborhood gossip, or community service; again the definition must satisfy the individual himself. He may even redefine as achievement his mere survival. On the other hand, he may *inhibit* the internalized norm or *reduce its salience.* Thus, he may bring into salience the norm of consummatory activity which was formerly (when the achievement norm had precedence) admissible only during recreation periods.

Defense and deviance.   Third, failing such a resolution, he may handle the dissonance by resorting (Type C) to a variety of possible modes of defense or deviance (cf. Parsons, 1951; Merton, 1957). Repressing his underlying ambivalence, he can refuse to admit that the former role (his work) is closed to him, assert that other goals (his health, or being with his family) are more important, place the blame on others, and the like. He may act compulsively to restore his former role (as by endless job-seeking) or over-conform to the new role (as by ritualistic performance of recreational activities, or by hedonistic pleasure-seeking as a *summum bonum*). He may show alienation toward work, or nihilistic denial of all moral principles. Or—more predictably in view of his early lifetime of assumedly good behavior—he may simply withdraw from activities generally (cf. Cloward, 1959). To be sure, this withdrawal is by no means always a deviant adaptation for the individual; it can eventuate because the individual is simply conforming to the expectation that he relinquish key roles. But, given the ambivalence of an unresolved conflict, his compulsion to withdraw may take various extreme forms, such as motivated illness, despondency or suicide.

Some portion of the illness and disability of the very old may constitute motivated deviance of this kind. The sick role of the aged appears similar in certain respects to the sick role in general (cf. Parsons, 1951). It legitimates withdrawal from active participation. It may also legitimate dependency—serving as a means of recovering close attachments with offspring, for example, or of permitting regression to childlike behavior. Nevertheless, unlike the illness of younger people, it does not imply the expectation of getting well. Hence it is a preparation for death, rather than for re-entry into life. It fosters disengagement.

Unemployment

This paradigm is useful for classifying the responses manifested by older people when the roles of worker or of spouse become closed, including their withdrawal which may occur either with or without feelings of unresolved conflict. To be certain, however, that such responses are not peculiar to the aged, let us now examine responses to another situation involving—not merely the old—but adults of all ages: let us consider the situation of unemployment during the Great Depression.

This situation, though unique in certain respects, closely parallels the inadequate societal contributions for socializing older people today. At that time, as in the case of retirement today, loss of the work role was imposed upon the individual quite apart from his own choice, and was so widespread and of sufficient duration to become a form of institutionalized deviance. Here, too, few positive contributions were provided at the societal level to help the individual learn the new role of "unemployed"—although there were various negative proscriptions (e.g., against stealing, or claiming relief allowances illegally); free time, rather than serving as a reward, became oppressive; and even the family, losing confidence, tended to withdraw its support.

Some types of responses.   Several studies probed intensively into the attempts of workers to adjust to this situation—efforts especially poignant among those who had best epitomized the achievement norm (e.g., Bakke, 1940; Jahoda-Lazarsfeld & Zeisel, 1933; Komarovsky, 1940; Pilgrim Trust, 1938). These responses prove strikingly similar to those of older people under the circumstances cited above.

First, comparatively few individuals (less than 10 per cent in one of Bakke's samples of unemployed) found activities that served even partially as *substitutes* (Type A) for the lost employment—activities such as home repair, gardening, gathering wood, or small game hunting. For some, the search for a job, and learning how to go about it, became in itself a central pursuit.

Second, there are various instances of the apparently successful *restructuring* of orientations (Type B) so as to redefine the roles involved or to bring new norms into salience. The women in one community, accustomed to working, became reconciled to unemployment and found fresh virtues in life at home. In another community, the men espoused betting as a major activity that offered prestige to the winner, an opportunity to make decisions and to maintain social contacts, and the feeling that they stood "as good a chance as anybody else" (Pilgrim Trust, 1938). In Marienthal, an Austrian community under pervasive unemployment, one type of individual maintained an unbroken spirit by temporarily renouncing the expectation of success, while he maintained home, children, and hope for the future (Jahoda-Lazarsfeld & Zeisel, 1933).

Third, responses that appear to be *defensive* or *deviant* (Type C) also occur in the several communities studied. Scapegoating arose, for example, as some individuals felt they were victimized, placing the blame on former employers or on minority groups. Some refused to acknowledge their unemployed status, or to associate with others who were unemployed (Pilgrim Trust, 1938). For others, morale was completely broken, self-esteem lost (Komarovsky, 1940). In Marienthal, certain workers evidenced deep despair (depression, hopelessness, a sense of futility). Finally, some individuals resorted to activity that was directly harmful to themselves, their families, or their communities, such as criminality, informing, drinking, marital unfaithfulness, or extreme irritability.

Withdrawal.   Of all the responses observed under these widely varied conditions of national background and severity of the unemployment crisis, withdrawal was by far the most common—though whether or not, in any particular case, withdrawal reflected ambivalence or conflict cannot be determined. Doing nothing dominated the day. Restlessness and hopelessness disrupted leisure activities. Borrowing from the library or walking in the park became less frequent. Thousands of men hung around on street corners, unable to settle down into any activity. The Austrian researchers classified some two-thirds of all their cases as "resigned"—typified by marked reductions in expectations of self and of society, and (though they managed to maintain home and children) by absence of plans or future orientations.

At the extreme, withdrawal gave way to retreatism (cf. Merton, 1957) and deterioration. Some 5 per cent of the Marienthal sample evidenced complete apathy, with indolence and inactivity displacing even the care of home and children. Those longest out of work were the most likely to become depressed. For some, physical and mental illness ensued. And for many, deterioration of skills and gradual acceptance of the unemployed status tended to result in complete unemployability (Pilgrim Trust, 1938; Komarovsky, 1940).

Thus it seems clear that, at all age levels, social structural barriers can destroy the motivation to perform in accustomed roles or to learn new ones. It is the rare individual who, like a Bettelheim focusing upon his work as scientist in the midst of a concentration camp, can maintain his self-esteem against massive assaults from the environment.

IV. SOME IMPLICATIONS

The examples in the foregoing sections suggest that much socialization today fails to realize the interlocking between individual goals and social goals postulated in the ideal model. Instead, a predominant current tendency is for many mature individuals, given the deficits of aging and the socially structured barriers to central roles, to respond to socialization pressures in a particular fashion—through withdrawal. Herein lies the irony: the older person today who conforms most closely to social expectations of relinquishment is thereby most likely to enter the ranks of those generally defined by society as deviant. The very fact that he complies with social mandates that shift as he ages destroys the original meshing between the social expectations for people in general and the particular expectations for him; for withdrawal, even though it may constitute conformity to expectations for the aging individuals, runs counter nevertheless to the dominant activist values of our culture. It has thus become a form of institutionalized deviance, tolerated for older people, though not positively approved. In this respect, aging is similar to illness, save for one major difference: the sick person is expected to get well and to renew his active participation, but the withdrawn older person is tacitly expected to die.

Withdrawal as a Consequence of Contemporary Socialization

The prevalence of withdrawal responses among the aged has implications both for the individual and for society.

Implications for the individual. Socialization for withdrawal may be viewed in the abstract as either functional or dysfunctional for the aging individual, depending upon the intrinsic state of his health and capacities. To the extent that aging, apart from social pressures, may restrict a person's energies and competence, institutionalized withdrawal provides a legitimate escape. It reduces the guilt he might otherwise feel if he must slack off or retire from his job, diminish his responsibilities to offspring, or curtail his participation in voluntary associations. But how many people suffer such intrinsic organic decrements, and at how early an age?

This question, though presently unanswerable, is critical. For, to the extent that the individual, though aging, remains capable and motivated to participate, socialization for withdrawal from former roles, *without substitution of adequate new ones,* can lead only to frustration. His enforced retreat from active participation in society no longer elicits approval from himself or from other people, who now tend to deprecate his status.

Implications for the society. For society, as for the individual, the current tendency to relegate masses of older people to socially deviant roles seems to entail both positive and negative consequences. Where roles are scarce (as in upper echelons of the bureaucracy, in power positions in the family, or in the labor force as a whole), removal of the old operates—like death—to make room for the young. Indeed, the effect of socializing older people to withdraw approximates the effect of speeding up the processes of mortality; it allows the continual renewal of the active population and thus fosters change (cf. Ryder, 1965). It is as if the successes of medical science in reducing mortality and prolonging human lives had produced a surfeit of human abilities, beyond the absorptive capacity of the present structure of established roles; so that socialization is operating—at least temporarily—to divert these excess abilities out of circulation.

At the same time, the social desirability of millions of unproductive citizens is certainly questionable. Since by no means all of them are incapacitated, their withdrawal constitutes at best a waste of human resources. At worst, those who manifest psychopathic symptoms, motivated illness, and other forms of extreme retreatism and evasion can add substantially to society's burden of dependency.

Repercussions on Society: The Reciprocity of Socialization

In a dynamic society, however, it seems unlikely that such a situation will persist, so that extensive withdrawal of mature members may not remain the predominant pattern. Indeed, the conceptual model as we have so far applied it, is asymmetric: though assuming an interplay between society and individual, it has appeared to locate the entire process of *change* at the level of the individual—as if he alone were required to restructure his orientations and to adapt to a set of social roles which we have treated as givens. Yet socialization has repercussions on the society as well (cf. Rosow, 1965).

Some additions to the model. Socialization processes involve, for the social system as well as for the individual, a continuing adjustment between the established norms and rules (the institutionalized expectations as to how the members should act and think) and the specific application of these norms to new situations. Thus it seems obvious that, if large numbers of individuals respond to socialization in new or deviant fashion, the norms and role definitions may themselves adapt. Just as the individual (Types B and C in Figure 23.2 above) may attempt—successfully or unsuccessfully—to resolve the conflicts of socialization by restructuring his norms and definitions in various ways, so too societal roles, norms and definitions may become rearranged (cf. Dubin, 1959). The social structure of roles, then, affected as it is by larger currents of stability and change, may also be affected through certain processes inherent in the socialization of individual members.

A paradigm of possible changes in the social structure—parallel to that for individual responses in Figure 23.2 except that it deals at the system level with *collective* responses of the many individuals being socialized—is outlined in Figure 23.3. There is, first, the possibility (Type D) of opening to older people

FIGURE 23.3

POSSIBLE CHANGES IN STRUCTURE OF ROLES
AVAILABLE TO MATURE INDIVIDUALS

(*Compare Figure 23.2, p. 971*)

D. Provision of additional *substitute* roles similar to those closed to individuals in later life.

E. Restructuring of roles and role definitions *within* the established normative pattern.

F. The spread of deviant roles and role definitions.

---

additional *substitute* roles essentially similar to those previously closed. For unemployed men during the Depression, for example, national governments provided jobs through relief agencies, thus enabling men to regain a sense of mastery and to perform in a socially respected fashion (Bakke, 1940) ; or clubs were formed to help the unemployed keep fit for work, maintain contacts with workmates, and plan for a future community (Pilgrim Trust, 1938). More recently, New York City appealed to persons who are already retired to be trained and hired as teachers (*New York Times,* April 4, 1966). New roles for old people have also been provided as temporary parent-surrogates to sick or orphaned children. Such substitute roles involve only minor variations in the established social structure, or in the related mechanisms for socialization.

Still more far-reaching changes are possible if the roles become restructured—either toward the spread of deviance or toward the restructuring of conformity. The establishment of new roles *outside* the existing value system (Type F) may occur in some instances because subcultures develop to reinforce the mature individual's deviance. Thus, in those social sectors where unemployment was most pervasive during the Depression, unemployment came to be accepted as inevitable; and the rumors with which friends consoled one another took on a defensive character—asserting, for example, that only those with influence, or only the Irish, could get jobs (Pilgrim Trust, 1938).

Deviance can also spread through society even when—as is more often the case—the withdrawn individuals are largely isolated from social supports. The typical unemployed man in the Depression was not a member of a subculture, but was cut off from neighbors, friends, political groups, recreational activities, and even from religion except where it might solve problems of daily living (Bakke, 1940). Within the family itself, divisive strains emanated from the employed male's withdrawal (Komarovsky, 1940)—just as they may also appear among retired couples if the wife finds it difficult to have her husband at home all day. The process whereby such pervasive isolation can lead to social disorganization or anomie is suggested by Durkheim's discussion of the "detachment" of certain individuals from their social relationships. As a consequence of the vague doubts which the isolated develop about the goals of their own activity, he says, "metaphysical and religious systems spring up which, by reducing these obscure sentiments to formulae, attempt to prove to men the senselessness of life" (Durkheim, 1951). Hence, previously institutionalized norms may become changed or weakened. In such fashion, the deviance of persons in middle or later life—their retreatist, hedonistic or nihilistic adaptations—even though presently insulated, might filter from the smaller deviant group through the larger society, fostering in oncoming generations such excessive manifestations as denial of moral principles, doctrines of pleasure seeking, or drug addiction (cf. Merton, 1957).

Alternatively (Type E), social change can occur because the roles available to older people become restructured and redefined *within* the existing value framework. New functions may be assigned to presently vacuous roles, or the activity content of the role may be redefined as socially useful. A few examples will suggest the potential for such positive changes that avoid anomie or threats to societal values.

Woman's changing occupational role. The development over recent decades of the woman's occupational role is a dramatic instance of an already established change in the social structure for which increasing numbers of individuals are now being socialized. (Since 1940 the rate of labor force participation among married women has more than *doubled*.) The new role, given impetus by manpower demands in World War II, appears to have crystallized as one individual woman after another—especially the better educated—learned to avail herself of the emerging opportunities.

Several traditional norms have become regrouped here to provide a new set of expectations—expectations of a career combined with marriage for the mature, educated woman whose children are grown. These expectations fit together (1) the achievement norm; (2) recognition of the woman's primary role in the family—for her, the work role is secondary and temporally succeeds the parental role; and (3) the male's function as major provider for the family, since the newly defined woman's role emphasizes the expressive, noneconomic aspect, in contrast to conventional instrumental dimensions of work (Riley, Johnson & Boocock, 1963).

How is such an emerging role diffused through the social system? Clues from exploratory research suggest that adolescent cohorts are now being socialized in anticipation for this redefined role, partly through formal education which prepares girls for occupations much as it does boys, but partly through parental influence. Working mothers serve as models for their daughters; and more importantly, girls tend to see their parents as expecting them to utilize their education and training in careers combined with marriage. That is, girls tend to espouse the career norm in families where their mothers are working, but are even more favorable where they perceive their parents as expecting them to work (Johnson, 1964).

Possible future changes. Are further new roles likely to develop for the retirement years as well? Here there are two desiderata to be met. First, any new roles should be compatible with existing norms: the roles should accept retirement from the lifetime career as institutionalized, should safeguard that mechanism which frees the failing older person from a sense of personal guilt and which opens the occupational system to the rising generations. Might not extension of optional, part-time jobs for retirees meet such a criterion? Second, new roles should be compatible with the short life-span and the diminishing skills remaining to the retired person. He cannot be made responsible for critical functions in a complex division of labor. Thus, for example, the role of teacher may be better suited to the oldster than the role of administrator.

Apart from occupational possibilities, are roles of other types likely to crystallize? Is there perhaps a new type of *achieved family solidarity* open to the aged parent or grandparent, an earned friendship and intimacy with descendant kin, to replace the ascribed solidarity to which the younger parent has a right whether or not he earns it? Or is there a potential for the gradual redefinition of achievement so as to embrace *leisure* activities as well as work in a calling? If so, retirement may in itself come to be regarded as worthwhile— much as the pursuit of the arts or of knowledge for its own sake were valued in the leisure classes of ancient Athens, the Renaissance, or 17th Century England.

Such questions may sound like idle speculation. Yet there is a suggestive parallelism with a paragraph once written about housewives:

> There must be a fundamental readjustment of the social division of labor. Today mature women have been cut loose from it. They no longer find a full life in the home, their traditional place. If we are ever to have a good society, housewives, as well as every other category within the population, must have a place in which they can feel secure, with ample opportunity for earning the social approbation which man, apart from the animals, so desperately needs (M. W. Riley, unpublished).

Written before World War II, at a time when talk of new roles for married women also seemed like idle speculation, this paragraph now seems merely descriptive of today's conditions. At least in this one instance, the quest of many individuals seeking personal fulfillment resulted in the creation of a new position in society.

Moreover, several contemporary changes may well foster future crystallization of new roles for adults—even for the retired or the widowed. Each new cohort of older people, better educated and more economically secure than the one before, is thus better prepared for retirement. Husbands and wives now enjoy an extended middle-life period, with peak incomes and freedom from child-rearing, in which to develop new patterns of leisure time interests and of relationship to family and friends. And finally, the entire role structure of industrial society is becoming increasingly complex and differentiated—opening up wider ranges of choices to individuals generally, stressing human relationships in contrast to purely productive goals (Parsons & White, 1961).

In sum, the learning tasks assigned to the mature individual in contemporary society are great. As early as his middle years, he must begin to face the loss—threatened or actual—of dependent children and the function of rearing them, of job, of spouse, and finally of life itself. Furthermore, many of the new roles he must learn are themselves shut off from society. In effect, he is often required to learn to withdraw. Hence his very success in learning often constitutes deviation from our dominant value patterns, depriving him at once of goals invested with wider social meaning and of esteem in his own eyes and in the eyes of others. Yet, according to the evidence, the spirit of many older people is indestructible; typically, they withdraw with grace.

Would the outcome of adult socialization be more positive if valued roles were provided and social supports to learning increased? The answer awaits empirical study of individuals with widely varied backgrounds within widely varied sociotemporal contexts. It is possible that the current situation may prove to be merely a temporary and unique phase in the history of industrial society. In an increasingly complex environment, new functions, appropriate to the successive stages of middle and later life, may well be assigned to mature individuals. For, as Winston White (1961) puts it, "American values conceive of the ideally good society as one that continually seeks to develop the capacities of all its members and to provide them with the opportunities for exercising these capacities."

REFERENCES

Back, K. W., & Gergen, K. J. Personal orientation and morale of the aged. In Ida H. Simpson & J. C. McKinney (Eds.), *Social aspects of aging*. Durham, N. C.: Duke Univer. Press, 1966. Pp. 296–305.

Bakke, E. W. *Citizens without work*. New Haven: Yale Univer. Press, 1940.

Becker, H. S. Notes on the concept of commitment. *American Journal of Sociology*, 1960, 66, 32–40.

Benedict, Ruth. Continuities and discontinuities in cultural conditioning. *Psychiatry*, 1938, 1, 161–167.

Birren, J. E. Adult capacities to learn. In R. G. Kuhlen (Ed.), *Psychological backgrounds of adult education*. Chicago: Center for the Study of Liberal Education for Adults, 1963. Pp. 8–42.

Blau, Zena S. Structural constraints on friendships in old age. *American Sociological Review*, 1961, 26, 429–439.

BOTWINICK, J. *Cognitive processes in maturity and old age.* New York: Springer, 1967.

BREDEMEIER, H. C., & STEPHENSON, R. M. *The analysis of social systems.* New York: Holt, Rinehart & Winston, 1962.

BRIM, O. G., JR. Socialization through the life cycle. In O. G. Brim, Jr. & S. Wheeler, *Socialization after childhood: Two essays.* New York: Wiley, 1966. Pp. 1–49.

BRIM, O. G., JR. Adult socialization. In J. A. Clausen (Ed.), *Socialization and society.* Boston: Little, Brown, 1967.

CAIN, L. D., JR. Life course and social structure. In R. L. Faris (Ed.), *Handbook of modern sociology.* Chicago: Rand McNally, 1964. Pp. 272–310.

CLAUSEN, J. A. Introduction. In J. A. Clausen (Ed.), *Socialization and society.* Boston: Little, Brown, 1967.

CLOWARD, R. A. Illegitimate means, anomie, and deviant behavior. *American Sociological Review,* 1959, 24, 164–176.

CUMMING, ELAINE. Further thoughts on the theory of disengagement. *UNESCO International Social Science Journal,* 1963, 15, 377–393.

CUMMING, ELAINE, & HENRY, W. E. *Growing old: The process of disengagement.* New York: Basic Books, 1961.

DUBIN, R. Deviant behavior and social structure: Continuities in social theory. *American Sociological Review,* 1959, 24, 147–164.

DURKHEIM, E. *Suicide.* (J. A. Spaulding & G. Simpson, translators) Glencoe, Ill.: Free Press, 1951.

EPSTEIN, LENORE A. Income of the aged in 1962: First findings of the 1963 survey of the aged. *Social Security Bulletin,* 1964, 27, 3–24, 28.

FESTINGER, L. *A theory of cognitive dissonance.* Evanston, Ill.: Row, Peterson, 1957.

GLASS, D. C. *Theories of consistency and the study of personality.* Unpublished manuscript, 1966.

GLICK, P. C., & PARKE, R., JR. New approaches in studying the life cycle of the family. *Demography,* II. Chicago: The Population Assn. of America, 1965. Pp. 187–202.

GOFFMAN, E. On cooling the mark out: Some aspects of adaptation to failure. In A. Rose (Ed.), *Human behavior and social processes.* Boston: Houghton Mifflin, 1962.

GOLDNER, F. H. Demotion in industrial management. *American Sociological Review,* 1965, 30, 714–724.

GORER, G. *Death, grief and mourning in Britain.* New York: Doubleday, 1965.

GURIN, G., VEROFF, J., & FELD, SHEILA. *Americans view their mental health: A nationwide interview survey.* New York: Basic Books, 1960.

HARRIS SURVEY. *The Washington Post,* November 28, 1965, 29.

HEIDER, F. *The psychology of interpersonal relations.* New York: Wiley, 1958.

HERON, A., & CHOWN, SHEILA M. Expectations of supervisors concerning older workers. In R. H. Williams, C. Tibbitts & Wilma Donahue (Eds.), *Processes of aging.* Vol. I. New York: Atherton Press, 1963. Pp. 273–285.

HOMANS, G. C. *Social behavior: Its elementary forms.* New York: Harcourt, Brace & World, 1961.

JAHODA-LAZARSFELD, MARIE, & ZEISEL, H. *Die arbeitslosen von Marienthal.* Leipzig: S. Hirzel, 1933.

JOHNSON, MARILYN E. Socialization of adolescents to the norm of women working. Unpublished master's thesis, Rutgers Univer., 1964.

JOHNSTONE, J. W. C., & RIVERA, R. J. *Volunteers for learning.* Chicago: Aldine, 1965.

KOMAROVSKY, MIRRA. *The unemployed man and his family.* New York: Dryden Press, 1940.

KUTNER, B. The social nature of aging. *The Gerontologist,* 1962, 2, 5–8.

KUTNER, B., ET AL. *Five hundred over sixty: A community survey on aging.* New York: Russell Sage Foundation, 1956.

LINDEMANN, E. Symptomatology and management of acute grief. In R. Fulton, *Death and identity.* New York: Wiley, 1965. Pp. 186–200.

LIPSET, S., ET AL. The psychology of voting: An analysis of political behavior. In L. Gardner (Ed.), *Handbook of social psychology.* Vol. II. Cambridge, Mass.: Addison & Wesley, 1954. Pp. 1124–1175.

MADDOX, G. L., JR. Disengagement theory: A critical evaluation. *The Gerontologist,* 1964, 4, 80–82, 103.

MERTON, R. K. *Social theory and social structure.* Glencoe, Ill.: Free Press, 1957.

MERTON, R. K., & ROSSI, ALICE S. Contributions to the theory of reference group behavior. In R. K. Merton, *Social theory and social structure.* Glencoe, Ill.: Free Press, 1957.

MILLER, D. R., & SWANSON, G. E. *The changing American parent.* New York: Wiley, 1958.

MOORE, W. E. *Man, time and society.* New York: Wiley, 1963.

NEUGARTEN, BERNICE. Personality changes during the adult years. In R. G. Kuhlen (Ed.), *Psychological backgrounds of adult education.* Chicago: Center for the Study of Liberal Education for Adults, 1963. Pp. 43–76.

NEWCOMB, T. M. *The acquaintance process.* New York: Holt, Rinehart & Winston, 1961.

PARSONS, T. *The social system.* Glencoe, Ill.: Free Press, 1951.

PARSONS, T., & BALES, R. F. The dimensions of action-space. In T. Parsons, R. F. Bales & E. A. Shils, *Working papers in the theory of action.* Glencoe, Ill.: Free Press, 1953.

PARSONS, T., & LIDZ, V. Death in American society. In E. S. Shneidman (Ed.), *Essays in self-destruction.* New York: Science House, Inc., 1967.

PARSONS, T., & SHILS, E. A. Values, motives, and systems of action. In T. Parsons & E. A. Shils (Eds.), *Toward a general theory of action.* Cambridge, Mass.: Harvard Univer. Press, 1951. Pp. 3–29.

PARSONS, T., & WHITE, W. The link between character and society. In S. M. Lipset & L. Lowenthal (Eds.), *Culture and social character.* New York: Free Press, 1961.

PILGRIM TRUST. *Men without work: A report made to the Pilgrim Trust.* London: Cambridge Univer. Press, 1938.

PITTS, J. R. Introduction: Personality and the social system. In T. Parsons et al., *Theories of society.* New York: Free Press, 1961. Pp. 685–716.

RILEY, J. W., JR. Death and bereavement. In *International encyclopedia of the social sciences.* New York: Macmillan, 1968.

RILEY, M. W., & COHN, R. Control networks in informal groups. *Sociometry,* 1958, 21, 30–49.

RILEY, M. W., FONER, ANNE, ET AL. *Aging and society: I. An inventory of research findings.* New York: Russell Sage Foundation, 1968.

RILEY, M. W., JOHNSON, MARILYN E., & BOOCOCK, SARANE S. Woman's changing occupational role. *American Behavioral Scientist,* 1963, VI, 33–37.

ROSE, A. M. A current theoretical issue in social gerontology. *The Gerontologist,* 1964, 4, 46–50.

ROSOW, I. Forms and functions of adult socialization. *Social Forces,* 1965, 44, 35–45.

ROSOW, I. *Social integration of the aged.* New York: Free Press, 1967.

RYDER, N. B. The cohort as a concept in the study of social change. *American Sociological Review,* 1965, 30, 843–861.

SHANAS, ETHEL. *The health of older people: A social survey.* Cambridge, Mass.: Harvard Univer. Press, 1962.

SIMMONS, L. W. Aging in preindustrial societies. In C. Tibbitts (Ed.), *Handbook of social gerontology.* Chicago: Univer. of Chicago Press, 1960. Pp. 62–91.

SMITH, M. W. Evidences of potentialities of older workers in a manufacturing company. *Personnel Psychology,* 1952, 5, 11–18.

STREIB, G. F. Morale of the retired. *Social Problems,* 1956, 3, 270–276.

THOMPSON, W. E., & STREIB, G. F. Situational determinants: Health and economic deprivation in retirement. *The Journal of Social Issues,* 1958, 14, 18–34.

TOBY, J. Some variables in role conflict analysis. *Social Forces,* 1952, 30, 323–327.

TOWNSEND, P. *The family life of old people: An inquiry in East London.* London: Routledge & Kegan Paul, 1957.

VAN GENNEP, A. *The rites of passage.* (M. B. Vizedom & G. L. Caffee, translators) Chicago: Univer. of Chicago Press, 1960.

WHEELER, S. The structure of formally organized socialization settings. In O. G. Brim, Jr. & S. Wheeler, *Socialization after childhood: Two essays.* New York: Wiley, 1966. Pp. 51–116.

WHITE, W. *Beyond conformity.* New York: Free Press, 1961.

WIRTZ, W. W. *The older American worker: Age discrimination in employment.* 2 vols. Report of the Secretary of Labor. Washington: Government Printing Office, 1965.

CHAPTER **24**

The Three Faces Of Continuity In Human Development

Jerome Kagan

Harvard University

Faith in the permanence of selected psychological structures lies at the base of most psychological theories, even those which demand that the child passes through discrete stages of development. Psychoanalytic theory insists that harsh socialization of cleanliness at age 3 will taint the behavior of the adult. Piaget (1932) acknowledges that fragments of preoperational thought can mar the reasoning of the adolescent. Even the less historically oriented behaviorist affirms that overlearning or partial reinforcement of a habit can result in remarkable resistance to extinction. Loyalty to a principle of continuity recruits additional strength from the naturalistic observations of the clinician and educator, as well as the laboratory findings of the comparative psychologist. The enthusiasm for preschool enrichment programs is nurtured by the belief that the dyslexia of a fifth-grade boy can be traced to particular experiential deficits during the preschool years or earlier. The commitment to continuity is most clearly supported by empirical inquiry into the effect of early experience in animals. The mildest of manipulations of an infant mouse appear to be amplified internally and eventually affect significant molar behaviors 100 days later.

There is a general consensus favoring belief in selected islands of continuity of process and behavior. The troublesome problem centers on designating the specific dimensions that remain stable and the reasons for their preferential status.

THE FALLACY OF THE PHENOTYPE

Although most theories neither demand nor assume that continuities refer only to phenotypically similar responses, the practicing empiricist is sometimes more cautious than necessary and searches for stability of behaviors that look alike.

Preparation of this paper was supported in part by research grant MH-8792 from NIMH, contract number PH 43-65-1009 from NICHD, United States Public Health Service and a grant from the Carnegie Corporation of New York.

983

We have sought evidence for the long term stability of intelligence test quotients, academic achievement, activity level, irritability, social responsiveness, depression, dominance or dependency. This strategy derives from the implicit assumption that a particular behavior is maintained over time by the same forces that promote its initial acquisition. This assumption is not always defensible. An 8-month-old infant usually cries when he is hungry, or confronted by a strange stimulus that is discrepant from an existing schema. An 8-year-old child cries when he wants to be freed from a coercive parental restriction, is afraid of physical harm, or anticipates punishment. The act of crying, although characterized by salty tears and facial grimaces at each age, is emitted in the service of dramatically different forces. There is no reason to expect any dramatic continuity of "predisposition to cry" from infancy to early childhood.

Preliminary results from our on-going longitudinal study affirm this proposition. Forty-four boys and forty-three girls, first born and Caucasian, have been observed at 4, 8, and 13 months of age in a variety of situations. There is no relation between amount of crying to visual representations of regular and disfigured human faces at 4 and 13 months of age. However, crying at 4 months does have psychological significance. The girls who cried to the "faces" at 4 months displayed significantly more original nonstereotyped play at 13 months than their nonirritable counterparts matched on social class. Specifically, there were 12 girls, 4 months of age, who were so irritable they could not be shown a complete series of faces because each time a stimulus was shown they would begin to cry and could not be placated. The crying seemed to be elicited by being in the crib and shown a stimulus, a context that was obviously strange to them. These girls showed between two and three unusual and nonstereotypic play activities at 13 months of age in contrast to the nonirritable girls who showed an average of one such act ($p < .05$). Moreover, when one examined the data from the girls who were only moderately fretful at 4 months the correlation between amount of time fretting or crying to the facial representations and the number of unusual nonstereotyped acts at 13 months was .56 ($p < .01$). However these infants who were irritable at 4 months were not more or less irritable than the other children when they were seen at 13 months of age.

This association is interpreted as evidence for continuity of a dimension we can call "relative precocity of cognitive development." The girls who cried at 4 months had a finely articulated schema of a human face and the representations were recognized as discrepant from their schema and elicited crying. The crying in this particular situation at this particular time indexed perceptual precocity. The display of nonstereotyped play at 13 months, it is argued, also indexed precocity of intellectual development. It is reasonable to believe that these two variables might be related. But there is no reason why crying at 4 months should be related to crying at 13 months, for at the older age presentation of "odd faces" typically elicits smiling or laughter. The most likely cause of crying in the year-old child in our laboratory situation is a refusal to be restricted in the high chair, fatigue, or boredom. There is no strong theoretical rationale that suggests that girls who were precocious at 4 months would be unusually restless, tired or bored at one year. Therefore one would not expect phenotypic continuity of the crying behavior over this 9-month period.

Some responses, on the other hand, should display stability of external form. The act of boasting by a 12-year-old boy or a 32-year-old man is often an attempt to maintain behavioral congruence with sex-role standards for masculinity. In this instance, there is theoretical cause to expect this category of behavior to show moderate stability over a 20-year period, for the motivating conditions that elicit "boasting" are likely to remain stable.

Some behaviors display stability of phenotype, others do not. Some processes remain stable but find expression in different actions at different times. Can we predict when we shall see each type? We shall deal with this issue in detail later. Let us explore further the meaning of genotypic continuity.

THE CRYPTOGRAPH OF
THE PSYCHOLOGICAL GENOTYPE

The more intriguing form of continuity bears close resemblance to the physicist's principle of energy conservation. A liter of water in a closed system is converted to steam and recondensed to liquid. Although the manifest character of the substance has changed profoundly, the physicist assures us that neither the number of molecules of water nor the amount of energy in the system has been altered. A copper bar placed in a clear acid solution turns the liquid into the deep blue of copper sulfate, but the chemist knows that the amount of copper remains unchanged. Many social scientists believe in the conservation of selected motivational and affective processes that assume different behavioral disguises. But when the scientist begins to gather data, he usually searches for behavioral similarities, rather than continuities in expectancies, motives, standards, or sources of anxiety that are expressed in different behavioral forms. Let us call this phenomenon "continuity of the psychological genotype," in contrast to continuity of the behavioral phenotype.

Convincing examples of genotypic continuity of psychic processes with behavioral change are few in number, but sufficiently persuasive to warrant more confident study of this brand of continuity. Emmerich (1964) has reported that aggressive, extroversive three-year-old children become socially poised five-year-olds, whereas the "well-behaved" three-year-olds often become anxious and withdrawn kindergarten children. The aggressive behavior of the three-year-old was not stable but perhaps his *expectancy of acceptance from both peer and adult* was the stable underlying dimension that produced the manifestly different responses at three and five years.

Behavioral passivity with adults in a ten-year-old boy is not conserved in the 25-year-old adult. But the passive ten-year-old is likely to avoid selection of a traditionally masculine vocation or masculine interests. The genotypic process that may have been conserved was anxiety over ability to assume the masculine role. The public forms of this process were different at 10 and 25 years of age.

CLASSES OF CONTINUITY

Postulation of three different types of continuity is, altogether, intuitively reasonable and empirically testable. Let us call these categories (a) complete continuity, (b) genotypic continuity, and (c) phenotypic continuity.

When continuity is complete both basic psychological process and manifest form of behavior remain stable. This class of stability is most likely to occur after puberty when the rate of change of basic components of personality organization is slowing down. The motives for group acceptance and mastery have become established and the desire to match behavior to internalized standards is usually strong by early adolescence. The 13-year-old boy who is competitive and involved in athletics because of a desire to match behavior to a sex-role standard is likely to display phenotypically similar behavior a decade later. The desire to maintain congruence with sex-role standards as well as the specific instrumental behaviors that gratify this desire remain stable for a long period of time.

Complete continuity between times t_1 and t_2 is most likely to occur when (a) the t_1 observation occurred sometime after puberty, (b) the genotypic construct was operative at both ages (e.g., desire to maintain congruence with sex-role standards; desire for social recognition; expectancy of hostility from others), and (c) the overt behaviors were not subject to inhibition or suppression because they violated societal norms for age or sex-role appropriate action.

When the psychological process remains stable but the form of the behavior changes we have an instance of *genotypic continuity*. A 6-year-old child who has strong anxiety over potential rejection or abandonment by his mother may be afraid to leave home and, as a result, refuse to go to school. At age 12, when display of a phobic reaction to school is regarded as regressive by both child and parent, the child may substitute excessive obedience to parents as a way of retaining a close tie to the parent and minimizing threat of rejection. If the parents value school achievement, the child may exhibit intense efforts at academic mastery. Anxiety over loss of nurturance was a basic component of the child's repertoire of fears at both ages. However, at age 6 the desire to reduce anxiety over possible rejection led to avoidance of school; whereas, at age 10 it elicited a zealous attitude toward school work.

Continuity of a psychological genotype can occur during any era of development if one believes that a core set of basic dimensions ties one epoch of development to the next. The absence of phenotypic continuity to match the stability of the genotype is most likely during the first decade of development when the child is learning more effective ways of gratifying motives; and family and peers are insisting that the child inhibit responses inappropriate to his age and sex role.

The third species of continuity, that of the behavioral phenotype, is a form of "fool's gold." In this case the topography of the behavior remains stable, but the response is issued in the service of different motives, standards, expectancies or sources of anxiety. There are several varieties of this species. Allport's (1961) concept of the functional autonomy of behavior is one variant. The story of the man who goes to sea to avoid the stress of a harried home life and comes to adopt the mariner's way for twenty years contains, as its moral, the idea that one motive may initiate a particular act, but a different motive can maintain that act with no obvious break in display of the behavior. A related dynamic includes instances in which a behavior is initially learned and maintained in the service of one motive, drops out of the behavioral repertoire for a period, and reappears at a later date in the service of a different set of forces. Our earlier example of "crying" is illustrative of this class. The 6-month-old child typically cries in response to strange events. The 6-year-old uses the cry as an instrumental strategy to avoid a coercive restriction; the 36-year-old cries as a result of task failure. The events that released the act of crying are markedly different at each of these ages, and there is no compelling theoretical basis for expecting that the infant who cries easily in response to novel events will be the adult who will cry at task failure.

It may seem gratuitous to endow any theoretical status to phenotypic stabilities that are not based on the same genotypic processes. However, this is a rash judgment. The public reacts more to the behaviors it witnesses than to the hidden intentions it may infer. Behaviors are maintained for long periods of time by social reward and punishment, despite important shifts in basic expectancies, standards, motives and sources of anxiety within the person. The uneasiness we feel toward the mica-thin mask of sincerity that dresses our culture reflects an acknowledgment that behavioral veneers can remain stable despite marked psychic changes within the individual.

DOMAINS OF CONSISTENCY AND CONTINUITY

The belief that a person carries some cognitive and behavioral dispositions for a reasonably long time is part of the catechism of psychological theory. The murky idea of "personality" is of no meaning without a commitment to the notion of enduring structures. We can speak of enduring structures for the infant in the crib, the preschooler with his parent, the youngster with his peers, or the mother with her child. The sections that follow are a selective summary of some recent studies of these varied faces of continuity. The sampling is intended to cover those domains that are of maximal interest to students of the socialization process.

Continuity from Childhood to Early Adulthood

A recent study of stability of behavior used the longitudinal population studied by the staff of the Fels Research Institute (Kagan & Moss, 1962). The investigation yielded evidence for both genotypic and phenotypic continuity. Each of 71 adults (36 men and 35 women) was interviewed and observed in his early twenties by one psychologist. A second psychologist quantified behavioral observations gathered on these subjects from their birth through age 14. The details of the procedure are summarized elsewhere (Kagan & Moss, 1962). The major conclusions were based on the correlations between behavior during each of four childhood periods (0–3, 3–6, 6–10, 10–14 years of age) and the adult test and interview protocols. These correlations furnished evidence for genotypic and complete continuity. The relation between behavior during the age period 6–10 and adulthood suggested genotypic continuity. School age boys who were passive in time of stress were not necessarily passive in most stress situations as adults. But as adults, these passive boys were not involved in heterosexual relationships (neither engaged nor married) ($r = .57$), avoided competitive activities and vocations ($r = .58$), and adopted interests that were not concordant with traditional standards for masculinity. Although there was no strong evidence for stability of the phenotypic behavior of passive-withdrawal to stress, one might infer that anxiety over lack of congruence with traditional sex-role standards did remain stable. During the early childhood years such anxiety might lead to a passive posture with other boys and in adulthood to an avoidance of heterosexual relations and reluctance to select masculine vocations or avocational pursuits. Among females there was greater evidence of phenotypic stability of passive-withdrawal from childhood to adulthood. Since the overt passivity seemed to be the product of similar forces at both ages, it is an example of complete continuity.

Aggressive behavior, on the other hand, showed an opposite pattern. Aggressive behavior during the early school years predicted similar responses in adulthood for males. The correlation between the "tendency to display tantrums" during age 6–10 and ease of anger arousal in adulthood was .37 for males but only .03 for adult women. However, the data for women argued for genotypic continuity. Women who displayed frequent tantrums at 6–10 were more likely to be highly motivated in high school and college, reluctant to be dependent on other people, and likely to be masculine in their interests but not usually openly aggressive. As with the male, the genotype that seemed to endure was a tendency to avoid adoption of normative feminine-role behaviors.

A fundamental determinant of the degree of complete continuity was the degree to which the behavior was congruent with sex-role standards. When the behavior met sex-role standards there tended to be phenotypic or complete continuity over time. When the behavior did not meet sex-role standards, complete continuity was attenuated and there was evidence for genotypic continuity. Aggressive behavior, which is appropriate for males, showed complete continuity for the men but seemed to display genotypic continuity for the female. Passive-withdrawal behavior, on the other hand, which is not sex-role appropriate for males, showed genotypic continuity for men but complete continuity for women. This argument is supported by the fact that the tendency to adopt behaviors congruent with sex-role standards was stable from the early school years to adulthood ($r = .63$ for men and $r = .44$ for women).

Evidence for complete continuity was most relevant for mastery behavior, especially high levels of performance in school. Achievement orientation toward intellectual mastery during the period 10–14 years predicted phenotypically similar behavior in adulthood ($r = .66$ for men and $r = .49$ for women).

These results suggest an hypothesis related to the likelihood of obtaining genotypic or complete continuity. When a specific behavior is congruent with the traditional definition of sex-role appropriate behavior it will be predictive of phenotypically similar behavior in adulthood. When it conflicts with traditional sex-role standards there is likely to be genotypic continuity in which the child's behavior finds expression in a substitute response that is socially more acceptable.

A study by Emmerich (1964) furnishes additional support for the notion of genotypic continuity during the preschool years. Each of the 38 middle-class preschool children was observed for 5-minute time samples during each of four consecutive semesters of nursery school attendance. The average age of children was 3.1 years at the beginning of the first semester. The observers classified the children's actions within one of seven categories and thirty-four subcategories. The variables within semesters were correlated and subjected to four independent factor analyses. There seemed to be complete continuity for an introversion-extroversion dimension, or what Emmerich calls an interpersonal-impersonal dimension. This behavioral category was relatively stable across the four consecutive semesters of nursery school attendance. However, an interesting transformation occurred during the fourth semester. The child who previously had been extroversive and mildly hostile in behavior became socially poised and nonaggressive. The child who had been introversive and socially cooperative became socially insecure and awkward. The lack of phenotypic continuity for a behavior one might label "hostile extroversion" was compensated by evidence for genotypic continuity. The "hostile extroversion" may have been the behavioral result of a high expectancy of adult acceptance. The child who trusted adults and viewed them as nurturant might be a bit wild at age 3 but easily persuaded to eliminate this behavior if adults requested it. Thus by age 5 this child might appear to be mature. The child who was overly cooperative at 3 years of age may have been anxious over adult acceptance. This anxiety grew and may have expressed itself in insecurity two years later. The developmental transformation during the fourth semester, when a previously interpersonal negative child became poised, whereas his previously impersonal counterpart showed social insecurity illustrates how a child's profile of behavior can change while covert processes may remain stable.

A second study, akin to Emmerich's investigation, also produces evidence for genotypic continuity (Byram, 1966). The subjects were 43 preschool children, 21 girls and 22 boys, who had been observed at the Fels Research Institute. The protocols consisted of 5-minute observations made on each child by a trained observer. The observations covered three different time periods, each spaced about six months apart. The subjects were about $3\frac{1}{2}$ years of age during the first observation period and about 5 years during the third. Aggression among 3-year-old boys (teasing, tattling, toy-taking, name-calling, and shoving) was not phenotypically stable from age $3\frac{1}{2}$ to 5 ($r = .08$). However, aggressive behavior at $3\frac{1}{2}$ predicted masculine-role play at age 5 ($r = .49$,

$p < .05$), and assertiveness with others ($r = .50$, $p < .05$). Similarly, social isolation (staring out the window, playing with one's back to the room, lying on one's back alone, or sucking one's thumb) was not predictive of similar indexes of social isolation at age 5 ($r = .09$). Isolated activity at $3\frac{1}{2}$, however, predicted feminine-role behavior at age 5 ($r = .50$, $p < .05$). The genotype of outgoing-masculine behavior versus introversive-feminine behavior seemed to be stable, although it found different behavioral expression at $3\frac{1}{2}$ than at 5 years. These data, together with those of Emmerich, and Kagan and Moss, argue for the occurrence of transformations in the external form of responses while underlying dimensions remain stable over time.

Genotypic Continuities in Cognitive Process

The traditional wall isolating studies of cognitive processes from affective and interpersonal dynamics has been scaled and we are searching for and expecting to find lawful links between these two domains of functioning that appear so different. A just-published study by Pedersen and Wender (1968) furnishes encouragement for those engaged in this search. A group of 30 middle-class boys were observed in a nursery school setting when they were about 30 months old. Their behavior was rated on eleven scales and the scales yielded four clusters— physical contact with adults; seeking attention from adults; oral behavior such as licking, drooling, or sucking; and sustained involvement in a play sequence.

Four years later each boy was tested individually on a cognitive battery that included: (a) verbal subscales from the WISC; (b) performance subscales from the WISC (block design, picture arrangement, mazes); (c) a conceptual sorting test designed to assess preference for relational, categorical, and analytic concepts; and (d) a children's form of the Embedded Figures Test to assess field independence.

The most important results indicated that while the verbal ability of the 6-year-old was independent of any of the four preschool behavior variables (r ranged from $-.24$ to $+.15$), the child's performance on the blocks, picture completion, and mazes was meaningfully related to his earlier social behavior. Specifically, the children who sought physical contact and attention did poorly on the performance tests ($r = -.31$, $p < .05$; $r = -.42$, $p < .05$); whereas the children who did well on the performance scale had displayed sustained involvement with the toys four years earlier ($r = .43$, $p < .01$).

The boys who had sought physical contact were more likely to use relational concepts on the sorting test ($r = .46$, $p < .01$); whereas the involved play subjects preferred categorical concepts ($r = .34$, $p < .05$).

How shall we explain this association between molar behavior with toys and adults at $2\frac{1}{2}$ years of age and performance on problems at age 6? Clearly there is no obvious phenotypic similarity between these behavioral dimensions. There are, admittedly, several *post hoc* interpretations that might be imposed upon these intriguing associations. The author favors the notion of a genotypic conservation of a tendency toward an impulsive-rapid tempo versus a reflective-slower tempo. That is, the child who displays long periods of sustained involvement with a toy can be said to have a high threshold for satiation. He does not become bored easily with a task and he seems capable of a reflective and pensive attitude. The child who is constantly seeking out others is likely to be less capable of such a posture. The negative correlation between attention-seeking and sustained play at 2½ $(r = -.48)$ supports this contention.

It is well known that quality of performance on the Kohs blocks, mazes, or picture arrangement tests is impaired by an impulsive attitude. These problems have response uncertainty and the child who offers an answer quickly or implements an hypothesis without sufficient consideration for its validity will get a poorer score on these tests. The use of the relational concepts on the sorting test is also correlated with an impulsive attitude—an initially quick selection of the first hypothesis that occurs to the child. Thus, one might argue that the pattern of associations in the Pedersen-Wender study reflects genotypic continuity of a conceptual tempo variable.

Recent results from our longitudinal investigation add important support to this speculative notion. It will be recalled that one of our samples consists of 44 boys and 43 girls, first born, Caucasian, who have been observed at 4, 8 and 13 months of age. One of the procedures at 4 months assesses the child's pattern of fixations to a set of achromatic slides of human faces that are illustrated in Figure 24.1. The child lies on his back in a crib and the stimuli are presented 20 inches from the plane of the child's face. Each of the four different stimuli is presented for 30 seconds with a 15 second interstimulus interval during which the visual field is blank. Each stimulus is presented four times (16 trials in all) in a random order that is the same for all infants. We shall be concerned here with the *length of the child's first fixation to each of the stimuli*. This variable is independently coded by two observers (intercoder reliability .97). Study of the change in first fixation times over the 16 trials reveals that some children show dramatic decreases in fixation time as the trials proceed; others show little change in fixation time, and are looking at the faces as long on trial 16 as they did on trials 1 or 2. We shall call the former group *rapid habituators* and the latter group *slow habituators*. The semantic link to the notion of rapid versus slow tempo is obvious. Some infants did not fit easily into either habituation group. When we eliminated these infants and those who did not complete the visual episode due to extreme irritability, we were left with 26 boys and 24 girls (ten rapid-tempo and six slow-tempo boys; eleven rapid- and thirteen slow-tempo girls).

One of the procedures at 8 months of age was a free-play session in which the child's behavior was observed for 15 minutes in a room 11 × 11 feet square. The mother was seated in a corner of the room and a standard set of toys was arranged in a given order (toys were a wooden bug, plastic dog, pail, wooden blocks, mallet, peg board, shaft of quoits, toy lawnmower, and furry dog). A complete account of the child's actions was recorded. We were concerned primarily with the frequency with which the child changed activities. The play of an 8-month-old infant in this context is relatively stereotyped. He

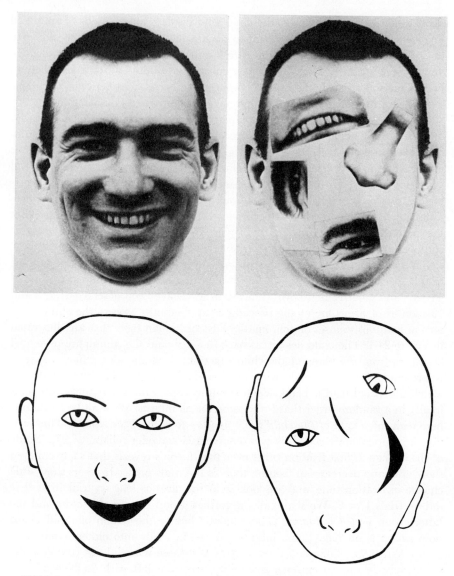

FIGURE 24.1.   Achromatic stimuli shown to 4-month-old infants.

sucks, manipulates, and pushes objects. The tempo is generally slow and there is minimal locomotor movement. The index of "tempo of play" was number of act changes, where an act change was tallied each time the infant changed his manipulative involvement from one toy to another. For example, if a child began the session by playing with the blocks and then put them down and began to play with the pegboard, an act change would be scored. Since the children spent most of their time interacting with the toys, number of act changes is a good index of the rate at which the child habituated or satiated on a particular activity. We expected, therefore, that the infants who displayed rapid habituation to the faces at 4 months would show the greatest number of act changes at 8 months. A 2 × 2 analysis of variance (with sex and tempo of habituation as the two factors) revealed no main effect, but a highly significant interaction ($F = 27.6$, $p < .001$). The rapid-habituating boys displayed more act changes than slow-habituating boys (29.6 vs. 16.3 acts, $t = 2.95$; $p < .01$); but rapid-habituating girls had fewer act changes than the slow-habituating girls (12.4 vs. 28.9 acts, $t = 3.03$; $p < .01$). Biserial correlations between rate of habituation at four months ($1 =$ rapid; $2 =$ slow) and number of acts at eight months revealed coefficients of $-.53$ ($p < .01$) for boys and $+.63$ ($p < .01$) for the girls.

Although rate of habituation was correlated with absolute length of fixation time (that is, slow habituators had longer fixation times ($r = .50$ for boys; .63 for girls), there was no significant association between length of fixation at four months and number of acts at eight months. Rate of habituation was a better predictor of tempo of play at eight months than was length of fixation.

Results from two independent studies are congruent with this finding and will be briefly summarized. A sample of predominately later-born children (12 boys and 10 girls) was also seen at 4 and 8 months of age under similar conditions. At 4 months the infants were shown four different three-dimensional sculptured faces. However, the procedures of administration were identical. These infants were also observed in the 8-month free-play situation described above. Rapid-habituating boys showed more act changes than the slow-habituating boys; there was no relation between these variables for girls. A final investigation was cross-sectional in design and involved 13-month-old children. The subjects were 24 lower-middle-class and 24 middle-class infants (half boys and half girls in each group).[1] Most of the lower-middle-class parents had not completed high school and none had entered college; the occupations of the fathers were unskilled and semiskilled. The middle-class parents were all high school or college graduates and the fathers in white collar or professional vocations.

Each infant was presented with a set of visual stimuli and observed in a free-play session. Each of six achromatic stimuli was presented three times in a fixed order and for a total of 18 presentations. The stimuli were three human faces (photograph of a man's face, photograph of a woman's face, and a schematic drawing of a man's face) and three non-facial stimuli (a bull's eye, a checker board and a nursing bottle). Each stimulus was presented for twelve seconds and the interstimulus interval was twelve seconds. Following the visual episode the mother and baby were brought to the same playroom described

---

[1] The lower-class infants were tested by Stanley Messer at Harvard University; the middle-class infants were seen by Michael Lewis and the author at the Fels Research Institute.

earlier and the child's behavior was observed for fifteen minutes during which number of act changes was coded.

Since the sample sizes were small and the fixation times generally short, it was difficult to construct two discrete habituation groups. It was decided, therefore, to use per cent change in first fixation time from the first six to the last six trials as the index of habituation. This index was derived by subtracting the first fixation times to the last six trials from the first fixation times to the first six trials and dividing this difference by the latter value. This ratio was correlated with the number of acts during the free play. There was a positive correlation between number of acts and a rapid rate of habituation for the boys ($r = .61$, $p < .05$ for the lower-middle-class group and .59, $p < .05$ for the middle-class group). Among the girls, the correlations were $r = -.81$ ($p < .01$) for the lower-middle-class and $-.15$ for the middle-class. The same pattern that emerged in the earlier two experiments with younger infants appeared again with 1-year-old children.

The results of these three studies suggest that, among boys, a rapid rate of habituation to meaningful stimuli is predictive of a rapid rate of satiation in play. It should be noted that a rapid rate of habituation at 4 months did not predict rate of habituation or fixation time at 8 months; there was minimal phenotypic continuity between looking patterns at 4 and 8 months. But an attribute which we like to call "tempo of information processing" seems to display continuity. This psychological dimension expressed itself in rate of habituation at 4 months and in number of acts in a free-play situation 4 months later. It is tempting to suggest that the children with many acts per unit time at 8 months, the fast-tempo children, are similar to the 2½-year-old children in the Pedersen and Wender study who sought attention from adults and did not become involved in long periods of sustained play. These are the children, it will be recalled, who at 6 years of age obtained poor scores on the performance scales of the Wechsler intelligence test. It is reasonable to predict that there may be genotypic continuity of a "tempo of processing" dimension that spans the era from 4 to 72 months and displays itself in different ways at different ages.

The fact that this bond of continuity is more striking for boys than for girls argues that this dimension may be biologically based, or that biological factors are more influential for this attribute for boys than for girls. This notion is supported by the fact that there is a moderately strong association between rate of habituation among boys at 4 months and subsequent weight at 8 months of age. Rapid-habituating boys weighed less than the slow-habituating boys at 8 months ($t = 2.71$; $p < .01$). Rapid-habituating boys were also slightly lighter than the slow-habituating infants at 4 months of age, but this difference was not significant. If length and weight are looked at jointly (mean z score on each dimension), 53 per cent of the slow-habituating boys fell in the quadrant labeled heavy and long; they were the largest boys in the sample. Only 10 per cent of the rapid-habituating boys were in this quadrant. On the other hand, 40 per cent of the rapid-habituating boys versus only 29 per cent of the slow-habituating were in the category light and short. There is a suggestion that the small boys were rapid habituators; the large heavy boys were the slow habituators. Among girls there was no difference in weight, length, or body size between rapid- versus slow-habituating infants.

The "tempo of processing" dimension furnishes a particularly good illustration of genotypic continuity. Man's description of man has always contained reference to this type of dimension from Hippocrates' postulation of the phlegmatic versus sanguine types through Jung's suggestion of the introversion-extroversion dimension. But the external behavioral signs of this attribute have varied for different developmental stages. Students of the young infant have differentiated the active from the passive baby. Observers of preschool children typically distinguish between the hyperkinetic, restless youngster and the child who can sit quietly for long periods of time. We are not suggesting that these behavioral dimensions are all indexes of the same process. That would be theoretically foolish and empirically unsound. We are implying, however, a more modest conclusion; namely that existing evidence is strong enough to warrant the suggestion that some of the variance in these complex behaviors may be attributable to a "tempo" construct—a process that may have long term stability despite changes in the manifest behaviors that serve it.

Continuity in Mother's Behavior with Child

The relationship between mother and child is a delicate ballet. We used to believe that a mother's behavior was purely a function of her motives and conflicts and thus, continuity was assumed to be dependent upon continuities in her own personality. We now recognize this to be too simple a belief. Some of the mother's behavior is guided by her motives and anxieties, but much is under the control of her child.

The two basic dimensions that have been studied with greatest fervor are the dimensions of maternal acceptance—hostility and restriction-autonomy. Studies of the continuity of these behaviors have not been impressive although there has been some evidence to suggest more continuity for an accepting-hostile attitude than a restrictive-autonomy-giving attitude. However, let us analyze the meaning of these words. The operational definitions for maternal rejection obviously cannot be the same for all cultural groups. Mothers in the isolated rural areas of Northern Norway do not talk to their children as much as American parents and they will be observed to move them away from doorways with an indifference that is characteristic of the treatment shown a pair of shoes that is out-of-place. An American psychologist would be prone to label this behavior as rejecting if he saw it in a middle-class Chicago mother. It may be a mistake, however, to view this act as indicative of rejection in this population. Rejection has two meanings: it is an attitude of dislike of mother toward child or the child's perception that he is not valued. It is not immediately obvious which specific behaviors should be regarded as the best operational indexes of either concept. Thus, studies of continuity of a rejecting or accepting parental attitude will have to accept the fact that there may be minimal phenotypic continuity, despite the possible presence of genotypic continuity.

The restrictive-permissive dimension in maternal behavior bears a closer resemblance to concrete behavioral events than the acceptance-hostility continuum. The controlling mother consistently punishes deviations from her standards, prevents the child's exploration of new areas, and punishes excessive independence of action. However, the degree to which a mother controls her child must be, in part, a function of the degree to which he requires control. The mother-child dyad is a feedback system in which the mother typically tends to react to the child in a way that is congruent with her internalized ideal for him. Maternal control will be governed, in part, by the child's behavior. A mother's contemporaneous behavior with her 5-year-old is often the reaction to his behavior at that time or during the previous twelve months, rather than an early antecedent of the behavior he is displaying.

Aside from the suggestion that an attitude of affection-hostility is more stable from infancy through preadolescence than an attitude of control-permissiveness (Schaefer & Bayley, 1963), there have been no detailed studies that have involved observations of the mother over relatively short periods of time in order to establish the forms that continuity might take. A rare exception is a longitudinal study being conducted at the National Institute of Mental Health. Howard Moss observed mothers and infants at 3 weeks and 3 months in the natural context of the home. He recorded a variety of discrete behavioral categories during a typical day. The maternal behaviors that showed the greatest stability between 3 weeks and 3 months involved social contact with the infant (affectionate contact yielded a correlation of .64; looks at infant, .37; talks to infant, .58; smiles at infant, .66). A common dimension implicit in these acts is communicative contact with the infant. The maternal behaviors that showed minimal stability were: holding the infant distant, total amount of holding of the infant, burping the infant, and stressing the musculature of the infant. These reactions were not stable over time and they became less frequent with age. The infant becomes a dramatically different organism between 3 weeks and 3 months, for the 12-week-old requires much less close physical handling than the 3-week-old infant. The decrease in close physical contact is a function of the child's decreasing needs for such caretaking actions. These maternal behaviors are controlled in large measure by the behavior of the infant, rather than by the mother's motives. As a result, there is little phenotypic continuity for these acts. The tendency to smile and vocalize to the infant, however, seems more closely tied to the mother's motives and standards and these show phenotypic continuity.

The mother's actions are shaped by her child in many domains. At 3 weeks the boys cried more than the girls, and, as a result, boys elicited more maternal physical contact than girls. However, the mother had extinguished her "tending" behavior by the time the boy was 3-months old, presumably because she learned that her son was not easily quieted by her nurturance. The boy's refusal to quiet led her to desist in her attempts to placate him.

There is a complex dialogue between mother and infant. Stabilities in maternal behavior depend on the degree to which the child's behavior controls the mother and the degree to which these infant acts change over time. If the child's behavior remains relatively stable, the mother's behavior will do the same. Since the child undergoes dramatic shifts during the opening years of life, one should not expect marked phenotypic stability for many maternal behaviors during this period.

CONDITIONS FAVORING CONTINUITY OR DISCONTINUITY

Let us consider in the penultimate section of this chapter some heuristic guides for predicting the three classes of continuity listed earlier.

Principle 1. Phenotypic continuity is likely to be minimal during the opening decade of development and especially during the first five years. The form and eliciting conditions of behavior change so dramatically during the early years of life that phenotypic or complete continuity of early behaviors such as crying in response to separation, tantrums to frustration, or withdrawal from a stranger is not to be expected. The major motives and sources of anxiety of 2-year-olds center around the mother and the preservation of the familiar. The 10-year-old is principally concerned with power, sex-role standards, mastery of instrumental competencies, and acceptance by peers. These critical developmental differences in psychological structure militate against strong evidence for complete or phenotypic continuity. However, biologically derived or early acquired predispositions toward rapid or slow tempo—for which evidence is beginning to accumulate—would lead to expectations of some genotypic continuity in information-processing situations, despite the different forms these behaviors might take.

Principle 2. Discontinuity in behavior and process is most likely to follow major changes in the psychological ecology of the child. These changes are usually linked with the birth of a sibling, alteration in the family structure (i.e., divorce, separation), change in the physical integrity of the child, or entrance into a new social context, such as school.

Principle 3. There are critical juncture points in development where reorganizations of behavior and process are likely to occur. Genotypic discontinuities are most likely to occur at these nodal points. One such node is the period before the second birthday. Language becomes a dominant mode of interaction with the environment between 18 and 24 months of age. The child's commerce with objects and people becomes dominated by his symbolic labeling of them and assimilation of new experience demands language resources. The child up to age 2 who has been motorically advanced and psychologically alert has usually been well-adapted to his environment. This child may suddenly appear less adaptive if he is growing in an environment that does not stimulate his language development. On the other hand, a child who has been motorically retarded, and even listless, may suddenly become alert and appear more adaptive because he is in an environment where his language development has been accelerated. There is no strong relation between level of precocity of sensory-motor schemas during the first eighteen months and language resources or IQ at age 3, 6, or 12 years, and the discontinuity in the phenotype is clear. It is not obvious, however, if there is any genotype continuity before and after the emergence of language and what the flavor of these genotypic processes might be.

A second focus of discontinuity occurs between 5 and 7 years of age. Most children undergo a marked increase in their tendency to inhibit irrelevant acts and to select appropriate ones. S. H. White has summarized some of the major behaviors that undergo change during this era (White, 1965). The child stops adopting position habits in his solution of problems and develops his own sense of left and right. Reversals in letters and forms become less frequent and the child is now able to detect the simultaneous touching of both face and hand. He becomes more planful in his play and in his attack upon problems. One of the processes common to many of these changes is an increase in reflection, an increased tendency to pause to consider the differential validity or appropriateness of a response, the ability to select the right response rather than emitting the one that happens to sit on top of the hierarchy when an incentive stimulus appears. This natural shift toward reflection and selection in behavior is demanded by the school environment as well as the family, and the child who is not capable of adopting this reflective posture will encounter more negative sanctions for his impulsive actions than he did during preschool years. The child who has difficulty maintaining appropriate inhibition because of central nervous system deficit or intense psychological conflict will have to develop a new set of defenses to attenuate the anxiety that will inevitably occur. These new defenses are likely to lead to phenotypic discontinuities.

A second characteristic of the period between 5 and 7 years is the common observation that the 5-year-old child's veneer of defenses against anxiety is thin, and evidence of serious sources of anxiety is usually visible. The preschool child who is anxious over separation shows it by clinging to his parent and protesting his reluctance to leave the home or the familiar. The children who are anxious over violation of cleanliness, sexual or aggressive standards will exhibit a tension that is obvious to most observers. During the next three or four years, however, defenses grow rapidly, and although the basic conflict may still exist, the behavioral topography of the child does not always reveal the hidden problem. Children who are seriously frightened, withdrawn, or regressed at age 5 may appear relatively mature and minimally anxious at 10 years of age. The phenotype has changed dramatically. For some, however, the genotype has not been altered to an appreciable degree. When a serious stress is imposed, the genotype is revealed. One of the cases from the Fels longitudinal study illustrates this point. This girl was seriously rejected by her mother during the early years of life and showed extreme lability of mood and excessive tantrums during the early years. At age 5 she was a shy, withdrawn, and frightened child. There were elements of autism in her speech and she appeared suspicious and seriously withdrawn. But after she began school, her behavior began to change. She became more friendly, happier, and less concerned with potential physical harm than she had been during the prekindergarten era.

She was an excellent pupil in elementary school and highly motivated to do well. She appeared to many to be a relatively mature, self-contained child who was not conspicuously different from her peers. Excellence in school became her defense against the hostilities of the world. It gave her power over people she feared and acquired praise from her mother. Thus, the school situation provided this child with a way to attenuate her basic conflicts and her manifest behavior changed markedly. Phenotypic continuity was absent. But when stress was imposed, as during the psychological examination at Fels or following graduation from college, her pathology was revealed. Excerpts from the interview when she was 22 years old betrayed the basic anxiety and fragile defenses which were seen when she was a 5-year-old but which were partially hidden during the interim years.

Louise was 22 years old when she appeared for the adult assessment. She was fairly attractive, single, and recently graduated from college. Initially, she was cooperative and superficially relaxed, but bursts of inappropriate laughter punctuated the interviews.

One of the most striking aspects of Louise's verbal behavior was her inability to answer questions directly. She was usually seduced into reporting tangential associations and many of her answers lasted several minutes, but were unrelated to the interviewer's questions.

> E: "We would like to know what has been happening to you since high school, and the various reasons for your doing the things you did. So go back to your senior year in high school. . . ."

> S: "Well the senior year in high school I was the art editor of our Yearbook and one of my ambitions was to, ah, was to be that of art editor of the Yearbook and I had wanted to be for quite a long time and I, ah, don't remember whether it was the senior year or before that I worked on the paper in the funny paper, for a very short term, it didn't go over too big, but we did have a lot of fun doing it and, ah, I was in the class play and, ah, Cheaper by the Dozen, I was the mother and so, ah, well ah, this that and the other thing, pretty active in things, mostly the things I was active in were the more scholastic things and never was too, ah, I was never too active in the physical ed—education part because I think it was due to the fact that, ah, I, I couldn't make it when I was farther down in high school, I couldn't make it living on a farm to, to ah, get to all the meetings and the kids that lived in town all went down to the court and played and because of that, they kept the ball and wouldn't play with me so I just went ahead in the parts that I could go with. And it was more scholastic and, ah, more of the, ah, ah, different things like—I became

pretty popular and won all the things that they hand to you and so forth, as far as beauty queen (laugh)."

This open-ended question was the first inquiry of the interview. Louise replied to this initial, general probe by reporting that she had a status position in high school. The intrusion of the irrelevant phrase "they kept the ball and wouldn't play with me" illustrates the way concrete experience broke the coherence of her narrative. This behavior was frequent during the interview.

A second anomaly in Louise's behavior was her preoccupation with physical harm and the integrity of her body. In discussing her choice of a major in college, she mentioned her defective eyesight.

> S: "I had gone up with my, ah, zoology professor and seven other girls and we went through a lab and saw the medical technologists at work. At the hospital up there, I saw the apparatus and understood that there are three or four different fields of medical technology and I always worried about my eyesight a little bit because I always heard there was quite a bit of microscopic work and, ah, then I talked to my optometrist about that and he said that I needn't worry. He wore glasses and that if I ever go into a hospital that I planned to work on for any, any length of time that they grind the top lens for you according to your eyes and so, ah, that sort of abolished that and I felt free to go into the field as far as my eyesight was concerned."

Finally, Louise showed a paranoid suspicion of the social environment and she spoke repeatedly about the jealousy and petulant aggression of others and of her attempt to maintain a wall between herself and other people.

Louise's adult behavior reflected serious personality and cognitive disorganization that seemed to have an historical link to her preschool status. It is to be noted that her manifest behavior during the pre- and early-adolescent years was not as publically disorganized as her preschool patterns. Louise's development is to be contrasted with a more common pattern in which symptomatic behavior develops first during early adolescence. The adolescent becomes preoccupied with death and sexuality, tries out drugs, engages in a delinquent act. The majority of these adolescents do not manifest the severity of pathology in adulthood that we saw in Louise. It is possible that open signs of psychological disturbance during the preschool years are more indicative of serious disturbance and, therefore, more predictive of adult pathology than symptomatic signs surrounding the adolescent era in children who have not shown any prior pathology.

SUMMARY

The desire to know the stable components of an individual's psychological organization is merely one exemplar of our more general need to know what is real and continuous; to ascertain the invariant attributes that define an object.

Science is man's institutionalized attempt to detail the constant in a sea of random change. The broad appeal of Erikson's (1950) term "identity" borrows its attractiveness from our insatiable requirement for believing in islands of personal continuity.

Earlier generations turned their attention to continuities in behavior. This prejudice was necessary because of the absence of any theory that gave direction to other places to look. When we know nothing we have no choice but to code what we see and to infuse those public events with theoretical meaning. Although we still lack a formal and forceful theory of human behavior, we are not completely bankrupt. Most behavioral scientists can be persuaded to agree that motives, standards, beliefs, sources of anxiety, and defenses are critical processes, and that biological predispositions give differential direction to behavioral stability and change.

There is often an implicit assumption that the potential for variety in behavior is equal to that of the possible diversity in covert processes; that there is sufficient variety in overt behavior to match the interactions of motives, standards, beliefs, anxieties, and defenses and their permutations in different situational contexts. I do not believe this assumption is reasonable. There seems to be less freedom or possible variability in the behavioral system than there is in the complex covert forces that shape it. Each response must serve different forces. The act of crying must serve, at the minimum, fear, happiness, requests for help, protest, and sadness, if not other less common needs. Smiling must serve comprehension, happiness, the need for social acceptance, and revenge. We have a situation in which a small troupe of actors must put on all of Shakespeare's plays and each actor must play several roles. The greater variability of covert process in comparison with manifest response must produce a disruption of phenotypic continuity for many behaviors. Moreover, there are developmental changes in the prepotency of the tie of particular behaviors to particular processes. Crying is the strongest reaction to frustration at 5 years but not at 15; hitting is a primary reaction to hostile feelings at 6 years but not at 26. If responses change we may or may not have a change in underlying structure.

A particular overt behavior is only a moderately reliable guide to structure. Some may see this position as specious and remark that the psychologist is only interested, after all, in understanding and predicting behavior. If the behavior changes, that is all we need to know or be concerned about. But there is a need to be concerned with continuities and discontinuities in motives, conflicts, beliefs, and sources of anxiety. Each class of behavior is typically ambiguous as to its meaning and it is likely that the inflection points for discontinuity in phenotypic responses may not resemble those that mark changes in genotypic process. In the decades ahead we must discover the inflection points and begin to map behaviors on processes as we map attributes on genes. This task will require much more rigorous theory than we have and more careful longitudinal observations. Only then will we attain this exasperatingly difficult goal.

REFERENCES

ALLPORT, G. W. *Pattern and growth in personality.* New York: Holt, Rinehart & Winston, 1961.

BYRAM, C. Longitudinal study of aggressive and self-assertive behavior in social intention. Unpublished honors thesis, Radcliffe College, 1966.

EMMERICH, W. Continuity and stability in early social development. *Child Development,* 1964, 35, 311–332.

ERIKSON, E. H. *Childhood and society.* New York: Norton, 1950.

KAGAN, J., & MOSS, H. A. *Birth to maturity.* New York: Wiley, 1962.

PEDERSEN, F. A., & WENDER, P. H. Early social correlates of cognitive functioning in six-year-old boys. *Child Development,* 1968, 39, 185–194.

PIAGET, J. *The origins of intelligence in children.* London: Kegan Paul, Trench, Trubner, 1932.

SCHAEFER, E. S., & BAYLEY, N. Maternal behavior, child behavior, and their interactions from infancy through adolescence. *Monograph for Research in Child Development,* 1963, 28, Serial No. 87, 1–127.

WHITE, S. H. Evidence for a hierarchical arrangement of learning processes. In L. P. Lipsitt & C. C. Spiker (Eds.), *Advances in child behavior and development.* (Vol. 2) New York: Academic Press, 1965.

PART IV
SPECIAL CONTEXTS
OF SOCIALIZATION

CHAPTER **25**

Socialization
In Correctional Institutions

Stanton Wheeler

Yale University

One of the most obvious but important features of socialization processes is that they take place within a broader social context. The structure of that social context may be expected to have an important effect upon the nature of the socialization process itself. A potential contribution of sociologists to the study of socialization processes, therefore, may be made through the analysis of the settings within which socialization takes place.

Increasingly in modern societies, those settings are large scale formal organizations. Just as industrialization has brought on the development of massive industrial and business organizations, so has it led to the development of organizations for the processing of people: the school, the university, the mental hospital and prison, as well as a variety of related organizations (Brim & Wheeler, 1966). And increasingly, such organizations are thought of not merely as places to train or contain people, but as sources of fundamental change in their attitudes, beliefs, and conceptions of themselves and their place in society. The prison is one such setting. It differs from more traditional socializing organizations in many ways. But like the school or university, socialization processes do indeed go on there, whether they follow the patterns intended by the prison staff or not.

It is my purpose in this chapter to examine socialization processes within the prison, with emphasis on the social organization and culture of the prison as it has an impact on socialization, and particularly on the relationship between what an inmate experiences within the prison, and his attachments to the outside world. Although these problems could be discussed in the standard fashion of a review article, I find it easier to get into them through the tracing of the changes that have occurred in my own thinking about socialization processes in the prison over the course of some ten or twelve years during which I have been reading and reflecting on the work of others in this area, and conducting research projects

I am indebted to Hugh F. Cline, Howard E. Freeman, Anne Romasco and David Ward for helpful criticism of an early draft of this chapter.

of my own. Over the course of that period of time, I have been forced to modify my own thoughts on the process in response to new data and observations from studies my colleagues and I have conducted, and in response to the ideas generated and developed by others in our field. Very largely, these changes have required moving beyond the immediate experiences to which inmates are exposed in the prison, to the nature of its culture and social organization, and finally to its connection with the external world.

SOCIALIZATION IN A STATE REFORMATORY

Until the decade of the 1950's the most serious effort to understand the process of socialization in prison was that of Donald Clemmer (1958). Clemmer was a sociologist with many years of experience behind the walls of prisons and he produced the first book-length study of a prison as a community. Clemmer described the culture and social organization of the prison, and noted that most of the characteristics he found suggested a system distinctly harmful to anything that might be regarded as a process of rehabilitation: The norms and codes of the inmate world appear to be organized in opposition to those of conventional society. He then turned his attention to the process by which inmates become a part of that world. He used the concept of *prisonization* as a summarizing concept revealing the consequences of exposure to inmate society. He defined prisonization as "the taking on, in greater or lesser degree, of the folkways, mores, customs and general culture of the penitentiary." And while he felt that no inmate could remain completely "unprisonized," he devoted a good deal of attention to variables that he thought probably influenced both the speed and the degree of prisonization. Some of these variables reflected the inmates' participation in conventional society. Thus prisonization would be lowest, he felt, for inmates who had positive relationships during pre-penal life, and for those who continued their positive relationships with persons outside the walls during the time they were in prison. But the feature that he thought was most important in determining the degree of prisonization was simply the degree of close interpersonal contact that inmates had with other inmates within the institution. Those who became affiliated with inmate primary groups and those whose work and cell assignments placed them in very close contact with other inmates were likely to show the greatest degree of prisonization.

It was possible to put these ideas to a fairly direct empirical test in a survey research study of Washington State Reformatory (Wheeler, 1961b). An attitude measure of attitudinal conformity versus non-conformity to the values of the staff (and presumably, those of the conventional world) was developed to serve as an empirical indicator reflecting Clemmer's concept of prisonization. And although the study utilized a cross-sectional design rather than a panel design in which we could actually trace changes in attitudes over time, we could at least approximate the temporal aspect of imprisonment by comparing inmates who had been in the institution for varying lengths of time in order to test Clemmer's hypothesis that the longer the duration of stay, the more likely one was to become "prisonized."

The result of this analysis provided strong support for Clemmer's hypotheses. There was a general trend toward greater nonconformity to staff values with increase in length of time in the prison. And the trend was much stronger for those inmates who had made many friends in the institution than for those who were relatively isolated.

But one of the interesting features of Clemmer's account is that he had little to say about what happens to inmates as they prepare to leave the institutions. Many of his ideas about the socialization process in prison were drawn from studies of assimilation of ethnic groups into American life, and since by and large those groups were here to stay, the problem of what happens to them as they prepare to return to a former way of life does not arise. Perhaps for this reason, Clemmer's account has much to say about the early stages of imprisonment and about the general effects of being in prison, with no systematic attention devoted to the process of leaving the prison, and particularly to the possibility that the impact of prison culture is short-lived.

These concerns led us to consider the time measure in studies of prisonization in a manner different from that conceived by Clemmer. Very simply, we divided inmates into three groups: those who had been in only a short time, those who had only a short time remaining to serve, and those who were near neither entry nor release. The general results of this analysis suggested important modifications in Clemmer's original hypotheses. While we found a larger percentage of inmates who were strongly opposed to staff norms during the last stage of their confinement than during the first, we also found a U-shaped distribution of high conformity responses over the three time periods: there were fewer than half as many high conformity respondents during the middle phase than during the early and later phases of imprisonment. These findings suggest that while some inmates might become increasingly alienated during the course of their stay, an even larger number may exhibit the process of prisonization until the middle of their stay, when it is replaced by a process of resocialization to the more conventional values of the outside world. And there was further evidence in support of the latter pattern: The U-shaped pattern of conforming responses was found both for inmates who had developed many friends in the institution and for those who had not, though it was stronger for the former group. It was also found both for first offenders and for recidivists. The clear suggestion from the evidence, then, was that this may well be a systematic feature of response to imprisonment, and not simply a minor deviation from the prisonization theme.

It would be simple enough to add the idea of "anticipatory socialization" to that of prisonization in an effort to make sense of both patterns of data. Indeed, Robert K. Merton (1957) had already written about the process of anticipatory socialization, and in retrospect, there was good reason to assume that such a process would operate, even though it had not been formally incorporated into Clemmer's scheme. But while this would have given us two descriptive labels for two different patterns of empirical results, it would not have moved us very far toward understanding the conditions under which one or the other pattern would be expected to occur. In attempting to move toward the latter aim we were forced to ask questions about the nature of the inmate culture itself, and particularly about the sources that give rise to it.

Almost all accounts of close custody prisons in the United States are in agreement on the fundamental qualities of the inmate world in such institutions (Sykes & Messinger, 1960). Very briefly, three features seem most important:

1. There is a normative order defined largely in opposition to the staff and placing great emphasis on loyalty to other inmates.
2. There is a system of informal social differentiation that is reflected in the series of social types or argot roles noted by Sykes (1958), Schrag (1944) and many others. Special labels are assigned to inmates depending on their mode of response to prison life and expressing the quality of their interaction with staff and inmates. The system of informally defined social types gives evidence both of the dominant values of the inmate world—for the pejoratives always apply to those inmates who support the staff or who exploit other inmates for their own benefit—and of the range of subcultures that form within the walls of the institutions.
3. Accounts of everyday life in American prisons point to numerous struggles for power, frequent involvement in illicit activities, and a fair amount of violence behind the walls. Every institution has its share of fist-fights and occasional knifings, with force used as a means of social control. Though it would be easy to exaggerate such matters, it seems clear that the American prison is not a particularly warm, tolerant or congenial cultural setting. Almost every institution finds that it needs, in addition to the unit designed to hold the assault-minded or escape-risk inmates, a special segregation unit to protect some inmates from others who are out to get them.

Why does the prison so typically show these patterns of inmate response? Two conflicting views can be found. One interpretation is along the lines of "cultural diffusion" theories in anthropology. Very briefly, inmate society is what it is because inmates have imported their antagonism toward law and order from the outside world. The single trait held in common by all inmates is participation in criminal activity. The capacity to engage in criminal acts suggests at least some degree of withdrawal of support from conventional values, and indeed can be viewed as indicating an opposition to conventional norms and values. By bringing together in a twenty-four-hour living establishment individuals who have deviated from conventional norms, the prison offers opportunities for mutual reinforcement of criminal values. Those inmates who occupy prominent positions within the inmate hierarchy and who spend the most time in interaction with their fellows should be the ones whose values are most likely to serve as the basis for the organization and culture of inmate life. And these same inmates, we know from other sources, are those who are likely to be most committed to a criminal value system—those who have followed systematic criminal careers, those who are most hostile and aggressive in their expression of opposition to the staff (Schrag, 1954; Wheeler, 1961a). And if the culture is viewed as an outgrowth of the dominant sort of attitudes entering inmates bring with them, it is reasonable to expect a reinforcement process operating throughout the duration of their confinement. This is consistent with the image of correctional institutions as "crime schools" and with a theory that accounts for the socialization processes in prison largely in terms of a concept such as "prisonization." And this is very much the sort of process hinted at by Clemmer, although he very largely took the values of the inmate system for granted, and did not set out to explain them.

An alternative interpretation of the sources for the inmate culture emerged in the years following Clemmer's work, and received its fullest expression in an analysis of the inmate's social system presented by Gresham Sykes and Sheldon Messinger (1960). Instead of viewing inmate culture as a simple expression, and perhaps extension, of the individual values inmates may bring to the prison, Sykes and Messinger saw the inmate culture as a response to the adjustment problems posed by imprisonment itself, with all of its frustrations and deprivations. Among the important deprivations include the low and rejected status of being an inmate, the material and sexual deprivations of imprisonment, the constant social control exercised by the custodians of the prison, and the presence of other offenders who may be perceived as dangerous and threatening. The normative order and the system of social differentiation discussed above can be seen as responses to the series of deprivations. The normative order may reinstate self-esteem by providing a meaningful reference group that will support an inmate's attack on the staff, and it may lessen the dangers of exploitation on the part of other inmates. Further, the system of social differentiation itself reflects the variety of individual adaptations to the deprivations in question. In short, an alternative to the cultural diffusion scheme is a functional theory in which inmate culture is seen as a response to the conditions of imprisonment rather than an extension of the values men bring to prison.

If this interpretation is valid, we might expect that inmate culture would exert its major impact on inmates during the middle of their stay in prison, at the point in time when they are farthest removed from the outside world. And if the inmate value system is a response to the deprivations of imprisonment, it would seem only natural that as men prepare to leave the prison, those deprivations begin to wane in their significance. Thus they move away from adherence to the inmate value system and toward the values of the conventional society to which they are soon returning. Furthermore, the deprivations themselves may be objectively less severe as men approach release, when they are likely to be allowed more freedom within the walls, and somewhat more of the few amenities prison life may offer.

This provides us with a more substantial theoretical underpinning for the empirical finding of a U-shaped socialization and resocialization cycle within the prison. We are left, then, with two different patterns of change over time in the prison, and with two different and conflicting ideas regarding the sources of inmate culture itself, ideas that might possibly explain one or another of the patterns of adjustment to the prison over time.

SOCIAL ORGANIZATION IN SCANDINAVIAN PRISONS[1]

A clear opportunity to further refine and test these ideas would be provided by a setting in which the prisons are relatively much like those found in the United States, with all their accompanying deprivations, but where the culture of the country as a whole is different. If the primary source of inmate culture lies in the deprivations of imprisonment themselves, the same inmate culture should be found wherever the deprivations are present, and should not vary widely with differences in the nature of the criminal and non-criminal world outside the walls. If differences in the external culture are very important, then we should find that despite a relatively uniform pattern of deprivations, inmate life sharply reflects the culture of the world outside the prison.

Some of the prisons in the Scandinavian countries provide a relevant case in point. In what follows, I shall present two different types of evidence from studies of Scandinavian prisons that enable us to elaborate on the themes developed above. The first is based upon a case study of a single institution in Norway, where we have both observational data and survey research data concerning the nature of inmate organization. The second type of evidence consists of survey data from some fifteen prisons spread throughout the Scandinavian countries, institutions which differ in the composition of their inmate population as well as in the nature of the goals and organization of the prisons themselves.

The major institution for normal long-term adult offenders in Norway is the Botsfengslet in Oslo. The prison houses about 200 offenders serving from six months to life, for crimes ranging from simple theft to treason and murder. It is a particularly interesting case for comparative analysis because its design and philosophy are modeled after American institutions based on the Pennsylvania system of prison architecture, and it is quite similar to Trenton prison, where Sykes' observations were made. Prison design was apparently one of the first elements of American culture to penetrate Norway, coming by way of English prison reformers of the early 19th century. Indeed, the deprivations mentioned in most functional accounts, such as the constant presence of guards, lack of women, attacks on self-esteem, and material deprivations, were clearly present at Botsfengslet, and were apparently felt as strongly by men there as they are by American inmates.

The most striking feature of inmate organization in Botsfengslet is the

[1] The materials in this section are derived from a broader study of Scandinavian prisons being conducted by Hugh F. Cline and the author. We are indebted to many Scandinavian sociologists, but will not attempt to give full acknowledgment of that help here.

apparent weakness of the normative order and the lack of cohesive bonds. Almost all respondents volunteered that the inmates "lacked cohesion." Intensive interviews with a few of the inmates revealed that there was indeed general agreement regarding a minimal normative order, including the injunction not to rat or inform. But the inmates agreed that even this rule was never enforced by coercive pressures. For example, two inmates offered the same story about a former inmate who upon his release had informed the staff about the presence of narcotics and alcohol in the prison. He did the same thing at another institution, and later was returned to Botsfengslet. There was some talk among the prisoners of doing something to him, but in fact after his return no one made a move to harm him. Other examples were given of a similar unwillingness to sanction inmates for violations of inmate norms.

Neither the interviews nor the survey data gave any evidence of organized opposition to the staff. In the questionnaire, for example, only 15 per cent of the inmates said that other inmates often put pressure on them to work less hard than they otherwise would, and only 9 per cent said that inmates often put pressure on other inmates to oppose the staff. One inmate, perhaps a bit extreme, suggested something of the lack of organization and clear opposition: "If someone unlocked all the cells and opened the front gate, not more than three inmates would take off. Most would run to the guard and ask what was happening."

It is important to note that the lack of organization was not due to any sense of being well-treated and therefore having nothing to fight against. In fact, a larger percentage of inmates in this institution than in any others in Norway and Sweden felt that their stay was going to hurt them. Individually, they indicated no great warmth of feeling for their keepers. But the individual complaints had not led to collective resistance. Rather, they seemed to be an atomized and depressed mass.

A similar deviation from the expected strong inmate culture characterizes the special vocabulary found at Botsfengslet. Unlike the American case, there has been almost no development of nouns with a special meaning to depict an inmate's social role in the prison. Patterns of behavior can be described which are similar to those for which a vocabulary has developed in American prisons, but there is no jargon, no institutional shorthand, to refer to them. Three exceptions, however, should be noted. There is a word for "rat," and an expression that literally means "noisemaker," referring to the occasional inmate who disturbs both staff and prisoners by talking too much, gossiping, and in general making a verbal nuisance of himself. Also, there are terms referring to the various roles involved in homosexual relations. But for the most part there is only an embryonic development of a special argot describing behavior patterns in the prison.

This may be due in part to the small number of inmates in Norwegian prisons at any one time. In Norway no more than 500 inmates are serving sentences of more than six months, and it may take a much larger base community to support a separate vocabulary. But this explanation seems doubtful, for there definitely are many terms which have special meaning only to prisoners. Most of these, however, refer not to behavioral patterns and social roles, but to the crime committed by the inmate or the nature of his life outside the institution. Thus, there is a special word for offenders who committed indecent acts with children (as there is in the United States), and a clear distinction between those who committed their acts against boys or against girls (unlike the United States). Another expression, meaning "traveler," characterizes those inmates who were nomadic and wandering in their pre-institutional life. Indeed, if any aspect of the typical American behavior pattern is present at Botsfengslet to a strong degree, it is the norms against asking persons about their pre-prison background or their offense—not the norms against ratting or other pro-staff behavior. The special language draws much more from the everyday vocabulary, and more frequently refers to life outside the institution than is the case in American prisons.

Finally, observations on characteristic behavior patterns in the institution reveal more deviations from the typical American case. I know of no way of getting an adequate picture of the amount of illicit activity in Norwegian institutions, but my impression is that the amount of gambling and homosexual activity, and probably the amount of drinking, is less than it is in comparable American institutions. And one fact is clear: there is almost no violence within the walls. Inmates and staff agreed that there had not been as much as a fist-fight between two Botsfengslet inmates for at least nine months preceding my contact with the institution. One inmate remembered a small fight in the short-term jail in which he had served some time before, but apparently this was remembered simply because fights are so unusual. As a Norwegian colleague expressed it: "Our institutions are like Sunday Schools compared to yours."

In short, the deprivations usually pointed to may be necessary conditions for the emergence of a strong and resistive inmate value system, but the Norwegian evidence suggests that they are not sufficient. Although the deprivations were present at Botsfengslet, the strong inmate culture was lacking. There are, however, four respects in which this is not a complete test of the functional argument.

First, it may be that *other* deprivations are more important than those usually cited, and that these deprivations vary from country to country. One major difference is length of sentence. The average stay in most American institutions is from two to five years. At Botsfengslet, it is much shorter, averaging slightly more than a year. Only life-termers are likely to be sentenced for more than two or three years. It is possible, then, that the differences in sentence length alone would account for much of the variation in the inmate culture.

A second condition concerns the rate of incarceration in Norway compared to the United States. Probation is used more, the crime rate is lower anyway, and officials are reluctant to give prison sentences if there is any alternative. As a result, a much smaller proportion of the criminal population is institutionalized. It may be that the inmate system fails to receive the type of inmate who is best at organizing and generating group opposition.

Third, the apparent normlessness at Botsfengslet may be partially accounted for by the structural constraints on interaction in the prison. One major way in which Botsfengslet departs from current American patterns is that the inmates there are more isolated. As in the American institutions of the turn of the century, inmates at Botsfengslet are locked in at 5 p.m., at the close of the work-day. They eat in their own cells, rather than in the dining hall. Those who go out in the evening must have a special task or assignment, such as band or a school course. Although inmates work together in the shops (as the American prisoners did after the industrial revolution had penetrated into the prison), the general policy is still against fraternization.

All these features make for a much greater degree of isolation than is found in modern American prisons. Indeed, 43 per cent of the inmate population at Botsfengslet report that they have made no friends among other inmates. The comparable figure for the American prison described above is 10 per cent. Thus the constraints on communication and interaction at Botsfengslet may well prevent formation of a solidary inmate culture.

Fourth, and perhaps most important, although it is possible to show that most of the deprivations in American prisons are also objectively present at Botsfengslet, it is not so easy to know whether they are subjectively defined as deprivations by Norwegian prison inmates. It may well be, for example, that inmates from a society that lacks some of the material abundance of the United States do not experience confinement in the same ways that American inmates do. A warm shelter, a clean bed, and three square meals a day—features that both prison systems provide—may have relatively greater value in Norway, with the result that prison itself is experienced as less depriving. Unfortunately, we do not have evidence on these matters of relative deprivation.

Based solely upon the case study of Botsfengslet, however, the most plausible explanation of the difference between inmate culture in Norway and in the United States is that general features of Norwegian society are imported into the prison, and that they operate largely to offset tendencies toward the formation of a solidary inmate group united in its opposition to the staff. The most important element seems to be the virtual absence, in Norway, of a subculture of violence and antagonism. Few offenders use weapons. The police do not carry guns. There are only three or four offenders in the entire country who fit our model of a professional criminal. Younger offenders have not participated extensively in organized delinquent gangs, as have many in this country. Consequently, the thought of using violence as a means of social control simply does not arise. Even the fact that boxing is an important recreational activity in American prisons was surprising and dismaying to the Norwegian inmates. In short, the value American inmates place on being tough, being smart, seeing society in "we-they" terms, is characteristically absent. This in turn would seem to reflect the relatively narrow range of the stratification system, the virtual absence of American-style slums, and the greater homogeneity of Norwegian society.

The relatively greater sense of isolation in Norwegian life, and the related tendency to be more inward-looking, may yield personality components which also work against the formation of social bonds with other inmates. One gets the strong impression that many prisoners, like their counterparts outside, would rather not get deeply enmeshed in an extended social circle. They are more likely to go their own way.

This extended set of observations on a Norwegian prison may seem out of place in a paper intended to deal generally with problems of socialization in prison communities. They are included here simply to indicate in the clearest possible way how much the cultural environment surrounding the prison is likely to influence the internal life of the institution, and along with it the processes of socialization that go on there.

Botsfengslet was one of fifteen institutions in the Scandinavian countries where we were able to collect systematic survey data relating to inmate culture and social organization. One way to examine further the relationship between influences from outside the prison versus the deprivations from within is to find out which of these possible sources of influence bears the strongest relationship to the formation of an anti-staff culture and set of attitudes among the inmates (Cline & Wheeler, 1968). We developed an index of the degree to which inmates felt that others held attitudes in opposition to those of the staff, an index which could be applied across the fifteen institutions. The range of responses on that index, without presenting the evidence here, indicates clearly that there is a wide variation in the extent to which an anti-staff climate tends to develop in different institutions. It is thus a perpetuation of a stereotype to assume that all prisons are alike.

What is most striking is that the variation in anti-staff culture and attitudes can be accounted for much better by examining the type of inmate that flows into the system than it can by examining the nature of the prison itself. The best single predictor of the anti-staff climate in these fifteen prisons is the median age of their inmates at first arrest. The older the median age of first arrest, the less the climate of the institution is one that is polarized in opposition to the staff (−.80). The youth institutions in our sample tend to be the highest in anti-staff climate scores and, of course, they have the institutions where the average age of first arrest is lowest. But even when those institutions are removed, other indicators of the criminal background inmates bring to prison continue to show the strong relationship to the nature of the climate that forms within. For example, if we order the institutions according to the percentage of men who have previously served a sentence in prison, the correlation between that index and the anti-staff climate scores is +.73.

Relationships between anti-staff climate scores and various indexes of deprivation, on the other hand, tend to be either inconsistent or nonexistent. Indeed, the one measure of deprivation that seems consistently related to the kind of attitudinal climate that forms behind the walls is a measure that reflects the extent of *social* deprivation faced by the inmates: the extent to which the institutions keep inmates from contacts with each other, with friends and relatives outside the prisons, and with prison officials. But this is a special kind of deprivation, for while it assuredly is generally discomforting for the inmates, and in that sense is a true "deprivation," it is the kind of deprivation that may well preclude the development of a strong culture of opposition to the staff. For to the extent that inmates are not free to associate with one another, it is clearly difficult for such a culture to emerge. Indeed, the direction of the relationship in our fifteen institutions is just the opposite from what one might anticipate given a simple deprivation model: in these institutions, the greater the degree of social deprivation, the less the extent to which the inmate culture is formed in opposition to the staff $(-.36)$.

These data, then, point again to the importance of experiences inmates bring into the prison when they enter as a determinant of the general climate within the institution. But two important qualifications have to be noted. First, there is great danger of generalizing far beyond the particular institutions contained in this study. One qualification concerns the actual range in the nature of the deprivations presented in different prisons. Even though we have institutions that were constructed as long ago as 1859 and as recently as 1959, even though they differ in many aspects of their organization, and even though these differing aspects can be shown to be related systematically to inmate feelings and attitudes on many issues, there remains a basic similarity in the degree to which a prison is likely to be perceived as a depriving experience from the perspective of the inmates. This is perhaps the one basic feature of prisons, and the one that is most difficult to change by altering prison organization, design, and program. And it may take a truly radical departure from traditional patterns if the socialization setting known as the prison is to produce major variations in the patterning of socialization itself. In a later section of this chapter, we turn to some examples of efforts to modify the general pattern of prison life through very intensive kinds of programs. Here I want simply to underscore the fact that our sense of the importance of external rather than internal features of imprisonment may be a limited historical judgment, rooted in the kinds of prisons our Western nations have so far developed.

The second qualification has to do with the nature of the materials themselves. The kind of survey data reported here is far from the intimate life experiences of individual inmates. When we get closer to those lives, as in autobiographies of individual prisoners, we get a much more dramatic feeling for the meaning of imprisonment in the personal lives of offenders. Whatever else such experiences reveal, they need to be viewed against a background of the general character of the prison. A most important quality of that general character, it appears from the above, is the nature of the ties its members have had with the outside world, and the nature of that outside world itself.

SOCIALIZATION IN AN
INSTITUTION FOR JUVENILE OFFENDERS[2]

A detailed analysis of feelings and experiences of young inmates as they move through their first stay in a correctional institution for juveniles provides the empirical base for the observations that follow. These boys are between 14 and 16

[2] The following materials are drawn from a study currently in progress being carried out by Martha Baum, Brendan Maher, Anne Romasco and the author.

years of age, and they have all been committed to youth institutions in the State of Massachusetts. Our study design called for them to be interviewed at the beginning of their stay in a correctional institution, at a point roughly in the middle, again just before they were released, and after they had been out in the community for three or four months. In this case, because of the panel design, we are in a better position to assert something about the changes the inmates undergo as they experience the correctional system. (For further details, see Baum & Wheeler, 1968.)

Our aim in this study was to attempt to capture the experience of imprisonment through the direct reports of the boys studied. Thus we asked relatively simple and straightforward questions in an open-ended fashion, and treated the boys as respondents about the setting rather than as "subjects" in a more traditional sense. The observations here will be limited to describing some central themes that emerge from our interview data and that have direct bearing on the nature of the relationship between the world inside the prison and the world outside.

One of our central lines of questioning concerns whether the boys think their stay in a correctional institution will be helpful or harmful to them in terms of their ability to get along in the world after they get out. After asking about the general direction of their feeling, we probed in detail as to why they felt that way. Somewhat over half of the boys feel that their stay will be helpful to them, and the vast majority of those who feel this way see the help largely in a classic free-will deterence framework. Being put away is helping them, they feel, because it is teaching them a lesson. Institutions are pretty lousy places, and it is very rough being away from home and family. In brief, it is an experience to be avoided and it will help them remain free from criminal activity after their release, because they don't want to come back again. They do not feel it is helping them because of the therapeutic qualities of the institutions, the warm and kind character of the staff, the education and trade-training opportunities, or most of the other reasons associated with current correctional philosophies and programs. Indeed, these reasons loom as relatively insignificant in comparison with the general status of being removed from the outside world.

Those who feel the stay will be harmful (and this constitutes a smaller proportion of the respondents) likewise do not attribute the harm to the dynamics of life within the institution, but rather to the way in which the institution is perceived by the outside world. It is not the institution's effect on *them* that they perceive as most important, but rather the effect of their having been there on others. It will harm them because it will make employment opportunities more difficult to find, because it may prevent them from being accepted by the armed services, and for a few, because of the general stigma attached to institutional confinement by community members. There is little mention of such factors as turning bitter while they are in confinement, learning crime from others, and the like. In other words, it is the fact of imprisonment per se that looms as most important, rather than any specific events that happen during confinement.

These are experiences reported by the boys at an early point in their stay. As they move through to the period just before their release, the only major change in response is that those who originally saw the institution as primarily harmful in its effect move to viewing it as neutral. This movement is apparently occasioned by their learning that juvenile records are handled differently from adult criminal records and that they may be able to conceal the fact of confinement from employers and others. Among those who still feel that their stay will help them, there is a slight increase in the number who attribute the help to something specific about institutional programs, but the main thrust of their responses remains the same as before: they don't like being away from home and are motivated to stay out of trouble so that they won't come back.

It could be argued that these are only verbal mouthings and that they only serve to conceal the real dynamics of the socialization process within the institution. Indeed, the boys may be observed to fight and argue vigorously, to jockey for position in the status hierarchy among the boys, to play up to the staff in their presence while verbally attacking them in their absence, and in other ways to be going through the routines we have come to expect from persons in closed institutions. These observations might all be correct, but they would give only a partial indication of the significance of life within the institution for the boys in question. For when we ask them what they spend most of the time thinking about while they are in the institution, even during the middle of their stay, about twice as many report thinking most about the outside world as report thinking about what is going on within the institution. Their minds are likely to be on family, friends, activities they used to enjoy but now can't, and the like. And when asked what are the worst and the best times while they are in, the great majority report that their high points and their low points center around visits and contacts from the outside, rather than around activities within the institution. They are happiest when they get a visit, when they receive letters, when they go on weekend furloughs to their home community. They are lowest when a planned visit does not materialize, or when it is time for a visit to end, or when no one writes.

We might expect these feelings to be strongest among young offenders who are separated from free community life for the first time and whose length of separation is relatively short, and both of these characteristics are present for those we studied. But coupled with the other observations regarding their sense of the impact of the institution on them, these data on juvenile offenders show clearly how life outside the institution has real cognitive and motivational significance for those inside.

It may seem that we have been wandering through the vineyards of several unrelated studies, but a consistent theme appears to emerge from each additional piece of empirical data. There is a hint of the importance of the external world in our earliest finding regarding the "U-shaped curve," for it suggests the ease with which inmates can begin adapting to the world beyond the prison even before they have emerged from behind the walls. The case study of a Norwegian prison pointed clearly to the importance of the culture outside the prison as a determinant of the life that forms within. The survey data from fifteen Scandinavian institutions shows the relatively great impact of inmates' prior backgrounds outside the prison, the lesser importance of prison deprivations themselves. Finally, the reports of juvenile offenders give further evidence of the powerful impact of life outside while they are inside. Taken together, these observations force a redirection of interest from life in the inner regions of the prison to the world of experience that lies beyond its boundaries.

DISCUSSION

The concept of socialization, like so many of the concepts in behavioral science, has been subject to a wide variety of definitions and interpretations. The definition suggested in the introduction to this volume, "the process by which individuals acquire the knowledge, skills and dispositions that enable them to participate as more or less effective members of groups and the society" can be given either a narrow or a broad interpretation. As applied to the prison, for example, it can be taken to refer to the ways in which inmates learn how to manage their lives within the institution at some minimal level of effectiveness. A substantive focus on this concern would lead to an effort to answer the questions: What does an inmate need to know, in addition to what he already knows, that will enable him to make a minimal adjustment to the prison? What skills must he develop that he does not already have? What attitudinal or behavioral dispositions will be needed?

There are abundant documentary materials to suggest that, in terms of these questions, adaptation to the prison is not greatly different from adaptation to any other setting. The inmate will learn from others what the guards expect of him as a routine matter, what the inmates expect, and how he can successfully negotiate between these two conflicting sets of expectations. He may also learn how to achieve those minimum creature comforts that make life tolerable within the institution (Goffman, 1961b). What is learned will depend upon the local culture of the institution in question, and on the degree to which an individual inmate becomes involved in that culture. The chief difference between the prison and many other social settings in this connection is that, as a "total institution," the pains resulting from failure to become socialized are particularly severe for there is literally no escape from the norms and role demands of the setting. As Goffman has pointed out, the prison shares this quality with many other forms of organization, including the ship, the mental hospital, the private boys' school, and the monastery (Goffman, 1961a). But aside from the "total" character of such settings, and the special importance that attaches to getting along, there is not a lot that distinguishes the total institution from other settings where socialization, in this narrow sense, goes on.

A more inclusive view of the socialization process would place less emphasis on problems of surface adjustment, more emphasis on deeper, more fundamental changes. It would emphasize the internalization of norms, rather than overt compliance with the setting in question. It might give less attention to external features of adjustment, more to possible changes in one's basic conception of himself, his sense of worth and dignity. Many who speak of socialization within the prison indeed have these latter qualities in mind. The typical assumption has been that the harsh and dramatic circumstances of imprisonment as a form of human existence are likely to lead to deep-seated and fundamental changes in values, ideologies and personal styles. And the assumption has typically been that these changes will have long-lasting effects. Similarly, when persons have talked about "rehabilitation" or "resocialization" they have been concerned with more than establishing a new surface adaptation to conventional ways of life. They have had in mind some relatively basic reconstruction or reconstitution of one's values, beliefs, and way of life (Studt, Messinger & Wilson, 1968).

It is this broader meaning of socialization that has been implicit in the matters discussed in this chapter. The prison is often viewed as a setting within which fundamental changes in attitudes and values are likely to take place. A growing body of both evidence and thought suggests that this view may be incorrect. Indeed, the central argument of this chapter may be put as follows:

1. Persons do not enter prison motivated to seek a basically new and different vision of themselves.

2. To the extent that they do change, the change is produced as much by the reaction to being confined and separated from the free community as it is by the dynamics of life within the institution.

3. The values and attitudes expressed by prison inmates are shaped in important ways by the circumstances to which inmates have been exposed prior to their period of incarceration.

4. In addition to its impact on the values held by entering inmates, the external world influences the kind of culture and social organization that is formed within the prison, and which serves as the social context within which adaptation to imprisonment takes place.

5. As a result of these conditions, whatever impact the experience of imprisonment itself might have on inmates, either positive or negative, is sharply attenuated. *It is the social definition of the prison in society, rather than the social status of the inmate within the prison, that appears to be most relevant for the future life and career of prison inmates.*

6. It follows from all of the above that a full understanding of processes of socialization and resocialization within the prison requires much greater attention than has heretofore been given to the relationship of both the prison and the prisoner to the external world.

The remainder of this chapter will examine other studies of the prison to assess their bearing upon this argument.

Inmates obviously differ in the roles they come to play within the prison, and these differences are related to the backgrounds they bring to prison.

Further, such differences have been shown to be related to the way men change as they experience prison life (Garabedian, 1963; Wellford, 1967). But often, the divergent sociocultural backgrounds men bring to the institution are forgotten as analysts attempt to untangle the nature of prison life. This fact is noted clearly in the one report that is most closely related to the argument of this paper (Irwin & Cressey, 1962). Irwin and Cressey call attention to the existence of three separate subcultures within the prison: a "convict" subculture, whose participants are oriented inward toward the internal life of the prison; a "thief" subculture, whose participants are oriented to the criminal culture outside the prison; and finally, there are prisoners oriented toward the legitimate culture in the broader society. To understand the prison behavior of the second and third types of men, it is crucial to understand the nature of their ties outside the prison. Although Irwin and Cressey make their case by examining individual differences within any one institution, their argument is entirely consistent with our findings on the degree to which inmate life generally reflects broader cultural conditions.

There are several studies of correctional communities that attempt to draw the link between the social organization of the prison and the individual adaptation of the inmates. Most of these studies focus on the nature of the formal authority system. For example, Street, Vinter and Perrow (1966) are able to show that inmates in youth institutions ranged along a continuum from custody and discipline to group and individual treatment responded rather differently to the staff and to their fellow inmates. From their data, they are able to argue effectively that the "solidary opposition" model of inmate culture in prisons does not adequately describe institutions that develop a fairly rich and complex set of treatment goals and programs. Related studies of prison camps by Grusky (1959) and by Berk (1966) point to substantially the same conclusion, as do comparative studies of adult institutions where some are operating within a traditional custodial model and others within a psychiatrically oriented version of the correctional process (Mathiesen, 1965; Wheeler, 1968).

It is clear from all these studies that different patterns of formal organization and structure may produce differences in inmate organization and in attitudes toward the prison experience. But these studies have not gone on to demonstrate the relationship between participation in inmate society and future behavior. Thus, as much as these studies tell us about the different patterns of organization within the prison and potentially different socialization processes, they have not yet shown whether changes occur that are deep and long lasting enough to produce real differences in rates of recidivism.

A number of other studies have examined rates of recidivism for men housed in different types of institutions. This has been part of a long-term series of studies supported by the California Correctional System. And if there is any one conclusion that appears to be safely drawn from those studies, it is that differences in prison organization themselves apparently produce relatively little difference in recidivism rates. Once one takes account of the nature of the inmate population in the different prisons, the institutional differences in recidivism rates tend to disappear. Relatively small effects may be shown for one or another aspect of prison programs, but the overall sense one gets from such studies is that the differences attributable to institutions are small relative to the differences attributable to the prior backgrounds of individual inmates. A recent Danish investigation lends cross-national support to this finding. Larsen (1967-68) has produced one of the few studies that has both recidivism data, and data on inmate attitudes and perspectives toward the institutions. He is able to show that institutions ranging along a treatment-custody dimension do indeed produce differences in the perspectives inmates have with regard to their life within the prison. But, again, once one controls for the differences in type of inmate, there are only small differences in the rates of recidivism among those released from the institutions. Indeed, the one current study in the field of correction that has been successful in demonstrating what appears to be the real impact of an experimental program is a project which compares inmates in traditional institutions with those who remain outside the institutions entirely, and are subject to a special and intensive treatment program on the outside (Warren, 1967). And even in this case, it remains unclear whether the results are due to merely not going to prison, to a more lenient recommitment policy for those in the treatment group, or to the effects of the treatment program itself.

Again, it is necessary to interpret these studies with caution, for in many respects the institutions do not offer really radical differences in their form of organization or in the kinds of treatment programs used with inmates. For the most part, it is a matter of providing more of what is already present in a minimum "treatment" model—more psychiatrists per inmate, more counseling facilities, more group therapy, better trade-training programs, and so forth. It may be that a much more radical reorientation of prison organization will be necessary in order to produce institutions that really make a difference. That such a reorientation is difficult to establish is suggested by the experiences of Elliot Studt and her colleagues (Studt et al., 1968).

Glaser's (1964) study of federal institutions provides further data that is relevant to the argument made above. He found a U-shaped pattern of response to prison life quite similar to that described for the State Reformatory, thus again suggesting that the changes that take place during the middle of imprisonment may not remain until the time of release. Further, when inmates in the institutions he studied were questioned regarding the effect of imprisonment on them, the responses were quite similar to those given in the study of juvenile institutions: inmates thought the primary impact of imprisonment was a deterent effect, rather than anything specific about institutional programs, although there were a minority who felt that they benefited from the trade-training program of the federal prison system. And to the extent they felt the institution had a bad effect, they were likely to see it primarily in terms of what it meant to have a "record" when they returned to civilian life.

A final study that has bearing upon our argument is Giallombardo's (1966) recent research in the federal women's prison at Alderson, West Virginia. She too found functional theory wanting as an explanation of the nature of inmate society. She observed that the same general deprivations are present in women's institutions as in men's but that the form of inmate society is radically different. The difference has to do with differences in what inmates bring into the institution as a result of role definitions provided by the broader society:

> The deprivations of imprisonment may provide necessary conditions for the emergence of an inmate system, but our findings clearly indicate that the deprivations of imprisonment in themselves are not sufficient to account for the form that the inmate social culture assumes in the male and female prison communities. Rather, general features of American society with respect to the cultural definition and content of male and female roles are brought into the prison setting and function to determine the direction and focus of the inmate cultural systems (Giallombardo, 1966, p. 187).

CONCLUSION

The argument presented above is clearly based on partial and fragmentary evidence. Despite the growing number of studies of prison environments over the past score of years, there is still a relative absence of a truly cumulative body of knowledge about the prison as a social environment, and about the changes inmates undergo as they experience imprisonment. On the basis of that partial evidence, we argue that studies of the formal and informal social organization of the prison and its effects on new inmates need to be supplemented by a stronger concern for the relationship between both prison and prisoner and the external world. When such studies are completed, we should be in a better position to assess the relative impact of the external and internal world on the conduct of offenders both during and after imprisonment.

REFERENCES

BAUM, M., & WHEELER, S. Becoming an inmate. In S. Wheeler (Ed.), *Controlling delinquents.* New York: Wiley, 1968.

BERK, B. B. Organizational goals and inmate organization. *American Journal of Sociology,* 1966, 71 (5), 522-534.

BRIM, O. G., JR., & WHEELER, S. *Socialization after childhood.* New York: Wiley, 1966.

CLEMMER, D. *The prison community.* New York: Rinehart & Co., 1958. (First published in 1940.)

CLINE, H. F., & WHEELER, S. The determinants of normative patterns in correctional institutions. In N. Christie (Ed.), *Scandinavian studies in criminology.* Vol. 2. Oslo: Universitetsforlaget, 1968.

GARABEDIAN, P. C. Social roles and processes of socialization in the prison community. *Social Problems,* 1963, 11, 139-152.

GARRITY, D. L. The effect of length of incarceration upon parole adjustment and estimation of optimum sentences; Washington State Correctional Institution. Unpublished doctoral dissertation, Univer. of Washington, 1956.

GIALLOMBARDO, R. *A study of a women's prison.* New York: Wiley, 1966.

GLASER, D. *The effectiveness of a prison and parole system.* Indianapolis: Bobbs-Merrill, 1964.

GOFFMAN, E. On the characteristics of total institutions. In E. Goffman, *Asylums.* New York: Doubleday, 1961. Pp. 1-124. (a)

GOFFMAN, E. The underlife of a public institution: A study of ways of making out in a mental hospital. In E. Goffman, *Asylums.* New York: Doubleday, 1961. Pp. 171-320. (b)

GRUSKY, O. Organizational goals and the behavior of informal leaders. *American Journal of Sociology,* 1959, 67 (1), 59-67.

IRWIN, J., & CRESSEY, D. R. Thieves, convicts, and the inmate culture. *Social Problems,* 1962, 10 (Fall), 142-155.

LARSEN, F. B. Aspects of a strategy for research in criminology. *Sociologiske Meddelelser: A Danish Sociological Journal,* hoefte 1967/68, 12, serie 1, 25-52.

MATHIESEN, T. *The defense of the weak.* London: Tavistock, 1965.

MERTON, R. K. *Social theory and social structure.* Rev. Ed. Glencoe, Ill.: Free Press, 1957.

SCHRAG, C. C. Social types in a prison community. Unpublished master's thesis, Univer. of Washington, 1944.

SCHRAG, C. C. Leadership among prison inmates. *American Sociological Review,* 1954, 19 (1), 37-42.

STREET, D., VINTER, R. D., & PERROW, C. *Organization for treatment.* New York: Free Press, 1966.

STUDT, E., MESSINGER, S. L., & WILSON, T. P. *C-unit: Search for community in prison.* New York: Russell Sage Foundation, 1968.

SYKES, G. M. *The society of captives.* Princeton, N. J.: Princeton Univer. Press, 1958.

SYKES, G. M., & MESSINGER, S. L. The inmate social system. In R. A. Cloward, D. R. Cressey, G. H. Grosser, R. McCleery, L. E. Ohlin, G. M. Sykes, & S. L. Messinger (Eds.), *Theoretical studies in social organization of the prison.* New York: Social Science Research Council, 1960. Pp. 11-13.

WARREN, M. Q. The community treatment project after six years. *Bulletin of the California Youth Authority,* 1967.

WELLFORD, C. Factors associated with adoption of the inmate code: A study of normative socialization. *The Journal of Criminal Law, Criminology and Police Science,* 1967, 58 (2), 197-203.

WHEELER, S. Role conflict in correctional communities. In D. R. Cressey (Ed.), *The prison: Studies in institutional organization.* New York: Holt, Rinehart & Winston, 1961. (a)

WHEELER, S. Socialization in correctional communities. *American Sociological Review,* 1961, 26 (5), 697-712. (b)

WHEELER, S. Legal justice and mental health in the care and treatment of deviants. In M. Levitt & B. Rubenstein (Eds.), *Orthopsychiatry and the law.* Detroit: Wayne State Univer. Press, 1968.

CHAPTER **26**

The Socialization
Of Blind Children

Robert A. Scott

Princeton University

Blindness is among the most severe of all forms of physical disability. Without vision the individual is cut off from a major segment of the social and physical environment to which he must adapt. He cannot easily relate to the distant environment; he can only infer, and, therefore, often misses meanings and intentions which are created when words are combined with the rich vocabulary of expressive gestures; he is forced to use a language which consists of words and phrases heavily saturated with visual imagery. Blindness therefore inevitably creates formidable social and psychological problems for an individual. These problems are compounded by the awesome fear which this handicap calls forth in others. There are few, if any physical disabilities which are more profoundly dreaded than blindness (Gowman, 1957), and certainly none about which there is more misinformation and misunderstanding. These two facets of blindness— the social and psychological limitations inherent in the condition, and the unreasoning reactions of sighted persons to it—comprise the basic contingencies of the socialization of children who are born without vision. The purpose of this chapter will be to examine certain aspects of the process of socialization as it occurs in blind children, and to formulate a series of theoretical and practical research questions which are suggested by the case of the blind child.[1]

Few aspects of a blind child's early socialization are not profoundly affected by his disability. The development of language and of the ability to communicate meaningfully with others, the emergence of a clear body image, role learning, imitation, self-concept development, participation in interpersonal relationships —all of these things are markedly altered when vision is absent. From the point

---

I wish to acknowledge the support of Russell Sage Foundation and the New York Association for the Blind of a larger study (Scott, 1968) from which materials for this paper were obtained. I am also indebted to Bruce Bassoff, Dorothy Burlingham, Berthold Lowenfeld, Frank Furstenberg, John Clausen, Dorothy Gordon, and Robbie Robinson for reading earlier drafts of this paper.

[1]For a discussion of the effects of other physical handicaps on socialization, see Chapter 27 by Stephen A. Richardson.

of view of the scientific study of socialization—the process of inculcating new values and behavior which are appropriate to social position and group membership (Rosow, 1963)—perhaps the most basic of these processes is the development of self. For this reason, I will devote a major portion of my attention to an analysis of the impact which blindness has upon the emergence of self-concept. This analysis is contained in Part II. Part III explores some of the consequences of blindness for other aspects of socialization. In order to completely appreciate the effects which blindness has upon socialization, it is important to have some basic understanding of the nature of blindness, and the implications which this disability has for cognitive functioning.

PART I: BACKGROUND INFORMATION

Two aspects of blindness are of special relevance for an analysis of the socialization of blind children. The first concerns a clarification of the various meanings of the term "blindness;" the second concerns certain characteristics of tactile apprehension and its consequences for cognitive and language development.

Definition of blindness. From a legal point of view blindness is defined as "visual acuity of 20/200 or less in the better eye after correction; or visual acuity of more than 20/200 if there is a field defect in which the widest diameter of the visual field subtends an angle distance not greater than 20 degrees" *(Blindness,* 1963, p. 1). Basically, this means that a person with about one-tenth or less of normal vision is legally blind. A person may be defined as blind even though he is able to read ink print and get about on the street with relative ease. For the purposes of this chapter, it is important to distinguish between persons with no vision or only enough to permit light, form, or motion perception and those with enough visual acuity to focus upon and identify an object even though it may require the viewer to come within inches of it. Another important distinction concerns the age of onset of blindness. It is customary to differentiate between those who are born blind and those whose vision is lost after birth. The former group is usually called the "congenitally blind" or simply the "blind," whereas the latter group is referred to as the "adventitiously blinded" or simply the "blinded." Conceptions of the environment based on the sensory information available to these groups differ according to whether or not a given person has seen, and, if so, for how long a period of time before he lost his sight. For those whose sight is lost adventitiously a few years after birth, there remains some conception of the external world, in terms of objects and their spatial relations, that can only be gotten from sight. Immediately after losing his sight, the blind person continues to use visual imagery to integrate information he gets through his remaining sense modalities. This visual imagery may be inaccurate and may disappear eventually, but this visualization is a significant part of the child's development. Our major concern will be with children who have been blind from birth or whose vision was lost not later than one year of age, when it is unlikely that any visual imagery is retained. While our comments have relevance for other blind children as well, care should be taken in extrapolating to those whose visual impairment does not meet the two criteria we have established.

The nature of tactile impressions. In the absence of vision and of the experience of seeing, the tactile-sense modality dominates. Touch is to the blind person what vision is to the sighted individual. The information which a blind person receives from remaining sensory modalities is used to supplement touch; it is by means of haptic impressions that the blind person confirms initial impressions which he has received through taste, smell, and sound. Haptic sensations are not used to construct crude visual images that the blind person is trying to apprehend. Haptic apprehension is an end in itself, and the blind person considers an object identified when he recognizes its tactile features.

Tactile apprehension of an object is guided by the same basic principles which determine the character of visual apprehension. The sighted person identifies an object by its shape because it is this which makes it different from all other objects. The blind person attempts to identify that which makes the object tactually unique. He seeks to isolate those touch sensations which will help him to distinguish the object from all others, and he then uses these sensations to identify the object at a later time. When the word referring to the object is used, it is its tactile features which are called to mind. What makes an object tactually unique is the sequence of touch sensations which are given by an object when an individual explores it with his hands.

When we are able to see, we use visual stimuli to construct an image of an object—that is, a picture of it having the properties of space, structure, and shape. The counterpart of visual imagery for a blind person is the schema. The schema of an object is determined by the nature of haptic stimuli. Unlike visual stimuli which are given simultaneously, haptic stimuli are given singly. In order for a person to apprehend an object tactually, he must resolve everything into succession. This is the case because from a single tactile impression one can learn almost nothing about an object. A multiplicity of impressions is required. From this fact, the schema derives its principal characteristics. A schema is a series of haptic impressions and the temporal changes among them as a hand passes over an object. The schema of an object is based upon the succession, change, and order, among properties of a tactile nature. It provides a temporal plan of the various impressions in one's mind. The objective for someone trying to identify an object haptically is to unify all of the impressions he receives and combine them into a kind of closed system.

Visual stimuli are experienced as images in the mind's eye. The schema is experienced as a sequence of variations in muscle tension which are occasioned by the passage of one's fingers over the surface of an object which is to be apprehended. Each separate tactile impression which is experienced is related to the next and mentally strung out in an orderly fashion. To the blind person, a tree is a set of tactile impressions beginning with the base of the trunk and extending on to branches, twigs, and leaves These tactile impressions, which are experienced as neuromuscular excitations of the arms and hands, are then mentally strung together in time. When the word "tree" is used, the person reproduces in a compressed form the tactile plan of his sensory experience. This reproduction is the touch sequence or schema for the tree.

Schematic apprehension has a number of important characteristics which differentiates it from ordinary visual apprehension. First, the schema for an object is lacking in spatiality since conceptions of spatial location are given only by sight. To a lesser degree the conception of an object's structure and shape as given by touch are not comparable to those given by sight. The conception one develops of an object based upon touch is, therefore, different from that based upon sight. This fact has obvious significance for shared meanings, which are the basis for language.

Second, in ordinary visual perception an individual pays attention to only those visual properties of an object which he needs to have in order to identify its shape. To concentrate on all of its properties would be wasteful and unduly time-consuming. The blind person, by the same token, does not have to explore an object in its entirety in order to create a schema for it. He needs only to identify that particular touch sensation, or sequence of sensations, which give an object its unique haptic identity. The nature of tactile stimuli leads the blind person to attempt to isolate those limited touch perceptions which permit him to distinguish the object from all others. A tree may be identified by the touch of its bark, a desk by the sharp edge of its corner, or a chair by the curve of its arm. Therefore, visual and tactile apprehension are different, with the result that the blind and the sighted person do not share meanings when they use the same words.

A third consequence of schematic apprehension is that the blind person often employs the same schema to identify broad classes of objects, but draws no distinction between objects within the same class. A common educational tool for blind children is the plastic or clay model of an object such as a tree. Unlike its counterpart in nature, the child can manipulate a model of a tree and obtain a much clearer impression of its total structure. The impression which is gained from manipulating the model then becomes the schema for all trees. In actual experience, of course, the child identifies real trees by a few simple tactile sensations. His impression of the entire object is based, however, upon his experience with the model. The result of this is a failure to differentiate within broad classes of objects, and to assume that the schema for one object can be applied to all objects of the same class. The blind child loses the tremendous richness of detail which is given by sight.

Fourth, since it is necessary for him to explore each object directly in order to schematize it, the blind child is limited in terms of what he can apprehend because there are some objects for which no schema can exist. The child cannot develop a schema for boiling water, for the moon, for a mirror image, or for objects of motion. He is limited to those objects and events which are stationary, or relatively so, from which he will incur no physical harm as a result of touching them, and for which there are no cultural taboos concerning direct contact.

Finally, schematic apprehension often results in misleading impressions about objects. Deutsch (1940, p. 125) for example, reports the case of a teacher who was familiarizing a class of blind children with various animals. She passed around the room a stuffed squirrel which was mounted on a tree branch, and let the students study it tactually. When they had familiarized themselves with it, she then removed the squirrel from the branch and passed around the branch. Most of the students identified it as the squirrel. The reasons for the error in identification are not important. What is important here is that there are many similar situations which arise, and their combined effect is to give the blind child a great many erroneous and distorted impressions of the world.

Thus, by its very nature, schematic apprehension of an environment and the objects in it is different from visual apprehension. It is clear that the sensory basis of language for the blind person and the sighted is different, and to that extent the common ground of shared meanings between them is limited. One obvious question for research concerns the areas in which shared meanings do occur between sighted and blind persons. One conclusion is clear: The blind child is seriously hampered in developing knowledge and experience about the world which is comparable to the knowledge and experience of sighted persons. Language is a poor substitute for vision during the early years of life.

There is a second sense in which schematic apprehension creates problems for shared meanings. We have indicated that the sensory basis for words is different between sighted and blind persons. It is also the case that since the blind person integrates far fewer perceptions than the sighted person does, the universe of potentially shared meanings is thereby delimited. As Lowenfeld (1949) observes, "Tactual perception has distinct limitations as compared with visual perception because it requires direct contact with the object to be observed. . . . [Because of this], the blind person is limited in his acquisition of knowledge" (p. 1). Since the amount of information a blind person obtains about any event or object is limited as compared to that obtained by sight, the potential meanings which can be shared are thereby limited.

The combined impact of these factors is that the sensory impressions upon which the meaning of words is based are fundamentally different in blind than in sighted children; and that shared meanings, which are the basis of language, correspondingly suffer. These facts lead us to reject out of hand common-sense notions about the use of language by the blind as an equivalent of sight. Indeed, it would appear that the sensory experience upon which language is based is so fundamentally different for blind than for sighted or blinded persons that language may actually have detrimental consequences for self-image formation in blind children. The sense in which I mean this will become clear in the next part.

PART II: THE IMPACT OF BLINDNESS
UPON DEVELOPMENT OF SELF

During the first weeks of life, the congenitally blind child presumably experiences his environment very much as his sighted counterpart does. Both are bewildered by the deluge of raw sensations, the difference being, of course, that the blind child has no experience with light or movement. Nevertheless, stimuli are equally diffuse and undifferentiated for both, so that at this point in their development there are few major differences between them. According to Sandlar (1963, p. 346), major differences between sighted and blind infants do not appear until about the twelfth or sixteenth week after birth.

The first major differences in development between the blind and sighted child begin to appear when the child's neuromusculature develops to the point where he is capable of controlled body movements. The sighted child is attracted by his environment, as he begins to have direct sensory experience of it. The differentiation between self and environment begins to emerge at this point. By differentiating objects from one another, by manipulating them, and by observing his impact upon them, the child is slowly able to distinguish the boundary between self and non-self. This process is greatly frustrated in the blind child. Whereas his sighted peer actively seeks out objects in his environment, the blind child must have that environment brought to him before he can experience it directly. This fact imposes a number of restrictions upon him. First, the amount of the environment which he can know and experience directly is limited. It ordinarily consists of small toys, such as rattles or a ball with a noise maker inside of it. Moreover, whereas the sighted child can relate to his environment at a distance, observing objects and people beyond his reach, the blind child's world is confined to his bed or playpen. The scope of the known environment is correspondingly circumscribed. Second, that part of his environment which is within his reach does not have the same stimulus value to the blind child that it has for the sighted one. Since he is often not aware of its existence, he is not attracted to it. This environment must be brought to him in order for him to become aware of it. Third, the blind child's appreciation of his impact upon the objects which he manipulates is limited. The sighted child can both feel an object and observe his impact upon it. The blind child is limited to touching it. In addition, direct experience of the environment is less sustained for a blind child because it too easily vanishes from his awareness. If a toy is dropped, it is lost unless it falls within his reach and he happens upon it. Otherwise, he must wait for someone to bring it to him again. Under these circumstances, the child quickly loses interest in his environment. As it is organized, it simply does not have the stimulus value for him that it has for sighted children.

This fact has been noted by many persons who have studied and worked with blind children. Lowenfeld (1949), for example, comments that "blind infants do not reach out or crawl toward objects because they do not attract them" (p. 3). Burlingham (1961) places great importance on the fact that in the absence of vision "the blind baby is not stimulated in the same manner to reach out toward people or inanimate objects" (p. 123). Wilson and Halverson (1947), who studied the development of a blind child from birth, commented on "the lack of spontaneity in the subject's movement and lack of inclination to initiate movements" (p. 160). Sandlar (1963), who also attributes this tendency toward passivity to a lack of environmental stimulation, believes that it has the effect of retarding the child's growth and development. She comments,

One of the first characteristics that is noted in observing a blind child is the tendency of the child, no matter how much he is stimulated by his teacher, to lack any sort of real creative drive toward or interest in progressive mastery of the outside world. The child seems to be abnormally content to be left alone and to indulge in repetitive self-stimulating movements or stereotypic, non-adaptive activities, and he continues to evidence a continual constant and powerful pullback toward the self-centeredness and limitation of interest in the outside world (Sandlar, 1963, p. 345).

In addition, the physical environment is organized on the assumption that those who live in it can see. Most toys are stimulating because one can see them; most objects are attractive to a child because of their visual properties. Those things which might stimulate the blind child are either unrecognized or located in the environment in such a way that they are not readily available to him. If his environment were more carefully organized around the sense of touch, perhaps the blind child would be aided in overcoming some of the difficulties which he faces.[2]

The lack of stimulation in the environment is not limited to inanimate objects; it includes people as well. Burlingham (1961) comments that the blind baby "is not guided by the mother's expression of interest in his activity, and therefore, lacks some of the incentive to repeat achievement. The lack of muscular response on the part of the baby again diminishes the mother's wish to stimulate the child by her own actions so that a vicious cycle is set up" (p. 123). In the same vein, Sandlar (1963) reports that "there is no visual exploration of the environment, no exploration of his world, and he is deprived of continual visual feedback of emotional response from his mother, a reward which stimulates and rewards his efforts" (p. 353).

Hearing, which is for the blind child the major sensory mechanism for relating to the environment at a distance, does not provide compensatory information. The consensus of people who have commented on the role which hearing plays in conveying information about the environment to the blind child is that in early self-image development its utility is very limited. Lowenfeld (1949) reports from his experience with blind children that "hearing has its greatest value as a means of verbal communication and information, as a social contact medium and as an indicator of conditions and changes in the environment. It does not, however, convey any concrete ideas of objects as such" (p. 1). He adds, "The sense of hearing which serves the blind as the main source of information brings to them only an abstract form of emanation which must be supplemented by tactual perception in order to become a concrete experience" (Lowenfeld, 1938, p. 6). From her experience with blind babies, Burlingham (1961) concluded that "hearing does not seem to give the same impetus to turning toward

---

[2]One interesting program in this vein is being conducted by Dorothy Burlingham at the Mayfair Clinic in London, England. Mrs. Burlingham has been attempting to construct a special physical environment for preschool blind children which is especially stimulating to the tactile, olfactory and auditory sense modalities.

the source of sound as sight does" (p. 123). From this observation she concluded that hearing was of only limited value in conveying meaningful information about the environment to the blind child. Similarly, Sandlar (1963) feels that "sound can only replace vision to a very limited extent in the life of the blind child" (p. 349). Cole and Taboroff (1955) report that "hearing, which gives certain clues in regard to distance and direction, does not convey any concrete ideas of objects as such, but remains valuable as a means of verbal communication and an aid to locomotion" (p. 629). Consequently, while sounds may be a source of stimulation in and of themselves, they are of only limited value as a means for conveying information about the environment to the blind child. As such, sound is no effective substitute for vision at this stage of development.

The fact that objects and persons in the environment of the blind child are not sufficiently stimulating to him has enormous consequences for his growth and development. The first concerns the nature of his conception of the difference between himself and his environment. One of the principal problems which the blind child has is in developing a clear impression of non-self which he can contrast with self. The blind child cannot very easily make this distinction because it is not readily apparent without sight. To the blind child, non-self consists of a confusing, ill-defined, diffuse something that comes and goes. It lacks sharpness and contrast and, as such, provides a poor background against which to draw the distinction between it and self. As a result, a conception of self in the blind child is very slow to emerge. Blank (1957) commented on this fact when he noted that "vision serves more efficiently than the other senses for differentiation of external objects from one another and of the self from others . . ." (p. 7). He concluded that ego development in blind children would inevitably be retarded because of the difficulty which they had in sharply differentiating between self and environment.

A second consequence which blindness has for self-image development concerns the self as a source of stimulation. While the environment of the blind child may fade in and out of his awareness, his own body remains constant. The child may be unable to experience the impact which his manipulations have on the toy which he holds, but he can experience the impact which he has upon his own body. If he grasps his ears, he not only experiences this with his hands, but he feels on the surface of his ear the hand which is grasping it. His own body becomes the vehicle for feedback. Consequently, as Lowenfeld (1962) has observed, "The blind child finds in himself the stimulation and motivation to action that the seeing child finds in the visually objective environment" (p. 97). The blind child turns to himself for stimulation, whereas the sighted child incorporates an ever-widening and broadening range of stimuli. The blind child explores his body, whereas his sighted counterpart explores his environment. As one incorporates more and more experiences of a new and different variety, the other inevitably becomes more and more self-contained.

A third consequence which blindness has for development of self-image concerns the conception which a child develops of the relative scope of self and environment. Because he is stimulated to explore the environment, a sighted child quickly learns that he is but a small part of the environment he lives in; that non-self is vaster and more complex than self. As Cole and Taboroff (1955) remark, "By progressively enlarging the seeing horizon, the 'I' or self becomes smaller in the determination of its relationship to the environment . . ." (p. 629). In contrast to this process, the blind child's direct experience with his environment extends only to the tips of his fingers. It is encompassed in that arc which is formed by his outstretched fingers and toes. Within that arc the most prominent and stimulating object is his own body. Consequently, the blind child's conception of self assumes greater magnitude and significance than that of non-self. It is this fundamental difference between the blind and the sighted child in the conception of the magnitude of self and environment that is so important in the early stages of a blind child's development. As his sighted peers reach the stage when they begin to share meanings with others, the blind child diverges in his development toward an inordinate egocentricity.

The sighted child responds to the gestures of others and begins to initiate interchanges of gestures at a very young age. The child learns these gestures by observing his parents in their interaction with him. Since the blind child is unable to observe those gestures which are mediated visually, he cannot learn to respond to them. The blind child is, therefore, largely deprived of the important experience provided by conversations of gestures between himself and his parents. Lowenfeld (1962) has placed great emphasis on this fact, commenting that the child "cannot acquire behavior patterns by imitation because he does not visually observe (them)" (p. 97). As we have noted Burlingham (1961) observes that the baby is not guided by his mother's look or expression and therefore loses the incentive to repeat his achievements. He does not always know how she responds and therefore loses the shared meanings which ordinarily result from this activity. Sandlar (1963) similarly reports that the child is deprived of the visual feedback of emotional response from his mother. Consequently, those conversations of gestures which are mediated through sight are lost to the blind child.

To be sure, there are types of gestures which are mediated through touch, particularly those signifying the warmth and affection of the parent, which are expressed through coddling, holding, and caressing. When parents convey their warmth and affection by means of direct contact with the child, he is given one type of gesturing experience from which he can learn shared meanings. Moreover, he will eventually respond to vocal gestures or make sounds himself which call out responses in others. In this case, of course, the meaning behind the gesture is not as clear as when that gesture is mediated through vision. A majority of gestures are visual in nature and require sight for their appreciation. Thus, initially at least, the blind child is cut off from the experience of gesturing, an experience which is of fundamental significance for the early growth and development of self. Whereas his sighted counterpart is inevitably drawn into more complete involvement with his environment, especially with the persons in it, the blind child almost inevitably tends to withdraw into himself. As the sighted child learns through gestures with others that bodily movement or facial expressions mean the ideas which are behind them, the blind child remains ignorant of this whole range of experience.

Since the blind child has never seen a bodily gesture or facial expression, he cannot imitate one. He hasn't the ability, therefore, to initiate interaction with others, i.e., to become a gesturer. It is frequently reported by the parents of these children that they are "so content, they just lie in bed for hours without making a sound." Whereas this behavior may be convenient for the parent, it should be clear that its consequences for the child's socialization are unfortunate and profound. The child is essentially unable to instigate social interaction because he is largely ignorant of how to do so, and, indeed, he is largely ignorant of why he should do so. However, because he cannot gesture properly, we must not assume that the child does not gesture at all. Unwittingly, he becomes a gesturer, and these gestures are responded to by others. But the gestures do not signify those emotions or meanings which one usually identifies with these gestures. They are gestures such as poking the eyes or mouth, pulling the ears and nose, rolling and swaying the body. These "blindisms" come from a desire for stimulation, which comes primarily from the blind child's own body. They are critical kinds of stimulation but we must not overlook the fact that they also serve as gestures; and as gestures they are interpreted by most persons to signify what they would indicate in the average person. The child's blindisms become gestures which mean mental retardation or emotional deprivation or some developmental deficiency. The sighted child who acts this way is labeled "brain damaged" and is treated accordingly. So it is with the blind child. He not only cannot gesture appropriately, but his movements are interpreted as gestures which only further reinforce his isolation and separateness.

The primary mechanism by which a child learns to internalize the behavior of others is play. The important fact about play, insofar as development of self is concerned, is that the individual comes to act toward himself as the person whose role he plays has acted toward him. Blindness poses two fundamental limitations upon this process. First, each social role has many facets of behavior. The more of these facets a child can internalize, the more completely he is able to evaluate himself from the point of view of the other whose role he mimics. Blindness markedly reduces the number of facets of role behavior of which a child can be aware. He knows only that part of a parent's role which involves direct verbal communication or direct bodily contact with him. He does not benefit from observing how Mommy or Daddy relates to Brother or Sister. He only *hears* them relating, and, insofar as play is concerned, he loses a great deal of the meaning of their relationships. He can, therefore, only play at those aspects of the parental roles which directly involve him.

It should also be noted that the blind child is limited in terms of his opportunity to observe how other fathers and mothers relate to their children. Largely because of his physical disability, parents tend to protect, and thereby isolate, the visually impaired child from sighted children. Because he misses many facets of other paternal and maternal interactions, his experience with the role of father or mother is limited to one person in each case until a much later date in his life.

This inherent problem may be compounded by unfortunate parental feelings toward the child. For if they are repulsed or frightened by the child, and unsure of how to handle him, they may find it most comfortable to simply let the child alone. He tends, therefore, to remain passive and undemanding, so that he may "play" in his crib for hours without a noise. If the parents let him do this, he may very well end up knowing little or nothing about the parental role except insofar as it relates to the satisfaction of his basic needs for food and cleanliness.

At the same time, the blind child is often limited in his knowledge of other nonfamilial roles which most children can observe and play at. For instance, his contact with such persons as policemen, grocery men, milkmen, and so on are so abbreviated and transitory, that few if any cues to their behavior are gotten by the blind child. Lowenfeld graphically illustrates this point in the following way:

> Let us assume that a blind child is taken along by his mother on a shopping tour of the grocery store. Johnny enters the store; a wave of mixed odor sensations accompanies his entrance. If he has previously been in a grocery store, he probably identifies the place on the basis of former odor associations. He holds his mother's hand and walks with her until she stops in front of the counter. If he is an alert blind child, who has been encouraged to explore, his free hand probably reaches out while he is walking and may touch one or the other objects. He cannot identify any of them because the contacts are too fleeting. If he is less alert or active, he will just cling to his mother, making no attempt to explore. Now he stands in front of the counter listening to the orders given to the clerk, hearing him walk behind the counter and placing things upon it. His hands may reach out and get hold of some objects, perhaps some wrapped packages, some bottles or some boxes which he also cannot identify. When his mother has finished her shopping which the child tried to interrupt with questions that she had no time to answer satisfactorily, they leave the store (Lowenfeld, 1962, pp. 92-93).

On the basis of information which he receives from encounters such as these, it is very difficult for him to play at the role of grocer in a way that corresponds to the grocer's actual behavior. The common result is that the blind child fails to develop a repertoire of roles and a consequent ability to understand how persons in these roles evaluate him. It is a slow and tedious process by which the child finally comes to understand what a policeman does; it is even more tedious for him to put himself in that role and evaluate himself from the point of view of the policeman.

We see then that blindness poses major limitations upon a child's role playing. As a consequence, the blind child misses the important experience of putting himself into the position of another person and of evaluating his own behavior from that point of view. It is important to recognize that, as we consider each of the stages in the development of self-image, blindness creates increasingly greater difficulties for the young child; and that as a result, during the early years of life, he drops further and further behind his sighted peers. This point becomes even clearer when we consider the consequences of blindness for the crucial socializing functions of games.

Before he participates in game-like activities, the ordinary child has no unified conception of himself and no general standpoint from which he is able to view his own behavior. The development of a child's ability to participate in game-like activities leads to a distinct, unified, and organized conception of self and a reference point for evaluating his own behavior.

Blindness will very likely preclude participation in a great many of the activities from which the average child learns so much. While there are some individual variations, the majority of game-like activities which sighted children enjoy cannot be enjoyed by blind persons because of the nature of their handicap. Unlike play, moreover, participation in game-like activities requires of the individual that he have the attitudes of all other players in mind. Blindness creates certain major barriers to such awareness. A blind child is usually limited in his awareness of what is going on to interactions which directly involve him. It is difficult for him to follow interactions between other players, since he must depend upon voice identification and the localization of sound as his basic sources of information. The basic problem is that of indicating to the blind person the nature of such interactions between other players. The blind child's participation in game-like activities is limited to direct contact and physical interaction with others. Unless someone tells him, he is unable to know what others are doing or how what they are doing affects the whole.

There are several important consequences of this pattern. First, the child experiences a great deal of difficulty constructing in his mind the concept of a whole social game. He grasps individual rules and norms, and he understands the actions of particular players; but his greater difficulty arises in organizing these impressions in a systematic fashion and from the point of view of the activity as a whole. He knows only that segment of the activity which directly involves himself, and his ability to evaluate himself from the point of view of others is seriously limited as a consequence.

In summary, blindness seriously hampers development in the child of an awareness of and participation in activities which are essential for acquiring knowledge about specific social roles as well as what George Herbert Mead calls a "generalized other"—the body of opinions of those engaged in the same social activity. The formation and growth of self in blind youngsters is correspondingly retarded, so that at this stage of their development, self-concept in blind children is fragmented and diffuse.

This conclusion reveals an important fact about symbolic interaction theory: It is based upon the fundamental but generally unrecognized assumption that *during the formative years of life, vision is a necessary condition for development of a self-image.* In addition, *these data also indicate that we can no longer assume that development of a self-image is inevitable.* The development of a self-image is problematic, apparently depending upon the presence of a number of factors which are adversely affected by blindness. These facts suggest a number of research questions: What are the effects of other sensory and motor impairments upon the development of a self-concept? What consequences do different kinds of social environments have for such development in ordinary children? Do certain environments inhibit the process? Are there certain environments which are especially conducive to it? The unusual case of the blind child serves to call our attention to important and heretofore unrecognized questions about variations in the socialization experiences of ordinary children.

Our primary concern thus far has been with the effects of blindness on the development of self-concept. Later we will examine the ways in which other aspects of the socialization process are affected by this disability. First, however, we will consider the ways in which the retardation of self-conception manifests itself. We will also consider the extent to which such retardation can be ameliorated.

Blind children have several characteristics which are symptomatic of retardation in self-conception. None of them is more dramatic than the tendency which they have to mistake for their own the ideas and experiences of others. There is, of course, a tendency for all children to present the ideas of parents and friends as though they were original to themselves. Except for the very young, however, this tendency is usually accompanied by an awareness of the fact that these ideas and experiences are borrowed. It is this awareness which is absent in many blind children.

This inability to differentiate between self and other is dramatically illustrated by an experience which occurred to Helen Keller. In 1891, when Miss Keller was a young girl of 11, she composed a short story entitled "The Frost King" for the Superintendent of the Perkins School for the Blind. The Superintendent was so impressed with her story that he had it published in the Perkins Institution Report of 1892. A reader of the report was struck by the style of the story and the familiarity of its plot. Investigation revealed that it was strikingly similar to a short story entitled "The Frost Fairies" which had been written by a prominent children's writer of the day. Since the whole matter was embarrassing for everyone, an extensive investigation was conducted by authorities at the school. At first there was no evidence to be found that Helen had even had the story read to her; and indeed, she vehemently denied any knowledge of it. It was eventually determined, however, that a woman with whom Miss Keller and her teacher had spent the summer had read the story to Helen one afternoon when Miss Sullivan, her regular teacher, was away. Helen retained the story in her mind and later mistook it for her own (Keller, 1954).

Some persons attributed this event to Miss Keller's unusually retentive mind; others felt that it was caused by the whims and fancies of a young child. But whatever the explanation of this event, it was the reaction which Miss Keller and her teacher had to it which is perhaps most important. For some time both were deeply despondent. Miss Sullivan was disturbed because it called into serious question the very foundation upon which she had based Helen's education. To Helen, however, the wound went far deeper, for, as she later remarked, "I have ever since been tortured by the fear that what I write is not my own. For a long time, when I wrote a letter, even to my mother, I was seized with a sudden feeling of terror, and I would spell the sentences over and over, to make sure that I had not read them in a book" (Keller, 1954, p. 66). In fact, these fears were not unjustified, for in the light of this episode, Miss Sullivan restudied many of Helen's papers and discovered that a great many of the ideas which Miss Keller expressed as her own were in reality those of others with whom she had spoken or about whom she had read. Miss Keller herself recognized this fact later, when she wrote that "this habit of assimilating what pleased me, and giving it out again as my own appears in much of my early correspondence and my first attempts at writing" (Keller, 1954, p. 67).

The exact prevalence of this quality among blind children is unknown. The only available data on the subject come from a study which I have done on the reactions of blind youngsters to an Asch-type situation, in which they are asked to make judgments about unambiguous auditory stimuli (Scott, 1967). The children, who are between the ages of 12 and 16, are all totally blind and congenitally blind and have no handicaps other than blindness. I have found that thirty per cent of them completely conformed on all confederate trials. More striking is the fact that one-quarter of the subjects not only conformed on all confederate trials but gave absolutely no indication that they were in any way aware of a discrepancy between what they heard and the answers which they later gave. These data provide strong presumptive evidence that the confusion of self and other among blind children is comparatively common. The findings are particularly important when it is recalled that the persons who were tested were already into the teenage years at the time of the study. It is reasonable to expect that an even greater occurrence of this phenomenon would be found among groups of younger blind children.

A second attribute which is commonly found among blind children has been termed "verbal unreality" or "verbalism." This term, in fact, describes two quite distinct aspects of language development. One aspect is the tendency of blind children to derive stimulation from words independent of their meaning. Often the adults who socialize the child mistakenly believe that sound, and not touch, is the dominant and most meaningful sense modality. As a result, the child is often saturated with auditory stimuli, with the effect that words and sounds acquire a stimulation value which is independent of their meanings. The fact that this stimulation may be more significant than the meaning of a word results in linguistic behavior that is autistic in character. Words and phrases which in combination are nonsensical may be endlessly repeated; words which have a special stimulus value to the child are employed in order to convey meanings which are not shared by the sighted listener. As a result, language among blind children often manifests the "word salad" quality which, in other contexts, is associated with certain autistic and schizophrenic syndromes.

The second aspect of linguistic development subsumed under the term "verbal unreality" is to describe events and experiences in visual rather than tactile terms. To some extent, of course, this is an inevitable tendency since our language is so heavily saturated with words conveying visual imagery, and so barren of words which convey tactile and kinesthetic experiences. The practicalities of communication require the blind child to use words and phrases for which he cannot possibly have shared sensory experiences. At the same time, this inevitable tendency is magnified in the course of the child's socialization. By listening to adults and by reading, the blind child learns to imitate visual descriptions of events and experiences and to invoke them in appropriate situations. The child, for example, learns to visually describe his home or his school by imitating the words and phrases which are used by his parents and teachers. These descriptions are then recited to others when the child speaks about the events and experiences of home and school. This subtle process is unwittingly reinforced by adults who reward the child with approval because his linguistic imitation makes him appear to be normal. The result of this process is that blind children come to use words to describe objects and events for which they can have no direct sensory experience. In this sense, much of the communication between sighted persons and blind children is somewhat illusory in that the blind child merely imitates and responds appropriately in conversations with others. To the extent that there is no underlying sensory experience, the communication is not genuine.

Blind children are often described as self-centered and egocentric (Cutsforth, 1951). A blind child may appear to be impervious to others, often failing to appreciate the nature of the impact which he has upon them. He may bluntly intrude himself into a situation with no apparent awareness of the consequences of his actions for others in that situation. He initiates complex patterns of self-stimulation in response to his own internal impulses, without any comprehension of the appropriateness of the activity for the situation in which it occurs. Persons who have tried to work with blind children in groups report that activities quickly degenerate into individual and uncoordinated efforts, and that the behavior of each child varies independently of the desired activities of the group. Behavior of this kind in sighted children is appropriately termed egocentric; in blind children, however, the basis of the behavior as well as its dynamics are different. Unfortunately, although such behavior stems from the dynamics of the socialization blind children undergo, it is interpreted by most adults in the same way that such behavior in average children is interpreted: as evidence that the child is spoiled.

Egocentricity, verbal unreality, and a confusion between self and other are the most apparent attributes to be found among young blind children. A great deal of systematic, conceptually meaningful research is required in order to document the prevalence of these attributes, and to determine what other, more subtle differences exist between blind and sighted youngsters.

The degree to which these qualities persist into the adolescent or teenage years is problematic. The results of my own study suggest that the self-other confusion is by no means rare among blind youths of this age. Their tendency to imitate the responses of others is indicative of a dramatic problem of self-conception. With regard to most of the other youngsters, who conformed on confederate trials but were aware of the fact that they had done so, we can infer that among this group the problem of self-other confusion is not nearly so serious. A critical research question which is suggested by these findings concerns differences between the two groups with respect to the types of personal, family, and social experiences which they have had.

There are almost no data on the persistence of verbal unreality among adolescent and teenage blind youths. The fundamental condition which is responsible for verbal unreality is the absence of meaningful tactile or visual stimuli. It is to be expected that through time the blind child will begin to acquire a pool of basic tactile experiences with common objects and events in his environment. Although the process of acquiring such experience is admittedly slow and fragmentary, there is no *a priori* reason to believe that blind children will not acquire sufficient sensory experience to ameliorate at least a substantial portion of the problem of verbal unreality by the time that the child has reached the end of the teen years.

Finally, as the environment is made more stimulating to the child, and especially that portion of it involving persons, we can expect some of the symptoms of egocentricity to abate. The need for bodily stimulation diminishes as the external environment is brought to the child through reading and social exchange with others. At the same time, the social disapproval which his egocentric tendencies often produce makes this behavior unrewarding. As a result, we can expect that some of the more blatant symptoms of egocentricity will abate over time.

While the basic problem of self-awareness probably loses its severity by the time that most blind youngsters reach the mid- or late teens, it does not follow therefore that the self-attitudes which they acquire will be comparable to those which are acquired by average sighted youths of the same age. The very nature of the disability leads us to expect a number of differences to occur between blind and sighted youths in terms of self-attitudes. I will briefly indicate what I believe to be the most important of these differences.

Much of a child's knowledge about common social roles is visually acquired. His awareness of the role as a meaningful social phenomenon, as well as his comprehension of the expectations attached to particular roles, depends largely upon his ability to see. In the absence of vision, a child acquires meaningful information about social roles by means of intensive, sustained interaction with a role incumbent. When such interaction is not possible, the only meaningful conception of the role which a blind child has is acquired by word of mouth or from the printed word. These facts, which modify the process of viewing oneself from the points of view of given social attitudes, lead us to expect differences in self-attitude between blind and sighted adolescent and teenage youths.

First, the most intensive, sustained interpersonal relationships that a blind child has are ordinarily with members of his immediate family. Problems of physical mobility coupled with the fact that blindness is a socially stigmatizing trait result in a kind of social isolation of blind children. As a result, we can expect blind children to have a much clearer conception of familial than of nonfamilial social roles. The social roles of the mother, father, brother, and sister will be more comprehensible to him than the social roles of friend, teacher, neighbor, minister, businessman, lawyer, or doctor. Consequently, the blind child's ability to assume social roles will be much better with regard to familial than to nonfamilial roles. As a result, his self-attitudes will derive largely from the attitudes which family members hold about him.

Two sets of attitudes and feelings toward blind children are commonly found among family members. On the one hand, there are some parents who are so disturbed by the idea of blindness, and who have such deep-seated fears about it, that they overtly reject the child. This rejection, of course, results in extremely negative self-attitudes in the child. Other parents appear to accept the fact of the child's disability, but they do not provide him with reliable feedback about himself and his performance. He is continually rewarded, regardless of how meagre his achievements are. Praise is heaped on him for the slightest effort. The tendency to assume that blindness totally incapacitates a child, and that anything he does is therefore amazing, can produce grossly distorted self-attitudes in the child. It is ironical that there are some blind youths who suffer from the illusion that their performance is extraordinary by any standards and that it is consistently so.

In short, the disability of blindness sharply diminishes the number of social roles that the child is able to meaningfully comprehend. Consequently the range and variety of self-attitudes which the child can assimilate are correspondingly limited. With regard to those roles which he is able to grasp, he faces the problem that the evaluation which he receives is notably distorted. The polar reactions which are common among parents of blind children lead us to expect that self-attitudes among populations of blind youths will tend to form a bi-modal distribution, while among sighted youths the distribution will approximate the standard bell-shaped curve.

Finally, there are a number of other factors in the environment which also affect the development of self-concept in blind youngsters. We would expect blind youths with brothers and sisters to have more elaborate self-attitudes than visually impaired youngsters who have no siblings. We would expect substantial variations in the kinds of attitudes which blind youngsters assimilate according to whether they go to residential schools for the blind or to ordinary public schools. Reading provides the blind youngster with an important means for acquiring knowledge about his distant environment which is independent of some of the distortions to which we have referred. We would expect, therefore, to find more advanced development in self-concept among blind youngsters who are able to read with some proficiency than among those who cannot. Family environments in which physical contact is an integral part of communication will result in a more clearly differentiated self-image for blind youngsters than family environments in which words and verbal gestures prodominate. The identification and study of these factors is a pressing research problem in this area.

PART III: OTHER EFFECTS OF BLINDNESS ON SOCIALIZATION

In this last part of the chapter we will consider a number of additional consequences which blindness has for the process of socialization. The role learning that goes on in childhood has three dimensions: The social role that the child is expected to play during the process of his socialization; the roles which are associated with common social statuses that he will be expected to occupy later in his life; and social roles which he will not necessarily play, but about which a certain basic knowledge is essential in order to participate effectively in the social process. Blindness interferes with developments in each of these areas.

One of the most important role-learning experiences of childhood concerns social and physical differentiation of the sexes. Blindness interferes with the learning of these differences in very important ways. The ordinary blind child is almost completely ignorant about physiological differences between himself and persons of the opposite sex. Awareness of sex differences depends basically upon sight. In the absence of sight there are no socially approved means for understanding what these differences are. The fact that there are physiological differences between men and women will not ordinarily occur to the young blind child because there is no reason why the question of these differences should ever arise. Unless parents deliberately call sex differences to the child's attention, he will be unaware that they exist until he becomes much older. When he is made aware of the fact of these differences, there are no socially approved means by which to meaningfully communicate them. The child is not permitted to physically explore the genitals of the parent or siblings of the opposite sex; open and free discussion among children about sexual differences is restricted by cultural taboos. As a result, the blind child possesses only the most rudimentary conception of physiological differences between men and women. The child's basic ignorance in this regard is compounded by the fact that he also experiences major difficulties comprehending fundamental role traits which are associated with sexual differences. Qualities of femininity and masculinity are not easily conveyed in the absence of vision.

The resulting uncertainty gives rise to a puzzling question: Does the blind child experience the basic Oedipal conflict which is presumed to be an inevitability in ordinary children? In order for an Oedipal conflict to arise, the child must possess an awareness of sexual differences between himself and his mother, and he must be able to appreciate qualitative differences in his and his father's relationship to the mother. It would appear that a child's awareness of these relationships is inhibited by blindness. As a result, we would expect to find basic differences between blind and sighted children in terms of the characteristic symptoms of this type of conflict.

The blind child's conception of social roles is distorted in another way. As we have noted, children who cannot see have a much more limited exposure to the larger world of people and interpersonal relationships than sighted youngsters do. Blind children may acquire a comparatively sophisticated conception of the social roles which their parents play, but they are likely to have only a rudimentary knowledge of the manner in which other children's parents fulfill their parental obligations. The only vehicle by which the child can learn about parental behavior is through experiences with his own parents, from word-of-mouth communications, and from books. The chief difference between the blind and the sighted child is that the latter has greater exposure to the behavior of parents of other children. As a result, he is able to compare the information which he acquires from his culture and from his experiences in his family with the range of actions he observes among other parents. From this comparison emerges a comprehensive conception of parental roles, including not only the ideal parental role but the kinds of acceptable deviations from it. Vision is the most important vehicle by which such deviations are learned; books and word-of-mouth communications will tend to reflect the ideal more than the real. As a result, we would expect to find that blind children stereotype parental roles. Their conception of these roles will be more limited and more rigid than those of sighted children. This same point can be made about other common social roles. As a rule, blind children will acquire a more rigid and delimited conception of these social roles.

In addition to its implications for the child's conception of common social roles, blindness also has important consequences for the child's ability to physically act out the social roles which he is required to play. Appropriate social conduct requires not only a comprehension of the behavior that is expected, but also the ability to include in performance appropriate gestures, postures, and related physical conduct. It is difficult, and in some ways even impossible, for the blind child to acquire this dimension of social role behavior. He does not associate bodily posture and facial gestures with appropriate role behavior. Indeed, as we have seen, his posturing and gestures are basically responsive to the requirements of internal stimulation and not to the requirements of social relationships. This fact results in an unfortunate anomaly. On the one hand, the child learns at least the basic rudiments of verbal behavior required by his role; on the other hand his physical conduct is inappropriate. This jarring discrepancy serves to heighten the perceived "differentness" between blind and sighted persons, thereby further isolating the blind youngster in his social contacts with others.

The fact that the blind child must rely so heavily upon words in order to acquire knowledge about his social environment has a number of consequences for his development. For the major part of his formative years, the child must depend entirely upon sighted persons to interpret for him the nature and meaning of tactile and auditory stimuli. As a rule, the child relies more heavily on his parents than on other children for this knowledge. The important fact about this process is that virtually his entire knowledge about the external world is mediated through adults. As a result, blind children—even very young ones—are very adult-like and seemingly grown-up in their behavior, attitudes, and interests. This quality has unfortunate consequences for the child. Because he has been given a distinctly adult view of the world, the blind child is often better at communicating with adults than with sighted children. He is consequently deprived of a very important type of social experience—that of sustained interaction with peers. At the same time, the interpretation by adults of the child's ability to communicate with them serves to reinforce the misconception that blind children are basically normal.

A number of intriguing questions about the nature of social attitudes can be explored in relation to blind children. One can study in blind children the role of language in the acquisition of common social, ethnic, and cultural sterotypes; as well as the more common social attitudes. While all children rely to some extent on words in order to acquire stereotypic conceptions of others, there is a tendency to modify these conceptions on the basis of repeated observations of individuals to whom they are applied. The blind child, however, learns these stereotypes almost completely by word of mouth. By studying the nature of his social attitudes and of his stereotypic conceptions of social, cultural, religious, and ethnic groups, it would be possible to isolate the role which language plays in their development. Similarly, studies of blind children can also illuminate such basic questions as the role which language plays in the formation of our conception of the nature of the physical and social environment; its role in acquiring common conceptions about the nature of people, objects and events; and its contribution to the fundamental assumptive world of our culture.

In this chapter we have tried to emphasize the adverse effects which blindness has for the process of socialization. We have focused on those qualities which make blind children different from sighted children. This approach is essential if we are to understand the kinds of questions concerning socialization which are raised by this limited case. At the same time, however, this focus tends to obscure one of the most critical facts raised by the case of the blind: that socialization is even possible in the first place. The fact that the blind child is able to communicate at all, or that he learns anything about the society to which he must adapt is testimony to the effectiveness and strength of the socialization process. In one respect, it is this similarity to sighted children, rather than the above differences, which is the basic theoretical question raised by our consideration of this case.

REFERENCES

BLANK, R. H. Psychoanalysis and blindness. *Psychoanalytic Quarterly,* 1957, 26, 1–24.

Blindness: Some facts and figures. New York: American Foundation for the Blind, 1963.

BURLINGHAM, DOROTHY. Notes on the development of the blind. In Ruth S. Eissler et al. (Ed.), *Psychoanalytic study of the child.* Vol. 16. New York: International Universities Press, 1961.

COLE, M. J., & TABOROFF, L. H. The psychological problems of the congenitally blind child. *American Journal of Orthopsychiatry,* 1955, 25, 627–639.

CUTSFORTH, T. *The blind in school and society.* New York: American Foundation for the Blind, 1951. P. 16.

DEUTSCH, F. The sense of reality in persons born blind. *Journal of Psychology,* 1940, 10, 121–140.

GOWMAN, A. *The war blind in American social structure.* New York: American Foundation for the Blind, 1957. Pp. 64-93.

KELLER, HELEN. *The story of my life.* Garden City: Doubleday, 1954. Pp. 63-66; 165-166; 349-355; 359-361.

LOWENFELD, B. The blind child and his world. In *What of the blind.* Vol. II. New York: American Foundation for the Blind, 1938.

LOWENFELD, B. A psychological approach to blindness. *Exceptional Children,* 1949, 16 (1), 1–6.

LOWENFELD, B. Psychological foundation of special methods in teaching blind children. In P. A. Zahl, *Blindness: Modern approaches to the unseen environment.* New York: Hafner, 1962.

Rosow, I. Forms and functions of adult socialization. A paper prepared for the SSRC Conference on Socialization, New York, 1963.

SANDLAR, ANNE-MARIE. Aspects of passivity and ego development in the blind infant. In Ruth S. Eissler et al. (Ed.), *Psychoanalytic study of the child.* Vol. 18. New York: International Universities Press, 1963.

SCOTT, R. Social competence and conformity. A paper presented at the meeting of the American Sociological Association, 1967.

SCOTT, R. *The making of blind men.* New York: Russell Sage Foundation, 1968.

WILSON, J., & HALVERSON, M. Development of a young blind child. *Journal of Genetic Psychology,* 1947, 71, 155–175.

CHAPTER **27**

The Effect Of
Physical Disability On
The Socialization Of A Child

Stephen A. Richardson

Association for the Aid of Crippled Children

The social consequences of physical disability as a focus of systematic investigation is a relatively recent concern. The number of World War II veterans with permanently handicapping conditions accelerated the development of rehabilitation services for the fitting of prostheses and training in their use, for training in activities of daily living, and for special vocational training. The frequency with which psychological problems developed as these men tried to adapt to their handicapping conditions and to negative attitudes and prejudices toward handicapping led to the establishment of psychological services as part of rehabilitation programs.

Rehabilitation services expanded to include children with physical disabilities, the orientation being primarily medical, with orthopedics and, later, physical medicine predominant. The frequency and range of problems encountered by handicapped children and their parents gave impetus to the growth of psychological, social work, and special educational services. One of the first systematic reviews of social research on the handicapped was initiated by the Social Science Research Council, which, in 1946, published the Barker, Wright, and Gonick monograph, *Adjustment to Physical Handicap and Illness*. Since then there has been a steady increase in both the amount and scope of research dealing with the consequences of physical disability. This chapter is not intended as a comprehensive review of this research but deals with only one segment.

A consideration of the concept of physical disability is a necessary prelude to a consideration of its effects. The essential elements of a physical disability are the extent to which it (1) results in some impairment of function, and (2) causes a visible deviation from generally expected physical appearance. Each of these elements may vary in its degree of severity.

A child may be born with a disability or acquire one at any age; although there is a dearth of studies on the significance of the time of onset, it is likely to have important consequences for the child's development. Disabilities may also be the unintended consequences of medical treatment. These iatrogenic effects may be seen in the thousands of children born in Europe with limb deformities as a result of the widespread use of thalidomide (Swinyard, 1969). They may be seen also in children with retrolental fibroplasia who become blind as a result of incorrect amounts of oxygen administered in the neonatal period. These are direct and dramatic illustrations of how environment or, more specifically, technology contributes to the causes of physical disability.

Although the commonly held notion of neat single effects of disability has been fostered by such administrative classifications as physical handicap, mental subnormality, psychiatric abnormality, blindness, etc., a physical disability may actually impair not only motor functioning but one or several other functional capacities—sensory, intellectual, or behavioral. By focusing on one function the classifications imply mutual exclusivity. It has also been common for the most easily detectable functional impairment, especially if it is severe, to attract primary attention, thereby diverting attention from less apparent ones. For example, the motor impairment of cerebral palsy has long been the dominant concern of physicians, and treatment is often prescribed by orthopedists, who specialize in the treatment of motor impairment. Only recently has more widespread attention centered on the question of whether the same neurological damage that causes motor defects can also cause intellectual and sensory impairments (Birch, 1964).

The cosmetic elements and related functional impairments constitute the initial physiological basis of physical disability.[1] People's reactions toward bodily impairment may, in turn, modify the degree of impairment. The consequences of a cosmetic disability are well known. In many cases, facial plastic surgery is performed even when the disfigurement does not cause any bodily impairment of function. The primary purpose of the surgery is to remove—to the greatest possible extent—a disfigurement which seriously interferes with social relationships and is a stigma that can cause severe social and psychological damage (Macgregor, 1951; Macgregor, Abel, Bryt, Lauer & Weissman, 1953).

The primary focus of this chapter will be on the less easily detected but nonetheless important consequences of the child's physical disability on his socialization.

In the early stages of a child's socialization, his caretakers—usually the parents—have a mandatory and continuous responsibility for the child. If for any reason they cannot fulfill their obligations, an attempt is made to find substitutes —relatives, foster parents, institutions, etc. More specialized and limited responsibilities will be assumed by physicians, teachers, and, in some cases, social workers. Seldom do the parents or the child have any choice in these given mandatory relationships. With increasing age, autonomy, and independence, the child begins to develop social relationships which are voluntary or optional—that is, they can

---

[1]There seems to be no term in general use which separates the physiological from the social elements of a physical impairment. The term "biological" in its full meaning includes the interaction between the organism and the environment and, therefore, is not appropriate. The term "bodily" will be used in this chapter to emphasize the physiological and anatomical aspects of the disability. In rehabilitation, this distinction is made by the terms "impairment," which denotes a physiological or anatomical change from the normal, and "disability," which refers to the social and economic sequelae.

be initiated, developed, or terminated, depending upon the degree of satisfaction they provide.

The first part of this chapter will be devoted to a consideration of the mandatory relationships between parents and other adults and the child, and the second part to the child's later, voluntary social relationships.

HOW MANDATORY SOCIAL RELATIONSHIPS WITH A CHILD ARE INFLUENCED BY THE EXISTENCE OF A PHYSICAL DISABILITY

During the first few months of life, the bodily needs of a baby—feeding, sleeping, elimination, physical appearance, motor activities, and growth—are primary objects of adult attention. If the child's appearance, functioning, and growth are within normal limits, as defined by social experience and expectations and as confirmed by relatives, friends, and physicians, there is no need for special concern. As a result, the parental focus of attention broadens to encompass other functions as they develop. Manifestations of intellectual, sensory, and behavioral ability, and social skills are observed, stimulated, and encouraged by the parents, siblings, and other adults involved in a social relationship with the child.

When a physical abnormality is identified at birth there is some evidence that the parents' initial attention to the baby's bodily appearance and functioning will be enormously intensified. Even before its birth, parents are sometimes fearful that something will be wrong with their child. Immediately after birth, it is not uncommon for the mother to ask whether the baby is physically whole— whether, for example, it has the correct number of fingers and toes. In cases in which the child is born with a handicap, there have been reports of the mother's violent reactions of grief, depression, and guilt feelings. In a study of 100 families in Germany in which a child was born with limb deformities, Strasser and Sievert (1969) found such reactions in varying intensity and duration in almost all families. Parents' reactions to having a handicapped child and the effects of different reactions on the child's early socialization merit further study.

The disability also will be unexpected and shocking for the physician and others who have assisted at the birth. Physicians are often inadequately trained to cope with their own or the parents' feelings, and their behavior may upset parents who seek their help and guidance. A handicap at birth also disrupts the social rituals associated with a new baby, and there are no generally known alternative patterns of behavior for use at such times.

Although the disability might have been caused before birth, in some cases it will not be evident at birth and will become apparent only as the infant's development does not take its expected course—as, for example, in some cases of cerebral palsy. In other cases, the disability may occur after birth, being caused by such factors as viral infection or accident.

The parents' primary concern, common to all forms of disability, will center on what is wrong with the child; and the predominant emphasis of the medical profession on pathological functioning will reinforce this concern. As the infant grows and the discrepancy between normal development and the handicapped child's development increases, the nature and extent of the physical impairment become increasingly apparent. The learning of motor skills such as self-feeding, walking, dressing, and toileting may develop later than is normal or not at all. The additional attention and care needed as the result of the physical impairment require time and energy which could otherwise be devoted to the child's intellectual and social development. If the child is apathetic or unresponsive, he provides less stimulation to the parent; this in turn reduces the amount and kinds of behavior to which the child is exposed.

A great deal of time and effort will also be spent by the parents in seeking a cure or amelioration for the child's disability. Their aspirations for the child may be unrealistic because of their expectations of what modern medicine can do, and they may persist in believing that a cure is possible. In the absence of a cure which has been systematically evaluated and found effective, a physician is unable to meet their unrealistic expectations of what he can achieve. One who claims he can do so becomes very attractive to such parents and may be asked to treat their child.

The parents' continued preoccupation with their child's handicap may be harmful to his social and intellectual development. The child, for example, may be given few opportunities for play with his family or with other children and his education may be disrupted by long periods of treatment and attempts at a cure. During this time he may be removed from his parents and may be subjected to painful, lengthy, or tiresome treatments whose purpose he cannot understand.

There may be many reasons for this continued preoccupation with the physical impairment at the expense of fulfilling the overall needs of the child. It may provide a rationale for the parents' lack of a more human relationship with the child, or it may result from feelings of guilt for having produced a handicapped child.

A study of a series of twins (Shere, 1956), one of whom had cerebral palsy, suggests that handicapped children are sometimes treated as though they were "sick," with all the social role connotations that have become associated with sickness. The child is given less responsibility; fewer limits are placed on his behavior, with increased tolerance for deviant behavior; and his personal whims are indulged, often at the expense of other children in the family. The effects of such treatment on the child's socialization merit study.

The same preoccupation with bodily aspects of disability and treatment of the child as though he were "sick" are reflected also in the practices of some residential institutions responsible for the daily care of handicapped children. Tizard (1964) reports that, in a large residential institution for mentally subnormal children (some of whom had associated physical disabilities) administered in a traditional hospital fashion, care of the children was largely in the hands of nurses, many of whom were untrained in the management of children. The nursing timetable did not take much account of the need for continuity of care—that is, care by the same nurses for the same children. Toileting and bathing the children, for example, were conducted on an assembly-line basis.[2] Children were placed in wards of 60 beds and grouped together according to their sex, age, and degree of handicap. Nurses were preoccupied with the physical needs of the children and had little opportunity to get to know individual children. Working conditions were such that there was a large turnover and a shortage of nurses.

> The older, higher grade children came off best, but the younger ones, living in an environment in which there was virtually no conversation, failed to learn from older children and adults elements of social living which they might in other circumstances have been able to pick up. As will be shown, they were in consequence very backward in speech—and in other aspects of behaviour also. Rocking and head-banging were commonly observed; they crowded round strangers, clutching and pawing them. The children were apathetic, and given to tantrums. They rarely played. Most striking of all, they were quite unsocialized. Outside the narrow limits of ward routines, they did not know how to behave (Tizard, 1964, p. 79).

Tizard established a small experimental unit, Brooklands, for some of the children who had previously been in the large institution. The unit was organized along "... principles of child care that today are regarded as meeting the needs of normal children deprived of normal home life" (p. 85). In other words, Tizard de-emphasized the children's disabilities and "sickness" and trained the staff to focus primarily on their functional capabilities and to encourage any signs of interest and growth. This required long-term consistent day-to-day contact with the same children—as opposed to rotating shifts, which make the development of personal relations between the staff and children difficult or impossible. The following account of the children gives an indication of some of the changes that were apparent after two years:

> They kept in good physical health and, living much of the time out of doors engaged in gross motor activities, they looked healthy, sun-tanned and alert. They ate and slept well, and we had little sickness. They became adept in using equipment such as swings and tricycles, climbing nets and parallel bars, and in kicking a ball and throwing. They were often eager, active and purposeful, and in this way presented a striking contrast to their behaviour on arrival. They became able to play socially and constructively, at a level approaching that of their mental age. Emotionally they became much less maladjusted. Tantrums were fewer, and lasted for a shorter time. The children could be comforted and talked out of them, in a way that was not at first possible. They developed strong attachments to members of the staff and to other children. They were able to play co-operatively with other children, to take turns with as much grace as comparable normal children, and to share. They were thus affectionate and happy children, usually busy and interested in what they were doing, confident, and full of fun (p. 133-134).

---

[2]Personal communication from Dr. Jack Tizard.

Some parents develop an awareness and perspective to their handicapped child's need for adequate socialization and respond to this need with appropriate behavior. To the extent that they develop a broader perspective they become different from other adults who have not had their experience, and they must learn to cope with the behavior of others who may be embarrassed and awkward in the presence of their handicapped child. Parents' skills in handling these encounters vary, as do the ways in which they are affected by the encounters (Killilea, 1952). Some will withdraw or avoid such meetings and pattern their family activities so as to reduce outside social relationships (Schaffer, 1964).

It is to be expected that a child with a disability will have had less experience in social relations than a nonhandicapped child and will become deeply concerned about his physical disability (Barker & Wright, 1955; Wright, 1960; Richardson, Hastorf & Dornbusch, 1964). Unless he is unusually sheltered, he will learn the negative values associated with physical disability and, as a result, he may tend to deprecate himself (Richardson, Goodman, Hastorf & Dornbusch, 1961). Such self-deprecation was demonstrated in 10- to 13-year-old children with physical disabilities who preferred a picture of a nonhandicapped child to five pictures of the same child portrayed with different physical handicaps (Richardson et al., 1961; Goodman, Richardson, Dornbusch & Hastorf, 1963).

HOW VOLUNTARY SOCIAL RELATIONSHIPS WITH A CHILD ARE INFLUENCED BY THE EXISTENCE OF A PHYSICAL DISABILITY

During the school years, the child's social relationships are determined increasingly on a voluntary rather than on a mandatory basis. The child moves outside the limited sphere of parents, siblings, relatives, and immediate neighbors to a wide range of social relationships in which he makes his own peer and adult friends in school and in recreational activities. These voluntary relationships—involving two people—may be initiated, sustained, or broken off by either person, and their continuation requires a degree of mutual congeniality and some continuing rewards for each person.

A child's skills in social relations develop as he gains experience with a diversity of people at all levels of social intimacy—from brief, superficial encounters to long-term close friendships. In these encounters, the child learns his repertory of interpersonal behavior and the skills of information and feeling exchange.

Direct Ways in Which a Disability Influences Social Relations

Implicit in some of the writing on physical disability is the premise that a non-handicapped person who is disturbed by a person who is handicapped is acting on the basis of irrational beliefs, stereotypes, or prejudice, and that if these could be changed there would be no further difficulty in the relationship. Such a premise diverts attention from examining ways in which a handicap may have rather direct effects on social relations. For example, functional restrictions inherent in the disability will place limits on mobility and on the range of activities, such as sports or dancing, which may be important in nurturing and sustaining a particular social relationship. For both the deaf and blind, the disability interferes directly with communication, whereas for the blind, it also interferes with mobility and certain physical activities.

Handicaps such as facial disfigurement, the absence or deformity of a limb, a bent spine, involuntary drivelling and grimaces, awkwardness of gait, and involuntary unusual movements lead to differences in static appearance, movement, and nonverbal behavior. Common to these is a disturbance of expectation of appearance because of the strangeness and unfamiliarity. This may have powerful effects on the person's social reactions. Kagan, Henker, Hen-Tov, Levine and Lewis (1966) have shown that 4-month-old children smiled less often when shown abnormal three dimensional models of faces than when shown a normal face. Kagan has also shown that children will react with moderate anxiety to stimuli that are discrepant from schema or images that are familiar. Thus, for example, eight-month-old children may show anxiety to a face in which the component parts are disarranged but will not show anxiety to a regular representation of a human face.[3]

In initial encounters with handicapped and nonhandicapped peers, high school students were more emotionally aroused (as measured by the galvanic skin response) by the students who were handicapped (Kleck, Ono & Hastorf, 1966).

Abnormalities of appearance and function may also interfere with nonverbal communication—e.g., facial expression or gesture. These factors do not constitute insuperable obstacles to social relationships between the handicapped and nonhandicapped and should not be dismissed as irrational in examining the behavior of the nonhandicapped toward the handicapped.

Indirect Ways in Which Disability Influences Social Relations

There is an array of evidence that personal characteristics are attributed to an individual on the basis of physical appearance. Beauty is often associated with good and ugliness with evil. Literature is replete with references to the cruelty of people with thin lips and the sensualness of wide lips, the strength of people with large chins and the weakness of those with receding chins. Shakespeare attributes dangerous qualities to "a lean and hungry look." An elaborate folklore has developed in phrenology and palmistry (Maisel, unpublished manuscript). In some cases, the beliefs may in part create the attributed characteristic through the mechanism of self-fulfilling prophecies.

Despite the lack of empirical evidence to support them, associations between personal characteristics and physical appearance continue to exist, perhaps because they serve a number of purposes in the initial social encounter. They

---

[3]Personal communication from Dr. Jerome Kagan.

provide a basis for classifying people and thereby serve as a guide—especially in the absence of other information—in the selection and initiation of new social relationships. In initiating social encounters, there is a general need for cues with which to label a person in order to provide a starting point for social intercourse. Physical appearance is a convenient first approximation, which is then modified by the feedback of new information as social interaction develops. For those with less social competence, labeling from physical cues may determine behavior which will continue with little modification, additional behavioral and verbal cues being selected which reinforce the initial simplified stereotype. The more limited the persons' social skills, the more need there probably is for simplifying devices such as stereotyping. Attributing derogatory characteristics to others may serve to reinforce the perceiver's sense of his own worth and importance, especially if he lacks self-confidence or talents which bring him social approval.

In his more general analysis of stigma, Goffman (1963) includes the following characteristics:

> While the stranger is present before us, evidence can arise of his possessing an attribute that makes him different from others in the category of persons available for him to be (p. 2-3).
>
> . . . an individual who might have been received easily in ordinary social intercourse possesses a trait that can obtrude itself upon attention and turn those of us whom he meets away from him, breaking the claim that his other attributes have on us (p. 5).
>
> We tend to impute a wide range of imperfections on the basis of the original one (p. 5).

The characteristics also have consequences for the person who is handicapped. Goffman suggests that the person who is stigmatized ". . . tends to hold the same beliefs about identity that we do" (p. 7). Also, ". . . he may perceive . . . that whatever others profess, they do not really 'accept' him and are not ready to make contact with him on 'equal grounds'."

How will these postulated functional and stigmatizing characteristics of physical disability influence voluntary social relationships?

THE INITIATION OF SOCIAL ENCOUNTERS

Initiation by the Nonhandicapped

There is a wide range of social encounters in which the potential participants have some degree of choice as to whether to initiate or avoid. Let us first consider the situation in which a nonhandicapped person has some choice in whether to initiate a social relationship with a physically disabled person. There are very few studies that focus on the effect the handicap may have in this situation, but the following have some pertinence.

In studies we have conducted, children were shown six pictures of the same child, the only variation being that in one picture the child had no disability and in each of the remaining five the child was portrayed with a different visible physical handicap. Children 9 to 11 years old were told to look at each picture carefully and were then asked, "Which boy (or girl) do you like best?" When the child indicated his preference, this picture was removed. This procedure was repeated until only one picture remained. Many different groups of children showed a remarkable consistency in the preference order they expressed. Because a value is essentially a preference ordering, we called the average rank order a value. Without exception, the nonhandicapped child was most liked (Richardson et al., 1961; Goodman et al., 1963). This finding was confirmed in Britain, Germany, Israel, and Mexico.[4]

The widespread value toward disability found among children suggested a study of the characteristics of children who learn the value accurately—i.e., whose rankings of the six pictures agree closely with the average—and those who learn it inaccurately—i.e., whose rankings disagree markedly with the average. In a study of children from high-income families, we tested the hypothesis that a child who learns a value accurately will be a central figure in his peer group, whereas one who learns a value inaccurately will be isolated from his peers. Using the value toward disability derived from the average picture ranking of the children and the number of times a particular child was chosen in answer to the question, "Who are the four children you play with most in your class?" we confirmed the hypothesis for boys aged 9-11 but not for girls. To the extent that the boys' preference for children with and without handicaps, as shown in their response to the pictures, reflects preferences they will exhibit in real life situations, the results suggest that the boy who is isolated from his peers is most likely to become friends with a child with a handicap.

In a study of 5- to 12-year-old children, Centers and Centers (1963) asked a series of social discrimination questions to elicit attitudes about appearance, social relationships, and popularity in school classes, some of which contained children with upper-extremity amputations. They found that peer-group children express more rejecting attitudes toward amputees than they do toward non-amputees.

In another study—at a camp for 8- to 14-year-old children from low socio-economic backgrounds, half of whom were handicapped—we found that when nonhandicapped children were asked at the beginning of the camp season who their best friend was, they chose nonhandicapped children proportionally more often than they chose children with visible physical handicaps. Furthermore, it was found, using the same picture ranking test described above, that those non-handicapped children who chose handicapped children gave a rank ordering that differed more from the average rank or value than did those who chose nonhandi-capped children.

These studies suggest that the nonhandicapped child who is likely to initiate contact with a handicapped child is more isolated, has less general social experience, and has learned the values of his peers less accurately. The arousal of

---

[4]In personal communications from Drs. D. H. Stott, Helmut Strasser, E. Chigier, and Joaquin Cravioto.

anxiety—probably a reaction of the nonhandicapped person in considering whether to initiate a social encounter with the handicapped—may influence the decision in the direction of avoiding the social encounter. Goffman (1963) has suggested: "In general, the tendency for a stigma to spread from the stigmatized individual to his close connections provides a reason why such relations tend either to be avoided or to be terminated where existing" (p. 30). Empirical studies are needed to test this suggestion.

In speaking about their behavior in initiating contacts with the handicapped, nonhandicapped young adults have indicated hesitation based on their belief that handicapped people are often lonely and socially rebuffed. They feel, therefore, that initiating a social relationship involves a higher degree of social commitment and one from which it would be more difficult to disengage. How generally this view is held and at what age it may develop is not known.

The extent to which nonhandicapped people perceive the handicapped as being more dependent than the nonhandicapped will be a factor in initiating a social relationship. Those who enjoy the dependency of others upon themselves will find this perceived characteristic of dependency attractive, whereas those who do not will find it unattractive. This may be a selective factor in those who initiate social relations with the handicapped.

A person who is threatened by competence, especially in physical skills, or who is not fully accepted by his peers may initiate social relationships with a person who is handicapped because he feels the latter is less threatening and competitive and more likely to accept him.

For some nonhandicapped persons the perceptual cue of a physical handicap may be irrelevant or have little salience compared to other cues, such as dress, age, sex, or known or presumed personal characteristics.

Initiation by the Handicapped

For the physically handicapped person, the impairment may increase the difficulty of initiating a social relationship. For example, a blind person will be unaware that other people are present unless he has auditory cues. When he is aware of someone's presence, he lacks all visual cues of a person's characteristics. In situations which would normally result in mutual recognition and some social interaction— e.g., sharing an elevator—a sighted person known to the blind person can avoid an encounter by remaining silent.

There is evidence (Barker & Wright, 1955) that physically handicapped children do not get around as much and are not involved in as a wide range of physical and social settings as nonhandicapped children. This reduces their opportunities for initiating social relationships. If the physically handicapped person has felt unwanted or rebuffed in social encounters, he may be discouraged from initiating further relationships.

A handicapped person may, for functional or social reasons, adopt devices to reduce the prominence of his disability as a physical cue. A person with one hand, for example, may use an artificial hand, which is more cosmetic but less functional than a hook (Dembo, Leviton & Wright, 1956). Viscardi (1952) reported that his handicapped legs drew less attention and became less of a social obstacle when he began to use prostheses which gave him normal stature. The eyes are an important nonverbal cue in social encounters, and, because the blind person cannot use his eyes and may move them inappropriately, he may choose to wear dark glasses.

When there is no way of modifying his appearance, the handicapped person may so manipulate the initial contact as to reduce the salience of his disability or to give the other person time to adapt to it. For example, the initial contact may be made by telephone or letter. The person with a severe facial disfigurement may arrange his initial meeting so that he is able to approach slowly from a distance in order to allow the other person to compose himself after the first impact of the disfigurement (Davis, 1961). The purpose of these strategies in the initial social encounter is to diminish the prominence of the handicap so that it does not obscure the personal characteristics which normally form the basis of first impressions.

These considerations of the initiation of social relationships suggest that a person with a physical handicap may have fewer initial social relationships than a nonhandicapped person and that the kinds of people who initiate social relations with him will be those who are less successful in social relations, those who hold atypical values, those for whom physical disability cues have low perceptual salience, or those who like others to be dependent upon them.

HOW THE BEHAVIOR OF A
NONHANDICAPPED PERSON IS MODIFIED
IN THE PRESENCE OF A HANDICAPPED PERSON

Once engagement occurs in the initial social relationship between persons with and without a physical disability, certain effects can be postulated for the non-handicapped person (Kelley, Hastorf, Jones, Thibaut & Usdane, 1960). Many people feel some ambivalence when they first meet a person with a handicap. Because they are fearful of revealing their negative feelings, they may be inhibited and not behave spontaneously. Their behavior tends to become more formal because of this unfamiliar situation in which they have had little prior experience. One can postulate from this that the nonhandicapped person will be formal, more anxious, inhibited, and overcontrolled in his behavior toward a handicapped person.

There is a widely held attitude that one should be kind and considerate toward others especially if they are less fortunate than ourselves. From this one can postulate that a nonhandicapped person will distort information in the direction in which he thinks the handicapped would like to hear it (Kelley et al., 1960).

In a standardized social relationship, Kleck et al. (1966) compared the behavior of high school students toward handicapped and nonhandicapped peers whom they had not previously met. For the nonhandicapped subjects in contact with the handicapped as compared with the nonhandicapped person they found:

1. more distortion of opinion;
2. less variability in the opinions offered;
3. shorter responses to questions; and
4. considerable variability among subjects on the three findings above.

These results suggest that the handicapped person does not receive accurate or spontaneous feedback from others who feel they must be especially considerate of him. Absence of accurate feedback makes it difficult for the person who is handicapped to learn appropriate behavior and, therefore, makes it more difficult for him to develop social skills and to know what others really think of him. In a study comparing the self image of adolescents with and without communication handicaps, Goodman (1964) found that the adolescents with communication disorders placed a great deal of importance on their school work, the only area in which they felt that they received an objective evaluation of their performance. The results also suggest that inhibition combined with anxiety on the part of the nonhandicapped person reduces the repertory of behavior to which the person with a handicap is exposed, thus limiting his range of experience in social relationships.

There is no good evidence of how aware handicapped children are of the extent to which they are responded to differently. However, evidence available from introspective accounts by handicapped adults (Henrich & Kriegel, 1961) certainly shows this awareness, although written accounts may be strongly biased because they reflect the experience of unusually articulate and sensitive people. Persons who have acquired a disability after years of being without a handicap—e.g., those disabled by war, polio in adolescence, etc.—have a body of experience by which they can compare the behavior of others toward them before and after they became disabled.

Davis (1961), on the basis of interviews with handicapped adults, suggests that there are three characteristic stages in the development of a social relationship between a handicapped and a nonhandicapped person. The first is "fictional acceptance," in which the norm of our society operates so that when we first meet people we function on the basis of equality and normalcy, irrespective of how different the other person may be from us. This norm provides the handicapped person with the initial opportunity to establish a social relationship although, as the Kleck et al. (1966) experiment shows, the nonhandicapped person's behavior is, in fact, often influenced by the presence of the handicap even though he may be unaware of his modifications in behavior. The second stage that Davis postulates is "breaking through," when the nonhandicapped person ceases to be aware of the handicap and reacts to the other's personal characteristics. The third stage, "amending and qualifying the normal relationship," is one in which the nonhandicapped person is aware of the functional impairment and takes it into account but does not allow it to interfere with the social relationship.

In regard to these stages, some issues that need investigation are: (1) how generally the postulated stages occur in the development of social relationships;

(2) how the stages may vary; (3) how quickly these stages are passed through; and (4) the extent to which they are applicable to children at different ages.

For the person who is handicapped, the development of a social relationship is complicated by his uncertainty as to the object of the other person's response—that is, the extent to which the handicap is primary or secondary. Should the handicapped person act as though the handicap is or is not present? How far can the social relationship proceed without the person with the handicap mentioning his disability? When there is evidence that the nonhandicapped person is unsure as to whether he can or should help the handicapped person, how can the latter reduce the ambiguity and uncertainty by indicating whether he wants help and what form the help should take?

Although parallels have been drawn, using the concept of stigma, between persons who are handicapped and minority groups, there is an important difference between the two. People are born into minority groups and in their socialization they learn from their minority culture how to deal with the majority culture. In addition, because they develop social skills primarily with adults and peers within their minority group, the behavior inhibitions common to minority-majority social interaction are operating only a small part of the time. It is unlikely that the child born with a handicap will have parents, neighbors, sibs, and peers who have the same handicap and from whom he can gain experience in dealing with others. Generally he will be surrounded by nonhandicapped people and share the general negative values of the culture toward handicap. Furthermore, he is unlikely to have an opportunity to develop social skills freely with people who share his handicap. If these postulates are reasonable, the child with a physical handicap will have more difficulty than a child from a minority group in gaining experience in behavioral skills in general and, specifically, in the skills for social relations with the majority group. Because of these differences between persons with disabilities and minority groups, the cumulation of the social inventions and experience in how to cope with minority-majority social relations, which is possible in minority groups, is much less likely to occur for handicapped people.

Where the social barriers created by the handicap are severe, adults with a common disability often seek one another out and spend considerable time together. Among the deaf, intermarriage is common. Children with similar handicaps are often placed together in hospitals and in special educational or recreational settings. Parents of handicapped children have formed parent organizations one of whose functions is the exchange of experience. Despite the existence of these social mechanisms, there is still an important need for investigating the kinds of special skills devised by handicapped people in dealing with the social barriers with which they are confronted (Gussow, 1964; Gussow & Tracy, 1965; Hathaway, 1943; Henrich & Kriegel, 1961; Katz, 1961; Sills, 1957).

The postulate that physical disability provides only an initial barrier to social relationships and that continued proximity between handicapped and nonhandicapped children overcomes these barriers can be examined in situations in which children with and without disabilities live in close contact with one another over a period of time. At the camp referred to earlier, the effects of living together for approximately three-week periods were studied among 8- to 14-year-old children. It was found that:

1. Using the preference order expressed for pictures of children with and without disability, children's values toward disability did not change.

2. When the children's choice of best friend obtained after about 36 hours in the camp was compared with the choice 12 days later, in general the nonhandicapped boys gave fewer best-friend choices to handicapped children late in the camp season than they had done earlier, and the girls gave slightly more best-friend choices to the handicapped.

3. In general, nonhandicapped children received a higher proportion of friendship choices both early and late in the camp season.

These findings do not support the postulate that a handicap presents only an initial barrier to social relations.

4. For both children with and without handicaps, the cumulative effect of social relationships is reflected in the way the children talk about themselves in response to the request to "Tell me about yourself." The handicapped children gave less evidence of social experience or involvement than the nonhandicapped children (Richardson et al., 1964).

At present our knowledge of the consequences of disability is more extensive for older children and adults than for young children. Age-specific knowledge is important, for without it generalization for all age levels may occur. For example, our initial studies of values toward disability focused on 9- to 11-year-old children. When we later studied values from age 5 to adulthood, we found that, although there was no change in the most preferred being nonhandicapped, the preference order of some of the five handicapping conditions shifted markedly. For first grade children who came from high socioeconomic-status families, the picture of the child with a slight facial disfigurement was the second most liked after the non-handicapped child. This preference position dropped with increasing age, the drop being earlier for girls than boys and most rapid around the onset of adolescence. High school seniors and their parents ranked the facial disfigurement in the same position—the sixth or lowest ranking position for females and the fourth position for males. The picture of the child with a forearm amputation, which was fourth in preference for children up to the sixth grade, dropped to sixth position between the seventh and ninth grades and then rose again to fourth position for high school seniors and parents.

The experimental finding that a forearm amputation becomes a more severe social handicap during adolescence is corroborated by an observation made by Dr. Henry Kessler[5] on the basis of his clinical experience in rehabilitation with young people with arm amputation. Because the children had developed satisfactory alternative functional mechanisms for coping with their arm amputations, it was difficult for him to persuade these pre-adolescents to use a prosthetic arm.

---

[5]In personal communication from Dr. Henry Kessler.

When these children reached adolescence they became very conscious of the amputation as a severe social handicap and asked for prosthetic arms. By this time, however, they had lost several years of experience in the use of the device. In order to anticipate this problem, he tried to persuade young children to use prostheses.[6] Although his efforts were unsuccessful, he found it was possible for adolescents with arm amputations to persuade his younger patients to use a prosthetic arm.

From a number of sources (e.g., Coleman, 1961) there is suggestive evidence that concern over physical appearance and physical disability increases with adolescence and that there may be less emphasis on physical appearance after the twenties. There are also indications that physical disability has somewhat different meaning and consequences for boys than for girls. Boys uniformly show more concern than girls for the functional consequences of disability, whereas girls show more concern for the cosmetic consequences (Richardson et al., 1961).

The evidence which has been brought together suggests that a physical handicap impoverishes the experiences necessary for a child's socialization. There is a cumulative loss in the types of experience a child obtains in both mandatory and voluntary social relationships. Thus far, rehabilitation and medical services have focused primarily on bodily pathology—that is, on the prevention of further deterioration, amelioration through treatment and prostheses, and, in some cases, on methods of cure. A second, more recent focus has been on the problem of education for children and on prevocational and vocational counseling for adolescents. A number of welfare and voluntary agencies are engaged in recreational programs for handicapped children, but these are hampered by the lack of specific knowledge of the kinds of experience the children have had, the kinds of skill they most need to learn, and how these skills can best be taught.

The studies and concepts reviewed in this chapter suggest several more specific ways of helping children with disabilities. Early awareness and provision for social experiences which the child would not otherwise obtain may prevent some of the consequences of social impoverishment. Older children may benefit from learning how to deal with some of the special problems of social relationships with the nonhandicapped. Training for parents and others who are in frequent contact with the children may be valuable in preventing some of the modifications of behavior which may be detrimental to the handicapped child and of which adults are unaware.

At present our knowledge of the social consequences of disability is partial and fragmentary, and there is a wide range of questions that require further investigation. The following are illustrative.

Does impoverishment of social relationships have more important consequences at one age level than at another? To what extent can training reverse the effects of early social impoverishment?

What actually takes place between handicapped and nonhandicapped

---

[6]Today, in part to avoid this difficulty, children begin to use prostheses before the age of one provided there is good cooperation from the parents.

children of different ages when they spend time together for longer and shorter periods of time? What are the kinds of adult intervention that take place and what are their consequences for the children?

At present there are very few detailed descriptions of children's institutions of any kind, the predominant focus being on institutions for adults. What are the kinds of institutions that provide care for children with handicaps and what are the effects of different patterns of care?

For issues involving the very young child who is handicapped, research may more profitably be focused on the adults responsible for him. What are the nature and variation of parents' and physicians' responses to the birth of a child with a handicap? To what extent and for how long does the physical pathology remain paramount in the thinking of those who care for the child? What are the mechanisms that produce a change in viewpoint?

To what extent and how does the parents' view of others become influenced by their own reaction to disability? For example, does the parent who feels repulsion for the child see others as behaving in the same way?

It is often implied that the concept of stigma operates rather generally across a wide range of social contexts. Less attention has been given to the circumstances and conditions which increase and decrease stigma and how they may be manipulated. For example, what kind of summer recreational program is most likely to provide handicapped children with a valuable social experience? What should be the composition of the groups in terms of age, the proportions of children with and without handicaps, and adults? What should be the personal characteristics of the adults and children? What kind of program would be most beneficial? What kinds of specific training in social skills might be of value?

The further development of knowledge about the social consequences of disability and carefully evaluated applications of this knowledge can provide the experiences necessary for the more effective socialization of children with physical disabilities. This knowledge can also contribute more generally to an understanding of the socialization processes of all children.

REFERENCES

BARKER, R. G., & WRIGHT, H. F. *Midwest and its children: The psychological ecology of an American town.* Evanston, Ill.: Row Peterson, 1955.

BARKER, R. G., WRIGHT, H. F., & GONICK, M. R. *Adjustment to physical handicap and illness.* New York: Social Science Research Council, 1946.

BIRCH, H. G. (Ed.) *Brain damage in children: The biological and social aspects.* Baltimore, Md.: Williams & Wilkins, 1964.

CENTERS, L., & CENTERS, R. Peer group attitudes toward the amputee child. *Journal of Social Psychology,* 1963, 61, 127-132.

COLEMAN, J. S. *The adolescent society.* New York: Free Press, 1961.

DAVIS, F. Deviance disavowal and normalization. *Social Problems,* 1961, 9 (2), 120-132.

DEMBO, T., LEVITON, G. L., & WRIGHT, B. A. Adjustment to misfortune: A problem of social psychological rehabilitation. *Artificial Limbs,* 1956, 3, 4-62.

GOFFMAN, E. *Stigma: Notes on the management of spoiled identity.* Englewood Cliffs, N. J.: Prentice-Hall, 1963.

GOODMAN, N. The adolescent with a communication impairment—special report. *Rehabilitation Literature,* 1964, 25 (2), 45–47.

GOODMAN, N., RICHARDSON, S. A., DORNBUSCH, S. M., & HASTORF, A. H. Variant reactions to physical disabilities. *American Sociological Review,* 1963, 28 (3), 429-435.

GUSSOW, Z. Behavioral research in chronic disease: A study of leprosy. *Journal of Chronic Diseases* (Great Britain), 1964, 17, 179–189.

GUSSOW, Z., & TRACY, G. S. Strategies in the management of stigma: Concealing and revealing by leprosy patients in the U.S. Unpublished mimeographed paper, October, 1965.

HATHAWAY, K. B. *The little locksmith.* New York: Coward-McCann, 1943.

HENRICH, E., & KRIEGEL, L. *Experiments in survival.* New York: Association for the Aid of Crippled Children, 1961.

KAGAN, J., HENKER, B. A., HEN-TOV, A., LEVINE, J., & LEWIS, M. Infants' differential reactions to familiar and distorted faces. *Child Development,* 1966, 37 (3), 518-532.

KATZ, A. H. *Parents of the handicapped.* Springfield, Ill.: Charles C Thomas, 1961.

KELLEY, H. H., HASTORF, A. H., JONES, E. E., THIBAUT, J. W., & USDANE, W. M. Some implications of social psychological theory for research on the handicapped. In L. H. Lofquist (Ed.), *Psychological research and rehabilitation.* Report of a conference of the American Psychological Association, Miami Beach, November, 1960. Pp. 172-204.

KLECK, R., ONO, H., & HASTORF, A. H. The effects of physical deviance upon face-to-face interaction. *Human Relations,* 1966, 19 (4), 425-436.

KILLILEA, M. *Karen.* Englewood Cliffs, N. J.: Prentice-Hall, 1952.

MACGREGOR, F. C. Some psycho-social problems associated with facial deformities. *American Sociological Review,* 1951, 16, 629–638.

MACGREGOR, F. C., ABEL, T. M., BRYT, A., LAUER, E. & WEISSMAN, S. *Facial deformities and plastic surgery: A psychosocial study.* Springfield, Ill.: Charles C Thomas, 1953.

MAISEL, E. Meet a body. Unpublished manuscript.

RICHARDSON, S. A., GOODMAN, N., HASTORF, A. H., & DORNBUSCH, S. M. Cultural uniformity in reaction to physical disabilities. *American Sociological Review,* 1961, 26 (2), 241-247.

RICHARDSON, S. A., HASTORF, A. H., & DORNBUSCH, S. M. The effects of a physical disability on a child's description of himself. *Child Development,* 1964, 35 (3), 93–97.

SCHAFFER, H. R. The too-cohesive family: A form of group pathology. *International Journal of Social Psychiatry,* 1964, 10 (4), 44–53.

SHERE, M. O. Socio-emotional factors in the family of twins with cerebral palsy. *Exceptional Children,* 1956, 22, 196-199, 206-208.

SILLS, D. L. *The volunteers: Means and ends in a national organization.* Glencoe, Ill.: Free Press, 1957.

STRASSER, H., & SIEVERT, G. Some psycho-social aspects of ectromelia: A preliminary report of a research study. In C. A. Swinyard (Ed.), Proceedings of a Conference on Human Limb Development and Maldevelopment with Special Reference to Experimental Teratogenesis and Medical Management of Limb Deficiencies, Kasteel Oud Wassenaar, The Hague, Holland, September, 1963. New York: Association for the Aid of Crippled Children, 1969.

SWINYARD, C. A. (Ed.) Proceedings of a Conference on Human Limb Development and Maldevelopment with Special Reference to Experimental Teratogenesis and Medical Management of Limb Deficiencies, Kasteel Oud Wassenaar, The Hague, Holland, September, 1963. New York: Association for the Aid of Crippled Children, 1969.

TIZARD, J. *Community services for the mentally handicapped.* London: Oxford Univer. Press, 1964.

VISCARDI, H., JR. *A man's stature.* New York: John Day Co., 1952.

WRIGHT, B. A. *Physical disability—a psychological approach.* New York: Harper & Bros., 1960.

CHAPTER **28**

The Socialization
Of The Mentally Retarded

Edward F. Zigler and Susan Harter

Yale University

Mental retardation has long been a problem of serious social concern. The history of this concern has witnessed rather marked shifts in thinking with regard to the socialization potential of the retarded. Inspired by the rehabilitative efforts of Itard and Seguin, with their great faith in the educability of the mentally deficient, and by Binet's belief in "mental orthopedics," workers in the mid-nineteenth century set out to improve the intellectual and social adjustment of the retarded. Their zealous spirit of reform led to the rapid establishment of numerous training schools in this country and abroad. Intensive educational programs provided by these schools were designed to train the retarded to a level of adjustment whereby they could function as relatively self-sufficient, productive members of society. However, the optimism of this movement was rather short-lived, since the disappointing results of these attempts soon became apparent. Thus, these institutions turned their attention to the provision of custodial care, and, with resignation, workers adopted the view that little more could be done for the retarded than provide them with a comfortable domicile. The marked shift in attitude which characterized this transition has implications for contemporary approaches to the retarded, since it suggests that undue optimism is dangerous to the extent that it may breed undue pessimism. (The reader is referred to Doll, 1962, for an excellent historical review of research and changing social philosophy concerning the management of the mentally retarded.)

The general attitude toward the retarded early in the present century was unmistakably pessimistic. The development of the intelligence test led to the identification of considerable numbers of retarded individuals, and the further suggestion of heredity as an etiological factor created rather widespread alarm. For example, Goddard's (1910, 1912) family charts demonstrat-

Preparation of this chapter was facilitated by Research Grant MH-0609 from the National Institute of Mental Health, United States Public Health Service, and the Gunnar Dybwad Award of the National Association for Retarded Children.

ing the recurrence of feeblemindedness extending several generations in a single family were viewed as particularly compelling evidence. Furthermore, under the influence of the mental-testing movement, institutions for the delinquent began to amass statistics which led them to the conclusion that since a large percentage of these inmates were revealed to be feebleminded, the retarded, as a group, were predisposed to a life of crime (cf., Crafts, 1916; Goddard, 1914; Knollin & Terman, 1918). Thus, the view became dominant that the retarded were essentially defective individuals whose condition was largely hereditary, by implication incurable, and that it produced a life style characterized as immoral, degenerate, and depraved. This social indictment is dramatically illustrated in the following quote from an address given in 1912 by one of the nation's leading figures in the area of mental retardation, Fernald:

> The social and economic burdens of uncomplicated feeblemindedness are only too well known. The feebleminded are a parasitic, predatory class, never capable of self-support or of managing their own affairs. The great majority ultimately become public charges in some form. They cause unutterable sorrow at home and are a menace and danger to the community. Feebleminded women are almost invariably immoral and ... usually become carriers of venereal disease or give birth to children who are as defective as themselves. ... Every feebleminded person, especially the high-grade imbecile, is a potential criminal, needing only the proper environment and opportunity for the development and expression of his criminal tendencies (reported in Davies & Ecob, 1959).

The impact of such indictments was profound, leading to the rather radical movement both to segregate and sterilize the retarded. It was thought that these practices would protect normal members of society, as well as establish a means of controlling the birth rate of potentially defective children. However, the effectiveness of these measures in dealing with the widespread problem of mental retardation was meager and disappointing. Not too many years ago this extremely pessimistic approach gave way to a third era of social policy concerning the retarded. This era, which includes the contemporary period, has been characterized by a more measured approach to the social problem of mental retardation. In the wake of this reassessment, a number of issues of general theoretical as well as practical interest have been raised. Not the least important of these are the implications for a general theory of socialization that may be derived from the social behavior of retarded individuals. Stated somewhat differently, the social behavior of many of the retarded poses the question for the general socialization theorist of whether such individuals are or are not socialized.

The answer to this question depends to a considerable extent on the theorist's conception of socialization. Whereas certain of the more traditional formulations lead to the conclusion that the retarded are, either by definition or implication, unsocialized, alternative conceptions of the socialization process suggest a quite different picture. In the more traditional camp (cf., Blatz, 1944; Dager, 1964) are those for whom socialization represents the relatively passive transmission of cultural norms from one generation to the next. Within such a framework, socialization is conceptualized as an end state, defined in terms of the acquisition of social values and conformity to certain norms. This point of view leaves little room for a consideration of individual differences in the socialization process and leads to the view that the mentally retarded, as well as others such as the psychopath, are unsocialized.

The narrowness of this general position has been criticized on several grounds. Brown (1965) and others (cf., Kohlberg, 1966b) have indicated the inadequacy of those treatments in which socialization has been conceptualized to be simply the control of impulses, the acquisition of values, conformity to norms, or the internalization of the parental superego. These workers have argued that the developing child plays a more active role than that of a passive recipient of the culture's mores and folkways.

Once one considers the biological characteristics of the species, the unique genetic inheritance of the individual, and the everchanging developmental processes available to the child as he encounters his environment, then the socialization process can no longer be viewed as the simple inculcation of, and conformity to, the cultural norms. Our emphasis here shifts to the complexities of the socialization process itself, rather than the end state of some abstract modal man against which each person's socialization is to be assessed. This difference in approach has been articulated by Wrong (1961) in his distinction between socialization as the "transmission of culture" and socialization as the "process of becoming human." According to the first definition, many retarded individuals would be considered unsocialized.

If one ascribes to the second and broader definition, however, socialization is considered to be a process applicable to every individual, including the retarded, since every individual somehow "becomes human." Such a viewpoint would seem to be the most fruitful approach to our understanding of socialization in general, as well as the particular problems presented by the retarded. It is of some interest that Durkheim (1938) acknowledged such a position some 30 years ago in his insistence that sociological theory be broad enough in scope to treat any pattern of human behavior as an essentially "normal phenomenon."

We come here to the crux of the matter, namely the issue of whether retarded individuals are best conceptualized as being "like" individuals of normal intellect, or as being immutably "different" from the more intelligent members of society. According to the similarity position, the retarded individual would be viewed as an essentially normal person, whose ultimate socialization pattern would be influenced by his low intelligence, but whose socialization process is mediated and/or influenced by precisely the same variables as influence the socialization of more intelligent individuals.

Within the difference orientation, the retarded individual would be viewed as one whose very nature was characterized by deficiencies which forever set him apart from more intelligent people. It is but a short step from this difference orientation to a dichotomy in which intelligent individuals are viewed as socialized and intellectually retarded individuals are viewed as somewhat less than human, and therefore unsocializable. The difference orientation, which generates the view that retarded individuals are unsocialized, can be traced to historical antecedents, as well as to contemporary theorizing concerning the functioning of the retarded. As noted earlier, the disappointing rehabilitative efforts with the retarded early in the century, and the ensuing social alarm, did much to foster the view that retardates were inherently different. The evidence revealing the inordinately high incidence of socially unacceptable behaviors such as crime and illegitimacy among the retarded served to perpetuate the notion that the retarded suffer from a moral or character defect. The subsequent application of psychoanalytic principles to the problem of mental retardation served to provide this view with theoretical respectability in considering the basic defect of the retarded as a deficiency in the organization and function of the ego (Pearson, 1942). Thus, not only did the retarded child show impaired development of those ego functions such as reality-testing, problem-solving, and ability to profit from past experience, but his ego was seriously handicapped in its capacity to control the demands of the id, e.g., the ability to control aggressive impulses, and to delay gratification.

In respect to contemporary theorizing, it should be noted that most theorists view all of the retarded as suffering from some specifiable defect over and above their generally lower level of cognitive functioning (see Zigler, 1967a, for a review of these theories). Whereas the earlier workers viewed the inherent defect as residing in the moral or character structure, contemporary theorists view the defect as inhering in the physical or cognitive structures of the retarded. While there is certainly a sizable group of retardates who suffer from one of a variety of known physiological defects, e.g., phenylketonuria, chromosomal defects, cerebral trauma, the majority of retardates, conventionally diagnosed as familial, do not manifest any such type of known physiological anomaly. Nevertheless, many workers in the area insist that even these retardates suffer from a specifiable defect, although these theorists differ among themselves as to the exact nature of the defect. Thus, the retarded have been described as suffering from a relative impermeability of the boundaries between regions of the cognitive structure (Kounin, 1941a, 1941b; Lewin, 1936); primary and secondary rigidity caused by subcortical and cortical malformations, respectively (Goldstein, 1942–43); malfunctioning disinhibitory mechanisms (Siegel & Foshee, 1960); dissociation of the verbal and motor systems (Luria, 1963); impaired attention-directing mechanisms (Zeaman & House, 1963); brevity of the stimulus trace (Ellis, 1963); and inadequate neural satiation (Spitz, 1963).

The diversity in the type of defects represented in this list is in part a reflection of the fact that the existence of such defects is inferred from differences in performance between retardates and normals, rather than on the basis of physiological evidence. The very number of different defects postulated attests to the etiological problem posed by familial retardation, which has been the object of the most heated disputes in the area. While a complete discussion of this dispute is beyond the scope of this paper (see Zigler, 1967a), the implications of the general defect position are critical to the consideration of the socialization of the retarded. Such an orientation, with its emphasis on the inherent differences between retarded and normal individuals, tends to perpetuate the rather pessimistic outlook which constitutes the heritage of workers in the area of mental retardation. Within such a frame of reference, research is directed toward the repeated demonstration of performance *differences* between the normal and the retarded, as further evidence in support of the existence of the particular defect postulated. There can be little question that this theoretical approach has lent tangential credence to the view that retardates, by their very nature, are unsocializable.

In contrast to this approach is the position that familial retardates are not essentially different from individuals of greater intellect, but represent, rather, the lower portion of the intellectual curve which reflects normal intellectual variability. This view is bolstered by the recent work of a number of authorities (see Gottesman, 1963; Hirsch, 1963; Penrose, 1963) who have emphasized the need for employing polygenic models of inheritance in an effort to understand the familial retardate. Within this framework, the familial retardate is seen as a perfectly normal expression of the population gene pool, of slower and more limited intellectual development than the individual of average intellect.

This view generates the proposition that retardates and normals at the same cognitive level, i.e., the same mental age, are similar with respect to their cognitive functioning. However, such a proposition runs headlong into the findings that retardates and normals of the same mental age frequently differ in performance. But such differences need not be attributed to any defect which inheres in familial retardation. Rather, those that support the similarity position have argued that performance on any experimental and real-life task is never the single inexorable product of the retardate's cognitive structure, but reflects a wide variety of relatively nonintellective factors as well. Thus, many of the reported behavioral differences between normals and retardates are seen as products of motivational and experiential differences between these groups, rather than as the result of any inherent cognitive deficiency in the retarded.

Such an approach emphasizes the systematic evaluation of the role of experiential, motivational, and personality factors. It is precisely an understanding of these factors, and their relationship to intelligence level, which will provide a better understanding of the socialization process in the retarded. For while the majority of the efforts and environmental manipulations designed to improve the quality of cognitive functioning in the retarded have been relatively unsuccessful (see reviews by Jones, 1954; Zigler, 1967a), there is a growing body of evidence indicating that certain motivational and personality factors relevant to social adjustment are considerably more modifiable. As Penrose (1963) noted, after a lifetime of work with the retarded,

> The most important work carried out in the field of training defectives is unspectacular. It is not highly technical but requires unlimited patience, good will and common sense. The reward is to be expected not so much in scholastic improvement of the patient as in his personal adjustment to social life. Occupations are found for patients of all grades so that they can take part as fully and usefully as possible in human affairs. This process, which has been termed socialization, contributes greatly to the happiness not only of the patients themselves, but also of those who are responsible for their care (p. 282).

It is perhaps within this area of socialization that we can do a great deal to enhance the everyday effectiveness of the retarded. Both Burks (1939) and Leahy (1935) discovered that personality and character traits were more influenced by environment than was intellectual level. Such findings bolster the argument that there are many modifiable factors which are important in the determination of social adjustment. It is not rare to encounter individuals with the same intellectual make-up demonstrating quite disparate social adjustments. Perhaps, then, the important question concerning the socialization potential of retarded individuals centers less on the problem of how to improve their cognitive functioning than on the issue of how to maximize their adjustment whatever their intellectual capacity may be. That considerable change in performance can result from the manipulation of nonintellective, i.e., motivational, factors will be made clear in a subsequent section of this chapter.

MENTAL RETARDATION, SOCIAL COMPETENCE, AND THE PROBLEM OF DEFINITION

Implicit in the foregoing discussion is the notion that mental retardation per se refers primarily to subnormal intellectual functioning and is diagnosed on the basis of intelligence test performance, which results in a score between zero and some upper limit or cut-off point, traditionally set at 70 or 75. However, in practice, the decision as to whether a person is considered retarded is often based not upon his intellectual characteristics but upon legal and occupational factors as well as his general level of social adjustment. The matter has been put most succinctly by Maher (1963) who stated:

> What constitutes mentally retarded behavior depends to a large extent upon the society which happens to be making the judgment. An individual who does not create a problem for others in his social environment and who manages to become self-supporting is usually not defined as mentally re-

tarded no matter what his test IQ may be. Mental retardation is primarily a socially defined phenomenon, and it is in large part meaningless to speak of mental retardation without this criterion in mind (p. 238).

The widespread acceptance of this view is reflected in the most recent definition and classification of mental retardation officially adopted by the American Association on Mental Deficiency in 1960. According to this definition, "Mental retardation refers to subaverage general intellectual functioning which originates during the developmental period and is associated with impairment in adaptive behavior" (Heber, 1962, p. 70). With regard to intelligence test performance, the statistical criterion established is such that all those at least one standard deviation below the population mean IQ are considered retarded. However, the critical factor in this concept of mental retardation is the "inclusion of the dual criteria of reduced intellectual functioning *and* impaired social adaptation" (Heber, 1962, p. 71).

The official adoption of this definition should not be taken to indicate that prior to this time, inferior intellectual performance was considered to be the sole or definitive criterion. On the contrary, as both Heber (1962) and Maher (1963) have noted, the social, administrative, and legal aspects of mental retardation have long been of critical significance. However, this emphasis on social factors in defining mental retardation may lead to more confusion than clarity, as indicated by the discrepancies found among various incidence and survey studies. If mental retardation is defined strictly in terms of IQ, and a certain constancy of the IQ score is assumed, no difference in the incidence of mental retardation would be expected at different ages, i.e., approximately three per cent of the population would be classified as retarded, using the 70 IQ cut-off. The incidence figures reported in Table 28.1 do not support this contention, however, since they indicate that the incidence of mental retardation fluctuates not only across age categories, but also according to the locality and even the date at which the data were collected.

TABLE 28.1

PERCENTAGE OF PERSONS CLASSIFIED AS MENTALLY RETARDED

	Locality		
Age	England (1929)	Baltimore, Maryland (1941)	Syracuse, New York (1955)
Under 5	0.12	0.07	0.45
5– 9	1.55	1.18	3.94
10–14	2.65	4.36	7.76
15–19	1.08	3.02	4.49

Sources: ENGLAND, Report of the Mental Deficiency Committee. London: His Majesty's Stationery Office, 1929; BALTIMORE, MARYLAND, Lemkau, P., Tietze, C., & Cooper, M. Mental-hygiene problems in an urban district. *Mental Hygiene*, 1941, 25, 624; and SYRACUSE, NEW YORK, New York State Department Mental Hygiene Technical Report, 1955.

These figures become understandable if one realizes that they reflect classifications based on some combination of IQ and the success of the individual in meeting social demands. For example, the extremely low incidence under five years of age may reflect the minimal social demands made on young children. The highest incidence obtained at the 10–14 age level occurs when the child is faced with school and more demanding intellectual tasks. It is probably in this age range that the relationship between IQ scores and meeting societal expectancies, i.e., successful school performance, is greatest. Stated somewhat differently, within this age range, employing either the IQ test or the child's success in meeting social demands would probably result in his classification as mentally retarded.

The use of social competence as a criterion for mental retardation would appear to be even more predominant in diagnosing adult populations. According to Heber (1962), "Social adjustment is the most important qualifying condition of mental retardation at the adult level where we are concerned with how well the individual conforms to the standards of personal and social responsibilities set by the community" (p. 73). Perhaps the most extreme argument for the reliance on social criteria has been presented by Tredgold (1952), who rejects the criteria of both educational and intelligence test performance on the grounds that a person capable of holding a job and managing his personal affairs should not be stigmatized as defective simply because he is either an educational failure or has an IQ below some arbitrary cut-off point. Instead, Tredgold favors a "biological and social criterion," based on the assumption that the essential purpose of the intellect is to enable the individual ". . . to adapt himself to his environment and to maintain an independent existence." According to Tredgold, the person who can meet this criterion should be considered normal, whereas those whose mental endowment does not permit such adjustment are to be regarded as defective.

In making this assertion, Tredgold recognizes the need to separate the psychological or intellectual from the environmental aspects of social adequacy. In this regard, he has stated that "to constitute abnormality and defect, the failure must be due to psychological and not to economic and social causes; and there is usually little difficulty in distinguishing between the two." However, as Clarke (1958) has noted, Tredgold provides no criteria for making such a distinction, and Clarke has further criticized Tredgold's formulation on the grounds "that social criteria (particularly those which are not operationally defined) are just as arbitrary as the IQ, if not more so, and have not even the advantage of being based on norms for an entire population" (p. 49). The inadequacy of the social competence construct as a necessary component in the definition of retardation has been noted by other investigators as well. Even Heber (1962), who has made the strongest case for employing social competence, has admitted that objective measures of adaptive behavior are presently unavailable. He has also stated that the present ambiguity of the social competence construct is such that in practice intelligence test performance must remain "the most important and heavily weighted of the criteria used."

The arbitrariness involved in the use of social criteria has other implications as well. For example, suppose social competence is defined in terms of occupational employment. Thus, if the individual, whatever his IQ, is dutifully employed, he is not considered mentally retarded. Now let us imagine an economic recession during which this hypothetical individual is laid off. At this point in time he becomes a mental retardate, by definition. Of course, from a practical point of view such an individual would not be considered retarded, since either explicitly or implicitly the criteria would change as a function of the socioeconomic conditions. However, one might well question both the value as well as the validity of such a classification system in which reliance on such an ephemeral concept as social competence guarantees that the system will be an unstable one. As Clarke (1958) has noted in a similar vein, "to the extent that mental deficiency is a social concept, with fluctuating thresholds of community tolerance, classification is bound to be somewhat arbitrary, and no system is likely to be either comprehensive or permanent" (p. 64).

The hypothetical example cited above is more relevant to a consideration of social competence as a criterion than may be immediately apparent. For example, Charles (1953) followed up a group of special class retarded pupils previously studied by Baller (1936) who had initially found that during the Depression, 42 per cent of this mentally subnormal group were on relief. Charles' subsequent study revealed that during the more prosperous period between 1941 and 1950 less than ten per cent of this same group of retarded were on relief.

A related theme commonly encountered in recent discussions of the social and occupational adjustment of the retarded is that because of society's trend toward increasing mechanization, technology, and mobility, fewer jobs are available to the retarded (Dexter, 1958; Ginzberg, 1965; Goldstein, 1964). These writers note that technical changes have resulted in the creation of many skilled jobs which the typical retarded individual is incapable of performing, and this trend has simultaneously reduced the amount of unskilled labor required. Dexter (1958) has expanded this point in his delineation of the detrimental effects of this trend on the adjustment of the retarded who must cope in a society which places increasing emphasis on formal skills. Dexter proposed what he terms a "social theory of mental deficiency," and while he himself presents no direct evidence, his thesis is indirectly supported by the fact that the majority of those follow-up studies revealing a high level of adjustment on the part of adult retardates in the community were conducted at a time when jobs were relatively plentiful (e.g., Bijou, Ainsworth & Stockey, 1943; Charles, 1953; Kennedy, 1948). Such social and economic factors are and should be considered important to the adjustment problems which individuals of lowered intellectual capacity have in meeting the demands of a changing society. However, these factors should not be considered as potentially fluctuating criteria which may demand a reclassification with regard to whether a person is judged to be mentally retarded.

Clarke (1958) has rejected the criterion of social incompetence on other grounds as well. He describes it as both scientifically invalid and administratively dangerous since it will necessarily result in the classification of considerable numbers of neurotics, psychopaths, and criminals as mentally defective. In this same regard, Benton (1962) has discussed the concept of pseudofeeble-mindedness as a false diagnosis in which lack of capacity for social adjustment is confused with intellectual inadequacy. He notes that there are factors in the diagnostic situation which may attenuate the efficiency of performance during a test or interview, e.g., hostility, distrust, resistance, anxiety, or more blatant antisocial behavior. Such factors may lead to the erroneous diagnosis of mental deficiency, "when in reality the child's social incompetence is determined by motivational and attitudinal factors rather than by intellectual inadequacy" (Benton, 1962, p. 85).

What should be emphasized is that social competence does not inevitably reflect normal intellectual functioning any more than its absence in the emotionally unstable, the criminal, or the social misfit reflects intellectual subnormality. Conversely, as Davies and Ecob (1959) pointed out, "A mental age of nine, ten, eleven, or twelve years does not, of necessity, imply social inadequacy any more than a mental age which indicates superior intelligence guarantees that the person will not be antisocial" (p. 225). What should be clear is that social competence is much too heterogeneous a phenomenon and reflects too many nonintellectual factors to be of great value in understanding mental retardation. The basic problem is that the concept of social competence is so value-laden and its definition so vague that it has little heuristic utility. Windle (1962) has pointed out that perhaps the social competence definition of mental retardation is applicable only to institutionalized populations, whereas quite different definitional criteria must be employed with the noninstitutionalized retarded. The applicability of the social competence criterion here would seem to inhere in its use as a valid index in the determination of commitment to an institution, as opposed to its function as a defining characteristic of mental retardation per se. Such considerations suggest that perhaps the most clear and acceptable operational definition of social competence is related to whether the individual has managed to function outside of an institutional setting.

With this in mind, we might legitimately ask what are the intellectual demands of such social competence? Phrased in this way, the question more appropriately directs our attention toward an assessment of both intellectual and nonintellectual determinants of social adjustment and their role in the socialization process. To date, we have made relatively little headway in exploring these issues. In the area of mental retardation social competence usually means the ability to maintain oneself without too frequent contact with state schools, state hospitals, welfare agencies, and police officers. Though social competence defined in this way reflects certain cognitive abilities, it may also reflect a variety of factors reminiscent of nonintellectual aspects of intelligence test performance. We refer here to factors such as social values, attitudes toward other people, and emotional needs that are relatively independent of intellectual level. Thus, present intelligence tests may predict social competence better than an ideal intelligence test because of the overlap of nonintellectual variables which influence both intelligence test scores and social competence.

There is a further problem with the social competence construct related to a fallacy which has permeated much of our thinking concerning the retarded. We have somehow come to believe that it is impossible for anyone who is "truly" retarded to meet the complex demands of our society. The bulk of retardates who have mental ages in the 9–12 range (remembering that a mental age of 16 is the upper limit for an individual of average IQ) have the intellectual wherewithal to meet the minimal demands of our society. This becomes immediately apparent if one raises the question of how much intellectual ability is required to arise in the morning, dress oneself, catch a bus or walk to a single location, perform some undemanding sort of labor, and return home. Indeed in the 1920's and 30's it was discovered that there were no less than 118 occupations in our society suitable for individuals having mental ages from 5–12 (Beckham, 1930; Burr, 1925). As late as 1956, DeProspo (Whitney, 1956) noted that 54 per cent of jobs require no schooling beyond the elementary level.

Another major aspect of social competence is the ability of the individual to abide by the values of the society, i.e., obey laws, etc. While the incidence of crime among the retarded is higher than among the nonretarded, this elevation in incidence is not terribly great, especially if one controls for the social class factor (see Goldstein, 1964). Here again it is an error to view obedience to the law as somehow beyond the ability of the retarded. One simply has to apply the concept of the stages of moral development as investigated by Piaget (1948) and Kohlberg (1966a) that fairly young children are capable of a morality based on absolutism, i.e., the rules inhere in the very fabric of existence and are not to be broken under any circumstances. Individuals who never achieve a higher stage of moral development are certainly not developmentally superior, but neither are they likely to break many laws.

In order to make social competence a meaningful construct, we must thus abandon some simplistic notion of social competence in favor of a variety of continua theoretically based upon the cognitive demands of the social requirements involved. Such indices could then be considered independent indicators of intellectual functioning. Empirical efforts of this sort may be seen in the Vineland Social Maturity Scale and the Worcester Scale of Social Attainment. A more theoretical effort may be found in the work of Phillips and Zigler (1961, 1964) in which both intelligence test scores and conventional social competence indices are combined into an index of developmental or maturational level.

LONGITUDINAL AND FOLLOW-UP STUDIES OF
THE OCCUPATIONAL AND SOCIAL ADJUSTMENT
OF THE RETARDED

Despite the theoretical ambiguities which continue to inhere in the social competence construct, studies of the social and occupational adjustment of the retarded would appear to shed some light on their socialization potential (see reviews by Goldstein, 1964; Tizard, 1958; Windle, 1962). One of the earliest follow-up studies of the adjustment of retarded individuals was conducted by Fernald (1919), whose pessimistic outlook toward the potential socialization of this group was noted at the outset of this chapter. Following up those who had been discharged from Waverly State School between 1890 and 1914, Fernald found that 51 per cent of the females and 64 per cent of the males had remained in the community. Of these, 58 per cent of the females and better than 80 per cent of the males had no record of difficulty and were judged to have made a satisfactory adjustment. Despite the fact that almost half of the original sample had to be reinstitutionalized, and approximately one-third of those remaining in the community did have records of difficulty, these findings were viewed with guarded optimism and surprise. As Davies (1930) related, "Dr. Fernald told the writer that he had hesitated for two years to publish the results of this study because they seemed so much at variance with the then accepted theories dealing with mental deficiency" (p. 196).

Following Fernald's lead, a number of similar studies began to appear (e.g., Foley, 1929; Matthews, 1922; Storrs, 1924). These studies were consistent in their findings that the majority of the paroled retarded did adjust relatively successfully to the community. However, the significance of these findings is somewhat difficult to assess, since typically these investigators employed gross or ambiguous measures of community adjustment, and the characteristics of the samples are not described, nor are the criteria for release; furthermore, the extent of prior training or rehabilitation is often not specified, and there are few data on such factors as community tolerance, availability of jobs, etc. (See Goldstein, 1964, for a complete review and critique of these and subsequent follow-up studies.)

More recent follow-up studies of the adjustment of the retarded paroled from institutions presents a similar and slightly more complete picture. Goldstein (1964) notes that perhaps the only broad generalization which may be derived with any degree of confidence is that the majority of higher grade mentally retarded inmates paroled will probably make a relatively successful adjustment in their communities when training, selection, placement, and supervision are all at an optimum. However, he also notes one other consideration of interest, namely that there seems to be little relationship between the mental status of these retarded and their earning capacity. Windle (1962), in his comprehensive review of over 100 studies dealing with the prognosis for the adjustment of retardates discharged from institutions, has come to a similar conclusion. The tendency to overemphasize the importance of intelligence in adjustment is made clear by his survey. Windle found that most institutions presume that intelligence is the critical factor in adjustment after release. He points out that the vast majority of studies on outcome "after release from institutions have reported no relation between intellectual level and later adjustment."

Windle goes on to state that there is some evidence (Grant, 1956; Krishef, 1957) which suggests a curvilinear relation between outcome after discharge and IQ level, where the IQ range is between 40 and 85. The tentative explanation for such findings is that among the high IQ institutionalized retarded there is a high incidence of personality problems which are more detrimental to extrainstitutional adjustment than is mild intellectual retardation in the absence of personality problems. Grant (1956), in examining the histories of his retarded subjects, found that the incidence of "character disorders," which he defined as persistent misconduct, was positively correlated with IQ. Tarjan and Benson (1953) have presented similar indirect evidence that the more intelligent subnormals released from the institution may have the most severe adjustment problems. Some understanding of this relationship may be gained from a consideration of the evidence indicating the atypical social histories of this particular group; these findings will be reviewed in the next section of this chapter.

That personality factors are as important in the retardate's adjustment as are intellective factors has been noted by numerous investigators, e.g., Davies and Ecob, 1959; Penrose, 1963; Sarason, 1953; Tizard, 1953. In fact, many of the early workers in this country, such as Fernald and Potter, felt that the difference between social adequacy and inadequacy in that large group of borderline retardates was a matter of personality rather than intelligence. One of a number of studies which seem to confirm this view is a comprehensive survey by Weaver (1946) of the adjustment of 8,000 retardates inducted into the United States Army, most of whom had IQs below 75. Of the total group, 56 per cent of the males and 62 per cent of the females made a satisfactory adjustment to military life. The median IQs of the successful and unsuccessful groups were 72 and 68, respectively. Weaver's conclusion was that "personality factors far overshadowed the factor of intelligence in the adjustment of the retarded to military service."

It has only been quite recently, however, that the specific personality factors relating to adjustment have been the object of more direct and systematic study. Shafter (1957), in attempting to ascertain those characteristics which best predicted successful adjustment of retardates after release, first compiled a list of 66 variables which had been described in the literature and which he could objectify. He then compared the records of a group of 111 parolees who had been successful in adjusting to the community with a group of 94 who had been unsuccessful, i.e., had been returned to the institution. Included among those characteristics which contributed nothing toward predicting successful adjustment were IQ, age at discharge, length of institutionalization, and behavior record while an inmate. Among those twelve characteristics which significantly differentiated the successful from the unsuccessful parolees were truthfulness, obedience, attention to details and personal habits, (less) predisposition toward quarrelsomeness, and (less) display of aggressiveness in the institution.

While Shafter's (1957) study represents a commendable attempt to delineate those characteristics which predict adjustment to community life, his effort suffers from the gross nature of the measure of successful adjustment, i.e., complete discharge from the institution versus return to the institution as a result of some difficulty or misconduct in the community. This same criticism can be made of the majority of studies designed to assess adjustment to the community in that they tend to employ rather gross measures of adjustment, i.e., per cent who are employed, married, or have had no contact with the law. By far, the most frequent criterion used is that of employment record, and the degree to which an individual is self-sufficient.

Kennedy's (1948) follow-up studies of 256 noninstitutionalized retarded persons is a typical example, although his study merits more attention than most since he compared their adjustment with that of a control group of nonretarded subjects who had initially attended the same public school. Kennedy found no significant differences between the groups in the proportion employed, the salaries earned, or the proportion on relief. However, significantly more of the retarded adults were in laboring occupations, received lower job ratings from their employers, and failed to save money. Furthermore, there were more violations of conventional codes of behavior among the retarded group, although their offenses were mostly misdemeanors. As a group, however, the retarded were largely self-supporting and socially adequate.

The importance of the particular criteria of adjustment selected is highlighted by another follow-up study by Saenger (1957) of noninstitutionalized severely retarded adults who had attended trainable classes in public school. The adjustment of this group is described very positively in terms of such criteria as their alertness, self-confidence, good relationships with family, helpfulness around the house, and absence of delinquent behavior. However, of this group of severely retarded adults, 73 per cent had no form of employment, and of those that did, none were self-sufficient. While this is certainly not surprising, in view of the degree of retardation manifest by this group, it has implications for our understanding of the relationship between intelligence and social competence. Saenger's (1957) findings lead us to qualify the conclusions derived from those studies which found no simple relationship between IQ and social competence.

The failure to find a simple and striking relationship between social competence and intelligence would appear to hold when the range of IQs is between approximately 50 and 75. Within this range, social adjustment would seem to be determined more by personality and motivational factors than by the intellective factors reflected in intelligence test performance. However, the positive relationship between intelligence test performance and social competence, defined by such measures as employability, becomes striking and predictable if one includes in their assessment more severely retarded (IQs of 0–40) individuals. It should be noted that this numerically smaller group of retarded demands the continual support and care of families and agencies, and will never be self-supporting, responsible, productive citizens. In many respects, the severely retarded individual is not really an independent, fully-functioning member of the mainstream of society. This does not mean that he is not a human being, manifesting those aspects of socialization characteristic of the very young child. Evaluating the socialization of the severely retarded simply requires quite different criteria, and involves different expectations, than with the mildly or moderately retarded. All of this is by way of saying that retarded individuals represent an extremely heterogeneous group in respect to their final socialization patterns, and any understanding of these patterns must consider both the intellective and nonintellective factors which play a role in the socialization process.

In general, the findings of those follow-up studies on the social adjustment of noninstitutionalized groups underscore the importance of those personality factors emphasized in the discussion of institutionalized populations. As Robinson and Robinson (1965) noted in their review of these studies, "Success in obtaining and keeping a job is related to a large number of psychological and work-habit variables, including initiative, self-confidence, co-operation, cheerfulness, social mixing with other employees, respect for the supervisor, and understanding and efficiency in work" (p. 545). Those factors which would seem to determine failure on the job have been studied by Collman and Newlyn (1956, 1957). Among a group of retarded individuals who had been former special class pupils in England, those few who failed to keep their jobs were most often described by their employers as having some character deficiency, e.g., temperamental instability, inefficiency, and/or poor home conditions.

These findings, taken with the general literature on factors relating to the adjustment of the retarded, reveal that those characteristics associated with poor social adjustment include anxiety, jealousy, overdependency, poor self-evaluation, hostility, hyperactivity, emotionality, resistance, and failure to follow orders even when requests are well within the range of intellectual competence. To date, however, relatively little attention has been directed toward an examination of the processes through which such characteristics are developed in the maturing retarded child. Tizard (1958) makes a similar point in his review of the longitudinal and follow-up studies of the retarded, which he criticizes as being largely descriptive. He concludes with a plea that we "learn more about the basic psychological processes of the mentally subnormal, and the laws which govern their interaction and development." Similarly, Windle (1962) notes the narrowness of those studies which tend to focus on the total IQ score as the major prognostic indicator; he urges a more meaningful research approach in which a broader range of variables, e.g., personality factors, based on psychological theory are examined.

The follow-up studies would appear to present compelling evidence for the general role of personality factors in the performance of the retarded. However, there has been too little attention given to the precise identification of these factors, their relative importance, and the socialization histories which give rise to such characteristics. We are certainly in agreement with the philosophy behind Davies and Ecob's (1959) statement that "The constructive efforts of (community) agencies are especially directed toward those elements of personality which have been shown not to be fixed, which are susceptible to improvement, and which are more decisive factors in socialization than intelligence alone" (p. 216). However, from their discussion of these rehabilitative efforts it would seem that much of this work is being conducted on the basis of little established evidence; in the absence of such information, it appears that often, and perhaps necessarily, policy decisions are based on common sense, intuition, vague generalizations, and stereotypic beliefs about the retarded, e.g., the mentally retarded are "notably impressionable and easily influenced" (Davies & Ecob, 1959). In the following section, we will review those more rigorous research efforts which have been directed toward the discovery of the ontogenesis of those characteristics important to the retardate's socialization. This review should make it clear that those characteristics which interfere with the socialization of the retarded are as much a product of the unique experiences of the retarded as they are of the retardation itself.

PERSONALITY AND MOTIVATIONAL FACTORS IN THE SOCIALIZATION OF THE RETARDED

A recurring theme in this chapter has been the importance of a variety of nonintellective factors as determinants of the level at which the retarded function. We shall never fully comprehend the behavior of the retarded if we assume that every behavior he manifests is the immutable product of his low intelligence alone. Indeed, a striking feature encountered when groups of retardates are observed is the variety of behavior patterns displayed. Clearly, we are not dealing with a homogeneous group of simple organisms. Once we concern ourselves with the total behavior of the retarded individual, we find him an extremely complex psychological system. To the extent that his behavior deviates from the norms associated with his mental age, he is even more difficult to understand than the normal individual. It is unfortunate that so little work emanating from a personality point of view has been done with the retarded. Some progress has been made, however, and much of the recent work supports the view that it is not necessary to employ constructs other than those used to account for the behavior of normal individuals in explaining the behavior of the familial retarded. It appears that many of the reported differences between retardates and normals are a result of motivational and emotional differences which reflect differences in environmental histories, and are not a function of innate deficiencies.

It is hardly surprising that the retarded evidence certain difficulties in social adjustment, given their atypical social histories. The specific atypical features of their socialization histories, and the extent to which they are atypical, may vary from child to child. Two sets of parents who are themselves familially retarded may provide quite different socialization histories for their children. At one extreme we may find a familially retarded child who is ultimately institutionalized, not due to lack of intelligence, but because his own home represents such a poor environment. That many borderline retardates are institutionalized for just such reasons has been confirmed by Kaplun (1935) in a study of 642 high-grade retardates. More recently, Saenger (1960) has reported that while level of intelligence is a major determinant of institutional commitment in New York City, other important factors determine such placement for the high-grade defective in particular; these include his having gotten into trouble, coming from a family of low socioeconomic status, having incompetent parents, and coming from a broken home. Zigler's finding (1961) that a positive relationship exists between the institutionalized familial retardate's IQ and the amount of preinstitutional deprivation he experienced provides further support for this claim. This latter finding does not indicate that social deprivation produces greater intelligence but rather that our institutions for the retarded contain individuals of borderline intelligence who would not be institutionalized except for their extremely poor home environments.

At the other extreme, a familially retarded set of parents may provide their children with a relatively normal home even though it might differ in certain important respects, e.g., values, goals and attitudes, from the typical home in which the families are of average or superior intelligence. In the first example, the child not only experiences a quite different socialization history while still living with his parents, but also differs from the child in the second situation to the extent that institutionalization affects his personality structure (see Yarrow, 1964). Given the penchant of many investigators for comparing institutionalized retardates with children of average intellect who live at home, the factor of institutionalization becomes an extremely important one. One cannot help but wonder how many differences discovered in such comparisons reflect the effects of institutionalization, the factors that led to the child's institutionalization, or some complex interaction between these factors and institutionalization, as opposed to some cognitive aspect of mental retardation.

To add even more complexity, the socialization histories of both institutionalized and noninstitutionalized familial retardates differ markedly from the history of the brain-damaged retardates. The brain damaged do not show the same gross differences from normals in the frequency of good versus poor early environments. In the face of such complexity, we need not consider the problem unassailable nor need we assert that each retarded child is so unique that it is impossible for us to isolate the ontogenesis of those factors which we feel are important in influencing the retardate's level of functioning. Once we conceptualize the retardate as occupying a position on a continuum of normalcy, we can allow our knowledge of normal development to give direction to our efforts.

This does not mean that we ignore the importance of the lowered intelligence per se, since personality traits and behavior patterns do not develop in a vacuum. However, in some instances the personality characteristics of the retarded will reflect environmental factors that have little or nothing to do with intellectual endowment. For example, many of the effects of institutionalization may be constant regardless of the person's intelligence level. In other instances, we must think in terms of an interaction, that is, given his lowered intellectual ability, a person will have certain experiences and develop certain behavior patterns differing from those of a person with greater intellectual endowment. An obvious example is the greater amount of failure which the retardate typically experiences. But again what must be emphasized is that the behavior pattern developed by the retardate as a result of such a history of failure may not necessarily differ in kind or ontogenesis from those developed by an individual of normal intellect who, by some environmental circumstance, also experiences an inordinate amount of failure. By the same token, if the retardate can somehow be guaranteed a more typical history of success, we would expect his behavior to be more normal, independent of his intellectual level. Within this framework, the personality factors which have been known to influence the performance of the retarded will be discussed.

Anxiety

Considerable evidence has now been collected indicating the importance of anxiety on performance for a wide variety of tasks (Sarason, Davidson, Lighthall, Waite & Ruebush, 1960; Spence, 1958; Taylor, 1963). The attenuating effects of anxiety on performance appear to be a function of both the task-irrelevant defensive responses employed by the person to alleviate his anxiety (Mandler & Sarason, 1952; Sarason et al., 1960), and the drive features of the anxiety itself. The drive approach to anxiety (Spence, 1958; Taylor, 1963), which has received considerable confirmation, conceptualizes high anxiety as beneficial on extremely nondemanding tasks, e.g., classical eyelid conditioning, but detrimental on complex tasks where a variety of responses are available to the person. The higher anxiety level of retardates, as compared to normals, has been noted by several investigators (see Berkson, 1963; Cantor, 1963; Garfield, 1963; Spradlin, 1963; Stevenson, 1963), who have either demonstrated or suggested that their heightened anxiety level could well have produced certain of the reported differences between retardates and mental age-control normals. Work with retardates that has either focused on anxiety or raised the anxiety issue in a *post hoc* manner is of considerable value "in that it applies concepts and techniques to the study of retarded individuals, which for the most part had not been applied or seen as relevant for this group" (Garfield, 1963, p. 594).

The evidence that anxiety level affects the performance of retardates much as that of normals, and that retardates might have higher levels of anxiety than normals, tells us little about the ontogenesis of anxiety in retardates. To understand their atypical anxiety levels, we must examine the relatively atypical experiences of the retarded, as well as a variety of other motivational states which influence their performance.

Social Deprivation

It has become increasingly clear that our understanding of the performance of the institutionalized familial retardate will be enhanced if we consider the inordinate amount of preinstitutional social deprivation he has experienced (Clarke & Clarke, 1954; Kaplun, 1935; Saenger, 1960; Zigler, 1961). Another series of studies (Green & Zigler, 1962; Shepps & Zigler, 1962; Zigler, 1961, 1963a; Zigler, Hodgden & Stevenson, 1958; Zigler & Williams, 1963) has indicated that one result of such early deprivation is a heightened motivation to interact with a supportive adult. (In the process of conducting these studies, a social deprivation scale was constructed which promises to bring some added objectivity to the social deprivation concept.) These studies suggest that given this heightened motivation, retardates exhibit considerable compliance with instructions when the effect of such compliance is to increase or maintain the social interaction with the adult. Compliance is apparently reduced in those instances where it leads to terminating the interaction.

It now appears that the perseveration so frequently noted in the behavior of the retarded is primarily a function of this motivational factor rather than the inherent cognitive rigidity suggested by Lewin (1936) and Kounin (1941a, 1941b). Evidence on this latter point comes from findings indicating that: (a) the degree of perseveration is directly related to the degree of preinstitutional deprivation experienced (Zigler, 1961), and (b) institutionalized children of normal intellect are just as perseverative as institutionalized retardates, while noninstitutionalized retardates are no more perseverative than noninstitutionalized children of normal intellect (Green & Zigler, 1962; Zigler, 1963a). The heightened motivation to interact with an adult, stemming from a history of social deprivation, would appear to be consistent with the often-made observation of certain behaviors in the retarded, i.e., they seek attention, desire affection, etc. (Cruickshank, 1947; Doll, 1962; Hirsh, 1959; Wellman, 1938). Hirsh (1959) has urged that we should consider such characteristics as perseveration and verbal parroting in terms of their adaptive significance rather than as "signs" of retardation. He notes, for example, that the behavior of the retarded child who repeats words of adults or questions extensively may be understood, in part, as his best effort to establish communication.

It is impossible to place too much emphasis on the role of overdependency in the institutional familial retarded and on the socialization histories that give rise to such overdependency. Given some minimal intellectual level, the shift from dependency to independence is perhaps the single most important factor necessary for the retardate to become a self-sustaining member of our society. It appears that the institutionalized retardate must satisfy certain affectional needs before he can cope with problems in a manner characterized by individuals whose affectional needs have been relatively satiated. These affectional needs can best be viewed as ones which often interfere with certain problem-solving activities. Evidence on this point comes from a recent study by Harter (1967), in which institutionalized retardates took significantly longer to solve a concept-formation problem in a social condition, where they were face-to-face with a warm supportive experimenter who praised their performance, than in a standard condition, where the experimenter was silent and out of view. The retarded subjects in the social condition appeared highly motivated to interact with an approving supportive adult, so much so that it seemed to compete with their attention to the learning task. Such findings suggest that because the retardate is highly motivated to satisfy such needs through maximizing interpersonal contact he is relatively unconcerned with the specific solution to such problems. Of course, the two goals will not always be incompatible, but in many instances they will be. Some evidence that this attenuating aspect of retarded behavior can be overcome has been presented by McKinney and Keele (1963), who found improvement in a variety of behaviors in the mentally retarded following an experience of increased mothering.

Crucial to this motivational interpretation is the view that institutionalized retardates have been deprived of adult social reinforcement and are therefore highly motivated to obtain this particular class of reinforcers. Evidence offering further support for this view is contained in a recent study (Harter & Zigler, 1968) in which it was found that an adult experimenter is a more effective social reinforcer than a peer experimenter for institutionalized retardates. Thus, it would appear that the institutionalized retardate's motivation to obtain social reinforcement is relatively specific to attention and praise dispensed by an adult, rather than a more generalized desire for reinforcement dispensed by any social agent, e.g., a peer. This differential effectiveness of peer and adult social reinforcement further argues against the popular view that retardates are inherently rigid and will therefore perseverate on a dull monotonous task. Rather, how perseverative the retarded child is would appear to depend on the valence of the social reinforcers dispensed during the task. That peer reinforcement was not highly valued by the institutionalized child is not particularly surprising, in view of the general availability of this type of reinforcer in the institutional setting (Balla, 1966).

Zigler and Williams (1963) have provided some evidence that the child's motivation for social interaction and support is influenced by an interaction between preinstitutional social deprivation and institutionalization. It was found that although institutionalization generally increased this motivation, it was increased much more for children coming from relatively nondeprived homes as compared to those coming from more socially deprived backgrounds.

An unexpected finding of the Zigler and Williams study was that when subjects were retested following three more years of institutionalization, a general decrease in IQs (on individually administered intelligence tests) of the retardates had occurred between the two testings. This change in IQ, discovered in the context of a study employing the amount of preinstitutional social deprivation as an independent variable, is reminiscent of a finding by Clarke and Clarke (1954). These investigators found that changes in the IQs of retardates following institutionalization were related to their preinstitutional histories. They discovered that children coming from extremely poor homes showed an increase in IQ which was not observed in children coming from relatively good homes. Zigler and Williams, however, found that the magnitude of the IQ change in their subjects was not significantly related to preinstitutional deprivation. Although this finding appears inconsistent with that of Clarke and Clarke, it should be noted that some support for a relationship was suggested since the only subjects in the Zigler and Williams study who evidenced an increase in IQ were in the high-deprived group. The failure of Zigler and Williams to replicate the findings of Clarke and Clarke may be due to two factors: the subjects used by Clarke and Clarke were older and had been institutionalized at a later age than the retardates employed by Zigler and Williams; and the IQ changes reported by Clarke and Clarke took place during two years of institutionalization, while the IQ changes reported in the Zigler and Williams study were based on five years of institutionalization. This latter factor becomes increasingly important in view of Jones and Carr-Saunders' (1927) finding that normal institutionalized children show an increase in IQ early in institutionalization and then a decrease in IQ with longer institutionalization.

The work of Clarke and Clarke, Jones and Carr-Saunders, and others (e.g., Guertin, 1949), dealing with changes in IQ following institutionalization, has given central importance to the degree of intellectual stimulation provided by the institution in contrast to that provided by the original home. This orientation suggests that it is the actual intellectual potential of the person which is altered. The Zigler and Williams study, however, suggests that the change in IQ reflects a change in the child's motivation for social interaction. That is, as social deprivation, resulting from increased length of institutionalization, increases, the desire to interact with the adult experimenter increases. Thus, for the deprived child the desire to be correct must compete in the testing situation with the desire to increase the amount of social interaction. This argument would appear to provide the conceptual framework for Clarke and Clarke's finding that highly deprived subjects evidence an increase in IQ with relatively short institutionalization, while the less deprived subjects demonstrate no greater increase than a test-retest control group. One would further expect that with continued institutionalization all children would exhibit a decrease in IQ, the phenomenon found by Jones and Carr-Saunders (1927), and one that appears in the Zigler and Williams study. Direct support for this view comes from the finding in the Zigler and Williams study of a positive relationship between the magnitude of the decrease in IQ and the child's motivation for social interaction.

It should be noted that the Jones and Carr-Saunders (1927) study involved institutionalized children of approximately average intellect, thus indicating that the dynamics under discussion here are the same for both normal and retarded children. Furthermore, the position advanced here is quite consistent with the findings for normal children obtained by Barrett and Koch (1930) and Krugman (1939); these investigators found that the greatest increase in IQ was obtained by children who showed the greatest improvement in their personality traits and/or by children who evidenced a marked change in the nature of their relationship with the examiner. Conversely, what must be emphasized in respect to lowered IQs is not the lowered test score per se, but rather that the factors which attenuate these test scores will, in all probability, reduce the adequacy of many problem-solving behaviors performed in a social situation.

More direct evidence indicating the effects of motivational and social factors on IQ test performance is contained in a recent study by Zigler and Butterfield (unpublished manuscript) of IQ change in children attending nursery school programs for the culturally deprived. This study indicates that the typical IQ gain found among such nursery school children is due largely to the effects that the nursery school experience has on attenuating debilitating motivational factors, rather than changing the child's formal cognitive structure.

Positive- and Negative-Reaction Tendencies

Although there is considerable observational and experimental evidence that social deprivation results in a heightened motivation to interact with a supportive adult, it appears to have other effects as well. The nature of these effects is suggested in those observations of the retarded that have noted their fearfulness, wariness or avoidance of strangers, or their suspicion and mistrust (Hirsh, 1959; Wellman, 1938; Woodward, 1960). The experimental work done by Zigler and his associates on the behavior of the institutionalized retarded has indicated that social deprivation results both in a heightened motivation to interact with supportive adults (positive-reaction tendency) and in a reluctance and wariness to do so (negative-reaction tendency).

The construct of a negative-reaction tendency has been employed to explain certain differences between retardates and normals reported by Kounin, differences that have heretofore been attributed to the greater cognitive rigidity of retarded individuals. As one measure of rigidity, Kounin employed a task in which the subject is instructed to perform a response which he may continue until he wishes to stop; he is then instructed to perform a highly similar response until again satiated. A recurring finding in studies employing such a two-part task (Kounin, 1941a; Zigler, 1958; Zigler et al., 1958) has been that retardates have a much greater tendency than normals to spend more time on task two than on task one. Zigler (1958) suggested that this was due to the greater negative-reaction tendency of retarded subjects which was an outgrowth of the more negative encounters that institutionalized retardates experienced at the hands of adults. His reasoning was that the high negative-reaction tendency of retardates was reduced as a result of the pleasant experiences encountered on task one which, in turn, resulted in a longer playing time on task two. Normals tend not to show such a pattern since there is relatively little negative-reaction tendency that can be reduced during task one.

This view was tested in a study (Shallenberger & Zigler, 1961) in which normal and retarded subjects, matched on mental age, were compared on a two-part experimental task similar to those used in the earlier studies. In addition to the basic procedure employed in these studies, three experimental games, given under two conditions of reinforcement, preceded the two-part criterion task. In a positive reinforcement condition all of the subject's responses met with success, and he was further rewarded with verbal and nonverbal support from the experimenter. It was assumed that this reinforcement condition reduced the subject's negative-reaction tendency. In a negative reinforcement condition, all of the subject's responses met with failure, and the experimenter further punished the subject by commenting on his lack of success. It was assumed that this condition increased the negative-reaction tendency. Half of the normals and half of the retardates were given the games in the positive experimental condition, while the other half of each group received the negative condition. All subjects were given the identical two-part criterion task in which they were consistently praised for all responses.

The most striking finding of this study was that, as predicted, both negatively reinforced groups spent more time on Part II than on Part I of the criterion task, while the two groups receiving the positive condition played Part I longer than Part II. The findings of this study offer further validation for the general motivational hypothesis, while also indicating a need for its extension. Future research should be concerned with the isolation of those specific events which give rise to each of these opposing motivational factors, i.e., the desire to interact and the wariness to do so. One recent study (Harter & Zigler, 1968) has shed additional light on the nature of these tendencies. Employing the measure of wariness validated by Shallenberger and Zigler (1961), it was found that institutionalized retardates were more fearful or wary than noninstitutionalized retardates in both an adult and a peer experimenter condition. Thus, contrary to the view that reluctance or wariness is a general characteristic of all the retarded (Hirsh, 1959; Wellman, 1938; Woodward, 1960), the findings suggest that this reaction to strangers is encountered only among the institutionalized retarded, and that it has its genesis in the institutionalization experience.

Further investigation of such positive- and negative-reaction tendencies, their interactions, and the specific events which give rise to them may clarify issues much more important to our understanding of the socialization process than the troublesome finding that under certain conditions retarded individuals will play a second part of a two-part cosatiation task longer than the first part. Specifically the authors have in mind the current controversy over whether social deprivation leads to an increase in the desire for interaction or to apathy and withdrawal (Cox, 1953; Freud & Burlingham, 1944; Goldfarb, 1953; Irvine, 1952; Spitz & Wolf, 1946; Wittenborn & Myers, 1957).

This issue has been followed up in a series of studies with children of normal intellect (Berkowitz, Butterfield & Zigler, 1965; Berkowitz & Zigler, 1965; McCoy & Zigler, 1965) directed at further validation of the "valence position." Stated simply, this position asserts that the effectiveness of an adult as a reinforcing agent depends upon the valence he has for the particular child whom he is reinforcing. This valence is determined by the child's history of positive and negative experiences with adults. The studies noted above have produced considerable evidence that prior positive contacts between the child and the adult increase the adult's effectiveness as a reinforcer, while negative contacts decrease it. If the experimentally manipulated negative encounters in these experiments are conceptualized as the experimental analogue of what institutionalized retardates actually have experienced, then the often-reported reluctance and wariness with which such children interact with adults becomes understandable. A logical conclusion here is that wariness of adults, and of the tasks that adults present, leads to a general attenuation in the retarded child's social effectiveness. Failure of institutionalized retardates on tasks presented by adults is therefore not to be attributed entirely to intellectual factors. The high negative-reaction tendency motivates him toward behaviors, e.g., withdrawal, that reduce the quality of his performance to a level lower than that which one would expect on the basis of his intellectual capacity alone.

FAILURE
AND THE PERFORMANCE OF THE RETARDED

Another factor frequently mentioned as important in the socialization of the retarded is their high expectancy of failure (Cromwell, 1963; Heber, 1964). This failure expectancy has been viewed as an outgrowth of a lifetime characterized by frequent confrontations with tasks for which the retarded are intellectually ill-equipped to deal. Robinson and Robinson (1965), for example, note that the retarded child is particularly likely to develop a sense of incompetence or inferiority when he begins school; this is derived not only from comparisons of himself with other children but from the personal failures which he experiences in dealing with the world outside his home. Dexter (1958) has elaborated on this theme and its implications for the adjustment of the adult retarded in modern society. He writes:

> The self image of the mentally defective in society which stresses aptitude
> at intellectual achievement is likely to be negative because the "looking-

glass self" principle operates and they learn from their social contacts and experiences to look down upon and distrust themselves; in consequence difficulties are created, derived from the social role of the defectives rather than from anything inherent in the bio-psychological nature of the defectives (p. 924).

Dexter goes on to hypothesize that the less the mental defective is exposed to conventional pressure for social or equivalent success, and the less he is exposed to ridicule, the greater will be the adult social and economic success experienced.

The results of experimental work employing the success-failure dimension with retardates are still somewhat inconsistent. The work of Cromwell and his colleagues (Cromwell, 1963) has lent support to the general proposition that retardates have a higher expectancy of failure than do normals. This results in a style of problem-solving for the retardate which causes him to be much more motivated to avoid failure than to achieve success. However, the inconsistent research findings suggest that this fairly simple proposition is in need of further refinement. One investigator (Gardner, 1957) found that retardates performed better following success and poorer following failure as compared to a control group. Another investigator (Heber, 1957) found that the performance of normals and retardates was equally enhanced following both a failure and a success condition, although in the success condition the performance of retardates was enhanced more than that of normals.

Conversely, Kass and Stevenson (1961) found that success enhanced the performance of normals more than that of retardates. Another study has also demonstrated that failure had a general enhancing effect for both normals and retardates, but that failure enhanced the performance of normals more than that of retardates (Gardner, 1958). In a recent study by Butterfield and Zigler (1965), one factor which may have produced this type of inconsistency was isolated. These investigators found that both normal and retarded children reacted differentially to success and failure experiences as a function of their responsivity to adults, i.e., their desire to gain an adult's support and approval. The nature of the difference between normals and retardates in their reaction to success or failure experiences appeared to be determined by this latter variable. Among high-responsive subjects, failure, as compared to success, attenuated the performance of retarded while improving the performance of normal subjects. Among low-responsive subjects, failure, as compared to success, attenuated the performance of normals while improving the performance of retardates.

The debilitating effects of prolonged failure on the performance of the retarded have been found by Zeaman and House (1963). These investigators discovered that following such failure, retardates were unable to solve a simple problem although they had previously been able to do so. Assuming a failure set in retardates, Stevenson and Zigler (1958) confirmed the prediction that retardates would be willing to "settle for" a lower degree of success than would normal children of the same mental age. The fear of failure in the mentally retarded also appears to be an important factor in differences that have been found between normals' and retardates' achievement motivation (Jordan & DeCharms, 1959).

OUTER-DIRECTEDNESS

Studies (Green & Zigler, 1962; Turnure & Zigler, 1964; Zigler et al., 1958) have indicated that the high incidence of failure experienced by retardates generates a style of problem-solving characterized by outer-directedness. That is, the retarded child comes to distrust his own solutions to problems and therefore seeks guides to action in the immediate environment. Such a style manifests itself in a greater sensitivity to external or environmental cues, particularly those provided by social agents, in the belief that these cues will be more reliable indicators than those provided by the child's own cognitive resources. This outer-directedness may explain the great suggestibility so frequently attributed to the retarded child (e.g., Davies & Ecob, 1959). Evidence has now been presented indicating that compared to normals of the same mental age the retarded child is more sensitive to verbal cues emitted by an adult, is more imitative of the behaviors of both adults and peers, and engages in more visual scanning.

Two additional studies (Hottel, 1960; Lucito, 1959), both demonstrating that duller pupils showed more frequent conformity to group decisions than did brighter subjects under ambiguous stimulus conditions where the group made the wrong decision, tend to support this general notion. Lucito's interpretation of these findings was that as a result of their previous experiences, the brighter children see themselves as successful in interpreting objective reality and as definers of social reality for others; however, the dull children have more frequently failed at interpreting objective reality and therefore have looked to others to define social reality for them.

Findings (Green & Zigler, 1962) have further suggested that the noninstitutionalized retardate is more outer-directed in his problem solving than the institutionalized retardate. This makes considerable sense if one remembers that the noninstitutionalized retardate does not reside in an environment adjusted to his intellectual shortcomings, and should therefore experience more failure than the institutionalized retardate. The findings of Rosen, Diggory and Werlinsky (1966) provide further evidence that residential care is more likely to foster the retardate's optimism and self-confidence than is the non-sheltered school in the community setting. These investigators found that, compared to noninstitutionalized retardates, institutionalized retardates set higher goals, predicted better performance for themselves, and actually performed at a higher level. Edgerton and Sabagh (1962) have also pointed out certain positive features of the sheltered institutional setting for the high-level retardate. They note certain "aggrandizements" of the self which are available, such as the presence of inferior low-level retardates with whom they can compare themselves favorably, their far greater social success within the institution, and mutual support for face-saving rationales concerning their presence there. This argument is similar to that presented by Johnson and Kirk (1950), who favor special classes for those retarded children in public schools since they tend to be isolated and rejected in regular classes.

What should be emphasized in this discussion is that the retarded child is not more outer-directed than a normal child simply because he has a lower IQ. The crucial variable would seem to be not just the level of cognitive ability but also the success or failure experienced by the child when employing his cognitive resources. It would appear that certain age expectancies are firmly built into our child-training practices and that society reacts to a child more on the basis of chronological age than mental age. The normal child's mental age is commensurate with his chronological age, and he is continuously presented problems that are in keeping with his cognitive resources. With increasing maturity he experiences more and more success in utilizing these resources in dealing with problems. The retarded child, on the other hand, is continuously confronted with problems appropriate to his chronological age but inappropriate to his mental age. These problems are too difficult for him and he does not experience that degree of success which would lead him to discard his outer-directedness in favor of reliance on his own cognitive abilities. That success, as compared to failure, leads the child to become less outer-directed was demonstrated in Turnure and Zigler's first experiment.

It may be hypothesized that outer-directedness, which is learned relatively early due to the rather effective cues provided by adults and peers, would generalize to a multiplicity of other external stimuli. This generalization would impel the child to attend to a wide variety of stimuli impinging upon him since such behavior has been conducive to more successful problem solving. Such a style should be given up relatively early in the development of the typical child but should continue to be characteristic of the retarded child, due to the inordinate amount of failure he experiences when relying on his own resources. One would probably describe a child utilizing such a style as being distractible, and, in fact, distractibility has often been attributed to the retarded child (Cruse, 1961; Goldstein & Seigle, 1961). The outer-directedness hypothesis suggests that distractibility, rather than being an inherent characteristic of the retarded, actually reflects a style of problem solving emanating from the particular experiential histories of these children. Employing this view, one would expect to find this style of problem solving and the trait of distractibility in normal children whose self-initiated solutions to problems have often been inadequate (e.g., the very young child), or the inappropriately reinforced child (e.g., the child whose parents make intellectual demands not in keeping with the child's cognitive ability).

THE REINFORCER HIERARCHY

Another nonintellective factor important in understanding the socialization of the retarded is their motivation for various types of incentives. That performance by normals and retardates on a variety of tasks is influenced by the nature of the incentive is certainly well documented (Cantor, 1963). The social deprivation work discussed earlier indicates that retardates have an extremely high motivation for attention, praise, and encouragement. Several investigators (Beller, 1955; Cromwell, 1963; Gewirtz, 1954; Heathers, 1955; Zigler, 1963b) have suggested that in normal development, the effectiveness of attention and praise as reinforcers diminishes with maturity, and is replaced by the reinforcement inherent in the information that one is correct. This latter type of reinforcer appears to serve primarily as a cue for the administration of self-reinforcement. The importance of this reinforcement in the socialization process cannot be overestimated, since the fully socialized individual must be able to maintain socially desirable patterns of behavior without the continuous application of external reinforcers.

Zigler and his associates (Zigler, 1962; Zigler & deLabry, 1962; Zigler & Unell, 1962) have argued that a variety of experiential factors in the history of the retarded cause them to be less motivated to be correct, simply for the sake of correctness, than normals of the same mental age. Stated somewhat differently, these investigators have argued that the position of various reinforcers in the reinforcer hierarchies of normal and retarded children of the same mental age differs. To date, the experimental work of this group on the reinforcer hierarchy construct has centered around the reinforcement which inheres in being correct. It is this reinforcer that is the most frequently encountered, immediate incentive in most real-life tasks. Furthermore, it is a frequently used incentive in many experimental cognitive and perceptual tasks on which retardates and normals are compared, and it also seems to be the most important incentive in the typical test situation. When such an incentive is employed in experimental studies, one wonders how many of the differences found are attributable to differences in capacity between retardates and normals, rather than to differences in performance which result from the different values that such incentives might have for the two types of subjects.

Clearest support for the view that the retardate is much less motivated to be correct than is the middle-class child, so typically used in comparisons with the retarded, is contained in a study by Zigler and deLabry (1962). These investigators tested middle-class, lower-class, and retarded children equated on mental age on a concept-switching task (Kounin, 1941a) under two conditions of reinforcement. In the first condition, similar to that employed by Kounin, the only reinforcement dispensed was the information that the child was correct. In the second condition, the child was rewarded with a toy of his choice if he switched from one concept to another. In the "correct" condition these investigators found, as Kounin did, that retardates were poorer in their concept switching than were middle-class children. That this was not a simple matter of cognitive rigidity was indicated by the finding that lower-class children equated with the middle-class children on mental age were also inferior to the middle-class children. In the toy condition this inferiority disappeared, and retarded and lower-class children performed as well as the middle-class children. This study highlights an assumption that has been noted as erroneous by many educators; namely, that the lower-class and retarded child are motivated by the same incentives that motivate the typical middle-class child. An intriguing avenue of further research is the degree to which the position of various reinforcers in the hierarchy can be manipulated.

Much of this work on motivational and emotional factors in the performance of the retarded is very recent. The research conducted on several of the factors discussed in this section is more suggestive than definitive. It is clear, however, that these factors are extremely important in determining the retardate's general level of functioning. Furthermore, these factors seem much more open to environmental manipulation than do cognitive processes. An increase in knowledge concerning motivational and emotional factors, and their ontogenesis and manipulation, holds considerable promise for alleviating much of the social ineffectiveness displayed by that rather sizable group of persons who must function at a relatively low intellectual level.

MENTAL RETARDATION, SOCIETY, AND VALUES

One final note concerning the socialization of the retarded is in order. As pointed out in the introduction, a measured approach to the socialization potential of the retarded demands that we be neither overly optimistic nor overly pessimistic. The foregoing section was devoted to an examination of those experiential factors important in determining the level of social functioning that the retarded can attain. Knowledge and further examination of these factors should lend additional credence to the proposition that the majority of the retarded can maintain themselves at a socially acceptable level if their family and society provide them with those experiences which optimize their potential for social behavior. The optimism inherent in this point of view should nevertheless be guarded.

Those interested in the socialization of the retarded must never lose sight of the intellectual limitations of retarded individuals. We must continually think in terms of optimizing the socialization of the retarded, rather than in terms of transforming the retarded into individuals of average or superior intellect. In other presentations (e.g., Zigler, 1967b) the authors have insisted on the need for workers in the area of mental retardation to take seriously the biological law of human variability as it pertains to the important trait of intelligence. In considering the socialization of the retarded, one should remember that differences in intellectual potential and resulting socialization patterns are probably an inevitable outcome of the very nature of the genetic pool of our population.

Students of the socialization of the retarded are in some ways handicapped by the fact that such considerations impinge on the area of our culture's values and social philosophy. This relationship between the study of the retarded and our culture's values has certain important implications for our knowledge-gathering efforts concerning the retarded. Mental retardation is an intriguing problem for the medical and behavioral sciences. It is also more than that. It is a "social problem" in the sense that poverty and race relations are social problems. Mental retardation thus becomes the province of federal and state officials, and it becomes involved in social action. Once having entered this social sphere, mental retardation invariably becomes involved with questions concerning social philosophy and personal values. The reader should be aware that science simply does not operate well in such an arena. Dilution of the quality of science can most clearly be seen in those instances where authoritarian states have made science a handmaiden, employing it to support social philosophies and to rationalize political actions. The scientific enterprise has rather strict ground rules, but there is a tendency to hold these rules in abeyance when personal values enter the picture. Nature is completely neutral in respect to men's inherent intelligence. Men, on the other hand, are anything but neutral with regard to issues such as intelligence. What must be remembered is that science is conducted by men and in much of the scientific enterprise that one encounters in the area of mental retardation, it is difficult to extricate the objective findings from the value-laden interpretive account of the data.

In the area of racial differences in intelligence, we have already reached the point where certain investigators (e.g., Klineberg, 1963) have laid down such criteria for an "adequate" investigation that it becomes manifestly impossible to demonstrate racial differences. Antithetically, others (e.g., Garrett, 1962) have argued that there is evidence which clearly supports the existence of racial differences in intelligence. Implicit in such an argument is the view that once a difference has been demonstrated in the population means of two races, every member of the population having the higher mean is superior to every member of the population having the lower mean. In this same vein, the entire issue of individual differences in intelligence has been influenced by personal, political, and social values. Progress in the area of mental retardation will be impeded to the extent that a distinction is not made between fact and value. What we must come to realize is that a 5-, 10-, or even 30-point difference in IQ has little or nothing to do with the rights a society bestows on its members, nor should it influence the general social treatment that is every person's due.

The insidious encroachment of values on the theory and practice of investigators in the area of mental retardation is easily seen. Pastore (1949), in an interesting exercise, has shown that there is a relationship between the political and social philosophies of leading scientists in the area of mental retardation and which position they championed in the nature-nurture controversy. Any evidence available is employed as a vehicle to advance a particular position. As Burks (1928) has noted, "Nearly every study published in the field has been seized upon by both the hereditarian and the environmentalist and interpreted as favorable to the point of view of their own school" (p. 219).

The role of social values in making the environmentalistic position a popular one in our society has been commented on by McClearn (1962) as follows:

> From the beginning, there have been vigorous opponents to any suggestion that the composition of a man's chromosomes could have any determining effect upon his intelligence, personality, emotional stability, or any other "mental or moral" characteristic.... Arguments that some men are inherently wiser than others have appeared to some to be inimical to the democratic ideal, and to imply the rightness of a rule by the elite. The dominant political philosophy of a large part of Western culture during much of the nature-nurture controversy has insisted, on the contrary, that education and socioeconomic reform can improve the lot of individuals and thereby the stature of a culture (p. 235f).

A rather novel, and therefore refreshing point of view on this issue has been presented by Davies and Ecob (1959), who consider individual differences in intelligence as basic to harmonious social organization. Davies argues that a society made up of persons all similar in intelligence, aptitude, or ability would function very poorly indeed. He states: "Cooperation inheres in the differences which exist among individuals. Were all men created with the intelligence and aptitude of leaders and with the will to lead, the result would not be social organization but social disruption" (p. 227).

Davies makes this point by way of reminding us that our solution to the problems of retardation will not be aided if we either ignore or deplore the fact that there is a certain proportion of individuals in society of relatively low intelligence. Thus, one can appreciate their individual differences in intelligence without denying the basic humanness of every individual whatever his intellectual potential may be. This essential humanness, rationality, and effort toward social adjustment on the part of the retarded has been a major theme of this chapter. Research in the area of mental retardation has recently entered a vigorous phase. The coming decade should witness a considerable advance in our knowledge of how the intellectual features of the retarded interact with their life experiences in producing the various patterns of socialization encountered among individuals of lowered intellect.

REFERENCES

BALLA, D. The verbal action of the environment on institutionalized and non-institutionalized retardates and normal children of two social classes. Unpublished doctoral dissertation, Yale Univer., 1966.

BALLER, W. R. A study of the present social status of a group of adults who, when they were in elementary schools, were classified as mentally deficient. *Genetic Psychology Monograph,* 1936, 18, 165–244.

BARRETT, H. E., & KOCH, H. L. The effect of nursery-school training upon the mental test performance of a group of orphanage children. *Journal of Genetic Psychology,* 1930, 37, 102–122.

BECKHAM, A. S. Minimum intelligence levels for several occupations. *Personnel Journal,* 1930, 9, 309–313.

BELLER, E. Dependency and independence in young children. *Journal of Genetic Psychology,* 1955, 87, 25–35.

BENTON, A. L. The concept of pseudofeeblemindedness. In P. E. Trapp & P. Himelstein (Eds.), *Readings on the exceptional child.* New York: Appleton-Century-Crofts, 1962. Pp. 82-95.

BERKOWITZ, H., BUTTERFIELD, E. C., & ZIGLER, E. The effectiveness of social reinforcers on persistence and learning tasks following positive and negative social interactions. *Journal of Personality and Social Psychology,* 1965, 2, 706–714.

BERKOWITZ, H., & ZIGLER, E. Effects of preliminary positive and negative interactions and delay conditions on children's responsiveness to social reinforcement. *Journal of Personality and Social Psychology,* 1965, 4, 500–505.

BERKSON, G. Psychophysiological studies in mental deficiency. In N. R. Ellis (Ed.), *Handbook of mental deficiency.* New York: McGraw-Hill, 1963. Pp. 556–573.

BIJOU, S. W., AINSWORTH, M. H., & STOCKEY, M. R. The social adjustment of mentally retarded girls paroled from the Wayne County Training School. *American Journal of Mental Deficiency,* 1943, 47, 422–428.

BLATZ, W. *Understanding the young child.* New York: Morrow, 1944.

BROWN, R. *Social psychology.* New York: Free Press, 1965.

BURKS, B. S. The relative influence of nature and nurture upon mental development: A comparative study of foster parent–foster child resemblance and true parent–true child resemblance. *Yearbook of the National Society for the Study of Education,* 1928, 27 (I), 219–316.

BURKS, B. S. Review (*Children in foster homes: A study of mental development,* by Marie Skodak). *Journal of Educational Psychology,* 1939, 30, 548–555.

BURR, E. T. Minimum intellectual levels of accomplishment in industry. *Personnel Journal,* 1925, 3, 207–212.

BUTTERFIELD, E. C., & ZIGLER, E. The effects of success and failure on the discrimination learning of normal and retarded children. *Journal of Abnormal Psychology,* 1965, 70, 25–31.

CANTOR, G. N. Hull-Spence behavior theory and mental deficiency. In N. R. Ellis (Ed.), *Handbook of mental deficiency.* New York: McGraw-Hill, 1963. Pp. 92–133.

CHARLES, D. C. Ability and accomplishment of persons earlier judged mentally deficient. *Genetic Psychology Monograph,* 1953, 47, 3–71.

CLARKE, A. D. B., & CLARKE, A. M. Cognitive changes in the feebleminded. *British Journal of Psychology,* 1954, 45, 197–199.

CLARKE, A. M. Criteria and classification of mental deficiency. In A. M. Clarke & A. D. B. Clarke (Eds.), *Mental deficiency: The changing outlook.* Glencoe, Ill.: Free Press, 1958. Pp. 43–64.

COLLMAN, R. D., & NEWLYN, D. Employment success of educationally subnormal expupils in England. *American Journal of Mental Deficiency,* 1956, 60, 733–743.

COLLMAN, R. D., & Newlyn, D. Employment success of mentally dull and intellectually normal expupils in England. *American Journal of Mental Deficiency,* 1957, 61, 484–490.

COX, F. The origins of the dependency drive. *Australian Journal of Psychology,* 1953, 5, 64–73.

CRAFTS, L. W. Bibliography of feeblemindedness in relation to juvenile delinquency. *Journal of Juvenile Research,* 1916, 1, 195–208.

CROMWELL, R. L. A social learning approach to mental retardation. In N. R. Ellis (Ed.), *Handbook of mental deficiency.* New York: McGraw-Hill, 1963. Pp. 41–91.

CRUICKSHANK, W. M. Qualitative analysis of intelligence test responses. *Journal of Clinical Psychology,* 1947, 3, 381–386.

CRUSE, D. Effects of distractions upon the performance of brain-injured and familial retarded children. *American Journal of Mental Deficiency,* 1961, 66, 86–92.

DAGER, E. Z. Socialization and personality development in the child. In H. T. Christenson (Ed.), *Handbook of marriage and the family.* Chicago: Rand McNally, 1964.

DAVIES, S. P. *Social control of the mentally deficient.* New York: Crowell, 1930.

DAVIES, S. P., & ECOB, K. G. *The mentally retarded in society.* New York: Columbia Univer. Press, 1959.

DEXTER, L. A. A social theory of mental deficiency. *American Journal of Mental Deficiency,* 1958, 62, 920–928.

DOLL, E. E. A historical survey of research and management of mental retardation in the United States. In P. E. Trapp & P. Himelstein (Eds.), *Readings on the exceptional child.* New York: Appleton-Century-Crofts, 1962. Pp. 21–68.

DURKHEIM, E. *The rules of sociological method.* Chicago: Univer. of Chicago Press, 1938.

EDGERTON, R. B., & SABAGH, G. From mortification to aggrandizement: Changing self-conception in the careers of the mentally retarded. *Psychiatry,* 1962, 25, 263–272.

ELLIS, N. R. The stimulus trace and behavioral inadequacy. In N. R. Ellis (Ed.), *Handbook of mental deficiency.* New York: McGraw-Hill, 1963. Pp. 134–158.

FERNALD, W. E. After-care study of the patients discharged from Waverly for a period of twenty-five years. *Ungraded,* 1919, 5, 25–31.

FOLEY, R. W. A study of patients discharged from the Rome State School for the twenty year period ending Dec. 31, 1924. *Journal of Psycho-Asthenics,* 1929, 34, 180–207.

FREUD, A., & BURLINGHAM, D. *Infants without families.* New York: International Press, 1944.

GARDNER, W. I. Effects of interpolated success and failure on motor task performance in mental defectives. Paper read at Southeastern Psychological Association, Nashville, Tenn., 1957.

GARDNER, W. I. *Reactions of intellectually normal and retarded boys after experimentally induced failure: A social learning theory interpretation.* Ann Arbor, Mich.: Universal Microfilms, 1958.

GARFIELD, S. L. Abnormal behavior and mental deficiency. In N. R. Ellis (Ed.), *Handbook of mental deficiency.* New York: McGraw-Hill, 1963. Pp. 574–601.

GARRETT, H. E. In Letters, *Science,* 1962, 135, 982.

GEWIRTZ, J. Three determinants of attention seeking in young children. *Monographs of the Society for Research in Child Development,* 1954, 19, No. 59.

GINZBERG, E. The mentally handicapped in a technological society. In S. F. Osler & R. E. Cooke (Eds.), *The biosocial basis of mental retardation.* Baltimore: Johns Hopkins Press, 1965.

GODDARD, H. H. Heredity of feeble-mindedness. *American Breeders Magazine,* 1910, 1, 165–178.

GODDARD, H. H. *The Kallikak family.* New York: Macmillan, 1912.

GODDARD, H. H. *Feeblemindedness, its causes and consequences.* New York: Macmillan, 1914.

GOLDFARB, W. The effects of early institutional care on adolescent personality. *Journal of Experimental Education,* 1953, 12, 106–129.

GOLDSTEIN, H. Social and occupation adjustment. In H. A. Stevens & R. Heber (Eds.), *Mental retardation.* Chicago: Univer. of Chicago Press, 1964. Pp. 214–258.

GOLDSTEIN, H., & SEIGLE, D. Characteristics of educable mentally handicapped children. In W. Rothstein (Ed.), *Mental retardation: Readings and resources.* New York: Holt, 1961.

GOLDSTEIN, K. Concerning rigidity. *Character and Personality,* 1942–1943, 11, 209–226.

GOTTESMAN, I. L. Genetic aspects of intelligent behavior. In N. R. Ellis (Ed.), *Handbook of mental deficiency.* New York: McGraw-Hill, 1963. Pp. 253–296.

GRANT, J. R. Results of institutional treatment of juvenile mental defectives over a 30-year period. *Canadian Medical Association Journal,* 1956, 75, 918–921.

GREEN, C., & ZIGLER, E. Social deprivation and the performance of feebleminded and normal children on a satiation-type task. *Child Development,* 1962, 33, 499–508.

GUERTIN, W. H. Mental growth in pseudo-feeblemindedness. *Journal of Clinical Psychology,* 1949, 5, 414–418.

HARTER, S. Mental age, IQ, and motivational factors in the discrimination learning set performance of normal and retarded children. *Journal of Experimental Child Psychology,* 1967, 5, 123–141.

HARTER, S., & ZIGLER, E. The effectiveness of adult and peer social reinforcement on the performance of institutionalized and noninstitutionalized retardates. *Journal of Abnormal Psychology,* 1968, 73, 144–149.

HEATHERS, G. Emotional dependence and independence in nursery school play. *Journal of Genetic Psychology,* 1955, 87, 37–57.

HEBER, R. F. *Expectancy and expectancy changes in normal and mentally retarded boys.* Ann Arbor, Mich.: Universal Microfilms, 1957.

HEBER, R. F. Mental retardation: Concept and classification. In P. E. Trapp & P. Himelstein (Eds.), *Readings on the exceptional child.* New York: Appleton-Century-Crofts, 1962. Pp. 69–81.

HEBER, R. F. Personality. In H. A. Stevens & R. F. Heber (Eds.), *Mental retardation.* Chicago: Univer. of Chicago Press, 1964. Pp. 143–174.

HIRSCH, J. Behavior genetics and individuality understood. *Science,* 1963, 142, 1436–1442.

HIRSH, E. A. The adaptive significance of commonly described behavior of the mentally retarded. *American Journal of Mental Deficiency,* 1959, 63, 639–646.

HOTTEL, J. V. The influence of age and intelligence on independence-conformity behavior of children. Unpublished doctoral dissertation, George Peabody College for Teachers, 1960.

IRVINE, E. Observations on the aims and methods of child rearing in communal settlements in Israel. *Human Relations,* 1952, 5, 247–275.

JOHNSON, G. O., & KIRK, S. A. Are mentally handicapped children segregated in the regular grades? *Exceptional Children,* 1950, 17, 65–68.

JONES, D., & CARR-SAUNDERS, A. The relation between intelligence and social status among orphan children. *British Journal of Psychology,* 1927, 17, 343–364.

JONES, H. E. The environment and mental development. In L. Carmichael (Ed.), *Manual of child psychology.* (2nd Ed.) New York: Wiley, 1954. Pp. 631–696.

JORDAN, T. E., & DeCHARMS, R. The achievement motive in normal and mentally retarded children. *American Journal of Mental Deficiency,* 1959, 64, 457–466.

KAPLUN, D. The high-grade moron: A study of institutional admissions over a ten year period. *Proceedings of the American Association on Mental Deficiency,* 1935, 40, 68–89.

KASS, N., & STEVENSON, H. W. The effect of pretraining reinforcement conditions on learning by normal and retarded children. *American Journal of Mental Deficiency,* 1961, 66, 76–80.

KENNEDY, R. J. R. *The social adjustment of morons in a Connecticut city.* Willport, Conn., Commission to Survey Resources in Connecticut, 1948.

KLINEBERG, O. Negro-white differences in intelligence test performance: A new look at an old problem. *American Psychologist,* 1963, 18, 198–203.

KNOLLIN, H. E., & TERMAN, L. W. A partial psychological survey of the prison population of San Quentin, California. In *Surveys in mental deviation.* Sacramento, Calif.: State Printing Office, 1918.

KOHLBERG, L. Sex differences in morality. In E. E. Maccoby (Ed.), *Sex role development.* New York: Social Science Research Council, 1966. (a)

KOHLBERG, L. A cognitive-developmental approach to socialization—morality and psychosexuality. Paper presented at the 1966 Midwestern Meeting of the Society for Research in Child Development, Bowling Green State Univer., Bowling Green, Ohio. (b)

KOUNIN, J. Experimental studies of rigidity: I. The measurement of rigidity in normal and feeble-minded persons. *Character and Personality,* 1941, 9, 251–272. (a)

KOUNIN, J. Experimental studies of rigidity: II. The explanatory power of the concept of rigidity as applied to feeblemindedness. *Character and Personality,* 1941, 9, 273–282. (b)

KRISHEF, C. H. An analysis of some factors in the institutional experience of mentally retarded dischargees from the Owatonna State School that influence their successful or unsuccessful community adjustment. Unpublished manuscript, School of Social Work, Univer. of Minnesota, 1957.

KRUGMAN, M. Some impressions of the Revised Stanford-Binet Scale. *Journal of Educational Psychology,* 1939, 30, 594–603.

LEAHY, A. M. Nature-nurture and intelligence. *Genetic Psychology Monographs,* 1935, 17, 236–308.

LEWIN, K. *A dynamic theory of personality.* New York: McGraw-Hill, 1936.

LUCITO, L. J. A comparison of independence-conformity behavior of intellectually bright and dull children. Unpublished doctoral dissertation, Univer. of Illinois, 1959.

LURIA, A. R. Psychological studies of mental deficiency in the Soviet Union. In N. R. Ellis (Ed.), *Handbook of mental deficiency.* New York: McGraw-Hill, 1963. Pp. 353–387.

McCLEARN, G. E. The inheritance of behavior. In L. Postman (Ed.), *Psychology in the making.* New York: Knopf, 1962. Pp. 144–252.

McCOY, N., & ZIGLER, E. Social reinforcer effectiveness as a function of the relationship between child and adult. *Journal of Abnormal and Social Psychology,* 1965, 1, 604–612.

McKINNEY, J. P., & KEELE, T. Effects of increased mothering on the behavior of severely retarded boys. *American Journal of Mental Deficiency,* 1963, 67, 556–562.

MAHER, B. A. Intelligence and brain damage. In N. R. Ellis (Ed.), *Handbook of mental deficiency.* New York: McGraw-Hill, 1963. Pp. 224–252.

MANDLER, G., & SARASON, S. B. A study of anxiety and learning. *Journal of Abnormal and Social Psychology,* 1952, 47, 166–173.

MATTHEWS, M. One hundred institutionally trained male defectives in the community under supervision. *Mental Hygiene,* 1922, 6, 332–342.

PASTORE, N. *The nature-nurture controversy.* New York: King's Crown Press, 1949.

PEARSON, G. H. J. The psychopathology of mental defect. *Nervous Child,* 1942, 2, 9–20.

PENROSE, L. S. *The biology of mental defect.* London: Sidgwick & Jackson, 1963.

PHILLIPS, L., & ZIGLER, E. Social competence, the action-thought parameter and vicariousness in normal and pathological behaviors. *Journal of Abnormal and Social Psychology,* 1961, 63, 127–146.

PHILLIPS, L., & ZIGLER, E. Role orientation, the action-thought parameter and outcome in psychiatric disorder. *Journal of Abnormal and Social Psychology,* 1964, 68, 381–389.

PIAGET, J. *The moral judgment of the child.* Glencoe, Ill.: Free Press, 1948.

ROBINSON, H. B., & ROBINSON, N. M. (Eds.) *The mentally retarded child: A psychological approach.* New York: McGraw-Hill, 1965.

ROSEN, M., DIGGORY, J. C., & WERLINSKY, B. E. Goal-setting and expectancy of success in institutionalized and noninstitutionalized mental subnormals. *American Journal of Mental Deficiency,* 1966, 71, 249–255.

SAENGER, G. *The adjustment of severely retarded adults in the community.* Albany: New York State Interdepartmental Health Resources Board, 1957.

SAENGER, G. *Factors influencing the institutionalization of mentally retarded individuals in New York City.* Albany: New York State Interdepartmental Health Resources Board, January, 1960.

SARASON, S. B. *Psychological problems in mental deficiency.* New York: Harper, 1953.

SARASON, S. B., DAVIDSON, K. S., LIGHTHALL, F. F., WAITE, R. R., & RUEBUSH, B. K. *Anxiety in elementary school children.* New York: Wiley, 1960.

SHAFTER, A. J. Criteria for selecting institutionalized mental defectives for vocational placement. *American Journal of Mental Deficiency,* 1957, 61, 599–616.

SHALLENBERGER, P., & ZIGLER, E. Rigidity, negative reaction tendencies, and cosatiation effects in normal and feebleminded children. *Journal of Abnormal and Social Psychology,* 1961, 63, 20–26.

SHEPPS, R., & ZIGLER, E. Rigidity and the effectiveness of social reinforcers in familial and organic retardates. *American Journal of Mental Deficiency,* 1962, 67, 262–268.

SIEGEL, P. S., & FOSHEE, J. G. Molar variability in the mentally defective. *Journal of Abnormal and Social Psychology,* 1960, 61, 141–143.

SPENCE, K. W. A theory of emotionally based drive (D) and its relation to performance in simple learning situations. *American Psychologist,* 1958, 13, 131–141.

SPITZ, H. H. Field theory in mental deficiency. In N. R. Ellis (Ed.), *Handbook of mental deficiency.* New York: McGraw-Hill, 1963. Pp. 11–40.

SPITZ, R., & WOLF, K. Anaclitic depression: An inquiry into the genesis of psychiatric conditions in early childhood. *Psychoanalytic Study of the Child,* 1946, 2, 313–342.

SPRADLIN, J. E. Language and communication of mental defectives. In N. R. Ellis (Ed.), *Handbook of mental deficiency.* New York: McGraw-Hill, 1963. Pp. 512–555.

STEVENSON, H. W. Discrimination learning. In N. R. Ellis (Ed.), *Handbook of mental deficiency.* New York: McGraw-Hill, 1963. Pp. 424–438.

STEVENSON, H. W., & ZIGLER, E. Probability learning in children. *Journal of Experimental Psychology,* 1958, 56, 185–192.

STORRS, H. C. A report on an investigation made of cases discharged from Letchworth Village. *Journal of Psycho-Asthenics,* 1924, 34, 220–232.

TARJAN, G., & BENSON, F. Report on the pilot study at Pacific Colony. *American Journal of Mental Deficiency,* 1953, 57, 453–462.

TAYLOR, J. A. Drive theory and manifest anxiety. In N. T. Mednick & S. A. Mednick (Eds.), *Research in personality*. New York: Holt, Rinehart & Winston, 1963. Pp. 205–222.

TIZARD, J. The prevalence of mental subnormality. *Bulletin of the World Health Organization,* 1953, 9, 423–440.

TIZARD, J. Longitudinal and follow-up studies. In A. M. Clarke & A. D. B. Clarke (Eds.), *Mental deficiency: The changing outlook*. New York: The Free Press of Glencoe, 1958.

TREDGOLD, A. F. *A textbook of mental deficiency*. (8th Ed.) Baltimore, Md.: Williams & Wilkins, 1952.

TURNURE, J., & ZIGLER, E. Outerdirectedness in the problem solving of normal and retarded children. *Journal of Abnormal and Social Psychology,* 1964, 69, 427–436.

WEAVER, T. R. The incidence of maladjustment among mental defectives in military environment. *American Journal of Mental Deficiency,* 1946, 51, 238–246.

WELLMAN, B. L. Guiding mental development. *Childhood Education,* 1938, 15, 108–112.

WHITNEY, E. A. Mental deficiency—1955. *American Journal of Mental Deficiency,* 1956, 60, 676–683.

WINDLE, C. Prognosis of mental subnormals. *American Journal of Mental Deficiency Monograph Supplement,* 1962, 66, No. 5.

WITTENBORN, J., & MYERS, B. *The placement of adoptive children*. Springfield: Thomas, 1957.

WOODWARD, M. Early experiences and later social responses of severely subnormal children. *British Journal of Medical Psychology,* 1960, 33, 123–132.

WRONG, D. H. The oversocialized conception of man in modern sociology. *American Sociological Review,* 1961, 26, 183–193.

YARROW, L. J. Separation from parents during early childhood. In M. L. Hoffman & L. W. Hoffman (Eds.), *Review of child development research*. Vol. I. New York: Russell Sage Foundation, 1964. Pp. 89–136.

ZEAMAN, D., & HOUSE, B. J. The role of attention in retardate discrimination learning. In N. R. Ellis (Ed.), *Handbook of mental deficiency*. New York: McGraw-Hill, 1963. Pp. 159–223.

ZIGLER, E. The effect of preinstitutional social deprivation on the performance of feebleminded children. Unpublished doctoral dissertation, Univer. of Texas, 1958.

ZIGLER, E. Social deprivation and rigidity in the performance of feebleminded children. *Journal of Abnormal and Social Psychology,* 1961, 62, 413–421.

ZIGLER, E. Rigidity in the feebleminded. In P. E. Trapp & P. Himelstein (Eds.), *Readings on the exceptional child*. New York: Appleton-Century-Crofts, 1962. Pp. 141–162.

ZIGLER, E. Rigidity and social reinforcement effects in the performance of institutionalized and noninstitutionalized normal and retarded children. *Journal of Personality,* 1963, 31, 258–269. (a)

ZIGLER, E. Social reinforcement, environment and the child. *American Journal of Orthopsychiatry,* 1963, 33, 614–623. (b)

ZIGLER, E. Mental retardation: Current issues and approaches. In M. L. Hoffman & L. W. Hoffman (Eds.), *Review of child development research,* Vol. 2. New York: Russell Sage Foundation, 1967. (a)

ZIGLER, E. Familial mental retardation: A continuing dilemma. *Science,* 1967, 155, 292–298. (b)

ZIGLER, E., & BUTTERFIELD, E. Motivational factors and IQ-changes in culturally deprived children attending nursery school. Yale Univer., unpublished manuscript.

ZIGLER, E., & DELABRY, J. Concept-switching in middle-class, lower-class, and re-tarded children. *Journal of Abnormal and Social Psychology,* 1962, 65, 267–273.

ZIGLER, E., HODGDEN, L., & STEVENSON, H. The effect of support on the performance of normal and feebleminded children. *Journal of Personality,* 1958, 26, 106–122.

ZIGLER, E., & UNELL, E. Concept-switching in normal and feebleminded children as a function of reinforcement. *American Journal of Mental Deficiency,* 1962, 66, 651–657.

ZIGLER, E., & WILLIAMS, J. Institutionalization and the effectiveness of social re-inforcement: A three-year follow-up study. *Journal of Abnormal and Social Psychology,* 1963, 66, 197–205.

CHAPTER **29**

The Socialization
Of American Minority Peoples

Donald R. Young

The Rockefeller University

Bearing in mind that socialization is the process which enables individuals to participate effectively as members of interest groups, local communities and the larger society, it is obvious that the process for American minority peoples in the abstract is similar to that for the general population. The fundamental observations in earlier chapters about the theory of socialization and its content and development through the stages of an individual's life apply to all elements in the population. Yet, it is no less obvious that the distinctively ascribed inferior status and the differentiating characteristics of minorities must be of significance in minority socialization. Differences of consequence in background, in environmental circumstances, in group influenced individual traits and expectations and in the agencies of socialization themselves do exist. These differences are both general in their basic nature for all minorities and specific in detail for each minority and its subgroupings. The manner in which they influence minority socialization is significant for the welfare of society as a whole as well as for that of the minorities themselves.[1]

MINORITY GROUPS DEFINED

Before beginning discussion of the nature of the special problems of minority socialization, brief indication of the diversity and numerical importance of the peoples to be considered is desirable.[2] Reference to "minorities" in the United States, for most people familiar with the word as it is used here, brings to mind population elements of relatively recent foreign origin, particularly if they are

---

[1] The socialization of members of the dominant majority insofar as it teaches and supports attitudes and behavior prejudicial to minorities is of no less importance but does not come within the scope of this chapter.

[2] Simpson and Yinger (1965) is recommended to those who wish more substantive detail; and P. Rose (1964) offers a brief, more popularly written overview of the field and includes a useful appendix note on significant research publications and an annotated list of selected readings. Bibliographies in most of the references also provide many other good general publications on minorities.

not Protestants or not of northern and western European origin, and members of a variety of colored peoples, mainly Negroes. Although this is much too inclusive a conception of minorities, the gross 1960 Bureau of the Census count of these population elements may be noted. In that year there were in the United States a total of 9,738,000 persons of foreign birth, of whom 9,294,000 were classified as white. The number of persons born in this country of foreign or mixed native and foreign parentage was 23,784,000. The countries contributing more than 1,000,-000 to the "foreign white stock," the Census term for the 33,078,000 white persons who were either foreign born or of foreign or mixed parentage, were Italy (4,540,000), Germany (4,313,000), Canada (3,154,000), Poland (2,778,000), U.S.S.R. (2,287,000), United Kingdom (2,288,000), Ireland (1,771,000), Mexico (1,725,000), Austria (1,098,000) and Sweden (1,046,000). It is estimated that there were 5,509,000 members of Jewish congregations and 43,848,000 Roman Catholics in the United States in 1962, estimates supplied by the religious bodies themselves; in the one case counting all Jews in communities having congregations, and in the other all persons baptized as Roman Catholics.

There were 18,872,000 Negroes and 1,620,000 members of other colored races in the United States in 1960. Those listed as members of other colored races included 523,000 American Indians, 465,000 of Japanese origin, 238,000 with Chinese forebears, 176,000 of Filipino extraction and 218,000 of "all other" colored groups such as Asian Indians, Koreans, Polynesians, Indonesians, Hawaiians, Aleuts and Eskimos. It should be noted that there are numerous colored persons in the United States not included in the groups just listed, such as many of those of Mexican, Puerto Rican, Cuban and other national origins (Statistical Abstract, 1964).

Characteristics of Minority Groups

Obviously not all individuals included in the totals given above may be classed as members of a minority. Also, there are persons of minority status not included in the totals, such as third and later American generation individuals still identified with a nationality group of restricted social status. For example, there are Spanish-speaking citizens in the southwest whose ancestors were residents there before the area became part of the United States who still have the attributes of a minority. Inadequate as they are for our purposes, the gross foreign stock, religious and racial counts are helpful as a broad indication of the population elements among whom or in association with whom minority individuals and groups are to be found. Minority status does not necessarily coincide with any classification of national origin nor is it automatically ascribed simply on the basis of divergent color. Only those elements within the foreign stock, the non-Protestant faiths and colored races in the United States with readily distinguishable members who are regarded as in some way competitive by a significant proportion of the dominant population, have been relegated to or long continued in minority status (see Young, 1932; Williams, 1947).

The group membership visibility necessary if ascription of minority status is to be effective in establishing and maintaining a hierarchical social system in intergroup relations may be a consequence of either cultural or genetic variance. Divergent cultural traits, including language, dress, form of worship and a wide range of behavior patterns such as manner and freedom of emotional expression, or intra-family relations and responsibilities vary greatly from one country to another and serve to distinguish unassimilated immigrant stocks. This is especially true for those stocks from other than northern and western Europe, the major source of the core cultural features and values of the dominant population in the United States. Although some European stocks do have distinguishable genetic features, as in the case of some Irish, Italians and Slavs, these do not seem to be sufficient by themselves for ready group membership identification in the heterogeneous population of the country. White minorities are identified primarily by their divergent cultural attributes.

Minorities distinguished by inherent racial features include Negroes, various Oriental peoples, American Indians, Puerto Ricans and Mexicans. They are distinguishable from the majority, however, not only by race but also by cultural traits. This is obvious for all except the Negro, but even the American Negro has distinctive cultural traits in spite of his long history in the United States. Slavery not only rooted out African ways of life except for a few insignificant cultural survivals but also imposed not the complete European-American pattern but a modified variant of it. For example, the more stable central role of the Negro mother in comparison with that of the father commonly found among Negroes probably can be traced, in part, back to the mother's role in slavery.[3] In the years since slavery, limited opportunity and segregation have required as well as permitted cultural variance, as, for example, in language, recreational patterns and interpersonal relations. As a result, American Negro culture can be described as, first of all, in the general European-American tradition, but with significant adaptations to the Negro's unique American background and circumstances. The cultures of all other American minorities, colored or white, are a mixture of what they and their ancestors brought with them and what they have acquired in this country, or something between the two, depending on how long they have been in this country, where they live, where they work and their penchant for or against assimilation.

The competitive group threat, real or fictitious, which also is a necessary condition for the maintenance of minority status, may be believed to be disadvantageous to the undiluted continued existence of the dominant stock, its values and accepted ways of life or to minority advantage in competition for a desired end. Thus the population element in power may believe that it has a superior genetic endowment which would be lowered in quality by miscegenation, that its religious and other values would suffer in the absence of social

---

[3]Although there is general agreement that the remarkable tendency of the Negro mother to be a more stable and important element in the Negro family than the father is related to the slave mother's predominant role, the influence of slave tradition commonly has been overemphasized in comparison with the influence of modern employment and related circumstances of Negroes (Moynihan, 1966; Bernard, 1966).

barriers to free intergroup association, or that the good things in life would be more difficult of attainment if employment, housing, education, recreation and government participation were unrestricted and freely open to all. As Robin M. Williams, Jr. (1964), has put it,

> If for any reason two clearly distinguished social categories or selectivities are so situated in a society that their members frequently come into competition, the likelihood is high that negative stereotyping (a common variety of prejudice) will reinforce a sense of difference and that hostile attitudes will tend to restrict interaction and/or cause conflict. Whether competition is economic, political, sexual or for prestige, if one group perceives another as a threat, prejudice results (p. 24).

The significance of group competition in minority-majority relations becomes clear when discrimination and the countercharge of prejudice are described in plain words for what they are: a demand for prescribed advantage by the dominant group and the denial of any valid basis for that demand.

In historical illustration of the dual requirement of ready group identification and belief in a competitive threat, it may be noted that American Indians and residents of Oriental ancestry in the United States, both once holding very low minority status but now largely relieved of minority restrictions, are still easily identified but so few in number that they cannot be regarded as a serious threat by the majority except in a few areas of concentration, the present areas of major tension and discrimination against them. Immigrant nationalities once held in low esteem, such as the Germans and the Irish, now largely are no longer casually identifiable and, although they and their descendants number in the millions, are not generally thought of as minorities except for those who have continued social visibility because of emphasis on Jewish or Roman Catholic identification and particularly if their religious affiliation is associated with some other country such as Israel or Italy. The status of Sephardic and German Jews in the country suffered when both the number and the social visibility of members of that faith were greatly increased by later arrivals of co-religionists from eastern Europe. Anti-Semitism in Germany under Hitler was deliberately based on measures which both increased the identifiability of Jews and the belief that they were a threat to the nation and its non-Jewish citizens. Minorities do not come into existence nor can they long survive in inferior and circumscribed statuses and roles without being both distinctively marked for recognition and regarded as a danger to majority objectives.

Seeming exceptions to this generalization are a consequence of the tendency of folk beliefs and ways to persist after the circumstances of their origin have ceased to exist and sometimes of their diffusion beyond the area of origin. An established intergroup relationship may continue for quite a while after the conditions of its initiation have changed, but not indefinitely. Also, discriminatory attitudes and patterns of behavior may be adopted from elsewhere by individuals and groups not directly or seriously involved in any competitive intergroup relationship and in parts of the country where members of the ethnic or racial group in question may hardly be found. Such extrasituational derivative group status beliefs and attitudes may be influential for a period, but they tend to lose significance and disappear in the absence of an evident and real or supposedly threatening group within the community or region. As long as they exist, however, they are a disturbing factor in the socialization of the group against whom they are directed.

These three basic factors in the development and maintenance of ethnic and racial inferior group status, i.e., visibility of members, attributed competitive threat and extrasituational derivative denigrating beliefs, are not alone adequate as broadly stated for the understanding of the special problems of socialization of a particular group of minority individuals. They are helpful, however, first, in specifying which subgroups and individuals of the ethnic and racial components of the population are most likely to be relegated to minority status and by whom; second, in making manifest the inadequacy of references to alleged group genetic differential qualities or to sheer human perversity as possible prime bases for the ascription of minority status; and third, in providing a framework for a rational approach to the analysis of the unique problems of minority socialization.

Exceptions to Minority Group Identification

As suggested earlier, it is a common practice, even among those who should and often do know better, to speak of some foreign stocks, members of other than Protestant religious bodies and colored peoples as though they constituted minorities in their entirety. Yet it is well known that not all members of such elements in the population are held, in fact, in equal minority status, if at all, by all members of the dominant majority. Exemptions range from broad acceptance of individuals and varying fractions of divergent population elements only in part treated as minorities through all degrees of invidious social restriction. There are great variations in the attribution of minority status and in patterns of restrictive intergroup relations. The seemingly chaotic variations, however, become understandable when the concurrent variations in the three underlying factors in group discrimination are kept in mind. In each specific subgroup situation of intergroup relations the conditions of visibility and competitive threat need to be examined with reference to the degree of cultural assimilation, physical distinctiveness, relative numbers of the groups involved, group concentration in a geographic area, community activities, the level of the economy, particularly in relation to available manpower, and other situational matters affecting group identification and relative opportunities for goal achievement. Should items of these kinds turn out not to be significant in a situation where minority discrimination is practiced, the explanation should be sought in the continuation of traditional beliefs and practices beyond the survival of the conditions of their origin or in the borrowing of group status beliefs from areas other than those of their original relevance. Such a shift from designating an entire ethnic or racial population element as a minority as though it were in a unitary situation to emphasizing the conditions at the locus of discriminating behavior permits orderly perspective and specificity in place of the prevailing current tendency toward overly broad generalization in the definition of minorities and in consideration of their relations with the dominating population. It recognizes the well-known fact that no statement beginning "all Chinese," "all Indians," "all Jews," "all Negroes," or all any other nationality or racial population element is true without implying that there is no commonality and order in intergroup relations when specific local situations are compared.

Alleged group genetic differentials in ability and personality traits clearly become irrelevant in minority socialization when it is realized that inferior status is ascribed unevenly over time, by different communities and in varying segments of the majority population to subgroups and individuals of ethnic, religious and colored peoples not as totalities but in correlation with specific but unstable situational factors. This is in conflict with the widespread conviction that differentiated statuses and roles for minorities, including some white as well as colored groups, are required and justified by genetic inadequacies for full participation in American civilization. It is a not unnatural assumption that recognizable group differences in appearance may be taken as indices of less tangible but socially significant qualitative distinctions. There are, in fact, some genetic differences between human population groups other than the external features commonly used as indices of race, as in the distribution of color blindness and of blood systems and types, which may suggest to the incautious the existence of still others more significant for achievement in modern society but not yet definitely identified. It is also understandable that there is a common tendency to ascribe group levels of achievement or failure to genetic endowment. In contradiction of these two misinterpretations, the following quotation from a statement on the biological aspects of race signed by twenty-two distinguished specialists in the field called together in 1964 by the United Nations Educational, Scientific and Cultural Organization to consider the question is offered as representing present scientific consensus:

> Neither in the field of hereditary potentialities concerning the overall intelligence and the capacity for cultural development, nor in that of physical traits, is there any justification for the concept of "inferior" and "superior" races (International Social Science Journal, 1965, p. 160).

All peoples of the world exhibit great variations in the qualities of their individual members. Assuming only for the sake of argument that it might some time be established, as is not now the case, that qualities significant for participation in modern complex civilization are varied in distribution or even in nature in the population groupings now inaccurately referred to by laymen as "races," such a finding would not have any relevance to group discrimination, let alone justify the maintenance of inferior status for any minority in our society. Democratic principles and law are concerned with the rights and duties of all individuals, the bright and the dull, the craftsman and the unskilled, the educated and the ignorant and even the pathologically incompetent, on the basis of individual capacity and performance, not group membership.

Analysis of minority-majority relations in terms of situational factors demonstrates not only the irrelevance of a genetic approach, but also the inadequacy of reliance for their understanding on simple charges of ignorance, evil intent or personalities so warped as to justify being regarded as "sick" from a mental hygiene point of view. Granted that people with such traits do exist, they are traits which exacerbate intergroup tensions but do not explain their origin and persistence or offer a sound basis for improving the process of minority socialization. If the problem is regarded mainly as one of ignorance, attention is drawn away from minority socialization needs to whatever education the majority is deemed to need, not an easy matter to decide. If it is evil intent, exhortation to reform and punishing sanctions seem called for. If the origin is in individual personalities, then socialization is faced with the presently impossible task of mass personality change. Unfortunately for these simple explanations, discrimination and prejudice are found in minorities as well as in the majority at all levels of educational sophistication, in individuals of otherwise high moral standards and in persons who may only be described as otherwise well balanced and socially adequate in the communities and interest groups within which they live and function. There is, of course, an element of truth in all three of these charges, and it may be agreed that all justify corrective efforts, but they are inadequate in themselves and do not get at the heart of the problem.

Fruitful analysis of minority socialization in terms both of current situational needs and of longer term integrative objectives becomes possible when misleading theories of minority genetic qualities and allegations of majority ignorance and perversity are replaced by attention to the items contributing to group visibility and to the nature of competing desires as the core factors in minority-majority relations. Both categories of factors vary in detail from group to group, place to place and from time to time, changes which in some measure may be anticipated on the basis of demographic and social trends. They also may be influenced in direction by planned effort. The variability in ascription of minority status to which attention already has been called, the rapid pace of social change in the United States and the disparity between American democratic ideals and intergroup practice necessitate situational specificity in relating socialization objectives and processes both to immediate and to projected needs. By way of illustration, this becomes evident when one considers the obviously widely differing conditions affecting social participation by such minority subgroups as American Indians on the extensive Navajo reservation in Arizona in comparison with those scattered on farms in Montana, by Puerto Ricans in New York City and those remaining in their home Commonwealth, by recently arrived professionally skilled Jewish immigrants and the families of earlier co-religionist arrivals now in manufacture, commerce and the professions, or by long established Negro families in northern cities, recent migrants to the same cities and those remaining in a rural Mississippi community. Socialization for each such group clearly needs to be concerned distinctively and in detail with both day-to-day existence and longer run improvement of prospects and to be based on each group's unique marks of affiliation and its apparent conflicts with the members of the majority most directly concerned.

SOURCES OF SOCIALIZATION EXPERIENCES

With the foregoing all too brief delineation of American minorities and again emphasizing the individuality of each one of their multitudes of subgroups, attention may be turned to four major sources of their differentiating socialization experiences and problems, namely, (1) their distribution within the country, (2) cultural distinctiveness, (3) position in the American social structure, and (4) man-made environment. These four categories, of course, overlap and interlock. They are here offered as though separable items only as matter of convenience in discussion. Similarly, in the interest of simplicity in presentation, each category will be related to the particular factor in socialization of major, although not exclusive, relevance to it.

Distribution of Minorities

First, the distribution of minorities within the total population obviously is a prime factor in the determination of their intra- and intergroup associations and may intensify or minimize competitive relations. Minorities are far from evenly distributed by geographic region, urban and rural areas, and location of residence within local population aggregations. For example, immigrant stocks, that is, immigrants and children of immigrant or mixed immigrant and native born parents, in 1960 were located predominantly in the most industrialized regions of the United States. About one-third of them were in New York, New Jersey and Pennsylvania; slightly more than one-fifth in Ohio, Indiana, Illinois, Michigan and Wisconsin; over one-ninth in California. Of the 9,738,000 persons of foreign birth as reported by the 1960 Census, 8,510,000 were living in urban areas and only 1,228,000 in rural districts. Over 70 per cent of the Indians in the country are concentrated on or close to reservations. About 75 per cent of those of Japanese ancestry are in Hawaii and California. Well over half of those of Chinese ancestry and over three-fourths of those counted as Filipinos also are in Hawaii and California. Negro distribution likewise is far from random. At one extreme, Negroes constitute only a fraction of 1 per cent of the population of Vermont (519), North Dakota (777), Montana (1,467) and Minnesota (22,263); between 5 per cent and 10 per cent in New York (1,417,511), Pennsylvania (852,750), New Jersey (514,875), California (883,861), Oklahoma (153,084), Indiana (269,275) and Ohio (786,097); between 10 per cent and 20 per cent in Illinois (1,037,470), Tennessee (586,876), Texas (1,187,125) and Florida (880,186). At the other extreme, in Mississippi their proportion rises to 42 per cent (915,743) and in the District of Columbia to 54 per cent (411,737).[4]

---

[4]The percentage distributions of colored groups are from Schmid and Nobbe (1965); other quantitative items are from *Statistical Abstract,* 1964.

Concentrations of foreign stock and colored minorities within urban areas have long been with us. Most striking today are the growing concentrations of colored minorities in cities of all regions of the United States. All cities with more than 250,000 inhabitants had marked increases in the proportion of colored to white residents between 1950 and 1960, as did also 148 of the 211 Bureau of the Census Standard Metropolitan Statistical Areas.[5] The growth of urban colored populations, of course, has been overwhelmingly Negro, but it is also true that all colored peoples in the United States, with the exception of American Indians, live mostly in cities.

The extent to which intra- and intergroup contacts are facilitated or limited by minority distributional characteristics may aid or hinder integrative socialization. It is also correlated with the minority individual's immediate need for special integrative effort and with the nature of the most suitable socialization orientation and substantive content. Regional differences in values and ways of life need to be taken into account. By way of illustration, the Negro, Italian immigrant or American of Japanese origin who is able to participate effectively in a community in Maine or Oregon would not be likely routinely to be similarly effective if he moved to Louisiana or New Mexico. With regard to urban-rural differentials, rural minorities have an advantage because social change tends to proceed at a slower pace on the farm than in the city where intergroup contacts ordinarily are more frequent and pressing.

Local concentrations of minority groups, whether in a city or in a rural district, have countervailing influences on socialization. On the one hand, they tend to retard integration with the larger society because they reduce intergroup contacts and constitute a differentiated community in which the individual can function effectively and at relative ease a goodly portion of his time. Group solidarity and continuity encourage withdrawal into the community of one's fellows. On the other hand, such communities are never self-contained with the result that there is always need for some degree of integrative socialization. Further, their existence as distinctive aggregates increases both the visibility of their members and the appearance of intergroup conflict of interest with the consquence that participation in the activities of the larger community, unavoidable if only for economic reasons, takes on extra difficulty. In urban areas there is special urgency for integration, yet housing pressures, majority attitudes and other external influences, together with the general human tendency to prefer to be a part of a community of people with whom one has the most in common, may be expected to continue to create and maintain minority subcommunities whose members must participate in two social systems varying in norms of behavior. At the same time, the very mobility which has facilitated the growth of minority concentrations in American cities may be counted on to become increasingly a factor in their dispersal because of increased differentiating

---

[5] Schnore, 1965, pp. 256 ff., offers a sound basis for appreciation of the extent and significance of recent changes in the proportion of urban colored to white populations. For a penetrating analysis of minorities in a specific urban setting, see Glazer and Moynihan, 1963.

socialization consequent to varying individual capabilities, experiences, needs and opportunities. This has been the common experience in earlier concentrations of European immigrants and Orientals and is in accord with man's desire for congenial associations.

It may be noted in passing that population distribution is not the only differentiating demographic factor influencing minority socialization. Minorities commonly have ratios of men to women, proportions married, birth rates, morbidity and mortality experience, age distributions and mobility records differing from those of the majority and of other minorities. These differences are consequences of early history and the conditions of their minority status. They are both major determinants of patterns of population distribution and in part consequences of those patterns. Their influence on the process of socialization, although significant, is less directly apparent than, and secondary to, that of spatial distribution.

Cultural Distinctiveness

A second source of minority socialization problems lies in the cultural distinctiveness characteristic of all minorities. In view of the fact that the details of cultural variance of any minority are beyond recounting here, reliance must be on the fact that their impact may be gauged by focus on the value conflicts for which they are responsible. These conflicts occur in intergroup relations, within minorities and in the personality organization of the minority individual.[6] The dominant population element in the United States and its modal or "hard core" values mainly are of northern and western European origin. American immigrant minority groups mainly are of southern and eastern European origin, including those from Latin American countries such as Cuba, whose basic values derive from southern Europe. In the main, European stocks in the United States have been rapidly losing whatever minority status they may have had because of cultural assimilation and intermarriage and in consequence of growing relativistic sophistication concerning divergent peoples and cultures. The most persistent cultural characteristic serving today to identify any group of European stock as of minority status is religion, particularly when correlated with southern and eastern European origins and cultures.

It is significant for minority-majority relations that more than any other social institution the church is concerned with the inculcation and maintenance of the traditional values of its members, values which apply to behavior in other institutional settings such as the school, economy, government and home. One need only call attention to the schools maintained by Lutherans, Jews, Quakers, Roman Catholics, and members of other denominations to demonstrate the strength with which values associated with religion are held. Conflicting value

---

[6]The relation between culture systems and modal personality structure is an intriguing aspect of minority cultural variance of probable important consequence in the socialization process. However, it is still too speculative a subject for confident practical generalization. For a review of studies and theory of the relationship, see Inkeles and Levinson, 1954.

systems of Protestant denominations no longer are regarded, as some once were, as sufficiently significant to justify the ascription of minority status, although this is still the case with some small, greatly divergent sects. Anti-Semitism and anti-Catholicism survive, but neither is strong except when the faith is associated with an eastern or southern European culture. Both have diminished in salience and extent in recent years.[7] Although Judaism and Roman Catholicism may seem to be the foci of antagonism in these cases, just how much discrimination against persons of any European stock may be accounted for on the basis of religion, alleged racial differences, secular cultural divergence or the persistence of traditional prejudice remains an unanswered question. In any event, it is their values in relation to those of the significant others with whom they interact that are of basic concern in consideration of their problems of socialization.

As has been mentioned, colored minorities all are distinguished not only by racial origin, but also by cultural traits. In the case of the Negro, cultural conflict arises primarily from the fact that his acceptance of European-American culture and values necessarily has been in modified form because of his ascribed status. The very modifications forced by the white majority, which, of course, have been far from uniform from place to place and from person to person because of varying conditions and experiences, are the main source of value conflict in Negro-white relations. An example is the relatively low modal value on male family responsibility as related to such contributing factors as substandard and crowded housing, low wages and high unemployment rates, inferior schooling, religious exclusion, the absence of corrective social pressures, and so on. Another example is the common low value on self-sufficiency in contrast with dependency on either private or public sources of largess, a value level which can be understood as of historical and situational derivation (by most Americans) without detailed explanation. The socialization problem in this respect, consequently, is how to bring such values into consonance with the requirements of effective social participation as defined by the white majority while, in fact, they remain in large measure in reasonable consonance with the actual circumstances of life for many Negroes.

Other colored minorities are confronted with culture and value conflicts mainly because of the persistence of beliefs and ways of life of the earlier homeland of their people, perhaps Japan, China, the Philippines, Mexico or, in the case of the American Indian, the United States itself. These beliefs and ways once were part of integrated cultural systems, but now are in varying degrees warped, fragmented and in process of revision under the influence of new circumstances. They are not just adaptations to minority necessity but survivals, however changed by American experience, which may or may not be handicaps in adaptive socialization. For example, the traditional views of health and illness of the

---

[7]Morris Janowitz (1964) has convincingly stated on the basis of a review of national sample surveys of attitudes and research of his own that "Research evidence since the close of World War II documents that the level and intensity of prejudice towards Jews and Negroes has declined during this period. . . . This is not to overlook important short-term countertrends, new manifestations of latent hostility, or the persistence of a 'hard core' of extremist attitudes" (p. 373).

Spanish-speaking people of the southwest are not consonant with those of English-speaking physicians and other health personnel (cf. Saunders, 1954, p. 317). The original pattern of division of labor on a sex basis of those American Indian tribes who assigned hunting and warfare to the men and most of the rest of the work to the women left the men with nothing suitable to do with the coming of enforced peace and the disappearance of game. Thus the Indian male who adhered to traditional values was defined by the white man as lazy, irresponsible and brutal in his treatment of women whose burden increased as his declined. On the other hand, the imported occupational and economic values of Chinese and Japanese origin are, in the main, well adapted to the opportunities encountered in this country. The problem of socialization under such circumstances is centered on value changes which require the elimination or modification of cherished ideals rather than of externally imposed and denigrating adaptations to inferior status. Of course, these colored minorities, as the Negro, have to some varying extent also modified their values in response to the pressures of ascribed status, but this is of lesser concern in their socialization because of survivals from an original culture in which pride can be taken and of greater opportunity for individual escape from many if not all of the limitations of minority membership on the basis of achievement.

Value conflicts also are found universally within minorities. Although American Indians have been thought of and treated as though all of a kind, they are of many tribes and cultures, a fact ignored with unfortunate consequences when a wide variety of tribes were assigned to residence in Indian Territory. Jews descended from early Sephardic and German arrivals have had their difficulties with later east-European immigrants. Separate churches understandably have developed for Roman Catholics of different national origins such as Poles, Germans, Irish and French Canadians because of cultural divergencies more value-laden than language or place of residence. Barriers of caste native to Japan have been carried to the United States to the disadvantage of the low-born Eta. Today, however, intra-minority value conflicts usually are less a matter of group tradition than of differential acculturation. Residential location, education, occupation and other factors in socialization have not been and cannot be uniform for a mobile minority in a changing social order. The upward but individually uneven social mobility of immigrant stocks long has been a cause of value differentiation within each. A similar but less free process has expanded and accelerated in the Negro population since the beginning of mass migration of Negroes to cities and to the north and west at the time of World War I.[8]

Thus, the minority individual is faced with an array of incongruent values from which he must make choices. Usually this is done without conscious thought about the matter. The dominant majority presents him with an idealized series of values which may be characterized as democratic and duty oriented, but at the same time makes it plain that they apply to him only within vague and

---

[8]The development of value and behavior differentiation within the Italian, Jewish and Negro American population elements is well portrayed and interpreted by Boroff, 1961 ; Himes, 1961 ; and Ianni, 1961, 1964.

punishing limits. These values encourage him to strive for education and economic advancement and to participate in government and community affairs, but he is also kept aware of his contradictory ascribed low status. From within the minority with which he is identified there are opposing pressures to hold firmly to traditional group values, to refuse to compromise for anything not consonant with the highest values of democracy, to resign himself to objectives in accord with his majority ascribed status and roles, or to be guided by momentary opportunity and personal whim. The result for many, of course, is a set of values inconsistent with each other to an unfortunate degree, with the requirements of day-to-day existence, and with the aims of the larger society.

Under such conditions of group and individual value disparities, the task of minority socialization needs to include corrective emphasis on the advancement of both intergroup and intragroup cultural congruity and also on internalized personal value congruity. This does not mean that the objective should be the elimination of diversity either in cultural patterns or in individual values, only improved consonance of items within the widest practical range of variation. Meanwhile, it is fortunate for sanity and the general social order that inconsistencies in information, attitudes and practices can be lived with without disastrous consequences most of the time by most people. Such inconsistency is the central theme of Gunnar Myrdal's (1944) monumental study of the American Negro, *An American Dilemma*. It is the basic concern in the sociopsychological theories of cognitive and attitudinal incongruity, dissonance and imbalance and their counterconditions (Secord & Backman, 1964, pp. 108-126; Newcomb, Turner & Converse, 1965). The potential disruptive influence of such inconsistencies can be limited by the way the individual defines the situation, no matter how illogical it may seem to someone else. Inconsistent facts may be deemed irrelevant in particular situations. Conflicts in values can become unimportant by not entering conscious thought. What one may metaphorically refer to as mental compartmentalization is quite easy for most people under ordinary conditions. Commonly the logical conflict of democratic ideals and the practices of minority discrimination simply do not come to the surface in people's minds or, if they do, are readily rationalized into irrelevance. There is, nevertheless, a question of how long such circumventions can remain effective in a growing industrialized and urbanized society undergoing the leveling influences of modern mass media of communication.

Position in the Social Structure

The ascription of inferior status and roles in the social structure is a third source of minority socialization problems. Minorities identified by racial or cultural divergencies are a variety of social class. That is, they are groups of persons to whom a particular social status in the hierarchical social structure, with attendant role expectations and limitations, has been assigned. Within each minority there are always a number of subclasses which also have hierarchical status. These correspond roughly to similar stratification distinctions within the majority, but generally are fewer in number. Furthermore, each individual also has distinctive social status in consequence of his identification with a variety of groupings of associates such as fellow employees, neighbors, political workers, social club members, his family and others. Everyone, of course, has similar multiple status positions, but in the case of the minority member there is the distinction that each such relationship is affected by the limitations of his over-riding minority class status.

It must be kept in mind, however, that the word "class" represents an abstraction, a concept of convenience for the analysis of social organization but not representing a hard and fast categorization of individuals. Social classes overlap and shade into each other. Individuals may move up or down in the social hierarchy. Yet the members of any society may be grouped with analytical profit in terms of their relative position in the social structure. Some sociologists have preferred the term "caste" to "class" when minority status is ascribed to an endogamous group distinguished by racial ancestry, with escape by assimilation consequently a practical impossibility for most, as in the case of the American Negro. This use of "caste" has been disputed by other behavioral scientists as inappropriate in view of the meaning of the word in India and also because of its opprobrious connotations. Whatever the merits of the dispute, there is less objection to the term "caste-like" to distinguish those minorities whose barriers to integration are most strict and lasting from others who are more readily absorbed by the majority. Regardless of whether we are considering a form of social class or a caste-like element in the social structure, the primary socialization relevance of minority group inferior status lies in its restrictions on the economic, political and social roles of minority individuals and attendant unhappy personality problems.

Majority role ascriptions and minority role expectations are ever-present factors in minority achievement. Minority individuals, as all others, have concern for their future, whether only for the next day or for their entire lives, possibly for the easiest way to get along or, at the other extreme, for a career of high achievement. Their objectives are as varied as the aspirations which may be found in a selection of the general population of relatively similar education, income and locality. Overwhelmingly, the chief and most common desires of minorities are for respect, for economic well-being in accordance with the demands of their self-images and for the means for obtaining these basic human requirements. These are the grossly defined needs of anyone. The distinguishing characteristics of minority aspirations are: first, the group-specific variants which influence self-images; and second, the exceptional difficulties of achievement in accordance with aspirations because of cultural differentials and ascribed status.

Aspirations are the individual's conception of the role in the social order which he would find most satisfactory. One thing minority individuals are practically certain to have in common is awareness of their special social status. This they learn about early in life and are reminded of as long as they live (Mussen, Conger & Kagan, 1963). Thus they either must restrict aspirations in accordance with ascribed roles, or suffer the uncertainties of attempting to overcome the majority concept of their proper place in society. There is also the possibility that fellow minority members may not approve of their aspirations because of conflict with group goals and standards. Further, unpleasant experiences may be anticipated as a reaction even by friends to exceptional desires and achievement. Success in the milieu of the dominant majority may be viewed as contempt or desertion by militant and less successful minority individuals. Broadly generalized, the variety and inconsistencies of role expectations for minority individuals is a cause of role strain and makes the choice and accomplishment of personal objectives especially troublesome.

A further difficulty is that minority career aspirations are subject to the conflicting influences of the emphasis in the American culture on upward mobility and the restraining force of inferior social status. These opposing forces make it not a simple matter to decide upon realistic personal goals and paths for advancement. Those who do choose high aspirations are in danger of exceptionally high discrepancy between goal and achievement. There is a general tendency in the United States for goals to be somewhat higher than actual achievement. Moderate discrepancy is common and ordinarily not devastating. However, failure to come reasonably close to goal achievement can have unfortunate results such as abandonment of even a reasonably feasible goal or self-fulfilling expectation of overall failure and rejection of the social order as unfit for participation.

Achievement in spite of handicaps of a minority individual's goal of advancement, such as occupational proficiency, high intellectual attainment or financial success, is not the end of the problem. It well may not carry with it all the supplementary rewards that were anticipated. Skilled employment, administrative and executive positions and professional opportunities are likely to continue to have ceilings lower than justified by the individual's proficiency and accomplishments. Many attractive recreational facilities will still be unavailable. Social acceptance by the general population on a par with that offered majority individuals of no greater or even lesser accomplishment may not be expected. Individual achievement does not lead to unqualified integration in the social structure of the dominant population.[9] Failure to receive desired and anticipated status rewards has been a punishing experience of minority individuals who achieved or approximated goals in advance of majority role expectations for them.

Under such circumstances, that is, with the prevalence of both external and internal conflicting role and status expectations with frequently consequent ambivalence, exceptional aspiration-achievement discrepancy and status-limited rewards for accomplishment, it is clear that ordinary socialization aims, resources and programs may not be relied upon with hope for satisfactory results.[10] They may easily be damaging to the individual because of their incongruence and in

---

[9]"The United States . . . is a multiple melting pot in which acculturation for all groups beyond the first generation of immigrants, without eliminating all value conflict, has been massive and decisive, but in which structural separation on the basis of race and religion—structural pluralism, as we have called it—emerges as the dominant sociological condition" (Gordon, 1964, pp. 234 ff.).

[10]See the discussion of minority status incongruity in Williams, 1964, pp. 372 ff.; and of the ways in which role strain may be reduced in Secord and Backman, 1964, pp. 504 ff.

extreme cases lead to a form of martyrdom of possible advantage in the democratizing of intergroup relations but demoralizing for the individual. On the other hand, realistic adaptation of the socialization process insofar as it affects individual aspirations could retard integration and would be certain to be regarded by many as designed to uphold the status quo.

Man-Made Environment

The man-made environment of minorities is the fourth and final category in the classification of major sources of socialization problems here adopted for convenience in the presentation of an otherwise unmanageable wide variety of factors. For minorities, it may be characterized as a restrictive environment in that its tendency is to deny to minority individuals equal access to material goods and to limit severely both cultural experience and associational range.

The material restriction of minorities as indexed by occupation, housing and income is too well known to need documentation. It is highly visible to the ordinary citizen and easily measured by the specialist in such matters. For immigrant minorities the most severe restrictions have been in the earlier years after arrival but they have commonly continued in significant degree beyond the immigrant generation. Invariably, however, they have eased with adaptation to American patterns and with replacement in the lower paid occupations by newer immigrant arrivals or less advantaged migrants from other parts of the country, particularly Negroes and very poor and poorly educated white elements such as disadvantaged rural southerners.

Immigrant economic advance has not invariably eliminated all material restrictions. There may still be relative material deprivation after any degree of economic advance. Not all residential areas or apartment buildings are available to immigrant stocks with continuing minority status, regardless of ability to pay, nor are all occupations equally open to all. Furthermore, residential occupancy, employment or the use of recreational facilities may be on a token basis or on reluctant uncongenial sufferance. It is this type of limitation on material benefits, the partial restricted availability of facilities and services and the partially closed occupations, that currently largely has replaced the earlier immigrant problem of making a living.

Economic restrictions, it need hardly be mentioned, are most severe for Negroes, Puerto Ricans and Spanish-speaking individuals of Mexican descent. For many the problem is one of obtaining basic material necessities. Dependence on charitable aid for food, housing and health needs is unavoidably high. It is, of course, true that minimal needs for food, shelter and medical care generally are met in one way or another. No one need starve, freeze or be without care in illness except through malfunction in welfare administration. It is also true that the level of living of American minorities is appreciably higher than in many of the less advantaged regions of their ancestral homes. Such statements, however, do not cancel out the fact that the minorities in question are subjected to gross material disadvantages. Subsistence for many is substandard even though it sustains life. For many it is obtained by wages from the lowest paid and most uncertain occupation or by charity. This and the fact that nothing much better is anticipated creates a more difficult socialization problem than is the case for immigrant minorities other than the relatively few with the darkest skin.

Progress has been made in recent decades in the material welfare of all minorities, a trend which may be expected to continue. Material welfare, however, must be measured on two scales, one in terms of physical needs and comfort, the other in terms of sociopsychological requirements. The latter requirements are crucial in socialization and also most neglected and least understood. In addition, the manner in which material requirements are met, whether by valued individual accomplishment or by largess, also is a matter of prime concern in socialization. The first practical concern, of course, must be with individual adequacy for obtaining basic physical requirements. Too often this has been the point at which humane interest in minorities has ended. Viewed in terms of the individual and his development, adequacy is always relative, a matter of comparison with reference models and self-images. Minority status and the accompanying demand for majority advantage always restrict both the acquisition and the enjoyment of material goods.

Minority status also restricts cultural experience and limits the range of personal associations. In part these latter restrictions necessarily follow material restrictions. In part they are consequences of such matters as minority language handicaps, inferior education, isolation, group preferences related to distinctive traditions and lack of interest in the unfamiliar. Such factors are not peculiar to minorities, although they are likely to be more common among them than in the general population. Practically unique to minorities, however, is the fact that cultural experience and growth and associations with persons not fellow minority members may be externally enforced regardless of material achievement, desire and readiness for expanded horizons. The range of such restrictions may be from the seemingly trivial to devastatingly near totality. There may be no more than occasional discourtesy or rejection by a snobbish hotel or restaurant, social group or higher status individual, incidents which may seem minor to a member of the majority who most likely has experienced similar rejection for snobbish reasons, but probably more punishing to the minority individual for whom they are not just incidents but manifestations of continuing and inescapable ascribed low status. The more extreme restrictions, as by segregated schools, libraries, theatres and other recreational facilities, stores and other commercial institutions, today are predominantly phenomena of Negro-white relations. Minority segregation no longer is legally enforceable except by agencies not offering goods or services to the public, such as churches, religious schools, clubs and other private voluntary associations, and is diminishing in rigidity and extent even where legally permissible. Nevertheless, segregation in fact still is quite common in all types of institutions, especially so if trivial token desegregation is recognized for what it is. It may not be anticipated that present restrictions on Negro cultural development and associational range will be reduced soon nearly as much as they have been for other minorities.

The restrictive social environment in which minorities live poses two most difficult socialization problems. First, to the extent that the environment is restrictive, preparation for participation in economic, political and other social activities of the individual's community and the larger society is complicated by the problem of weighing the relative merits of unrealistic disregard of the practicalities of the situation and undemocratic accommodation to the limited opportunities permitted by ascribed status. The problem is one which few individuals are able or willing to resolve by deliberately choosing one horn of the dilemma and rejecting the other. Second, the process of socialization is made extremely difficult because of the varied and practically unpredictable reactions of minority individuals to social restrictions imposed on the basis of group identification. For some it may be a spur to intellectual effort, material achievement or the adoption of a leadership role. For others the result may be low achievement motivation, resignation, frustration, animosity towards the more advantaged, open revolt, self-hatred or a variety of other socially disadvantageous reactions. Just what the reaction will be depends on an unmanageable multitude of factors such as the experience and culture of the group to which an individual belongs, on his personal qualities, his background, his self-image and reference models and the details of the situation in which he finds himself.[11] The net effect is not likely to be wholly satisfactory either for the individual or for society, particularly if the individual's reach materially exceeds his possible grasp.

The impact on minority individuals of the materially and sociopsychologically restrictive man-made environment needs to be considered both by simple, factual description of what is or is not ordinarily attainable and in comparison with what is more readily attained by members of the dominant majority and a few exceptionally fortunate minority individuals. Deprivation can be, and too often is, measured only in comparison with some conception of a level or standard of living limited to "necessities." Television sets, automobiles, party clothes, theatre tickets, foods of choice, vacation trips and many other items generally regarded as commonplace in an affluent society have low values in such measurements if they are counted at all. This procedure neglects the fact that all persons measure their own extent of deprivation by comparison with what is attainable by others, by their reference models or even by individuals and groups of such high achievement that emulation is practically inconceivable. This is in accord with the American democratic pattern which strongly encourages upward leveling and offers little respect for those who do not strive for more than the so-called necessities. As minorities have increasingly recognized this pattern as

---

[11] Currently there is considerable speculation supported by very little convincing research about the effect of experiential deprivations on personality development of minority individuals. This seems to have been stimulated by intriguing reports of the results of sensory and social deprivation experiments with animals, including primates. There also has been suggestive research with children under experimentally established conditions of deprivation, uncertainty and anxiety and in socially depriving institutions. No reliable generalization about the personality consequences of minority limitations on experience has been established, but the subject does seem to justify rigorous research exploration. For a suggestive review of experiments with animals, see Solomon et al., 1961.

applying to themselves and internalized its values, they inevitably have raised their sights. Their achievement problem today is less one of a bare living, or even a physically comfortable one, than of their relative lacks, their relative deprivation, as participants in the body politic, the economy and the community.[12]

ULTIMATE OBJECTIVES

The problems of minority socialization resulting from demographic patterns, disparities of values, limited role ascriptions and a restricting social environment are especially difficult to resolve because of disagreement within the majority and also within minorities themselves about the most desirable and feasible long-run group objectives toward which minorities should strive. Here reference is to the ultimate group goals for minorities and not immediately to the individual roles for which their members are to be prepared. The advocated group objectives include avoidance by departure from the country or from areas of greatest stress within it, continuation of group identity involving some degree of externally- or self-imposed segregation, disappearance through integration either voluntarily or under strong compulsion, or reliance on meeting each troublesome situation opportunistically as it arises from day to day and from place to place while hopefully waiting for one or another overall final solution to appear. Effective patterns of participation in the community and nation may hardly be developed in the absence of clear understanding of which of these general objectives is to prevail.

Removal of a minority in whole or in part to some distant area as a way of eliminating or reducing intergroup conflict has a long history and still has advocates. The notion that Negroes as well as the country would be better off if as many as possible moved to Africa has been held by many. It was the view of President Lincoln, among many others of his time, and had sufficient strength to lead to the establishment of Liberia. It has had appeal not only to members of the white majority, but also to some Negroes, relatively few in number, as in the abortive movement between World Wars led by Marcus Garvey and, more recently, in the call of the Black Muslims for a Negro nation, preferably within the boundaries of the United States but possibly in the Arab East. Lincoln (1961) gives a factual account and analysis of "Negro nationalism" movements. There has been no consequential Negro emigration result. Immigrants in large numbers, however, have left the country, mainly in voluntary return to their places of origin, as in the case of hundreds of thousands of Italians and others. The now scattered and sporadic existence of the idea that removal from the country is a practical means for the reduction of minority-majority troubles, let alone their elimination, is of little, if any, current significance beyond the fact that it adds a minor confusing note to discussions of socialization aims and impedes integration of the relatively few minority individuals who take it seriously.

---

[12]For a concise review of the absolute gains of the American Negro in recent years in contrast with the growing gap between accomplishment and increasing aspirations, see Pettigrew, 1964, pp. 178-192.

The belief that minority movement away from concentrations within the United States would be a desirable objective, e.g., Negroes out of the south and out of urban concentrations, Jews out of the big cities, Cubans out of Miami, Orientals away from California, Puerto Ricans out of New York City to dispersal throughout the country, has considerable validity, as was suggested earlier in the discussion of the geographic distribution of American minorities. The early government policy and practice of removal of American Indians to reservations in distant areas of no great interest to the white man at the time is the only American example of forced mass migration for the purpose of reducing intergroup conflict. Both official and voluntary agency encouragement of minority dispersal has been given in the cases of European and Cuban refugees since World War II. The mobility of minorities which thus far have shown a sedentary tendency may be expected to increase with their inevitable acculturation. To the extent that this increases dispersal and does not merely create or enlarge existing minority concentrations, improvement in status and attendant gains may be anticipated, as may also new and improved socialization influences and facilities. Nevertheless, there is practically always a difficult problem of reorientation involved in moving into a new community.

Segregation, a desired continuing condition of a minority, usually is argued on the basis of a belief in inherent incapacity for full participation in the dominant society or on the grounds of social and moral incompatibility. Rarely, however, is there intended to be anything as close to complete physical segregation as in the case of those American Indians who were removed to western reservations. Even then, not all Indians were removed; it was possible to leave a reservation and white men were not kept out. The policy of apartheid in South Africa does not contemplate total separation of Negroes and whites, far from it (van den Berghe, 1965). European segregation of Jews in ghettoes was not nearly total. Negro segregation in the United States, of course, never has been intended by its strongest advocates to be more than fractional. However strong and prevailing the conviction that a minority is genetically, socially or morally inferior to the dominant group, the possibilities of exploitation have prevented serious advocacy of even the approximation of absolute isolation.

Advocates of segregation actually want a caste-like system with advantageously restricted contacts. As previously suggested, the Negro now occupies a modified caste-like position in the American social structure. His status is hereditary, with relatively few exceptions marriage is endogamous and the highest individual achievement does not dissolve all status barriers. With far less extensive and stringent restrictions than in the case of the Negro, a caste-like element persists in the status ascribed by many members of the dominant majority to other colored minorities and to Jews. However, the present tendency is for the status of all American minorities to become less and less caste-like in that opportunities in all still limited areas of economic, political and social activity are expanding. Yet the lines of status and role distinction are not nearly erased in the minds and behavior of the majority as a whole. Majority permissiveness most commonly is consequent to the absence of any more self-advantageous choice or to relative indifference rather than the result solely of democratic conviction. Also, the number who would prefer to tighten or at least hold present restrictions, although they may be reticent about saying so, is appreciable. While there seems to be no chance of their prevailing, the elements in favor of strengthening or indefinitely continuing the present structure can and do slow down integrative trends.

Although the prevailing sentiment among minorities favors integration, or at least the removal of majority barriers to integration, there are a few individuals, and sometimes many, in all minorities who hope to restrict cultural assimilation and intermarriage in order to preserve their traditional values and stock. They are supported by a considerable number of members of the majority who are convinced that society as a whole is enriched by a diversity of peoples. This should not be mistaken for that form of antiquarianism in which successfully integrated individuals take satisfaction in reclaiming and glorifying their previously discarded origins. Here reference is to the desire to retain a significant measure of a traditional way of life and identity of stock with confidence in its suitability for the present place and day and the conviction that this may be done without harm to the larger community and with benefit to all. In support of cultural pluralism, as this form of self-segregation has been named by its advocates, Switzerland often is cited as demonstrating both its feasibility and advantage in that three major languages and cultures with different original national associations are successfully maintained there. Russia has stressed the desirability of maintaining the several distinctive cultures to be found within its boundaries. Cultural enclaves exist within many other countries. Within the United States, some Cajuns of Louisiana and some Pennsylvania German sects have retained an appreciable fraction of their respective French and German languages and cultures, although with increasing difficulty in recent years. Cultural enclaves, however, have not usually existed in perfect harmony with their neighbors. Also, it is relevant that such enclaves usually have enjoyed a considerable degree of isolation now becoming increasingly difficult to continue. Cultural pluralism in its extreme form clearly is impossible as a way of life for any minority in the United States. It rarely has been considered seriously, except for some isolated reservation Indian tribes and a few small religious sects, as involving anything approximating a total minority culture; rather only selected but traditionally important segments of the culture not in sharp conflict with basic American values are maintained, a compromise between the old ways and the new.

Integration to the extent necessary for effective functioning (but, beyond that, no more than desired by minority individuals), of course, is the only ultimate socialization objective not in logical conflict with the principles of democracy.[13] Including opportunity both for achieving cultural compatibility and for biological amalgamation as individually desired, integration is the most widely accepted

---

[13]An integrated society, as the concept is here used, is one in which inferior status is not ascribed on the basis of alleged racial or ethnic origin. Nevertheless, groups of such origin, if they wish, can retain, indeed may hardly avoid retaining for several generations, their identity insofar as compatible with the effective functioning of the social order. This conception is in harmony with the first but not the second of the two definitions in the following:

"The term integration sometimes refers to the openness of society, to a condition in which every individual can make the maximum number of voluntary contacts with others

goal for minorities of European origin. Cultural compatibility, but not biological amalgamation, also is generally recognized as the desirable aim for American Negroes. For other colored minorities, such as American Indians and Orientals, even amalgamation today is accepted as at least minimally objectionable and permissible, albeit with reluctance and reservation in areas of their greatest concentration.

Judging by experience in other parts of the world as well as in the United States, integration is an end which in the long run is not likely to be avoided by any minority under any foreseeable circumstances, nor are the problems and patterns of minority-majority relations in the United States unique (Wagley & Harris, 1958; Rose & Rose, 1965; Shibutani & Kwan, 1965). There is no known instance in any land where two peoples, no matter in what proportion or how divergent in appearances, have long lived in the same area and communities without a blending of cultures at least to the point of operational compatibility. That biological intermixture also may be anticipated is evident from the fact that there is no biologically pure human race in the modern world.

Jews commonly are cited as challenging generalization about inevitable ultimate integration because they have lived in all parts of the world and not lost Jewish identity. The fact is, however, that adherents of the Jewish faith have mixed with the populations among whom they have lived and they have largely adopted the cultures of those populations. Judaism as a religion, together with some associated secular traits, has survived, but with major modifications, as is evident in the fact that American Jews who are still religiously faithful worship in three distinctive major denominational groups, Orthodox, Reform and Conservative (cf. Glazer, 1957). The original stock and ways of life long since have been blended beyond recognition except for quantitatively, if not qualitatively, minor survivals. What has happened in the course of Jewish history has happened in the history of all minority peoples in long continuing contact with others, and is happening to all American minorities. The question is not whether integration will be the eventuality but whether it should be facilitated or, as some would argue, retarded. There is every reason in history and current experience to believe that it cannot be stopped. Purposeful retardation of minority integration no doubt is possible, but at a great price in the effective functioning of an urbanized, industrially oriented society with otherwise democratic ideas and structure.

TRENDS IN MINORITY SOCIALIZATION

Facilitation of integration, of course, is the purpose of socialization in a democratic society. Care needs to be taken, however, not to confuse facilitation with

---

without regard to qualifications of ancestry. In that sense, the object is a levelling of all barriers to association other than those based on ability, taste, and personal preference.

"But integration sometimes also refers to a condition in which individuals of each racial and ethnic group are randomly distributed through the society so that every realm of activity contains a representative cross section of the population. In that sense, the object is the attainment, in every occupational, educational, and residential distribution, of a balance among the constituent elements in the society" (Handlin, 1966, p. 661).

compulsion. It is going too far to stretch the meaning of facilitation to cover the use of practically every conceivable form of pressure from severe employment restriction to social ostracism to compel the abandonment of cultural differences and the adoption of something vaguely called "the American way of life." This kind of forced integration was attempted in the "Americanization" programs of the federal, state and local governments, the schools, industry and many welfare agencies when the dislike of anything "alien" was heightened by World War I and immediate post-war conditions. These programs did have integrative results, but there also was much lip service, resentment and negative response to the ill-advised and unnecessary denigration and penalization of cherished traditional ways and beliefs categorized as "un-American." Permissive encouragement with guidance and opportunity for integration is more in accord with American ideals and also less resistance-arousing and consequently a more effective pattern for procedure towards inevitable ultimate integration.

Regardless of the advocacy of reduction in numbers, continuation as minorities, or integration as the objective, for some years to come practical attention must be given to more immediate circumstances in any discussion of minority socialization. Even most of those whose slogan is "integration now" recognize the need, however temporary, for adaptation to the urgencies of the present and the proximate future. Few are happy with the current inconsistencies in everyday practices and between present practices and professed democratic social values. Transitional compromise measures are unavoidable on the way to the resolution of conflicting ends. Many who have no confidence that a solution to the conflict will be found soon or who are doing well enough as things are, show little or no active concern in more than fractional progressive changes in minority status and conditions. This seems to be the overall attitude of the majority and is far from absent within minorities. Such an attitude easily is stigmatized as "gradualism," apathy, selfishness or callousness, but it is understandable and it presently prevails. There would be less impatience with compromising adjustments if they were more clearly defined and recognized as steps toward the goal of integration, a goal which cannot be reached by just a few immediate giant strides.

Minority Reference Groups

Quite possibly the resolution of the minority socialization dilemma of unhappy choice between idealism and realism will come from the continuation and expansion of the current integrative trend of all minorities in shifting and multiplying the reference groups and individuals from whom they derive their personal role aspirations and expectations. Reference groups and individuals are models, sources of personal ambitions and standards, the admired types accepted as patterns to be followed as closely as possible, bases for self-comparison, guides in the choice of goals and means for achievement. The individual may or may not be a member of his chosen reference group. He may be striving for acceptance or hopeful of no more than unassociated emulation. There are also negative reference groups and individuals, models for avoidance, as were the so-called "shanty Irish" to their "lace curtain" fellow immigrants. Each individual has several such sources of guidance in rough relation to his diversity of social roles, although one reference group commonly provides patterns for more than one role. Such reference groups and individuals are basic socialization agencies. The extent and direction of change by minority individuals of their group and individual models is the historical and present main index of assimilative role improvement and social integration.

Immigrant stocks in the main have been relatively prompt and facile in adopting new reference models as American circumstances permitted. The major exceptions have been small and compact religious groups committed to their ways of life and those immigrants intending to remain in the United States only long enough to save a little money to take care of their needs after returning to their country of origin, notably Italians and Chinese. No minority, of course, has shifted models suddenly and completely. Traditional foreign models can continue to serve advantageously in this country during the transitional integrative period and later. This follows from the fact that the fundamental aspiration, achievement, and behavior standards of the United States stem from Europe and are to be found in all major civilizations. Distant and even unrelated groups and individuals can be used for self-comparison and emulation as well as neighbors and persons of the same ethnic stock. Inevitably, however, allegiance to traditional foreign models has become attenuated and has been replaced by reference groups and individuals in the United States, chosen in varying proportions, partially related to a minority's residential concentration or dispersion, from within the dominant majority and from integrative leaders of the individual's minority stock itself. Choice of reference models from within an individual's own minority has the advantage of likelihood of no more than tolerable goal-achievement discrepancy and of appreciable recognition and supplementary rewards, albeit perhaps not as full as might be granted a similarly successful member of the majority. By definition, minority status carries with it some degree of goal restriction and achievement limitation. Nevertheless, the potential range of achievement is large and the ceiling high for striving individuals of nearly all minorities of immigrant origin, Oriental and Latin-American as well as European.

The choice of advantageous reference models is most crucially limited for Negroes. The most rewarded ideals are set by white models. The extent to which ideals impossible of achievement are nevertheless accepted may be illustrated by reference to Negroes' adoption of white standards of desired physical appearance in spite of the frustrating inability of all but a few to approximate idealized white features, color, and hair appearance even with the best of cosmetics. From the founding of the nation it has been impossible for Negroes to match the accomplishments of their white reference groups and individuals except for fractional emulation. The relatively few Negroes who have overcome barriers in universities and schools of first rank, in the professions, in business, in government, and in the arts have not generally been free of lowered ceilings and have not usually received all the customary supplementary rewards. All too frequently barriers have been partially removed merely to permit individuals to serve as tokens of democratic good faith, as so-called "show Negroes." Also, not unusually, achievement standards have been lowered to facilitate token recognition. Under the circumstances, white reference models may be regarded as offering attenuated and confusing guidance. Nevertheless, they continue to predominate as they must if integration is the goal.

Negro reference models for emulation by individuals in efforts at upward social mobility are in relatively short supply. Not only is there a poverty of high level achievers in roles regarded as superior, there is also a disproportionately small Negro middle class from which Negro youth may select reference models (Frazier, 1957, and Edwards, 1966, give detailed illustration and discussion of the significance of the numerical and other inadequacies of middle- and upper-class Negroes for reference model purposes). Furthermore, the criteria for classification in the middle and upper ranges of Negro social stratification are not as demanding as those applied to the similarly designated white positions in the social structure. Yet standards are being raised and the numbers and the achievement diversification of the members of Negro upper and middle classes are growing, with the result that there is an improving range and quality of available reference groups for those who hesitate to rely on white models for self-comparison and emulation. Changes in dress and behavior, in spread of employment, in avoidance of segregated schools, colleges and other institutions and in extent of government participation are the most prominent evidences that there is an integrative trend in Negro selection of reference models. A likely corollary of this trend which may be inferred but less readily demonstrated is an increasing influence of negative reference groups, the groups whose goals and characteristics are to be avoided. Of these, the "Uncle Toms," "handkerchief heads" and "hat-in-hand" Negroes long have been characterized as avoidance figures by those ambitious to be first-class citizens in their own right and by their own achievement. Such avoidance now has spread and gained intensity in criticism of those who passively accept inferior status and lack ambition for advancement.

The optimistic observation that there definitely is a trend in the direction of increasing Negro dependence on model groups and individuals encouraging and supporting more effective participation in community and national life must be tempered by emphasis on the fact that concern with socialization needs to take into account much more detailed knowledge of the subject than is presently available. The extent, speed and detailed nature of the trend are not known. Nor is it known what proportion of Negroes are basing their ambitions and behavior on models with contrary influence, such as juvenile delinquents and adult criminals, passive accepters of lowly status, protesters of their lot by destructive and illegal violence or merely by words, just plain quitters or other negative elements. Also, it should not be overlooked that white models who offer no positive socialization guidance may be excessively chosen because significant Negro contacts are disproportionately likely to be with the least advantaged white population elements. Social status and its corresponding roles and achievement levels may neither be fully understood nor improved by rational effort without better information about the prevalence and attractiveness of advantageous model groups and individuals and their use.

By now it should be clear that there can be no simple formula for the improvement of minority socialization. It is hoped that it also may be clear that dispassionate analysis of the complex of factors involved can be helpful in the development of more effective socialization procedures than now prevail. The drastic simplification of the nature and problems of the process of minority socialization attempted in the previous pages of this chapter has not been intended to minimize its complexity but rather to provide a general structure facilitating orderly consideration of its many facets. To recapitulate, emphasis has been, first, on the need to recognize the specificity of the nature and circumstances of the numerous subgroups within each minority; second, on the underlying influence of group visibility, attributed competitive threat and denigrating majority beliefs sometimes outlasting the situation of origin or borrowed from elsewhere; third, on the major broad sources of socialization problems; and, fourth, on the several long-run conflicting advocated group objectives. The remainder of the chapter will be concerned with questions of policy and procedure in socialization practice designed to meet transitional problems of individuals and groups on the way to ultimate integration.

REACTIONS TO
HANDICAPPING CIRCUMSTANCES

Minority socialization has supported three distinct patterns of behavior for countering the special handicapping circumstances of social participation. All three have been simultaneously practiced throughout the history of the country and no doubt will be continued so long as a minority exists. These are: first, avoidance of inter-group issues insofar as possible where no clear purpose in bringing them to the fore can be seen; second, forcefully joining the issues when it is judged that advantage might be gained; and third, the preparation for filling more advantageous roles than generally available in the expectation that greater opportunities will be afforded those prepared to take advantage of them.

Avoidance of Intergroup Issues

Avoidance of minority-majority issues may seem less strange as an objective of socialization if it is defined as a form of accommodation to an unavoidable unhappy status relationship. Reference here is not to withdrawal or self-isolation from intergroup contacts but to behavior which recognizes and accommodates to a status relationship. The strains in interpersonal relations across the barriers of varying and uncertain social status can be relieved by the development of behavior patterns whereby the sensitive and considerate majority member avoids words, subjects and behavior which he thinks may have offensive connotations for a minority individual. The trouble-avoiding minority individual on his part ostensibly accepts his ascribed role by acting in accordance with his idea of majority expectations. Thus, Negro socialization has taught that it is helpful in avoiding trouble and in gaining one's ends to respond to a white man's question either by giving the answer gauged most likely to be pleasing or by pretending ignorance or stupidity. Genteel white people, in turn, tend to overpraise Negro achievement in such fields as art, music, literature, and science and to avoid reference to, or excuse as a consequence of discrimination, Negro crime and delinquency, inadequate skills and work habits or low educational levels. The etiquette of Negro-white relations, as this most common technique was termed by Bertram Doyle (1937) thirty years ago, has had a long and varied history.

Similar tension-reducing and trouble-avoiding behavior is characteristic of all other minority-status groups in their relations with members of the dominant majority. It is rare, for example, for Christians to discuss anti-Semitism and its possible relation to differing cultural backgrounds and value systems with Jews or for Protestants to talk about birth control or the merits of parochial schools with devout Roman Catholics. This is not a phenomenon unique to minority-majority relations but rather a general practice in relations between members of any two groups with differential social status. It eases intergroup contacts, but it also symbolizes and supports status differentials and tends to slow integration. It also can be a device for facilitating the avoidance of giving thought to present problems and long-run objectives. Insofar as avoidance of sensitive items and issues is no more than recognition that life would be intolerable in the absence of kindly intended social amenities and white lies, it may be regarded as temporarily necessary and helpful in intergroup relations. Carried to the point of interference with objective research, publication, and discussion in school or on public platform, as is presently commonly the case, it is a serious obstruction to minority integration.

The Use of Pressure to Gain Advantages

Minority socialization may encourage active conflict as well as accommodation as means for achieving desired ends. Differing situations may require differing measures for correction, and even a single situation may be judged differently by more than one person. Some individuals may be more inclined to direct forceful action than others. In the past and also currently, minority socialization has relied overwhelmingly on accommodation as the technique for getting along under the handicap of inferior status, but throughout American history there always have been some minority individuals and groups convinced that strong action directed to improved status and opportunity is an unavoidable necessity. Indian attacks and slave revolts may be cited as early examples of the use of force by minorities. Until the present decade, minority violence has been rare and mainly in the form of rioting initiated by a majority element. After all, physical conflict may hardly be expected to be a reliable technique for minority gain, if only because of the relative numbers involved. It may, however, serve the purpose of educating the majority by dramatizing complaint and thus lead by other paths to later improvements even though the immediate battle was lost. Negro rioting in New York, Los Angeles, Detroit and other cities in recent years, for example, seems to have had such an influence, but this is as difficult to demonstrate with precision and assurance as it is to establish the extent of the alleged countervailing "boomerang" or "white backlash" effect. Encouragement of physical force undoubtedly will continue to be an element in the socialization of minorities if only because "standing up and fighting for one's rights" is highly valued in American culture. Nevertheless, its general low practical utility even as a means for dramatizing injustice in relation to its potential costs and repercussions should be obvious even to the most intransigent minority leader (cf. Coser, 1966).

Interpretation of the increasingly open, insistent and compelling efforts by Negroes in the 1960's to improve their lot as a "revolution" has a retarding influence on integrative socialization. It supports the view that the interests of Negroes and the rest of the population are in fundamental conflict, strengthens conflict-oriented group solidarity, and hampers Negro-white cooperative action. It is not merely a semantic quibble to stress the importance of understanding that the desire and drive of Negroes is not for a revolution but for full citizenship, for full participation in the life of the country as promised by the Constitution, supporting legislation and the ideals of American democracy (cf. Pettigrew, 1964, pp. 192 ff.). The objective certainly is not revolutionary. It must also be recognized that all but a few Negroes are staying within the law in their use of political, economic, and protest demonstration pressures to achieve their legal rights. As a social phenomenon, the movement is akin to that in earlier years for women's rights, to the long struggle for the improvement of the lot of labor, and to the still-continuing campaign against anti-Semitism. The thoughtless designation of the Negro movement for reform as a "revolution," based on its stepped-up tempo and unprecedented intensity and on the lawless behavior of a relatively very small number of individuals, is a serious disservice to integrative socialization effort.

Common forms of minority conflict techniques such as economic pressure, political action and nonviolent protest and obstructionism have been strikingly effective. Severe economic pressure can be exerted by boycotting stores, sometimes euphemistically referred to as "selective buying," and refusing to patronize segregated busses and other commercial facilities. Disregard of union wage scales and working standards can be punishing to discriminating unions. The slogan "Don't buy where you can't work" has had increasing power as minority income has grown. Not only the Negro but all minorities have resorted to such devices with significant results. The impact throughout the history of the country of minority bloc voting both by European as well as colored groups, especially effective where a minority holds the numerical balance of power between the two major political parties, is too well known to require illustration. More recent is the extensive organized utilization of nonviolent group protest and obstructionism by Negroes in the form of interference with business in segregated restaurants by merely sitting quietly at tables or counters, by similar sit-ins in public and commercial recreational facilities and in exclusive white churches, by picketing and mass demonstrations at segregated schools and places of business, by shows of strength in "marches" as on Washington in 1963 and, in general, a wide variety of forms of peaceful noncompliance with majority behavior expectations.

The effectiveness of such pressure techniques, of course, depends on particular, suitable circumstances, but these today are common and well known to minority leaders and even the rank and file. Currently they are generally thought of as Negro protest techniques. They are, in fact, today most widely used by Negroes (Marvick, 1965; Rose, 1965). It should not be overlooked, however, that they have been used and still are being used, although to a much more limited extent, by other minorities. They are, of course, in the American tradition and have ample precedent in majority behavior dating back to colonial times.

Nonviolent protest action may be spontaneous, but it is more likely to be successful if guided by organized leaders. There are literally hundreds of minority voluntary associations capable of offering such guidance, some of which have been organized expressly for the purpose. Among those with primary concern for improving the status of the Negro by challenging existing conditions are the Congress of Racial Equality, the Student Nonviolent Coordinating Committee, the Southern Christian Leadership Conference, the National Association for the Advancement of Colored People and the National Urban League. Similar in purpose but with distinctive approaches because of the differing circumstances of the groups involved are such agencies as the American Jewish Committee, the American Jewish Congress, the Anti-Defamation League of B'nai B'rith, the American Council for Judaism, the Japanese-American Citizens League, the National Congress of American Indians, the Political Association of Spanish-Speaking Americans, the National Conference of Christians and Jews, and many others. Most minority voluntary associations have been organized for social, recreational, political, educational, welfare, religious, historical, or ego-enhancing purposes, the same purposes for which a vast number of majority dominated associations have been created. The fact that for minorities such associations have the distinguishing bonds of common stock, differentiating culture and a status handicap makes them potential protest agencies, a role many of them take on as situations warrant or even continuously as a secondary concern. All minority voluntary associations are influential socialization agencies. Insofar as all give emphasis to the need for group solidarity they contribute to the internalization of an attitude of intergroup competition and conflict.[14] With full recognition that such associations have served and are serving an important function for the nation as well as for minorities, nevertheless, there is an unavoidable contradiction involved when stress is placed on conflict techniques and their requisite of group solidarity for accomplishing integration. The internaliza-

---

[14]Minority voluntary associations not only tend to contribute to a sense of competition and conflict, but also at the same time may support either resignation to social disadvantage or encourage active protest. For example, a church, like any other voluntary association, may either serve as an "opiate" or as an "action agency," cf. Marx, 1957.

tion of means not congruent with the end, as observed earlier, is bound to be disturbing and disruptive to some minority individuals even though such incongruence can be rationalized or ignored by mental "compartmentalization" by most.

Development of Motivation and Competence

The opening sentence of this chapter defined socialization as the process which enables individuals to participate effectively as members of their interest groups, communities, and the larger society. Accommodation to an unhappy situation or battling one's way out are forms of such participation. The heart of socialization, however, is the development of both motivation and competence to meet role responsibilities. The socialization of European immigrant and Japanese stocks has effectively, if unevenly (as between culturally differing minorities such as the Irish, Italians and Jews), attended to preparation for acceptance of the entire range of active and potential social roles. This has been appreciably less true for Mexicans and the relatively small and predominantly male Chinese and Filipino minorities, especially in earlier years. It has also been less true for American Indians, particularly those on or near reservations. For the bulk of all these minorities, but excepting the Negro, it has been taken for granted and emphasized that transcendence of the limitations of inferior status beyond ascribed minority roles required the development of motivation, values, behavior patterns, occupational competence and responsibility acceptance not necessarily identical but compatible with those of their majority associates.

In the case of the Negro, attacks on prejudice and discrimination and demands for political, economic and social advancement have not been effectively balanced by free expression of the need for preparation for meeting wider opportunities and responsibilities. True, there are those who argue persuasively that limitations of inferior status must first be removed before any minority can prepare properly for unaccustomed roles and that new levels of achievement must come from within an emancipated group rather than through paternalistic guidance while social restrictions are still in force. This is the argument for "full freedom now" with secondary regard for preparation for its exercise. Its kernel of truth obscures the practical needs of current conditions. The rights of membership in a democratic society carry with them role responsibilities which must be met. However, in recent years, Negro leaders and white champions have given secondary attention at most to the obligations that always accompany rights, to the difficulty of adapting to social change and to the preparatory effort necessary for functioning in new roles. It is understandable that there is growing impatience with what has come to be known as "gradualism" and widely regarded as obstructionism in the effort for Negro improvement. No doubt the position that a high proportion of Negroes are not yet ready to take advantage of the opportunities they demand frequently has been taken for obstructionist purposes, but that does not change the fact that preparation for change is needed and that it takes effort and time. The direction of Negro socialization inevitably must remain unclear while the vocal leaders most widely heard and most loudly publicly applauded direct their major efforts to the achievement of equal status now and speak in guarded terms of concurrent requirements and responsibilities.

It should not be assumed that the reiterated goal of prompt and full integration demanded by white and colored spokesmen for Negroes is accepted by a majority of Negroes much beyond the verbal level, as a slogan or tactic, or wishfully. There is general awareness that there are too many white people of the contrary opinion to be ignored and that the practicalities of the situation presently require a compromise pattern of participation in American society. Some Negroes, comparatively few, are fully committed to prompt integration without compromise. Others adjust to inferior status and make the best of it, perhaps with resignation based on hopelessness or on mere habit and convenience. Most live in accord with a policy of gradualism, working quietly or openly fighting for advancement as chance offers, or doing nothing at all to improve conditions in spite of distaste for delay in change. A number attempt rejection of the white man and his civilization, as in the case of the Black Muslims. No matter what choice is made, the socialization of every Negro in any American community is complicated by such conflicts of views and by reticence to consider them frankly.

The subject of reticence in reference to minority shortcomings for effective participation in American communities may not be dropped without noting that it also is to be found in discussions of the problems of minorities other than the Negro. Commonly they are not shortcomings in minority eyes. There is reluctance to discuss the extent to which anti-Semitism is stimulated by subtle differences of East European, German, or religious origin in such matters as emotional patterns of reaction and expression, in intellectual and economic values, family patterns or conversational manners. As has been noted, Mexican peasant health concepts and practices cause problems for U.S. medical practitioners, hospitals and community agencies. Aspects of Italian or French Canadian culture, such as lesser interest in higher education and more on children's contribution to the family budget than is regarded as ideal by many in the United States, may be regarded as shortcomings. Incomprehension and resentment are ordinary reactions to any challenge to traditional minority ways and values. Such reactions are understandable and at least partially justifiable in that there is, in fact, nothing inherently "wrong" about such differences other than that they are "different." However, the persistence of even minor divergent cultural traits helps keep alive anti-minority sentiment. Often they are not known to minorities as different or widely recognized by the majority as significant. Those who do see their significance in intergroup relations hesitate to call attention to them because of likely embarrassment and resentment. Another cause of hesitation is the understanding on the part of persons sensitive to the role of cultural differences in social interaction that there is no intrinsic qualitative distinction involved.

The modification of minority traditional aims and patterns of behavior has been left mostly to fumbling trial and error. Why this is so may be seen by considering, for example, the complexity of the problems of socialization of one relatively small group, the Cuban refugees who have come to the United States in recent years. Their adaptation for participation in pre-Castro Cuban society proved unsuited for life under his regime or presumably they would have stayed where they were. Now their values and accustomed life patterns need to be modified to meet the basic requirements of the new environment and social system within which they must function. Will it do to advise them and for them to resolve to become "Americans"? What about those who expect to return to Cuba after another change in government? What kind of Americans? How can it be done and at what cost even if suitable models are agreed upon? Are the socialization agencies of their own and of their new communities adequate for the task? Can the multiplicity of agencies involved direct their aims at consonant goals and adhere to harmonious policies and strategies? Should they try to do so? How may the problems consequent to differential socialization of children and their elders and of earlier and later arrivals be minimized? How may the receptivity of the native American community be maximized? These are all pressing problems of socialization, but only a beginning list, stripped of multiple details, of those which face the refugees and their neighbors. They are no more extensive or complex than the quite similar problems in the socialization of minorities in general.

MINORITY SOCIALIZATION AGENCIES

In the abstract, the main socialization agencies for minorities are the same as those for the general population. However, minority socialization agencies, for reasons mentioned earlier (demographic characteristics, cultural distinctiveness, status in the social structure, and the man-made environment of minorities), are imperfectly adapted either for integrative or socially static socialization objectives. As emphasized earlier, interests, institutions, values, and behavior patterns are far from uniform within any minority. There is consequent necessity for considering the socialization process with care for variations within subgroupings and between individuals. Although abstract generalizations about the nature of minority-majority relations are necessary for understanding and effective action in the field, as with all theory, their application to a particular problem situation must take into account the conditions specific to the situation. It is, of course, not possible here to detail or even outline the multiplicity of variations in minority socialization agencies, situations, and programs. In fact, reliable knowledge about them exists only in fragments. However, a few illustrative items may be offered as suggestive of the range and kind of questions involved and of needed further research.

The family ordinarily is the first socialization influence in the life of the individual and for most is of the greatest formative importance. Significant variations in family structure and activity from what is generally regarded as well within the range of normality in the United States are found in the prevalence of incomplete families because of illegitimacy, desertion or divorce, in the authoritarian, economic and training roles of the father and mother, and in the child-rearing practices concerning nutrition and other physical care, discipline, behavior as a family member and life-goal and moral guidance.

The second decisive socialization agency chronologically is the school. Here there is need to know the extent and likely minority-majority differences in such characteristics of teachers and fellow students as race, national origin, religion, and economic and social status; in the attitudes and behavior of fellow students and their families regarding minority acceptance, active rejection or isolating indifference; in minority students' self-concepts, goals, motivation and general readiness for integrated education; in textbook content; in the qualifications and attitudes of teachers and administrators; and, of course, in the adequacy of physical facilities. Information is woefully lacking about the influence on minority intellectual and personality development of compulsory and voluntary group-supported school segregation or of integration in varying proportions and in differing situations.

Mass communication media (newspapers, radio, television, magazines, books, and public assemblies) exert a socializing influence throughout life. Dominatingly controlled and supported by members of the white majority, they naturally tend to reinforce the beliefs and attitudes of their audiences. The extent of their reinforcing influence, of their power as change agents when minority news and information in them is directed to this purpose and the relative integrative and divisive impact of media specifically designed for minority audiences, such as foreign language broadcasts and Negro and foreign language newspapers and other publications, is highly debatable.

Similar items in all other areas of social activity need to be investigated, e.g., the economic, political, religious, welfare, health, and recreational areas. Research focused on the particularistic components of socialization agencies in specific situations currently is increasingly common; much more urgently is needed.

In broad generalization, two significant distinctions between the functioning of minority and majority socialization agencies must be noted. First, there is likely to be excessive disagreement among minority agencies concerning objectives and proper paths to be followed. Second, minority socialization is a concern not only of their own social institutions and interest groups but also of agencies controlled by the majority. Social control through the internalization of social norms functions effectively in direct relation to the degree of agreement of the institutional agencies with which the individual is in contact. Because minority individuals are especially subject to the influence of a partially incongruent variety of agencies attempting to internalize conflicting norms, their socialization commonly is excessively fragmentary and inadequate.

There is disagreement about strategies to be followed as well as about norms to be internalized. First, there is a fundamental difference of opinion among integrationists about the relative emphasis which should be placed on the integration of the individual for his own benefit or on the advancement of the minority as a whole. Should major attention be on the emancipation of the individual from limited status regardless of consequences for the group from which he may become alienated and for the individual himself in the not likely event of alienation from the minority without acceptance by the majority? This approach can deprive a minority of needed leadership and weaken group solidarity in the struggle for advancement. It can also make marginal, frustrated misfits. The opposing position also may be criticized in that it suggests the sacrifice of individuals for wider group benefit. Obviously neither position is a practical absolute; something of both must guide minority socialization, as is, in fact, the case at present. Nevertheless, there are influential leaders who are strongly, even emotionally, of one view or the other and who subject those who choose a middle ground to criticism and obstruction.

Second, there is also disagreement about the attention which should be given to minority cultural heritage, achievement and commonality of interest. Emphasis on such items is claimed to have an anti-integration influence, yet they may not be denigrated without loss of solidarity needed both for improvement of living conditions and status, and for individual self-esteem and confidence in potentiality. Furthermore, in general minorities prefer their customary ways of life and tend to interpret suggestions for change, particularly if they come from external sources, as prejudiced criticism. There is also a general preference on the part of minority individuals for residential, recreational and predominant association with congenial fellow minority members which limits the gains in lowered visibility and reduction of apparent competitive threat otherwise possible through wider dispersion. The perplexing situation is that individual preference and need, and also group advantage are in some very important respects best served by emphasis on differentiating behavior and group cohesion while the objectives of full social status and equality of opportunity would be better advanced by stress on cultural assimilation and dispersal.

Turning to schools for illustration of the quandry in which minority socialization agencies find themselves, to what extent can the public schools increase instruction in Negro and immigrant history, culture and current problems, as urged by many, without sharpening the distinction between minorities and "old Americans" with consequent confusion for the children? There is good reason to question the integrative influence of attention to distinctive cultural traits, however praiseworthy, such as unique contributions to music and the arts, to the minority identification of outstanding individuals, or to the problems of prejudice and discrimination encountered by minorities. The question is especially difficult to answer positively when the minority contribution has been unjustifiably upgraded, as has often been the case in the past. There is also a question concerning the extent to which parochial schools and other educational facilities privately maintained by religious bodies with ethnic associations, because of desire to preserve values at variance with those prevailing in public school instruction, negatively influence status and opportunity. Similar questions could be asked about minority-oriented socialization influences of parents, the clergy, mass media and other agencies of social control. Each has the problem of helping individuals achieve the most satisfactory balance possible between the conflicting ideals of economic, political, and social equality of opportunity and living as much as one pleases in accord with the values and patterns of a minority.[15]

The necessity for considering schools as minority socialization agencies as just one factor operating interdependently with all the others is demonstrated in two recent large scale studies, one of Catholic parochial schools and the other concerned with Negro-white comparisons in public schools. The parochial school study reports among its conclusions that "No confirmation was found for the notion that Catholic schools are 'divisive.' There is divisiveness in American society, but it is apparently based more on religion than on religious education." It also reports that "There is a weak but persistent association between Catholic education and economic and social achievement (usually about .1)" (Greeley & Rossi, 1966, p. 220). The public school study based the following statement on information gathered about 600,000 Negro and white children in segregated and mixed schools throughout the United States:

> Taking all these results together, one implication stands out above all: That schools bring little influence to bear on a child's achievement that is independent of his background and general social context; and that this very lack of an independent effect means that the inequalities imposed on children by their home, neighborhood, and peer environment are carried along to become the inequalities with which they confront adult life at the end of school (Coleman et al., 1966, p. 325).

The findings of these two outstanding research projects suggest that the role of formal education in minority socialization, whether the objective is integration or some degree of pluralism, is more severely limited by the other socialization forces than is widely understood.

CONCLUSION

The conflict involved in concurrent concerns for cultural permissiveness and also for assimilation may be difficult for logical resolution, but it is nevertheless capable of practical adjustment. Argument for one extreme or the other, while still heard, has declined to comparatively minor importance. The concept of relativity of cultural norms for a broad range of behavior extending from table manners to family standards has gained wide acceptance at the expense of the absolutist view. At the same time, advantageous cultural adaptation has become easier because of rising levels of living, the growth of mass communication facilities and modern mobility. Both freedom of choice and facility for change are continuing to expand. Society requires and minority socialization needs only a core of common values and behavior patterns clearly helpful to individuals in

---

[15]Thought-provoking debate at a four-day conference of Negro and white educators, behavioral scientists and specialists in community development about the school as a socialization agent for Negro youth is reported in Kavaraceus et al., 1965. The reported discussion illustrates very well the existing sharp diversity of opinion concerning school intergroup functions and techniques, and the lack of available data needed for rational consideration of the issues.

the satisfactory performance of their various social roles. Uniformity would be disastrous if demanded beyond the minimum necessary for cooperation in moving towards the broader objectives of interest groups, the community, and the larger society. Conformity in the overriding principles of American democracy with compatible diversity in the details of belief and behavior is a practical aim for minority socialization. It applies no less to the majority.

Paul Weiss has written that "If there is any lesson in the study of organic nature, it is that there is order in the gross with freedom of excursion in the small. . . . Freedom within the law: responsible freedom to move within an orbit as wide as, but no wider than, what is compatible with the preservation of the overall order that defines the harmony of relationships on which effective living and survival depend" (Weiss, 1960, pp. 189f.). Although a biological generalization may not be offered as proof of a social principle, the quoted words can felicitously define the cultural setting in which the peoples of the United States might participate most fully in all aspects of society, not as minorities but as individuals.

REFERENCES

BERNARD, JESSIE. *Marriage and family among Negroes*. Englewood Cliffs, N. J.: Prentice-Hall, 1966.

BOROFF, D. Jewish teen-age culture. *The Annals of the American Academy of Political and Social Science,* 1961, 338, 79-90.

COLEMAN, J. S., CAMPBELL, E. Q., HOBSON, CAROL J., McPARTLAND, J., MOOD, A. M., WEINFELD, F. D., & YORK, R. L. *Equality of educational opportunity*. Washington, D. C.: U.S. Government Printing Office, 1966.

COSER, L. A. Some social functions of violence. M. E. Wolfgang (Ed.), Patterns of violence. *The Annals of the American Academy of Political and Social Science,* 1966, 364, 8-18.

DOYLE, B. *The etiquette of race relations in the south*. Chicago: Univer. of Chicago Press, 1937.

EDWARDS, G. F. Community and class realities: The ordeal of change. In T. Parsons & K. B. Clark, *The Negro American*. Boston: Houghton Mifflin, 1966. Pp. 280-302.

FRAZIER, E. F. *Black bourgeoise, the rise of a new middle class in the United States*. Glencoe, Ill.: Free Press, 1957.

GLAZER, N. *American Judaism*. Chicago: Univer. of Chicago Press, 1957.

GLAZER, N., & MOYNIHAN, D. P. *Beyond the melting pot, the Negroes, Puerto Ricans, Jews, Italians and Irish of New York City*. Cambridge, Mass.: M.I.T. Press, 1963.

GORDON, M. M. *Assimilation in American life*. New York: Oxford Univer. Press, 1964.

GREELEY, A. M., & ROSSI, P. H. *The education of Catholic Americans*. Chicago: Aldine, 1966.

HANDLIN, O. The goals of integration. In T. Parsons & K. B. Clark, *The Negro American*. Boston: Houghton Mifflin, 1966.

HIMES, J. S. Negro teen-age culture. *The Annals of the American Academy of Political and Social Science,* 1961, 338, 91-101.

IANNI, F. A. J. The Italo-American teenager. *The Annals of the American Academy of Political and Social Science,* 1961, 338, 70-78.

IANNI, F. A. J. Minority group status and adolescent culture. In D. Gottlieb & C. E. Ramsey, *The American adolescent.* Homewood, Ill.: Dorsey Press, 1964. Pp. 219-247.

INKELES, A., & LEVINSON, D. J. National character: The study of modal personality and sociocultural systems. In G. Lindzey, *Handbook of social psychology.* Vol. II. Reading, Mass.: Addison-Wesley, 1954. Pp. 977-1020.

International Social Science Journal, UNESCO, Paris, 1965, 17 (1).

JANOWITZ, M. Social change and prejudice. In E. W. Burgess & D. J. Bogue, *Contributions to urban sociology.* Chicago: Univer. of Chicago Press, 1964. Chapter 24.

KAVARACEUS, W. C. ET AL. *Negro self-concept: Implications for school and citizenship.* New York: McGraw-Hill, 1965.

LINCOLN, C. E. *The Black Muslims in America.* Boston: Beacon Press, 1961.

MARVICK, D. The political socialization of the American Negro. Roberta Sigel (Ed.), Political socialization: Its role in the political process. *The Annals of the American Academy of Political and Social Science,* 1965, 361, 112-127.

MARX, G. T. Religion: Opiate or inspiration of civil rights militancy among Negroes. *American Sociological Review,* 1957, 32 (1), 64-72.

MOYNIHAN, D. P. Employment, income, and the ordeal of the Negro family. In T. Parsons & K. B. Clark (Eds.), *The Negro American.* Boston: Houghton Mifflin, 1966. Pp. 134-159.

MUSSEN, P. H., CONGER, J. J., & KAGAN, J. *Child development and personality.* (2nd Ed.) New York: Harper & Row, 1963. Pp. 409 ff.

MYRDAL, G. *An American dilemma: The Negro problem and American democracy.* New York: Harper & Bros., 1944.

NEWCOMB, T. M., TURNER, R. H., & CONVERSE, P. E. *Social psychology.* New York: Holt, Rinehart & Winston, 1965. Pp. 121-136.

PETTIGREW, T. F. *A profile of the American Negro.* Princeton, N. J.: Van Nostrand, 1964.

ROSE, A. M. The Negro protest. *The Annals of the American Academy of Political and Social Science,* 1965, 357, passim.

ROSE, A. M., & ROSE, CAROLINE B. *Minority problems, a textbook of readings in intergroup relations.* New York: Harper & Row, 1965. Pp. 67-139.

ROSE, P. I. *They and we: Racial and ethnic relations in the United States.* New York: Random House, 1964.

SAUNDERS, L. *Cultural differences and medical care.* New York: Russell Sage Foundation, 1954.

SCHMID, C. F., & NOBBE, C. E. Socioeconomic differentials among nonwhite races. *American Sociological Review,* 1965, 30 (6), 909-922.

SCHNORE, L. F. The changing color composition of metropolitan areas. Part 5. *The urban scene.* New York: Free Press, 1965.

SECORD, P. F., & BACKMAN, C. W. *Social psychology.* New York: McGraw-Hill, 1964.

SHIBUTANI, T., & KWAN, K. M. *Ethnic stratification, a comparative approach.* New York: Macmillan, 1965.

SIMPSON, G. E., & YINGER, J. M. *Racial and cultural minorities: An analysis of prejudice and discrimination.* (3rd Ed.) New York: Harper & Row, 1965.

SOLOMON, P., ET AL. (Eds.) *Sensory deprivation.* Cambridge, Mass.: Harvard Univer. Press, 1961.

Statistical Abstract of the United States. (85th Ed.) Bureau of the Census, U.S. Department of Commerce, 1964. Pp. 25, 26, 28, 29, 42.

VAN DEN BERGHE, P. Socio-political conflicts: "Native policy." *South Africa, a study in conflict*. Middleton, Conn.: Wesleyan Univer. Press, 1965.

WAGLEY, C., & HARRIS, M. *Minorities in the new world, six case studies*. New York: Columbia Univer. Press, 1958.

WEISS, P. Organic form: Scientific and aesthetic aspects. *Daedalus*, 1960, Winter.

WILLIAMS, R. M., JR. *The reduction of intergroup tensions*. Bulletin 57. New York: Social Science Research Council, 1947. Pp. 54 ff.

WILLIAMS, R. M., JR. *Strangers next door: Ethnic relations in American communities*. Englewood Cliffs, N. J.: Prentice-Hall, 1964.

YOUNG, D. *American minority peoples, a study in racial and cultural conflicts in the United States*. New York: Harper & Bros., 1932. Pp. 586 ff.

Author Index

* Page numbers in italics are reference pages.

Subject Index

PRINTED IN U.S.A.